Microsoft® Office 2010

INTRODUCTORY

by Pasewark and Pasewark*

William R. Pasewark, Sr., Ph.D.
Professor Emeritus, Business Education,
Texas Tech University

Scott G. Pasewark, B.S.
Occupational Education, Computer Technologist

William R. Pasewark, Jr., Ph.D., CPA
Professor, Accounting, Texas Tech University

Carolyn Denny Pasewark, M.Ed.
National Computer Consultant, Reading and Math
Certified Elementary Teacher, K-12 Certified Counselor

Jan Pasewark Stogner, MBA
Financial Planner

Beth Pasewark Wadsworth, B.A.
Graphic Designer

**Rachel Biheller Bunin, Jessica Evans,
Katherine T. Pinard, Robin M. Romer**
Contributing Authors

*Pasewark and Pasewark is a trademark of the Pasewark LTD.

COURSE TECHNOLOGY
CENGAGE Learning™

Australia • Brazil • Japan • Korea • Mexico • Singapore • Spain • United Kingdom • United States

COURSE TECHNOLOGY
CENGAGE Learning™

Microsoft Office 2010 Introductory
Pasewark and Pasewark

Contributing Authors: Rachel Biheller Bunin, Jessica Evans, Ann Fisher, Fran Marino, Katherine T. Pinard, Robin M. Romer, Danielle Shaw, Barbara Waxer

Executive Editor: Donna Gridley

Product Managers: Allison O'Meara McDonald, Amanda Lyons

Development Editor: Fran Marino

Associate Product Manager: Amanda Lyons

Editorial Assistant: Kim Klasner

Senior Content Project Manager: Catherine DiMassa

Associate Marketing Manager: Julie Schuster

Director of Manufacturing: Denise Powers

Text Designer: Shawn Girsberger

Photo Researcher: Abigail Reip

Manuscript Quality Assurance Lead: Jeff Schwartz

Manuscript Quality Assurance Reviewers: Green Pen QA, Serge Palladino, Susan Pedicini, Jeff Schwartz, Danielle Shaw, Marianne Snow, Susan Whalen

Proofreader: Kim Kosmatka

Indexer: Sharon Hilgenberg

Art Director: Faith Brosnan

Cover Designer: Hannah Wellman

Cover Image: © Neil Brennan / Canopy Illustration / Veer

Compositor: GEX Publishing Services

For product information and technology assistance, contact us at
Cengage Learning Customer & Sales Support, 1-800-354-9706
For permission to use material from this text or product, submit all requests online at **www.cengage.com/permissions**.
Further permissions questions can be e-mailed to
permissionrequest@cengage.com.

Hardcover:
ISBN-13: 978-0-538-47539-6
ISBN-10: 0-538-47539-0

Hardcover spiral-bound:
ISBN-13: 978-0-538-47551-8
ISBN-10: 0-538-47551-X

Softcover:
ISBN-13: 978-0-538-47550-1
ISBN-10: 0-538-47550-1

Course Technology
20 Channel Center Street
Boston, Massachusetts 02210
USA

Cengage Learning is a leading provider of customized learning solutions with office locations around the globe, including Singapore, the United Kingdom, Australia, Mexico, Brazil, and Japan. Locate your local office at:
international.cengage.com/region

Cengage Learning products are represented in Canada by Nelson Education, Ltd.

To learn more about Course Technology, visit **www.cengage.com/coursetechnology**

To learn more about Cengage Learning, visit **www.cengage.com**

Any fictional data related to persons or companies or URLs used throughout this book is intended for instructional purposes only. At the time this book was printed, any such data was fictional and not belonging to any real persons or companies.

Printed in the United States of America
1 2 3 4 5 6 7 14 13 12 11 10

ABOUT THIS BOOK

Microsoft Office 2010 Introductory is designed for beginning users of Microsoft Office 2010. Students will learn to use Word, Excel, PowerPoint, Access, Outlook, and Publisher through a variety of activities, simulations, and case projects. *Microsoft Office 2010 Introductory* demonstrates the basic tools and features for each of these programs in an easy-to-follow, hands-on approach.

This self-paced, step-by-step book with corresponding screen shots makes learning easy and enjoyable. End-of-lesson exercises reinforce the content covered in each lesson and provide students with the opportunity to apply the skills they have learned. It is important to work through each lesson within a unit in the order presented, as each lesson builds on what was learned in previous lessons.

Illustrations provide visual reinforcement of features and concepts, and sidebars provide notes, tips, and concepts related to the lesson topics. Step-by-Step exercises provide guidance for using the features. End-of-lesson projects concentrate on the main concepts covered in the lesson and provide valuable opportunities to apply or extend the skills learned in the lesson. Instructors can assign as many or as few of the projects at the end of the lesson as they like.

The **Introductory** unit contains two lessons. The Microsoft Office 2010 Basics and the Internet lesson introduces students to this integrated software package by teaching Office, including starting and exiting programs; using the Ribbon and other common tools; saving files; using the Office Help system; and using Web browsers. The Microsoft Windows 7 Basics lesson teaches students the basics of the operating system and the devices that aid in its navigation. Students learn the components of the Windows 7 desktop, how to navigate around the computer using the Control Panel, managing files, using the Help system, and managing the security and maintenance of the computer's Action Center.

The lessons in the **Word** unit start by teaching the basics of document creating and editing, and then move on using Word commands to apply formatting, styles, and themes, and create elements such as numbered and bulleted lists and tables. Then students learn how to create specialized documents with multiple columns and graphics, and how to work with longer documents by adding headers, footers, and page numbers and working with document properties. Finally, students learn how to use the Mail Merge feature, how to review documents using tracked changes and comments, and how to combine different versions of a document.

The lessons in the **Excel** unit teach students spreadsheet basics, how to enter and edit data, and how to change the appearance of worksheets; how to organize a worksheet, how to prepare a worksheet for printing, and how to enter formulas and functions. They learn how to enhance a worksheet with graphics, conditional formatting, and comments. Finally, students learn how to work with multiple worksheets and workbooks, and how to create and modify charts.

The lessons in the **Access** unit teach students how to develop, design, and create tables with primary keys and field properties set for fields. They work with the program to learn how to create queries based on one or more tables and set criteria. They learn how to develop and create forms to display the data in one or more tables and use the form to find, enter, and view data. Students learn how to create reports to present data in an efficient, organized way. Finally, they learn how to use Access to merge records stored in a database with a Word document.

The lessons in the **PowerPoint** unit introduce students to presentation graphics software and teach them how to create professional-looking PowerPoint presentations. Working with the program, they learn how to enter text and graphics to create slides they can use when delivering a presentation. Students learn how to edit and enhance slides. They insert and link information from other programs such as Word and Excel, insert sound and video to enhance the slides, and create SmartArt and WordArt on the slides. Students learn how to animate objects on the slides and add transitions to the slide show to create exciting presentations. They learn how to run slide shows and deliver custom shows as well as share presentations through email and broadcasting on the Internet.

The lessons in the **Outlook** unit introduce students to e-mail basics. They learn how to create, edit, and use a Contacts list and Address Book; and how to create a signature, attach files to e-mail messages, and manage e-mail messages. Students also learn the basics of the Calendar, including how to schedule, alter, and delete appointments and events, and how to create and respond to meeting requests. They learn how to customize and print Calendars. Finally, students learn how to use the To-Do Bar; how to create, manage, and assign tasks and the Tasks list; and how to use the Journal and Notes features.

The lessons in the **Publisher** unit teach students how to create a document from a pre-designed template. Students learn how to create a business information set for use in current and future publications. Students learn how to modify a template by adding clip art, changing the font and color schemes, and inserting a building block. They learn how to create a brochure, about guides, and how to remove elements from a template, place artwork, crop pictures, and format text. Finally, students learn how to insert text from Microsoft Word, and how to use the Find and Replace feature and the spell checker.

To complete all lessons and End-of-Lesson material, this book will require approximately 75 hours.

Start-Up Checklist

Hardware

- Computer and processor 500-megahertz (MHz) processor or higher
- Memory: 256 megabytes (MB) of RAM or higher
- Hard disk: 3.5 gigabyte (GB) available disk space
- Display 1024 × 768 or higher-resolution monitor

Software:

- Operating system: Windows XP with Service Pack 3, Windows Vista with SP1, or Windows 7

INSIDE THIS BOOK

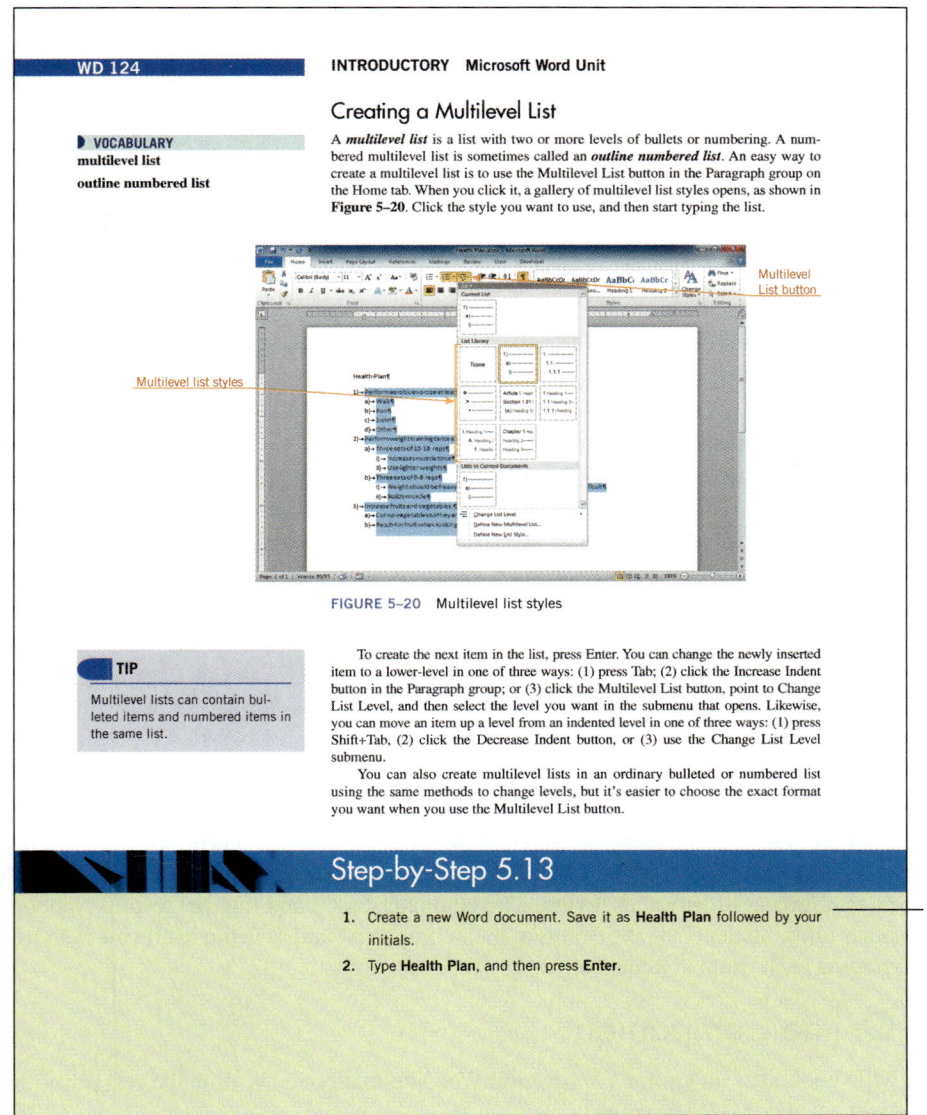

INTRODUCTORY   Microsoft Word Unit

Creating a Multilevel List

multilevel list

outline numbered list

A *multilevel list* is a list with two or more levels of bullets or numbering. A numbered multilevel list is sometimes called an *outline numbered list*. An easy way to create a multilevel list is to use the Multilevel List button in the Paragraph group on the Home tab. When you click it, a gallery of multilevel list styles opens, as shown in **Figure 5–20**. Click the style you want to use, and then start typing the list.

Multilevel List button

Multilevel list styles

FIGURE 5–20   Multilevel list styles

TIP

Multilevel lists can contain bulleted items and numbered items in the same list.

To create the next item in the list, press Enter. You can change the newly inserted item to a lower-level in one of three ways: (1) press Tab; (2) click the Increase Indent button in the Paragraph group; or (3) click the Multilevel List button, point to Change List Level, and then select the level you want in the submenu that opens. Likewise, you can move an item up a level from an indented level in one of three ways: (1) press Shift+Tab, (2) click the Decrease Indent button, or (3) use the Change List Level submenu.

You can also create multilevel lists in an ordinary bulleted or numbered list using the same methods to change levels, but it's easier to choose the exact format you want when you use the Multilevel List button.

Step-by-Step 5.13

1. Create a new Word document. Save it as **Health Plan** followed by your initials.

2. Type **Health Plan**, and then press **Enter**.

Step-by-Step Exercises offer "hands-on practice" of the material just learned. Each exercise uses a data file or requires you to create a file from scratch.

Lesson opener elements include the **Objectives, Suggested Completion Time**, and **Vocabulary Terms**.

End of Lesson elements include the **Summary, Vocabulary Review, Review Questions, Lesson Projects**, and **Critical Thinking Activities**.

Instructor Resources Disk

ISBN-13: 978-0-538-47523-5
ISBN-10: 0-538-47523-4

The Instructor Resources CD or DVD contains the following teaching resources:

The Data and Solution files for this course
ExamView® tests for each lesson
Instructor's Manual that includes lecture notes for each lesson and references to the end-of-lesson activities and Unit Review projects
Answer Keys that include solutions to the end-of-lesson and unit review questions
Critical thinking solution files that provide possible solutions for critical thinking activities
Copies of the figures that appear in the student text
Suggested Syllabus with block, two quarter, and 18-week schedule
Annotated Solutions and Grading Rubrics
PowerPoint presentations for each lesson
Spanish glossary and Spanish test bank
Appendices that include models for formatted documents, an e-mail writing guide, and a letter writing guide
Proofreader's marks

ExamView®

This textbook is accompanied by ExamView, a powerful testing software package that allows instructors to create and administer printed, computer (LAN-based), and Internet exams. ExamView includes hundreds of questions that correspond to the topics covered in this text, enabling students to generate detailed study guides that include page references for further review. The computer-based and Internet testing components allow students to take exams at their computers, and save the instructor time by grading each exam automatically.

Online Companion

This book uses an Online Companion Web site that contains valuable resources to help enhance your learning.

- Student data files to complete text projects and activities
- Key terms and definitions for each lesson
- PowerPoint presentations for each lesson
- Additional Internet boxes with links to important Web sites
- Link to CourseCasts

CourseCasts

CourseCasts—Learning on the Go. Always Available…Always Relevant.

Want to keep up with the latest technology trends relevant to you? Visit our site to find a library of podcasts, CourseCasts, featuring a "CourseCast of the Week," and download them to your mp3 player at http://coursecasts.course.com.

Our fast-paced world is driven by technology. You know because you're an active participant—always on the go, always keeping up with technological trends, and always learning new ways to embrace technology to power your life.

Ken Baldauf, a faculty member of the Florida State University Computer Science Department, is responsible for teaching technology classes to thousands of FSU students each year. He knows what you want to know; he knows what you want to learn. He's also an expert in the latest technology and will sort through and aggregate the most pertinent news and information so you can spend your time enjoying technology, rather than trying to figure it out.

Visit us at http://coursecasts.course.com to learn on the go!

SAM 2010

SAM 2010 Assessment, Projects, and Training version 1.0 offers a real-world approach to applying Microsoft Office 2010 skills. The Assessment portion of this powerful and easy to use software simulates Office 2010 applications, allowing users to demonstrate their computer knowledge in a hands-on environment. The Projects portion allows students to work live-in-the-application on project-based assignments. The Training portion helps students learn in the way that works best for them by reading, watching, or receiving guided help.

- SAM 2010 captures the key features of the actual Office 2010 software, allowing students to work in high-fidelity, multi-pathway simulation exercises for a real-world experience.

- SAM 2010 includes realistic and explorable simulations of Office 2010, Windows 7 coverage, and a new user interface.

- Easy, web-based deployment means SAM is more accessible than ever to both you and your students.

- Direct correlation to the skills covered on a chapter-by-chapter basis in your Course Technology textbooks allows you to create a detailed lesson plan.

- SAM Projects offers live-in-the-application project-based assignments. Student work is automatically graded, providing instant feedback. A unique cheating detection feature identifies students who may have shared files.

- Because SAM Training is tied to textbook exams and study guides, instructors can spend more time teaching and let SAM Training help those who need additional time to grasp concepts

Note: This textbook may or may not be available in SAM Projects at this time. Please check with your sales representative for the most recent information on when this title will be live in SAM Projects.

About the Pasework Author Team

Pasework LTD is a family-owned business with more than 90 years of combined experience authoring award-winning textbooks. They have written over 100 books about computers, accounting, and office technology. During that time, they developed their mission statement: To help our students live better lives.

Pasework LTD authors are members of several professional associations that help authors write better books. The authors have been recognized with numerous awards for classroom teaching and believe that effective classroom teaching is a major ingredient for writing effective textbooks.

From the Contributing Authors

With deep appreciation, I would like to thank my professional and talented co-authors; Kitty, Jess, and Robin for their support, friendship, expertise, and laughs as well as the team at Course Technology-Cengage Learning for working tirelessly to produce this excellent book. Thanks to Donna Gridley for making this all happen. Thanks to the editorial and production team, Allison O'Meara McDonald, Amanda Lyons, Kim Klasner, and Cathie DiMassa for their management and production skills. A special thanks to my family—David, Jennifer, Emily, and Michael—for their endless support, love, and good humor through it all.
— **Rachel Biheller Bunin**

It has been a privilege to be a part of this project and the talented group of people who have worked on it. Thank you Donna Gridley, Allison O'Meara McDonald, Amanda Lyons, and Cathie DiMassa of Course Technology for managing the many details of this project; thank you to my co-authors Kitty, Robin, and Rachel for their support and friendship while we were all busy writing; and special thanks to Rachel for her thoughtful edits of my lessons. Finally, thank you Richard and Hannah for your patience, understanding, humor, and support during this book's development. When I count my blessings, you share the top spot on my list. — **Jessica Evans**

I'd like to thank Amanda Lyons, Allison O'Meara McDonald, and Donna Gridley for inviting me to be part of this great team as well as Fran Marino for her wonderful editing of my work, Kim Klasner for juggling the many day-to-day details, Cathie DiMassa for her guidance throughout the production process, and Jeff Schwartz for managing quality control. Finally I would like to thank Rachel Biheller Bunin and Kitty Pinard for helping me out whenever I had questions. This was truly an enjoyable project. — **Ann Fisher**

Thank you especially to Donna Gridley for again giving me the opportunity to contribute to this book. Thank you to my co-conspirators, Robin, Jess, and Rachel for putting up with me. As always, the talented team at Course Technology worked together to create a fantastic book under impossible deadlines. Thanks to Cathie DiMassa, our production editor, and Allison O'Meara McDonald and Amanda Lyons, our product managers, for their tireless efforts. And as always, thank you to my family for picking up the slack while I was chained to my desk. — **Katherine T. Pinard**

Many thanks to my talented co-authors and the dedicated editorial and production team at Course Technology. Thank you Donna Gridley for the continued opportunity to be part of your team. Thank you Allison O'Meara McDonald, Amanda Lyons, and Cathie DiMassa for keeping everything on track. Thank you Jess Evans for the detailed, thorough edit. Much love to my family for their constant support. A special thank you to Brian and Jake for your patience and endurance. — **Robin M. Romer**

Kudos to a talented and gracious authoring and production team. Special thanks to Fran Marino for a superb editing job.
— **Barbara Waxer**

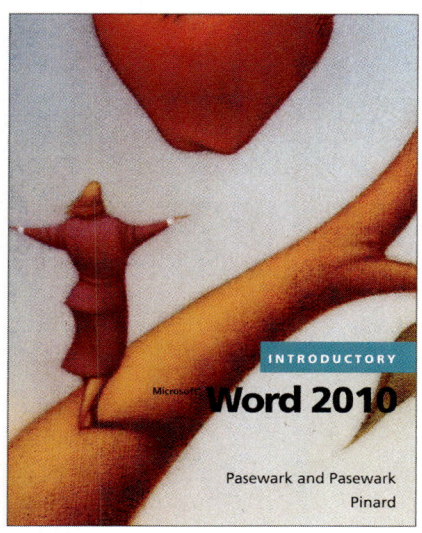

Microsoft Word 2010 Introductory
Top spiral easel back
ISBN–13: 978-0-538-47522-8
ISBN–10: 0-538-47522-6

Microsoft Access 2010 Introductory
Top spiral easel back
ISBN–13: 978-0-538-47520-4
ISBN–10: 0-538-47520-X

Microsoft Excel 2010 Introductory
Top spiral easel back
ISBN–13: 978-0-538-47521-1
ISBN–10: 0-538-47521-8

Microsoft PowerPoint 2010 Introductory
Top spiral easel back
ISBN–13: 978-0-538-47519-8
ISBN–10: 0-538-47519-6

CONTENTS

INTRODUCTORY UNIT

MICROSOFT WORD 2010

MICROSOFT EXCEL 2010

MICROSOFT ACCESS 2010

MICROSOFT POWERPOINT 2010

MICROSOFT OUTLOOK 2010

MICROSOFT PUBLISHER 2010

CAPSTONE SIMULATION

Appendix E: Models for Formatted Documents, Appendix F: E-Mail Writing Guides, and Appendix G: Letter Writing Guides are available on the Instructor Resources Disk.

OFFICE 2010 INTRODUCTORY DATA FILES GRID

APPLICATION	LESSON	DATA FILE	SOLUTION FILE
OFFICE	1	Employees\Abbott	Employees\Abbott\May Work Schedule.xlsx
		Employees\Browne	Employees\Browne\May Work Schedule.xlsx
		Employees\Gomez	Employees\Gomez\May Schedule.xlsx
		Employees\Kamnani	Employees\Gomez\May Work Schedule.xlsx
		Employees\Perez\Memo.docx	Employees\Gomez\Memo.docx
		Employees\Perez\Schedule.xlsx	Employees\Kamnani\May Work Schedule.xlsx
		Employees\Reid	Employees\Perez\Memo.docx
		Employees\Tam	Employees\Perez\Schedule.xlsx
		Employees\Wong	Employees\Reid\May Work Schedule.xlsx
			Employees\Tam\May Work Schedule.xlsx
			Employees\Wong\June Work Schedule.xlsx
WORD	1	Interview.docx	Cosmic Connections Flyer.docx
		Lecture.docx	Holiday Sale Flyer.docx
		Sale.docx	Interview Tips.docx
			\My Letters\Thank You Letter.docx
			\My Tasks\My To Do List.docx
WORD	2	Interview.docx	Customer Letter.docx
		Letter.docx	Interview Preparation.docx
		Tournament.docx	Spelling List.docx
		Web Site.docx	Tournament Notice.docx
		Workshop.docx	Web Site Tips.docx
			Workshop Checklist.docx
WORD	3	Application.docx	Application Letter.docx
		Lancaster Memo.docx	Club Minutes.docx
		Memo.docx	Fall Classes Memo.docx
		Minutes.docx	Lancaster Voting Memo.docx
		Museum.docx	Museum Visit.docx

APPLICATION	LESSON	DATA FILE	SOLUTION FILE
WORD	4	Certificate.docx	Break Room Poster.docx
		Checking Account.docx	Checking Account Info.docx
		Flyer.docx	Employee Certificate.docx
		Golf Tournament 2.docx	Employee Handbook.docx
		Handbook.docx	Formatted Golf Tournament Notice.docx
		Poster.docx	Race Track Flyer.docx
WORD	5	Diet Guidelines.docx	Agenda.docx
		Diet.docx	American Diet.docx
		Interview 2.docx	American Diet Guidelines.docx
		Invitation.docx	American Diet Title Page.docx
		NADA Memo.docx	Break Room Poster 2.docx
		Poster 2.docx	Exercise Plan.docx
		Shipping.docx	Government.docx
			Health Plan.docx
			Interview Preparation Tips.docx
			NADA Office Supplies Memo.docx
			Overnight Shipping.docx
			Resume for Jeffrey.docx
			Wedding Invitation.docx
WORD	6	Invitation2.docx	Garage Sale.docx
		Memo2.docx	HH Newsletter.docx
		Newsletter.docx	Holiday Invitation.docx
		Shelter.docx	Org Chart Memo.docx
			Park Map.docx
			Shelter News.docx
WORD	7	Diet2.docx	Correspondence Guidelines.docx
		Guidelines.docx	Diet Final.docx
		References.docx	References Formatted.docx
		Sales.docx	References Unformatted.docx
			Sales Leaders.docx
WORD	8	Bank Customers.docx	Bank Fax.docx
		Checking.docx	Bank Letter.docx
		Subscription.docx	Bank New Customer Letters.docx

APPLICATION	LESSON	DATA FILE	SOLUTION FILE
		Telephone 2.docx	Bank Template.dotx
		Telephone.docx	Combined Bank Letter.docx
			Envelope.docx
			Final Bank Letter.docx
			Hodges Envelope.docx
			Hodges Labels.docx
			Journal Addresses.docx
			Journal Subscription.dotx
			Labels.docx
			Letter with Changes Accepted.docx
			Letter with Comments.docx
			Merged Journal Letters.docx
			My Resume.docx
			Telephone Combined Solution.docx
			Telephone Etiquette 2.docx
			Telephone Etiquette.docx
WORD	Unit Review	Bagels.docx	Bagel Mania.docx
		Internet.docx	Ergonomics.docx
		Menu.docx	Greeting Card Sample.docx
		Properties.docx	Internet Terms.docx
		Recycling.docx	Island West Properties.docx
		Tenses.docx	Java Menu.docx
			Recycling Flyer.docx
			Star Contacts.docx
			Star Envelope.docx
			Star Letter.docx
			Star Merge.docx
			Star Template.dotx
			Verb Tenses.docx
EXCEL	1	Frogs.xlsx	Activity 1-1.docx
		Homes.xlsx	Activity 1-2.docx
		Names.xlsx	Frogs Census.xlsx

APPLICATION	LESSON	DATA FILE	SOLUTION FILE
		Properties.xlsx	Home Ownership.xlsx
			Last Names.xlsx
			Properties Estimates.xlsx
EXCEL	2	Birds.xlsx	Activity 2-1.docx
		Cassidy.xlsx	Activity 2-2.docx
		Central.xlsx	Birds Census.xlsx
		Mileage.xlsx	Cassidy Budget
		Shop.xlsx	Central Conference.xlsx
		TechSoft.xlsx	Mileage Chart.xlsx
		Wireless.xlsx	Technology Shop.xlsx
			TechSoft Balance Sheet.xlsx
			Wireless Bill.xlsx
EXCEL	3	Assets.xlsx	Activity 3-1.xlsx
		Chemistry.xlsx	Assets Statement.xlsx
		Club.xlsx	Chemistry Grades.xlsx
		Creston.xlsx	Club Equipment.xlsx
		Inventory.xlsx	Creston Pool.xlsx
		Time.xlsx	Inventory Purchase.xlsx
		Trade.xlsx	Time Sheet.xslx
		Utilities.xlsx	Trade Balance.xlsx
			Utilities Expenses.xlsx
EXCEL	4	Formula.xlsx	Activity 4-1.xlsx
		Investment.xlsx	Formula Practice.xlsx
		Juice.xlsx	Investment Record.xlsx
		Mackenzie.xlsx	Investment Record Updated.xlsx
		Operation.xlsx	Juice Sales.xlsx
		Zoo.xlsx	Mackenzie Development.xlsx
			Operation Results.xlsx
			Zoo Invoice.xlsx
EXCEL	5	Coyotes.xlsx	Activity 5-1.xlsx
		Exam.xlsx	Activity 5-3.xlsx
		Finances.xlsx	Coyote Stats.xlsx
		Functions.xlsx	Exam Scores.xlsx

		Golf.xlsx	Finances for *Student Name*.xlsx
		National.xlsx	Functions Worksheet.xlsx
		Reynolds.xlsx	Golf Tryouts.xlsx
		Xanthan.xlsx	National Bank.xlsx
			Reynolds Optical.xlsx
			Xanthan Promotion.xlsx
EXCEL	6	Bamboo.png	Activity 6-1.xlsx
		Beautiful.xlsx	Activity 6-2.xlsx
		Bus.bmp	Beautiful Blooms.xlsx
		City.xlsx	Bus Records.xlsx
		Creative.xlsx	City Facts.xlsx
		Eco.xlsx	Compact Cubicle.xlsx
		Logo.docx	Eco Container.xlsx
		Salary.xlsx	Roberts Statement.xlsx
		Stock.xlsx	Salary List.xlsx
		Tax.xlsx	Stock Quotes.xlsx
		Titus.xlsx	Tax Estimate.xlsx
		Top.xlsx	Time Card.xlsx
		Travel.xlsx	Titus Oil.xlsx
		Tulips.jpg	Top Films.xlsx
		Zoom.xlsx	Travel Expenses.xlsx
			Travel Expenses 2003.xlsx
			Travel Expenses Web.mht
			Zoom Salaries.xlsx
EXCEL	7	Alamo.xlsx	Activity 7-1.docx
		Annual.xlsx	Alamo Industries.xlsx
		Crystal.xlsx	Annual Income.xlsx
		Delta.xlsx	Crystal Sales.xlsx
		March.xlsx	Delta Circuitry.xlsx
		Rain.xlsx	March Income.xlsx
		Vote.xlsx	Rain Records.xlsx
			Vote Tally.xlsx
EXCEL	8	Cash.xlsx	Activity 8-1.docx
		Chico.xlsx	Activity 8-2.xlsx
		Concession.xlsx	Cash Surplus.xlsx

DATA FILES

APPLICATION	LESSON	DATA FILE	SOLUTION FILE
		Coronado.xlsx	Chico Temperatures.xlsx
		Education.xlsx	Concession Sales.xlsx
		Great.xlsx	Coronado Foundries.xlsx
		Largest.xlsx	Education Pays.xlsx
		McDonalds.xlsx	Great Plains.xlsx
		Red.xlsx	Largest Cities.xlsx
		Run.xlsx	McDonalds Report.xlsx
		Starburst.xlsx	Red Cross.xlsx
		Study.xlsx	Run Times.xlsx
			Starburst Growth.xlsx
			Study and Grades.xlsx
EXCEL	Unit Review	Club.xlsx	Club Members.xlsx
		CompNet.xlsx	Coffee Prices Job 1.xlsx
		Computer.xlsx	Coffee Prices Job 2.xlsx
		Gas.xlsx	CompNet Expenses.xlsx
		Java.docx	Computer Prices Job 1.xlsx
		Organic.xlsx	Computer Prices Job 2.xlsx
			Gas Sales.docx
			Java Menu.docx
			Java Menu Revised.docx
			Organic Financials.xlsx
ACCESS	1	Employees.accdb	Employees Solution.accdb
		Members.accdb	Members Solution.accdb
		Restaurants.accdb	Restaurants Solution.accdb
		Stores.accdb	Stores Solution.accdb
ACCESS	2	Company.accdb	Company Solution.accdb
			Interviews Solution.accdb
			Music Solution.accdb
			RetailStores Solution.accdb
			Database.accdb (student supplies filename)

DATA FILES

APPLICATION	LESSON	DATA FILE	SOLUTION FILE
ACCESS	3	Agents.accdb	Agents Solution.accdb
		Listings.accdb	Listings Solution.accdb
		Product.accdb	Product Solution.accdb
		Properties.accdb	Properties Solution.accdb
		Realtors.accdb	Realtors Solution.accdb
ACCESS	4	Broker.accdb	Broker Solution.accdb
		Class.accdb	Class Solution.accdb
		Recreation.accdb	Recreation Solution.accdb
		Teacher.accdb	Teacher Solution.accdb
ACCESS	5	Agencies.accdb	Agencies Solution.accdb
		Office.gif	
		Supplies.accdb	Supplies Solution.accdb
		Teacher.gif	
		Staff.accdb	Staff Solution.accdb
		Sales.accdb	Sales Solution.accdb
ACCESS	6	Abbott.docx	Abbott Solution.docx
		Clubs.txt	Club Officials Solution.xlsx
		InfoTech.accdb	InfoTech Solution.accdb
		Inventory.accdb	Inventory Solution.accdb
		Items.accdb	Items Solution.accdb
		Lakewood.docx	Lakewood Solution.docx
		Officials.xlsx	
		Products.xlsx	Products Solution.txt
		Sales.docx	Sales Solution.docx
		School.accdb	School Solution.accdb
		Student.txt	Student Solution.rtf
		Student Excel.xlsx	Student Word Solution.xlsx
			Swimming Solution.accdb
ACCESS	Unit Review	Dining.accdb	Dining Solution.accdb
		Favorites.accdb	Favorites Solution.accdb
		Java.accdb	Java Solution.accdb
		Meals.accdb	Meals Solution.accdb

DATA FILES

APPLICATION	LESSON	DATA FILE	SOLUTION FILE
		Personnel.accdb	Personnel Solution.accdb
		Price.accdb	Price Solution.accdb
		Reminder.docx	Reminder Solution.docx
POWERPOINT	1	Tornadoes.pptx	Tornado Report Solution.pptx
		Network.pptx	Network Summary Solution.pptx
			Critical Thinking 1-1 Sample Solution.pptx
			Critical Thinking 1-2 Sample Solution.pptx
POWERPOINT	2	EMT.potx	EMT Rosewood Solution.pptx
		EMT Class.pptx	EMT Class Spring Session Solution.pptx
		FirstAid.jpg	EMT Class Spring Session– Copy Solution.pptx
		Rose.jpg	Critical Thinking 2-1 Sample Solution.pptx
		911.wav	Critical Thinking 2-2 Sample Solution.pptx
POWERPOINT	3	DogsAndCats.pptx	Animal Shelter - Solution.pptx
			DogsAndCats Palace.pptx
		History of Cotton.pptx	History of Cotton Report Solution.pptx
		Cotton Gin.jpg	Internet Company Research Sample Solution.pptx
		Highway.jpg	My New Company Sample Solution.pptx
		Potato Chip Plant.jpg	
		Sky.jpg	
		Truck.jpg	
		cribbedding.mpg	
POWERPOINT	4	Planet Facts.docx	Astronomy Club Solution.pptx
		Planet Number of Moons.docx	Many Moons Solution.pptx
		The Moons of Jupiter.docx	Our Solar System Solution.pptx
		Planets.xlsx	Solar System Handouts Solution.docx
		Sun Facts.pptx	Critical Thinking 4-1 Sample Solution.pptx
			Critical Thinking 4-1 Sample Solution.pptx
			Package Solar System – Solution (not provided-this is a CD file)

DATA FILES

APPLICATION	LESSON	DATA FILE	SOLUTION FILE
POWERPOINT	Unit Review	Coffee Prices.xlsx	Java Cafe Info.pptx
		Java Cafe.pptx	Project 3 Template Presentation.pptx
			Project 4 Template Presentation.pptx
			States Project 1.pptx
			States Project 2.pptx
OUTLOOK	1	Alien Lecture.docx	
PUBLISHER	1	Yoga.pub	New Card solution.pub
		Yoga solution.pub	My Card solution.pub
		Coupon.pub	Birthday Card solution.pub
		Coupon solution.pub	My Letter solution.pub
	2	Ballet Classes.pub	Brochure solution.pub
		Ballet Classes solution.pub	Guides solution.pub
		Flyer.pub	Bookmarks solution.pub
		Flyer solution.pub	
		Layers.pub	
		Layers solution.pub	
CAPSTONE SIMULATION		Potential Customers.txt	Billing Solution.xlsx
		Presentation.pptx	Form Letter Solution.docx
			GWFlyer Solution.pub
			Income Statement Solution.xlsx
			Invoice Solution.docx
			Letterhead Template Solution.dotx
			May Invoice Solution.docx
			Neighbors Solution.accdb
			Presentation Solution.pptx
			Resident Letters Solution.docx

Estimated Time for Unit:
2.5 hours

INTRODUCTION UNIT

LESSON 1   **1.5 HRS.**

Microsoft Office 2010 Basics and the Internet

LESSON 1   **1 HR.**

Microsoft Windows 7 Basics

🕐 **Estimated Time:**
1.5 hours

LESSON 1

Microsoft Office 2010 Basics and the Internet

▪ OBJECTIVES

Upon completion of this lesson, you should be able to:

- Explain the concept of an integrated software package.
- Start an Office program from Windows.
- Explain the features of the program window.
- Know how to use the Ribbon and contextual tools.
- Open an existing Office file.
- Save and close an Office file.
- Know the shortcut for opening recently used files.
- Use the Office Help system.
- Exit an Office program.
- Use a Web browser to visit a Web site.

▪ VOCABULARY

Backstage view

contextual tab

gallery

home page

Internet

link

Live Preview

Microsoft Office 2010 (Office)

Mini toolbar

Ribbon

ScreenTip

SharePoint

shortcut menu

SkyDrive

tab

task pane

toolbar

Uniform Resource Locator (URL)

Web browser

World Wide Web (Web)

Introducing Microsoft Office 2010

Microsoft Office 2010 (or ***Office***) is a collection of software programs. Word is the word-processing program. It enables you to create documents such as letters and reports. Excel, the spreadsheet program, lets you work with numbers to prepare items such as budgets or to calculate loan payments. Access, the database program, organizes information such as addresses or inventory items. The presentation program is PowerPoint. It is used to create electronic slides that usually accompany a verbal presentation. Outlook is the program used to send and receive e-mail messages and to organize information about people, appointments, and to-do lists. Publisher, the desktop-publishing program, helps you design professional-looking documents such as newsletters and brochures. OneNote is a notes program that you can use to store your thoughts, ideas, or other information.

Office is available in many suites, each of which includes a different combination of programs. For example, the Professional suite includes Word, Excel, Access, PowerPoint, Outlook, Publisher, and OneNote. Other Office suites include additional or fewer programs.

Because Office is an integrated program, the programs can be used together. For example, numbers from a spreadsheet can be included in a letter created in the word processor or in a presentation. This ability to share information between programs ensures consistency and accuracy. It also saves time because you don't have to reenter the same information in several programs.

Starting an Office Program

To start an Office program, click the Start button on the taskbar, click All Programs, and then click Microsoft Office. A list of the Office programs available on your computer appears, as shown in **Figure 1–1**. Click the name of the program you want to start.

Click the Microsoft Office folder to see all the programs

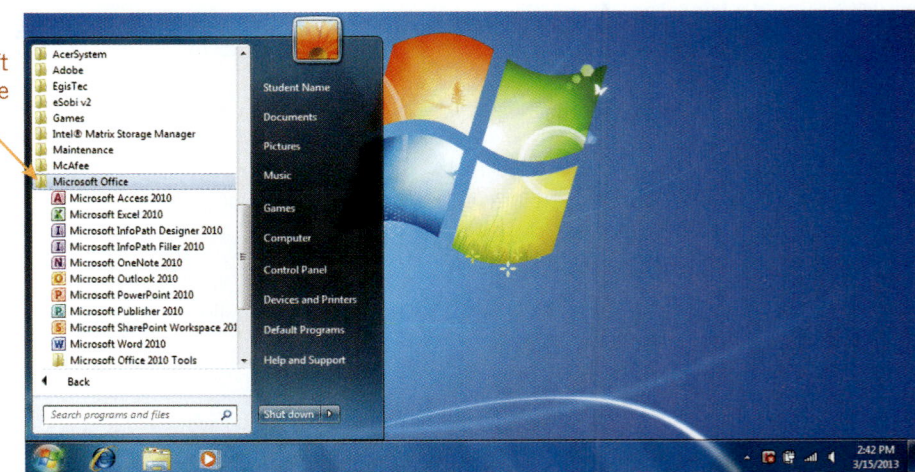

FIGURE 1–1   Microsoft Office folder

Step-by-Step 1.1

1. On the taskbar, click the **Start** button. The Start menu appears.

2. Click **All Programs**. The left side of the Start menu changes to show the All Programs menu.

3. Click **Microsoft Office**. The Microsoft Office folder expands to show all the Office programs installed on the computer, as shown in Figure 1–1.

4. Click **Microsoft PowerPoint 2010**. PowerPoint starts and opens a blank presentation.

5. Click the **Start** button, and then click **All Programs**.

6. Click **Microsoft Office**, and then click **Microsoft Word 2010**. Word starts and opens a blank document, as shown in **Figure 1–2**.

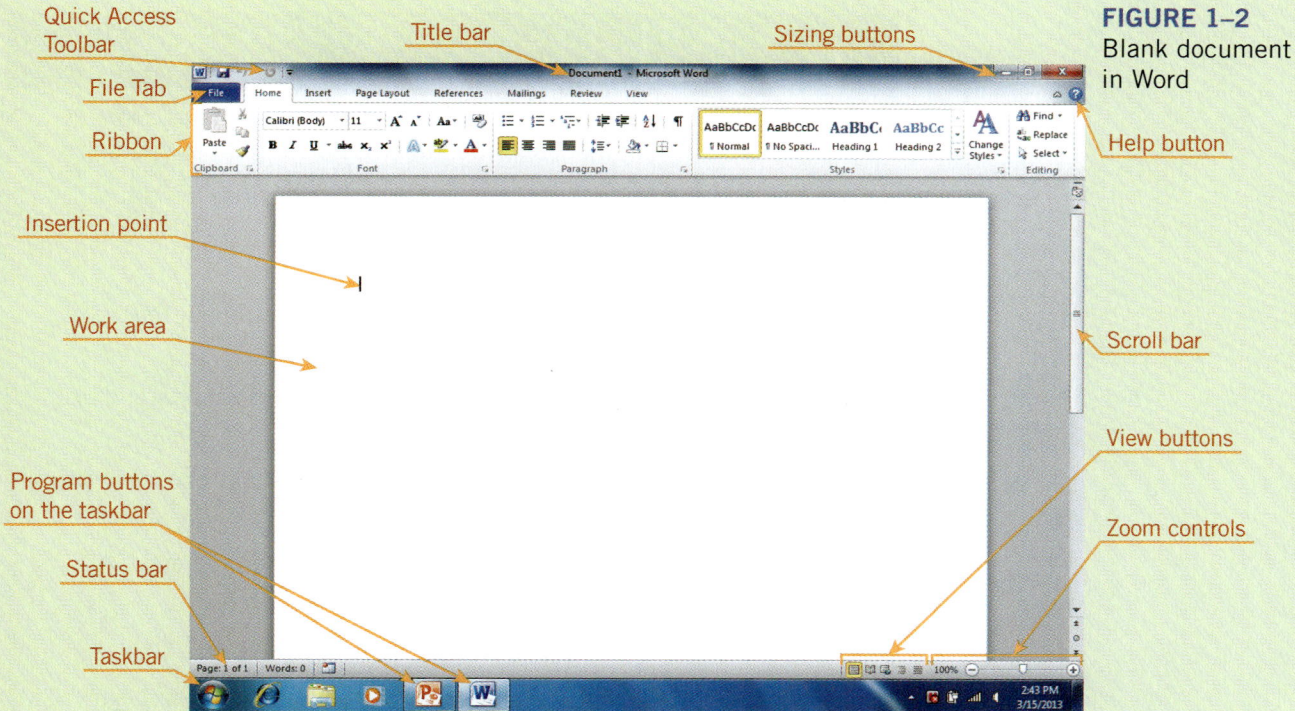

Quick Access Toolbar

Title bar

Sizing buttons

File Tab

Ribbon

Insertion point

Work area

Program buttons on the taskbar

Status bar

Taskbar

Help button

Scroll bar

View buttons

Zoom controls

FIGURE 1–2
Blank document in Word

7. Leave Word and PowerPoint open for the next Step-by-Step.

When working in Office programs, you can open more than one file at a time. You can open multiple files in the same program and you can open files in different Office programs, such as Word and Excel. To move between the open files, just click the taskbar button for the file you want to display.

▶ **VOCABULARY**

program window

Ribbon

tab

Exploring the Program Window

A **program window** is the rectangle that contains the open program, tools for working with the file, and the work area. Look carefully at the parts of the Word program window labeled in Figure 1–2. These parts are similar in all of the Office programs and are described in **Table 1–1**.

TABLE 1–1 Items in the program window

ITEM	FUNCTION
File tab	Opens Backstage view, which contains commands for working with files, such as opening, saving, printing, and creating new files
Quick Access Toolbar	Provides access to commonly used commands
Title bar	Shows the names of the program and the current file
Sizing buttons	Change the size of the program window and exit the program
Ribbon	Contains tabs from which you can choose a variety of commands
Microsoft Office Help button	Opens the Help window for the program
Work area	Displays the file you are working on
Insertion point	Shows where text will appear when you begin typing
Scroll bars	Shift other areas of the file into the work area
Status bar	Provides information about the current file and process
View buttons	Change how a file is displayed in the work area

TIP

You can shrink the Ribbon to one line that shows the tab names by double-clicking any tab or clicking the Minimize the Ribbon button. You can then see more of the work area. To redisplay the entire Ribbon, double-click any tab or click the Expand the Ribbon button.

Using the Ribbon

The **Ribbon** is "command central" for the Office programs. The **tabs** on the Ribbon organize the commands into related tasks. The commands on each tab are organized into groups. Each group contains buttons that you click to choose a command. By clicking a **button** to choose a command, you give the program instructions about what you want to do. Each button has an icon (a small picture) or words to remind you of its function. **Figure 1–3** labels the different parts of the Ribbon.

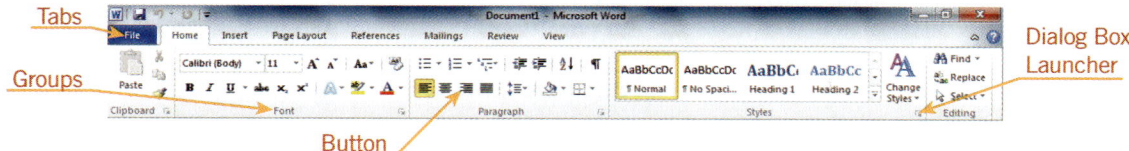

FIGURE 1–3   Parts of the Ribbon

To use the buttons on the Ribbon, you need to click them. When a step instructs you to click a button or something else on the screen, it means to do the following: Move the mouse until the pointer is positioned on top of the item, press the left mouse button, and then release it.

Generally, when you click a button, something happens. Some buttons are like light switches: one click turns on the feature and the next click turns it off. This is often referred to as a *toggle*. Other buttons have two parts: a button that you can click to choose the command and an arrow that you can click to open a **menu**, or list, of other commands related to the button. **Figure 1–4** compares these different types of buttons.

> **▶ VOCABULARY**
>
> **button**
>
> **menu**
>
> **gallery**
>
> **Live Preview**

> **● TIP**
>
> If you do not know a button's function, move the pointer to the button, but do not click. A ScreenTip with the button's name and a short description of its function appears below the button. You'll learn more about ScreenTips later in this lesson.

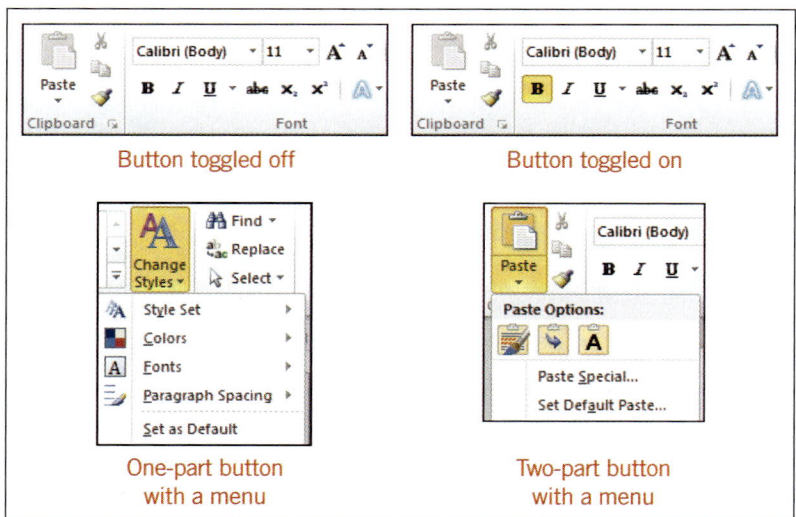

FIGURE 1–4   Buttons on the Ribbon

Some buttons open galleries. A **gallery** shows the options available for a command. Galleries can also appear directly on the Ribbon. If a gallery on the Ribbon has more options than can be displayed on the Ribbon, you click its More button to open the full gallery. **Live Preview** lets you see how a gallery option affects your file without making the change. Point to an option in a gallery, but do not click it. Your file shows the results of selecting that option. After you find the option you want, you click that option to make the change in your file. See **Figure 1–5**.

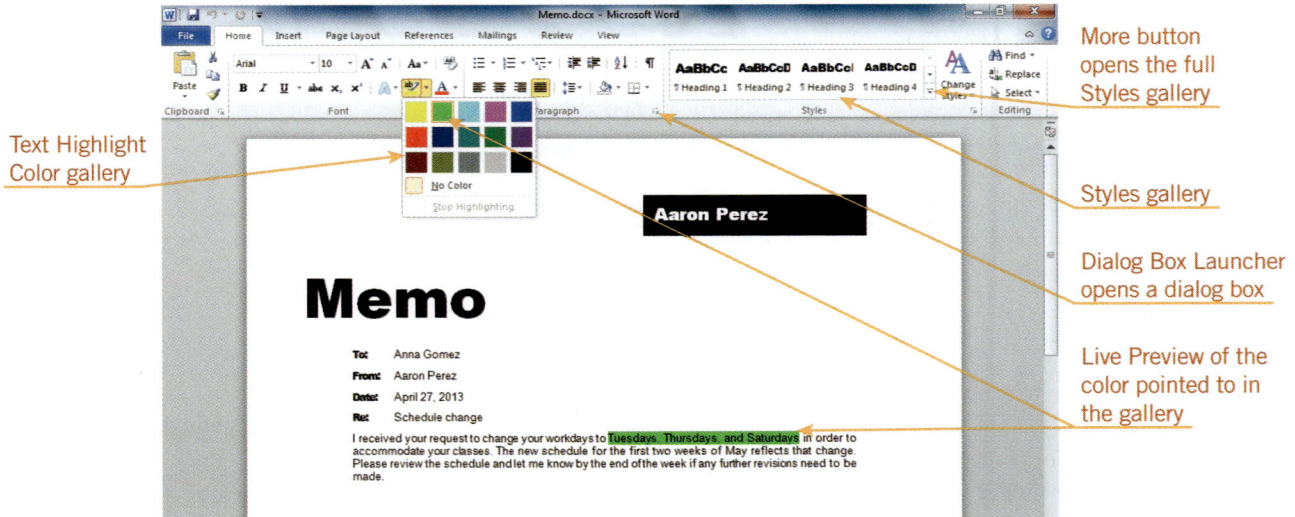

FIGURE 1–5   Text Highlight Color gallery

▶ **VOCABULARY**

dialog box

task pane

The Ribbon has one other type of button—the Dialog Box Launcher, which you click to open a dialog box or task pane to choose additional settings. A *dialog box* is a window that opens on top of the program window. A *task pane* is a pane, like a windowpane, that opens on the right or left side of the program window. The Dialog Box Launcher appears in the lower-right corner of any group that has a related dialog box or task pane, as shown in Figure 1–5.

The buttons on the Ribbon change depending on settings in your computer and on how big the program window is. For example, the Home tab on the Ribbon in Word might look like the one shown in **Figure 1–6a** or the one shown in **Figure 1–6b**. If the Ribbon on your screen looks like the one shown in Figure 1–6b, you will need to make some adjustments as you follow the steps in this book. For example, look at the Editing group in both figures. A step might say "In the Editing group, click the Find button." If your screen looks like the one shown in Figure 1–6b, you will need to click the Editing button on the Ribbon first to expand the group, as shown in Figure 1–6b. Then you can click the Find button.

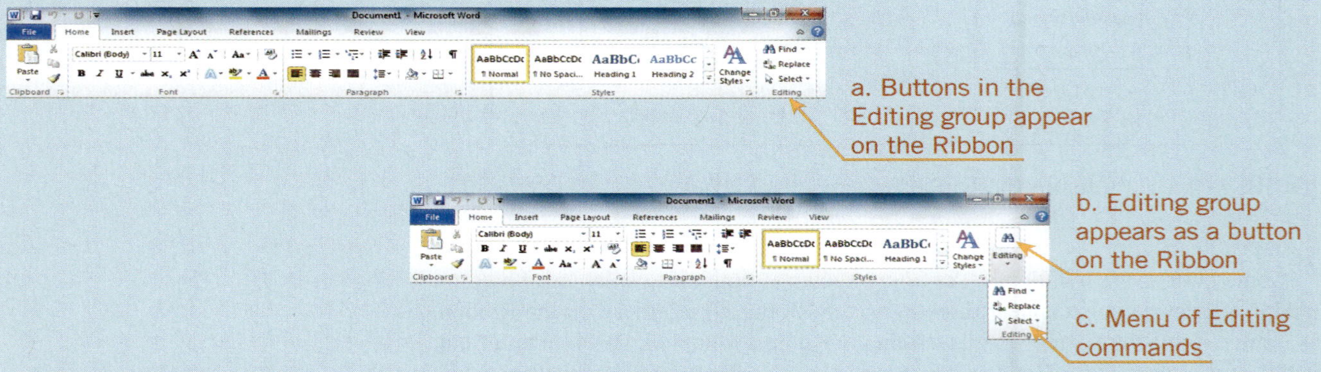

a. Buttons in the Editing group appear on the Ribbon

b. Editing group appears as a button on the Ribbon

c. Menu of Editing commands

FIGURE 1–6   Ribbons with different computer settings

Understanding Contextual Tools

Some tools appear as you work. Because they appear only when you need them, the workspace stays neat and uncluttered. This type of tool is called a contextual tool.

Contextual tabs appear on the Ribbon only when you select certain items in a file, and they contain commands related to that item. The contextual tabs work the same way as the standard tabs, but they disappear when you click somewhere else on the screen. **Figure 1–7** shows the Drawing Tools contextual tabs. In this case, there is only one—the Format tab. This tab appears when you click a drawing in a Word document.

▶ **VOCABULARY**
contextual tabs
toolbar
Mini toolbar

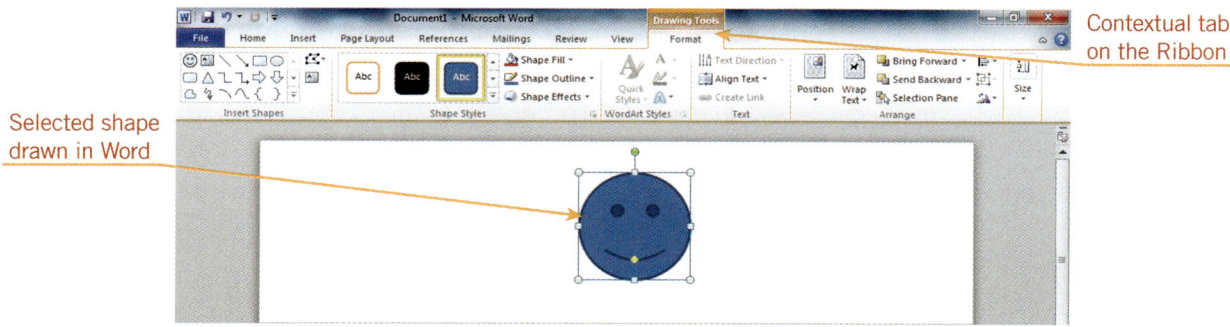

FIGURE 1–7   Drawing Tools Format contextual tab

A *toolbar* contains buttons that you can click to perform common tasks. The Ribbon is actually a large toolbar. Office also has a special contextual toolbar called the Mini toolbar. It contains buttons you click to choose common formatting commands. The *Mini toolbar* appears in the work area after you drag the pointer over text while holding down the left mouse button. (This is called *selecting* text.) The Mini toolbar is transparent when you first select text. After you move the pointer over the Mini toolbar, it comes into full view and you can click buttons on it to format the selected text. The Mini toolbar disappears when you move the pointer off the toolbar, press a key, or press a button on your mouse. All of the commands on the Mini toolbar are also available on the Ribbon. **Figure 1–8** shows the Mini toolbar in both transparent and full view.

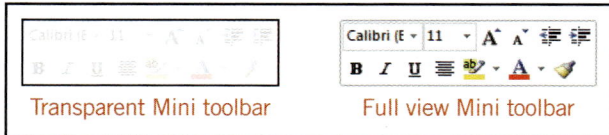

Transparent Mini toolbar   Full view Mini toolbar

FIGURE 1–8   Mini toolbar

TIP

If the Mini toolbar disappears, you can right-click the selected text to show it again.

shortcut menu

Backstage view

Another contextual tool available in Office is the shortcut menu. *Shortcut menus* appear when you right-click something in the program window. They contain lists of commands that you are most likely to use with the item or text you right-clicked. The shortcut menu can be a faster way to get to these commands than the Ribbon. **Figure 1–9** shows the shortcut menu that opens when you right-click selected text. Notice that the Mini toolbar appears at the top of this shortcut menu. (It does not appear on all shortcut menus; only on those shortcut menus that appear when you right-click selected text.)

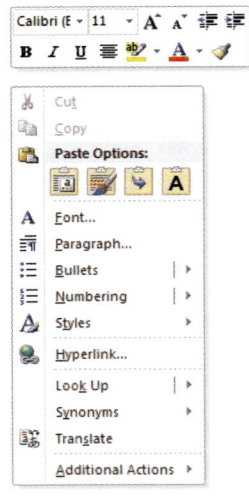

FIGURE 1–9   Shortcut menu with Mini toolbar

Using Backstage View to Open, Save, and Close Files

In all Office programs, you open, save, and close files in the same way—in Backstage view. *Opening* a file means loading a file from a disk into the program window. *Saving* a file stores it on a disk. *Closing* a file removes it from the program window. A disk can be an internal storage location, such as a hard drive, or an external storage location, such as a Flash drive, a CD-ROM, or a DVD.

Backstage view, shown in **Figure 1–10**, is where you do "behind the scenes" tasks such as getting information about the current file, creating new files, printing the current file, sharing files with others, and defining file properties. The specific tasks available change depending on the program you are using. To display or hide Backstage view, you click the File tab on the Ribbon. The banner along the left side of the window is called the navigation bar. From the navigation bar, you can click frequently used commands or open the tabs to see commands related to that task.

WARNING

The Close button in the upper-right corner of the title bar and the Exit command at the bottom of the navigation bar in Backstage view both exit the program, closing the file that is open. To return to the current file, click any tab on the Ribbon.

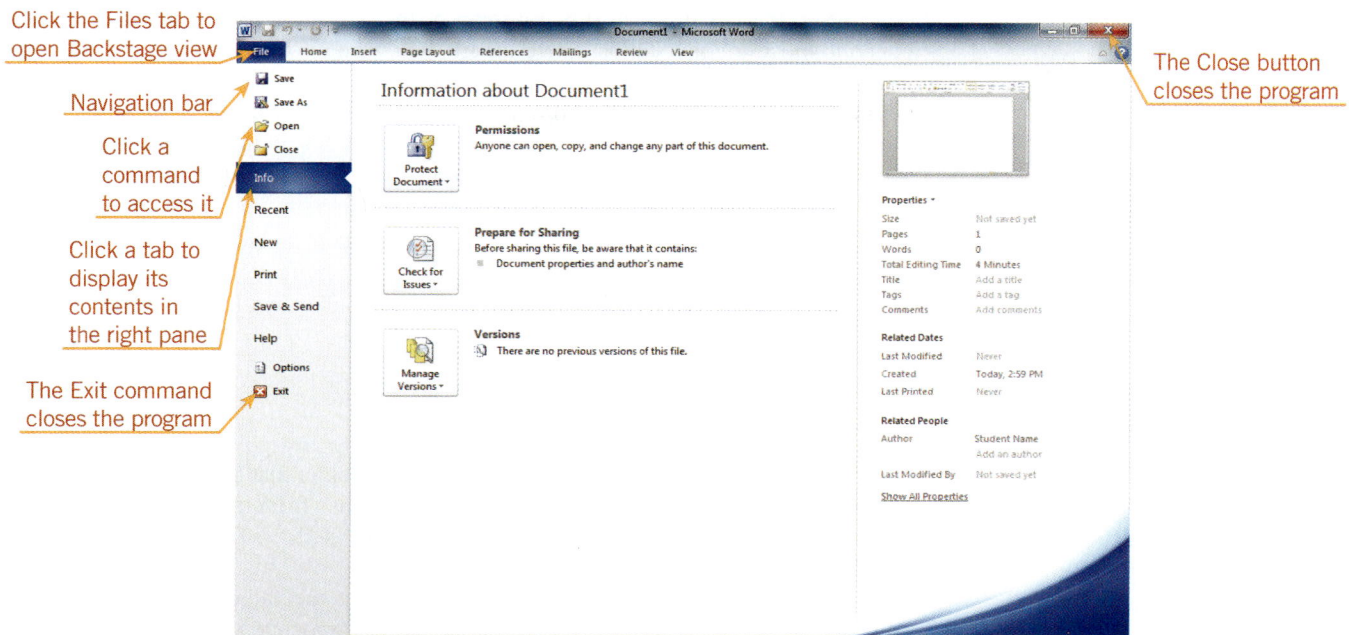

Click the Files tab to open Backstage view

Navigation bar

Click a command to access it

Click a tab to display its contents in the right pane

The Exit command closes the program

The Close button closes the program

FIGURE 1–10   Backstage view

Opening an Existing File

To open an existing file, you can click the File tab on the Ribbon, and then, in Backstage view, click Open. The Open dialog box appears, as shown in **Figure 1–11**.

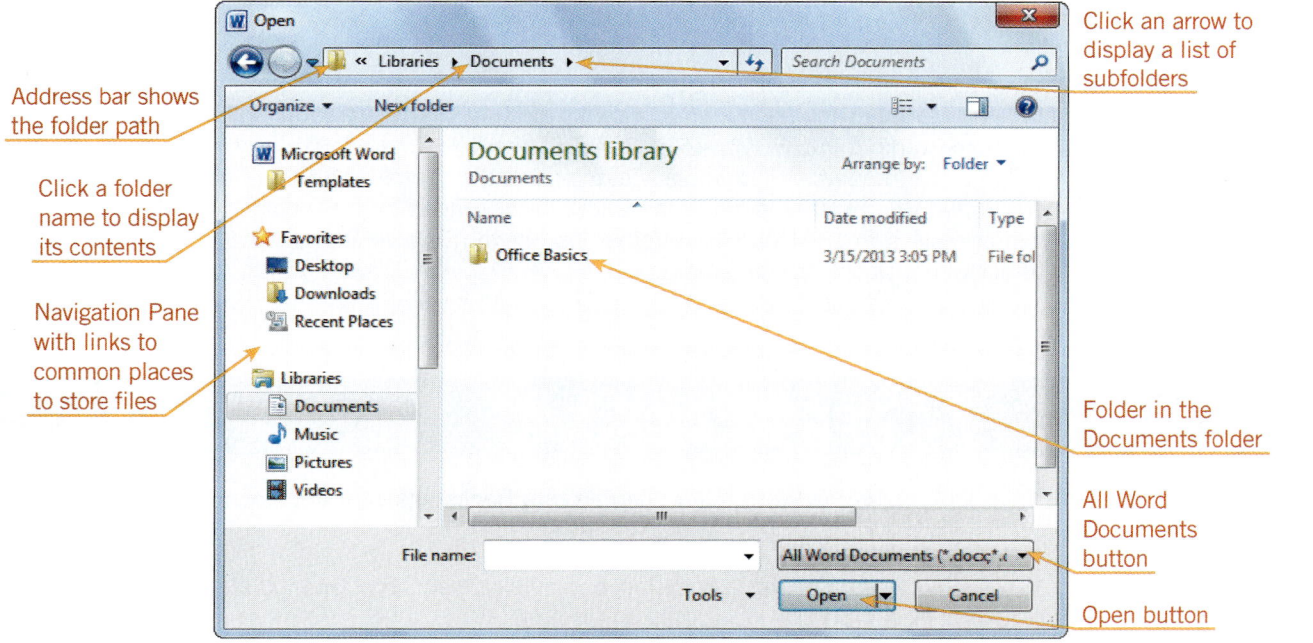

Address bar shows the folder path

Click a folder name to display its contents

Navigation Pane with links to common places to store files

Click an arrow to display a list of subfolders

Folder in the Documents folder

All Word Documents button

Open button

FIGURE 1–11   Open dialog box

TIP

To create a new, blank file in any Office program, click the File tab on the Ribbon, and then click New. In the New tab that appears in the right pane, double-click the type of new file you want to create.

EXTRA FOR EXPERTS

In the Open dialog box, you can double-click a file to open it in the program without clicking Open.

From the Open dialog box, you can open a file from any available disk. You need to move to the location where the file you want to open is stored. The Address bar, near the top of the dialog box, shows the path of the drive and folders to your current location. Below the Address bar, a list shows the folders or files that are in the current location. The Navigation Pane, on the left side of the dialog box, provides links to common places on your computer to store files. To change the path, you can use a combination of the following methods:

- Click a link in the Navigation Pane.
- Click a location in the Address bar to see the folders and files in that location.
- Click a location arrow in the Address bar to see a list of folders in that location, and then click the folder you want to see.
- Double-click a folder to see its folders and files.

The Open dialog box shows all the files in the folder that the active program can open. To see all the files in the folder, choose All Files from the Files of type button located above the Open button. After you have located the file you want to open, click the file to select it and then click Open.

Any file you open that was downloaded from the Internet, accessed from a shared network, or received as an e-mail attachment may open in a read-only format, called Protected View. In Protected View, you can see the file contents, but you cannot edit, save, or print them until you enable editing. To do so, click the Enable Editing button on the Information Bar, as shown in **Figure 1-12**.

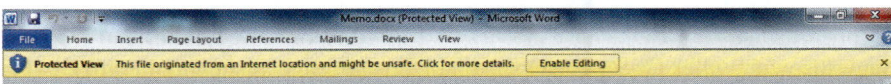

FIGURE 1–12   File in Protected View

The files you need for each lesson in this book are stored in a series of folders. The main folder shows the name of the program whose unit you are working on. For example, *Office Basics* is the main folder for this unit. The next folder lists the current lesson in the unit. For example, *Lesson 01* is the subfolder for this lesson. Your instructor will tell you where to find the folders that store the Data Files you need for this book. The following Step-by-Step includes steps for moving to this location. All other lessons in this book instruct you to open the *File name* from the drive and folder where Data Files are stored.

Step-by-Step 1.2

1. In Word, click the **File** tab. Backstage view appears in the work area, as shown in Figure 1–10.

2. On the navigation bar, click **Open**. The Open dialog box appears, as shown in Figure 1–11.

3. Use the Navigation Pane and Address bar to move to the location of your Data Files.

4. Double-click the **Office Basics** folder, and then double-click the **Lesson 01** folder. The Employees folder is stored in the Lesson 01 folder, as shown in **Figure 1–13**.

Employees folder in the Office Basics\Lesson 01 folder

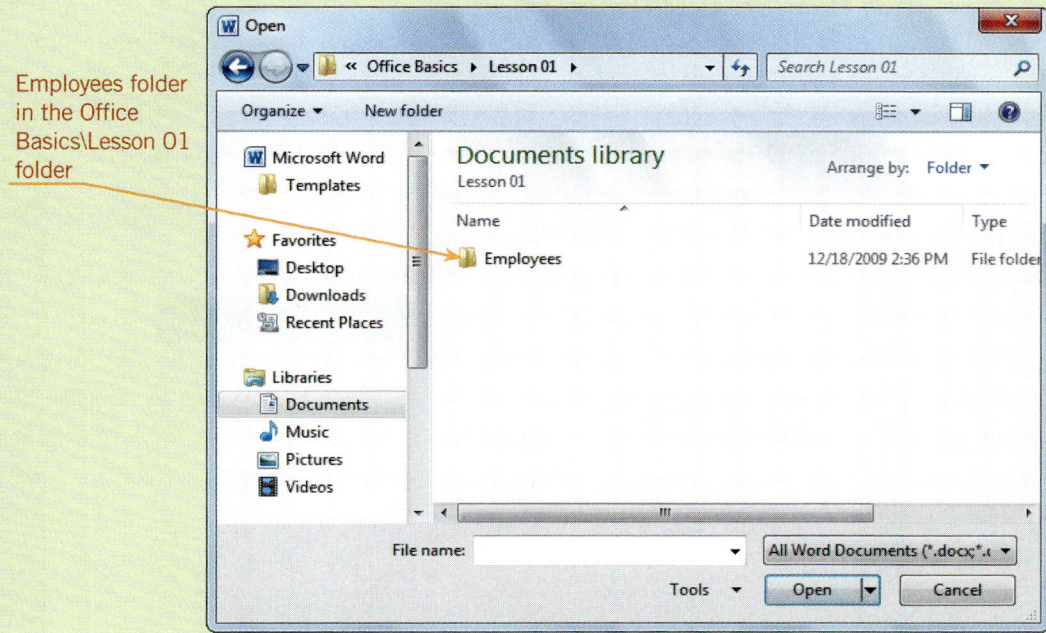

FIGURE 1–13
Employees folder

5. Double-click the **Employees** folder. The folders within the Employees folder appear, as shown in **Figure 1–14**.

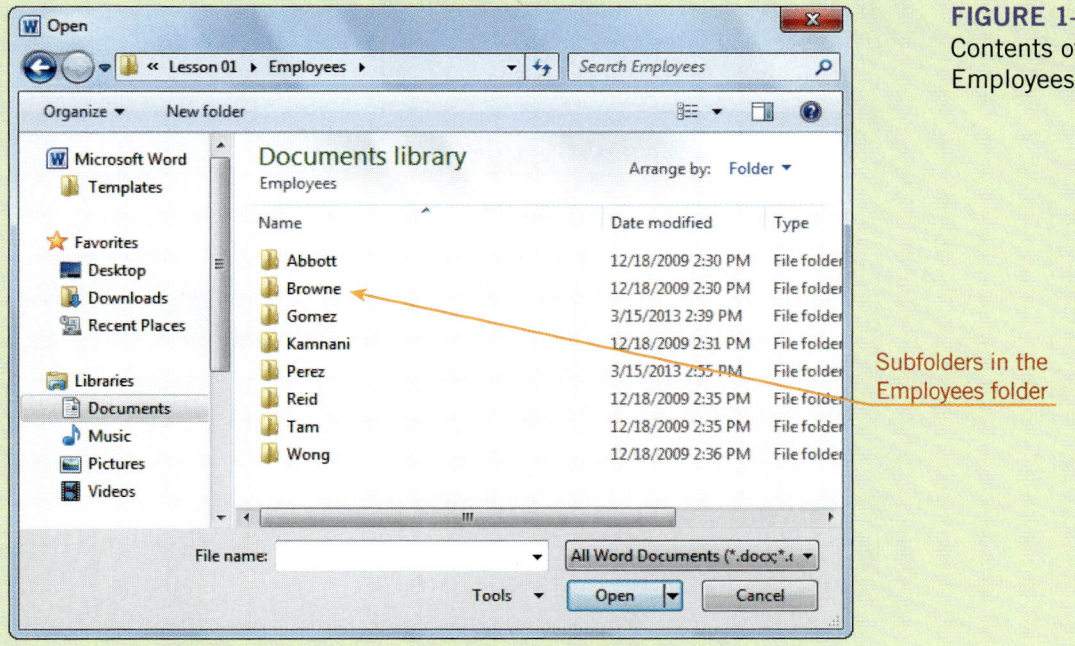

Subfolders in the Employees folder

FIGURE 1–14
Contents of the Employees folder

6. Double-click the **Perez** folder. The Word document named Memo.docx appears in the Perez folder.

7. Click the **All Word Documents** button to display the list of file types. Click **All Files** to display all the files in the Perez folder. In addition to the *Memo.docx* file, there is also an Excel file named Schedule.xlsx.

8. Click **Memo.docx** to select it, and then click **Open**. The document appears in the work area of the Word program window, as shown in **Figure 1–15**.

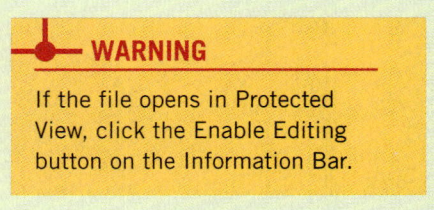

FIGURE 1–15
Memo.docx document

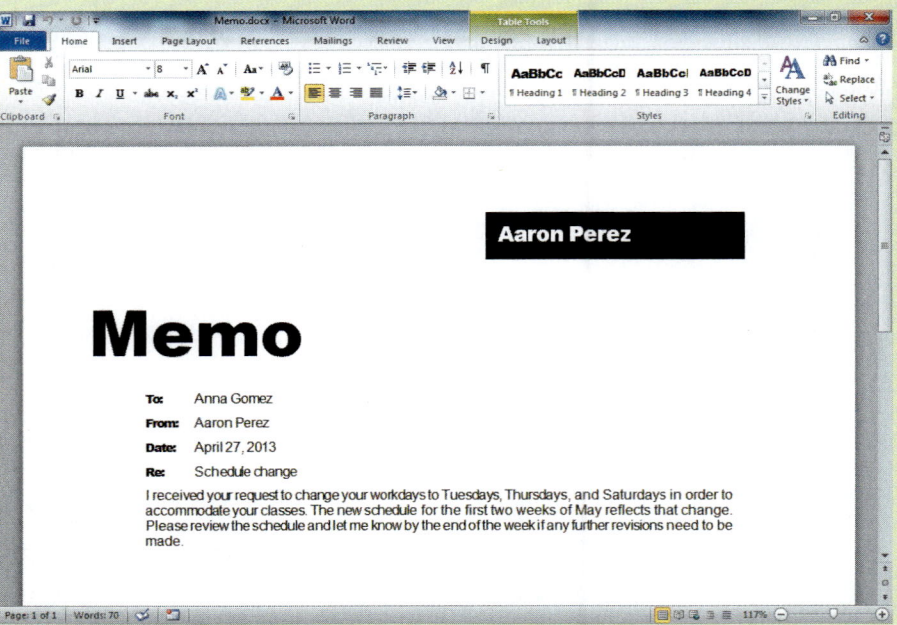

WARNING

If the file opens in Protected View, click the Enable Editing button on the Information Bar.

9. Leave the file open for the next Step-by-Step.

You can see how folders help organize and identify files. The *Perez* folder also contains the spreadsheet referenced in the memo that includes the work schedule for the first two weeks in May.

Step-by-Step 1.3

1. On the taskbar, click the **Start** button, click **All Programs**, click **Microsoft Office**, and then click **Microsoft Excel 2010**. Excel starts and a blank spreadsheet appears.

2. On the Ribbon, click the **File** tab, and then on the navigation bar, click **Open**. The Open dialog box appears.

3. Use the Navigation Pane and Address bar to display the **Employees** folder.

4. Double-click the **Employees** folder, and then double-click the **Perez** folder.

5. Double-click **Schedule.xlsx**. The Schedule.xlsx workbook appears in the Excel work area, as shown in **Figure 1–16**.

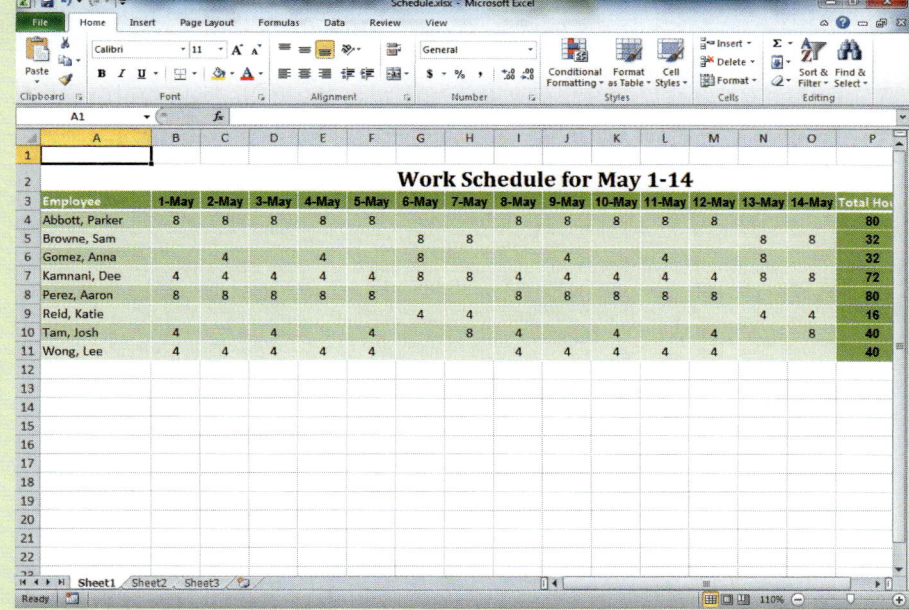

FIGURE 1–16
Schedule.xlsx workbook

Employee	1-May	2-May	3-May	4-May	5-May	6-May	7-May	8-May	9-May	10-May	11-May	12-May	13-May	14-May	Total Hours
Abbott, Parker	8	8	8	8	8			8	8	8	8	8			80
Browne, Sam						8	8						8	8	32
Gomez, Anna		4		4		8			4		4		8		32
Kamnani, Dee	4	4	4	4	4	8	8	4	4	4	4	4	8	8	72
Perez, Aaron	8	8	8	8	8			8	8	8	8	8			80
Reid, Katie						4	4						4	4	16
Tam, Josh	4		4		4		8	4		4		4		8	40
Wong, Lee	4	4	4	4	4			4	4	4	4	4			40

Work Schedule for May 1-14

6. Leave the workbook open for the next Step-by-Step.

► **VOCABULARY**
file extension

Saving a File

Saving is done using one of two methods. The Save command saves a file on a disk using its current name and save location. The Save As command lets you save a file with a new name. You can also use the Save As command to save a file to a new location.

Each program has a different *file extension*, which is a series of letters Office adds to the end of a file name that identifies in which program that file was created. **Table 1–2** lists the file extensions for the four main Office programs. Depending on how your computer is set up, you might not see file extensions.

TABLE 1–2   File extensions for the main Office programs

PROGRAM	FILE EXTENSION
Word	.docx
Excel	.xlsx
PowerPoint	.pptx
Access	.accdb

Step-by-Step 1.4

1. On the Ribbon, click the **File** tab, and then on the navigation bar, click **Save As**. The Save As dialog box appears, as shown in **Figure 1–17**.

FIGURE 1–17
Save As dialog box

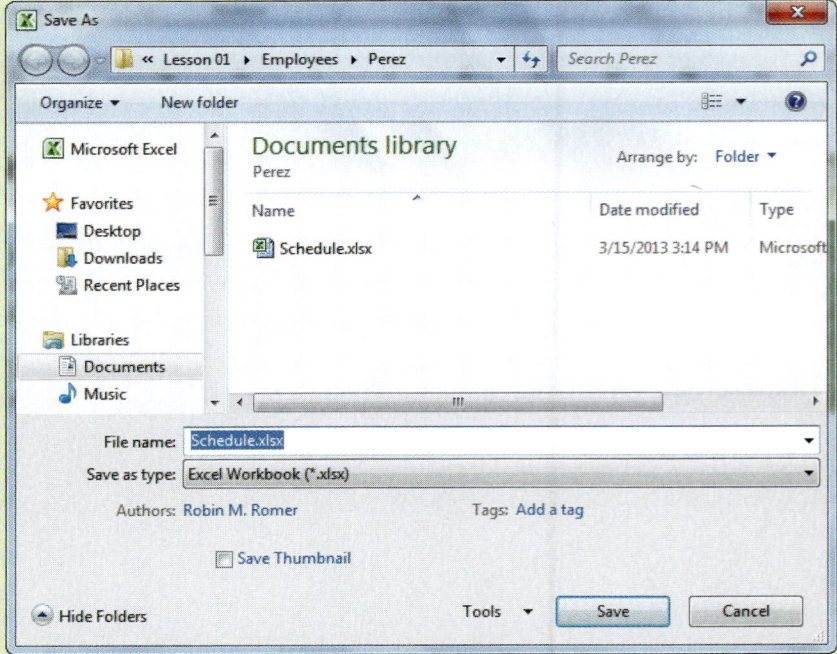

2. In the File name box, type **May Schedule** followed by your initials.

3. In the Address bar, click the **Employees** location arrow. The list of folders in the Employees folder appears, as shown in **Figure 1–18**.

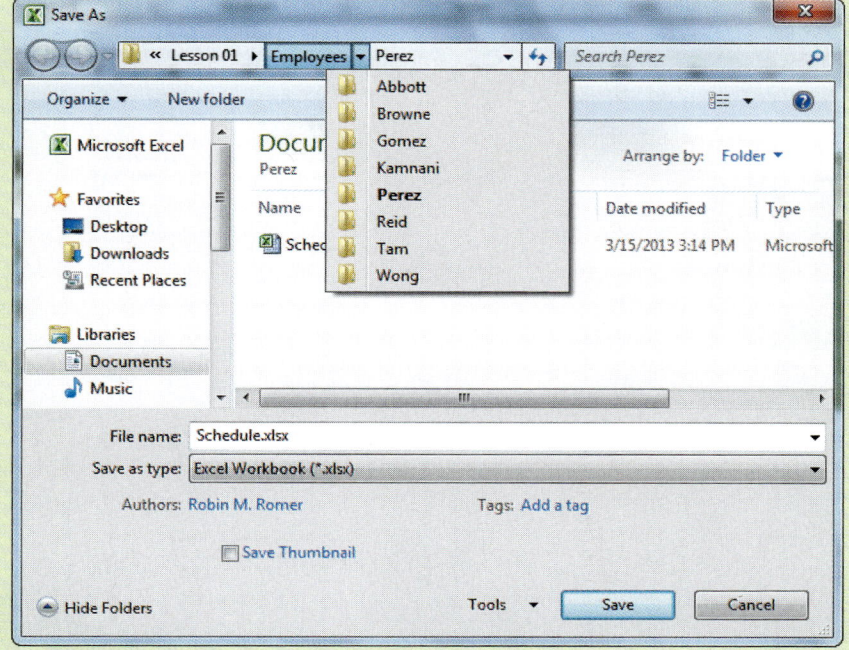

4. Click **Gomez**.

5. Click **Save**. The workbook is saved with the new name in the Gomez folder.

6. Leave the workbook open for the next Step-by-Step.

TIP

To save changes to a file using the same name and location, you can click the Save button on the Quick Access Toolbar.

Sharing a File

Often the purpose of creating a file is to share it with others—sending it attached to an e-mail message for someone else to read or use, collaborating with others on the same document, posting it for others to review. You can do all of these things in Background view from the Save & Send tab, as shown in **Figure 1–19**.

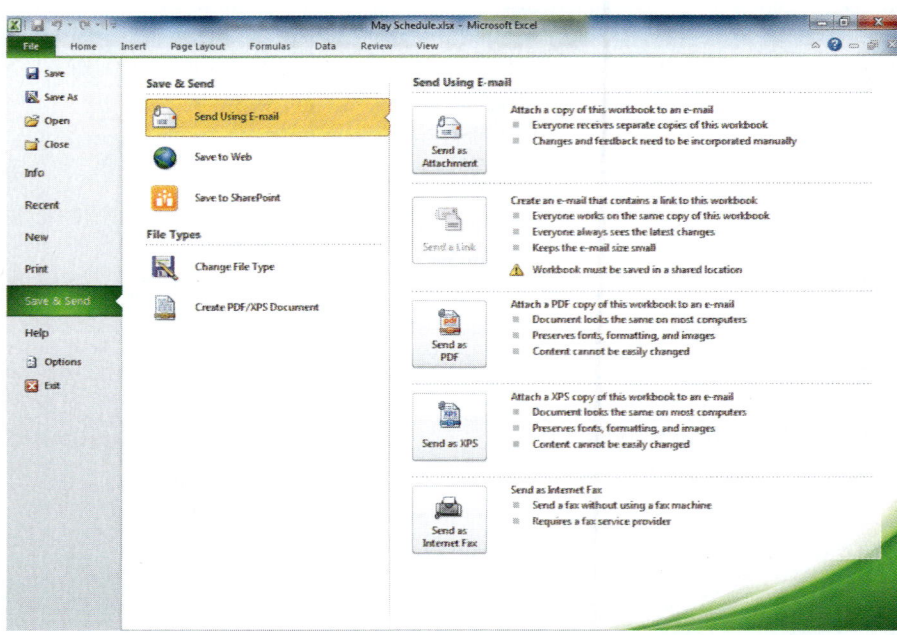

FIGURE 1–19   Save & Send tab

▶ **VOCABULARY**
SkyDrive

SharePoint

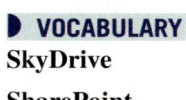 **EXTRA FOR EXPERTS**

SkyDrive is a folder on the Internet that you can access with your Windows Live ID. You can also use your Web browser to access your SkyDrive folder.

When you send a file using e-mail, you can attach a copy of the file, send a link to the file, or attach a copy of the file in a PDF or another file format. You can also save to Windows Live SkyDrive or SharePoint, which are online workspaces where you can make the file available to others for review and collaboration. *SkyDrive* is a Web site provided by Microsoft. (SkyDrive is not available from Backstage view in Access.) To use SkyDrive, you need a Windows Live ID. *SharePoint* is a site set up by an organization, such as school, business, or nonprofit group. Files saved to either location can be worked on by more than one person at the same time. The changes are recorded in the files with each author's name and the date of the change. A Web browser is used to access and edit the files. You choose who can have access to the files.

Step-by-Step 1.5

1. On the Ribbon, click the **File** tab. Backstage view opens, showing the Info tab.

2. On the navigation bar, click **Save & Send**. The Send Using E-mail options appear, as shown in Figure 1–19.

3. In the center pane, click **Save to Web**. The Save to Windows Live options appear, as shown in **Figure 1–20**.

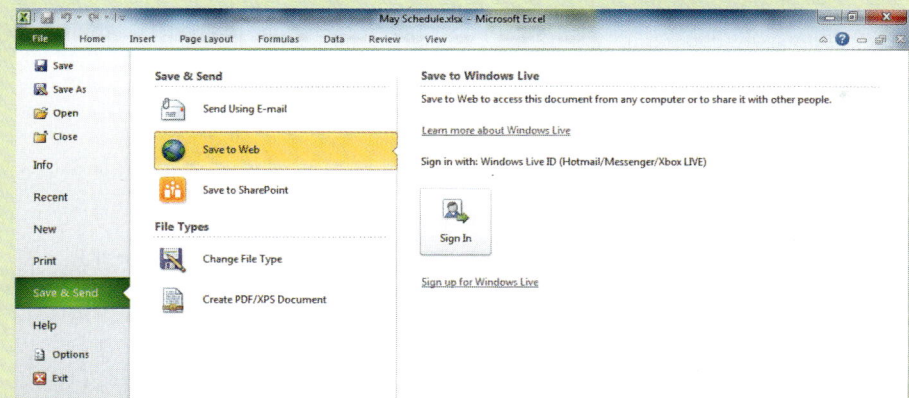

FIGURE 1–20
Save to SkyDrive options

4. Click **Save to SharePoint**. The Save to SharePoint options appear.

5. Leave the workbook open for the next Step-by-Step.

Closing a File

You can close an Office file by clicking the File tab on the Ribbon, and then clicking Close. If you use the Close command in Backstage view to close a file, the program remains open and ready for you to work on another file. You can also close the file by clicking the Close button on the right side of the title bar. If you close a file with the Close button, and no other file is open in that program, the program also closes.

Another way to quickly open recently used files is to click the Start button, point to the name of the program that you used to work on the recently opened file, and then click the name of the file in the list that appears. Keep in mind that you must be working on the same computer you recently used to work on that file. If the file you want to open on doesn't appear in the list, you might have worked on too many other files more recently and need to use another method to open the file.

TIP

If you try to close a file that contains changes you have not saved, a dialog box appears, asking whether you want to save the file. Click Save to save and close the file. Click Don't Save to close the file without saving. Click Cancel to return to the program window without saving or closing the file.

Step-by-Step 1.6

1. In Backstage view, on the navigation bar, click **Close**. The May Schedule.xlsx workbook closes, and Excel remains open.

2. On the taskbar, click the **Microsoft Word** button to make the window active. The Memo.docx document appears.

3. Click the **File** tab, and then click **Close**. The Memo.docx document closes, and Word remains open.

4. Leave Word, Excel, and PowerPoint open for the next Step-by-Step.

Opening Recently Used Files

⊶ **WARNING**

If the file you want to open from a shortcut is on an external storage device such as a Flash drive, make sure that the correct device is in the drive before you click the shortcut.

Office provides a shortcut for opening recently used files: Click the File tab in any of the Office programs, and then click Recent in the navigation bar. The Recent Documents list appears in the right pane and shows the names of the files that were most recently opened in that program. The most recently opened file appears at the top of the list, as shown in **Figure 1–21**. When a new file is opened, each file name moves down to make room for the new most recently opened file. To open one of the files, you simply click it. You can click a pin next to a file in the Recent Documents list to keep that file "pinned" to the list. If the file you are looking for is not in the Recent Documents list, use the Open command to locate and select the file.

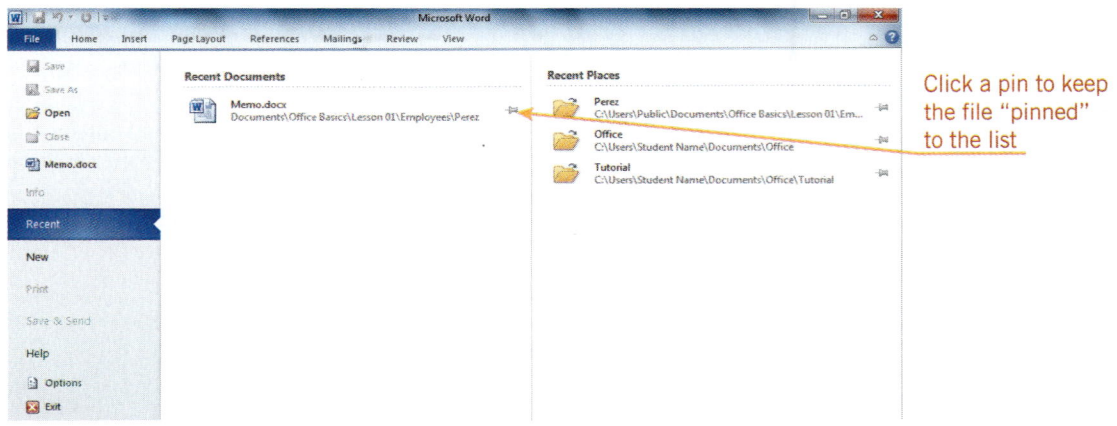

Click a pin to keep the file "pinned" to the list

FIGURE 1–21   Recent Documents list

Getting Help in Office

This lesson has covered only a few of the many features of the Office programs. You will learn more about each of these programs in their individual units later in this text. But you can always learn more by using the Office Help system, which includes ScreenTips and the Help window.

Using ScreenTips

A *ScreenTip* is a box that appears when you point to a button. As shown in **Figure 1–22**, it contains the button's name and a description of its function. It can also include a link to more information and a keyboard shortcut if the command has one. To view a ScreenTip, you just point to a button—do not click it. If the ScreenTip includes a link to more information, you can press the F1 key to open the Help window with that topic displayed.

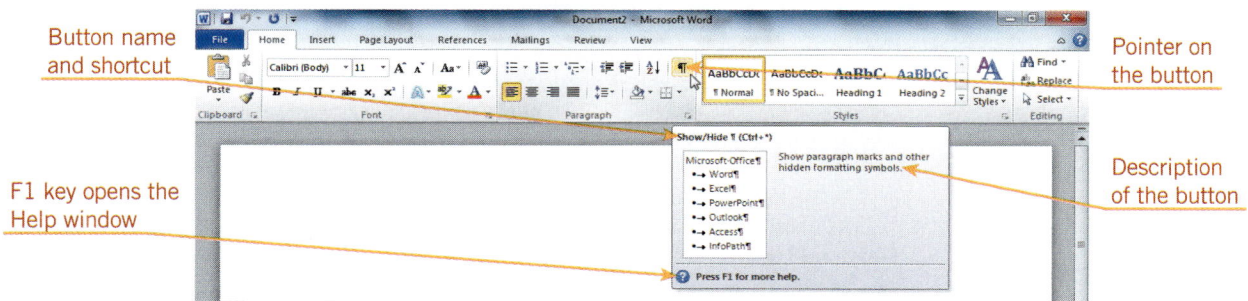

FIGURE 1–22   ScreenTip for the Show/Hide ¶ button

Using the Help Window

To get specific help about topics relating to the program you are using, you use the Help window, as shown in **Figure 1–23**. To open the Help window, click the Microsoft Office Help button located near the upper-right corner of the program window. Each program has its own Help window.

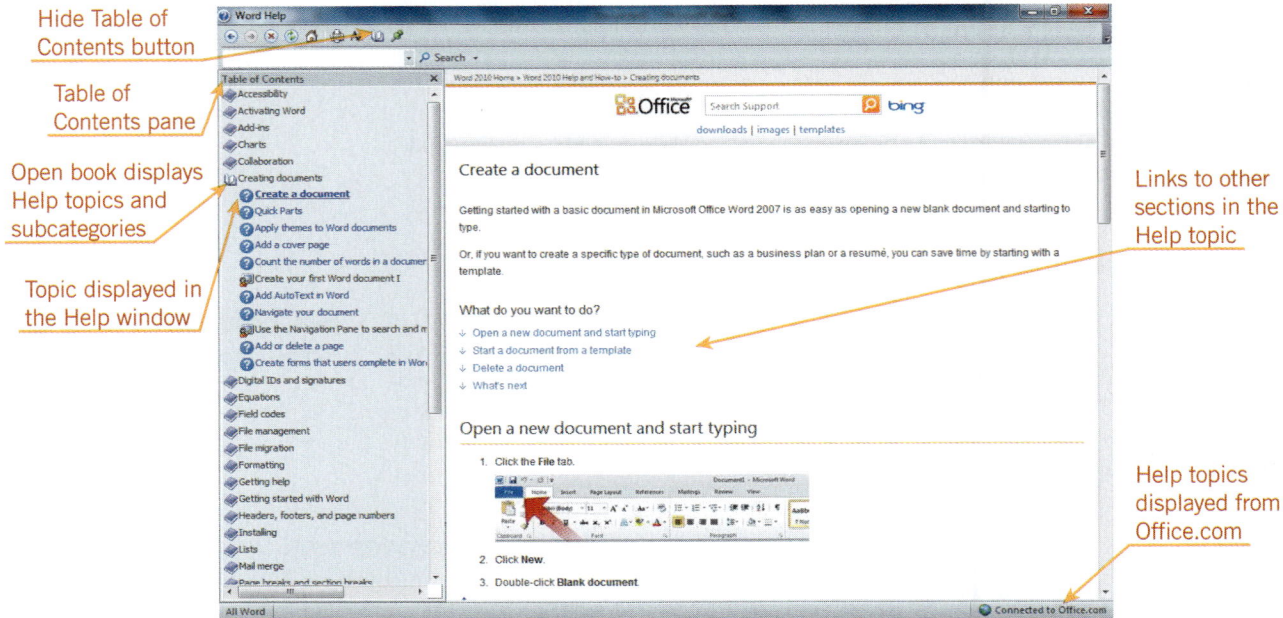

Hide Table of Contents button

Table of Contents pane

Open book displays Help topics and subcategories

Topic displayed in the Help window

Links to other sections in the Help topic

Help topics displayed from Office.com

FIGURE 1–23   Word Help window with Table of Contents

You can search the Help system by browsing topics or using keywords. The Help and How-to window lists general categories of topics in the Help system. You can also display the Table of Contents and browse topics from that list. To see the information in a category, click the text link.

When you want to search for help on a particular topic, you can type a word or phrase in the *Type words to search for* box. After you click the Search button, a list of Help topics that include the keyword appears in the Help window, and you can click a topic to display it in the Help window.

Step-by-Step 1.7

1. On the Ribbon, click the **File** tab. Click **New** on the navigation bar. Click the **Create** button in the right pane. A new document opens.

2. In the Clipboard group, point to the **Show/Hide ¶** button, resting the pointer on the button. The button's ScreenTip appears, as shown in Figure 1–22.

3. Read the button's name and a description of its function in the ScreenTip.

4. On the Ribbon, point to the **Microsoft Word Help** button and read its ScreenTip.

5. Click the **Microsoft Word Help** button. The Help topics are listed in the window.

6. If the Word Help window that appears does not fill the screen, click the **Maximize** button on the title bar.

7. On the Help window toolbar, click the **Show Table of Contents** button if necessary to display a list of Help topic categories. If you have Internet access, this information is downloaded from Office.com rather than only the Help topics stored on your computer.

8. In the Table of Contents pane, click the **Creating documents** book, and then click the **Create a document** topic. The topic appears in the right side of the Word Help window, as shown in Figure 1–23. If you are not connected to Office.com, the list of topics and the topic content you see may differ.

9. Read the contents of the Help window.

10. On the Word Help window toolbar, click the **Hide Table of Contents** button to hide the pane.

11. In the Word Help window, click the **Type words to search for** box.

12. Type **print**, and then click the **Search** button to display the list of search results shown in **Figure 1–24**. If you are not connected to the Internet, your list of search results will differ.

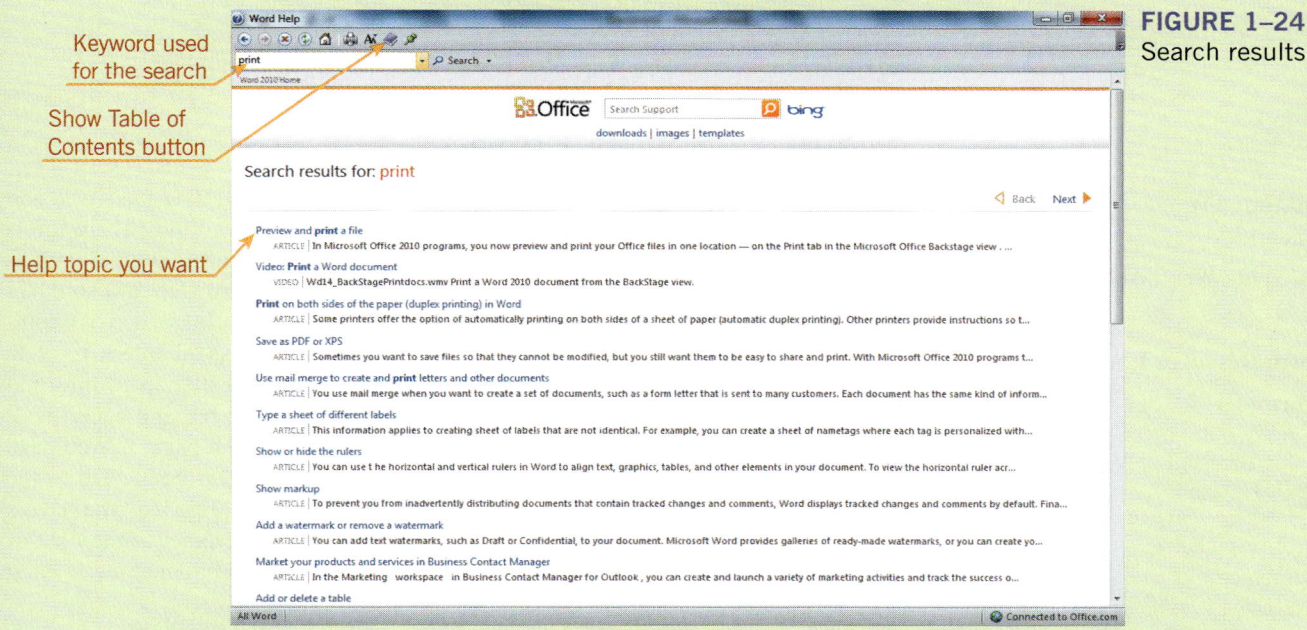

Keyword used for the search

Show Table of Contents button

Help topic you want

FIGURE 1–24
Search results

13. Search the list of results until you find **Preview and print a file**. Click it to display information in the Word Help window.

14. Read the information, clicking links as needed to learn how to print in Word.

15. On the Word Help window title bar, click the **Close** button. The Help window closes.

Exiting an Office Program

The Exit command, which is located in Backstage view, closes the open Office program. If you have only one file open in that program, you can also click the Close button on the right side of the title bar. If you have not saved the final version of your file, a dialog box opens, asking whether you want to save your changes. Click Yes to save and close the file and exit the program. When you exit an Office program, the program window closes.

Step-by-Step 1.8

1. Click the **File** tab. Notice the files listed on the right side of the menu. These are the most recently used files mentioned previously in this lesson.

2. Click **Exit**. Word closes and Excel appears on the screen.

3. On the Excel title bar, click the **Close** button [x]. Excel closes, and PowerPoint appears on the screen.

4. Click the **File** tab, and then click **Exit** button. The desktop reappears on the screen.

Viewing a Web Page

▶ **VOCABULARY**

Internet

World Wide Web (Web)

link

Uniform Resource Locator

Web browser

◗ **INTERNET**

You can connect your computer to the Internet in a variety of ways. You might use a telephone line (called a dial-up connection) or a high-speed connection through your local cable company or a special telephone service called DSL. You might also connect without any phone lines or cables by using a wireless connection. The connection you have depends on your service provider, how much you are willing to spend, and the way your computer is connected to the provider.

The **Internet** is a vast network of computers that are located all over the world and linked to one another. The Internet allows people around the world to share information and ideas using Web pages, blogs, e-mail, chat or text messaging, as well as other services. Connecting to the Internet requires special hardware and software and an Internet service provider (ISP). Before you can use the Internet, your computer needs to be connected, and you should know how to access the Internet.

The **World Wide Web** (or **Web**) is a system of computers that share information by means of links on Web pages. A **link** is text (often colored and underlined) or a graphic that you click to "jump" to another location or Web page. A Web page is a document specially formatted to be displayed on computers connected to the Internet. To find a Web page, the Web uses an address system. Just like you have a home address, each Web page has an address on the Web. The fancy name for this type of address is **Uniform Resource Locator** (**URL**—you pronounce each letter separately: U-R-L). Examples of URLs are:

http://www.senate.gov

http://www.microsoft.com

http://www.cengage.com

To view Web pages, you need special software called a **Web browser**. Internet Explorer is the Web browser that is packaged with computers that run Windows. **Figure 1–25** shows a Web page using Internet Explorer as a browser.

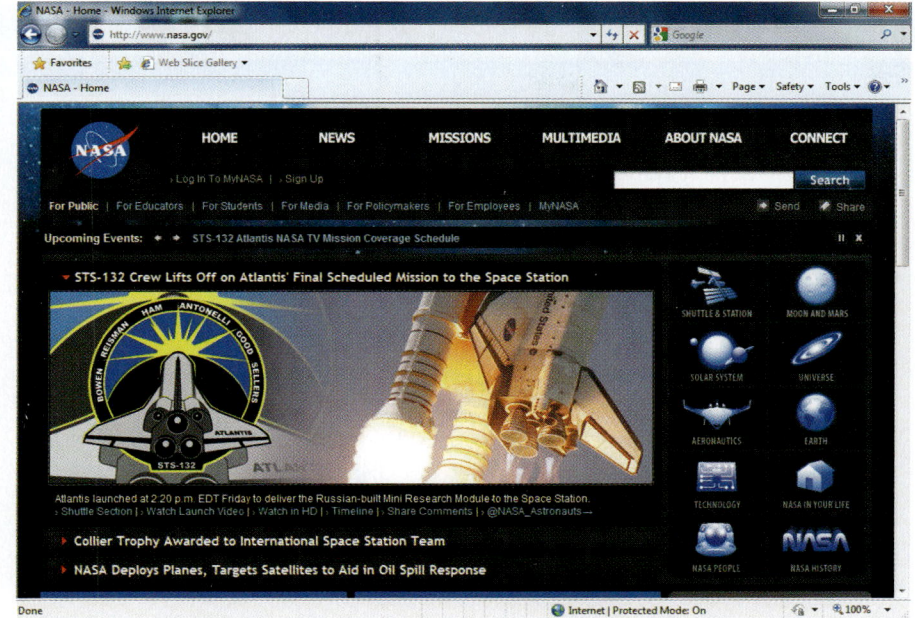

FIGURE 1–25 Internet Explorer Web browser

INTERNET

The length of time it takes to load a page depends upon the speed of your connection as well as the file size of the page you are viewing. If you want to go to a different address or click a link you can see on the page, you do not have to wait for the page to finish loading. Even when you cannot see the entire page, you can type a different URL in the Address bar or click a link on the partially loaded page.

To go to a specific Web page, you click the Address bar in your browser, type the URL, and then press Enter. You can jump to other pages by clicking links on the page you are viewing. Click the Back button to move back to previous pages you viewed, and click the Forward button to move to subsequent pages you viewed. Click the Home Page button to load your ***home page*** (or *start page*), which is the first page that opens when you start your browser.

▶ VOCABULARY
home page

TECHNOLOGY CAREERS

You can use the Internet to research different careers in business. Find out about careers in business by typing the following URL in the Address bar in your browser: *www.careers-in-business.com*.

Step-by-Step 1.9

1. On the taskbar, click the **Internet Explorer** taskbar button . The home page begins loading.

2. Click the **Address bar**, type **www.nasa.gov**, and then press **Enter**. The NASA home page appears in the browser, as shown in Figure 1–25.

3. Click a link to see more information.

4. Click the **Back** button  to return to the previous page.

5. Click another link to display a different page.

6. Click the **Home** button 🏠 to return to the home page for your computer.

7. On the title bar, click the **Close** button ❌. Internet Explorer closes.

SUMMARY

In this lesson, you learned:

- Microsoft Office 2010 is a combination of programs that can include a word-processor program, a spreadsheet program, a database program, a presentation program, a schedule/organizer program, a desktop publishing program, and a notes program. The files of these programs can be used together.

- Office programs can be started by clicking the Start button, clicking All Programs, clicking Microsoft Office, and then clicking the program name.

- The basic parts of the program window are similar in all of the Office programs.

- The Ribbon is "command central" for all the Office programs. Commands are organized in groups on tabs on the Ribbon. You click a button to choose the command you want. Some buttons open a menu of additional commands or a gallery of options.

- Contextual tabs on the Ribbon, the Mini toolbar, and shortcut menus are tools that appear when you work with a specific object in the program window.

- No matter which Office program you are using, the files are opened, saved, and closed the same way.

- You can open an existing file from the Backstage view. The Open dialog box enables you to open a file from any available disk or directory. You can open recently used files quickly by clicking the file name in the Recent Documents list in Backstage view.

- To exit an Office program, click the Exit button in Backstage view, or click the Close button on the program window title bar.

- The Office Help system provides additional information about the many features of the Office programs. In the Help window, you can browse topics, use the Table of Contents or use the *Type word to search for* box to get information. If your computer is connected to the Internet, you see Help topics and additional information from Office.com.

- Internet Explorer is a Web browser. You can use it to view Web pages.

◼ VOCABULARY REVIEW

Define the following terms:

Backstage view	Microsoft Office 2010 (Office)	tab
contextual tab	Mini toolbar	task pane
gallery	Ribbon	toolbar
home page	ScreenTip	Uniform Resource Locator (URL)
Internet	SharePoint	Web browser
link	shortcut menu	World Wide Web (Web)
Live Preview	SkyDrive	

■ REVIEW QUESTIONS

WRITTEN QUESTIONS

Write a brief answer to each of the following questions.

1. List the four main programs that are included in Office 2010.

2. How do you start an Office program?

3. What are the location and the function of the following: title bar, Ribbon, and status bar?

4. What is the difference between the Save and Save As commands?

5. Describe two ways to get help in an Office program.

TRUE / FALSE

Circle T if the statement is true or F if the statement is false.

T   F   **1.**   Excel is the spreadsheet program in Office.

T   F   **2.**   You must type a file extension if you want to include it in the file name.

T   F   **3.**   To save a file with a different name and to a different location, click the Save button on the Quick Access Toolbar.

T   F   **4.**   Live Preview lets you see how an option affects your file without making the change.

T   F   **5.**   When you point to a button on the Ribbon, a gallery appears that shows the button's name and a description of its function.

FILL IN THE BLANK

Complete the following sentences by writing the correct word or words in the blanks provided.

1. A(n) _____ is the rectangle that contains the open program, tools for working with the file, and the work area.

2. _____ appear when you right-click something in the program window. They contain lists of commands that you are most likely to use with the item or text you right-clicked.

3. _____ is where you do "behind the scenes" tasks such as getting information about the current file, creating new files, printing the current file, and sharing files with others.

4. You can save a file to _____, which is an online workspace provided by Microsoft where you can make the file available to others for review and collaboration.

5. To view Web pages, you need special software called a(n) _____.

■ PROJECTS

PROJECT 1–1

1. Start Word.

2. Start Excel. Use the Open dialog box to locate the **Employees** folder in the Data Files. Open the **Schedule.xlsx** Data File from the **Perez** folder.

3. Use the Save As command to save the workbook in the **Abbott** folder as **May Work Schedule** followed by your initials.

4. Repeat the process to save the file in the **Browne**, **Gomez**, **Kamnani**, **Reid**, **Tam**, and **Wong** folders.

5. Close the **May Work Schedule** workbook and exit Excel. Word remains on the screen.

6. Use the Open dialog box to open the **Memo.docx** Data File from the **Perez** folder.

7. Save the document in the **Gomez** folder with the same name followed by your initials.

8. Close the document, and then exit Word.

PROJECT 1–2

1. Start Word and open the Word Help window.

2. Search for how to minimize the Ribbon, and then open the *Minimize the ribbon* Help topic.

3. Read the information in the Help topic, and then follow the directions to minimize the Ribbon.

4. Click the Insert tab to display the full Ribbon.

5. In the Pages group, click the Blank Page button. A new page is added to the document, and the Ribbon minimizes again.

6. Follow the directions in the Help topic to expand the Ribbon.

7. Close the Word Help window, and then exit Word. If prompted to save changes, click No.

PROJECT 1–3

1. Open your Web browser.

2. Go to the Microsoft Web site at *www.microsoft.com*.

3. Search for information about at least two Microsoft programs.

4. Return to your home page.

5. Close your Web browser.

■ CRITICAL THINKING

ACTIVITY 1–1

The Office Professional suite can include Word, Excel, Access, PowerPoint, Outlook, Publisher, and OneNote. Describe how you could use each of these Office programs in your personal life. Imagine you are a business owner. Describe how each of these Office programs would help you increase productivity. When you run a business, you need to correspond with clients, vendors, and employees; you need to track income and spending; you need to keep track of items, such as inventory, documents, and so on; and you need to market and advertise your business.

ACTIVITY 1–2

Use the Office Help system to find out more about keyboard shortcuts. If you are connected to the Internet, you can click the Training Keyboard shortcuts in the 2010 Office system. Write a description of the different types of shortcuts. List one advantage of using shortcuts. Then list the three shortcuts you think you would use most frequently.

ACTIVITY 1–3

Start your Web browser. Describe the function of all the buttons you see. Remember to point to each button to see its ScreenTip. Then describe the steps to print a Web page. Use the Help system as needed.

Estimated Time:
1 hour

LESSON 1

Microsoft Windows 7 Basics

■ OBJECTIVES

Upon completion of this lesson, you should be able to:

- Start Windows.
- Use a pointing device.
- Understand the desktop.
- Navigate in Windows.
- Use Windows.
- Manage files and folders.
- Delete files using the Recycle Bin.
- Use Windows Help.
- Manage your computer.

■ VOCABULARY

Action Center

Address bar

Close button

Computer folder

Control Panel

desktop

Explorer window

Favorites

jump list

Libraries

Notification area

operating system

pin

pointer

pointing device

Recycle Bin

Start button

taskbar

window

Windows Aero

VOCABULARY

operating system

Windows Aero

pointing device

pointer

WARNING

Aero is not included in Windows 7 Home Basic or Windows 7 Starter.

This lesson will familiarize you with the Windows 7 operating system. An *operating system* is software that controls the basic operations of your computer. In this lesson, you will learn to control your computer's components, move around your desktop, and manage the files, folders, and other resources you work with every day. You will also learn about the Windows Help system and the basics of managing your computer.

Starting Windows

If Windows is already installed, it should start automatically when you turn on the computer. If your computer is on a network, you may need some help from your instructor. Remember, there are many versions of Windows 7 available. While your educational institution may have hardware that supports all the Windows 7 features, your personal copy of Windows 7 may not. Be aware that some tasks in this lesson may not be applicable. For example, most Windows 7 editions support *Windows Aero*, a graphic interface feature that gives a translucent quality to windows, dialog boxes, and other items. Aero is turned on automatically, which allows you to see through one window to the next or scan through thumbnails and other miniatures in what is known as Flip or Flip 3D. For this lesson, Windows Aero is turned on.

Step-by-Step 1.1

1. Turn on the computer and the monitor, if necessary.

2. If prompted for login information, click your **username**.

3. If prompted for a password, type your **password**, then click the **Go** button .

4. After a few moments, the Windows 7 desktop appears.

EXTRA FOR EXPERTS

Some touch screens and mice not only emulate typical mouse functions, they also support multi-touch functionality, such as matching the speed of your finger movements to actions on the screen.

Using a Pointing Device

A *pointing device* allows you to interact and communicate with your computer. A pointing device can be a mouse, trackball, touch pad or screen, pointing stick, digital pen, or even a joystick. All pointing devices share the ability to point to and manipulate graphics and text on the screen. The *pointer*, which appears as an arrow on the screen, indicates the position of the pointing device. **Table 1–1** describes the five most common mouse operations.

TABLE 1–1   Common pointing device actions

ACTION	DESCRIPTION	USE TO
Point	Positions the pointing device on a specific object on the screen	highlight options or short descriptions
Click	Press and release the left button once while pointing to an object on the screen	select or open an item
Double-click	Quickly press and release the left button twice to initiate an action	open programs, folders, or files
Drag	Point to an object on the screen, press and hold the left button, move the object, and then release the button	move objects, such as icons or folders
Right-click	Press and release the right button to view file properties or a menu of functions	display a context-sensitive menu of options

Understanding the Desktop

When Windows starts up, and depending on current settings, icons, shortcuts, folders, and files might appear on the desktop. Files and *folders*, directories that contain files or other folders, are displayed in a small framed work area known as a **window**. The **desktop** is the main work area in Windows. It contains Windows program elements, other programs, and files. **Figure 1–1** illustrates a typical desktop screen when Windows is first installed. More commonly, your desktop may contain different icons, shortcuts, or gadgets, shown in **Figure 1–2**. An *icon* is a small picture that represents a file, folder, program, or program shortcut. You use shortcuts to open files and folders and start applications. You can also drag icons to a new location on the desktop, copy, or delete them. *Gadgets* are mini-programs that provide information or tools. They are readily available in a transparent panel that is attached to one side of the screen.

The **taskbar** appears at the bottom of the screen and displays icons of the programs that you can open. You can change the order of icons by clicking and dragging them to a new location. To easily access programs, you can attach, or **pin** a program icon directly to the taskbar or Start menu. On the Start menu, you can right-click the icon to view recently used files in a **jump list**. You can further customize and organize your desktop by creating files, folders, and shortcuts.

> ▶ **VOCABULARY**
>
> **window**
>
> **desktop**
>
> **taskbar**
>
> **pin**
>
> **jump list**

> **TIP**
>
> Aero themes have multiple images associated with them. You can select your desktop background to play as slide show by right-clicking the desktop, clicking Desktop Background Slideshow, and then selecting the options you want.

Recycle Bin

Desktop

Taskbar buttons

Start button

Taskbar

Notification area

FIGURE 1–1 Typical Windows 7 desktop

Shortcut icons

Nature theme

Gadgets

FIGURE 1–2 Customized Windows 7 desktop

The main features of the desktop screen are labeled on Figure 1–1 and Figure 1–2, and discussed below:

1. The **Recycle Bin** stores the files you want to delete and allows you to restore them if needed.

2. Icons appear on the desktop and are visual representations of a program, file, folder, or operation.

3. A *desktop background* is a theme that uses images, patterns, or colors as the background on the desktop. Aero themes also include colors, sounds, and screen-saver images.

4. The **Start button** brings up menus that give you a variety of options, such as starting a program, opening a document, searching for items on your computer, finding help, or shutting down the computer.

5. Taskbar buttons start frequently used programs or display the desktop.

6. The taskbar, located at the bottom of the screen, lets you access open programs and files.

7. **Notification area** task icons run in the background; you can use these to check the time and date, adjust speaker volume, and access other network or system features.

8. Gadgets on the Windows Sidebar are mini-programs that have specific functionality, such as displaying the time, weather, news feeds, slide shows, and other frequently accessed information.

Click the Start button to open the Start menu. The Start menu is divided into two panes. On the left, you can view recently opened programs, search for any file or folder, and easily access programs installed on your computer by pinning them to the Start menu. The right pane lists links to popular functions and features, and contains the Power button menu, where you select an option for ending a session.

▶ **VOCABULARY**
Recycle Bin
Start button
Notification area

Step-by-Step 1.2

1. On the taskbar, click the **Start** button 🪟. The Start menu appears in two panes, as shown in **Figure 1–3**.

FIGURE 1–3
Start menu

Pinned items list (your list will differ)

Recently opened programs (your list will differ)

Common features and folders

Search programs and files text box

Shut down and log off options

2. In the left pane, click **All Programs**. The list of programs installed on your computer appears in the left pane, as shown in **Figure 1–4**.

FIGURE 1–4
Start menu showing list of All Programs

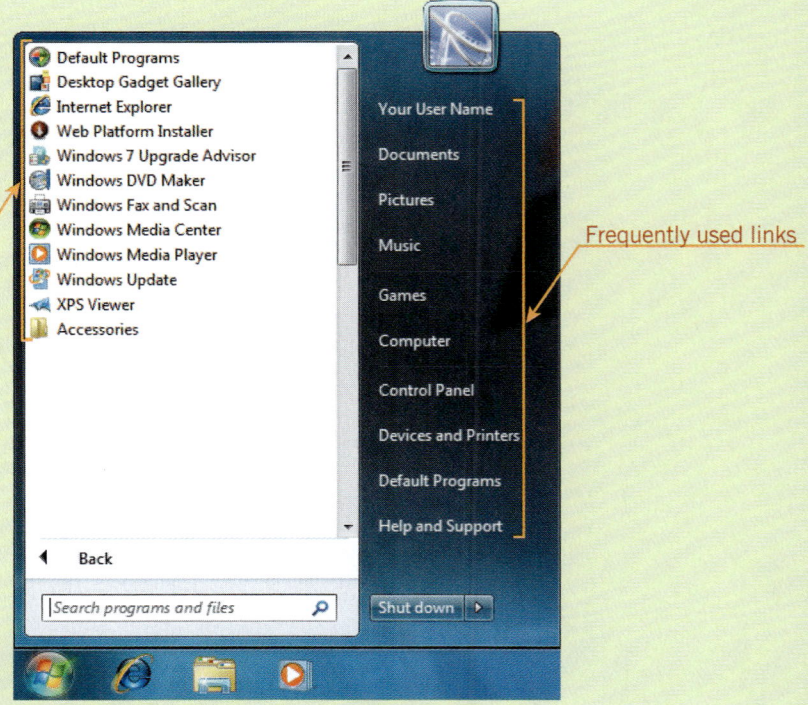

Installed programs (your list will differ)

Frequently used links

TIP

To pin a program to the taskbar or Start menu, right-click a program icon in the Start menu, and then click Pin to Taskbar or Pin to Start Menu. To pin a favorite item to a jump list so you can always access it, point to a program on the Start menu or taskbar to open its jump list, point to the item, and then click the Pin to this list icon. The item will appear at the top of the jump list.

3. In the Programs list in the right pane, click **Computer**. The Computer window opens.

4. On the taskbar, click the **Internet Explorer** button .

5. In the upper-right corner of the Internet Explorer title bar, click the **Close** button ![X] to return to the open window on the desktop. Leave the Computer window open for the next Step-by-Step.

WARNING

If prompted to take a tour of Internet Explorer 8, click the Close button.

Navigating in Windows

Windows offers many features that allow you to easily locate and open the files you need. *Explorer windows* are used to navigate to items on your computer. Most windows share common navigation tools such as a Navigation pane, Address bar, toolbar, or *Close button*, even if their specific function varies.

Viewing Open Windows

Many windows you work with share similar features, so you can work effortlessly and efficiently no matter the task you need to perform. Each window has a *toolbar*, controls, or links that contains functions specific to the window. **Figure 1–5** shows navigation features in three windows. You can use Windows Flip to move to an open window, program, or file by pressing and holding Alt, and then pressing Tab. As you press Tab, an icon representing the open window appears highlighted in a bar with icons of the other open windows. You can continue pressing Tab until the window you want to view is highlighted. When you release Alt, the selected window appears on the screen.

▶ **VOCABULARY**
Explorer windows
Close button

TIP

To customize your view of an open Computer or Windows Explorer window, right-click a blank part of the main pane, and then select the options you want from a menu.

TIP

You can use Flip 3D to view open windows in a 3D telescoped display. To do so, press and hold the Windows logo key on the keyboard, and then press Tab. Do not release the Windows logo key; then continue pressing Tab to flip through each open window.

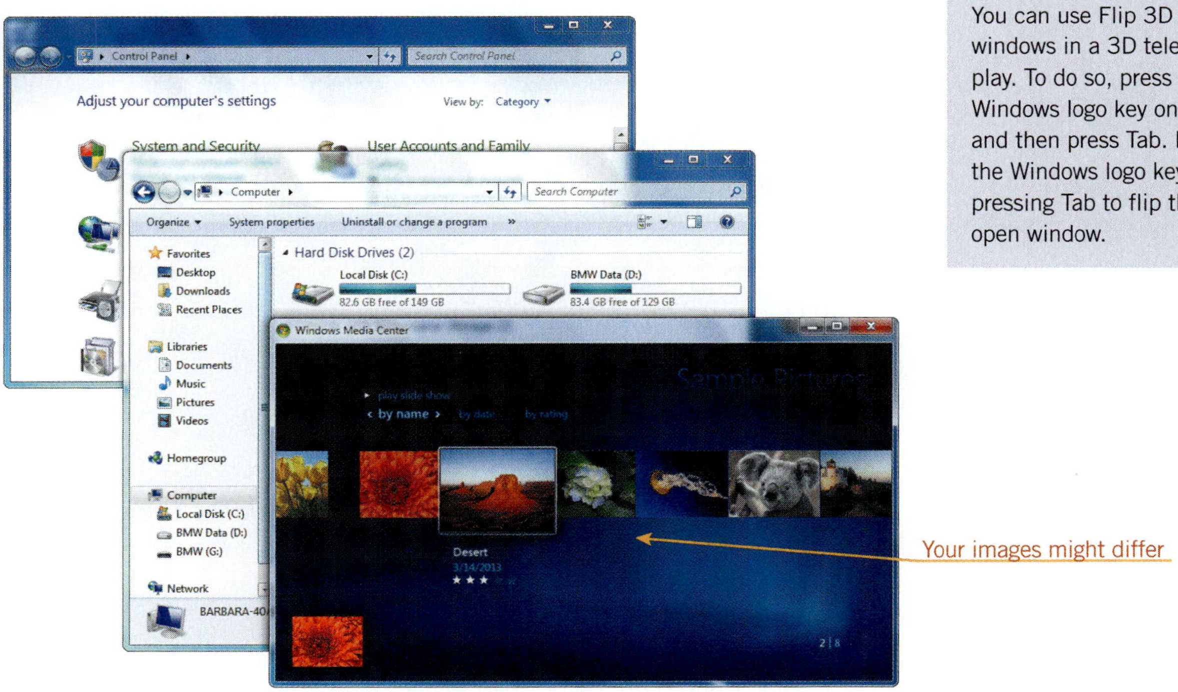

Your images might differ

FIGURE 1–5   Viewing window features

Step-by-Step 1.3

1. Make sure the Computer window is open, click the **Start** button , and then click **Control Panel** in the right pane. The Control Panel window opens on top of the Computer window.

2. On the taskbar, click the **Start** button, and then click **Windows Media Center**. The Windows Media Center appears on top of the Control Panel. All three windows are open, but they overlap each other, making it difficult to view them all at once.

3. Press and hold **Alt**, and then press **Tab** once. The Control Panel is on top.

4. Press and hold **Alt**, and then press **Tab** twice. The Computer window Gallery is now on top.

5. Press and hold **Alt**, and then press **Tab** twice. The Windows Media Center is on top. Compare your screen to **Figure 1–6**. Leave the Computer window open for the next Step-by-Step, and then click the **Close** button in the Control Panel and Windows Media Center windows.

> **TIP**
>
> Aero Peek lets you view thumbnails of open files from the taskbar by pointing to a pinned icon on the taskbar. To view the file full size, point to a thumbnail. To work on the file, click the thumbnail.

FIGURE 1–6
Viewing open windows

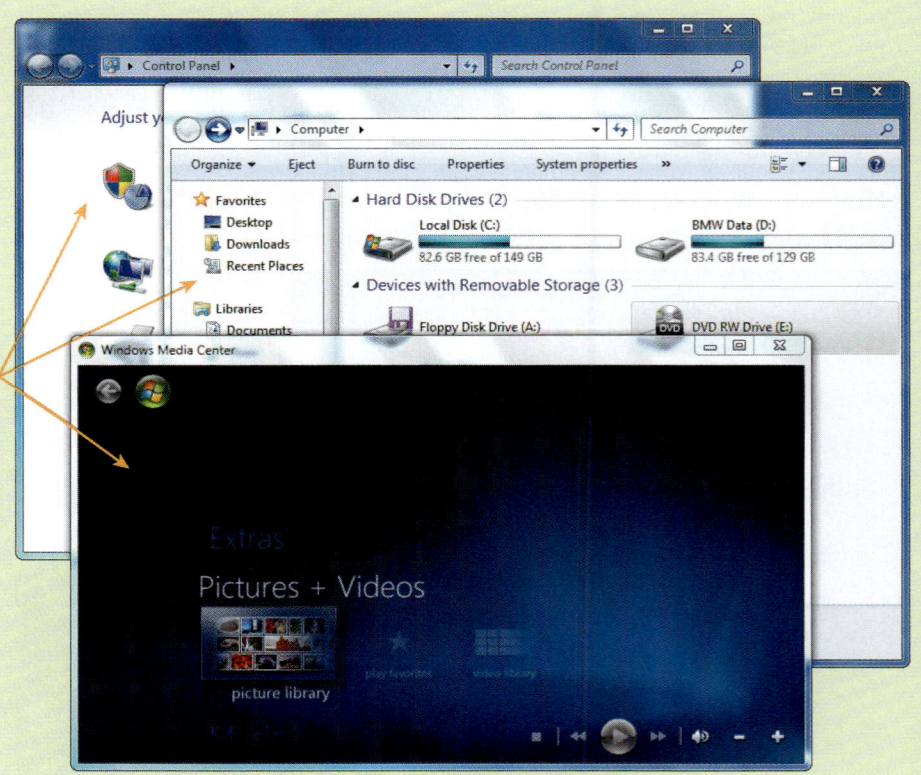

The location and size of your windows will differ

> **TIP**
>
> Aero Peek also lets you see through all your open windows directly to the desktop. To do so, on the taskbar, point to the Show desktop button, or press and hold the Windows logo key, and then press the Spacebar.

Navigating Using the Address Bar

The Address bar in Windows is a dynamic tool and shares some functionality with the Address bar in Internet Explorer. The *Address bar* identifies the path for the currently open folder, as shown in **Figure 1–7**. Each folder name in the path is a link that you can click to display that folder's contents, which is useful when working with subfolders within a main folder. To navigate to recently visited locations, click the Back button and the Forward button to the left of the Address bar. You can also view previous locations by clicking the Previous Locations arrow button at the end of the Address bar. The Search text box searches the contents of the open folder for the search term you entered.

▶ **VOCABULARY**
Address bar

 TIP

Windows performs searches incrementally; it begins searching as soon as you type a character in the text box and refines the search as you add more text.

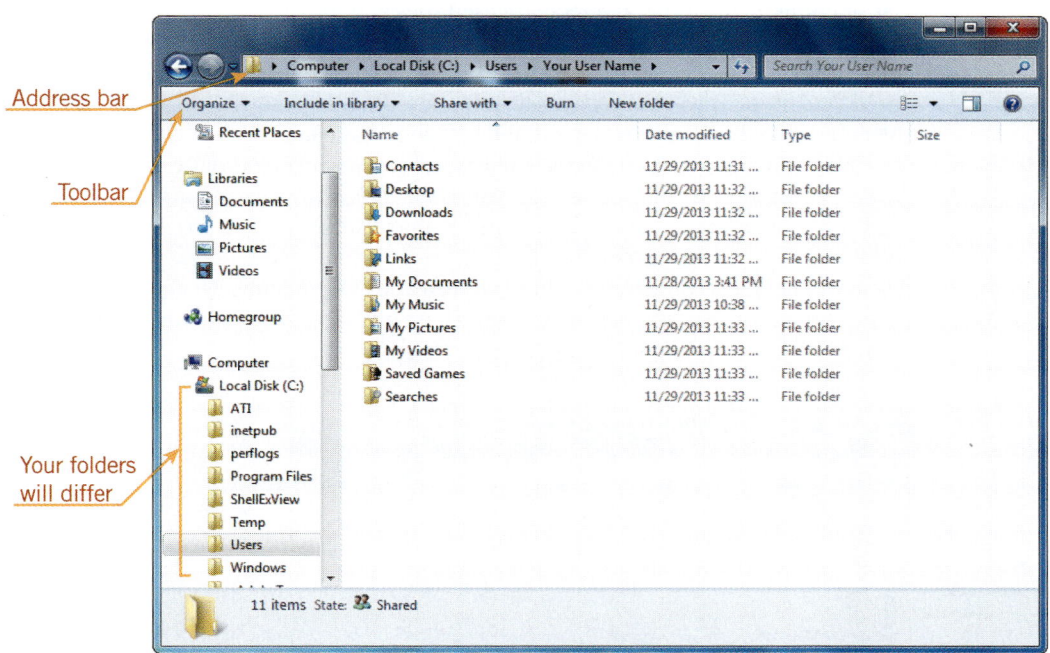

FIGURE 1–7   Viewing a path in the Address bar

Step-by-Step 1.4

1. Make sure the Computer window is open, and then double-click the **Local Disk (C:)** icon. (*Note*: Select another disk or device if this disk is not available. Because your computer setup might vary, complete as many of these steps as you can.)

2. In the Main pane, double-click the **Users** folder, if necessary, double-click your **User Name** folder, and then compare your window to Figure 1–7. The Address bar shows the path to your folder.

3. In the Address bar, click **Computer**. The Main pane shows the disks and removable devices in the Computer folder.

4. Click the **Back** button 🔙 next to the Address bar. The Main pane shows the files in your User Name folder.

5. Click the **Forward** button  next to the Address bar. The Main pane shows the files in the Computer folder. Keep this window open for the next Step-by-Step.

Navigating Using the Navigation Pane

▶ **VOCABULARY**
Favorites

Libraries

EXTRA FOR EXPERTS

You can further personalize the look of a Windows Explorer window by clicking Organize on the toolbar, pointing to Layout, and then selecting the options you want to be visible or hidden.

Windows Explorer windows have a Navigation pane to help you find your files, which you can also customize. You can use the *Navigation pane* to navigate to popular or common locations and recently used files and folders.

Favorites link to folders containing the items you use the most, including the desktop, downloads, and recently opened files and folders. You can add frequently used folders or files to the Favorite Links by dragging the file or folder from the Main pane to the Favorites section in the Navigation pane.

You may find that you store content in folders throughout your computer, which makes it difficult to find the pieces you need. *Libraries* provide a view of related files and folders by assembling them in a single location. The folders in a library do not actually store the content. Instead, they contain links to files, so you can see them in one place. By default, Microsoft provides Documents, Music, Pictures, and Videos libraries, but you can also select where each folder opens or create a custom library with your own folders, as shown in **Figure 1–8**.

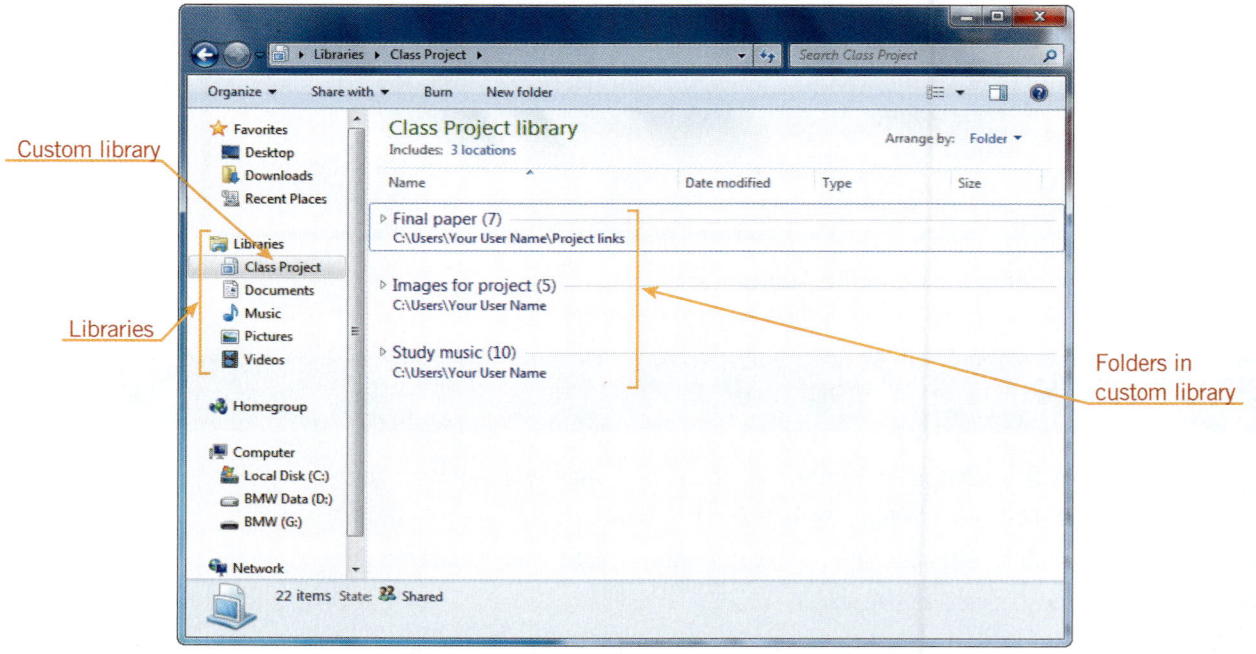

FIGURE 1–8   Viewing Libraries

Step-by-Step 1.5

1. Make sure the Computer window is open, in the Libraries section of the Navigation pane, click **Pictures**, and then click a **photo** if one is available. Photos that you have downloaded to your computer appear in the Main pane, and a preview of the selected image appears in the Preview pane and in the Details pane, if those panes are visible.

2. In the Navigation pane, click **Computer**, click the **drive** containing your files, and then view its contents in the Main pane.

3. Click a **folder** to view its contents, and then in the Address bar, click **Computer**. Close all open windows.

> **TIP**
>
> You can display a list of textual or graphic choices, known as a menu. To do so, click Organize on the toolbar, point to Layout, and then click Menu bar.

Using Windows

Windows are essential to using the Windows 7 operating system. They display and store information and run programs. It is important to understand how to adjust and use them so you can optimize your efficiency.

Moving and Resizing Windows

Sometimes you will have several windows open on the screen at the same time. To work more effectively, you may need to move or change the size of a window. To move a window, click the *title bar*, the bar at the top of the window, and drag the window to another location. You can adjust the height, width, or overall size of a window by dragging a sizing handle on a window's border or corner. Depending on where you position the pointer on a border or corner, the pointer changes to a two-headed arrow that is configured horizontally, vertically, or diagonally. When you adjust a corner border, the window is resized proportionately smaller or larger.

You can also resize a window using the Maximize button, Minimize button, and Restore Down button, located in the upper-right corner of the window. See **Figure 1–9**. The *Maximize button* enlarges a window to the full size of the screen. The *Minimize button* reduces a window to an icon on the taskbar. The button on the taskbar is labeled, and you can click it any time to redisplay the window. When a window is maximized, the Maximize button is replaced by the Restore Down button. The *Restore Down button* returns the window to the size it was before the Maximize button was clicked.

You use the ***Close button*** to close a window, which would include any file you have open in a program. If you are in a program, clicking the Close button will exit the program and you will be prompted to save or discard any changes in an open file.

> **VOCABULARY**
> **Close button**

> **TIP**
>
> You can eliminate clutter and view a single open window by using Windows Shake. Click and hold a window taskbar, then joggle it back and forth. Repeat to redisplay all the open windows.

Minimize button — Maximize button — Close button — Restore Down button

FIGURE 1–9   Window resizing buttons

Step-by-Step 1.6

1. On the taskbar, click the **Start** button , and then click **Control Panel**. The Control Panel window opens.

2. Point to the bar at the top of the window, click and hold the **left mouse** button, and then drag the **Control Panel window** until it appears to be centered on the screen. Release the mouse button.

3. Point to the border at the right edge of the Control Panel window. When the pointer turns into a **horizontal two-headed** arrow ⟷, drag the right border farther to the right to expand the window.

4. Point to the lower-right corner of the window border. When the pointer turns into a **two-headed diagonal** arrow ⤡, drag the border up and to the left to resize the width and height at the same time until the window appears similar to **Figure 1–10**.

FIGURE 1–10
Resizing a window

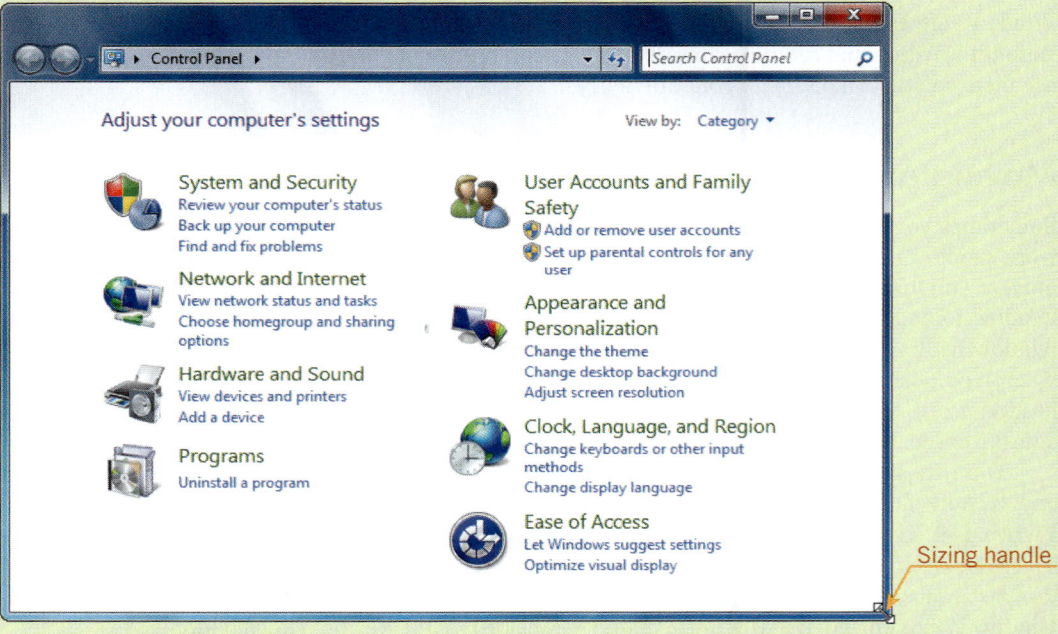

Sizing handle

5. In the upper-right corner of the window, click the **Maximize** button . The Control Panel window is maximized and you cannot adjust its borders.

6. In the upper-right corner of the window, click the **Restore Down** button . The Control Panel window returns to its previous size and approximate position on the desktop.

7. In the upper-right corner of the window, click the **Minimize** button . The Control Panel window is no longer visible on the desktop, but it is still open. The minimized window is shown as an icon on the taskbar.

8. On the taskbar, point to the **Control Panel** icon. A thumbnail of the Control Panel appears, as shown in **Figure 1–11**.

TIP

You can use the Snap feature to instantly resize a window to fill half the desktop when you drag it to the left or right edge of the screen. This makes it easy to maximize your view of two windows and compare them side-by-side.

Control Panel
minimized on
the taskbar

Thumbnail

FIGURE 1–11
Minimized window on
the taskbar

9. On the taskbar, click the **Control Panel** button to restore the window.
Leave the Control Panel open for the next Step-by-Step.

Scroll Bars

A *scroll bar* appears on the edge of a window any time there is more content than can appear in the window at its current size, as shown in **Figure 1–12**. A scroll bar can appear along the bottom edge (horizontal) and along the right side (vertical) of a window.

Scroll bars are a convenient way to bring another part of the window's contents into view. The scroll bar contains a scroll box and two scroll arrows. The *scroll box* is a slider that indicates your position within the window. When the scroll box reaches the bottom of the scroll bar, you have reached the end of the window's contents. *Scroll arrows* are located at the ends of the scroll bar. Clicking a scroll arrow moves the window content in that direction one line at a time. You can move to the end of a window's content by clicking a blank area of the scroll bar on either side of the scroll box.

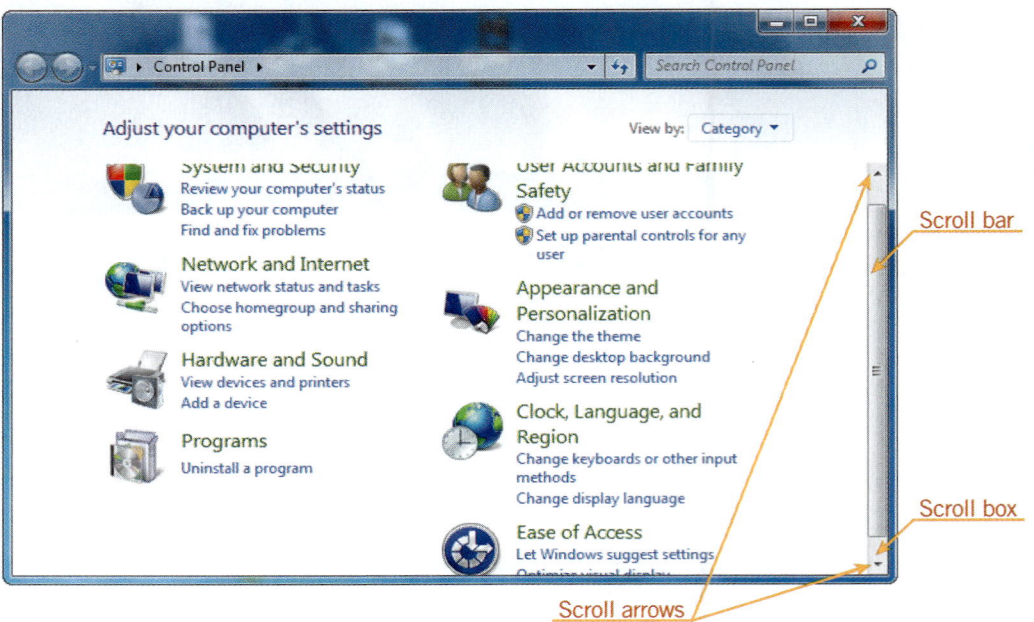

FIGURE 1–12   Scroll bar, arrows, and boxes

Step-by-Step 1.7

1. Make sure that the Control Panel window is open, and then, if necessary, resize the window vertically until the vertical scroll bar is visible on the right side of the window.

2. On the vertical scroll bar, click the **down scroll** arrow twice. The contents of the window shift downward one line at a time, as shown in Figure 1–12.

3. On the vertical scroll bar, drag the **scroll box** all the way up, and then the all the way down. You can drag the scroll box anywhere in the scroll bar to keep certain content in view.

4. Click the blank space above the vertical scroll box but beneath the scroll arrow. The contents scroll all the way to the top.

> **TIP**
>
> To scroll quickly through a window, point to a scroll arrow in a window, and then click and hold the mouse button.

5. Resize the Control Panel window until the scroll bar is no longer visible. Click the **Close** button ![X button] in the Control Panel window.

Using Toolbars, Menus, and Dialog Boxes

You perform many tasks by clicking commands and buttons. These functions are usually contained on a menu, a toolbar, or in a dialog box. A *toolbar* contains buttons that execute a function or open a command menu. A *menu* contains commands for initiating certain actions or tasks. For example, when you click the Start button, a menu appears with a list of options. A *dialog box* or an interactive message window appears when more information is required before the command can be performed. You may have to enter information, choose from a list of options, or simply confirm that you want the command to be performed. To back out of a dialog box without performing an action, press Esc, click the Close button, or choose Cancel (or No).

Step-by-Step 1.8

1. On the taskbar, click the **Start** button 🪟, click **All Programs**, click **Acccessories**, and then click **Paint**. The Paint program window opens.

2. On the Home tab, click the **Brushes button** arrow, and then click **Airbrush** ![airbrush icon].

3. Slowly draw **WIN 7** on the drawing area, in the Image group, click the **Select button** arrow, and then point to **Select all** until the keyboard shortcut screentip appears, as shown in **Figure 1–13**.

> **TIP**
>
> Instead of clicking commands, you can use a keyboard shortcut to perform a task, which is pressing a combination of keys on the keyboard. If available, a keyboard shortcut is shown when you highlight a command.

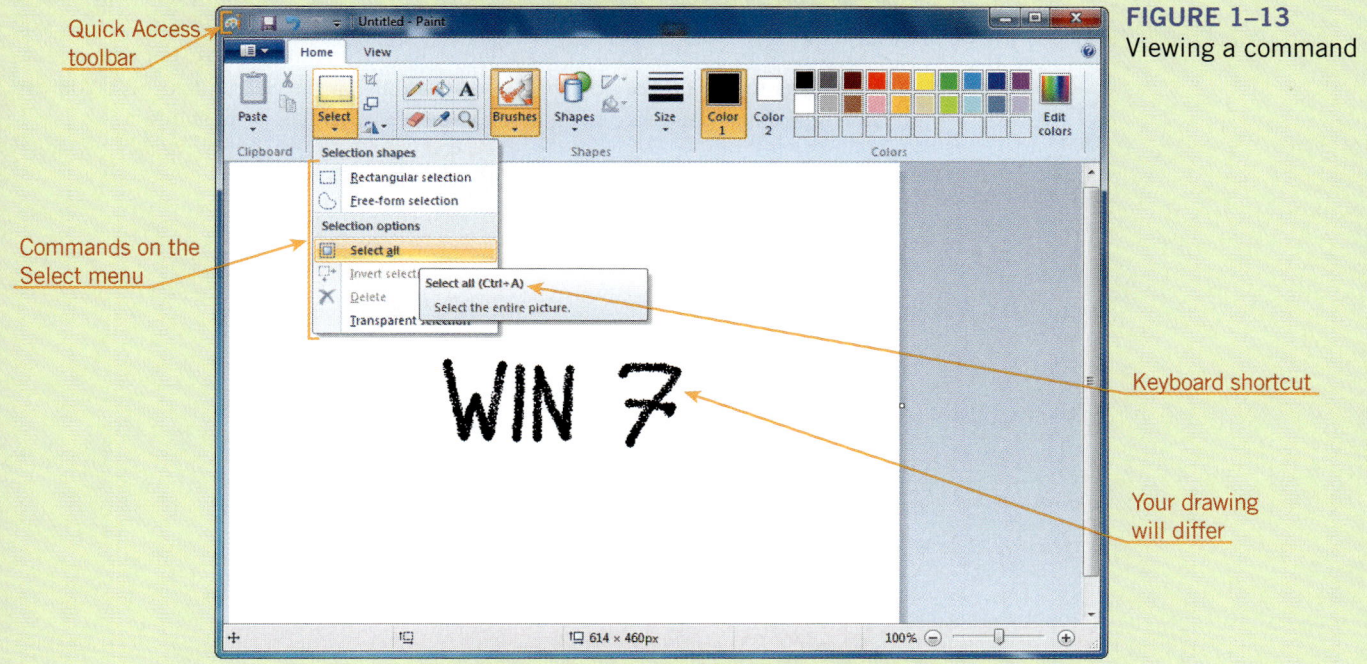

Quick Access toolbar

Commands on the Select menu

Keyboard shortcut

Your drawing will differ

FIGURE 1–13
Viewing a command

4. Beneath the title bar, click the **Paint button** 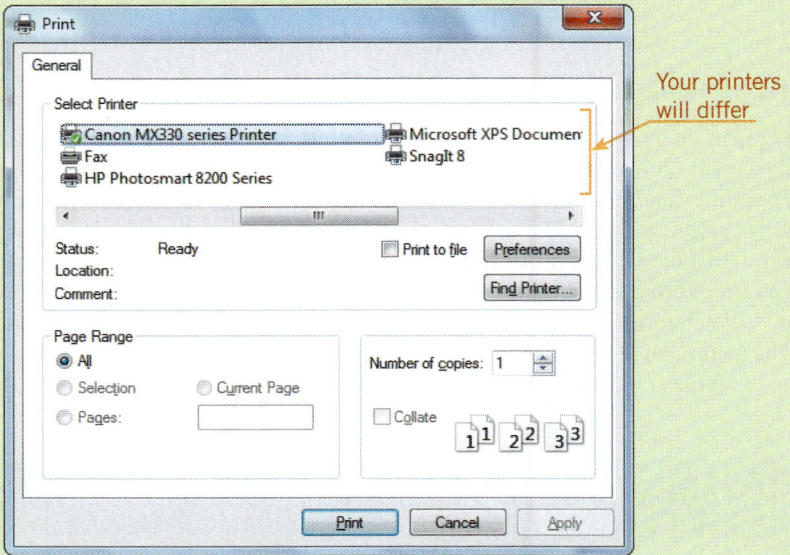, and then click **Print**. The Print dialog box opens, as shown in **Figure 1–14**.

FIGURE 1–14
Print dialog box

5. Click **Cancel** to close the Print dialog box.
6. Beneath the title bar, click the **Paint** button, click **Exit**, and then click **Don't Save**. Paint closes.

Using the Control Panel

The *Control Panel*, shown in **Figure 1–15**, is the command center for configuring Windows settings. You can customize settings for appearance, sound, and performance. The number of categories and links can be overwhelming and may not be descriptive enough for you to find exactly what you want. To find the settings you are interested in, type a word or search term in the Search text box. For example, to find gadgets to use on the desktop, type "gadgets" in the Search text box. You can search in ordinary language without knowing the official or technical term.

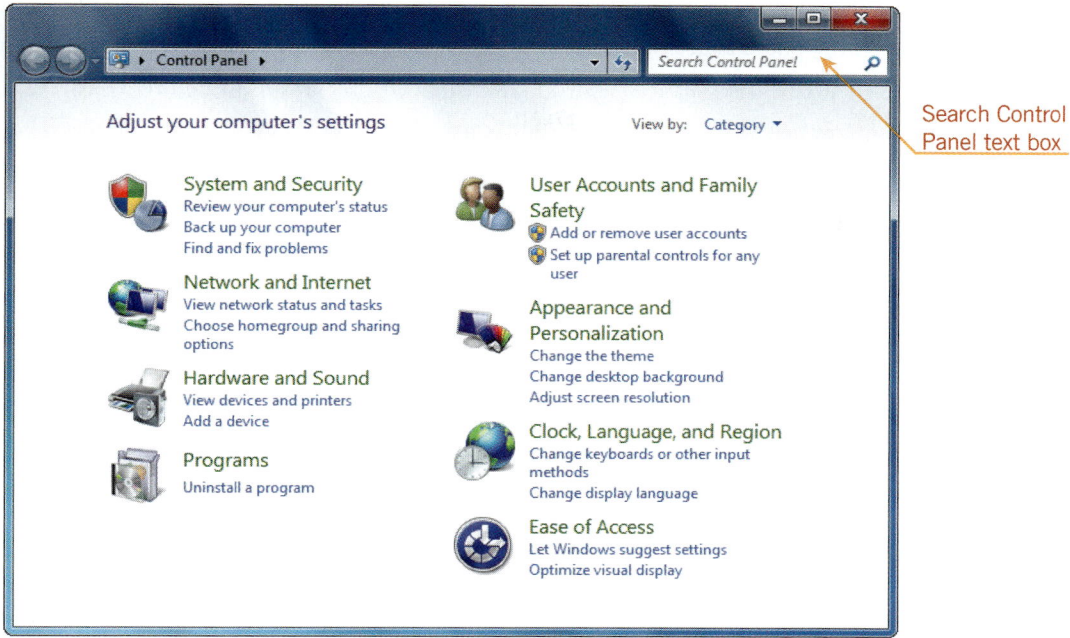

Search Control
Panel text box

FIGURE 1–15   Control Panel

Step-by-Step 1.9

1. On the taskbar, click the **Start** button, click **Control Panel**, and then resize the window so that the scroll bar is not visible.

2. Click **Appearance and Personalization**, then if necessary, resize the Control Panel window to view all the topics. Notice that topics pertaining to appearance and personalization appear.

3. In the left pane, click **Control Panel Home** to return to the main Control Panel page.

4. In the Search Control Panel text box, type **sound**. Search results related to "sound" appear as you type the word, as shown in **Figure 1–16**. Your results may differ depending on your connection to the Internet.

FIGURE 1–16
Viewing search results in the Control Panel

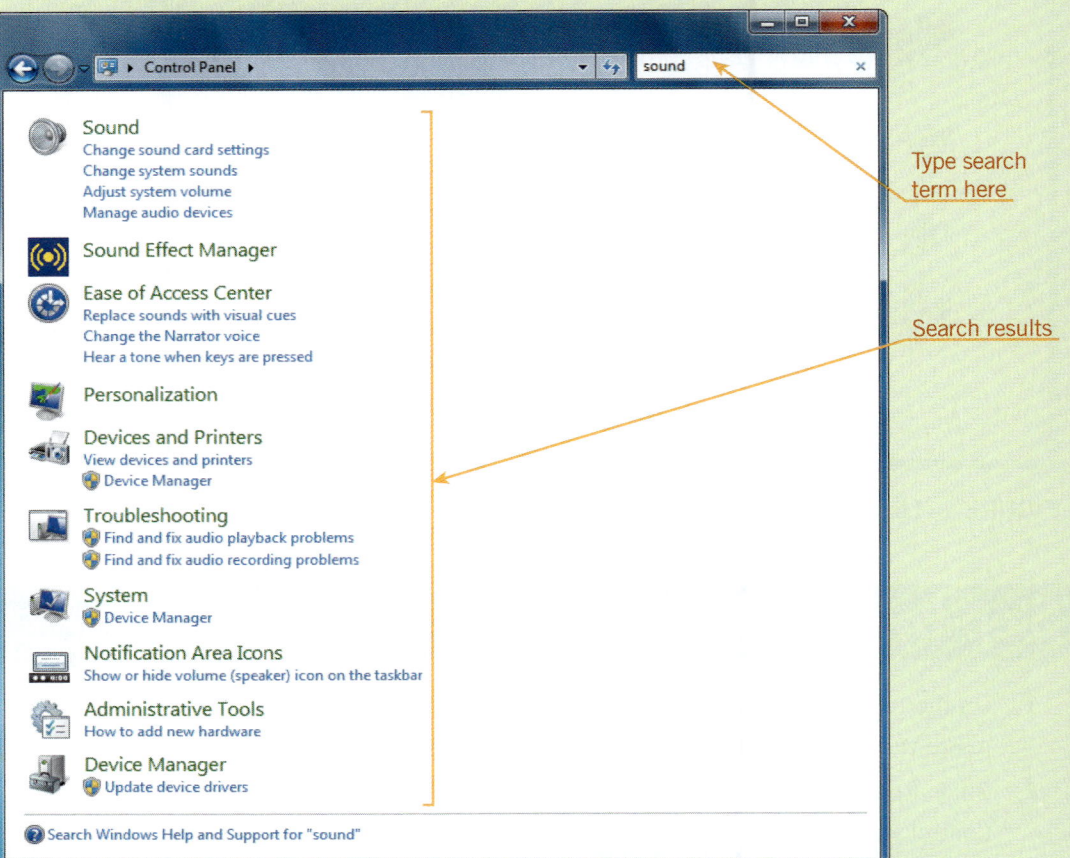

Type search term here

Search results

5. In the Sound section, click **Change system sounds**, review the options on the Sounds tab, click the **Sound Scheme** list arrow to view the available themes, click **Cancel** in the Sound dialog box to close the Sound Scheme list, and then click **Cancel** again to close the dialog box.

6. Next to the Address bar, click the **Back** button ⬅ to return to the previous screen, Control Panel Home.

7. Close the Control Panel.

TIP

When typing a search term, often less is better. Not all Help systems are designed to retrieve words similar to the keyword, even if the difference is minor. Compare searching in Control Panel for "sound" versus "sounds."

Managing Files and Folders

It is important to understand the file and folder structure of Windows 7. Each registered user has the same default Library folders, such as Documents, Pictures, and Music, which you can easily access on the right pane of the Start menu. For example, the *Documents folder* stores the files you use for your projects, such as documents, presentations, and spreadsheets. The **Computer folder** is where you access hard disk drives, removable drives and media, CD and DVD drives, network locations, and other removable media such as cameras and scanners.

▶ **VOCABULARY**
Computer folder

> **TIP**
>
> When you click the More options button on the toolbar of the Computer or Windows Explorer window, you can select whether to view folder contents as Extra Large Icons, Large Icons, Medium Icons, Small Icons, List, Details, Tiles, or Content.

Step-by-Step 1.10

1. On the taskbar, click the **Start** button 🪟, and then click **Documents**. The Documents library window opens with sample folders, as shown in **Figure 1–17**.

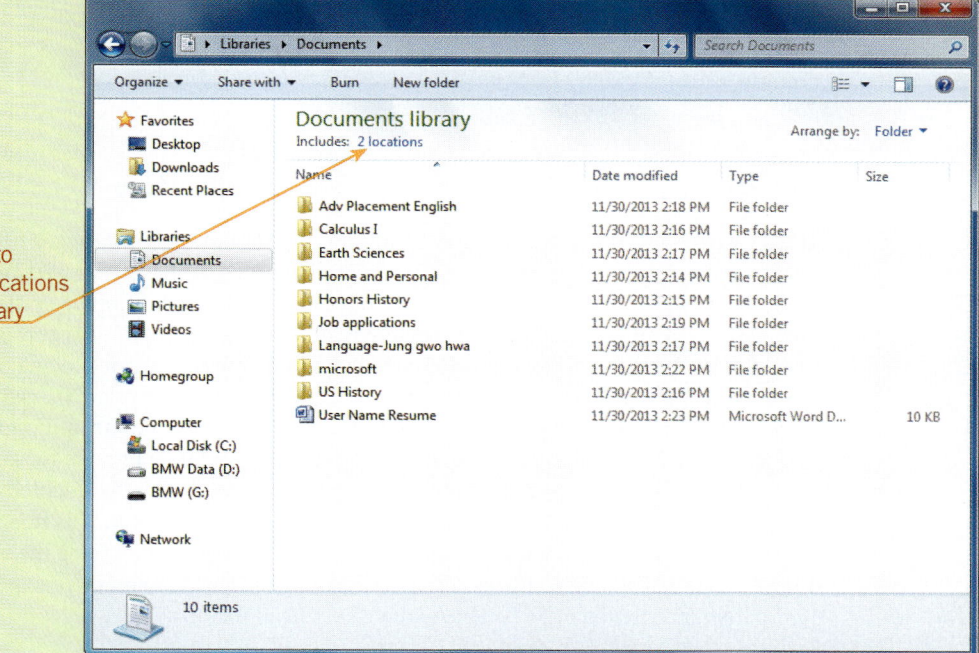

FIGURE 1–17
Viewing folders in the Documents library folder

2. On the Documents library toolbar, click the **New folder** button New folder, type **Resume**, and then press **Enter**. A new folder is created.

> **TIP**
>
> To open multiple Windows Explorer windows, right-click the Start button, and then click Open Windows Explorer.

3. Right-click the **Resume** folder, click **Rename**, type **My Resume**, and then press **Enter**. The folder is renamed, as shown in **Figure 1–18**.

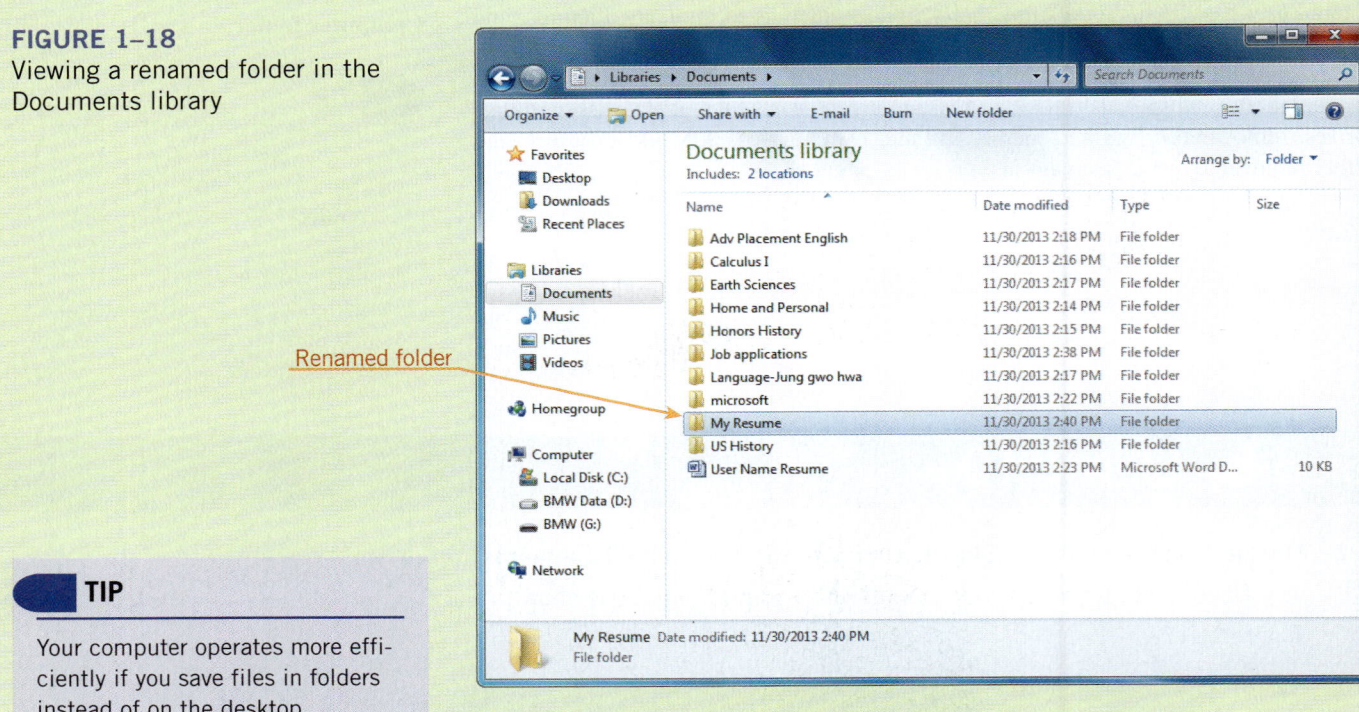

Renamed folder

4. Close the Documents library window.

Deleting Files Using the Recycle Bin

As you work with different files, there will always be some you no longer need and want to delete. When you delete a file from a window, its name is removed from the window's content and the file is physically moved to the Recycle Bin, the wastebasket icon on the desktop. However, while the item is stored for deletion, it is not permanently deleted. The Recycle Bin icon changes depending on whether or not it contains files, as shown in **Figure 1–19**. To permanently delete files in the Recycle Bin, right-click the Recycle Bin icon, and then click Empty Recycle Bin from the menu. Fortunately, just like a regular wastebasket, you can retrieve items before they're gone for good. To restore a deleted item from the Recycle Bin, open the Recycle Bin by double-clicking the icon, select the file you want to restore, and then click the Restore this item button on the toolbar. Note that once you permanently delete an item by emptying the Recycle Bin, you cannot restore it using another Windows 7 function, although you can purchase third-party software that may be able to recover deleted files.

With items
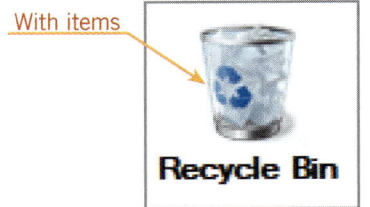
Empty

FIGURE 1–19   Comparing the Recycle Bin when it contains items or is empty

Step-by-Step 1.11

1. On the desktop, double-click the **Recycle Bin** icon. If there are files in the Recycle Bin, it will look similar to **Figure 1–20**; if not, it will be empty.

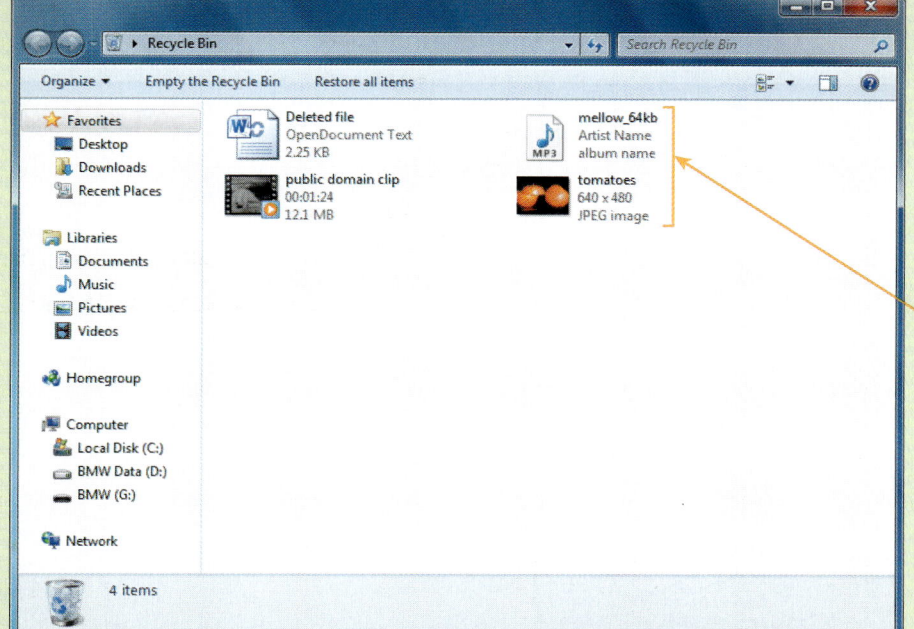

FIGURE 1–20
Viewing items in the Recycle Bin

2. On the toolbar, click **Empty the Recycle Bin** to delete the files, and then click **No** in the Delete File or Delete Multiple Items dialog box. (*Note*: Unless you work on your own computer, you should not permanently delete files without first checking with your instructor or computer lab manager.)

3. Close the Recycle Bin.

Using Windows Help

This lesson has covered only a few of the many features of Windows. For additional information, Windows has an easy-to-use Help system. Use Help as a quick reference when you are unsure about a function. You can access Windows Help by clicking *Help and Support* on the Start menu. Then, from the Windows Help and Support window, you can choose a category in the Find an answer section, such as Windows Basics or Troubleshooting. You can continue to click topics or you can type a search term, just like you can in the Control Panel. You can also print topics, browse Help,

EXTRA FOR EXPERTS

If you are working in a Windows program, you can access Help for the program by clicking the Help button on the toolbar.

INTRODUCTORY   Introduction Unit

and access online and other types of help. Note that if you are connected to the Internet, your searches can include Help results from the Windows Help online Web site. See **Figure 1–21**.

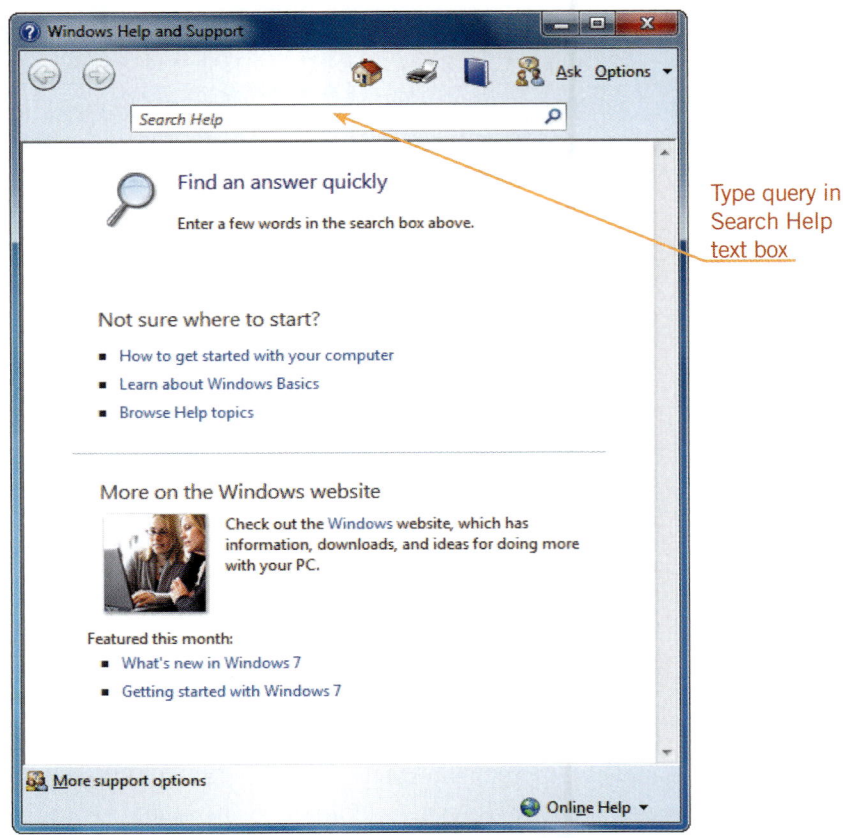

Type query in Search Help text box

FIGURE 1–21   Windows Help and Support window

Step-by-Step 1.12

1. On the taskbar, click the **Start** button , click **Help and Support**, and then maximize the window, if necessary. The Windows Help and Support window opens, as shown in Figure 1–21.

2. Click **Learn about Windows Basics**, on the Windows Basics: all topics page, scroll down to the Internet, e-mail, and networking section, click **Setting up a wireless network**, and then review the topic.

3. Click the **Help and Support Home** button to return to the main Windows Help and Support page.

4. Click the **Search Help** text box, type **camera**, and then click the **Search Help** button . A list of search results appears for the keyword you typed, as shown in **Figure 1–22**.

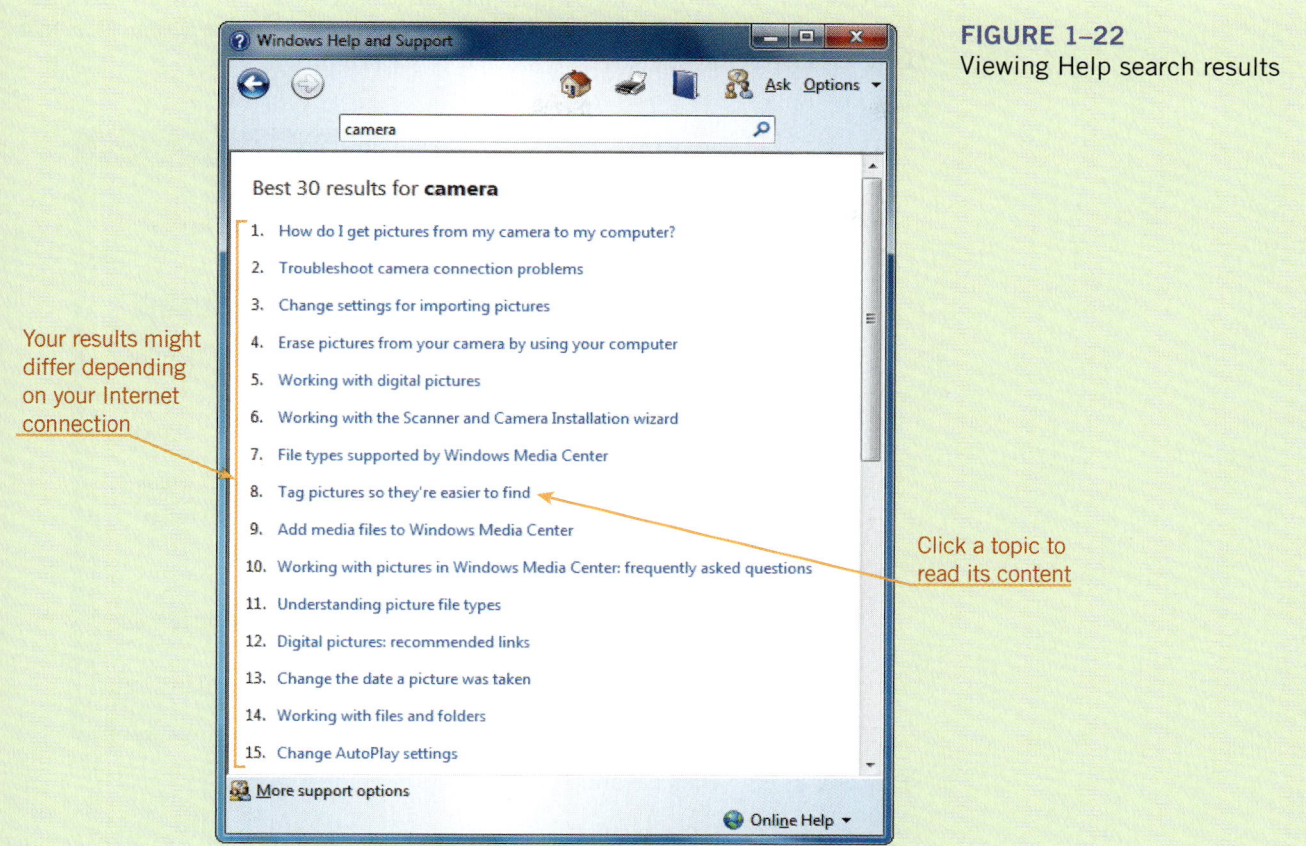

Your results might differ depending on your Internet connection

Click a topic to read its content

FIGURE 1–22
Viewing Help search results

5. Click a topic that interests you, read it, and then close the Windows Help and Support window.

Managing Your Computer

Like any machine, a computer requires maintenance to keep it running smoothly. Windows provides utilities designed to keep your computer optimized and safe.

Using Disk Cleanup

A computer handles thousands of files to do its job. Reducing the number of files on your hard disk frees up space and helps improve your computer's speed. Windows provides *Disk Cleanup,* a utility that deletes temporary files created when you surf the Web, watch videos, edit files, or perform other actions, such as opening e-mail attachments from the message window instead of first saving the attachment to your hard disk. To run Disk Cleanup, click the Start button, click All Programs, click the Accessories folder in the left pane, click the System Tools folder, and then click Disk Cleanup. Specify the drive you want to clean. You can choose to clean up the files in your account or you can click the Clean up system files button to clean up all the files on the computer. Disk Cleanup describes the categories of files it can delete and you check the boxes of the files you want to include, as shown in **Figure 1–23**. Click OK to begin the cleanup, and then click Delete Files to confirm the action. Note that Disk Cleanup closes automatically when it is finished.

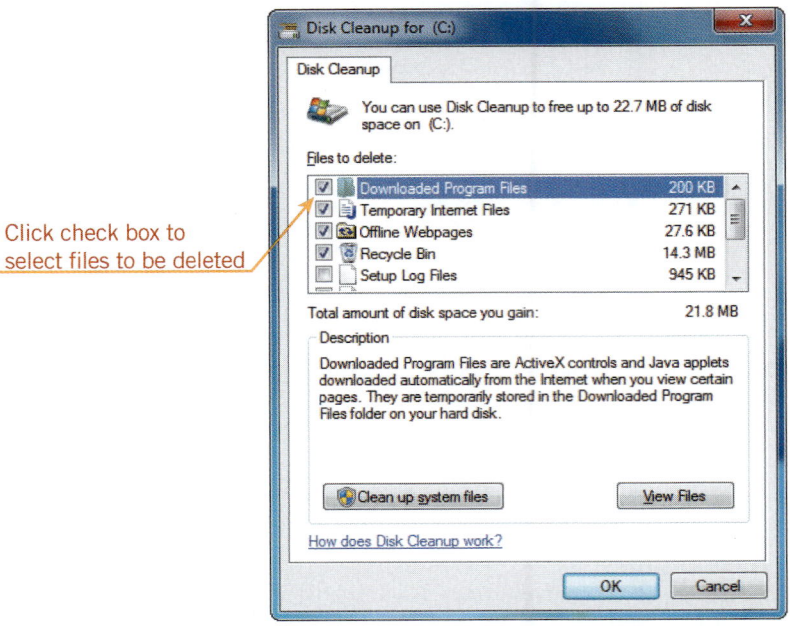

FIGURE 1–23   Disk Cleanup

Understanding the Action Center

The *Action Center* provides important messages about critical security and maintenance components on your computer, such as the firewall, antivirus protection, and spyware protection. You can also link to other features such as Windows updates and User Account Control. Click the Action Center icon in the Notification area to see security and maintenance alerts, as shown in **Figure 1–24**, and then click Open Action Center to display the window. You can also open the Action Center from the Control Panel. From the main page of the Control Panel, click System and Security, and then click Action Center.

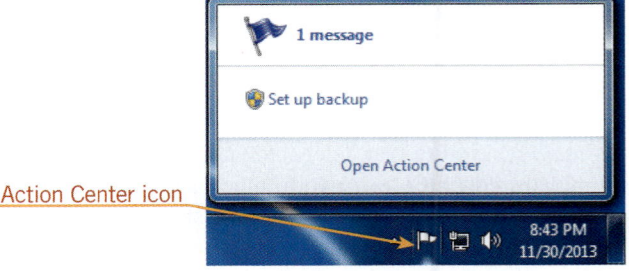

FIGURE 1–24   Action Center icon and message window

Protecting your computer from unauthorized access, malicious code, and software that collects information about your Web-surfing habits is essential. The Action Center is shown in **Figure 1–25**. To view the components of the Security and

Maintenance sections, click the expand arrow. If a component requires attention, an area will be marked red for important and yellow for suggestions.

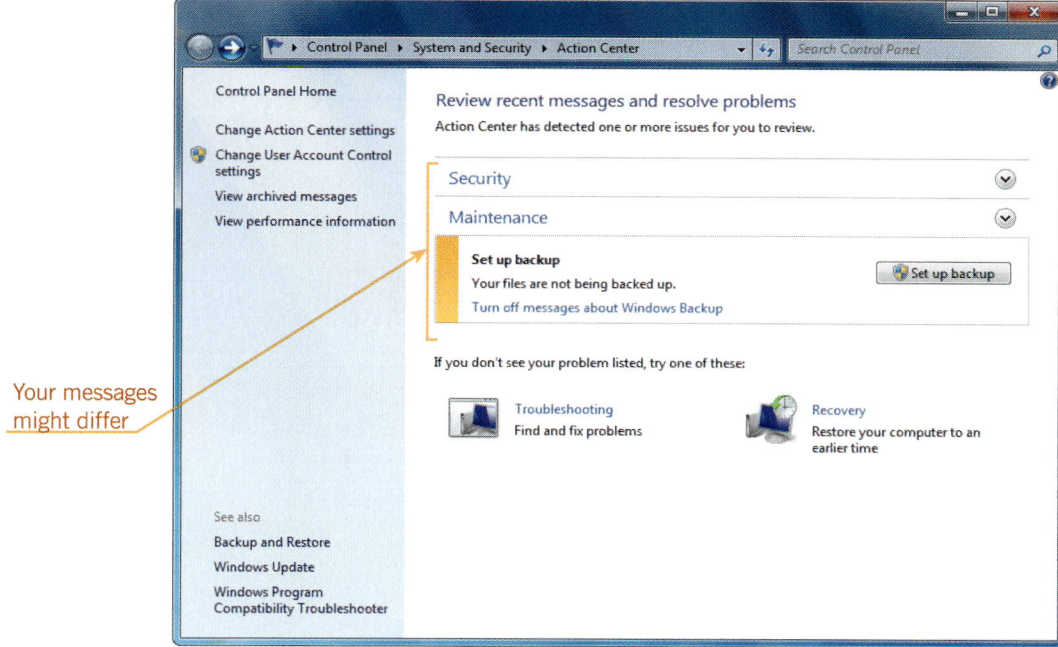

FIGURE 1–25   Viewing the Action Center

SUMMARY

In this lesson, you learned that:

- Starting Windows brings up the desktop, and possibly a prompt to enter a password depending on your settings. Several different versions of Windows 7 are available.

- A pointing device, such as a mouse, trackball, touch pad, or pointing stick, is a device you use to interact with and navigate your computer. You can use a touch screen to interact with the computer.

- The desktop is the main work area, and contains access to Windows elements such as files, folders, and programs, all of which are represented by icons. The main features of the desktop are the Start button, Recycle Bin, desktop theme, taskbar, notification area, and gadgets.

- Windows contains toolbars, controls, or links for a specific function. You can switch between open windows, open different folders by clicking folders in a path on the Address bar, and using the Navigation pane to open and organize folders.

- Windows can be moved, resized, opened, and closed. If you are unable to display all the contents of a window as it is currently sized, scroll bars appear to allow you to move to the

part of the window that you want to view. Windows can be maximized to fill the screen or minimized to appear as a button on the taskbar. You can use toolbars and menus in windows to perform tasks or actions, and input information in dialog boxes. The Control Panel contains searchable links for configuring Windows settings.

- Windows provides several default library folders for storing and organizing files on your computer and for viewing similar files, sharing files, or accessing frequently used files.

- The Recycle Bin stores files you have deleted from your computer. You can restore deleted files that are placed in the Recycle Bin or delete them permanently from your computer.

- The Windows Help and Support window provides additional information about the many features of Windows. You can access the Help program from Start menu or from any Windows program.

- Windows provides several utilities you can use to clean up unnecessary files on your computer and check your computer's security settings.

VOCABULARY REVIEW

Define the following terms:

Action Center	Favorites	pointing device
Address bar	jump list	Recycle Bin
Close button	Libraries	Start button
Computer folder	Notification area	taskbar
Control Panel	operating system	window
desktop	pin	Windows Aero
Explorer window	pointer	

 # REVIEW QUESTIONS

TRUE / FALSE

Circle T if the statement is true or F if the statement is false.

T   F   **1.**   You can view topics on adjusting your monitor in the Documents library.

T   F   **2.**   You can restore items moved to the Recycle Bin.

T   F   **3.**   Pressing Alt and Tab minimizes all open windows.

T   F   **4.**   You can use the path in the Address bar to navigate to a folder.

T   F   **5.**   You can automatically share files in your Personal folder with other users.

MATCHING

Match the correct Term in column 1 with the Description in column 2.

Term

_____ 1. taskbar

_____ 2. jump list

_____ 3. Address bar

_____ 4. operating system

_____ 5. Libraries

Description

a. Identifies the path for the currently open folder in a window

b. Software that control's your computer's operations

c. Assembles related files and folders in a single view

d. A bar at the bottom of the screen that contains icons

e. Recently used files, viewable by right-clicking a program icon

WRITTEN QUESTIONS

Write a brief answer to each of the following questions.

1. What happens to a window when you minimize it?

2. Describe two ways you can find information in Windows Help and Support.

3. What does right-clicking a pointing device, such as a mouse, do?

4. Describe one way you can switch between open windows using the keyboard?

5. What is the difference between a toolbar and a menu?

■ PROJECTS

PROJECT 1–1

1. Start Windows.
2. Use the Start menu to open the Music library.
3. Use the Start menu to open the Control Panel.
4. Open the Clock, Language, and Region window from the Control Panel.
5. Open the Date and Time dialog box from the Control Panel.
6. Make the Music library active.
7. Close the Date and Time dialog box.
8. Go to Control Panel Home from the Control Panel.
9. Close all open windows.

PROJECT 1–2

1. Open the Recycle Bin.
2. Double-click a file, if available, and then close the Properties dialog box.
3. Restore the file.
4. Delete the contents of the Recycle Bin, if there are any, and if you are the sole user of the computer.
5. In the Recycle Bin, use the toolbar to change the view to Details.
6. Close the Recycle Bin.

PROJECT 1–3

1. Open Windows Help and Support.
2. Find information about **print**, and then display search results for printing using Windows.
3. Print the page, then close the Windows Help and Support window.
4. Open the Windows Media Center from the Start menu.
5. Click Music, then play a song if one is available.
6. Click the Pause button, click the Back button in the upper-left corner of the window, then play another song if one is available.
7. Click the Back button, view the music by genre, then view the music by artists.
8. Close the Windows Media Center.
9. Exit Windows.

CRITICAL THINKING

ACTIVITY 1–1

You want to add a photograph to your Web page, but first you need to edit the image. Use Windows Help and Support to find information about editing a photo in Paint and read several topics. Print the topic that lists tips for editing pictures. If you have a photo on your computer, open Paint, edit the image, and then save it and exit Paint. (*Note*: You can rotate, resize, add a shape or draw in the image.)

ACTIVITY 1–2

Your supervisor has asked you to prepare a handout on using keyboard shortcuts. Use Windows Help and Support to find information keyboard shortcuts. Read several topics, expand the one about Windows logo key keyboard shortcuts, select the table with your mouse, then print the selection in the Print dialog box.

ACTIVITY 1–3

You want to see how Windows can help you learn about burning a CD. Open Computer, Windows Help and Support, and the Control Panel. Search for "CD" in each window and write down the search results on a sheet of paper. Search for "burn CD" and compare the search results to the first search. Where possible, print the search results in each window.

INTRODUCTORY UNIT

MICROSOFT WORD 2010

LESSON 1

Microsoft Word Basics

■ OBJECTIVES

Upon completion of this lesson, you should be able to:

■ Start Word and understand the ways to view your document.

■ Enter text in a document and navigate a document.

■ Use Backspace and Delete to correct errors.

■ Save a document.

■ Open an existing document.

■ Use Full Screen Reading view.

■ Change the page orientation of a document. Preview and print a document.

■ Exit Word.

■ VOCABULARY

Draft view

Full Screen Reading view

insertion point

landscape orientation

Outline view

portrait orientation

Print Layout view

Quick Access Toolbar

Ribbon

status bar

toolbar

view buttons

Web Layout view

word processing

word wrap

Zoom

Introduction to Word Processing

▶ **VOCABULARY**
word processing

Word processing is the use of computer software to enter and edit text. When using word-processing software such as Word, you can easily create and edit documents such as letters and reports. You can even create more complex documents such as newsletters with pictures and other graphics. These documents can be used in your school, career, personal, and business activities.

The lessons in this unit contain step-by-step exercises for you to complete using a computer and Word. You'll learn how to start Word, enter and edit text, save and open a document, and switch among the various ways to view a document. You'll also learn how to change the orientation of a page, preview and print a document, and exit Word.

Starting Word

To start Word, click the Start button on the taskbar. Click All Programs on the Start menu, and then click Microsoft Office on the submenu. Click Microsoft Word 2010. A screen displaying copyright information appears briefly, followed by a window containing a blank page in which you can create and edit documents. See **Figure 1–1**.

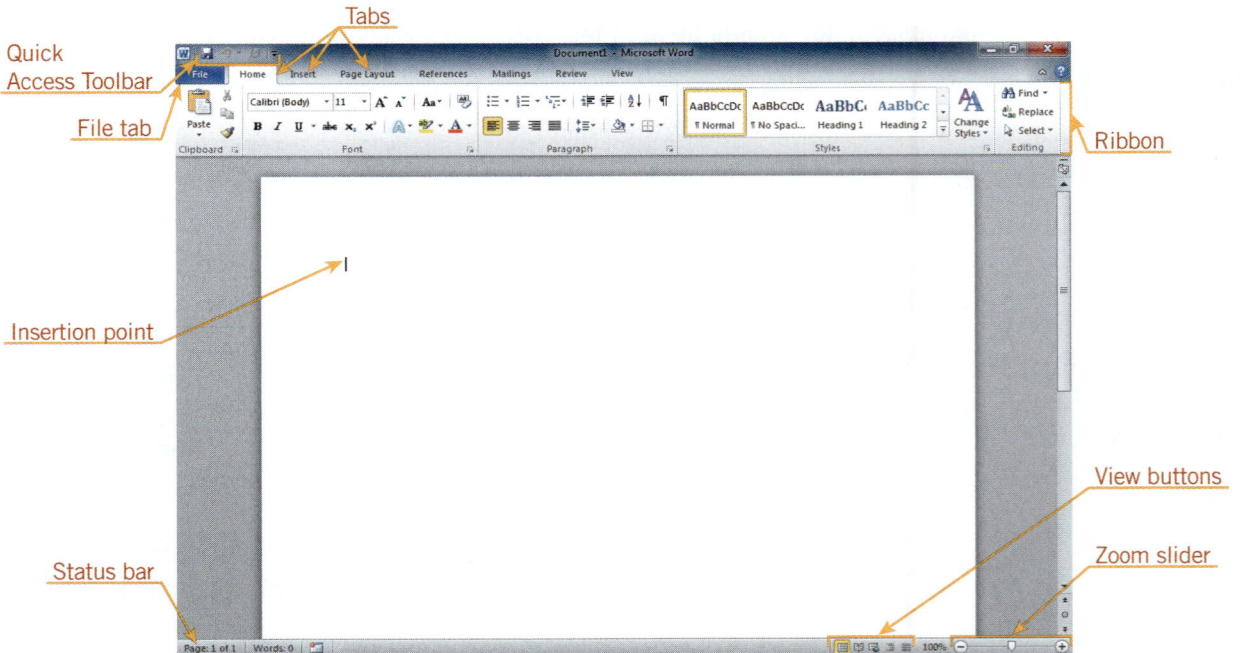

FIGURE 1–1   Opening screen in Word

Step-by-Step 1.1

1. Click the **Start** button 🪟 on the taskbar.

2. Click **All Programs**. The Start menu changes to show all the programs installed on the computer.

3. On the Start menu, click the **Microsoft Office** folder. The list of programs in the folder appears. Click **Microsoft Word 2010** on the submenu. Word starts and a blank document appears in the program window, as shown in Figure 1–1.

4. Leave the blank Word document open for the next Step-by-Step.

Identifying Parts of the Word Program Window

Look carefully at the parts of the Word program window labeled in Figure 1–1, and find them on your screen. Many of these elements appear in other Office applications. **Table 1–1** describes some of the commonly used elements of the program window.

TABLE 1–1   Understanding the Word program window

ELEMENT	FUNCTION
Ribbon	Contains commands for working with the document, organized by tabs.
Quick Access Toolbar	Contains buttons (icons) for common commands.
Insertion point	Shows where text will appear when you begin typing.
Status bar	Displays information about the current document and process.
View buttons	Allows you to change views quickly.
Zoom slider	Allows you to increase or decrease the size of the document on-screen.

When the pointer is in the document window, it looks like an uppercase letter *I* and is called the I-beam pointer. When you move the pointer out of the document window toward the Ribbon or the status bar, it turns into an arrow to allow you to point to and click the buttons. The pointer changes into other shapes for performing certain tasks.

Understanding Document Views

As you work with a document, you might want to change the way it looks on the screen. Word provides five ways to view a document on the screen: Print Layout, Full Screen Reading, Web Layout, Outline, and Draft. **Table 1–2** describes each view.

TABLE 1–2   Document views

VIEW	DESCRIPTION
Print Layout	Shows how a document will look when it is printed
Full Screen Reading	Shows text on the screen in a format that is easy to read and hides the Ribbon
Web Layout	Simulates the way a document will look when it is viewed as a Web page; text and graphics appear the way they would in a Web browser
Outline	Displays headings and text in outline form so you can see the structure of your document and reorganize easily
Draft	Displays only the text of a document without showing the arrangement of the text; if your document includes any pictures, they would not appear

To switch between views, on the Ribbon, click the View tab, and then in the Document Views group, click the button that corresponds to the view you want. You can also click one of the *view buttons* at the bottom-right of the document window, to the left of the Zoom slider. Switching views changes only the way the document looks on the screen. It does not change the way it looks when you print it. You will work in Print Layout view most of the time.

▶ **VOCABULARY**

view buttons

insertion point

word wrap

Inserting Text and Understanding Word Wrap

To enter text in a new document, you begin typing. The text appears in the document window at the *insertion point*. As you type, the insertion point moves to the right and the word count indicator in the status bar changes to show the number of words in the document. If the text you are typing extends beyond the right margin, it automatically moves to the next line. This feature is called *word wrap* because words are "wrapped around" to the next line when they do not fit on the current line.

When you press Enter, a blank line is inserted automatically and you start a new paragraph. Most documents in the business world are typed with a blank line between paragraphs, rather than indenting the first line of each paragraph. The settings in Word help you do this easily.

Step-by-Step 1.2

1. Type the following text. As you type, watch how the words at the end of lines wrap to the next line. If you type a word incorrectly, just continue typing. You learn how to correct errors later in this lesson.

   You should take the time to plan and organize your work. To help you meet your goals, it can be helpful to list the tasks you need to accomplish, and then you can rank them by importance.

2. Press **Enter**. The insertion point skips a line and appears blinking at the left margin, as shown in **Figure 1–2**.

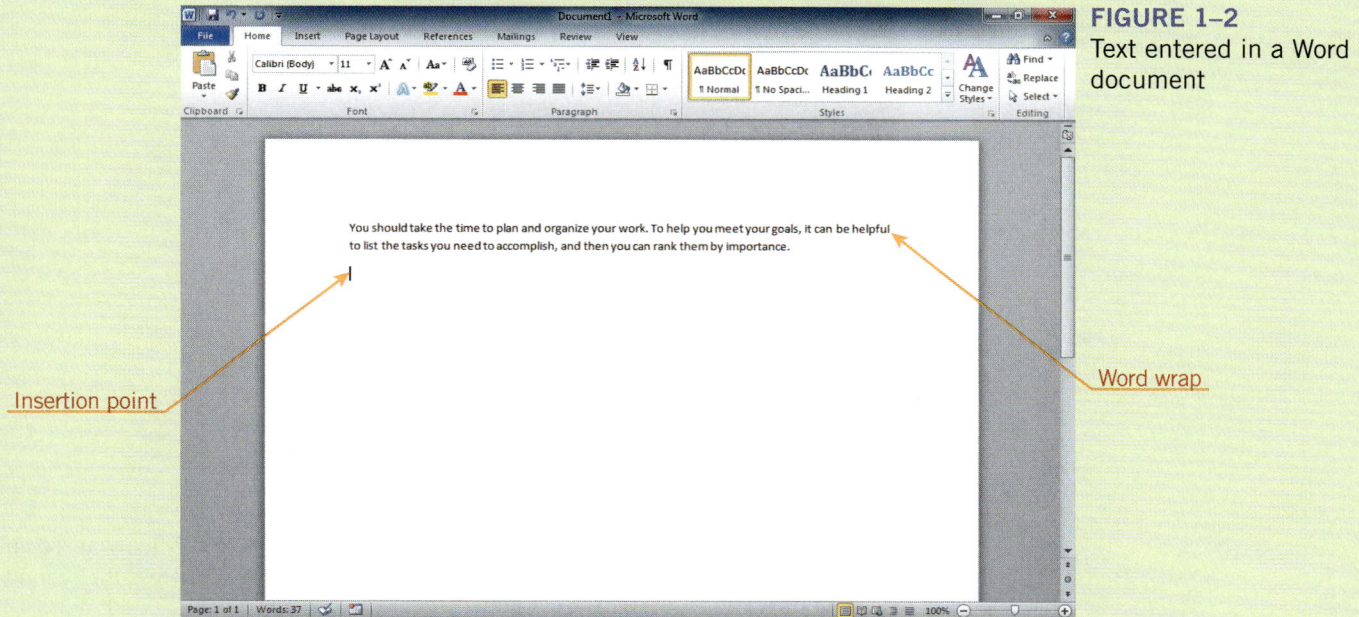

FIGURE 1–2
Text entered in a Word document

Insertion point

Word wrap

3. Type the following text. Press **Enter** at the end of each paragraph.

   Start by listing everything you need to accomplish today. Include both tasks that you must complete, as well as tasks you would like to complete.

   Next, examine the tasks you listed, and then number them in order of importance. Once you have the items in order, you have a plan!

4. Leave the document open for the next Step-by-Step.

Navigating a Document

To correct errors, insert new text, or change existing text, you must know how to reposition the insertion point in a document. You can move the insertion point in a document by using the mouse or the keyboard. To reposition the insertion point using the mouse, move the mouse so that the pointer moves to the position where you want the insertion point to appear, and then click the left mouse button. The blinking insertion point appears at the point you clicked.

When working with a long document, it is faster to use the keyboard to move the insertion point. **Table 1–3** lists the keys you can press to move the insertion point.

TABLE 1–3 Keyboard shortcuts for moving the insertion point

PRESS	TO MOVE THE INSERTION POINT
Right arrow	Right one character
Left arrow	Left one character
Down arrow	To the next line
Up arrow	To the previous line
End	To the end of the line
Home	To the beginning of the line
Page Down	To the next page
Page Up	To the previous page
Ctrl+right arrow	To the beginning of the next word
Ctrl+left arrow	To the beginning of the previous word
Ctrl+End	To the end of the document
Ctrl+Home	To the beginning of the document

In Table 1–3, two keys are listed for some of the movements. When you see an instruction to press two keys at once, press and hold the first key, press the second key, and then let go of both keys.

Step-by-Step 1.3

1. Press **Ctrl+Home**. The insertion point jumps to the beginning of the document.

2. Press **Ctrl+right arrow** four times to move to the fourth word (*time*) in the first line.

3. Press **End**. The insertion point moves to the end of the first line.

4. Press **down arrow** to move to the end of the next line.

5. Press **Ctrl+End**. The insertion point jumps to the end of the document.

6. Press **Ctrl+Home** to move back to the beginning of the document.

7. Leave the document open for the next Step-by-Step.

Using Backspace and Delete

If you make a mistake typing, or you just want to change text, you might need to delete characters or words. There are two ways to delete characters: Use Backspace or Delete. Pressing Backspace deletes the character to the left of the insertion point. Pressing Delete deletes the character to the right of the insertion point.

Step-by-Step 1.4

1. Position the insertion point after the word *should* in the first sentence of the document.

2. Press **Backspace** until the words *You should* are deleted.

3. Press **Delete** twice to delete the space and the lowercase letter *t* in the word *take*, and then type **T**.

4. In the second sentence of the first paragraph, position the insertion point before the third word instance of the word *you* (after the word *then*).

5. Press **Delete** until the words *you can* and the space after *can* are deleted.

6. Look over the document. Position the insertion point as needed, and then use Backspace or Delete to correct any typing errors you made.

7. Leave the document open for the next Step-by-Step.

Saving a Document

When you save a document for the first time, you can click the Save button on the **Quick Access Toolbar**. You can also click the File tab, and then on the navigation bar, click the Save or Save As command. In all three cases, the Save As dialog box

▶ **VOCABULARY**
Quick Access Toolbar

appears, as shown in **Figure 1–3**. This is where you name your file and choose a location to save it in.

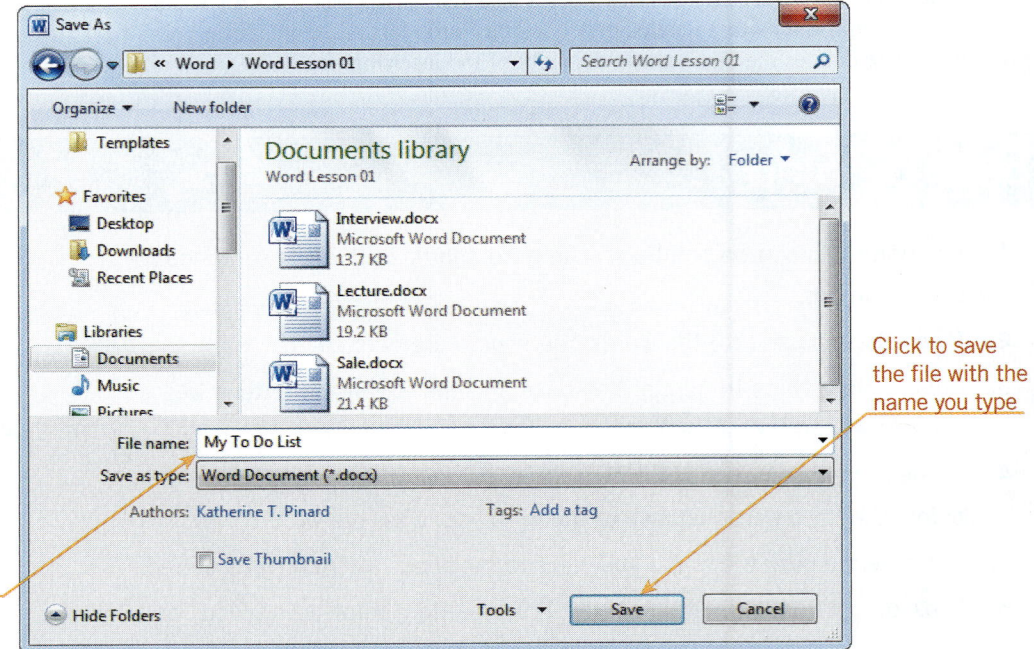
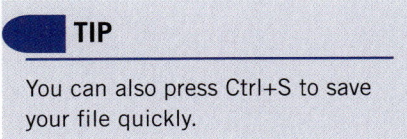

FIGURE 1–3   Save As dialog box

TIP

You can also press Ctrl+S to save your file quickly.

Once you have saved a document for the first time, you can click the Save button on the Quick Access Toolbar, or you can click the File tab, and then on the navigation bar, click the Save command, and Word saves the changes you made in the document by copying over the previous version. If you don't want to copy over the original version of your document, you can use the Save As command to open the Save As dialog box and save it using a different name or to a new location.

Creating Folders

EXTRA FOR EXPERTS

You can rename a folder by right-clicking the folder, and then clicking Rename on the shortcut menu.

Folders can help you organize files. You can create a new folder in the Save As dialog box. To create a new folder within your current folder, click the New folder button on the toolbar in the Save As dialog box. A new folder appears in the list with the temporary name "New folder" highlighted in blue, as shown in **Figure 1–4**. Because the name is highlighted, you can just type the new folder name, and the text you type will replace the old name. When you are finished, press Enter. The folder name is changed and the folder opens to become the current folder.

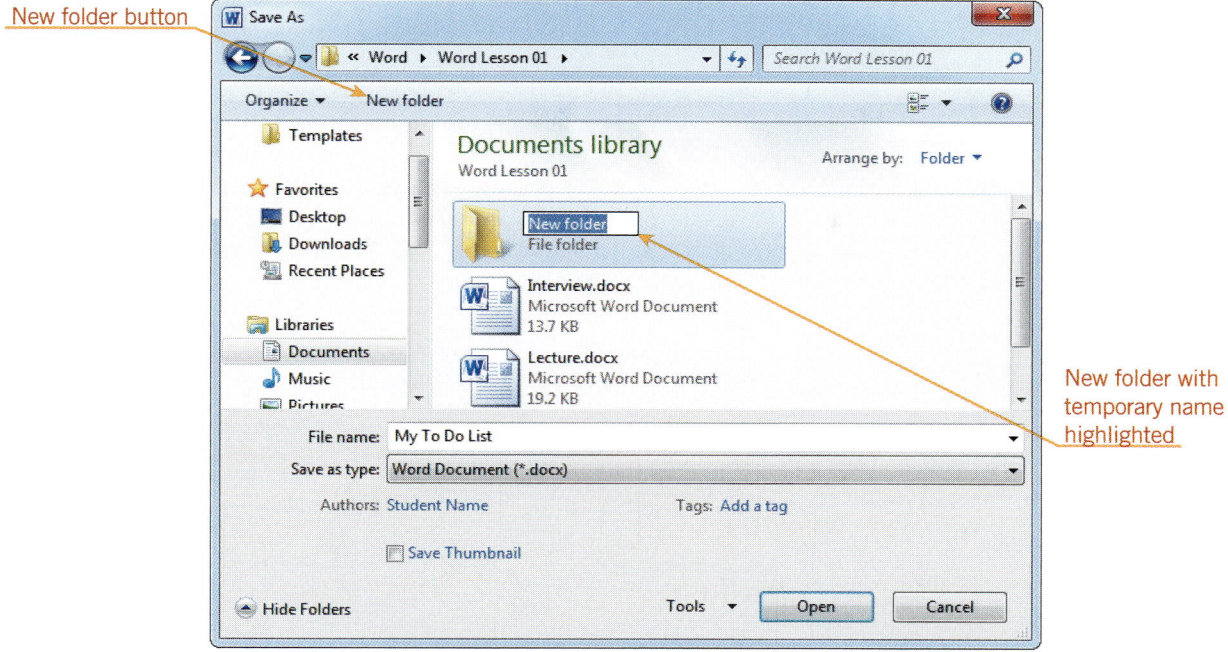

New folder button

New folder with temporary name highlighted

FIGURE 1–4   Save As dialog box after creating a new folder

Step-by-Step 1.5

1. On the Ribbon, click the **File** tab, and then on the navigation bar, click the **Save As** command. The Save As dialog box appears. Refer back to Figure 1–3.

2. Navigate to the drive and folder where your Data Files are stored.

3. Double-click the **Word** folder, and then double-click the **Word Lesson 01** folder.

4. On the toolbar, click the **New folder** button. A new folder appears in the list in the dialog box with the name highlighted. Refer back to Figure 1–4.

5. Type **My Tasks**, and then press **Enter**. Click **Open**. The Address bar at the top of the Save As dialog box changes to indicate that My Tasks is the current folder.

6. In the File name box, select the entire name of the file, if necessary. Type **My To Do List** followed by your initials.

7. Click **Save**. Word saves the file in the folder you created, and the dialog box closes. The new file name appears at the top of the document window.

8. Click the **File** tab, and then on the navigation bar, click the **Close** command to close the document without exiting Word.

9. Keep Word open for the next Step-by-Step.

Locating and Opening an Existing Document

You can open an existing document by clicking the File tab, and then on the navigation bar, clicking the Open command. This displays the Open dialog box, as shown in **Figure 1–5**, where you can open a file from any available disk and folder. If you worked on the document recently, you can click the File tab, on the navigation bar, click Recent, and then in the middle pane, click the name of the document in the list of recently opened and saved documents.

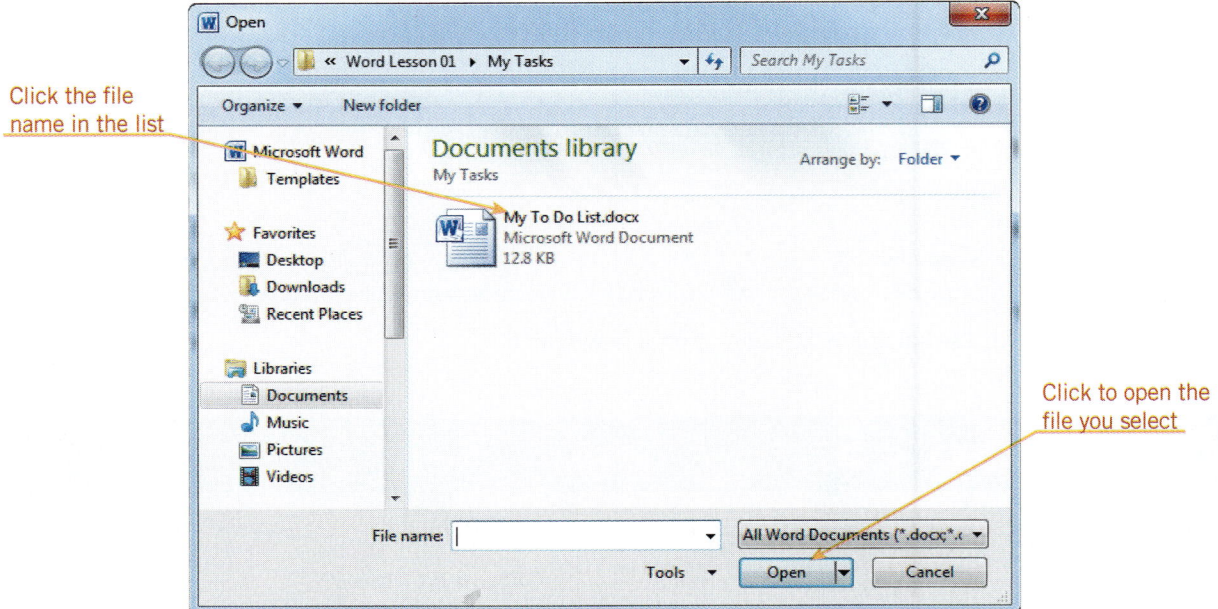

FIGURE 1–5   Open dialog box

Opening a New, Blank Document

You can open a new, blank document by clicking the File tab, and then on the navigation bar, clicking New. This opens the New tab in Backstage view, as shown in **Figure 1–6**. In the Available Templates list in the center, the Blank document button is selected. Click the Create button in the pane on the right to close Backstage view and open a new, blank document.

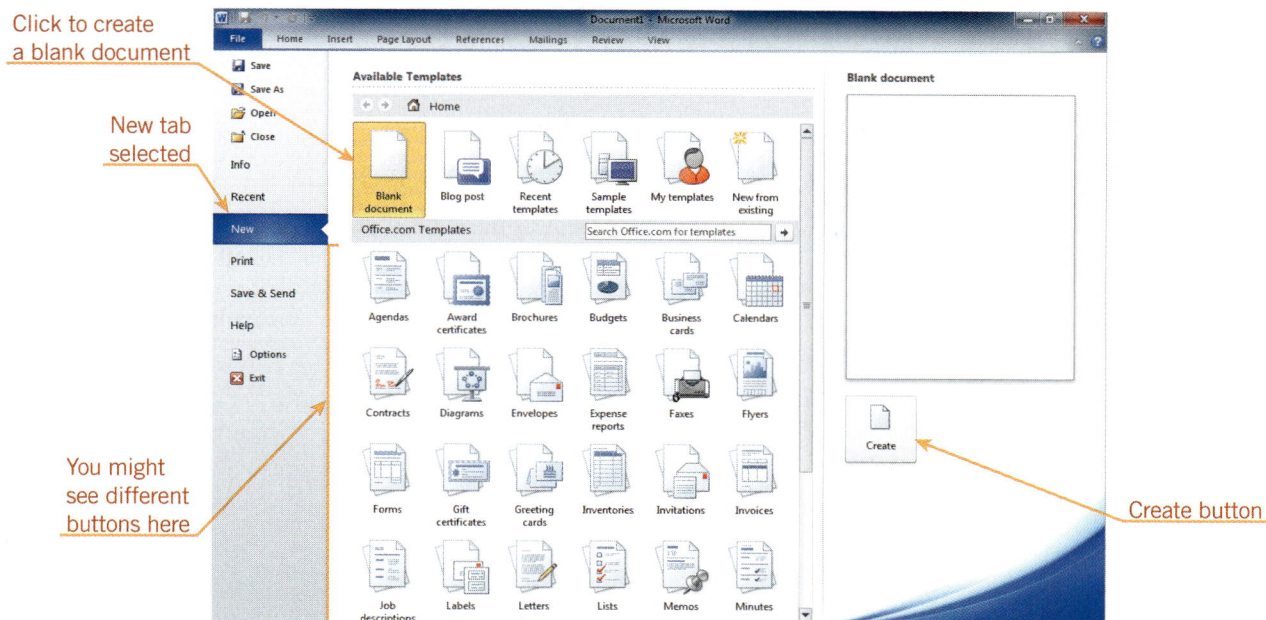

Click to create
a blank document

New tab
selected

You might
see different
buttons here

Create button

FIGURE 1–6   New tab in Backstage view

Step-by-Step 1.6

1. With Word still running, click the **File** tab, and then on the navigation bar, click the **Open** command. The Open dialog box appears.

2. If necessary, navigate to the drive and folder where your Data Files are stored.

3. If necessary, double-click the **Word** folder. Double-click the **Word Lesson 01** folder. Finally, double-click the **My Tasks** folder. The saved file My To Do List.docx appears in the dialog box.

4. Click **My To Do List.docx** in the list. Click **Open**. The My To Do List document appears on the screen.

5. Leave the document open for the next Step-by-Step.

TIP

You can also open a file by double-clicking it in the Open dialog box.

WARNING

If the yellow Protected View bar appears at the top of the document window when you open the document, click the Enable Editing button, and then continue with Step 5.

Zooming a Document

You can use the *Zoom* feature to magnify and reduce your document on the screen. Zoom is measured in percentage. A zoom percentage of 100% shows the document at its normal size. The higher the percentage, the larger the document appears; the lower the percentage, the smaller the document appears. The easiest way to change the percentage is to drag the Zoom slider at the bottom-right of the screen, or to click the Zoom In or Zoom Out buttons on either end of the Zoom slider. You can also click the Zoom level

VOCABULARY
Zoom

percentage to the left of the Zoom slider to open the Zoom dialog box. Finally, you can click the View tab on the Ribbon, and then click one of the buttons in the Zoom group to zoom to a preset percentage, or click the Zoom button to open the Zoom dialog box.

Switching to Full Screen Reading View

Full Screen Reading view removes the Ribbon and the status bar from the screen. It leaves only the document and, in place of the Ribbon, a small bar called a *toolbar* that contains buttons for performing commands. See **Figure 1–7**. Full Screen Reading view is useful for reading the document on the screen. It does not show how the document will look when printed on paper.

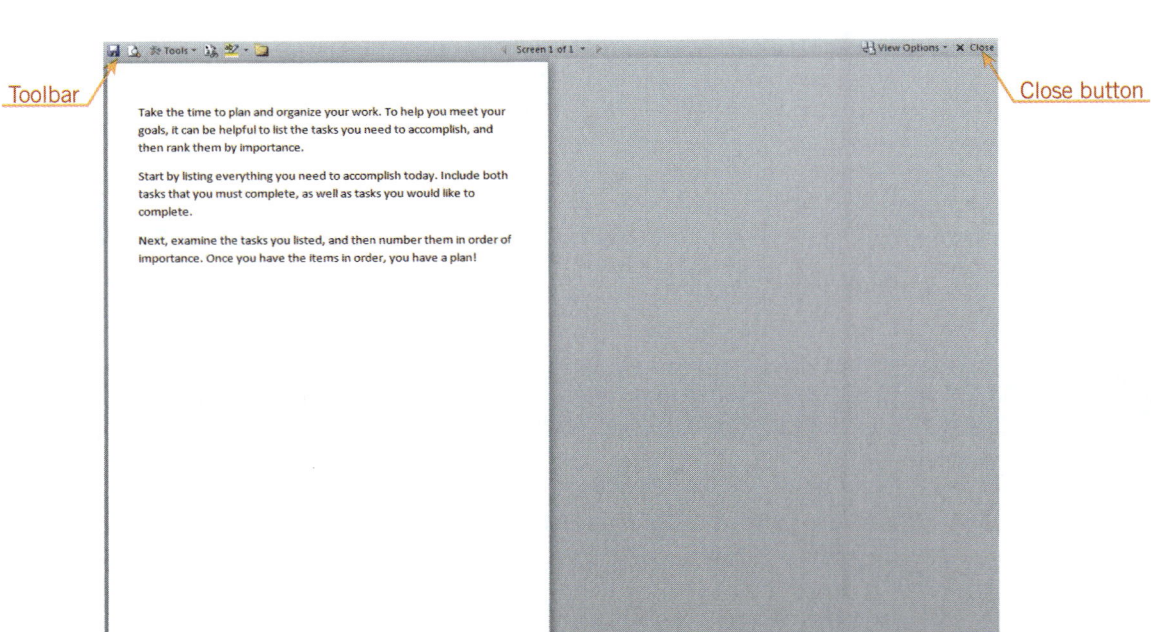

FIGURE 1–7   Document in Full Screen Reading view

To use Full Screen Reading view, click the View tab on the Ribbon, and then in the Document Views group, click the Full Screen Reading button. You can also click the Full Screen Reading button on the status bar to the left of the Zoom slider. To return to Print Layout view, click the Close button on the toolbar at the top of the screen.

Step-by-Step 1.7

1. At the lower-right of the document window, drag the **Zoom slider** all the way to the left. The zoom percentage is changed to 10% and the document appears as a small piece of paper in the upper-left of the document window.

2. At the right end of the Zoom slider, click the **Zoom In** button ⊕ five times. The zoom percentage increases by 10 each time you click the Zoom In button. The zoom percentage is now 60%.

3. On the Ribbon, click the **View** tab. The Ribbon changes to show the View commands. In the Zoom group, click the **Page Width** button. The document just about fills the screen. See **Figure 1–8**.

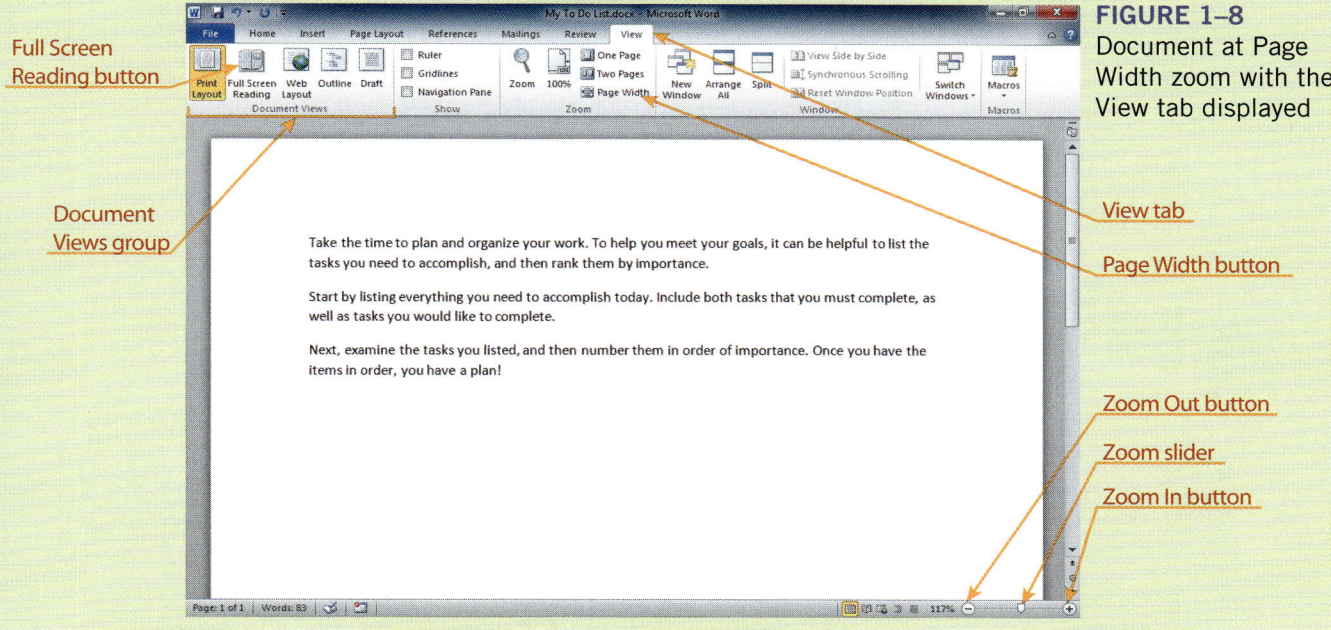

FIGURE 1–8
Document at Page Width zoom with the View tab displayed

Full Screen Reading button

Document Views group

View tab

Page Width button

Zoom Out button

Zoom slider

Zoom In button

4. On the View tab, in the Zoom group, click the **One Page** button. The zoom changes to show the whole page on the screen.

5. On the View tab, locate the Document Views group. Click the **Full Screen Reading** button. The view changes to Full Screen Reading view.

6. At the right end of the toolbar, click the **Close** button. You return to Print Layout view.

7. Leave the document open for the next Step-by-Step.

Selecting a Page Orientation

Word has two ways to print text on a page. Documents printed in *portrait orientation*, as shown in **Figure 1–9**, are longer than they are wide. By default, Word is set to print pages in portrait orientation. In contrast, documents printed in *landscape orientation*, as shown in **Figure 1–10**, are wider than they are long. Most documents are printed in portrait orientation. Some documents, such as documents with graphics or numerical information, look better when printed in landscape orientation.

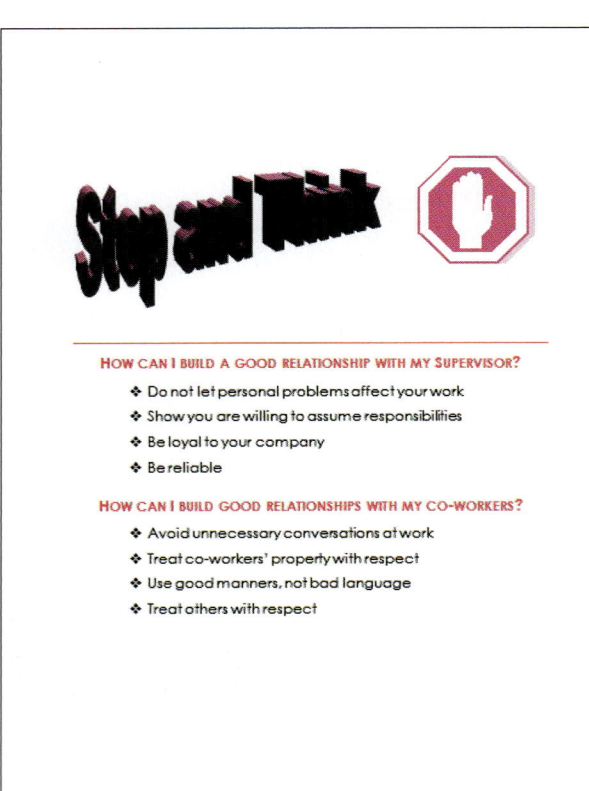

FIGURE 1–9   Portrait orientation

FIGURE 1–10   Landscape orientation

You can change the orientation of the document you want to print. To do this, click the Page Layout tab on the Ribbon, and then, in the Page Setup group, click the Orientation button, as shown in **Figure 1–11**. On the menu, click the option you want.

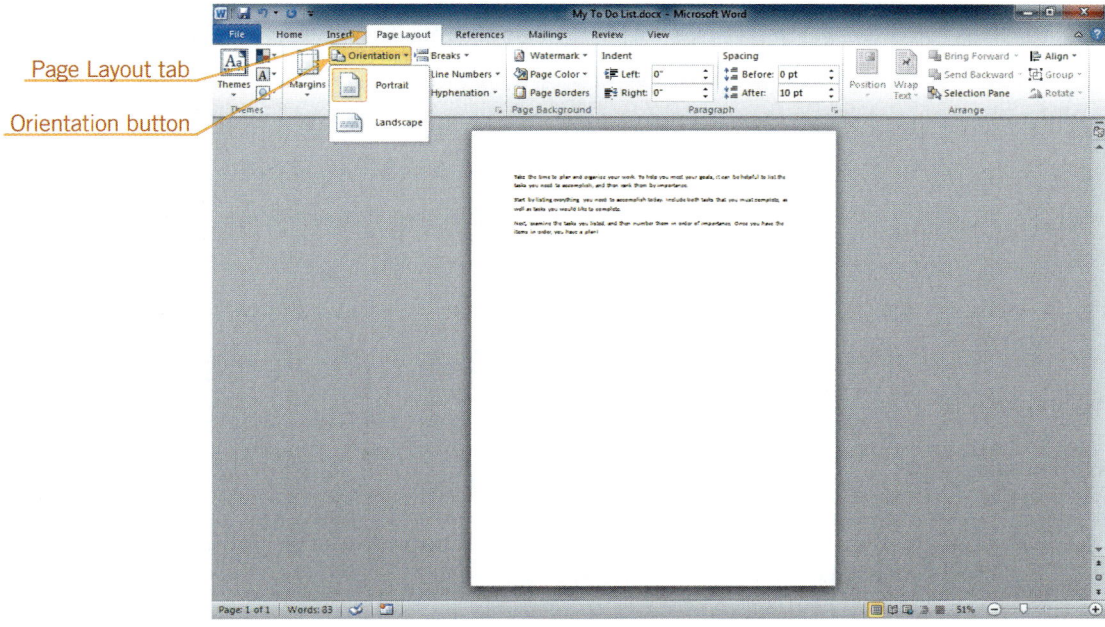

FIGURE 1–11   Changing page orientation on the Page Layout tab

You can also change the orientation on the Print tab in Backstage view. After displaying the Print tab, click the Portrait Orientation button or the Landscape Orientation button in the Settings section, and then click the orientation you want to use on the menu.

Step-by-Step 1.8

1. On the Ribbon, click the **Page Layout** tab. The Page Layout commands appear on the Ribbon.

2. In the Page Setup group, click the **Orientation** button. Notice that Portrait is selected. Because the document is in One Page zoom, you can clearly see this.

3. Click **Landscape** on the menu. The page orientation of the document changes to landscape.

4. On the Ribbon, click the **File** tab, and then on the navigation bar, click **Print**. Notice in the preview that the page orientation of the document is landscape.

5. In the Settings section in the center pane, click the **Landscape Orientation** button. A menu opens.

6. On the menu, click **Portrait Orientation**. The orientation of the document changes back to portrait.

7. On the Ribbon, click the **File** tab. Backstage view closes and the Page Layout tab is selected again. You can see the entire page in portrait orientation.

8. On the Quick Access Toolbar, click the **Save** button 🖫.

9. Leave the document open for the next Step-by-Step.

Previewing and Printing a Document

The Print tab in Backstage view enables you to look at a document as it will appear when printed before you actually print it. To open the Print tab, click the File tab on the Ribbon, and then on the navigation bar, click Print. The Print tab appears as shown in **Figure 1–12**. A preview of how the document will print using the current settings appears on the right. You should always look at the preview to make sure the document will print as you expect.

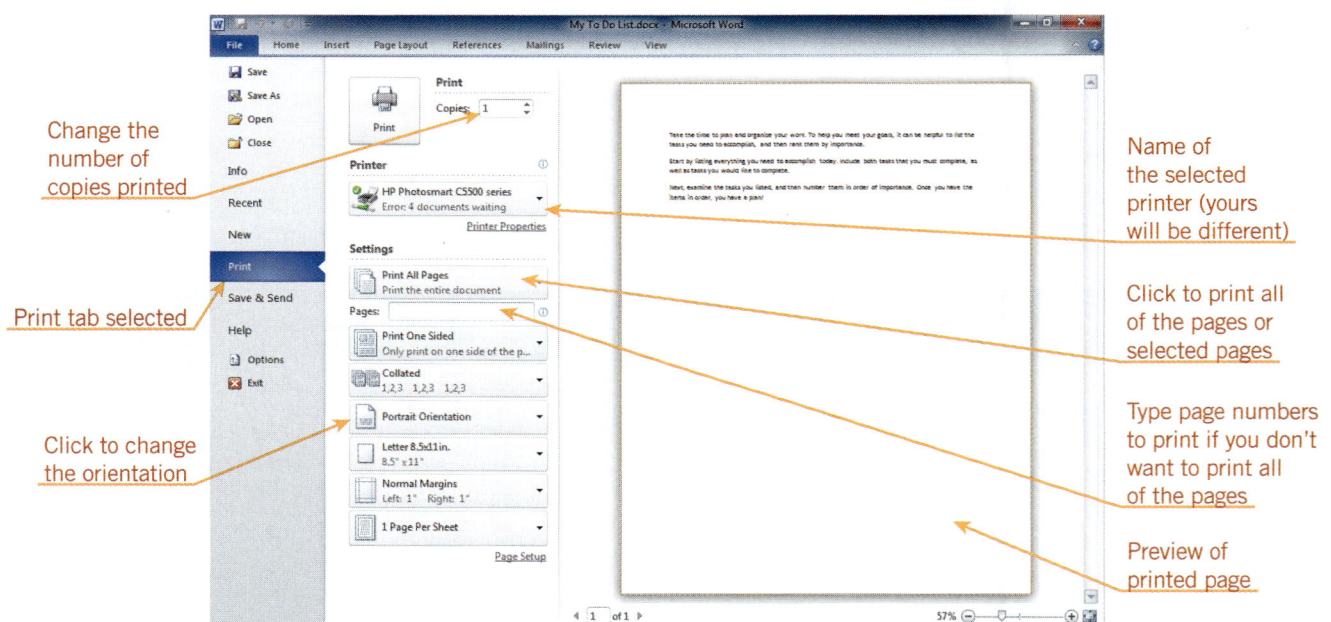

Change the number of copies printed

Print tab selected

Click to change the orientation

Name of the selected printer (yours will be different)

Click to print all of the pages or selected pages

Type page numbers to print if you don't want to print all of the pages

Preview of printed page

FIGURE 1–12   Print tab in Backstage view

The Print tab contains settings for printing your document. You can change the orientation, paper size, margins, and whether to print more than one page per sheet of paper or automatically shrink text to fit it on a page. You can zoom in on the document using the Zoom slider in the lower-right corner of Backstage view.

After you select the settings you want, to print a document, click the Print button in the center pane on the Print tab in Backstage view.

Step-by-Step 1.9

1. Use the **Zoom slider** ▽ to return to 100% view.

2. Press **Ctrl+End** to jump to the end of the document, press **Enter**, and then type your name.

3. On the Ribbon, click the **File** tab, and then on the navigation bar, click **Print**. The Print tab appears in Backstage view.

4. At the top of the center pane, click the **Print** button to print the document using the default settings.

5. Leave the document open for the next Step-by-Step.

Exiting Word

When you are finished working, you can close your document and exit Word. To close the document without exiting Word, click the File tab, and then on the navigation bar, click the Close command. To exit Word, click the Close button in the upper-right corner of the document window. You can also click the File tab on the Ribbon, and then on the navigation bar, click the Exit command.

Step-by-Step 1.10

1. On the Ribbon, click the **File** tab.

2. On the navigation bar, click the **Close** command. A dialog box opens asking if you want to save any changes.

3. Click **Save**. The document closes, but Word is still running.

4. In the upper-right corner of the window, click the **Close** button [X]. Word exits and the Word program window closes.

SUMMARY

In this lesson, you learned:

- You can view the document screen in Print Layout view, Full Screen Reading view, Web Layout view, Outline view, and Draft view. The key elements of the screen in Print Layout view are the Ribbon, Quick Access Toolbar, insertion point, status bar, view buttons, and Zoom slider.

- When text is entered, the word wrap feature automatically wraps words to the next line if they will not fit on the current line.

- When corrections or additions need to be made, you can place the insertion point anywhere within a document using the mouse or keyboard, and then delete text using Backspace and Delete.

- When you save a document for the first time, the Save As dialog box opens. This is where you name your file and choose a location in which to save it. After you have saved a document the first time, you use the Save command to save your changes in the document or use the Save As command to save it with a different file name or to a new location.
- You can create new folders for storing documents in the Save As dialog box.
- You can locate and open an existing document using the Open dialog box.

- You can use the Zoom slider to magnify or reduce the size of your document on the screen.
- Full Screen Reading view makes it easier to view the entire document on the screen by removing the Ribbon and status bar and displaying only the text, not the layout, of the document.
- You can use the Orientation command to change the page orientation to portrait orientation or landscape orientation.
- You can preview and print a document by using the Print tab in Backstage view.

 ## VOCABULARY REVIEW

Define the following terms:

Draft view	Print Layout view	Web Layout view
Full Screen Reading view	Quick Access Toolbar	word processing
insertion point	Ribbon	word wrap
landscape orientation	status bar	Zoom
Outline view	toolbar	
portrait orientation	view buttons	

 ## REVIEW QUESTIONS

MULTIPLE CHOICE

Select the best response for the following statements.

1. In Full Screen Reading view, which of the following is visible?

   A. Ribbon
   B. Zoom slider
   C. toolbar
   D. status bar

2. Which dialog box do you use to save a file for the first time?

   A. Save
   B. Save As
   C. Save File
   D. Locate File

3. Dragging the Zoom slider to the left

   A. magnifies the document on-screen.
   B. reduces the size of the document on-screen.
   C. switches the document to Full Screen Reading view.
   D. changes the way the document will look when it is printed.

4. The feature that causes text you type to automatically move to the next line when it does not fit on the current line is called

   A. paragraphing.
   B. word processing.
   C. jumping.
   D. word wrap.

5. Commands for working with the document are organized into tabs on the

   A. Ribbon.
   B. status bar.
   C. Zoom slider.
   D. Quick Access Toolbar.

FILL IN THE BLANK

Complete the following sentences by writing the correct word or words in the blanks provided.

1. _____ view shows how a document will look when it is printed.

2. The _____ shows where text will appear when you begin typing.

3. Pressing Enter starts a new _____ in a document.

4. _____ can help you organize files on your disks.

5. Documents printed in _____ orientation are wider than they are tall.

TRUE / FALSE

Circle T if the statement is true or F if the statement is false.

T   F   **1.**   When the pointer is positioned in the document window, it takes the shape of the I-beam pointer.

T   F   **2.**   Word provides seven different views, including Web Layout view.

T   F   **3.**   Pressing Delete deletes the character immediately to the left of the insertion point.

T   F   **4.**   Pressing Ctrl+Home moves the insertion point to the beginning of the document.

T   F   **5.**   You can preview a document on the Preview tab in Backstage view.

■ PROJECTS

If you have a SAM 2010 user profile, your instructor may have assigned an autogradable version of the indicated project. If so, log into the SAM 2010 Web site at *www.cengage.com/sam2010* to download the instruction and start files.

PROJECT 1–1

Match the key or keys in the first column to the description in the second column.

Column 1

_____ 1. Right arrow

_____ 2. Left arrow

_____ 3. Down arrow

_____ 4. Up arrow

_____ 5. End

_____ 6. Home

_____ 7. Page Down

_____ 8. Page Up

_____ 9. Ctrl+right arrow

_____ 10. Ctrl+left arrow

_____ 11. Ctrl+End

_____ 12. Ctrl+Home

Column 2

A.   Moves to the end of the document

B.   Moves left one character

C.   Moves to the previous page

D.   Moves to the next line

E.   Moves to the beginning of a line

F.   Moves to the end of the line

G.   Moves right one character

H.   Moves to the beginning of the document

I.   Moves to the previous word

J.   Moves to the previous line

K.   Moves to the next page

L.   Moves to the next word

 **PROJECT 1–2**

1. Start Word. Open the **Lecture.docx** document from the drive and folder where your Data Files are stored. This is a flyer announcing an upcoming program at the planetarium.

2. Save the document as **Cosmic Connections Flyer** followed by your initials.

3. Scroll down so you can see the lines of text below the drawing. Place the insertion point at the end of the first sentence (after *galaxy.*), press the spacebar, and then type: **Dr. Scott Wycoski will be the guest lecturer.**

4. Place the insertion point after the word *Park* in the next line, and then use Backspace to delete that word and the extra space.

5. Create a new paragraph after *Green Hills Planetarium*. Type the following: **Thursday, May 9, 7 p.m. to 8 p.m.**

6. Change the view to Full Screen Reading.

7. Close Full Screen Reading view.

8. Change the zoom to One Page.

9. Change the orientation of the document to landscape.

10. Change the zoom back to 100%, press Ctrl+End, press Enter, and then type your name.

11. Save, print, and close the document. Exit Word.

PROJECT 1–3

1. Start Word. You will write a letter thanking Dr. Wycoski for his presentation.

2. Type today's date, using the format *May 10, 2013*.

3. Press Enter twice, and then type the following text:

Dear Dr. Wycoski,

Thank you for participating in our lecture series. Your presentation was very interesting! Thanks to your clear explanations, we now understand much more about the origins of the galaxy. Thank you again for helping to make our lecture series a great success.

Sincerely,

4. Press Enter twice to insert enough blank space after *Sincerely* for you to sign your name, and then type your name.

5. Change the document to Full Screen Reading view.

6. Close Full Screen Reading view.

7. Change the zoom to One Page.

8. Open the Save As dialog box. Navigate to the drive and folder where you want to save the file. Create a new folder in this location. Name the folder **My Letters**.

9. Make sure the My Letters folder is the current folder. Save the document as **Thank You Letter** followed by your initials.

10. Print and close the document. Exit Word.

PROJECT 1–4

1. Start Word, and then open the **Sale.docx** document from the drive and folder where your Data Files are stored. You will modify this advertisement for a department store sale.

2. Save the document as **Holiday Sale Flyer** followed by your initials.

3. Change the Zoom percentage to 110%.

4. Scroll down, and then position the insertion point in front of the sentence starting with *These great bargains*. Type: **Hurry now to Carville's for sale prices on all holiday products.** Press the spacebar.

5. Position the insertion point before the word *now* in the sentence you just typed, and then use Delete to delete that word and the space after it. Position the insertion point to the right of the word *products* in the second line in the document. Use Backspace to delete that word, and then type **items**.

6. Press Ctrl+End to move the insertion point to the end of the last sentence.

7. Press Enter, and then type your name.

8. Change the orientation of the document to **portrait**.

9. Save the document.

10. Preview and print the document. Close the document, and exit Word.

PROJECT 1–5

1. Start Word. Open the **Interview.docx** document from the drive and folder where your Data Files are stored. Save the document as **Interview Tips** followed by your initials. You will revise a page in this informational pamphlet provided as a resource for people seeking employment.

2. Change the zoom to Page Width.

3. Change to Full Screen Reading view.

4. Read the document to become familiar with it.

5. Close Full Screen Reading view.

6. Press Ctrl+Home to position the insertion point at the beginning of the document, if necessary.

7. Press Ctrl+right arrow five times to move the insertion point after the word *job* and before the word *ahead*. Type **interview**, and then press the spacebar.

8. Press Ctrl+End to position the insertion point at the end of the document. Press the spacebar, and then type: **The third thing you should do is to prepare a list of questions about the position for which you are interviewing. Make sure you do not ask about the salary at this point.**

9. Start a new paragraph and type: **After the interview, write a thank you note as soon as possible to the person who conducted the interview. A handwritten note will make a better impression than an e-mail. In addition to being good manners, it reminds the interviewer who you are, and it sets you apart from the other candidates.**

10. Proofread the document. Use Backspace or Delete to correct any errors.

11. Jump to the end of the document, insert a new paragraph, and then type your name.

12. Save, preview, print, and close the document. Exit Word.

CRITICAL THINKING

ACTIVITY 1–1

Thank you notes are easier to write when done promptly, preferably the day you receive a gift or attend an event. Using what you have learned in this lesson, start Word and write a thank you note to someone who has done something special for you recently. Save the document with a file name of your choice, print it, and then close the document and exit Word.

ACTIVITY 1–2

With Windows, a file name may contain up to 255 characters and include spaces. You should use a descriptive file name that will remind you of what the file contains, making it easy to find.

Read each item below. From the information given, create a file name for each document. Create a new Word document and type the file name next to the appropriate number in a list. Each file must have a different name. Strive to develop descriptive file names. Choose a file name for the document you created, and then save the document. Print and close your document, and then exit Word.

1. A letter to Binda's Boutique requesting a catalog.

2. A report entitled "Possible Problems Due to Global Warming" written by the environmental foundation, Earth!. The report will be used to develop a grant proposal.

3. A letter that will be enclosed with an order form used to place an order with Binda's Boutique.

4. A letter of complaint to Binda's Boutique for sending the wrong merchandise.

5. An announcement for a reception to be given in honor of a retiring executive, Serena Marsh.

6. A memo to all employees explaining new vacation time policies at Sheehan Global Enterprises.

7. Minutes of the November board of directors' meeting of Eastern Seaboard Insurance Company.

8. A press release written by Earth! to the media about a one-day event called *Live in Harmony with Nature*.

9. A mailing list for sending newsletters to all employees of Sheehan Global Enterprises.

10. An agenda for the December board of directors' meeting of Eastern Seaboard Insurance Company.

ACTIVITY 1–3

When you open the New tab in Backstage view, you see a variety of options for creating a new document. In addition to creating a blank document, you can create a document based on a template, which is a special type of document that contains sample text and formatting. When you open a template, it opens as a new document that you need to save with a file name.

Use the Help system in Word to find out more about creating a document from a template, and then use this information to create a new document based on one of the templates located in the Sample Templates folder (at the top of the New tab in Backstage view). Save the new document you create with the file name **Document Based on Template** followed by your initials. Close this document when you are finished.

Next, create a new, blank Word document, and then type the answer to the following questions based on the information presented in this Activity and in Help. Save the document you create using an appropriate file name, and then preview and print it. Close the document and exit Word.

- What is a template and why would you use one?
- Can a template contain text?
- How do you create a new document based on a template?

LESSON 2

Basic Editing

■ OBJECTIVES

Upon completion of this lesson, you should be able to:

- Show and hide formatting marks.
- Select text.
- Create paragraphs without blank space between them.
- Undo, redo, and repeat recent actions.
- Move and copy text using drag-and-drop and the Clipboard.
- Use the Office Clipboard.
- Find and replace text, and use the Go To command.
- Identify the number of words in a document or a selection.

■ VOCABULARY

Clipboard

copy

cut

drag

drag-and-drop

format

Office Clipboard

paste

select

toggle

Editing Text

Word's features and tools make it easy to edit documents. In this lesson, you will learn how to show and hide formatting marks, select text, and remove extra space after paragraphs. You will also undo and redo actions, move and copy text, and locate and replace text. Finally, you will learn how to jump to a specific location in the document, and count the number of words in a document or a selection of text.

Showing Formatting Marks

Many times it is easier to select and edit sentences and paragraphs if you can view the paragraph marks and other formatting symbols. The Show/Hide ¶ command allows you to see these hidden formatting marks, as shown in **Figure 2–1**. To view the formatting marks, click the Show/Hide ¶ button in the Paragraph group on the Home tab. The formatting marks do not appear when you print your document.

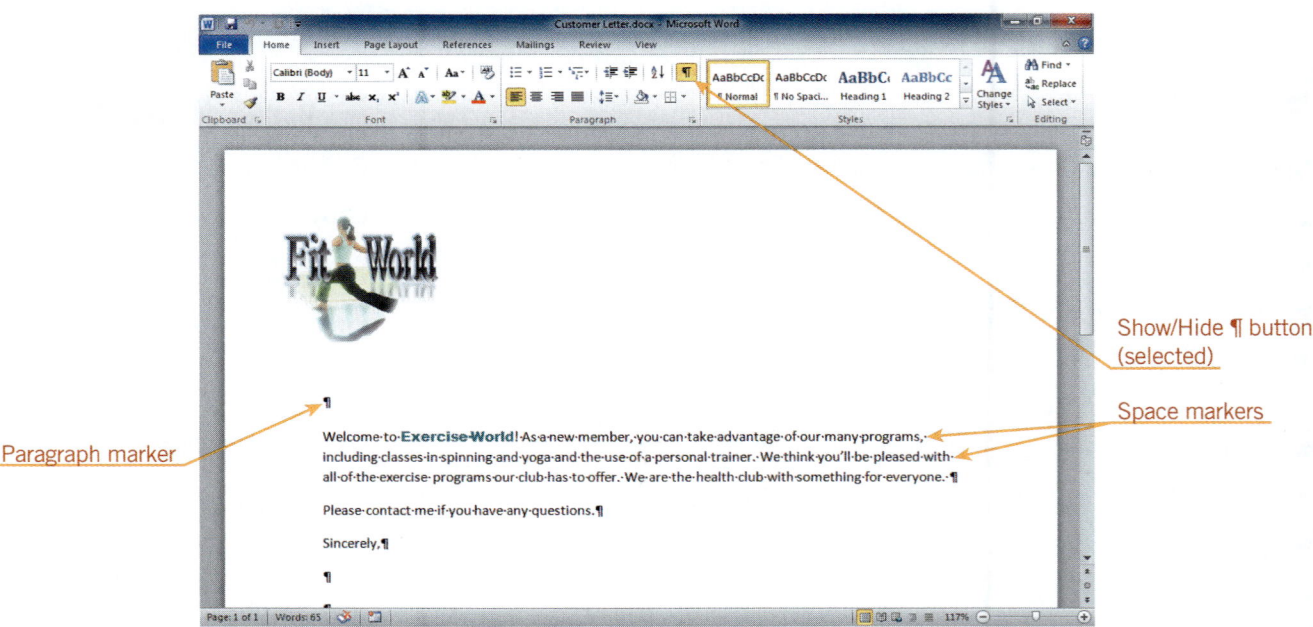

FIGURE 2–1   Formatting marks displayed

Understanding Toggle Commands

Clicking the Show/Hide ¶ button once displays paragraph and formatting marks; clicking the button again hides them. Switching between two options in this manner is known as ***toggling***, so a command that you use by turning a feature on or off is sometimes known as a toggle command. Word contains several toggle commands that turn a feature on or off. When a toggle command on the Ribbon is selected, it is orange. Toggle commands can also appear on a menu. When a toggle command on a menu is selected, a check mark appears next to it.

▶ **VOCABULARY**
toggle

Selecting Text

To *select* text means to highlight a block of text. Blocks can be as small as one character or as large as an entire document. After selecting a block of text, you can work with the entire block of text as a whole. You can select text using the mouse, using the keyboard, or using the keyboard in combination with the mouse.

To select text with the mouse, position the I-beam pointer to the left of the first character of the text you want to select. Hold down the left button on the mouse, drag the pointer to the end of the text you want to select, and release the button. This is called *dragging*. To remove the highlight, click the mouse button.

To select text with the keyboard, press and hold down Shift, and then press an arrow key in the direction of the text you want to select. Pressing Shift extends the selection in the direction of the arrow key you press. To select a word at a time, press and hold Shift+Ctrl, and then press the left or right arrow key. To select a paragraph at a time, press and hold Shift+Ctrl, and then press the up or down arrow key. **Table 2–1** summarizes additional ways to select text.

▶ **VOCABULARY**

select

drag

 TIP

To quickly select everything in a document, press and hold Ctrl+A or on the Home tab, in the Editing group, click the Select button, and then click Select All.

▦ **EXTRA FOR EXPERTS**

To select blocks of text that are not next to each other, select the first block of text, press and hold down Ctrl, and then use the mouse to select additional blocks of text.

TABLE 2–1   Selecting blocks of text

TO SELECT THIS	DO THIS
Characters	Click to the left of the first character you want to select, press and hold Shift, and then click to the right of the last character you want to select.
Word	Double-click the word.
Line	Position the pointer in the left margin next to the line so that it changes to ⇗, and then click.
Multiple lines	Position the pointer in the left margin next to the first line so that it changes to ⇗, press and hold the left mouse button, and then drag down or up in the margin to select as many lines as you want.
Sentence	Press and hold down Ctrl, and then click anywhere in the sentence.
Paragraph	Triple-click anywhere in the paragraph. Or Position the pointer in the left margin next to the paragraph so that it changes to ⇗, and then double-click.
Entire document	Triple-click in the left margin. Or Position the pointer in the left margin next to any line so that it changes to ⇗, press and hold down Ctrl, and then click in the left margin

Step-by-Step 2.1

1. Open the **Letter.docx** document from the drive and folder where your Data Files are stored. Save the document as **Customer Letter** followed by your initials.

2. On the Home tab, in the Paragraph group, click the **Show/Hide ¶** button ⊞. The paragraph marks and other hidden formatting marks appear on your screen, and the Show/Hide ¶ button on the Ribbon changes to orange to show that it is selected, as shown in Figure 2–1.

3. Position the pointer in the left margin to the left of the word *Welcome* so that it changes to ⟋. Click once. The first line in the document is selected, as shown in **Figure 2–2**.

FIGURE 2–2
A selected line of text

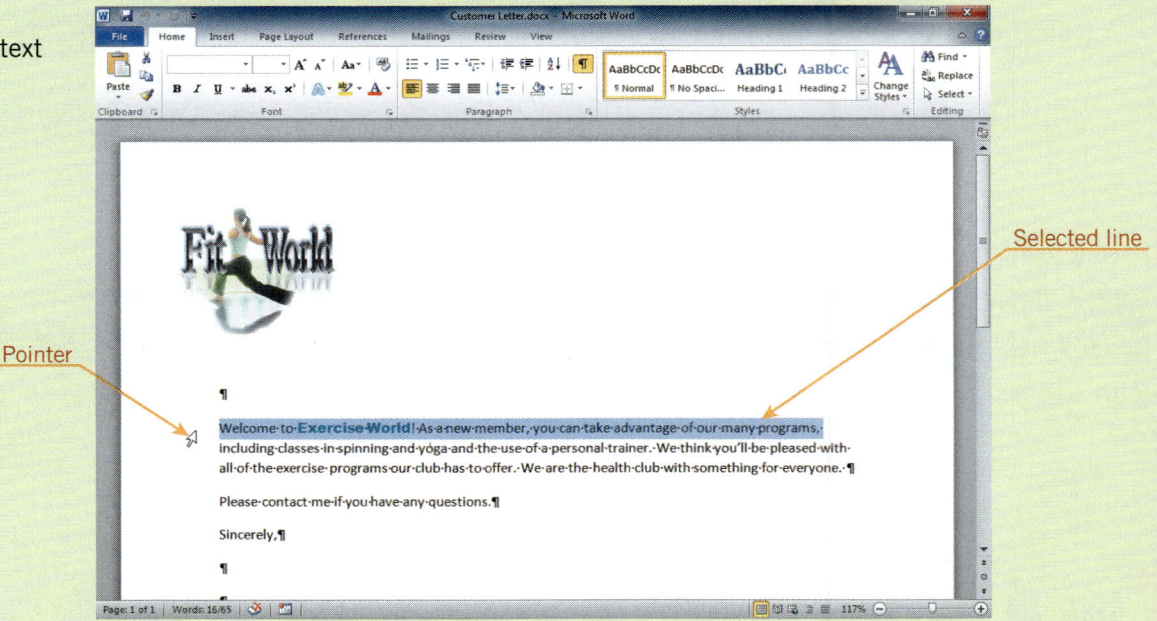

Pointer

Selected line

4. Click anywhere in the document. The text is deselected.

5. Double-click the word **Welcome** at the beginning of the first paragraph. The word is selected.

6. Click anywhere in the document to deselect the text.

7. Triple-click anywhere in the first paragraph. The entire paragraph is selected. Deselect the text.

8. In the first paragraph at the beginning of the second sentence, position the I-beam pointer before the letter *A* in the word *As*. Press and hold the left mouse button, and then drag to the right and down to just before the last sentence in the first paragraph (just before *We are the health club...*). Release the mouse button. The text you dragged the pointer over is selected.

TIP

You can also press an arrow key to deselect text.

9. On the Home tab, in the Editing group, click the **Select** button, and then click **Select All**. The entire document is selected. Deselect the text.

10. Press **Ctrl+A**. The entire document is selected again. Deselect the text.

11. Click the **Show/Hide ¶** button ¶. The formatting characters are hidden again.

12. Leave the document open for the next Step-by-Step.

Creating Paragraphs Without Blank Space Between Them

When you press Enter, you create a new paragraph. When you create a new paragraph, the default style is for extra space to be added after the original paragraph. The extra space is helpful when you are typing because you don't need to press Enter twice to insert space between paragraphs. But there may be times when you don't want that extra space to appear. For example, when you type a letter, extra space should not appear between the lines in the inside address.

You can format a paragraph so that it does not have extra space after it. To *format* text or paragraphs means to change its appearance. To do this, you can use the Line and Paragraph Spacing button, which is located in the Paragraph group on the Home tab. When you click this button, a gallery opens, as shown in **Figure 2–3**. To remove the space after the selected paragraphs, click Remove Space After Paragraph at the bottom of the menu. Notice that the command above this lets you add space before the paragraph. These commands change depending on the settings applied to the selected paragraphs. For example, if the selected paragraphs did not have space after them, the bottom command would be Add Space After Paragraph.

▶ **VOCABULARY**
format

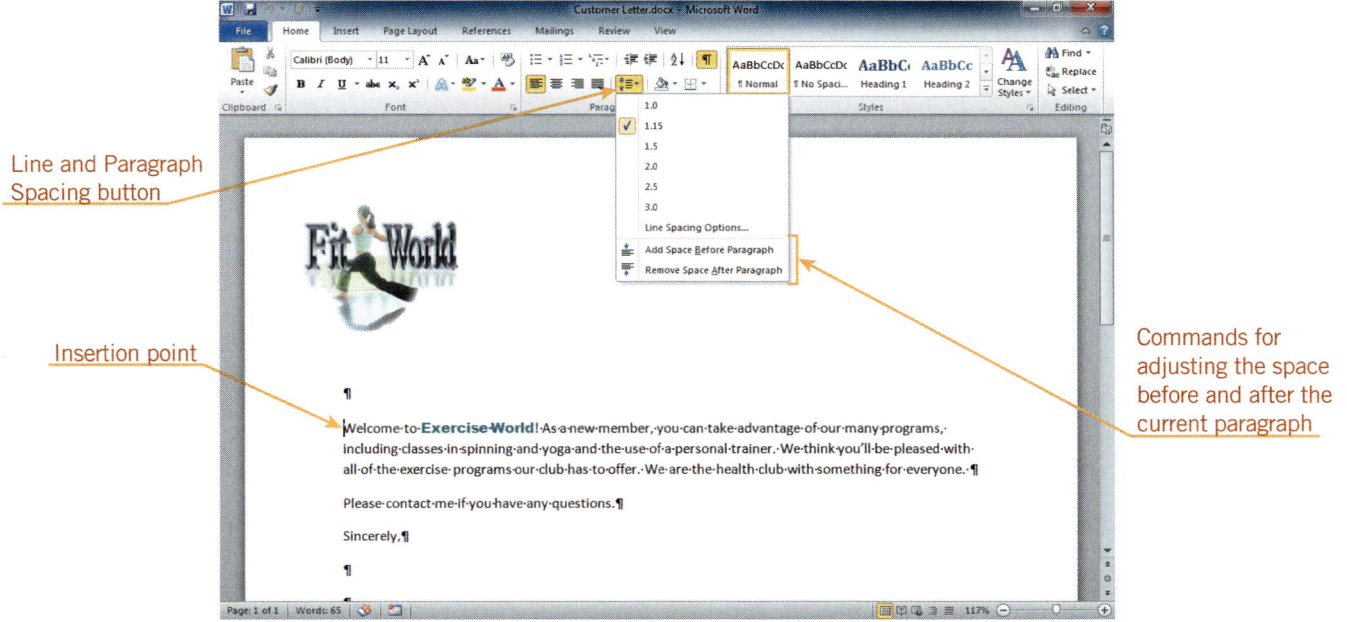

Line and Paragraph Spacing button

Insertion point

Commands for adjusting the space before and after the current paragraph

FIGURE 2–3   Line and Paragraph Spacing button menu

Step-by-Step 2.2

1. Click the **Show/Hide ¶** button ¶. The formatting marks are displayed.

2. In the vertical scroll bar, drag the scroll box to the top. Position the insertion point in the blank paragraph below the logo and above the first paragraph. Type **May 13, 2013**. Press **Enter**. A blank line is inserted and the insertion point is blinking at the beginning of a new paragraph.

3. Type **Karen DeSimone**.

4. On the Home tab, in the Paragraph group, click the **Line and Paragraph Spacing** button. A gallery opens as shown in Figure 2–3.

5. At the bottom of the menu, click **Remove Space After Paragraph**. The space after the current paragraph is removed. See **Figure 2–4**.

FIGURE 2–4
Paragraph with spacing after removed

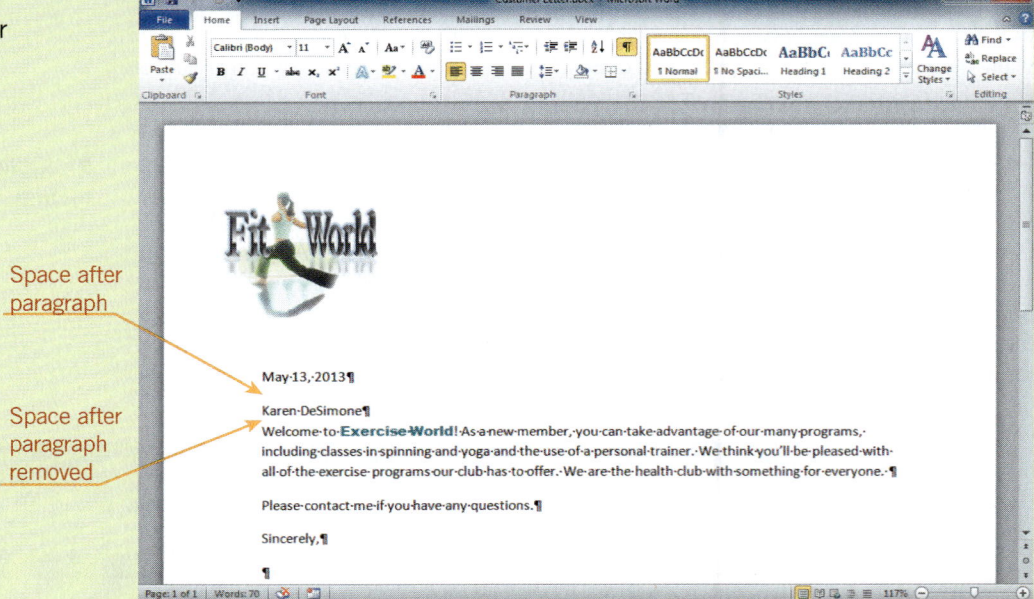

Space after paragraph

Space after paragraph removed

6. Press **Enter**. A new paragraph is created, but no space appears between the two paragraphs. Type **47 Bradford St.**, press **Enter**, and then type **Salem, RI 02922**. The inside address is complete.

7. In the Paragraph group, click the **Line and Paragraph Spacing** button, and then click **Add Space After Paragraph**. Space is inserted below the current paragraph.

8. Press **Enter**. A new paragraph is created. Because you changed the paragraph formatting before you pressed Enter, space was added after the previous paragraph.

9. Type **Dear Ms.**

10. On the Quick Access Toolbar, click the **Save** button to save your changes to the document. Leave the document open for the next Step-by-Step.

Using the Undo, Redo, and Repeat Commands

When working on a document, you might delete text accidentally or change your mind about editing or formatting changes that you made. The Undo command is useful in these situations because it reverses recent actions. To use the Undo command, click the Undo button on the Quick Access Toolbar.

You can keep clicking the Undo button to continue reversing recent actions, or you can click the arrow next to the Undo button to see a list of your recent actions. The most recent action appears at the top of the list, as shown in **Figure 2–5**. Click an action in the list, and Word will undo that action and all the actions listed above it.

TIP

You can also press Ctrl+Z to execute the Undo command.

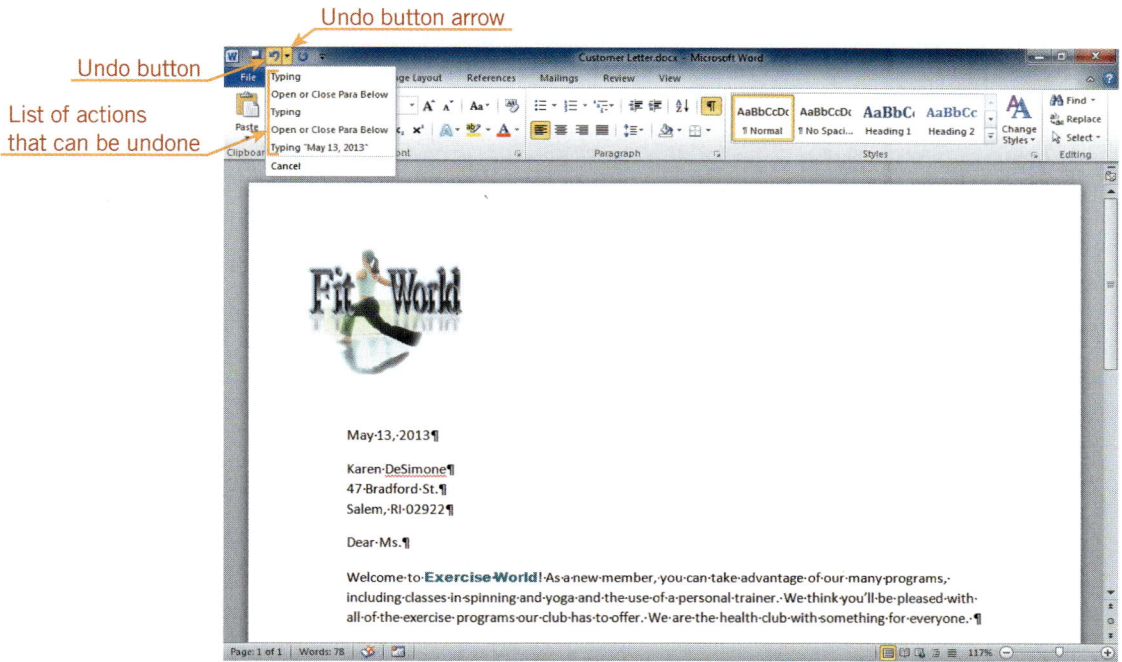

FIGURE 2–5   List of actions on the Undo button

The Redo command is similar to the Undo command. The Redo command reverses an Undo action. To use the Redo command, click the Redo button on the Quick Access Toolbar. Unlike the Undo command, you cannot open a list of actions to redo.

The Redo button does not appear on the Quick Access Toolbar until you have undone something. Until then, the Repeat button appears next to the Undo button. The Repeat command repeats the most recent action. For example, if you type something, and then click the Repeat button, the same text will appear on the screen. If you select text, delete it, and then select more text, clicking the Repeat button deletes the selected text. To use the Repeat command, click the Repeat button on the Quick Access Toolbar. The Repeat button is sometimes visible but light gray, which means that it is unavailable; that is, you can't repeat the most recent action.

TIP

You can also press Ctrl+Y to execute the Redo or Repeat command.

Step-by-Step 2.3

1. On the Quick Access Toolbar, click the **arrow** next to the Undo button. The list of actions that can be undone appears, similar to Figure 2–5. You might see additional actions on your list.

2. Point to the third item in the list. The action you point to as well as all of the actions above it are selected. The command at the bottom of the list changes from Cancel to Undo 3 Actions.

3. Click the third item on the Undo list. The last three actions are undone, and some of the text you typed disappears from the letter. Also note that the Redo button now appears next to the Undo button on the Quick Access Toolbar.

4. On the Quick Access Toolbar, click the **Redo** button three times. The actions you undid are redone and all the text is restored to the document. The Redo button on the Quick Access Toolbar changes to the Repeat button, which is now light gray, so clicking it will have no effect.

5. Double-click the word **Ms** in the salutation to select it. Press **Delete**. The selected word is deleted. On the Quick Access Toolbar, the Repeat button is now available.

6. Double-click the word **Dear** in the salutation to select it. On the Quick Access Toolbar, click the **Repeat** button. The last action is repeated and the selected word is deleted.

7. On the Quick Access Toolbar, click the **arrow** next to the Undo button. Click the second **Clear** in the list. The salutation is restored.

8. Deselect the text, and then save your changes to the document. Leave the document open for the next Step-by-Step.

Using Drag-and-Drop to Move and Copy Text

At some point when you are editing a document, you will probably want to move or copy text to a different location. The easiest way to move text is to select it, position the pointer on top of the selected text, and then drag the selected text to the new location. This is called *drag-and-drop*. As you drag the selected text, a vertical line follows the pointer indicating where the text will be positioned when you release the mouse button, as shown in **Figure 2–6**. If you want to copy the text instead of move it, you must press and hold Ctrl while you drag it.

▶ **VOCABULARY**
drag-and-drop

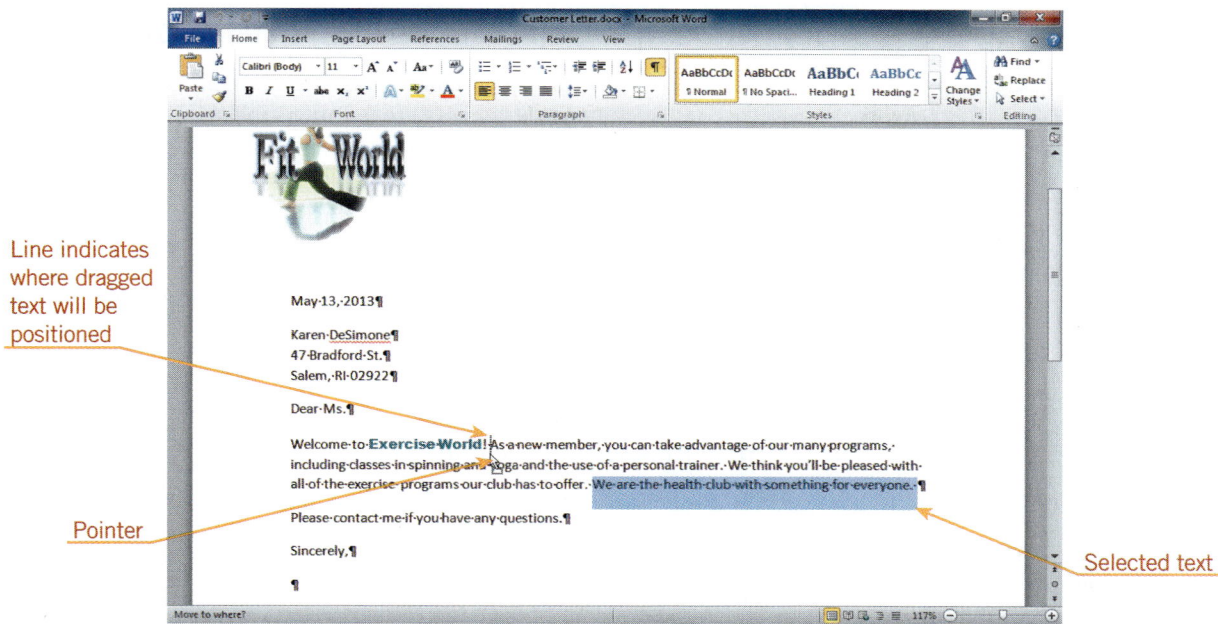

Line indicates where dragged text will be positioned

Pointer

Selected text

FIGURE 2–6   Using drag-and-drop to move selected text

Step-by-Step 2.4

1. Press and hold **Ctrl**, click the last sentence of the first paragraph to select it, and then release Ctrl.

2. Position the insertion point on top of the selected text. The pointer changes to ⌖.

3. Press and hold the left mouse button, and then drag the pointer up to the first line in the first paragraph until the vertical line following the pointer is positioned just before the word *As*, as shown in Figure 2–6. Release the mouse button. The selected sentence moves from the end of the first paragraph to become the second sentence in the first paragraph.

4. In the inside address, double-click **DeSimone**. The last name is selected.

5. Press and hold down **Ctrl**, and then drag the selected text to the salutation line so that the vertical indicator line is positioned between the period after Ms. and the paragraph mark. Release the mouse button and Ctrl. A copy of the selected text is positioned in the salutation line, and the original text is still in the inside address.

6. Press the **right arrow** key to deselect the text and move the insertion point after *DeSimone*, and then type **:** (a colon).

7. Save your changes to the document. Leave it open for the next Step-by-Step.

Using the Clipboard to Move and Copy Text

Another way to move or copy text is to use the Clipboard. The **Clipboard** is a temporary storage place in the computer's memory. To use the Clipboard, you cut or copy text. When you **cut** selected text, it is removed from the document and placed on the Clipboard. When you **copy** selected text, it remains in its original location and a copy of it is placed on the Clipboard. Once you have placed text on the Clipboard, you can then **paste** whatever is stored on the Clipboard into the document.

The Clipboard can hold only one selection at a time, so each time you cut or copy text, the newly cut or copied text replaces the text currently stored on the Clipboard. The Clipboard is available to all the programs on your computer, and it is sometimes called the system Clipboard.

Cutting and Pasting to Move Text

To move text from one location to another using the Clipboard, you need to use the Cut command and then the Paste command. First, select the text you want to move. Then, on the Home tab, in the Clipboard group, click the Cut button.

To paste the text stored on the Clipboard to a new place in the document, position the insertion point at the location where you want the text to appear. On the Home tab, in the Clipboard group, click the Paste button. The text currently stored on the Clipboard is pasted into the document. Moving text in this manner is referred to as *cutting and pasting*.

Copying and Pasting Text

To copy text in one location to another location, you need to use the Copy command. Select the text you want to copy. On the Home tab in the Clipboard group, click the Copy button.

To paste the copied text, you use the Paste command in the same manner as when you move text. This procedure is sometimes referred to as *copying and pasting*.

Using the Paste Options Button

When you use the Paste command, the Paste Options button appears below and to the right of the pasted text. Click this button to open a gallery of options. You can also click the arrow below the Paste button in the Clipboard group on the Home tab to see the Paste Options buttons. You can point to the buttons to see the effect using each one would have on the pasted text. See **Figure 2–7**. The Paste Options buttons change depending on what you pasted in the document. Usually when text is on the Clipboard, you can choose to paste the text so its appearance matches the original appearance (source formatting), so its appearance matches or merges with the text in the location where it is being pasted (destination formatting), or so it is pasted as text only, with no custom formatting. This means that it will match the formatting of the location where it is being pasted.

TIP

When you press Delete or Backspace, the text you delete is not placed on the Clipboard; it is simply removed from the document.

TIP

Press Ctrl+X to cut selected text; press Ctrl+C to copy selected text; and press Ctrl+V to paste text from the Clipboard into the document at the insertion point.

Arrow below the
Paste button

Paste Options
buttons

ScreenTip
identifying button
being pointed to

Live Preview of
text to be pasted

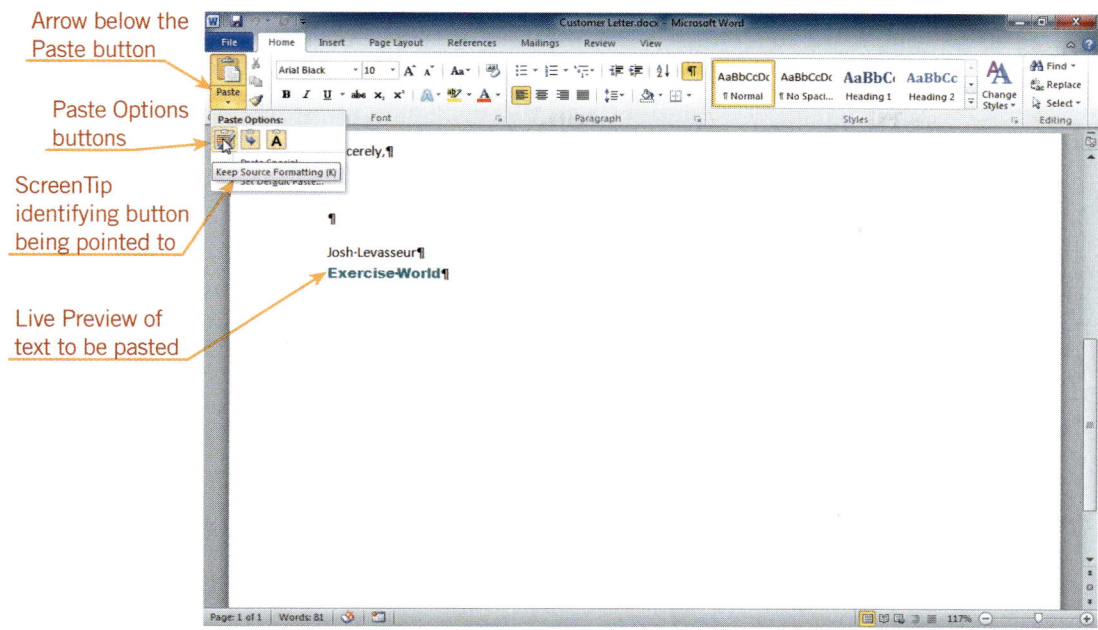

FIGURE 2–7   Paste Options buttons

Step-by-Step 2.5

1. Select the last sentence in the first paragraph (*We think you'll be pleased...*). On the Home tab, in the Clipboard group, click the **Cut** button ✂. The selected sentence disappears from the screen and is placed on the Clipboard.

2. Position the insertion point at the beginning of the second sentence in the first paragraph (immediately to the left of *We are the health club...*).

3. On the Home tab, in the Clipboard group, click the **Paste** button 📋. The sentence you cut is pasted at the location of the insertion point. The Paste Options button 📋 (Ctrl) ▾ appears just below the pasted text.

4. In the first sentence in the first paragraph, select the blue text **Exercise World**. On the Home tab, in the Clipboard group, click the **Copy** button 📄. The text stays in the document and is also placed on the Clipboard, replacing the sentence that you had previously cut and placed on the Clipboard.

5. Press **Ctrl+End**. The insertion point moves to the end of the document, in the blank paragraph below the closing.

6. On the Home tab, in the Clipboard group, click the **arrow** below the Paste button. The Paste Options buttons appear.

7. Position the pointer on top of the **Keep Source Formatting** button 📝. The text you copied appears in the document with the same formatting as the original. See Figure 2–7.

💬 EXTRA FOR EXPERTS

You can also access the Cut, Copy, and Paste commands by right-clicking the selected text, and then choosing the commands from the shortcut menu.

8. Position the pointer on top of the **Merge Formatting** button . The formatting of the text to be pasted changes to match the formatting of the text in the current paragraph.

9. Position the pointer on top of the **Keep Text Only** button . The formatting of the text to be pasted is plain, unformatted text. This formatting looks exactly the same as the formatting that appears when you pointed to the Merge Formatting button. This is what happens most of the time with these two options.

10. Click the **Merge Formatting** button .

11. Save your changes to the document. Leave it open for the next Step-by-Step.

Using the Office Clipboard

If you want to collect more than one selection at a time, you can use the Office Clipboard. The **Office Clipboard** is a special clipboard on which you can collect up to 24 selections. It is available only to Microsoft Office programs.

Unlike the system Clipboard, which is available all the time, you must activate the Office Clipboard to use it. On the Home tab, in the Clipboard group, click the Clipboard Dialog Box Launcher. (Remember, the Dialog Box Launcher for a group is the small square with an arrow in the lower-right corner of the group.) This opens the Clipboard task pane on the left side of the window. Once the Clipboard task pane is open, each selection that you cut or copy is placed on it. See **Figure 2–8**. The task pane displays up to 24 items. When you cut or copy a twenty-fifth item, it replaces the first item.

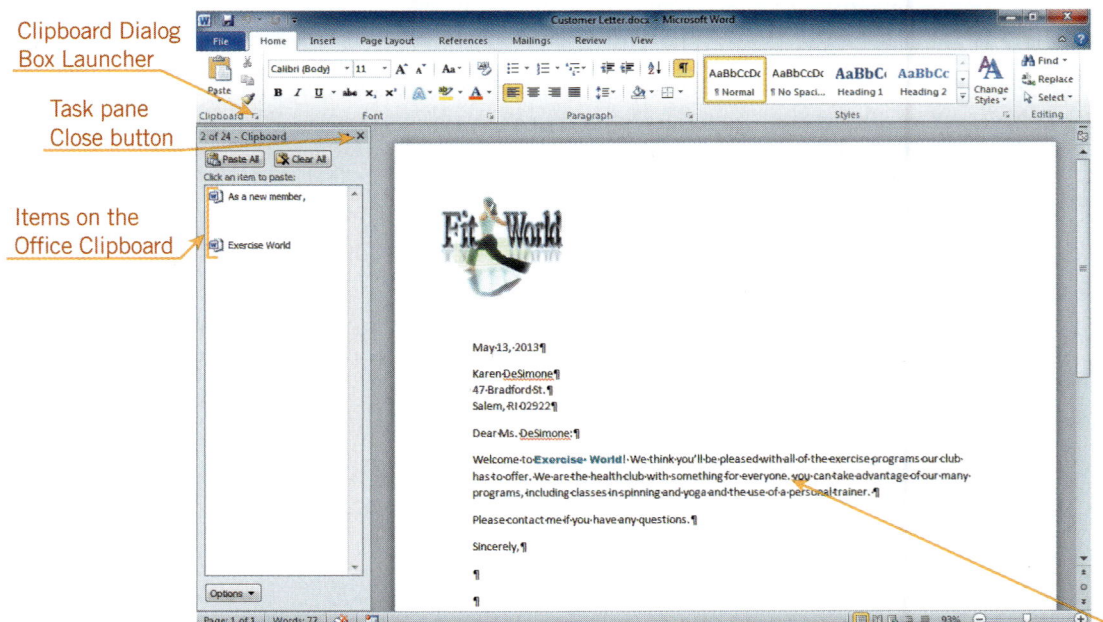

Clipboard Dialog Box Launcher

Task pane Close button

Items on the Office Clipboard

Text deleted from letter

FIGURE 2–8   Clipboard task pane with two items collected on it

Step-by-Step 2.6

1. Press **Ctrl+Home** to jump to the beginning of the document.

2. On the Home tab, in the Clipboard group, click the **Clipboard Dialog Box Launcher**. The Clipboard task pane opens on the left side of the window. The item currently on the system Clipboard, the text *Exercise World*, is the first item in the task pane.

3. In the first paragraph of the letter, at the beginning of the fourth sentence, select the text **As a new member,** (including the comma).

4. On the Home tab, in the Clipboard group, click the **Cut** button ✂. The text is deleted from the paragraph and appears in the Clipboard task pane, as shown in Figure 2–8.

5. Position the insertion point in the first paragraph at the beginning of the second sentence (it begins with *We think you'll be pleased...*).

6. In the Clipboard task pane, click **As a new member,**. The text is pasted at the location of the insertion point.

7. Press **Delete**, and then type **w**. If there is no space between the comma after the word *member* and the word *we*, press the **left arrow** key, and then press the **spacebar**.

8. Position the insertion point in the first paragraph at the beginning of the fourth sentence (it begins with *you can take advantage*). Type **At**, and then press the **spacebar**.

9. In the Clipboard task pane, click **Exercise World**. If there is no space between *World* and *you*, press the **spacebar**.

10. In the title bar at the top of the Clipboard task pane, click the **Close** button ✖. The task pane closes.

11. Save your changes to the document. Leave it open for the next Step-by-Step.

> **TIP**
>
> You can clear the Office Clipboard by clicking Clear All at the top of the Clipboard task pane, and you can paste all of the items on the Office Clipboard at once by clicking Paste All.

> **WARNING**
>
> Clicking the Paste button or pressing Ctrl+V pastes the contents of the system Clipboard into the document, not the contents of the Office Clipboard.

Using the Find and Replace Commands

Find and Replace are useful editing commands that let you locate specific words in a document quickly and, if you wish, change them instantly to new words. Both commands are located in the Editing group on the Home tab.

Finding Text with the Navigation Pane

When you click the Find button, the Navigation pane appears on the left side of the program window, as shown in **Figure 2–9**. The tab whose ScreenTip is "Browse the results from your current search" is selected. To find every occurrence of a specific word or phrase in a document, click in the Search Document box in the Navigation Pane, and then type the word or phrase. All of the occurrences of the text for which you are searching appear in a list in the Navigation pane, and they are highlighted in yellow in the document. If you continue typing in the Search Document box, the list and highlighting change to match what you type.

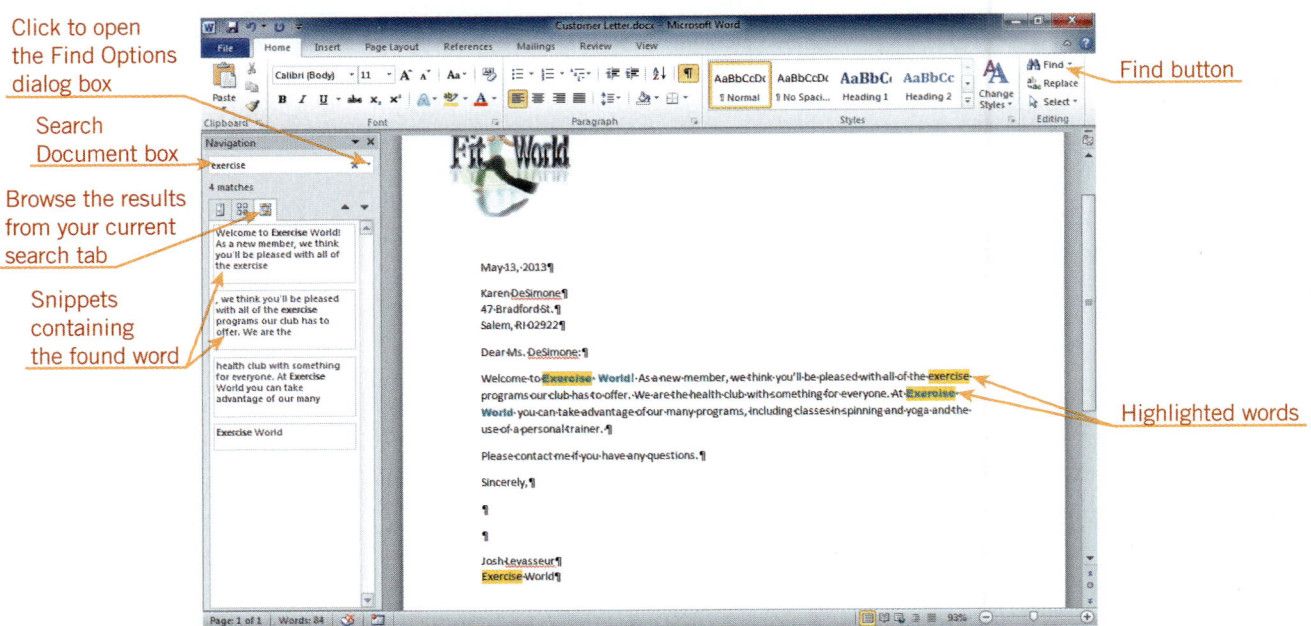

Click to open the Find Options dialog box

Search Document box

Browse the results from your current search tab

Snippets containing the found word

Find button

Highlighted words

FIGURE 2–9   Navigation Pane after searching for text

The highlighting and the list of items in the Navigation Pane matches the exact text you type in the Search Document box, even if it's in the middle of another word. For example, you can find the word *all* or any word with *all* in it, such as *fall*, *horizontally*, or *alloy*. Find also ignores capitalization when finding words. For example, if you search for *run*, the list of results will include *Run* as well as *run*.

You can make your search more specific. Click the small arrow on the right end of the Search Document box in the Navigation Pane. (The ScreenTip identifies this as the "Find Options and additional search commands" button.) Click that button, and then click Options on the menu that appears to open the Find Options dialog box. The options in this dialog box are described in **Table 2–2**.

TABLE 2–2 Find options

OPTION	DESCRIPTION
Match case	Searches for words with the same capitalization as the text that you type.
Find whole words only	Finds only the exact word or phrase you entered in the Find what box. (For example, choose this option if you want to find the word *all*, but not words with all in them, such as *fall*, *horizontally*, or *alloy*.)
Use wildcards	Makes it possible to search for words using **wildcards**, which are special characters that represent other characters. The most common wildcards are ? (the question mark), which represents any one character, and * (the asterisk), which represents any number of characters. For example, *a??* finds all three-letter words that begin with the letter *a*, including *all* and *ask*, and *a** finds all words of any length that begin with the letter *a*, including *all*, *apple*, or *arithmetic*.
Sounds like (English)	Locates homonyms—words that sound alike but are spelled differently. For example, if you type the word *so*, Word would also find the word *sew*.
Find all word forms (English)	Finds different forms of the entered word. For example, if you search for the word *run*, Word would also find *ran*, *runs*, and *running*.
Highlight all	Highlights all the found words in the document. This is selected by default.
Incremental find	Finds the text as you type. This is selected by default. If you deselect this, you need to click the Search button in the Search Document box in the Navigation Pane to find the text.
Match prefix	Finds words that begin with the text you type in the Search Document box.
Match suffix	Finds words that end with the text you type in the Search Document box.
Ignore punctuation characters	Finds words that match the text in the Search Document characters box, but ignores any punctuation in the words in the document. For example, if you type *its* in the Search Document box, it will find *it's* as well as *its*.
Ignore white-space characters	Finds text that matches the text in the Search Document box even if there is a space between some of the characters in the document. For example, if you type *Maryellen* in the Find what text box, it will also find *Mary Ellen*.

Step-by-Step 2.7

1. On the Home tab, in the Editing group, click the **Find** button. The Navigation Pane appears. The insertion point is blinking in the Search Document box at the top of the Navigation Pane.

2. Type **exercise**. All four instances of the word *exercise* are highlighted in the document, and the four snippets of text containing the word appear in the Navigation Pane.

3. If necessary, drag the scroll box in the vertical scroll bar up until you can see all four instances of highlighted text in the window, similar to Figure 2–9.

4. In the Navigation Pane, click the **top snippet**. The first highlighted word in the document is selected.

5. In the Navigation Pane, click in the **Search Document** box. The text in the box is selected.

6. Press the **right arrow** key, press the **spacebar**, and then type **w**. One of the snippets in the list in the Navigation Pane is removed, the yellow highlighting disappears from the instance of the word *exercise* in the document that is not followed by a space and the letter *w*, and the highlighting on the other three instances is extended to the *W* in the word *World*.

7. Click anywhere in the document, and then press **Ctrl+Home** to move the insertion point to the beginning of the document.

8. In the Navigation Pane, click the **Close** button ✖. The Navigation Pane closes.

9. Save the document, and leave it open for the next Step-by-Step.

Replacing Text

If you want to replace text you find with other text, you can use the Replace command. To do this, click the Replace button in the Editing group on the Home tab to open the Find and Replace dialog box with the Replace tab selected, as shown in **Figure 2–10**. To replace a word or phrase, type it in the Find what box, and then type the replacement word or phrase in the Replace with box. The Find what box has the same purpose as the Search Document box in the Navigation Pane. The replacements can be made one at a time by clicking Replace, or all at once by clicking Replace All. To make the search more specific, click More to see the same options that appear in the Find Options dialog box.

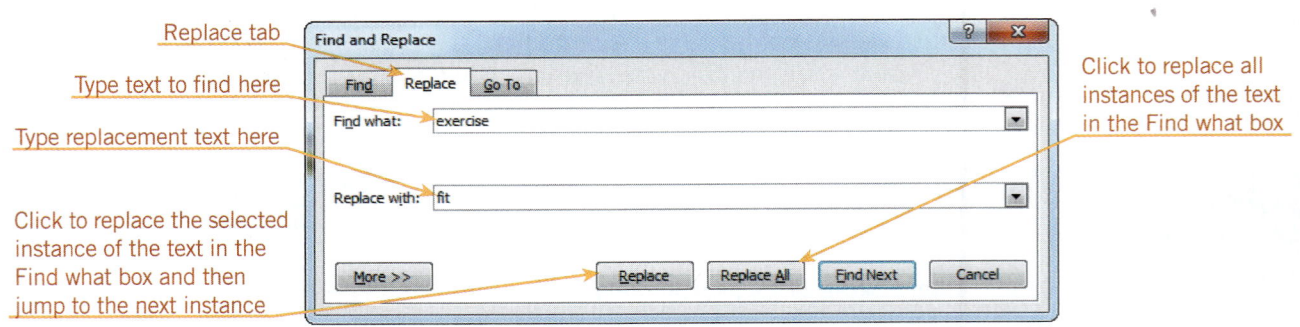

FIGURE 2–10   Replace tab in the Find and Replace dialog box

Step-by-Step 2.8

1. On the Home tab, in the Editing group, click the **Replace** button. The Find and Replace dialog box opens with the Replace tab selected. The text you typed in the Search Document box in the Navigation Pane, *exercise w*, appears in the Find what box in the dialog box.

2. Click in the **Find what** box to the right of the *w*, and then press **Backspace** twice to delete the *w* and the space after *exercise*.

3. Click in the **Replace with** box, and then type **fit**. See Figure 2–10.

4. Click **Find Next**. The first instance of the word *exercise* is selected in the document.

5. Click **Replace**. The selected word is replaced with *fit*, and the next instance of the word *exercise* is selected. Notice that the first letter of the word *fit* was automatically changed to an uppercase letter to match the case of the word it replaced. Also note that because this instance of the word *exercise* was formatted in blue and italics, the replacement word is formatted in the same way. The instance of the word *exercise* that is now selected should not be replaced with *fit*.

6. Click **Find Next**. The next instance of *exercise* is selected.

7. Click **Replace**. The selected text is replaced with the word *fit* and the next instance of *exercise* is selected. Click **Replace** to replace this instance of the word. A dialog box opens telling you that Word has completed its search of the document.

8. Click **OK** to close this dialog box. The Find and Replace dialog box is still open.

9. Click **Close**. The Find and Replace dialog box closes.

10. Save your changes to the document, and leave it open for the next Step-by-Step.

> **TIP**
>
> To replace all instances of the Find what text with the Replace with text, click Replace All. But watch out for replacements of words that contain the text you are replacing rather than whole words.

Using the Go To Command

One of the quickest ways to move through a long document is to use the Go To command. Go To allows you to jump to a specific part of a document. On the Home tab, in the Editing group, click the arrow next to the Find button, and then click Go To on the menu. The Find and Replace dialog box opens with the Go To tab on top. See

Figure 2–11. In the Go to what list, select the type of location you want to move to, and then enter the corresponding number or other information in the box on the right. After you click Next, Word moves the insertion point to the location you specified.

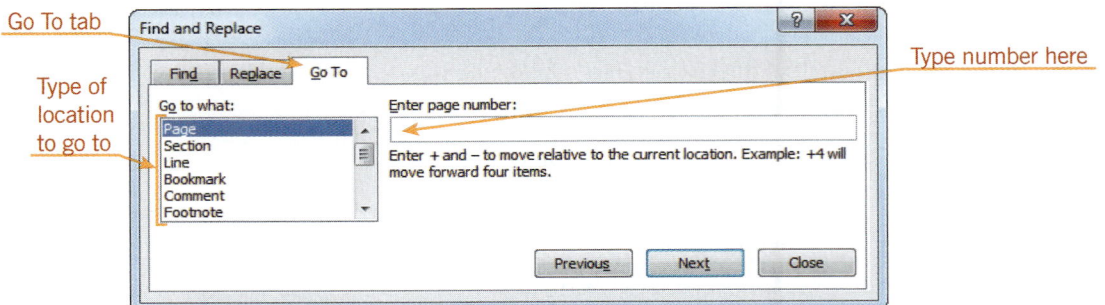

FIGURE 2–11   Go To tab in the Find and Replace dialog box

Step-by-Step 2.9

1. On the Home tab, in the Editing group, click the **arrow** next to the Find button. Click **Go To**. The Find and Replace dialog box appears with the Go To tab on top, as shown in Figure 2–11.

2. In the Go to what box, click **Line**. The box to the right of the Go to what box changes to the Enter line number box.

3. Click in the **Enter line number** box, and then type **10**.

4. Click **Go To**. The insertion point jumps to the tenth line in the document (the paragraph above the closing, which begins *Please contact me...*).

5. Click **Close**. The Find and Replace dialog box closes.

6. Save your changes to the document, and leave it open for the next Step-by-Step.

Identifying the Number of Words in a Document or Selection

As you type and edit a document, you may want to know how many words it contains. The number of words in a document appears in the status bar and is updated as you type. If you select text, the status bar displays the number of words in the selection. You can also find out the number of characters, paragraphs, and lines in a document by opening the Word Count dialog box. To do this, you can click the number of words in the status bar, or you can click the Review tab on the Ribbon, and then, in the Proofing group, click the Word Count button. See **Figure 2–12**.

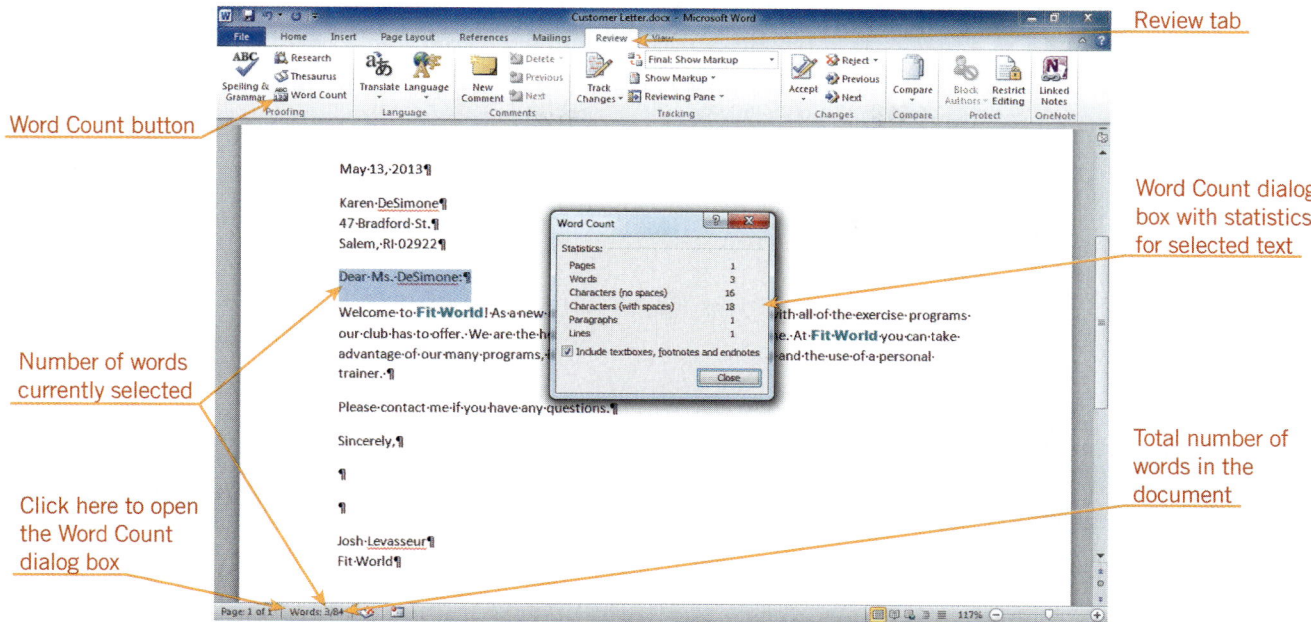

FIGURE 2–12 Word count on the status bar and in the Word Count dialog box

Step-by-Step 2.10

1. Scroll up so that you can see all the text in the document. Look at the word count in the status bar. The document contains 84 words.

2. Select the entire salutation (**Dear Ms. DeSimone:**). The word count indicator in the status bar shows that three out of a total of 84 words are selected in the document.

3. In the status bar, click the word count indicator. The Word Count dialog box opens, as shown in Figure 2–12. Because text is currently selected, this dialog box displays information about the selected text. The selected text consists of 16 characters if you don't count spaces, and 18 if you do.

4. In the dialog box, click **Close**. The Word Count dialog box closes.

5. Deselect the text in the document.

6. On the Ribbon, click the **Review** tab. In the Proofing group, click the **Word Count** button. The Word Count dialog box opens again. Because no text is selected, it tells you that the document contains 383 characters not including spaces, 458 characters if you do count the spaces, 10 paragraphs, and 15 lines. (Remember that a new paragraph is created every time you press Enter.) Because you might have inserted or removed a space when you cut or copied text, the character count with spaces in the dialog box on your screen might be slightly higher or lower than 458.

7. Click **Close**. The Word Count dialog box closes.

8. On the Ribbon, click the **Home** tab. In the Paragraph group, click the **Show/Hide ¶** button ¶. The button is deselected, and the formatting marks disappear from the screen.

9. At the bottom of the document, select the name **Josh Levasseur**, and then type your name.

10. Save, print, and close the document.

SUMMARY

In this lesson, you learned:

- You can select blocks of text to perform operations on the entire block of text at once, such as cutting, copying, and pasting.

- The Show/Hide ¶ command allows you to view hidden formatting marks. The Show/Hide ¶ button is a toggle command, which means you can turn the feature on or off.

- You can change the space before and after a paragraph by using the Line and Paragraph Spacing button in the Paragraph group on the Home tab.

- You can undo recent actions by using the Undo command. When you click the arrow next to the Undo button, a list of your recent actions appears. You can redo an action using the Redo button and repeat an action using the Repeat button.

- You can drag selected text to a new location in the document. You can press and hold the Ctrl key to copy the selected text rather than move it when you drag.

- You can send text to the Clipboard by using either the Cut or Copy command. You can paste text stored on the Clipboard by

using the Paste command. If you want to collect more than one item at a time to paste, you can use the Office Clipboard.

- The Find command opens the Navigation Pane with the "Browse the results from your current search" tab selected. You type a word or phrase in the Search Document box to highlight every instance of the word in the document and display a list of snippets containing the word in the Navigation Pane.

- The Replace command opens the Replace tab in the Find and Replace dialog box, finds the next occurrence of the word or phrase for which you are searching and replaces it with the word or phrase you type in the Replace with box.

- The Go To command moves the insertion point to a part of the document that you specify.

- You can see the number of words in a document or a selection by checking the status bar. You can see the number of characters, paragraphs, and lines in a document or selection by opening the Word Count dialog box.

VOCABULARY REVIEW

Define the following terms:

Clipboard	drag-and-drop	select
copy	format	toggle
cut	Office Clipboard	
drag	paste	

REVIEW QUESTIONS

TRUE / FALSE

Circle T if the statement is true or F if the statement is false.

T   F   **1.**   You can hide formatting marks.

T   F   **2.**   You can undo more than one action at a time.

T   F   **3.**   You can remove the extra space that normally appears after a paragraph.

T   F   **4.**   The Office Clipboard can store up to 48 items.

T   F   **5.**   The only way to find out how many words are in a document or selection is to open the Word Count dialog box.

WRITTEN QUESTIONS

Write a brief answer to each of the following questions.

1. How do you use the keyboard to select text?

2. How do the Cut and Copy commands differ?

3. Describe how to move and copy text using drag-and-drop.

4. Describe the Paste Options button and how to use it, including how to preview the effects.

5. Which dialog box contains the Go To tab?

FILL IN THE BLANK

Complete the following sentences by writing the correct word or words in the blanks provided.

1. The _____ is a special clipboard on which you can collect up to 24 selections.

2. The _____ opens when you click the Find button in the Editing group on the Home tab.

3. To jump to a specific part of a document, use the _____ command.

4. Commands that turn a feature on or off are known as _____ commands.

5. To automatically replace a word or phrase with another one, use the _____ command.

■ PROJECTS

If you have a SAM 2010 user profile, your instructor may have assigned an autogradable version of the indicated project. If so, log into the SAM 2010 Web site at *www.cengage.com/sam2010* to download the instruction and start files.

PROJECT 2–1

1. Open a new Word document. Show hidden formatting marks. Remove the space after the current paragraph.

2. Type the list of commonly misspelled words shown below.

   Committee

   Occurrence

   Occasional

   Collectible

   Received

   Jewelry

   Correspondence

   Judgment

   Absence

   Accommodate

3. Type **Until** below *Occurrence*.

4. Undo the last action. The word *Until* disappears.

5. Redo the undone action. The word *Until* reappears.

6. Use the Go To command to move the insertion point to line 5.

7. Use the drag-and-drop technique to alphabetize the word list.

8. Hide formatting marks.

9. Press Ctrl+End, press Enter twice, and then type your name.

10. Save the document as **Spelling List** followed by your initials. Print and close the document.

SAM PROJECT 2–2

1. Open the **Workshop.docx** Data File. Save the document as **Workshop Checklist** followed by your initials.

2. Show hidden formatting marks.

3. Use the Go To command to move the insertion point to line 2.

4. Type the following sentence at the beginning of line 2:

   We are pleased that you have applied to be part of the Summer Language Workshop at Granville University.

5. Use the drag-and-drop technique to move the line *Nonrefundable $15 application fee* to the end of the checklist.

6. Select the entire document. Copy the selection to the Clipboard.

7. Press Ctrl+End to move to the end of the document. Paste the contents of the Clipboard. Press Backspace to remove the second blank paragraph at the end of the document.

8. Use the Find command to find all instances of the word *items*. Then change the word you are looking for to *necessary*. Close the Navigation Pane.

9. Use the Replace command to replace all instances of the word *necessary* with *needed*.

10. Jump to the end of the document, and then type your name in the blank paragraph at the end of the document. Hide formatting marks.

11. Print, save, and close the document.

PROJECT 2–3

1. Open the **Web Site.docx** Data File. Save the file as **Web Site Tips** followed by your initials.

2. Highlight all instances of the word *sight* in the document. Replace them with the word **site**. There should be 10 replacements.

3. Make the insertions and deletions indicated by the proofreader's marks in **Figure 2–13**.

4. Display formatting marks. Move to the blank paragraph below tip number 6, type **Document word count:**, press the spacebar, and type the number of words currently in the document.

5. Remove the space after the current paragraph, and then press Enter. Type **Introductory paragraph word count:**, and then press the spacebar.

6. Create another paragraph. Type **Introductory paragraph character count with no spaces:**, and then press the spacebar.

7. Select all of the text in the introductory paragraph, and determine the number of words in the selection. Move to the end of the document, and then type this number after the phrase you typed in Step 5.

8. Determine the number of characters without counting spaces, in the introductory paragraph, and then type this number after the phrase you typed in Step 6.

9. Add space after the last paragraph, press Enter twice, and then type your name. Hide formatting marks.

10. Save, print, and close the document.

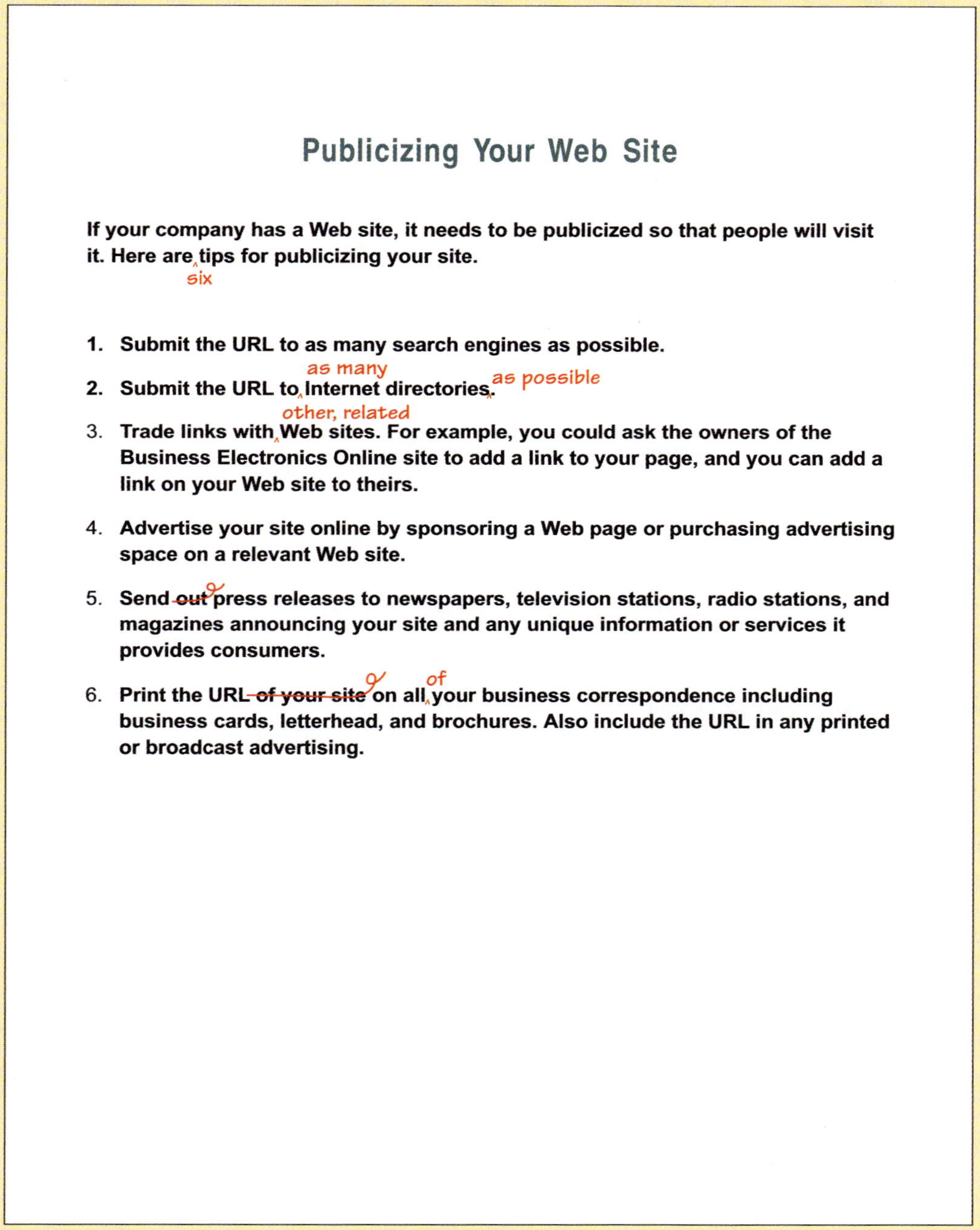

Publicizing Your Web Site

If your company has a Web site, it needs to be publicized so that people will visit it. Here are *six* tips for publicizing your site.

1. Submit the URL to as many search engines as possible.

2. Submit the URL to *as many* Internet directories *as possible*.

3. Trade links with *other, related* Web sites. For example, you could ask the owners of the Business Electronics Online site to add a link to your page, and you can add a link on your Web site to theirs.

4. Advertise your site online by sponsoring a Web page or purchasing advertising space on a relevant Web site.

5. Send ~~out~~ press releases to newspapers, television stations, radio stations, and magazines announcing your site and any unique information or services it provides consumers.

6. Print the URL ~~of your site~~ *of* on all your business correspondence including business cards, letterhead, and brochures. Also include the URL in any printed or broadcast advertising.

FIGURE 2–13

PROJECT 2–4

1. Open the **Tournament.docx** Data File. Save the document as **Tournament Notice** followed by your initials.

2. Display formatting marks. Position the insertion point in the blank paragraph between the document heading and the first paragraph. Type the following:.
   Where: Forest Hills Golf Club
   When: August 10–11
   Time: Tee times begin at 8:00 a.m.
   Cost: $50 entry fee per person

3. Select the first three lines you typed (from the line staring with *Where* through the line starting with *Time*). Remove the space after these paragraphs.

4. Select the word *Where*. Type **Location**.

5. Undo the change you made in Step 4.

6. Open the Office Clipboard. Cut the four lines you typed at the beginning of the document. Cut the last sentence in the first paragraph.

7. Copy all the text in the heading, but do not copy the paragraph marker in the paragraph.

8. Paste the four lines you typed below the paragraph in the document. Paste the *For more information* sentence in a paragraph below the four lines you typed.

9. Paste the heading at the end of the first sentence in the document, after **Sixth Annual**. Use the Paste Options button to match the format of the first paragraph. Close the Clipboard task pane.

10. Use the Find command to find the text *Robert Shade*, and then replace it with your name. Close the Navigation Pane.

11. Hide formatting marks. Save, print, and then close the document.

PROJECT 2–5

1. Open the **Interview.docx** Data File. Save the document as **Interview Preparation** followed by your initials.

2. Replace all instances of the word *notes* with the word **information**. You should have two replacements.

3. Use the Find command to find the word *these*. Select the word *these*, and then type **this**. Close the Navigation Pane.

4. In the second paragraph, in the first line, cut the text *be sure to*.

5. Use the Repeat command to cut the second paragraph.

6. Paste the paragraph you just cut below the last paragraph in the document.

7. At the end of the document, type your name in the empty paragraph.

8. Save, print, and close the document.

◼ CRITICAL THINKING

ACTIVITY 2–1

Work with a classmate to create a new Word document listing qualities employers look for in a job applicant. Some examples are a person who is responsible, detail-oriented, and cooperative. Then, each of you create another document, and list a personal inventory of your strengths and weaknesses as a potential applicant for a job of your choice.

ACTIVITY 2–2

A coworker asks you the following questions about using the Office Clipboard to copy and paste items. Use Help to answer the questions.

1. Can I use the Office Clipboard without displaying the Clipboard task pane?

2. Is there another way to display the Office Clipboard?

3. How do I delete an item from the Office Clipboard? How do I delete all the items from the Office Clipboard?

LESSON 3

Helpful Word Features

■ OBJECTIVES

Upon completion of this lesson, you should be able to:

- Use AutoCorrect.
- Use AutoFormat As You Type.
- Create, insert, and delete Quick Parts.
- Use AutoComplete.
- Insert the current date and time.
- Check the spelling and grammar in a document.
- Use the Thesaurus.
- Insert symbols.

■ VOCABULARY

AutoComplete

AutoCorrect

AutoFormat As You Type

automatic grammar checking

automatic spell checking

building block

contextual spell checking

format

Quick Part

Thesaurus

Using Automatic Features

Word provides many helpful features and commands. For example, as you type, some types of errors correct automatically, and some text is formatted automatically. You can also take advantage of a feature that completes the month names and the days of the week after you type a few letters, or you can simply insert the current date using a button on the Ribbon. If there's text you use all the time, you can save the text as a special item that you can insert with a few clicks. Word provides a feature that checks the spelling and grammar in a document, and you can use a built-in feature to find a synonym for a word. You can also insert symbols that aren't on the keyboard. In this lesson, you will learn how to take advantage of all of these features.

Understanding Automatic Features

Word provides many types of automated features that can help you create documents. The AutoCorrect feature corrects errors as you type, and AutoFormat As You Type, as the name implies, applies built-in formats as you type. You can create and use Quick Parts to insert frequently used text. The AutoComplete feature "guesses" days of the week and month names as you type, and then suggests the complete word.

Using AutoCorrect

▶ **VOCABULARY**
AutoCorrect

AutoCorrect corrects common capitalization, spelling, grammar, and typing errors as you type. You can also customize AutoCorrect by adding or removing words or by changing the types of corrections made.

Using AutoCorrect in a Document

When you type something that is in the AutoCorrect list, the automatic correction occurs after you press the spacebar or Enter. For example, you can specify that when you type the letters *nyc,* they will always be replaced with *New York City*. Or if you start typing a new sentence after some ending punctuation, and you forget to capitalize the first letter of the first word in the new sentence, it will be capitalized automatically when you press the spacebar.

Step-by-Step 3.1

1. Start Word. Open the **Memo.docx** Data File from the drive and folder where your Data Files are stored. Save the document as **Fall Classes Memo** followed by your initials. Ignore the words in the document that are misspelled for now.

2. Position the insertion point at the end of the second paragraph in the memo (immediately following the period after *time*).

3. Press the **spacebar**, type **if**, and then press the **spacebar** again. Notice that as soon as you pressed the spacebar, the word *if* was capitalized because the AutoCorrect feature recognized it as the first word in a new sentence.

4. Type the following (with the lowercase *i* and the misspelled word *accomodate*): **possible, i will accomodate**, and then press the **spacebar**. AutoCorrect recognized that you meant to type *I* and automatically changed it, and automatically corrected the misspelled instance of *accommodate*.

5. Type **you.** (Be sure to type the period.)

6. Save the document and leave it open for the next Step-by-Step.

Customizing AutoCorrect

You can add or remove words from the AutoCorrect list and change the AutoCorrect options. To do this, you need to open the AutoCorrect dialog box. Click the File tab, and then in the navigation bar, click Options. This opens the Word Options dialog box. You can customize many Word features using this dialog box. Clicking a category on the left side of the Word Options dialog box changes the commands displayed on the right side of the dialog box. To open the AutoCorrect dialog box, click Proofing in the list on the left side of the dialog box. The right side of the dialog box changes to display commands for customizing tools you use to help proofread your document in Word. See **Figure 3–1**.

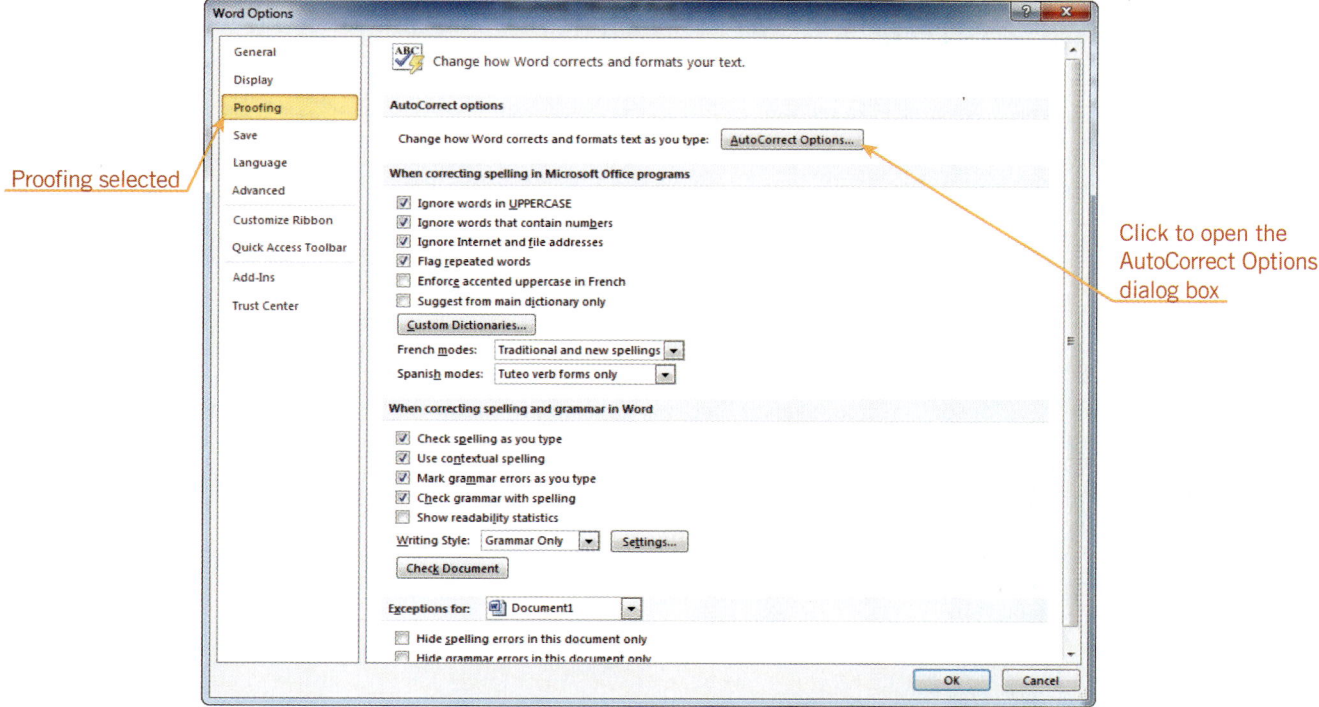

FIGURE 3–1   Proofing options in the Word Options dialog box

On the right side of the dialog box, click AutoCorrect Options. The AutoCorrect dialog box opens with the AutoCorrect tab on top, as shown in **Figure 3–2**. The check boxes at the top of the tab control the AutoCorrect options. Commonly misspelled or mistyped words are listed in the box at the bottom of the tab. The correct spellings that AutoCorrect inserts in the document when you press Enter appear on the right side of the list. Notice in the figure that the first few items listed in the box are not misspellings but are characters that represent a symbol. If you type the sequence of characters, AutoCorrect automatically inserts the symbol in place of the characters.

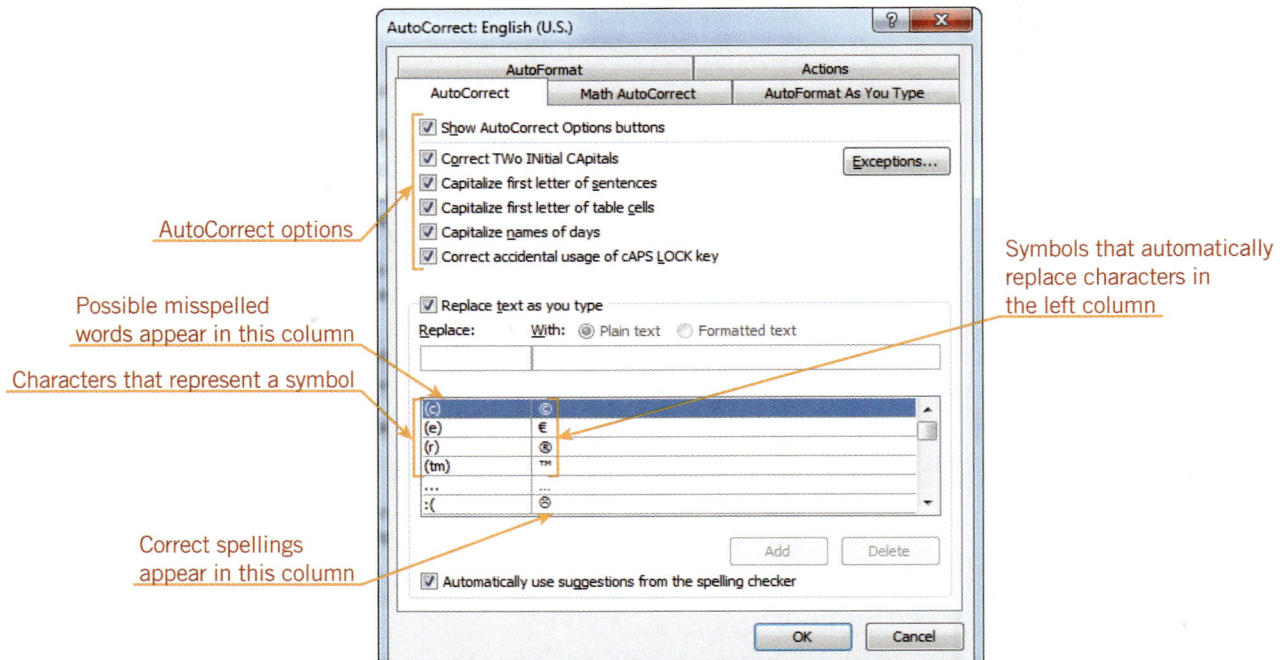

FIGURE 3–2   AutoCorrect tab in the AutoCorrect dialog box

You can also open the AutoCorrect dialog box using the AutoCorrect Options button. When you position the pointer over text that has been automatically corrected, a small blue box appears just below the first character in the word or below the symbol. When you point to the box, it changes to the AutoCorrect Options button. You can click the AutoCorrect Options button to open a menu of commands for changing the AutoCorrect action. Click Control AutoCorrect Options to open the AutoCorrect dialog box.

Step-by-Step 3.2

1. Click the **File** tab, and then in the navigation bar, click **Options**. The Word Options dialog box opens.

2. In the list on the left, click **Proofing**. The commands for customizing proofing tools in Word appear in the right side of the dialog box, as shown in Figure 3–1.

3. On the right side of the dialog box, click **AutoCorrect Options**. The AutoCorrect dialog box opens, as shown in Figure 3–2.

4. In the Replace box, type your initials. If the list under the Replace box scrolls and displays an entry that is the same as your initials, add another letter to your initials.

5. Press **Tab** to move to the With box. In the With box, type your name. Near the bottom of the dialog box, click **Add**. AutoCorrect is now customized with your name.

6. Click **OK** to close the AutoCorrect dialog box, and then click **OK** to close the Word Options dialog box.

7. In the memo, next to the word *From:*, select **David Chofsky**. Type your initials, and then press the **spacebar**. AutoCorrect replaces the initials with your name.

8. Move the pointer on top of your name. A small blue box appears below the first part of your name. Point to the **blue box**. The box changes to the AutoCorrect Options button.

9. Click the **AutoCorrect Options** button 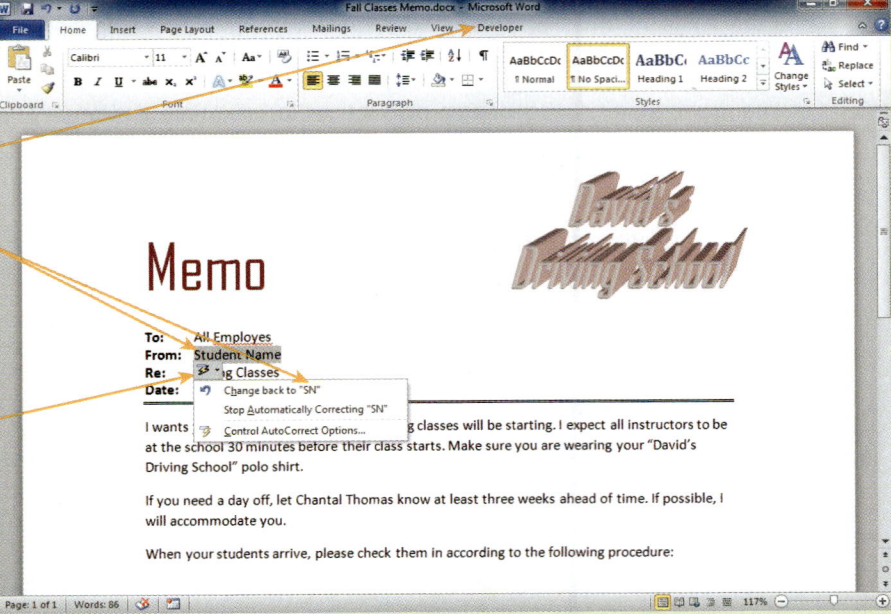. A menu opens, as shown in **Figure 3–3**. The top two commands on the menu allow you to undo the correction or stop making that particular type of correction. The last command opens the AutoCorrect dialog box.

FIGURE 3–3
AutoCorrect Options button in a document

You might not see the Developer tab on your screen

Your name and initials appear here

AutoCorrect Options button

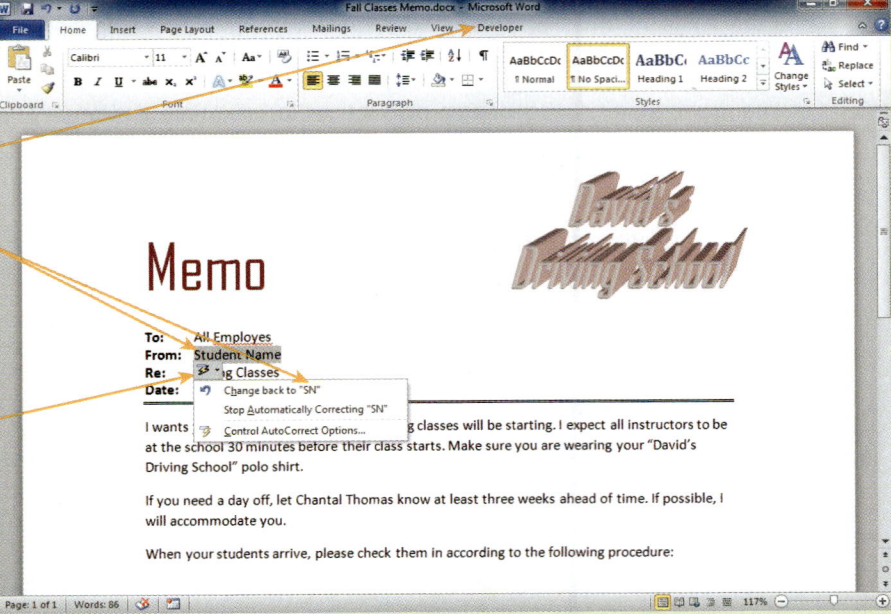

10. On the menu, click **Control AutoCorrect Options**. The AutoCorrect dialog box opens with the AutoCorrect tab on top.

11. In the list at the bottom, scroll down until you see your initials. (Note that the list is organized so that the Replace column is in alphabetical order.)

12. In the list, click your initials. The whole line is selected. Below the list, click **Delete**. Your initials and your name are removed from the list.

13. Click **OK** to close the AutoCorrect dialog box. Save the document and leave it open for the next Step-by-Step.

TIP

To quickly jump to an item in the list, start typing it in the Replace with box.

Understanding Formatting

VOCABULARY
format

Formatting means to change the look of text. You can format specific words or entire paragraphs. Examples of text formatting are adding bold, italics, or underlining to words to emphasize them. Examples of paragraph formatting are indenting the first line of a paragraph or double-spacing the lines of text in a paragraph. A paragraph format can also include text formatting. For example, a paragraph format for headings (like the preceding "Understanding Formatting" heading) can include extra space above and below it (paragraph formatting), as well as formatting the text as blue and in a larger font size.

Using AutoFormat As You Type

The *AutoFormat As You Type* feature automatically applies built-in formats to text as you type. In a new paragraph, for example, if you type the number *1* followed by a period, and then press Tab, Word assumes that you are trying to create a numbered list. The AutoFormat As You Type feature changes the text you just typed and the new paragraph you just created to the List Paragraph Quick Style and formats it as a numbered list. If you type something in the list, and then press Enter, the number *2* followed by a period and a tab space is automatically inserted on the next line. Another example of text automatically formatted by the AutoFormat As You Type feature is certain fractions. For example, when you type *1/2*, it changes it to ½.

You can choose which automatic formatting options you want to use on the AutoFormat As You Type tab in the AutoCorrect dialog box, shown in **Figure 3–4**.

> **VOCABULARY**
> **AutoFormat As You Type**

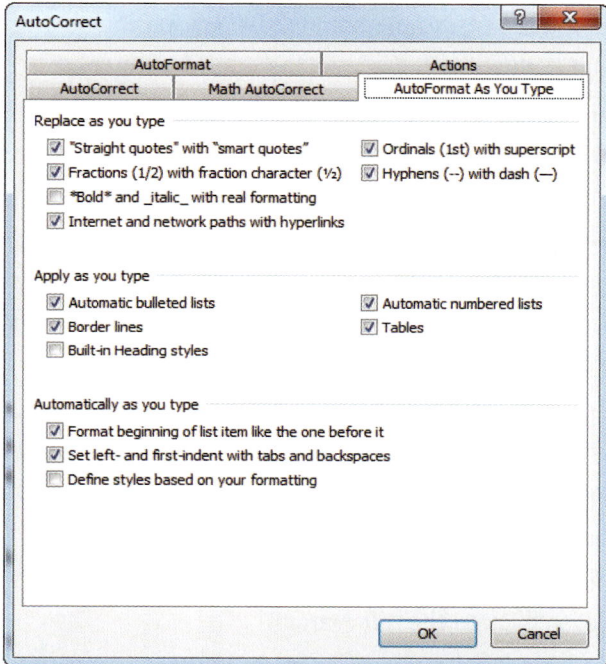

FIGURE 3–4   AutoFormat As You Type tab in the AutoCorrect dialog box

Step-by-Step 3.3

1. On the Home tab, in the Paragraph group, click the **Show/Hide** button ¶. Formatting marks appear in the document. (Remember, this button is a toggle button, so if you don't see formatting marks in your document, click the button again to select it.) This will make it easier to see AutoFormat As You Type in action.

2. Press **Ctrl+End** to position the insertion point in the blank paragraph below the last paragraph. Type **1.**, and then press **Tab**. Pressing Tab moves the insertion point to the right approximately one-half inch. The formatting mark that indicates a tab is an arrow that points to the right. The AutoCorrect Options button appears to the left of the text you typed.

3. Point to the **AutoCorrect Options** button ⬚. It changes to the same AutoCorrect Options button you saw earlier. Click the **AutoCorrect Options** button ⬚ to open the menu. The second command on the menu identifies the type of automatic correction that was made; in this case, the paragraph was changed to a numbered list. On the Ribbon, you can see in the Paragraph group that the Numbering button is selected.

4. Press **Esc** to close the AutoCorrect Options menu without choosing a command. You want to create a numbered list.

5. Type **Check each student's name on the class list.** Press **Enter**. Because this text is formatted as a numbered list, the number *2* followed by a period and a tab mark automatically appear on the next line. The insertion point is blinking in the new line after the tab mark.

6. Type **On the 1st**. Press the **spacebar**. When you press the spacebar, AutoFormat As You Type changed *st* to superscript—text that is formatted much smaller than the rest of the text and raised up to the top of the line.

7. Type **day of class, check the list from the accounting office to see if the student has paid for the class.** When this line wraps, the second line is automatically indented so that it aligns with words after the tab mark in the line above it. This formatting is part of the numbered list style.

8. Press **Enter**. The next line is formatted as part of the numbered list. Type **Give any student who has not paid a green slip, and then send him or her to the office.** Press **Enter**. The fourth item in the list is created.

9. Press **Enter** again. Because you didn't type any text as part of the fourth item, the item is removed, the numbered list is ended, and the insertion point moves back to the left margin.

10. Type **If you have any questions, refer to the Instructor's page on our Web site at www.davidsdriving.biz.** Press **Enter**. A new paragraph is created and the Web page address you typed (www.davidsdriving.biz) is formatted in blue and underlined. In addition, it is changed to a hyperlink to that Web site on the Internet.

11. Position the pointer over the blue underlined text. A ScreenTip appears telling you to press Ctrl and click to follow the link (which means to jump to that Web page on the Internet). The small blue AutoCorrect box appears just below the beginning of the URL.

12. Point to the blue AutoCorrect box. The AutoCorrect Options button appears. Click the **AutoCorrect Options** button ⬚, and then click **Undo Hyperlink** on the menu. The link is removed and the text is no longer formatted as blue and underlined.

EXTRA FOR EXPERTS

To change the paragraph from a numbered list to normal text, you also can click the Normal button in the Styles group on the Home tab.

WARNING

The Web page address that you typed is not the address of a real Web page, so following the link will open a dialog box telling you that the page could not be opened.

13. On the Home tab, in the Paragraph group, click the **Show/Hide ¶** button ¶ to turn formatting marks off, and then save the document and leave it open for the next Step-by-Step.

Using Quick Parts

Building blocks are document parts that are stored and reused. *Quick Parts* are building blocks you create from frequently used text, such as a name, address, or slogan, and then save so that you can access them by clicking the Quick Parts button in the Text group on the Insert tab.

▶ VOCABULARY
building block
Quick Part

Creating and Inserting a Quick Part

To create a Quick Part, select the text that you want to save as a Quick Part. Click the Insert tab on the Ribbon, and then, in the Text group, click the Quick Parts button. The Quick Parts menu opens. If any Quick Parts are stored on your computer or in your document, they will appear at the top of this menu. On the menu, click Save Selection to Quick Part Gallery. The Create New Building Block dialog box opens, as shown in **Figure 3–5**.

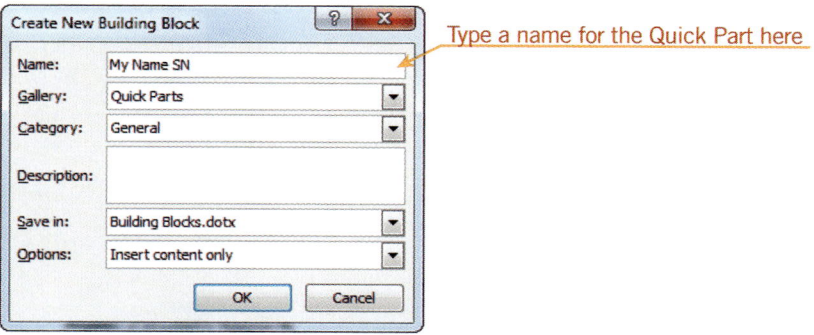

Type a name for the Quick Part here

FIGURE 3–5   Create New Building Block dialog box

The first few words of the selected text appear as the default name for the Quick Part in the Name box. You can change this name if you want. Click OK to save the Quick Part. After you create a Quick Part, it appears at the top of the Quick Parts menu.

Step-by-Step 3.4

1. In the *From* line in the memo header, select your name.

2. On the Ribbon, click the **Insert** tab. In the Text group, click the **Quick Parts** button, and then click **Save Selection to Quick Part Gallery**. The Create New Building Block dialog box opens.

3. In the Name box, type **My Name** followed by your initials. You don't need to click in the box first because the text in the Name box is selected when the dialog box appears, and your typing automatically replaces the selected text.

4. Click **OK**. The dialog box closes.

5. In the first line of the second paragraph in the memo, select the text **Chantal Thomas**. Press **Delete** to delete her name.

6. On the Insert tab, in the Text group, click the **Quick Parts** button. The Quick Part you created appears at the top of the menu, similar to the one shown in **Figure 3–6**. If other *My Name* entries appear on this menu, scroll down until you see the one you created.

FIGURE 3–6
Quick Parts menu with a new Quick Part on it

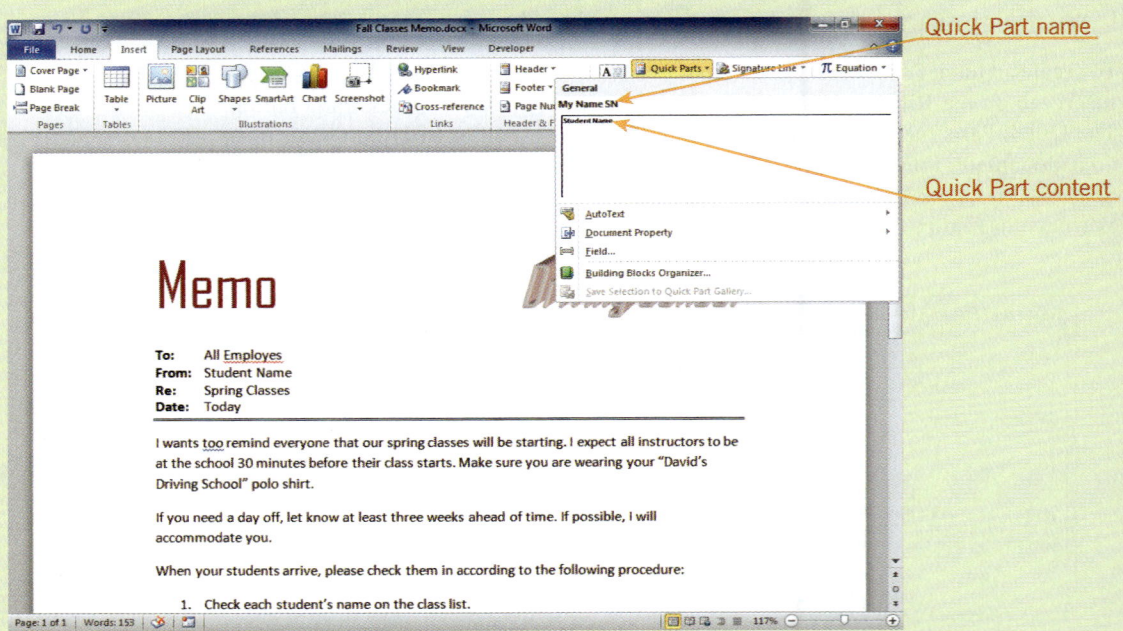

7. On the menu, click the **My Name** Quick Part that you created. The menu closes and your name appears in the document at the insertion point.

8. If there is no space between your last name and the word *know*, press the **spacebar** to insert a space.

9. Save the document and leave it open for the next Step-by-Step.

> **TIP**
>
> A Quick Part can consist of text several paragraphs long and it can also contain formatted text.

Deleting a Quick Part

To delete a Quick Part, you need to open the Building Blocks Organizer dialog box. To do this, on the Ribbon, click the Insert tab. In the Text group, click the Quick Parts button, and then click Building Blocks Organizer. The Building Blocks Organizer dialog box opens, similar to the one shown in **Figure 3–7**.

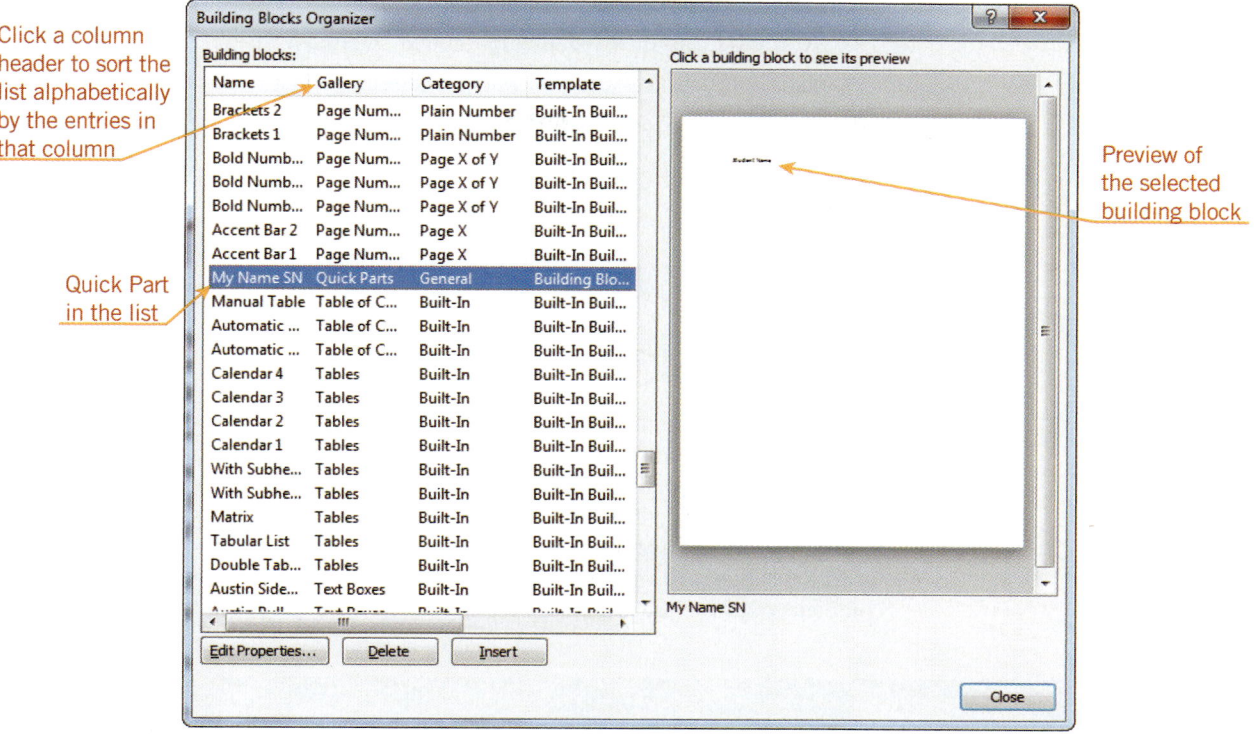

FIGURE 3–7   Building Blocks Organizer dialog box

As you see, Word comes with quite a few built-in building blocks. Building blocks are organized into galleries. By default, the list is sorted alphabetically by gallery name. You can sort the building blocks in this list by any of the column headings in the dialog box. The Quick Part you created is stored in the Quick Parts gallery. To see building blocks in the Quick Parts gallery, scroll down the list. To delete a Quick Part, select it, and then click Delete.

EXTRA FOR EXPERTS

You can use the built-in building blocks just as you used the Quick Part you created. Click a building block in the list in the Building Blocks Organizer dialog box, and then click Insert. The building block is inserted into the document.

Step-by-Step 3.5

1. On the Insert tab, in the Text group, click the **Quick Parts** button, and then click **Building Blocks Organizer**.

2. If the list of building blocks is not sorted alphabetically by Gallery name (you might see a few AutoText entries, and then two Bibliographies entries, followed by several Cover Pages entries), click the **Gallery** column header.

3. Use the scroll bar to scroll down the list until you see Quick Parts in the Gallery column. Locate the Quick Part you created. Remember its name is *My Name* followed by your initials. Click the Quick Part you created to select it.

EXTRA FOR EXPERTS

You can also click the Quick Parts button, right-click the Quick Part, and then click Organize and Delete to open the Building Blocks Organizer with that Quick Part already selected.

4. At the bottom of the dialog box, click **Delete**. A warning dialog box opens asking if you are sure you want to delete the selected building block.

5. Click **Yes**. The selected Quick Part is deleted from the list.

6. Click **Close** to close the dialog box.

7. Save the document and leave it open for the next Step-by-Step.

Using AutoComplete

▶ **VOCABULARY**
AutoComplete

AutoComplete is a feature in Word that automatically completes the spelling of days of the week and months of the year that have more than five letters in their names. After you type the first four letters, AutoComplete suggests the complete word. For example, if you type *Febr*, the word *February* appears in a ScreenTip above the insertion point. **Figure 3–8** shows an example of an AutoComplete suggestion. To insert the suggested word, press Enter, and AutoComplete automatically inserts the complete word for you. To ignore the suggested word, just keep typing.

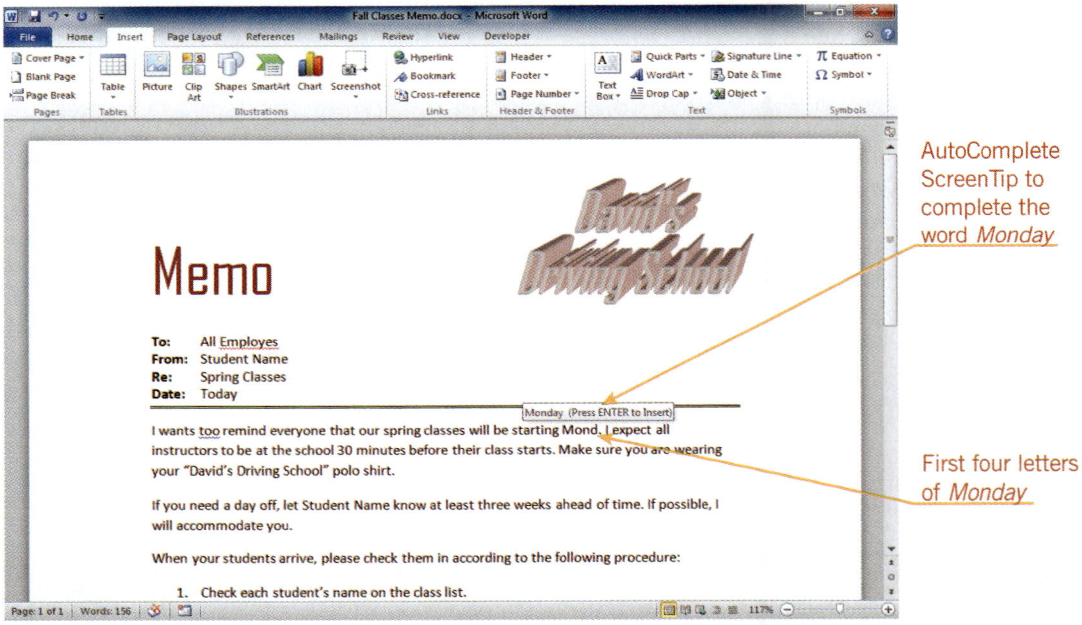

AutoComplete ScreenTip to complete the word *Monday*

First four letters of *Monday*

FIGURE 3–8   Inserting a day of the week with AutoComplete

Step-by-Step 3.6

1. In the first paragraph, at the end of the first sentence, position the insertion point between the word *starting* and the period. Press the **spacebar**.

2. Type **Mond**. A ScreenTip appears telling you to press Enter to insert *Monday*, as shown in Figure 3–8.

3. Press **Enter** to accept the AutoComplete suggestion. *Monday* appears in the document.

4. Save the document and leave it open for the next Step-by-Step.

Inserting the Date and Time

You can easily insert the current date and time into a document. To do this, on the Ribbon, click the Insert tab. Then, in the Text group, click the Date & Time button. The Date and Time dialog box opens, as shown in **Figure 3–9**. Select one of the available formats in the list. Some of the formats display only the date, and others display the date and time.

Dates and times shown are the current date and time, so your date will probably differ

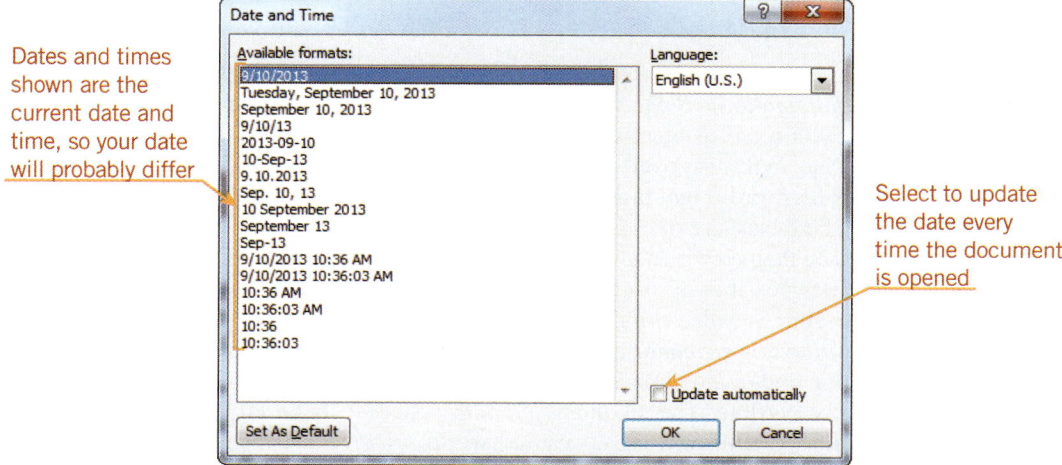

Select to update the date every time the document is opened

FIGURE 3–9   Date and Time dialog box

If you want to display the current date whenever you open the document, you would click the Update automatically check box to select it. For example, if you create a template or a report on a regular basis, you would probably want to have the current date displayed each time you opened the document. If you want a date inserted in the document to always show the date you inserted it, leave the Update automatically check box unselected. For example, when you create a letter or memo, you would want the date to remain unchanged for record keeping purposes.

Step-by-Step 3.7

1. In the *Date* line in the memo header, select the text **Today**, and then press **Delete**.

2. On the Insert tab, in the Text group, click the **Date & Time** button. The Date and Time dialog box opens.

3. In the Available formats box, click the third format, which shows today's date in a format similar to *September 10, 2013.*

4. If the **Update automatically** check box has a check mark in it, click it to remove the check mark. This will prevent the date from updating to the current date every time this document is opened.

5. Click **OK**. The dialog box closes and the current date is inserted in the letter.

6. Save the document and leave it open for the next Step-by-Step.

Checking Spelling and Grammar as You Type

Word has the capability to identify misspelled or misused words or incorrect grammar. *Automatic spell checking* flags words that might be misspelled by underlining them with a red or blue wavy line immediately after you type them. A red, wavy underline indicates Word cannot find that word in its built-in dictionary, which means the word might be misspelled. A blue, wavy underline indicates a word that might be misused. For example, if you type *We came form the store*, the word *form* would be flagged with a blue, wavy underline as a word that might be misused. Word identifies possible misusage by examining the context in which the word is used. This feature is called *contextual spell checking*.

　　Automatic grammar checking examines your document for grammatical errors. When it finds a possible error, the word, phrase, or sentence is underlined with a green, wavy line. The automatic grammar checker looks for capitalization errors, commonly confused words, misused words, passive sentences, punctuation problems, and other types of grammatical problems.

　　To correct a spelling, contextual, or grammatical error that has been identified with a wavy underline, right-click the flagged word or phrase to open a shortcut menu with a list of suggestions to replace the possible error. See **Figure 3–10**. Click a suggestion on the shortcut menu to select it and replace the flagged word or phrase.

VOCABULARY

automatic spell checking

contextual spell checking

automatic grammar checking

── WARNING

The automatic spell checker sometimes incorrectly identifies words as being misspelled, because the word is not in the built-in dictionary. This frequently occurs with proper names.

TIP

Although automatic grammar checking is a helpful tool, you still need a good working knowledge of English grammar. The grammar checker can identify a possible problem, but you must decide if the change should be made.

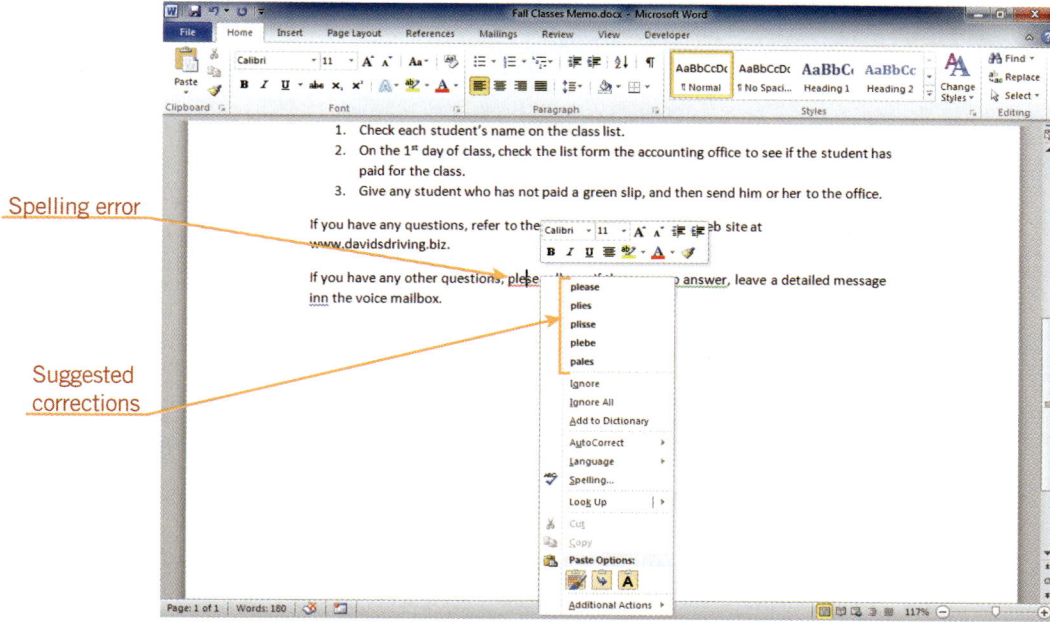

Spelling error

Suggested corrections

FIGURE 3–10   Correcting a spelling error using the shortcut menu

Automatic spelling and grammar checking can be turned on and off or adjusted in the Proofing section of the Word Options dialog box, as shown in **Figure 3–11**. The options in the spelling and grammar section of the dialog box are described in **Table 3–1**.

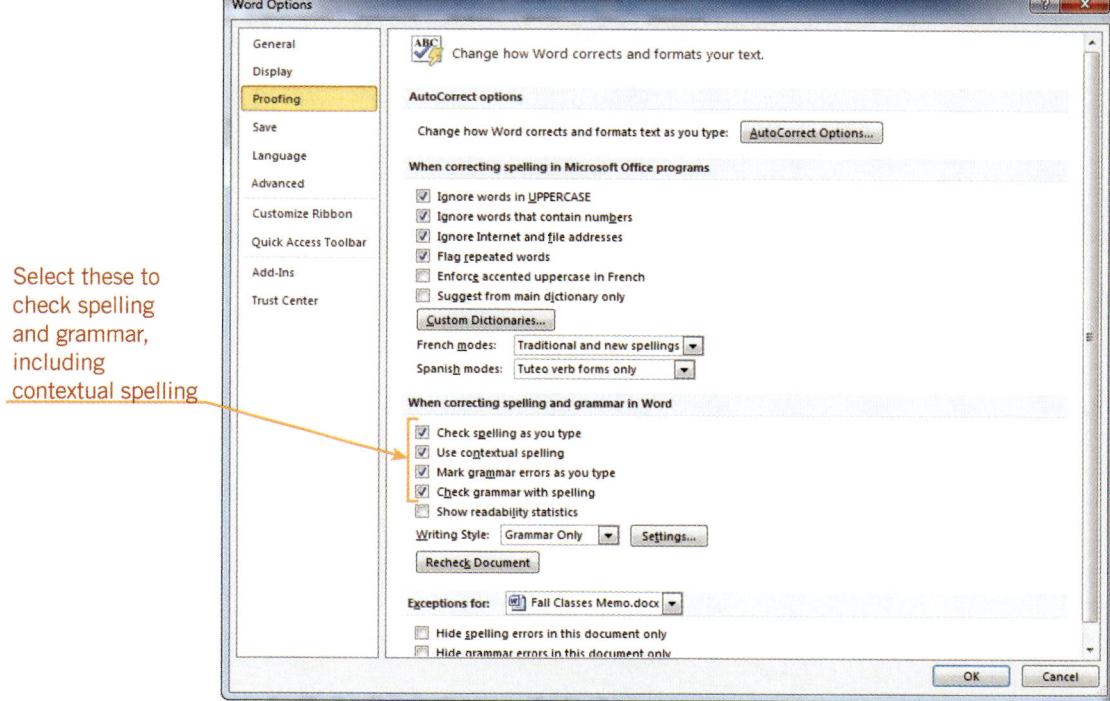

Select these to check spelling and grammar, including contextual spelling

FIGURE 3–11   Proofing options in Word Options dialog box

TABLE 3–1   Spelling and grammar options in the Word Options dialog box

OPTION	ACTION
Check spelling as you type	Flags possible misspelled words in the document with a red, wavy underline.
Use contextual spelling	When checking the document for spelling errors, flags possible misused words with a blue, wavy underline.
Mark grammar errors as you type	Flags possible grammatical errors in the document with a green, wavy underline.
Check grammar	When checking the document for spelling errors, also checks for spelling grammatical errors.
Show readability	Opens the Readability Statistics dialog box when the spelling and statistics grammar check is complete. The Readability Statistics dialog box provides information about the reading level of the document.
Writing Style	If you turn on the grammar checker, allows you to check for grammar errors only or for writing style errors, such as use of the passive voice. The default is to check for grammar only.
Settings	Opens the Grammar Settings dialog box, in which you can select the grammar and writing style rules the grammar checker uses as it checks the document.
Recheck Document	Resets the spelling and grammar checker so that words you previously chose to ignore will be flagged in the document again.

Step-by-Step 3.8

 TIP

The options in the "When correcting spelling in Microsoft Office programs" section in the dialog box apply to all Microsoft Office programs installed on your computer, not just to Word.

1. On the Ribbon, click the **File** tab, and then in the navigation bar, click **Options**. In the list on the left side of the Word Options dialog box, click **Proofing**. The right side of the dialog box changes to display options for customizing the proofing tools in Word.

2. In the section labeled "When correcting spelling and grammar in Word," the first four check boxes should be selected. If any of these check boxes does not contain a check mark, click it to insert a check mark. Click **OK** to close the dialog box.

3. Press **Ctrl+End**. The insertion point moves to the end of the document.

4. Type the following sentences *exactly* as they appear here: **If you have any other questions, plese call me. If there are no answer, leave a detailed message inn the voice mailbox.** The three intentional errors are flagged by Word with wavy underlines.

5. Right-click **plese**, the word flagged with a red, wavy underline indicating a possible misspelled word. (Remember, right-click means to position the mouse pointer over the word or words specified, and then click the *right* mouse button.) A shortcut menu opens.

6. With the left mouse button, click **please** on the shortcut menu. The incorrect spelling is replaced with the correct spelling, and the red, wavy underline disappears.

7. Right-click anywhere on the words **are no answer**. This phrase is flagged with a green, wavy underline indicating a possible grammatical error. (If the green, wavy underline is not showing, click in a different paragraph, and then click in the sentence that you typed.)

8. On the shortcut menu that opens, click **is no answer**. This is the correct phrase to use in this instance. The incorrect phrase is replaced with the correct phrase, and the green, wavy underline disappears.

9. Right-click **inn**, the word flagged with a blue, wavy underline indicating that it might be used incorrectly in this context.

10. On the shortcut menu that opens, click **in**. The incorrectly used word is replaced with the correct word, and the blue, wavy underline disappears.

11. Save the document and leave it open for the next Step-by-Step.

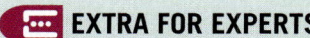 **EXTRA FOR EXPERTS**

When you right-click a grammar error, you can click Grammar on the shortcut menu to learn more about the grammar error that has been identified.

Using the Spelling and Grammar Checker

In addition to checking your spelling and grammar as you type, you can use the Spelling and Grammar dialog box to check a document's spelling and grammar after you finish typing. You can check an entire document or a selected portion of a document. To do this, on the Ribbon, click the Review tab. Then, in the Proofing group, click the Spelling & Grammar button. The Spelling and Grammar dialog box opens, displaying the first flagged error identified in the document.

The options in the Spelling and Grammar dialog box change depending on the nature of the current error. When a spelling error is detected, the Spelling and Grammar dialog box appears similar to the one shown in **Figure 3–12**. When a contextual spelling error is detected, the dialog box that appears is the same as the one shown in Figure 3–12, but only the Ignore Once and Change commands are available. When a grammar error is identified, the Spelling and Grammar dialog box appears similar to the one shown in **Figure 3–13**.

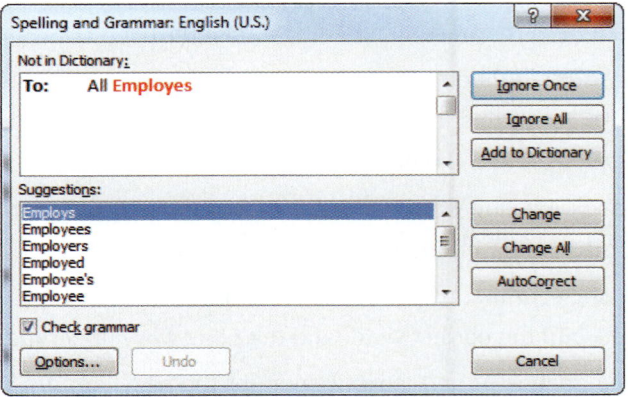

FIGURE 3–12   Spelling error flagged in the Spelling and Grammar dialog box

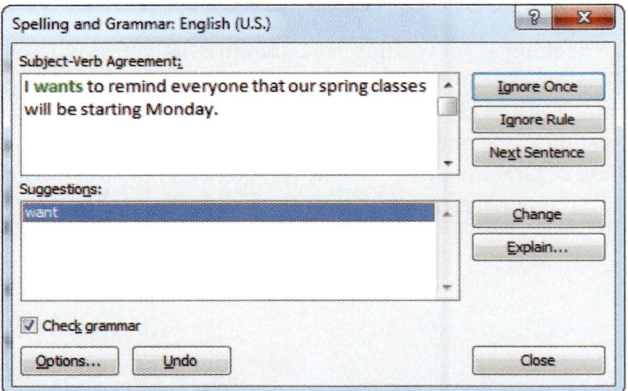

FIGURE 3–13   Grammatical error flagged in the Spelling and Grammar dialog box

When an error is found, it is highlighted in the document and listed in the top box in the dialog box. Suggestions for correcting the error are listed in the bottom box. For some grammar errors, only a description of the type of error appears in the bottom box.

You can click in the document and correct the error, click in the top box in the dialog box and correct the error, or click a suggestion in the Suggestions box to correct the error. If you click in the document to correct the error, the Ignore Once command in the dialog box changes to Resume. If you correct the error by clicking in the top box in the dialog box, the Ignore Once command changes to Undo Edit. When you are finished working in the document, click in the dialog box, and then click Resume. **Table 3–2** and **Table 3–3** explain the options in the Spelling and Grammar dialog box.

> **TIP**
>
> If a word appears twice in a row, the second word will be underlined with a red, wavy underline. To delete the repeated word, click Delete Repeated Word on the shortcut menu or, in the Spelling and Grammar dialog box, click Delete (which replaces Change).

TABLE 3–2   Spelling and Grammar dialog box commands for spelling errors

COMMAND	ACTION
Ignore Once	Leaves the word in the document unchanged and jumps to the next flagged error; changes to Resume if you click in the document to correct the error; and changes to Undo Edit if you correct a change in the top box.
Ignore All	Leaves all instances of the word unchanged in the document and jumps to the next flagged error.
Add to Dictionary	Leaves all instances of the word unchanged in the document, adds the word to the built-in dictionary, and jumps to the next flagged error.
Change/Delete	The Change command changes the flagged word to the selected suggestion or to the correction you type in the top box in the dialog box, and then jumps to the next flagged error. The Delete command appears when a word appears twice in a row; click it to delete the repeated word.
Change All	Changes all instances of the flagged word in the document to the selected suggestion or to the correction you type in the top box in the dialog box, and then jumps to the next flagged error.
AutoCorrect	Changes the flagged word to the selected suggestion, adds the word and its correction to the AutoCorrect list, and jumps to the next flagged error.
Options	Opens the Proofing section in the Word Options dialog box so you can change default spelling and grammar check settings.
Undo/Undo Edit	Reverses the last decision you made in the dialog box.
Cancel/Close	Before you make a decision on the first spelling change, Cancel stops the spelling check. After you make a decision on the first error, it changes to Close, and clicking it stops the spelling and grammar check.

TABLE 3–3   Spelling and Grammar dialog box commands for grammar errors

COMMAND	ACTION
Ignore Once	Leaves the flagged error untouched and jumps to the next flagged error; changes to Resume if you click in the document to correct the error; and changes to Undo Edit if you correct a change in the top box.
Ignore Rule	Leaves all instances of errors that violate the identified grammar rule untouched and jumps to the next flagged error.
Next Sentence	Leaves the flagged error untouched or changes the flagged error to the correction you type in the top box in the dialog box, and then jumps to the next flagged error.
Change	Changes the flagged error to the selected suggestion or to the correction you type in the top box in the dialog box, and then jumps to the next flagged error.
Explain	Opens a Word Help window with an explanation of the grammar or style rule being applied.
Options	Opens the Proofing section in the Word Options dialog box to allow you to change default spelling and grammar check settings.
Undo/Undo Edit	Reverses the last decision you made in the dialog box.
Cancel/Close	Before you make a decision on the first grammar change, Cancel stops the grammar check. After you make a decision on the first error, it changes to Close, and clicking it stops the spelling and grammar check.

Step-by-Step 3.9

> **TIP**
>
> To check only spelling in the document, click the Check grammar check box in the Spelling and Grammar dialog box to deselect it, or, in the Proofing section of the Word Options dialog box, click the Check grammar with spelling check box to deselect it.

1. Press **Ctrl+Home**. This ensures that the spelling and grammar check starts from the beginning of the document.

2. On the Ribbon, click the **Review** tab. The Ribbon changes to display the commands on the Review tab.

3. In the Proofing group, click the **Spelling & Grammar** button. The Spelling and Grammar dialog box opens. The first error it finds in the document, *Employes*, is highlighted in the document and appears in red in the Not in Dictionary box in the dialog box. The Suggestions box at the bottom of the dialog box contains several possible alternatives for the flagged word.

4. In the Suggestions box, click **Employees**, and then click **Change**. The word is corrected in the document, and the next possible error is flagged.

5. If your first or last name is selected as the next error, click **Ignore All**, and then watch as the next error is flagged. It finds the misused word *too*.

6. Click in the box at the top of the dialog box, and then use the arrow keys to position the insertion point after the word *too*. Press the **Backspace** key to delete the second *o*.

7. Click **Change**. Word replaces the misused word and continues checking. The next error, a Subject-Verb Agreement grammatical error in the first sentence, *wants*, is highlighted.

8. In the Suggestions box, make sure **want** is selected, and then click **Change**. If you made any typing errors, additional words might be highlighted next in the dialog box. If this happens, use the commands in the dialog box to correct these errors. When the spelling and grammar check is finished, the Spelling and Grammar dialog box closes and a dialog box opens telling you that the spelling and grammar check is complete.

9. Click **OK**. The dialog box closes. The insertion point returns to the beginning of the document.

10. Save the document and leave it open for the next Step-by-Step.

Using the Thesaurus

The **Thesaurus** is a useful feature for finding a synonym (a word with a similar meaning) for a word in your document. For some words, the Thesaurus also lists antonyms, or words with opposite meanings. You can use the Thesaurus to find the exact word to express your message or to avoid using the same word repeatedly in a document.

To use the Thesaurus, select the word you want to look up. On the Ribbon, click the Review tab. Then, in the Proofing group, click the Thesaurus button. The Research task pane opens on the right side of the window, as shown in **Figure 3–14**. The word you selected in the document appears in the top box, and *Thesaurus: English (U.S.)* appears in the second box. A list of synonyms and antonyms appears in the third box. The main entries in the list are bold. To replace the selected text, point to a word underneath a main entry, click the arrow that appears, and then click Insert. If you click a word underneath a main entry, that word is looked up in the Thesaurus for you.

▶ **VOCABULARY**
Thesaurus

EXTRA FOR EXPERTS

You can also look up a word in the Thesaurus or dictionary by right-clicking a selected word and choosing Synonyms on the shortcut menu.

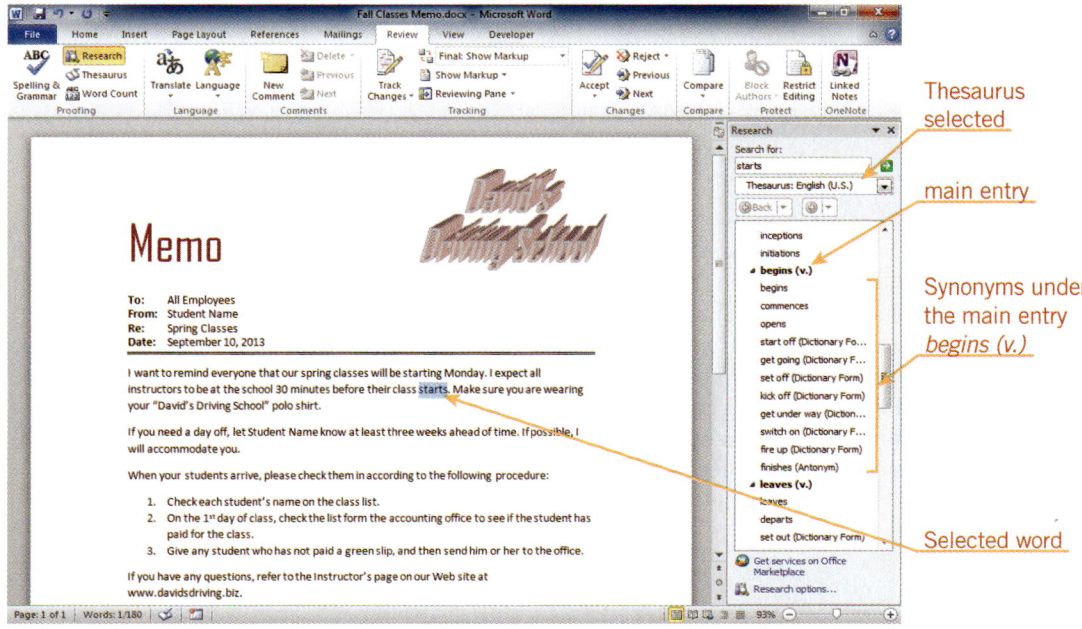

FIGURE 3–14 Thesaurus in the Research task pane

📧 **EXTRA FOR EXPERTS**

To look up the definition of a word, select the word, click the Thesaurus button to open the Research task pane, click the arrow next to the second box (the one that contains *Thesaurus: English (U.S.)*), and then click Encarta Dictionary: English (North America).

If you select a plural noun or a verb in a form other than its base form (the infinitive form), a list of related words appears in the list in the task pane. For example, if you select the word *walked* in the sentence *he walked to the park*, the Research task pane would display the word *walk* under the heading "Related Words" in the task pane. You click the correct related word in the list, and the task pane changes to show the related word in the top box and its synonyms in the third box. If this happens, make sure you edit the word you insert in the document so it is in the same form as the original word.

Step-by-Step 3.10

1. In the first paragraph in the body of the memo, select the word **starts** at the end of the second sentence.

2. On the Review tab, in the Proofing group, click the **Thesaurus** button. The Research task pane opens on the right side of the window with Thesaurus: English (U.S.) in the second box. The task pane displays a list of words organized under main entries.

3. Scroll down the list until you see the main entry *begins (v.)*.

4. Under the main entry, point to the first synonym, **begins**, click the **arrow** that appears, and then click **Insert**. The word *begins* replaces *starts* in the document.

5. In the task pane title bar, click the **Close** button  to close the task pane.

6. Save the document and leave it open for the next Step-by-Step.

⚠ **WARNING**

If you click the word in the task pane instead of clicking the arrow, the word you clicked is looked up in the thesaurus and a new set of results appears. Close the task pane, and then repeat the steps.

Inserting Symbols

At times, you may need to use a letter or symbol that is not on the keyboard. For example, you might want to insert a symbol used in a foreign language, such as the tilde over the *n* in Spanish (ñ), or a currency symbol such as the euro symbol (€) for currency in the European Union.

To insert a symbol, on the Ribbon, click the Insert tab. Then, in the Symbols group, click the Symbol button. Commonly used symbols appear on the menu. See **Figure 3–15**. To insert a symbol located on the menu, click it. If you don't see the symbol you want on the menu, click More Symbols to open the Symbol dialog box, as shown in **Figure 3–16**.

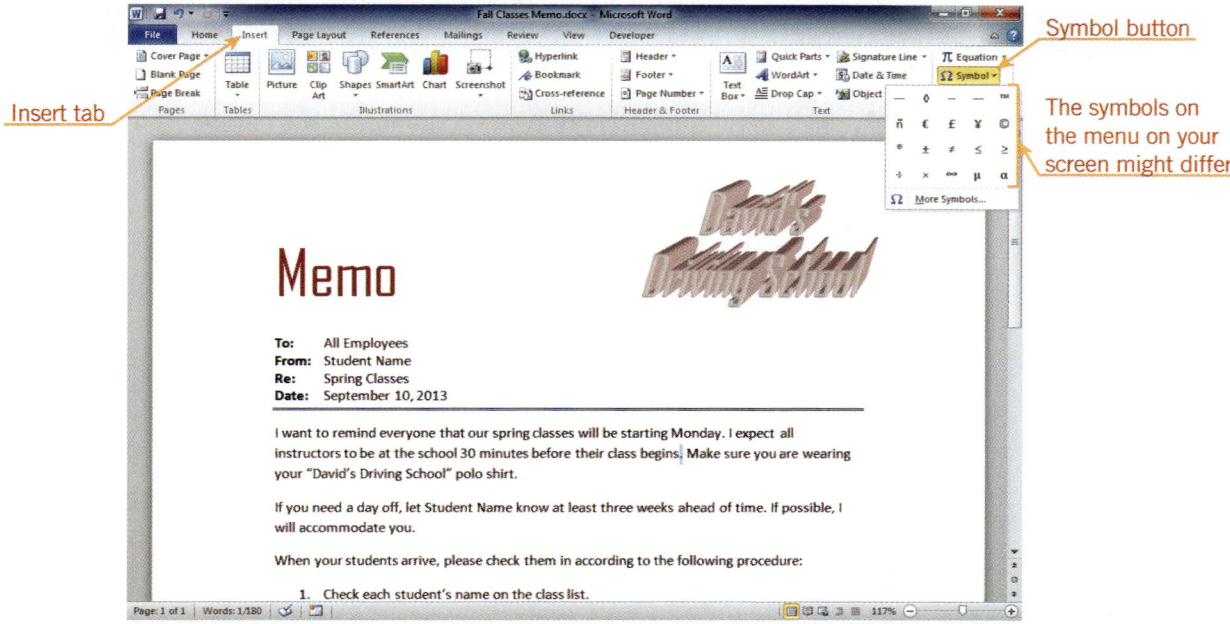

FIGURE 3–15 Symbols on the Symbol menu

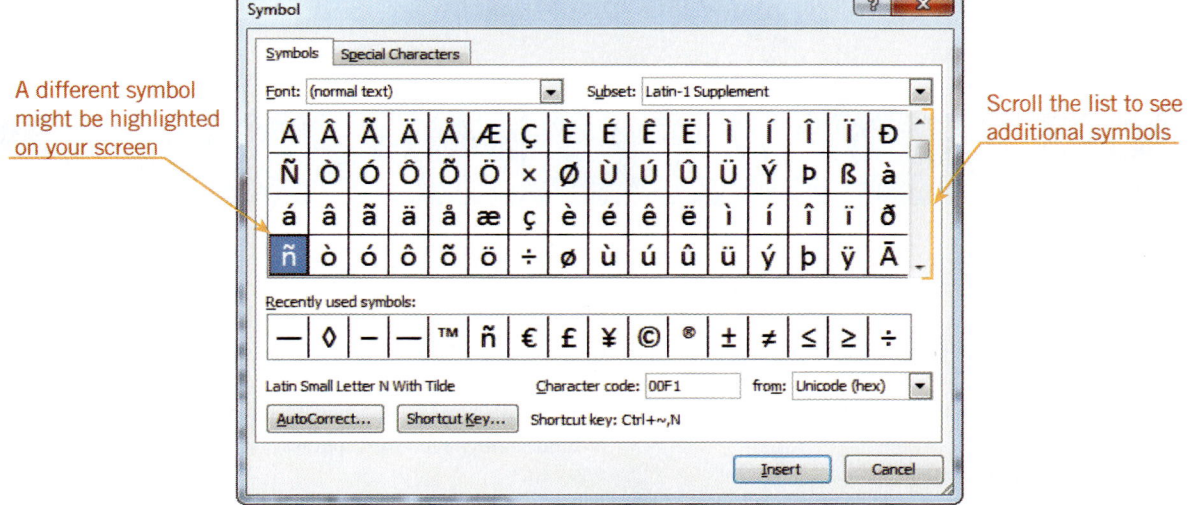

FIGURE 3–16 Symbol dialog box

Click the symbol you want in the dialog box, and then click Insert. The symbol you selected appears in the document. You then need to click Close to close the dialog box. If the symbol you inserted from the dialog box was not on the Symbol menu, it will replace one of the other symbols on the menu to make it easier for you to insert it again.

Step-by-Step 3.11

1. In the last line of the first paragraph in the body of the memo, position the insertion point between the *l* in *School* and the quotation marks.

2. On the Ribbon, click the **Insert** tab. In the Symbols group, click the **Symbol** button to open the Symbols menu. See Figure 3–15. Position the pointer on top of several of the symbols in the menu to see the ScreenTip identifying each of them.

3. Position the pointer over ™. This is the trademark symbol. The ScreenTip identifies it as TRADE MARK SIGN. (If you don't see the trademark symbol on the menu, click **More Symbols** to open the Symbol dialog box. In the Symbol dialog box, drag the scroll box to the bottom of the scroll bar, scroll up a few rows until you see the trademark symbol, click the trademark symbol, click **Insert**, and then click **Close**.)

4. Click ™. The menu closes and the trademark symbol is inserted into the document at the insertion point.

5. Save, print, and close the document.

SUMMARY

In this lesson, you learned:

- AutoCorrect automatically corrects common capitalization and spelling errors as you type. The AutoFormat As You Type feature automatically applies built-in formats to text as you type.

- You can create Quick Parts to store frequently used text so you don't have to retype the text each time. Quick Parts are a type of building block.

- AutoComplete automatically completes the spelling of days of the week and months with more than five letters in their names.

- You can automatically insert the date and time in a document using the Date & Time button.

- Automatic spell checking identifies misspelled words and words that are not in Word's dictionary by underlining them with a red, wavy underline immediately after you type them.

- Contextual spell checking identifies words that might be used incorrectly by underlining them with a blue, wavy line.

- Automatic grammar checking identifies grammatical errors by underlining the word, phrase, or sentence with a green, wavy line.

- The Spelling and Grammar dialog box contains options that allow you to check the spelling and grammar of words, make changes, and add words to your own custom dictionary.

- You can use the Thesaurus to find a synonym for a word in your document. For some words, the Thesaurus also lists antonyms.

- You can insert symbols and special characters not found on the keyboard using the Symbol button on the Insert tab.

VOCABULARY REVIEW

Define the following terms:

AutoComplete

AutoCorrect

AutoFormat As You Type

automatic grammar checking

automatic spell checking

building block

contextual spell checking

format

Quick Part

Thesaurus

REVIEW QUESTIONS

FILL IN THE BLANK

Complete the following sentences by writing the correct word or words in the blanks provided.

1. The _____ feature corrects common capitalization, spelling, grammar, and typing errors as you type.

2. All document parts that are stored and reused are called _____.

3. A blue, wavy underline in a document indicates a possible _____ error.

4. A green, wavy underline in a document indicates a possible _____ error.

5. To check the entire document for spelling and grammar errors, use the _____ dialog box.

MATCHING

Match the correct term in Column 2 to its description in Column 1.

Column 1

_____ 1. A building block of text frequently use.

_____ 2. Changes fractions and numbers as you type, such as *3/4* to ¾.

_____ 3. Corrects common capitalization, typing, spelling, and grammatical errors when you press Enter or the spacebar.

_____ 4. Identifies possible grammatical errors with green wavy underlines.

_____ 5. Displays synonyms for a selected word.

Column 2

A. Thesaurus

B. Quick Part

C. AutoCorrect

D. Automatic grammar checking

E. AutoFormat As You Type

TRUE / FALSE

Circle T if the statement is true or F if the statement is false.

T   F   **1.** To insert letters, symbols, and characters not found on the keyboard, you use the Symbol button in the Symbols group on the Insert tab.

T   F   **2.** To accept an AutoComplete suggestion, you press the spacebar.

T   F   **3.** You cannot add or delete entries from the AutoCorrect list.

T   F   **4.** The AutoFormat As You Type feature automatically applies built-in formats to text as you type.

T   F   **5.** You can right-click a word or phrase with a colored, wavy line under it and then select a correction from a list of suggestions.

■ PROJECTS

If you have a SAM 2010 user profile, your instructor may have assigned an autogradable version of the indicated project. If so, log into the SAM 2010 Web site at *www.cengage.com/sam2010* to download the instruction and start files.

PROJECT 3–1

1. Open the **Minutes.docx** document from the drive and folder where your Data Files are stored. Save the document as **Club Minutes** followed by your initials.

2. Check the document's spelling and grammar, and correct any errors.

3. Near the top of the document, insert the current date in the blank paragraph beneath *Minutes of the Business Meeting* in the format *Thursday, March 21, 2013*. Do not update the date automatically.

4. Insert your name at the beginning of the list of members who attended the meeting, and then create an AutoCorrect entry for your name.

5. In the second to last paragraph, position the insertion point between *recognized* and *as*. Use the AutoCorrect feature to insert your name. Insert any necessary spaces or delete extra spaces.

6. In the last sentence in the Old Business paragraph, find a synonym for the word *aim* that makes sense in context.

7. In the last sentence in the first New Business paragraph, find a synonym for the word *arrange* that makes sense in context.

8. At the end of the Announcements paragraph, type **The next meeting will be held on the 24th of April.**

9. Delete the AutoCorrect entry you added.

10. Save, print, and close the document.

 PROJECT 3–2

1. Open the **Lancaster Memo.docx** document from the drive and folder where your Data Files are stored. Save the document as **Lancaster Voting Memo** followed by your initials.

2. Turn on formatting marks, and then position the insertion point after the tab mark in the *From* line in the memo header.

3. Type **Dinah Muñoz.** (If the letter *ñ* is not on the Symbol menu, open the Symbol dialog box. Make sure the scroll box is at the top of the list, and then click the down scroll arrow eight times to see the row containing the character.)

4. Insert the current date after the tab mark in the *Date:* line in the format that looks like 9/29/13. Do not update the date automatically.

5. In the body of the memo, position the insertion point after the word *for* at the end of the first sentence. Use the AutoComplete and AutoFormat As You Type features to insert the text **September 31st**. Insert any necessary spaces. (*Hint*: You will need to press the spacebar after typing the date, and then remove the extra space before the period.)

6. Create a Quick Part named **Chamber** from the text *Chamber of Commerce* in the second sentence of the first paragraph. Insert the Chamber Quick Part at the end of the *To* line in the memo header.

7. Use the AutoFormat As You Type feature to create the following numbered list after the second paragraph in the body of the memo:

   1. **G. W. Carter Elementary School**
   2. **Kennedy Middle School**
   3. **Lancaster High School**

8. Use the Thesaurus to replace the word *personal* in the last paragraph with a word that makes sense in context.

9. Delete the Chamber Quick Part.

10. Correct the spelling and grammatical errors in the document.

11. Jump to the end of the document, press Enter twice, and then type your name.

12. Turn off formatting marks, and then save, print, and close the document.

PROJECT 3–3

1. Open the **Museum.docx** document from the drive and folder where your Data Files are stored. Save the document as **Museum Visit** followed by your initials.

2. Use the Thesaurus to change as many words as you can without changing the meaning of the text.

3. Jump to the end of the document, press Enter twice, and then type your name.

4. Save, print, and close the document.

PROJECT 3–4

1. Open the **Application.docx** document from the drive and folder where your Data Files are stored. Save the document as **Application Letter** followed by your initials.

2. Insert the current date in the format *September 29, 2013* in the blank paragraph above the inside address. Set the date to update automatically.

3. In the third paragraph in the body of the letter, position the insertion point in front of the last sentence (just before *These*), and then type the following sentence. (If you don't see the symbols on the Symbol menu, open the Symbol dialog box, click the Subset arrow, and then click Greek and Coptic to jump to the Greek alphabet.)

   I have also been active on campus, holding various leadership positions in the service organization Omega Delta Psi ($\Omega\Delta\Psi$).

4. In the last line of the document, replace *Sarah Summers* with your name**.**

5. Check the document's spelling and grammar, and correct any errors.

6. Save, print, and close the document.

■ CRITICAL THINKING

ACTIVITY 3–1

It is important for students to begin to develop a personal portfolio for employment before they graduate from high school or college. A personal portfolio contains a resume, well-written application letters, a list of references, and a list of achievements. Write an application letter for a job that interests you. Team up with a few classmates, and then edit and critique each other's application letters. Be careful to provide constructive criticism.

ACTIVITY 3–3

Word has many helpful editing features. Some Word features are more helpful as you type your text, and some are more useful after you have finished typing. Make one list of the Word features you would use as you type a document, and then make another list of Word features you would use after you finished typing the document. If a feature can be listed in both lists, decide when it is the most useful.

ACTIVITY 3–2

You are the regional vice president for Candlelight Time, a chain of candle stores. A new store will be opening soon, and you need to type a letter to potential customers announcing the grand opening and offering three free scented candles to the first 100 customers. Make the letter at least three paragraphs long. Use any helpful automatic features. Insert the current date (set it to update automatically), and then check the spelling and grammar.

LESSON 4

Formatting Text

■ OBJECTIVES

Upon completion of this lesson, you should be able to:

■ Change the font.

■ Change the size, color, and style of text.

■ Use different underline styles and font effects and highlight text.

■ Copy formatting using the Format Painter.

■ Understand styles and apply Quick Styles.

■ Change the theme.

■ Create new Quick Styles.

■ Clear formatting.

■ VOCABULARY

attribute

color palette

font

font effect

font size

font style

Format Painter

point

Quick Style

style

text effect

theme

Formatting Text

Once you have typed text in a document, you can format the text to change its appearance and make an impact on the reader.

In this lesson, you will learn how to change the appearance, size, color of text, and how to apply several formats at once using styles. You will learn how to copy formats and clear formatting. You will also learn how to change a document's theme and how to modify and create new styles.

To change the format of text, you must first select the text you want to change. If you are changing the format of a single paragraph, the insertion point must be located somewhere in that paragraph. If you are changing the format of multiple paragraphs, you must select at least part of each paragraph you want to format. You can also change the format before you start typing, and all the text you type from then on will have the new format applied until you change to another format.

Changing the Font

Designs of type are called *fonts*. Just as clothing comes in different designs, fonts have different designs. For example, the font used for this text is Times LT Std Roman and the font used for the blue *Changing the Font* heading above is Futura Std Medium.

Like clothing, fonts can be dressy or casual. When you are creating a document, you should consider what kind of impression you want the text to make. Do you want your document to look dressy and formal? Or do you want it to look casual and informal? Using the fonts shown in **Figure 4–1** would result in very different looking documents.

This font is called Calibri.

This font is called Times New Roman.

This font is called Arial.

This font is called Broadway.

This font is called Old English Text MT.

This font is called Comic Sans MS.

This font is called Lucida Handwriting.

FIGURE 4–1   Examples of different fonts

To change the font, locate the Font group on the Home tab on the Ribbon. Click the arrow next to the Font box, as shown in **Figure 4–2**, and then scroll to the font of your choice. If you have selected text in the document first, you can point to each font to use Live Preview, the Microsoft Office feature that enables you to watch the selected text change in the document without actually making the change. When you find the font you want, click it. The menu closes and the new font is applied to the selected text.

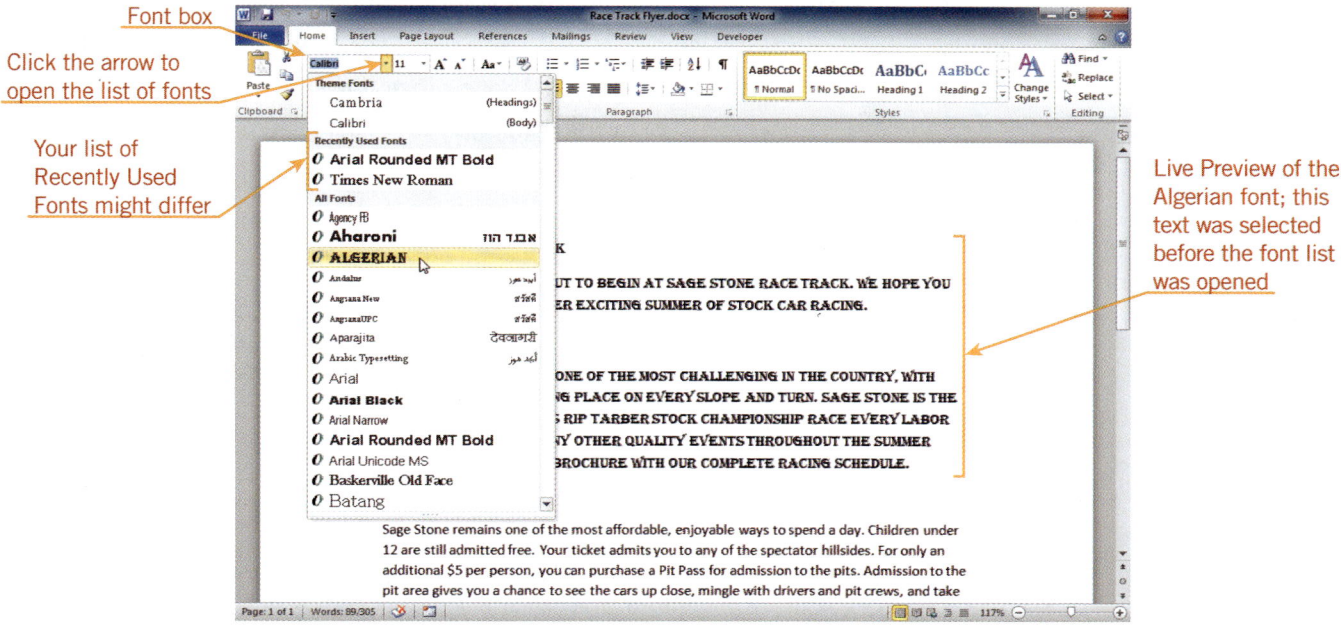

FIGURE 4–2   Live Preview of the Algerian font

You can change the font of text already in the document by selecting it first, and then choosing a new font. To change the font of text not yet typed, first choose the font, and then type the text. The new font will be applied until you change to another font.

Step-by-Step 4.1

1. Open the **Flyer.docx** document from the drive and folder where your Data Files are stored. Save the document as **Race Track Flyer** followed by your initials.

2. On the Home tab, in the Editing group, click the **Select** button, and then click **Select All**. All the text in the document is selected.

3. On the Home tab, in the Font group, click the **arrow** next to the Font box `Calibri (Body)`. The list of fonts opens. The font currently applied to the selected text, Calibri, is listed in the Font box and is selected at the top of the list.

4. Point to **Algerian** (but don't click it). The Live Preview feature changes the selected text in the document to the Algerian font so you can see what it would look like.

5. Point to a few other fonts in the list and watch how the Live Preview feature changes the selected text.

6. Click a blank area of the document. The Font list closes and the font of the selected text stays the same.

TIP

If you use the mouse to select text, the Mini toolbar will appear. To choose a different font using the Mini toolbar, move the mouse toward it to make it fully visible, and then click the arrow next to the Font box on the Mini toolbar.

7. In the paragraph below the heading *Sage Stone Race Track*, in the first line of text, select the text **Sage Stone Race Track**.

8. In the Font group, click the **arrow** next to the Font box . Click **Arial Rounded MT Bold**. The Font list closes and the selected text is changed to Arial Rounded MT Bold.

9. Click a blank area of the document to deselect the text.

10. Save the document and leave it open for the next Step-by-Step.

Changing Font Attributes

▶ **VOCABULARY**
attributes
font size
points

Once you have decided on a font, you can change its *attributes*, or how it looks. For example, you can change the size of the font or change its style by making the font bold, italic, or underlined. You can also add color and apply special effects.

Changing Font Size

TIP

You can also use the Grow Font and Shrink Font buttons in the Font group on the Home tab or on the Mini toolbar to increase or decrease the font size.

Font size is determined by measuring the height of characters in units called *points*. Standard font sizes for text are 10, 11, and 12 points. Font sizes for headings are usually larger. For example, this text is 10 points, and the blue *Changing Font Attributes* heading above is 18 points. The higher the point size, the larger the characters. **Figure 4–3** illustrates the Calibri font in different sizes. You can change font size by using the Font Size box on the Formatting toolbar or on the Mini toolbar.

This is 10-point Calibri.

This is 11-point Calibri.

This is 12-point Calibri.

This is 16-point Calibri.

This is 20-point Calibri.

FIGURE 4–3   Examples of font sizes

Step-by-Step 4.2

1. In the paragraph below the heading *Sage Stone Race Track*, in the first line of text, select **Sage Stone Race Track**.

2. On the Home tab, in the Font group, look at the Font Size box 11 ▾. The selected text is 11 points. See **Figure 4–4**.

Font Size box

Font group

Selected text

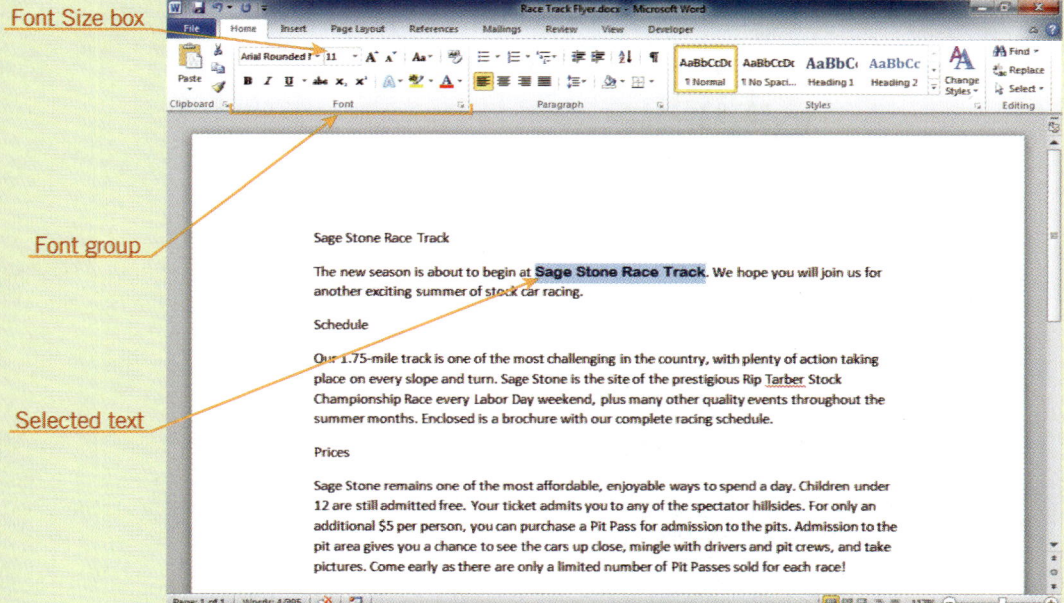

FIGURE 4–4
Font size of selected text

3. In the paragraph below the heading *Sage Stone Race Track*, select the second line of text, and then look at the Font Size box 11 ▾. This text is also 11 points. Although these characters look smaller than *Sage Stone Race Track* in the first line of this paragraph, all of the text in the document is 11 points.

4. Scroll to the bottom of the document, and then select all the text in the last paragraph (*We can't wait to see you!*).

5. Click the **arrow** next to the Font Size box 11 ▾. A list of font sizes appears.

6. Click **16**. The Font Size list closes, and the selected text is changed to 16 points.

7. Deselect the text.

8. Save the document and leave it open for the next Step-by-Step.

TIP

Point size tells you the size of text relative to text in other point sizes in the same font. But, 11-point text in one font might be larger or smaller than 11-point text in another font.

EXTRA FOR EXPERTS

If you want to use a font size that is not on the Font Size list, type the point size directly in the Font Size box, and then press Enter.

Changing the Color of Text

You can change the color of text to make it stand out or to add interest to a document. To change the color of text, click the arrow next to the Font Color button in the Font group on the Home tab. This opens a gallery that includes the *color palette*, a coordinated set of colors available for use in the document. See **Figure 4–5**.

▶ **VOCABULARY**
color palette

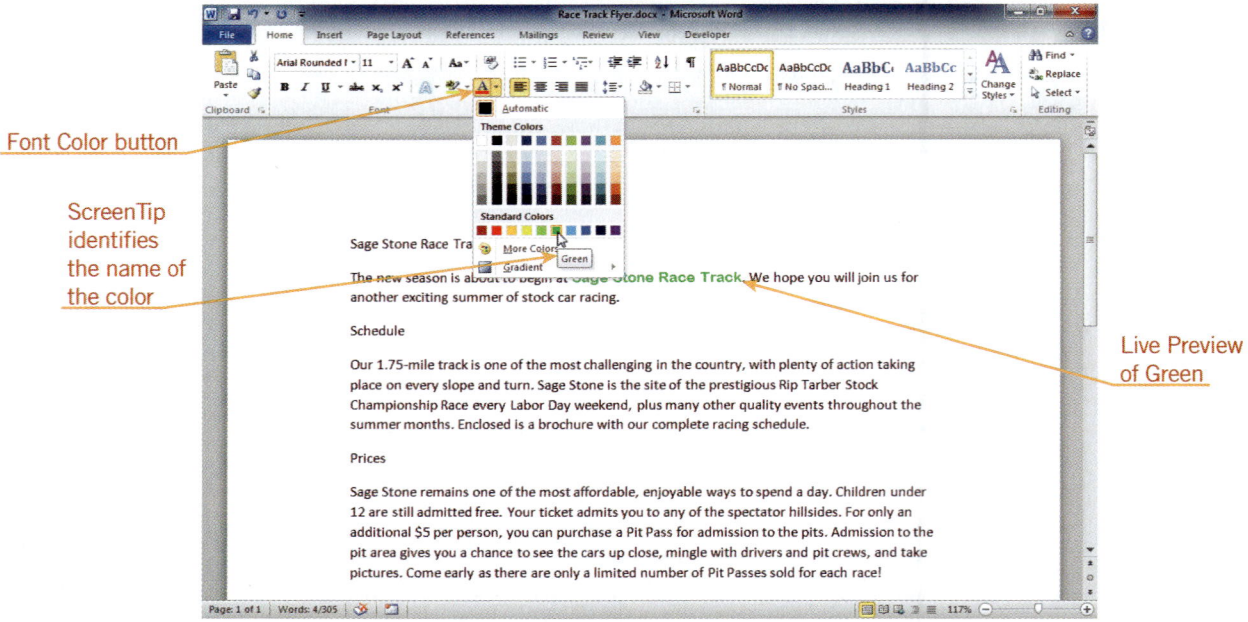

Font Color button

ScreenTip identifies the name of the color

Live Preview of Green

FIGURE 4–5   Color palette on the Font Color button gallery

The gallery has four sections. The top section contains the Automatic color for the current text; this is usually black. The middle section contains the color palette of Theme Colors, which are colors specifically designed to work with the current document. The bottom section contains the palette of Standard Colors, which are colors that are always available. Finally, the More Colors command below the color palette, opens the Colors dialog box in which you can choose many more colors.

The colors in the palette all have names. You can see the names by pointing to each color to see its ScreenTip, as shown in Figure 4–5. The Standard Colors have simple names, such as Red, Yellow, and Light Green. The Theme Colors have more complex names that identify the color, shade, and other information.

Step-by-Step 4.3

▶ **TIP**

The colored bar on the Font Color button changes to reflect the last color selected. If you want to apply the color shown in the colored bar, you can simply click the Font Color button.

1. In the bulleted list at the end of the document, in the second bulleted item, select **recycle**.

2. On the Home tab, in the Font group, click the **arrow** next to the Font Color button . A gallery containing the color palette opens.

3. In the Standard Colors row, click the **Green** color. The color palette closes and the selected text is now green.

4. Press **Ctrl+Home** to jump back to the beginning of the document, and then in the paragraph below the heading *Sage Stone Race Track*, select the text **Sage Stone Race Track** again. (This is the text you formatted with the Arial Rounded MT font.)

5. On the Home tab, in the Font group, click the **arrow** next to the Font Color button , and then in the first row under Theme Colors, click the **Olive Green, Accent 3** color. The color palette closes and the color you selected is applied to the selected text.

6. Deselect the text.

7. Save the document and leave it open for the next Step-by-Step.

Changing Font Style

Font style is a formatting feature you can apply to a font to change its appearance. Common font styles are bold, italic, and underlining. These styles can be applied to any font. **Figure 4–6** illustrates these styles applied to the Calibri font.

> **This text is bold.**
>
> *This text is italic.*
>
> This text is underlined.
>
> ***This text is bold, italic, and underlined.***

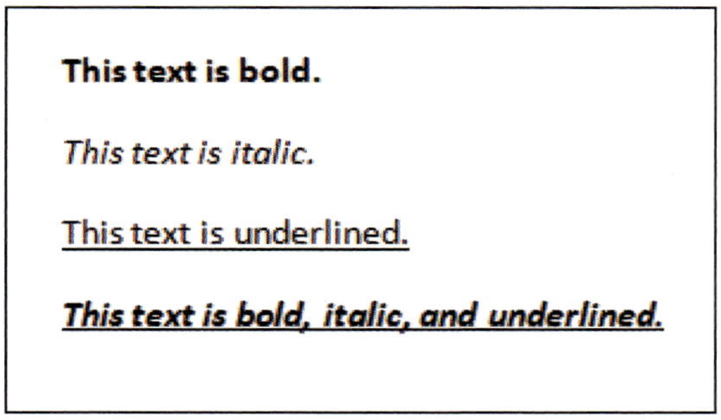

FIGURE 4–6   Examples of font styles

The easiest way to change the font style is to select the text, and then click the Bold, Italic, or Underline buttons in the Font group on the Home tab. The Bold and Italic buttons are also available on the Mini toolbar. All three of the style commands are toggle commands, so to turn a style off, you click the button again.

Changing Underline Style and Color

When you underline text, you can underline with one line or change the style to multiple lines, dotted lines, dashed lines, or another style. You can also change the color of the underline. To change to another underline style or color, click the arrow next to the Underline button. See **Figure 4–7**.

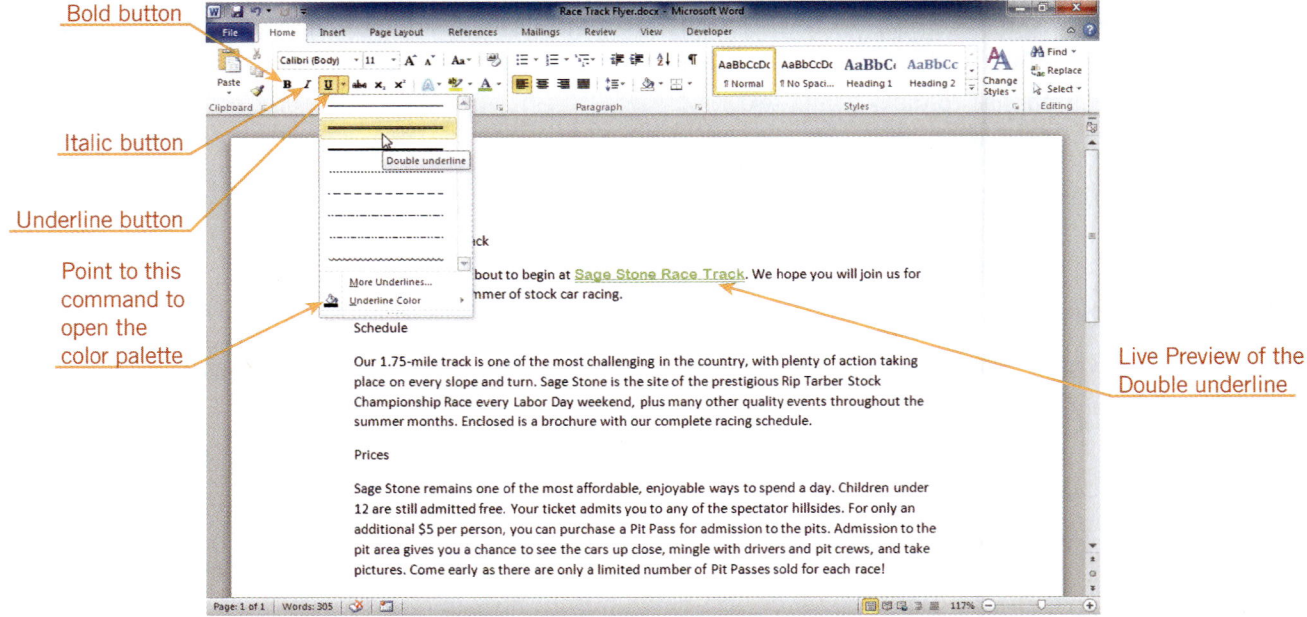

FIGURE 4–7   Underline menu to choose underline style and color

You can click one of the styles on the menu, or click More Underlines to open the Font dialog box. In the Font dialog box, click the Underline style arrow, and then scroll down the list to see additional underline styles. To change the color of the underline, click the arrow next to the Underline button, and then point to Underline Color. This opens the same palette of colors available when you click the Font Color button arrow.

Step-by-Step 4.4

> **⚠ WARNING**
>
> Remember that you create a new paragraph every time you press Enter, so a paragraph can be a single line or even one word.

1. Select the text **Sage Stone Race Track** once more in the paragraph below the heading *Sage Stone Race Track*.

2. On the Home tab, in the Font group, click the **Bold** button **B**. The selected text becomes bold. The Bold button is orange to indicate that it is toggled on selected and bold formatting is turned on.

3. In the fourth paragraph (the paragraph under "Schedule"), at the end of the second line, select the text **Rip Tarber Stock Championship Race**.

4. In the Font group, click the **Italic** button **I**. The selected text is italicized and the Italic button is selected.

5. Press **Ctrl+End** to jump to the end of the document. In the bulleted list, in the second bulleted item, select the green text **recycle**. In the Font group, click the **Underline** button. Deselect the text. The text *recycle* is underlined.

6. Select **recycle** again. In the Font group, click the **Underline** button. The selected text is no longer underlined.

7. With *recycle* still selected, in the Font group, click the **arrow** next to the Underline button. The Underline menu opens. Click the **Double underline**. The selected text is underlined with a double underline.

8. In the Font group, click the **arrow** next to the Underline button. Point to **Underline Color**. A gallery containing the color palette opens.

9. Under Standard Colors, click the **Blue** color. The color palette closes and the color of the double underline changes to blue.

10. Deselect the text.

11. Save the document and leave it open for the next Step-by-Step.

Changing Text Effects

Text effects, sometimes called *font effects*, are similar to font styles and can help enhance or clarify text. To apply a text effect—such as, strikethrough, subscript, or superscript—to selected text, click the button corresponding to that effect in the Font group on the Home tab. Many more text effects are available on the Text Effects button gallery and menu shown in **Figure 4–8**. Like font styles, font effects are toggle commands—a font effect is either turned on or off.

VOCABULARY
text effects
font effects

Text Effects button

Point to commands to open submenus and galleries

Selected text effect

Preview of selected text effect

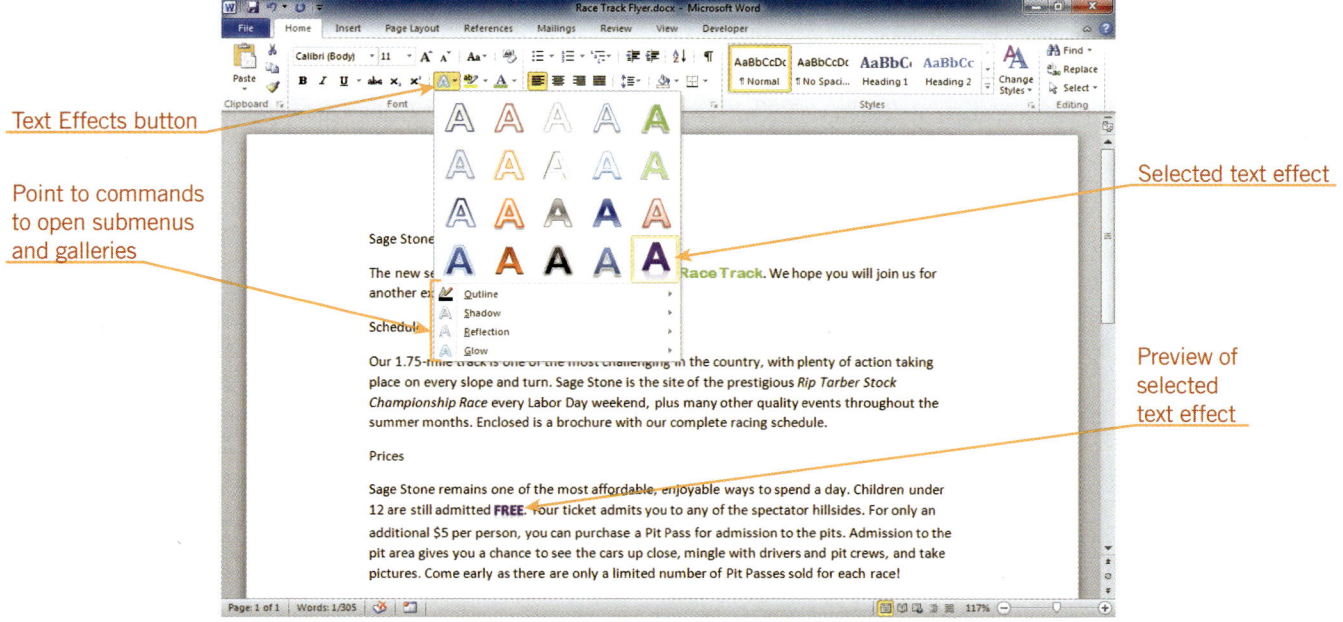

FIGURE 4–8   Text Effects button gallery and menu

Step-by-Step 4.5

1. In the sixth paragraph (the paragraph under *Prices*), in the second line, select the text **free**.

2. On the Home tab, in the Font group, click the **Text Effects** button. The Text Effects gallery and menu opens.

3. Point to a few of the effects to see the Live Preview.

4. Click the **Gradient Fill – Purple, Accent 4, Reflection** effect (the last effect in the last row). See Figure 4–8. The text is formatted so it is all uppercase, purple, and has a reflection.

5. On the Home tab, in the Font group, click the **Text Effects** button again. In the menu, point to **Reflection**. A submenu showing a gallery of reflection options appears.

6. In the gallery, click the **No Reflection** effect (in the first row under No Reflection). The reflection effect is removed from the selected text.

7. Deselect the text. Save the document and leave it open for the next Step-by-Step.

Highlighting Text

When you read a paper document, you sometimes use a highlighting marker to draw attention to an important part of the document. You can highlight text in a Word document for the same effect. To highlight text, click the arrow next to the Text Highlight Color button in the Font group on the Home tab. A gallery of colors opens. Click one of the colors.

If text is selected in the document, the text becomes highlighted with the color you chose. If no text is selected, the pointer changes to the Highlight pointer, an I-beam pointer with a marker on it, when you position it on top of text in the document. You can drag the pointer over any text you want to highlight. See **Figure 4–9**. When you are finished, click the Text Highlight Color button again to toggle this command off.

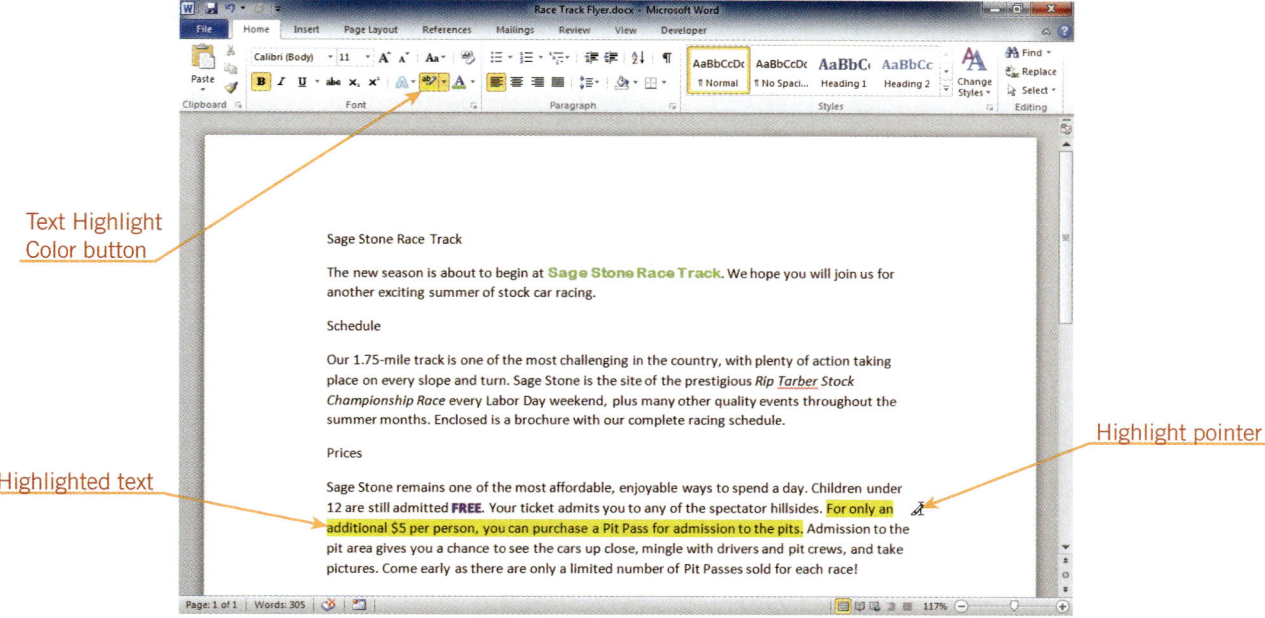

Text Highlight Color button

Highlighted text

Highlight pointer

FIGURE 4–9   Text highlighted with the Highlight pointer

If text is highlighted and you want to remove the highlight, select the highlighted text, and then click the Text Highlight Button. If you'd rather drag over each selection of highlighted text to "erase" the highlighting, you can click the arrow next to the Text Highlight Color button, and then click No Color. The pointer changes to the Highlight pointer, and when you drag over highlighted text, you remove the highlight.

Step-by-Step 4.6

1. On the Home tab, in the Font group, locate the **Text Highlight Color** button. The colored bar near the bottom of the button indicates the current highlighter color.

2. Click the **arrow** next to the Text Highlight Color button. A gallery of colors opens. Click the **Yellow** box (even if the button already indicates that the current color is yellow). The Text Highlight Color gallery closes. The colored bar on the Text Highlight Color button is yellow to reflect the color you chose, and the button is colored orange to indicate that it is selected.

3. Move the pointer so it is positioned anywhere on top of text. The pointer changes to the Highlight pointer.

4. In the sixth paragraph (the paragraph under *Prices*), near the end of the second line, position the pointer in front of the fourth sentence (in front of the word *For*). Click and drag to select the entire sentence (finishing at *admission to the pits.*), releasing the mouse button when you have selected the whole sentence. The fourth sentence is highlighted with yellow. See Figure 4–9.

5. In the Font group, click the **Text Highlight Color** button. The button is no longer selected, and the pointer returns to normal.

6. In the same paragraph, select the last sentence (it starts with *Come early*).

7. In the Font group, click the **arrow** next to the Text Highlight Color button. Click the **Bright Green** color. The selected text is highlighted with bright green. The pointer does not change to the Highlighter pointer.

8. Select the green highlighted sentence.

9. In the Font group, click the **arrow** next to the Text Highlight Color button. Click **No Color**. The highlighting is removed from the selected text.

10. Save the document and leave it open for the next Step-by-Step.

Copying Formatting

Often you will spend time formatting text and then find that you need the same format in another part of the document. You can copy the format of selected text to other text by using the ***Format Painter***. To access the Format Painter, click the Format Painter button in the Clipboard group on the Home tab or on the Mini toolbar.

To use the Format Painter, select the text with the format you want to copy, and then click the Format Painter button. When you move the pointer over text, it changes to the Format Painter pointer, which is the I-beam pointer with a paintbrush to its left. Drag the Format Painter tool across the text you want to format. The text changes to the copied format. If you want to copy the format to more than one block of text, double-click the Format Painter button. The button will remain selected and the Format Painter stays active until you click the button again to deselect it. See **Figure 4–10**.

▶ **VOCABULARY**
Format Painter

TIP

You can also press Esc to turn off the Highlighter or the Format Painter.

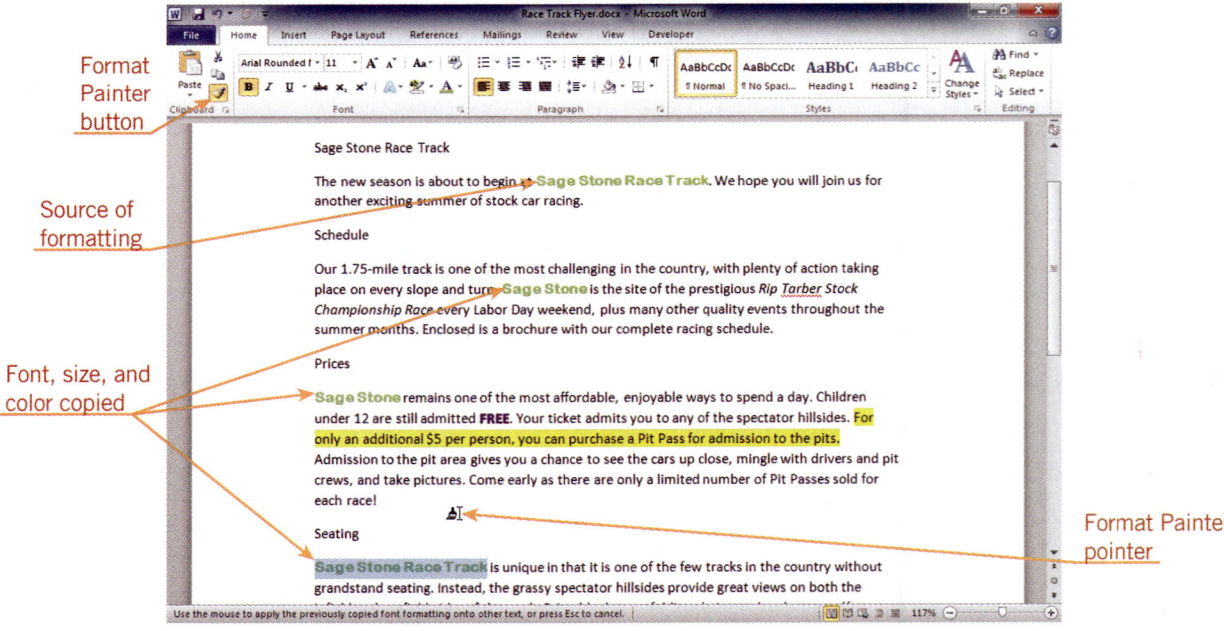

FIGURE 4–10   Text after using Format Painter

Step-by-Step 4.7

1. In the paragraph below the heading *Sage Stone Race Track*, select the green **Sage Stone Race Track**. Remember, this text is formatted with the Arial Rounded MT Bold font, and you added the bold font style and changed the color to Olive Green.

2. On the Home tab, in the Clipboard group, click the **Format Painter** button. The Format Painter button is selected. Move the pointer so it is on top of any text in the document. The pointer changes to the Format Painter pointer.

3. In the fourth paragraph (under *Schedule*), in the second line, drag across the text **Sage Stone**. The text is formatted with the same formats as the text in the second paragraph.

4. Move the pointer on top of the text. It is the normal pointer again. The Format Painter button is no longer selected.

5. With *Sage Stone* still selected, in the Clipboard group, double-click the **Format Painter** button.

6. In the sixth paragraph (the paragraph under *Prices*), drag across **Sage Stone**. The copied format is copied to the text.

7. Move the pointer on top of the text to see that the Format Painter pointer is still active. The Format Painter button is still selected.

8. In the eighth paragraph (under *Seating*), drag across **Sage Stone Race Track**. The formatting is applied to the selected text, as shown in Figure 4–10.

9. Press **Ctrl+End** to jump to the end of the document. In the last bulleted item, drag across **Sage Stone**. The format is copied again.

10. In the Clipboard group, click the **Format Painter** button. The button is no longer selected and the pointer returns to normal.

11. Save your changes to the document and leave it open for the next Step-by-Step.

Understanding Styles

In Word, a *style* is a set of formatting options that have been named and saved. Character styles affect only selected text; paragraph styles affect entire paragraphs.

Using styles can save time and add consistency to a document. For example, if you are working on a long document, such as a research paper that contains headings, you would want to format the headings to stand out from the regular (the Normal) text. You could do this manually by selecting each heading, changing the font size, and applying font styles, such as bold. You might also change the color of the headings. If your document contained many headings, you would need to do this

▶ **VOCABULARY**
style

for each heading, or use the Format Painter to copy the format to each heading. If you changed your mind about the look of the headings, for example, if you decide to use red text instead of bold purple text, you would need to change each heading again.

If you used a style to format your headings, the style could define this type of heading as 14-point bold, purple text. You could then apply that style with the click of the mouse to each heading. If you changed your mind and wanted the headings in red, you could change the style definition to format the text as red instead of purple, and the headings formatted with that style would change red to reflect the new definition.

Applying Quick Styles

A **Quick Style** is a style that is available by clicking a button in the Styles group on the Home tab. If you want to see the additional Quick Styles available in the Quick Styles gallery, click the up or down arrows to scroll the gallery, or click the More button in the Styles group to open the Styles gallery. See **Figure 4–11**.

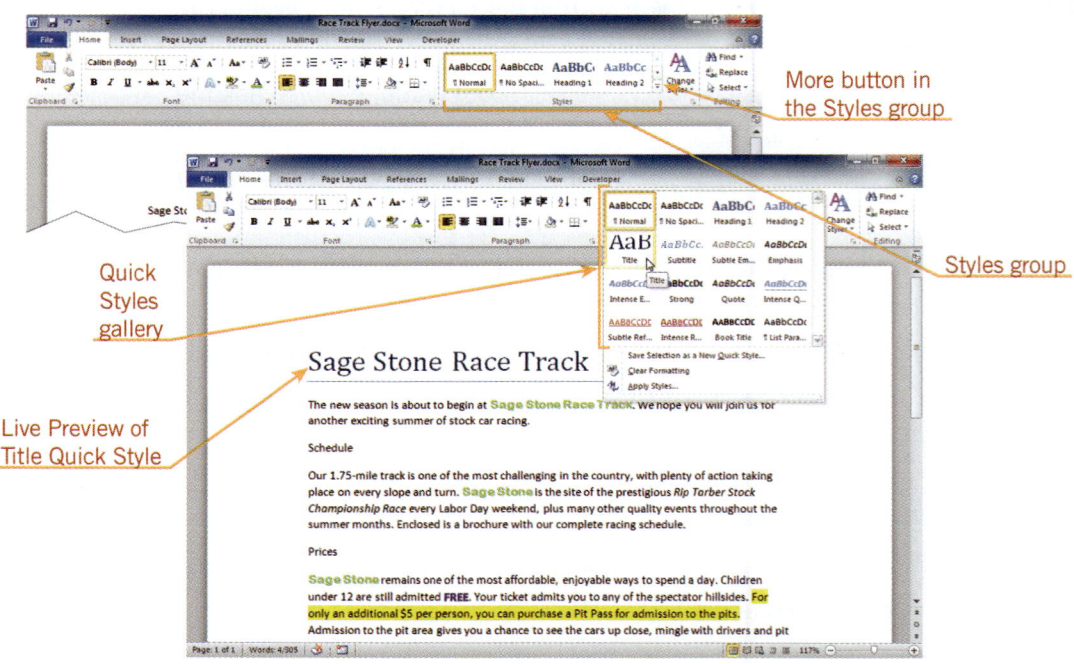

FIGURE 4–11   Quick Styles gallery

When the Quick Styles gallery is open, you can point to a Quick Style to see a Live Preview of the formatting in the document. The default style for text is the Normal Quick Style. It is used for ordinary text.

Step-by-Step 4.8

1. Scroll to see the beginning of the document, and then click anywhere in the first line of text. On the Home tab, locate the Styles group. The Normal style has a yellow box around it indicating that it is selected.

2. In the Styles group, click the **More** button. The Quick Styles gallery opens.

3. In the second row, first column, click the **Title** style. Refer back to Figure 4–11. The Quick Styles gallery closes and the Title Quick Style is applied to the current paragraph. The text is formatted with the font, color, and size defined by the Title Quick Style. The Title Quick Style also includes a light blue horizontal line under the paragraph.

4. Select the heading **Schedule**. In the Styles group, click the **More** button to open the Quick Styles gallery. In the first row, third column, click the **Heading 1** style. The Heading 1 Quick Style is applied to the paragraph. In addition to changing the text to medium-blue 14-point Cambria, the Heading 1 Quick Style removed the extra space after the paragraph.

5. Apply the **Heading 1** Quick Style to the **Prices** and **Seating** headings.

6. In the paragraph under the Schedule heading, select the italicized text **Rip Tarber Stock Championship Race**.

7. In the Styles group, click the **More** button. Locate the style with the name *Intense E...*, and then point to it. The ScreenTip labels this style *Intense Emphasis*. Click the **Intense Emphasis** style. The italic formatting you applied earlier is removed and the formats associated with the Intense Emphasis Quick Style are applied. The selected text is now light blue, bold, and italic.

8. Select the yellow-highlighted sentence. Open the Styles gallery. In the second row, last column, click the **Emphasis** style. The text is formatted with the Emphasis Quick Style, which is the Normal style plus italics.

9. Deselect the text. Note that the highlighting was not removed when you applied the Quick Style. Highlighting can be part of a style definition, but manual highlighting is not removed when you apply a different style.

10. Save the document and leave it open for the next Step-by Step.

> **WARNING**
>
> When you apply a Quick Style, any manual formatting that you've already applied to the text is overridden by the Quick Style formats (except highlighting).

Changing Themes

A *theme* is a coordinated set of fonts, styles, and colors. The theme determines the default font, the color of headings formatted using the Heading Quick Styles, and other features of the document. To see the available themes, click the Page Layout tab, and then, in the Themes group, click the Themes button. A gallery of themes

> **VOCABULARY**
> theme

opens, as shown in **Figure 4–12**. Word comes with 40 built-in themes. They are arranged in alphabetical order except that the default theme, the Office theme, appears first.

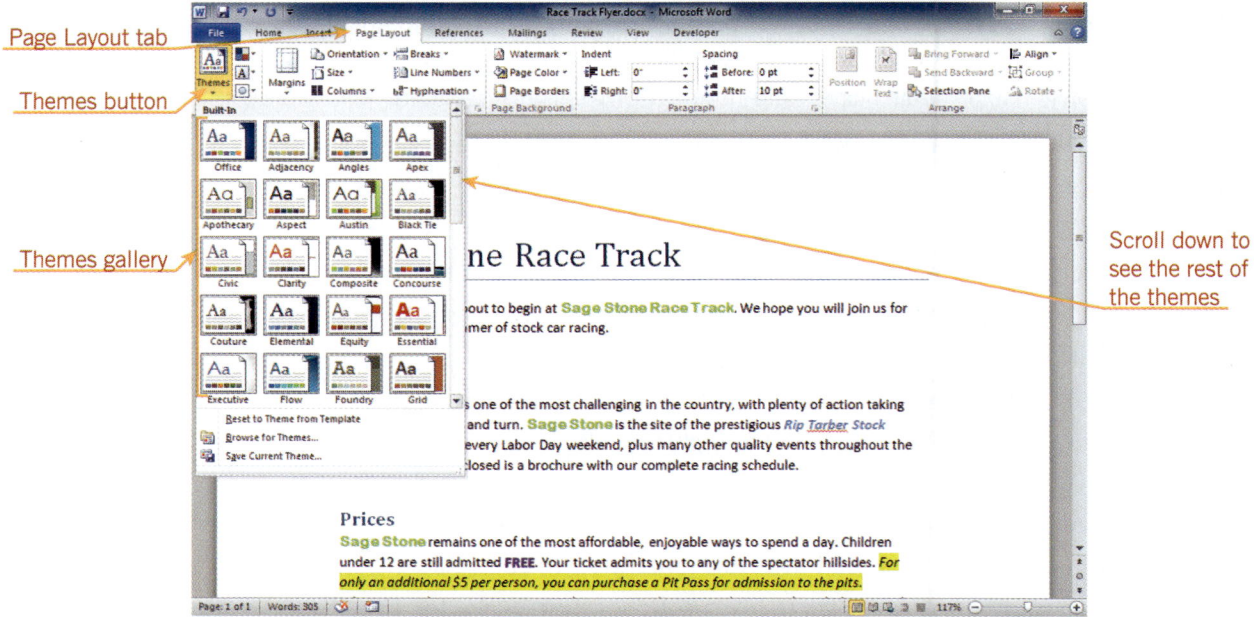

FIGURE 4–12   Themes gallery

The definitions of Quick Styles are tied to the themes. For example, in the previous section, the text that you formatted with the Heading 1 Quick Style appeared in bold, medium blue, 14-point Cambria. If you changed to the Apex theme, text formatted with the Heading 1 Quick Style would change to bold, yellow-brown, 14-point Lucida Sans. If you changed to the Verve theme, the Heading 1 text would change to bold, dark pink, 14-point Century Gothic.

The fonts used in a document are tied to the theme as well. Text formatted with the Normal style and other text tied to that style use the font labeled "(Body)" in the Font list on the Font button. Text formatted with heading styles use the font labeled "(Headings)" in the Font list.

Step-by-Step 4.9

TIP

Point to the Themes button on the Page Layout tab to see a ScreenTip that identifies the current theme.

1. On the Ribbon, click the **Page Layout** tab. In the Themes group, click the **Themes** button. The Themes gallery opens. The Office theme is the default theme for new documents and is the current theme. You might see orange highlighting on the Office theme in the Themes gallery.

2. In the first row, third column, point to the **Angles** theme. Live Preview shows the changes to the document; the title changes to black text, the headings change to gray, and the *FREE* text you formatted with using the effect on the Text Effects button gallery changes to green. In addition, the fonts change to Franklin Gothic Medium for the headings and Franklin Gothic Book for the rest of the text.

3. Point to several other theme buttons, and watch the Live Preview to see each change.

4. In the third row, third column, click the **Composite** theme. The Themes gallery closes and the Composite theme is applied to the document.

5. Save the document and leave it open for the next Step-by Step.

TIP

If you apply a style and then apply manual formatting, when you change to a new theme, the manual formatting will still be applied.

Redefining an Existing Quick Style

What if none of the Quick Styles formats the text exactly the way you want it to look? You can create your own style. The easiest way to create your own style is to format text with an existing Quick Style, and then make changes until you are satisfied with the final look. To redefine an existing Quick Style, select the formatted text you want to use as the style, right-click the Quick Style you want to redefine to open a shortcut menu, and then click the Update command on the shortcut menu. In the example shown in **Figure 4–13**, you would click Update Intense Emphasis to Match Selection. The selected text doesn't change, but the Quick Style is redefined to match it. The redefined Quick Style is available only in the current document.

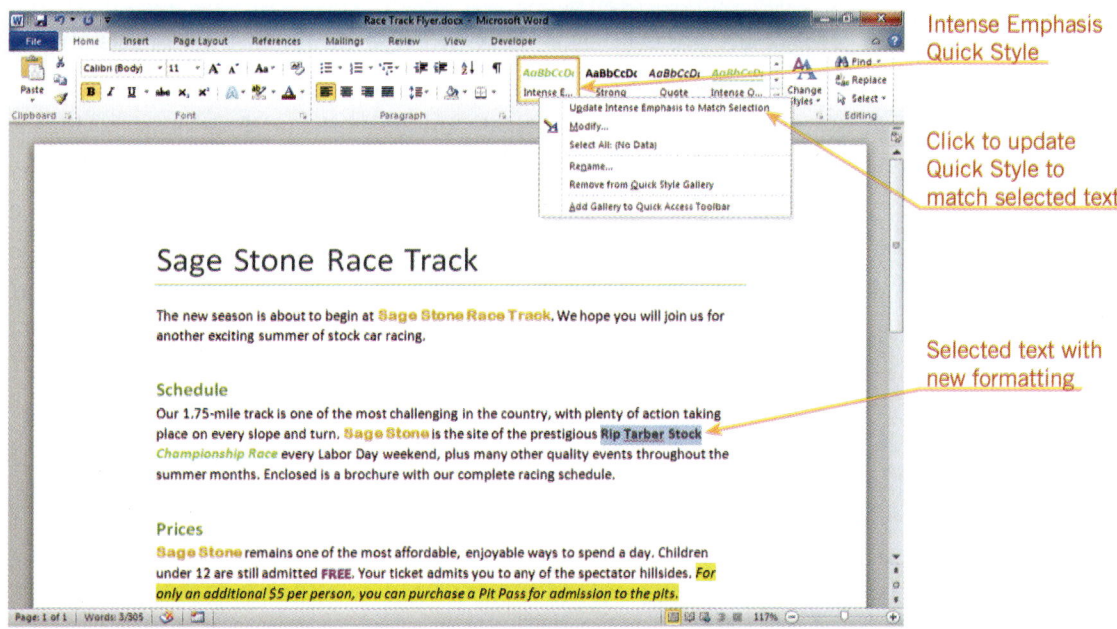

FIGURE 4–13 Redefining a Quick Style

Step-by-Step 4.10

1. In the paragraph under the Schedule heading, select the text **Rip Tarber Stock**. (Do not select *Championship Race*.)

2. On the Ribbon, click the **Home** tab. In the Font group, click the **arrow** next to the Font Color button ⬛. In the color palette, note the red box around the Lime color in the top row under Theme Colors. This is the color of the selected text.

3. In the last row of the color palette under Theme Colors, in the second to last column, click the **Orange, Accent 5, Darker 50%** color.

4. In the Font group, click the **Italic** button ☐ to deselect it.

5. In the Font group, click the **arrow** next to the Font Size box ☐, and then click **12**. The selected text is changed to 12-point, dark orange, bold text that is not italicized.

6. In the Styles group, click the **More** button. Right-click the **Intense Emphasis** style. A shortcut menu opens. You're going to redefine the Intense Emphasis style. As you do the next step, keep an eye on the rest of the phrase that is formatted with the Intense Emphasis style—*Championship Race*.

7. On the shortcut menu, click **Update Intense Emphasis to Match Selection**. The Quick Styles gallery closes. The selected text retains the formatting you applied, and the Intense Emphasis style is redefined to match the formatting of the selected text. This means that *Championship Race* is now 12-point dark orange and is no longer italicized.

8. Save the document and leave it open for the next Step-by-Step.

Creating a New Quick Style

You can also create a brand new Quick Style. Again, the easiest way to do this is to first format text with the font, style, and any other characteristics that you want. To name your style and add it to the Quick Styles gallery, open the Quick Styles gallery, and then click Save Selection as a New Quick Style on the menu at the bottom of the gallery. This opens the Create New Style from Formatting dialog box. Type a name for your new Quick Style in the Name box, as shown in **Figure 4–14**. The new Quick Style is available only in your document.

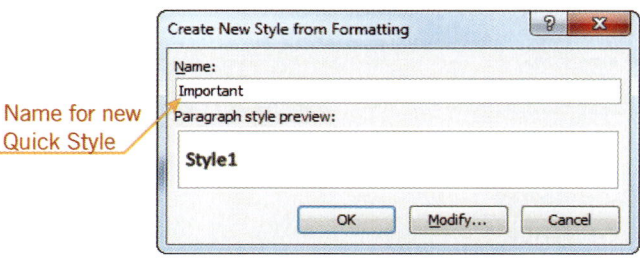

Name for new Quick Style

FIGURE 4–14   Create New Style from Formatting dialog box

Step-by-Step 4.11

1. Select all of the text in the first paragraph in the document under the title.

2. In the Font group, click the **Text Effects** button 🅰, and then point to **Outline**. The color palette for the Composite theme appears.

3. In the second column under Theme Colors, click the **Black, Text 1, Lighter 35%** color (in the third row). The gallery closes and the selected text is formatted with a dark gray outline effect.

4. With the first paragraph still selected, in the Styles group, click the **More** button. On the menu below the gallery, click **Save Selection as a New Quick Style**.

5. In the Create New Style from Formatting dialog box, type **Important** in the Name box, as shown in Figure 4–14. Click **OK**. The dialog box closes. The new Quick Style appears in the first position in the Styles group. If you don't see the new style, click the up arrow in the Styles gallery as many times as needed to scroll up and display the first row in the gallery on the Ribbon.

6. Scroll down to the end of the document, and then select the last paragraph.

7. In the Styles group, click the **up scroll arrow** twice, and then click the **Important** style. The new Quick Style is applied to all of the text in the last paragraph.

8. Save the document and leave it open for the next Step-by-Step.

Clearing Formatting

You can use the Clear Formatting command to remove manual formatting and styles. To do this, first select the formatted text to be cleared. You can then click the Clear Formatting button in the Font group on the Home tab. Or, you can open the Quick Styles gallery, and then click Clear Formatting on the menu at the bottom of the gallery. See **Figure 4–15**. When you remove a style, the Normal Quick Style is automatically applied.

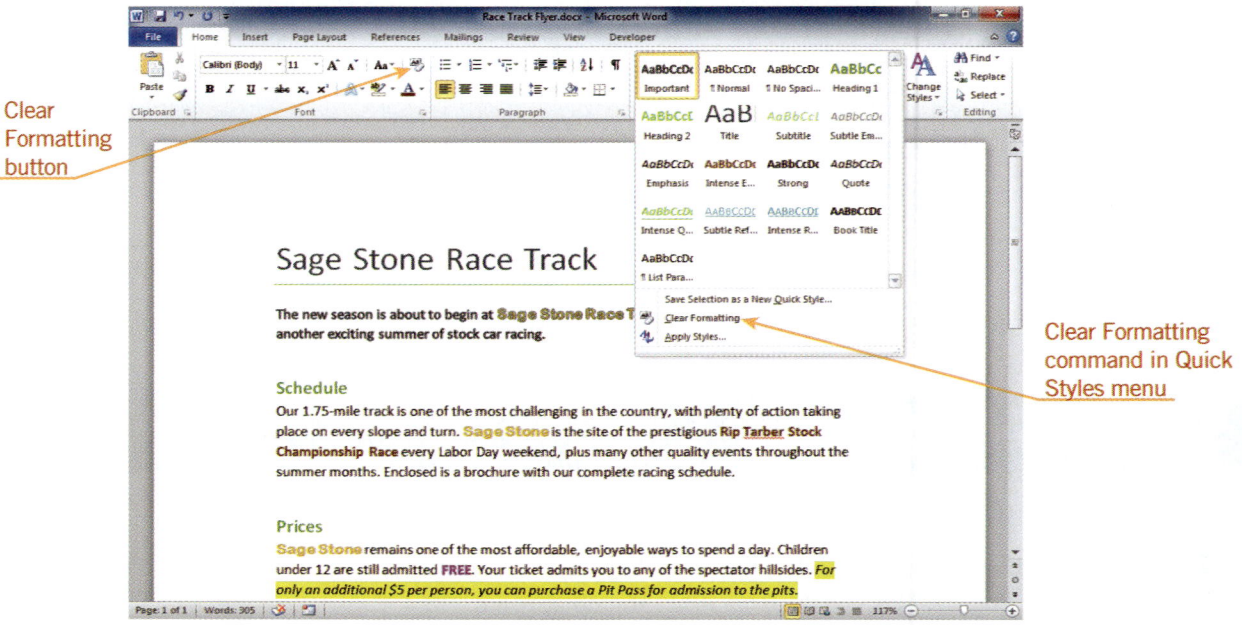

Clear Formatting button

Clear Formatting command in Quick Styles menu

FIGURE 4–15   Clear Formatting command

Step-by-Step 4.12

WARNING

To apply or clear a paragraph style, the insertion point can be located anywhere in the paragraph. To apply or clear a character style, all of the text that you want to affect must be selected.

1. If necessary, click anywhere in the last paragraph in the document.

2. In the Font group, click the **Clear Formatting** button. The Important Quick Style is removed from the current paragraph, and the Normal style button in the Styles gallery is selected.

3. In the second item in the bulleted list, select the word **recycle**.

4. In the Styles group, click the **More** button. At the bottom of the Quick Styles gallery, click **Clear Formatting**. The color and double underline is removed from the selected word.

5. Click after the last word in the document (after *We can't wait to see you!*). Press **Tab** three times, and then type your name.

6. Save, print, and close the document.

SUMMARY

In this lesson, you learned:

- Fonts are designs of type that can be used to change the appearance of a document.

- Font size is measured in points. The higher the point size, the larger the characters.

- Common font styles are bold, italic, and underline. These styles can be applied to any font. You can change the color and style of underlines.

- The look of text can be changed by changing its color and adding text effects.

- Highlighting can be used to emphasize important text.

- The Format Painter copies the format and style of blocks of text.

- Styles are predefined sets of formatting options that save time and add consistency to a document. A Quick Style appears in the Styles gallery on the Home tab.

- A theme is a coordinated set of fonts, styles, and colors. When you change the theme, all text that has a Quick Style applied to it, including the Normal Quick Style, changes to the fonts, colors, and styles in the new theme.

- You can create new Quick Styles by redefining existing Quick Styles or by creating an entirely new Quick Style.

- The Clear Formatting command clears all formatting and styles from selected text.

 **VOCABULARY REVIEW**

Define the following terms:

attribute	font size	Quick Style
color palette	font style	style
font	Format Painter	text effect
font effect	point	theme

REVIEW QUESTIONS

TRUE / FALSE

Circle T if the statement is true or F if the statement is false.

T F **1.** Highlighting text has the same effect as using the Italic button.

T F **2.** A point is the unit of measurement for fonts.

T F **3.** A font attribute is its name.

T F **4.** When you change the document theme, you change only the colors used for text.

T F **5.** You can create a new Quick Style, but you cannot change the definition of an existing Quick Style.

WRITTEN QUESTIONS

Write a brief answer to each of the following questions.

1. What does the Format Painter do?

2. What are three common font styles?

3. What is the color palette in a document?

4. Why would you use a style?

5. What is a Quick Style?

FILL IN THE BLANK

Complete the following sentences by writing the correct word or words in the blanks provided.

1. The design of type is called the _____.

2. A(n) _____ is a set of formatting options that have been named and saved.

3. A(n) _____ is a coordinated set of fonts, styles, and colors.

4. Text that does not have any other Quick Style applied to it is actually formatted with the _____ Quick Style.

5. The _____ command clears manual formatting and styles.

■ PROJECTS

If you have a SAM 2010 user profile, your instructor may have assigned an autogradable version of the indicated project. If so, log into the SAM 2010 Web site at *www.cengage.com/sam2010* to download the instruction and start files.

PROJECT 4–1

1. Open the **Certificate.docx** Data File. Save the document as **Employee Certificate** followed by your initials.

2. Change all text to 20-point Castellar. If the font is not available, choose another one.

3. Apply the Gradient Fill - Purple, Accent 4, Reflection text effect.

4. Change the color of all the text to the Light Blue standard color.

5. Remove the Reflection text effect, and then add the Blue, 8 pt glow, Accent color 1 glow effect. (*Hint:* Click the Text Effects button, and then point to Glow.)

6. Select the first paragraph and change its size to 36 points.

7. Create a new Quick Style named **Certificate Heading** based on the first paragraph.

8. Change *Joe Harrington* to 36-point Edwardian Script ITC. Replace *Joe Harrington* with your name.

9. Preview the document. Save, print, and close the document.

PROJECT 4–3

1. Open the **Checking Account.docx** Data File. Save the document as **Checking Account Info** followed by your initials.

2. Apply the Title Quick Style to the title *New Checking Account*.

3. Apply the Heading 2 style to the three headings in the document.

4. Near the bottom of the document, highlight all four lines of the address with Gray-25% from the Text Highlight Color palette.

5. In the last line, format the phone number with bold formatting.

6. Change the theme to Horizon.

7. In the last paragraph of the document, replace *the Customer Service Department* with your name. Highlight your name with yellow.

8. Preview the document. Save, print, and close the document.

SAM PROJECT 4–2

1. Open the **Handbook.docx** Data File. Save the document as **Employee Handbook** followed by your initials.

2. In a new paragraph after the last paragraph, type the following: **This Data File had the theme applied.** Click immediately before *theme* in the sentence you just typed. Identify the current theme, and then type its name. Press the Spacebar.

3. Select all the text and clear the formatting.

4. Apply the Heading 1 Quick Style to the first line of text, *Employee Handbook*, and then change the font size to 22 points.

5. Add a Wavy underline to the first line of text using the same color as the text.

6. Create a new Quick Style called Handbook Title based on the first line of text.

7. Apply the Heading 2 Quick Style to the other four headings in the document.

8. Apply the Subtle Emphasis Quick Style to the last line in the document (the line you typed).

9. Change the theme to Adjacency. Go to the end of the document, create a new paragraph, and then type **It now has the Adjacency theme applied.** Create another new paragraph, and then type your name.

10. Select the heading *Regular Attendance*. Change the font size to 16 points. Change the color to Gray-50%, Accent 4 (in the first row under Theme Colors in the color palette).

11. Redefine the Heading 2 Quick Style to match the *Regular Attendance* heading.

12. In the paragraph under the *Confidential Information* heading, italicize the word *Never* in the third line.

13. Preview the document. Save, print, and close the document.

PROJECT 4–4

1. Open the **Poster.docx** Data File. Save the document as **Break Room Poster** followed by your initials.

2. Apply the Title Quick Style to the first line of text.

3. Change the second line of text so it is 16 points, and has an Offset Right shadow effect. (*Hint*: Click the Text Effects button, and then point to Shadow.)

4. Change the theme to Opulent.

5. Change the color of the second line of text to Pink, Text 2 (in the first row under Theme Colors in the color palette).

6. Use the Format Painter to copy the style of the second line of text to the seventh line of text (*How can I build good relationships with my co-workers?*).

7. Apply the List Paragraph Quick Style to the four lines of text under both headings.

8. Change the font size of the four lines of text under both headings to 14 points.

9. Jump to the end of the document, and then type your name. Format your name with italics.

10. Preview the document. Save, print, and close the document.

PROJECT 4–5

1. Open the **Golf Tournament 2.docx** Data File. Save the document as **Formatted Tournament Notice** followed by your initials.

2. Choose a different theme. Be sure your choice is appropriate for a golf tournament information sheet and that the colors go with the colors in the image at the top of the sheet.

3. In the four lines at the bottom of the sheet, change the format of the word in front of the colon to a different font and color, and then add a style or text effect. (Use the same formatting for each of the four words.) Format all four lines in a larger text size.

4. Underline the title. Use the style and color of your choice, but do not underline with the same color as the title text and do not use the single underline style.

5. Apply a Perspective Shadow effect to the title.

6. In the third line under the title, replace Robert Shade with your name. Format your name with a Quick Style that looks attractive.

7. Preview the document. Save, print, and close the document.

CRITICAL THINKING

ACTIVITY 4–1

Create a certificate honoring a person in an organization to which you belong.

ACTIVITY 4–2

You work for a photo lab. In addition to film developing, the lab also offers reprints, enlargements, slides, black-and-white prints, copies and restorations, posters, and passport photos. Your manager wants to include a list of services available with each customer's order, and he asks you to create it. List each service, how much it costs, and how much time it takes to complete. Choose an appropriate theme, and make effective use of Quick Styles, fonts, font sizes and style, colors, and effects. Print and close the document.

ACTIVITY 4–3

Hidden text is text formatted with the text effect "Hidden." You can only access this formatting if you open the Font dialog box by clicking the Font Dialog Box Launcher. Hidden text can be useful if you want to insert text in a document that won't print by default. But what if you forgot that you included hidden text in a file you sent to someone? Use Help to find out how to remove hidden data from a document, and then describe what you learned.

LESSON 5

Formatting Paragraphs and Documents

■ OBJECTIVES

Upon completion of this lesson, you should be able to:

- Show and hide the ruler.
- Set the margins of a document.
- Align text and adjust paragraph indents.
- Adjust line and paragraph spacing.
- Change vertical alignment.
- Set and modify tab stops.
- Create and modify bulleted, numbered, and outline numbered lists.
- Organize a document in Outline view.

■ VOCABULARY

alignment

bullet

center

first-line indent

hanging indent

indent

inside margin (gutter margin)

justify

leader

left-align

margin

mirrored margin

multilevel list

negative indent (outdent)

outline numbered list

outside margin

right-align

tab stop (tab)

vertical alignment

Formatting Paragraphs and Documents

Just as you apply formatting to text, you can also use Word features to format paragraphs and entire documents. Formatting presents a consistent and attractive style throughout a document, allowing readers to understand your message more easily.

In this lesson, you will learn how to use the ruler, and set margins. You will also learn how to align paragraphs, adjust paragraph indents and line spacing. Next, you will learn how to change the spacing before and after paragraphs, change the vertical alignment of a paragraph, adjust tab stops, and create lists. Finally, you will learn how to use Outline view.

Viewing the Ruler

Word provides rulers along the top and left margins to help you as you format your documents. The ruler is hidden by default. To display it, you can click the View Ruler button located at the top of the vertical scroll bar on the right side of the window. You can also click the View tab on the Ribbon, and then, in the Show group, click the Ruler check box.

Setting Margins

▶ **VOCABULARY**

margin

Margins are the blank areas around the top, bottom, and sides of a page. Word sets predefined, or default, margin settings, which you can keep or change. To change margin settings, click the Page Layout tab on the Ribbon, and then in the Page Setup group, click the Margins button. You can choose from one of the preset margin settings, as shown in **Figure 5–1**, or you can click Custom Margins at the bottom to open the Margins tab of the Page Setup dialog box, as shown in **Figure 5–2**.

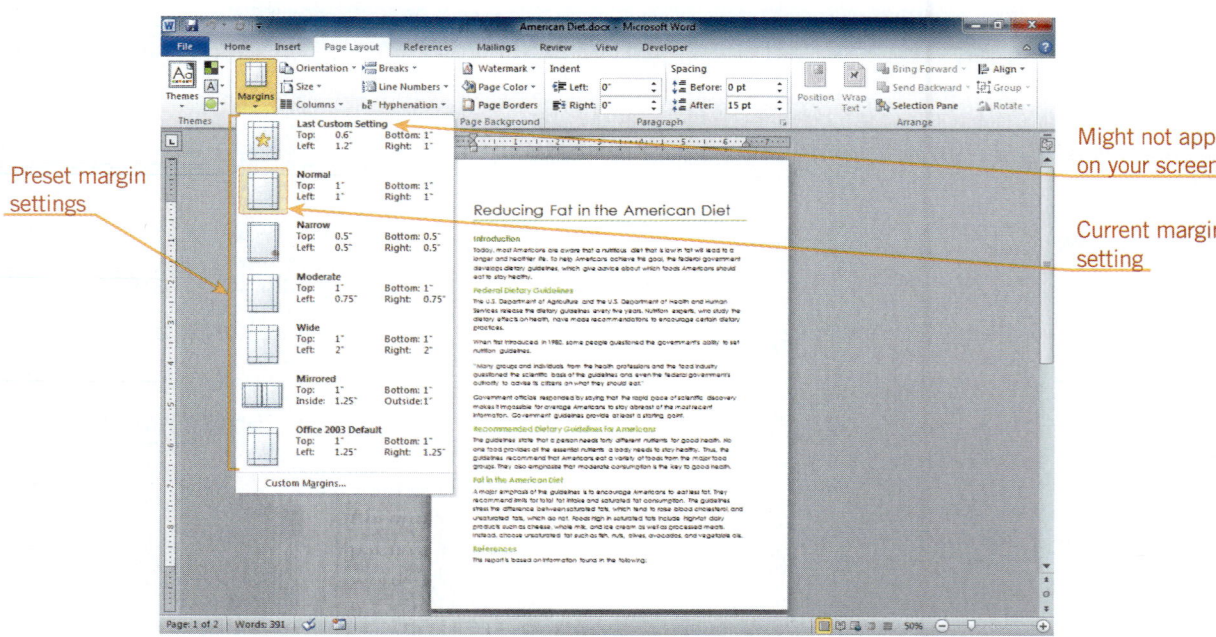

FIGURE 5–1   Margins menu

Margins tab

Click arrows to change measurement one-tenth of an inch at a time

Margins section

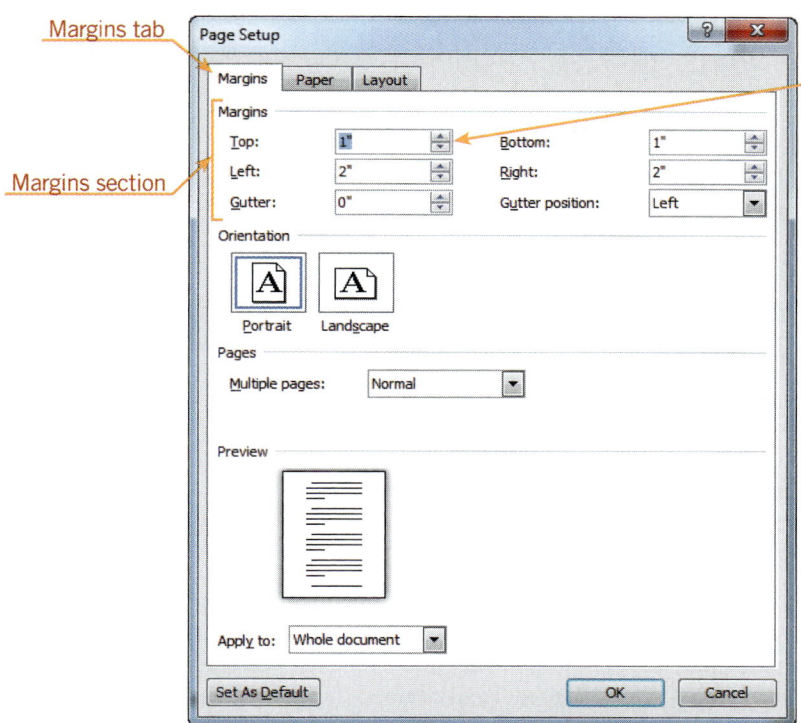

FIGURE 5–2   Margins tab in the Page Setup dialog box

▶ **VOCABULARY**
mirrored margin
inside margin (gutter margin)
outside margin

Step-by-Step 5.1

1. Open the **Diet.docx** document from the drive and folder where your Data Files are stored. Save the document as **American Diet** followed by your initials.

2. If the ruler is not displayed below the Ribbon, above the vertical scroll bar, click the **View Ruler** button 🔲 to display the ruler.

3. On the Ribbon, click the **View** tab. In the Zoom group, click the **One Page** button. Note that the current margins are one inch on all sides.

4. On the Ribbon, click the **Page Layout** tab. In the Page Setup group, click the **Margins** button. The current margin, Normal, is selected. See Figure 5–1.

5. Click **Wide**. The left and right margins increase to two inches.

6. In the Page Setup group, click the **Margins** button. Wide is selected on the menu. Click **Custom Margins** at the bottom of the menu. The Page Setup dialog box opens with the Margins tab on top. See Figure 5–2.

7. In the Top box, click the **down arrow** three times to change the number to 0.7".

8. Press **Tab**. The value in the Bottom box is selected. Type **.7**.

📟 **EXTRA FOR EXPERTS**

Pages in books and magazines are often formatted with **mirrored margins**. The **inside margins** (also called the **gutter margins**) are the margins closest to the inside of the page, near the binding. The **outside margins** are the margins closest to the edge of the page.

9. Click **OK**. The dialog box closes and the top and bottom margins are changed.

10. In the Page Setup group, click the **Margins** button again. Notice that **Last Custom Setting** is selected at the top of the menu and that the settings match the custom settings you chose. Click a blank area of the document window to close the Margins menu without changing the current setting.

11. On the Ribbon, click the **View** tab, and then in the Zoom group, click **Page Width**.

12. Save the document and leave it open for the next Step-by-Step.

Aligning Text

▶ **VOCABULARY**

alignment

left-align

center

right-align

justify

Alignment refers to the position of text between the margins. As **Figure 5–3** shows, you can *left-align*, *center*, *right-align*, or *justify* text. Left-aligned and justified are the two most commonly used alignments in documents. For invitations, titles, and headings, text is often center-aligned. Page numbers and dates are often right aligned.

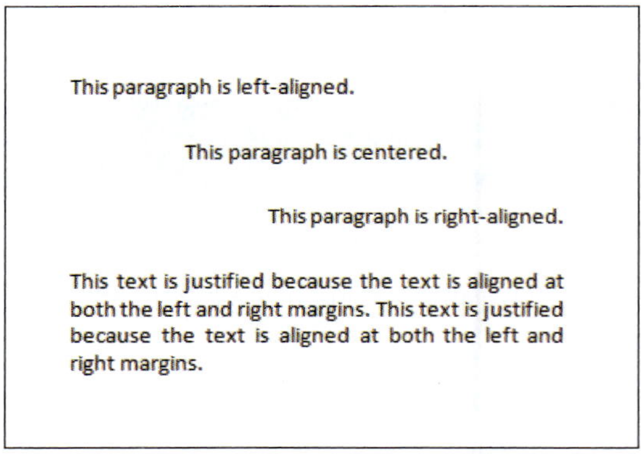

This paragraph is left-aligned.

This paragraph is centered.

This paragraph is right-aligned.

This text is justified because the text is aligned at both the left and right margins. This text is justified because the text is aligned at both the left and right margins.

FIGURE 5–3   Examples of different text alignments

To align text, you click one of the Alignment buttons in the Paragraph group on the Home tab, as shown in **Figure 5–4**. Alignment settings affect the current paragraph or currently selected paragraph.

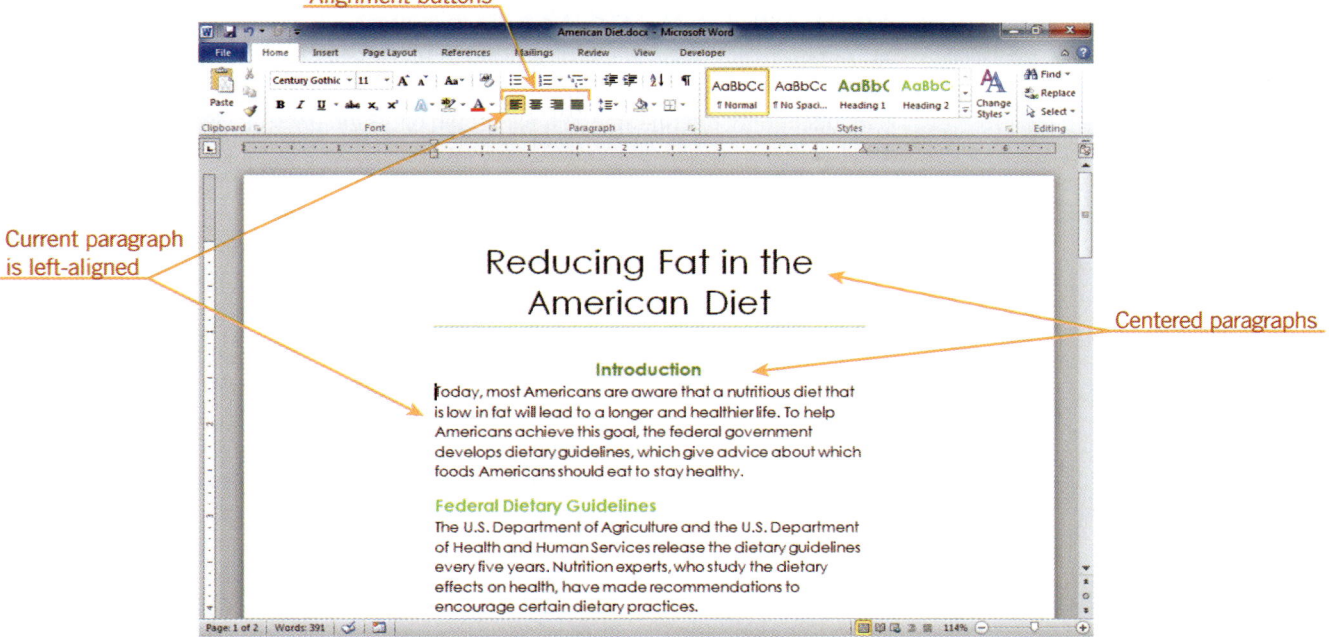

FIGURE 5–4 Alignment buttons

Step-by-Step 5.2

1. If necessary, click anywhere in the title at the beginning of the document.

2. On the Ribbon, click the **Home** tab. In the Paragraph group, notice that the Align Text Left button ▤ is selected. Only one alignment button can be selected at a time.

3. In the Paragraph group, click the **Center** button ▤. The title is centered.

4. Click anywhere in the *Introduction* heading. In the Paragraph group, click the **Center** button ▤.

5. Click anywhere in the third paragraph under the *Federal Dietary Guidelines* heading (it starts with *"Many groups and individuals*). In the Paragraph group, click the **Justify** button ▤. The paragraph is justified.

6. Press **Ctrl+End**. The insertion point moves to the end of the document.

7. Select the last two paragraphs (*Prepared by Roberta Sanchez*). In the Paragraph group, click the **Align Text Right** button ▤. The last two paragraphs are right-aligned.

8. Save the document and leave it open for the next Step-by-Step.

> **TIP**
>
> You can also click the Center button on the Mini toolbar.

▶ **VOCABULARY**
indent

Changing Indents

An *indent* is the space between text and a document's margin. You can indent text either from the left margin, from the right margin, or from both margins. You can also indent only the first line of a paragraph or all the lines in a paragraph *except* the first line.

Indenting Entire Paragraphs

To quickly change the indent of an entire paragraph one-half inch at a time, click the Increase Indent or Decrease Indent buttons in the Paragraph group on the Home tab.

To change the indent by different amounts, you can drag the Left and Right Indent markers on the ruler. To change the left indent, drag the Left Indent marker, which is the small rectangle at the bottom of the icon at the left margin. Note, however, that the entire icon will move when you drag it. See **Figure 5–5**. Indenting from both margins sets off paragraphs from the main body of text. You might use this type of indent for long quotations.

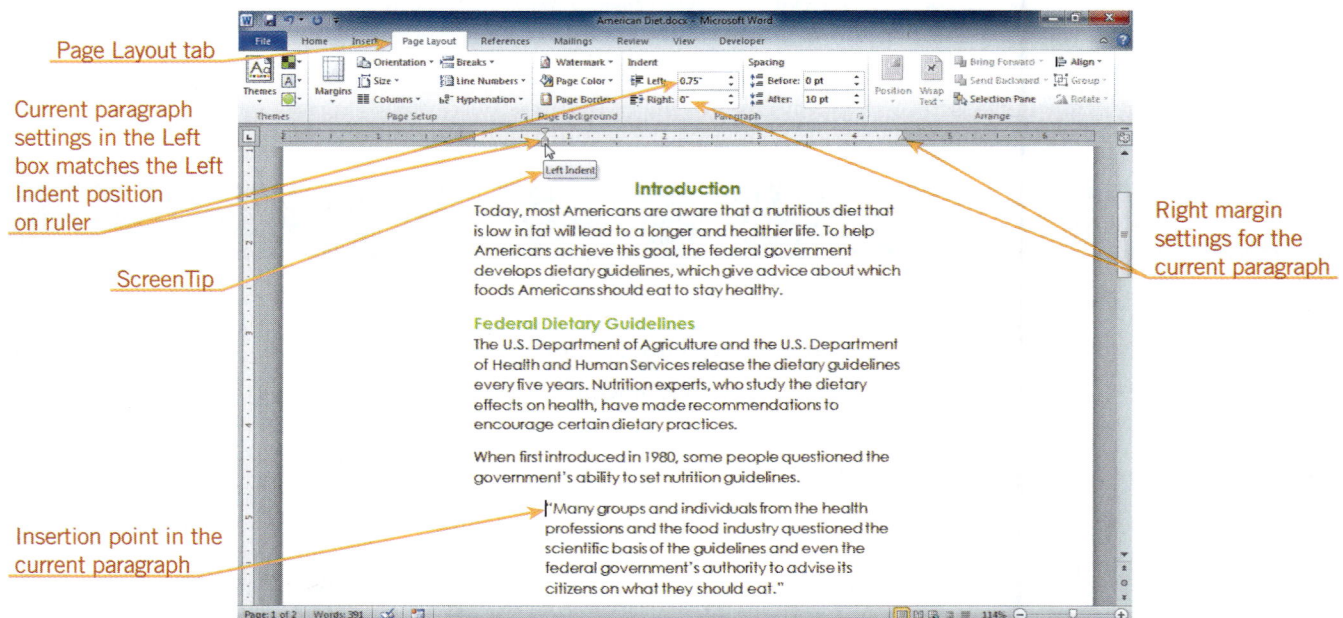

FIGURE 5–5   Examining paragraph indents

You can also change the left and right indents by clicking the Page Layout tab, and then setting the exact measurement of the indents in the Left and Right boxes in the Paragraph group, as shown in Figure 5–5.

Step-by-Step 5.3

1. Scroll up in the document, and then position the insertion point in the third paragraph under the *Federal Dietary Guidelines* section (it starts with *"Many groups and individuals"*).

2. In the Paragraph group, click the **Increase Indent** button ⊞ twice. The entire paragraph indents one inch, and the Indent marker on the left end of the ruler moves to the one-inch mark on the ruler.

3. In the Paragraph group, click the **Decrease Indent** button ⊞. The paragraph indent moves back to the one-half-inch mark.

4. On the ruler, position the pointer on top of the **rectangle** ▢ at the bottom of the Left Indent marker so that the Left Indent ScreenTip appears.

5. Drag the **Left Indent marker** ▢ to the three-quarter-inch mark on the ruler, as shown in Figure 5–5. The paragraph indents another quarter of an inch.

6. On the ruler, drag the **Right Indent marker** △ to the left to the 4-inch mark. The paragraph with the quote is indented three-quarters of an inch from the left margin and one-half inch from the right margin.

7. Save the document and leave it open for the next Step-by-Step.

Setting a First-Line Indent

A ***first-line indent*** is just what it sounds like—only the first line of a paragraph is indented. You are familiar with this because it is the usual format for paragraphs set in type in books, newspapers, and magazines. To indent the first line of a paragraph, you can drag the First Line Indent marker on the ruler, as shown in **Figure 5–6**. After you set a first-line indent in one paragraph, all subsequent paragraphs you type will have the same first-line indent.

▶ **VOCABULARY**
first-line indent

TIP

It's better to set first-line indents than to use Tab because each time you press Enter, the new paragraph will automatically have a first-line indent.

First-line indent set for the selected paragraphs

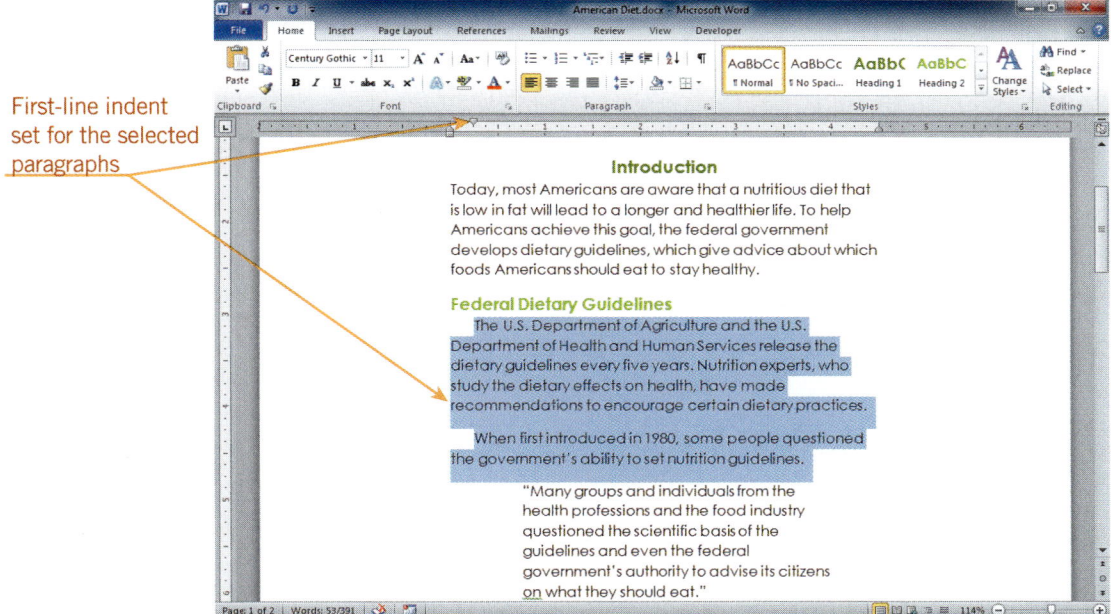

FIGURE 5–6 Examining a first-line indent

Step-by-Step 5.4

1. Select the first two paragraphs under the *Federal Dietary Guidelines* heading.

2. On the ruler, position the pointer over the **top triangle** ⬇ on the Left Indent marker so that the First Line Indent ScreenTip appears.

3. Drag the **First Line Indent marker** ⬇ to the one-quarter-inch mark on the ruler. The first line of the two selected paragraphs is indented one-quarter inch. See Figure 5–6.

4. Select the paragraph above the *Recommended Dietary Guidelines for Americans* heading. Press and hold **Ctrl**. Use the mouse to select the paragraphs under the *Recommended Dietary Guidelines for Americans* and the *Fat in the American Diet* headings. Release **Ctrl**. The three paragraphs are selected.

5. On the ruler, drag the **First Line Indent marker** ⬇ to the one-quarter-inch mark. The first line of the three selected paragraphs is indented one-quarter inch. Click a blank area of the document to deselect the text.

6. Save the document and leave it open for the next Step-by-Step.

Setting a Hanging Indent

You can also create *hanging indents* in which the first full line of text is not indented but the following lines are, as shown in **Figure 5–7**. To set a hanging indent, drag the Hanging Indent marker on the ruler to the right of the First Line Indent marker. Hanging indents appear commonly in lists and documents such as glossaries and bibliographies.

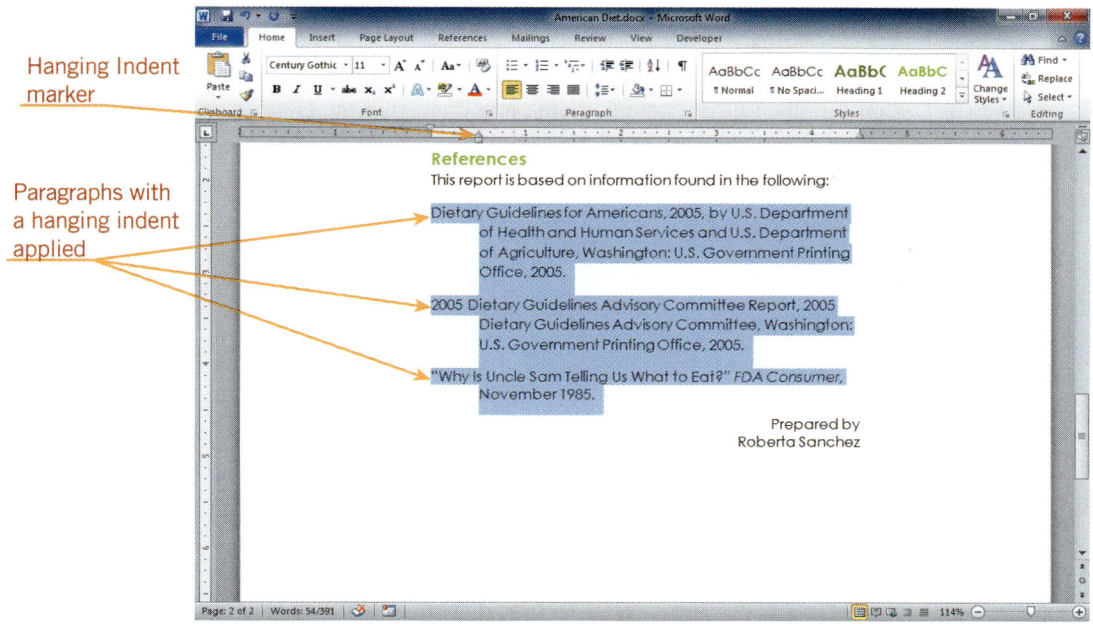

Hanging Indent marker

Paragraphs with a hanging indent applied

FIGURE 5–7 Examining a hanging indent

Step-by-Step 5.5

1. Select the three paragraphs above the *Prepared by* line.

2. On the ruler, position the pointer over the **bottom triangle** 🔻 on the Left Indent marker so that the Hanging Indent ScreenTip appears.

3. Drag the **Hanging Indent marker** 🔻 to the one-half-inch mark. All the lines except for the first line of the three selected paragraphs are indented one-half inch. See Figure 5–7.

4. Save the document and leave it open for the next Step-by-Step.

> **WARNING**
>
> If the wrong triangle moves, release the mouse button, and then try again.

Using the Paragraph Dialog Box to Set Indents

You can set indents on the Indents and Spacing tab in the Paragraph dialog box. You can open the Paragraph dialog box both from the Home tab and from the Page Layout tab by clicking the Paragraph Dialog Box Launcher in the Paragraph group. See **Figure 5–8**.

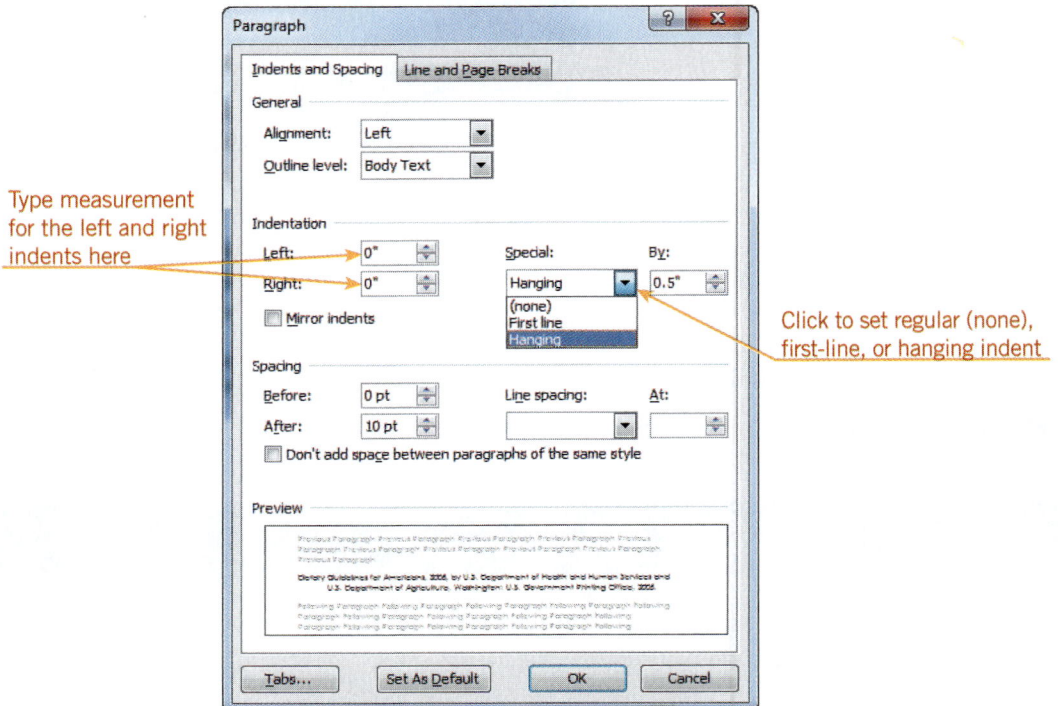

FIGURE 5–8   Paragraph dialog box

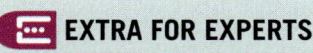
In the Indentation section on the Indents and Spacing tab, type measurements in the Left and Right boxes to change the left and right indents. This is similar to using the Left and Right boxes in the Paragraph group on the Page Layout tab. To set a first-line or hanging indent, click the Special arrow, choose the type of indent you want, and then adjust the measurement in the By box.

Adjusting Line Spacing

You can adjust line spacing in a document, which is the amount of space between lines of text. Single-spaced text has no extra space between each line; double-spaced text has an extra line of space between each line of text. You might be surprised to learn that the default setting in a Word document is 1.15 lines, not single spaced. The little bit of extra space makes text easier to read on the screen. See **Figure 5–9** for examples of different spacing.

The line spacing in this paragraph is 1.0 lines. This means the paragraph is single-spaced.

The line spacing in this paragraph is 1.15 lines This is the default line spacing for the Normal Quick Style.

The line spacing in this paragraph is 1.5 lines. This is another common line spacing.

The line spacing in this paragraph is 2.0 lines. This

means the paragraph is double-spaced.

FIGURE 5–9   Different line spacing

To change line spacing, you can click the Line and Paragraph Spacing button in the Paragraph group on the Home tab, and then choose a new line spacing option on the menu.

Step-by-Step 5.6

1. Press **Ctrl+Home**, and then click anywhere in the paragraph under the *Introduction* heading. Notice that the Normal Quick Style button is selected in the Styles group on the Home tab.

2. On the Home tab, in the Paragraph group, click the **Line and Paragraph Spacing** button. A check mark appears next to 1.15, the current line spacing, as shown in **Figure 5–10**. The 1.15 line spacing is part of the Normal Quick Style definition.

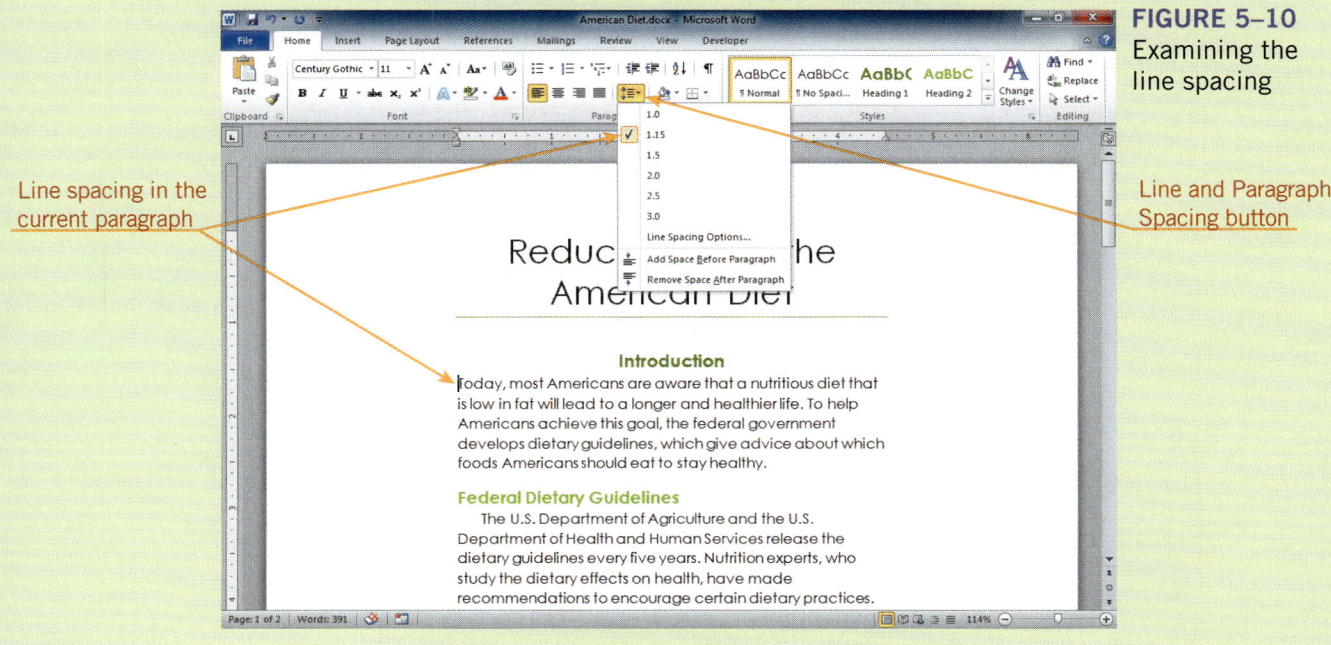

FIGURE 5–10
Examining the line spacing

Line spacing in the current paragraph

Line and Paragraph Spacing button

3. Click a blank area of the document to close the menu without making a selection.

4. Click anywhere in the title. In the Styles group, click the **down arrow** to scroll the gallery down one row. Notice that the Title Quick Style button is selected.

5. In the Paragraph group, click the **Line and Paragraph Spacing** button again. The line spacing for the title is 1.0 (single-spaced). Single spacing is part of the Title Quick Style definition. Click a blank area of the document to close the menu.

6. Press **Ctrl+A**. All the text in the document is selected. In the Paragraph group, click the **Line and Paragraph Spacing** button. Click **1.0**. All the text in the document is now single-spaced.

7. Save the document and leave it open for the next Step-by-Step.

Adjusting Paragraph Spacing

Another way to increase the readability of a page is to modify the paragraph spacing—the amount of space between paragraphs. You've seen this already because the default in Word is to add 10 points of space after each paragraph, and you used the Remove Space After Paragraph command on the Line and Paragraph Spacing menu to remove the space after the paragraphs in the letter you worked on in Lesson 2. Often heading styles include space before or after the heading paragraph as part of the style definition. For example, in this book, the format of the *Step-by-Step* headings include 30 points of space above them, and the format of the blue headings, such as the *Adjusting Paragraph Spacing* heading above, includes 42 points of space before and 10 points of space after. If you want to precisely adjust the space before or after a paragraph, you can use the Before and After boxes in the Paragraph group on the Page Layout tab. See **Figure 5–11**.

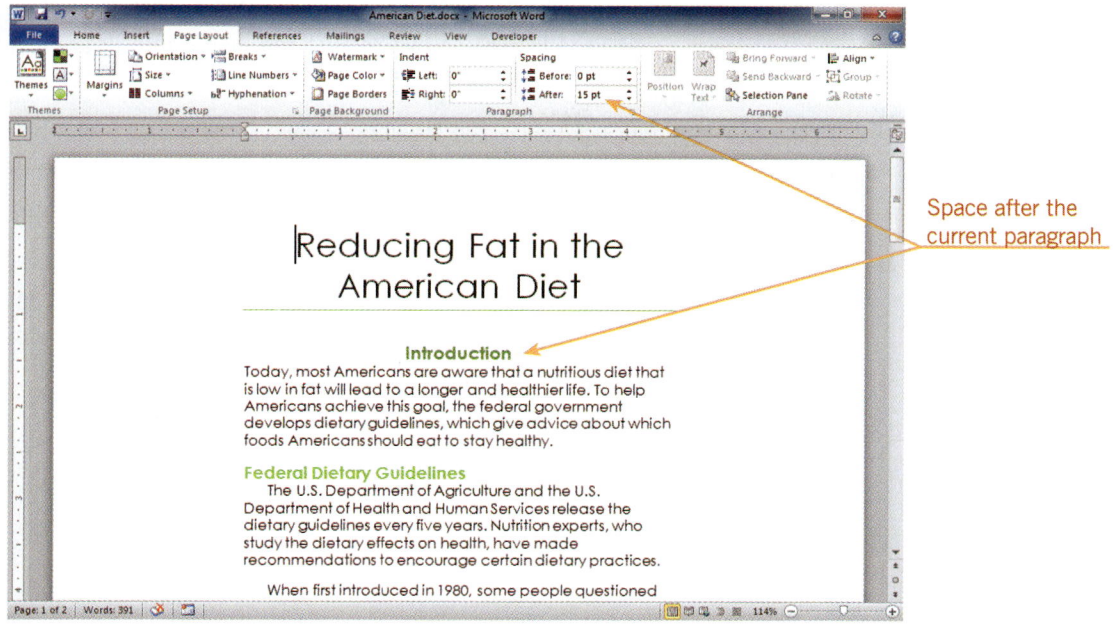

FIGURE 5–11   Examining the paragraph spacing

Step-by-Step 5.7

1. Click anywhere in the paragraph under the *Introduction* heading.

2. On the Ribbon, click the **Page Layout** tab. Locate the Spacing section in the Paragraph group, and notice that 10 pt appears in the After box. This is the default for the Normal Quick Style.

3. Click anywhere in the title, which is formatted with the Title Quick Style. The value in the After box changes to 15 pt.

4. Click anywhere in the *Introduction* heading. This paragraph is formatted with the Heading 1 Quick Style. The value in the Before box changes to 24 pt and the value in the After box changes to 0 pt.

5. Click anywhere in the *Federal Dietary Guidelines* heading. This is formatted with the Heading 2 Quick Style, which has 10 pt before and 0 pt after the paragraph.

6. In the Paragraph group, click the **up arrow** next to the Before box twice to change the value to 18 pt.

7. If necessary, scroll down in the document so that you can see both the *Federal Dietary Guidelines* and the *Recommended Dietary Guidelines for Americans* headings. The *Recommended Dietary Guidelines for Americans* heading is also formatted with the Heading 2 Quick Style, as are the other two headings in the document.

8. On the Ribbon, click the **Home** tab. Make sure the insertion point is still in the *Federal Dietary Guidelines* heading.

9. In the Styles group, right-click the **Heading 2** style button, and then click **Update Heading 2 to Match Selection**. Each paragraph formatted with the Heading 2 style is modified so that there are 18 points of space before it.

10. Click in the third paragraph under the *Federal Dietary Guidelines* heading (the paragraph that is indented from both the right and left margins). On the Ribbon, click the **Page Layout** tab. Change the space before and after the paragraph to **12 points**.

11. Press **Ctrl+End**. Select **Roberta Sanchez**, and then type your name.

12. Save, print, and close the document, but leave Word open for the next Step-by-Step.

Changing Vertical Alignment

Vertical alignment refers to positioning text between the top and bottom margins of a document. You can align text with the top of the page, center the text, distribute the text equally between the top and bottom margins (justify), or align the text with the bottom of the page. To vertically align text, select the text, click the Page Setup Dialog Box Launcher on the Page Layout tab, and then click the Layout tab in the Page Setup dialog box, which is shown in **Figure 5–12**. In the Page section, click the arrow next to the Vertical alignment box and choose Top, Center, Justified, or Bottom.

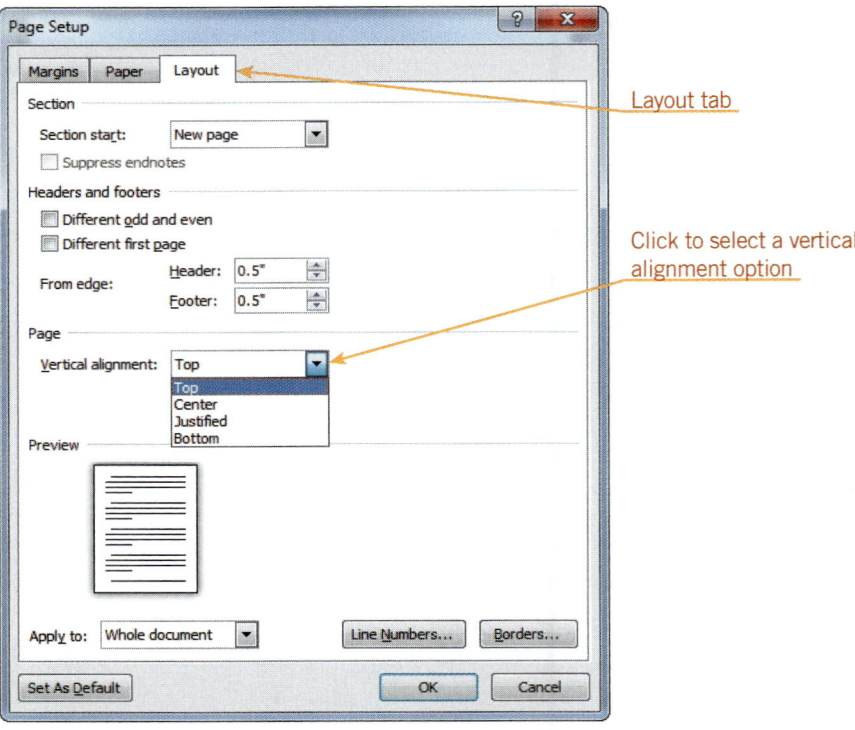

FIGURE 5–12 Layout tab in the Page Setup dialog box

Step-by-Step 5.8

1. Create a new Word document. Save the document as **American Diet Title Page** followed by your initials.

2. Type your name, and then press **Enter**. Type the following:

   Health and Nutrition 101

   Reducing Fat in the American Diet

3. On the Ribbon, click the **View** tab. In the Zoom group, click the **One Page** button.

4. Select all the text. On the Ribbon, click the **Home** tab. In the Font group, click the **arrow** next to the Font Size button `11 ▾`, and then click **20**.

5. In the Paragraph group, click the **Center** button ▤. Deselect the text.

6. On the Ribbon, click the **Page Layout** tab. In the Themes group, click the **Themes** button, and then click **Austin**. This is the same theme that is used in the American Diet document.

7. In the Page Setup group, click the **Page Setup Dialog Box Launcher**. The Page Setup dialog box opens with the Margins tab on top.

8. At the top of the dialog box, click the **Layout** tab. The dialog box changes to show the commands on the Layout tab.

9. In the Page section, click the **arrow** next to the Vertical alignment box. See Figure 5–12.

10. Click **Center**. Click **OK**. The dialog box closes and the text is centered vertically on the page.

11. Save, print, and close the document, but leave Word open for the next Step-by-Step.

Understanding Tab Stops

Tab stops, or *tabs*, mark the place where the insertion point will stop when you press Tab. Tab stops are useful for creating tables or aligning numbered items. In Word, default tab stops are set every half inch and are left-aligned. Text alignment can be

▶ **VOCABULARY**
tab stop (tab)

set with left, right, center, or decimal tab stops. **Figure 5–13** shows examples of some of these tab stops. (You'll learn about the dotted leader in the next section.) **Table 5–1** describes each of the tab stops.

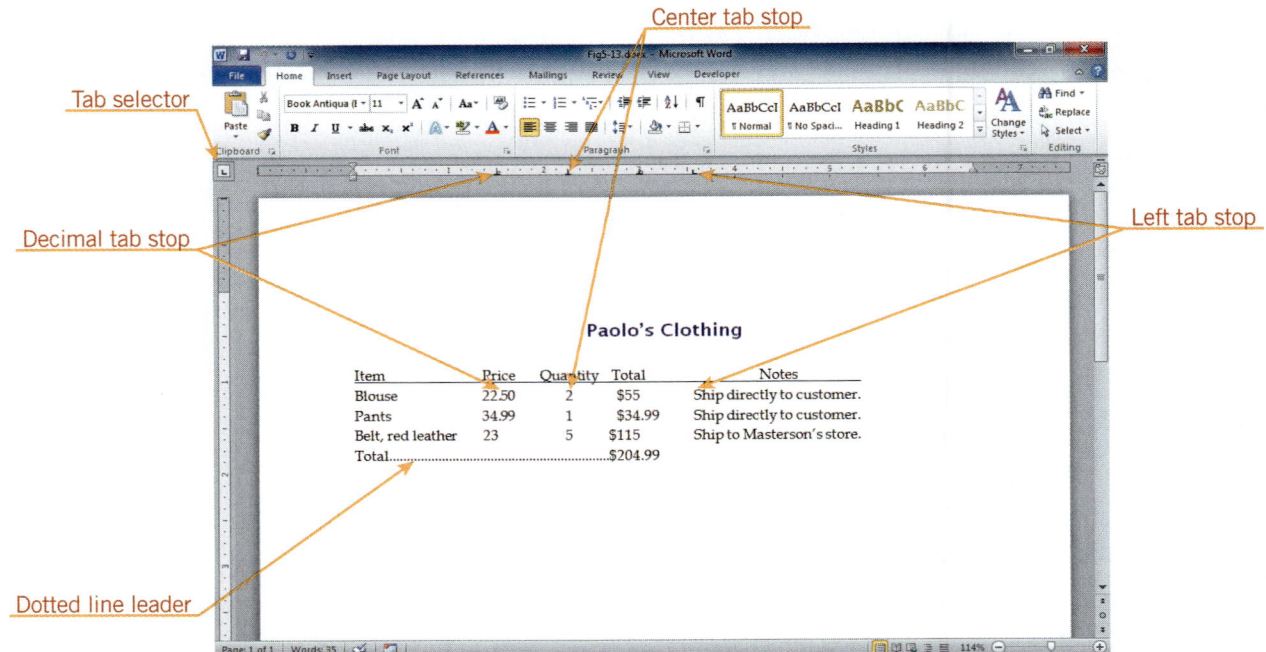

FIGURE 5–13   Types of tabs

TABLE 5–1   Tab stops

TAB	TAB NAME	FUNCTION
⌞	Left Tab	Left-aligns selected text at the point indicated on the horizontal ruler. This is the default tab.
⌟	Right Tab	Right-aligns selected text at the point indicated on the horizontal ruler. This is useful for aligning page numbers in a table of contents.
⊥	Center Tab	Centers selected text at the point indicated on the horizontal ruler. This is used with titles and announcements.
⊥.	Decimal Tab	Aligns selected text on the decimal point at the point indicated on the horizontal ruler. This is helpful when preparing price lists, invoices, and menus.

Setting, Modifying, and Clearing Tab Stops

To set a tab stop, select the paragraph, and then click the ruler at the location you want to set the tab. A tab stop marker appears on the ruler at the location you clicked. If you want to insert a tab stop other than a left tab stop, click the tab selector at the far left of the ruler. Each time you click, the tab selector changes to another type of tab—left, right, center, or decimal. When you insert a tab stop, all of the default tab stops before that tab stop marker are erased. To move a tab stop, drag the tab stop marker to a new location on the ruler. To remove a tab, drag the marker off the ruler.

> **TIP**
>
> The tab selector has additional options—Bar, First Line Indent, and Hanging Indent. Keep clicking the tab selector to return to the Left Tab icon.

> **EXTRA FOR EXPERTS**
>
> The Bar Tab is not a tab stop. It inserts a vertical line in the paragraph.

Step-by-Step 5.9

1. Open the **NADA Memo.docx** document from the drive and folder where your Data Files are stored. Save the document as **NADA Office Supplies Memo** followed by your initials.

2. If paragraph marks are not displayed, in the Paragraph group on the Home tab, click the **Show/Hide ¶** button ¶. If the ruler is not displayed, on the Ribbon, click the **View** tab. In the Show group, click the **Ruler** check box to select it. Notice that there are tab marks in each line in the memo header. The tab marks position the text after the tab mark at the next default tab stop. For all the lines except the *From* line, this is one-half inch. Because the text *From:* extends to the one-half-inch mark, the text after the tab mark is moved to the next default tab stop, one inch.

3. In the memo header, select all four paragraphs (from *To* through *Date*).

4. Locate the **tab selector** to the left of the ruler below the Ribbon. If it is not displaying the Left Tab icon ⌞, click it as many times as necessary to display the Left Tab icon.

5. On the ruler, click the **three-quarter-inch mark**. A Left Tab marker is inserted on the ruler. In the selected paragraphs, the text after the tab mark moves over to left-align at the tab marker you inserted.

6. Scroll down until you can see all the items in the list below the paragraph in the body of the memo (from *Inkjet printer* through *Total*). Select all of the items in the list. The items in the first column are left-aligned at the one-half-inch mark, the first default tab stop. The items in the second column appear at the next available default tab stop in that line.

7. To the left of the ruler, click the **tab selector** twice. It changes to the Right Tab icon ⌟.

> **TIP**
>
> Position the pointer over the tab selector or the tab stop marker on the ruler to see a ScreenTip labeling the type of tab.

8. On the ruler, click the **3½-inch mark**. The first column in the list right-aligns at 3½ inches. You wanted the prices to right-align.

9. Click the **tab selector** five times to return to the Left Tab icon 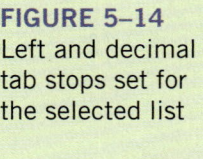. On the ruler, click the **one-half-inch mark**. The first column in the list again left-aligns at one-half inch on the ruler, and the second column in the list right-aligns at the 3½-inch mark on the ruler. The price of the second item, *Surge protector*, doesn't have a decimal point, so the dollar amount doesn't align with the other dollar amounts.

10. On the ruler at the 3½-inch mark, drag the **Right Tab stop marker** off the ruler. The tab stop marker disappears and the prices shift left to align at the next default tab stop marker.

11. Click the **tab selector** three times. It changes to the Decimal Tab icon.

12. On the ruler, click the **3½-inch mark**. The dollar amounts align on the decimal point, as shown in **Figure 5–14**. (The dollar amount for the second item in the list doesn't have a decimal point, but it is understood that it is the same as *29.00*.)

FIGURE 5–14
Left and decimal tab stops set for the selected list

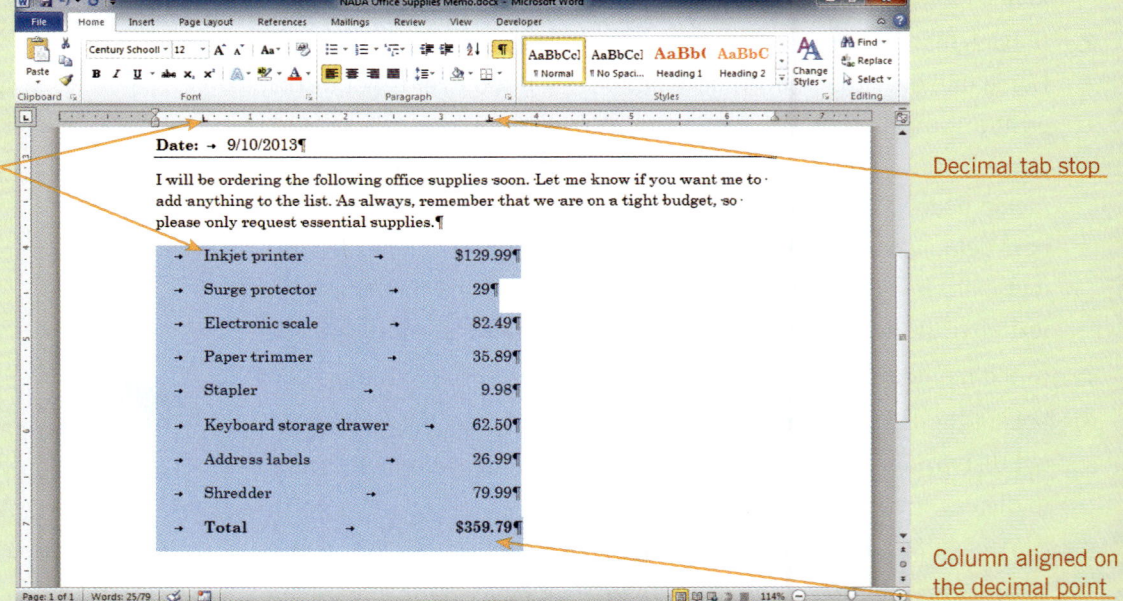

Left tab stop

Decimal tab stop

Column aligned on the decimal point

13. Save the document and leave it open for the next Step-by-Step.

Setting Leaders

Leaders are solid, dotted, or dashed lines that fill the blank space before a tab setting. Leaders are often used in tables of contents. To insert a leader, open the Tabs dialog box, as shown in **Figure 5–15**. To do this, double-click a tab stop marker on the ruler, or on the Home or Page Layout tabs, click the Paragraph Dialog Box Launcher, and then click Tabs in the Paragraph dialog box. In the Tab Stop Position list, click the tab stop to which you want to apply the leader. Then, in the Leader section, click the option button next to the leader you want to use. If you want to set leaders for more than one tab stop, click Set, and then select the next tab stop and the leader you want to set. If you are finished, you can simply click OK.

TIP

In the Tabs dialog box, click a tab to select it, and then click Clear to remove that tab stop. Click Clear All to remove all the tabs in the current paragraph.

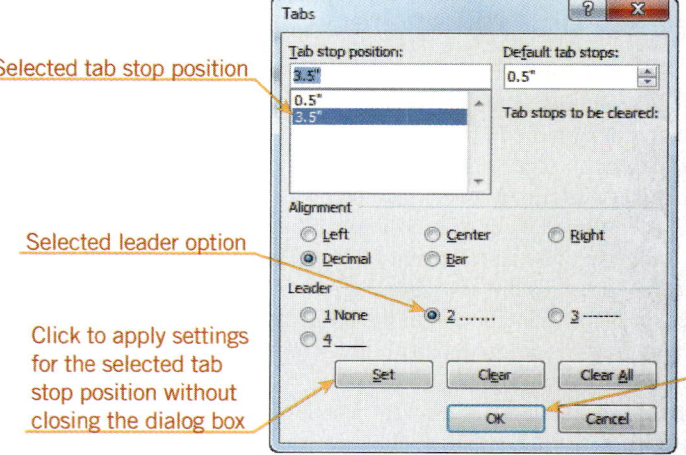

Selected tab stop position

Selected leader option

Click to apply settings for the selected tab stop position without closing the dialog box

Click to apply the settings for the selected tab stop position and close the dialog box

FIGURE 5–15 Tabs dialog box

Step-by-Step 5.10

1. Make sure the list under the first paragraph in the body of the memo is still selected.

2. On the ruler, double-click the **tab stop marker** at the 3½-inch-mark. The Tabs dialog box opens. You want to set a leader in front of the tab at the 3½-inch mark. (If the Page Setup dialog box opened instead, click Cancel and try again. If you inserted a new tab stop marker on the ruler, drag it off the ruler, and then try again.)

3. In the Tab stop position list, click **3.5"**. The value is selected.

4. In the Leader section, click the **2 ....** option button. You are setting the leader for only one tab stop, so you do not need to click Set. See Figure 5–15.

5. Click **OK**. The dialog box closes and dotted leaders are inserted in front of the items aligned at the 3½-inch mark.

6. In the *To* line in the memo header, position the insertion point after the tab mark. Type your name.

7. Save, print, and close the document, but leave Word open for the next Step-by-Step.

Using Bulleted and Numbered Lists

Sometimes you may want to create a bulleted or numbered list in a document. A numbered list is useful when items appear sequentially, such as instructions. A bulleted list often is used when the order of items does not matter. A *bullet* is any small character that appears before an item. Small, solid circles are often used as bullets, but other symbols and icons, as well as pictures, may serve as bullets.

Creating Bulleted and Numbered Lists

You have already used the AutoFormat As You Type feature to create a numbered list. Another way to create a numbered list as you type is to create a new paragraph, and then, in the Paragraph group on the Home tab, click the Numbering button. Likewise, to create a bulleted list as you type, click the Bullets button in the Paragraph group.

When you are finished adding items to the list, press Enter twice. Pressing it the first time inserts a new bulleted or numbered item. When you press Enter a second time without typing anything, the AutoFormat As You Type feature assumes you are finished with the list and changes the new paragraph to a Normal paragraph. You can also click the Bullets or Numbering button in the Paragraph group to turn the feature off, or if the next paragraph is formatted with the Normal style, you can click the Normal style button in the Quick Styles gallery.

You can also change a list that you already typed to a bulleted or numbered list by selecting all the items in the list, and then clicking either the Bullets or Numbering button in the Paragraph group.

> **VOCABULARY**
> **bullet**

> **TIP**
>
> You can also click the Bullets button on the Mini toolbar.

Step-by-Step 5.11

1. Open the **Diet Guidelines.docx** document from the drive and folder where your Data Files are stored. Save the document as **American Diet Guidelines** followed by your initials.

2. Select the two paragraphs in the first indented list.

3. On the Home tab, in the Paragraph group, click the **Numbering** button ▦. Numbers are inserted in front of each item, and the extra space after each paragraph is removed.

4. In the list, click at the end of the first line (after *healthy weight*). Press **Enter**. A new numbered item 2 is created. Type **Be physically active each day**. See **Figure 5–16**.

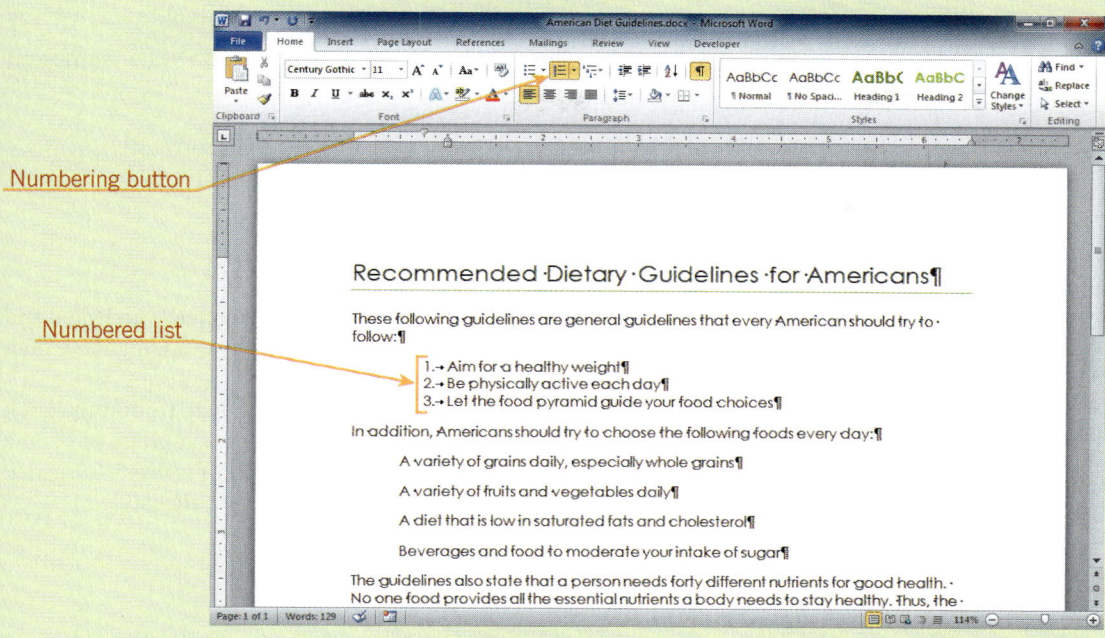

FIGURE 5–16
Numbered list

Numbering button

Numbered list

5. Select all the items in the second indented list. On the Home tab, in the Paragraph group, click the **Bullets** button. The paragraphs are changed to a bulleted list.

6. Click after the last item in the list (after *sugar*). Press **Enter**. A new bulleted item is created. Type **Food with less salt**. See **Figure 5–17**.

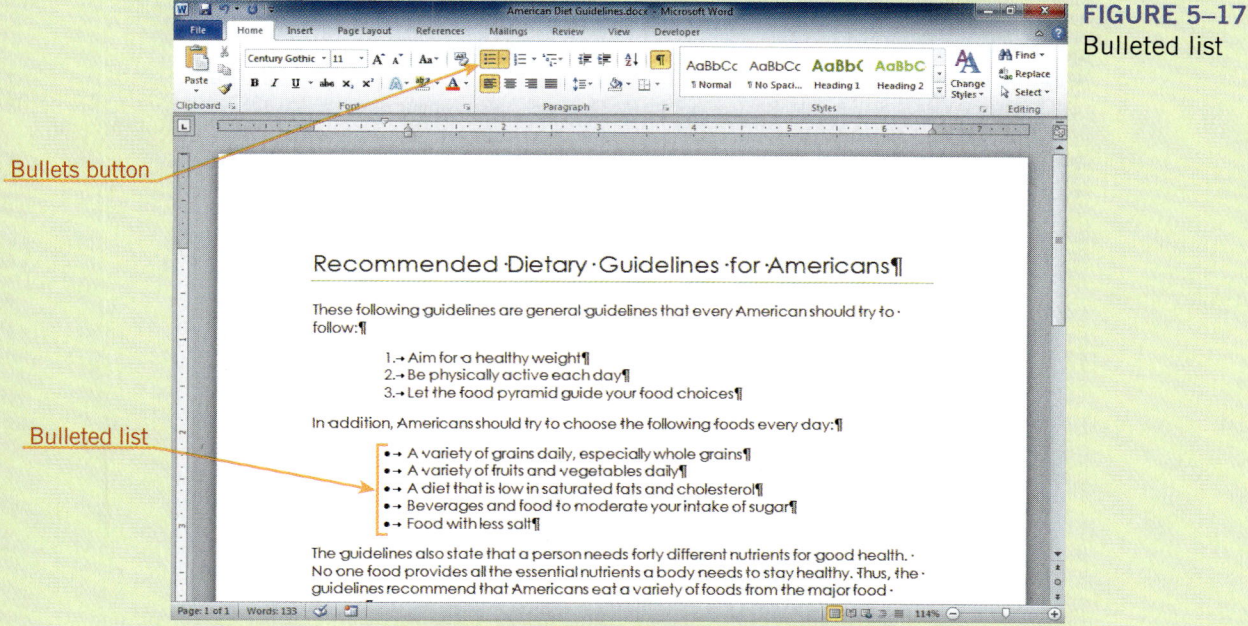

FIGURE 5–17
Bulleted list

Bullets button

Bulleted list

7. Press **Enter**. A new bulleted item is created.

8. Press **Enter** again. The bullet is removed and a new blank paragraph is created. Type **These guidelines emphasize that moderate consumption is the key to good health.**

9. Save the document and leave it open for the next Step-by-Step.

Customizing Bulleted and Numbered Lists

You can customize bulleted and numbered lists. Lists are automatically indented and formatted with a hanging indent. You can change the indents by dragging the indent markers on the ruler.

You can also customize the bullets and the numbers in a list. To do this, click the arrow next to the Bullets or Numbering button in the Paragraph group to open a gallery of bullet or number styles, as shown in **Figure 5–18** and **Figure 5–19**. Click a different style in the gallery to change the bullets or numbers to that style.

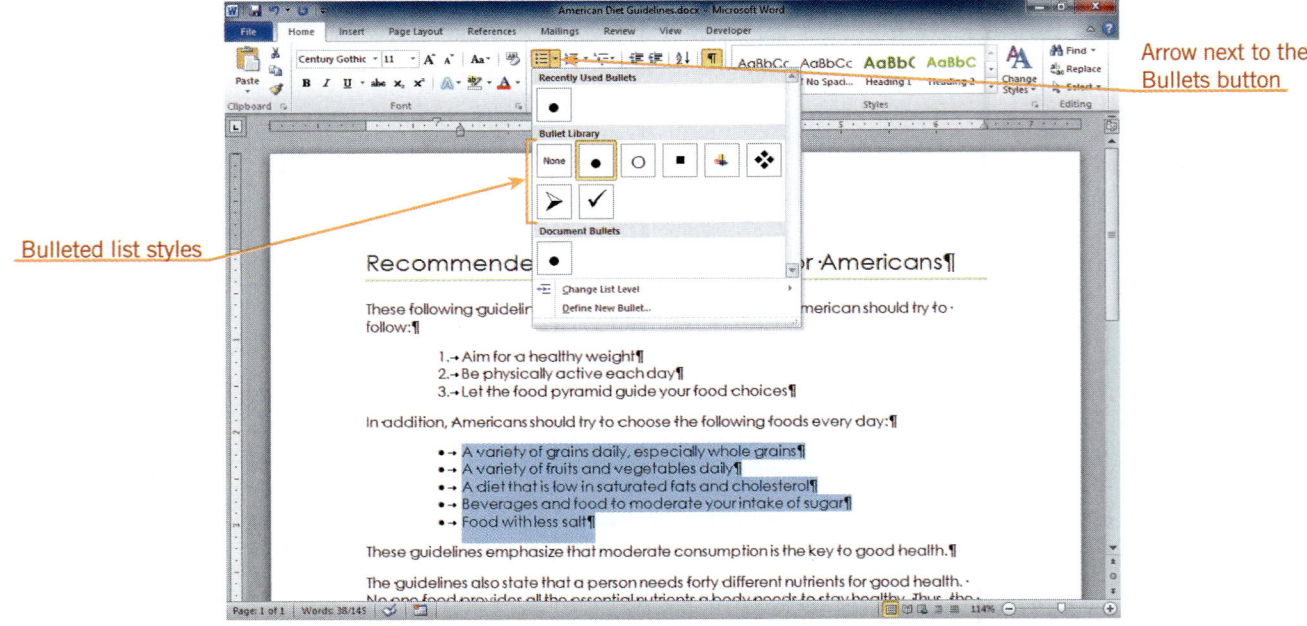

FIGURE 5–18   Bullets gallery

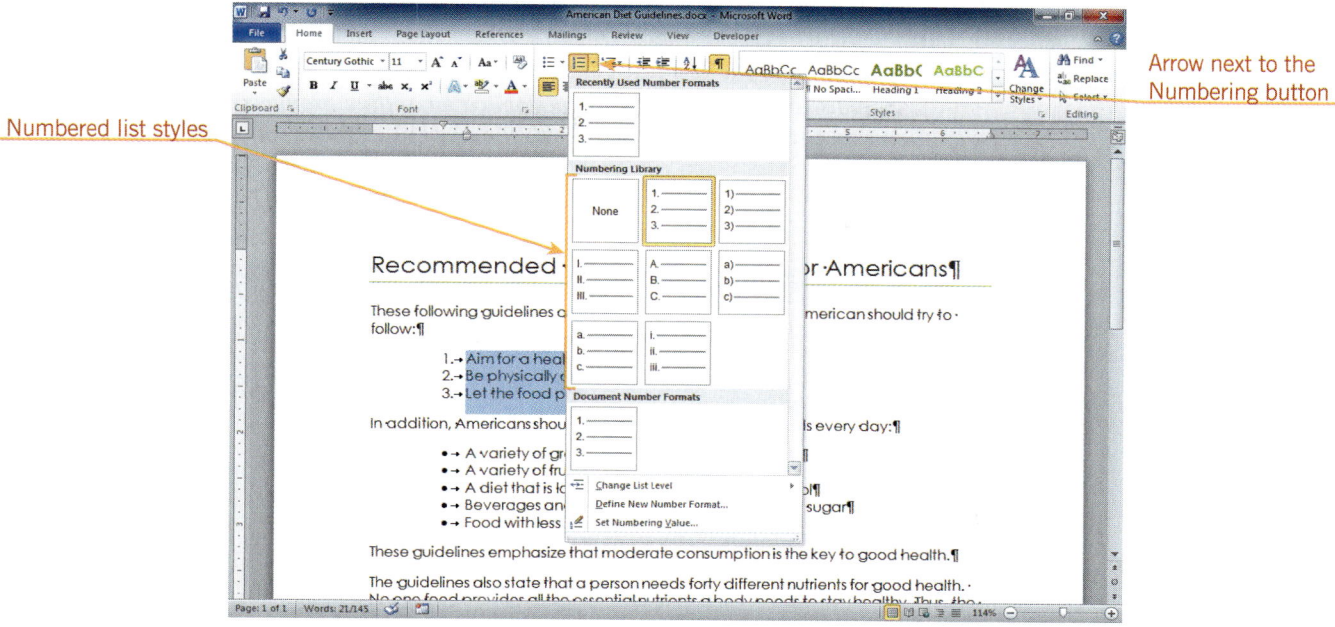

Numbered list styles

Arrow next to the Numbering button

FIGURE 5–19 Numbering gallery

Step-by-Step 5.12

1. Select the three numbered list items. (The numbers themselves will not be selected.)

2. On the Home tab, in the Paragraph group, click the **arrow** next to the Numbering button.

3. Click the uppercase Roman numerals style. The numbers in the list change to Roman numerals.

4. On the ruler, drag the **Left Indent marker** to the 1¼-inch mark. Notice that the other indent markers followed the Left Indent marker to keep the indents set the same distance apart. The indents change so that the numbers are aligned at the one-inch mark and the text after the numbers aligns at the 1¼-inch mark.

5. Select the bulleted list. (The bullets will not be selected.)

6. On the Home tab, in the Paragraph group, click the **arrow** next to the Bullets button.

7. Click the arrow pointing to the right and shaded half black and half white. The bullets in the list change to right-pointing arrows.

8. On the ruler, drag the **Left Indent marker** to the 1¼-inch mark.

9. Press **Ctrl+End**, press **Enter**, and then type your name.

10. Save, print, and close the document, but leave Word open for the next Step-by-Step.

Creating a Multilevel List

▶ **VOCABULARY**
multilevel list
outline numbered list

A *multilevel list* is a list with two or more levels of bullets or numbering. A numbered multilevel list is sometimes called an *outline numbered list*. An easy way to create a multilevel list is to use the Multilevel List button in the Paragraph group on the Home tab. When you click it, a gallery of multilevel list styles opens, as shown in **Figure 5–20**. Click the style you want to use, and then start typing the list.

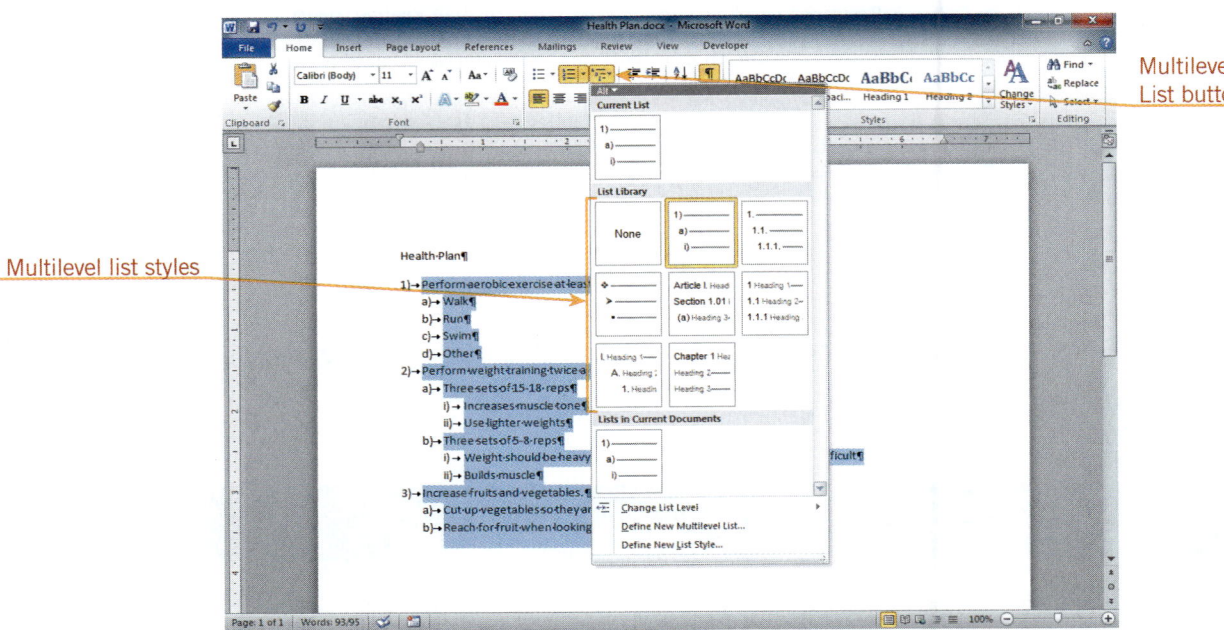

Multilevel list styles

Multilevel List button

FIGURE 5–20   Multilevel list styles

TIP

Multilevel lists can contain bulleted items and numbered items in the same list.

To create the next item in the list, press Enter. You can change the newly inserted item to a lower-level in one of three ways: (1) press Tab; (2) click the Increase Indent button in the Paragraph group; or (3) click the Multilevel List button, point to Change List Level, and then select the level you want in the submenu that opens. Likewise, you can move an item up a level from an indented level in one of three ways: (1) press Shift+Tab, (2) click the Decrease Indent button, or (3) use the Change List Level submenu.

You can also create multilevel lists in an ordinary bulleted or numbered list using the same methods to change levels, but it's easier to choose the exact format you want when you use the Multilevel List button.

Step-by-Step 5.13

1.   Create a new Word document. Save it as **Health Plan** followed by your initials.

2.   Type **Health Plan**, and then press **Enter**.

3. On the Home tab, in the Paragraph group, click the **Multilevel List** button ⬛. In the gallery, click the list style that uses Arabic numbers (*1.*) as the first level, lowercase letters (*a.*) as the second level, and lowercase Roman numerals (*i.*) as the third level. The numbers and letters should be followed by a close parenthesis.

4. Type **Perform aerobic exercise at least three times a week.**, and then press **Enter**. A second item at the first level is created.

5. On the Home tab, in the Paragraph group, click the **Increase Indent** button ⬛. The paragraph is changed to a second-level item.

6. Type the following, pressing **Enter** after you type each item:

Walk

Run

Swim

Other

7. If you didn't press **Enter** after entering the last item, press it now. In the Paragraph group, click the **Decrease Indent** button ⬛. The current paragraph is changed to a first-level item.

8. Type **Perform weight training twice a week.**, and then press **Enter**. Press **Tab**. The new item is changed to a second-level item.

9. Type **Three sets of 15–18 reps**, and then press **Enter**. Press **Tab**. The item is changed to a third-level item.

10. Type **Increases muscle tone**, and then press **Enter**. Type **Use lighter weights**, and then press **Enter**.

11. Press **Shift+Tab**. The blank item is changed to a second-level item.

12. Type the rest of the items in the list, as shown below:

    b.   **Three sets of 5–8 reps**

       i. **Weight should be heavy enough that the last rep in each set is very difficult**

       ii. **Builds muscle**

3.   **Increase fruits and vegetables.**

    a.   **Cut up vegetables so they are easy to grab when looking for a snack**

    b.   **Reach for fruit when looking for something sweet**

13. At the top of the vertical scroll bar, click the **View Ruler** button ⬛ to hide the ruler.

14. At the top of the document, position the insertion point at the end of the first line (*Health Plan*), press **Enter**, and then type your name.

15. Save, print, and close the document, but leave Word open for the next Step-by-Step.

Organizing a Document in Outline View

In Outline view, you can type topic headings and subheadings for a document. You could use a multilevel list to do this, but when you use Outline view, you can switch to Normal view and the headings are all set up for you. To switch to Outline view, click the View tab on the Ribbon, and then in the Document Views group, click the Outline button. You can also click the Outline button to the left of the Zoom slider at the bottom-right of the document window.

When you switch to Outline view, a new tab, the Outlining tab, appears as the active tab on the Ribbon to the left of the Home tab. A round symbol with the minus sign in it appears in the document, as shown in **Figure 5–21**. When you type a heading, the text appears to the right of the circle. The minus sign indicates that there are no subheadings or body text below the heading. A plus sign in the circle before a heading indicates that there are subheadings or body text below the heading.

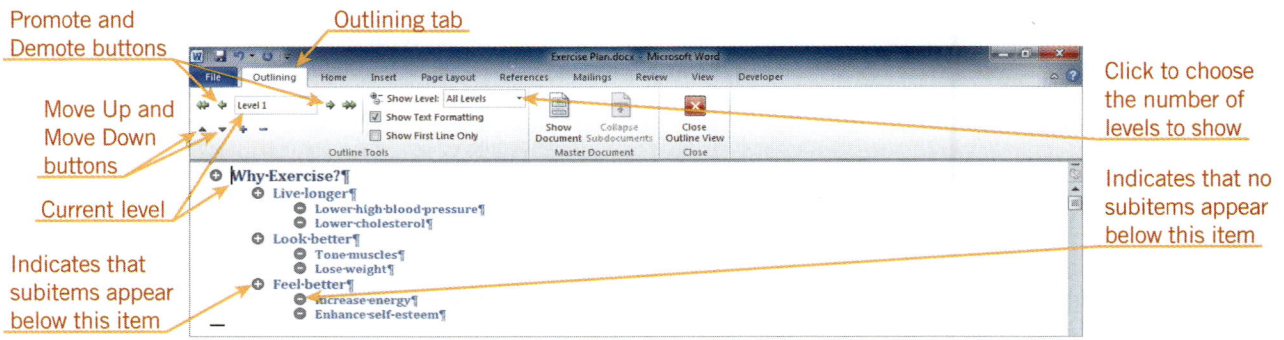

FIGURE 5–21   Text in Outline view

Creating an Outline

When you switch to Outline view in a blank document, the first line of the document is ready for you to type the first heading. Word formats this heading with the Heading 1 style. When you press Enter, a new Level 1 heading, formatted with the Heading 1 style, is created. As with bulleted and numbered lists, if you press the Tab key, you create a Level 2 heading. In Outline view, you can also click the Demote button in the Outline Tools group to demote the text to Level 2. Likewise, if you want to change a heading from a lower level to a higher level, you can press the Shift+Tab keys or click the Promote button.

Step-by-Step 5.14

1. Create a new Word document. Save the document as **Exercise Plan** followed by your initials.

2. On the Ribbon, click the **View** tab. In the Document Views group, click the **Outline** button. The Outlining tab appears on the Ribbon to the left of the Home tab and is the active tab. The insertion point is blinking next to a circle containing a minus sign. In the Outline Tools group on the Outlining tab, the level is identified as Level 1 in the Outline Level box.

3. Type **Why Exercise?**. Press **Enter**. A new Level 1 paragraph is created.

4. In the Outline Tools group, click the **Demote** button ➡ to indent the paragraph to Level 2. The Outline Level box indicates that the item is a Level 2 item.

5. Type **Live longer**. Press **Enter**, and then press **Tab**. The next item indents more to become a Level 3 item.

6. Type **Lower high blood pressure**, and then press **Enter**. Type **Lower cholesterol**, and then press **Enter**.

7. In the Outline Tools group, click the **Promote** button ⬅. The blank paragraph moves up to become a Level 2 item.

8. Type the following:

   Feel better

      Enhance self-esteem

9. If you didn't press **Enter** after typing the last item, press it now. Press **Shift+Tab**. The blank item moves up a level to Level 2.

10. Type the following:

    Look better

       Lose weight

       Tone muscles

       Increase energy

11. Save the document and leave it open for the next Step-by-Step.

Modifying an Outline

Once you have typed an outline, you can easily modify it. You can drag a heading to a different position in the outline by dragging the circle with the plus or minus sign in it. You can also click the Move Up and Move Down buttons in the Outline Tools group. When you move a heading, all the subordinate text underneath it moves too. To make it easier to reorganize the outline, you can click the Expand or Collapse buttons in the Outline Tools group or you can click the arrow next to the Show Level box in the Outline Tools group to view only the headings you want.

Closing Outline View

If you want to add text to your document below the headings you create in Outline view, it's easier to work in Print Layout view. To close Outline view, you click the Close Outline View button in the Close group on the Outlining tab.

Step-by-Step 5.15

1. On the Outlining tab, in the Outline Tools group, click the **arrow** next to the Show Level box. Click **Level 2**. The outline changes to display only the Level 1 and Level 2 items.

2. Double-click the **plus sign** next to *Feel better.* The item expands to display the subitems below it.

3. In the Outline Tools group, click the **arrow** next to the Show Level box. Click **All Levels**. All the levels are shown in the document again.

4. In the subitems under *Look better*, position the pointer on top of the **minus sign** next to *Increase energy.* Press and hold the left mouse button and start dragging the minus sign up the list. As you drag, the pointer changes to a double-headed arrow ↕ and a horizontal line appears. Drag until the line is above *Enhance self-esteem* and below *Feel better*. Release the mouse button. The *Increase energy* item is repositioned as the first subheading under *Feel better*.

5. Click the **minus sign** next to *Lose weight*. The item is selected.

6. In the Outline Tools group, click the **Move Down** button . The item moves down one line so it is the second Level 3 item in the *Look better* section.

7. Click the **plus sign** next to the *Look better* heading. The item and its subitems are selected.

8. In the Outline Tools group, click the **Move Up** button three times. The item and its subitems move up above the *Feel better* item.

9. Insert a new Level 1 heading at the end of the document, and then type your name.

10. In the Close group, click the **Close Outline View** button. Outline view closes and you are returned to Print Layout view. You can see that the headings are formatted with the Headings Quick Styles. (You might need to scroll up.)

11. Switch back to Outline view. Hide the formatting marks.

12. Save, print, and close the document.

TIP

You can also click the Expand button in the Outline Tools group to expand an item.

TIP

The outline symbols on the screen in Outline view show you the document's structure. They will not appear when you print.

EXTRA FOR EXPERTS

To print only the headings (outline) of a document, switch to Outline view, display the level of headings you want to print, and then print the document.

SUMMARY

In this lesson, you learned:

- You can show and hide the ruler to suit your working style by clicking the View Ruler button at the top of the vertical scroll bar, or by clicking the View tab, and then selecting the Ruler check box in the Show/Hide group.

- Margins are the blank areas around the top, bottom, and sides of a page. You can change the margin settings by clicking the Margins button in the Page Setup group on the Page Layout tab.

- You can align text by clicking one of the alignment buttons in the Paragraph group on the Home tab.

- You can indent text either from the left margin, from the right margin, or from both margins. You can also set first-line and hanging indents.

- You can change the line spacing of text from the default of 1.15 lines to 1.0 (single-spaced), 2.0 (double-spaced), or greater. You can change the paragraph spacing by changing the measurements in the Before and After boxes in the Paragraph group on the Page Layout tab.

- You can change the vertical alignment of text by opening the Page Setup dialog box, clicking the Layout tab, and selecting an alignment option from the Vertical alignment list in the Page section.

- Text alignment can be set with left, right, centered, or decimal tabs. Leaders can be used with any kind of tab.

- You can use the Bullets or Numbering buttons in the Paragraph group on the Home tab to create bulleted or numbered lists. To change the appearance of a list, click the arrow next to the Bullets or Numbering button to choose a different bullet or numbering style.

- You can use the Multilevel list button in the Paragraph group on the Home tab to create a list with a hierarchical structure.

- You can work in Outline view to set up the outline of a document.

VOCABULARY REVIEW

Define the following terms:

alignment	justify	negative indent (outdent)
bullet	leader	outline numbered list
center	left-align	outside margin
first-line indent	margin	right-align
hanging indent	mirrored margin	tab stop (tab)
indent	multilevel list	vertical alignment
inside margin (gutter margin)		

REVIEW QUESTIONS

TRUE / FALSE

Circle T if the statement is true or F if the statement is false.

T   F   **1.**   Documents are normally left-aligned or justified.

T   F   **2.**   Line spacing is the amount of space between paragraphs.

T   F   **3.**   Double-spaced text has a full blank line between each line of text.

T   F   **4.**   You can change the bullet used for bulleted lists.

T   F   **5.**   The only way to change an indent is to use the Indent markers on the ruler.

MULTIPLE CHOICE

Select the best response for the following statements.

1. Which of the following margins can you customize in a document?

   A. Top and bottom

   B. Right and left

   C. Top, bottom, right, and left

   D. You cannot customize margins in a document.

2. When you change the vertical alignment of text, you change the position of text between:

   A. two sentences

   B. all margins

   C. the left and right margins

   D. the top and bottom margins

3. The small rectangle marker below the two triangle markers at the left edge of the ruler indicates the:

   A. left indent marker

   B. first-line indent marker

   C. hanging indent marker

   D. decrease indent marker

4. Text can be aligned using all of the following types of tab stops except:

   A. decimal

   B. right

   C. center

   D. justified

5. In Outline view, which button do you click to move an item up to a higher level?

   A. Plus

   B. Promote

   C. Demote

   D. Expand

FILL IN THE BLANK

Complete the following sentences by writing the correct word or words in the blanks provided.

1. The blank areas around the top, bottom, and sides of a page are the _____.

2. A(n) _____ indents the lines that follow the first full line of text.

3. The position of text between the margins is called the _____.

4. _____ mark where the insertion point will stop when you press Tab.

5. In _____ view, you can type topic headings and subheadings for a document.

■ PROJECTS

If you have a SAM 2010 user profile, your instructor may have assigned an autogradable version of the indicated project. If so, log into the SAM 2010 Web site at *www.cengage.com/sam2010* to download the instruction and start files.

PROJECT 5–1

1. Open the **Poster 2.docx** document from the drive and folder where your Data Files are stored. Save the document as **Break Room Poster 2** followed by your initials.

2. Center the title.

3. Change the line spacing of the four items after each heading to 1.5 lines.

4. Change the four items under each heading into a bulleted list. Use any bullet symbol except the solid, round bullet symbol.

5. Press Ctrl+End, and then create a new paragraph that is not part of the second bulleted list. Type your name, press Tab, and then insert the current date. Display the ruler, if necessary, and then use a tab stop to right-align the date at the 6½-inch mark. (*Hint:* You'll have to click to position the tab stop near the 6½-inch mark on the ruler, and then drag the tab stop on top of the Right Indent marker.)

6. Vertically center the text on the page.

7. Hide the ruler, and then save, print, and close the document.

SAM PROJECT 5–2

1. Open the **Shipping.docx** document from the drive and folder where your Data Files are stored. Save the document as **Overnight Shipping** followed by your initials.

2. Center the heading *Overnight Shipping*.

3. Change the spacing of the paragraph under the heading so that there are 6 points of space before it and 18 points of space after it.

4. Indent the first line of the paragraph under the *Overnight Shipping* heading one-quarter inch.

5. Single space the paragraph under the heading.

6. Jump to the end of the document, and then press Enter. Change the spacing before and after this paragraph to zero, and then change the first-line indent to zero (that is, remove the first line indent).

7. In the new paragraph, set left tabs at **1.75** inches, **3** inches, and **4.75** inches.

8. Type the headings **Company**, **Cost**, **Weight Limit**, and **Delivery Time**, using tabs to separate the four columns. Underline the headings without underlining the spaces between the headings.

9. Press Enter. In the new paragraph, remove all of the tabs from the ruler and turn off underlining.

10. Set a decimal tab at **2** inches.

11. Set a center tab at **3.5** inches.

12. Set a right tab at **5.63** inches (the tick mark on the ruler between the 5½- and 5¾-inch marks).

13. Open the Tabs dialog box. In turn, select each of the measurements in the Tab stop position list, click the 2 .... option button, and then click Set. Click OK to close the dialog box after all three of the tab stops have been formatted with the dotted line leader.

14. Using the tabs you just set, type the following information:

Company	Cost	Weight Limit	Delivery Time
Zippy	**$20.50**	**2 lbs.**	**10:00 a.m.**
Lightning	**$15.75**	**1 lb., 4 oz.**	**1:00 p.m.**
Speed Air	**$11.95**	**none**	**3:00 p.m.**
Pronto	**$10.99**	**10 oz.**	**12:30 p.m.**

15. Create a new paragraph at the end of the document with 42 points of space before it. Type your name.

16. Save, print, and close the document.

PROJECT 5–3

1. Create a new Word document. Save it as **Resume for Jeffrey** followed by your initials.

2. Set all margins at 1.2 inches.

3. Type the resume shown in **Figure 5–22**. Use alignment commands, indenting, and tabs to format the text. The theme is the Office theme with the default font and font size. The name at the top is 14 points. All the text is single spaced. The text is centered vertically on the page. The final resume should not contain any blank paragraphs (in other words, adjust the paragraph spacing as needed).

4. Preview the document.

5. Insert a new paragraph at the end of the document, type **Prepared by** followed by your name. Right-align this paragraph.

6. Save, print, and close the document.

PROJECT 5–5

1. Open the **Interview 2.docx** document from the drive and folder where your Data Files are stored . Save the document as **Interview Preparation Tips** followed by your initials.

2. Change all the text except the title to double-spaced. Change the space after all the paragraphs except the title to 24 points.

3. Center the title. Justify the rest of the text.

4. Indent the first line of all the paragraphs except the title ¼ inch.

5. At the end of the second paragraph, position the insertion point after the colon after the words *such as*. Insert a new paragraph and then type the following as a bulleted list. Use a bullet character of your choice.

   Names and addresses of former employers

   Names and addresses of references

   Social Security card

   A copy of your resume

   School records

6. Create a new paragraph at the end of the document, right-align it, and then type your name.

7. Save, print, and close the document.

PROJECT 5–4

1. Open the **Invitation.docx** document from the drive and folder where your Data Files are stored. Save the document as **Wedding Invitation** followed by your initials.

2. Change the font of all the text to 24-point, bold Vivaldi. (If this font is not available, choose another font.) Change the color to Black, Text 1, Lighter 25%.

3. Center all the text vertically and horizontally on the page.

4. Create a new paragraph at the end of the document. Change the font to 11-point Calibri, not bold. Format the paragraph so that there are 36 points of space before it and 10 points after it. Type your name.

5. Save, print, and close the document.

JEFFREY WEBSTER
5524 Grand View Road
Clearwater, FL 33759-9047
727-555-9613

GOAL   An entry-level administrative assistant position with an opportunity for advancement.

WORK EXPERIENCE

Assistant to the Sales Manager, Four Winds Sales, Clearwater, Florida
September 2011 to present
Duties: Use computer to enter data, greet visitors, and answer telephone.

Recreation Assistant, Clearwater Summer Sports Camp
Summer, 2011
Duties: Taught soccer to third and fourth graders.

Cashier (Part-time), Classics Videos, Clearwater, Florida
October 2010 to May 2011
Duties: Assisted customers and operated cash register.

EDUCATION

Prescott Junior College, Clearwater, Florida
September 2011 to present
Business Subjects: Accounting, Office Administration, Word, Excel, PowerPoint, and Access

West High School, Clearwater, Florida
Graduated May 31, 2008
Grade Point Average: 3.5

EXTRACURRICULAR ACTIVITIES

Secretary, Future Business Leaders of America
National Honor Society
Varsity Soccer team
Quill and Scroll, Journalism Honor Society

Habitat for Humanity
Friends of the Library

REFERENCES

Furnished upon request.

FIGURE 5–22

PROJECT 5–6

1. Create a new Word document. Save it as **Agenda** followed by your initials.

2. Set the top margin to two inches and the bottom, left, and right margins to one inch.

3. Type the agenda shown in **Figure 5–23**. Format all the paragraphs in the list so there is no space before or after them. Format the third paragraph in the heading (it starts with *7:00 p.m.*) so there are 48 points of space after it. All the lines are single spaced, and the font color of all the text is black.

4. Insert a new paragraph at the end of the document. Deselect the Multilevel List button. Format the new paragraph with 36 points of space above it, and then type your name.

5. Save, print, and close the document.

PROJECT 5–7

1. Create a new Word document. Save it as **Government** followed by your initials.

2. In Outline view, type the list shown below.

3. Change the Senators item so that it is a Level 2 item with subitems, and then move it so that it is the first item under *Legislative Branch*.

4. Press Ctrl+Home. Type **U.S. Federal Government** as a new Level 1 heading. Insert your name as a new Level 2 heading.

5. Save, print, and close the document.

Executive Branch
    President
        Elected by Electoral College
        Term - Four years
Judicial Branch
    Supreme Court Justices
        Appointed by President
        Term - Life
Senators
    Elected by Direct Vote - Statewide
    Term - Six Years
Legislative Branch
    Representatives
        Elected by Direct Vote - Congressional District
        Term - Two Years

 # CRITICAL THINKING

ACTIVITY 5–1

Create your own resume using the format of the resume in Project 5-3. Trade your resume with a classmate. Edit each other's resume, and then make corrections to your resume if you feel they are warranted.

ACTIVITY 5–2

Make a bulleted list of your three favorite songs, three favorite books, and three favorite movies. Choose a different bullet symbol for each list by clicking Define New Bullet on the Bullets menu, and then click Symbol in the Define New Bullet dialog box. Click the arrow next to the Font box at the top of the dialog box, and then click one of the Wingdings fonts. Search for just the right bullet character for each list.

ACTIVITY 5–3

Use Help to learn how to change a single-level list into a multilevel list style. Create a new Word document and describe the process.

LANCASTER INDEPENDENT SCHOOL DISTRICT
Agenda for Board of Trustees Meeting
7:00 p.m., Monday, April 22, 2013

I.   **Verify quorum**
II.   **Approve minutes for March 25, 2013 meeting**
III.   **Approve the Tax Report for January, 2013**
IV.   **Committee Reports**
     A.   **Curriculum**
     B.   **Textbooks**
     C.   **Construction**
     D.   **Building Maintenance**
V.   **Old Business**
     A.   **Maintenance Contracts**
     B.   **Cafeteria**
VI.   **New Business**
     A.   **Recognition of students participating in School Clean-up Week**
     B.   **Short-term Borrowing**
VII.   **Next Meeting, Monday, May 20, 2013**

FIGURE 5–23

LESSON 6

Working with Graphics

■ OBJECTIVES

Upon completion of this lesson, you should be able to:

- Create and balance columns.
- Add borders and shading.
- Insert clip art and pictures.
- Insert, resize, and move inline and floating objects.
- Recolor graphics.
- Draw and modify shapes.
- Add text and callouts to drawings.
- Create and modify SmartArt and WordArt.

■ VOCABULARY

aspect ratio

callout

chart

clip art

crop

diagram

floating object

graphic

inline object

keyword

object

pull quote

rotation handle

selection rectangle

sidebar

sizing handle

SmartArt

text box

WordArt

Working with Graphics

▶ **VOCABULARY**
graphic

You can enhance documents by adding graphics. *Graphics* are pictures that help illustrate the meaning of the text and make the page more attractive. You can add predefined shapes, diagrams, and charts as well as photographs and drawings. You can also use the drawing tools in Word to create your own graphics and add them to your documents.

Creating Columns

Sometimes a document can be more effective if the text is formatted in multiple columns. A newsletter is an example of a document that often has two or more columns. Columns are easy to create in Word. You click the Page Layout tab on the Ribbon, and then, in the Page Setup group, click the Columns button. The Columns menu opens, as shown in **Figure 6–1**.

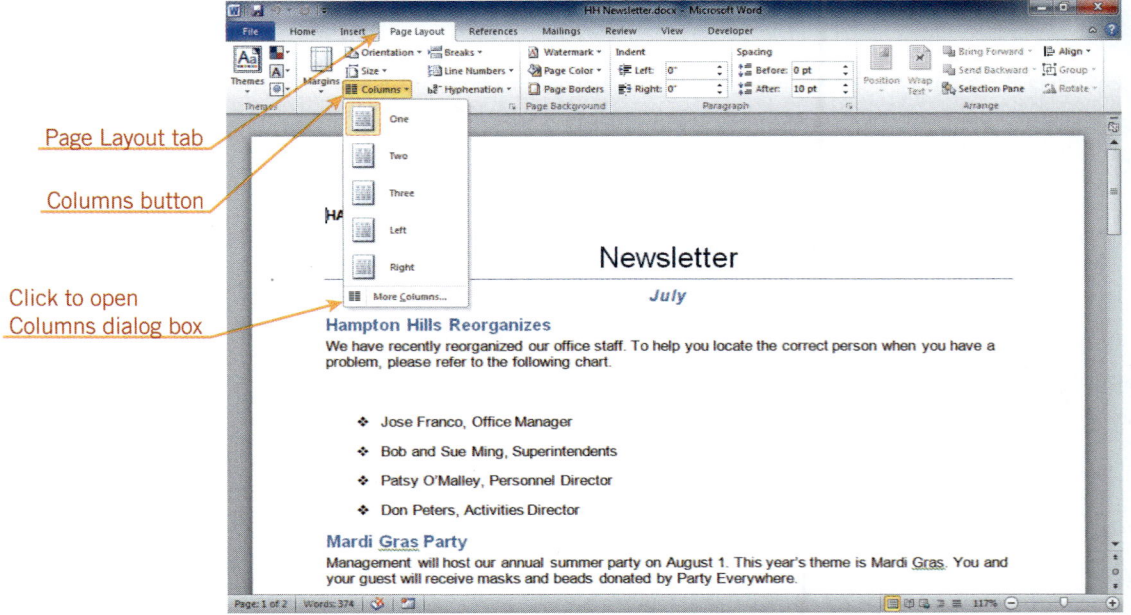

FIGURE 6–1   Columns menu

You can choose one, two, or three columns of equal width. You can also choose Left or Right, which creates two columns with either the left or the right column a little less than half the size of the other column. If none of these options suits you, you can click More Columns at the bottom of the Columns menu to open the Columns dialog box. See **Figure 6–2**. In this dialog box, you can create columns of custom widths, or you can add a vertical line between columns. You can also click the Apply to arrow and choose to apply the columns to the whole document (the default) or from the location of the insertion point to the end of the document.

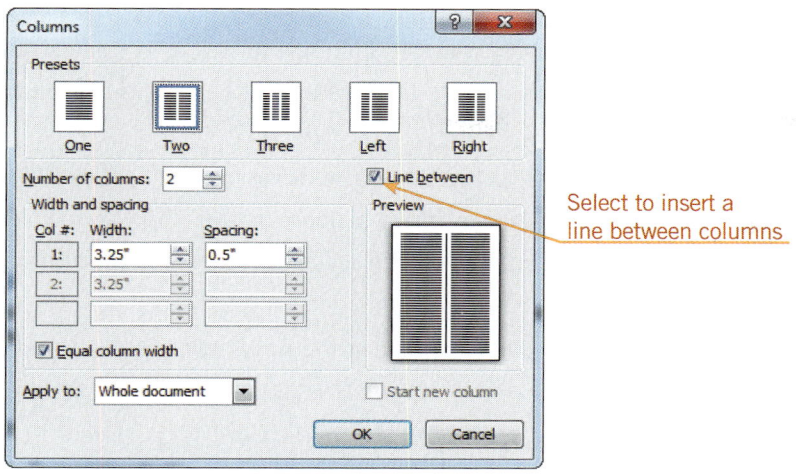

FIGURE 6–2   Columns dialog box

After you create columns, you might need to change the point at which a new column starts. You can do this using either of two methods. First, you can automatically create columns that are the same length. This is called balancing columns. To do this, click at the end of the columns you want to balance, click the Page Layout tab, and then, in the Page Setup group, click the Breaks button. On the menu that opens, click Continuous. Second, you can insert a column break to force a column to start at the point where you insert the break. To do this, position the insertion point immediately in front of the text you want to start the next column. In the Page Setup group on the Page Layout tab, click the Breaks button, and then click Column.

Step-by-Step 6.1

1. Open the **Newsletter.docx** document from the drive and folder where your Data Files are stored. Save the document as **HH Newsletter** followed by your initials.

2. On the Ribbon, click the **Page Layout** tab. In the Page Setup group, click the **Columns** button. The Columns menu opens as shown in Figure 6–1. On the menu, click **Two**. The entire document is formatted in two columns. But you want the newsletter title and date to be centered across the page, not placed in the first column.

3. On the Quick Access Toolbar, click the **Undo** button 🔄. The document returns to its original format.

4. Position the insertion point before the *H* in the *Hampton Hills Reorganizes* heading. You want everything after this point to be formatted in two columns and everything before this point to remain formatted as one column.

5. In the Page Setup group, click the **Columns** button, and then click **More Columns**. The Columns dialog box opens. Notice that the Preview section shows one column.

6. In the Presets section at the top of the dialog box, click **Two**. Click the **Line between** check box to insert a check mark. The Preview section changes to show two columns with a line between the columns. Refer back to Figure 6–2.

7. At the bottom of the dialog box, click the **Apply to** arrow, and then click **This point forward**. The Preview box changes to reflect this setting.

8. Click **OK**. The dialog box closes, all the text in the document from the first heading to the end is formatted in two columns, and a line appears between the two columns.

9. On the Ribbon, click the **View** tab. In the Zoom group, click the **One Page** button. The document appears in One Page view.

10. At the bottom of the second column, click immediately after the last period after the last word in the column, *month*. On the Ribbon, click the **Page Layout** tab. In the Page Setup group, click the **Breaks** button, and then click **Continuous**. Some of the text in the first column shifts to the second column and the two columns are now the same length.

11. On the Ribbon, click the **Home** tab. In the Paragraph group, click the **Show/Hide ¶** button to display formatting marks. Notice at the top of the document, after *July*, a double dotted line and the words *Section Break (Continuous)* appear. This is the point in the document at which the two-column format starts. At the bottom of the second column, a double dotted line appears. This is the continuous break you inserted.

12. In the Paragraph group, click the **Show/Hide ¶** button again to hide the formatting marks. Save your changes to the document. Leave it open for the next Step-by-Step.

TIP

To format only part of the document in columns without opening the Columns dialog box, select the paragraphs you want to format in columns. Then, click the Columns button in the Page Setup group on the Page Layout tab, and use any of the commands on this menu.

Adding Borders and Shading to Paragraphs

Borders around a paragraph draw the reader's attention to the paragraph. You can specify whether the border appears on all four sides (like a box), on two sides, or on only one side of the paragraph. You can also specify the border style, for example, whether the border consists of a single or a double line, is thick or thin, or includes a shadow or a 3-D effect.

To add a border, first select the text around which you want the border to appear. On the Home tab on the Ribbon, click the arrow next to the Borders button in the Paragraph group. A menu of border choices opens, as shown in **Figure 6–3**. You can click a command on the menu to add a border. Note that you can then click the arrow next to the Borders button again and click another command to add a second border to the selected text. For example, if you wanted to add a border above and below a paragraph, you would click Bottom Border on the menu, open the menu again, and then click Top Border. If you opened the menu again, both commands would be selected. Note that the icon for the Borders button and the exact name of the ScreenTip changes to reflect the most recent choices made.

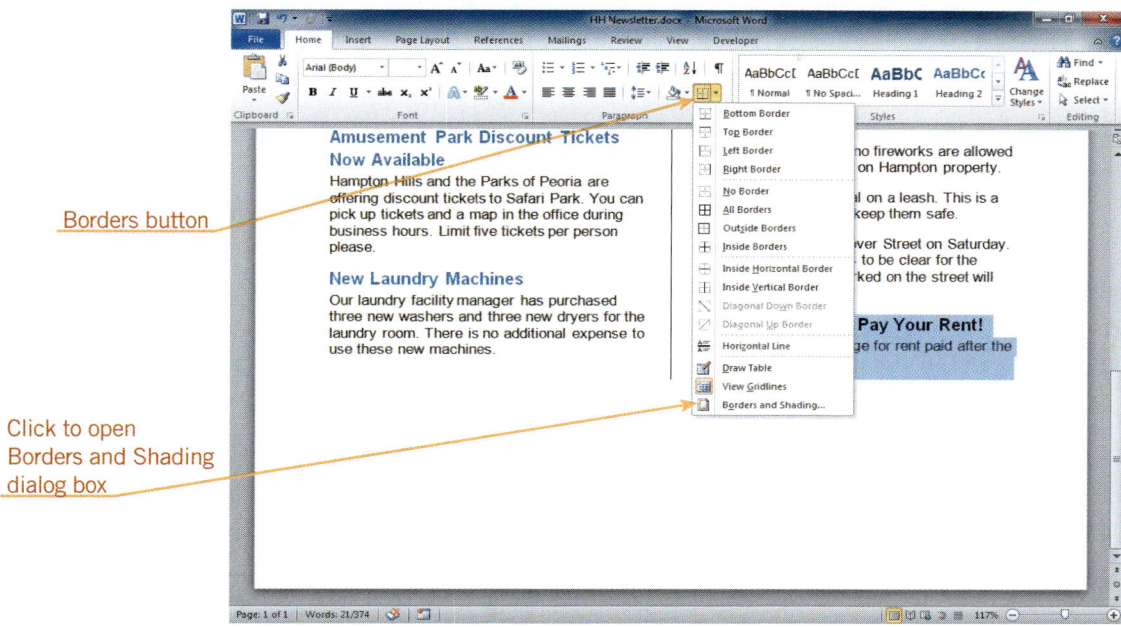

FIGURE 6–3 Borders menu

If you want to change the border style, you need to click Borders and Shading on the menu to open the Borders and Shading dialog box. In the dialog box, click the Borders tab if it is not the top tab. See **Figure 6–4**. Here you can specify the border setting, style, color, and width of the border line. To insert or remove borders, you click the sides of the paragraph preview on the right.

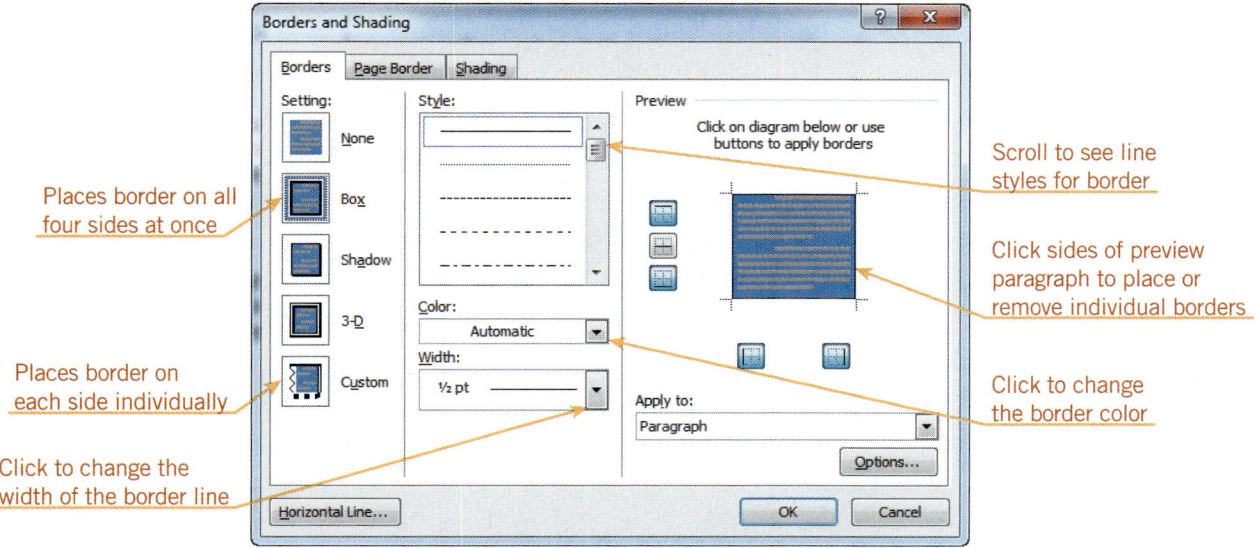

FIGURE 6–4 Borders tab in the Borders and Shading dialog box

You can also add shading or patterns to a paragraph or lines of text to emphasize the text. To do this, select the text you want to shade. In the Paragraph group on the Home tab, click the arrow beside the Shading button, and then click a color in the palette that opens.

To add a pattern, open the Borders and Shading dialog box, and then click the Shading tab, as shown in **Figure 6–5**. You can click the Fill arrow to choose a shading color from the same palette available on the Shading button. To add a pattern, click the Style arrow to choose a style or pattern for the shading (a percentage of the selected color, dots, or stripes), and then click the Color arrow to choose a color for the pattern. The Preview box shows you a sample of what your shading choices will look like.

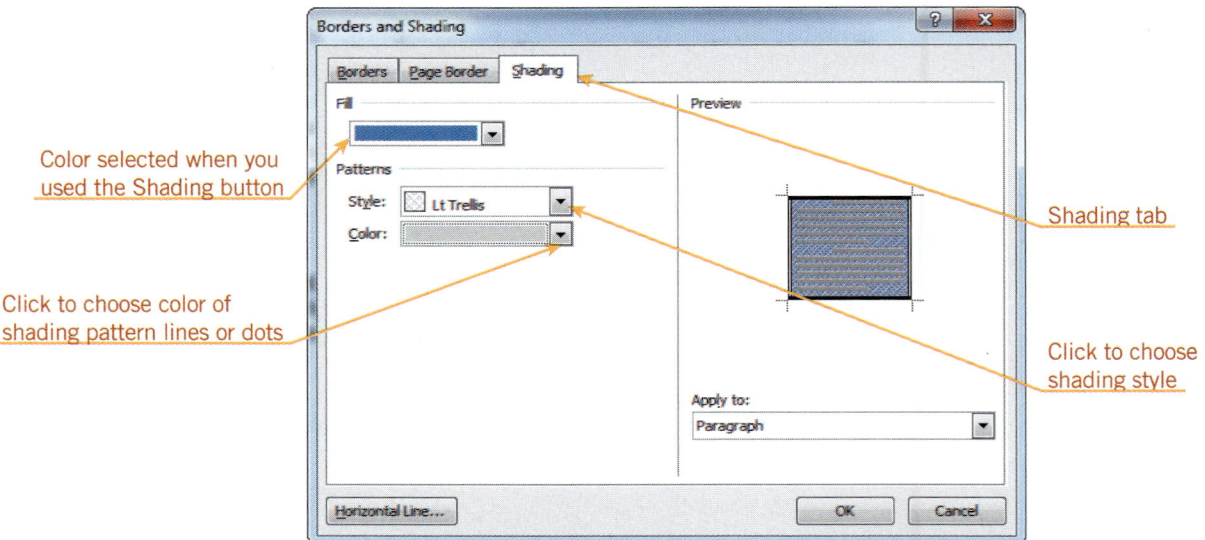

FIGURE 6–5   Shading tab in the Borders and Shading dialog box

Step-by-Step 6.2

1. Click the **View** tab, and then in the Zoom group, click the **Page Width** button. At the bottom of the page, select the heading **Don't Forget to Pay Your Rent!** and the sentence below it.

2. On the Ribbon, click the **Home** tab. In the Paragraph group, click the **arrow** next to the Borders button. The Borders menu opens. (Refer back to Figure 6–3.) Notice that none of the border commands are selected on the menu. Click **Outside Borders**. The menu closes and borders are added on all four sides of the selected text.

3. In the Paragraph group, click the **arrow** next to the Shading button ⬛▾. In the palette, click the **Dark Blue, Text 2, Lighter 40%** box (fourth row, fourth column). The selected paragraphs are shaded with a medium blue color.

4. In the Paragraph group, click the **arrow** next to the Borders button ⬛▾. Notice that the top four commands as well as the Outside Borders command are selected on the menu. At the bottom of the menu, click **Borders and Shading**. The Borders and Shading dialog box opens, with the Borders tab on top. Refer back to Figure 6–4. In the Setting section on the left, the Box button is selected. On the right, the Preview section shows the borders on all four sides of the paragraph.

5. In the center column in the dialog box, click the **Width** arrow, and then click **2 ¼ pt**. Because the Box button is selected, all four borders are changed to 2¼ points wide.

6. In the Setting section, click the **Custom** button. When the Custom button is selected, you need to click a border in the Preview section to apply the new border.

7. In the Style list, click the **down scroll arrow** twice, and then click the **double line** at the bottom of the list. In the Preview section, click the **left**, and then the **right** border. The borders you clicked change to double lines.

8. Click the **Shading** tab. Notice that the color in the Fill box is the same color you chose when you used the Shading button.

9. Click the **Style** arrow, scroll down to the bottom of the list, and then click **Lt Trellis**. The Preview section shows a trellis pattern.

10. Click the **Color** arrow, and then click the **White, Background 1, Darker 15%** box (third row, first column). Now the trellis pattern is much lighter.

11. Click **OK**. The selected paragraphs are formatted with the borders, shading, and pattern you chose.

12. Save your changes to the document. Leave it open for the next Step-by-Step.

Adding Borders and Shading to Pages

EXTRA FOR EXPERTS

To specify the amount of space between the border and the text or edge of the page, click the Options button on the Borders or Page Border tab in the Borders and Shading dialog box.

Just as you can add borders to paragraphs, you can add borders and shading to entire pages. To do this, click the Page Layout tab on the Ribbon, and then, in the Page Background group, click the Page Borders button. This opens the Borders and Shading dialog box with the Page Border tab on top, as shown in **Figure 6–6**. This is the same Borders and Shading dialog box you opened to add borders and shading to paragraphs. Everything is the same except the default in the Apply to box is Whole document, and there is an additional box at the bottom of the middle section of the dialog box. This is the Art box, from which you can choose graphics to use as a border. As with a paragraph, you can add page borders to any or all sides of a page.

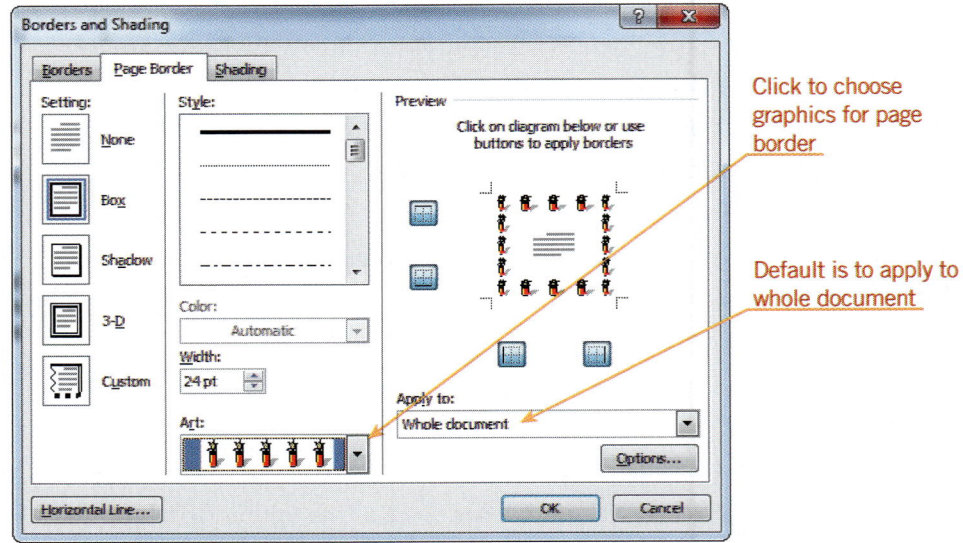

FIGURE 6–6   Page Border tab in the Borders and Shading dialog box

To add shading to an entire page, in the Page Background group on the Page Layout tab, click the Page Color button. The palette of theme colors opens. Click a color in the palette. The entire page is shaded with that color.

Step-by-Step 6.3

1. Switch to One Page view.

2. On the Ribbon, click the **Page Layout** tab. In the Page Background group, click the **Page Borders** button. The Borders and Shading dialog box opens, with the Page Border tab selected.

3. At the bottom of the middle section of the dialog box, click the **Art** arrow. Scroll down the list until you see the row of **red firecrackers**, and then click it. The Preview section changes to show a border of red firecrackers around the edge of the page.

4. Click **OK**. The dialog box closes and the firecracker border appears around the page.

5. In the Page Background group, click the **Page Color** button. In the color palette, click the **Red, Accent 2, Lighter 80%** square (second row, sixth column). The page is shaded with a light red color.

6. Save your changes to the document. Leave it open for the next Step-by-Step.

WARNING

If there is a white box at the bottom of the first column after applying the page background color, click in it, and then use the Shading button in the Paragraph group on the Home tab to fill the paragraph with the same color as the page background.

Understanding Objects

An *object* is anything that can be manipulated as a whole, such as clip art or another graphic that you insert in a document. You can insert, modify, resize, reposition, and delete objects in documents. You can cut, copy, and paste objects the same way you do text, using either the Cut, Copy, and Paste commands or by dragging and dropping the selected object.

▶ VOCABULARY
object
clip art
keywords

Inserting Clip Art

Graphics that are already drawn or photographed and available for use in documents are called *clip art*. To insert clip art, click the Insert tab, and then, in the Illustrations group, click the Clip Art button. This opens the Clip Art task pane to the right of the document window. See **Figure 6–7**. In the Search for box, type a word or words that describe the type of clip art you want to insert. These words are called *keywords*. By default, Word searches all clip art on your computer as well as on Microsoft Office Online, a Web site maintained by Microsoft that stores thousands of pieces of clip art. When Word finds clip art that matches the keywords you typed, it displays the images in the task pane. You can scroll to view the images and click the one you want. Word inserts the clip art at the insertion point in your document.

TIP

The term *clip art* refers not only to drawn images, but also to photographs, video clips, and sound files. To restrict your search to specific types of clip art, click the Results should be arrow in the Clip Art task pane, and then select the check boxes next to the type of clip art you want.

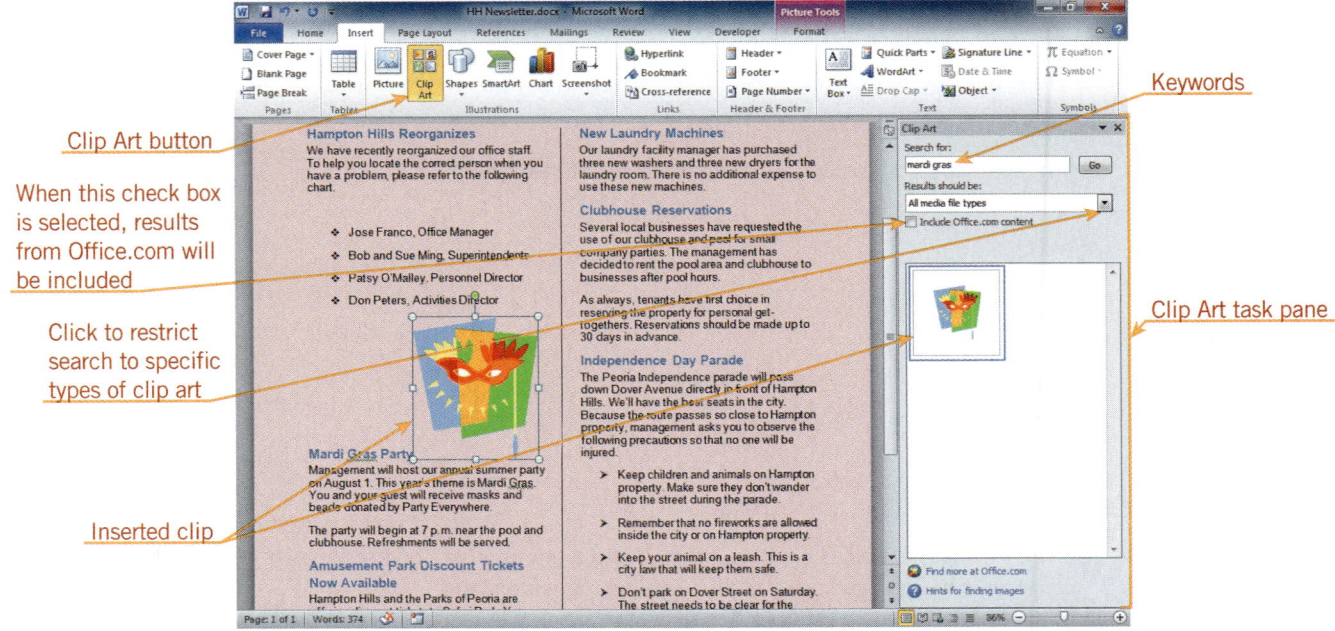

FIGURE 6–7　Inserting clip art

Step-by-Step 6.4

1. Click the **View** tab, and then in the Zoom group, click **Page Width**. Scroll up so that you can see the heading *Mardi Gras Party* in the first column.

2. In the first column, position the insertion point after the word *Party* in the heading *Mardi Gras Party*. On the Ribbon, click the **Insert** tab. In the Illustrations group, click the **Clip Art** button. The Clip Art task pane appears to the right of the document window.

3. At the top of the Clip Art task pane, click in the **Search for** box and select the text in the box if there is any. Type **mardi gras**, and then click **Go**. Clips relating to Mardi Gras appear in the task pane. Refer back to Figure 6–7. (Note: If you are connected to the Internet and if the Include Office.com content check box is selected, you will see more results in the task pane.)

4. In the task pane, point to the clip of a mask on top of colored panels. An arrow appears on the right side of the clip and a ScreenTip listing key words that describe the clip and other information about the clip appears.

> **WARNING**
>
> If your search does not return the clip shown in Figure 6–7, click the Results should be arrow, and then select any check boxes that are not selected.

5. Click the **arrow**, and then on the menu, click **Insert**. The clip is inserted in the document.

6. In the document window, position the insertion point immediately after the heading *Independence Day Parade*.

7. In the task pane, replace the text in the Search for box with **flag**. You need to find a photograph of a flag.

8. Click the **Results should be** arrow. Click the **All media types** check box to deselect it, and then click the **Photographs** check box to select it. The Photographs check box should be the only check box with a check mark in it. Click the **Results should be** arrow to close the menu. To find a clip art photograph of a flag, you need to search Office.com.

9. Click the **Include Office.com content** check box to select it if it is not already selected, and then click **Go**. Clip art photographs of flags appear in the task pane. (Note: If you are not connected to the Internet, delete the text in the Search for box, and then click Go. Choose any one of the photographs to insert in place of the flag.)

10. In the task pane, scroll down until you see photos of American flags. Point to one, click the **arrow** on the clip, and then click **Insert**. The clip art photo of the flag is inserted into the document.

11. In the title bar of the Clip Art task pane, click the **Close** button . The task pane closes. Save the document and leave it open for the next Step-by-Step.

TIP

You can also simply click a clip in the Clip Art task pane to insert it into the document.

TIP

You can press Enter instead of clicking Go in the task pane to search for clips matching the keywords.

Selecting an Object

To manipulate or modify an object, you must select it first. To select an object, position the pointer over the object, and then click. A box with small circles at the corners and small squares on each side appears around the object, as shown in **Figure 6–8**. The box appears when the object is selected and is called the *selection rectangle*. The squares and circles are called *sizing handles*; you drag the sizing handles to resize the object. The green circle is the *rotation handle*; you can drag it to rotate the object. To deselect an object, click a blank area of the document window, just as you would to deselect selected text.

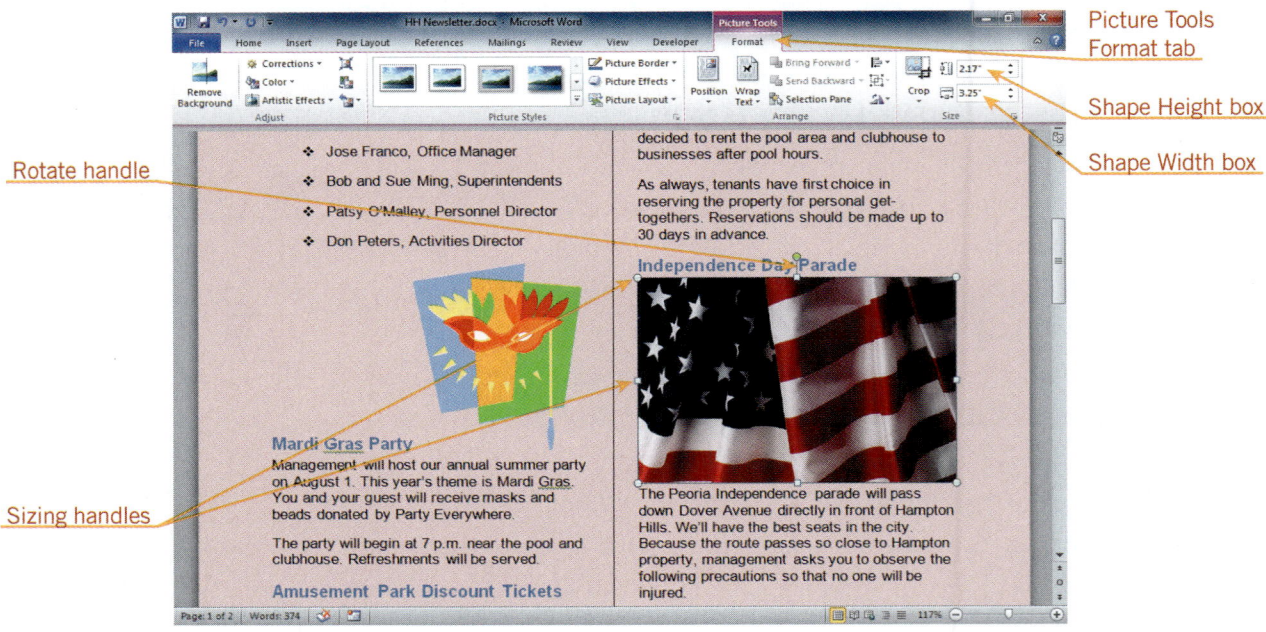

FIGURE 6–8　Selected picture

When you select a clip art image, the Picture Tools Format tab appears, as shown in Figure 6–8. Remember, contextual tabs contain commands that are available only when a particular type of object is selected. For example, after you insert clip art, you can change its height and width or recolor it. These commands appear on the Picture Tools Format tab because you cannot perform either of these actions on regular text.

Resizing an Object

Once an object has been inserted, you can resize it to fit better on the page. To resize an object, first select it, and then drag a sizing handle. When you position the pointer directly on top of one of the sizing handles, it changes to a two-headed arrow. Drag the handle inward or outward to make the object smaller or larger.

The relationship of the object's height to its width is called the *aspect ratio*. If you drag a corner sizing handle (one of the circles), you change the size of the object without changing the aspect ratio; in other words, you change the object's height and width proportionately. If you drag a side sizing handle (one of the squares), you change the size of the object without maintaining the aspect ratio. You can also change the size of an object by selecting it, clicking the Picture Tools Format tab, and then adjusting either of the measurements in the Size group. The default is to maintain the aspect ratio, so if you change the measurement in one box, the measurement in the other box adjusts automatically.

Step-by-Step 6.5

1. If the clip art of the flag is not selected, click to select it. If the rulers are not displayed on your screen, at the top of the vertical scroll bar, click the **View Ruler** button so that the rulers are displayed.

2. Using the ruler as a guide, drag the **upper-right sizing handle** on the flag until the faint outline of the clip indicates that it is approximately two inches tall.

3. Click the clip art of the mask.

4. On the Ribbon, click the **Format** tab under Picture Tools, if necessary. In the Size group, click the **up arrow** in the Shape Width box (the bottom box) as many times as necessary until the measurement in the box is **2"**. Note that the measurement in the Shape Height box changed as well.

5. In the Size group, click in the **Shape Height** box (the top box). The measurement is selected. Type **1.15**, and then press **Enter**. The height of the clip is changed to 1.15 inches, and the width automatically changed to one inch. Now both clips are resized smaller. See **Figure 6–9**.

> **EXTRA FOR EXPERTS**
>
> If you don't want part of a graphic to appear in the document, you can **crop** off (cut off) the part you don't want. Select the graphic, click the Format tab, and then, in the Size group, click the Crop button to change the pointer to the Crop pointer. Drag a sizing handle on the graphic toward the center of the graphic until the indicator box that appears includes only the section of the graphic you want to use. Click the Crop button again to turn off this feature.

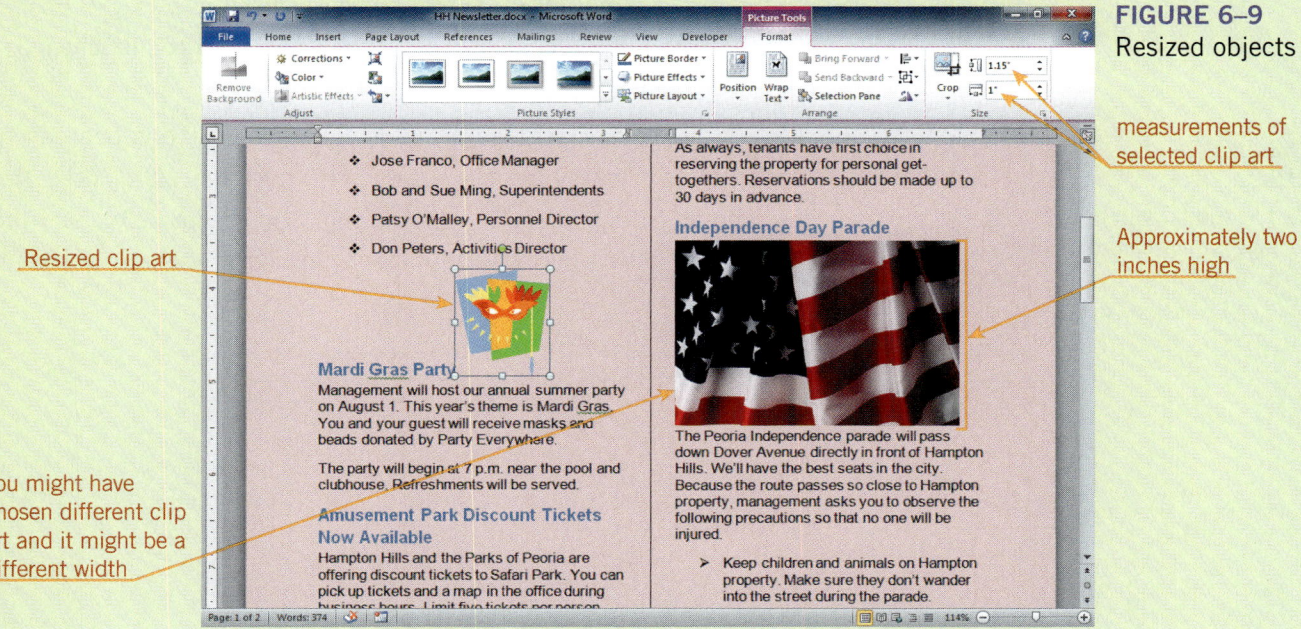

FIGURE 6–9
Resized objects

measurements of selected clip art

Approximately two inches high

Resized clip art

You might have chosen different clip art and it might be a different width

6. Save the document and leave it open for the next Step-by-Step.

Repositioning and Removing an Inline Object

When you insert an object, it is inserted as an *inline object* in the text, which means it is treated as if it were a character in the line of text. You can apply paragraph formatting commands to the paragraph that contains the inline object; for example, you can use the Align commands to change its alignment or set a specific amount of space before or after the paragraph. If you want to move or copy an inline object to another line in the document, click it to select it, and then use drag-and-drop or the Cut, Copy, and Paste commands to move or copy it, just as you would with text. If you want to delete an object, select it, and then press the Delete or the Backspace key, again, just as you would with text.

Step-by-Step 6.6

1. In the second column, click the picture of the flag to select it.

2. On the Ribbon, click the **Home** tab. In the Paragraph group, click the **Center** button ☰. The flag and the heading above it are centered in the column. Why did the heading become centered as well as the selected clip art of the flag?

3. In the Paragraph group, click the **Show/Hide ¶** button ¶. Because there is a paragraph mark after the flag but not after the heading, the flag is in the same paragraph as the heading, so any paragraph formatting you apply to the inline clip art of the flag also applies to the heading.

4. In the Paragraph group, click the **Align Text Left** button ☰. The paragraph, including the heading, is again left-aligned.

5. In the first column, click the clip art of the mask to select it. Position the pointer directly on top of the selected object. The pointer changes to the Move pointer ⭥.

6. Drag the selected image down until the indicator line is between the period at the end of the first paragraph under the *Mardi Gras Party* heading and the paragraph mark, as shown in **Figure 6–10**, and then release the mouse button. The image is moved to the end of the first paragraph.

TIP

Just as you do with text, if you want to copy rather than move an object using drag-and-drop, press and hold Ctrl while you drag the object.

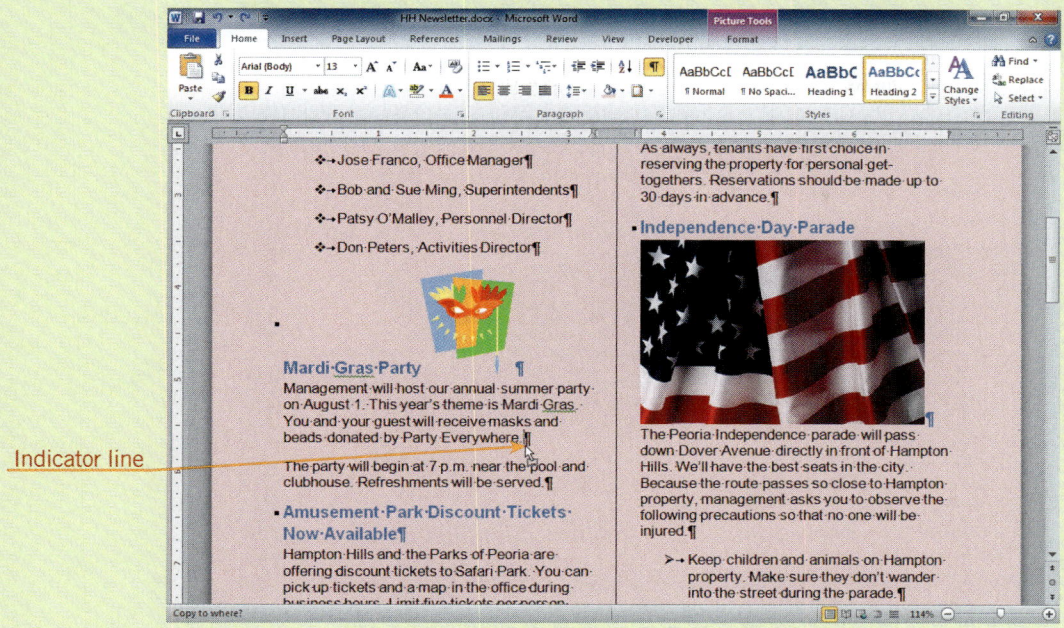

FIGURE 6–10
Moving an object

Indicator line

7.   Save the document and leave it open for the next Step-by-Step.

Wrapping Text Around an Object

To save space and make a document look more professional, you may want to wrap text around an object. To do this, you need to change the inline object to a *floating object*, an object that acts as if it were sitting in a separate layer on the page. You can drag a floating object anywhere on the page. To do this, click the contextual Format tab, and then in the Arrange group, click the Wrap Text button to open a menu of wrapping options, as shown in **Figure 6–11**. **Table 6–1** describes these options.

> **VOCABULARY**
> **floating object**

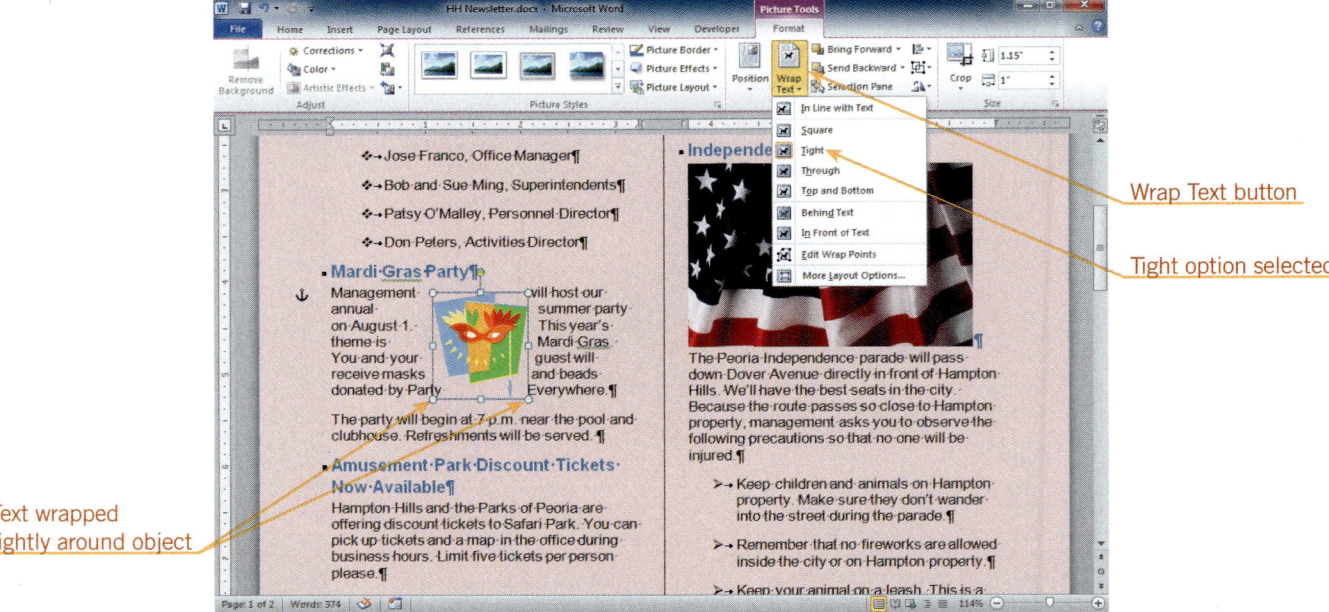

FIGURE 6–11   Wrapping text around an object

TABLE 6–1   Text wrapping commands

COMMAND	ACTION
In Line with Text	Changes a floating object to an inline object
Square	Wraps text around top, bottom, and both sides of an object
Tight	Wraps text around all sides of an object no matter what shape the object is
Through	Wraps text around all sides of an object—no matter what shape the object is—more tightly than the Tight command
Top and Bottom	Wraps text around the top and bottom of an object and leaves the space on either side of the object empty
Behind Text	Places the object behind the text
In Front of Text	Places the object in front of (on top of) the text
Edit Wrap Points	Displays small squares around the perimeter of an object, which you can drag to change the perimeter for objects wrapped with the Tight or the Through option
More Layout Options	Opens the Layout dialog box with the Text Wrapping tab on top, displaying options for adjusting the distance between the text and the sides of the object

To change the object to a floating object that is positioned in a predetermined location on the page (centered in the top, middle, or bottom, one of the corners, or in the middle of the left or right side), on the Format tab in the Arrange group, click the Position button, and then click one of the options in the gallery under With Text Wrapping. See **Figure 6–12**.

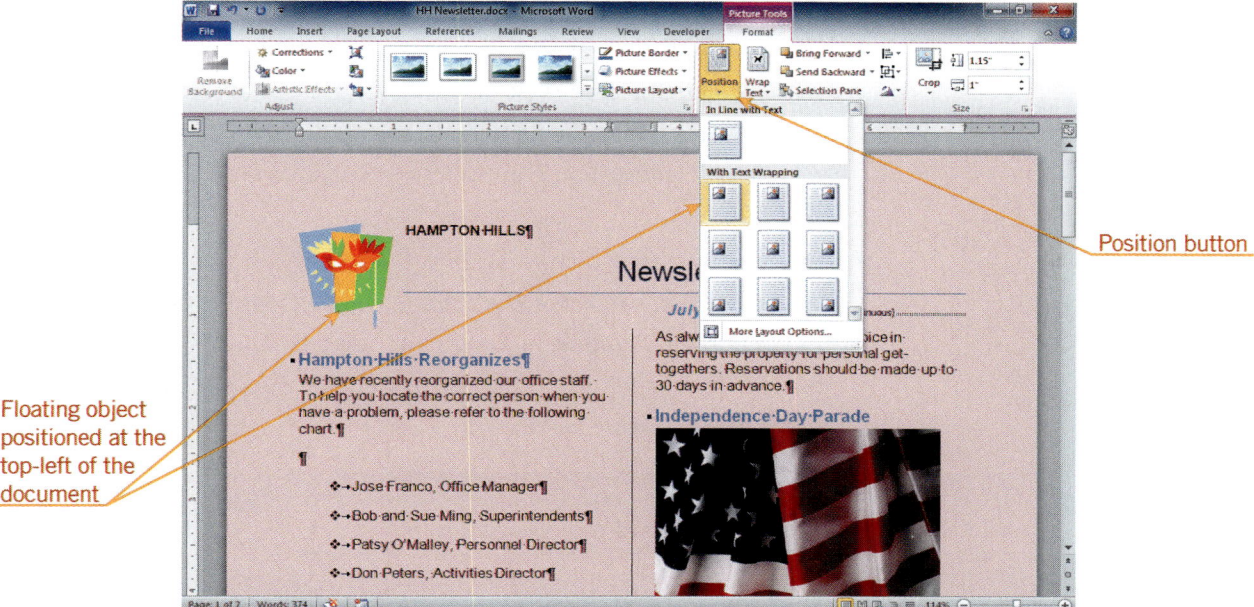

FIGURE 6–12   Positioning text in a predetermined position using the Position button

Step-by-Step 6.7

1. If the clip art of the mask is not already selected, click it.

2. On the Ribbon, click the **Picture Tools Format** tab. In the Arrange group, click the **Wrap Text** button, and then click **Tight**. The text in the first column under the *Mardi Gras Party* heading shifts and wraps around the clip art.

3. Drag the clip art up to approximately center it in the first paragraph under the *Mardi Gras Party* heading so that all the text in that paragraph wraps around the clip art. Refer to Figure 6–11.

4. In the second column, click the clip art of the flag. On the Ribbon, click the **Picture Tools Format** tab. In the Arrange group, click the **Wrap Text** button, and then click **Behind Text**. Deselect the picture. The text in the second column flows on top of the picture.

5. Click anywhere on the heading **Independence Day Parade**. The insertion point is placed in the paragraph on top of the picture; the picture does not become selected. You might be able to click directly on the flag, but sometimes when you send an image behind text, it is impossible to select it simply by clicking.

6. In the Editing group on the Home tab, click the **Select** button, and then click **Select Objects**. Click directly on the heading **Independence Day Parade**. This time, the picture is selected. When the Select Objects option is selected, you can select only objects on a page; you cannot select text.

7. Drag the selected picture so that the top of the image is just at the top of the *Independence Day Parade* heading. On the selected picture, drag the **bottom middle** and the **right sizing handles** until the picture is as wide and as tall as all the text under the Independence Day Parade heading. See **Figure 6–13**.

FIGURE 6–13
Clip art
behind text

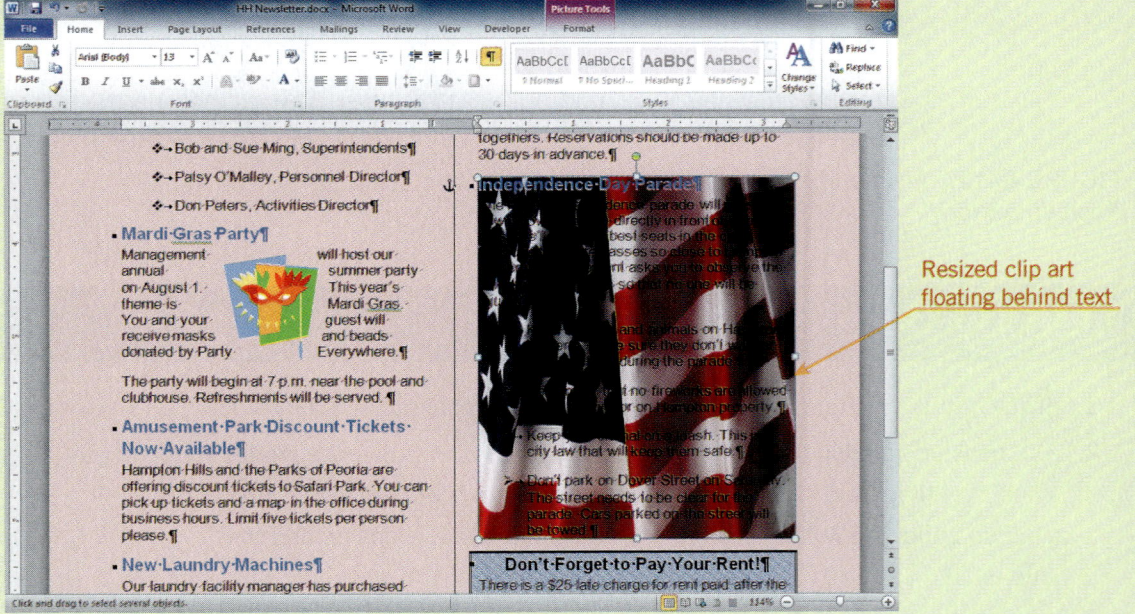

Resized clip art
floating behind text

8. In the Editing group, click the **Select** button, and then click **Select Objects**. Now you will be able to select text again.

9. Save the document and leave it open for the next Step-by-Step.

Recoloring Pictures

Sometimes you need to adjust the color of an image. You can change the brightness or contrast, or recolor an image all in one shade or with a washout (very light) style. To do this, click the contextual Format tab. In the Adjust group, click the Corrections button, and then click a button to adjust the settings. The Corrections gallery is shown in **Figure 6–14**. Also in the Adjust group, you can click the Color button, and then click a style to recolor the image all in one shade. See **Figure 6–15**.

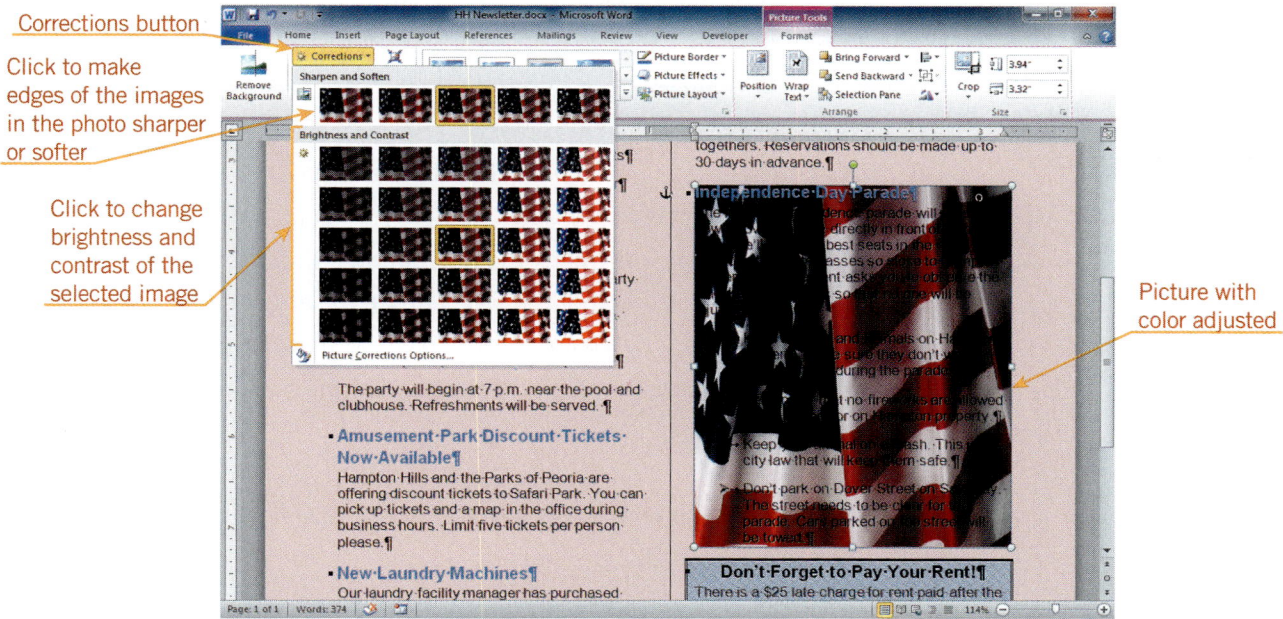

FIGURE 6–14   Corrections gallery

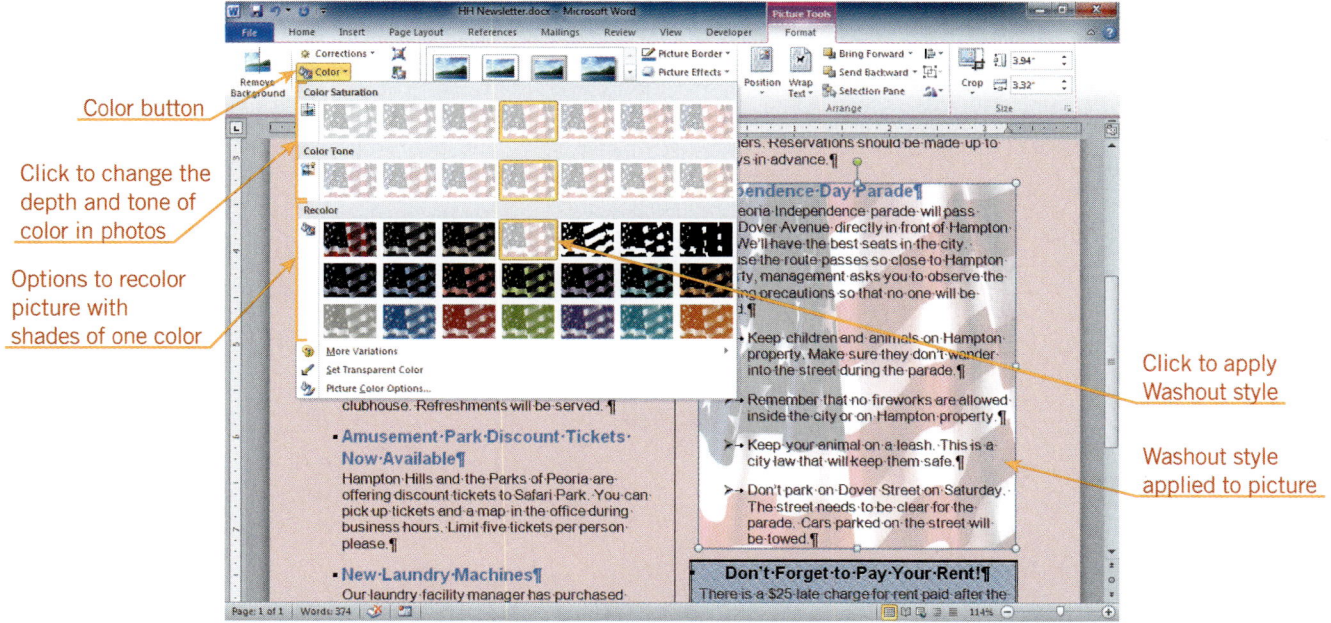

FIGURE 6–15   Color gallery

Step-by-Step 6.8

1. In the second column, select the picture of the flag, if necessary.

2. On the Ribbon, click the **Picture Tools Format** tab. In the Adjust group, click the **Corrections** button.

3. In the Sharpen and Soften section, point to the first style, and watch the Live Preview of the picture. Point to the last style in the Sharpen and Soften section, and watch the Live Preview again.

4. In the Brightness and Contrast section, point to the first style in the last row and watch the Live Preview of the picture. Point to the last style in the last row, and watch the Live Preview again. Press **Esc** to close the menu without selecting a command.

5. In the Adjust group, click the **Color** button. In the Color Saturation section, point to several of the styles to see the effect on the image. In the Color Tone section, point to several of the styles to see the effect.

6. In the Recolor section, point to several of the styles to see the effect on the picture.

7. In the first row under Recolor, click the **Washout** style (fourth style in the row). The picture is recolored in the Washout style, and the text is now readable on top of the image.

8. Save the document and leave it open. You will not use it in the next Step-by-Step, but you will use it later.

Inserting Pictures

In Word, pictures are graphic files stored on your computer. To insert a picture in a document, click the Insert tab, and then in the Illustrations group, click the Picture button to open the Insert Picture dialog box. See **Figure 6–16**. This dialog box is similar to the Open and the Save As dialog boxes. You can navigate to the folder that contains the picture you want to insert, click the file, and then click Insert. The picture is inserted as an inline object at the location of the insertion point. You can then change the object to a floating object if you want, as well as resize and reposition it, in the same manner as clip art.

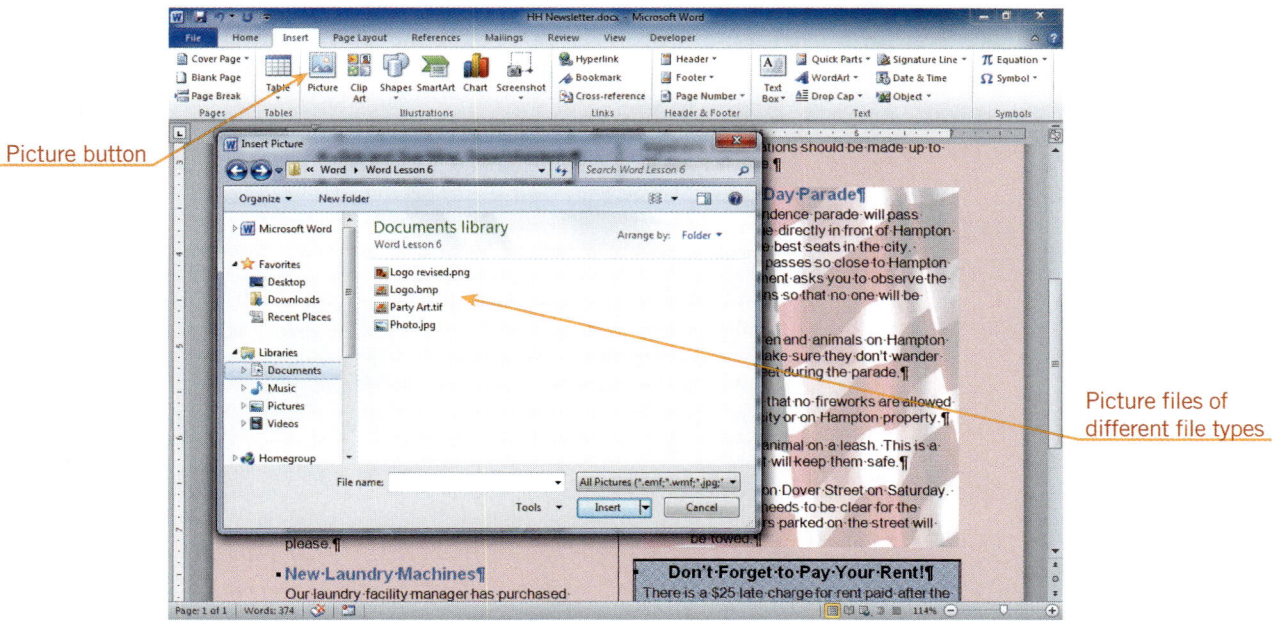

Picture button

Picture files of different file types

FIGURE 6–16 Insert Picture dialog box

Adding Shapes

Word provides tools for you to create your own graphic images. To access these tools, click the Insert tab, and then, in the Illustrations group, click the Shapes button to open a menu of choices. See **Figure 6–17**. **Table 6–2** summarizes the types of drawing tools available on the menu.

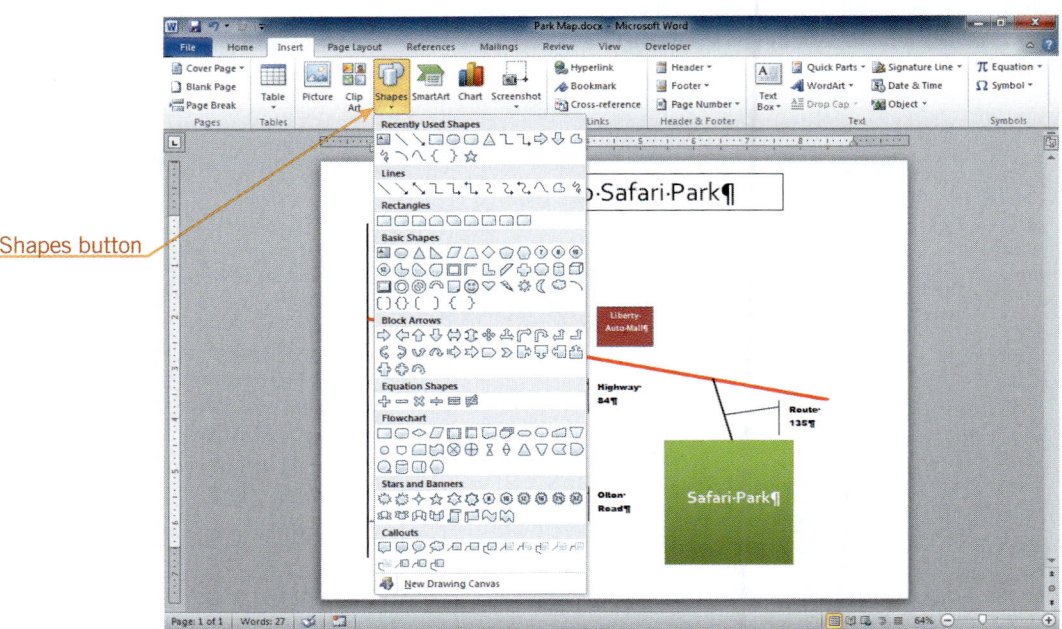

FIGURE 6–17   Shapes gallery

TABLE 6–2   Types of drawing tools

CATEGORY	DESCRIPTION
Lines	Draw straight or curved lines
Rectangles	Draw rectangles with different corner styles
Basic Shapes	Draw many basic shapes, including rectangles, ovals, triangles, and several more interesting shapes, such as a smiley face and a lightning bolt
Block Arrows	Draw various forms of block arrows
Equation Shapes	Draw shapes used in mathematical equations
Flowchart	Draw shapes used to create a flow chart
Stars and Banners	Draw star and banner shapes
Callouts	Draw boxes with lines that point to something to highlight or "call out" the item being pointed to

Drawing Shapes

To draw a shape, click the shape you want to draw on the menu. The pointer changes to the crosshairs pointer. Drag the pointer on the document to draw the shape. Drawn shapes are inserted as floating objects by default. As with clip art objects, you can cut, copy, and paste drawn shapes as well as move and resize them.

Step-by-Step 6.9

1. Create a new, blank Word document. Save it as **Park Map** followed by your initials. Study the map in **Figure 6–18**. You will be drawing a map similar to this one.

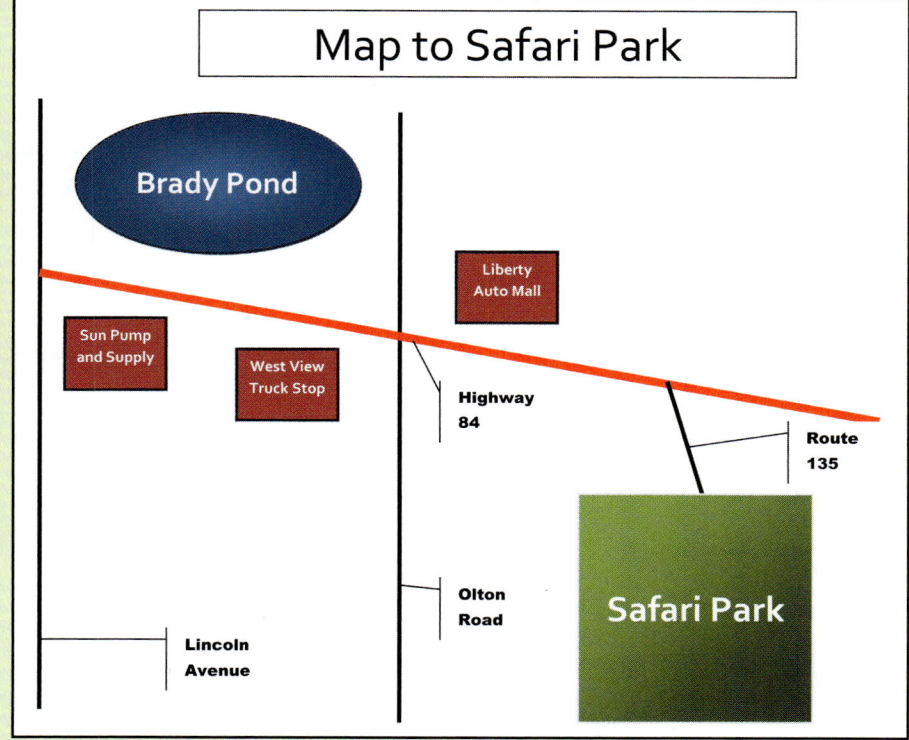

FIGURE 6–18
Map created with drawn shapes

TIP

To draw a square instead of a rectangle, a circle instead of an oval, or an equilateral triangle instead of an isosceles triangle, press and hold Shift while you drag to draw the shape.

2. If formatting marks are showing, in the Paragraph group, click the **Show/Hide ¶** button to hide them. If the ruler is not visible, at the top of the vertical scroll bar, click the **View Ruler** button to display the rulers. On the Ribbon, click the **Page Layout** tab. In the Page Setup group, click the **Orientation** button, and then click **Landscape**. On the Ribbon, click the **View** tab. In the Zoom group, click the **One Page** button. You're ready to draw the map now.

3. On the Ribbon, click the **Insert** tab. In the Illustrations group, click the **Shapes** button. The Shapes menu opens.

4. Under Basic Shapes on the menu, click the **Oval** button (second button in the top row under Basic Shapes). The mouse pointer changes to $+$.

5. Position the pointer on the blinking insertion point, press and hold the mouse button, and then drag to draw an oval approximately 3 inches wide and 1½ inches high. When the oval is approximately the same size as the pond shown in Figure 6–18, release the mouse button. The Drawing Tools Format tab is active on the Ribbon.

6. On the Ribbon, click the **Insert** tab. In the Illustrations group, click the **Shapes** button, and then under Lines, click the **Line** button (first button under Lines).

7. Position the pointer just above and about one-half inch to the left of the oval. Press and hold Shift, and then drag to draw a line down to the 6½-inch mark on the vertical ruler. Release the mouse button when your line is positioned similar to *Lincoln Avenue* in Figure 6–18.

8. Click the line you drew to select it. On the Ribbon, click the **Home** tab. In the Clipboard group, click the **Copy** button 📋, and then click the **Paste** button. A copy of the line appears in the document. Drag the line to position it to the right of the circle you drew, similar to *Olton Road* in Figure 6–18.

9. Use the **Line** button to create the road that is colored red on the map and the road labeled *Route 135*.

10. Use the **Rectangle** button under Rectangles on the Shapes menu (first shape under Rectangles) to draw the rectangle labeled *Sun Pump and Supply* in Figure 6–18. Copy the rectangle twice, and then place one copy in the position labeled *West View Truck Stop* on the map and the other copy in the position labeled *Liberty Auto Mall* on the map.

11. Click the **Rectangle** button again, press and hold **Shift**, and then draw the square labeled *Safari Park* on the map. Pressing Shift at the same time you drag creates a square.

12. Compare your document to the map shown in Figure 6–18. You have drawn the basic shapes for the map. Resize and reposition any shapes as needed to make your drawing match the map as closely as possible. You will add color and style to these shapes in the next Step-by-Step. (Ignore the labels that identify the street names.)

13. Save the document and leave it open for the next Step-by-Step.

Adding Color and Style to Drawings

Color adds life to your drawings. Word has tools that you can use to fill objects with color and change the color of lines. To change the color, select the object you want to fill or the line you want to change, and then click the Drawing Tools Format tab. This tab contains the same Arrange group of commands as on the Picture Tools Format tab as well as additional commands for working with a drawn object.

To fill the object with a different color, use the Shape Fill button on the Drawing Tools Format tab (see **Figure 6–19**). To change the line or outline color of a drawing, use the Shape Outline button on the Drawing Tools Format tab (see **Figure 6–20**). These buttons are similar to the Font Color button. You can click the arrow next to either of these buttons to open the color palette, or you can click the button itself to quickly apply the color that appears in the bar at the bottom of the button.

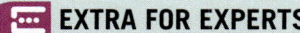

EXTRA FOR EXPERTS

Additional commands for modifying lines or shape outlines and the shape fill are available using the commands at the bottom of the menu that opens when you click the arrow next to either the Shape Outline or Shape Fill button.

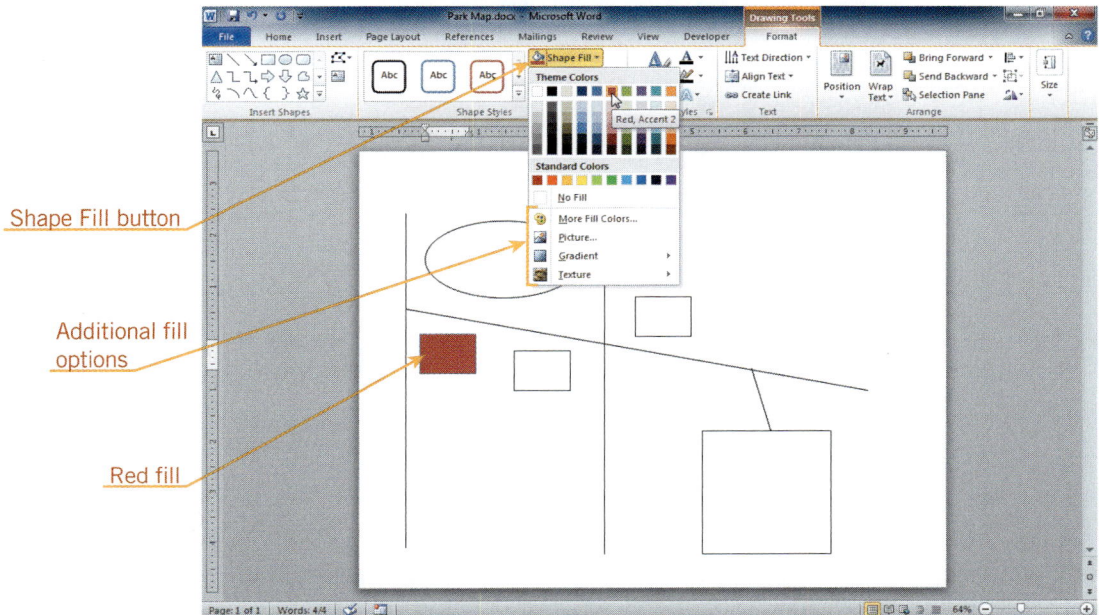

Shape Fill button

Additional fill options

Red fill

FIGURE 6–19   Applying a fill color to a shape

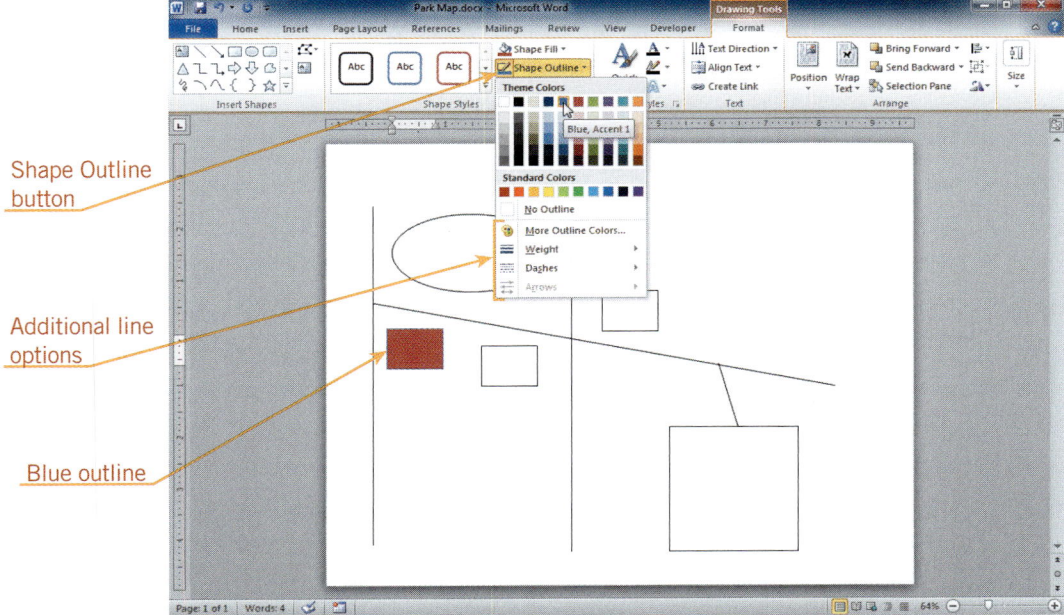

Shape Outline button

Additional line options

Blue outline

FIGURE 6–20   Applying a line or outline color to a shape

You can also use the Shape Styles gallery to add color to your drawings. To open the Shape Styles gallery, in the Shape Styles group, click the More button. See **Figure 6–21**. The gallery provides various options for quickly formatting your shapes with styles and colors associated with the current theme.

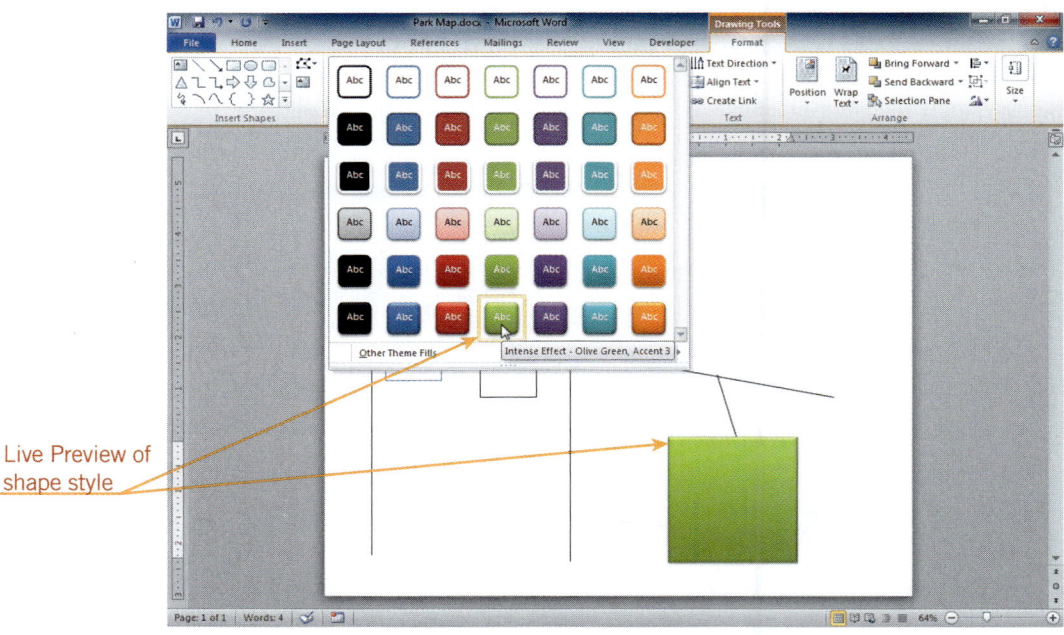

Live Preview of shape style

FIGURE 6–21   Shape Styles gallery

Finally, you can also change the line weight, or thickness, of lines or shape outlines in your drawing. To do this, select the object. In the Shape Styles group, click the Shape Outline button, and then point to Weight on the menu. A submenu of line thicknesses measured in points opens. See **Figure 6–22**. Click the line weight you want to use.

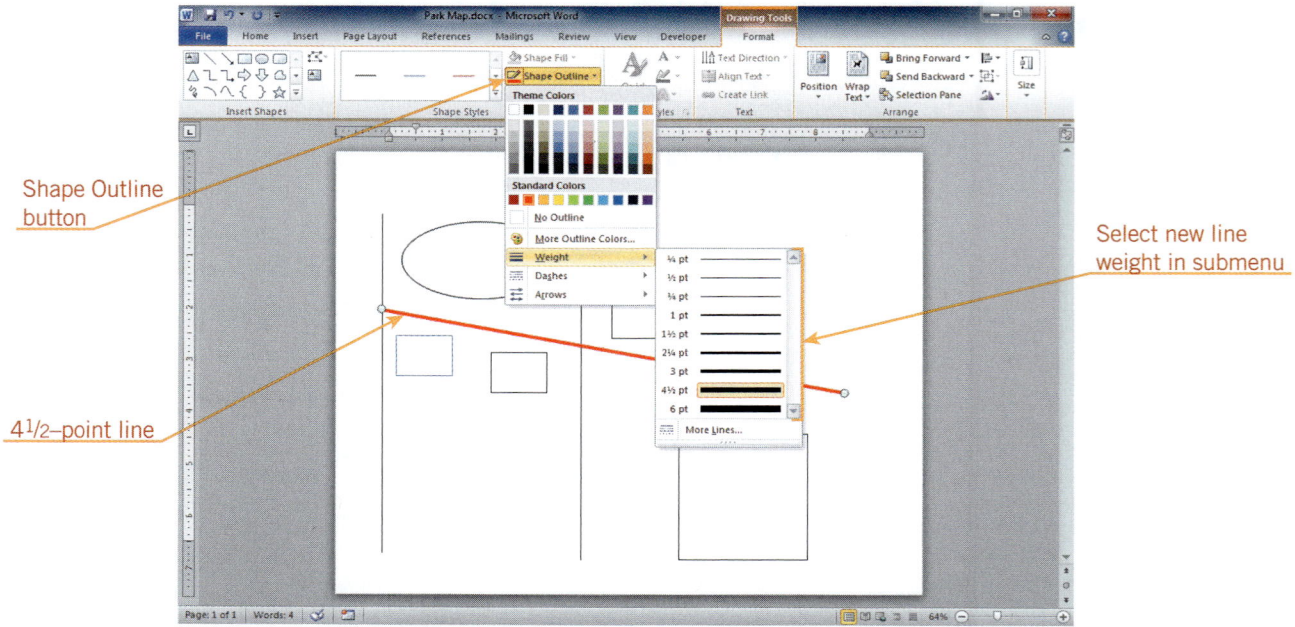

Shape Outline button

Select new line weight in submenu

$4\frac{1}{2}$–point line

FIGURE 6–22   Changing a shape's line thickness

Step-by-Step 6.10

1. Click the **line** in the drawing that slants diagonally from the left edge of the page to the lower-right to select it.

2. If necessary, on the Ribbon, click the **Drawing Tools Format** tab. In the Shape Styles group, click the **arrow** next to the Shape Outline button. In the palette under Standard Colors, click the **Red** box. The selected line is recolored red.

3. Click one of the three rectangles in the drawing. In the Shape Styles group, click the **arrow** next to the Shape Fill button. In the palette under Theme Colors, click the **Red, Accent 2** box (first row, sixth column). The selected rectangle is filled with a dark red color.

4. With the same rectangle selected, in the Shape Styles group, click the **arrow** next to the Shape Outline button. In the palette under Theme Colors, click the **Blue, Accent 1** box (first row, fifth column). The outline color is changed to blue.

5. With the same rectangle selected, on the Ribbon, click the **Home** tab. In the Clipboard group, double-click the **Format Painter** button. Click the two other rectangles in the drawing. Press **Esc** to deselect the Format Painter button. All three rectangles are formatted the same way.

6. Select the oval in the drawing. Click the **Drawing Tools Format** tab. In the Shape Styles group, click the **More** button. The gallery of Shape Styles opens. Below the gallery, point to **Other Theme Fills**, and then click **Style 11** box (the third style in the last row). The oval is formatted with the selected style.

7. Select the square in the drawing. In the Shape Styles group, click the **More** button, and then click the **Moderate Effect – Olive Green, Accent 3** style (second to last row, fourth column). The square is formatted with the selected style. Notice that this style includes a small shadow below the shape.

8. On the **Format** tab, in the Shape Styles group, click the **Shape Effects** button. Point to **Shadow**, and then under No Shadow, click the **No Shadow** style. The shadow effect is removed from the shape.

9. Click the **red diagonal line** in the drawing. In the Shape Styles group, click the **arrow** next to the Shape Outline button, point to **Weight**, and then click **4½ pt**. The weight of the red line is now 4½ points.

10. Click one of the other lines in the drawing, press and hold **Shift**, and then click the other two lines to select all three of them. Change the weight of the selected lines to **2¼ points**.

11. Select all three maroon rectangles, and then change the weight of the outline to **1½ points**.

12. Save the document and leave it open for the next Step-by-Step.

Adding Text to Your Drawings

Often your drawings will require labels. Word provides several ways to add text to a drawing. The easiest way is to click an object, and then start typing. You can format your text as usual.

Another way to add text to your drawing is to insert text boxes. A ***text box*** is a shape specifically designed to hold text. To add a text box, click the Insert tab, and then, in the Illustrations group, click the Shapes button. Click the Text Box button in the Basic Shapes section of the menu. Or, on the Insert tab, in the Text group, click the Text Box button, and then click Draw Text Box. The pointer changes to the cross-hair pointer. Position the pointer where you want the text box to appear, and then click and drag to create a text box. An insertion point appears inside the text box so you can type the text you want. Text within a text box can be formatted in the same way you format ordinary text in a document.

A text box can be treated like any other object. You can format, resize, or change the position of a text box using the commands on the Text Box Tools Format tab that appears when you select the text box.

📰 **EXTRA FOR EXPERTS**

Text copied from the document and set off in a text box is called a **pull quote**. Text that does not appear in a document but adds extra information for the reader and is set off in a text box is called a **sidebar**.

TIP

To insert formatted text boxes, click the Text Box button on the Insert tab, and then click one of the text box styles in the gallery. The formatted text box appears as a floating object in the position indicated by the text box style in the gallery.

Step-by-Step 6.11

1. Click the oval, and then type **Brady Pond**.

2. Click the dotted line border of the shape so that the border changes to a solid line. Click the **Home** tab on the Ribbon. Format the text as bold, white, 24-point Corbel. The default is for the text to be centered in the shape. You can check this.

3. Click the **Drawing Tools Format** tab, and then in the Text group, click the **Align Text** button. Notice on the menu that Middle is selected.

4. Add the following text to the three maroon rectangles, using Figure 6–18 as a guide: **Sun Pump and Supply**, **West View Truck Stop**, and **Liberty Auto Mall**. Format the text in each text box as bold, white, 12-point Corbel, and then center it horizontally and vertically in the text boxes.

WARNING

You cannot use the Format Painter to copy the format of the text because the Painter copies the format of the shape.

5. Add the text **Safari Park** to the large square. Change the style to **No Spacing**. Format the text as bold, white, 28-point Corbel, and then center it horizontally and vertically in the text box.

6. On the Ribbon, click the **Insert** tab. In the Illustrations group, click the **Shapes** button. Under Basic Shapes, click the **Text Box** button (first row, first column under Basic Shapes). In the document, click at the top, above the drawing. A square text box appears with the insertion point inside it.

7. Type **Map to Safari Park**.

8. Drag the **right, middle sizing handle** to the right until the text box is approximately six inches wide. Format the text as 36-point Corbel, and then center it in the text box.

9. Drag the **bottom, middle sizing handle** of the text box up to resize the text box so it is approximately one-half inch high.

10. Position the pointer on the edge of the text box so that it changes to ⬚, and then drag the text box to center it between the left and right margins.

11. On the Ribbon, click the **Insert** tab, if necessary. In the Text group, click the **Text Box** button. The Text Box gallery opens. At the bottom of the gallery, click **Draw Text Box**. Click in the document below the map, and then, in the text box that appears, type your name.

12. If necessary, resize the text box so that your name fits on one line. Reposition the text box so it appears in the lower-left corner of the map.

13. Save the document and leave it open for the next Step-by-Step.

> **EXTRA FOR EXPERTS**
>
> To quickly create a text box from existing text, select the text, click the Text Box button in the Text group on the Insert tab, and then click Draw Text Box. The selected text is removed from the document and placed inside the text box.

Adding Callouts to Your Drawings

A *callout* is a special type of label in a drawing that consists of a text box with an attached line to point to a detail in the drawing. Many of the figures in this book have callouts identifying items on the screen. To add a callout, click one of the callout buttons on the Shapes menu, and then type the callout text in the callout shape.

> ▶ **VOCABULARY**
> callout

Step-by-Step 6.12

1. On the Ribbon, click the **Insert** tab. In the Illustrations group, click the **Shapes** button. Under Callouts, click the **Line Callout 1 (Accent Bar)** button (first row under Callouts, fifth button from the right).

2. To create a label for Highway 84, click to the right of the center line below the red diagonal line, as shown on the map in Figure 6–18. A callout appears on the map, with the insertion point inside the text box.

> **EXTRA FOR EXPERTS**
>
> To add an arrow to the end of a callout line (or any other drawn line), click the Format tab. In the Shape Styles group, click the Shape Outline button, point to Arrows, and then click the style of arrow you want to add.

3. Type **Highway 84**. Format the text as **12-point Arial Black**, change the font color to **Black**, **Text 1**, and then change the shape fill to **No Fill**. (Make sure you format the text.)

4. Repeat Steps 2 and 3 to insert the callouts for **Lincoln Avenue**, **Olton Road**, and **Route 135** as shown on the map.

5. Compare your map to Figure 6–18. Make adjustments as needed.

6. Save, print, and close the document.

Creating Diagrams and Charts with SmartArt

Diagrams and **charts** are visual representations of data. They organize information in illustrations so readers can better understand relationships among data. In Word, you can insert diagrams and charts quickly using predesigned drawings called **SmartArt**. You can create many types of diagrams using SmartArt, including List, Process, Cycle, Hierarchy, Relationship, Matrix, Pyramid, and Picture. Organization Charts, a common chart in business, are hierarchical charts.

To create a SmartArt graphic, click the Insert tab, and then, in the Illustrations group, click the SmartArt button. The Choose a SmartArt Graphic dialog box opens, as shown in **Figure 6–23**. You can click a category in the list on the left to narrow the available choices in the middle pane in the dialog box. To insert a SmartArt graphic, click the one you want in the pane in the middle of the dialog box, and then click OK. The graphic appears in the document with a border around it, and two SmartArt Tools tabs—Design and Format—appear on the Ribbon. You can use the commands on these tabs to add elements (shapes) and text to a diagram and to change its size and color.

EXTRA FOR EXPERTS

To change a SmartArt graphic to another shape, click the More button in the Layouts group on the SmartArtTools Design tab, and then click More Layouts to open the Choose a SmartArt Graphic dialog box again.

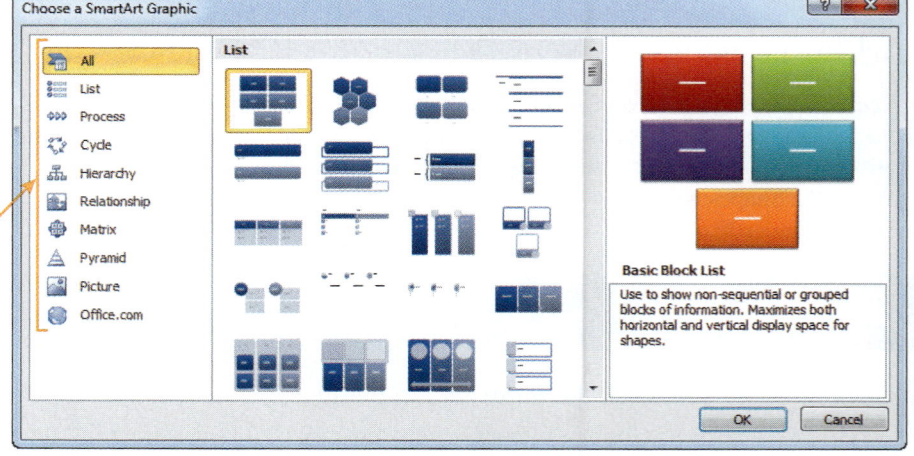

FIGURE 6–23　Choose a SmartArt Graphic dialog box

Step-by-Step 6.13

1. If the **HH Newsletter.docx** document that you worked on earlier in this lesson is not open, open it now. If formatting marks are not visible, display them. Press **Ctrl+Home** to jump to the top of the document.

2. In the first column in the newsletter, click in the blank paragraph above the bulleted list. On the Ribbon, click the **Insert** tab. In the Illustrations group, click the **SmartArt** button. The Choose a SmartArt Graphic dialog box opens.

3. In the category list on the left side of the dialog box, click **Hierarchy**. The middle section of the dialog box changes to display only charts that show hierarchical relationships. In the middle section of the dialog box, click the **Organization Chart** style (first row, first column). Click **OK**. An organization chart appears in the document as an inline object at the insertion point.

4. Save the document and leave it open for the next Step-by-Step.

Add Text to a SmartArt Graphic

When you create a SmartArt graphic, placeholder text appears in each shape. To insert text in a SmartArt graphic, click in each box in the graphic and start typing. The text you type replaces the placeholder text.

Step-by-Step 6.14

1. Click in the top box in the organization chart. The placeholder text disappears and the insertion point blinks in the box.

2. Type **Jose Franco**. The placeholder text is replaced with your text. Press **Enter**. Type **Office Manager**. Notice that the font size adjusted automatically as you typed so that all the text fits in the box.

3. Replace the text in the three boxes in the third row in the chart with the names and titles in the last three bullets in the bulleted list under the chart. Make sure you press Enter before typing the job titles.

4. Select the four names and titles in the bulleted list below the chart, and then delete them. You will have one extra box in the SmartArt graphic.

5. Save the document and leave it open for the next Step-by-Step.

TIP

You can click the Text pane control on the left side of the SmartArt graphic's border or the Text Pane button in the Create Graphic group to open the Text pane, which displays the text of the SmartArt graphic as a bulleted list. You can add items to the list in the Text pane as you would to a bulleted list in a document.

Modify a SmartArt Graphic

You can resize SmartArt graphics as you would resize any object. Instead of squares or circles, the sizing handles on a SmartArt graphic are three dots at each corner and in the middle of the sides of the selection rectangle. You can change a SmartArt graphic from an inline object to a floating object. You can also add an outline and a colored fill to the entire graphic.

In addition, you can change the look and structure of a SmartArt graphic by using some of the many commands available on the SmartArt Tools contextual tabs. On the Design tab (see **Figure 6–24**), you can add, move, or remove shapes to and from the diagram by using commands in the Create Graphic group. To change the layout of the graphic, click the More button in the Layouts group to display all the available layouts in the Layouts gallery. You can change the color scheme of the diagram by clicking the Change Colors button in the SmartArt Styles group. Or, you can change the style of the SmartArt, including choosing a 3-D look, by clicking the More button in the SmartArt Styles group to display the SmartArt Styles gallery.

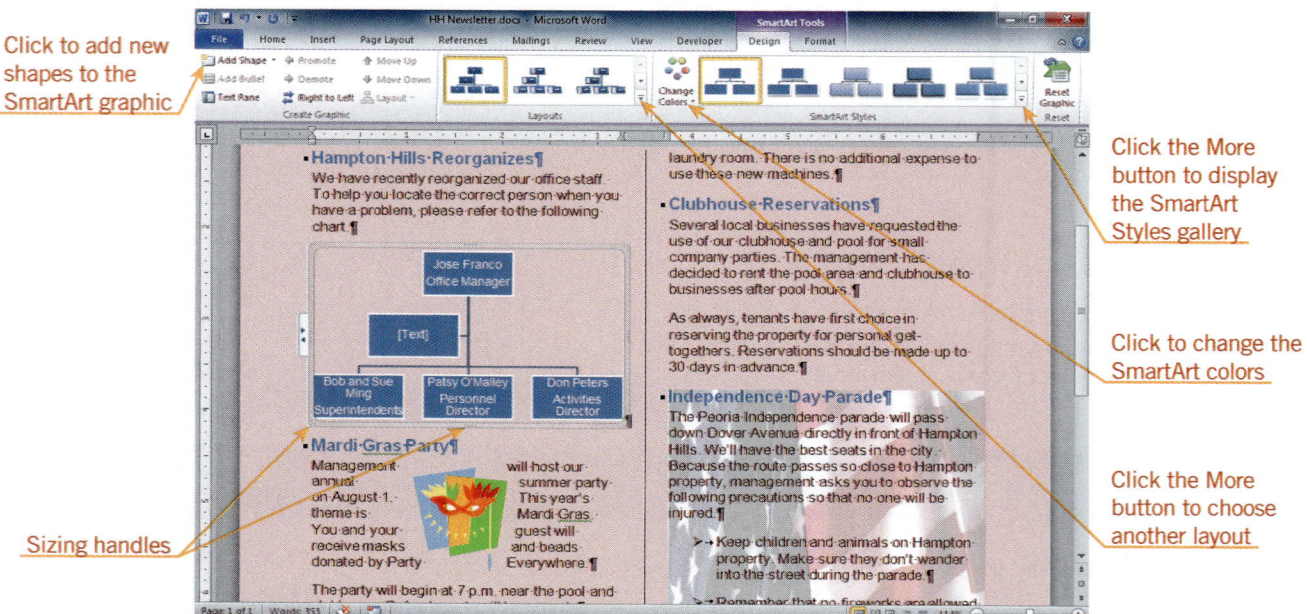

Click to add new shapes to the SmartArt graphic

Click the More button to display the SmartArt Styles gallery

Click to change the SmartArt colors

Sizing handles

Click the More button to choose another layout

FIGURE 6–24   Modifying SmartArt

Step-by-Step 6.15

1. In the organization chart, click the edge of the box in the second row. If a dashed line appears around the edge of the box, click the edge again to change it to a solid line. Press **Delete**. The box is deleted and the chart now contains only two rows of boxes.

2. Click the **Patsy O'Malley** box. On the Ribbon, click the **SmartArt Tools Design** tab, if necessary. In the Create Graphic group, click the **arrow** next to the Add Shape button.

3. On the menu, click **Add Shape Below**. A box appears in the chart below the Patsy O'Malley box. Type **Rosa Mendez**, press **Enter**, and then type **Assistant**.

4. On the Design tab, in the Layouts group, click the **More** button. Click the **Horizontal Organization Chart** style (third row, second column). The chart changes to the horizontal style.

5. In the SmartArt Styles group, click the **Change Colors** button. Under Accent 2 in the gallery, click **Colored Fill – Accent 2** (second style from the left). The chart colors change to dark red.

6. In the SmartArt Styles group, click the **More** button. Under Best Match for Document in the gallery, click **Intense Effect** (last style in the row under Best Match for Document). The chart style changes so that boxes have some shading.

7. Save the document and leave it open for the next Step-by-Step.

Creating WordArt

WordArt is stylized text that is formatted and placed in a text box. To create WordArt, click the Insert tab, and then, in the Text group, click the WordArt button. A gallery of WordArt styles opens, as shown in **Figure 6–25**. Click one, and a text box appears. if you select text before you click the WordArt button, the text you selected appears in the text box; otherwise *Your text here* appears in the text box, and you can type the text you want to use as the WordArt text.

▶ **VOCABULARY**
WordArt

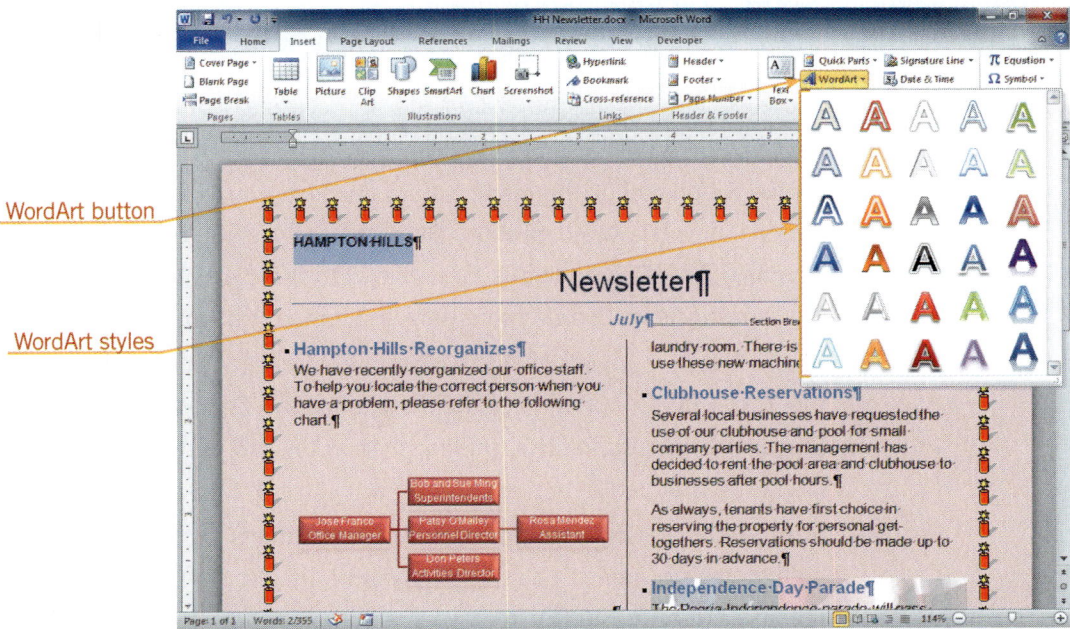

FIGURE 6–25   Inserting WordArt

You can change the WordArt style, color, and outline color by clicking the appropriate buttons in the WordArt Styles group on the Drawing Tools Format tab. See **Figure 6–26**. In addition, you can click the Text Effects button in the same group, and then apply shadow, reflection, glow, bevel, and 3-D effects. You can also use the Text Effects button to change the shape of the WordArt by selecting an option on the Transform submenu. As with any other object, you can drag the sizing handles or use the boxes in the Size group on the Format tab to resize WordArt.

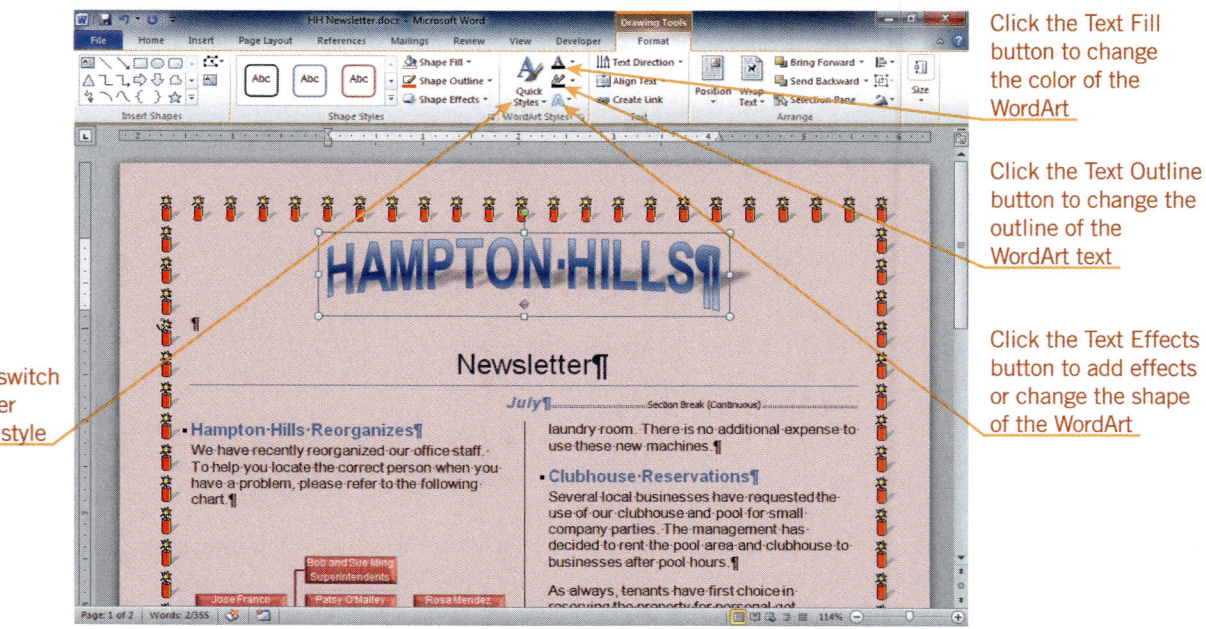

Click to switch to another WordArt style

Click the Text Fill button to change the color of the WordArt

Click the Text Outline button to change the outline of the WordArt text

Click the Text Effects button to add effects or change the shape of the WordArt

FIGURE 6–26   Modifying WordArt

Step-by-Step 6.16

1. Scroll to the top of the document, if necessary. Select **HAMPTON HILLS**. Do not select the paragraph mark.

2. On the Ribbon, click the **Insert** tab. In the Text group, click the **WordArt** button. Click the **Gradient Fill – Blue, Accent 1** style (third row, fourth column). The selected text is formatted with the style you selected, and the Drawing Tools Format tab is selected on the Ribbon.

3. In the WordArt Styles group on the Drawing Tools Format tab, click the **Text Effects** button. Point to **Shadow**. Click the **Perspective Diagonal Upper Right** style (middle style in the row under Perspective). A shadow is added to the text.

4. In the WordArt Styles group, click the **Text Effects** button. At the bottom of the menu, point to **Transform**. In the Warp section, click the **Can Up** style (fourth row under Warp, third column). The WordArt changes shape.

5. In the Arrange group, click the **Wrap Text** button. Click **Top and Bottom**. The text box is changed to a floating object and the newsletter text moves below the WordArt.

6. In the Arrange group, click the **Align** button, and then click **Align Center**. The WordArt title is centered between the left and right margins. See Figure 6–26.

7. On the Ribbon, click the **View** tab. In the Zoom group, click the **One Page** button. You need to adjust the SmartArt graphic so that the newsletter still fits on one page.

8. On the SmartArt graphic, drag the **bottom middle sizing handle** up a little. The scroll box in the vertical scroll bar disappears and you see a blank paragraph at the bottom of the first column. The newsletter fits on one page again. Compare your document to **Figure 6–27**, and make any adjustments necessary.

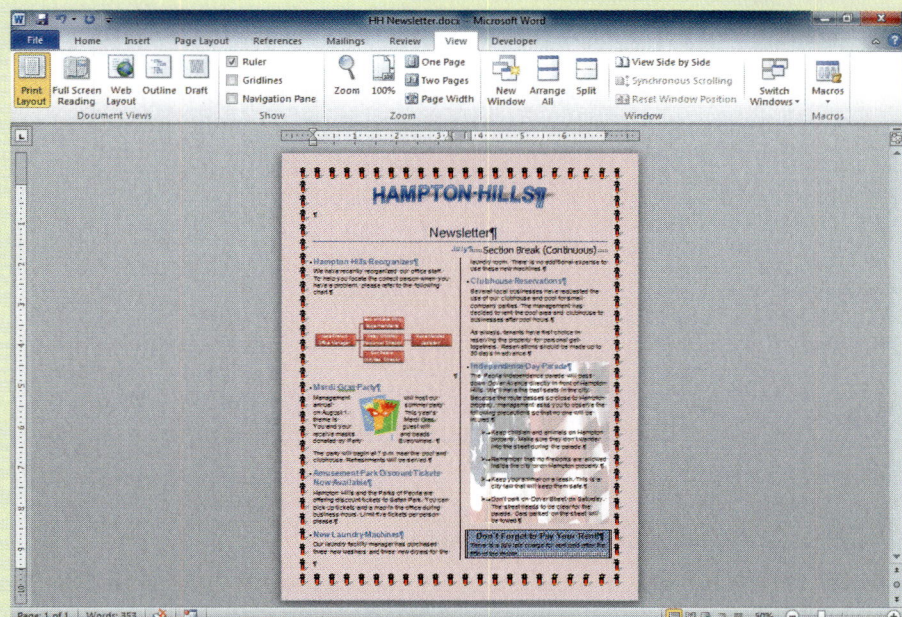

FIGURE 6–27
Completed newsletter document

9. Press **Ctrl+End** to jump to the blank paragraph at the end of the document, and then type your name.

10. Hide formatting marks and the ruler. Save, print, and close the document.

SUMMARY

In this lesson, you learned:

- Graphics add interest to documents.

- You can format all or part of a document in multiple columns.

- You can add borders and shading to selected text to emphasize it. You can also add a page border and shading to the entire page.

- An object is anything that can be manipulated as a whole. An inline object is inserted as if it were a character in a line of text. A floating object acts as if it is sitting in a separate layer on the page.

- You can insert clip art and resize and recolor it to fit your document. You can also insert and resize pictures in a document.

- You can draw shapes in a document. Drawn objects can be resized, moved, and colored.

- You can add text to drawn shapes or create a text box shape. Text boxes can be formatted, resized, or moved just like other drawn objects.

- Callouts are special text boxes that have a line attached to them to point to specific items in a document.

- Charts and diagrams organize your data in a manner that illustrates relationships among data. You can use SmartArt to add charts and diagrams to documents. You can change the structure and look of SmartArt.

- You can insert WordArt to create stylized text objects. As with other objects, you can resize, reposition, and format WordArt.

 ## VOCABULARY REVIEW

Define the following terms:

aspect ratio	graphic	selection rectangle
callout	inline object	sidebar
chart	keyword	sizing handle
clip art	object	SmartArt
crop	pull quote	text box
diagram	rotation handle	WordArt
floating object		

 ## REVIEW QUESTIONS

FILL IN THE BLANK

Complete the following sentences by writing the correct word or words in the blanks provided.

1. Choose the _____ tab on the Ribbon to add clip art, pictures, shapes, and WordArt to a document.

2. To automatically balance columns, insert a(n) _____ section break.

3. When text wraps around an object, the object is called a(n) _____ object.

4. Words that you use to search for clip art are _____.

5. The _____ is the relationship of an object's height to its width.

TRUE / FALSE

Circle T if the statement is true or F if the statement is false.

T   F   1.   You must carefully choose the type of SmartArt to create because you cannot change it to another type later.

T   F   2.   You can add a border to paragraphs, but you cannot add a border to a page.

T   F   3.   Borders can be placed on all four sides of a selected paragraph.

T   F   4.   Objects that you insert in a document can be placed only in a line of text in a paragraph.

T   F   5.   To find an appropriate piece of clip art, you must scroll through an alphabetized list of all the available clip art.

MATCHING

Match the correct term in Column 2 to its description in Column 1.

Column 1

_____ 1. Pictures that help illustrate the document and make the page more attractive

_____ 2. Anything that can be manipulated as a whole

_____ 3. An object that is inserted as if it were a character in the line of text

_____ 4. Squares and circles on a selected object that you drag to resize the object

_____ 5. Visual representation of data

Column 2

A. Diagram or chart

B. Object

C. Graphics

D. Inline object

E. Sizing handles

 # PROJECTS

If you have a SAM 2010 user profile, your instructor may have assigned an autogradable version of the indicated project. If so, log into the SAM 2010 Web site at *www.cengage.com/sam2010* to download the instruction and start files.

PROJECT 6–1

1. Open the **Shelter.docx** document from the drive and folder where your Data Files are stored. Save the document as **Shelter News** followed by your initials.

2. Format the text in the document below the phone number as two columns. Do not add a line between the two columns.

3. Center the headings in the columns.

4. Balance the columns.

5. Near the bottom of the first column, apply a 2¼-point border at the top and the bottom of the paragraph that contains *Thank you for your help!*. Change the color of the border to Tan, Accent 2, Darker 50%. Add shading using the Tan, Accent 2, Lighter 40% theme color and add a 10% pattern, changing the color of the pattern to White, Background 1, Darker 15%.

6. At the top of the second column, insert clip art of a person and a dog. Try using the keyword **pet** or **dog**. Use a photograph or an illustration.

7. Change the clip art to a floating object so that the text wraps tightly around it, and then resize it to approximately one-inch by one-inch. (If it is impossible to resize the clip art you chose to this size, click the Crop button in the Size group on the Format tab, and then drag one of the sizing handles on the side of the clip to crop off a portion of the clip so that the final size is close to one-inch by one-inch.) Position the clip art in the middle of the paragraph at the top of the second column.

8. At the top of the newsletter, change *Plains Animal Shelter* to WordArt. Use the Fill – Gold, Text 2, Outline – Background 2 style (the first style in the first row). Add a Tan, 8 pt glow, Accent color 2 glow text effect, and then use the Transform effect to change the WordArt to the Square effect in the Warp section.

9. Change the WordArt to a floating object and wrap the text around the top and bottom of the object.

10. View the document in One Page view. If necessary, adjust the clip art so that the entire newsletter fits on one page.

11. Insert a text box near the lower-left corner of the document. Type your name, and then resize the text box so your name fits on one line. Fill the text box with Yellow.

12. Save, print, and close the document.

SAM PROJECT 6–2

1. Create the poster shown in **Figure 6–28** using what you have learned in this lesson. The theme used is Clarity. Refer to the instructions shown in the figure.

2. Insert a text box near the upper-right corner of the document. Type your name in the text box. Change the border of the text box so it is 4½ points wide.

3. Save the document as **Garage Sale** followed by your initials.

4. Print and close the document.

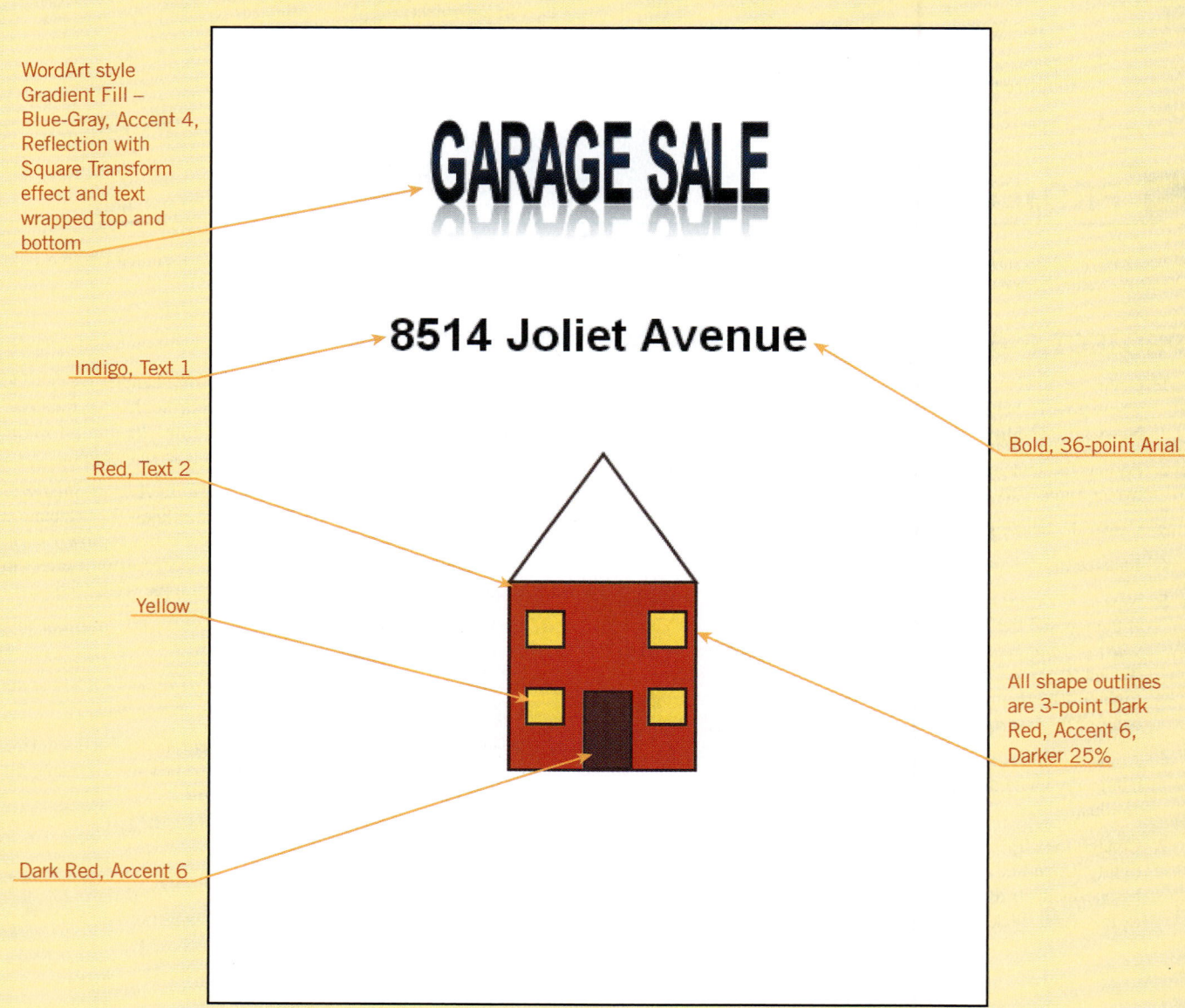

WordArt style Gradient Fill – Blue-Gray, Accent 4, Reflection with Square Transform effect and text wrapped top and bottom

Indigo, Text 1

Red, Text 2

Yellow

Dark Red, Accent 6

Bold, 36-point Arial

All shape outlines are 3-point Dark Red, Accent 6, Darker 25%

FIGURE 6–28

PROJECT 6–3

1. Open the **Invitation2.docx** document from the drive and folder where your Data Files are stored. Save the document as **Holiday Invitation** followed by your initials.

2. Insert clip art with a holiday theme above the text. Resize and align the graphic to fit the document.

3. Change the text to a color, font, and size of your choice. The entire document should fit on one page.

4. Apply an appropriate page border and page color.

5. Insert a text box near the lower-right corner of the document. Type your name, and then resize the text box so that your name fits on one line. Format the text as bold, 12-point Calibri. Fill the text box with red.

6. Save, print, and close the document.

PROJECT 6–4

1. Open the **Memo2.docx** Data File from the drive and folder where your Data Files are stored. Save the document as **Org Chart Memo** followed by your initials.

2. At the top of the document, change the color of *New World Marketing, Inc.* to Blue, Accent 2, Darker 25%. Change the color of the heading *MEMORANDUM* to the same color.

3. Add a border below *MEMORANDUM*. Choose a line style that has one thick line and one thin line on either side of the thick line. Apply the same color to the line as you used for *MEMORANDUM*.

4. At the top of the document, insert clip art. Use the keyword **world** to find an image of the earth.

5. Change the object to a floating object using the Behind Text wrapping option, and then resize it so it is approximately the same height as the header information at the top of the document (from the company name through the Web site address).

6. Change the object so that it appears behind the text. Recolor it or change the brightness or contrast so that the text is visible on top of the object.

7. At the end of the document, insert an organization chart using a SmartArt graphic.

8. Modify the organization chart and insert text so it matches the chart shown in Figure 6–29. The color is the Primary Theme Color Dark 2 Fill; the SmartArt style is Intense Effect under Best Match for Document; and the Layout style is Half Circle Organization Chart.

9. Add a callout in any style pointing to Rosa Molina's box. Type **Rosa was promoted to District Manager last week** as the text of the callout.

10. In the *From* line in the memo header, replace *Vera Thomas* with your name.

11. Save, print, and close your document.

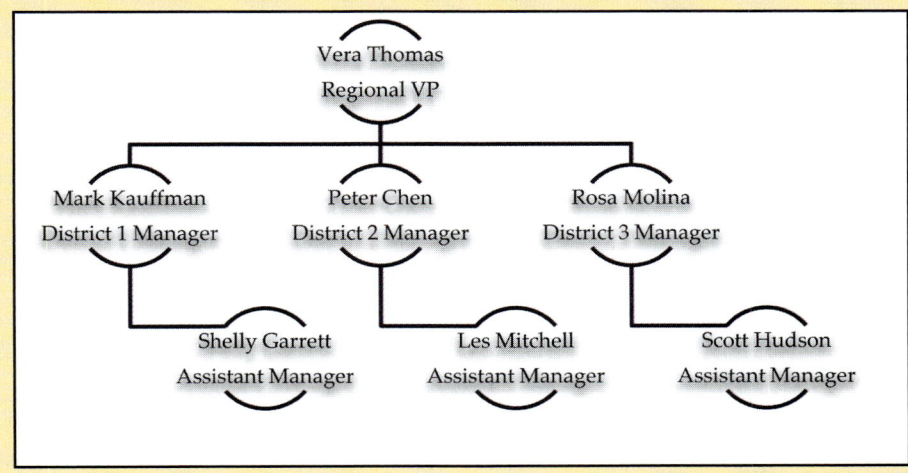

FIGURE 6–29

CRITICAL THINKING

ACTIVITY 6–1

You are having a birthday party for your friend. Create an invitation using clip art, borders, and shading. Use the drawing tools to create a map from your school to your house.

ACTIVITY 6–2

With a classmate, create a newsletter about your class. Decide on a name for the newsletter, what information should be included, a page design, and attractive clip art. Have the class vote for their favorite.

ACTIVITY 6–3

Use the Help system to find out how to insert a chart in a document. Create a new document, and insert a pie chart. Close the Excel window that opens, and then change the style to one that uses shades of all one color.

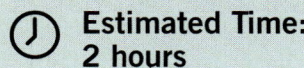

**Estimated Time:
2 hours**

LESSON 7

Working with Documents

■ OBJECTIVES

Upon completion of this lesson, you should be able to:

- Insert page breaks, headers, footers, and page numbers.
- Understand content controls.
- Modify document properties.
- Insert predesigned cover pages.
- Create a section with formatting that differs from other sections.
- Use the Research tool.
- Insert, modify, and format tables.
- Sort text.

■ VOCABULARY

cell

content control

footer

gridline

header

orphan

page break

property

section

sort

table

widow

As you work with longer documents, you can make the content clearer by creating pages and inserting information at the tops and bottoms of pages to identify the content, author, date, page number, and so on. Word also provides tools that help you insert content and conduct research online. You can also create tables of information.

Inserting Page Breaks

In a multipage document, Word determines the place to end one page and begin the next. The place where one page ends and another begins is called a ***page break***. Word automatically inserts page breaks where they are needed, but you can insert a page break manually. For example, you might want to do this to prevent an automatic page break from separating a heading from the text that follows, or you might want to start a new section of a document on a new page.

To insert a page break manually, click the Insert tab on the Ribbon, and then in the Pages group, click the Page Break button. You can also execute this command on the Page Layout tab—in the Page Setup group, click the Breaks button, and then click Page. Finally, you can also use the keyboard to insert a page break by pressing Ctrl+Enter. If formatting marks are displayed, a manual page break appears immediately after the last line of text on the page. It is indicated by a dotted line with the words *Page Break* in the middle of the line, as shown in **Figure 7–1**. To delete manual page breaks, select the page break line, and then press Backspace or Delete.

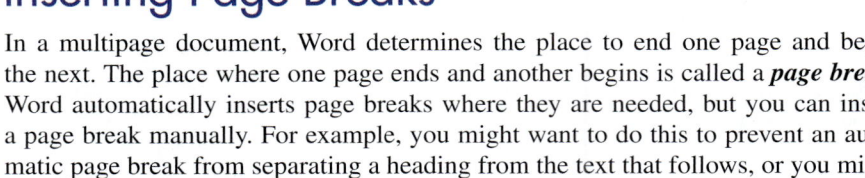
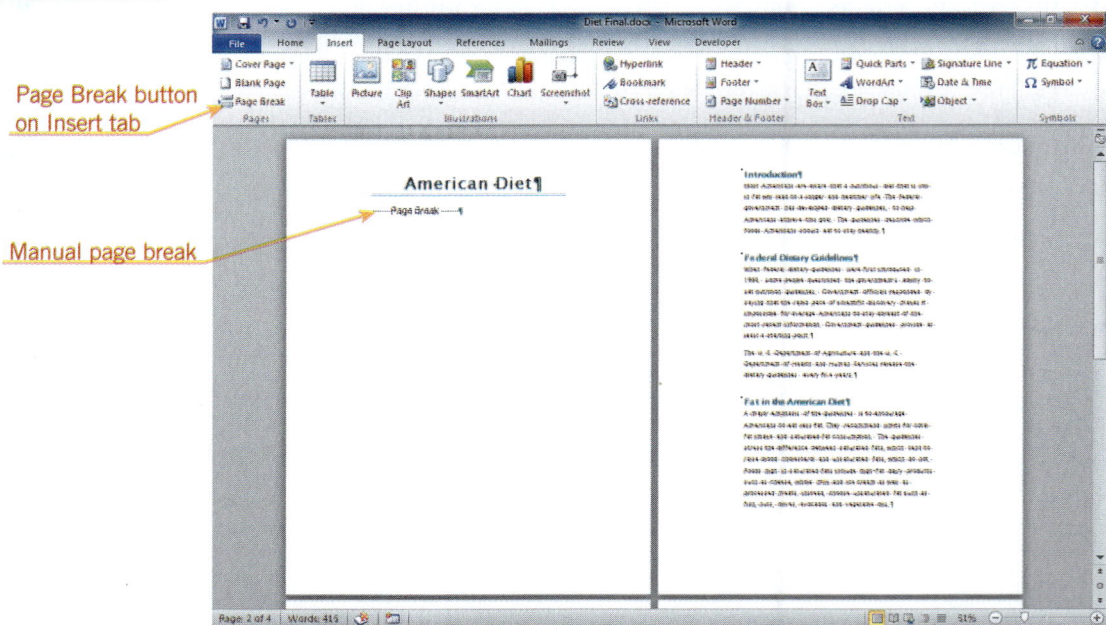

Page Break button on Insert tab

Manual page break

FIGURE 7–1   Manual page break in a document

Step-by-Step 7.1

1. Open the **Diet2.docx** from the drive and folder where your Data Files are stored. Save the document as **Diet Final** followed by your initials.

2. Display formatting marks. Position the insertion point at the beginning of the *Introduction* heading.

3. On the Ribbon, click the **Insert** tab. In the Pages group, click the **Page Break** button. A page break is inserted, and the document scrolls down so that the insertion point is blinking at the top of the new page 2. You created a new cover page for the document.

4. Scroll up so that you can see the text near the top of page 1. The manual page break is indicated by a dotted line below the last line of text on the page with the words *Page Break* in the middle of it.

5. Scroll down to page 4 in the document. Position the insertion point at the beginning of the heading *References*. Insert a page break.

6. Save your changes and leave the document open for the next Step-by-Step.

TIP

When you insert manual page breaks, you should try to avoid creating widows and orphans. A **widow** is when the first line of a paragraph appears at the bottom of a page; an **orphan** is when the last line of a paragraph appears at the top of a page. Widows and orphans are avoided when automatic page breaks are inserted.

The style definition for headings can include a setting to keep the heading on the same page as the first line in the next paragraph. You can also specify that there is always a manual page break before a heading. To change these settings, in the Paragraph group on the Home tab or the Page Layout tab, click the Paragraph Dialog Box Launcher, and then click the Line and Page Breaks tab in the Paragraph dialog box. The settings are at the top in the Pagination section.

► **VOCABULARY**

widow

orphan

content control

Understanding Content Controls

Many predesigned elements in Word contain ***content controls***, which are special placeholders designed to contain a specific type of text, such as a date or the page number. When you click a content control, the entire control is selected and a title tab appears at the top or to the left of the control. See **Figure 7–2**. The title tab can identify the type of information that appears in the control.

Title tab on content control with title of content control

Title tab on content control with no title

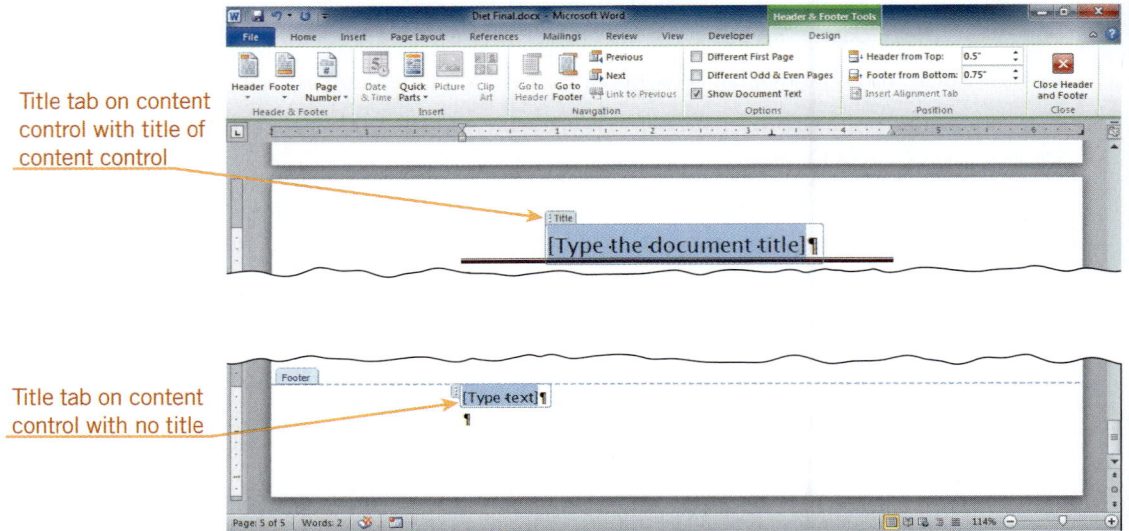

FIGURE 7–2   Content controls

For most controls, you simply start typing, and the text you type replaces the placeholder text. For some controls, an arrow appears when you click the control, and you click the arrow to choose an item from a list or a date from a calendar. Sometimes the content control is removed when you enter text, and sometimes the content control remains in the document (although only the contents of the control will appear in the printed document). If you decide you don't want to use a content control, you can delete it. Click the title tab to select the entire control, and then press Delete or Backspace.

Inserting Headers, Footers, and Page Numbers

Headers and footers allow you to include the same information, such as your name and the page number, on each page of a document. A **_header_** is text that is printed at the top of each page. A **_footer_** is text that is printed at the bottom of each page. **Figure 7–3** shows both a header and a footer.

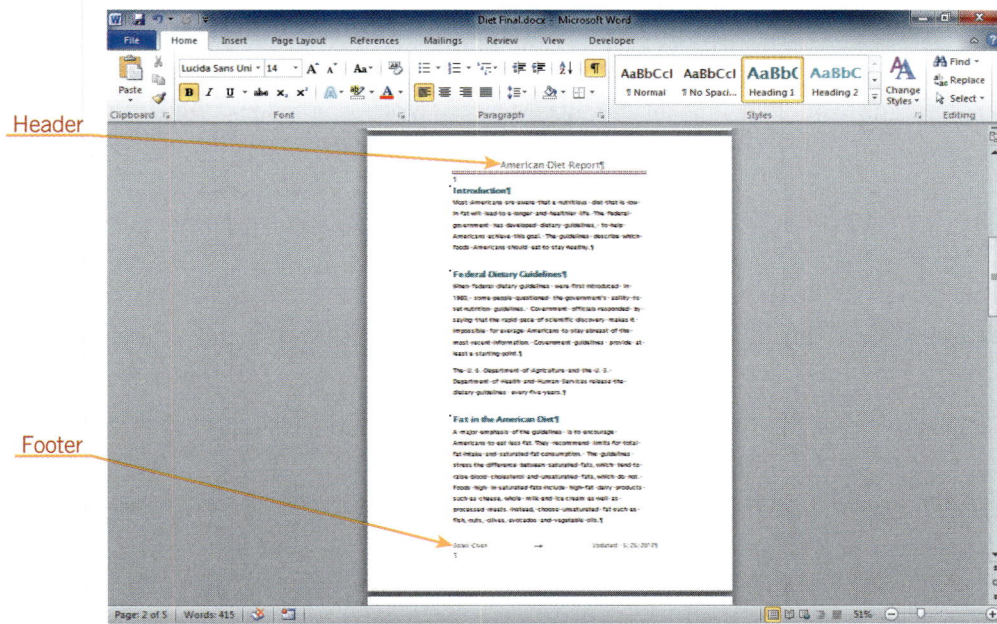

FIGURE 7–3   Page with header and footer

Inserting and Modifying Headers and Footers

Insert headers and footers by clicking the Insert tab, and then clicking the Header or Footer button in the Header & Footer group. When you click either of these buttons, a gallery of predesigned headers or footers opens, as shown in **Figure 7–4**. At the top of the list, two Blank styles are listed, and then additional styles are listed alphabetically. Each header and footer contains content controls.

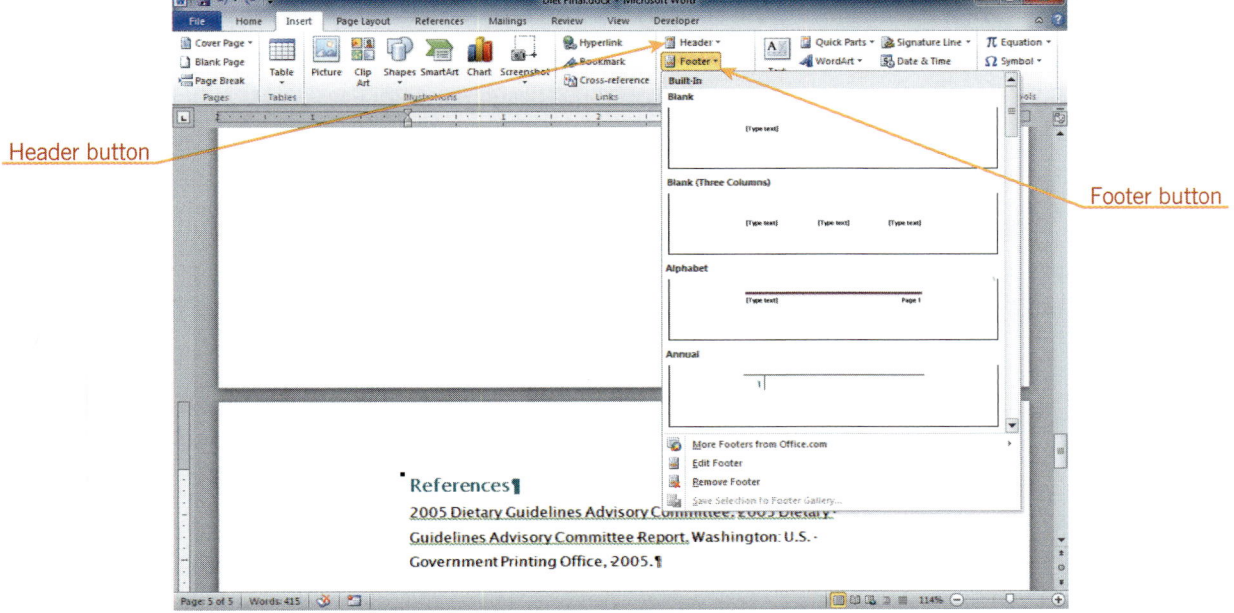

FIGURE 7–4   Footer gallery

When the header or footer area is active, the Header & Footer Tools Design tab appears on the Ribbon, as shown in **Figure 7–5**. This tab contains buttons you can use to insert elements such as the date, time, and page numbers. Other buttons allow you to set formatting options. In the Options group, you can select the Different First Page check box to remove the header and footer from the first page of the document.

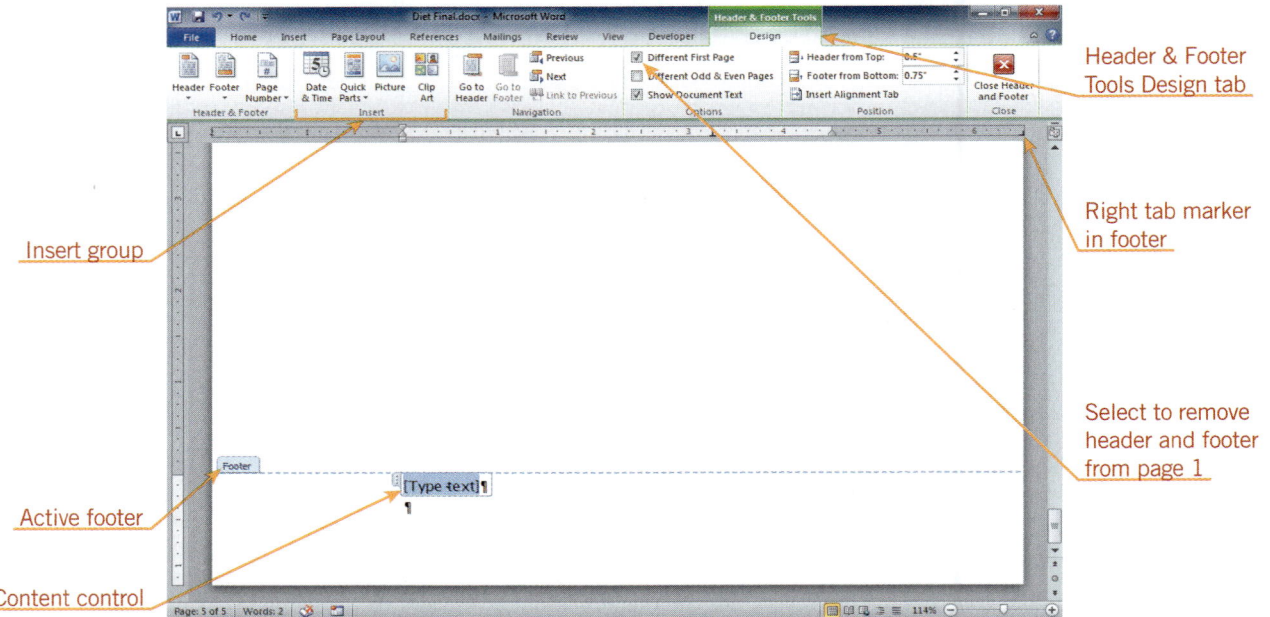

FIGURE 7–5   Footer with selected placeholder text

Step-by-Step 7.2

1. Display the rulers, if necessary.

2. On the Insert tab, in the Header & Footer group, click the **Footer** button. A gallery of footer styles appears. Refer back to Figure 7–4. Click **Blank**. The footer section appears at the bottom of the current page with placeholder text at the left margin. Refer back to Figure 7–5. Notice that the footer contains a center tab marker at the 3¼-inch mark on the ruler and a right tab marker at the 6½-inch mark. The Header & Footer Tools Design tab appears on the Ribbon and is the active tab. The content control in the footer is selected, ready for you to enter text.

3. In the footer section in the document, type your name. The text you type replaces the placeholder text in the content control. In this case, the content control is deleted as soon as you start typing.

4. On the ruler, drag the **right tab marker** positioned at the 6½-inch mark to the left so that it is directly on top of the right margin marker. Press **Tab** twice. The insertion point is at the right margin in the footer.

5. On the Design tab, in the Insert group, click the **Date & Time** button. In the Date and Time dialog box, deselect the **Update automatically** check box, if necessary, and then click **OK**. The current date is inserted in the footer in the format 5/25/2013.

6. On the Design tab, in the Header & Footer group, click the **Header** button, and then click the **Alphabet** style. The header section at the top of the page comes into view. The Alphabet style header with placeholder text is centered in the header. It includes a brown horizontal graphic line. A blue border appears around the placeholder text and a title tab appears at the top, identifying this as a Title content control, that is, a content control that contains the document title.

7. Type **American Diet Report**. The text you type replaces the placeholder text, but the content control stays in the document. See **Figure 7–6**.

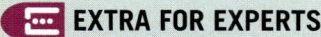
EXTRA FOR EXPERTS

You can insert an empty header and footer with no content controls. In the Header & Footer group on the Insert tab, click the Header or Footer button, and then click Edit Header or Edit Footer on the menu.

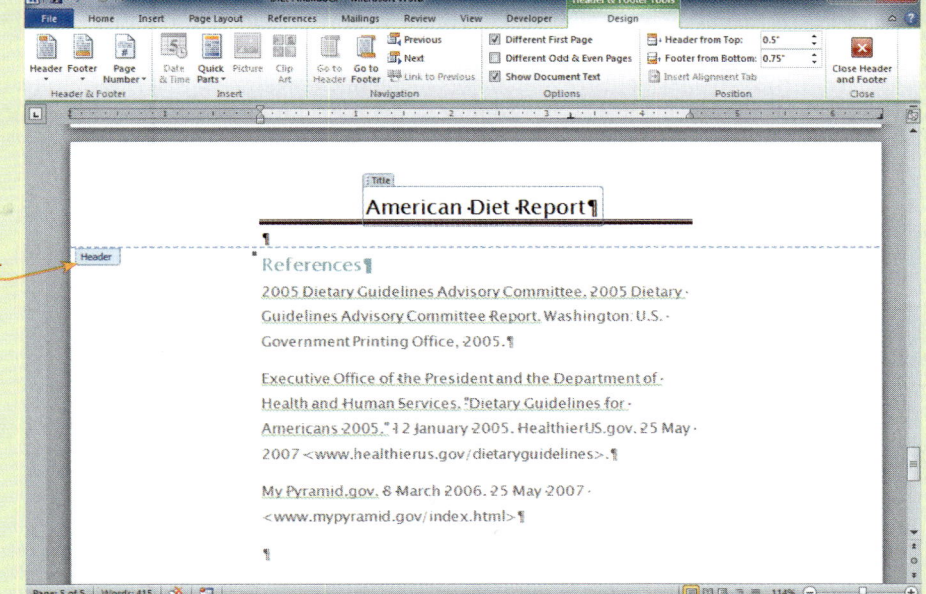

FIGURE 7–6
Header with text entered in Title content control

Active header

8. With the headers and footers still active, scroll up in the document so that you can see the top of page 2 and the bottom of page 1. Click in the header on page 2. On the Design tab, in the Options group, click the **Different First Page** check box, and then scroll up again so that you can see the bottom of page 1. The footer no longer appears on the first page of the document.

9. Scroll to the top of page 1. The header does not appear on the first page.

10. Scroll back down so you can see the insertion point in the header at the top of page 2. On the Design tab, in the Navigation group, click the **Go to Footer** button. The footer on page 2 comes into view with the insertion point blinking at the beginning of the line.

11. Position the insertion point in front of the date. Type **Updated:**, and then press the **spacebar**.

12. Double-click the document window above the footer section. The section of the document that was active before you started working on the header and footer (page 5) jumps into view. The headers and footers appear faded, and the insertion point is blinking in the document window. (If you clicked somewhere in the document before you started working on the header and footer, the current page will be different.)

13. Save your changes and leave the document open for the next Step-by-Step.

Inserting Page Numbers

Page numbers are included in some of the header and footer styles. If you choose a header or footer style that does not include page numbers, or if you want to insert page numbers without inserting anything else in a header or footer, you can use the Page Number button in the Header & Footer group on the Insert tab or on the Header & Footer Tools Design tab. A menu opens with choices for you to insert page numbers at the top or the bottom of the page, in the margin, or at the current position. When you point to any of these options, a gallery of choices appears. If you choose Top of Page or Bottom of Page, you automatically create a header or footer with only the page number as content. See **Figure 7–7**. If a header or footer already exists, the page number style you choose replaces it.

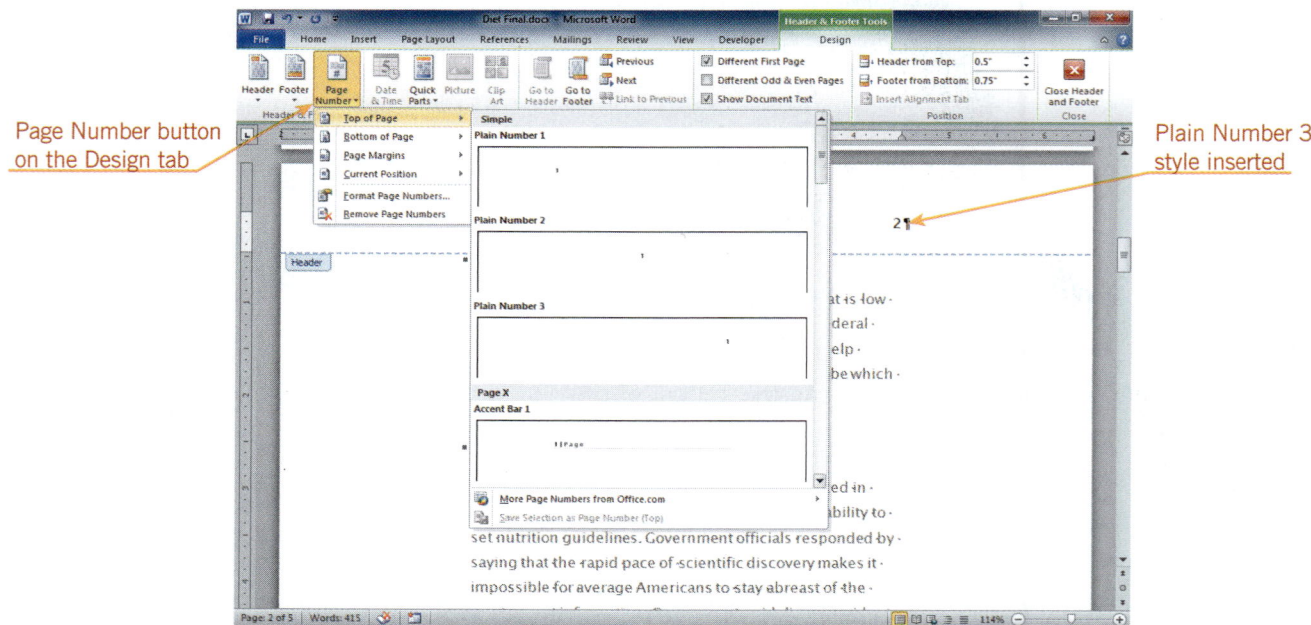

Page Number button on the Design tab

Plain Number 3 style inserted

FIGURE 7–7   Top of Page gallery on Page Number menu

If you want to insert the page number in an existing header or footer, first position the insertion point in the header or footer at the location where you want the page number to appear. Click the Page Number button, point to Current Position, and then choose a style.

Step-by-Step 7.3

1. Scroll so that you can see the top of page 2. Double-click anywhere in the header on page 2. The header becomes active and the insertion point blinks at the beginning of the content control.

2. On the Design tab, in the Header & Footer group, click the **Page Number** button, point to **Top of Page**, and then click **Plain Number 3**. Instead of adding the page number near the right margin, the page number header replaced the header you created.

3. On the Quick Access Toolbar, click the **Undo** button . The header you created reappears.

4. On the ruler, drag the **right tab marker** positioned at the 6½-inch mark to the left so that it is directly on top of the right margin marker. Drag the **center tab marker** positioned at the 3¼-inch mark off the ruler to remove it. Press **End**, and then press the **right arrow key**. The insertion point is positioned between the content control and the paragraph mark. Press **Tab**. The insertion point is positioned at the right margin.

5. In the Header & Footer group, click the **Page Number** button. Point to **Current Position**, and then click **Plain Number**. The page number appears at the location of the insertion point, formatted in the same style as the rest of the header text.

6. On the Design tab, in the Close group, click the **Close Header and Footer** button.

7. Save your changes and leave the document open for the next Step-by-Step.

TIP

To hide the margins and space between pages in a document, move the insertion point to the top of the page until it changes to a button with double arrows, and then double-click. To show the space again, position the insertion point on the top of the line between pages so that it changes, and then double-click.

Modifying Document Properties

When you save a file, identifying information about the file is saved along with it, such as the author's name and the date the file was created. This information is known as the file **properties**.

To view or add properties to a document, click the File tab, and then click Info. The properties appear in the right pane in Backstage view, as shown in **Figure 7–8**.

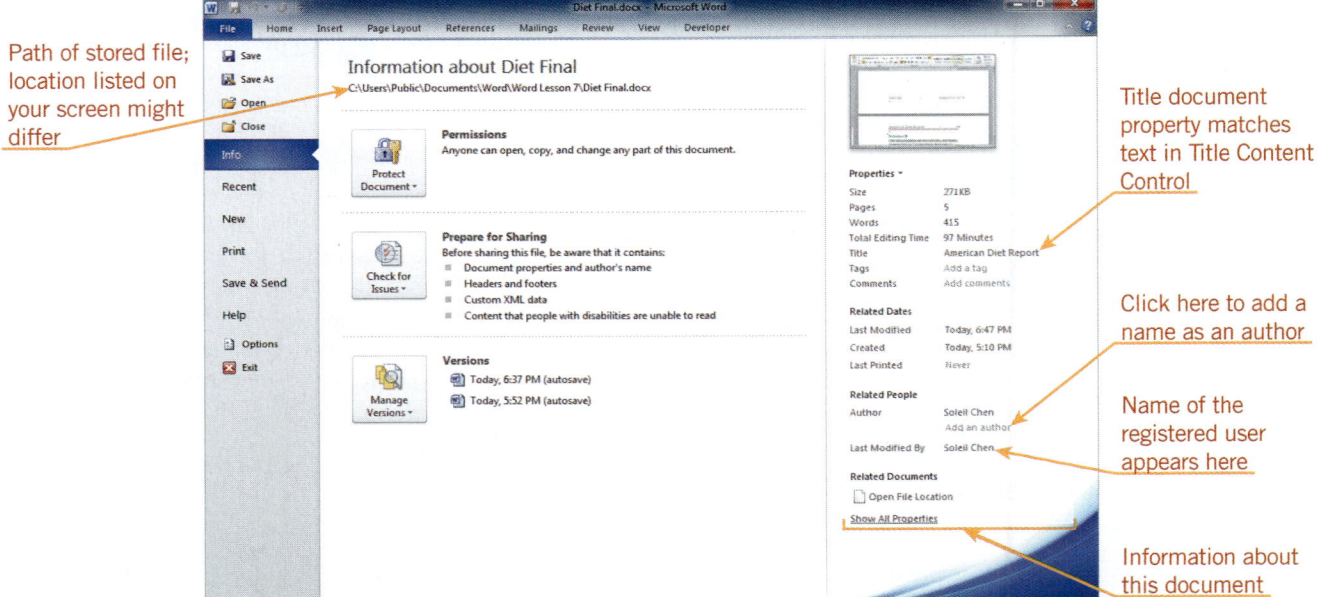

Path of stored file; location listed on your screen might differ

Title document property matches text in Title Content Control

Click here to add a name as an author

Name of the registered user appears here

Information about this document

FIGURE 7–8   Info tab in Backstage view

Content controls can be linked to document properties so that they pick up and display the information stored as a document property. For example, if a content control is tied to the Title document property, it displays the information stored in the Title box in the Properties section of the Info tab in Backstage view. The connection works both ways, so that if you change the Title in the content control, the change appears in the Title box in the Properties section and in every other Title content control in the document.

Step-by-Step 7.4

1. If necessary, scroll up so you can see the header at the top of page 2. Click the **File** tab, and then in the navigation bar, click **Info**, if it is not already selected. The document properties appear in the right pane in Backstage view. Refer back to Figure 7–8. Notice that *American Diet Report*, the title you typed in the Title content control in the header, appears as the Title property.

2. Click anywhere on *American Diet Report* next to Title, and then select **American Diet Report**. Type **Reducing Fat in the American Diet**. Click a blank area in Backstage view. The text in the Title content control in the header on page 2 also changed to the text you just typed.

3. On the Ribbon, click the **File** tab. Backstage view closes and your document appears again. Notice that the title in the header is changed to the new title you typed in Backstage view.

4. Click the **File** tab. Backstage view appears again with the Info tab selected.

5. Under Related People in the Backstage view, click **Add an author**. The placeholder text disappears and a box appears with the insertion point in it. Type your name in the box.

6. Right-click **Soleil Chen**. On the shortcut menu, click **Remove Person**. Now your name is the only name listed as the author of the document.

7. At the top of the right pane, click **Properties**, and then click **Advanced Properties**. The Diet Final.docx Properties dialog box opens. Click the **Summary** tab. See **Figure 7–9**.

TIP

To see the properties while you are working on the document, click Properties on the Info tab in Backstage view, and then click Show Document Panel.

TIP

To see contact information for an author, point to the author's name. If there is contact information for that author stored in Outlook, it will appear in the box that opens.

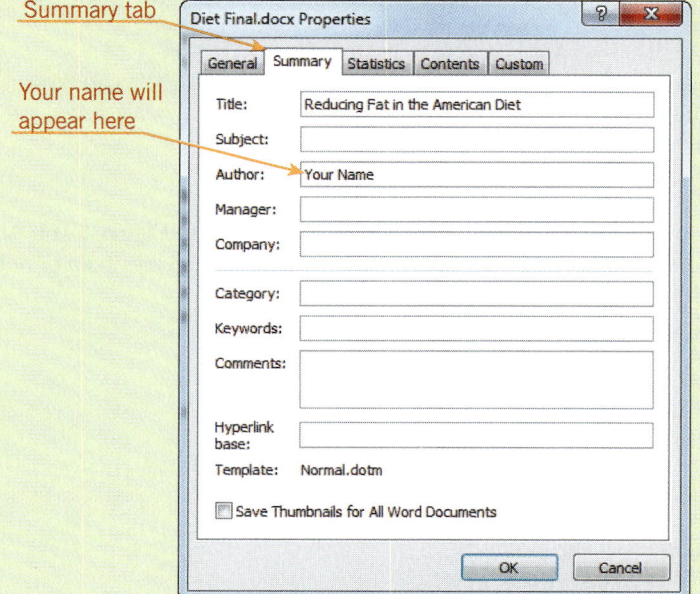

FIGURE 7–9
Summary tab in Diet Final.docx Properties dialog box

8. If there is any text in the Company box, select it. Type your school name in the Company box. Click **OK**.

9. Click the **Home** tab. Backstage view closes.

10. Save your changes and leave the document open for the next Step-by-Step.

Inserting a Cover Page

You can quickly create a cover page for your document by inserting one of the many predesigned cover pages available with Word. To insert a predesigned cover page, click the Insert tab, and then, in the Pages group, click the Cover Page button. A gallery of cover pages opens, as shown in **Figure 7–10**.

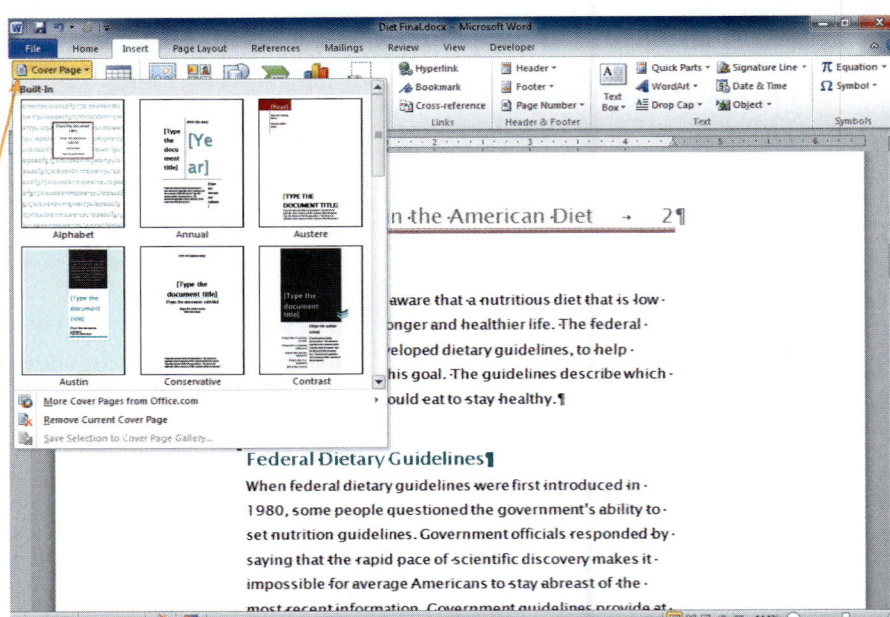

FIGURE 7–10   Cover Page gallery

The cover pages contain content controls, as shown in **Figure 7–11**. As with the content controls that appear in headers and footers, you can use them or delete them, and then insert your own content.

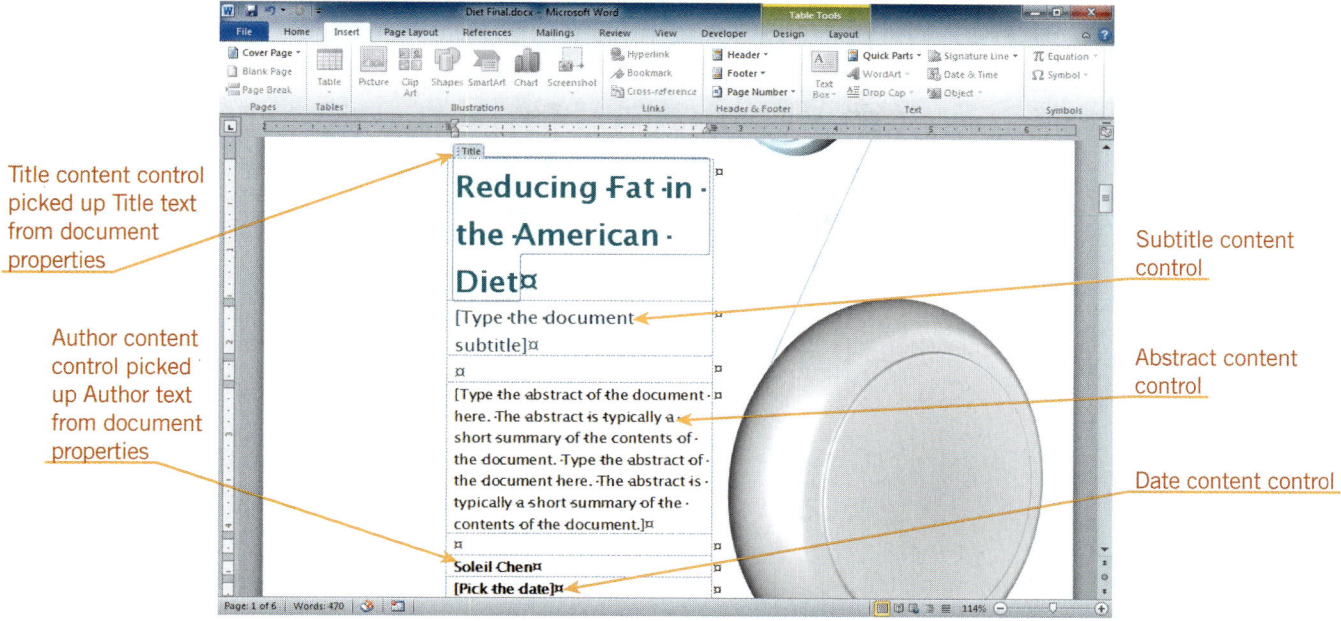

Title content control picked up Title text from document properties

Author content control picked up Author text from document properties

Subtitle content control

Abstract content control

Date content control

FIGURE 7–11 Mod cover page with information from document properties

Step-by-Step 7.5

1. On the Ribbon, click the **Insert** tab. In the Pages group, click the **Cover Page** button. In the gallery, scroll down until you see Mod, and then click **Mod**. A cover page is inserted at the beginning of the document.

2. Scroll up to see the title tab on the content control containing *Reducing Fat in the American Diet*. The word *Title* in the title tab identifies this as a content control that picked up the title from the document properties.

3. Click anywhere on your name. The word *Author* identifies this as a content control that picked up the author from the document properties.

4. Click the placeholder that says *Type the document subtitle*. Click the **Subtitle** title tab. The title tab darkens. Press **Delete**. The content control is deleted.

5. Delete the content control that contains the placeholder text *Type the abstract...* .

6. Scroll down to the bottom of the cover page, and then click the placeholder that says *Pick the date*. The Date title tab appears, and an arrow appears to the right of the control.

7. Click the **arrow**. A calendar appears displaying the current month and year with today's date in a red box. See **Figure 7–12**.

FIGURE 7–12
Selecting a date with a Date content control

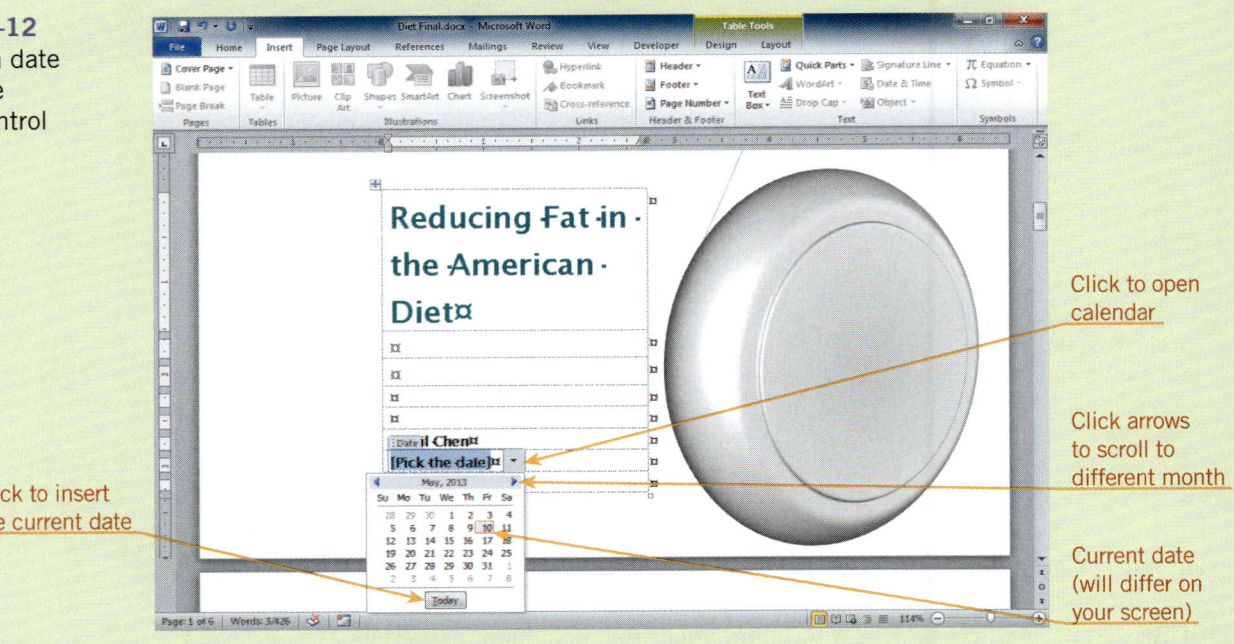

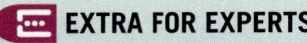
EXTRA FOR EXPERTS

To view two parts of a document at once, in the Window group on the View tab, click the Split button. Without pressing the mouse button, drag the horizontal gray bar that appears to position it, and then click. To remove the split, click the Remove Split button in the Window group on the View tab.

8. Click tomorrow's date in the calendar. Tomorrow's date appears in the document. (If you need to scroll to the next month, click the arrow to the right of the month name.)

9. Scroll down, if necessary, so that you can see the text and the page break on page 2. You don't need the temporary cover page any more.

10. On page 2, select **American Diet**, the paragraph mark at the end of the line, the Page Break formatting mark, and the paragraph mark at the end of the line. Press **Delete**. The text on the page and the page break are deleted, removing the entire page from the document. The first page in the document is numbered page 1 instead of page 2. This is because, like the cover of a book, the cover page is not included in the page count.

11. Save your changes and leave the document open for the next Step-by-Step.

Creating New Sections

▶ **VOCABULARY**
section

You can divide a document into two or more sections. A *section* is a part of a document where you can create a different layout from the rest of the document. For example, you might want to format only part of a page with columns, as you did in Lesson 6. You can also have different headers and footers, page numbers, margins, orientation, and other formatting features in different sections.

To create a new section, click the Page Layout tab, and then in the Page Setup group, click the Breaks button. A menu of choices for inserting breaks appears, as shown in **Figure 7–13**. The bottom half of the menu lists types of section breaks. To start the new section on the next page, choose Next Page. To start the new section on the same page, choose Continuous. To start the new section break on the next even-numbered or odd-numbered page, choose Even Page or Odd Page.

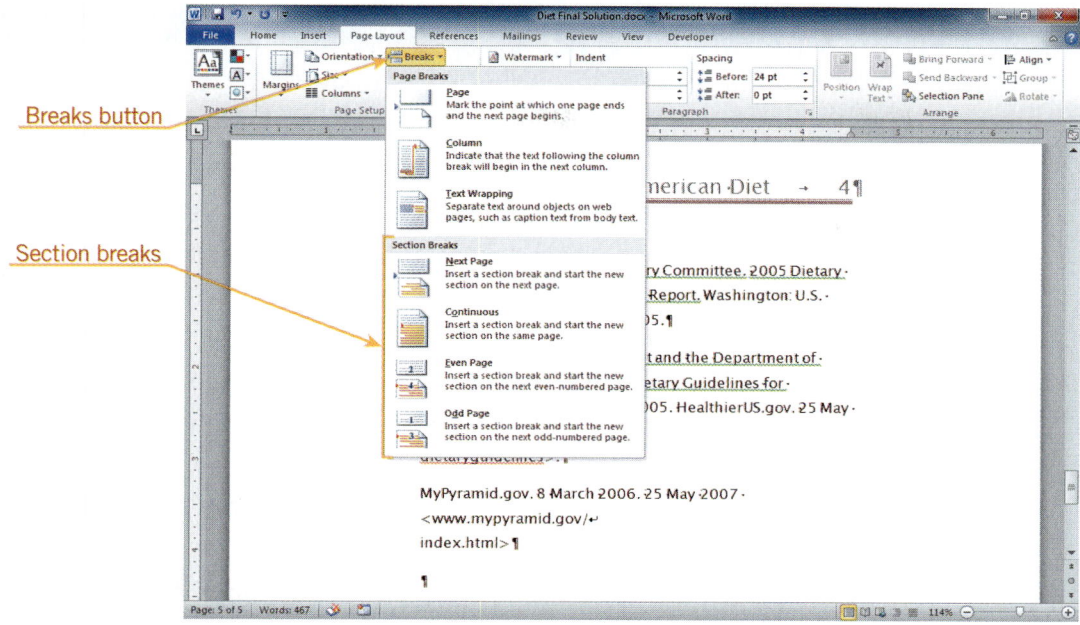

Breaks button

Section breaks

FIGURE 7–13   Breaks menu

When formatting marks are displayed, a section break is indicated by a double dotted line across the page with the words *Section Break* in the middle, as shown in **Figure 7–14**. To delete a section break, select the section break line, and then press Delete or Backspace.

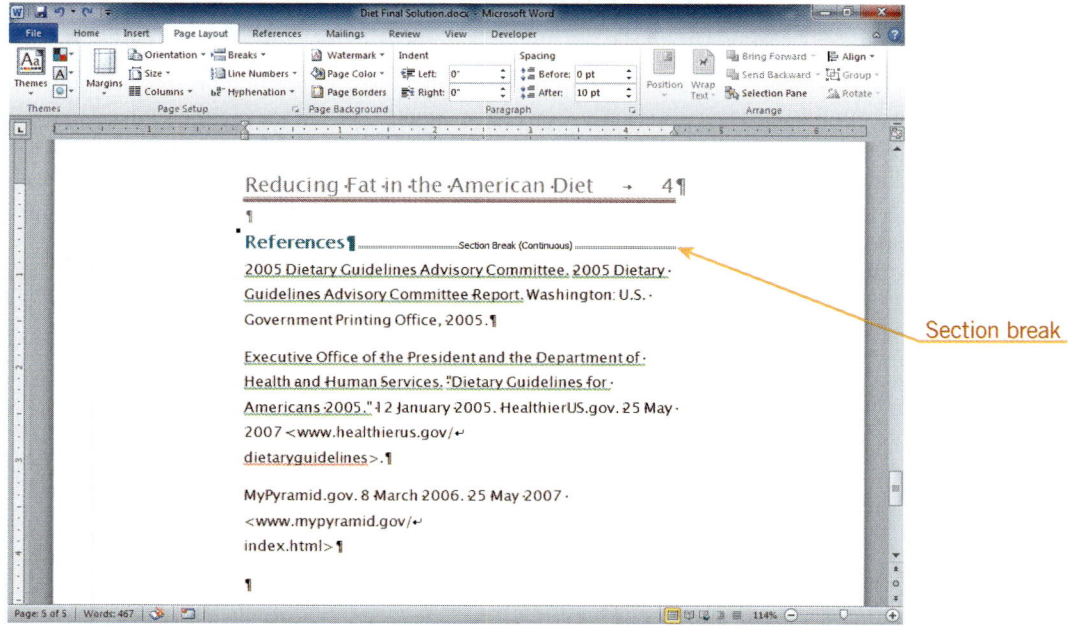

Section break

FIGURE 7–14   Continuous section break in a document

Step-by-Step 7.6

1. Go to the last page in the document. Position the insertion point in front of *2005 Dietary Guidelines Advisory Committee* in the first reference.

2. On the Ribbon, click the **Page Layout** tab. In the Page Setup group, click the **Breaks** button. Under Section Breaks, click **Continuous**. Because formatting marks are displayed, you can see that a continuous section break was inserted.

3. In the Page Setup group, click the **Columns** button, and then click **Two**. The current section is formatted in two columns. If the section break were not there, the entire document would have been formatted in two columns. You want to force the third reference to move to the top of the second column.

4. Position the insertion point in front of the third reference, *MyPyramid.gov*. In the Page Setup group, click the **Breaks** button, and then under Page Breaks, click **Column**. A column break is inserted below the last line in the *Executive Office of the President* reference.

5. Save your changes and leave the document open for the next Step-by-Step.

Using the Research Tool

Word provides online access to a dictionary, thesaurus, and other resources to help you research information. You need an Internet connection for all research resources except the dictionary, thesaurus, and some features of the translation tool. To use the Research tool, click the Review tab on the Ribbon. In the Proofing group, click the Research button. The Research task pane opens to the right of the document window. Type a word or phrase that describes the topic to be researched in the Search for box, and then click the arrow in the box below the Search for box to select the reference that you want to use. The search executes and the results appear in the task pane. See **Figure 7–15**. If the reference you want to use already appears in the Search for box, you can click the Start searching button to execute the search.

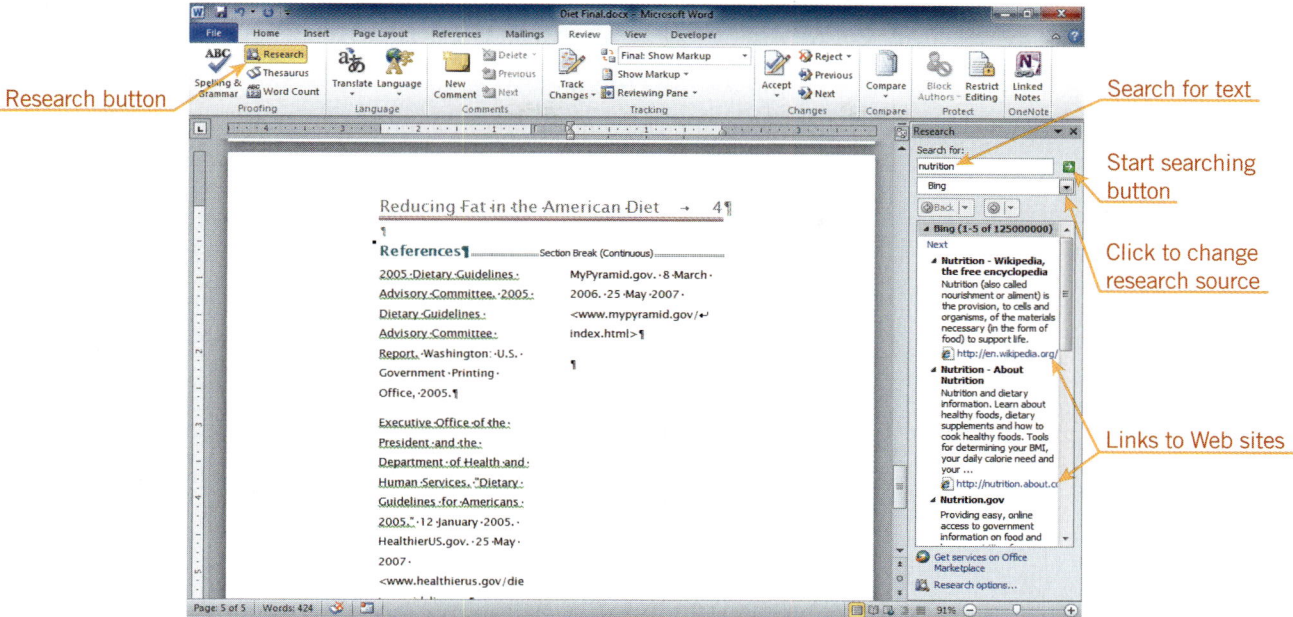

Research button

Search for text

Start searching button

Click to change research source

Links to Web sites

FIGURE 7–15   Research task pane open with results from Bing search engine

Step-by-Step 7.7

1. On the Ribbon, click the **Review** tab. In the Proofing group, click the **Research** button. The Research task pane opens to the right of the document window.

2. In the Research task pane, select all the text in the Search for box if there is any, or simply click in the Search for box if it is empty. Type **nutrition**.

3. Click the **arrow** next to the box below the Search for box. Click **Bing**. If the search doesn't start, click the Start searching button ⟶. The search starts and, after a moment, results appear in the task pane. This is a shortcut to using the Bing search engine in a browser. (*Note*: If you are not connected to the Internet, you will not get any results. Read the rest of the steps in this section and only complete Steps 7 through 10.)

4. Scroll down and look for the result *Nutrition.gov*. Click the link at the bottom of that result. Your browser starts, and the Nutrition.gov home page appears in the browser window. (If you don't see your browser window, look on the taskbar. The taskbar button for your browser should be blinking or appear orange. Click the browser taskbar button. If more than one button for your browser appears on the taskbar, click the orange button.)

5. Look in the Address bar at the top of the browser window. The address is very long, but to send someone to this home page, all you need is the part that starts with *www* and ends with *.gov*.—www.nutrition.gov.

TIP

If you need to translate a word or phrase, select Translation in the All Reference Books list.

6. In the upper-right corner of the browser window, click the **Close** button . The browser window closes, and the Diet Final document appears again. (If another browser window is open, click its Close button.)

7. In the document, go to page 2 (numbered page 1 in the header). In the paragraph under the *Fat in the American Diet* heading, position the insertion point at the end of the last sentence between the period and the paragraph mark. Press **spacebar**.

8. Type **For more information, go to www.nutrition.gov.**

9. In the Research task pane title bar, click the **Close** button .

10. Save your changes and leave the document open for the next Step-by-Step.

▶ VOCABULARY

table

cell

▬ TIP

If you know exactly how many rows and columns you want to create, you can also click the Table button in the Tables group on the Insert tab, and then click Insert Table on the menu. The Insert Table dialog box opens. Change the values in the Number of columns and the Number of rows boxes as needed.

Creating Tables

A *table* is an arrangement of text or numbers in rows and columns, similar to a spreadsheet. Tables are useful for organizing information. The intersection of a row and column is called a *cell*. Tables are sometimes easier to use than trying to align text with tabs.

Inserting a Table

To create a table, click the Insert tab, and then, in the Tables group, click the Table button. A menu opens with a grid in the top portion. As you move the pointer over the grid, the outline of the cells in the grid changes to orange, and the label at the top of the menu indicates the dimensions of the table. As you drag, the table appears in the document behind the grid. See **Figure 7–16**. Click when the grid and the label indicate the number of rows and columns you want to create. A table is inserted at the location of the insertion point. To enter text in a table, click in a cell, and then type. To move to the next cell to the right, press Tab or click in the cell. To move back one cell, press Shift+Tab.

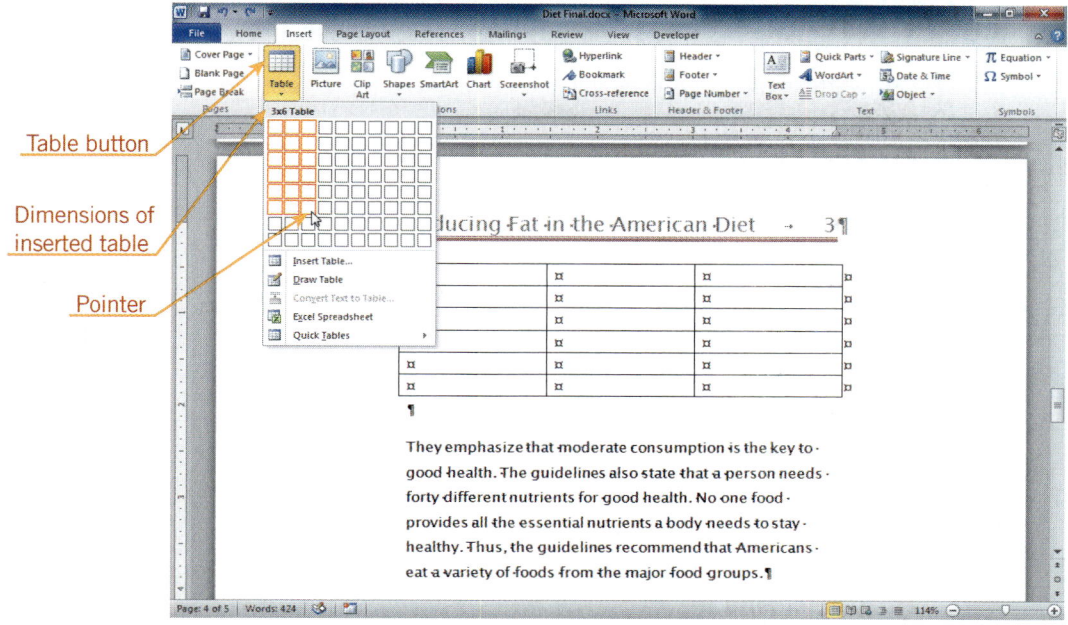

FIGURE 7–16   Inserting a table

Step-by-Step 7.8

1. Go to page 4 in the document (numbered page 3 in the header). Position the insertion point in the empty paragraph at the top of the page, above the paragraph that starts *They emphasize that*.

2. On the Ribbon, click the **Insert** tab. In the Tables group, click the **Table** button. A menu opens with a grid at the top of it. Insert Table appears above the top of the grid.

3. Without clicking the mouse button, drag the pointer over the grid. As you drag, the boxes in the grid change from black to orange outlines, and the text above the grid changes to the number of columns and rows you have selected.

4. Point to the cell that creates a **3×6 Table**, and then click. The menu closes and a table with three columns and six rows is inserted in the document. The insertion point is blinking in the first cell in the table.

5. Type **Food Groups**. The text you type appears in the first cell in the table. Press **Tab**. The insertion point moves to the next cell to the right.

6. Type **Daily Recommendations**, and then press **Tab** twice. The insertion point moves to the second cell in the first column.

7. Type the rest of the data in the table as shown in **Figure 7–17**. Leave the third column blank.

FIGURE 7–17
Data in table

Food Groups¤	Daily· Recommendations¤	¤	¤
Grains¤	3·oz whole grains¤	¤	¤
Vegetables¤	2·to·3·cups¤	¤	¤
Fruits¤	1–1/2 to·2·cups¤	¤	¤
Oils¤	5·to·7 teaspoons¤	¤	¤
Milk¤	3·cups¤	¤	¤

8. Click in the last cell in the table. Press **Tab**. A new row is created at the bottom of the table.

9. Type **Meat & beans**. Press **Tab**. Type **5 to 6-1/2 oz**.

10. Save your changes and leave the document open for the next Step-by-Step.

Modifying the Table Structure

You can modify the structure of a table by using commands on the Table Tools Layout tab on the Ribbon. To insert a row, click a cell in the table, and then in the Rows & Columns group, click the Insert Above or Insert Below button, depending on where you want the row to appear in relation to the insertion point. To insert a column, click the Insert Left or Insert Right button. To delete a row or column, position the insertion point in the row or column you want to delete. In the Rows & Columns group, click the Delete button, and then click the appropriate command to delete cells, columns, rows, or the entire table.

You can change the width of columns and the height of rows. Position the pointer on top of a gridline in the table so that it changes to a double-headed arrow. Drag the border line to resize the column or the row.

You can split cells to transform one column or row into two or more. You can merge cells to create one large cell out of several small cells. To merge cells, select the cells, and then click the Merge Cells button in the Merge group on the Table Tools Layout tab. To split cells, select a cell or cells, and then click the Split Cells button to open the Split Cells dialog box. Specify the number of columns and rows you want to create from the selected cell or cells, and then click OK. If the result is not what you expected, undo your change, open the Split Cells dialog box again, and then click the Merge cells before split check box.

Step-by-Step 7.9

1. Position the insertion point in any cell in the last column of the table. On the Ribbon, click the **Table Tools Layout** tab, if necessary. In the Rows & Columns group, click the **Delete** button. Click **Delete Columns**. The current column is deleted.

2. Position the insertion point in any cell in the first row of the table. In the Rows & Columns group, click the **Insert Above** button. A new row is inserted above the row containing the insertion point.

3. Click in the first cell in the new row. Type **USDA Food Pyramid Guidelines**.

4. Position the pointer over the column divider between the two columns. The pointer changes to a double-headed arrow ↔. Press and hold the mouse button, and then drag the column divider to the left until the left column is approximately 1¼ inches wide.

5. Drag the right border of the table to the right until the right column is approximately two inches wide and Daily Recommendations fits on one line in the cell.

6. Drag to select the two cells in the top row. On the Layout tab, in the Merge group, click the **Merge Cells** button. The two cells are merged into one cell. See **Figure 7–18**.

> **TIP**
>
> To select an entire row, click to the left of the row (outside the table). To select an entire column, position your pointer just above the column so that the pointer changes to a downward-pointing arrow, and then click.

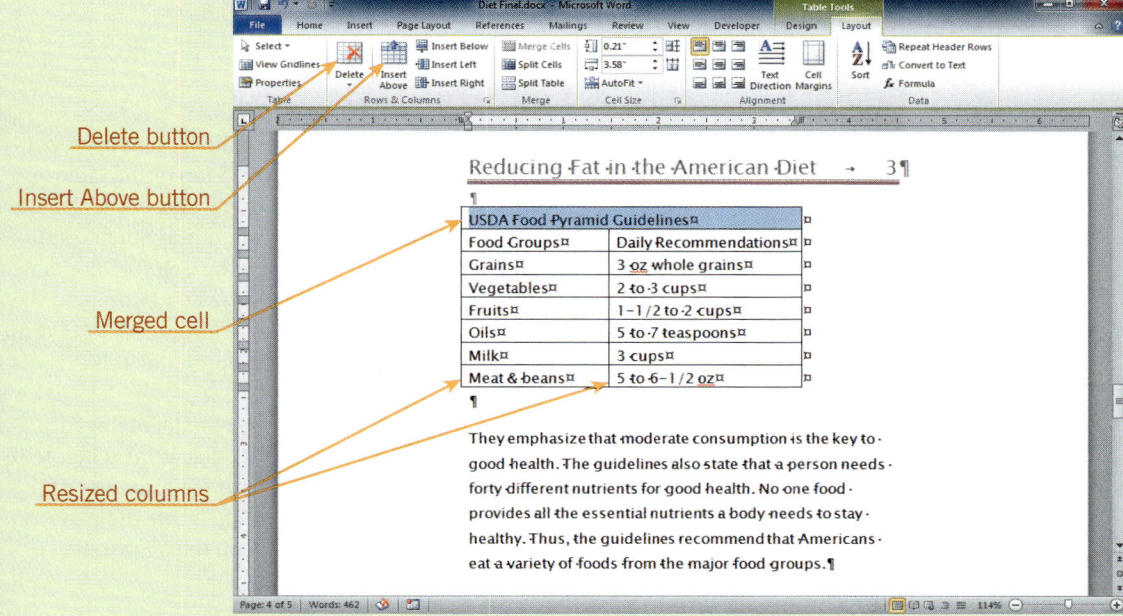

Delete button

Insert Above button

Merged cell

Resized columns

FIGURE 7–18
Modified table

7. Save your changes and leave the document open for the next Step-by-Step.

Formatting Tables

The easiest way to format a table is to use one of the many predesigned formats in the Table Styles group on the Table Tools Design tab. See **Figure 7–19**. If you want to treat the first and last rows or the first and last columns differently from the rest of the rows and columns in the table, you can select the Header Row, Total Row, First Column, and Last Column check boxes in the Table Style Options group on the Table Tools Design tab. To add shading to every other row or every other column, select the Banded Rows or Banded Columns check boxes in the same group.

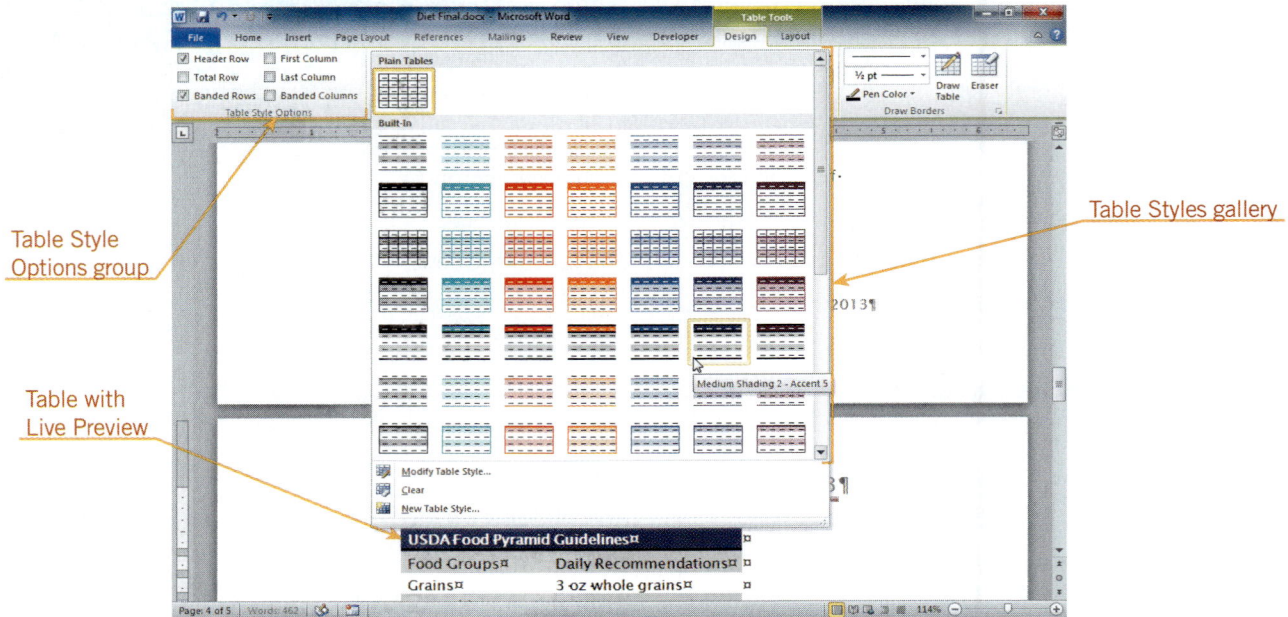

FIGURE 7–19   Live Preview of a table style

▶ **VOCABULARY**
gridline

You can manually format text in a table as you would format any text in a document. You can select the entire table by positioning the pointer on top of the table and then clicking the table move handle that appears above the upper-left corner of the table. Then you can position the table on the page by clicking an alignment button in the Paragraph group on the Home tab. You can also change the color of the table lines and the fill color of the cells by using the Shading and Borders buttons in the Table Styles group on the Table Tools Design tab. To change the alignment of text in a cell, click one of the alignment buttons in the Alignment group on the Table Tools Layout tab.

When you add color to borders, you need to make sure you are trying to format border lines, not table gridlines. Border lines are visible lines that print when you print your document. When a table is created, the *gridlines* form the structure of the table, the outline of the rows and columns. To make sure the table prints the way you expect, turn off the gridlines by checking the Gridlines button on the View tab.

Step-by-Step 7.10

1. Click anywhere in the table. On the Ribbon, click the **Table Tools Design** tab. In the Table Style Options group, notice that the Header Row, First Column, and Banded Rows check boxes are selected.

2. On the Design tab, in the Table Styles group, click the **More** button, and then in the gallery, click the **Medium Shading 2 – Accent 5** style (fifth row, second to last column under Built-In). The gallery closes and the table is reformatted with that style.

3. In the Table Style Options group, click the **First Column** check box to deselect it. The shading and bold formatting is removed from the first column.

4. Click in the first row of the table. On the Ribbon, click the **Table Tools Layout** tab. In the Alignment group, click the **Align Center** button 🔳. The text in the top row is centered in the cell.

5. Select all the text in the second row of the table. On the Ribbon, click the **Home** tab. In the Font group, click the **Bold** button **B**. The text in the second row is bold, and *Daily Recommendations* might wrap to two lines.

6. If *Daily Recommendations* is now on two lines, click in the table to position the insertion point without selecting any text. Drag the right border of the table to the right just enough so that *Daily Recommendations* fits on one line again.

7. Position the pointer over the table. The table move handle ⊕ appears above the upper-left corner of the table. Position the pointer over the table move handle ⊕ so that the pointer changes to a four-headed arrow, and then click the **table move handle** ⊕. The entire table is selected.

8. On the Home tab, in the Paragraph group, click the **Center** button 🔳. The table is centered on the page. Click anywhere in the table to deselect it and keep the table active.

> **TIP**
>
> You can double-click the right border of a column to automatically resize the column to accommodate the width of the longest entry in the column.

> **TIP**
>
> Using the table move handle, you can drag a table anywhere in a document.

9. On the Ribbon, click the **Table Tools Layout** tab. In the Table group, locate the View Gridlines button and determine if it is selected. If it is selected, it will be orange. See **Figure 7–20**. If it is selected, you will see a dotted gridline between the two columns in the table.

FIGURE 7–20
Formatted table
with gridlines visible

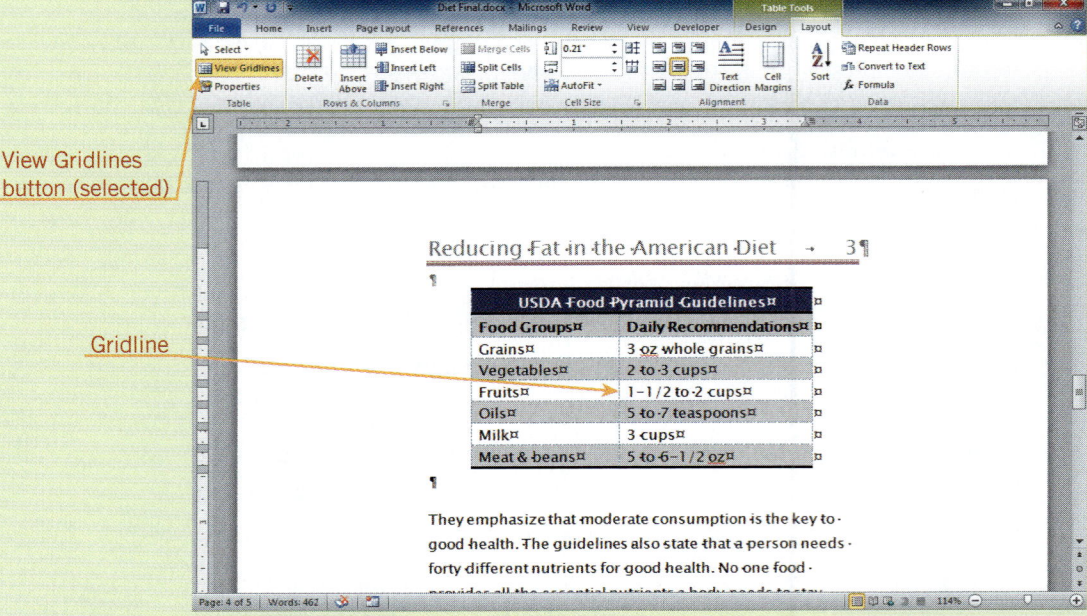

View Gridlines
button (selected)

Gridline

10. If the View Gridlines button is selected, click the **View Gridlines** button to deselect it. The dotted gridline between the two columns in the table disappears.

11. Drag to select all the rows in the table except the first row. On the Ribbon, click the **Table Tools Design** tab. In the Table Styles group, click the **arrow** next to the Borders button. Click **Inside Vertical Border**. A vertical line appears between the first and second columns in the table.

12. Save your changes and leave the document open for the next Step-by-Step.

Converting Text into Tables

You can convert text you have already typed into a table. Select the text you want to convert to a table. On the Insert tab on the Ribbon, click the Table button in the Tables group, and then click Convert Text to Table on the menu. The Convert Text to Table dialog box opens. Word converts the text to a table by creating columns from text separated by a comma or a tab, and by creating rows from text separated by a paragraph marker.

Sorting Text

Sorting arranges a list of words in ascending order (*a* to *z*) or in descending order (*z* to *a*). Sorting can also arrange a list of numbers in ascending order (smallest to largest) or descending order (largest to smallest). Sorting is useful for putting lists of names or terms in alphabetical order.

To sort text in a table, click anywhere in the table, click the Table Tools Layout tab, and then in the Data group, click the Sort button. The Sort dialog box opens, as shown in **Figure 7–21**. In this dialog box, you can choose the options for the sort.

▶ **VOCABULARY**

sort

Click to change column on which data is sorted

Select to indicate that the selected data includes a header row

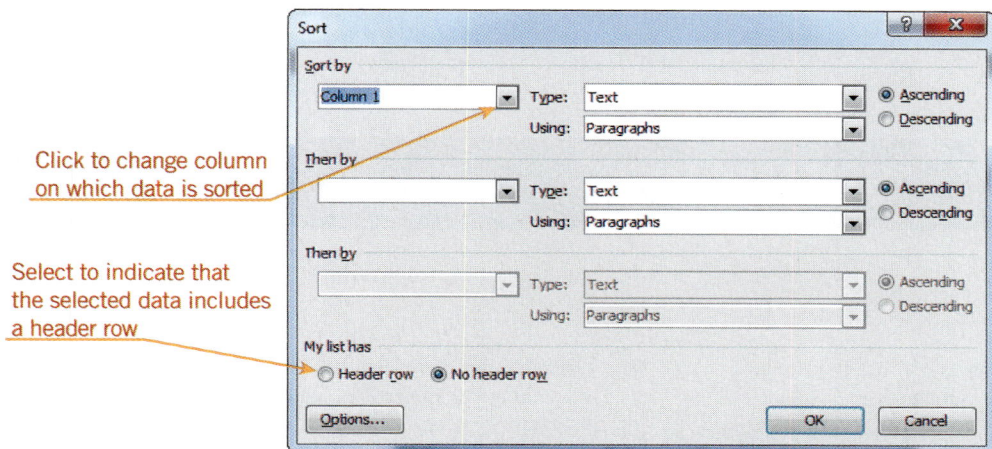
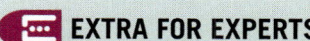

FIGURE 7–21   Sort dialog box

> **EXTRA FOR EXPERTS**
>
> If the table contains numbers, click the Type arrow in the Sort dialog box, and then click Number to sort the table numerically. Otherwise, it will sort the data using the first digit only, so that 10 would come before 2.

Step-by-Step 7.11

1. If necessary, drag to select all the rows in the table except the first row with USDA Food Pyramid Guidelines, and then click the **Table Tools Layout** tab.

2. In the Data group, click the **Sort** button. The Sort dialog box opens.

3. Make sure **Column 1** appears in the Sort by box. Make sure that the **Ascending** option button at the top of the dialog box is selected. The table will be sorted in alphabetical order by the values in the first column.

> **TIP**
>
> You can also sort a list that is not organized in a table. Select the list, and then, in the Paragraph group on the Home tab, click the Sort button.

WARNING

If a thick border line appears in the middle of the table, reapply the Medium Shading 2 – Accent 5 table style, add the vertical border between rows 2 through 8, and then center the table horizontally.

4. At the bottom of the dialog box, click the **Header row** option button. This will exclude the first row of the selected rows from being included in the sort.

5. Click **OK**. The dialog box closes and the data in the table is sorted in alphabetical order by the data in the first column.

6. Deselect the table. Turn off the rulers and hide formatting marks.

7. Save, print, and then close the document.

SUMMARY

In this lesson, you learned:

- Word automatically inserts page breaks where they are necessary. You also can insert page breaks manually.

- Content controls are special placeholders designed to contain a specific type of text. When you insert text, some content controls remain in the document and some are deleted.

- Headers appear at the top of every page in the document; footers appear at the bottom of every page. The Header & Footer Tools Design tab appears when a header or footer is active.

- You can insert page numbers in the header or footer area. The page number style can replace a header or footer, or you can use the Current Position command to insert a page number at the location of the insertion point.

- You can modify file properties in Backstage view. Some types of content controls are linked to document properties.

- You can insert a predesigned cover page with content controls by clicking the Cover Page button in the Pages group on the Insert tab.

- To create different page layouts within one document, divide the document into sections.

- The Research tool allows you to access the Internet to explore different sources for information.

- Tables show data in columns and rows. You can modify tables by adding and removing rows and columns and merging and splitting cells. You can format a table with styles as well as use manual formatting. You can convert text into a table with the Convert Text to Table command.

- You can sort text in a document alphabetically or numerically in ascending or descending order.

 VOCABULARY REVIEW

Define the following terms:

cell	header	section
content control	orphan	sort
footer	page break	table
gridline	property	widow

■ REVIEW QUESTIONS

MULTIPLE CHOICE

Select the best response for the following statements.

1. When formatting marks are displayed, a manual page break is indicated in the document by a:

A. series of dashes.

B. thick horizontal line.

C. dotted line with the words Page Break in the middle of the line.

D. row of paragraph marks with the words Page Break in the middle of the line.

2. To modify the document properties, you need to display the:

A. Summary dialog box.

B. Backstage view.

C. Properties task pane.

D. Document dialog box.

3. A part of a document that is formatted with a different page layout than the rest of the document is called a(n):

A. auto-orientation.

B. table.

C. section.

D. manual break.

4. To find information on the Web using a variety of sources, what button do you click in the Proofing group on the Review tab?

A. Proof

B. Encyclopedia

C. Research

D. Web

5. What is the intersection of a row and column in a table called?

A. box

B. cell

C. grid

D. content control

FILL IN THE BLANK

Complete the following sentences by writing the correct word or words in the blanks provided.

1. Text that is printed at the top of each page is called a(n) _____ .

2. Document or file _____ are identifying information about the file, such as the author's name and the date the file was created, that is saved along with the file.

3. To combine two or more cells into one, use the _____ command.

4. If a list of words is sorted alphabetically, it is listed in _____ order.

5. _____ form the structure of a table.

TRUE / FALSE

Circle T if the statement is true or F if the statement is false.

T   F   **1.**   The place where one page ends and another begins is called section break.

T   F   **2.**   Content controls are special placeholders designed to contain a specific type of information, such as a date or the page number.

T   F   **3.**   The only place you can insert page numbers in a document is in the header.

T   F   **4.**   Some content controls are linked to specific document properties.

T   F   **5.**   When you insert a section break, the text after the section break always appears on the same page as the section break.

PROJECTS

If you have a SAM 2010 user profile, your instructor may have assigned an autogradable version of the indicated project. If so, log into the SAM 2010 Web site at *www.cengage.com/sam2010* to download the instruction and start files.

PROJECT 7–1

1. Open the **Guidelines.docx** Data File from the drive and folder where you store your Data Files. Save the document as **Correspondence Guidelines** followed by your initials.

2. Create a header using the Annual style. Type **Guidelines** in the Title content control, and use the Date content control to insert the current year. (*Hint:* Just click the Today button.)

3. Insert the Stacks footer. Do not replace the placeholder text.

4. Do not display the header or footer on the first page of the document.

5. Open the Info tab in Backstage view. Add your name as the author, and then delete the current author. Add your school as the Company name. Change the title to **Guidelines for Correspondence**. Close Backstage view and verify that the Title property is displayed in the header and that the Company name property is displayed in the footer.

6. Position the insertion point to the right of the content control in the footer, and then press Tab. Insert the Accent Bar 2 page number style at the current position.

7. On page 1, insert a page break before the *Check Spelling* heading.

8. Select the words *commonly misspelled words* in the *Check Spelling* section. Open the Research pane to find other lists of commonly misspelled words. Change the source for the research to Bing.

9. If you are connected to the Internet, open the Web page associated with one of the search results. Click in the Address bar at the top of the window to select the entire Web address. Right-click the selected address, and then click Copy on the shortcut menu. Close the browser window. Position the insertion point before the period at the end of the second sentence in the paragraph under the *Check Spelling* heading. Press the spacebar, type (and then paste the contents of the Clipboard which contains the Web site address. Type) and then close the Research task pane. (If you do not have access to the Internet, skip this step.)

10. Add the following words to the list of misspelled words: **laboratory**, **beginning**, **maintenance**, **cooperate**, and **friend**. Use the Sort button in the Paragraph group on the Home tab to sort the list in ascending order.

11. Insert a continuous section break before the spelling list. Format the second section (the one containing the spelling list) in three columns. Insert another continuous section break after the spelling list, and then format the last section of the document in one column.

12. Save, print, and close the document.

 PROJECT 7–2

1. Open the **References.docx** Data File from the drive and folder where you store your Data Files. Save it as **References Formatted** followed by your initials.

2. Convert the text in the document into a table with two columns.

3. Use the Merge cells command to merge each cell containing a person's name with the two cells below it. Merge the three cells containing each address into one cell.

4. Enter the last row of information as shown in the table in **Figure 7–22**—the row containing *Wayne Parks*. Don't be concerned with the formatting yet.

References	
Dr. John Dugan, Chairperson	State University Department of Computer Science Santa Fe, NM 87501
Selma Hernandez, President	Sierra Computer Consultants 1734 Water Street Santa Fe, NM 87505
Wayne Parks	Parks Electronics 8755 Arbor, Suite A Santa Fe, NM 87509

FIGURE 7–22

5. Format the table as shown in Figure 7–22. The table style is Medium Grid 3 – Accent 2. The text in the first row is 14 points. Notice that the names of the references in the first column are in bold, but the titles of the references are not. This means the first column is not formatted differently from the rest of the table; you need to format the names and titles manually. Also note that the first row is just tall enough to fit the text.

6. Resize the columns to the widths shown in Figure 7–22.

7. Change the name *Wayne Parks* to your name. Save your changes, and then print (but do not close) the document.

8. Select the entire table. On the Design tab, use the Shading and Borders buttons to remove the shading and the borders. The text in the first row is formatted in white, so it looks like there's nothing there. Change the color of the text in the first row to black. Save the revised document as **References Unformatted** followed by your initials.

9. Delete the first row in the document. If the new first row was reformatted as white text, select it, and then change the color of the text in the new first row to black. If necessary, correct the bold formatting in the first row.

10. Insert any style cover page you want. Use the content controls on the cover page or use the Info tab in Backstage view to insert **References** as the Title property and your name as the Author. (Make sure you delete any other author names.) If the cover page includes a Date content control, insert the current date. Delete all other content controls in the cover page.

11. Save, print, and close the document.

PROJECT 7–3

1. Open the **Sales.docx** Data File from the drive and folder where you store your Data Files. Save the document as **Sales Leaders** followed by your initials.

2. Insert a new row at the top of the table. Type the following headings**: Name,** (skip the second column)**, Region, Manager**, and **Year–to-Date Sales**.

3. Merge the cell containing *Name* and the cell to its right. Merge each of the cells containing first and last names so that each person's name appears in one cell. Remove the paragraph mark after each first name, and then insert a space between the first and last names.

4. Widen the fourth column so that *Year-to-Date Sales* fits on one line.

5. Format the table with the Colorful List - Accent 6 style. Add special formatting for the header row, and use banded columns.

6. Sort the table by year-to-date sales in descending order.

7. Center the table horizontally. Center the column headings and everything in the last column.

8. In the memo header, replace *All Employees* in the To line with your name.

9. Save, print, and close the document.

CRITICAL THINKING

ACTIVITY 7–1

Using a table without borders, create your own list of references for your personal portfolio for employment.

ACTIVITY 7–3

You own a small company that sells used CDs and DVDs. To increase sales, you decide to develop a presence on the Web. To do this, you need to register a Web site address with a domain name registrar. Most registrars also offer to host your Web site, which means they store all the files that make up your Web site on a computer so that anyone using the Web can access your site.

Use the Internet to locate at least three registrars. (Try going to **www.internic.net** to find a list of registrars.)

Create a table in Word to compare the data you find on the Internet regarding each registrar company's services provided, cost per month (per service, if available), and any convenience factors such as setup or installation requirements, fees, and customer service. Which company or companies offer the best package or services for your company?

After you have determined which registrar would be able to best serve your needs, think of a possible Web site address for your company, and then use the registrar's search function to see if that Web site address is available. If the Web site address you want to register is already taken with *.com* as the top-level domain (the last three or four letters of a Web site address), try other top-level domains such as *.biz, .net,* or *.name*.

ACTIVITY 7–2

Use Help to learn how to insert a formula to add a column of numbers in a table. Use a formula to add the Year-to-Date Sales column in the Sales Leaders.docx document that you worked on in Project 7–3.

LESSON 8

Increasing Efficiency Using Word

■ OBJECTIVES

Upon completion of this lesson, you should be able to:

- Use and create templates.
- Use mail merge.
- Create and print envelopes and labels.
- Insert, view, edit, and print comments.
- Track changes.
- Accept and reject changes and delete comments.
- Combine different versions of a document.
- Customize Word.

■ VOCABULARY

data source

mail merge

main document

merge field

template

Track Changes

workgroup collaboration

Word provides many tools and customization that you can use to increase your efficiency when using the program. For example, you can create and use templates to help you create consistent looking documents that contain the correct information. You can merge a list of addresses with a form letter to create personalized form letters. You can also ask other people to review your documents and make changes and suggestions using features that display the changes as colored text and the suggestions in balloons. Finally, you can customize many options in Word to take advantage of the way you work.

Using Templates

Suppose you are a sales representative, and you must file a report each week that summarizes your sales and the new contacts you have made. Parts of this report will be the same each week, such as the format and the headings. Re-creating the document each week would be time consuming. You can solve this problem by creating a template in Word or using an existing Word template for documents that you create frequently.

A ***template*** is a file that contains the basic elements of a document, such as page and paragraph formatting, fonts, and text. You can customize the template to create a new document that is similar to but slightly different from the original. For example, a report template for a sales representative would save all formatting, font choices, and text that does not change, allowing you to fill in only the new information each week.

Using an Installed Template

Word contains many templates you can use to create documents. Some templates are installed on your computer, and others are available on the Microsoft Office Online Web site. To use an installed Word template, click the File tab, and then in the navigation bar, click New. In the Available Templates list, click Sample Templates. The middle pane in the dialog box changes to show all the templates installed on your computer. You can scroll down to see the various templates installed. See **Figure 8–1**.

▶ **VOCABULARY**

template

Sample templates are the templates installed on this computer

Preview shows the selected template

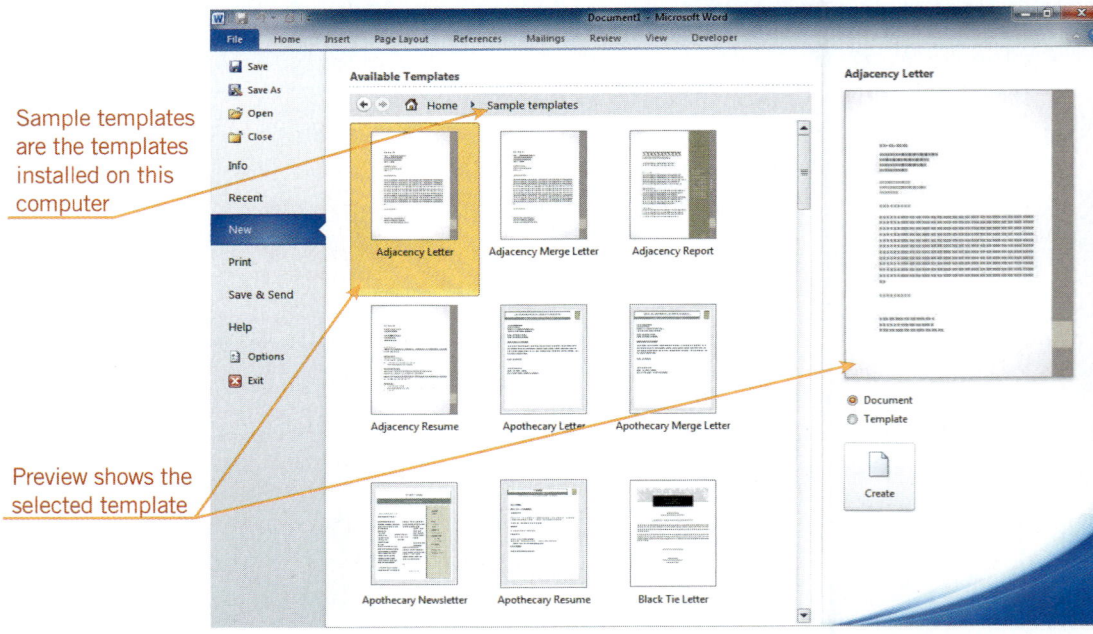

FIGURE 8–1   Sample templates on the New tab in Backstage view

To create a new document based on one of the templates, click it, and then in the right pane, click the Create button. Word opens a new blank document with the settings and text specified by the template already in place. As with any new document, the file name in the title bar is *Document* followed by a number. Replace the data in the template with your own data and save it.

TIP

To create a document based on a template from Office.com, click one of the categories under Office.com Templates in the center of the New tab, click a category folder as needed, select a template, and then click the Download button.

Step-by-Step 8.1

1. Start Word. On the Ribbon, click the **File** tab, and then in the navigation bar, click **New**. The New tab appears in Backstage view.

2. In the center under Available Templates, click **Sample templates**. The installed templates appear. Scroll down and then click the **Origin Fax** icon. The preview on the right shows the Origin Fax template.

3. In the right pane, make sure the **Document** option button is selected, and then click the **Create** button. The Origin Fax template appears on your screen as a new, unsaved document. Note that the title in the title bar is *Document* followed by a number, like all new documents.

4. On the Quick Access Toolbar, click the **Save** button 🔲. Navigate to the drive and folder where you save your files. Replace the text in the File name box with **Bank Fax** followed by your initials, and then click **Save**.

5. At the top of the document, on the right, click **[Pick a date]**. This is a date content control. Click the **arrow** to the right of the content control. Click **Today**.

6. Next to *From*, if placeholder text appears in the content control, click **[Type the sender name]**, and then type your name. If a name already appears in that location, select the name, and then type your name.

7. Next to *Phone* under *From*, click the placeholder text **[Type the sender phone number]**, and then type **(914) 555-7534**.

8. Next to *Fax* under *From*, replace the placeholder text **[Type the sender fax number]** with **(914) 555-6409**, and replace the placeholder text **[Type the sender company name]** with **White Plains National Bank**.

9. To the right of *To*, replace **[Type the recipient name]** with **Wyatt Brown**.

10. In the *To* section, replace **[Type the recipient phone number]** with **(914) 555-6430**, replace **[Type the recipient fax number]** with **(914) 555-6432**, and then replace **[Type the recipient company name]** with **Graphic Designers**.

WARNING

If the Template option button is selected, the file that you open will be a template file type, not a document file type.

11. Under *Comments*, click **[Type comments]** and then type:

    I reviewed the first draft of the checking account pamphlet and added my comments to the draft. Please revise the pamphlet by next Thursday. Thank you.

12. Save your changes. Print and close the document, but do not exit Word.

Creating a Template

You can create a customized template by modifying an existing template or document. To create a template, you need to save the document as a template. Click the File tab, in the navigation bar, click Save As, click the Save as type arrow, and then click Word Template (*.dotx). Type a file name in the File name box, and then click Save. Your document will be saved as a template in the current folder.

Step-by-Step 8.2

1. Create a new, blank document.

2. Type the following:

   White Plains National Bank

   309 Third Street

   White Plains, NY 10610

   (914) 555-7534

   www.whiteplainsnationalbank.com

3. Press **Enter** twice. Type **<Replace with current date>**. Press **Enter** again.

4. Change the theme to **Grid**. Change the style of the first five paragraphs to **No Spacing**, and then center those paragraphs.

5. Change the paragraph spacing of the *<Replace with current date>* paragraph so that it has 36 points of space before it and 10 points of space after it.

6. Right-click the Web site address at the top of the document, and then on the shortcut menu, click **Remove Hyperlink**.

7. Format the first line in the document as **14-point Copperplate Gothic Bold**. Change the font size of the rest of the lines in the header to **12 points**.

8. Position the insertion point in front of the word *White* in the first line of the header, and then search for clip art using the keyword **bank**. Insert a clip of a piggy bank. If you can't find that clip, use another appropriate clip. If you do not have access to Office.com, try the search using the keyword *money* instead, and use the clip with the dollar sign. Close the Clip Art task pane when you are finished.

9. Proportionately resize the image so that at least one side is one inch.

10. With the image still selected, on the Ribbon, click the **Picture Tools Format** tab, if necessary. In the Arrange group, click the **Position** button, and then click the first icon in the first row under With Text Wrapping. The image changes to a floating graphic and moves to the top-left corner of the document. Deselect the image. See **Figure 8–2**.

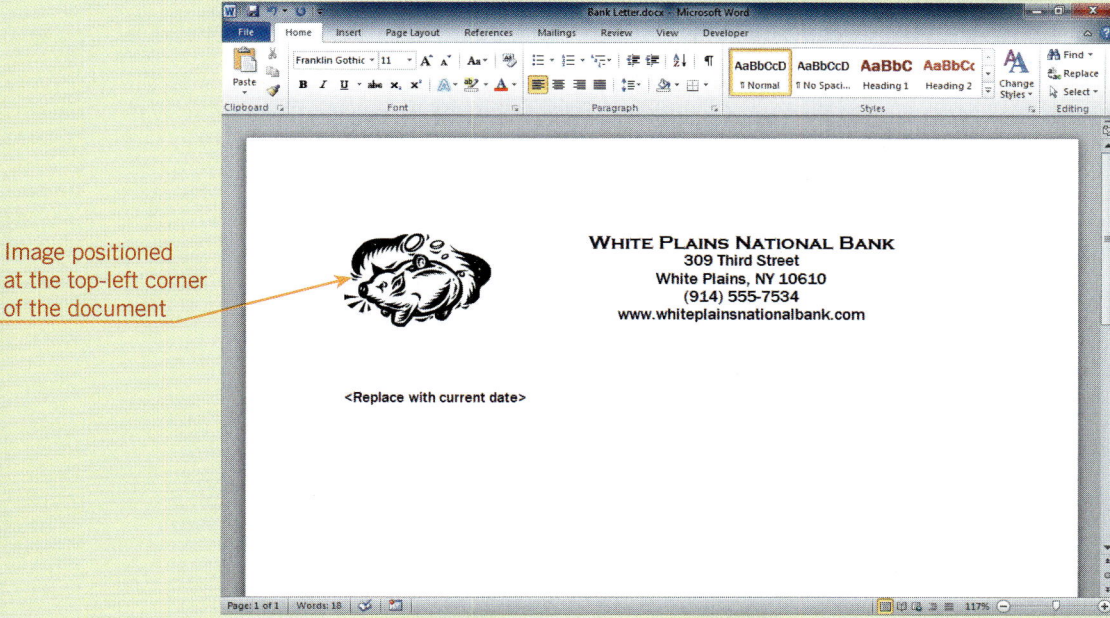

FIGURE 8–2
Completed Bank
Template document

Image positioned
at the top-left corner
of the document

11. Add your name in the paragraph below the date placeholder.

12. Click the **File** tab, and then in the navigation bar, click **Save As**. In the Save As dialog box, click the **Save as type** arrow, and then click **Word Template (.dotx)**.

13. Select the text in the File name box, and then type **Bank Template** followed by your initials. Click **Save**.

14. Close the file, but do not exit Word.

EXTRA FOR EXPERTS

To store your templates so that others can easily locate them, in the Save As dialog box, click Templates in the navigation pane, and then save the template in that folder. To access these templates, in the New tab in Backstage view, click My templates, and then select the template in the New dialog box that opens.

Creating a Document Using a Custom Template

You can use the template you created as many times as needed. To create a new document based on your template, open the New tab in Backstage view. Under Available Templates, click New from existing. The New from Existing Document dialog box opens, as shown in **Figure 8–3**.

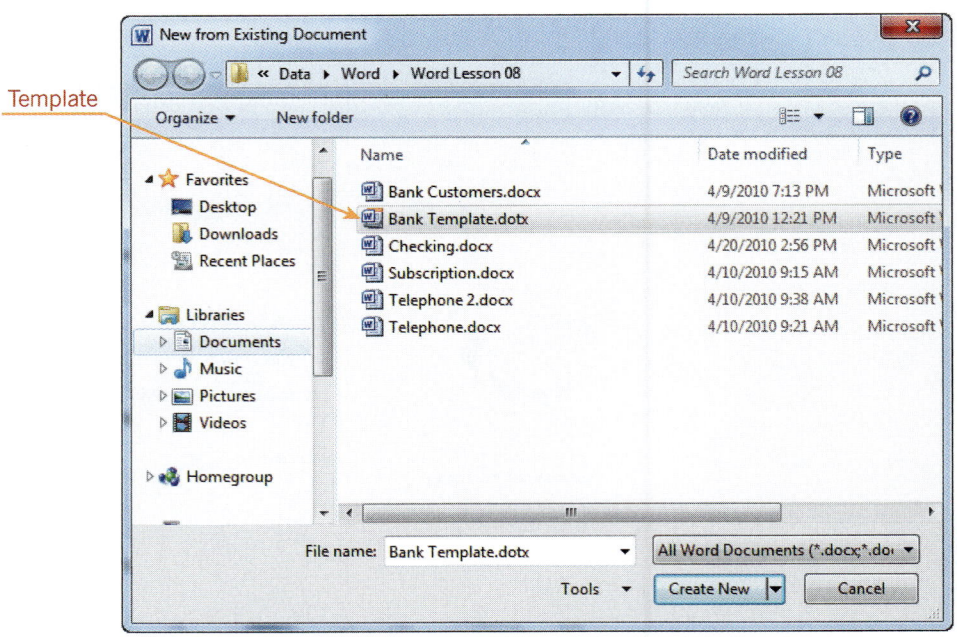

FIGURE 8–3   New from Existing Document dialog box

The files shown in the dialog box are both template and document files. Click the template or document you want to use, and then click Create New. A new document opens with all the text and formatting from the template or document you selected. As with the new document you created from the installed template, the file name in the title bar is *Document* followed by a number. After you make changes to this document, you can save the document as you normally would.

Step-by-Step 8.3

1. Click the **File** tab, and then in the navigation bar, click **New**. The New tab appears in Backstage view. Under Available Templates, click **New from existing**. The New from Existing Document dialog box opens. Notice that the command button on the left in the lower-right corner of the dialog box is Open.

2. Locate the folder in which you saved the Bank Template file. Click **Bank Template.dotx**. The Open button changes to Create New. Click **Create New**. The template opens as a new document.

3. Save the document as **Bank Letter** followed by your initials.

4. Position the insertion point at the beginning of the line containing your name, and then press **Enter** to insert a blank paragraph between the *<Replace with current date>* line and your name.

5. Open the **Checking.docx** file from the drive and folder where your Data Files are stored. Select all the text in the document, and then copy it to the Clipboard. Close the Checking.docx document.

6. Select your name in the Bank Letter document. In the Clipboard group on the Home tab, click the **Paste** button.

7. On the right end of the status bar, click the number to the left of the Zoom slider to open the Zoom dialog box. In the Percent box, select the value, and then type **77**. Click **OK**. Scroll down so that you can see the entire letter on the screen. Your screen should match **Figure 8–4**.

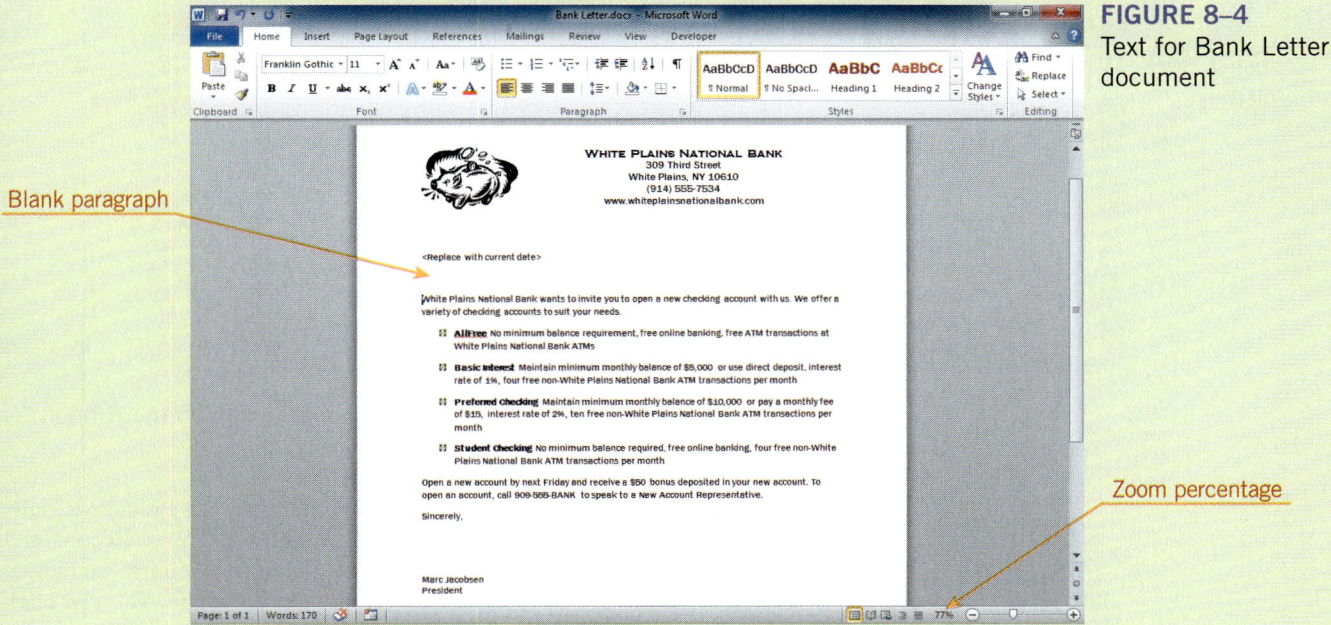

FIGURE 8–4
Text for Bank Letter document

Blank paragraph

Zoom percentage

8. On the Ribbon, click the **View** tab, and then in the Zoom group, click the **Page Width** button.

9. Save your changes, and leave the document open for the next Step-by-Step.

Using Mail Merge

▶ **VOCABULARY**

mail merge

main document

data source

merge fields

Mail merge combines a document with information that personalizes the document. For example, you might send a letter to each member of a professional organization. In each letter, the text is the same but the names of the recipients are different. For example, a letter may begin *Dear Mr. Montgomery* or *Dear Ms. Jansen*. The document with the information that does not change is called the *main document*. The *data source* is the file containing the information that varies in each document.

To perform a mail merge, you use the commands on the Mailings tab on the Ribbon. You start by clicking the Start Mail Merge button in the Start Mail Merge group, and then clicking the type of mail merge you want to do. The most common type is a letter. The second step is to choose the data source by clicking the Select Recipients button in the Start Mail Merge group. Next, you need to insert merge fields. *Merge fields* are placeholders that are replaced with data from the data source when you perform the merge. See **Figure 8–5**.

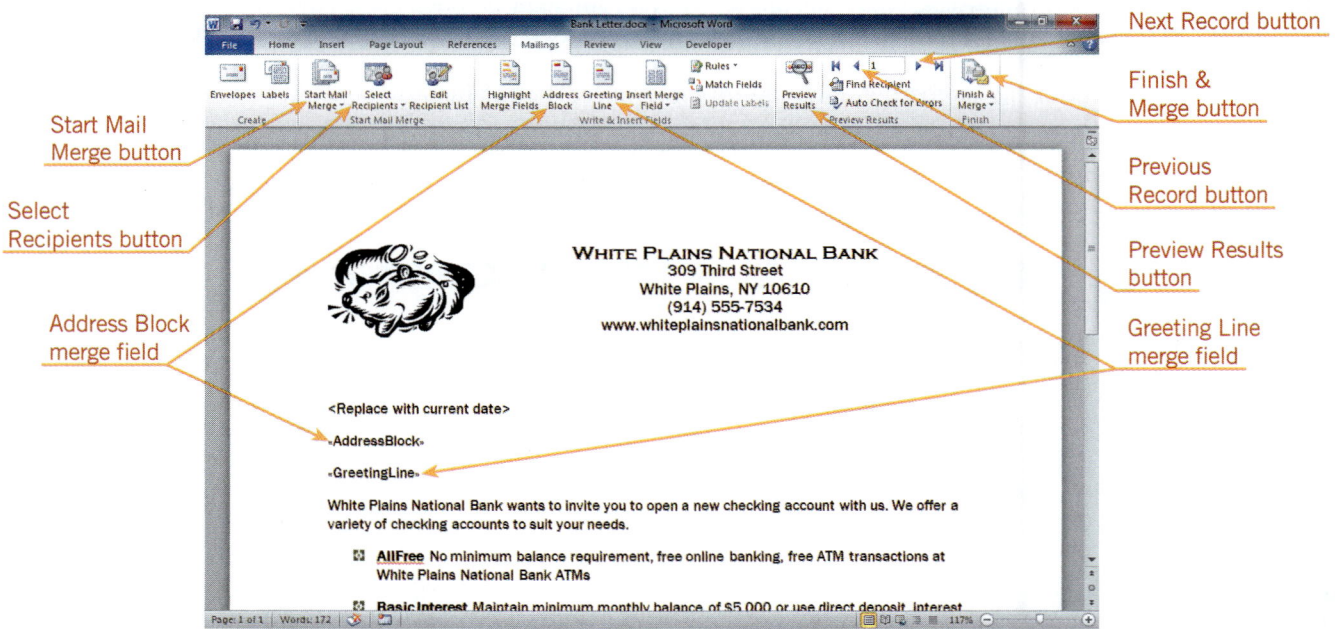

FIGURE 8–5   Merge fields inserted using the Mailings tab on the Ribbon

After you have inserted all the merge fields, you can click the Preview Results button in the Preview Results group. You can then click the Next Record and Previous Record buttons to scroll through the results preview. To finish the merge, click the Finish & Merge button in the Finish group. On the menu, you can click Print Documents to print the merged documents or click Edit Individual Documents to create a new document consisting of all the merged documents.

Step-by-Step 8.4

1. Open the **Bank Customers.docx** file from the drive and folder where your Data Files are stored. This file contains a table with a list of names and addresses. This is the data source for the merge. Notice that each person's title, first name, and last name are in separate columns. Close this file.

2. On the Ribbon, click the **Mailings** tab. In the Start Mail Merge group, click the **Start Mail Merge** button. Click **Letters**. The current document is identified as a letter you will merge with a data source. Notice that none of the buttons in the Write & Insert Fields, Preview Results, or Finish groups are available.

3. In the Start Mail Merge group, click the **Select Recipients** button. Click **Use Existing List**. The Select Data Source dialog box opens. This dialog box is similar to the Open dialog box.

4. Navigate to the drive and folder where you store your Data Files. Click **Bank Customers.docx**, and then click **Open**. Now the rest of the buttons on the Mailings tab are available.

5. Position the insertion point in the blank paragraph below the date placeholder text. First, you need to insert the Address Block merge field, which will be replaced with the inside address in the letter. In the Write & Insert Fields group, click the **Address Block** button. The Insert Address Block dialog box opens.

6. If necessary, in the list on the left, scroll down and then click the **Mr. Joshua Randall Jr.** name format, as shown in **Figure 8–6**.

EXTRA FOR EXPERTS

To create a new list of recipients, click the Select Recipients button, and then click Type New List to open the New Address List dialog box. Type your data, and then click OK. In the Save Address List dialog box, type a file name, and then click Save. The Save as type is Microsoft Office Address Lists (*.mdb).

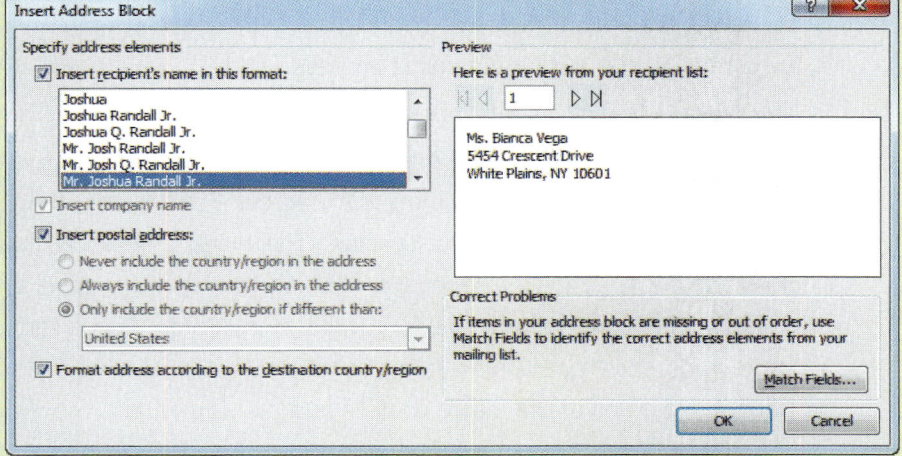

FIGURE 8–6
Insert Address Block dialog box

7. Click **OK**. The Address Block merge field is inserted in the document.

8. Press **Enter**. In the Write & Insert Fields group, click the **Greeting Line** button. The Insert Greeting Line dialog box opens.

9. If necessary, click the **arrow** next to the middle box in the row under Greeting line format, and then click **Mr. Randall** in the list. Click the **arrow** next to the comma (next to the rightmost box), and then click : (the colon). See **Figure 8–7**.

FIGURE 8–7
Insert Greeting Line dialog box

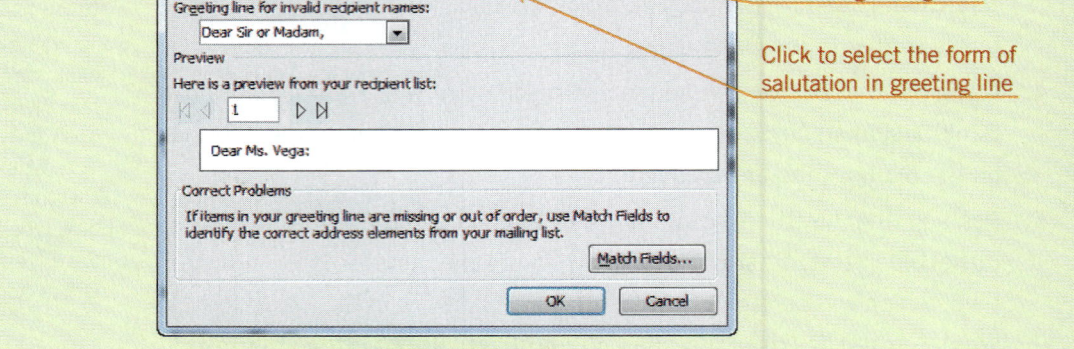

10. Click **OK**. The Greeting Line merge field is inserted in the document.

11. On the Mailings tab, in the Preview Results group, click the **Preview Results** button. The merge fields in the document are replaced with data in the first row in your data source (Bianca Vega's information). Notice that each line in the inside address has extra space after it. This is not normal formatting for the inside address.

12. In the Preview Results group, click the **Preview Results** button. The preview turns off and you see the merge fields again.

13. Click anywhere in the line containing the Address Block merge field, and then change the style to **No Spacing**. The blank line below the Address Block merge field disappears. Position the insertion point at the end of the Address Block line, and then press **Enter**. This inserts a single blank line (a paragraph formatted with the No Spacing style) between the last line of the inside address and the salutation.

14. On the Ribbon, click the **Mailings** tab, and then, in the Preview Results group, click the **Preview Results** button. Bianca Vega's information appears in the letter properly formatted. In the Preview Results group, to the right of the number 1, click the **Next Record** button ▶. The data from the recipient in the second row in the table in the data source (George Corrigan) appears in the document.

15. Replace the date placeholder text with the current date in the form June 27, 2013.

16. On the Ribbon, click the **Mailings** tab. In the Finish group, click the **Finish & Merge** button, and then click **Print Documents**. The Merge to Printer dialog box opens, in which you can specify the records you want to print. Click the **Current record** option button. This tells Word to print only the current letter (the letter addressed to George Corrigan) rather than all three letters. Click **OK**. The Print dialog box opens.

17. Click **OK**. The Print dialog box closes and the current letter prints.

18. In the Preview Results group, click the **Preview Results** button to display the merge fields again. In the Finish group, click the **Finish & Merge** button, and then click **Edit Individual Documents**. The Merge to New Document dialog box opens. Click the **All** option button, if necessary, and then click **OK**. A new document opens with the temporary name "Letters" followed by a number. This document contains one letter for each of the recipients listed in the data source.

19. Save the document as **Bank New Customer Letters** followed by your initials. Close the document. Close the Bank Letter document, and when the dialog box opens asking if you want to save changes, click **Don't Save**. Do not exit Word.

EXTRA FOR EXPERTS

You can insert customized information in the body of the letter. Add the data to the data source, and then use the Insert Merge Field button on the Mailings tab to insert the custom data.

Creating and Printing Envelopes

Addressing envelopes is easy using Word. Click the Mailings tab on the Ribbon. In the Create group, click the Envelopes button to open the Envelopes and Labels dialog box with the Envelopes tab on top, as shown in **Figure 8–8**.

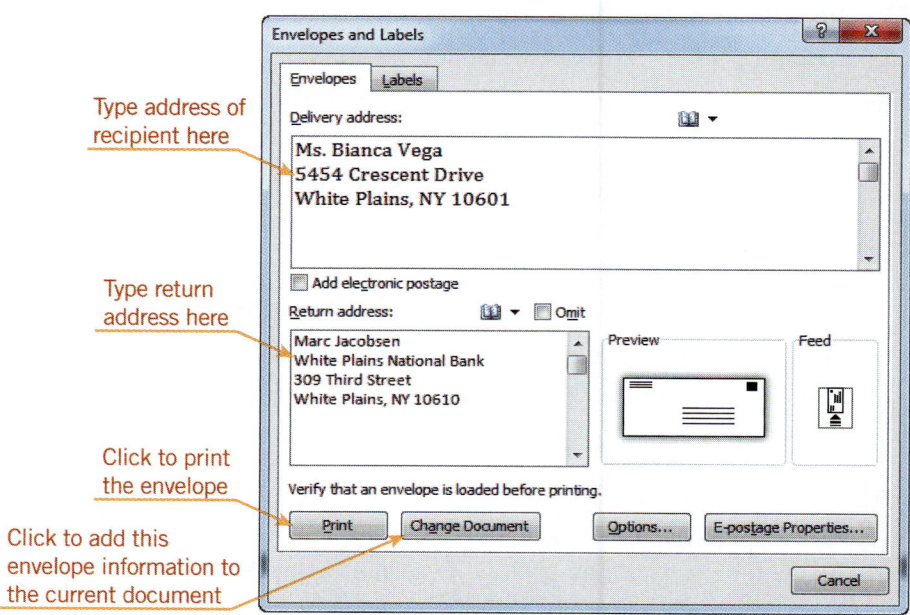

FIGURE 8–8 Envelopes tab in the Envelopes and Labels dialog box

If you select an address (such as the inside address in a letter) before you open the dialog box, the address appears in the Delivery address box in the dialog box, although you can replace the text in the address box with any address you like. If there is any text in the Return address box, select it, and then type your own name and address. To print the envelope, insert an envelope in your printer, and then click Print. To see the envelope layout before you print, click Add to Document. The envelope appears at the top of the current document, as shown in **Figure 8–9**. Then you can print the envelope as you would any document.

Envelopes button

Your name appears here

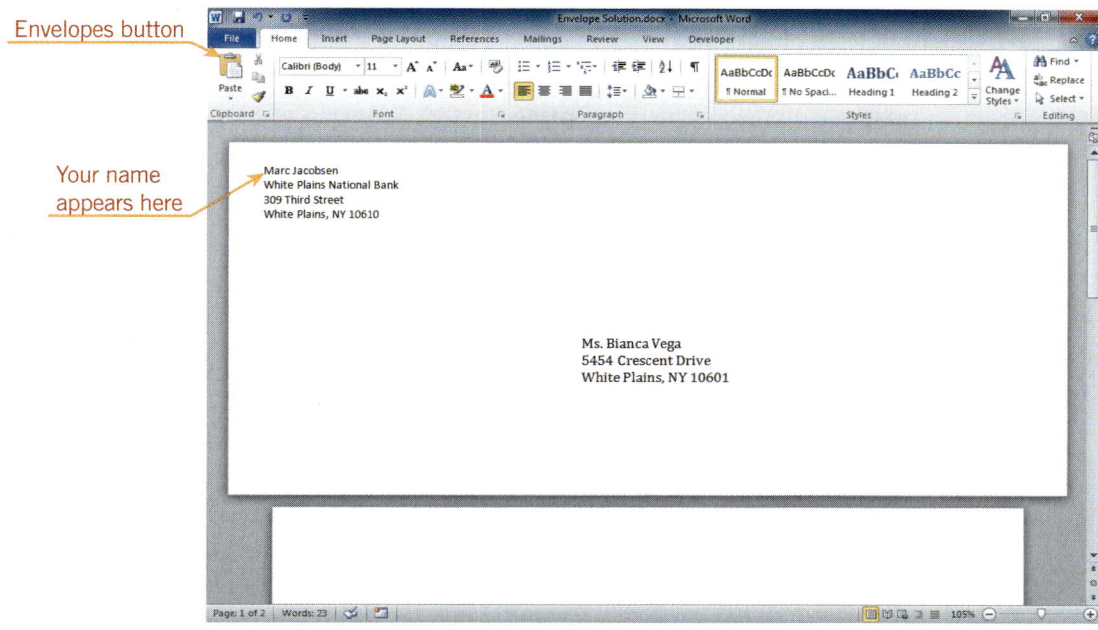

FIGURE 8–9   Completed envelope

Step-by-Step 8.5

1. Create a new, blank Word document.

2. On the Ribbon, click the **Mailings** tab. In the Create group, click the **Envelopes** button. The Envelopes and Labels dialog box opens with the Envelopes tab on top.

3. In the Delivery address box, type the following:

   Ms. Bianca Vega

   5454 Crescent Drive

   White Plains, NY 10601

4. Click in the **Return address** box, type your name, and then type the following address:

   White Plains National Bank

   309 Third Street

   White Plains, NY 10610

> **TIP**
>
> You can also perform a mail merge with a data source to print envelopes and labels. In the Start Mail Merge group on the Mailings tab, click the Start Mail Merge button, and then click Envelopes or Labels.

> **EXTRA FOR EXPERTS**
>
> To change the envelope size from the standard business-sized envelope, click Options on the Envelopes tab in the Envelopes and Labels dialog box.

5. Click **Add to Document**. A dialog box opens asking if you want to save the return address as the default return address. Click **No**. The dialog box closes and the setup of the document is changed to an envelope with the addresses you typed in the correct locations.

6. If you have an envelope, insert it into the printer; otherwise you can print on plain paper. Print the document.

7. Save the document as **Envelope** followed by your initials.

8. Close the document, but do not exit Word.

Creating and Printing Labels

Creating labels is similar to creating envelopes. On the Mailings tab, click the Labels button in the Create group. The Envelopes and Labels dialog box opens with the Labels tab on top, as shown in **Figure 8–10**.

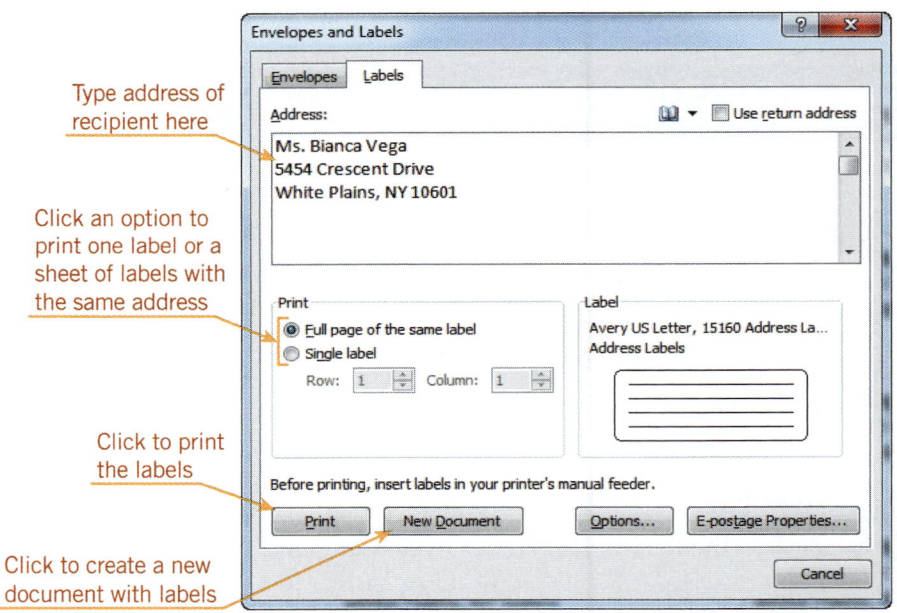

Type address of recipient here

Click an option to print one label or a sheet of labels with the same address

Click to print the labels

Click to create a new document with labels

FIGURE 8–10   Labels tab in the Envelopes and Labels dialog box

Type the address you want to appear on the labels. The default is to print a full page of the same label. If you want to print just one label, in the Print section, click the Single label option button.

The dimensions of the label are listed in the Label section. To print the labels, insert a sheet of labels in your printer, and then click Print. To see the layout of the labels before you print, click New Document. A new document opens with the labels, as shown in **Figure 8–11**. Then you can format and print the document as you would any document.

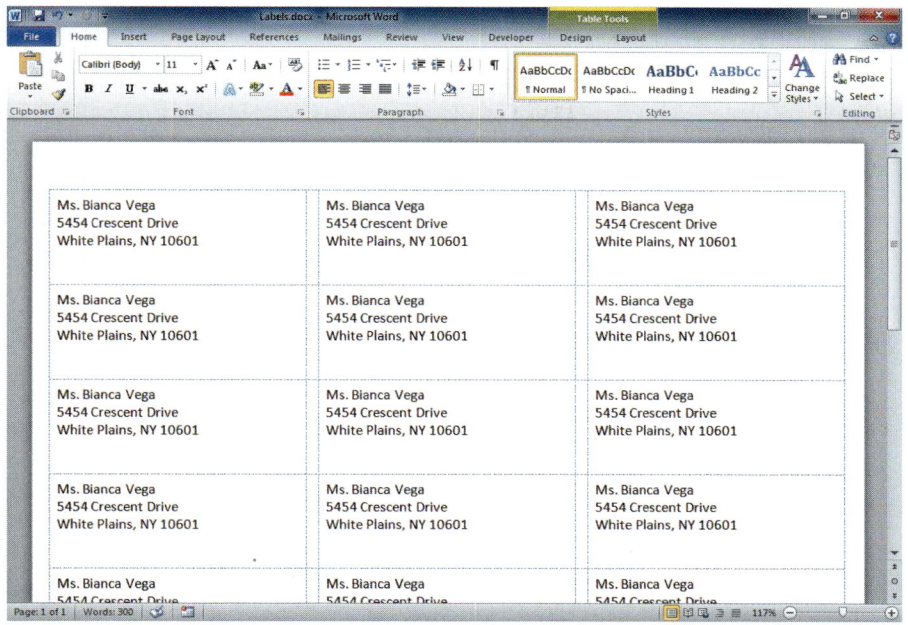

FIGURE 8–11   Completed Labels document

To choose a label type other than the one listed, click Options on the Label tab in the Envelopes and Labels dialog box. The Label Options dialog box opens. You can buy labels at an office supply store. Click the Label vendors arrow, and then click the manufacturer of the labels you purchased. Scroll down the Product number list, and then click the product number of the labels you bought (it will be on the box of labels).

Step-by-Step 8.6

1. Create a new, blank Word document.

2. On the Ribbon, click the **Mailings** tab. In the Create group, click the **Labels** button. The Envelopes and Labels dialog box opens with the Labels tab on top.

3. In the Address box, type your name and the following address. Notice that the address is inserted with either the No Spacing or the Normal style applied.

   5454 Crescent Drive

   White Plains, NY 10601

4. In the Print section, make sure the **Full page of the same label** option button is selected.

5. Click **Options** to open the Label Options dialog box, and then click the **Label vendors** arrow. A list of label manufacturers opens. Each manufacturer sells labels of different sizes. If you have labels that you bought at an office supply store, you could click the name of the manufacturer of your labels, and then, in the Product number list, scroll down if necessary and click the product number of your labels. For now, you'll print on ordinary paper.

6. Click **Avery US Letter** in the Label vendors list, scroll down the Product number list until you see 15160, and then click **15160 Address Labels**. The Label information on the right indicates that the document will be set up for mailing labels one inch high and 2.63 inches wide on 8.5" x 11" paper.

7. Click **OK**. The Label Options dialog closes. Click **New Document**. The Envelopes and Labels dialog box closes and a document opens with the name and address you typed inserted into cells in a table. Dotted lines indicate the borders of the table.

8. Save the document as **Labels** followed by your initials. Print the document.

9. Close the document, but do not exit Word.

Collaborating with a Workgroup Using Comments and Tracked Changes

> **VOCABULARY**
> **workgroup collaboration**

The process of working together in teams, sharing comments, and exchanging ideas for a common purpose is called *workgroup collaboration*. When you work in groups, the tasks are often divided among the team members. The team meets to review each other's work, comment on it, and suggest changes.

Word provides several ways team members can collaborate. Team members can circulate a document and add comments to the document. Each member can also make changes to the document and have those changes tracked so that it is easy for the owner of the document to see suggested insertions, deletions, and moved text.

Changing the User Name

When you make certain changes to a document, Word identifies the changes with the user name. To change the user name that appears for these changes, you need to open the Word Options dialog box. Click the File tab, and then in the navigation bar, click Options. The Word Options dialog box opens with General selected in the list on the left, as shown in **Figure 8–12**.

General options are displayed

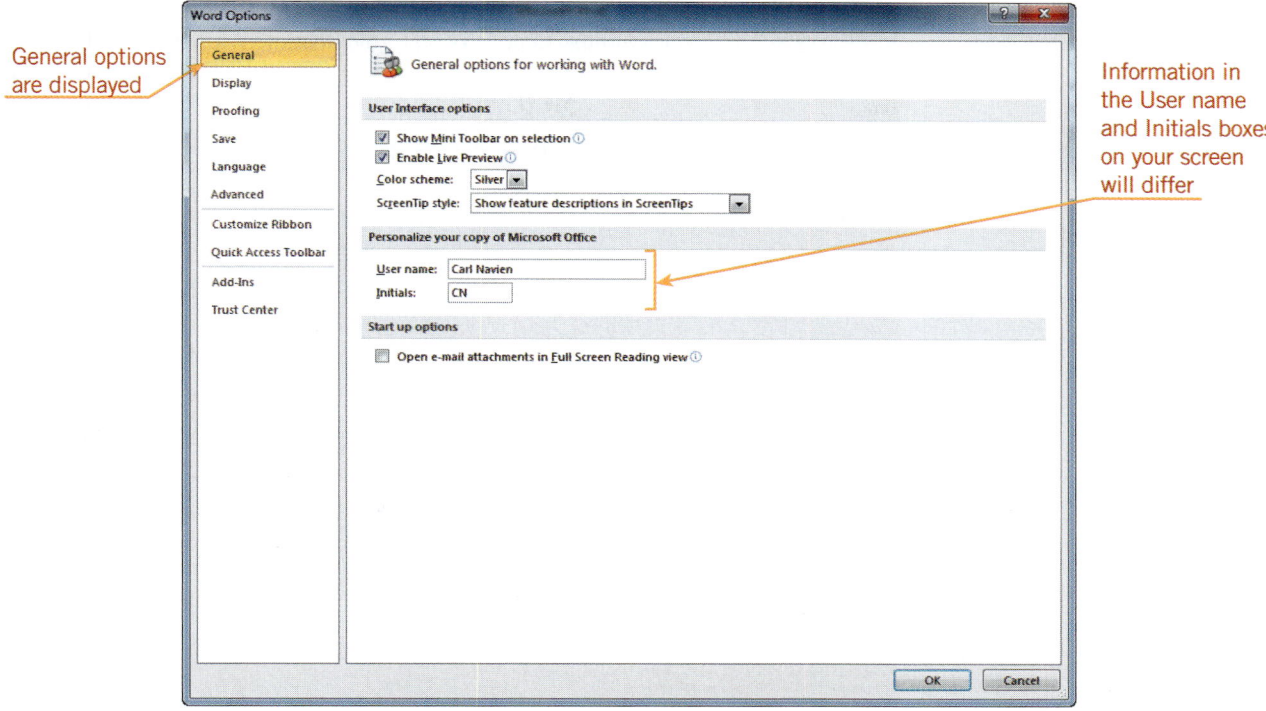

Information in the User name and Initials boxes on your screen will differ

FIGURE 8–12   Word Options dialog box with General selected

Under Personalize your copy of Microsoft Office, the User name and Initials boxes appear. You can change the name and initials in these boxes. When you are finished, click OK to close the dialog box and save your changes.

Using Comments

One way you can collaborate with others is to send a document out for review. Each person who reviews the document can insert comments in the document. To insert a comment, either position the pointer or select the text about which you wish to comment. On the Ribbon, click the Review tab, and then in the Comments group, click the New Comment button. A comment balloon appears to the right of the text. The comment balloon is connected to the text by a line. The initials from the General section of the Word Options dialog box and the comment number appear in the comment balloon. If you position the pointer on top of the comment balloon or the highlighted text in the document, the name of the person who made the comment as well as the date and time the comment was made appear in a ScreenTip, as shown in **Figure 8–13**. If you send the same version of the document to another person for review and that person inserts comments, their comments appear in a different color.

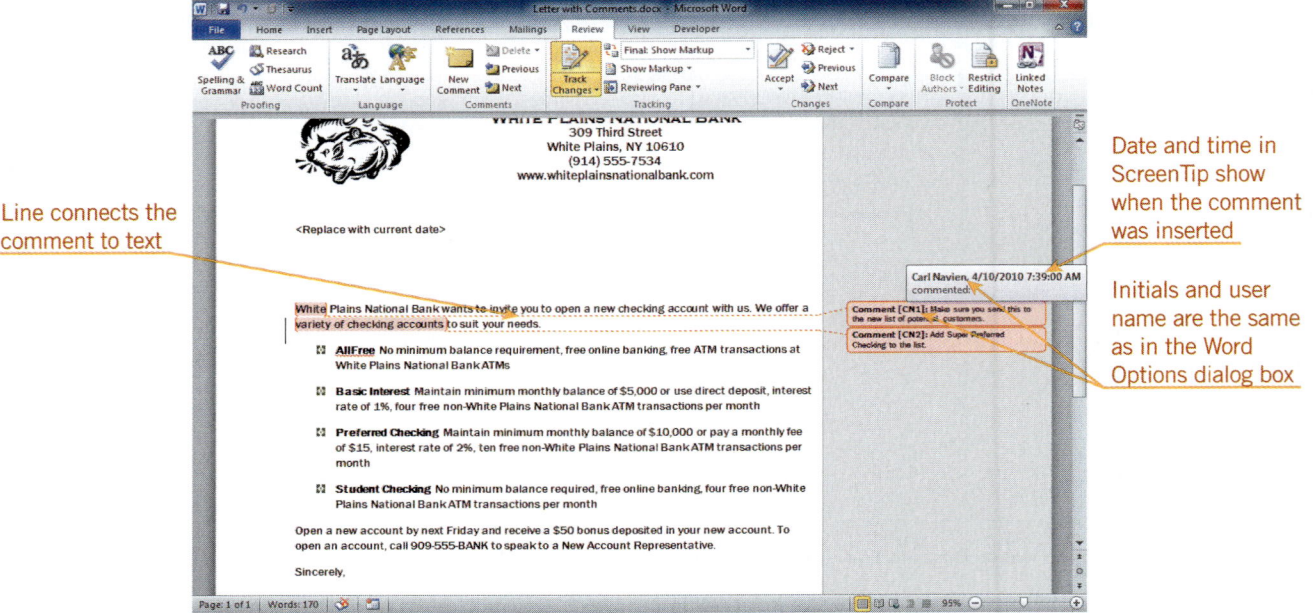

Line connects the comment to text

Date and time in ScreenTip show when the comment was inserted

Initials and user name are the same as in the Word Options dialog box

FIGURE 8–13   Comments in a document

EXTRA FOR EXPERTS

If a comment is very long, or if there are many comments on a page, only the first part of the comment appears in the comment balloon, and a button with three small dots appears in the lower-right corner of the comment balloon. To see the entire comment, click the button to open the Reviewing pane to the left of or below the document window. You can also click the Reviewing Pane button in the Tracking group on the Review tab.

After you have inserted your comments in a document, you can go back and make changes to them. To move from comment to comment, click the Next or Previous button in the Comments group on the Review tab. To edit a comment, click inside the comment balloon, and then make your changes.

Step-by-Step 8.7

1. Open the **Bank Letter.docx** file that you created earlier in this lesson. Save it as **Letter with Comments** followed by your initials. Change the zoom to **Page Width**.

2. Click the **File** tab, and then in the navigation bar, click **Options**. The Word Options dialog box opens with General selected in the list on the left. Write down the name and initials that appear in the User name and Initials boxes.

3. Select all the text in the User name box, and then type **Carl Navien**. Select the text in the Initials box, and then type **CN**. Click **OK**. The dialog box closes.

4. Position the insertion point at the beginning of the first paragraph in the body of the letter. On the Ribbon, click the **Review** tab. In the Comments group, click the **New Comment** button. The first word in the paragraph is highlighted in color and a comment balloon appears off to the right. The initials CN appear in the balloon, and the insertion point is blinking in the balloon.

5. Type **Make sure you send this to the list of potential customers.**

6. In the second sentence of the first paragraph in the body of the letter, select the phrase **variety of checking accounts**. In the Comments group, click the **New Comment** button. The phrase you selected is highlighted with your comment color, and another comment balloon appears.

7. In the comment balloon, type **Add Super Preferred Checking to the list.**

8. Click in the first comment balloon. Position the insertion point immediately in front of the word *list*. Type **new**, and then press the **spacebar**.

9. Click the **File** tab, and then in the navigation bar, click **Options**. Change the name in the User name box to **Stefanie E. Riposa**. Change the initials in the Initials box to **SER**. Click **OK**.

10. In the second item in the bulleted list (the *Basic Interest* item), select the word **four**. On the Review tab, in the Comments group, click the **New Comment** button. A new comment is inserted with Stefanie's initials and in a color different from the color used for Carl's comments. Type **This is now three transactions per month.** See **Figure 8–14**.

FIGURE 8–14
Document with comments from two people

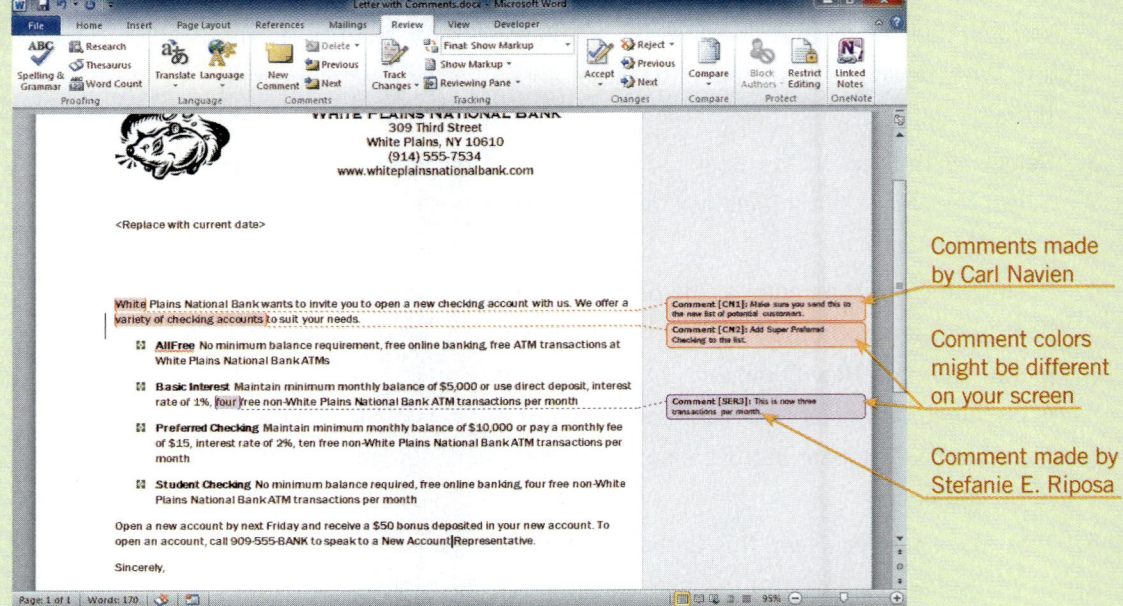

11. Position the pointer over the first comment. A ScreenTip appears identifying Carl Navien as the person who inserted the comment. The date and time the comment was inserted also appear in the ScreenTip.

12. Position the pointer over the last comment in the document. The ScreenTip identifies Stefanie E. Riposa as the author of this comment.

13. Save the document. Leave it open for the next Step-by-Step.

Tracking Changes

▶ **VOCABULARY**
Track Changes

Word provides a tool called **Track Changes** that keeps a record of any changes you or a reviewer makes in a document. If you turn this feature on, any changes made are marked in the document. Text that you insert is underlined and colored with the same color as your comments. Text you delete is put into a Deleted balloon similar to a comment balloon.

If you move text and it is at least a sentence long, the text you cut is marked with a Moved balloon. The pasted text is also marked with a Moved balloon and appears in green with a green double underline. Both Moved balloons have a Go button in them. You can click the Go button to jump back and forth between the cut and paste locations. The two Moved balloons associated with the first moved selection both have the number 1 in them. If you move a second selection, the two Moved balloons for the second move will have the number 2 in them.

You can position the pointer on top of inserted, deleted, or moved text, and as with comments, a ScreenTip identifies the person who made the change and the date and time the change was made.

To turn on the Track Changes feature, click the Review tab on the Ribbon, and then, in the Tracking group, click the Track Changes button.

EXTRA FOR EXPERTS

To show the document with all the changes, in the Tracking group, click the Final Showing Markup arrow, and then click Final. The insertions appear as normal text, and the Moved and Deleted balloons are removed.

Step-by-Step 8.8

1. On the Review tab, in the Tracking group, click the **Track Changes** button to turn on the Track Changes feature.

2. In the first item in the bulleted list (the *AllFree* item), delete the phrase **free online banking,**. Make sure you delete the comma and the space after the comma. A Deleted balloon appears to the right of the document, showing the deleted text. As with the comment balloons, a line connects the balloon to the location of the deleted text in the document. The line and the outline of the balloon are the same color as Stefanie Riposa's comment. (*Note*: If the deleted text appears with a line through it instead of in a Deleted balloon, in the Tracking group, click the **Show Markup** button, point to **Balloons**, and then click **Show Revisions in Balloons**.)

3. In the last paragraph at the bottom of the letter, select **New Account**, and then type **Customer Service**. Note that the new text is underlined and shown in the color of Stefanie's comment.

WARNING

If the Moved balloons do not appear, click the Review tab, click the arrow on the Track Changes button in the Tracking group, click Change Tracking Options, click the Use Balloons (Print and Web Layout) arrow in the Balloons section, click Always, and then click OK.

4. In the last paragraph, select the first sentence. (It starts with *Open a new account.*) Use drag-and-drop or the Cut and Paste commands to move the selected sentence to the end of the first paragraph. The moved text appears in green with a double underline, and a Moved balloon with a Go button appears next to the moved text and next to the paragraph where the text was located before you moved it. The two Moved balloons both have the number 1 in them. See **Figure 8–15**.

FIGURE 8–15
Document with tracked changes

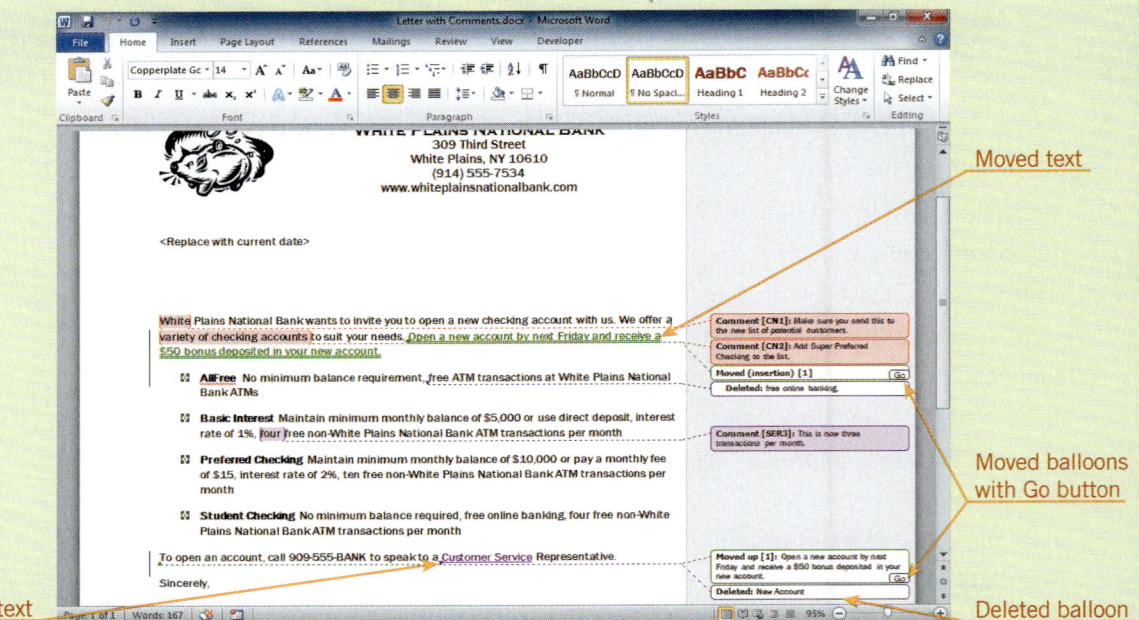

5. In the Moved balloon next to the first paragraph, click **Go**. The other Moved balloon associated with this Moved balloon is selected.

6. Click the **File** tab, and then in the navigation bar, click **Options**. Select the text in the User name box, and then replace it with the original name that you wrote down when you first opened the Word Options dialog box. Select the text in the Initials box, and then replace it with the original initials. Click **OK**.

7. Save the document, and leave it open for the next Step-by-Step.

Accepting and Rejecting Changes and Deleting Comments

Now that the changes have been made to the document, you have an opportunity to either accept or reject them. To accept or reject a change in the document, click the text that has been changed to select it, and then click the Accept or Reject button in the Changes group on the Review tab. The change is accepted or rejected, and the insertion point jumps to the next change in the document. If you don't want to jump to the next change in the document, click the arrow below the Accept or Reject button, and then click Accept Change or Reject Change.

Step-by-Step 8.9

1. Move the insertion point to the beginning of the document. On The Review tab, in the Comments group, click the **Next** button. The first comment in the document, Carl Navien's first comment, is selected. This comment is a reminder to send the letter to the new list of potential customers, so it would be helpful to leave it in the letter.

2. In the Comments group, click the **Next** button. The next comment is selected. You'll add the information requested after deleting the comment. In the Comments group, click the **Delete** button. The comment is deleted.

3. In the document, click after the last word in the *Preferred Checking* bullet (after *month*). Press **Enter**. Type **Super Preferred Checking**. Press **Ctrl+B** to turn off the automatic bold formatting that was picked up from the previous item in the list. Press the **spacebar** twice. Type **Maintain minimum monthly balance of $25,000 or pay a monthly fee of $25, interest rate of 2.5%, free transactions at all ATMs**. Because you changed the User name and Initials back to their originals, the inserted text appears in a third color.

4. Press the **left arrow key** to position the insertion point in the new bulleted item. In the Changes group, click the **Accept** button. The inserted text is accepted and changes to the normal black color, and the next change, the Moved balloon, is selected.

5. In the Changes group, click the **arrow** below the **Accept button**, and then click **Accept Change**. Both Moved balloons disappear, and the green underlined moved text in the first paragraph changes to black. The insertion point stays at the location of the Moved balloon that was selected.

6. In the Comments group, click the **Next** button. A dialog box opens asking if you want to start searching from the beginning of the document. Click **Yes**. The first comment is selected again.

7. In the Comments group, click the **Next** button to select the second comment in the document, Stefanie's comment. In the Comments group, click the **Delete** button. In the Tracking group, click the **Track Changes** button to turn off the Track Changes feature. In the Basic Interest bullet, replace the word *four* with **three**.

TIP

To delete all comments in a document, in the Comments group, click the arrow next to the Delete button, and then click Delete All Comments in Document.

TIP

To reject a tracked change, in the Changes group, click the Reject button or click the arrow next to the Reject button, and then click Reject Change.

8. In the Changes group, click the **Next** button. The deletion *New Account* is selected. In the Changes group, click the **Accept** button. Click the **Accept** button again to accept the insertion of *Customer Service*. In the dialog box, click **Yes** to continue searching from the beginning of the document. The CN1 comment is highlighted again.

9. In the Changes group, click the **Next** button. The space between the second and third sentences in the first paragraph is highlighted. When you moved the sentence, Word automatically inserted the space. The space wasn't accepted when you accepted the Moved text because the inserted space wasn't part of the moved text.

10. In the Changes group, click the **arrow** below the Accept button, and then click **Accept All Changes in Document**. The inserted space and the deletion in the bulleted list are accepted.

11. Save the document as **Letter with Changes Accepted** followed by your initials. Leave it open for the next Step-by-Step.

Print Comments and Tracked Changes

You can print a document with comments and tracked changes. To do this, click the File tab, and then in the navigation bar, click Print. In the Settings list click the Print All Pages button, and verify that Print Markup on the menu at the bottom of the list has a check mark next to it.

Step-by-Step 8.10

1. Click the **File** tab, and then in the navigation bar, click **Print**. The Print tab appears in Backstage view.

2. In the Settings list, click the **Print All Pages** button. Make sure **Print Markup** has a check mark next to it. Click the **Print All Pages** button again to close the menu without making a selection.

3. Click the **Print** button. The document prints with the comment.

4. Delete the comment in the document.

5. Save the document as **Final Bank Letter** followed by your initials. Leave the document open for the next Step-by-Step.

Combine Different Versions of a Document

The Compare and Combine commands are useful ways to see differences between documents. Suppose you send your document to several colleagues for review. They return their copies with changes and suggested revisions. Using the Compare or Combine command, you can merge their comments and changes into one document for easy review.

To combine documents, click the Review tab on the Ribbon. In the Compare group, click the Compare button. On the menu that opens, click Combine. The Combine Documents dialog box opens. The dialog box can display many or few options. The command button in the lower-left corner of the dialog box is *More* when no options are displayed in the dialog box, and *Less* when the dialog box is expanded. **Figure 8–16** shows the expanded dialog box.

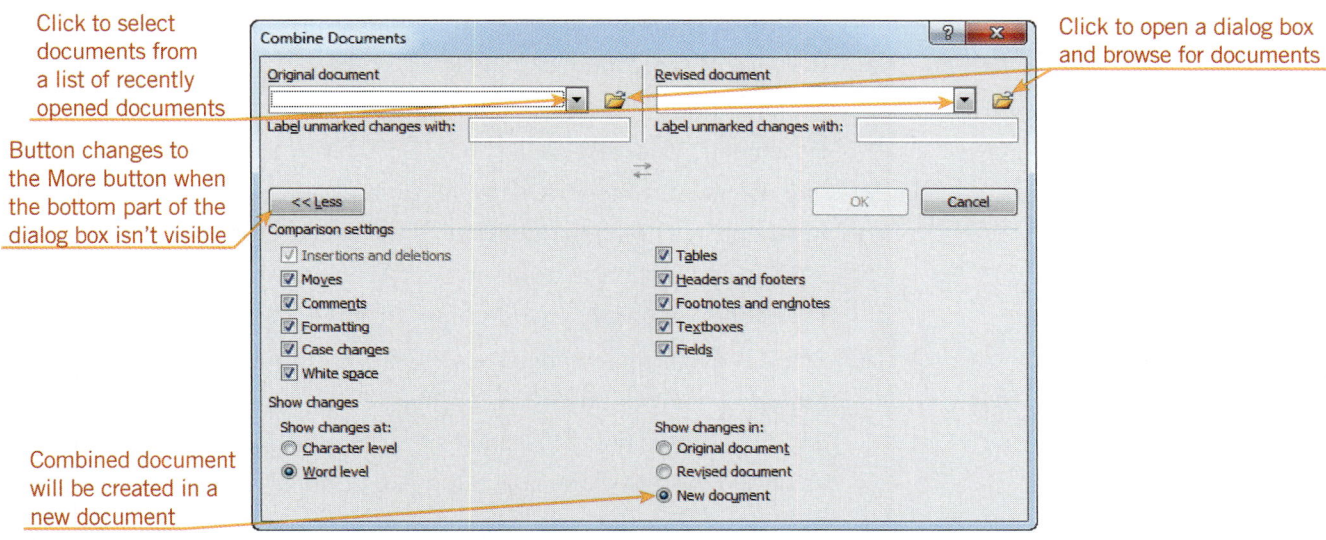
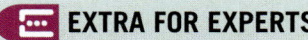

FIGURE 8–16   Combine Documents dialog box

Click the Original document arrow to display a list of recently opened documents or click the Browse button in the dialog box to use a dialog box similar to the Open dialog box to locate the original document. Click the original document in the list or double-click it in the Browse dialog box. Do the same in the Revised document section. The name that appears in the Label unmarked changes with box below the Original document box is the name that was in the User name box in the Word Options dialog box when the document was saved.

When you click OK, the dialog box closes, and a new document is created with the changes from the revised document marked. You can then choose to view just the combined document or view the combined document along with the original, the revised, or both the original and revised documents in a pane to the right of the combined document with the Revision pane open to the left. You should always look over the combined document carefully because the results might not be what you expect.

EXTRA FOR EXPERTS

To compare two documents side by side, close any other open documents. On the Ribbon, click the View tab, and then in the Window group, click the View Side by Side button. The two documents appear side by side, and when you scroll in one window, the other window scrolls as well. To scroll each window independently, click the Window button in either window, and then click Synchronous Scrolling to deselect it.

Step-by-Step 8.11

1. On the Review tab, in the Compare group, click the **Compare** button, and then click **Combine**. The Combine Documents dialog box opens. If the More button appears instead of the Less button, click **More** to expand the dialog box.

2. Click the **Original document** arrow. Locate and click **Bank Letter.docx**.

3. Click the **Revised document** arrow. Locate and click **Final Bank Letter. docx**. Notice that the New document option button is selected under Show changes in at the bottom of the dialog box.

4. Click **OK**. A new document with *Combine Result* in the document window title bar, followed by a number, opens.

5. In the Compare group, click the Compare button, point to **Show Source Documents**, and then click **Show Both** (even if it's already selected). The document window is divided into four panes. The combined document appears in the middle pane in the window. On the right, the original document appears at the top and the revised document appears on the bottom. The Revision pane appears on the left.

6. Scroll through the combined document in the middle pane. Note that the changes made to create the Final Bank Letter document are indicated in the combined document. The author of the changes is the name that currently appears in the Word Options dialog box.

7 Save the document as **Combined Bank Letter** followed by your initials. Print the document showing markup, and then close the document. Close the Final Bank Letter document.

TIP

If the document you want to compare or combine is not in the list, click the Browse button (the folder icon) to the right of the Original document or Revised document arrow.

Customizing Word

You can customize many features of Word by using the Word Options dialog box. You have already used this dialog box when you checked the spelling and grammar settings and when you changed the user name and initials.

To customize Word, click the File tab, and then click Options. The Word Options dialog box displays different options and commands depending on the category selected in the list on the left. The options that appear when General is selected are some of the most common options for customizing Word, including the User name and Initials boxes. The options that appear when Display is selected (see **Figure 8–17**) affect how the document looks on the screen and when printed.

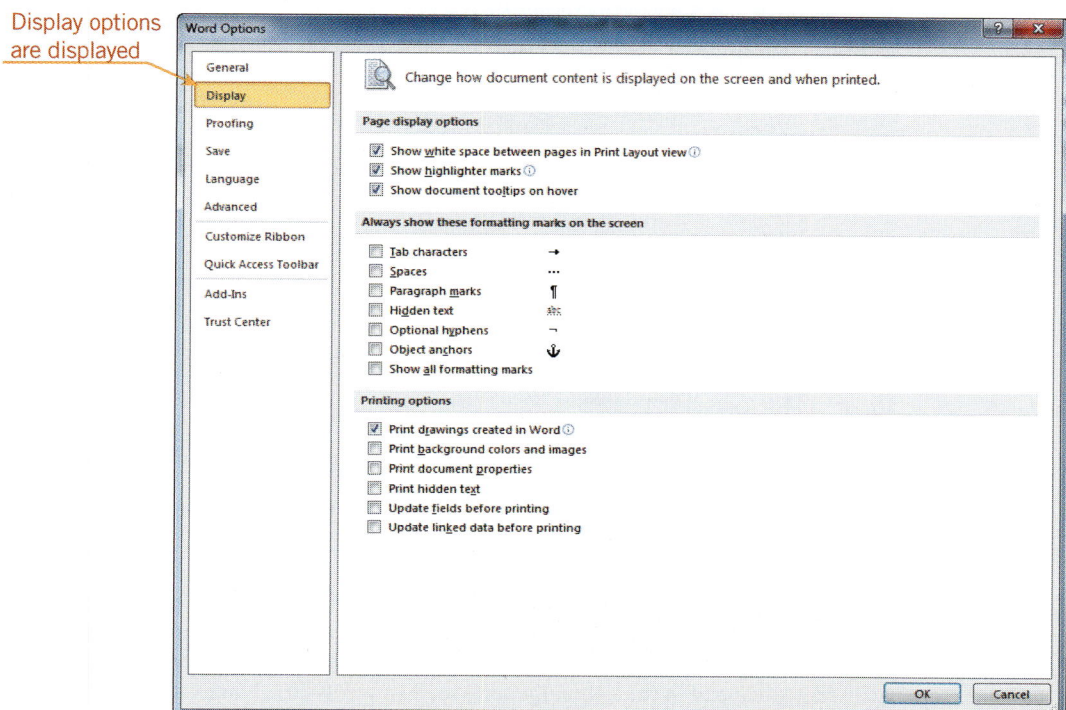

FIGURE 8–17   Word Options dialog box with Display selected

The Proofing options (see **Figure 8–18**) affect the spelling and grammar checker. You can also open the AutoCorrect dialog box when Proofing is selected in the list on the left.

Proofing options displayed

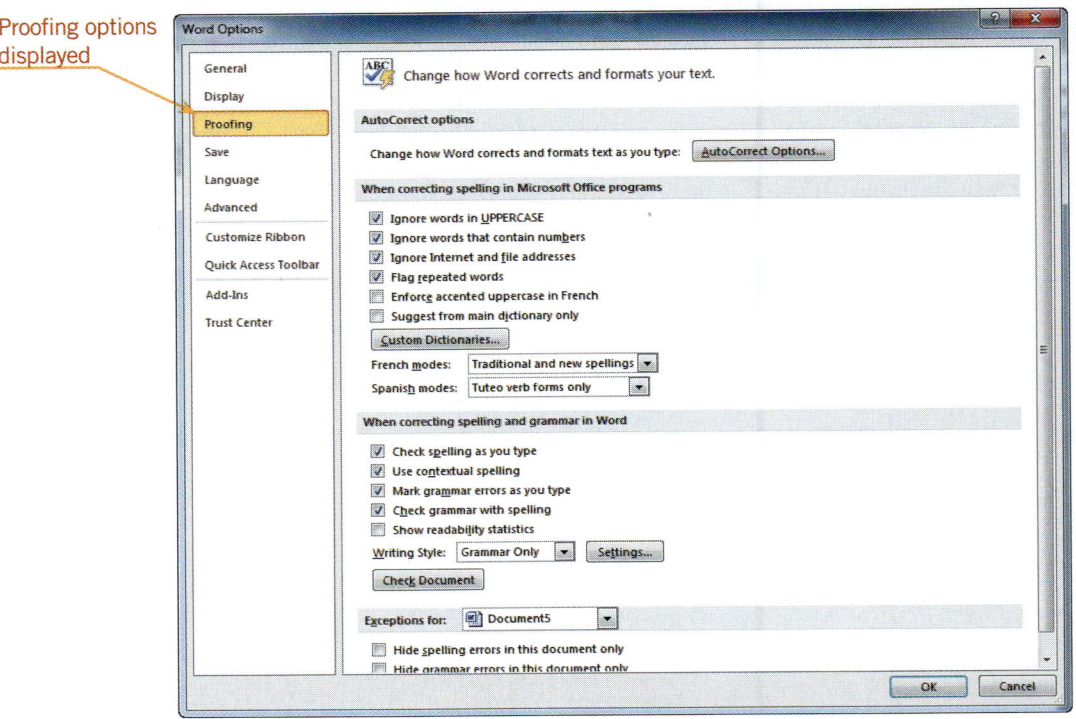

FIGURE 8–18   Word Options dialog box with Proofing selected

Clicking Save in the list on the left (see **Figure 8–19**) changes the dialog box so that you can change default save locations and behaviors. You can click Language in the list on the left to change the default language from English to another language. Clicking Advanced in the list on the left (see **Figure 8–20**) changes the dialog box so that it shows several categories of advanced options.

Save options
displayed

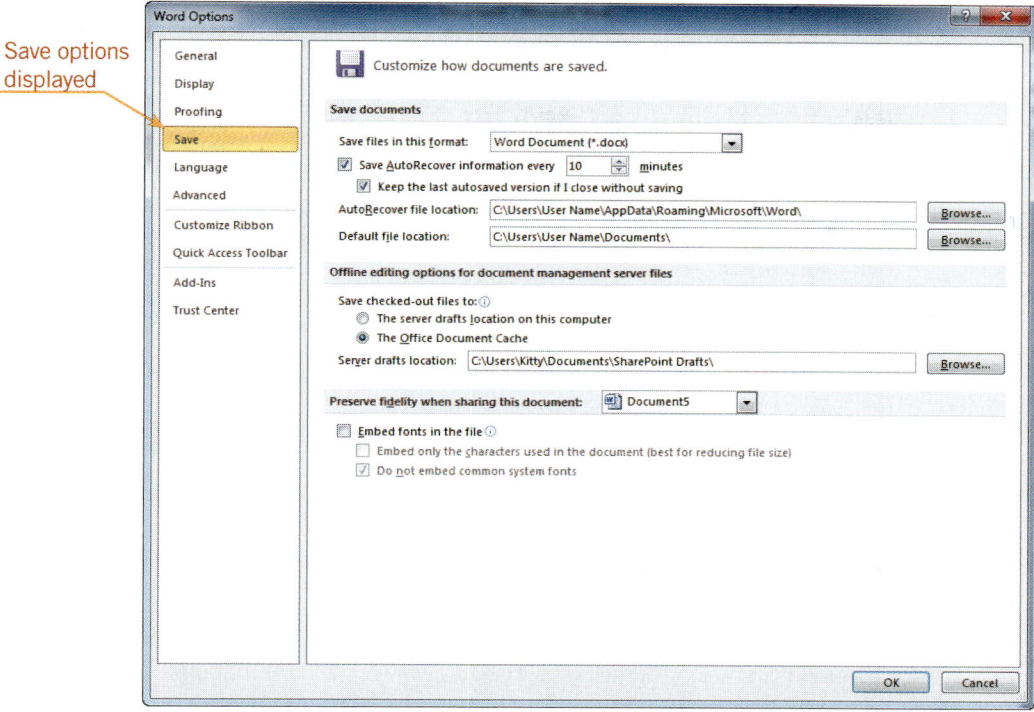

FIGURE 8–19   Word Options dialog box with Save selected

Advanced
options displayed

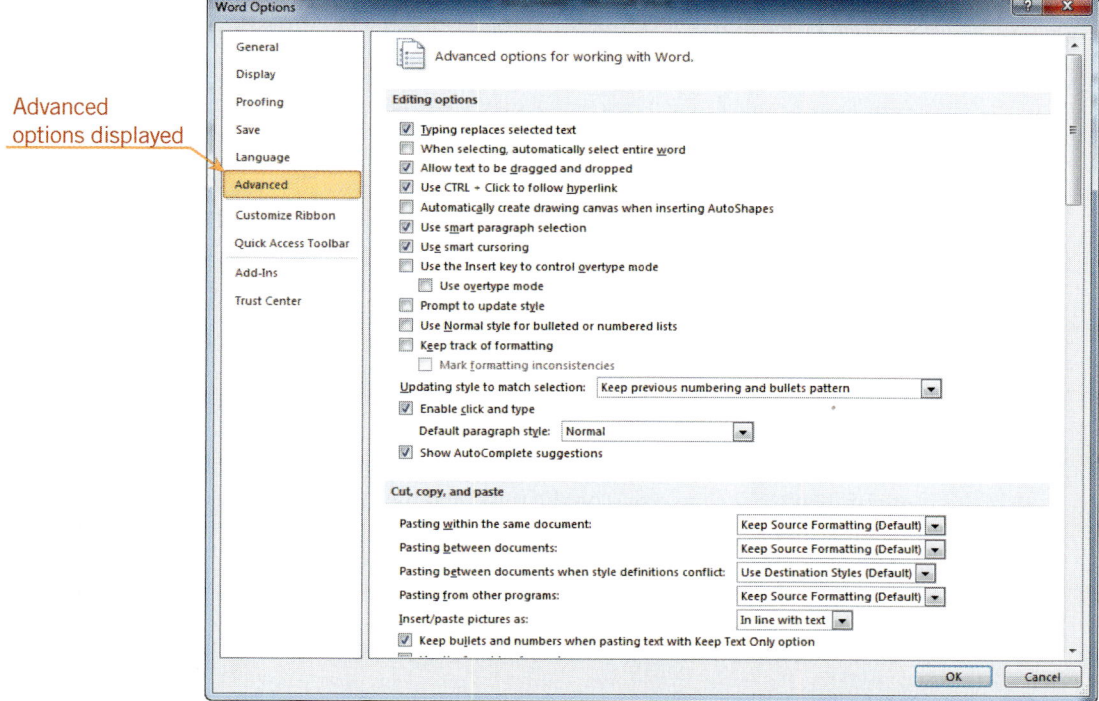

FIGURE 8–20   Word Options dialog box with Advanced selected

Finally, there are two options for customizing Word. You can customize the Ribbon and you can customize the Quick Access Toolbar. To do this, click Customize Ribbon or click Quick Access toolbar in the list on the left of the Word Options dialog box. The dialog box with Customize Ribbon selected is shown in **Figure 8–21**. The dialog box looks similar when Quick Access Toolbar is selected.

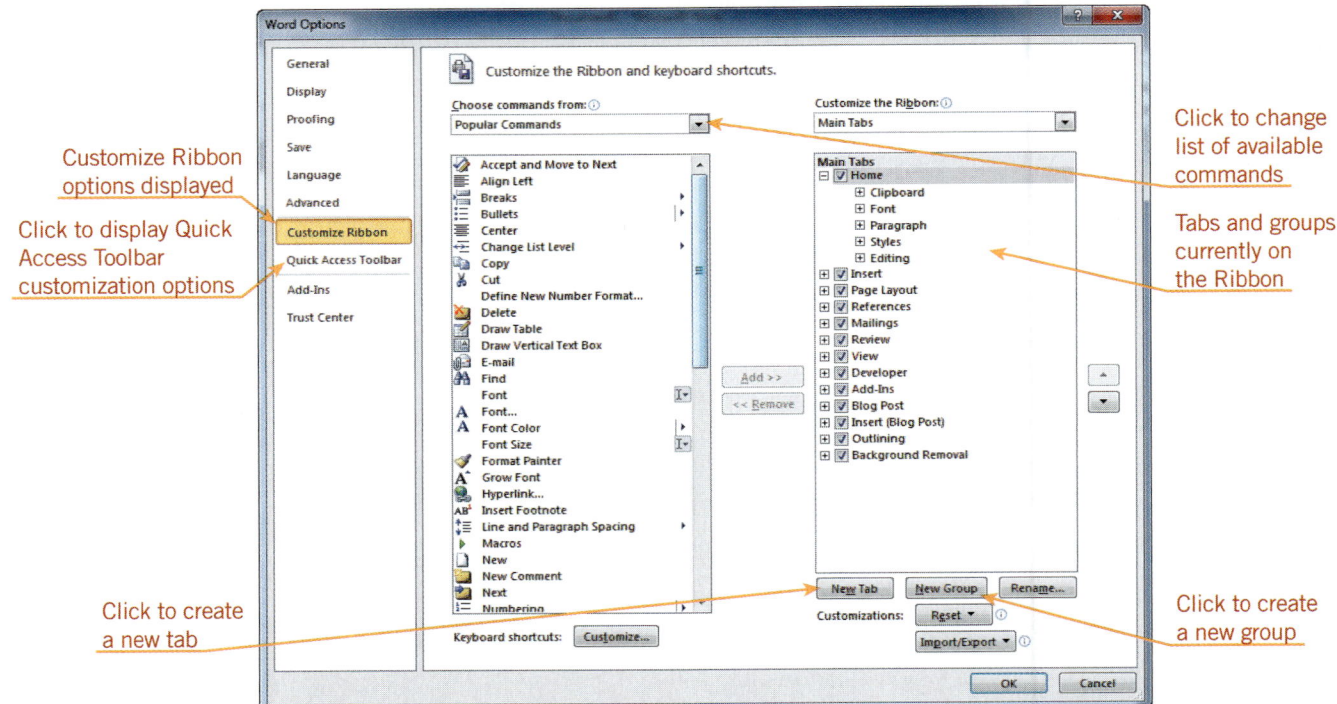

FIGURE 8–21   Word Options dialog box with Customize Ribbon selected

The tabs currently on the Ribbon are shown in the list on the right in the order they appear on the Ribbon. (For the Quick Access Toolbar, the list shows the commands on the toolbar.) The list on the left shows the commands available in Word. To filter the commands in this list, click the Choose commands from arrow at the top of the list, and then click a category of commands. The default is the set of Popular Commands. You can also choose to list all the commands and commands not in the Ribbon. The commands appear alphabetically in the list. To add a command to a group on a tab on the Ribbon or to the Quick Access Toolbar, in the list on the left, click the command you want to add. If you are adding the command to a group on the Ribbon, click the group on the right, and then click Add. To remove a command from a group or the toolbar, click the command in the list on the right, and then click Remove.

You can also create new tabs and new groups on the Ribbon. To create a new tab, click New Tab below the list on the right to create a new tab in that list. Likewise, click New Group to create a new group on the selected tab.

SUMMARY

In this lesson, you learned:

- Templates allow you to save the format, font choices, and text of commonly produced documents. You can use installed templates, templates available on Microsoft Office Online, or you can create your own.

- Mail merge lets you insert changing information into a standard document.

- You can quickly create envelopes and labels in Word.

- When working in a group, suggesting changes to a document is easily done by inserting comments, which are labeled with the person's name and the date and time the comment was made.

- Changes made by each person can be identified and labeled by using the Track Changes feature.

- You can accept or reject tracked changes and delete comments.

- You can print a document with tracked changes and comments, or you can print the document without the comments and as if all the tracked changes were accepted.

- You can combine documents with comments and changes into one document for easy review.

- You can customize Word by changing the options in the Word Options dialog box.

 VOCABULARY REVIEW

Define the following terms:

data source   merge field   Track Changes
mail merge   template   workgroup collaboration
main document

 REVIEW QUESTIONS

WRITTEN QUESTIONS

Write a brief answer to each of the following questions.

1. How does using a template to create documents increase your efficiency?

2. Describe *workgroup collaboration*.

3. How does Word indicate each of the following when the Tracked Changes feature is turned on?
   a. Inserted text

b. Deleted text

c. Moved text

4. Under what circumstances would you use Mail Merge?

5. What name appears in the ScreenTip associated with a comment?

TRUE / FALSE

Circle T if the statement is true or F if the statement is false.

T   F   **1.**   A template file can be used only once.

T   F   **2.**   If you want to create a sheet of labels with different names and addresses on each label, you should use the Labels button on the Mailings tab.

T   F   **3.**   Comments automatically show the name of the person typing the comment, regardless of the text in the User name box on the General tab in the Word Options dialog box.

T   F   **4.**   ScreenTips for comment balloons identify the date and time the comment was made.

T   F   **5.**   You can print comments.

MATCHING

Match the correct term in Column 2 to its description in Column 1.

Column 1

_____ 1. The file in a mail merge that contains the information that varies in each document

_____ 2. The process of combining a document with information that personalizes it

_____ 3. A file that contains the basic elements of a document, such as page and paragraph formatting, fonts, and text

_____ 4. The document in a mail merge that contains the information that does not change

_____ 5. A placeholder in a main document that is replaced with data from the data source when you perform a mail merge

Column 2

A. Main document

B. Data source

C. Merge field

D. Template

E. Mail merge

■ PROJECTS

If you have a SAM 2010 user profile, your instructor may have assigned an autogradable version of the indicated project. If so, log into the SAM 2010 Web site at *www.cengage.com/sam2010* to download the instruction and start files.

PROJECT 8–1

1. Create a new document based on the installed template **Adjacency Resume**. Save the document as **My Resume** followed by your initials.

2. Replace the name at the top of the document with your name, if necessary. Replace the appropriate placeholders with your address, phone number, and email address. (Note that some of the placeholder text in this template does not automatically select when you click the placeholder, therefore you need to drag to select it.)

3. Delete the date placeholder.

4. If you have a Web site, type the Web site address in the *Type your website* placeholder; otherwise, type **www .websiteplaceholder.com**. Press the spacebar after typing the Web site address. Remove the hyperlink formatting from the Web site address.

5. Below the *Education* heading, replace the placeholder with the name of your school.

6. Save, print, and close the document.

PROJECT 8–2

1. Open the **Subscription** Data File. Save the document as a template named **Journal Subscription** followed by your initials.

2. Create a new blank document. Save it as **Journal Addresses** followed by your initials. Create a table with seven columns and four rows. Type as the column names **First Name**, **Last Name**, **Company**, **Address**, **City**, **State**, and **Zip**. Enter the following data in the appropriate columns in table:

Barry Hodges
Pillar Shipping Company
1908 Queens Street
Los Angeles, CA 90025

David Norris
Unisource Marketing, Inc.
6421 Douglas Road
Coral Gables, FL 33134

Charlotte Smith
Accent Wireless
717 Pacific Parkway
Honolulu, HI 96813

3. Save and close the document.

4. Insert the current date in the appropriate position in the Journal Subscription template. Change the letter to a mail merge letter, and then select the Journal Addresses document as the recipient list. Insert the Address Block merge field with the recipient's name in the format *Joshua Randall Jr.* Insert the Greeting Line merge field with the greeting in the format *Dear Joshua,*. Adjust the spacing for the Address Block field.

5. In the closing, replace *Alan Dunn* with your name. Save your changes and close the document.

6. Create a new document based on the Journal Subscription template. When the dialog box opens asking if you want to continue using data from the database *Journal Addresses.docx*, click the Yes button.

7. Preview the results of the merge. Scroll through the three documents. Print the third document (the letter addressed to Charlotte Smith). Merge the documents in a new document, and then save the merged document as **Merged Journal Letters** followed by your initials. Close the document. Close the Journal Subscription document without saving changes.

8. Create a new document, and then create and print an envelope for Barry Hodges. Use your name and address as the return address. Save it as **Hodges Envelope**, and then print and close the document.

9. Create and print a sheet of labels with Barry Hodges's information. In the labels document, replace the name in the first cell with your name. Adjust the paragraph spacing, if necessary. Save it as **Hodges Labels**. Print and close the document.

PROJECT 8–3

1. Open the **Telephone.docx** Data File. Save the document as **Telephone Etiquette** followed by your initials.

2. Turn on the Tracked Changes feature. Change the User name and Initials in the Word Options dialog box to your own.

3. Click at the end of the first numbered item, after the text *Answer the telephone promptly*. Insert the following as a comment: **Add a note to answer the phone after the first ring.**

4. In the third sentence in the third item, delete the words **using** and **terms**.

5. In item 5, delete the last sentence. (Make sure you do not delete the paragraph mark.)

6. Move the sixth item under *Answering the Telephone* so it is the third item under *Taking Messages*. Change its number accordingly.

7. In the second item under *Taking Messages*, add the prefix **pre** to the word *determined*.

8. In a blank paragraph at the end of the document, type your name.

9. Print the document showing changes and comments.

10. Turn the Track Changes feature off. Change the User name and Initials in the Word Options dialog box back to their original values.

11. Save and close the document.

PROJECT 8–4

1. Open the **Telephone 2.docx** Data File. Save it as **Telephone Etiquette 2** followed by your initials.

2. Turn on the Tracked Changes feature. Change the User name and Initials in the Word Options dialog box to your own.

3. Make the changes suggested in the two comments.

4. Delete the comments.

5. In a blank paragraph at the end of the document, type your name.

6. Accept the changes in the first numbered item. Reject the changes in the third numbered item. Accept the rest of the changes in the document.

7. Save, print, and close the document, but do not exit Word.

8. Use the Combine command to combine the **Telephone 2.docx** Data File with the **Telephone Etiquette 2.docx** file you created. Show both documents.

9. Save the combined document as **Telephone Combined**. Print the document showing the changes and comments. Close the document.

■ CRITICAL THINKING

ACTIVITY 8–1

Write an application letter for a job that interests you. Save the document on a USB drive or other removable media and give it to a classmate. Have your classmate use Track Changes to add comments and propose changes. Review your classmate's suggestions, and accept or reject the changes and delete the comments.

ACTIVITY 8–2

Create a letterhead for an organization to which you belong. Save it as a template.

ACTIVITY 8–3

It is career week at your school, which gives students an opportunity to explore possible careers. Your faculty advisor asks you to prepare a list of jobs that interest you. Next, follow the steps outlined below.

1. Set up appointments with at least two people who currently are working in the field(s) that interest you.

2. Interview each person. Ask leading questions, such as:
   a. Why did you choose this career?
   b. What did you have to do to prepare for this career?
   c. What work habits did you have to form to succeed in your job?

Listen attentively to the answers. Make sure you take notes as well. Before leaving the interview, read back your responses to the person you are interviewing to make sure you captured the appropriate information.

3. Write a report in a Word document explaining the job responsibilities of the people you interviewed and disclose whether you would consider a career in that field.

4. Present your findings to the class.

UNIT REVIEW

Introduction to Microsoft Word

MATCHING

Match the correct term in Column 2 to its description in Column 1.

Column 1

_____ 1. Feature that lets you copy the format of selected text to other text

_____ 2. Feature that corrects common capitalization, spelling, grammar, and typing errors as you type

_____ 3. Text printed at the top of each page

_____ 4. Building block you create from frequently used text

_____ 5. File that contains formatting with text you can customize

Column 2

A. Quick Part

B. footer

C. hanging indent

D. AutoCorrect

E. Format Painter

F. template

G. header

WRITTEN QUESTIONS

Write a brief answer to the following questions.

1. What does the Undo command do?

2. How do you align text? What are the four text alignment positions?

3. Describe how to redefine an existing Quick Style, and then describe how to create a new Quick Style.

4. How do you automatically balance columns?

5. What is the difference between the system Clipboard and the Office Clipboard?

TRUE / FALSE

Circle T if the statement is true or F if the statement is false.

T   F   **1.**   The blank areas around the top, bottom, and sides of a page are called indents.

T   F   **2.**   Graphics help illustrate the meaning of the text and make the page more attractive.

T   F   **3.**   Content controls are special placeholders designed to contain a specific type of text, such as a date or the page number.

T   F   **4.**   A style is a coordinated set of fonts and colors applied to an entire document.

T   F   **5.**   Contextual spell checking is the process of identifying possible misusage by examining the context in which the word is used.

PROJECTS

PROJECT WD 1

1. Open the file **Properties.docx** from the drive and folder where your Data Files are stored.

2. Save the document as **Island West Properties** followed by your initials.

3. Check the document for spelling and grammar errors. Make corrections as needed.

4. Find the word *Property* and replace it with **Properties** each time it occurs in the document.

5. Move the heading *How do I get more information?* and the paragraph that follows to the end of the document.

6. Use the Find command to locate the word *excellent*, and then replace it with a synonym that makes sense in context.

7. Change the theme to Austin.

8. Select the first heading, *Are You in the Market for a New Home?*, and change its color to Olive Green, Accent 4, Darker 50%, then update the Heading 1 style so that it reflects this change.

9. Change the orientation to landscape.

10. Add an appropriate page border and page color.

11. Center align the text vertically on the page.

12. Change the title to 36 points, centered. Change the font of the title to one of your choice. Change the color to one that coordinates with the page border.

13. Change each of the headings to the Heading 1 Quick Style.

14. Indent the last paragraph one inch on each side.

15. Create a 3-point border around the last paragraph. Change the color of the border and paragraph shading to colors that match the page border.

16. Add your name in a blank paragraph under the paragraph with the border around it. Preview the document. Save, print, and close the document.

PROJECT WD 2

1. Open the file **Tenses.docx** from the drive and folder where your Data Files are stored. Save the document as **Verb Tenses** followed by your initials.

2. Apply any appropriate Quick Style to the title except for the Heading 1 Quick Style, and then, if necessary, center it and apply bold formatting. Change the font size to 28.

3. Select all the text in the document, set a left tab marker at the 1½-inch mark on the ruler, and then set a right tab marker at the 4¾-inch mark.

4. Modify the right tab so that there is a dotted line leader in front of it.

5. Format the *Present* heading so it is 18 points, Dark Blue, Text 2, Lighter 40%, centered, and bold.

6. Change the paragraph spacing before the *Present* heading to 12 points.

7. Redefine the Heading 1 Quick Style to match the style of the heading you just formatted, and then apply the new Heading 1 Quick Style to the other two headings.

8. Insert a formatted header that contains a date content control, and then insert a footer that has a content control that contains the company name. Add your name as the Company name in the document properties. Select the current date in the Date content control in the header. Delete any other content controls (including the page number) that appear in the header or footer.

9. Center the text vertically on the page.

10. Preview the document. Save, print, and close the document.

PROJECT WD 3

1. Open the file **Bagels.docx** from the drive and folder where your Data Files are stored.

2. Save the document as **Bagel Mania** followed by your initials.

3. Change the theme to Clarity, change the size of all the text to 14 points, and change the color of all the text to Dark Red, Accent 6, Darker 25%.

4. Format the title *Bagel Mania* with the Title Quick Style. Center the title, change it to 24-point Arial Black, and add a shadow font effect. Define a new Quick Style named Bagel Title based on this formatting.

5. Center the subtitle *"The Best Bagels in Town"*. Change the subtitle to Arial Black, 16-point, bold, and italic.

6. Indent the first line of the first paragraph under the subtitle one-half inch.

7. Change the list of bagels (from *Rye* to *Cinnamon-Raisin*) to a bulleted list, and then sort the list in alphabetical order. Make all the text in the list bold.

8. Format the list of bagels in three columns. The rest of the document should remain one column.

9. Format the *Breakfast Bagels* heading with the Heading 1 Quick Style. Add a double underline in the same color as the text. Redefine the Heading 1 Quick Style based on this formatting.

10. Apply the redefined Heading 1 Quick Style to the *Lunch Bagels* heading.

11. Change the left margin of the entire document to 1.25 inches, and the right margin to .75 inches.

12. Change the items in the breakfast and lunch bagel lists to numbered lists.

13. Change the line spacing of the paragraph under the subtitle to single-spacing and the types of bagels list to 1.5 lines.

14. Format the last line, *Come again!*, as 18-point, bold, italic Arial.

15. Add your name in 10-point type in a new line at the end of the document. Save, preview, and print the document, and then close the document.

PROJECT WD 4

1. Open a new Word document. Switch to Outline View.

2. Type the outline shown in **Figure UR–1**. (Note that the zoom in the figure is set at 120% zoom so that you can more easily read the text.)

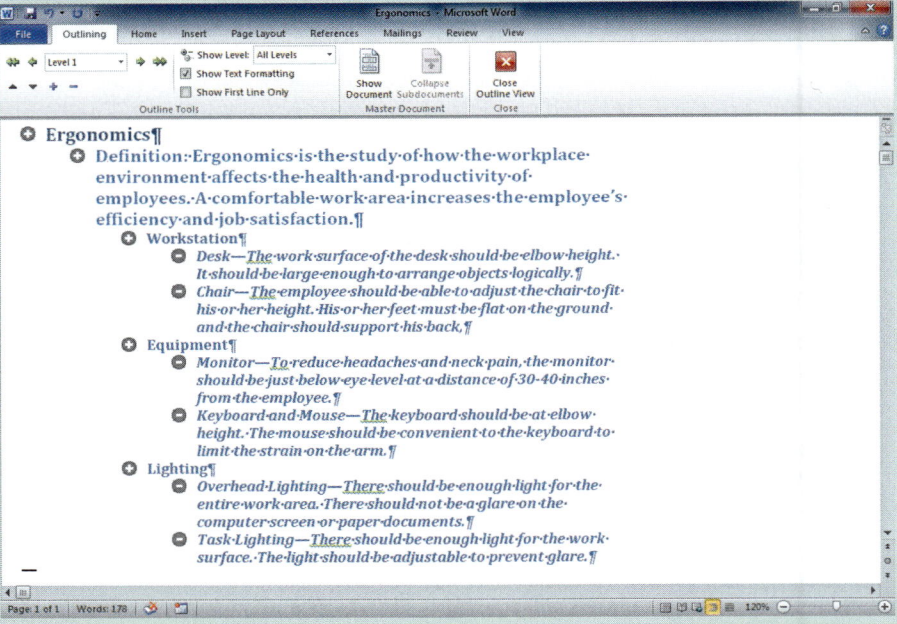

FIGURE UR–1

3. Collapse the outline to show only the heading levels 1-3.

4. Rearrange the Level 2 headings so that they are in the following order: *Equipment*, *Lighting*, *Workstation*.

5. Expand the outline.

6. Move the *Chair* heading (and its text) above the *Desk* heading.

7. Add your name in a new blank Level 1 paragraph at the end of the document. Save the document in Outline view as **Ergonomics** followed by your initials.

8. Preview the document. Print and close the document.

PROJECT WD 5

1. Open a new Word document. Create letterhead for Star Financial Group, as shown in **Figure UR–2**.

WordArt Style Fill – Orange, Accent 6, Warm Matte Bevel with Half Reflection, touching effect

Use different clip art if you can't find this one

Star Financial Group

550 CORNELL STREET
INDIANAPOLIS, IN 46202
(317) 555-0991

12-point Engravers MT

FIGURE UR–2

2. Save the document as a Word Template named **Star Template** followed by your initials.

3. Insert four blank paragraphs below the letterhead. Insert the current date so that it is updated automatically.

4. Press Enter twice, type **Sincerely,** press Enter three times, and then type your name. Save this as a Quick Part named **Closing** in the template only.

5. Save your changes. Close the file.

6. Create a new document based on the **Star Template** that you created.

7. After the date, press Enter three times. Type the letter shown in **Figure UR–3.**

This is to let you know that I have recently joined the professionals at the Star Financial Group. I am happy to be working with such a highly regarded company.

I would like to set up a meeting with you to discuss the type of services I can provide. This brief visit will not obligate you in any way, and it could result in an exchange of worthwhile ideas regarding your general financial strategy.

I plan to call you within the next few days to arrange an appointment at your convenience. Thank you for your consideration.

FIGURE UR–3

8. In a new paragraph below the body of the letter, insert four blank lines at the end of the letter. Insert the Closing Quick Part that you created.

9. Save the document as a Word document named **Star Letter** followed by your initials.

10. Create a new document. Create a table and type the following names as the contact list. Include columns for the title, first name, last name, address, city, state, and zip code. Format the table with a table style (choose any style you like). Save the contact list as **Star Contacts** followed by your initials, and then close the file.
    Mr. Adam McGuire
    717 Oakridge Avenue
    Indianapolis, IN 46225

    Ms. Sandra Novak
    5506 Douglas Street
    Indianapolis, IN 46216

Mr. Michael Lombardi
1908 Cameron Road
Indianapolis, IN 46206

11. Use the mail merge process to merge the Star Letter document with the Star Contacts data source. Use the recipient's title in the greeting line. Complete the merge to a new document, and then print the letter to Adam McGuire.

12. Save the document as **Star Merge** followed by your initials, and then close the document. Close the Star Letter document without saving changes.

13. Create an envelope in a new document addressed to Adam McGuire for the letter using your address as the return address. Save it as **Star Envelope** followed by your initials, and then print and close the document.

PROJECT WD 6

1. Open the file **Recycling.docx** from the drive and folder where your Data Files are stored. Save the document as **Recycling Flyer** followed by your initials.

2. Format all the text in the document as a multilevel list. Indent items so they make sense.

3. Switch to the theme of your choice. Add **Recycling** as the document title, and format it appropriately.

4. Add the title you typed in Step 3 as the Title document property. Add your name as an Author document property, and delete the placeholder *Your Name* author property.

5. Insert one of the Cubicles footers, type **Sage Stone Race Track** in the Company name content control, and then delete the empty content control in the footer. Insert one of the Cubicles headers. Delete the empty content control in the header.

6. Save, print, and close the document.

PROJECT WD 7

You need to have access to the Internet and Office.com in order to complete this project.

1. Open the New tab in Backstage view, click Greeting cards under Office.com Templates, and then click the category folders and scroll through the greeting card templates.

2. To see a preview of a template, click it to select it, and then look at the preview in the pane on the right.

3. When you find a greeting card you like, select it, and then click Download. The template appears in a new document window.

4. Replace the placeholder text with your own text.

5. If you don't like the colors used, adjust the text and page background colors.

6. Add clip art if you like. Resize and reposition the clip art to fit nicely on the page. Change it to a floating object if necessary.

7. Add your name in a text box in an appropriate place in the card. Use a font that looks like script (handwriting).

8. Save the document with a name of your choice, and then print and close it.

■ SIMULATION

You work at the Java Internet Café, which has been open only a few months. The café serves coffee, other beverages, and pastries, and offers Internet access. Seven computers are set up on tables along the north side of the store. Customers can come in, have a cup of coffee and a muffin, and explore the World Wide Web.

Because of your Microsoft Office experience, your manager asks you to create and revise many of the business's documents.

JOB WD 1

Some customers at Java Internet Café do not have much experience using computers or accessing the Internet. Your manager asks you to create a poster with definitions of the most common terms users encounter while surfing the Internet. The poster will hang near each computer.

1. Open the file **Internet.docx** from the drive and folder where your Data Files are stored. Save it as **Internet Terms** followed by your initials.

2. Create the poster shown in **Figure UR–4**. Use the Trek theme.

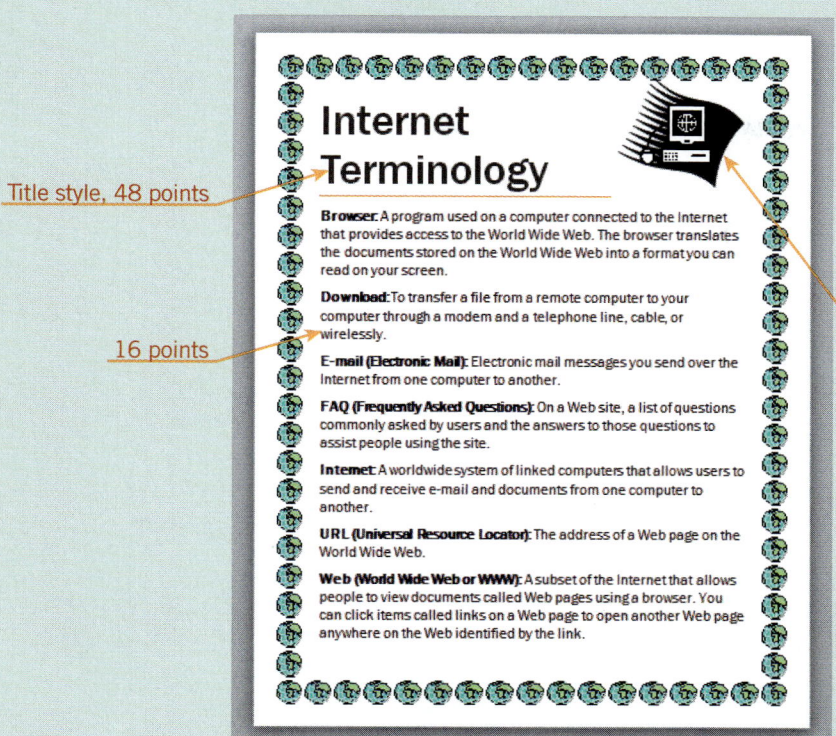

Title style, 48 points

16 points

Clip art is recolored with Black and White: 75%

FIGURE UR–4

3. Add your name in a text box at the bottom of the document. Save your changes.

4. Print and close the document.

JOB WD 2

Many customers become curious when they see computers through the window of the coffee shop. The café servers are often too busy to explain the concept to customers entering the store. Your manager asks you to revise the menu to include a short description of the café. These menus will be printed and placed near the entrance.

1. Open the **Menu.docx** Data File. Save the document as **Java Menu** followed by your initials.

2. Jump to the end of the document, and then type the following text:

> **Java Internet Café offers customers computers with high-speed Internet access as well as free Wi-Fi. Each of our computers has a special interface for new users to help you get started exploring the World Wide Web. You have heard about it; now you need to try it! Ask your server to help you get started.**

3. Change the font of the paragraph you just typed to Corbel, 11 point.

4. Change the left and right margins to 1½ inches.

5. Insert a new paragraph, and then type the title **Menu**.

6. Format *Menu* with the Title Quick Style.

7. Center the title.

8. Change the bottom border to the style that is a long dashed line followed by a short dashed line, change the color to Lavender, Accent 3, Darker 50%, and change the width to 1½ points. (*Hint*: Don't forget to reapply the border to the preview.)

9. Redefine the Title Quick Style to reflect the modified format.

10. Save, print, and close the document.

INTRODUCTORY UNIT

MICROSOFT EXCEL 2010

LESSON 1

Microsoft Excel Basics

■ OBJECTIVES

Upon completion of this lesson, you should be able to:

- Define the terms *spreadsheet* and *worksheet*.
- Identify the parts of a worksheet.
- Start Excel, open an existing workbook, and save a workbook.
- Move the active cell in a worksheet.
- Select cells and enter data in a worksheet.
- Edit and replace data in cells.
- Zoom, preview, and print a worksheet.
- Close a workbook and exit Excel.

■ VOCABULARY

active cell

active worksheet

adjacent range

cell

cell reference

column

formula

Formula Bar

landscape orientation

Microsoft Excel 2010 (Excel)

Name Box

nonadjacent range

portrait orientation

range

range reference

row

sheet tab

spreadsheet

workbook

worksheet

Numbers are everywhere. Spreadsheets make it simple to perform calculations with these numbers and resolve problems based on those calculations. People rely on numbers and spreadsheets to do such things as track inventories, set up budgets, determine grades, create invoices, evaluate attendance records, to name just a few examples.

Introduction to Spreadsheets

Microsoft Excel 2010 (or **Excel**) is the spreadsheet program in Microsoft Office 2010. A **spreadsheet** is a grid of rows and columns in which you enter text, numbers, and the results of calculations. The primary purpose of a spreadsheet is to solve problems that involve numbers. Without a computer, you could try to solve these types of problems by creating rows and columns on paper and using a calculator to determine the results (see **Figure 1–1**). Spreadsheets have many uses. For example, you can use a spreadsheet to calculate grades for students in a class, to prepare a budget for the next few months, or to determine payments for repaying a loan.

▶ **VOCABULARY**

Microsoft Excel 2010

Excel

spreadsheet

worksheet

workbook

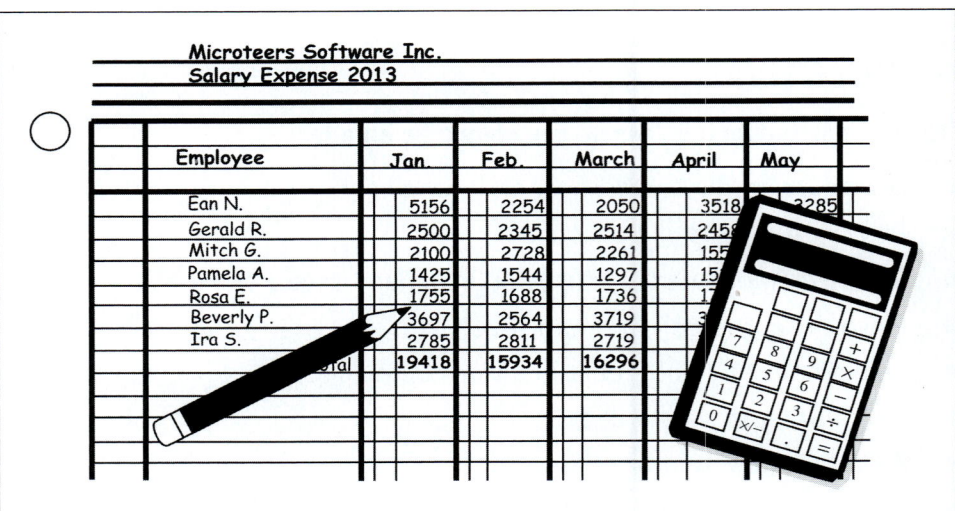

Employee	Jan.	Feb.	March	April	May
Ean N.	5156	2254	2050	3518	3285
Gerald R.	2500	2345	2514	2458	
Mitch G.	2100	2728	2261	155	
Pamela A.	1425	1544	1297	15	
Rosa E.	1755	1688	1736	1	
Beverly P.	3697	2564	3719	3	
Ira S.	2785	2811	2719		
Total	19418	15934	16296		

Microteers Software Inc.
Salary Expense 2013

FIGURE 1–1   Spreadsheet prepared on paper

Computer spreadsheets also contain rows and columns with text, numbers, and the results of calculations. But, computer spreadsheets perform calculations faster and more accurately than you can with spreadsheets you create on paper, using a pencil and a calculator. The primary advantage of computer spreadsheets is their ability to complete complex and repetitious calculations quickly and accurately.

Computer spreadsheets are also flexible. Making changes to an existing computer spreadsheet is usually as easy as pointing and clicking with the mouse. Suppose, for example, you use a computer spreadsheet to calculate your budget (your monthly income and expenses) and overestimate the amount of money you need to pay for electricity. You can change a single entry in the computer spreadsheet, and the computer will recalculate the entire spreadsheet to determine the new budgeted amount. Think about the work this change would require if you were calculating the budget by hand on paper with a pencil and calculator.

In Excel, a computerized spreadsheet is called a **worksheet**. The file used to store worksheets is called a **workbook**. Usually, a workbook contains a collection of related worksheets.

Starting Excel

You start Excel from the Start menu in Windows. Click the Start button, click All Programs, click Microsoft Office, and then click Microsoft Excel 2010. When Excel starts, the program window displays a blank workbook titled *Book1*, which includes three blank worksheets titled *Sheet1*, *Sheet2*, and *Sheet3*. The Excel program window has the same basic parts as all Office programs: the title bar, the Quick Access Toolbar, the Ribbon, Backstage view, and the status bar. However, as shown in **Figure 1–2**, Excel also has additional buttons and parts.

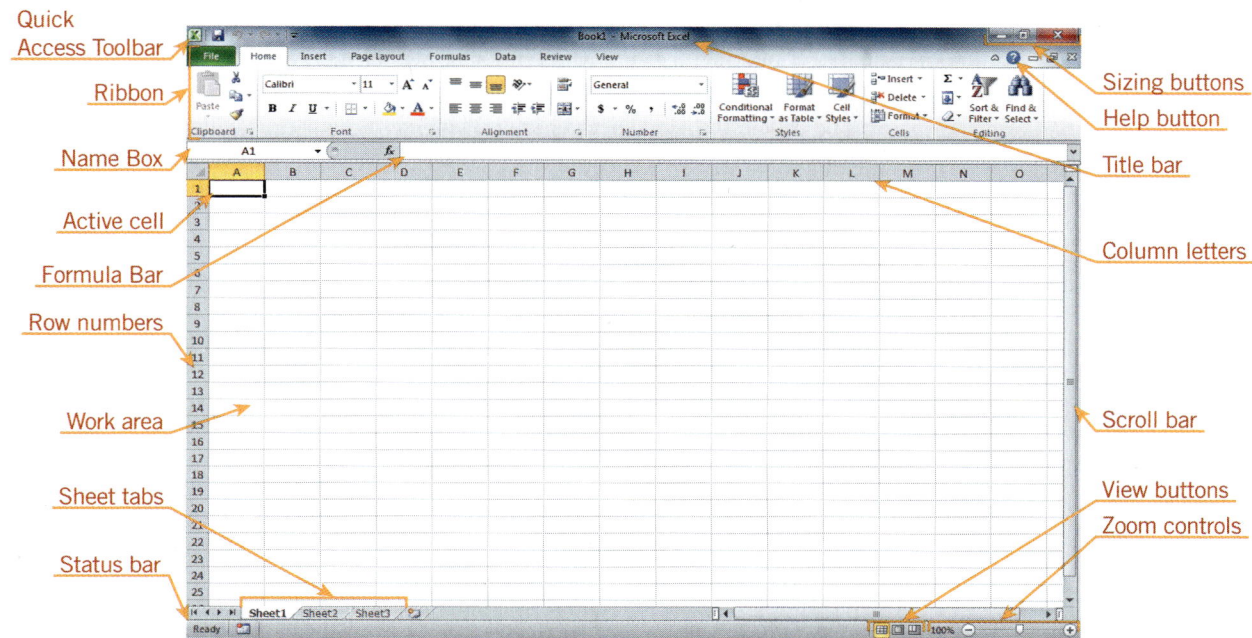

FIGURE 1–2   Excel program window

Step-by-Step 1.1

1. With Windows running, click the **Start** button on the taskbar.

2. Click **All Programs**. The Start menu shows all the programs installed on the computer.

3. Click **Microsoft Office** to display a list of programs in the folder, and then click **Microsoft Excel 2010**. Excel starts and opens a blank workbook, titled *Book1*, as shown in Figure 1–2.

4. If the Excel program window does not fill your screen, click the **Maximize** button in the title bar.

5. Leave the workbook open for the next Step-by-Step.

Exploring the Parts of the Workbook

Each new workbook contains three worksheets by default. The name of each worksheet appears in the *sheet tab* at the bottom of the worksheet window. The worksheet that is displayed in the work area is called the *active worksheet*. *Columns* of the worksheet appear vertically and are identified by letters at the top of the worksheet window. *Rows* appear horizontally and are identified by numbers on the left side of the worksheet window. A *cell* is the intersection of a row and a column. Each cell is identified by a unique *cell reference*, which is formed by combining the cell's column letter and row number. For example, the cell that intersects at column C and row 4 has the cell reference C4.

The pointer changes shape as you move it around the Excel window. The pointer becomes a thick white plus sign ✛ when it is in the worksheet. If you move the pointer to a button on the Ribbon, the pointer changes to a white arrow ⬡.

The cell in the worksheet in which you can type data is called the *active cell*. The active cell is distinguished from the other cells by a dark border. In your worksheet, cell A1 has the dark border, which indicates that cell A1 is the active cell. You can move the active cell from one cell to another. The *Name Box*, or cell reference area located below the Ribbon, displays the cell reference of the active cell.

The *Formula Bar* appears to the right of the Name Box and displays a formula when the cell of a worksheet contains a calculated value (or the results of the formula). A *formula* is an equation that calculates a new value from values currently in a worksheet, such as adding the numbers in cell A1 and cell A2.

Opening an Existing Workbook

Opening a workbook means loading an existing workbook file from a drive into the program window. To open an existing workbook, you click the File tab on the Ribbon to display Backstage view, and then click Open in the navigation bar. The Open dialog box appears. The Open dialog box shows all the workbooks in the displayed folder that you can open with Excel. When you open another workbook, the *Book1* workbook that opened when you started Excel disappears.

TIP

To open a workbook that you recently worked on, click the File tab on the Ribbon, and then click Recent in the navigation bar. The right pane contains the Recent Workbooks list. Click the workbook you want to open to open it in Excel.

Step-by-Step 1.2

1. On the Ribbon, click the **File** tab. Backstage view appears.

2. In the navigation bar, click **Open**. The Open dialog box appears.

3. Navigate to the drive and folder where your Data Files are stored, open the **Excel** folder, and then open the **Excel Lesson 01** folder.

4. Double-click the **Frogs.xlsx** workbook file. Depending on how Windows is set up on your computer, you might not see the file extension after the file name; in that case, double-click the **Frogs** workbook file. The workbook appears in the program window, as shown in **Figure 1–3**.

WARNING

If the workbook opens in the Protected View window, click the Enable Editing button to close the Protected View window.

FIGURE 1–3
Frogs workbook open in Excel

Current workbook name (you might not see the file extension)

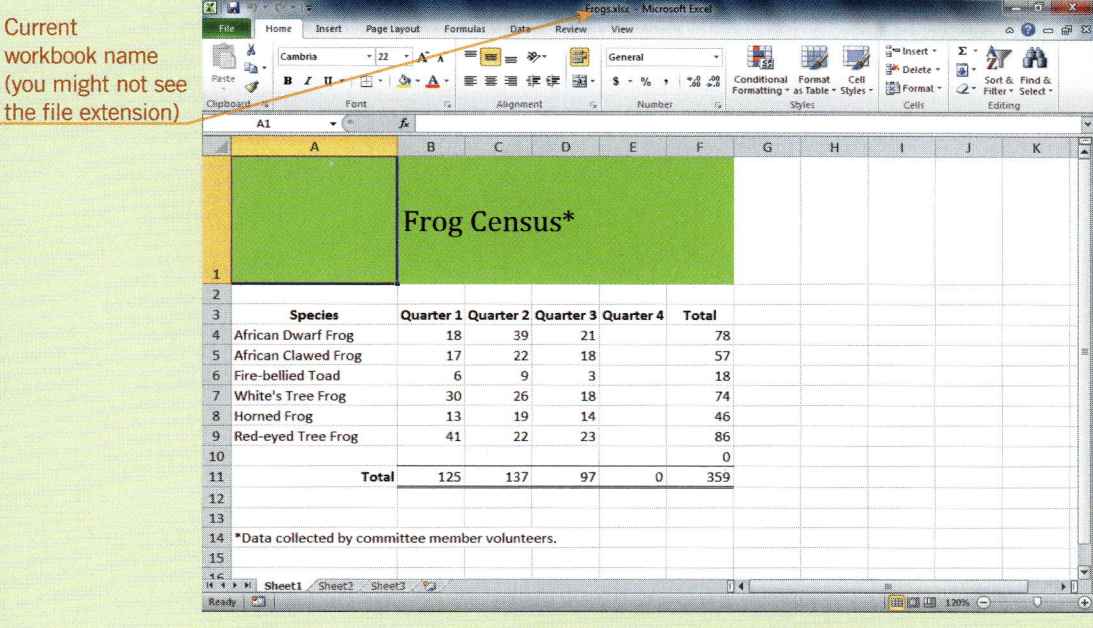

5. Leave the workbook open for the next Step-by-Step.

Saving a Workbook

Saving is done two ways. The Save command saves an existing workbook, using its current name and save location. The Save As command lets you save a workbook with a new name or to a new location.

The first time you save a new workbook, the Save As dialog box appears, as shown in **Figure 1–4**, so you can give the workbook a descriptive name and choose a location to save it. After you have saved the workbook, you can use the Save command in Backstage view or the Save button on the Quick Access Toolbar to periodically save the latest version of the workbook with the same name in the same location. To save a copy of the workbook with a new name or to a different location, you need to use the Save As dialog box. You'll use this method to save the Frogs workbook you just opened with a new name, leaving the original workbook intact.

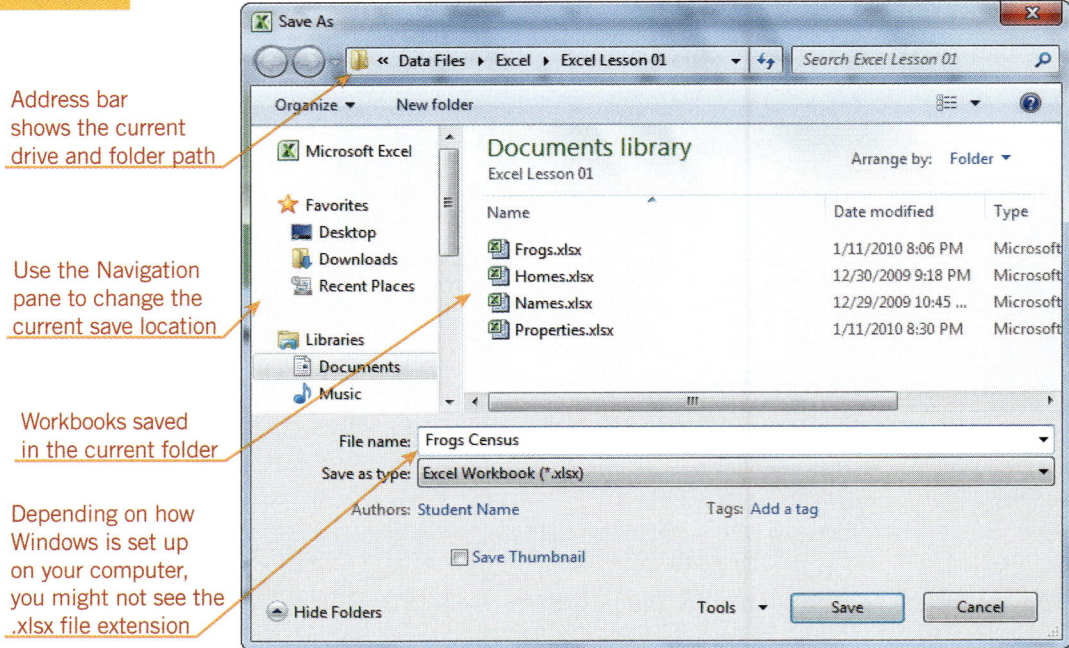

Address bar shows the current drive and folder path

Use the Navigation pane to change the current save location

Workbooks saved in the current folder

Depending on how Windows is set up on your computer, you might not see the .xlsx file extension

FIGURE 1–4   Save As dialog box

Step-by-Step 1.3

1. On the Ribbon, click the **File** tab. In the navigation bar, click **Save As**. The Save As dialog box appears.

2. Navigate to the drive and folder where you store the Data Files for this lesson, if necessary.

3. In the File name box, type **Frog Census** followed by your initials. Your dialog box should look similar to Figure 1-4.

4. Click **Save**.

5. Leave the workbook open for the next Step-by-Step.

Moving the Active Cell in a Worksheet

The easiest way to change the active cell in a worksheet is to move the pointer to the cell you want to make active and click. The dark border surrounds the cell you clicked, and the Name Box shows its cell reference. When working with a large worksheet, you might not be able to see the entire worksheet in the program window. You can display different parts of the worksheet by using the mouse to drag the scroll box in the scroll bar to another position. You can also move the active cell to different parts of the worksheet using the keyboard or the Go To command.

TIP

The column letter and row number of the active cell are shaded in orange for easy identification.

Using the Keyboard to Move the Active Cell

You can change the active cell by pressing the keys or using the keyboard shortcuts shown in **Table 1–1**. When you press an arrow key, the active cell moves one cell in that direction. When you press and hold down an arrow key, the active cell shifts in that direction repeatedly and quickly.

TABLE 1–1   Keys for moving the active cell in a worksheet

TO MOVE	PRESS
Left one column	Left arrow key
Right one column	Right arrow key
Up one row	Up arrow key
Down one row	Down arrow key
To the first cell of a row	Home key
To cell A1	Ctrl+Home keys
To the last cell of the column and row that contain data	Ctrl+End keys
Up one window	Page Up key
Down one window	Page Down key

Using the Go To Command to Move the Active Cell

You might want to change the active cell to a cell in a part of the worksheet that you cannot see in the work area. The fastest way to move to that cell is with the Go To dialog box. In the Editing group on the Home tab of the Ribbon, click the Find & Select button, and then click Go To. The Go To dialog box appears, as shown in

EXTRA FOR EXPERTS

You can change the active worksheet in a workbook to next worksheet by pressing the Ctrl+Page Down keys or to the previous worksheet by pressing the Ctrl+Page Up keys. You can also use the mouse to click the sheet tab of the worksheet you want to make active.

Figure 1–5. Type the cell reference in the Reference box, and then click OK. The cell you specified becomes the active cell.

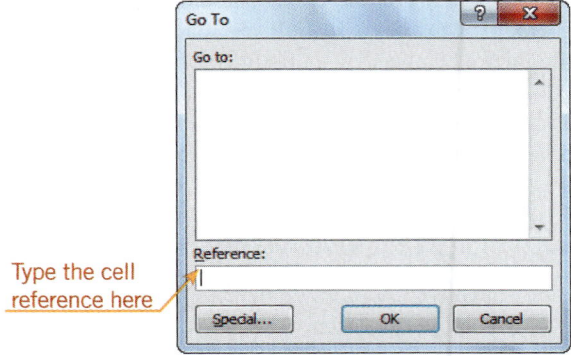

Type the cell reference here

FIGURE 1–5   Go To dialog box

Step-by-Step 1.4

1. Press the **Ctrl+End** keys. The active cell moves to cell F14, which is the cell that intersects the last column and row that contain data in the worksheet.

2. Press **Home**. The active cell moves to the first cell of row 14—cell A14, which contains the text *Data collected by committee member volunteers.*

3. Press the **Up arrow** key six times to move the active cell up six rows. The active cell is cell A8, which contains the words *Horned Frog.*

4. On the Ribbon, click the **Home** tab, if the tab is not already active.

5. In the Editing group, click the **Find & Select** button 🔍 to open a menu of commands, and then click **Go To**. The Go To dialog box appears, as shown in Figure 1–5.

6. In the Reference box, type **B4**.

7. Click **OK**. The active cell moves to cell B4, which contains the number *18*.

8. Leave the workbook open for the next Step-by-Step.

> **TIP**
>
> You can also open the Go To dialog box by pressing the Ctrl+G keys or by pressing the F5 key.

Selecting a Group of Cells

Often, you will perform operations on more than one cell at a time. A group of selected cells is called a *range*. In an *adjacent range*, all cells touch each other and form a rectangle. The range is identified by its *range reference*, which lists both the cell in its upper-left corner and the cell in its lower-right corner, separated by a colon (for example, A3:C5). To select an adjacent range, click the cell in one corner of the range, drag the pointer to the cell in the opposite corner of the range, and then release the mouse button. As you drag, the range of selected cells becomes shaded

> **VOCABULARY**
> **range**
> **adjacent range**
> **range reference**

(except for the first cell you selected), and the dark border expands to surround all the selected cells. In addition, the column letters and row numbers of the range you select change to orange. The active cell in a range is white; the other cells are shaded.

You can also select a range that is nonadjacent. A ***nonadjacent range*** includes two or more adjacent ranges and selected cells. The range reference for a nonadjacent range separates each range or cell with a semicolon (for example, A3:C5;E3:G5). To select a nonadjacent range, select the first adjacent range or cell, press the Ctrl key as you select the other cells or ranges you want to include, and then release the Ctrl key and the mouse button.

▶ **VOCABULARY**
nonadjacent range

Step-by-Step 1.5

1. Click cell **B3** to make it active.

2. Press and hold the left mouse button as you drag the pointer to the right until cell **F3** is selected.

3. Release the mouse button. The range B3:F3 is selected, as you can see from the shaded cells and the dark border. Also, the column letters B through F and the row number 3 are orange. See **Figure 1–6**.

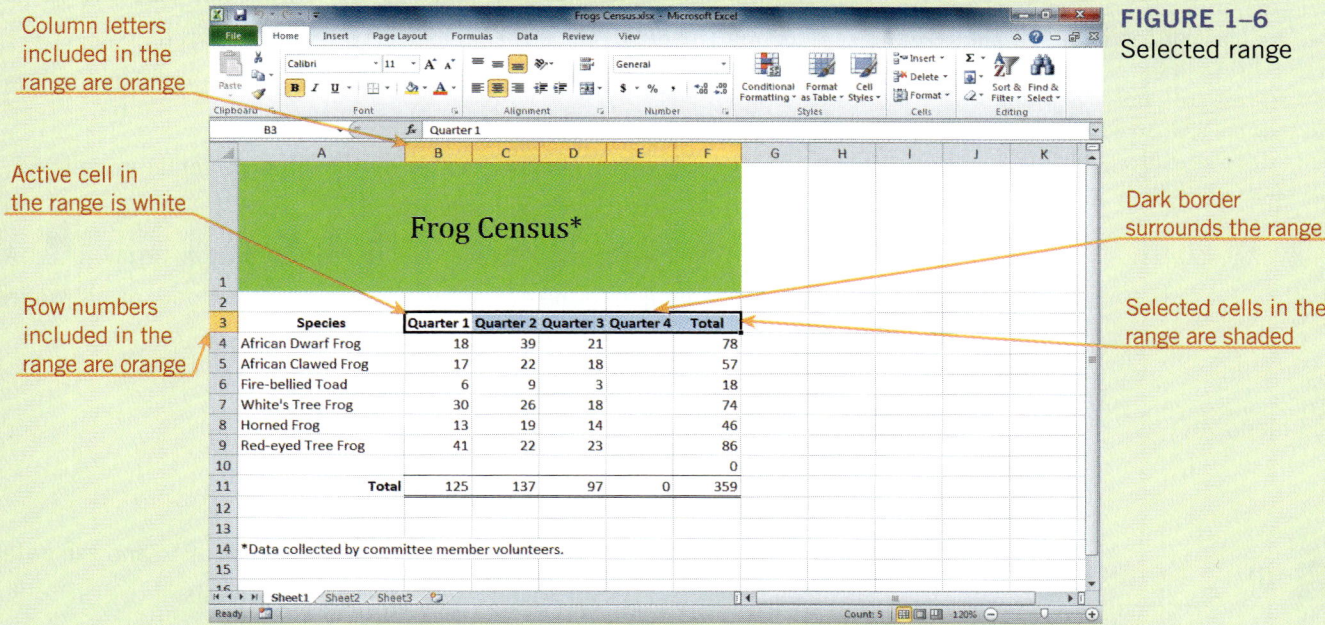

Column letters included in the range are orange

Active cell in the range is white

Row numbers included in the range are orange

FIGURE 1–6
Selected range

Dark border surrounds the range

Selected cells in the range are shaded

4. Click cell **B4**. The range B3:F3 is deselected when you select cell B4.

5. Press and hold the left mouse button as you drag down and to the right until cell **F11** is selected.

6. Release the mouse button. The range B4:F11 is selected.

7. Leave the workbook open for the next Step-by-Step.

Entering Data in a Cell

TIP

After you type data in a cell, the active cell changes, depending on how you enter the data. If you click the Enter button on the Formula Bar, the cell you typed in remains active. If you press the Enter key, the cell below the cell you typed in becomes active. If you press the Tab key, the cell to the right of the cell you typed in becomes active.

Worksheet cells can contain text, numbers, or formulas. Text is any combination of letters and numbers and symbols, such as headings, labels, or explanatory notes. Numbers are values, dates, or times. Formulas are equations that calculate a value.

You enter data in the active cell. First, type the text, numbers, or formula in the active cell. Then, click the Enter button ✔ on the Formula Bar or press the Enter key or the Tab key on the keyboard. The data you typed is entered in the cell. If you decide not to enter the data you typed, you can click the Cancel button ✖ on the Formula Bar or press Esc to delete the data without making any changes to the cell.

If you have already entered the data in the cell, you can undo, or reverse, the entry. On the Quick Access Toolbar, click the Undo button ↺ to reverse your most recent change. To undo multiple actions, click the Undo button arrow ↺▾. A list of your previous actions appears, and you can choose how many actions you want to undo.

Step-by-Step 1.6

1. Click cell **E4** to make it active.

2. Type **17**. As you type, the number appears in the cell and in the Formula Bar.

TIP

If a cell is not wide enough to display all the cell's contents, extra text extends into the next cells, if they are blank. If not, only the characters that fit in the cell appear, and the rest are hidden from view, but they are still stored. Numbers that extend beyond a cell's width appear as #### in the cell.

3. Press the **Enter** key. The number 17 is entered in cell E4, and the active cell moves to cell E5. The totals in cells F4, E11, and F11 change as you enter the data.

4. Type **24**. As you type, the number appears in the cell and in the Formula Bar.

5. On the Formula Bar, click the **Enter** button ✔. The totals in cells F5, E11, and F11 change as you enter the data.

6. On the Quick Access Toolbar, click the **Undo button arrow** ↺▾. A menu appears listing the actions you have just performed, as shown in **Figure 1–7**.

FIGURE 1–7
Undo menu

Click the Undo button
arrow to open the menu
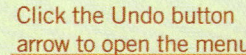
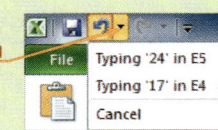
Any entries you select will
be reversed when you click

7. Click **Typing '24' in E5**. The data is removed from cell E5, and the data in cells F5, E11, and F11 return to their previous totals.

8. Click cell **A10**, and then enter **Pac Frog**. The Pac Frog species is added to the Frog Census.

TIP

The instruction to click a cell and then enter data means you should click the specified cell, type the data indicated, and then enter that data in the cell by pressing the Enter key, pressing the Tab key, or clicking the Enter button on the Formula Bar.

9. In the range **E5:E10**, enter the data, as shown in **Figure 1–8**, to include the number of frogs sighted for each species in Quarter 4.

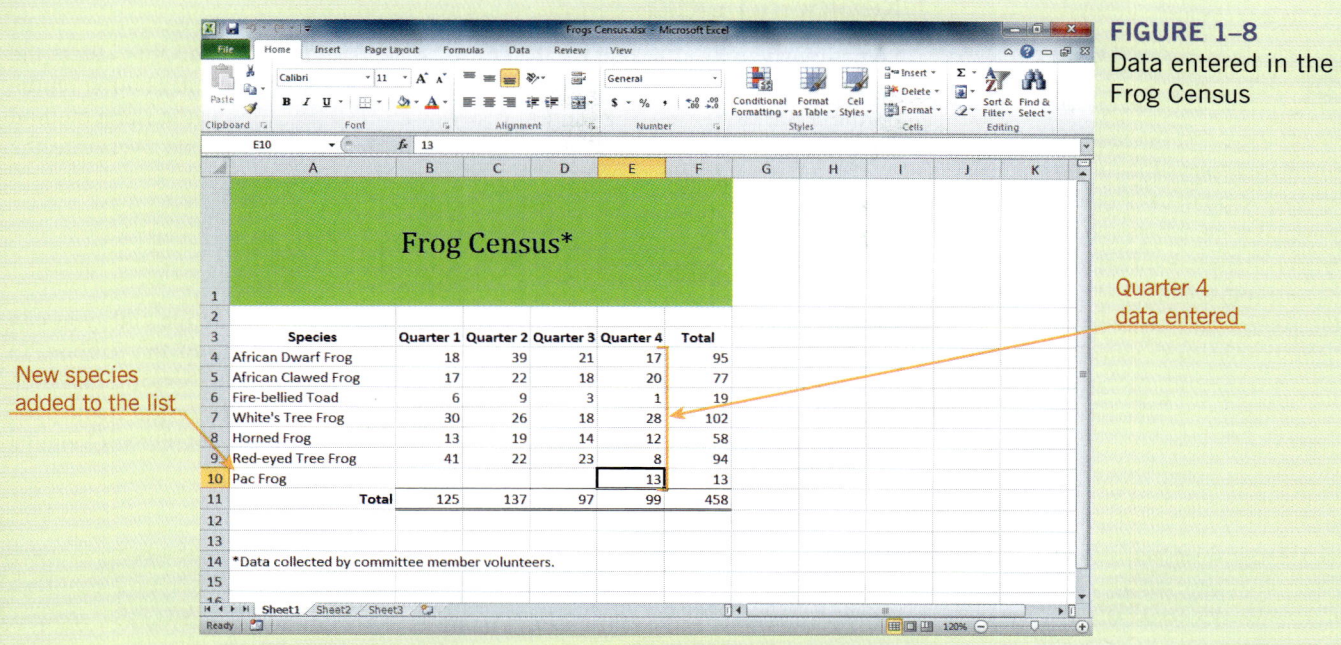

FIGURE 1–8
Data entered in the
Frog Census

New species
added to the list

Quarter 4
data entered

10. On the Quick Access Toolbar, click the **Save** button 🖫 to save the workbook.

11. Leave the workbook open for the next Step-by-Step.

Changing Data in a Cell

After you enter data in cells in the worksheet, you might change your mind or discover a mistake. If so, you can edit, replace, or clear the data.

Editing Data

When you need to make a change to data in a cell, you can edit it in the Formula Bar or in the cell. The contents of the active cell always appear in the Formula Bar. To edit the data in the Formula Bar, click in the Formula Bar and then drag the pointer to select the text you want to edit. You can also use the arrow keys to position the insertion point. Then, press the Backspace key or the Delete key to remove data, or type the new data. To edit the data directly in a cell, make the cell active and then press the F2 key or double-click the cell to enter editing mode, which places the insertion point within the cell contents. An insertion point appears in the cell, and you can make changes to the data. When you are done, click the Enter button on the Formula Bar or press the Enter key or the Tab key.

> **TIP**
>
> If you need help while working with any of the Excel features, use the Excel Help feature. Click the Microsoft Excel Help button. In the Excel Help window, type a word or phrase about the feature you want help with, and then click the Search button. A list of Help topics related to the word or words you typed appears. Click the appropriate Help topic to learn more about the feature.

Replacing Data

Sometimes you need to replace the entire contents of a cell. To do this, select the cell, type the new data, and then enter the data by clicking the Enter button on the Formula Bar or by pressing the Enter key or the Tab key. This is the same method used to enter data in a blank cell. The only difference is that you overwrite the existing cell contents.

Clearing Data

Clearing a cell removes all the data in the cell. To clear the active cell, you can use the Ribbon, the keyboard, or the mouse. On the Home tab of the Ribbon, in the Editing group, click the Clear button to display a menu with options, and then click Clear Contents. To use the keyboard, press the Delete key or the Backspace key. To use your mouse, right-click the active cell, and then click Clear Contents on the shortcut menu.

> **TIP**
>
> As you type, the AutoComplete function displays the full text entered in other cells that begins with the same letters you have typed. To make a different entry, keep typing the new data. To accept the entry, press the Enter key.

Step-by-Step 1.7

1. Click cell **A10** to make it the active cell.
2. Press the **F2** key. A blinking insertion point appears in cell A10.
3. Press the **left arrow** key five times to move the insertion point after *Pac*.
4. Type **Man**, and then press the **Enter** key. The contents of cell A10 are edited to *PacMan Frog*.
5. Click cell **D9**, and then type **19**.
6. On the Formula Bar, click the **Enter** button ✔. The number 19 is entered in cell D9, replacing the previous contents.
7. Click cell **A3**, and then press the **Delete** key. The contents are cleared from cell A3. Your screen should look similar to **Figure 1–9**.

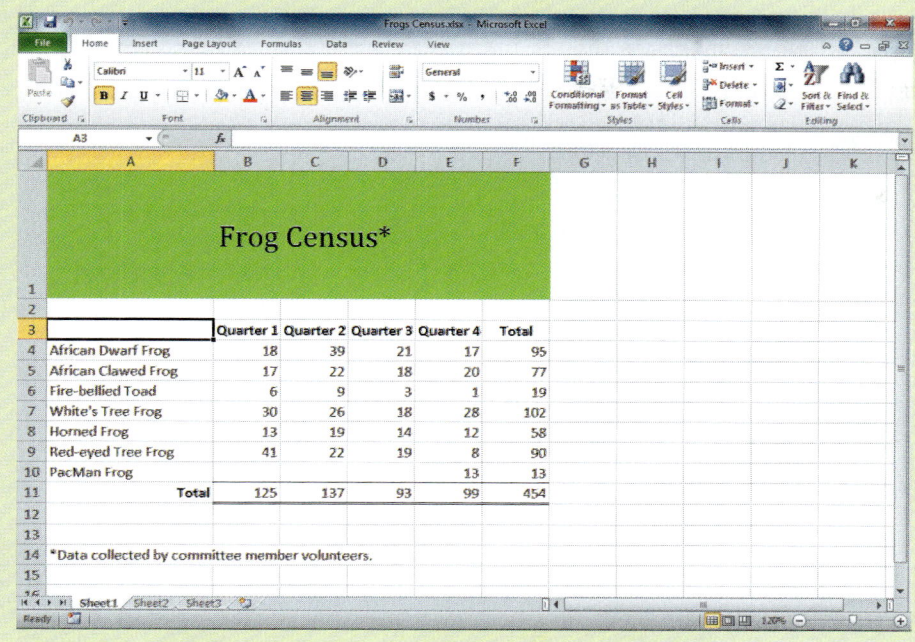

FIGURE 1–9
Data in cells changed and cleared

8. Save the workbook, and leave it open for the next Step-by-Step.

Searching for Data

The Find and Replace dialog box enables you to locate specific data in a worksheet. If you like, you can then change data you find.

Finding Data

The Find command locates data in a worksheet, which is particularly helpful when a worksheet contains a large amount of data. You can use the Find command to locate words or parts of words. For example, searching for *emp* finds the words *employee* and *temporary* It also finds Employee and TEMPORARY because the Find command doesn't match the uppercase or lowercase letters you typed unless you specify that it should. Likewise, searching for *85* finds the numbers *85*, *850*, and *385*. On the Home tab of the Ribbon, in the Editing group, click the Find & Select button, and then click Find. The Find and Replace dialog box appears, with the Find tab active.

Replacing Data

The Replace command is an extension of the Find command. Replacing data substitutes new data for the data that the Find command locates. As with the Find command, the Replace command doesn't distinguish between uppercase and lowercase letters unless you specify to match the case. On the Home tab of the Ribbon, in the Editing group, click the Find & Select button, and then click Replace. The Find and Replace dialog box appears, with the Replace tab active.

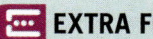 **EXTRA FOR EXPERTS**

You can use wildcard characters in the Find what box to search for data that matches a particular pattern. Use ? (a question mark) for a single character. Use * (an asterisk) for two or more characters. For example, Br?an finds Brian and Bryan, whereas Sam* finds Samuel, Samantha, Sammy, and Sammi.

You can perform more specific searches by clicking the Options button in the dialog box. **Figure 1–10** shows the Replace tab in the Find and Replace dialog box after clicking the Options button.

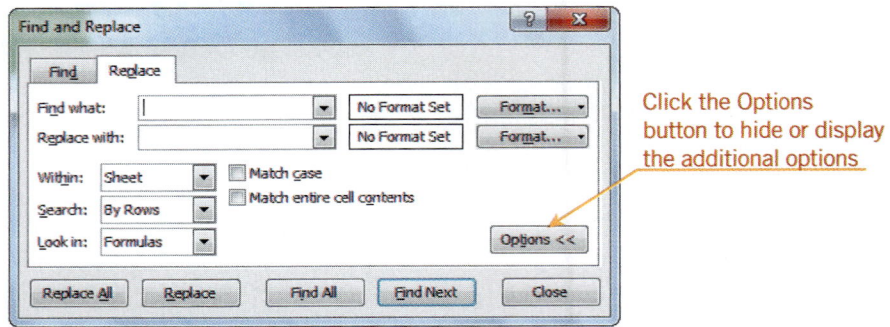

Click the Options button to hide or display the additional options

FIGURE 1–10   Find and Replace dialog box expanded

Table 1–2 lists the options you can specify in the Find and Replace dialog box.

TABLE 1–2   Find and Replace options

SEARCH OPTION	SPECIFIES
Find what	The data to locate
Replace with	The data to insert in place of the located data
Format	The format of the data you want to find or replace
Within	Whether to search the worksheet or the entire workbook
Search	The direction to search: across rows or down columns
Look in	Whether to search cell contents (values) or formulas
Match case	Whether the search must match the capitalization you used for the search data
Match entire cell contents	Whether the search should locate cells whose contents exactly match the search data

Step-by-Step 1.8

1. Click cell **A1**.

2. On the Home tab of the Ribbon, locate the **Editing** group.

3. Click the **Find & Select** button , and then click **Find**.

4. In the Find what box, type **Quarter**.

5. Click **Find Next**. The active cell moves to cell B3, the first cell that contains the search data.

6. In the Find and Replace dialog box, click the **Replace** tab. A Replace with box appears.

7. In the Replace with box, type **Month**.

8. Click **Replace**. The word *Quarter* is replaced by *Month* in cell B3, and the active cell moves to cell C3, which is the next cell that contains the search data.

9. Click **Replace All**. A dialog box appears, indicating that Excel has completed the search and made three additional replacements of the word *Quarter* with the word *Month*.

10. Click **OK**.

11. In the Find and Replace dialog box, click **Close**.

12. Save the workbook, and leave it open for the next Step-by-Step.

Zooming a Worksheet

You can change the magnification of a worksheet using the Zoom controls on the status bar. The default magnification for a workbook is 100%, which you can see on the Zoom level button. For a closer view of a worksheet, click the Zoom In button ⊕, which increases the zoom by 10% each time you click the button, or drag the Zoom slider to the right to increase the zoom percentage. The entire worksheet looks larger, and you see fewer cells in the work area. The Sheet1 worksheet you are working on is zoomed to 120% so you can more easily see the contents in the cells. If you want to see more cells in the work area, click the Zoom Out button ⊖, which decreases the zoom by 10% each time you click the button, or drag the Zoom slider to the left to decrease the zoom percentage. The entire worksheet looks smaller. To select a specific magnification, click the Zoom level button 100% to open the Zoom dialog box, type the zoom percentage you want in the Custom box, and then click OK. The Zoom level button shows the current zoom level percentage. **Figure 1–11** shows the Zoom dialog box and the zoom controls.

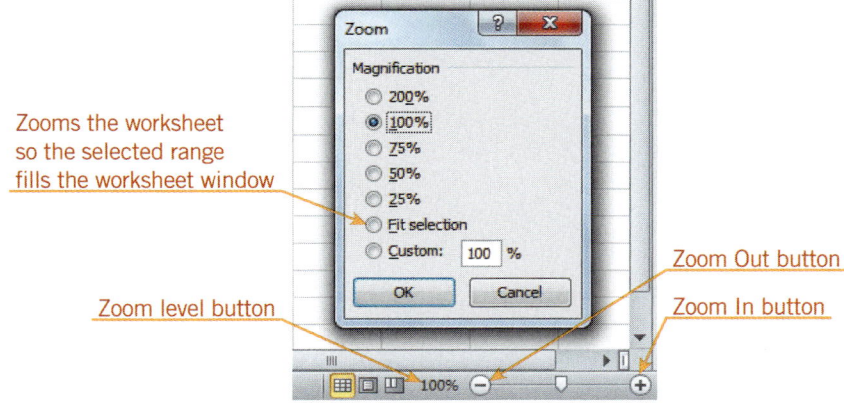

FIGURE 1–11   Zoom dialog box and controls

Step-by-Step 1.9

1. On the status bar, click the **Zoom In** button ⊕ two times. The worksheet zooms to 140%, and you see a closer view of fewer cells.

2. On the status bar, drag the **Zoom slider** ▽ right to approximately 200%. The view of the worksheet is magnified even more.

3. On the status bar, click the **Zoom level** button. The Zoom dialog box appears, as shown in Figure 1–11.

4. Click the **50%** option button, and then click **OK**. The view of the worksheet is reduced to half of its default size, and you see many more cells.

5. On the status bar, click the **Zoom In** button ⊕ seven times. The worksheet returns to zoom level of 120%.

6. Click cell **A16**, and then enter your name.

7. Save the workbook, and leave it open for the next Step-by-Step.

Previewing and Printing a Worksheet

▶ **VOCABULARY**
portrait orientation

landscape orientation

Sometimes you need a printed copy of a worksheet to give to another person or for your own files. You can print a worksheet by clicking the File tab on the Ribbon, and then clicking Print in the navigation bar to display the Print tab (see **Figure 1–12**). The Print tab enables you to select the number of copies to print, a printer, the parts of the worksheet to print, and the way the printed worksheet will look. The print settings include the page orientation (**portrait orientation** for a page turned so that its shorter side is at top and **landscape orientation** for a page turned so that its longer side is at top), the paper size, and the margins. For now, you will print the entire worksheet using the default settings.

Click to print the worksheet

Click to select the printer to use

Click to select what to print

Click to select the paper orientation

Click to select the margins

Click the Next Page and Previous Page buttons to scroll through the preview

Select the number of copies to print

Preview of the worksheet as a printed page

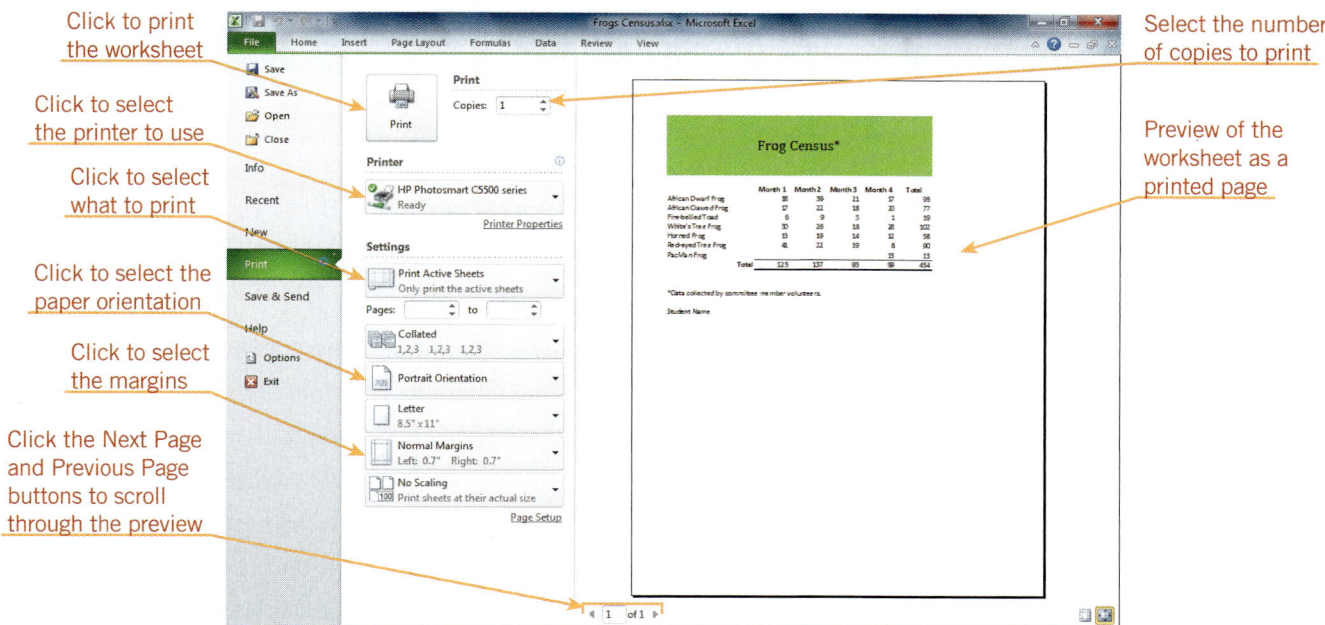

FIGURE 1–12   Print tab

The Print tab also shows you how the printed pages will look before you use the resources to print a worksheet. You can click the Next Page and Previous Page buttons to display other pages of your worksheet. You can click the Zoom to Page button, which shows a closer view of the page (see **Figure 1–13**). When you have finished previewing the printed pages and are satisfied with the print settings, you click the Print button.

Use the scroll bars to shift different parts of the page into view

Click to display other pages of a longer worksheet

Zoom to Page button

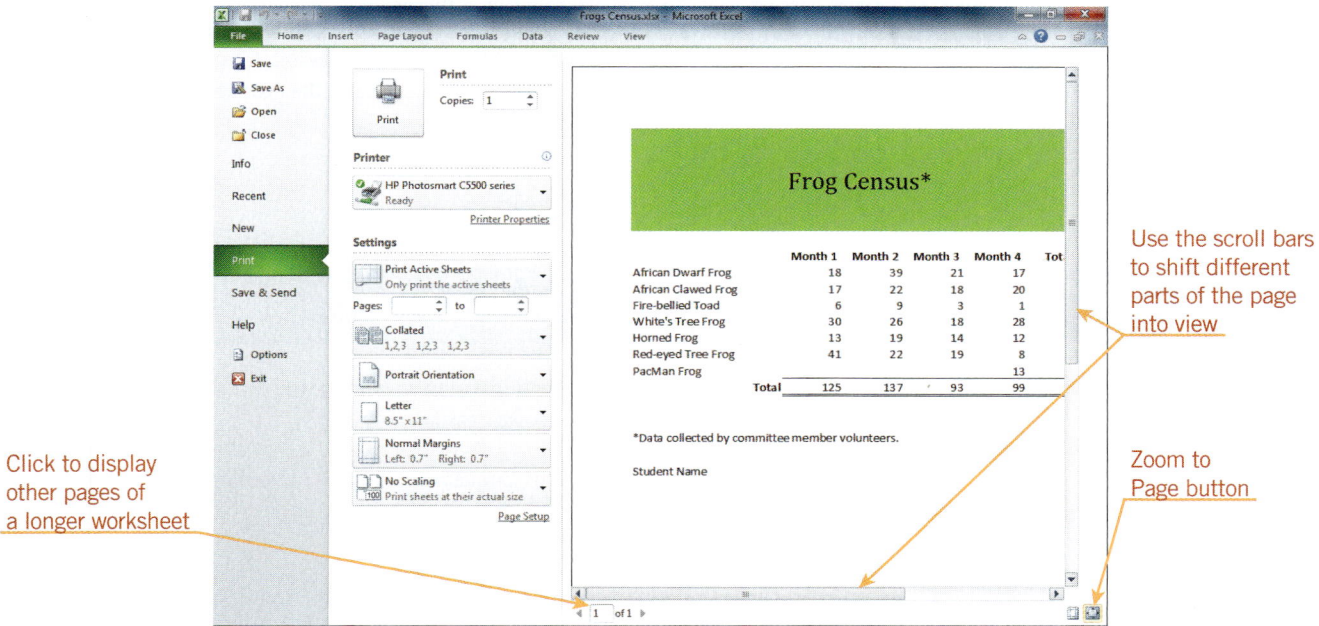

FIGURE 1–13   Zoom to Page

Step-by-Step 1.10

1. On the Ribbon, click the **File** tab. In the navigation bar, click **Print**. The Print tab appears, as shown in Figure 1–12.

2. Review the default settings on the Print tab. If the printer you want to use is not in the Printer button, click the **Printer** button, and then click the appropriate printer name.

3. Click **Zoom to Page** button 🖻. The previewed page becomes larger so you can examine it in more detail, as shown in Figure 1–13.

4. Drag the scroll bars to display different parts of the previewed page.

5. Click **Zoom to Page** button 🖻. The preview returns to its original size.

6. If your instructor asks you to print the worksheet, click the **Print** button 🖨. The active worksheet is printed. If you do not need to print, click the **File** tab on the Ribbon to return to the worksheet.

7. Leave the workbook open for the next Step-by-Step.

Closing a Workbook and Exiting Excel

TIP

You can also close the workbook and leave Excel open by clicking the Close Window button located below the sizing buttons in the title bar. To close the workbook and exit Excel, you can click the Close button in the title bar.

You can close a workbook by clicking the File tab on the Ribbon, and then clicking Close in the navigation bar. If you use the Close command to close a workbook, Excel remains open and ready for you to open or create another workbook. To exit the workbook, click the Exit command in the navigation bar.

If you try to close a workbook that contains changes you haven't saved, a dialog box opens, asking whether you want to save the file. Click Yes to save and close the workbook. Click No to close the workbook without saving. Click Cancel to return to the Excel program window without saving or closing the workbook.

Step-by-Step 1.11

1. On the Ribbon, click the **File** tab, and then in the navigation bar, click **Close**.

2. If you are asked to save changes, click **Save**. The workbook closes.

3. On the File tab, in the navigation bar, click **Exit**. The Excel program window closes.

SUMMARY

In this lesson, you learned:

- The primary purpose of a spreadsheet is to solve problems involving numbers. The advantage of using a computer spreadsheet is that you can complete complex and repetitious calculations quickly and accurately.

- A worksheet consists of columns and rows that intersect to form cells. Each cell is identified by a cell reference, which combines the letter of the column and the number of the row.

- The first time you save a workbook, the Save As dialog box opens so you can enter a descriptive name and select a save location. After that, you can use the Save command in Backstage view or the Save button on the Quick Access Toolbar to save the latest version of the workbook.

- You can change the active cell in the worksheet by clicking the cell with the pointer, pressing keys, or using the scroll bars. The Go To dialog box lets you quickly move the active cell anywhere in the worksheet.

- A group of selected cells is called a range. A range is identified by the cells in the upper-left and lower-right corners of the range, separated by a colon. To select an adjacent range, drag the pointer across the rectangle of cells you want to include. To select a nonadjacent range, select the first adjacent range, hold down the Ctrl key, select each additional cell or range, and then release the Ctrl key.

- Worksheet cells can contain text, numbers, and formulas. After you enter data or a formula in a cell, you can change the cell contents by editing, replacing, or deleting it.

- You can search for specific characters in a worksheet. You can also replace data you have searched for with specific characters.

- The zoom controls on the status bar enable you to enlarge or reduce the magnification of the worksheet in the worksheet window.

- Before you print a worksheet, you should check the page preview to see how the printed pages will look.

- When you finish your work session, you should save your final changes and close the workbook.

VOCABULARY REVIEW

Define the following terms:

active cell	Formula Bar	range reference
active worksheet	landscape orientation	row
adjacent range	Microsoft Excel 2010 (Excel)	sheet tab
cell	Name Box	spreadsheet
cell reference	nonadjacent range	workbook
column	portrait orientation	worksheet
formula	range	

REVIEW QUESTIONS

TRUE / FALSE

Circle T if the statement is true or F if the statement is false.

T   F   **1.**   The primary advantage of the worksheet is the ability to solve numerical problems quickly and accurately.

T   F   **2.**   A cell is the intersection of a row and a column.

T   F   **3.**   You use the Go To command to get a closer view of a worksheet.

T   F   **4.**   You can use the Find command to substitute *Week* for all instances of *Period* in a worksheet.

T   F   **5.**   Each time you save a worksheet, you must open the Save As dialog box.

WRITTEN QUESTIONS

Write a brief answer to the following questions.

1. What term describes a cell that is ready for data entry?

2. How are rows identified in a worksheet?

3. What term describes a group of cells?

4. What key(s) do you press to move the active cell to the first cell in a row?

5. If you decide not to enter data you just typed in the active cell, how do you cancel your entry without making any changes to the cell?

FILL IN THE BLANK

Complete the following sentences by writing the correct word or words in the blanks provided.

1. A(n) _____ is a computerized spreadsheet.

2. Each cell is identified by a unique _____, which is formed by combining the cell's column letter and row number.

3. The contents of the active cell always appear in the _____.

4. _____ a cell removes all the data in a cell.

5. You can increase or decrease the magnification of a worksheet with the _____ controls on the status bar.

◼ PROJECTS

If you have a SAM 2010 user profile, your instructor may have assigned an autogradable version of the indicated project. If so, log into the SAM 2010 Web site at *www.cengage.com/sam2010* to download the instruction and start files.

PROJECT 1–1

In the blank space, write the letter of the key or keys from Column 2 that correspond to the movement of the active cell in Column 1.

Column 1   Column 2

_____ 1. Left one column   A. Up arrow key

_____ 2. Right one column   B. Page Up key

_____ 3. Up one row   C. Left arrow key

_____ 4. Down one row   D. Home key

_____ 5. To the first cell in a row   E. Down arrow key

_____ 6. To cell A1   F. Right arrow key

_____ 7. To the last cell containing data G. Ctrl+End keys

_____ 8. Up one window   H. Ctrl+Home keys

_____ 9. Down one window   I. Page Down key

 PROJECT 1–2

1. Start Excel. Open the **Homes.xlsx** workbook from the drive and folder where your Data Files are stored.

2. Save the workbook as **Home Ownership** followed by your initials.

3. In cell A15, enter **Colorado**.

4. In cell B15, enter **67.30**.

5. In cell C15, enter **62.20**.

6. In cell A16, edit the data to **Connecticut**.

7. In cell B16, edit the data to **66.80**.

8. In cell A5, delete the data.

9. In cell A2, enter your name.

10. Change the page orientation to landscape orientation.

11. Save, preview, and print the workbook. Close the workbook and exit Excel.

PROJECT 1–3

1. Start Excel. Open the **Properties.xlsx** workbook from the drive and folder where your Data Files are stored.

2. Save the workbook as **Properties Estimates** followed by your initials.

3. Enter the square footages in the following cells to estimate the home costs. The estimated home cost in each neighborhood will change as you enter the data.

CELL	ENTER
C5	1300
C6	1550
C7	2200
C8	1500

4. After selling several houses in the Washington Heights neighborhood, Neighborhood Properties has determined that the cost per square foot is $71.25, rather than $78.50. Edit cell B7 to **$71.25**.

5. In cell A3, enter your name.

6. Save, preview, print, and then close the workbook. Exit Excel.

PROJECT 1–4

1. Start Excel. Open the **Names.xlsx** workbook from the drive and folder where your Data Files are stored.

2. Save the workbook as **Last Names** followed by your initials.

3. Use the Find command to locate the name *CRUZ*. The active cell should be cell A123.

4. Click in the worksheet outside the dialog box, and then press the Ctrl+Home keys to return to cell A1.

5. Click in the Find and Replace dialog box, and then locate the name *BOOTH*. The active cell should be cell A595. (*Hint*: The Find and Replace dialog box remains on-screen from Steps 3 and 4. You can simply enter the new search in the Find what box.)

6. Click in the worksheet, and then press the Ctrl+Home keys to return to cell A1.

7. Click in the Find and Replace dialog box, click the Replace tab, and then replace the name *FORBES* with **FABERGE**. The active cell should be cell A988.

8. Undo the last change you made to the workbook.

9. Search for your last name and the last names of three of your friends in the workbook. These names might not appear in the workbook.

10. Save and close the workbook. Exit Excel.

CRITICAL THINKING

ACTIVITY 1–1

The primary purpose of a spreadsheet is to solve problems that involve numbers. Identify two numerical situations in each of the following categories that might be solved by using a spreadsheet.

1. Business

2. Career

3. Personal

4. School

ACTIVITY 1–2

In your worksheet, you have selected a large range of adjacent cells that extends over several screens. You realize that you incorrectly included one additional column of cells in the range.

To reselect the range of cells, you must page up to the active cell (the first cell in the range) and drag through several screens to the last cell in the range. Is there a better way to remove the column from the range, without having to reselect the entire range? Also, is there a faster way to select such a large range—one that doesn't include dragging through several screens?

Start Excel, and use the Help system to learn more about how to select fewer cells without canceling your original selection. Then research how to select a large range without dragging. Use Word to write a brief explanation of the steps you would take to change the selected range and to select a large range without dragging.

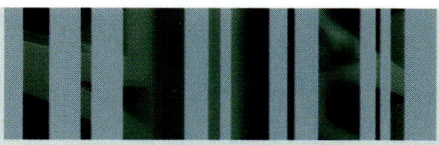

LESSON 2

Changing the Appearance of a Worksheet

■ OBJECTIVES

Upon completion of this lesson, you should be able to:

- Change column widths and row heights.
- Position data within a cell by aligning, wrapping, rotating, and indenting.
- Change the appearance of cells using fonts, font sizes, font styles, colors, and borders.
- Designate the number format used for data stored in a cell.
- Use the Format Painter to copy formatting from one cell to another.
- Apply and clear cell styles.
- Find and replace cell formats.

■ VOCABULARY

align
AutoFit
border
cell style
clear
column heading
fill
font
font size
font style
Format Painter
indent
merge
number format
orientation
row heading
style
theme
truncate
wrap text

Worksheet contents should be easy to read and attractive. You can use formatting to provide visual cues to help determine the purpose of different data in the worksheet as well as to make the data visually pleasing. Changing column widths and row heights ensures that all the contents are visible. How data is positioned in cells helps improve readability by lining up items, wrapping long entries onto multiple lines, rotating text for interest, and indenting subentries. You can also change fonts, sizes, colors, and borders to distinguish different parts of the worksheet and highlight key sections. Values are more understandable when the appropriate number format is applied. As you apply formatting to a worksheet, it's often faster to copy formatting with the Format Painter than to reapply several formats. You can also apply a variety of preset formatting using cell styles. If you want to change a specific format, you can quickly find and replace cell formats.

Resizing Columns and Rows

Worksheets are most valuable when the information they present is simple for the user to understand. Data in a worksheet must be accurate, but it is also important that the data be presented in a visually appealing way.

Changing Column Width

Sometimes the data you enter in a cell does not fit in the column. When you enter information that is wider than the column, one of the following situations occurs:

- Text that fits in the cell is displayed in the cell. The rest is stored but hidden when the next cell contains data.

- Text that does not fit in the cell extends into the next cell when that cell is empty.

- Numbers are converted to a different numerical form (for example, numbers with many digits are displayed in exponential form).

- Numbers that do not fit in the cell are displayed as a series of number signs (######).

You can resize a column to fit a certain number of characters. Place the pointer on the right edge of the ***column heading*** (the column letter) until the pointer changes to a double-headed arrow. Click and drag the column's edge to the right until the column expands to the width you want. Drag the column's edge to the left to reduce the column width. As you drag, a ScreenTip appears near the pointer, displaying the new column width measurement.

If you want to use a precise column width, it's easiest to enter that value in the Column Width dialog box shown in **Figure 2–1**. To access the dialog box, click any cell in the column you want to change. On the Home tab of the Ribbon, in the Cells group, click the Format button, and then click Column Width. In the Column width box, type the width you want, and then click OK. The column resizes to fit the number of characters you specified.

VOCABULARY
column heading

TIP

You can also open the Column Width dialog box by right-clicking the column heading of the column you want to resize, and then clicking Column Width on the shortcut menu.

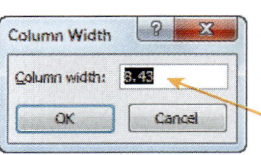

Type the number of characters to display in the column

FIGURE 2–1   Column Width dialog box

Changing Row Height

The process for changing row height is similar to how you change the column width. Place the pointer below the ***row heading*** (the row number) until the pointer changes to a double-headed arrow. Click and drag the border of the row heading down until the row has the height you want. You can also use the Row Height dialog box to specify an exact row height. Click a cell in the row you want to resize. On the Home tab of the Ribbon, in the Cells group, click the Format button, and then click Row Height to open the Row Height dialog box. In the Row height box, type the height you want, and then click OK.

Using AutoFit to Change Column Width or Row Height

Columns often contain data of varying widths. To make the worksheet easier to read, a column should be wide enough to display the longest entry, but no wider than necessary. ***AutoFit*** determines the best width for a column or the best height for a row, based on its contents. Place the pointer on the right edge of the column heading (or below the row heading) until the pointer changes to a double-headed arrow. Then, double-click to resize the column or row to the best fit.

EXTRA FOR EXPERTS

You can resize several columns or rows at once. Select the columns or rows to resize. Then, use the pointer to click and drag the right edge of a selected column heading or the bottom edge of a selected row heading to the desired width or height.

Step-by-Step 2.1

1. Open the **Cassidy.xlsx** workbook from the drive and folder where your Data Files are stored.

2. Save the workbook as **Cassidy Budget** followed by your initials. Notice that the text in some cells extends into the empty cells in the next column; for example, the month name in cell D3 extends into column E. Some text is hidden because the adjacent cell contains data, such as the text in cell A6.

3. Place the pointer on the right edge of the column D column heading. The pointer changes to a double-headed arrow ✛.

4. Click and drag to the right until the ScreenTip reads *Width: 10.00 (75 pixels)*, as shown in **Figure 2–2**. Release the mouse button. The entire word *September* now fits within column D.

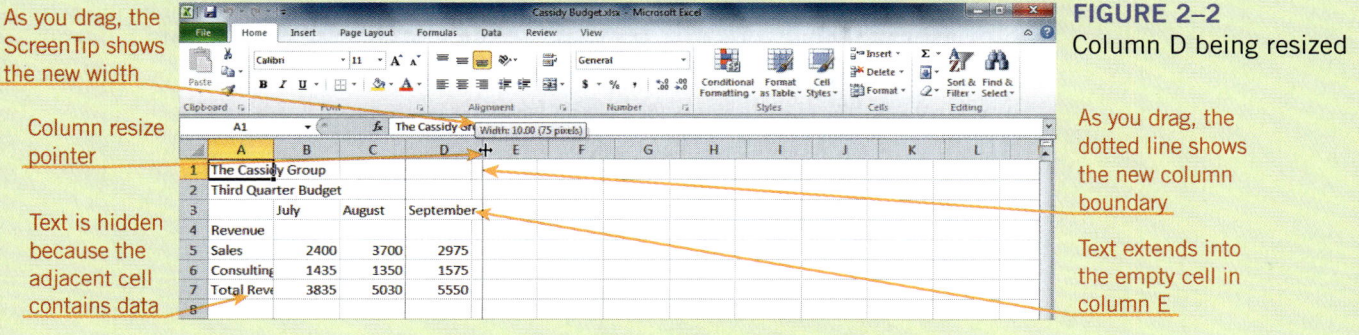

As you drag, the ScreenTip shows the new width

Column resize pointer

Text is hidden because the adjacent cell contains data

FIGURE 2–2
Column D being resized

As you drag, the dotted line shows the new column boundary

Text extends into the empty cell in column E

5. Point to the **column B** column heading. The pointer changes to the column selection pointer ↓. Click and drag across the **column B** and **column C** column headings. Both columns B and C are selected. Release the mouse button. You want the two selected columns to be the same width as column D.

6. On the Ribbon, click the **Home** tab, if necessary, and then locate the **Cells** group.

7. Click the **Format** button, and then click **Column Width**. The Column Width dialog box appears, as shown in Figure 2–1.

8. In the Column width box, type **10**. Click **OK**. The widths of the selected columns change to 10 characters.

9. Place the pointer on the bottom edge of the row 18 row heading. The pointer changes to a double-headed arrow ↨.

10. Click and drag down until the ScreenTip reads *Height: 18.00 (24 pixels)*, and then release the mouse button.

11. Look at the data in column A. Some cells are not wide enough to display all their contents.

12. Click cell **A19**. You see only a portion of the words *Cumulative Profit* in the cell. The Formula Bar shows the complete contents of the cell.

13. Double-click the right edge of the column A column heading. Column A widens to display the longest cell contents in the column, which, in this case is cell A2. You can now see all the contents in column A, and including the contents of cell A19.

14. Save the workbook, and leave it open for the next Step-by-Step.

Positioning Data Within a Cell

Unless you specify otherwise, text you enter in a cell is lined up along the bottom-left side of the cell, and numbers you enter in a cell are lined up along the bottom-right side of the cell. However, you can position data within a cell in a variety of ways, as described in **Table 2–1**. All of these positions are available on the Home tab of the Ribbon, in the Alignment group.

TABLE 2–1 Positioning data within a cell

POSITION	DESCRIPTION	BUTTON	EXAMPLE
Alignment	Specifies where data is lined up within the cell	▤	Align Text Left is the default for text
		▤	Align Text Right is the default for numbers
		▤	Center is often used for title text
Indent	Changes the space between the cell border and its content	▤	Increase Indent adds space; used for subheadings
		▤	Decrease Indent removes space
Orientation	Rotates cell contents to an angle or vertically	▧▾	Labels in a narrow column
Wrap Text	Moves data to a new line when the cell is not wide enough to display all the contents	▤	Long descriptions
Merge	Combines multiple cells into one cell	▤	Title across the top of a worksheet; Merge & Center centers contents in the merged cell

Aligning Text

You can *align* the contents of a cell horizontally and vertically within the cell. Horizontal alignments are left, centered, or right. Vertical alignments are top, middle, or bottom, as shown in **Figure 2–3**. Excel left-aligns all text and right-aligns all numbers. All data is bottom-aligned. You can select a different horizontal and vertical alignment for any cell.

▶ **VOCABULARY**
align
alignment

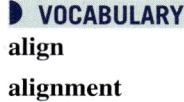

FIGURE 2–3 Horizontal and vertical alignments

To change the *alignment* of a cell, select the cell and then click an alignment button in the Alignment group on the Home tab of the Ribbon. For other alignment options, click the Format Cells: Alignment Dialog Box Launcher to display the Alignment tab in the Format Cells dialog box. In the Text alignment section, click the alignment you want in the Horizontal or Vertical boxes, and then click OK.

▶ **VOCABULARY**

merge

indent

Merging and Centering Data

You can also center cell contents across several columns. Select the cells, and then click the Merge & Center button in the Alignment group on the Home tab of the Ribbon. The selected cells *merge*, or combine into one cell, and the contents from the upper-left cell are centered in the newly merged cell.

Indenting Data

Data can be *indented* (or shifted to the right) within cells to help distinguish categories or set data apart. Instead of trying to indent data by pressing the spacebar, you should use the Increase Indent button in the Alignment group on the Home tab of the Ribbon. This way, all cells' contents are indented evenly. To move the indent in the other direction, click the Decrease Indent button.

Step-by-Step 2.2

1. Select the range **B3:D3**.

2. On the Home tab of the Ribbon, locate the **Alignment** group. All the positioning buttons are located in this group.

3. Click the **Center** button . The headings are centered horizontally in the cell.

4. Click cell **A7**.

5. On the Home tab, in the Alignment group, click the **Align Text Right** button . *Total Revenue* is aligned at the right of the cell.

6. Click cell **A16**, press and hold the **Ctrl** key, click cells **A18** and **A19**, and then release the **Ctrl** key. The nonadjacent range is selected.

7. On the Home tab, in the Alignment group, click the **Align Text Right** button . The contents of the three cells are right-aligned.

8. Select the range **A1:D1**.

9. On the Home tab, in the Alignment group, click the **Merge & Center** button . Cells A1 through D1 are combined into one cell, and the title *The Cassidy Group* is centered in the merged cell.

10. Select the range **A2:D2**. On the Home tab, in the Alignment group, click the **Merge & Center** button . Cells A2 through D2 are merged, and the subtitle *Third Quarter Budget* is centered in the merged cell.

11. Click cell **A5**. On the Home tab, in the Alignment group, click the **Increase Indent** button ⊞. The contents of cell A5 shift to the right.

12. Click cell **A6**. On the Home tab, in the Alignment group, click the **Increase Indent** button ⊞. The contents of cell A6 shift to the right and line up with the contents of cell A5.

13. Select the range **A10:A15**. On the Home tab, in the Alignment group, click the **Increase Indent** button ⊞. The contents of the cells in the range shift to the right.

14. Save the workbook, and leave it open for the next Step-by-Step.

Changing Text Orientation

Sometimes labels that describe the column data, or the data itself, are longer than the column widths. To save space in the worksheet, you can change each cell's text *orientation* to rotate its data to any angle. Changing the text orientation of some cells can also help give your worksheet a more professional look.

To change text orientation, select the cells whose contents you want to rotate. Then, on the Home tab of the Ribbon, in the Alignment group, click the Orientation button. A menu of orientation options appears, with commands for angling the text at 45-degree angles clockwise or counterclockwise, stacking the text vertically, or rotating the text up or down.

If you want to use a different angle, you need to use the Alignment tab in the Format Cells dialog box, as shown in **Figure 2–4**. Click the Format Cells: Alignment Dialog Box Launcher to display the Alignment tab in the Format Cells dialog box. In the Orientation box, click a degree point, drag the angle indicator, or type the angle you want in the Degrees box. Click OK.

▶ **VOCABULARY**
orientation

TIP

Rotated text is often used for labels on charts. Angled or vertical text fits more data in a label, while remaining readable.

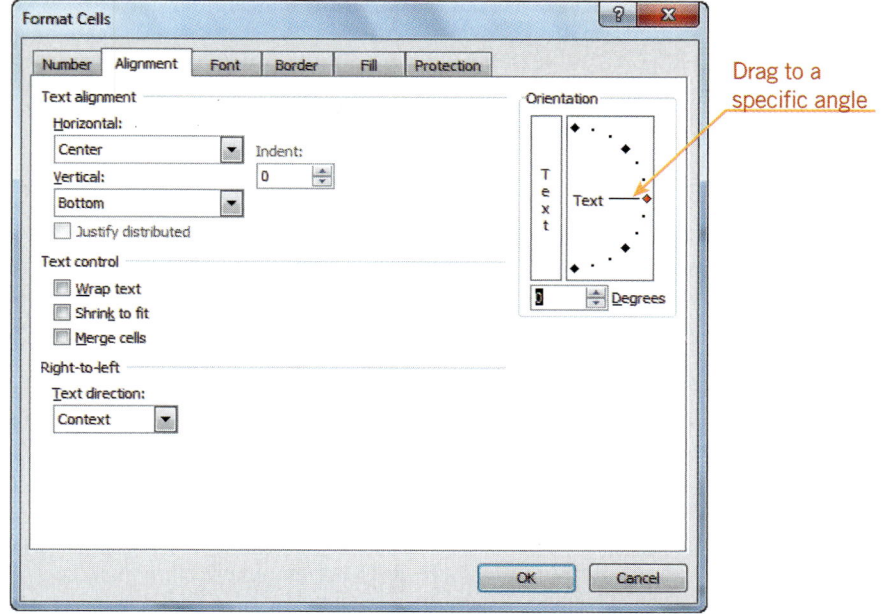

FIGURE 2–4   Alignment tab in the Format Cells dialog box

Step-by-Step 2.3

1. Select the range **B3:D3**.

2. On the Home tab, in the Alignment group, click the **Orientation** button
   . A menu appears with the most common orientations.

3. Click **Angle Counterclockwise**. The text in cells B3 through D3 shifts to
   a 45-degree angle, and the height of row 3 increases to accommodate
   the angled text, as shown in **Figure 2–5**.

FIGURE 2–5
Modified alignments

Positioning buttons

Angled text

Right-aligned text

Indented text

Format Cells:
Alignment Dialog
Box Launcher

Merged cells with
centered text

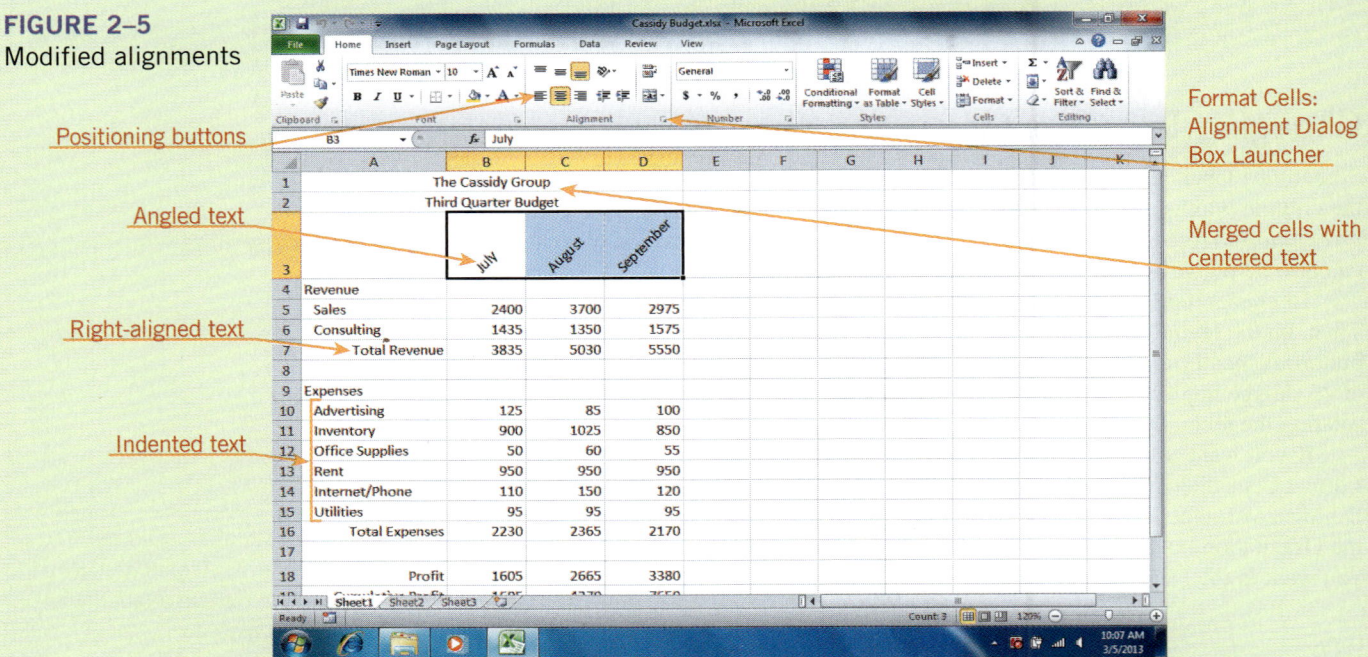

4. Save the workbook, and leave it open for the next Step-by-Step.

📰 **EXTRA FOR EXPERTS**

You can choose where a new line
begins in a cell. Double-click in the
cell to position the insertion point in
the cell. Use the arrow keys to move
the insertion point to where you
want the new line to begin. Press
the Alt+Enter keys to insert a line
break. Press the Enter key to accept
the change.

Wrapping Text

Text that is too long to fit within a cell is displayed in the next cell, if it is empty. If
the next cell already contains data, any text that does not fit in the cell is *truncated*,
or hidden from view. One way to see all the text stored in a cell is to *wrap text*. The
row height increases automatically to display additional lines until all the text is visible. When you wrap text, the column width is not changed.

To wrap text, select the cells in which you want to wrap text. Then, on the Home
tab of the Ribbon, in the Alignment group, click the Wrap Text button. If the cells
already contain text, the row height increases as needed to display all the content. If
you enter text after you turn on wrap text, the row height expands to fit the text as
you type. To turn off wrap text, click the Wrap Text button again.

If you change the column width for a cell with wrapped text, the contents readjust
to fit the new size. Be aware that row height does not automatically adjust, so you
might need to AutoFit the row height to eliminate extra blank lines within the cell.

Step-by-Step 2.4

1. Scroll the worksheet down until row 21 is visible.

2. Click cell **A21**. Type **Third Quarter Budget submitted**. Click the **Enter** button ☑ on the Formula Bar.

3. On the Home tab, in the Alignment group, click the **Wrap Text** button 🖼️. The text wraps in the cell, the row height adjusts to fit both lines of text, and the Wrap Text button remains selected, as shown in **Figure 2–6**.

Wrap Text button

Text wrapped to two lines within the cell

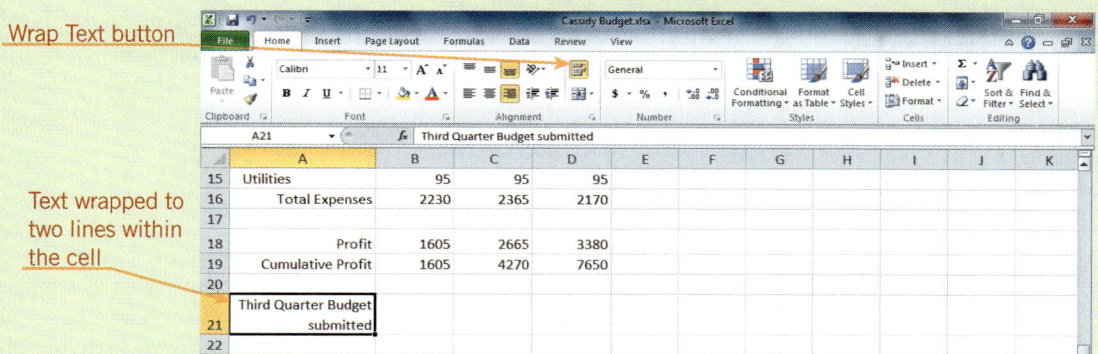

FIGURE 2–6
Wrapped text

4. Save the workbook, and leave it open for the next Step-by-Step.

Changing the Appearance of Cells

You can change the appearance of cells to make them easier to read, to differentiate sections in a worksheet, or to create a specific look and feel for the worksheet. To do this, you can modify the cell's default font, font size, font style, font color, fill color, and borders.

The fonts and colors used in each workbook are part of a theme. A *theme* is a preset collection of design elements, including fonts, colors, and other effects. By default, the Office theme is applied to each workbook. To change a workbook's appearance, you can select a different theme, or you can format cells with other fonts and colors. If you select another theme font or theme color, it will change when you apply a different theme. Or, you can choose non-theme or standard fonts and colors that stay the same no matter which theme is applied to the workbook.

As you format cells, *Live Preview* shows the results of the different formatting options you can choose. Select the cell or range you want to format, and then point to the formatting option you are considering. The cell or range changes to reflect that option. To accept that format, click the option.

Changing Fonts and Font Sizes

A *font* is the design of text. The default font for cells is Calibri. *Font size* determines the height of characters, as measured in *points*. The default font size for cells is 11 points. You can choose different fonts and font sizes in a worksheet to emphasize part of a worksheet or to distinguish worksheet titles and column headings from other data. The fonts and font sizes you use can significantly affect the readability of

▶ **VOCABULARY**
theme
Live Preview
font
font size
points

📧 **EXTRA FOR EXPERTS**

You can select a different theme for your workbook. Click the Page Layout tab on the Ribbon. In the Themes group, click the Themes button to display a gallery of themes. Point to different themes to see how your workbook changes. When you find a theme you like, click that theme to make the change.

TECHNOLOGY CAREERS

Excel workbooks are helpful to people and businesses in sales. Salespeople use worksheets to determine what items are available in inventories, to analyze sales performance, and to track customer orders.

TIP

You can also use the Mini toolbar to change the font, font size, font style, and font color. Double-click the cell, select the text in the cell to format, and then click the appropriate buttons on the Mini toolbar to apply the formatting.

VOCABULARY
font style

EXTRA FOR EXPERTS

You can quickly apply a font style to a selected cell or range. Press the Ctrl+B keys to apply bold. Press the Ctrl+I keys to apply italics. Press the Ctrl+U keys to apply underlining. Press the same keys to remove that font style from the selected cell or range.

the worksheet. Office comes with many fonts and sizes for text. However, the available fonts and sizes can change from one computer to another, depending on which fonts are installed on each computer.

To change fonts and sizes, you first select the cells you want to change. Then, on the Home tab of the Ribbon, in the Font group, click the Font arrow to display a gallery of available fonts or click the Font Size arrow, to display a gallery of available font sizes. When you point to a font or a size, Live Preview changes the cell contents to reflect that selection. Click the font or size you want to use.

Applying Font Styles

Bold, *italic*, and underlining can add emphasis to the contents of a cell. These features are referred to as ***font styles***. You can also combine font styles to change the emphasis, such as ***bold italic***. To apply a font style, select the cell or range you want to change. Then, on the Home tab of the Ribbon, click the appropriate button in the Font group. To remove a font style from the cell contents, simply click the button again.

Step-by-Step 2.5

1. Scroll the worksheet up until row 3 is displayed. Select the range **B3:D3**.

2. On the Home tab, in the Font group, click the **Font** arrow. A gallery appears, listing the fonts available on your computer, as shown in **Figure 2–7**.

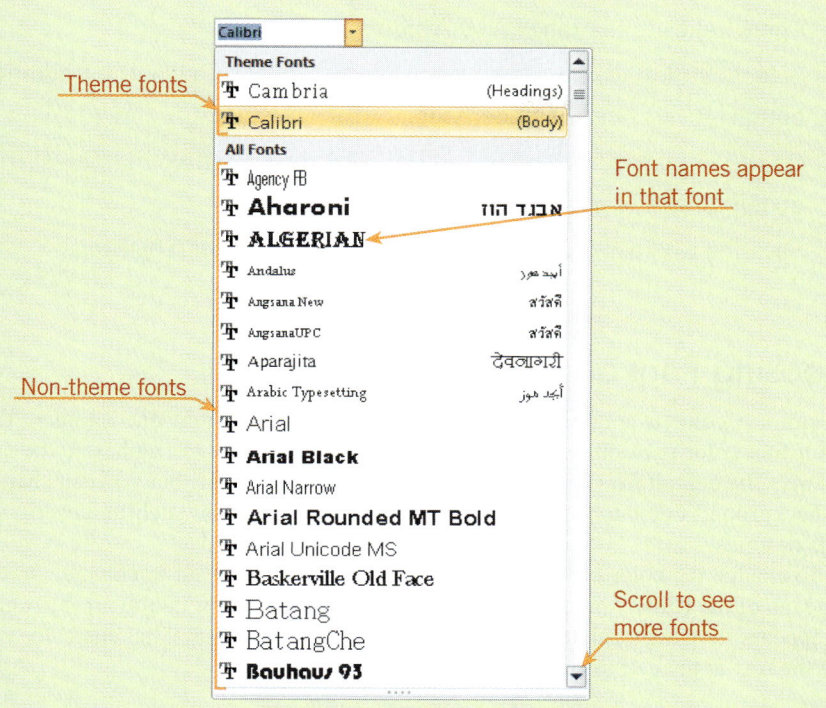

FIGURE 2–7
Font gallery

3. Scroll down the list and click **Times New Roman** (or a similar font). The font of the month names in cells B3, C3, and D3 changes from Calibri to Times New Roman.

4. On the Home tab, in the Font group, click the **Font Size** arrow. A gallery appears, listing the available font sizes. Click **10**. The font size of the month names in cells B3, C3, and D3 is reduced from 11 points to 10 points.

5. Click cell **A1** (the cell you merged from the range A1:D1). On the Home tab, in the Font group, click the **Font** arrow. Scroll down the list and click **Times New Roman**. The font of the company name in cell A1 changes to Times New Roman. Cell A1 remains active.

6. On the Home tab, in the Font group, click the **Font Size** arrow. Click **16**. The font size of the company name in cell A1 increases to 16 points. Cell A1 remains active.

7. On the Home tab, in the Font group, click the **Bold** button B. The text in cell A1 changes to bold, and the button remains selected to show it is toggled on.

8. Click cell **A2**. On the Home tab, in the Font group, click the **Bold** button B. The text in cell A2 changes to bold.

9. Apply bold to cells A4, A7, A9, A16, A18, and A19.

10. Select the range **A5:A6**. On the Home tab, in the Font group, click the **Italic** button I. The revenue items are italicized.

11. Apply italics to the range A10:A15.

12. Select cell **A4**. On the Home tab, in the Font group, click the **Underline** button ⊔. *Revenue* is underlined.

13. On the Home tab, in the Font group, click the **Underline** button ⊔. The underlining is removed from the text.

14. Save the workbook, and leave it open for the next Step-by-Step.

Choosing Font and Fill Colors

You can use color to emphasize cells or distinguish them from one another. The default font color is black, but you can select a different color to emphasize the cell contents. The default *fill* (or background) color of cells is white, but you can change this background color to help draw attention to certain cells, such as descriptive labels or totals.

To change the color of text in a cell, select the cell you want to change. On the Home tab of the Ribbon, in the Font group, click the Font Color button arrow. A gallery appears showing a palette of colors, as shown in **Figure 2–8**. Click the color you want the text in the cell to change to.

TIP

You can also change font and fill colors in selected cells using the Format Cells dialog box. On the Font tab, click the Color arrow, and then click a font color. On the Fill tab, use the Background Color section to select a color, click the Pattern Style arrow to select a pattern, or click the Pattern Color arrow to select a pattern color.

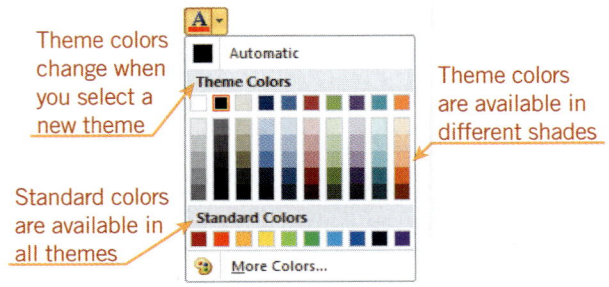

Theme colors change when you select a new theme

Theme colors are available in different shades

Standard colors are available in all themes

FIGURE 2–8   Font colors

To change the background color of a cell, select the cell you want to change. On the Home tab of the Ribbon, in the Font group, click the Fill Color button arrow. A gallery appears with a palette of colors, as shown in **Figure 2–9**. Click the color you want to fill the cell with.

EXTRA FOR EXPERTS

You can create contrasting headings by using a light font color with a dark fill color. For example, use white or yellow text on cells with green or blue backgrounds.

Theme colors change when you select a new theme

Theme colors are available in different shades

Click to remove a fill color from the selected cell or range

Standard colors are available in all themes

FIGURE 2–9   Fill colors

Step-by-Step 2.6

1. Click cell **A1**.

2. On the Home tab, in the Font group, click the **Font Color** button arrow . A gallery appears with a palette of colors, as shown in Figure 2–8.

3. Point to the **Red** color (the second color in the Standard Colors section). A ScreenTip displays the name of the color, and *The Cassidy Group*, the text in cell A1, changes to red, showing you a Live Preview of that selection.

4. Point to the **Dark Blue, Text 2** color (the fourth color in the first row of the Theme Colors section). A ScreenTip displays the name of the color, and Live Preview shows the company name in dark blue.

5. Click the **Dark Blue, Text 2** color. The gallery closes and the company name remains dark blue. Cell A1 is still the active cell.

6. On the Home tab, in the Font group, click the **Fill Color** button arrow . A gallery appears with a palette of colors, as shown in Figure 2–9.

7. Click the **Dark Blue, Text 2, Lighter 80%** color (the fourth color in the second row of the Theme Colors section). The cell background becomes light blue. Cell A1 is still the active cell.

8. Save the workbook, and leave it open for the next Step-by-Step.

Applying Cell Borders

You can add emphasis to a cell by applying a *border* (or line) around its edges. You can apply the border around the entire cell or only on certain sides of the cell. You can also select different border styles, such as a thick border or a double border.

▶ **VOCABULARY**
border

TIP

The Borders button shows the most recently selected border style. To apply that border style to a selected cell or range, click the Borders button (instead of the arrow).

To apply a border, select a cell or range. Then, on the Home tab of the Ribbon, in the Font group, click the Borders button arrow. A menu appears with border styles, as shown in **Figure 2–10**. Click the border style you want to add. You can remove the borders from a selected cell by clicking No Border in the border style menu.

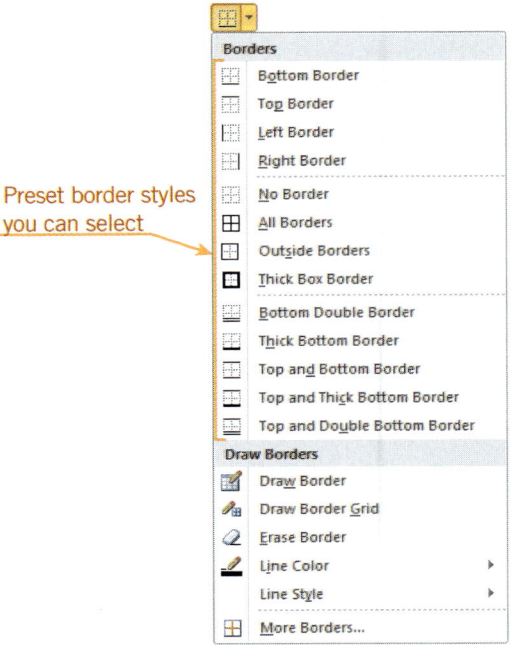

Preset border styles you can select

FIGURE 2–10   Borders styles

Step-by-Step 2.7

1. Select the range **B7:D7**.

2. On the Home tab, in the Font group, click the **Borders** button arrow. A menu of border styles appears, as shown in Figure 2–10.

3. Click **Top and Double Bottom Border**. Click cell **A8** to deselect the range. A single border appears above the range B7:D7 and a double border appears below the range. The Borders button changes to Top and Double Bottom Border.

4. Select the range **B16:D16**.

TIP

Standard accounting format uses a single border below a column of numbers and a double border below the total.

5. On the Home tab, in the Font group, click the **Top and Double Bottom Border** button . Click cell **A17** to deselect the range. A single border appears above the range B16:D16 and a double border appears below the range.

6. Save the workbook, and leave it open for the next Step-by-Step.

Selecting Number Formats

Number formats change the way data looks in a cell. The actual content you entered is *not* changed. The default number format is General, which displays numbers the way you enter them. However, you can select any of the number formats described in **Table 2–2**. Be aware that changing a number format affects only the appearance of the data in the cell. The actual value is not affected. The Formula Bar shows the actual value of the contents you see in the active cell. For example, the actual value shown in the Formula Bar might be 1000, whereas the number you see in the active cell is $1,000.00 if the cell uses the Currency number format.

> ▶ **VOCABULARY**
> **number formats**

TABLE 2–2 Number formats

FORMAT	EXAMPLE	DESCRIPTION
General	1000	The default format; displays numbers as entered; if the number doesn't fit in the cell, decimals are rounded, or the number is converted to scientific notation
Number	1000.00	Displays numbers with a fixed number of places to the right of the decimal point; the default is two decimal places
Currency	$1,000.00	Displays numbers with a dollar sign, a thousands separator, and two decimal places
Accounting	$1,000.00 $ 9.00	Displays numbers in the Currency format but lines up the dollar signs and the decimal points vertically within a column
Date	6/8/2013	Displays numbers as dates
Time	7:38 PM	Displays numbers as times
Percentage	35.29%	Displays numbers with two decimal places and a percent sign
Fraction	35 7/8	Displays decimal numbers as fractions
Scientific	1.00E+03	Displays numbers in exponential (or scientific) notation
Text	45-875-33	Displays text and numbers exactly as you type them
Special	79410-1234 (503) 555-4567	Displays numbers with a specific format: zip codes, zip+4 codes, phone numbers, and Social Security numbers
Custom	000.00.0	Displays data in the format you create, such as with commas or leading zeros

To change the number format for a selected cell or range, click the Number Format arrow in the Number group on the Home tab of the Ribbon, and then select the appropriate number format from the menu that opens. You can also change the number format for a selected cell or range by clicking the appropriate button in the Number group. The Accounting Number Format button quickly applies the Accounting number format; click the button arrow to select a different currency symbol, such as Euros. The other buttons let you choose whether the number includes a percent sign, whether it uses a thousands separator (a comma), and how many decimal places to show.

Copying Cell Formatting

▶ **VOCABULARY**
Format Painter

The **Format Painter** enables you to copy formatting from one worksheet cell and paste it to other cells without pasting the first cell's contents. This is especially helpful when the cell formatting you want to copy includes several formats. For example, after formatting a cell as a percentage with a white font, a green fill, and a double bottom border, you can use the Format Painter to quickly format other cells the same way.

To copy a cell's formatting, select the cell that has the format you want to copy. On the Home tab of the Ribbon, in the Clipboard group, click the Format Painter button. Then, click another cell or drag to select the range of cells you want to format in the same way.

TIP

You can use the Format Painter to copy the formatting to nonadjacent cells or ranges. Double-click the Format Painter button in the Clipboard group on the Home tab of the Ribbon. Select the cells or ranges to format. Click the Format Painter button again when you are done.

Step-by-Step 2.8

1. Select the range **B5:D5**, press and hold the **Ctrl** key, select the range **B7:D7**, and then release the **Ctrl** key. The nonadjacent range is selected.

2. On the Home tab, in the Number group, click the **Number Format** arrow. A menu of number formats appears.

3. Click **Accounting**. The numbers in the selected ranges include a dollar sign, a thousands separator, and two decimal places, which is the standard Accounting number format.

4. Click cell **B5**. Compare the value in the Formula Bar with the value in the active cell. The Formula Bar shows *2400*, which is the actual value stored in cell B5. Cell B5 shows *$2,400.00*, which is the stored value formatted for display.

5. On the Home tab, in the Clipboard group, click the **Format Painter** button. The pointer changes to a paintbrush next to the white plus pointer when placed over worksheet cells. A flashing dashed border surrounds cell B5 to remind you that the formatting from this cell is being copied.

6. Click and drag from cell **B10** to cell **D10**, and then release the mouse button. The format of the range B10:D10 changes to the Accounting number format.

7. Select the range **B11:D15**.

8. On the Home tab, in the Number group, click the **Number Format** arrow, and then click **Number**. The cells in the range are formatted with two decimal places.

9. On the Home tab, in the Number group, click the **Comma Style** button
    . A thousands separator is added to the number with four digits in
    cell C11 and the decimal points align with the values you formatted in
    row 10 with the Accounting number format.

10. On the Home tab, in the Clipboard group, click the **Format Painter** but-
    ton . The range B11:D15 is surrounded by a flashing dashed border.

11. Click and drag from cell **B6** to cell **D6**, and then release the mouse button.
    The format of the range B6:D6 is formatted with both the Number and
    Comma Style number formats that you applied to the range B11:D15.

12. Apply the **Accounting** number format to the ranges B16:D16 and B18:D19.

13. Click cell **A2** to deselect the range. Your screen should look similar to
    Figure 2–11.

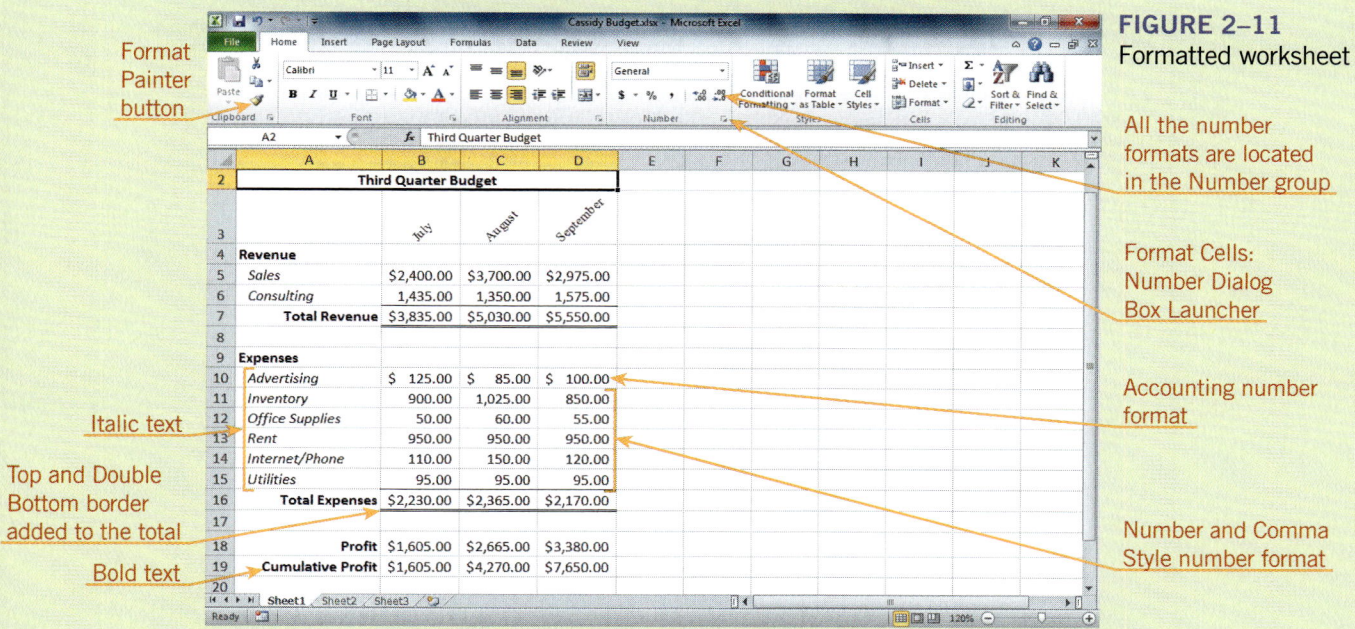

FIGURE 2–11
Formatted worksheet

14. Save the workbook, and leave it open for the next Step-by-Step.

Using the Format Cells Dialog Box

The Format Cells dialog box provides access to all the formatting options avail-
able on the Ribbon, as well as some additional formatting options. To open the
Format Cells dialog box, you can click the Dialog Box Launcher in the Font,
Alignment, or Number group on the Home tab of the Ribbon, or you can

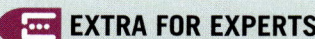 **EXTRA FOR EXPERTS**

The Format Cells dialog box also
includes a Protection tab, which
has options for locking and hiding
cells in a protected workbook. You
can protect a workbook to prevent
others from making changes to the
workbook.

press the Ctrl+1 keys. As shown in **Figure 2–12**, the Format Cells dialog box has Number, Alignment, Font, Border, and Fill tabs. You can use these tabs to change the number format, position of data, font options, borders, and cell background color as you have done so far.

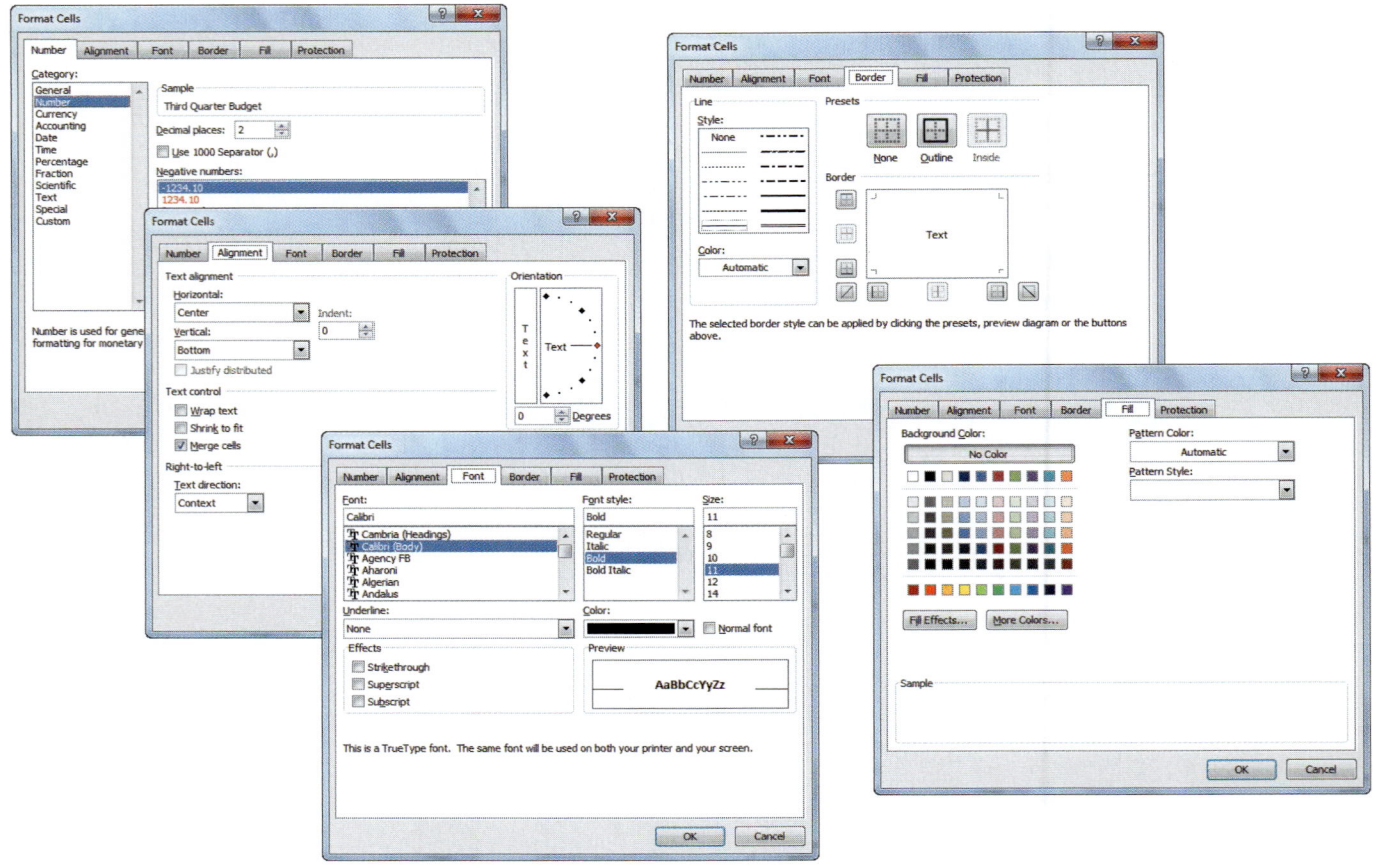

FIGURE 2–12   Format Cells dialog box

Using Styles to Format Cells

A *style* is a combination of formatting characteristics such as alignment, font, font size, font color, fill color, and borders. When you apply a style to a cell, you apply all the formatting characteristics simultaneously, saving you the time of applying the formats individually. Styles also help you format a worksheet consistently. When you use a style, you know that each cell with that style is formatted the same way.

Applying Cell Styles

A *cell style* is a collection of formatting characteristics you apply to a cell or range of data. To apply a cell style, select the cells you want to format. On the Home tab of the Ribbon, in the Styles group, click the Cell Styles button. The Cell Styles gallery appears, as shown in **Figure 2–13**. Point to a cell style in the gallery to see a Live Preview of that style on the selected cell or range in the worksheet. When you find a style you like, click the style to apply it. To remove a style from the selected cell, simply click Normal in the Good, Bad and Neutral section of the Cell Styles gallery.

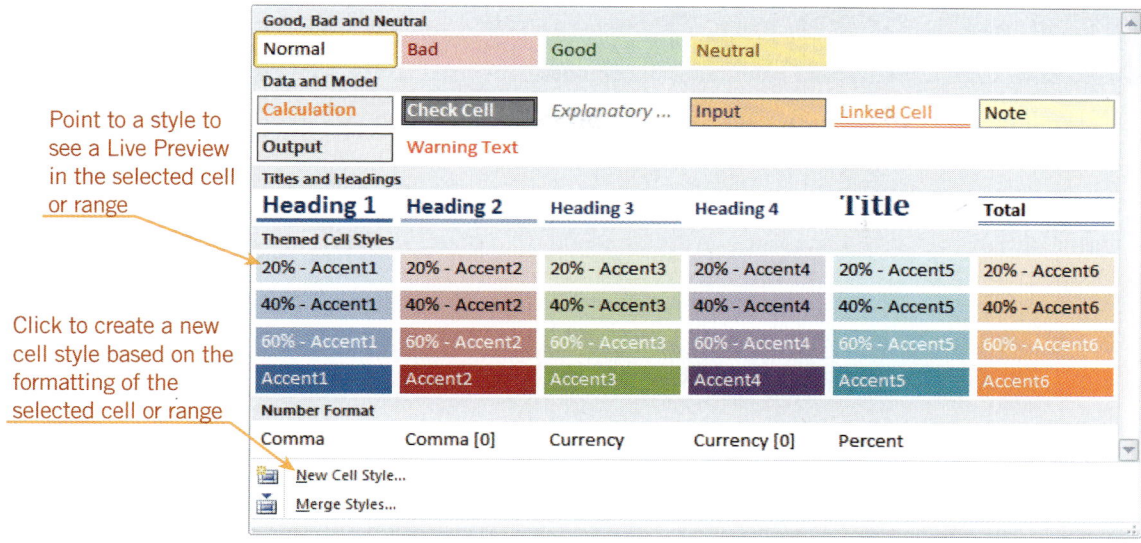

Point to a style to
see a Live Preview
in the selected cell
or range

Click to create a new
cell style based on the
formatting of the
selected cell or range

FIGURE 2–13   Cell Styles gallery

The Cell Styles gallery includes many predefined styles. However, if none of these styles meets your needs, you can define your own styles. First, format a cell with the exact combination of formats you want. Then, select the formatted cell, and click New Cell Style at the bottom of the Cell Styles gallery. In the Style dialog box that opens, shown in **Figure 2–14**, type a descriptive name for the style in the Style name box, verify the formatting in the Style Includes (By Example) section (uncheck any format you don't want to include), and then click OK. When you open the Cell Styles gallery again, the custom style you created appears in the Custom section at the top of the gallery.

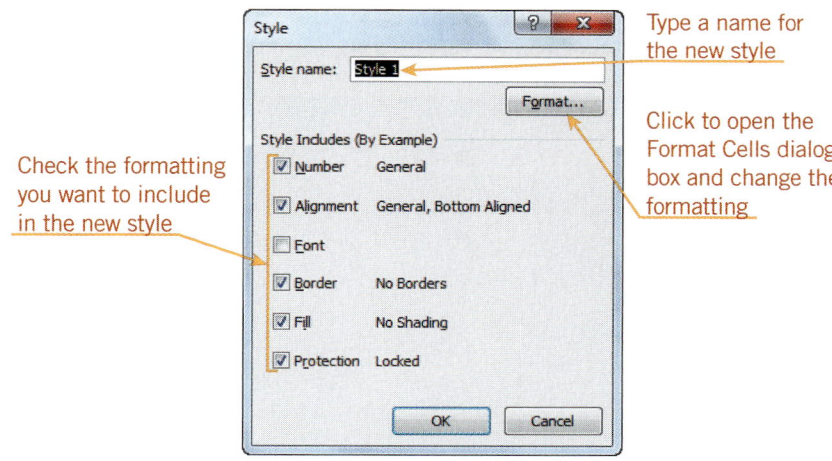

Type a name for
the new style

Click to open the
Format Cells dialog
box and change the
formatting

Check the formatting
you want to include
in the new style

FIGURE 2–14   Style dialog box

Clearing Cell Formats

You have learned how to change the appearance of cells in a worksheet by applying individual formats as well as cell styles. At times, you might need to remove, or *clear*, all the formatting applied to a cell or range of cells. Select the cell or range, click the Clear button in the Editing group on the Home tab of the Ribbon, and then click Clear Formats. Only the cell formatting is removed; the cell content remains the same.

VOCABULARY
clear

Step-by-Step 2.9

1. Select the range **A4:D4**.

2. On the Home tab, in the Styles group, click the **Cell Styles** button. The Cell Styles gallery appears, as shown in Figure 2–13.

3. In the Titles and Headings section, point to **Heading 2**. Live Preview shows the selected range with the font, font size, color, and border in that style.

4. In the Titles and Headings section, point to **Accent1** to see the Live Preview of the style applied to the cells in the selected range. Click **Accent1**. Blue fill and white font colors are applied to the cells in the selected range.

5. Select the range **A9:D9**.

6. On the Home tab, in the Styles group, click the **Cell Styles** button.

7. In the Cell Styles gallery, in the Titles and Headings section, click **Accent1**. Blue fill and white font are applied to the cells in the selected range.

8. Click cell **A1**. On the Home tab, in the Styles group, click the **Cell Styles** button.

9. In the Cell Styles gallery, in the Titles and Headings section, click **Heading 1**. Click cell **E1** to deselect the merged cell A1. The formatting for this style is added to the formatting you already applied to cell A1, as shown in **Figure 2–15**.

FIGURE 2–15
Cell styles applied to cells and ranges

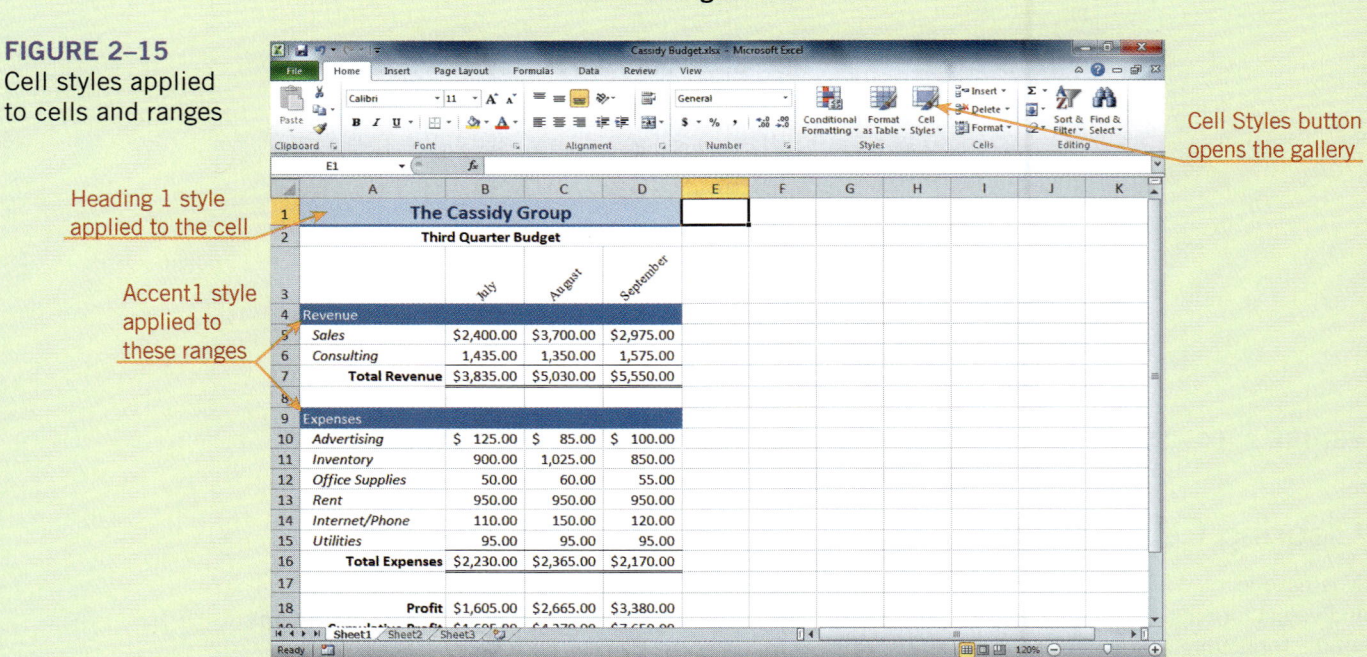

Heading 1 style applied to the cell

Accent1 style applied to these ranges

Cell Styles button opens the gallery

10. Scroll down until you can see row 21, and then click cell **A21**. On the Home tab, in the Styles group, click the **Cell Styles** button.

11. In the Cell Styles gallery, in the Titles and Headings section, click **Accent3**. The cell is formatted with the selected style.

12. On the Home tab, in the Editing group, click the **Clear** button. A menu appears with the Clear commands.

13. Click **Clear Formats**. All the formatting applied to cell A21 is removed. The cell returns to the default font color and fill color and text wrap.

14. Click cell **A22**, and then enter your name. Save, print, and close the workbook.

Finding and Replacing Cell Formatting

You have already learned to find and replace data in a workbook. You can also find and replace specific formatting in a workbook. For example, you might want to replace all italicized text with bold text, or you might want to change all cells with a yellow fill color to another color.

Step-by-Step 2.10

1. Open the **Central.xlsx** workbook from the drive and folder where your Data Files are stored.

2. Save the workbook as **Central Conference** followed by your initials.

3. On the Home tab, in the Editing group, click the **Find & Select** button, and then click **Replace**. The Find and Replace dialog box appears, with the Replace tab displayed.

4. Click the **Options** button to expand the Find and Replace dialog box, if it is not already expanded.

5. If any entries appear in the Find what or Replace with boxes, delete them.

6. Click the top **Format** button. The Find Format dialog box appears. This dialog box has all the same tabs and options as the Format Cells dialog box.

7. Click the **Font** tab if it is not the active tab. In the Font style list, click **Bold Italic**. This is the formatting you want to find.

8. Click **OK**. The Find Format dialog box closes, and the Find and Replace dialog box reappears. The Find what Preview box shows the bold italic formatting you want to find.

9. Click the lower **Format** button. The Replace Format dialog box appears. This dialog box has all the same tabs and options as the Format Cells dialog box.

> **WARNING**
>
> Clicking the Format button arrow opens a menu instead of the dialog box. If the menu appears, click Format to open the dialog box.

10. On the Font tab, in the Font style list, click **Regular**.

11. Click **OK**. The Replace Format dialog box closes, and the Find and Replace dialog box reappears. The Replace with Preview box shows the regular formatting you want to use instead of the bold italics, as shown in **Figure 2–16**.

FIGURE 2–16
Find and Replace dialog box

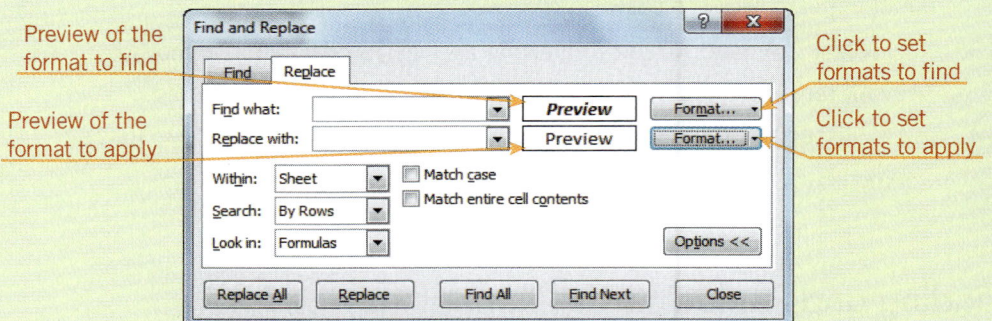

12. Click **Replace All**. A dialog box appears, stating that Excel has completed the search and has made 12 replacements.

13. Click **OK**. The dialog box closes.

14. Click **Close**. The Find and Replace dialog box closes. Your screen should look like **Figure 2–17**.

FIGURE 2–17
Worksheet with formatting replaced

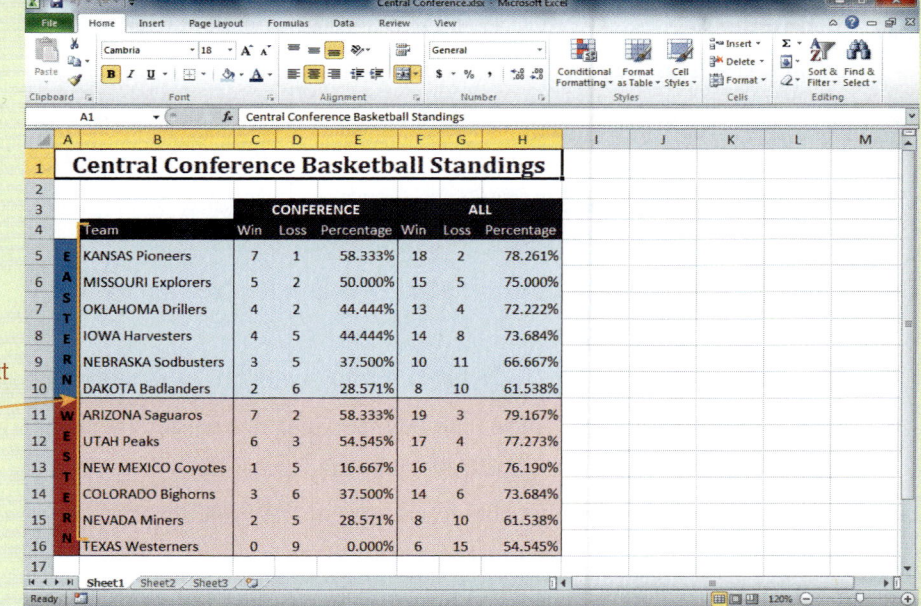

15. Click cell **B2**, and then enter your name.

16. Save, print, and close the workbook.

SUMMARY

In this lesson, you learned:

- If data does not fit in a cell, you can resize the columns and rows to make the data easier to read.

- You can align, indent, rotate, wrap text, and merge cells to reposition data in worksheet cells.

- You can change the appearance of cells to make the worksheet easier to read or to create a specific look and feel. Choose the appropriate fonts, font sizes, font styles, font and fill colors, and borders.

- Using a number format enables you to change how a number is displayed in a cell. No matter which number format you select, the actual value stored in the cell does not change. You can see this by comparing the formatted value in the active cell with the value displayed in the Formula Bar.

- Format Painter copies all the formatting from one cell and pastes it to another cell or range without copying the contents of the cell.

- The Format Cells dialog box provides all the number, alignment, font, border, and fill formatting options available on the Ribbon, as well as some additional options.

- A style is a combination of formatting characteristics, such as alignment, font, font size, font color, fill color, and borders that you can apply simultaneously. The Cell Styles gallery lets you quickly apply a style to selected cells or create a new style.

- You can use the Find and Replace dialog box to find and replace cell formatting.

■ VOCABULARY REVIEW

Define the following terms:

align	font	orientation
AutoFit	font size	row heading
border	font style	style
cell style	Format Painter	theme
clear	indent	truncate
column heading	merge	wrap text
fill	number format	

REVIEW QUESTIONS

TRUE / FALSE

Circle T if the statement is true or F if the statement is false.

T   F   **1.**   A series of number signs (######) in a cell indicates that the data entered in the cell is unformatted.

T   F   **2.**   AutoFit determines the best width for a column or the best height for a row based on its contents.

T   F   **3.**   The Merge & Center button combines several selected cells into one cell and places the data in the center of the merged cell.

T   F   **4.**   You can apply a border around the entire cell or on any side of the cell.

T   F   **5.**   The default number format for a cell is General.

WRITTEN QUESTIONS

Write a brief answer to each of the following questions.

1. Which cell formats display numerical data with a dollar sign?

2. What can you do if text is too long to fit within a cell?

3. What is one reason for changing the orientation of text in a cell?

4. What is the difference between fill color and font color?

5. What is an advantage of using cell styles?

FILL IN THE BLANK

Complete the following sentences by writing the correct word or words in the blanks provided.

1. Text that does not fit in a cell is _____ or hidden from view.

2. A(n) _____ is a preset collection of design elements, including fonts, colors, and other effects.

3. Bold, italic, and underlining are examples of font _____.

4. The default _____ (or background) color of cells is white.

5. The _____ copies all the formatting from one cell and pastes it to another cell or range without copying the contents of the cell.

■ PROJECTS

If you have a SAM 2010 user profile, your instructor may have assigned an autogradable version of the indicated project. If so, log into the SAM 2010 Web site at *www.cengage.com/sam2010* to download the instruction and start files.

PROJECT 2–1

Write the letter of the cell format option in Column 2 that matches the worksheet format described in Column 1.

Column 1

_____ 1. Displays data as entered

_____ 2. Displays numbers with a fixed number of decimal places

_____ 3. Displays numbers with a dollar sign, a thousands separator, and two decimal places; however, dollar signs and decimal points do not necessarily line up vertically within a column

_____ 4. Displays numbers with a dollar sign, a thousands separator, and two decimal places; dollar signs and decimal points line up vertically within a column

_____ 5. Displays numbers as dates

_____ 6. Displays numbers as times

_____ 7. Displays numbers with two decimal places and a percent sign

_____ 8. Displays the value of 0.5 as 1/2

_____ 9. Displays numbers in exponential (or scientific) notation

_____ 10. Displays numbers as zip codes, zip+4 codes, phone numbers, or Social Security numbers

_____ 11. Displays data in a format you design

Column 2

A.   Time

B.   Date

C.   Scientific

D.   Fraction

E.   Accounting

F.   General

G.   Special

H.   Number

I.   Currency

J.   Custom

K.   Percentage

 **PROJECT 2–2**

1. Open the **Birds.xlsx** workbook from the drive and folder where your Data Files are stored.

2. Save the workbook as **Birds Census** followed by your initials.

3. Change the width of column A to 25.00 characters.

4. Merge and center the range A1:F1 and the range A2:F2.

5. Format cell A1 with the Title cell style and change the fill color to Orange, Accent 6.

6. Change the fill color of cell A2 to Accent6.

7. Bold the range A6:F6.

8. Angle the data in the range B6:F6 counterclockwise.

9. Change the width of columns B through E to 6.00 characters.

10. Bold the range A14:F14.

11. Indent and italicize the range A7:A13.

12. Right-align the text in cell A14.

13. Format the range B14:F14 with a top and double bottom border.

14. Change the font color of the text in the range F6:F14 to Orange, Accent 6, Darker 25%.

15. In cell A4, type **Prepared by:** followed by your name.

16. Save, print, and close the workbook.

PROJECT 2–3

1. Open the **Shop.xlsx** workbook from the drive and folder where your Data Files are stored.

2. Save the workbook as **Technology Shop** followed by your initials.

3. AutoFit column A.

4. Change the width of columns B, C, and D to 12.00 characters.

5. Bold and center the text in the range B5:D6.

6. Bold the text in cell A6.

7. Indent the range A7:A10.

8. Change the text in cell A1 to 16-point Cambria. Merge and center the range A1:D1.

9. Change the fill color of cell A1 to Green (in the Standard Colors section).

10. Change the fill color of the range A2:D2 to Yellow (in the Standard Colors section).

11. Change the fill color of the range A3:D3 to Red (in the Standard Colors section).

12. Format the range C7:D10 and cell D11 with the Currency number format.

13. Format cell D11 with the Total cell style. Change the fill color of cell D11 to Yellow.

14. Add a thick bottom border to the range A6:D6.

15. In cell A3, enter your name.

16. Save, print, and close the workbook.

PROJECT 2–5

1. Open the **TechSoft.xlsx** workbook from the drive and folder where your Data Files are stored.

2. Save the workbook as **TechSoft Balance Sheet** followed by your initials. This workbook contains a *balance sheet*, which is a financial statement that lists a corporation's assets (resources available), liabilities (amounts owed), and equity (ownership in the company).

3. Change the column width of column C to 4.00 characters.

4. Format cell A1 with the Heading 1 cell style.

5. Format the range A2:A3 with the 40% - Accent1 cell style.

6. Merge and center the ranges A1:E1, A2:E2, and A3:E3.

7. Bold cells A5, A6, A20, D5, D6, D17, and D21.

8. Apply a bottom border to cells B8, B13, E11, and E19. Apply a top and double bottom border to cells B20 and E21.

9. Format cells B7, E7, B20, and E21 in the Accounting number format with no decimal places.

10. Format the ranges B8:B19, E8:E15, and E18:E20 in the Number format with a thousands separator and no decimal places.

11. In cell A4, enter your name, and then bold and italicize the text.

12. Save, print, and close the workbook.

PROJECT 2–4

1. Open the **Wireless.xlsx** workbook from the drive and folder where your Data Files are stored.

2. Save the workbook as **Wireless Bill** followed by your initials.

3. In cell A1, type **Wireless Bill Estimate**.

4. Bold the text in cell A1.

5. Change the font size of the text in cell A1 to 18.

6. Merge and center the range A1:D1.

7. Change the fill color of cell A1 to Dark Blue, Text 2.

8. Change the font color of the text in cell A1 to White, Background 1.

9. Underline the contents of cell A1.

10. Center the contents of the range B3:C3. Italicize the range B3:C3.

11. Format the range C4:D8 with the Currency number format.

12. Format cell D8 with a Thick Box Border.

13. Widen column A to 14.00 characters. In cell A4, wrap text.

14. Middle-align the range B4:D4.

15. Apply the 40% - Accent1 cell style to the range D4:D7. Apply the Accent1 cell style to cell D8.

16. In cell A2, enter your name.

17. Save, print, and close the workbook.

PROJECT 2–6

1. Open the **Mileage.xlsx** workbook from the drive and folder where your Data Files are stored.

2. Save the workbook as **Mileage Chart** followed by your initials.

3. Change the font size of the range A1:O15 to 8 points.

4. Format the range B2:O15 in the Number format with a thousands separator and no decimal places.

5. Bold the ranges B1:O1 and A2:A15.

6. Change the width of column A to 10.00 characters.

7. Right-align the content of the range A2:A15.

8. Change the orientation of the range B1:O1 to Angle Clockwise.

9. Change the width of columns B through O to 5.00 characters.

10. In cell A1, enter your name, and then change the font size to 12 points and wrap text.

11. Save, print, and close the workbook.

■ CRITICAL THINKING

ACTIVITY 2–1

To be useful, worksheets must convey information clearly, both on-screen and on the printed page. Identify ways to accomplish the following:

1. Emphasize certain portions of a worksheet.

2. Make data in a worksheet easier to read.

3. Distinguish one part of a worksheet from another.

4. Format similar elements in a worksheet consistently.

ACTIVITY 2–2

You have been spending a lot of time formatting worksheets. A friend tells you that you could save some time by using the Mini toolbar to apply formatting. Use Excel Help to research the following:

1. How do you access the Mini toolbar?

2. What formatting can you apply using the Mini toolbar?

3. How do you use the Mini toolbar to apply formatting to text in a cell?

4. How does the Mini toolbar save you time when formatting a worksheet?

LESSON 3

Organizing the Worksheet

■ OBJECTIVES

Upon completion of this lesson, you should be able to:

- Copy and move data in a worksheet.
- Use the drag-and-drop method and Auto Fill options to add data to cells.
- Insert and delete rows, columns, and cells.
- Freeze panes in a worksheet.
- Split a worksheet window.
- Check spelling in a worksheet.
- Prepare a worksheet for printing.
- Insert headers and footers in a worksheet.

■ VOCABULARY

automatic page break

copy

cut

fill handle

filling

footer

freeze panes

header

manual page break

margin

Normal view

Office Clipboard (Clipboard)

Page Break Preview

Page Layout view

paste

print area

print titles

scale

split

Data in a worksheet should be easy to locate, read, and interpret. You can reorganize data by moving it to another part of the worksheet. You can also reduce the time it takes for data entry time by copying or cutting data and pasting it in another part of the worksheet. If you no longer need certain data, you can delete entire rows or columns. If you want to include additional information within existing data, you can insert another row or column. You can also display different parts of the worksheet at one time. Before sharing a workbook, you should check and correct any spelling errors to present a positive impression. Finally, you can set up a worksheet to print attractively on paper and add headers or footers to provide summary information, such as page numbers or your name, on each worksheet.

Copying and Moving Cells

When creating or editing a worksheet, you might want to use the contents of one or more cells in another part of the worksheet. Rather than retyping the same content, you can copy or move the contents and formatting of a cell or range to another area of the worksheet. *Copying* duplicates the cell or range in another location, while also leaving the cell in its original location. *Cutting* removes a cell or range from its original location in the worksheet. *Pasting* places the cell or range in another location.

Copying and Pasting Cells

When you want to copy a cell or range, you first select the cell or range. Then, you use buttons in the Clipboard group on the Home tab of the Ribbon. To duplicate the cell or range without affecting the original cell or range, you click the Copy button. The selected data is placed as an item on the Office Clipboard. The *Office Clipboard* (or *Clipboard*) is a temporary storage area for up to 24 selections you copy or cut. A flashing border appears around the copied selection, as shown in **Figure 3–1**.

> ▶ **VOCABULARY**
> copy
> cut
> paste
> **Office Clipboard (Clipboard)**

> ⚠ **WARNING**
> Be sure to check the destination cells for existing data before moving or copying. Pasting replaces any content already in the cell.

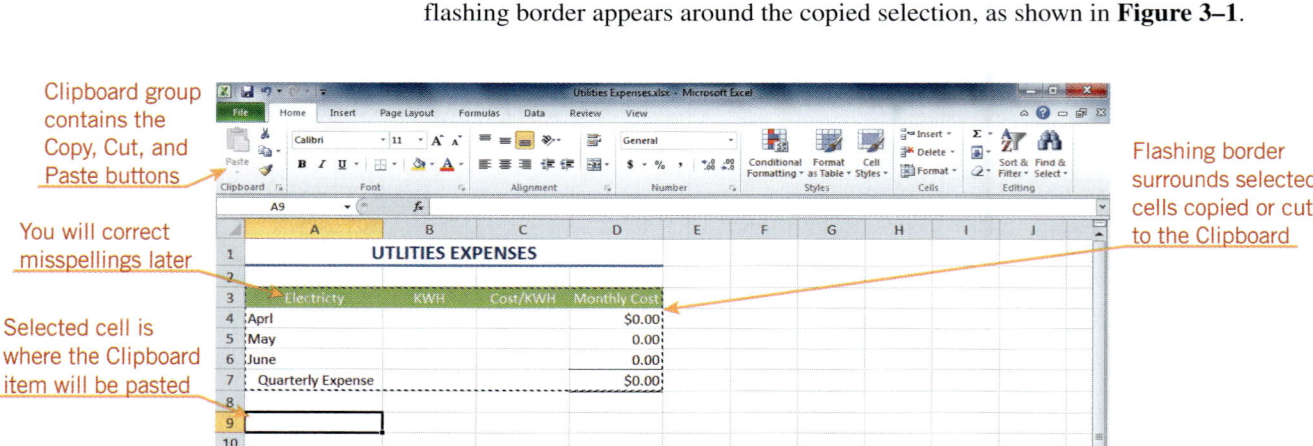

Clipboard group contains the Copy, Cut, and Paste buttons

You will correct misspellings later

Selected cell is where the Clipboard item will be pasted

Flashing border surrounds selected cells copied or cut to the Clipboard

FIGURE 3–1 Range copied to the Clipboard

Next, you select the cell or upper-left cell of the range where you want the copied item to appear in the worksheet. Click the Paste button in the Clipboard group on the Home tab. The Clipboard item is pasted into the selected cell or range. Pasting places the last item from the Clipboard into the selected cell or range in the worksheet. You can continue to paste that item in the worksheet as long as the flashing border appears around the copied cell or range. Just select the new destination cell or range, and then click the Paste button again.

Before pasting, you can click the arrow below the Paste button to open the Paste gallery, which provides additional commands. For example, the Formulas button pastes the actual formulas entered in the cells. The Values button pastes the formula results. The Transpose button pastes a row of cells into a column, or a column of cells into a row. For even more options, you can click the Paste Special command to open the Paste Special dialog box. As you point to a button in the Paste gallery, Live Preview shows the results of clicking that button.

Cutting and Pasting Cells

The process for moving a cell or range is similar to copying a cell or range. First, select the cell or range you want to move. Then, click the Cut button in the Clipboard group on the Home tab of the Ribbon. A flashing border appears around the selection, and the selected cell or range is placed as an item on the Clipboard. Next, select the cell or upper-left cell of the range where you want to move the cut item. Click the Paste button in the Clipboard group on the Home tab. When the cell or range is removed from its original position and placed in the new location, the flashing border disappears from the worksheet. Unlike copying, you can paste a cut cell or range only once.

EXTRA FOR EXPERTS

You can paste any of the last 24 items you cut or copied to the Clipboard. On the Home tab, click the Clipboard Dialog Box Launcher. The Clipboard task pane appears along the left side of the worksheet. In the worksheet, click the cell where you want to paste an item. In the Clipboard task pane, click the item you want to paste. When you are done, click the Close button on the task pane title bar.

TIP

You can use shortcut keys to quickly cut, copy, and paste cells. Click the Ctrl+X keys to cut selected cells. Click the Ctrl+C keys to copy selected cells. Click the Ctrl+V keys to paste the selected cells.

Step-by-Step 3.1

1. Open the **Utilities.xlsx** workbook from the drive and folder where your Data Files are stored.

2. Save the workbook as **Utilities Expenses** followed by your initials. Some words in the workbook are misspelled. Ignore them for now.

3. Select the range **A3:D7**.

4. On the Home tab of the Ribbon, locate the **Clipboard** group. This group includes all the buttons for cutting, copying, and pasting.

5. Click the **Copy** button. A flashing border surrounds the selected range to indicate that it has been placed on the Clipboard.

6. Click cell **A9**. Cell A9 is the upper-left cell of the range in which you want to paste the copied cells, as shown in Figure 3–1.

7. On the Home tab, in the Clipboard group, click the **Paste** button. The range A3:D7 is copied from the Clipboard to the range A9:D13. All the formatting from the range A3:D7 is copied along with the data. The flashing border surrounds the range A3:D7 until you click another button on the Ribbon or type in a cell.

TIP

After pasting, the Paste Options button appears next to the cell or range with the pasted item. Clicking the Paste Options button opens a gallery of options that you can use to choose how to format the pasted item.

8. In cell **A9**, enter **Natural Gas**. The flashing border disappears from the range A3:D7.

9. In cell **B9**, enter **100 cf** to indicate the number of cubic feet in hundreds. In cell **C9**, enter **Cost/100 cf** to indicate the cost per hundred cubic feet.

10. Select the range **A9:D13**.

11. On the Home tab, in the Clipboard group, click the **Cut** button. A flashing border surrounds the range you selected.

12. Click cell **A8**.

13. On the Home tab, in the Clipboard group, click the **Paste** button. The data moves to the range A8:D12.

14. Save the workbook, and leave it open for the next Step-by-Step.

Using the Drag-and-Drop Method

You can quickly move or copy data using the drag-and-drop method. First, select the cell or range you want to move or copy. Then, position the pointer on the top border of the selected cells. The pointer changes from a white cross to a four-headed arrow. To move the selected cells, drag them to a new location. As you move the selected cells, a dotted border shows where they will be positioned after you release the mouse button, and a ScreenTip lists the destination cell or range address, as shown in **Figure 3–2**. When the destination you want is selected, release the mouse button. To copy the cells, press and hold the Ctrl key to include a plus sign above the pointer as you drag the cells to a new location, release the mouse button, and then release the Ctrl key.

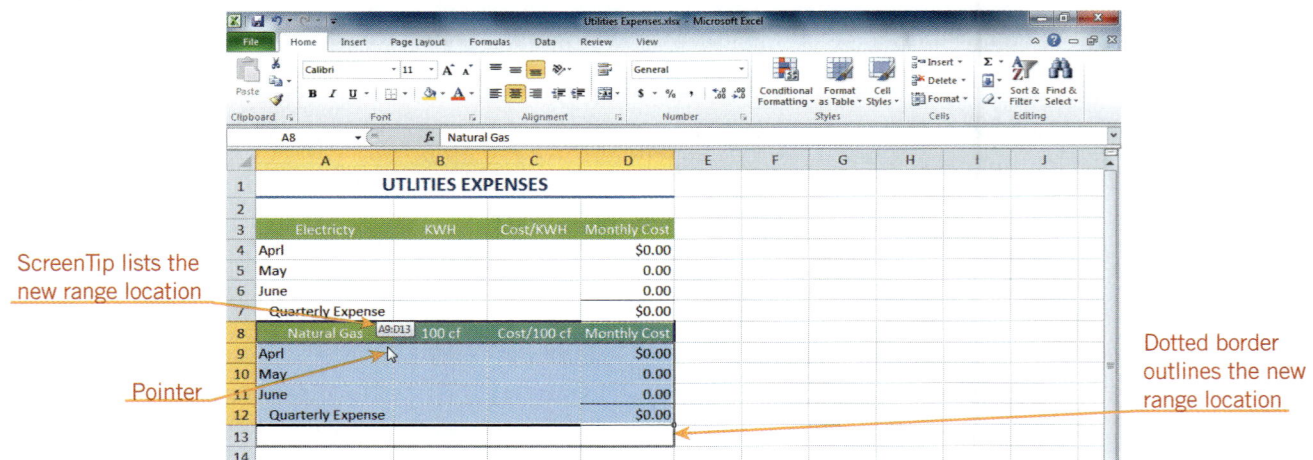

ScreenTip lists the new range location

Pointer

Dotted border outlines the new range location

FIGURE 3–2   Range during drag and drop

Step-by-Step 3.2

1. Make sure the range **A8:D12** is selected.

2. Move the pointer to the top edge of cell A8 until it changes to a white arrow with a black four-headed arrow ⇕.

3. Click the top border of cell **A8**, press and hold the **left mouse** button, and then drag down to cell **A9** until the ScreenTip reads *A9:D13*, as shown in Figure 3–2.

4. Release the mouse button. The data moves to range A9:D13 and remains selected.

5. Move the pointer to the top edge of cell A9 until it changes to a four-headed arrow ⇕.

6. Press and hold the **Ctrl** key. The pointer changes to a white arrow with a plus sign ⬈.

7. Click and drag down to cell **A15** until the ScreenTip reads *A15:D19*.

8. Release the mouse button, and then release the **Ctrl** key. The data is copied from range A9:D13 to range A15:D19.

9. In cell A15, enter **Water**.

10. In cell B15, enter **1000 gallons**.

11. In cell C15, enter **Cost/1000 gal** to indicate the cost per 1000 gallons of water.

12. Save the workbook, and leave it open for the next Step-by-Step.

Using the Fill Handle

Filling copies a cell's contents and/or formatting into an adjacent cell or range. Selecting the cell or range that contains the content and formatting you want to copy displays a *fill handle* in the lower-right corner of the selection. When you point to the fill handle, the pointer changes to a black cross. Click and drag the fill handle over the cells you want to fill. Then, release the mouse button. The cell contents and formatting are duplicated into the range you selected, and the Auto Fill Options button appears below the filled content. You can click the Auto Fill Options button to

▶ **VOCABULARY**
filling
fill handle

TIP

Be aware that you can fill data only when the destination cells are adjacent to the original cell.

open the menu shown in **Figure 3–3**. You choose whether you want to copy both the cell's formatting and the cell's contents (the default), only the cell's contents, or only the cell's formatting.

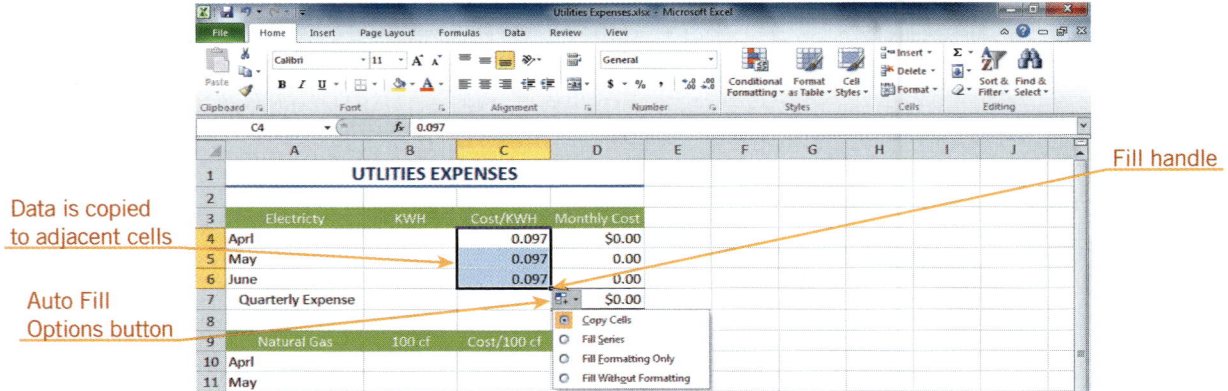

FIGURE 3–3   Auto Fill Options menu

You can also use the fill handle to continue a series of text items, numbers, or dates. For example, you might want to enter column labels of months, such as January, February, March, and so on, or row labels of even numbers, such as 2, 4, 6, and so forth. First, enter data in at least two cells to establish the pattern you want to use. Then, select the cells that contain the series pattern. Finally, drag the fill handle over the range of cells you want to fill. Excel enters appropriate data in the cells to continue the pattern.

Step-by-Step 3.3

1. Click cell **C4**, type **.097** to record the cost of electricity, and then press the **Enter** button ✔ on the Formula Bar. The cost of electricity for all three months is $0.097 per kilowatt hour. You want the amount entered in cell C4 to be entered in cells C5 and C6.

2. Point to the **fill handle** in the lower-right corner of cell C4. The pointer changes to a black cross **+**.

3. Click and drag the **fill handle** down to cell **C6**, and then release the mouse button. The contents of C4 are copied to cells C5 and C6.

4. Click cell **C10**, type **1.72** to record the cost per 100 cubic feet of natural gas, and then press the **Enter** button ✔ on the Formula Bar.

5. Click and drag the **fill handle** in the lower-right corner of cell C10 down to cell **C12**, and then release the mouse button. The data from cell C10 is copied to cells C11 and C12.

6. In cell C16, type **1.98** to record the cost per 1000 gallons of water, and then press the **Enter** button ✔ on the Formula Bar.

7. Click and drag the **fill handle** in the lower-right corner of cell C16 down to cell **C18**, and then release the mouse button. The data from cell C16 is copied to cells C17 and C18.

8. In column B, enter the utility usage data shown in **Figure 3–4**. The monthly costs in column D are calculated based on the data you entered.

Enter data in column B

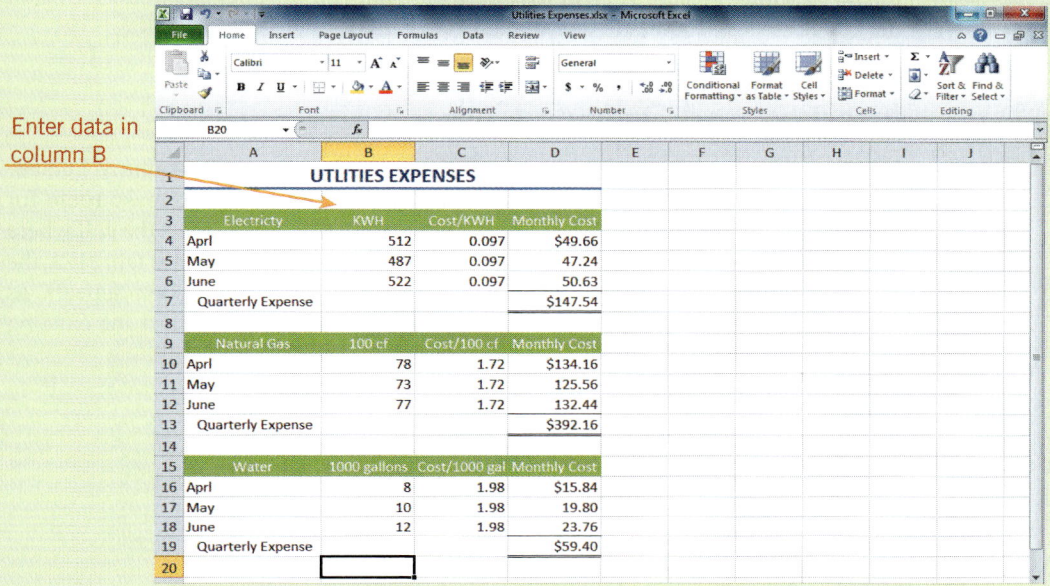

FIGURE 3–4
Utility usage data

9. Save the workbook, and leave it open for the next Step-by-Step.

Inserting and Deleting Rows, Columns, and Cells

As you build a worksheet, you may need to add rows or columns to store more data. Sometimes, you may need to remove a row or column of data. At other times, you may need to insert or delete specific cells. On the Home tab of the Ribbon, the Cells group includes buttons for inserting and deleting rows, columns, and cells.

Inserting Rows and Columns

To insert a row, click the row heading to select the row where you want the new row to appear. Then, click the Insert button in the Cells group on the Home tab. A blank row is added, and the existing rows shift down. To insert a column, click the column heading to select the column where you want the new column to appear. Then, click the Insert button in the Cells group. A blank column is added, and the existing columns shift to the right. The Insert Options button appears so you can choose to format the inserted row or column with the same formatting as the row or column on either side or clear the formatting.

 TIP

If you select more than one row or column, the same number of rows or columns you selected is inserted in the worksheet.

Deleting Rows and Columns

The process for deleting a row or column is similar to the process for inserting one. First, click the row or column heading of the row or column you want to delete. Then, in the Cells group on the Home tab, click the Delete button. The selected row or column disappears, removing all its data and formatting. The existing rows shift up, or the existing columns shift left.

If you accidentally delete the wrong column or row, you can click the Undo button on the Quick Access Toolbar to restore the data. You can click the Redo button on the Quick Access Toolbar to cancel the Undo action.

Inserting and Deleting Cells

When entering a long column of data, it is not unusual to discover an omitted number near the top of the column. Rather than moving the existing data to make room for entering the omitted data, you can insert a new, blank cell. First, select the cell where you want to insert the new cell. Then, in the Cells group on the Home tab, click the Insert button arrow, and then click Insert Cells. The Insert dialog box appears, as shown in **Figure 3–5**. In this dialog box, you choose whether to shift the existing cells down or to the right.

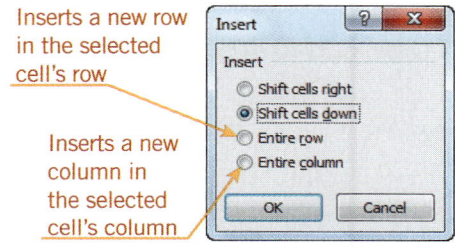

Inserts a new row in the selected cell's row

Inserts a new column in the selected cell's column

FIGURE 3–5   Insert dialog box

Another common problem is entering a number twice in a long column of data. To eliminate the duplicate data and reposition the rest of the data correctly, you can delete the cell that contains the duplicate value. First, select the cell you want to delete. Then, in the Cells group on the Home tab, click the Delete button arrow, and then click Delete Cells. The Delete dialog box appears so you can choose whether to shift the remaining cells up or to the left.

Step-by-Step 3.4

1. Click the **row 3** row heading. Row 3 is selected.

2. On the Home tab, in the Cells group, click the **Insert** button. A new, blank row appears as row 3. The original row 3 becomes row 4.

3. In cell B3, enter **Units Used**. In cell C3, enter **Unit Cost**. In cell D3, enter **Billed**. Select the range **B3:D3**, and then apply the **20% - Accent3** cell style to the range.

4. Click the **column B** column heading. Column B is selected.

5. On the Home tab, in the Cells group, click the **Insert** button. A new, blank column appears as column B. The original column B becomes column C and picks up the formatting used in column B.

6. Click cell **B3**. On the Home tab, in the Cells group, click the **Delete** button arrow, and then click **Delete Sheet Columns**. Column B is deleted, and the remaining columns shift left.

7. Click the **row 4** row heading. Row 4 is selected.

8. In the Cells group, click the **Delete** button. Row 4 disappears, and the remaining rows shift up.

9. On the Quick Access Toolbar, click the **Undo** button 🔄. Row 4 reappears in the worksheet.

10. Click cell **B18**. In the Cells group, click the **Insert** button arrow, and then click **Insert Cells**. The Insert dialog box appears, as shown in Figure 3–5.

11. Click the **Shift cells down** option button, if it is not selected. Click **OK**. The data in the range B18:B19 shifts to the range B19:B20. Cell B18 is still the active cell.

12. On the Home tab, in the Cells group, click the **Delete** button arrow, and then click **Delete Cells**. The Delete dialog box appears.

13. Click the **Shift cells up** option button, if it is not selected. Click **OK**. The data in the range B19:B20 shifts back to the range B18:B19.

14. Save the workbook, and leave it open for the next Step-by-Step.

Freezing Panes in a Worksheet

Often a worksheet includes more data than you can see on the screen at one time. As you scroll the worksheet, titles and labels at the top or side of the worksheet might shift out of view, making it difficult to identify the contents of particular columns. For example, the worksheet title *Utilities Expenses* in the previous Step-by-Step might have scrolled off the screen when you were working in the lower part of the worksheet.

You can view two parts of a worksheet at once by freezing panes. When you *freeze panes*, you select which rows and/or columns of the worksheet remain visible on the screen as the rest of the worksheet scrolls. For example, you can freeze the row or column titles so they appear on the screen no matter where you scroll in the

▶ **VOCABULARY**
freeze panes

TECHNOLOGY CAREERS

Business managers use Excel worksheets in a variety of ways. For example, human resource managers use worksheets to conduct performance reviews and to manage employee records. Production managers use worksheets to track machine production efficiency and to keep machine maintenance records.

worksheet. As shown in **Figure 3–6**, rows 1, 2, and 3 are frozen so they remain on-screen even when you scroll down to row 16 (hiding rows 4 through 15).

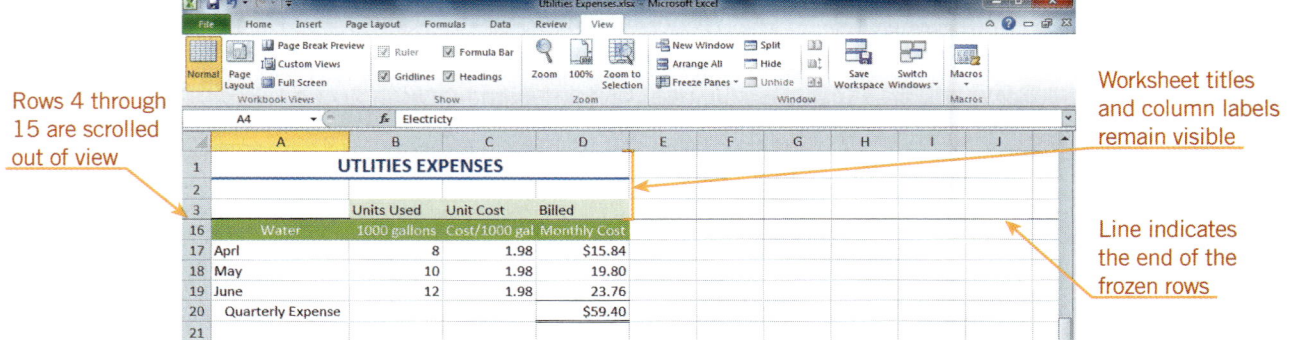

Rows 4 through 15 are scrolled out of view

Worksheet titles and column labels remain visible

Line indicates the end of the frozen rows

FIGURE 3–6   Worksheet with rows 1 through 3 frozen

When you freeze panes in a worksheet, the rows and columns that remain locked on screen depend on the location of the active row, column, or cell. **Table 3–1** describes the different selection options. On the View tab of the Ribbon, in the Window group, click the Freeze Panes button, and then click Freeze Panes. A black line appears between the frozen and unfrozen panes of the worksheet.

TABLE 3–1   Freeze panes options

TO FREEZE	DO THE FOLLOWING
Rows	Select the first row below the row(s) you want to freeze
Columns	Select the first column to the right of the column(s) you want to freeze
Rows and columns	Select the first cell below and to the right of the row(s) and column(s) you want to freeze

When you want to unlock all the rows and columns to allow them to scroll, you need to unfreeze the panes. On the View tab of the Ribbon, in the Window group, click the Freeze Panes button, and then click Unfreeze Panes. The black line disappears, and all rows and columns are unfrozen.

Splitting a Worksheet Window

You might want to view different parts of a large worksheet at the same time. *Splitting* divides the worksheet window into two or four panes that you can scroll independently. This enables you to see different parts of a worksheet at the same time. Splitting is particularly useful in a large worksheet when you want to copy data from one area to another. You can click in one pane and scroll the worksheet as needed while the other part of the worksheet remains in view in a different pane.

▶ VOCABULARY
split

You can split the worksheet window into horizontal panes, as shown in **Figure 3–7**, vertical panes, or both. Select a row to split the window into horizontal panes. Select a column to split the worksheet into vertical panes. Select a cell to split the worksheet into both horizontal and vertical panes. Then, on the View tab of the Ribbon, in the Window group, click the Split button. The Split button remains selected, and a split bar separates the panes you created. If you want to resize the panes, drag the split bar. When you want to return to a single pane, click the Split button again.

EXTRA FOR EXPERTS

You can use the mouse to add, resize, and remove panes. Drag the split box above the vertical scroll bar down to create horizontal panes. Drag the split box that appears to the right of the horizontal scroll bar to the left to create vertical panes. Drag a split bar to resize the panes. Double-click a split bar to remove it.

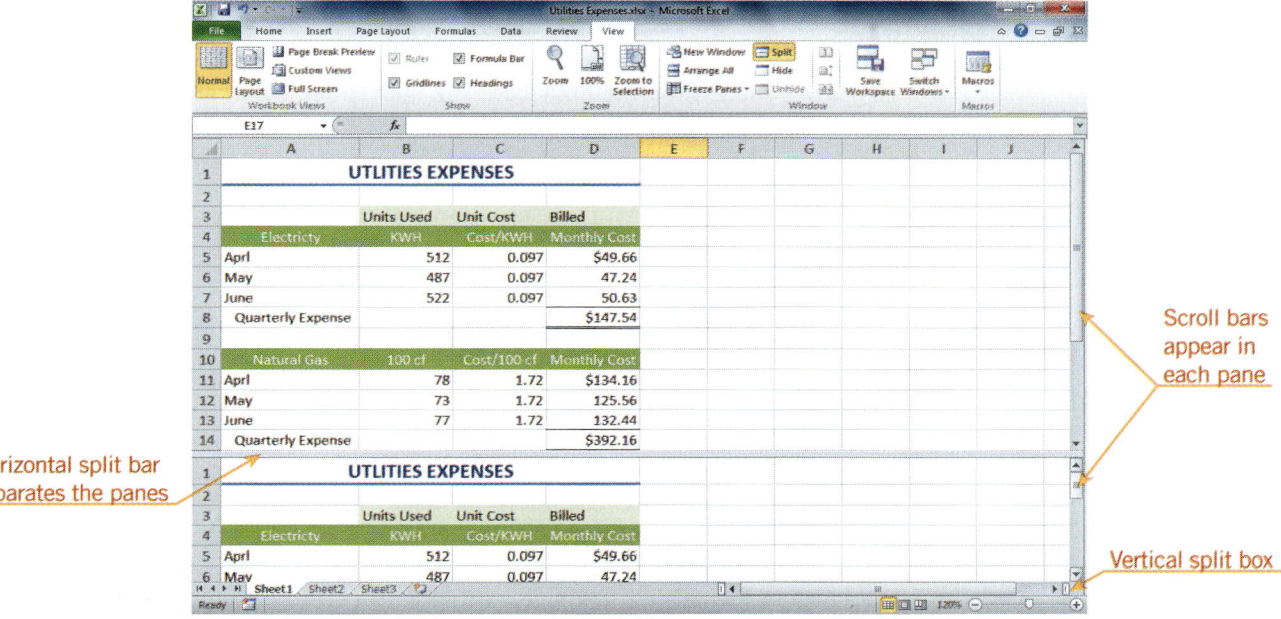

FIGURE 3–7   Worksheet window split into horizontal panes

Step-by-Step 3.5

1. Click cell **A4**.

2. Click the **View** tab on the Ribbon, and then locate the **Window** group. This group contains the buttons for freezing and splitting panes.

3. Click the **Freeze Panes** button, and then click **Freeze Panes**. The title and column headings in rows 1 through 3 are locked. A black line appears between rows 3 and 4.

4. Scroll the worksheet down until row **16** is at the top of the worksheet window. The worksheet title and column headings remain locked at the top of the screen, even as other rows scroll out of view, as shown in Figure 3–6.

5. On the View tab, in the Window group, click the **Freeze Panes** button, and then click **Unfreeze Panes**. The title and column headings are no longer frozen.

6. Click the **row 15** row heading.

7. On the View tab, in the Window group, click the **Split** button. A split bar appears above row 15, dividing the worksheet into two horizontal panes.

8. Click in the lower pane and scroll up to row **1**. The same part of the worksheet appears in both panes, as shown in Figure 3–7.

9. Double-click the **split bar**. The split is removed, and worksheet is displayed again one pane.

10. Save the workbook, and leave it open for the next Step-by-Step.

Checking Spelling in a Worksheet

An important step in creating a professional workbook is to correct any misspellings. Typographical errors can be distracting and can cause others to doubt the accuracy of the rest of the workbook's content. To help track down and correct spelling errors in a worksheet, you can use the Spelling command, which checks the spelling in the entire active worksheet against the dictionary that comes with Microsoft Office. To check the spelling in a worksheet, click the Review tab on the Ribbon, and then, in the Proofing group, click the Spelling button. The Spelling dialog box appears, as shown in **Figure 3–8**, and highlights the first potential spelling error shown in the Not in Dictionary box.

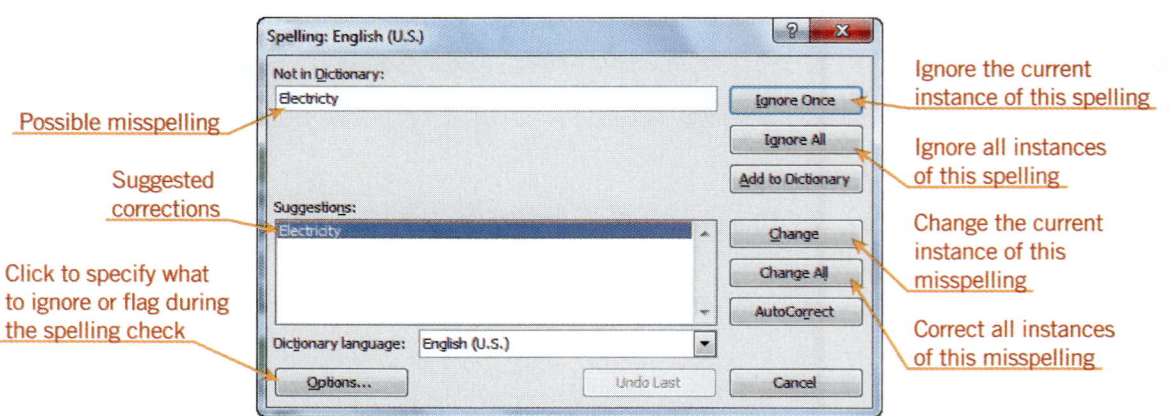

FIGURE 3–8   Spelling dialog box

The Spelling dialog box provides many ways to deal with a possible misspelling. If the word is mistyped, you can correct the spelling yourself or click the correct word in the Suggestions box. Then, click Change to replace the current instance of the misspelling with the correct word, or click Change All to replace every instance of the misspelling. If the word is correct (as often happens with company and product names), you can click Ignore to move to the next potential spelling error without making a change to the word, or click Ignore All to skip every instance of this word in the worksheet. After you have addressed all the possible misspellings in the worksheet, a dialog box appears to let you know that the spelling check is complete for the entire sheet.

Be aware that the spelling checker is not foolproof. The default spelling options are to ignore words that are capitalized, contain numbers, or are Internet addresses. As a final check, you should proofread the worksheet for any misspellings that the spelling checker ignored or missed. You might find words that are spelled correctly, but used incorrectly (such as *they're*, *their*, and *there*, or *hour* and *our*). In addition, you might discover a missing word (*and* or *the*, for instance). This final check helps to ensure that your worksheet is free from errors.

⊟ EXTRA FOR EXPERTS

If Excel incorrectly flags a word that you use frequently as a misspelling, you can add the word to a custom dictionary that resides on your computer by clicking the Add to Dictionary button. If the misspelling is a typo you make often, you can select the correct word in the Suggestions box, and then click the AutoCorrect button. Excel will automatically correct this mistake whenever you type it.

Step-by-Step 3.6

1. Press the **Ctrl+Home** keys. Cell A1 is the active cell in the worksheet.

2. Click the **Review** tab on the Ribbon, and then locate the **Proofing** group. The Spelling button is located here.

3. Click the **Spelling** button. The Spelling dialog box appears, as shown in Figure 3–8. The word *Electricty* is identified as a misspelled word. One correction appears in the Suggestions box.

4. In the Suggestions box, click **Electricity** if it is not selected, and then click **Change**. The spelling of the word in the worksheet is corrected, and *Aprl* appears in the dialog box as the next possible misspelled word.

5. In the Suggestions box, click **April**, if it is not selected, and then click **Change All**. All three instances of this misspelling are corrected, and *cf* appears in the Not in Dictionary box as the next possible misspelling. However, *cf* is being used as an abbreviation for cubic feet, so you will ignore all instances of this abbreviation in the worksheet.

6. Click **Ignore All**. A dialog box appears, indicating the spelling check is complete for the entire sheet. (If the spelling checker flags other possible misspellings, change or ignore them as necessary, until the dialog box appears.)

7. Click **OK**.

8. Proofread the worksheet. In cell A1, the word *UTLITIES* is misspelled. The spelling checker did not flag this word because the word is capitalized.

9. Click cell **A1**, and then, in the Formula Bar, click after *UT* to place the insertion point.

10. Type **I** to insert the missing letter in the word, and then press the **Enter** key.

11. Save the workbook, and leave it open for the next Step-by-Step.

Preparing a Worksheet for Printing

So far, you have worked in *Normal view*, which is the best view for entering and formatting data in a worksheet. Excel has other views as well. *Page Layout view* shows how the worksheet will appear on paper, which is helpful when you prepare a worksheet for printing. Excel has many options for changing how a worksheet appears on a printed page.

Setting Margins

The *margin* is the blank space around the top, bottom, left, and right sides of a page. The margin settings determine how many of a worksheet's columns and rows fit on a printed page. You can increase (widen) the margins in a worksheet to create extra blank space for jotting notes on the printed copy. Or, you can decrease (narrow) the margins in a worksheet when you want to print more columns and rows on a page. To change the margins of a worksheet, click the Page Layout tab on the Ribbon, and then, in the Page Setup group, click the Margins button. You can then choose among three preset margins—Normal (the default), Wide, and Narrow, as shown in **Figure 3–9**.

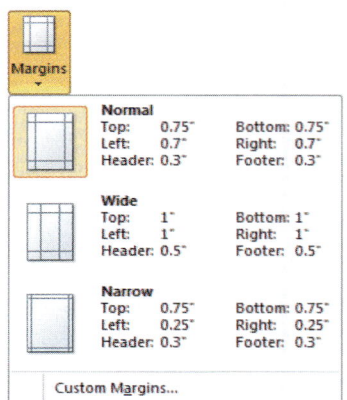

FIGURE 3–9   Margins menu

Changing the Page Orientation

You can print worksheets using different orientations to best display the data. Worksheets printed in portrait orientation are longer than they are wide. In contrast, worksheets printed in landscape orientation are wider than they are long. By default, Excel is set to print pages in portrait orientation. Many worksheets, however, include more columns of data than fit on pages in portrait orientation. These pages look better and are easier to understand when printed in landscape orientation. You can change the orientation of the worksheet by clicking the Page Layout tab on the Ribbon, and then, in the Page Setup group, clicking the Orientation button. As shown in **Figure 3–10**, you can then click Portrait or Landscape on the menu.

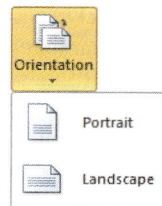

FIGURE 3–10   Orientation menu

Setting the Print Area

When you print a worksheet, Excel assumes that you want to print all of the data entered in the worksheet. If you want to print only a portion of the data in a worksheet, you need to set the print area. The ***print area*** consists of the cells and ranges designated for printing. For example, you might want to print only the range A1:A19, which shows the utility and month data, and the range D3:D19 (billed amount). To do this, first select the range. Then, click the Page Layout tab on the Ribbon. In the Page Setup group, click the Print Area button, and then click Set Print Area. Each time you print the worksheet, only the cells in the print area appear on the page. You must clear the print area to print the entire worksheet again. In the Page Setup group on the Page Layout tab, click the Print Area button, and then click Clear Print Area.

A print area can include multiple ranges and/or nonadjacent cells. For example, you might want to print the utility and month data as well as the billed amount. To do so, select the cells and ranges you want to print, and then set the print area. The selected cells and ranges will print until you clear the print area.

Inserting, Adjusting, and Deleting Page Breaks

When a worksheet or the print area doesn't fit on one printed page, you can use a page break to indicate where the next page begins. Excel inserts an ***automatic page break*** whenever it runs out of room on a page. You can also insert a ***manual page break*** to start a new page. To insert a manual page break, select the row below where you want to insert a horizontal page break, or select the column to the left of where you want to insert a vertical page break. Then, click the Breaks button in the Page Setup group on the Page Layout tab, and then click Insert Page Break.

▶ **VOCABULARY**
print area
automatic page break
manual page break

EXTRA FOR EXPERTS

You can center the print area on the printed page. On the Page Layout tab, click the Page Setup Dialog Box Launcher. Click the Margins tab. In the Center on page section, check Horizontally to center the print area between the left and right margins and/or check Vertically to center it between the top and bottom margins. Click OK.

The simplest way to adjust page breaks in a worksheet is in *Page Break Preview*, as shown in **Figure 3–11**. On the status bar, click the Page Break Preview button to switch the worksheet to this view. Dashed lines appear for automatic page breaks, and solid lines appear for manual page breaks. You can drag any page break to a new location.

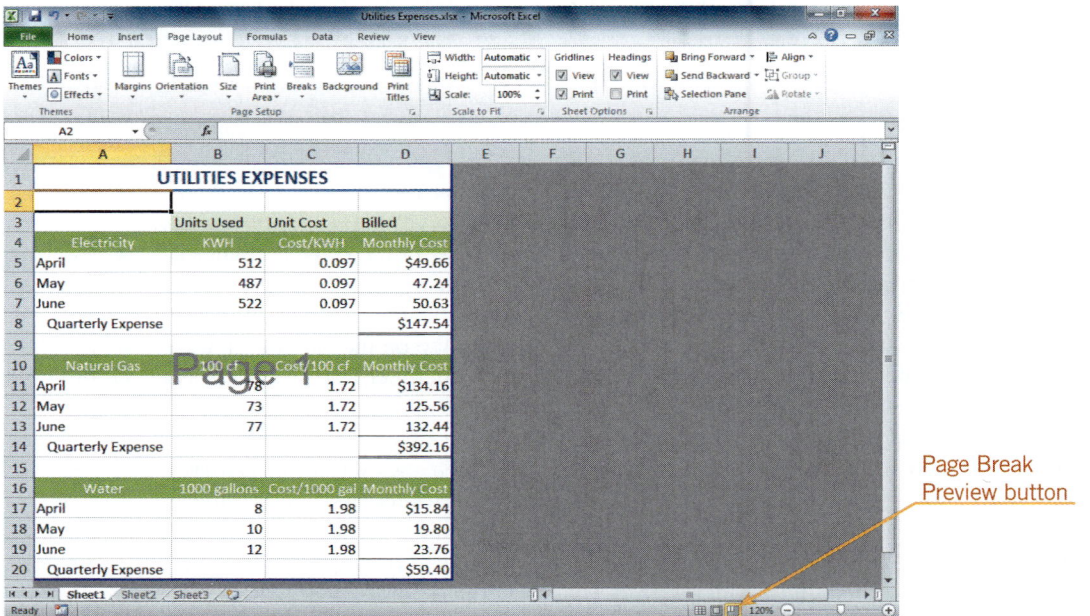

FIGURE 3–11   Page Break Preview

When you no longer need a manual page break any longer, you can delete it. Click below or to the left of the page break you want to remove. Click the Page Layout tab on the Ribbon. In the Page Setup group, click the Breaks button, and then click Remove Page Break.

Scaling to Fit

Scaling resizes a worksheet to print on a specific number of pages. The Scale to Fit group on the Page Layout tab contains three options for resizing a worksheet, as shown in **Figure 3–12**. You can fit the worksheet on the number of pages you specify for its width or height. Just click the Width arrow or the Height arrow, and then select the maximum pages for the printed worksheet's width or height. Another option is to set the percentage by which you want to shrink or enlarge the worksheet on the printed page. Click the Scale arrows to increase or decrease the percentage.

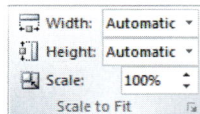

FIGURE 3–12   Scale to Fit group on the Page Layout tab

Choosing Sheet Options

By default, gridlines, row numbers, and column letters appear in the worksheet—but not on the printed page—to help you enter and format data. You can choose to show or hide gridlines and headings in a worksheet or on the printed page. The Sheet Options group, shown in **Figure 3–13**, contains check boxes for viewing and printing gridlines and headings. Check and uncheck the boxes as needed.

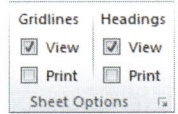

FIGURE 3–13 Sheet Options group on the Page Layout tab

Specifying Print Titles

Print titles are designated rows and/or columns in a worksheet that are printed on each page. Specified rows are printed at the top of each page. Specified columns are printed on the left of each page. To set print titles, click the Page Layout tab on the Ribbon, and then, in the Page Setup group, click the Print Titles button. The Page Setup dialog box appears with the Sheet tab displayed, as shown in **Figure 3–14 A**. Click the Collapse button next to the Rows to repeat at top box to shrink the dialog box, as shown in **Figure 3–14 B**. Click the row or rows to use as the print title. Then, click the Expand button to restore the dialog box to its full size. You use the same process to select columns to repeat at left. Click OK to add the print titles to the worksheet.

> **VOCABULARY**
> **print titles**

A. Expanded dialog box

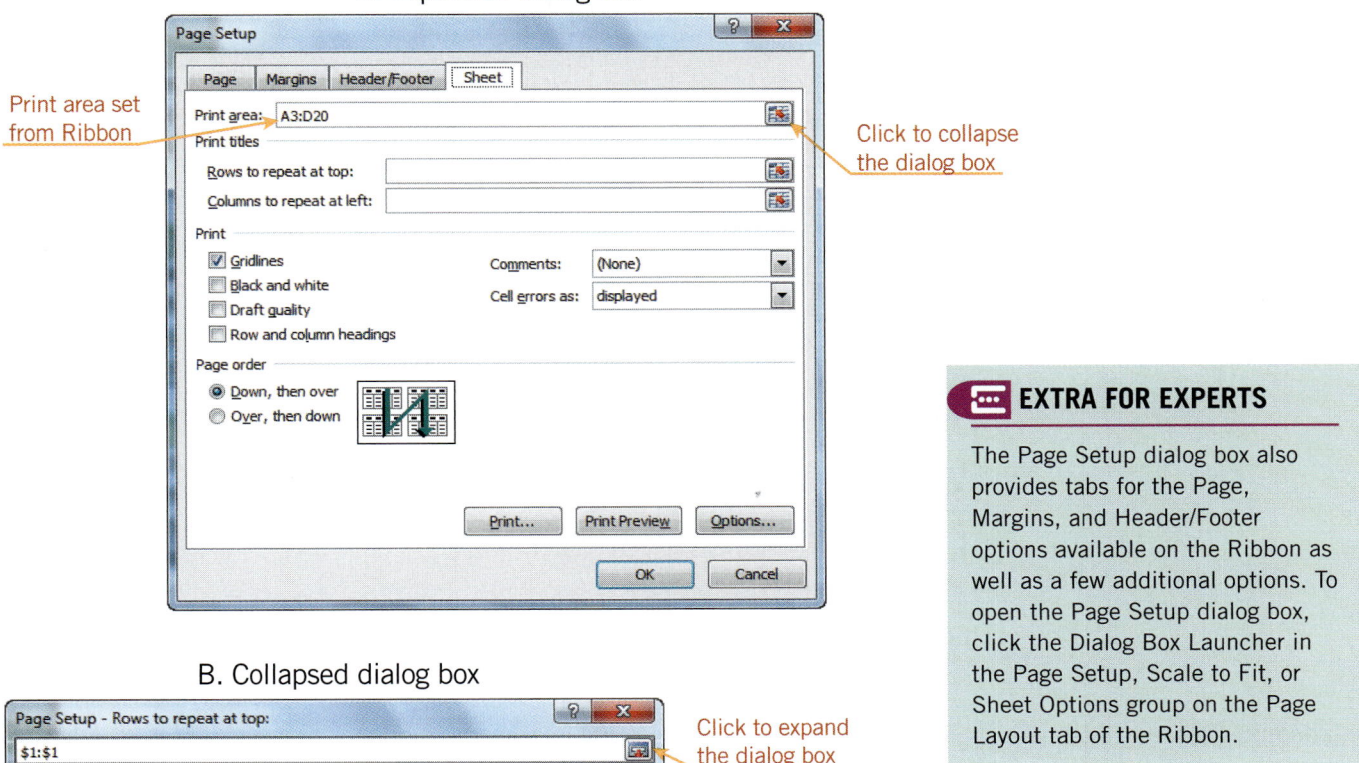

B. Collapsed dialog box

FIGURE 3–14 Sheet tab in the Page Setup dialog box

> ### EXTRA FOR EXPERTS
>
> The Page Setup dialog box also provides tabs for the Page, Margins, and Header/Footer options available on the Ribbon as well as a few additional options. To open the Page Setup dialog box, click the Dialog Box Launcher in the Page Setup, Scale to Fit, or Sheet Options group on the Page Layout tab of the Ribbon.

Step-by-Step 3.7

1. Click the **Page Layout** tab on the Ribbon. This tab contains many commands for preparing a worksheet for printing.

2. In the Page Setup group, click the **Margins** button to open the menu shown in Figure 3–9, and then click **Wide**. The margins are set to one inch on all sides. A dashed line, indicating an automatic page break, appears after column F.

3. On the Page Layout tab, in the Page Setup group, click the **Orientation** button to open the menu shown in Figure 3–10, and then click **Landscape**. The automatic page break moves to after column J, indicating that the printed workbook will be wider than it is tall.

4. Select the range **A3:D20**.

5. On the Page Layout tab, in the Page Setup group, click the **Print Area** button, and then click **Set Print Area**. Only the selected range will print on the page.

6. On the Page Layout tab, in the Scale to Fit group, click the **Scale** up arrow, shown in Figure 3–12, six times until **130** appears in the box. The printed data will be enlarged to take up more of the page.

7. On the Page Layout tab, in the Sheet Options group, click the **Gridlines Print** check box to insert a check mark. The gridlines will be printed on the page.

8. On the Page Layout tab, in the Page Setup group, click the **Print Titles** button. The Page Setup dialog box appears, as shown in Figure 3–14 A.

9. On the Sheet tab, in the Print titles section, click the **Collapse** button on the Rows to repeat at top box.

10. In the worksheet, click **row 1** row heading as the row to repeat at the top of each printed page. The row reference is added to the dialog box, as shown in Figure 3–14 B.

11. In the collapsed Page Setup dialog box, click the **Expand** button .

12. Click **OK**.

13. Press the **Ctrl+Home** keys. Cell A1 becomes the active cell.

14. Save the workbook, and leave it open for the next Step-by-Step.

Inserting Headers and Footers

▶ **VOCABULARY**
header

footer

Headers and footers are useful for adding identifying text to a printed page. A *header* is text that is printed in the top margin of each page, as shown in **Figure 3–15**. A *footer* is text that is printed in the bottom margin of each page. Text that is commonly included in a header or footer is your name, the page number, the current date, the workbook file name, and the worksheet name. Headers and footers are each divided into three sections, which you can use to organize the text.

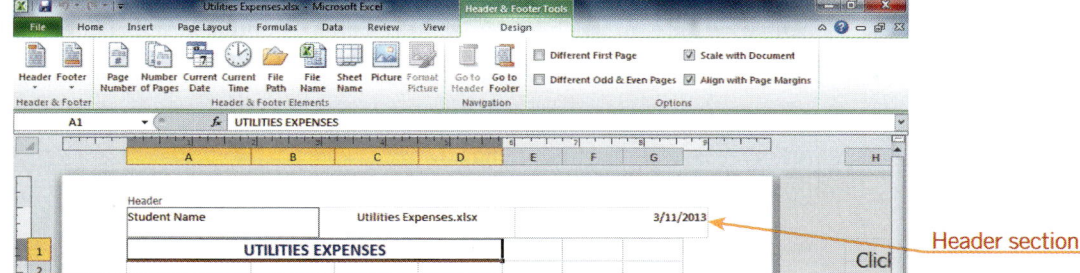

FIGURE 3–15   Completed Header section

To create a header or footer for a printed worksheet, click the Insert tab on the Ribbon, and then in the Text group, click the Header & Footer button. The worksheet switches to Page Layout view, and the Header & Footer Tools Design tab includes groups for working with headers and footers. The insertion point is in the center header box, but you can easily move to the left or right section by clicking a different box. Type the text you want to enter, or click a button in the Header & Footer Elements group on the Design tab. To enter a preset header or footer, in the Header & Footer group on the Design tab, click the Header or Footer button, and then click the header or footer you want to use. Click anywhere in the worksheet to close the headers and footers.

TIP

You can enter, edit, delete, and format the text in each header and footer section the same way you do for text in worksheet cells.

Step-by-Step 3.8

1. Click the **Insert** tab on the Ribbon, and then locate the **Text** group.

2. Click the **Header & Footer** button. The worksheet changes to Page Layout view. The insertion point is in the center header box.

3. On the Design tab, in the Header & Footer Elements group, click the **File Name** button. The code *&[File]* appears in the center header box.

4. Press the **Tab** key to move to the right header box. The code *&[File]* in the center header box is replaced with *Utilities Expenses.xlsx*, which is the current file name of the workbook. Remember, if your computer is not set to show file extensions, you see *Utilities Expenses* in the center header box.

5. On the Design tab, in the Header & Footer Elements group, click the **Current Date** button. The code *&[Date]* appears in the right header box.

6. Press the **Tab** key to move the insertion point to the left header box. The code *&[Date]* in the right header box is replaced with the current date.

7. In the left header box, type your name. The header is complete, as shown in Figure 3–15.

8. On the Design tab, in the Navigation group, click the **Go to Footer** button. The insertion point moves to the left footer box.

9. Click the center footer box.

10. On the Design tab, in the Header & Footer Elements group, click the **Page Number** button. The code *&[Page]* appears in the center footer box. After you move the insertion point out of the center footer box, the actual page number will appear.

11. Click the worksheet to close the headers and footers. Press the **Ctrl+Home** keys to make cell A1 the active cell. The worksheet appears in Page Layout view, as shown in **Figure 3–16**, giving a good sense of how it will be printed on the page.

FIGURE 3–16
Worksheet in Page Layout view

Column and row headings will not be printed

Print title

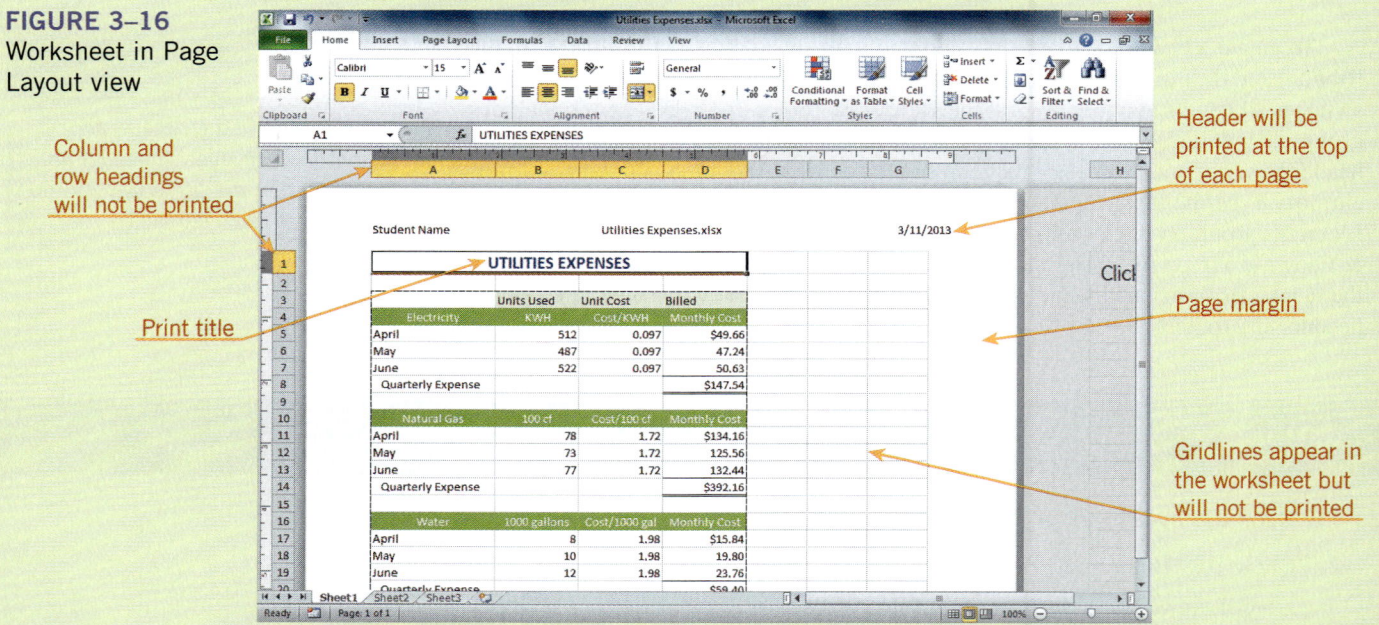

Header will be printed at the top of each page

Page margin

Gridlines appear in the worksheet but will not be printed

12. Save the workbook.

13. Click the **File** tab to open Backstage view. In the navigation bar, click **Print**. A preview of the printed worksheet and buttons to access many of the page layout settings are displayed, as shown in **Figure 3–17**.

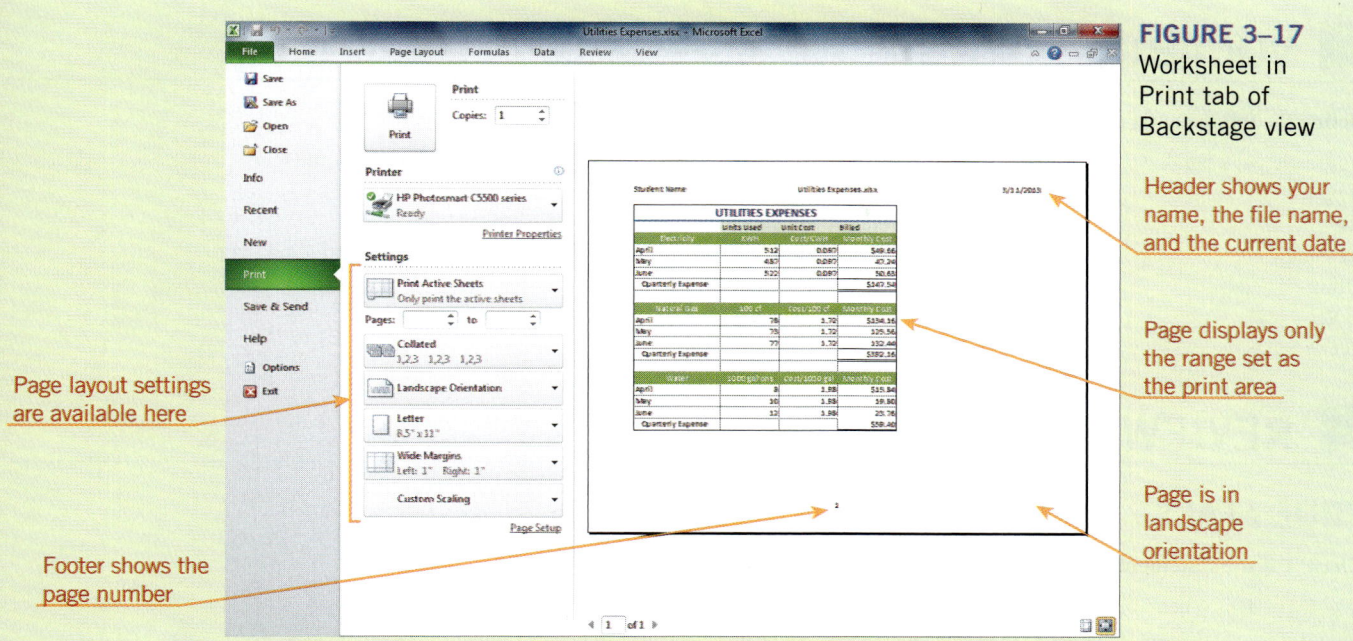

FIGURE 3–17
Worksheet in
Print tab of
Backstage view

Header shows your
name, the file name,
and the current date

Page displays only
the range set as
the print area

Page is in
landscape
orientation

Page layout settings
are available here

Footer shows the
page number

14. On the Print tab, click the **Print** button, and then close the workbook.
     The worksheet is printed.

SUMMARY

In this lesson, you learned:

■ You can copy or move data to another part of the worksheet. You can use the Copy, Cut, and Paste buttons, the drag-and-drop method, and the fill handle to copy and move data in a worksheet. These tools save time by eliminating the need to retype data.

■ As you build a worksheet, you may need to insert a row or column to enter more data, or delete a row or column of unnecessary data. You can also insert or delete specific cells within a worksheet.

■ When a worksheet becomes large, the column or row labels can scroll out of view as you work on other parts of the worksheet. To keep selected rows and columns on the screen as the rest of the worksheet scrolls, you can freeze panes.

■ Splitting a large worksheet enables you to view and work in different parts of a worksheet at once, in two or four panes that you can scroll independently.

■ You can check a worksheet for possible misspellings and correct them using the Spelling dialog box.

■ When you are ready to print a worksheet, switching from Normal view to Page Layout view can be helpful. You can modify how a worksheet appears on the printed page by increasing or decreasing the margins, changing the page orientation, designating a print area, inserting page breaks, scaling, showing or hiding gridlines and headings, and specifying print titles.

■ Headers and footers are useful for adding identifying text at the top and bottom of the printed page. Common elements include your name, the page number, the current date, the workbook file name, and the worksheet name.

VOCABULARY REVIEW

Define the following terms:

automatic page break	header	Page Layout view
copy	manual page break	paste
cut	margin	print area
fill handle	Normal view	print titles
filling	Office Clipboard (Clipboard)	scale
footer	Page Break Preview	split
freeze panes		

■ REVIEW QUESTIONS

TRUE / FALSE

Circle T if the statement is true or F if the statement is false.

T   F   **1.**   When you paste data into cells with existing data, the pasted data replaces the existing data.

T   F   **2.**   The Fill commands are available only when you are copying data to cells adjacent to the original cell.

T   F   **3.**   Deleting a row or column moves the data in that row or column to the adjacent row or column.

T   F   **4.**   Splitting creates two, three, or four panes in the worksheet.

T   F   **5.**   The spelling checker might not find all the misspellings or incorrectly used words in a worksheet.

WRITTEN QUESTIONS

Write a brief answer to each of the following questions.

1. What key do you press to copy data using the drag-and-drop method?

2. How do you paste multiple copies of data that has been copied to the Clipboard?

3. What should you do if you accidentally delete a column or row?

4. How do you keep the titles and column labels of a worksheet on the screen, no matter where the worksheet is scrolled?

5. What is the difference between a header and a footer?

FILL IN THE BLANK

Complete the following sentences by writing the correct word or words in the blanks provided.

1. _____ removes a cell or range from its original location in the worksheet.

2. _____ shows how the worksheet will appear on paper.

3. The _____ is the blank space around the top, bottom, left and right sides of a page.

4. The _____ consists of the cells and ranges designated for printing.

5. _____ are designated rows and/or columns in a worksheet that are printed on each page.

PROJECTS

If you have a SAM 2010 user profile, your instructor may have assigned an autogradable version of the indicated project. If so, log into the SAM 2010 Web site at *www.cengage.com/sam2010* to download the instruction and start files.

PROJECT 3–1

Match the correct command in Column 2 to the action indicated in Column 1.

Column 1

1. You are tired of typing repetitive data.

2. A portion of the worksheet would be more useful in another area of the worksheet.

3. You forgot to type a row of data in the middle of the worksheet.

4. You no longer need a certain column in the worksheet.

5. Column headings scroll out of view while you are working in the worksheet.

6. You want to be sure that all words are spelled correctly in the worksheet.

7. Your boss requests a printed copy of your worksheet.

8. You need to print only a selected area of the worksheet.

Column 2

_____ A. Fill or Copy

_____ B. Cut, Paste

_____ C. Insert Sheet Rows

_____ D. Delete Sheet Columns

_____ E. Print

_____ F. Print Area

_____ G. Freeze Panes

_____ H. Spelling

PROJECT 3–2

1. Open the **Assets.xlsx** workbook from the drive and folder where your Data Files are stored.

2. Save the workbook as **Assets Statement** followed by your initials.

3. Insert a column to the left of column B.

4. Change the width of column A to 45.00 characters.

5. Move the contents of the range D3:D16 to the range B3:B16.

6. Change the width of columns B and C to 10.00 characters.

7. Indent the contents of A9, A13, and A16.

8. Underline the contents of B3:C3.

9. Check the spelling in the worksheet, and then proofread the worksheet to correct any errors the spelling checker missed. (*Hint:* You will need to make three corrections with the spelling checker and one correction by proofreading.)

10. Insert a footer that includes your name in the left footer box and the current date in the right footer box.

11. Save, preview, and print the worksheet, and then close the workbook.

PROJECT 3–3

1. Open the **Trade.xlsx** workbook from the drive and folder where your Data Files are stored.

2. Save the workbook as **Trade Balance** followed by your initials.

3. Freeze rows 1 through 6.

4. Check the spelling of the countries listed in the worksheet. (*Hint*: You will need to make four corrections.)

5. Change the orientation of the worksheet to portrait.

6. Scale the worksheet to 80% of its original size.

7. Change the margins to Wide.

8. In cell A5, enter your name.

9. Save, preview, and print the worksheet, and then close the workbook.

PROJECT 3–4

1. Open the **Inventory.xlsx** workbook from the drive and folder where your Data Files are stored.

2. Save the workbook as **Inventory Purchase** followed by your initials.

3. Organize the worksheet so inventory items are grouped by supplier, as shown below. Be sure to insert suitable headings and format them appropriately. Some of the data is out of order and needs to be moved.

Item	Product Code	Quantity
Mega Computer Manufacturers		
Mega X-39 Computers	X-39-25879	24
Mega X-40 Computers	X-40-25880	18
Mega X-41 Computers	X-41-25881	31
Xenon Paper Source		
Xenon Letter Size White Paper	LT-W-45822	70
Xenon Letter Size Color Paper	LT-C-45823	16
Xenon Legal Size White Paper	LG-W-45824	20
Xenon Legal Size Color Paper	LG-C-45825	7
MarkMaker Pen Company		
MarkMaker Black Ball Point Pens	MM-Bk-43678	100
MarkMaker Blue Ball Point Pens	MM-Bl-43677	120
MarkMaker Red Ball Point Pens	MM-R-43679	45

4. The following inventory item was excluded from the worksheet. Add the item below the MarkMaker Red Ball Point Pens row by using the Fill command and then editing the copied data.

Item	Product Code	Quantity
MarkMaker Green Ball Point Pens	MM-G-43680	35

5. Delete the following item.

Item	Product Code	Quantity
Mega X-39 Computers	X-39-25879	24

6. Change the page orientation to landscape.

7. Hide the gridlines from view.

8. Insert a header that includes your name in the center header box and the current date in the right header box.

9. Save, preview, and print the worksheet, and then close the workbook.

PROJECT 3–5

1. Open the **Time.xlsx** workbook from the drive and folder where your Data Files are stored.

2. Save the workbook as **Time Sheet** followed by your initials.

3. Delete rows 4 and 5.

4. Enter the following data in rows 13 through 16 in the time record.

Date	From	To	Admin.	Meetings	Phone	Work Description
9-Oct	8:15 AM	12:00 PM	1.75		2.50	Staff meeting and called clients
10-Oct	7:45 AM	11:30 AM	2.00		1.75	Paperwork and called clients
11-Oct	7:45 AM	11:30 AM			3.75	Called clients
13-Oct	8:00 AM	12:00 PM	2.50		1.50	Mailed flyers and met w/KF

5. Freeze rows 1 through 7 in the worksheet.

6. Insert a blank row above row 16. Use Auto Fill to enter the formula in cell D16. Enter the following information:

Date	From	To	Admin.	Meetings	Phone	Work Description
12-Oct	7:45 AM	11:30 AM	2.00		1.75	Paperwork and called clients

7. Change the orientation of the worksheet to landscape.

8. In the range B1:D1, enter your first name, middle initial, and last name, replacing the data already in that range. Save the workbook.

9. Preview the worksheet in Backstage view. Click the Zoom to Page button in the lower-right corner of the window to zoom in to see the total hours worked.

10. Print the worksheet, and then close the workbook.

PROJECT 3–6

1. Open the **Chemistry.xlsx** workbook from the drive and folder where your Data Files are stored.

2. Save the workbook as **Chemistry Grades** followed by your initials.

3. Merge and center the range A1:H1. Merge and center the range A2:H2.

4. Insert a column between the current columns A and B.

5. In the range B3:B9, enter the following data:

Cell	Data
B3	First Name
B4	Max
B5	Aiden
B6	Cindy
B7	Raul
B8	Alicia
B9	Mika

6. Change the worksheet to landscape orientation.

7. Switch to Page Layout view. Click in the left header box and type your name.

8. Go to the footer, and insert *Page 1* in the center footer box. (*Hint*: On the Header & Footer Tools Design tab, in the Header & Footer group, click the Footer button, and then click Page 1.)

9. Save, preview, and print the worksheet, and then close the workbook.

PROJECT 3–7

1. Open the **Club.xlsx** workbook from the drive and folder where your Data Files are stored.

2. Save the workbook as **Club Equipment** followed by your initials.

3. Bold and center the column headings in row 2.

4. Insert a row above row 3.

5. Freeze the column headings in row 2.

6. Insert a row above row 8, and then, in cell A8, enter **Bats**.

7. Copy cell E4 to the range E5:E11.

8. Format the Cost (D4:D11) and Total (E4:E12) columns as currency with two decimal places.

9. In the Sport and Cost columns, enter the following data, and then widen the columns as needed to display all of the data:

Item	Sport	Cost
Basketballs	**Basketball**	32
Hoops	**Basketball**	60
Backboards	**Basketball**	135
Softballs	**Softball**	8
Bats	**Softball**	45
Masks	**Softball**	55
Volleyballs	**Volleyball**	35
Nets	**Volleyball**	155

10. In the Quantity column, enter the following data:

Basketballs	5	Bats	8
Hoops	2	Masks	2
Backboards	2	Volleyballs	7
Softballs	25	Nets	1

11. You have $1,785 to spend on equipment. Use any remaining cash to purchase as many basketballs as possible. Increase the number of basketballs and watch the dollar amount in the total. You should use $1,780 and have $5 left over.

12. In cell A16, enter **Prepared by:** followed by your name.

13. Change the worksheet to landscape orientation.

14. Save, preview, and print the worksheet, and then close the workbook.

PROJECT 3–8

1. Open the **Creston.xlsx** workbook from the drive and folder where your Data Files are stored.

2. Save the workbook as **Creston Pool** followed by your initials.

3. Move data as needed to better reorganize the worksheet.

4. Format the worksheet in an appropriate and appealing way.

5. Set appropriate margins and page orientation.

6. Check the spelling in the worksheet, and then proofread the worksheet to correct any errors the spelling checker missed. (*Hint:* You will need to make three corrections with the spelling checker and one correction by proofreading.)

7 Insert your name, the workbook file name, and the current date in the appropriate header and footer boxes.

8. Save, preview, and print the worksheet, and then close the workbook.

■ CRITICAL THINKING

ACTIVITY 3–1

As a zoo employee, you have been asked to observe a chimpanzee's behavior during a three-day period. You need to record the number of minutes the animal displays certain behaviors while the zoo is open to visitors. Create a worksheet to record the number of minutes that the chimpanzee participates in the following behaviors during each of the three days.

- Sleeping
- Eating
- Walking
- Sitting
- Playing

Format the worksheet to make it attractive and easy to read. Change margins, orientation, and other page setup options to prepare the worksheet for printing. Include appropriate headers and footers, including at least your name in one of the boxes. Save, preview, and print the workbook.

LESSON 4

Entering Worksheet Formulas

■ OBJECTIVES

Upon completion of this lesson, you should be able to:

- Enter and edit formulas.
- Distinguish between relative, absolute, and mixed cell references.
- Use the point-and-click method to enter formulas.
- Use the Sum button to add values in a range.
- Preview a calculation.
- Display formulas instead of results in a worksheet.
- Manually calculate formulas.

■ VOCABULARY

absolute cell reference

formula

manual calculation

mixed cell reference

operand

operator

order of evaluation

point-and-click method

relative cell reference

Sum button

You can use the numerical data in a worksheet to perform mathematical calculations. Rather than add specific numbers, you can use cell references in equations to make the calculation more flexible. As these equations become more complex, you will need to keep in mind the order of evaluation to be sure you obtain the intended results. You can create equations using the keyboard or the mouse. To enter common calculations quickly, you can use the Sum button. These mathematical calculations are what make Excel such a powerful tool for both personal and business use.

What Are Formulas?

One of the main advantages of Excel is that you can use numbers entered in cells to make calculations in other cells. The equation used to calculate values based on numbers entered in cells is called a *formula*. Each formula begins with an equal sign (=). The results of the calculation appear in the cell in which the formula is entered. The formula itself appears in the Formula Bar. For example, if you enter the formula =8+6 in cell A1, the value 14 appears in the cell, and the formula =8+6 appears in the Formula Bar when cell A1 is the active cell, as shown in **Figure 4–1**.

▶ **VOCABULARY**

formula

operand

operator

Formula in the active cell appears in the Formula Bar

Formula results appear in the cell

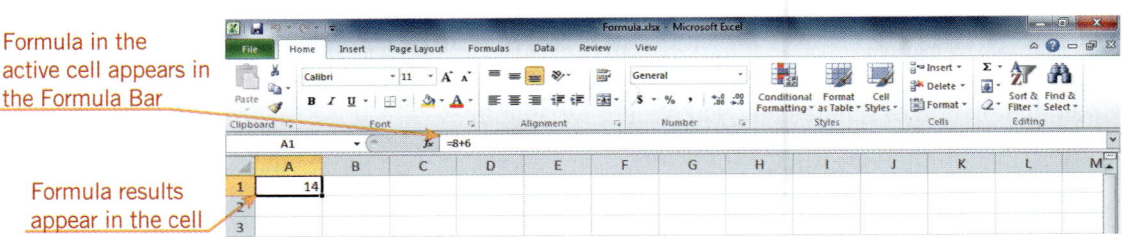

FIGURE 4–1   Formula and formula results

Entering a Formula

Worksheet formulas consist of two components: operands and operators. An *operand* is a constant (text or number) or cell reference used in a formula. An *operator* is a symbol that indicates the type of calculation to perform on the operands, such as a plus sign (+) for addition. **Table 4–1** shows the different mathematical operators you can use in formulas. Consider the formula =B3+5. In this formula, the cell reference B3 and the constant 5 are operands, and the plus sign (+) is an operator. This formula tells Excel to add the value in cell B3 to the value 5. After you finish typing a formula in a cell, you enter it by pressing the Enter key or the Tab key or by clicking the Enter button on the Formula Bar.

TABLE 4–1   Mathematical operators

OPERATOR	OPERATION	EXAMPLE	MEANING
+	Addition	B5+C5	Adds the values in cells B5 and C5
−	Subtraction	C8–232	Subtracts 232 from the value in cell C8
*	Multiplication	D4*D5	Multiplies the value in cell D4 by the value in cell D5
/	Division	E6/4	Divides the value in cell E6 by 4
^	Exponentiation	B3^3	Raises the value in cell B3 to the third power

In editing mode, each cell reference in a formula appears in a specific color. The corresponding cell in the worksheet is outlined in the same color. You can change a cell reference in a formula by dragging the outlined cell to another location in the worksheet. You can also change which cells are included in a reference by dragging any corner of the colored outline to resize the selected range.

Step-by-Step 4.1

1. Open the **Formula.xlsx** workbook from the drive and folder where your Data Files are stored.

2. Save the workbook as **Formula Practice** followed by your initials.

3. Click cell **C3**. You'll enter a formula in this cell.

4. Type **=A3+B3** and then press the **Enter** key. The formula result 479 appears in the cell. Cell C4 is the active cell.

5. In cell C4, type **=A4–B4** and then press the **Enter** key. The formula result –147 appears in the cell. Cell C5 is the active cell.

6. In cell C5, type **=A5*B5** and then press the **Enter** key. The formula result 13166 appears in the cell. Cell C6 is the active cell.

7. In cell C6, type **=A6/B6** and then press the **Enter** key. The formula result 18 appears in the cell. Compare your results to **Figure 4–2**.

> **TIP**
>
> You can type cell references in uppercase (A1) or lowercase (a1) letters.

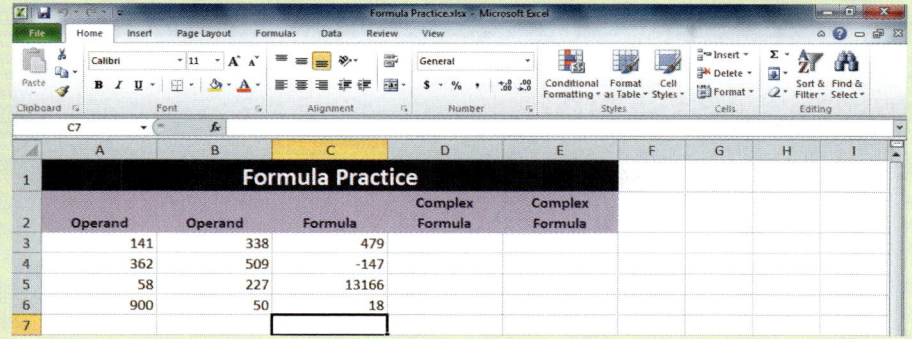

FIGURE 4–2
Formulas entered in worksheet

8. Save the workbook, and leave it open for the next Step-by-Step.

Order of Evaluation

Formulas can include more than one operator. For example, the formula =C3*C4+5 includes two operators and performs both multiplication and addition to calculate the value in the cell. The sequence used to calculate the value of a formula is called the ***order of evaluation***.

Formulas are evaluated in the following order:

1. Contents within parentheses are evaluated first. You can use as many sets of parentheses as you want. The innermost set of parentheses is evaluated first.

2. Mathematical operators are evaluated in the order shown in **Table 4–2**.

3. If two or more operators have the same order of evaluation, the equation is evaluated from left to right. For example, in the formula =20–15–2, first the number 15 is subtracted from 20, then 2 is subtracted from the difference (5).

> **VOCABULARY**
> **order of evaluation**

TABLE 4–2 Order of evaluation

ORDER OF EVALUATION	OPERATOR	SYMBOL
First	Exponentiation	^
Second	Positive or negative	+ or −
Third	Multiplication or division	* or /
Fourth	Addition or subtraction	+ or −

Step-by-Step 4.2

> **EXTRA FOR EXPERTS**
>
> If you start typing an entry that matches another cell entry, which happens in Step 1 after you type A and again after you type B, the AutoComplete features displays the complete contents of the existing entry in ScreenTip. If you want to insert the complete entry, press the Enter key. If not, continue typing.

1. Click cell **D3**, and then type **=(A3+B3)*20**. This formula adds the values in cells A3 and B3, and then multiplies the result by 20.

2. Press the **Tab** key. The formula results in the value 9580, which appears in cell D3. Cell E3 is the active cell.

3. In cell E3, type **=A3+B3*20**. This formula is the same as the one you entered in cell D3, but without the parentheses. The lack of parentheses changes the order of evaluation and the resulting value.

4. Press the **Enter** key. The formula in cell E3 results in the value 6901. This differs from the formula results in cell D3 because Excel multiplied the value in cell B3 by 20 before adding the value in cell A3. In cell D3, Excel added the values in cells A3 and B3, and then multiplied the sum by 20.

5. Save the workbook, and leave it open for the next Step-by-Step.

Editing Formulas

If you attempt to enter a formula with an incorrect structure in cell, Excel opens a dialog box that explains the error and provides a possible correction. You can accept that correction or choose to correct the formula yourself. For example, if you enter a formula with an opening parenthesis but no closing parenthesis, a dialog box appears, as shown in **Figure 4–3**, indicating that Excel found an error and proposing a correction that adds a closing parenthesis to the formula. Click Yes to accept the proposed correction. Click No to see a description of the error in another dialog box, and then click OK to return to the formula. You can correct the formula by editing it directly in the cell or by clicking in the Formula Bar.

Proposed correction

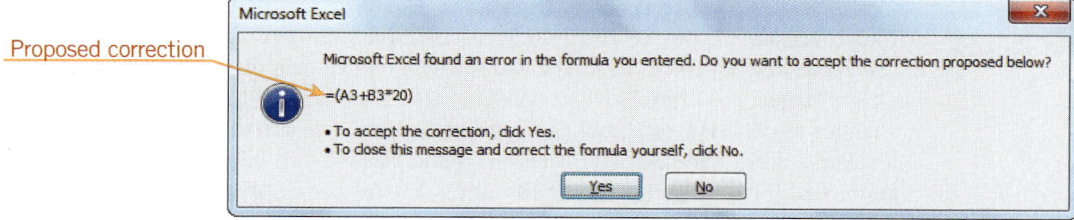

FIGURE 4–3   Formula error message

Although Excel checks the formula for the correct structure, it does not check the formula for the correct values or cell references. If you discover that you need to make a correction, you can edit the formula. Click the cell with the formula you want to edit. Press the F2 key or double-click the cell to enter editing mode or click in the Formula Bar. Move the insertion point as needed to edit the entry. Then, press the Enter key or click the Enter button on the Formula Bar to enter the formula.

Step-by-Step 4.3

1. Click cell **E3**. The formula is displayed in the Formula Bar.

2. In the Formula Bar, click after = (the equal sign).

3. Type **(** (an opening parenthesis). You will intentionally leave out the closing parenthesis.

4. Press the **Enter** key. The dialog box shown in Figure 4–3 appears, indicating that Excel found an error and offers a possible correction.

5. Read the message, and then click **No**. You will correct the error yourself. A dialog box appears, describing the specific error Excel found, as shown in **Figure 4–4**.

Description of the error Excel found in the formula

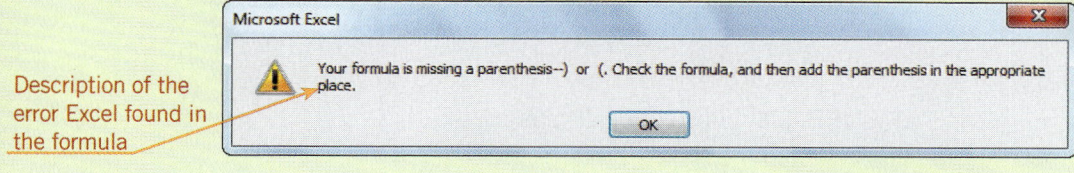

FIGURE 4–4
Formula error description message

6. Read the message, and then click **OK**.

7.   Move the insertion point in the Formula Bar between the 3 and the *.

8.   Type) (a closing parenthesis).

9.   Press the **Enter** key. The value in cell E3 changes to 9580.

10. Save the workbook, and leave it open for the next Step-by-Step.

Comparing Relative, Absolute, and Mixed Cell References

▶ **VOCABULARY**

relative cell reference

absolute cell reference

Excel has three types of cell references: relative, absolute, and mixed. A *relative cell reference* adjusts to its new location when copied or moved to another cell. For example, when the formula =A3+A4 is copied from cell A5 to cell B5, the formula changes to =B3+B4, as shown in **Figure 4–5**. How does Excel know how to change a relative cell reference? It creates the same relationship between the cells in the new location. In other words, the formula =A3+A4 in cell A5 instructs Excel to add the two cells directly above it. When you move this formula to another cell, such as cell B5, Excel uses that same instruction: to add the two cells directly above the cell with the formula. Notice that only the cell references change; the operators remain the same.

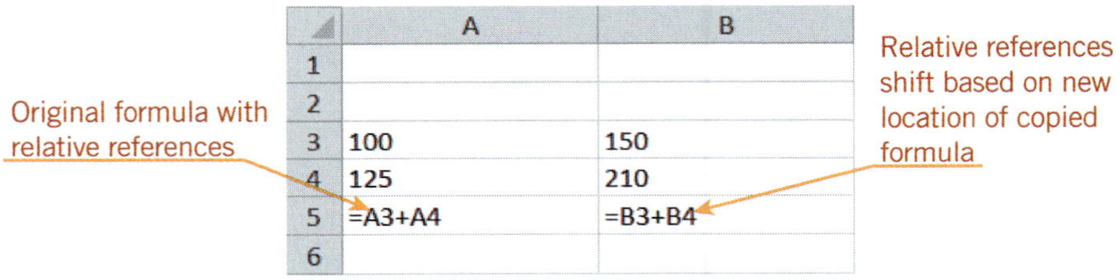

Original formula with relative references

Relative references shift based on new location of copied formula

FIGURE 4–5   Relative cell references

Absolute cell references* do not change when copied or moved to a new cell. To create an absolute cell reference, you insert a dollar sign ($) before the column letter and before the row number. For example, when the formula =$A$3+$A$4 in cell A5 is copied to cell B7, the formula remains unchanged, as shown in **Figure 4–6**.

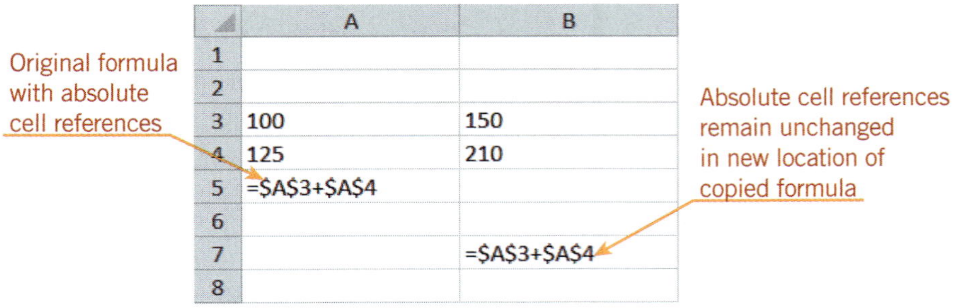

Original formula with absolute cell references

Absolute cell references remain unchanged in new location of copied formula

FIGURE 4–6   Absolute cell references

TECHNOLOGY CAREERS

Engineers use Excel worksheets to perform complex calculations in areas such as construction, transportation, and manufacturing. For example, Excel worksheets are used to fit equations to data, interpolate between data points, solve simultaneous equations, evaluate integrals, convert units, and compare economic alternatives.

Cell references that contain both relative and absolute references are called *mixed cell references*. When formulas with mixed cell references are copied or moved to another cell, the row or column references preceded by a dollar sign do not change; the row or column references not preceded by a dollar sign adjust to match the cell to which they are moved. As shown in **Figure 4–7**, when the formula =A$3+A$4 is copied from cell A5 to cell B7, the formula changes to =B$3+B$4.

▶ **VOCABULARY**
mixed cell reference

Original formula with mixed cell references (relative column references and absolute row references)

Relative column references shift based on new location of copied formula; absolute row references remain unchanged

▲	A	B
1		
2		
3	100	150
4	125	210
5	=A$3+A$4	
6		
7		=B$3+B$4

FIGURE 4–7   Mixed cell references

Step-by-Step 4.4

1. Click cell **D3**. The formula =(A3+B3)*20 (shown in the Formula Bar) contains only relative cell references.

2. Drag the fill handle to cell **D4** to copy the formula from cell D3 to cell D4.

3. Click cell **D4**. The value in cell D4 is 17420, and the formula in the Formula Bar is =(A4+B4)*20. The operators in the formula remain the same, but the relative cell references change to reflect the new location of the formula.

4. Click cell **D5**, type =$A$3*($B$3–200) and then press the **Enter** key. The value in cell D5 is 19458. The formula contains absolute cell references, which are indicated by the dollar signs that precede the row and column references.

5. Copy the formula in cell **D5** to cell **E6**. The value in cell E6 is 19458, the same as in cell D5.

6. Click cell **D5** and look at the formula in the Formula Bar.

▣ **EXTRA FOR EXPERTS**

You can press the F4 key to change a cell reference from a relative reference to an absolute reference to a mixed reference with an absolute row to a mixed reference with an absolute column and back to a relative reference.

7. Click cell **E6** and look at the formula in the Formula Bar. The formula in cell D5 is exactly the same as the formula in cell E6 because the formula you copied from cell D5 contains absolute cell references.

8. Click cell **E4**, type **=$A$4+B4** and then press the **Enter** key. This formula contains both relative and absolute cell references. The value in cell E4 is 871.

9. Copy the formula in cell **E4** to cell **E5**, and then click cell **E5**. The relative cell reference B4 changes to B5, but the absolute reference $A$4 stays the same. The value in cell E5 is 589.

10. Copy the formula in cell **E5** to cell **D6**. The relative cell reference B5 changes to A6, but the absolute reference $A$4 stays the same. The value in cell D6 is 1262.

11. Click cell **A8**, and then enter your name. Save, preview, print, and close the workbook.

Creating Formulas Quickly

So far, you have created formulas by typing the formula or editing an existing formula. You can also create formulas quickly by using the point-and-click method and the Sum button.

Using the Point-and-Click Method

Earlier, you constructed formulas by typing the entire formula directly in a worksheet cell. You can include cell references in a formula by using the *point-and-click method* to click each cell rather than typing a cell reference. The point-and-click method is particularly helpful when you need to enter long formulas that contain multiple cell references.

To use the point-and-click method, simply click the cell instead of typing its cell reference. For example, to enter the formula =A3+B3 with the point-and-click method, click the cell in which you want to enter the formula, press =, click cell A3, press +, click cell B3, and then press the Enter key.

Step-by-Step 4.5

TIP

A flashing colored border indicates that you can replace the current reference in the formula by clicking another cell or selecting a range. When the border stops flashing, the cell reference is "locked," and you must select the reference in the formula to replace it.

1. Open the **Juice.xlsx** workbook from the drive and folder where your Data Files are stored.

2. Save the workbook as **Juice Sales** followed by your initials.

3. Click cell **F6**, type **=(** to begin the formula, and then click cell **B6**. A flashing blue border surrounds cell B6 to indicate it is selected, and its cell reference in the formula is also blue.

4. Type *. The flashing border disappears, but the cell border and reference remain blue.

5. Click cell **C6**. A flashing green border appears around cell C6, and its cell reference in the formula is the same color.

6. Type **)+(** and then click cell **D6**. The cell border and reference in the formula are purple.

7. Type * and then click cell **E6**. The cell border and reference in the formula are red. **Figure 4–8** shows the color-coded formula and cell references.

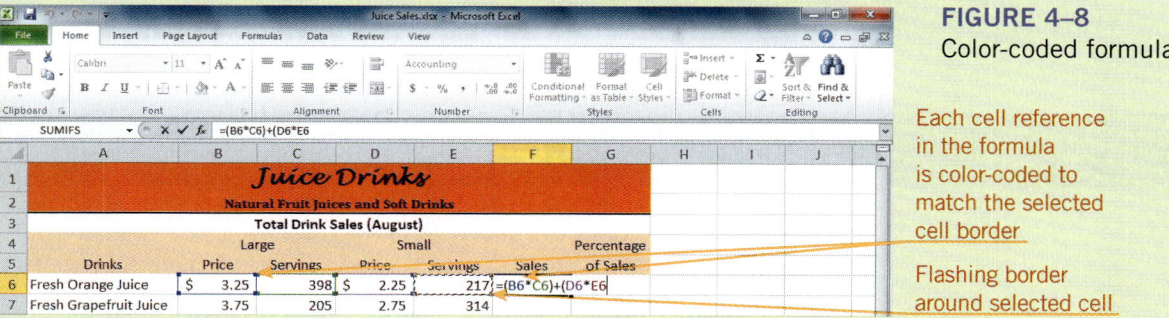

FIGURE 4–8
Color-coded formula

Each cell reference in the formula is color-coded to match the selected cell border

Flashing border around selected cell

8. Type **)** and then press the **Enter** button ☑ on the Formula Bar. The value $1,781.75 appears in cell F6.

9. Use the fill handle to copy the formula in cell F6 to the range **F7:F11**. Click cell **F12** to deselect the range. All the monthly sales are calculated for each type of drink, as shown in **Figure 4–9**.

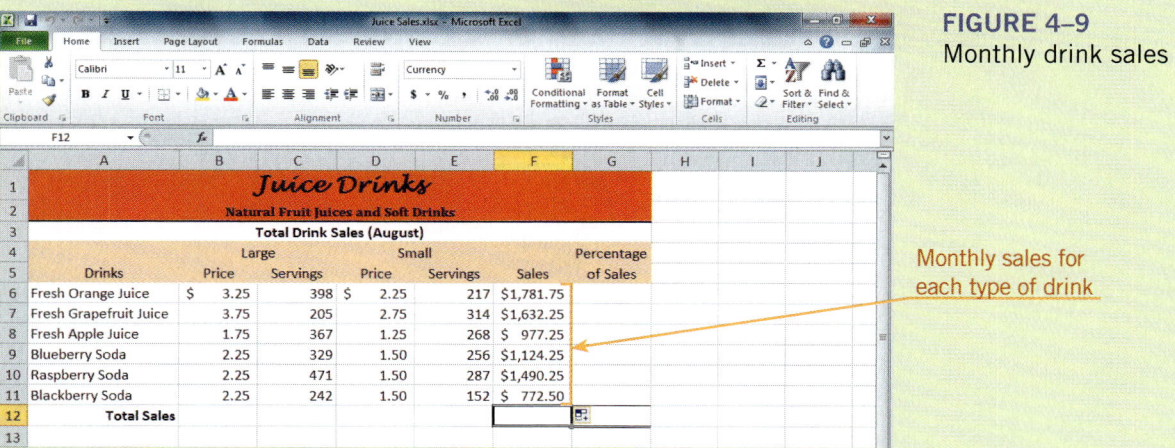

FIGURE 4–9
Monthly drink sales

Monthly sales for each type of drink

10. Save the workbook, and leave it open for the next Step-by-Step.

Using the Sum Button

Worksheet users frequently need to add long columns or rows of numbers. The ***Sum button***, located in the Editing group on the Home tab of the Ribbon, makes this operation simple. To use the Sum button, click the cell where you want the total

▶ **VOCABULARY**
Sum button

EXTRA FOR EXPERTS

Other commonly used functions are AVERAGE, MAX (maximum), MIN (minimum), and COUNT NUMBERS (counts how many entries in the range contain numbers). Click the cell in which you want to enter the function. On the Home tab, in the Editing group, click the Sum button arrow. A menu lists these common functions. Click the function you want to use. Verify the range, and then press the Enter key.

to appear, and then click the Sum button. Excel scans the worksheet to determine the most logical adjacent column or row of cells with numbers to add. An outline appears around the range it suggests, and the range reference appears in the active cell. If you want to add the numbers in a different range, drag to select those cells. Press the Enter key to complete the formula. The active cell displays the sum.

The Sum button enters a formula with the SUM function, which is a shorthand way to specify adding numbers in a range. The SUM function that adds the numbers in the range D5:D17, for example, is =SUM(D5:D17). Functions are discussed in greater detail in the next lesson.

Step-by-Step 4.6

1. Make sure cell **F12** is the active cell.

2. On the Home tab, in the Editing group, click the **Sum** button **Σ**. The suggested range F6:F11 is outlined. The formula =SUM(F6:F11) appears in the Formula Bar and cell F12. See **Figure 4–10**.

FIGURE 4–10
SUM function in the formula

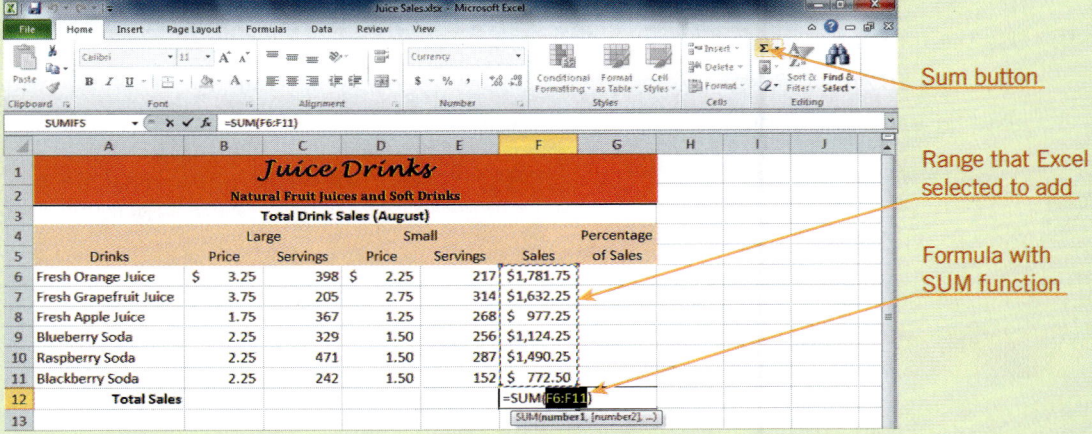

3. Verify that the range **F6:F11** is the selected range. Press the **Enter** key. The range is deselected and the formula results of $7,778.25 appear in cell F12, which is the sum of the numbers in column F.

4. Click cell **G6**, and then type **=**.

5. Click cell **F6**, and then type **/**.

6. Click cell **F12**, press the **F4** key to change the cell reference (F12) to an absolute reference ($F$12). You used an absolute reference to cell F12 because you want the cell reference to remain unchanged when you copy it to the rest of the range.

7. Press the **Enter** button ✓ on the Formula Bar. The formula results 22.91% appear in cell G6.

8. Copy the formula in cell G6 to the range **G7:G11**. The Percentage of Sales is entered for all of the drinks.

9. Click cell **G12**. On the Home tab, in the Editing group, click the **Sum** button Σ. Press the **Enter** key. The total percentage of sales is 100.0%. See **Figure 4–11**.

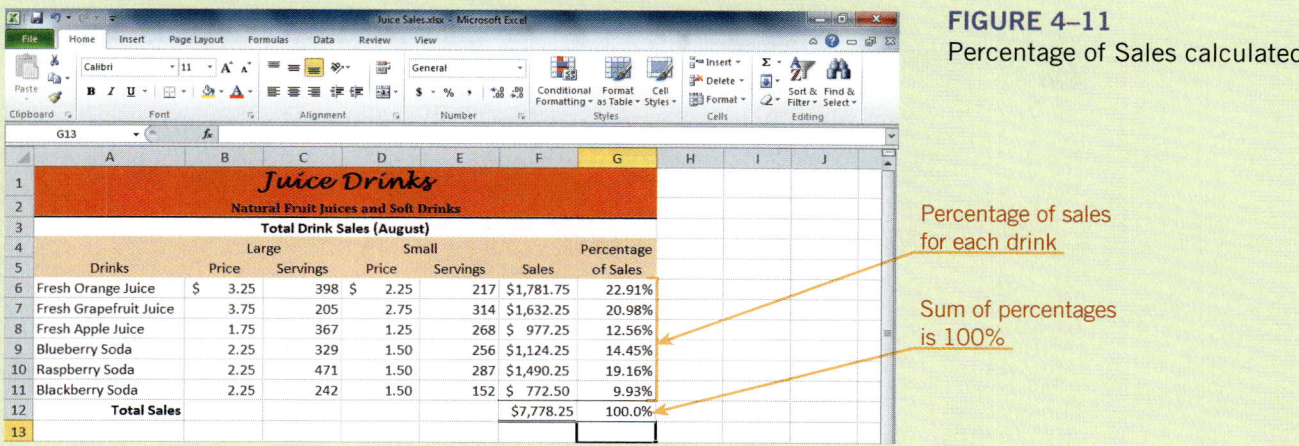

FIGURE 4–11
Percentage of Sales calculated

Percentage of sales for each drink

Sum of percentages is 100%

10. Save the workbook, and leave it open for the next Step-by-Step.

Previewing Calculations

When you select a range that contains numbers, the status bar shows the results of common calculations for the range, without you having to enter a formula. By default, these calculations display the average value in the selected range, a count of the number of values in the selected range, and a sum of the values in the selected range. For ranges that contain only text values, the status bar displays a count of the number of values in the range. You can also customize Excel to display a numerical count, minimum value, and maximum value for the selected range. **Table 4–3** describes each of these options.

TABLE 4–3   Summary calculation options for the status bar

CALCULATION	DESCRIPTION
Average	Displays an average of the values in the selected range
Count	Lists how many cells in the selected range contain values
Numerical Count	Lists how many of the cells in the selected range contain numbers
Minimum	Shows the smallest number in the selected range
Maximum	Shows the largest number in the selected range
Sum	Adds all the numbers in the selected range

To display the default calculations in the status bar, just select a range. You can change which summary calculations appear in the status bar. Right-click the status bar to open the Customize Status Bar menu shown in **Figure 4–12**. Options that are preceded by a check mark appear in the status bar. Options without a check mark are hidden. You can choose which calculations you want to show or hide. Click a checked option to hide it, or click an unchecked option to show it. Press Esc to close the menu. The checked summary calculations appear in the status bar for selected ranges until you change the displayed options.

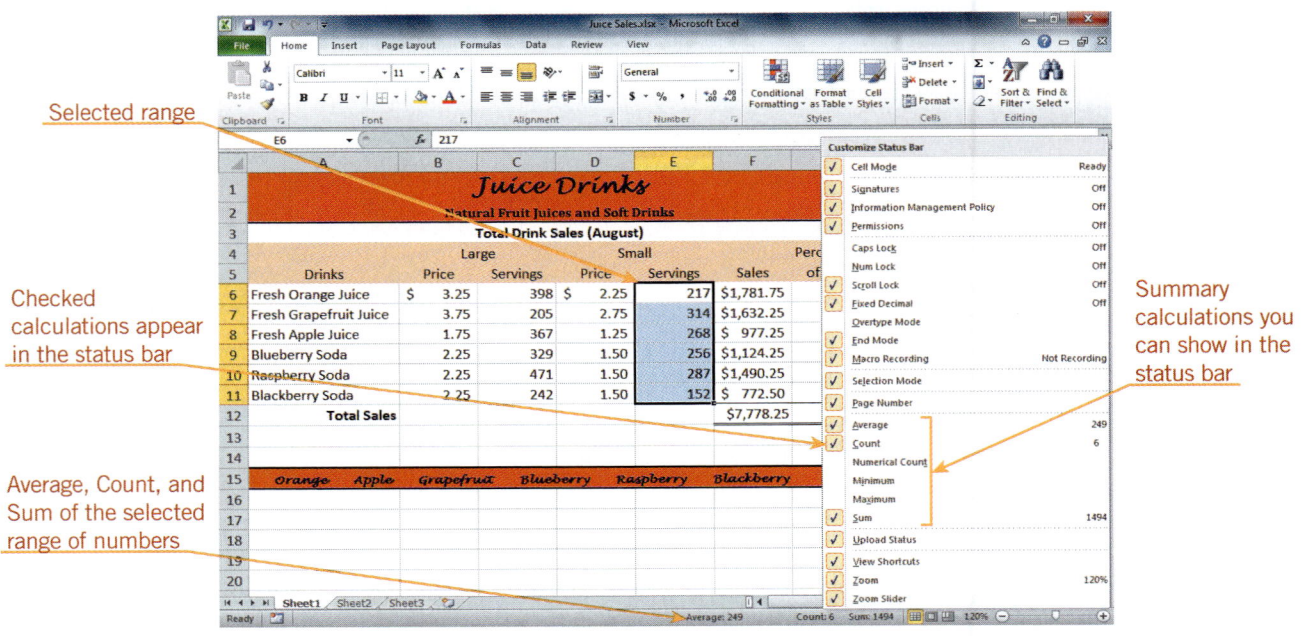

Selected range

Checked calculations appear in the status bar

Average, Count, and Sum of the selected range of numbers

Summary calculations you can show in the status bar

FIGURE 4–12   Customize Status Bar menu

Step-by-Step 4.7

EXTRA FOR EXPERTS

You can use the summary calculations in the status bar to confirm that the same formula in the worksheet is correct. Cell F12 contains the SUM function formula that adds the values in the range F6:F11. To confirm the formula is correct and the results are accurate, select the range F6:F11, then compare the Sum value in the status bar with the value in cell F12. The sum in the status bar should equal the value in cell F12.

1. Select the range **E6:E11**. Summary calculations for the small servings appear in the status bar, showing an Average of 249, a Count of 6, and a Sum of 1494.

2. Right-click the **status bar**. The Customize Status Bar menu appears, as shown in Figure 4–12.

3. Click **Minimum**. A check mark precedes Minimum on the menu, and the menu remains open so you can click additional options. The fewest number of small drinks served, 152, appears in the status bar. Depending on where you right-clicked, this or another calculation in the status bar might be covered by the shortcut menu.

4. Click **Minimum** to hide the calculation from the status bar, and then press the **Esc** key to close the menu.

5. Select the range **F6:F11**. Summary calculations for the sales appear in the status bar, showing an Average of $1,296.38, a Count of 6, and a Sum of $7,778.25.

6. Click cell **A13** to deselect the range.

7. Save the workbook, and leave it open for the next Step-by-Step.

Showing Formulas in the Worksheet

In previous Step-by-Steps, you viewed formulas in the Formula Bar or directly in the worksheet cells as you typed or edited the formulas. After you enter the formulas, the cells show the formula results rather than the formulas. Typically, the formula result is what you want to see. However, when creating a worksheet with many formulas, you may find it simpler to organize formulas and detect formula errors when all formulas are displayed in their cells. To do this, click the Formulas tab on the Ribbon, and then, in the Formula Auditing group, click the Show Formulas button. The formulas replace the formula results in the worksheet. If a cell does not contain a formula, the data entered in the cell remains displayed. The Show Formulas button remains selected until you click it again to redisplay the formula results. It can be helpful to print the worksheet showing formulas for reference.

> **TIP**
>
> You can also switch between showing formulas and showing formula results in a worksheet by pressing the Ctrl+` keys (the grave accent ` key is located above the Tab key on most standard keyboards).

Calculating Formulas Manually

Excel calculates formula results when you enter the formula and recalculates the results whenever the cells used in that formula change. If a worksheet contains many formulas, the calculation and recalculation process can take a long time. When you need to edit a worksheet with many formulas, you can specify *manual calculation*, which lets you determine when Excel calculates the formulas.

The Formulas tab on the Ribbon contains all the buttons you need when working with manual calculations. To switch to manual calculation, click the Calculation Options button in the Calculation group, and then click Manual. When you want to calculate the formula results for the entire workbook, click the Calculate Now button. To calculate the formula results for only the active worksheet, click the Calculate Sheet button. To return to automatic calculation, click the Calculation Options button, and then click Automatic.

> ▶ **VOCABULARY**
> **manual calculation**

Step-by-Step 4.8

1. Click the **Formulas** tab on the Ribbon. In the Formula Auditing group, click the **Show Formulas** button. All formulas appear in the worksheet cells instead of the formula results.

2. Scroll to the right as needed so that columns F and G appear on the screen and you can see the formula results.

3. On the Formulas tab, in the Calculation group, click the **Calculation Options** button. A menu of options appears, as shown in **Figure 4–13**.

FIGURE 4–13
Worksheet with formulas displayed

Button is a toggle; click it again to redisplay the formula results

Text and numbers remain unchanged

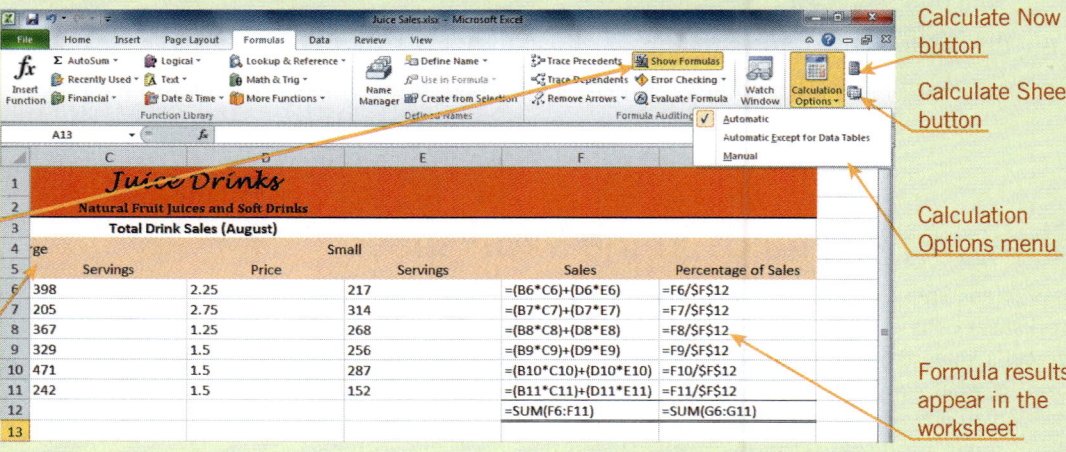

Calculate Now button

Calculate Sheet button

Calculation Options menu

Formula results appear in the worksheet

4. Click **Manual**. Automatic calculation is turned off.

5. Press the **Ctrl+`** keys. The formula results reappear.

6. Click cell **C6**, and then enter **402**. Click cell **C7**, and then enter **220**. Click cell **C10**, and then enter **305**. The worksheet values change, but Excel does not recalculate the formula results.

7. On the Formulas tab, in the Calculation group, click the **Calculate Sheet** button while watching the worksheet. Excel recalculates the formulas when you click the button. For example, the total sales amount in cell F12 is now $7,474.00.

8. On the Formulas tab, in the Calculation group, click the **Calculation Options** button, and then click **Automatic**.

9. Insert a header with your name in the left section and the current date in the right section.

10. Save, preview, print, and close the workbook.

TIP

You can also press the Shift+F9 keys to calculate the values in the worksheet.

SUMMARY

In this lesson, you learned:

- Formulas are equations used to calculate values and display them in a cell. Formulas can include values referenced in other cells of the worksheet. Each formula begins with an equal sign and contains at least two operands and one operator.

- Formulas can include more than one operator. The order of evaluation determines the sequence used to calculate the value of a formula.

- When you enter a formula with an incorrect structure, Excel can correct the error for you, or you can choose to edit it yourself. To edit a formula, click the cell with the formula and then make changes in the Formula Bar. You can also double-click a formula and then edit the formula directly in the cell.

- Relative references adjust to a new location when copied or moved to another cell. Absolute references do not change, regardless of where they are copied or moved. Mixed references contain both relative and absolute references.

- Formulas can be created quickly using the point-and-click method. With this method, you insert a cell reference in a formula by clicking a cell rather than typing its column letter and row number.

- The Sum button in the Editing group on the Home tab inserts a formula with the SUM function, which adds the value of cells in a specified range.

- The status bar shows a preview of common formulas, such as Average, Count, and Sum, when you select a range of cells. You can choose which formula previews to show or hide in a worksheet by right-clicking the status bar.

- You can view the formulas in a worksheet, instead of the formula results, by clicking the Show Formulas button in the Formula Auditing group on the Formulas tab.

- Excel calculates formula results in a worksheet when you enter the formula, and recalculates the results whenever the values in the cells used in that formula change. When you need to edit a worksheet with many formulas and don't want formulas to recalculate automatically, you can click the Calculation Options button in the Calculation group on the Formulas tab, and then click Manual. When you want to calculate the formula results for the current worksheet, click the Calculate Sheet button.

VOCABULARY REVIEW

Define the following terms:

absolute cell reference	operand	point-and-click method
formula	operator	relative cell reference
manual calculation	order of evaluation	Sum button
mixed cell reference		

REVIEW QUESTIONS

TRUE / FALSE

Circle T if the statement is true or F if the statement is false.

T   F   **1.**   An operator is a constant or cell reference used in formulas.

T   F   **2.**   In a formula, multiplication is performed before subtraction.

T   F   **3.**   In a formula, operations within parentheses are performed after operations outside parentheses.

T   F   **4.**   An absolute reference does not change when the formula is copied or moved to another cell.

T   F   **5.**   Manual calculation lets you control when Excel calculates formula results.

WRITTEN QUESTIONS

Write a brief answer to each of the following questions.

1. In a worksheet formula, which operator has the highest priority in the order of evaluation?

2. What type of cell reference will not adjust to its new location when it is copied or moved to another cell?

3. Write an example of a formula that contains a mixed cell reference.

4. Explain how to enter the formula =C4+B5+D2 in cell D3 using the point-and-click method.

5. How do you display formulas instead of formula results in a worksheet?

FILL IN THE BLANK

Complete the following sentences by writing the correct word or words in the blanks provided.

1. The equation used to calculate values based on numbers entered in cells is called a(n) _____.

2. The sequence used to calculate the value of a formula is called the _____.

3. The cell reference D4 is an example of a(n) _____ cell reference.

4. Default summary calculations for a selected range appear in the _____.

5. _____ calculation lets you control when Excel calculates the formulas in a worksheet.

■ PROJECTS

If you have a SAM 2010 user profile, your instructor may have assigned an autogradable version of the indicated project. If so, log into the SAM 2010 Web site at *www.cengage.com/sam2010* to download the instruction and start files.

PROJECT 4–1

Match the letter of the worksheet formula in Column 2 to the description of the worksheet operation performed by the formula in Column 1.

Column 1

_____ 1. Adds the values in cells A3 and A4

_____ 2. Subtracts the value in cell A4 from the value in cell A3

_____ 3. Multiplies the value in cell A3 by 27

_____ 4. Divides the value in cell A3 by 27

_____ 5. Raises the value in cell A3 to the 27th power

_____ 6. Divides the value in cell A3 by 27, and then adds the value in cell A4

_____ 7. Divides the value in cell A3 by the result of 27 plus the value in cell A4

_____ 8. Multiplies the value in cell A3 by 27, and then divides the product by the value in cell A4

_____ 9. Divides 27 by the value in cell A4, and then multiplies the result by the value in cell A3

_____ 10. Raises the value in A3 to the 27th power, and then divides the result by the value in A4

Column 2

A.   =A3/(27+A4)

B.   =A3/27+A4

C.   =A3^27/A4

D.   =(A3*27)/A4

E.   =A3*(27/A4)

F.   =A3^27

G.   =A3+A4

H.   =A3–A4

I.   =A3/27

J.   =A3*27

 **PROJECT 4–2**

1. Open the **Zoo.xlsx** workbook from the drive and folder where your Data Files are stored.

2. Save the workbook as **Zoo Invoice** followed by your initials.

3. In cells D6, D7, D8, and D9, enter formulas that multiply the values in column B by the values in column C.

4. In cell D10, enter a formula to sum the totals in the range D6:D9.

5. In cell D11, enter a formula to calculate an 8% sales tax of the subtotal in cell D10.

6. In cell D12, enter a formula to add the subtotal and sales tax.

7. Change the worksheet to manual calculation.

8. Format the range D6:D12 in the Accounting number format. The worksheet is ready to accept customer data.

9. A customer purchases two tiger T-shirts, three dolphin T-shirts, one sweatshirt, and four coffee mugs. Enter these quantities in column C and recalculate the values.

10. Insert a footer with your name in the left section and the current date in the right section.

11. Save the workbook, preview and print the worksheet, and then close the workbook.

PROJECT 4–3

1. Open the **Operation.xlsx** workbook from the drive and folder where your Data Files are stored.

2. Save the workbook as **Operation Results** followed by your initials.

3. Enter formulas in the specified cells that perform the operations listed below. After you enter each formula, write the resulting value in the space provided.

Resulting Value	Cell	Operation
a. _____	C3	Add the values in cells A3 and B3.
b. _____	C4	Subtract the value in cell B4 from the value in cell A4.
c. _____	C5	Multiply the value in cell A5 by the value in cell B5.
d. _____	C6	Divide the value in cell A6 by the value in cell B6.
e. _____	B7	Sum the values in the range B3:B6.
f. _____	D3	Add the values in cells A3 and B3, and then multiply by 3.
g. _____	D4	Add the values in cells A3 and A4, and then multiply by cell B3.
h. _____	D5	Copy the formula in cell D4 to cell D5.
i. _____	D6	Subtract the value in cell B6 from the value in cell A6, and then divide by 2.
j. _____	D7	Divide the value in cell A6 by 2, and then subtract the value in cell B6.

4. In cell A1, enter your name. Save, preview, print, and close the workbook.

PROJECT 4–4

1. Open the **Investment.xlsx** workbook from the drive and folder where your Data Files are stored.

2. Save the workbook as **Investment Record** followed by your initials.

3. In cells D6 through D8, enter formulas to calculate the values of the stocks. The formulas should multiply the number of shares in column B by the price of the shares in column C.

4. In cells D10 and D11, enter formulas to calculate the values of the mutual funds. As with the stocks, the formulas should multiply the number of shares in column B by the price of the shares in column C.

5. In cell D12, enter a formula that sums the values in cells D4 through D11. Format cell D12 with a Top and Double Bottom Border.

6. In cell E4, enter the formula **=D4/$D$12**. This formula determines the percentage of each investment value with respect to the total investment value.

7. Copy the formula in cell E4 to the ranges E6:E8 and E10:E11. Notice that the absolute reference to cell D12 in the formula remains unchanged as you copy the formula.

8. In cell E12, enter a formula that sums the percentages in cells E4 through E11. Format cell E12 with a Top and Double Bottom Border.

9. Insert a footer with your name in the left section, the file name in the center section, and the current date in the right section.

10. Save, preview, and print the workbook.

11. Save the workbook as **Investment Record Updated** followed by your initials.

12. Change the worksheet to manual calculation in preparation for updating the investment values.

13. Enter the following updated share price amounts in the appropriate cells:

Investment	Price
MicroCrunch Corp.	$17.25
Ocean Electronics, Inc.	$21.75
Photex, Inc.	$12.25
Prosperity Growth Fund	$ 6.50
Lucrative Mutual Fund	$24.00

14. Perform the manual calculation.

15. Save, preview, print, and close the workbook.

PROJECT 4–5

1. Open the **Mackenzie.xlsx** workbook from the drive and folder where your Data Files are stored.

2. Save the workbook as **Mackenzie Development** followed by your initials.

3. In cell D5, enter a formula that multiplies the square footage in cell B5 by the value per square foot in cell C5.

4. In cell D6, enter a formula that multiplies the number of bathrooms in cell B6 by the value per bathroom in cell C6.

5. In cell D7, enter a formula that multiplies the number of car garages in cell B7 by the value per car garage in cell C7.

6. In cell D8, enter a formula that calculates the increase in value in cell C8 if 1 is entered in cell B8.

7. In cell D9, enter a formula that calculates the increase in value in cell C9 if 1 is entered in cell B9.

8. In cell D10, use the Sum button to calculate the sum of the numbers in the range D5:D9.

9. A potential buyer inquires about the estimated price of a home with the following specifications:

Square Footage:	**2000**
Number of Bathrooms:	**3**
Number of Car Garage:	**2**
On a Cul-de-Sac?	**No**
With a Swimming Pool?	**Yes**

In the range B5:B9, enter this data to determine the estimated home cost.

10. Insert a footer with your name in the left section and the current date in the right section.

11. Save, preview, print, and close the workbook.

CRITICAL THINKING

ACTIVITY 4–1

You have been offered three jobs, each with a different salary. You know the gross pay (the amount before taxes), but not the net pay (the amount you receive after taxes have been taken out). Assume you will have to pay 10% income tax and 7% Social Security tax. Develop a worksheet with formulas to calculate your net pay. The format should be similar to that shown in **Figure 4–14**.

Your worksheet should include the following:

■ In the range C7:C9, formulas that multiply the gross pay in column B by the 10% income tax.

■ In the range D7:D9, formulas that multiply the gross pay in column B by the 7% Social Security tax.

■ In the range E7:E9, formulas that subtract the amounts in columns C and D from the amount in column B.

Format the worksheet appropriately and attractively. Insert a header with your name and the current date. Save, preview, print, and close the workbook.

ACTIVITY 4–2

One of the most difficult aspects of working with formulas in a worksheet is getting them to calculate the proper value when you copy and move them into other cells. Copying and moving formulas requires an understanding of the differences between relative and absolute cell references. Research the differences between absolute and relative cell references in the Excel Help system. Write a brief explanation of the differences in your own words, and give an example of a situation in which you would use each type of cell reference. List the name(s) of the Help topics you used for reference.

	A	B	C	D	E
1	Potential Net Pay				
2					
3	Income Tax	10%			
4	Social Security Tax	7%			
5					
6	Job Offer	Gross Pay	Income Tax	Social Security Tax	Net Pay
7	1	$24,500			
8	2	$26,200			
9	3	$27,100			
10					

FIGURE 4–14   Format for net pay worksheet

LESSON 5

Using Functions

■ OBJECTIVES

Upon completion of this lesson, you should be able to:

- Identify the parts of a function.
- Enter formulas with functions.
- Use functions to solve mathematical problems.
- Use functions to solve statistical problems.
- Use functions to solve financial problems.
- Use logical functions to make decisions with worksheet data.
- Use functions to insert times and dates in a worksheet.
- Use text functions to format and display cell contents.

■ VOCABULARY

argument

date and time functions

financial functions

Formula AutoComplete

function

logical functions

mathematical functions

statistical functions

text functions

trigonometric functions

In the previous lesson, you created formulas that used cell references and constants. A formula can also contain a function. Functions often simplify formulas that are long or complex. Excel includes functions to perform complex calculations in specialized areas of mathematics, including statistics, logic, trigonometry, accounting, and finance. Function formulas are also used to display and determine dates and times. You will work with all these different types of functions in this lesson.

What Are Functions?

▶ **VOCABULARY**
function

argument

A *function* is a shorthand way to write an equation that performs a calculation. For example, the SUM function adds values in a range of cells. A formula with a function has three parts: an equal sign, a function name, and for most functions at least one argument, as shown in **Figure 5–1**. The equal sign identifies the cell contents as a formula. The function name identifies the operation to be performed. The *argument* is the value the function uses to perform a calculation, including a number, text, or a cell reference that acts as an operand. The argument follows the function name and is enclosed in parentheses. If a function contains more than one argument, commas separate the arguments.

FIGURE 5–1   Parts of a function

In the previous lesson, you used the Sum button to enter a formula with the SUM function, =SUM(F6:F11). The equal sign specifies that the cell entry is a formula. The function name SUM identifies the operation. Parentheses enclose the argument, which is the range of cells to add—in this case, cells F6 through F11. The function provides a simpler and faster way to enter the formula =F6+F7+F8+F9+F10+F11.

Entering Formulas with Functions

To enter a formula with a function, you need to do the following. First, start the formula with an equal sign. Second, select or enter the function you want to use. Third, select or enter the arguments. Finally, enter the completed formula. The results appear in the cell.

Because Excel includes so many functions, the best way to select a function is to use the Insert Function dialog box. To open the Insert Function dialog box, click the Insert Function button on the Formula Bar. From this dialog box, you can browse all of the available functions to select the one you want. First, click a category in the Or select a category box, and then click the function you want in the Select a function box. A brief description of the selected function appears near the bottom of the dialog box, as shown in **Figure 5–2**. Click OK. The Function Arguments dialog box then appears.

TIP

If you know the function you want to enter, you can click the appropriate category button in the Function Library group on the Formulas tab of the Ribbon, click the function you want in the menu that appears, and then enter the arguments in the Function Arguments dialog box.

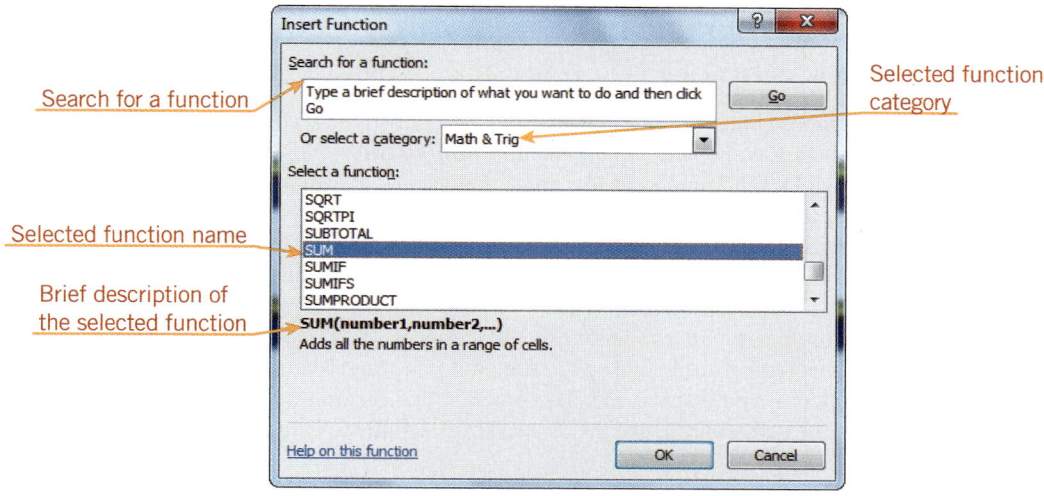

FIGURE 5–2   Insert Function dialog box

The Function Arguments dialog box, shown in **Figure 5–3**, provides a description of each argument you need to enter for the selected function. When an argument requires a cell or range, you can choose one of two ways to enter the reference. You can type the range directly in the appropriate argument box of the Function Arguments dialog box. Or, you can click in the appropriate argument box and then select the cell or range directly in the worksheet. When you select a range in the worksheet, the dialog box shrinks to show only the title bar and the argument box, so you can see more of the worksheet. It expands to the full size when you release the mouse button. You can also click the Collapse Dialog Box button on the right side of an argument box to shrink the dialog box so only its title bar and the argument box are displayed, and then click the Expand Dialog Box button to return the Function Arguments dialog box to its full size. After all the arguments are complete, click OK. The function is entered in the active cell.

> **EXTRA FOR EXPERTS**
>
> You can also use the Insert Function dialog box to find a specific function. In the Search for a function box, type a brief description of what you want to do. Then, click Go. A list of functions that match the description appears in the Select a function box. Double-click the appropriate function to open the Function Arguments dialog box.

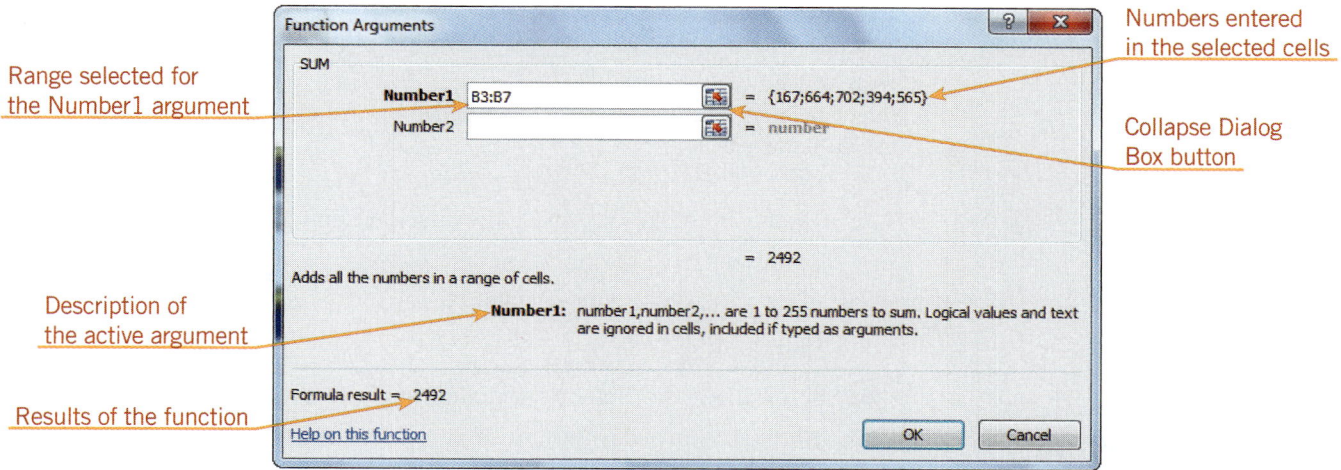

FIGURE 5–3   Function Arguments dialog box

Entering a Function Directly in a Cell Using Formula AutoComplete

▶ **VOCABULARY**

Formula AutoComplete

TIP

You can also use the arrow keys to select a function in the list, and then press the Tab key to enter the function.

You can also enter a formula with a function directly in a cell by typing an equal sign, the function name, and the argument. *Formula AutoComplete* helps you enter a formula with a valid function name and arguments, as shown in **Figure 5–4**. As you begin to type the function name, a list of function names appears below the active cell. The functions listed match the letters you have typed. For example, when you type *=s*, all functions that begin with the letter *s* appear in the list box, such as SEARCH, SECON, and SERISSUM. When you type *=su*, the list narrows to show only functions that begin with the letters *su*, such as SUBSTITUTE, SUBTOTAL, and SUM. Continue typing until you see the function you want. Then, double-click the name of the function you want to use. The function and its arguments appear in a ScreenTip below the cell. You can use the ScreenTip as a guide to enter the necessary arguments.

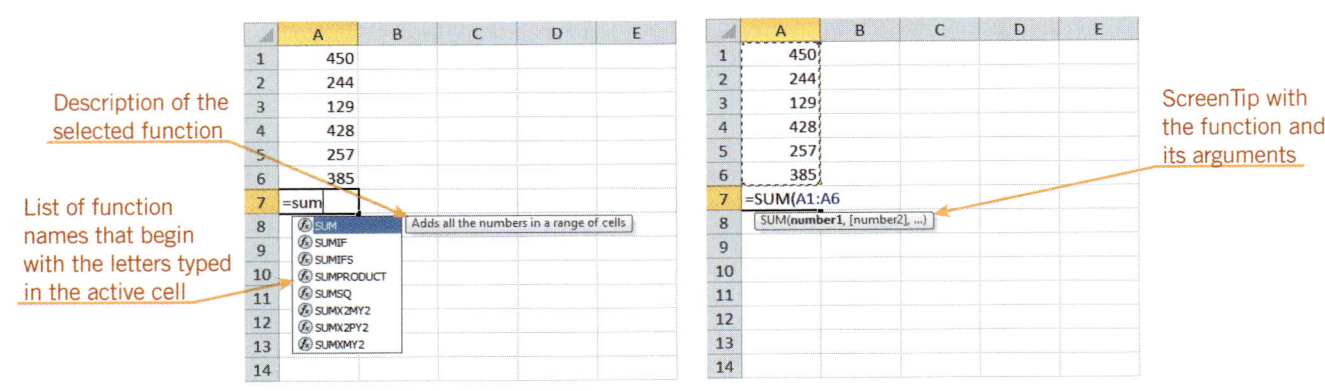

FIGURE 5–4   Formula AutoComplete

Step-by-Step 5.1

1. Open the **Functions.xlsx** workbook from the drive and folder where your Data Files are stored.

2. Save the workbook as **Functions Worksheet** followed by your initials.

3. Click cell **B10**.

4. On the Formula Bar, click the **Insert Function** button [fx]. The Insert Function dialog box appears.

5. Next to the Or select a category box, click the **arrow**, and then click **Math & Trig**.

6. Scroll down the **Select a function** list, and then click **SUM**. The SUM function and a description of its purpose appear below the Select a function box, as shown in Figure 5–2.

7. Click **OK**. The Function Arguments dialog box appears with a range reference selected in the Number1 box. The Number1 argument is the range of cells whose values you want to add. Excel tried to "guess" which cells you want to add. You want to add a different range.

📇 **EXTRA FOR EXPERTS**

The SUM function can total the values stored in up to 255 nonadjacent cells or ranges. Enter additional ranges in the Number2 through Number255 boxes.

8. In the worksheet, select the range **B3:B7**. The Function Arguments dialog box collapses when you click a cell in the worksheet and expands when you release the mouse button. The value that will appear in cell B10, 2492, appears below the SUM function section and at the bottom of the dialog box, as shown in Figure 5–3.

9. Click **OK**. The formula in cell B10 is =SUM(B3:B7). The formula appears in the Formula Bar, and the results of the formula (2492) appear in cell B10.

10. Save the workbook, and leave it open for the next Step-by-Step.

> **TIP**
>
> You can also enter the formula with the SUM function in cell B10 by typing *=SUM(B3:B7)* or clicking the Sum button in the Editing group on the Home tab.

Types of Functions

Excel provides many functions you can use in formulas. Each function has a different purpose. The functions are organized by category, such as Math & Trig, Statistical, Financial, Logical, Date & Time, and Text. The next sections introduce some of the most common functions in each of these categories.

Mathematical and Trigonometric Functions

Mathematical functions and *trigonometric functions* manipulate quantitative data in a worksheet. Some mathematical operations, such as addition, subtraction, multiplication, and division, do not require functions. However, mathematical and trigonometric functions are particularly useful when you need to determine values such as logarithms, factorials, sines, cosines, tangents, and absolute values.

You already used a mathematical and trigonometric function when you created a formula with the SUM function. **Table 5–1** describes two other mathematical functions, the square root and rounding functions, as well as one trigonometric function, the natural logarithm. Notice that the rounding operation requires two arguments, which are separated by a comma.

> ▶ **VOCABULARY**
> **mathematical functions**
> **trigonometric functions**

TABLE 5–1   Commonly used mathematical and trigonometric functions

FUNCTION	RETURNS
SQRT(number)	The square root of the number in the argument. For example, =SQRT(C4) returns the square root of the value in cell C4.
ROUND(number,num_digits)	The number in the first argument rounded to the number of decimal places designated in the second argument. For example, =ROUND(14.23433,2) returns 14.23, which rounds the number in the first argument to two decimal places. If the second argument is a negative number, the first argument is rounded to the left of the decimal point. For example, =ROUND(142.3433,–2) returns 100.
LN(number)	The natural logarithm of a number. For example, =LN(50) returns 3.912023.

Step-by-Step 5.2

1. Click cell **B11**. On the Formula Bar, click the **Insert Function** button 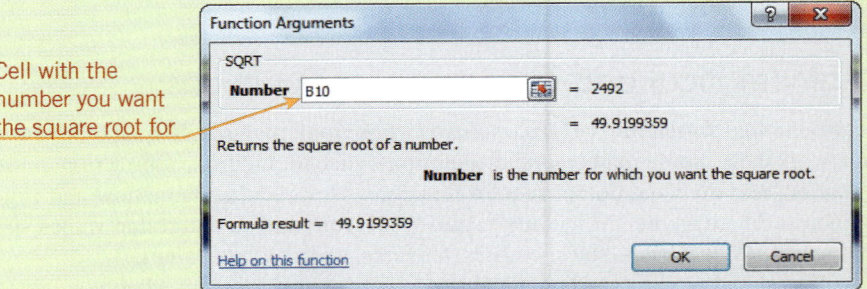. The Insert Function dialog box appears.

2. Next to the Or select a category box, click the **arrow**, and then click **Math & Trig**, if it is not already selected.

3. Click the **Select a function** box, and then press the **S** key five times until *SQRT* is selected. Read the description of the function.

4. Click **OK**. The Function Arguments dialog box appears. Read the description of the argument.

5. In the Number box, type **B10**. You want to calculate the square root of the value in cell B10, which is 2492, as shown to the right of the Number box. The number that will appear in cell B11, 49.9199359, appears under the function and at the bottom of the dialog box next to Formula result =, as shown in **Figure 5–5**.

FIGURE 5–5
SQRT function argument

Cell with the
number you want
the square root for

6. Click **OK**. The formula entered in cell B11 is =SQRT(B10), which calculates the square root of the value in cell B10—2492—and results in the value 49.9199359.

7. Click cell **B12**. On the Formula Bar, click the **Insert Function** button . The Insert Function dialog box appears with Math & Trig selected in the Or select a category box.

8. Click the **Select a function** box, and then press the **R** key five times to select ROUND.

9. Read the function's description. Click **OK**. The Function Arguments dialog box appears.

10. Read the description of the first argument. In the Number box, type **B11**.

11. Press the **Tab** key to place the insertion point in the Num_digits box. Read the description of the second argument.

12. Type **2**. The formula results appear below the function and at the bottom of the dialog box, as shown in **Figure 5–6**.

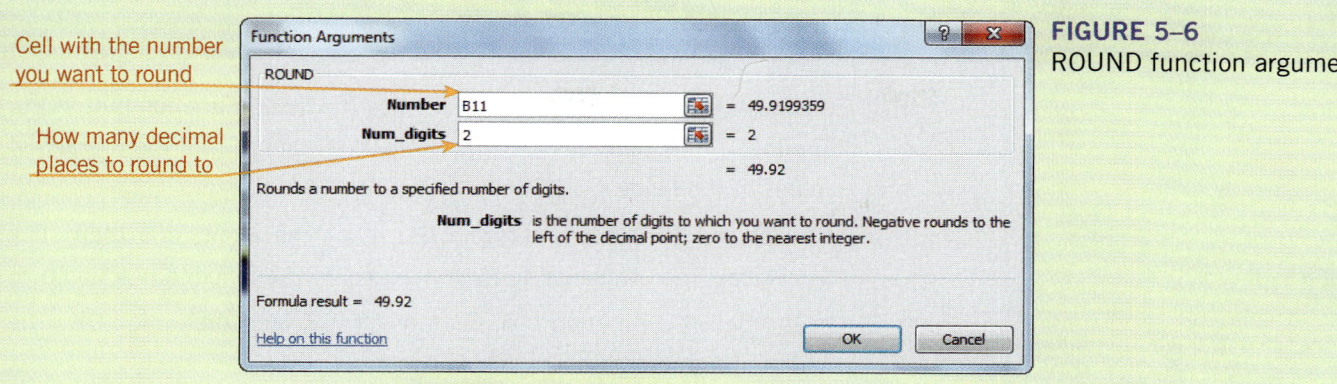

Cell with the number
you want to round

How many decimal
places to round to

FIGURE 5–6
ROUND function arguments

13. Click **OK**. The formula in cell B12 is =ROUND(B11,2), which rounds the value in cell B11 to two digits, displays the results of 49.92.

14. Save the workbook, and leave it open for the next Step-by-Step.

Statistical Functions

Statistical functions are used to describe quantities of data. For example, statistical functions can determine the average, standard deviation, or variance of a range of data. Statistical functions can also determine the number of values in a range, the largest value in a range, and the smallest value in a range. **Table 5–2** describes some of the statistical functions available in Excel. All the statistical functions contain a range for the argument. You can include multiple ranges by entering additional arguments. The range is the body of numbers the statistics will describe.

▶ **VOCABULARY**
statistical functions

TABLE 5–2   Commonly used statistical functions

FUNCTION	RETURNS
AVERAGE(number1,number2...)	The average (or mean) of the range; for example, =AVERAGE(E4:E9) returns the average of the numbers in the range E4:E9
COUNT(value1,value2...)	The number of cells in the range that contain numbers; for example, =COUNT(D6:D21) returns 16 if all the cells in the range contain numbers
COUNTA(value1,value2...)	The number of cells in the range that are not empty; for example, =COUNT(B4:B15) returns 11 if all the cells in the range contain data
MAX(number1,number2...)	The largest number in the range
MIN(number1,number2...)	The smallest number in the range
STDEV.P(number1,number2...)	The estimated standard deviation of the numbers in the range
VAR.P(number1,number2...)	The estimated variance of the numbers in the range

Step-by-Step 5.3

1. Click cell **B15**. On the Formula Bar, click the **Insert Function** button . The Insert Function dialog box appears. You want to find the average of values in the range B3:B7.

2. Next to the Or select a category box, click the **arrow**, and then click **Statistical**. The Statistical functions appear in the Select a function box.

3. In the Select a function box, click **AVERAGE**, and then click **OK**. The Function Arguments dialog box appears.

4. Next to the Number1 box, click the **Collapse Dialog Box** button. The Function Arguments dialog box shrinks to its title bar and Number1 box.

5. In the worksheet, drag to select the range **B3:B7**. The range reference appears in the Number1 box, as shown in **Figure 5–7**.

> **TIP**
>
> You can also enter a formula with the AVERAGE, COUNT, MAX, or MIN function in a selected cell by clicking the Sum button arrow in the Editing group on the Home tab, clicking the function name, selecting the appropriate range, and then pressing the Enter key.

FIGURE 5–7
Collapsed Function Arguments dialog box

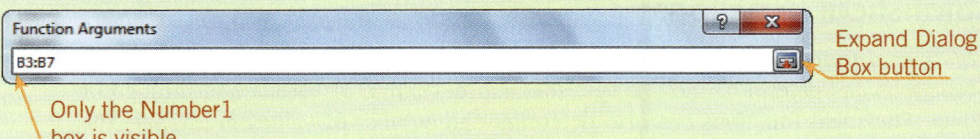

Expand Dialog Box button

Only the Number1 box is visible

6. Click the **Expand Dialog Box** button. The Function Arguments dialog box expands to its full size, as shown in **Figure 5–8**.

FIGURE 5–8
Expanded Function Arguments dialog box

Selected range in the Number1 box

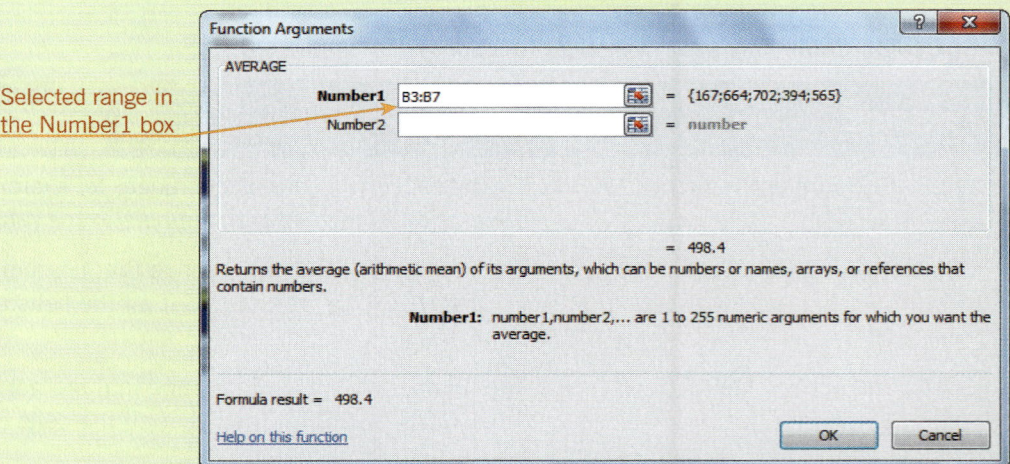

7. Click **OK**. The average of the values in the range B3:B7, which is 498.4, appears in cell B15.

8. Click cell **B16**. On the Formula Bar, click the **Insert Function** button. You want to find how many cells in the range B3:B7 contain numbers.

9. In the Or select a category box, click **Statistical**, if it is not already selected. In the Select a function box, double-click **COUNT**. The Function Arguments dialog box appears.

10. In the Value1 box, enter **B3:B7**, and then click **OK**. The number of cells in the range B3:B7 that contain numbers is 5.

11. Click cell **B17**, and then enter **=MAX(B3:B7)**. The largest number in the range B3:B7 is 702.

12. Click cell **B18**, and then enter **=MIN(B3:B7)**. The smallest number in the range B3:B7 is 167.

13. Click cell **B19**, and then enter **=STDEV.P(B3:B7)**. The standard deviation of the range B3:B7 is 196.9960406.

14. Click cell **B20**, and then enter **=VAR.P(B3:B7)**. The variance of the range B3:B7 is 38807.44.

15. Save the workbook, and leave it open for the next Step-by-Step.

Financial Functions

Financial functions are used to analyze loans and investments. Some commonly used financial functions are future value, present value, and payment, which are described in **Table 5–3**. Note that for these functions to return the correct value, the payment and the interest rate must have the same time period. For example, the payment period is usually expressed in months, whereas interest rates are commonly expressed in years. So, if the payment period is monthly, you must divide the annual interest rate by 12 to determine the monthly rate.

▶ **VOCABULARY**
financial functions

TABLE 5–3   Commonly used financial functions

FUNCTION	RETURNS
FV(rate,nper,pmt,pv,type)	The future value of an investment based on equal payments (third argument), at a fixed interest rate (first argument), for a specified number of periods (second argument). (The fourth and fifth arguments for the present value of the investment and the timing of the payments are optional.) For example, =FV(.08,5,–100) determines the future value of five $100 payments earning an 8% interest rate at the end of five years.
PV(rate,nper,pmt,fv,type)	The present value of a loan or an investment based on equal payments (third argument), at a fixed interest rate (first argument), for a specified number of payments (second argument). (The fourth and fifth arguments for the future value of the investment and the timing of the payments are optional.) For example, =PV(.1,5,–500) displays the current value of five payments of $500 at a 10% interest rate.
PMT(rate,nper,pv,fv,type)	The equal payments needed to repay a loan (third argument), at a fixed interest rate (first argument), in a specified number of periods (second argument). (The fourth and fifth arguments for the future value of the loan and the timing of the payments are optional.) For example, =PMT(.01,36,10000) displays the monthly payment needed to repay a $10,000 loan at a 1% monthly interest rate (12% annual interest rate divided by 12 months), for 36 months (three years multiplied by 12 months).

TECHNOLOGY CAREERS

Scientists use Excel workbooks to help them as they conduct research. They record collected data in worksheets. Then they use statistical function formulas to analyze experimental results.

Step-by-Step 5.4

1. Click cell **B24**, and then enter **.015**. The annual interest rate of 1.5% appears in the cell.

2. Click cell **B25**, and then enter **6**, which is the number of payment periods—one payment each year for six years.

3. Click cell **B26**, and then enter **–250**. The annual payment of $(250.00) appears in the cell.

4. Click cell **B27**. On the Formula Bar, click the **Insert Function** button 𝑓𝑥. In the Insert Function dialog box, next to the Or select a category box, click the **arrow**, and then click **Financial**. In the Select a function box, click **FV**. Click **OK**.

5. In the Rate box, type **B24**, the cell with the annual interest rate. In the Nper box, type **B25**, the cell that contains the number of payment periods. In the Pmt box, type **B26**, the cell that contains the annual payment amount. See **Figure 5–9**.

TIP

A negative number indicates a payment; a positive number indicates income. In this case, you use a negative number because you are making a payment to the bank.

FIGURE 5–9
FV function arguments

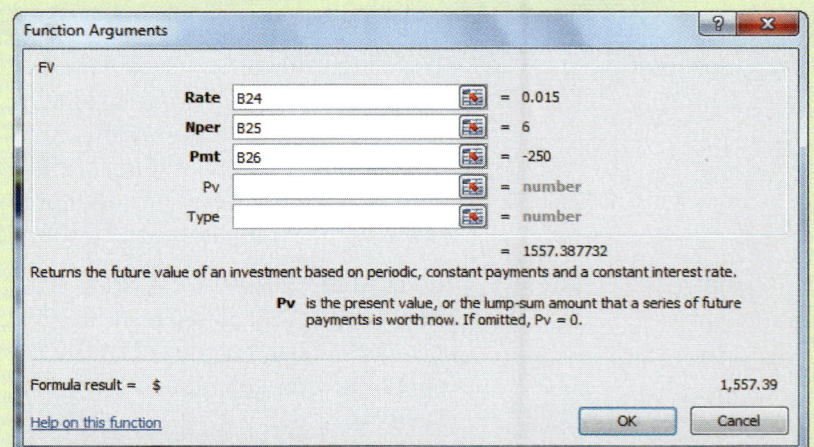

6. Click **OK**. As you can see in cell B27, the amount in the savings account will have grown to $1,557.39 after six years.

7. Click cell **B29**, and then enter **2.5**. The annual interest rate of 2.5% appears in the cell.

8. Click cell **B30**, and then enter **8**, which is the number of payment periods—one payment each year for eight years.

9. Click cell **B31**, and then enter **–210**. The annual payment of $(210.00) appears in the cell. (Remember, a negative number indicates a payment; a positive number indicates income. In this case, you use a negative number because you are making a payment.)

10. Click cell **B32**, and then enter **=PV(B29,B30,B31)** using Formula AutoComplete to help you enter the function accurately. The delayed payments are more profitable because the present value, $1,505.73, is greater than the immediate lump sum of $1,200.

11. Click cell **B34**, and then enter **1**. The monthly interest rate of 1.0% appears in the cell.

12. Click cell **B35**, and then enter **=5*12** to determine the number of monthly payment periods (the number of years, 5, multiplied by 12 months). The number of monthly payment periods, 60, appears in the cell.

13. Click cell **B36**, and then enter **6000**, which is the amount of the loan (the principal amount).

14. Click cell **B37**, and then enter **=PMT(B34,B35,B36)**, using Formula AutoComplete to help you enter the function accurately. The monthly payment ($133.47) appears in the cell in red. The parentheses around the number indicate that it is a negative number, and a payment.

> **TIP**
>
> The monthly interest rate is determined by dividing the annual interest rate by 12 months. In this case, the annual interest rate of 12% divided by 12 months equals 1%, which you entered in cell B34.

15. Click cell **B38**, and then enter **=(B37*B35)+B36** to determine the interest you will pay over the life of the loan. The formula multiples the monthly payment returned by the PMT function in cell B37 by the number of monthly payments stored in cell B35, and then adds the loan amount in cell B36. Because the payments are negative, you need to add the loan amount to calculate the difference between the total payments and the total principal. Under the conditions of this loan, you will pay a total of $2,008.00 in interest over the life of the loan, as shown in **Figure 5–10**.

FIGURE 5–10
Financial functions

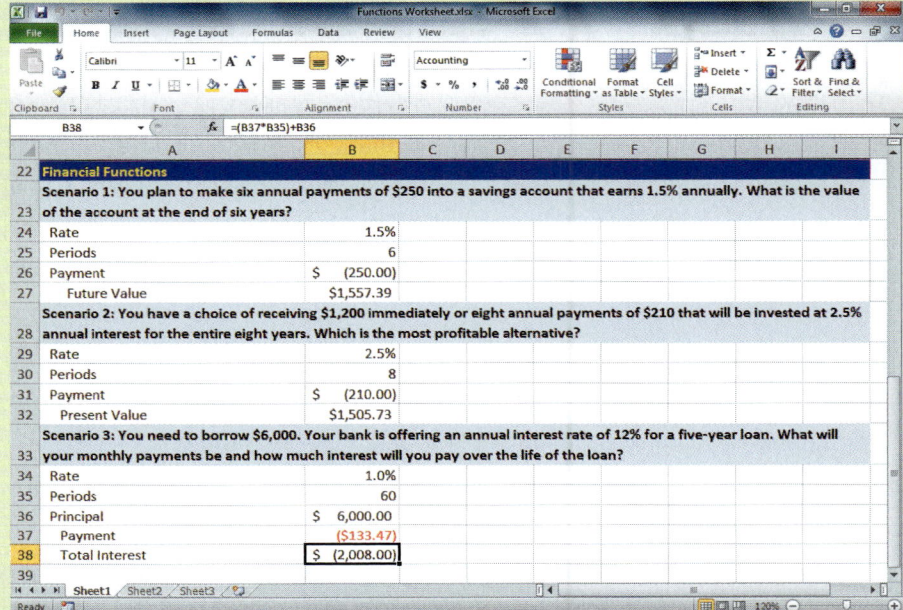

16. Insert a header with your name and the current date. Save, print, and close the workbook.

Logical Functions

Logical functions, such as the IF function, display text or values if certain conditions exist. In the IF function, the first argument sets a condition for comparison, called a *logical test*. The second argument determines the value that appears in the cell if the logical test is true. The third argument determines the value that appears in the cell if the logical test is false.

For example, a teacher might use the IF function to determine whether a student has passed or failed a course. The formula =IF(C4>60,"PASS","FAIL") returns *PASS* if the value in cell C4 is greater than 60; otherwise the formula returns *FAIL*.

Table 5–4 describes the IF, AND, OR, NOT, and IFERROR functions.

TIP

You must use quotation marks to enclose the text you want the IF function to return in the second and third arguments. For example, =IF(B10<100,"Low Result","High Result").

TABLE 5–4   Commonly used logical functions

FUNCTION	RETURNS
IF(logical_test,value_if_true,value_if_false)	One value if the condition in the logical test is true, and another value if the condition in the logical test is false; for example, =IF(2+2=4, "Over", "Under") returns *Over*
AND(logical1,logical2,...)	TRUE if all of the arguments are true, and FALSE if any or all of the arguments are false; for example, =AND(1+1=2,1+2=3) returns *TRUE*, but =AND(1+1=2,1+2=4) returns *FALSE*
OR(logical1,logical2,...)	TRUE if any of the arguments are true, and FALSE if none of the arguments is true; for example, =OR(1+1=2,1+2=3) returns *TRUE*, and =OR(1+1=2,1+2=4) returns *TRUE*, but =OR(1+1=3,1+2=4) returns *FALSE*
NOT(logical)	TRUE if the argument is false, and FALSE if the argument is true; for example, =NOT(2+2=1) returns *TRUE*, but =NOT(2+2=4) returns *FALSE*
IFERROR(value,value_if_error)	The formula results if the first argument contains no error, and the specified value if the argument is incorrect; for example, =IFERROR(2+2=1, "Error in calculation") returns *Error in calculation*

Step-by-Step 5.5

1. Open the **Reynolds.xlsx** workbook from the drive and folder where your Data Files are stored.

2. Save the workbook as **Reynolds Optical** followed by your initials.

3. Click cell **D6**, and then type **=IF(B6<5,22.5,0)**. This formula returns 22.50 (the shipping fee) if the quantity in cell B6 is less than 5. If the quantity in cell B6 is not less than 5, then the formula returns 0.

4. Press the **Enter** key. This order has no shipping fee because the order quantity is six, more than the five cartons needed for free shipping.

5. Copy the formula in cell **D6** to the range **D7:D15**, and then click cell **A18**. The shipping fee is calculated for all the orders, as shown in **Figure 5–11**.

FIGURE 5–11
Shipping fee calculated with the IF function

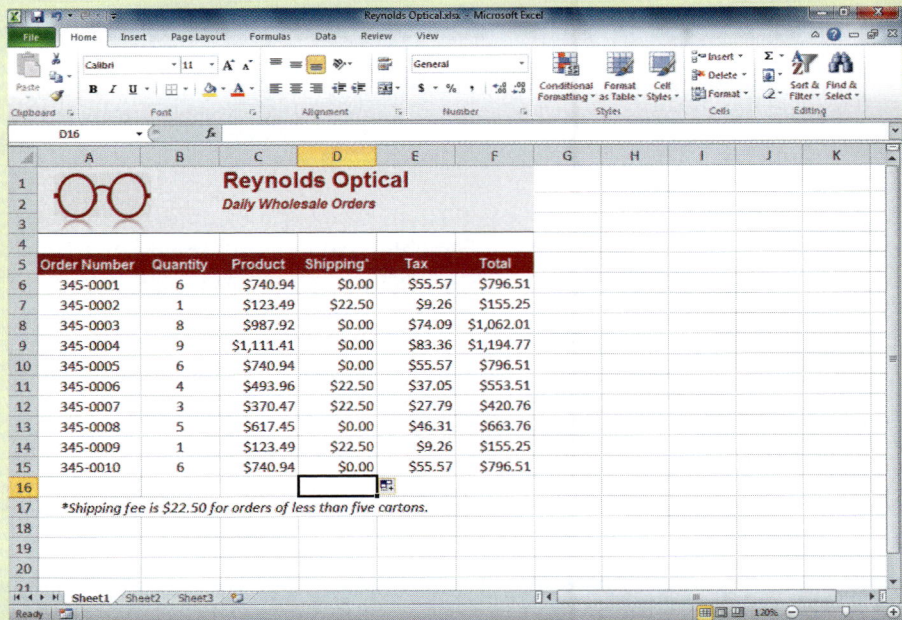

6. Insert a footer that includes your name and the current date. Save, print, and close the workbook.

Date and Time Functions

> **VOCABULARY**
> **date and time functions**

Functions can also be used to insert dates and times in a worksheet. For example, *date and time functions* can be used to convert serial numbers to a month, a day, or a year. A date function can also be used to insert the current date or the current date and time. **Table 5–5** describes the DATE, NOW, and TODAY functions.

TABLE 5–5   Commonly used date and time functions

FUNCTION	RETURNS
DATE(year,month,day)	The date specified in the year, month, and day arguments, which are entered as numbers. For example, =DATE(2013,5,23) returns 5/23/2013.
NOW()	The current date and time based on the computer's date and time settings. For example, =NOW() returns the current date and time, such as 5/23/2013 22:05. This function has no arguments.
TODAY()	The current date based on the computer's date setting and formatted as a date. For example, =TODAY() returns the current date, such as 5/23/2013. This function has no arguments.

Text Functions

Text functions are used to format and display cell contents. A text function can be used to convert text in a cell to all uppercase or lowercase letters. Text functions can also be used to repeat data contained in another cell. These functions are described in **Table 5–6**. Note that if you enter text instead of a cell reference in the argument, the text must be enclosed within quotation marks.

▶ **VOCABULARY**
text functions

TABLE 5–6   Commonly used text functions

FUNCTION	OPERATION
PROPER(text)	Converts the first letter of each word in the specified cell to uppercase and the rest to lowercase.
LOWER(text)	Converts all letters in the specified cell to lowercase.
UPPER(text)	Converts all letters in the specified cell to uppercase.
SUBSTITUTE(text,old_text,new_text,instance_num)	Replaces existing text (the second argument) in a specified cell (the first argument) with new text (the third argument). If you omit the optional fourth argument, instance_num, every occurrence of the text is replaced. For example, =SUBSTITUTE(C2,"Income","Revenue") replaces every instance of the word *Income* in cell C2 with the word *Revenue*.
REPT(text,number_times)	Repeats the text (first argument) in the specified cell a specified number of times (second argument). For example, =REPT(B6,3) repeats the text in cell B6 three times.

Step-by-Step 5.6

1. Open the **Finances.xlsx** workbook from the drive and folder where your Data Files are stored.

2. In cell **A1**, replace the word *NAME* with your name.

3. In cell **B13**, enter **=NOW()**. The current date and time appear in the cell.

4. Click cell **B13**. On the Home tab, in the Number group, click the **Number Format arrow**, and then click **General**. The date changes to the serial number Excel uses to express the current date and time.

5. On the Home tab, in the Number group, click the **Number Format arrow**, and then click **Short Date**. The date changes to the form 5/23/2013.

6. On the Quick Access Toolbar, click the **Undo** button 🔄 twice. The current date and time in cell B13 return to their original format.

7. Click cell **B14**. You want to repeat the text in cell A1 in cell B14.

8. Click the **Formulas** tab on the Ribbon. In the Function Library group, click the **Text** button, and then click **REPT**. The Function Arguments dialog box appears.

9. In the Text box, enter **A1**. In the Number_times box, enter **1**. The contents of cell A1 will be repeated once in cell B14.

10. Click **OK**. The title in cell A1 is repeated in cell B14.

11. Save the workbook using the contents of cell B14 as the file name. Your screen should look similar to **Figure 5–12**.

FIGURE 5–12
Date & Time and
Text functions

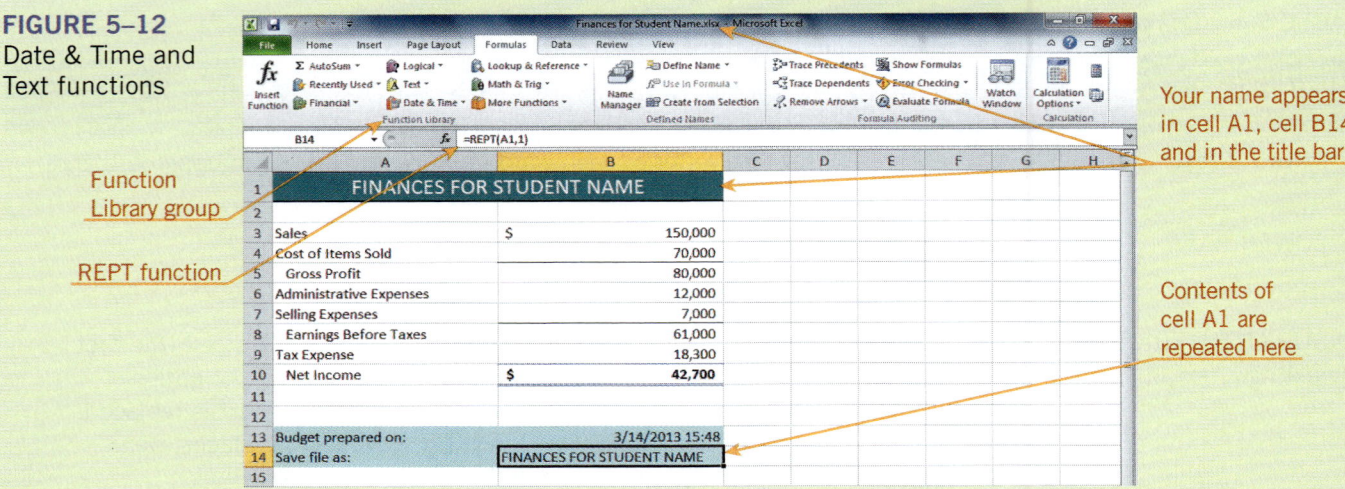

12. Print and close the workbook.

SUMMARY

In this lesson, you learned:

■ A function is a shorthand way to write an equation that performs a calculation. A formula with a function has three parts: an equal sign, a function name, and for most functions one argument, which acts as an operand.

■ The best way to select a function is from the Insert Function dialog box. The Function Arguments dialog box provides a description of each argument you enter for the function.

■ When you type a formula with a function directly in a worksheet cell, Formula AutoComplete helps you enter a formula with a valid function name and arguments.

■ Functions can be used to perform mathematical, statistical, financial, and logical operations. They can also be used to insert and calculate dates and times and to format text.

■ VOCABULARY REVIEW

Define the following terms:

argument	function	statistical functions
date and time functions	logical functions	text functions
financial functions	mathematical functions	trigonometric functions
Formula AutoComplete		

REVIEW QUESTIONS

TRUE / FALSE

Circle T if the statement is true or F if the statement is false.

T   F   **1.**   Formulas with functions have three parts: an equal sign, a function name, and usually an argument.

T   F   **2.**   The argument identifies the function to be performed.

T   F   **3.**   You select the function you want to use in the Function Arguments dialog box.

T   F   **4.**   The COUNTA function returns the number of cells in the range identified in the argument that contain data.

T   F   **5.**   The OR function displays one value if the specified condition is true and a different value if the condition is false.

WRITTEN QUESTIONS

Write a brief answer to each of the following questions.

1. What is a function?

2. Write the formula with a function that would add all the values in cells D6, D7, and D8.

3. Explain what happens when you click the Insert Function button on the Formula Bar.

4. What does the SQRT function return?

5. What does the TODAY function return?

FILL IN THE BLANK

Complete the following sentences by writing the correct word or words in the blanks provided.

1. The _____ is (are) enclosed in parentheses in a formula with a function.

2. The _____ dialog box specifies arguments to be included in the function.

3. _____ functions manipulate quantitative data in a worksheet.

4. _____ functions are used to analyze loans and investments.

5. _____ functions display text or values if certain conditions exist.

■ PROJECTS

If you have a SAM 2010 user profile, your instructor may have assigned an autogradable version of the indicated project. If so, log into the SAM 2010 Web site at *www.cengage.com/sam2010* to download the instruction and start files.

PROJECT 5–1

Write the appropriate formula to perform each of the described operations. Refer to Tables 5–1 through 5–6 to help you determine the function and its arguments.

_____ 1. Add all the values in the range F14:F42.

_____ 2. Determine the largest value in the range J45:J102.

_____ 3. Determine the average of the values in the range L29:L40.

_____ 4. Determine the smallest value in the range X14:X92.

_____ 5. Determine the standard deviation of the values in the range K4:K33.

_____ 6. Determine the yearly payments on a $4,500 loan at 8% for 7 years.

_____ 7. Determine the value of a savings account at the end of 5 years, after making five yearly payments of $475 each and earning 3%.

_____ 8. Round the value in cell E3 to the tenths place.

_____ 9. Determine the present value of a pension plan that will pay you 20 yearly payments of $7,000 each; the current rate of return is 7.5%.

_____ 10. Determine the square root of 375.

_____ 11. Determine the variance of the values in the range G9:G35.

_____ 12. Determine how many cells in the range H7:H24 contain numbers.

SAM PROJECT 5–2

1. Open the **National.xlsx** workbook from the drive and folder where your Data Files are stored.

2. Save the workbook as **National Bank** followed by your initials.

3. In cell B12, enter the PMT function to calculate the yearly payment for borrowers. The lending rate will be entered in cell B8, the term of the loan will be entered in cell B10, and the loan principal (or present value) will be entered in cell B6. (The formula results are *#NUM!*, indicating a number error because you haven't entered data in the argument's cell references yet.)

4. A potential borrower inquires about the payments on a $6,500 loan for four years. The current lending rate is 6%. Determine the yearly payment on the loan. (The number in cell B12 is a negative number because this amount must be paid.)

5. Insert a header with your name and the current date.

6. Print the portion of the worksheet that pertains to the loan (the range A2:C15) to give to the potential borrower.

7. In cell B25, enter the FV function to calculate the future value of periodic payments for depositors. The interest rate will be entered in cell B23, the term of the payments will be entered in cell B21, and the yearly payments will be entered in cell B19. (The formula results show *$0.00*, because you haven't entered data in the argument's cell references yet.)

8. A potential depositor is starting a college fund for her child. She inquires about the value of yearly deposits of $2,575 at the end of 18 years. The current interest rate is 4.5%. Determine the future value of the deposits. (Remember to enter the deposit as a negative number because the depositor must pay this amount.)

9. Print the portion of the worksheet that pertains to the investment (the range A15:C27) to give to the potential depositor.

10. Save and close the workbook.

PROJECT 5–3

1. Open the **Exam.xlsx** workbook from the drive and folder where your Data Files are stored.

2. Save the workbook as **Exam Scores** followed by your initials.

3. In cell B25, enter a formula with a function to determine the number of students who took the examination.

4. In cell B26, enter a formula with a function to determine the average exam grade.

5. In cell B27, enter a formula with a function to determine the highest exam grade.

6. In cell B28, enter a formula with a function to determine the lowest exam grade.

7. In cell B29, enter a formula with a function to determine the standard deviation of the exam grades.

8. Format cells B26 and B29 to display two digits to the right of the decimal.

9. Insert a header with your name and the current date. Save, print, and close the workbook.

PROJECT 5–4

The Tucson Coyotes have just completed seven preseason professional basketball games. Coach Patterson will soon be entering a press conference in which he is expected to talk about the team's performance for the upcoming season. Coach Patterson wants to be well informed about player performance before entering the press conference.

Part 1

1. Open the **Coyotes.xlsx** workbook from the drive and folder where your Data Files are stored.

2. Save the workbook as **Coyotes Stats** followed by your initials.

3. In cell J6, enter a function that adds the values in the range B6:I6.

4. Copy the formula in cell J6 to the range J7:J12.

5. In cell J19, enter a function that adds the values in the range B19:I19.

6. Copy the formula in cell J19 to the range J20:J25.

7. In cell B13, enter a function that averages the game points in the range B6:B12.

8. In cell B14, enter a function that calculates the standard deviation of the game points in the range B6:B12.

9. In cell B15, enter a function that counts the number of cells that contain data in the range B6:B12.

10. Copy the formulas in the range B13:B15 to the range C13:I15.

11. In cell B26, enter a function that averages the rebounds in the range B19:B25.

12. In cell B27, enter a function that calculates the standard deviation of the rebounds in the range B19:B25.

13. In cell B28, enter a function that counts the number of cells that contain data in the range B19:B25.

14. Copy the formulas in the range B26:B28 to the range C26:I28.

15. Insert a footer with your name and the current date. Save and print the workbook, and leave it open.

Part 2

Based on the Coyotes Stats workbook you prepared, indicate in the blanks the names of the players who are likely to be mentioned in the following interview. When you have finished filling in the blanks, close the workbook.

Reporter: You have had a very successful preseason. Three players seem to be providing the leadership needed for a winning record.

Patterson: Basketball teams win by scoring points. It's no secret that we rely on (1) _____, (2) _____, and (3) _____ to get those points. All three average at least 10 points per game.

Reporter: One player seems to have a problem with consistency.

Patterson: (4) _____ has his good games and his bad games. He is a young player and we have been working with him. As the season progresses, I think you will find him to be a more reliable offensive talent.

(*Hint*: One indication of consistent scoring is the standard deviation. A high standard deviation might indicate high fluctuation of points from game to game. A low standard deviation might indicate that the scoring level is relatively consistent.)

Reporter: What explains the fact that (5) _____ is both an effective scorer and your leading rebounder?

Patterson: He is a perceptive player. When playing defense, he is constantly planning how to get the ball back to the other side of the court.

Reporter: Preseason injuries can be heartbreaking. How has this affected the team?

Patterson: (6) _____ has not played since being injured in the game against Kansas City. He is an asset to the team. We are still waiting to hear from the doctors whether he will be back soon.

Reporter: It is the end of the preseason. That is usually a time when teams make cuts. Of your healthy players, (7) _____ is the lowest scorer. Will you let him go before the beginning of the regular season?

Patterson: I don't like to speculate on cuts or trades before they are made. We'll just have to wait and see.

PROJECT 5–5

1. Open the **Golf.xlsx** workbook from the drive and folder where your Data Files are stored.

2. Save the workbook as **Golf Tryouts** followed by your initials. A player must average a score of less than 76 to qualify for the team.

3. In cell I5, enter a function that displays *Made* if the average score in cell H5 is less than 76 and *Cut* if the score is not less than 76. (*Hint*: The IF function has three arguments. The first argument is the logical test that determines whether the value in cell H5 is less than 76. The second argument is the text that appears if the statement is true. The third argument is the text that appears if the statement is false. Because the items to be displayed are words rather than numbers, they must be entered within quotation marks.)

4. Copy the formula from cell I5 to the range I6:I16.

5. In cell B21, enter a function that displays today's date.

6. Click cell B22, and then enter your name.

7. Save, print, and close the workbook.

PROJECT 5–6

1. Open the **Xanthan.xlsx** workbook from the drive and folder where your Data Files are stored.

2. Save the workbook as **Xanthan Promotion** followed by your initials.

3. In cell B7, enter **75** as the supervisor rating of leadership potential. In cell B8, enter **80** as the supervisor rating of understanding of duties. In cell B9, enter **90** as the supervisor rating of willingness to work hard.

4. In cell B12, enter a function that determines the average of the values in the range B7:B10.

5. Format cell B12 in the Number format with no decimal places.

6. In cell B13, enter an IF function that displays *Promotion* if the average score in cell B12 is greater than or equal to 80 and *No Promotion* if the average score is less than 80.

7. Format the contents of cell B13 as bold and centered.

8. In cell B10, enter each of the following test scores, one at a time, and watch the average score: **70**, **78**, **82**, **85**, and **90**. Which scores will result in a promotion?

9. Insert a footer with your name and the current date. Save, print, and close the workbook.

CRITICAL THINKING

ACTIVITY 5–1

You are considering purchasing a car and want to compare prices offered by different dealerships. Some dealerships have cars that include the accessories you want; others need to add the accessories for an additional price. Prepare a worksheet similar to the one shown in **Figure 5–13**.

Perform the following operations to provide information that will be useful to making the car purchase decision.

- In the range D3:D7, enter formulas that add the values in column B to the values in column C.

- In cell D9, enter a function that determines the highest price in the range D3:D7.

- In cell D10, enter a function that determines the lowest price in the range D3:D7.

- In cell D11, enter a function that determines the average price in the range D3:D7.

	A	B	C	D
1	**Price Comparison by Dealership**			
2	**Dealer**	**Base Price**	**Accessories**	**Total**
3	Bernalillo New and Used	$ 19,900	$ 1,600	
4	Los Alamos Auto	$ 23,050	$ 2,300	
5	Mountain Auto Sales	$ 26,000	$ 2,200	
6	Sandia Car Sales	$ 27,900	$ 1,200	
7	Truchas Truck & Auto	$ 26,500	$ 3,000	
8				
9			Highest Price	
10			Lowest Price	
11			Average Price	

FIGURE 5–13

ACTIVITY 5–2

The Insert Function dialog box contains a Search for a function box, as shown in **Figure 5–14**. When you enter a brief description of what you want to do and click Go, Excel will list functions best suited for the task you want to perform.

Suppose you are preparing a large worksheet in which all cells in a range should contain data. You want to enter a function near the end of a range that displays the number of cells in the range that are blank. If a number other than zero appears as the function result, you will know that you must search for the cell or cells that are empty and enter the appropriate data.

Create a new workbook, and then open the Insert Function dialog box. Enter a description in the Search for a function box that will find a function to count the number of empty cells in a range. If more than one function is suggested, click each function in the Select a function box and read the description of the function that appears below the box. Which function is most appropriate to complete this task?

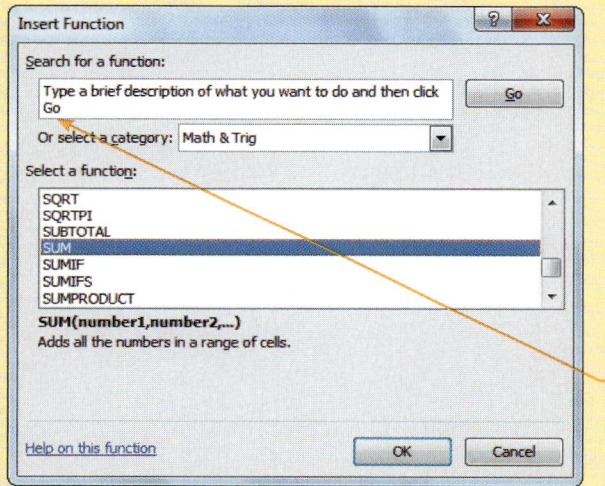

FIGURE 5–14

ACTIVITY 5–3

A manufacturing company prepares a budget each month. At the end of the month, the Accounting Department prepares a report similar to the one shown in **Figure 5–15**, which compares the actual amount spent to the budgeted amount.

Write an IF function you can use to draw attention to an item that exceeded its budget.

	A	B	C	D
1	**Manufacturing Expense Report**			
2		**Budget**	**Actual**	**Variance**
3	Labor	$64,000	$72,000	($8,000)
4	Raw Material A	$48,000	$47,900	$100
5	Raw Material B	$39,750	$42,000	($2,250)
6	Overhead	$125,000	$122,750	$2,250
7				

FIGURE 5–15

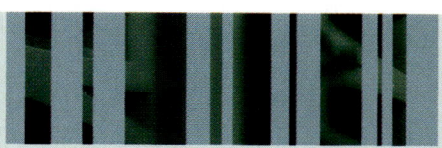

LESSON 6

Enhancing a Worksheet

■ OBJECTIVES

Upon completion of this lesson, you should be able to:

- Sort and filter data in a worksheet.
- Apply conditional formatting to highlight data.
- Hide worksheet columns and rows.
- Insert a shape, SmartArt graphic, picture, and screenshot in a worksheet.
- Use a template to create a new workbook.
- Insert a hyperlink in a worksheet.
- Save a workbook in a different file format.
- Insert, edit, and delete comments in a worksheet.
- Use the Research task pane.

■ VOCABULARY

ascending sort

comment

conditional formatting

descending sort

filter

filter arrow

hyperlink

object

picture

Research task pane

screen clipping

screenshot

shape

SmartArt graphic

sort

template

There are many ways to enhance the appearance of a workbook. You can arrange the data in a meaningful order, display only the data related to a specific question, or highlight data that meets certain criteria. You can hide rows or columns to help focus attention on specific data or results. You can add shapes, graphics, and pictures to a worksheet. You can use a template to create many worksheets with the same basic structure. You can add a link to a worksheet that jumps to another part of the worksheet, another file, or a Web site. You can save a workbook in a different format, making it available in other programs or versions of Excel. Finally, you can add comments to worksheet cells to document their contents. You will learn to do all these tasks in this lesson.

Sorting Data

Data entry often occurs in an order that is not necessarily best for understanding and analysis. ***Sorting*** rearranges data in a more meaningful order. For example, you might want to sort a list of names in alphabetical order. In an ***ascending sort***, data with letters is arranged in alphabetical order (A to Z), data with numbers is arranged from smallest to largest, and data with dates is arranged from earliest to latest. The reverse order occurs in a ***descending sort***, which arranges data with letters from Z to A, data with numbers from largest to smallest, and data with dates from oldest to newest. When you sort data contained in columns of a worksheet, Excel does not include the column headings.

To sort data, you first click a cell in the column you want to sort. Click the Data tab on the Ribbon. In the Sort & Filter group, click the Sort A to Z button for an ascending text sort or click the Sort Z to A button for a descending text sort. The button names change depending on what type of data you selected for sorting. For numerical data, the buttons are Sort Smallest to Largest and Sort Largest to Smallest. For date and time data, the buttons are Sort Oldest to Newest and Sort Newest to Oldest.

You can sort by more than one column of data. For example, you might want to sort a list of names in alphabetical order by last name and then within last names by first name. In this case, you need to create a sort with different levels of criteria. The last name is the first-level sort and the first name is the second-level sort. You set up a sort with multiple levels in the Sort dialog box, which is shown in **Figure 6–1**. To open the Sort dialog box, click the Sort button in the Sort & Filter group on the Data tab of the Ribbon. You set up the first-level sort by selecting the column to use in the Sort by row in the Sort dialog box. The Column box indicates the column that will be used for the first-level sort, such as Last Name. The Sort On box indicates the type of data to be sorted, which is usually Values. If data is formatted with different font or fill colors, you can sort the data by color. The Order box specifies whether the sort is ascending or descending. To create an additional sort level, such as for the First Name column, click Add Level. The Then by row is added to the dialog box. You set up the second-level (and each next-level) sort by selecting the sort column, the data type, and the sort order, just as you did for the first-level sort. After creating all the sort levels, click OK. The data is rearranged in the order you specified.

▶ **VOCABULARY**

sort

ascending sort

descending sort

TIP

The Sort commands are also available on the Home tab of the Ribbon and on a shortcut menu. On the Home tab, in the Editing group, click the Sort & Filter button to open a menu with the Sort commands. Or, right-click a cell in the column you want to sort, and then point to Sort on the shortcut menu to open a submenu of Sort commands. In either case, click the appropriate Sort command.

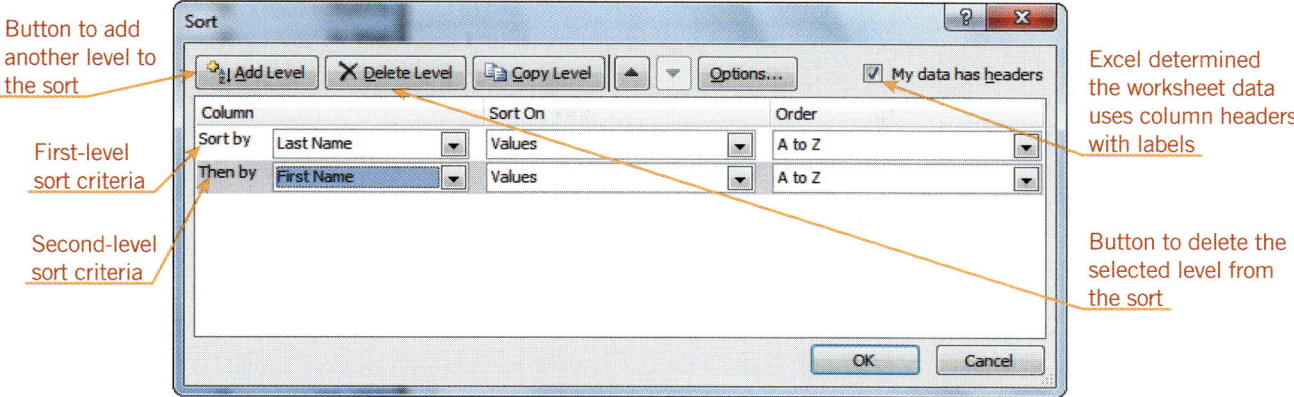

Button to add another level to the sort

First-level sort criteria

Second-level sort criteria

Excel determined the worksheet data uses column headers with labels

Button to delete the selected level from the sort

FIGURE 6–1   Sort dialog box

Step-by-Step 6.1

1. Open the **Salary.xlsx** workbook from the drive and folder where your Data Files are stored.

2. Save the workbook as **Salary List** followed by your initials.

3. Click cell **D4**. Clicking any cell in column D indicates that you want to sort by the Salary data in column D.

4. Click the **Data** tab on the Ribbon, and then locate the **Sort & Filter** group. This group includes the buttons for sorting in ascending or descending order and opening the Sort dialog box.

5. In the Sort & Filter group, click the **Sort Smallest to Largest** button. The data in the range A4:D29 is sorted in ascending order by the numerical values in column D.

6. On the Data tab, in the Sort & Filter group, click the **Sort** button. The Sort dialog box appears. The sort you just created appears as the first-level sort in the Sort by row.

7. In the Column column, click the **Sort by arrow**, and then click **Last Name**. Notice that the column headings from the Salary data appear in the Sort by list. Values is already selected in the Sort On column.

8. In the Order column, click the **arrow**, and then click **A to Z**, if it is not already selected.

9. Click **Add Level**. A Then by row is added so you can specify the second-level sort.

10. In the Column column, click the **Then by arrow**, and then click **First Name**. Values is already selected in the Sort On box.

11. In the Order column, click the **arrow**, and then click **A to Z**, if it is not already selected. Your Sort dialog box should match Figure 6–1.

12. Click **OK**. The data is sorted by last name and then by first name, as shown in **Figure 6–2**.

FIGURE 6–2
Data sorted by last name and then by first name

Sort buttons

Then data is sorted in alphabetical order by first name

Data is sorted first in alphabetical order by last name

Three employees with the last name *Brown* are sorted in alphabetical order by their first names

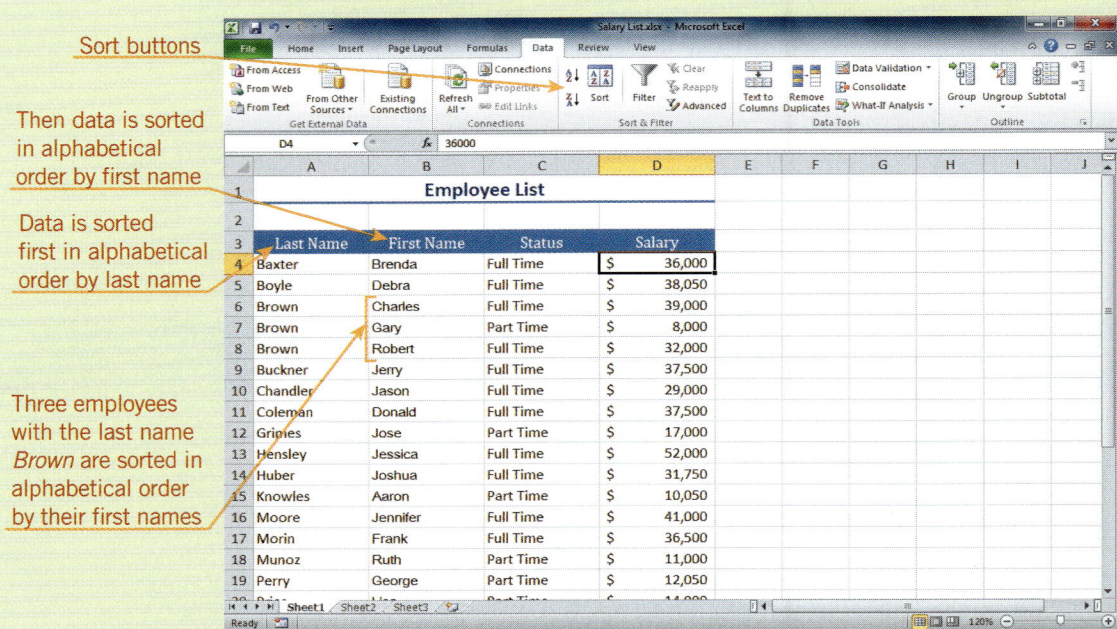

13. Save the workbook, and leave it open for the next Step-by-Step.

TIP

The Filter commands are also available on the Home tab of the Ribbon and on a shortcut menu. On the Home tab, in the Editing group, click the Sort & Filter button to access the Filter commands. Or, right-click the cell in the column you want to filter, and then point to Filter on the shortcut menu to open a submenu of Filter commands. In either case, click the appropriate command.

Filtering Data

Filtering displays a subset of data that meets certain criteria and temporarily hides the rows that do not meet the specified criteria. For example, you could filter a list of employees to show only those employees who work full time. The rows that contain part-time employees are then hidden, but these employees are not deleted from the worksheet.

You can filter by value, by criteria, or by color. On the Data tab of the Ribbon, in the Sort & Filter group, click the Filter button. *Filter arrows* appear in the lower-right corners of the cells with column labels. When you click a filter arrow, the AutoFilter menu for that column appears, as shown in **Figure 6–3**. The AutoFilter menu displays a list of all the values that appear in that column along with additional criteria and color filtering options. When you select one of the values, the filter is applied to the data to display only those rows in the worksheet in which that value is entered in the filtered column.

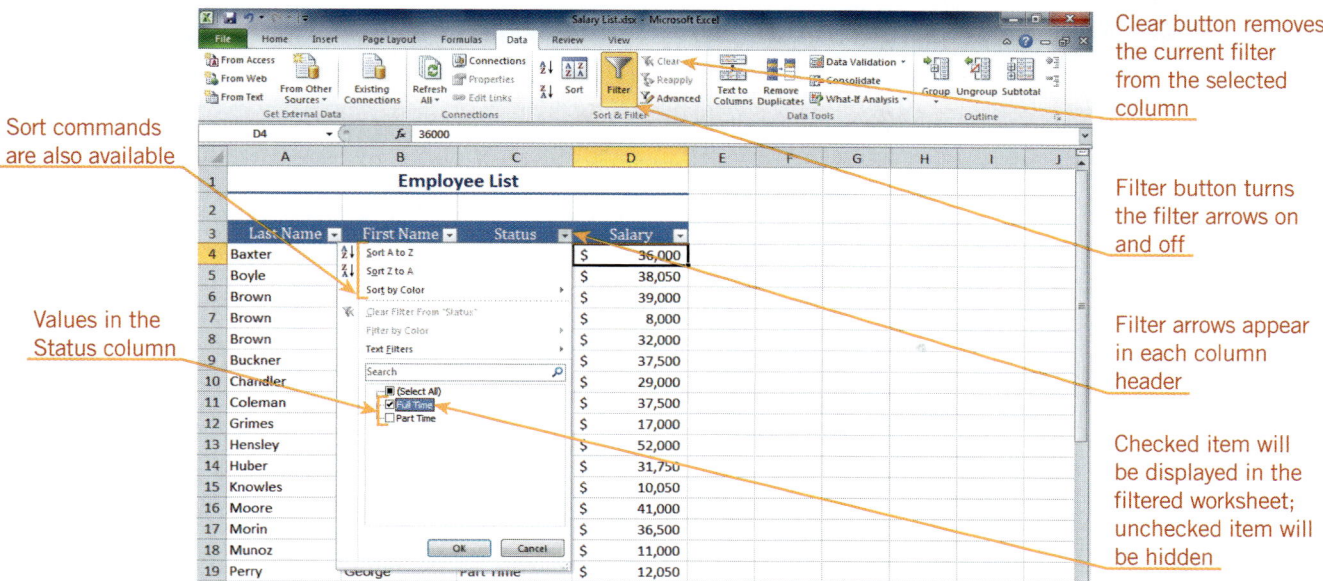

Clear button removes the current filter from the selected column

Sort commands are also available

Filter button turns the filter arrows on and off

Values in the Status column

Filter arrows appear in each column header

Checked item will be displayed in the filtered worksheet; unchecked item will be hidden

FIGURE 6–3   AutoFilter menu

The Number, Text, and Data AutoFilters provide different filtering options. For example, you can use comparison operators, such as equals, between, and begins with, to select data. You can also filter numbers based on their relative values, such as the top 10, above average, or below average. If you select the Top 10 number filter, the Top 10 AutoFilter dialog box appears, as shown in **Figure 6–4**. In the Top 10 AutoFilter dialog box, you can choose to show the largest (top) or smallest (bottom) values in the column. For example, you might show the rows with the 10 largest values in that column of the worksheet. However, you can change the specifications in the dialog box to show a different number of items or a percentage, such as the Bottom 50 Items or the Top 10 Percent.

The rank of items to show

The number of items or percentages to show

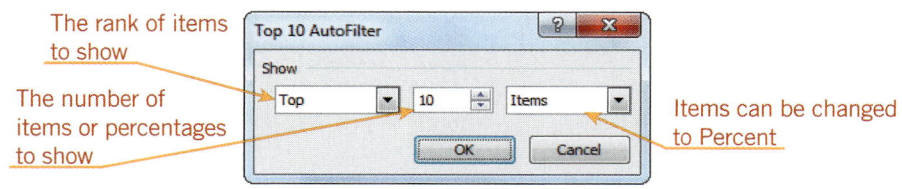

Items can be changed to Percent

FIGURE 6–4   Top 10 AutoFilter dialog box

When a column is filtered, the filter arrow icon changes from ⬇ to ⬇. When you want to see all the data in a worksheet again, you can restore all the rows by clearing the filter. Click the filter arrow, and then click the Clear Filter From command or click the Clear button in the Sort & Filter group on the Data tab of the Ribbon. To hide the filter arrows, click the Filter button in the Sort & Filter group.

Step-by-Step 6.2

1. Click cell **C4**.

2. On the Data tab, in the Sort & Filter group, click the **Filter** button. Filter arrows appear on cells A3 through D3, which are the cells with the column labels.

3. In cell C3, click the **filter arrow**. The AutoFilter menu appears.

4. Click the **(Select All)** check box. All of the column values are deselected.

5. Click the **Full Time** check box. The Part Time check box remains deselected on the AutoFilter menu, as shown in Figure 6–3.

6. Click **OK**. The list of employees is filtered to show only the full-time workers. All of the part-time employees are hidden.

7. In cell D3, click the **filter arrow**. You'll add a second filter to show the 10 full-time employees who earn the highest salaries.

8. On the AutoFilter menu, point to **Number Filters**, and then click **Top 10**. The Top 10 AutoFilter dialog box appears, as shown in Figure 6–4.

9. Click **OK**. The worksheet is filtered to show the 10 employees who work full time and earn the highest salaries.

10. Insert a footer that includes your name and the current date. Save and print the workbook. Switch to Normal view.

11. Click the **Data** tab on the Ribbon. In the Sort & Filter group, click the **Clear** button. The filter is removed from the worksheet, and all of the employees are visible.

12. On the Data tab, in the Sort & Filter group, click the **Filter** button. The filter arrows disappear from the cells with the column labels.

13. Save the workbook, and leave it open for the next Step-by-Step.

Applying Conditional Formatting

Conditional formatting changes the appearance of cells that meet a specified condition. Conditional formatting helps you analyze and understand data by highlighting cells that answer a question, such as "Which employees have worked for the company for more than three years?" The Highlight Cells Rules format cells based on comparison operators such as greater than, less than, between, and equal to. You can also highlight cells that contain specific text, a certain date, or even duplicate values. The Top/Bottom Rules format cells based on their rank, such as the top 10 items, the bottom 15%, or those that are above average compared to the rest of the values in the range. You specify the number of items or the percentage to include.

To add conditional formatting, select the range you want to analyze. On the Home tab, in the Styles group, click the Conditional Formatting button, point to Highlight Cells Rules or Top/Bottom Rules, and then click the condition you want. In the dialog box that appears, enter the appropriate criteria, select the formatting you want, and then click OK. The conditional formatting is applied to the selected range. To remove conditional formatting, click the Conditional Formatting button, point to Clear Rules, and then click Clear Rules from Selected Cells or Clear Rules from Entire Sheet.

> **▶ VOCABULARY**
> **Conditional formatting**

> **● TIP**
>
> If you update the data in a range, the conditional formatting changes to reflect the new values. Consider a worksheet that conditionally formats employee salaries to highlight the top five salaries. If an employee receives a raise that changes her salary rank from sixth to fifth, this employee's salary is conditionally formatted and the employee's salary previously ranked as fifth is cleared of conditional formatting.

Step-by-Step 6.3

1. Select the range **D4:D29**. These cells contain the salaries for each of the 26 employees.

2. Click the **Home** tab on the Ribbon. In the Styles group, click the **Conditional Formatting** button. The Conditional Formatting menu appears.

3. Point to **Top/Bottom Rules**. The Top/Bottom Rules submenu appears, as shown in **Figure 6–5**.

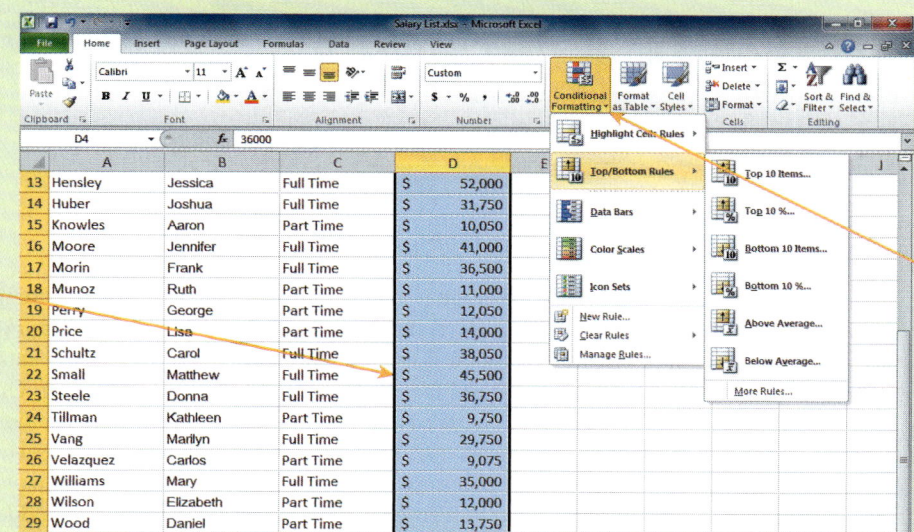

FIGURE 6–5
Top/Bottom Rules submenu on the Conditional Formatting menu

Button to open the Conditional Formatting menu

4. Click **Top 10 Items**. The Top 10 Items dialog box appears, as shown in **Figure 6–6**.

FIGURE 6–6
Top 10 Items
dialog box

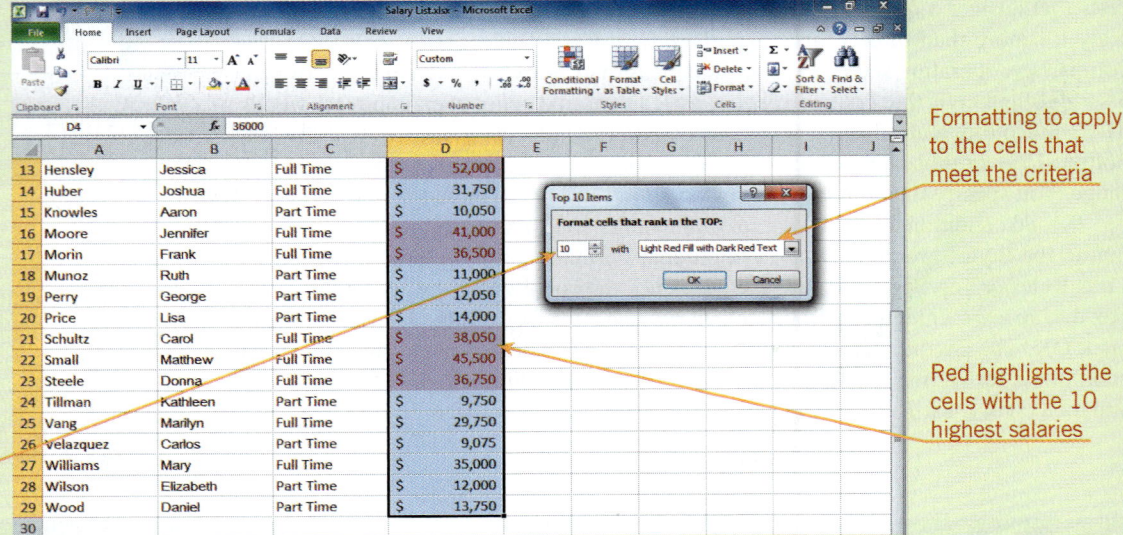

Formatting to apply to the cells that meet the criteria

Number of cells to format

Red highlights the cells with the 10 highest salaries

5. Type **5** in the left box to reduce the number of salaries to the top five.

6. Click **OK**. The five highest salaries appear in red text on a red background.

7. On the Home tab, in the Styles group, click the **Conditional Formatting** button.

8. On the Conditional Formatting menu, point to **Top/Bottom Rules**, and then click **Bottom 10 Items**. The Bottom 10 Items dialog box appears.

9. Type **5** in the left box, click the **arrow**, and then click **Yellow Fill with Dark Yellow Text**.

10. Click **OK**. Click any cell in column E to deselect the range. The five lowest salaries appear in yellow text on a yellow background.

11. Save, print, and close the workbook. Leave Excel open for the next Step-by-Step.

TIP

You can also display and hide selected rows and columns using the Ribbon. Click the Home tab. In the Cells group, click the Format button. On the Format menu that appears, in the Visibility section, point to Hide & Unhide. Use the commands on the submenu that opens to hide or unhide (display) the selected rows, columns, or sheet.

Hiding Columns and Rows

Hiding a row or column temporarily removes it from view. Hiding rows and columns enables you to use the same worksheet to view different data. For example, you can hide monthly data and display only the total values. To hide data, select the rows or columns you want to hide, and then right-click the selection. On the shortcut menu that appears, click Hide to remove the selection from view in the worksheet. You can repeat this process to hide as many rows and columns in the worksheet as you like. Hidden rows and columns remain out of sight until you redisplay them. To display hidden data, select the row or column on each side of the hidden rows or columns you want to redisplay. Right-click the selection, and then click Unhide on the shortcut menu.

Step-by-Step 6.4

1. Open the **Titus.xlsx** workbook from the drive and folder where your Data Files are stored.

2. Save the workbook as **Titus Oil** followed by your initials.

3. Select columns **B** through **G**. You'll hide the monthly data for the oil wells.

4. Right-click the selected columns. On the shortcut menu that appears, click **Hide**. Columns B through G are hidden.

5. Click cell **I1** to deselect the range. The worksheet shows the six-month production total for each well in the field, as shown in **Figure 6–7**.

Columns B through G are hidden

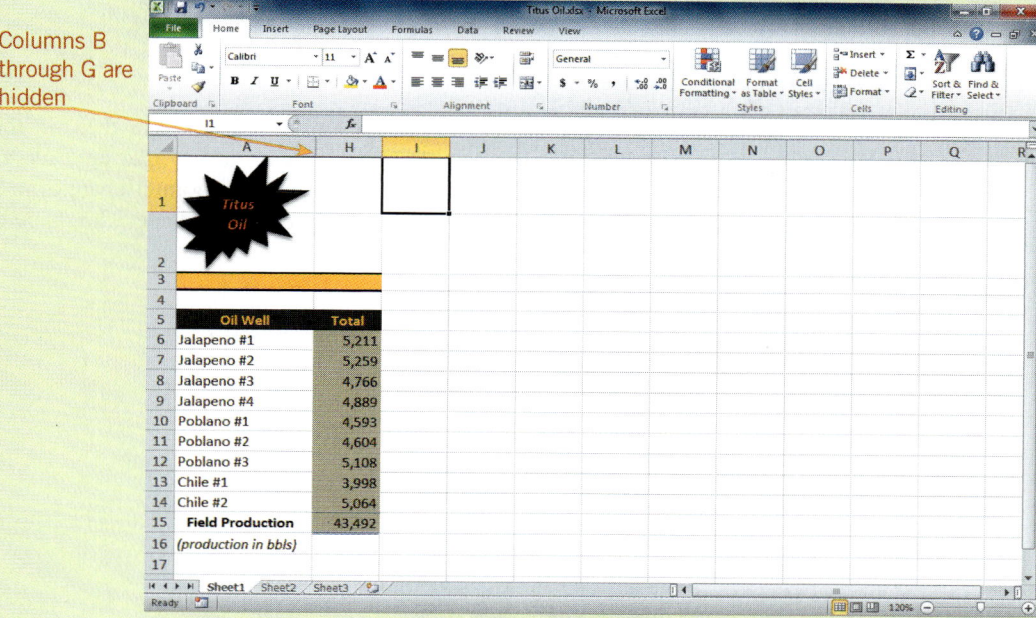

FIGURE 6–7
Worksheet with hidden columns

6. Insert a footer with your name and the current date. Save and print the workbook. Return to Normal view.

7. Select columns **A** and **H**. These columns surround the hidden columns.

8. Right-click the selected columns. On the shortcut menu that appears, click **Unhide**. Columns B through G reappear.

9. Select rows **6** through **14**. You'll hide individual oil well data, leaving only the monthly totals.

10. Right-click the selected rows, and then click **Hide** on the shortcut menu. Rows 6 through 14 are hidden.

11. Click cell **A19** to deselect the range. The worksheet shows only the field production totals for each month. Save and print the workbook.

12. Select rows **5** and **15**. These rows surround the hidden rows.

13. Right-click the selected rows, and then click **Unhide** on the shortcut menu. Rows 6 through 14 reappear in the worksheet. Click cell **A4** to deselect the rows.

14. Save the workbook, and leave it open for the next Step-by-Step.

Adding a Shape to a Worksheet

Shapes, such as rectangles, circles, arrows, lines, flowchart symbols, and callouts, can help make a worksheet more informative. For example, you might use a rectangle or circle to create a corporate logo. Or, you might use a callout to explain a value in the worksheet. Excel has a gallery of shapes you can use.

Inserting a Shape

To open the Shapes gallery, click the Insert tab on the Ribbon, and then, in the Illustrations group, click the Shapes button. In the Shapes gallery that appears, as shown in **Figure 6–8**, click the shape you want to insert. The pointer changes to a crosshair, which you click and drag in the worksheet to draw the shape. The shape is inserted in the worksheet.

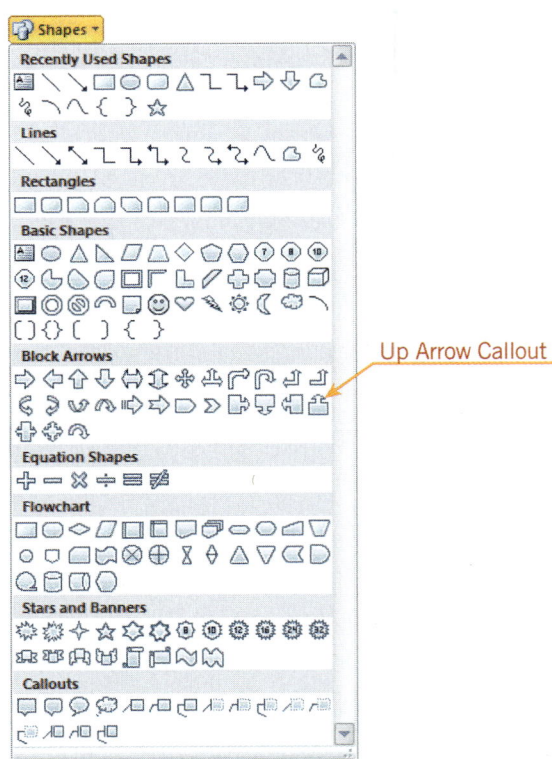

Up Arrow Callout

FIGURE 6–8   Shapes gallery

Modifying a Shape

Shapes are inserted in the worksheet as objects. An *object* is anything that appears on the screen that you can select and work with as a whole, such as a shape, picture, or chart. When the shape is selected, the Drawing Tools appear on the Ribbon and contain the Format tab, as shown in **Figure 6–9**. You use the tools on the Format tab to modify the shape. For example, you can change the shape's style, fill, and outline as well as add special effects, such as shadows. You can also move and resize the selected shape.

▶ **VOCABULARY**
object

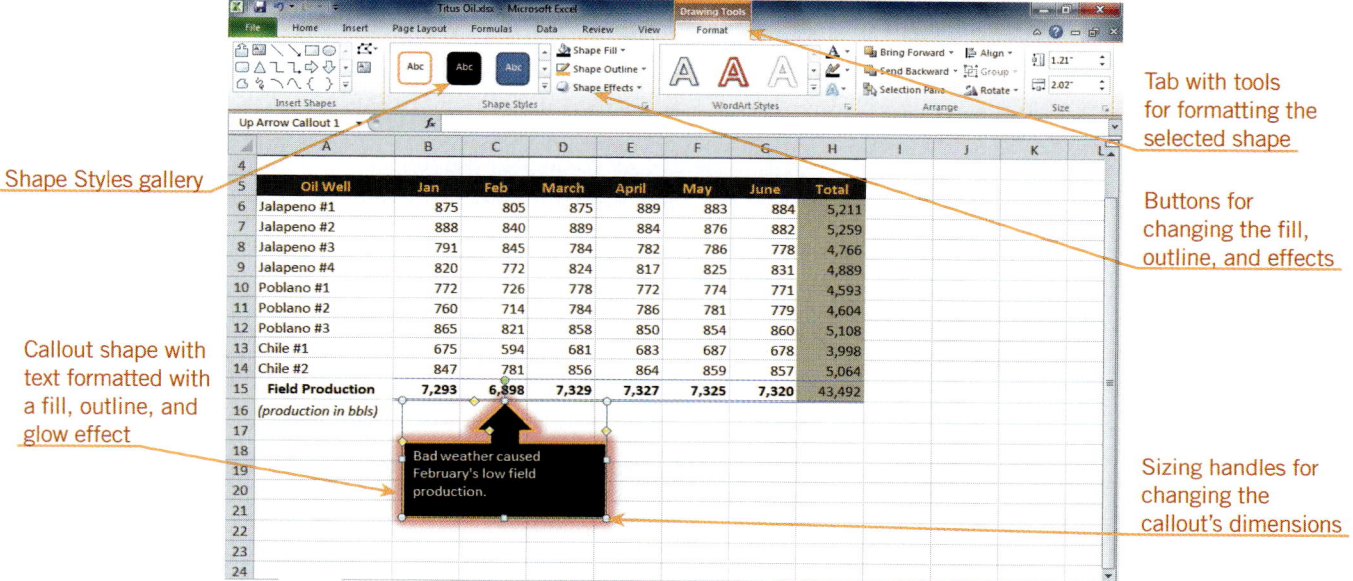

Shape Styles gallery

Callout shape with text formatted with a fill, outline, and glow effect

Tab with tools for formatting the selected shape

Buttons for changing the fill, outline, and effects

Sizing handles for changing the callout's dimensions

FIGURE 6–9 Formatted shape in the worksheet

Deleting an Object

When you no longer need a shape or any other object in a worksheet, you can delete it. First click the object to select it. Then press the Delete key. The object is removed from the worksheet.

Step-by-Step 6.5

1. Click the **Insert** tab on the Ribbon. In the Illustrations group, click the **Shapes** button. The Shapes gallery appears, as shown in Figure 6–8.

2. In the Block Arrows section, click the **Up Arrow Callout** button 🖾 (the last button in the second row). The pointer changes shape to a crosshair ✛.

3. Click and drag from cell **B17** to cell **E20**, and then release the mouse button. A callout with a light blue background and dark blue outline is inserted in the worksheet, with the upper-left corner in cell B17 and the lower-right corner in cell E20. The Format tab appears under Drawing Tools on the Ribbon.

4. Type **Bad weather caused February's low field production.** (including the period). The text is inserted in the callout.

5. Point to the lower-right sizing handle until the pointer changes to the diagonal resize pointer ↘, and then drag left to column D and down to row 22. The callout is narrower but longer.

6. Point to the callout to display the four-headed move pointer ⇞, and then drag the callout until its arrow points to the bottom of cell **C15**. The callout points to the correct cell and remains selected.

7. On the Format tab, in the Shape Styles group, click the **Shape Fill** arrow. A color palette appears.

8. In the Theme Colors section, click **Black, Text 1** (the second color in the first row). The callout background color changes to black.

9. On the Format tab, in the Shape Styles group, click the **Shape Outline** arrow. A color palette appears.

10. In the Standard Colors section, click **Orange** (the third color). The line around the callout changes to orange.

11. On the Format tab, in the Shape Styles group, click the **Shape Effects** button.

12. On the Shapes Effects menu, point to **Glow**. In the Glow Variations section, click **Red, 11 pt glow, Accent color 2** (the second effect in the third row). The callout is formatted as shown in Figure 6–9.

13. Click any cell in the worksheet to deselect the shape. The Format tab disappears from the Ribbon.

14. Save the workbook, and leave it open for the next Step-by-Step.

Adding a SmartArt Graphic to a Worksheet

▶ **VOCABULARY**
SmartArt graphic

SmartArt graphics enhance worksheets by providing a visual representation of information and ideas. SmartArt graphics are often used for organizational charts, flowcharts, and decision trees.

Inserting a SmartArt Graphic

To insert a SmartArt graphic, click the SmartArt button in the Illustrations group on the Insert tab. The Choose a SmartArt Graphic dialog box appears, as shown in **Figure 6–10**. You can select from a variety of layouts, including list, matrix, and pyramid. Click the SmartArt graphic you want to use in the center pane and read its description in the right pane. Click OK to insert the graphic in the worksheet as an object.

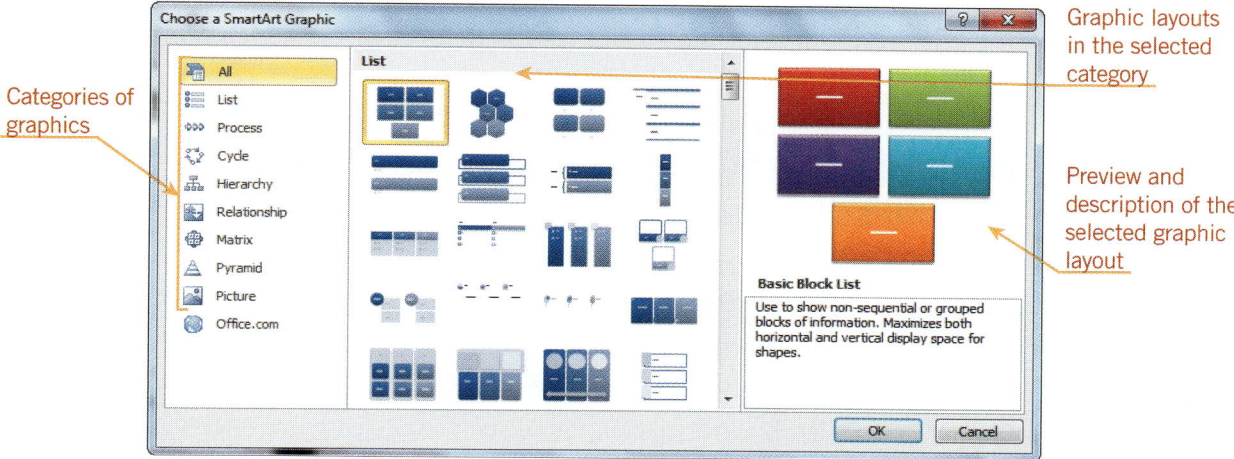

Categories of graphics

Graphic layouts in the selected category

Preview and description of the selected graphic layout

FIGURE 6–10   Choose a SmartArt Graphic dialog box

Modifying a SmartArt Graphic

When the SmartArt graphic is selected, SmartArt Tools appear on the Ribbon and contain the Design and Format tabs, as shown in **Figure 6–11**. You use the tools on the Design tab to select a layout, apply a style, and select the layout's color. The Format tab has tools to modify the shapes used in the selected layout by changing the shape, size, fill color, and outline color, as well as tools to apply shape styles and special effects such as shadows. You can also move and resize the selected shapes.

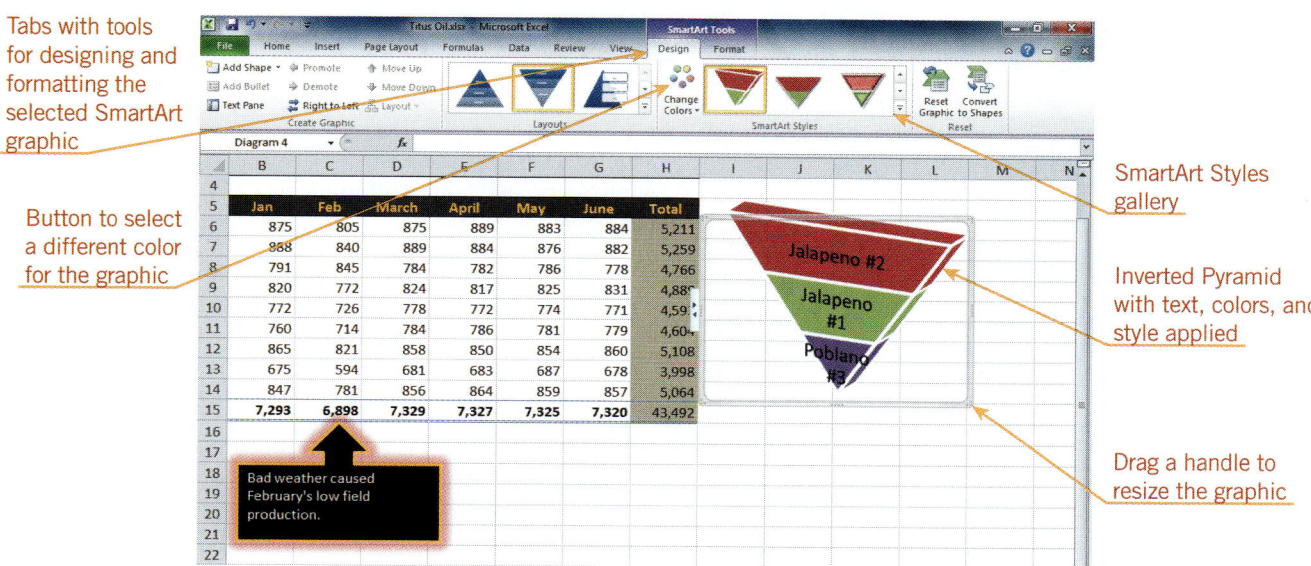

Tabs with tools for designing and formatting the selected SmartArt graphic

Button to select a different color for the graphic

SmartArt Styles gallery

Inverted Pyramid with text, colors, and style applied

Drag a handle to resize the graphic

FIGURE 6–11   Formatted SmartArt graphic

Step-by-Step 6.6

1. Click the **Insert** tab on the Ribbon. In the Illustrations group, click the **SmartArt** button. The Choose a SmartArt Graphic dialog box appears, as shown in Figure 6–10.

2. In the left pane, click **Pyramid**.

3. In the center pane, click **Inverted Pyramid** (the second graphic). A preview and description appears in the right pane.

4. Click **OK**. The SmartArt graphic appears in the worksheet, on top of the data. The SmartArt Tools appear on the Ribbon.

5. Type **Jalapeno #2**. The text appears in the top level of the pyramid.

6. Click **[Text]** in the second level of the pyramid, and then type **Jalapeno #1**. Click **[Text]** in the bottom level of the pyramid, and then type **Poblano #3**.

7. Click within the selection box to deselect the text box, but keep the SmartArt graphic selected. Drag the lower-right sizing handle up until the graphic is about four columns wide and nine rows high.

8. If the Type your text here box to the left of the SmartArt graphic is open, click the **Close** button ⊠.

9. Position the pointer on the selection box to change it to the move pointer ⌖. Drag the **selection box** until its upper-left corner is in cell I6. The pyramid covers the range I6:L14.

10. On the Design tab, in the SmartArt Styles group, click the **Change Colors** button. A gallery of color options appears.

11. In the Colorful section, click **Colorful – Accent Colors** (the first color option). Each of the top three oil well producers is a different color in the pyramid.

12. On the Design tab, in the SmartArt Styles group, click the **More** button ⤓. The gallery of SmartArt Quick Styles appears.

13. Point to each style to see its Live Preview. In the 3-D section, click **Brick Scene** (the second style in the second row). The pyramid changes to reflect the Quick Style, as shown in Figure 6–11.

14. Save, print, and close the workbook. Leave Excel open for the next Step-by-Step.

Adding a Picture to a Worksheet

▶ **VOCABULARY**
picture

You can use a picture to make the appearance of a worksheet more attractive. A *picture* is a digital photograph or other image file. Some organizations like to include their corporate logo on worksheets. Pictures can also be used to illustrate data in a worksheet. For instance, you might want to insert a picture of each product in an inventory list.

Inserting a Picture

You can insert a picture in a worksheet by using a picture file or by using the Clip Art task pane. If you have access to the Internet, you can also download pictures from Office.com to insert in your worksheets.

To insert a picture from a file, click the Picture button in the Illustrations group on the Insert tab of the Ribbon. The Insert Picture dialog box, which looks and functions like the Open dialog box, appears. Go to the drive or folder that contains the picture file, and then double-click the picture file you want to use.

The Clip Art task pane provides a wide variety of clip art, photographs, movies, and sounds that you can insert in a worksheet. To access the Clip Art task pane, click the Clip Art button in the Illustrations group on the Insert tab of the Ribbon. The Clip Art task pane appears on the right side of the program window, as shown in **Figure 6–12**. In the Search for box, type a brief description of the clip you want to find, and then click Go. Clips that match the search words appear in the results box. Click an image to insert it in the worksheet.

Brief description of the clip you want to find

The types of files you want to find—clip art, photographs, movies, and/or sounds

Search results; click a clip to insert it in the workbook

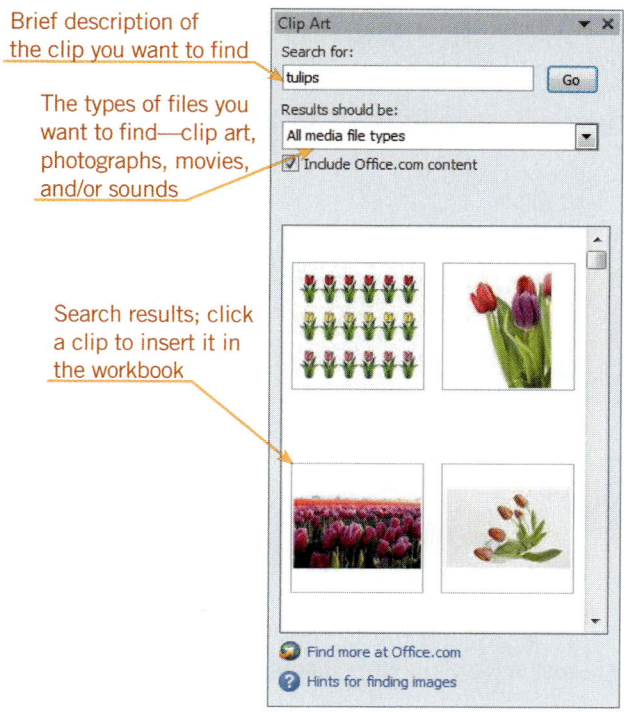

FIGURE 6–12 Clip Art task pane

Modifying a Picture

A picture is inserted in the workbook as an object. As with shapes, you can move, resize, or format the picture to fit your needs. When you click a picture to select it, the Picture Tools Format tab appears on the Ribbon. The Format tab contains tools to edit and format the picture. The tools in the Adjust group enable you to change a picture's appearance, such as its brightness, contrast, color, and background. The Picture Styles group includes the Picture Styles gallery as well as tools to change the picture's shape and border, and effects such as shadows and rotation. The Size group includes the Crop button, which you use to cut out parts of the picture you do not want to use, and options to change the picture's size.

Step-by-Step 6.7

1. Open the **Beautiful.xlsx** workbook from the drive and folder where your Data Files are stored.

2. Save the workbook as **Beautiful Blooms** followed by your initials.

3. Click the **Insert** tab on the Ribbon. In the Illustrations group, click the **Picture** button. The Insert Picture dialog box appears.

4. Click the **Tulips.jpg** file from the drive and folder where your Data Files are stored. This file contains the picture you want to insert.

5. Click the **Insert** button. The tulips picture is inserted in the worksheet. The Picture Tools Format tab appears on the Ribbon.

6. On the Format tab, in the Adjust group, click the **Remove Background** button. The Background Removal tab appears on the Ribbon, and all areas of the background to be removed are purple, as shown in **Figure 6–13**.

FIGURE 6–13
Picture background marked
for removal

Button to apply the
background changes

Drag a sizing
handle to change
background
removal area

Purple area will
be removed

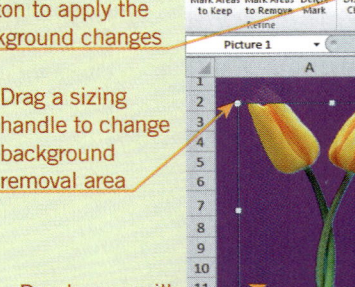
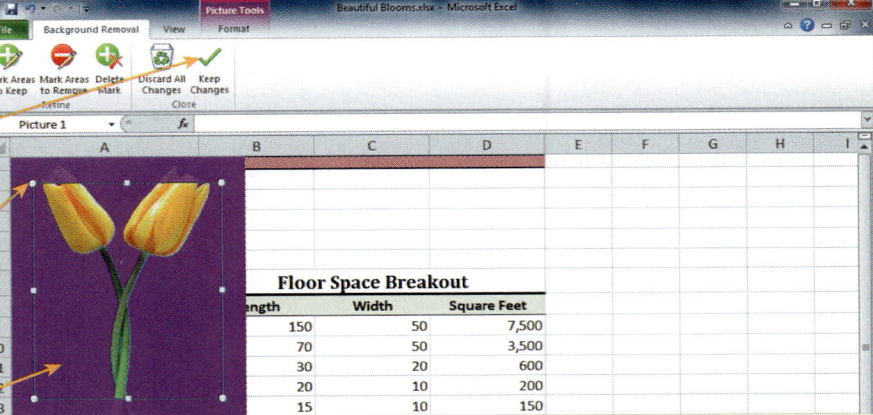

7. Drag the top-middle resize handle up so that all of the flowers are visible.

8. On the Background Removal tab, in the Close group, click the **Keep Changes** button. The picture's background is removed, leaving only the flowers.

9. Drag the lower-right sizing handle up to the bottom of row 6. The picture resizes proportionally and covers the range A1:A6.

10. On the Format tab, in the Picture Styles group, click the **More** button ▾. The gallery of Picture Styles appears.

11. Point to different picture styles to see the Live Preview, and then click **Snip Diagonal Corner, White** (the third style in the third row). The overall style of the picture changes to include a gray background and a white border with the upper-right and lower-left corners clipped.

12. Position the pointer on the picture to change it to the move pointer ⬉. Drag the picture until its upper-left corner is in cell A2. The picture covers the range A2:A7, as shown in **Figure 6–14**.

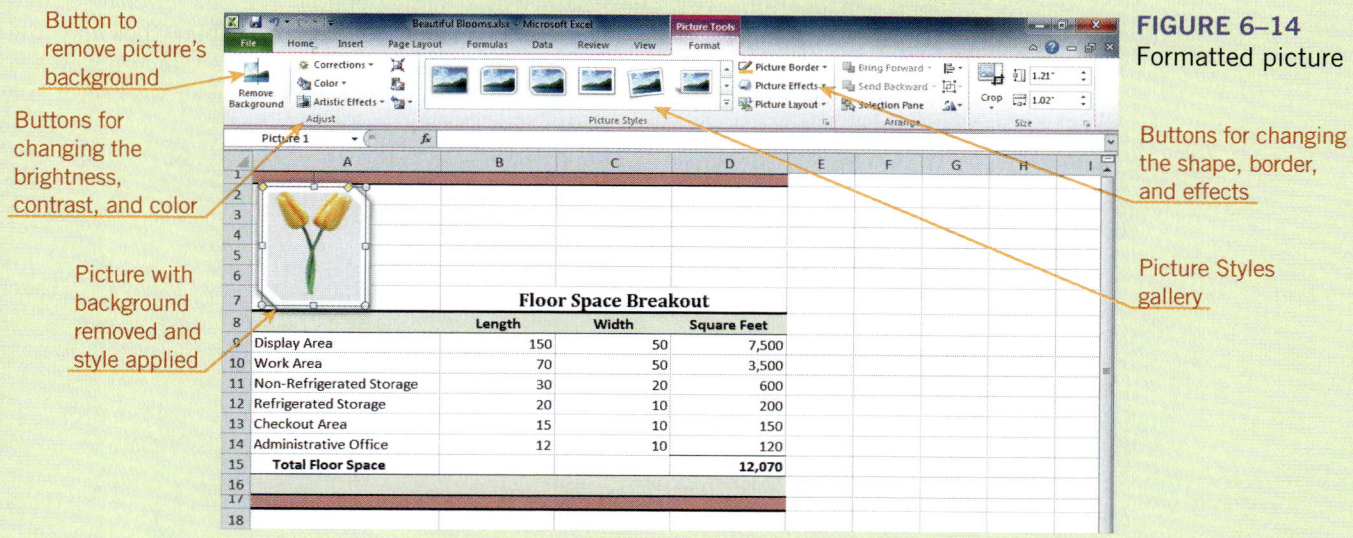

FIGURE 6–14
Formatted picture

13. Click the right side of cell **A1** to select that cell and deselect the picture.

14. Save the workbook, and leave it open for the next Step-by-Step.

Adding a Screenshot or Screen Clipping to a Worksheet

A *screenshot* is a picture of all or part of something you see on your monitor, such as a Word document, an Excel workbook, a photograph, or a Web page. When you take a screenshot, you can include everything visible on your monitor or a *screen clipping*, which is the area you choose to include. The screenshot is added to the worksheet as a picture object that you can resize and modify like any other picture. When you take a screenshot or screen clipping, the original file is not changed.

▶ **VOCABULARY**
screenshot

screen clipping

To take a screenshot, first open the file or Web page that you want to use. Then, switch to Excel and click the Insert tab on the Ribbon. In the Illustrations group, click the Screenshot button. The Screenshot gallery appears, as shown in **Figure 6–15**. To include the entire program window, click the appropriate thumbnail in the Available Windows section of the Screenshot gallery. To choose part of a window to include, click the Screen Clipping option. The pointer changes to a crosshair shape, and the first program window becomes available. Click and drag to select the portion of the window you want to include in the screenshot. When you release the mouse button, the selected portion is added to your worksheet as a picture object.

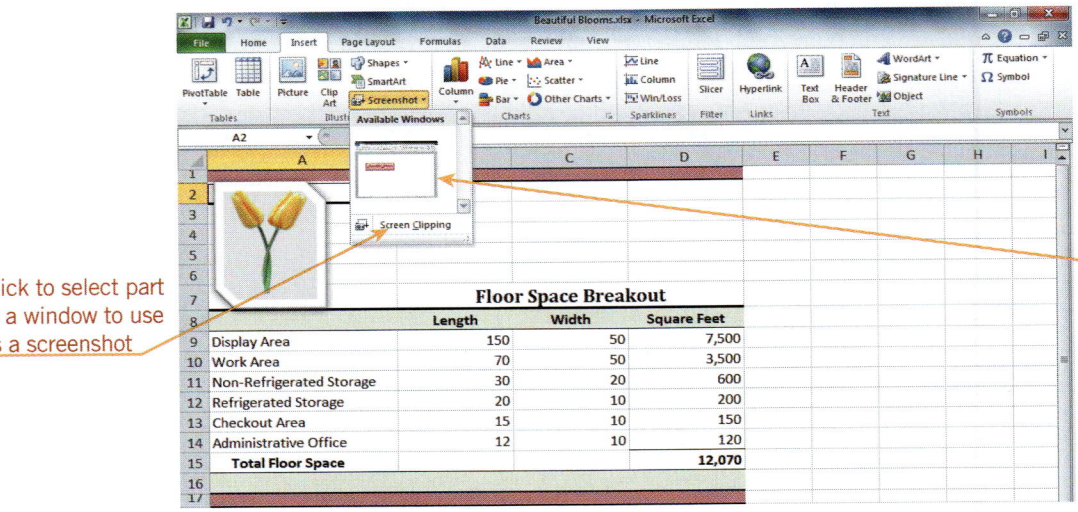

Click a thumbnail to use the entire window as a screenshot (you might see additional windows)

Click to select part of a window to use as a screenshot

FIGURE 6–15   Screenshot gallery

Step-by-Step 6.8

1. Open the **Logo.docx** document from the drive and folder where your Data Files are stored.

2. Switch to the **Beautiful Blooms** workbook.

3. In Excel, click the **Insert** tab on the Ribbon. In the Illustrations group, click the **Screenshot** button. The Screenshot gallery appears, as shown in Figure 6–15.

4. In the Screenshot gallery, click **Screen Clipping**. The Excel program window is minimized, the Word program window displaying the Logo document is activated and dimmed, and the pointer changes to a crosshair ✛.

5. Click just above the upper-left corner of the logo, drag to the lower-right corner of the logo, and then release the mouse button. The logo is copied from the document, the Excel program window becomes active, and a copy of the logo is added as a picture object in the worksheet.

6. Move the pointer to the **Beautiful Blooms** picture so it changes to a move pointer ✛, and then drag the picture so the upper-right corner is in the upper-right corner of cell D2. Release the mouse button. Your screen should look similar to **Figure 6–16**.

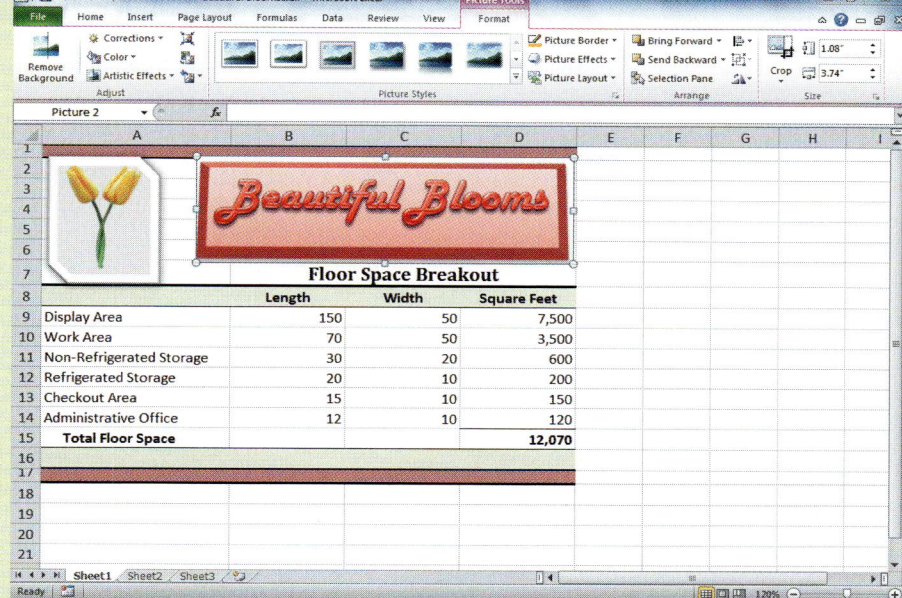

FIGURE 6–16
Screen clipping inserted in the worksheet

7. Close the Logo document.

8. Insert a footer with your name and the current date.

9. Save, print, and close the workbook. Leave Excel open for the next Step-by-Step.

Using a Template

Templates are predesigned workbook files that you can use as the basis or model for new workbooks. The template includes all the parts of a workbook that will not change, such as text labels, formulas, and formatting. You save a copy of the template as a workbook and enter the variable data. You can use a template again and again, entering different data in each new workbook you create from the template. For example, suppose your employer asks you to submit a weekly time sheet. Each week you use the same worksheet format, but the number of hours and dates you enter in the worksheet change. You can use a template to save the portion of the worksheet that is the same every week. Then, each week, you can create a new workbook based on the template and add the data for the current week.

▶ **VOCABULARY**
template

TIP

Each time you download a template from Office.com, Microsoft verifies that the version of the Office software on your computer is genuine. Depending on your setup, you might see a message explaining this feature.

Excel includes a variety of templates, which you access from the New tab in Backstage view, as shown in **Figure 6–17**. The Home templates are template files stored on your computer. The Office.com Templates, which are available when your computer is connected to the Internet, are organized by categories, such as Budgets, Forms, and Invoices. Click a template category to display the templates available for that category. Click a template to display a preview and description of the selected template in the right pane. To open a new workbook based on the selected template, click the Create button or the Download button. Templates have the file extension .xltx to differentiate them from regular Excel workbook files. After you open a workbook based on a template file, you need to save it with a descriptive name to the appropriate location.

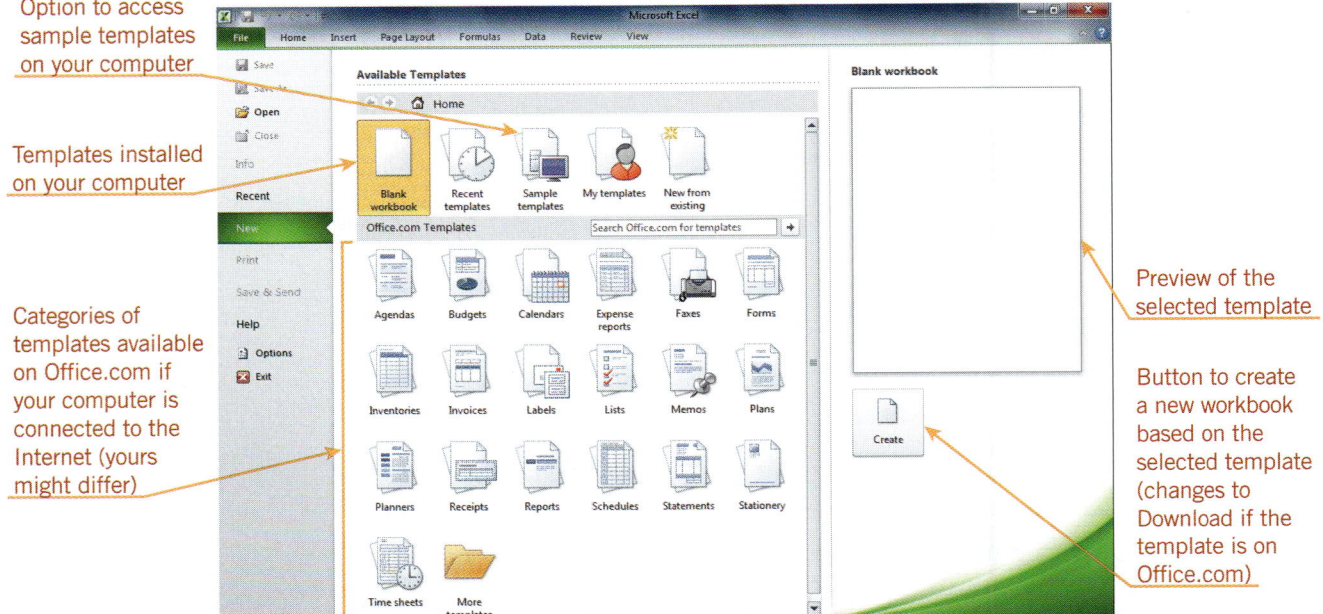

Option to access sample templates on your computer

Templates installed on your computer

Categories of templates available on Office.com if your computer is connected to the Internet (yours might differ)

Preview of the selected template

Button to create a new workbook based on the selected template (changes to Download if the template is on Office.com)

FIGURE 6–17   New tab in Backstage view

You can also create a workbook based on an existing file. Click the New from existing button. The New from Existing Workbook dialog box, which looks and functions like the Open dialog box, appears. Select the workbook you want to use as the basis for another workbook, and then click Create New. A copy of the selected workbook appears in the program window. You can modify the file as needed, and then save the workbook with an appropriate name and location, without overwriting the original workbook.

Step-by-Step 6.9

1. Click the **File** tab on the Ribbon, and then, in the navigation bar, click **New**. The New tab appears, as shown in Figure 6–17.

2. In the Home templates section, click **Sample templates**. A list of templates installed on your computer appears in the Available Templates pane.

3. In the Sample templates list, click **Time Card**. A preview of the Time Card template appears in the right pane.

4. Click the **Create** button. A workbook based on the Time Card template appears in the program window. The default name of the workbook is *Time Card1*.

5. Save the workbook as **Time Card** followed by your initials.

6. Zoom the worksheet to **85%** so you can see the entire width of the time card.

7. In cell **C7**, enter your name.

8. Click cell **C16**, and then enter **5/25/2013** as the week ending date. The dates for the specified week appear in the range C21:C27, the Date column in the time card.

9. Click cell **D21**, and then enter **7**. The total hours for the day appear in cell H21, and the total regular hours for the week appear in cell D28.

10. Click cell **D29**, and then enter **12.5**. The rate of $12.50 per hour for regular hours is entered. The total regular pay for the day appears in cell D30, and the total pay for the week appears in cell H30.

11. Click cell **E21**, and then enter **1.5**. The total hours for the day in cell H21 are updated to include the overtime hours, and the total overtime hours for the week appear in cell E28.

12. Click cell **E29**, and then enter **18.75**. The rate of $18.75 per hour for overtime hours is entered. The total overtime pay for the day appears in cell E30, and the updated total pay for the week appears in cell H30. Your worksheet should look similar to **Figure 6–18**.

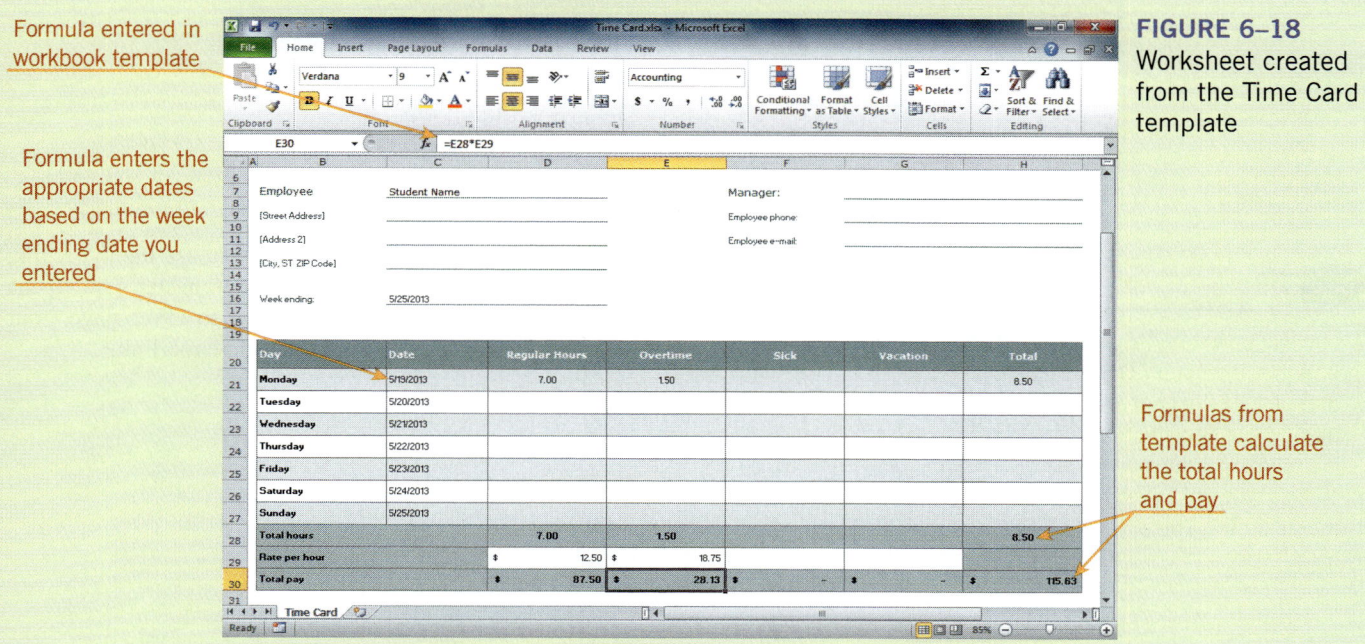

Formula entered in workbook template

Formula enters the appropriate dates based on the week ending date you entered

Formulas from template calculate the total hours and pay

FIGURE 6–18
Worksheet created from the Time Card template

13. Save, print, and close the workbook. Leave Excel open for the next Step-by-Step.

Inserting a Hyperlink

A *hyperlink* is a reference that opens a Web page, a file, a specific location in the current workbook, a new document, or an e-mail address when you click it. A hyperlink usually appears as text in a cell, but you can also use an object, such as a picture, as a hyperlink. For example, you can create a hyperlink in a worksheet to open a workbook that contains the source data for information used in the current worksheet. You can also create a hyperlink to open a company's Web page using the company's logo picture.

TIP

You can enter a custom ScreenTip that appears when a user points to a hyperlink. In the Insert Hyperlink dialog box, click ScreenTip. In the Set Hyperlink ScreenTip dialog box that appears, type the text in the ScreenTip text box, and then click OK. Use the Insert Hyperlink dialog box to finish creating the hyperlink, and then click OK.

Creating a Hyperlink

To create a hyperlink, first click the cell or object that you want to use for the hyperlink. On the Insert tab of the Ribbon, in the Links group, click the Hyperlink button. The Insert Hyperlink dialog box appears, as shown in **Figure 6–19**. Type the file name or Web page address in the Address box, and then click OK. The hyperlink is added to the worksheet.

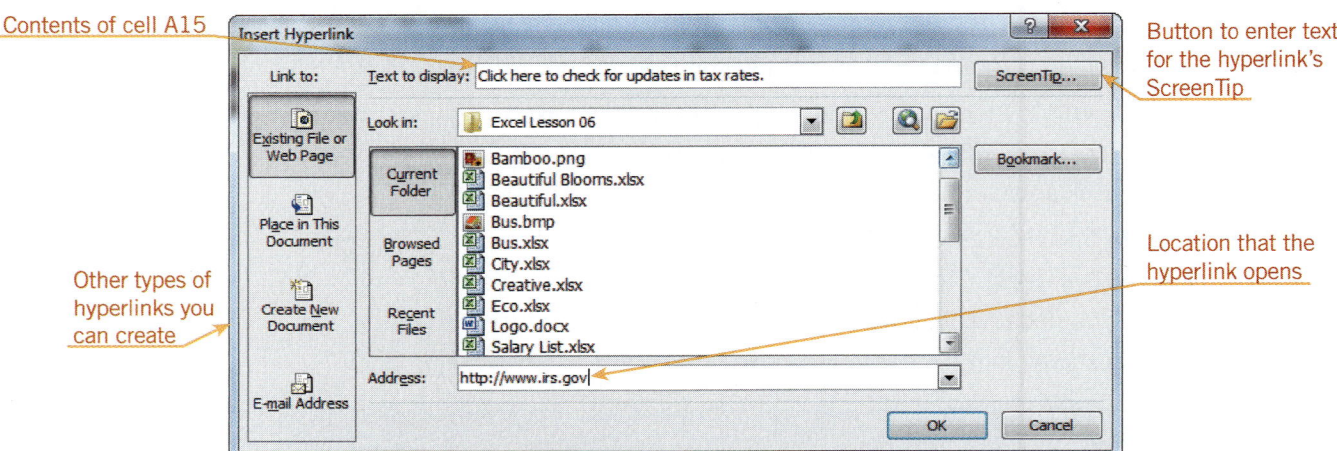

FIGURE 6–19   Insert Hyperlink dialog box

Using a Hyperlink

TIP

The worksheet cell is the hyperlink, not the contents entered in that cell. If the contents extend beyond the cell's border, the hyperlink will not work if the user clicks the text that extends into the next cell. The actual cell must be clicked.

When you point to a hyperlink, the pointer appears as a hand. To use the hyperlink, click the cell or object. If you created a hyperlink to a file, a program starts and opens the file when you click the hyperlink. If you created a hyperlink to a Web page, your Web browser starts and opens the Web page when you click the hyperlink.

Editing a Hyperlink

You can edit a hyperlink to change its displayed text, ScreenTip, the location it opens. Click the cell or object with the hyperlink, and then click the Hyperlink button in the Links group on the Insert tab. The Edit Hyperlink dialog box appears, and looks and functions just like the Insert Hyperlink dialog box. In addition, it contains the Remove Link button, which you can click to delete the hyperlink from the cell or object without changing the cell's contents or the object.

Step-by-Step 6.10

1. Open the **Tax.xlsx** workbook from the drive and folder where your Data Files are stored.

2. Save the workbook as **Tax Estimate** followed by your initials.

3. Click cell **A15**. You will use this cell as the hyperlink to open the Web site for the Internal Revenue Service (IRS).

4. Click the **Insert** tab on the Ribbon. In the Links group, click the **Hyperlink** button. The Insert Hyperlink dialog box appears.

5. In the Address box, type **www.irs.gov**. This is the Web site you want to open when a user clicks the hyperlink. Excel inserts *http://* before the Web address, as shown in Figure 6–19.

6. Click **OK**. Cell A15 is a hyperlink with blue and underlined text, which is a common format for indicating a hyperlink.

7. Point to **cell A15**. The pointer changes to 🖑 and the default ScreenTip appears, as shown in **Figure 6–20**.

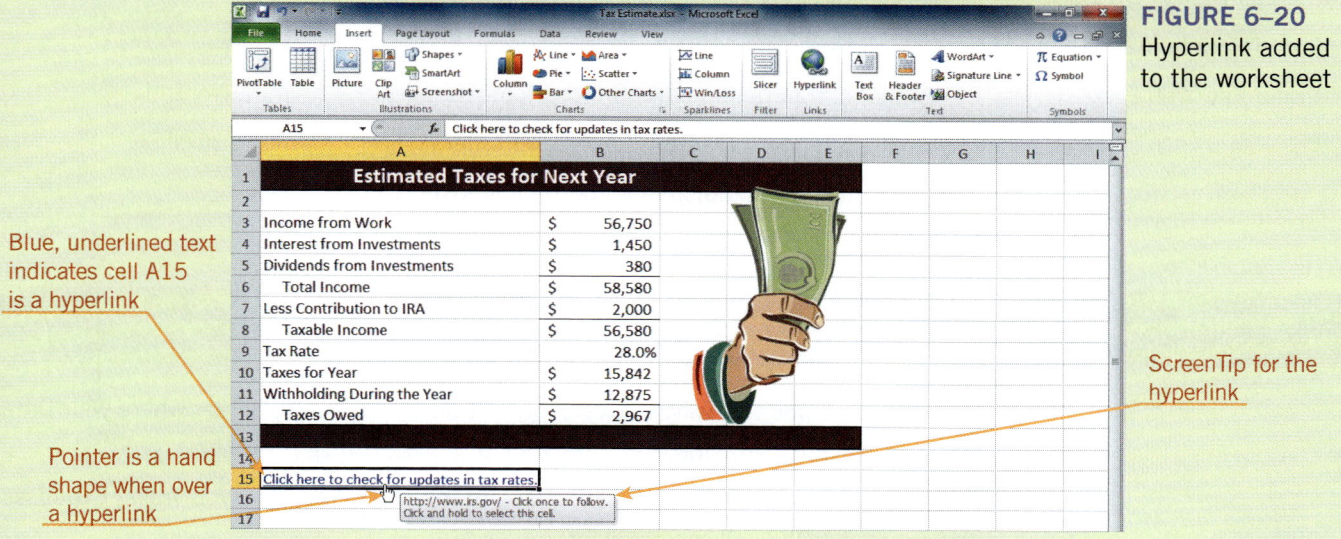

Blue, underlined text indicates cell A15 is a hyperlink

Pointer is a hand shape when over a hyperlink

FIGURE 6–20
Hyperlink added to the worksheet

ScreenTip for the hyperlink

8. If your computer is connected to the Internet, click cell **A15**. Your browser starts and opens the home page for the IRS. If your computer is not connected to the Internet, continue with Step 10.

9. Close your browser and return to the worksheet.

10. Insert a header with your name and the current date.

11. Save, print, and close the workbook. Leave Excel open for the next Step-by-Step.

Saving a Workbook in a Different Format

Excel workbooks can be saved in different file formats so that they can be opened in other programs. For example, if you want to share data with a coworker or friend who uses an earlier version of Excel, you can save your Excel file in a format that is readable by Excel 2003. You can also save the file in a format that can be viewed as a Web page on the Internet. **Table 6–1** describes some of the different formats in which you can save a workbook.

TABLE 6–1   Common file formats in which to save workbooks

FILE TYPE	DESCRIPTION	FILE EXTENSION
CSV (Comma delimited)	Data separated by commas	.csv
Excel Template	File used to create other similar files	.xltx
Formatted Text (Space delimited)	Data separated by spaces	.prn
Microsoft Excel 97-2003	Data created in an earlier version of Excel	.xls
Text (Tab delimited)	Data separated by tabs	.txt
Single File Web Page	File to be displayed on the Internet	.mht, .mhtml
Web Page	File to be displayed on the Internet	.htm, .html
XML Data	Data in Extensible Markup Language	.xml

Step-by-Step 6.11

1. Open the **Travel.xlsx** workbook from the drive and folder where your Data Files are stored.

2. Open the Save As dialog box. In the File name box, type **Travel Expenses 2003** followed by your initials.

3. Click the **Save as type** button. A list of file types you can use to save the workbook appears. Click **Excel 97-2003 Workbook (*.xls)**. You will save the Excel 2010 workbook in a format that Excel 2003 and earlier versions can open.

4. Click **Save**. The Microsoft Excel – Compatibility Checker dialog box appears, as shown in **Figure 6–21**, listing elements of the workbook that are not supported by earlier versions of Excel. In this case, some of the formatting in the current worksheet cannot be saved in the earlier file format. These formats will be converted to the earlier format.

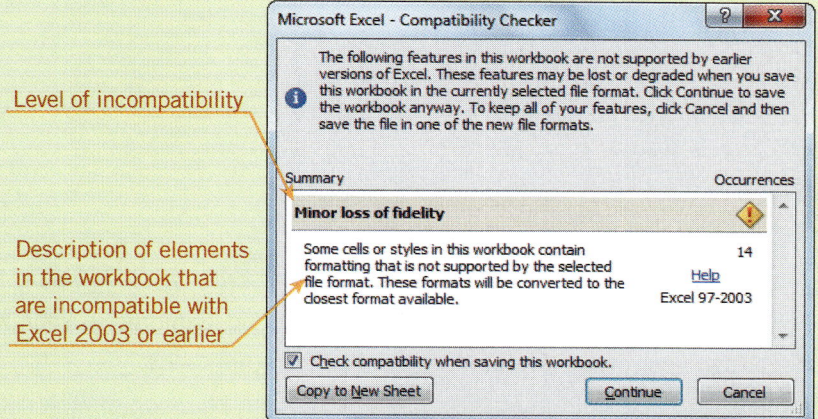

FIGURE 6–21
Microsoft Excel – Compatibility Checker dialog box

Level of incompatibility

Description of elements in the workbook that are incompatible with Excel 2003 or earlier

5. Click **Continue**. The dialog box closes and the workbook is saved as a file that can be opened in Excel 2003 and earlier versions. Close the **Travel Expenses 2003** workbook.

6. Open the **Travel.xlsx** workbook from the drive and folder where your Data Files are stored. Open the Save As dialog box. In the File name box, type **Travel Expenses** followed by your initials.

7. Click the **Save as type** button, and then click **Single File Web Page**. The Save As dialog box expands to show additional options.

8. Click **Change Title**. The Enter Text dialog box appears. In the Page title box, type **Expense Report for Sales Staff**, and then click **OK**. The page title will appear in the title bar of the browser.

9. Click **Publish**. The Publish as Web Page dialog box appears. Click the **Choose** arrow, and then click **Items on Sheet1**, if it is not already selected.

10. Click **Change**. The Set Title dialog box appears. Press the **Delete** key to delete the text in the Title box, and then click **OK**. You do not want the same text to appear in both the browser title bar and the browser window centered over the worksheet content.

11. In the File name box, change the file name to **Travel Expenses Web** followed by your initials. The full path shows the drive and folders in which the file will be saved.

12. Click the **Open published web page in browser** check box, if it is not already checked. The Publish as Web Page dialog box should match **Figure 6–22**.

FIGURE 6–22
Publish as Web Page dialog box

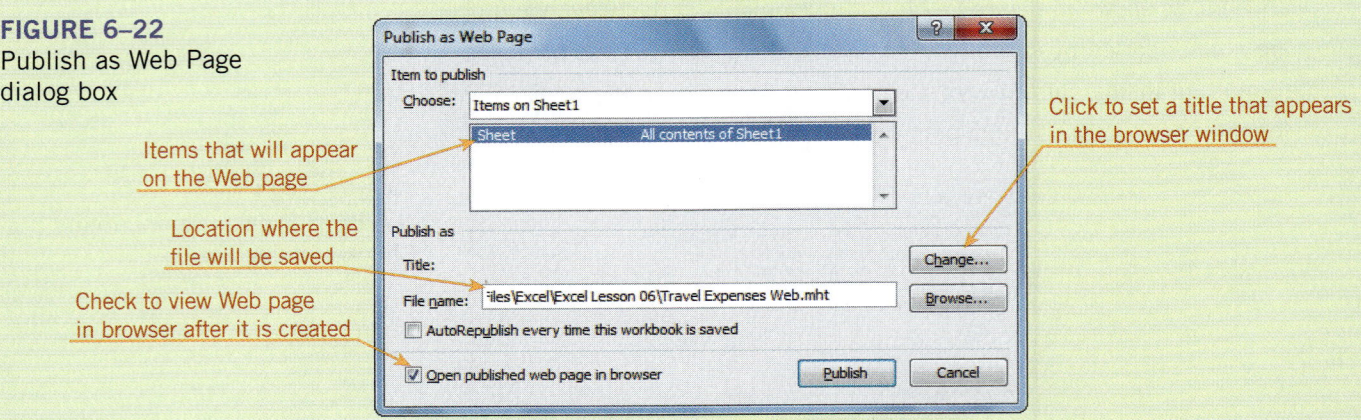

13. Click **Publish**. The Web page appears in your browser, as it would if it were published on the Web. If you use Internet Explorer as your Web browser, your screen should look similar to **Figure 6–23**.

FIGURE 6–23
Web page in Internet Explorer

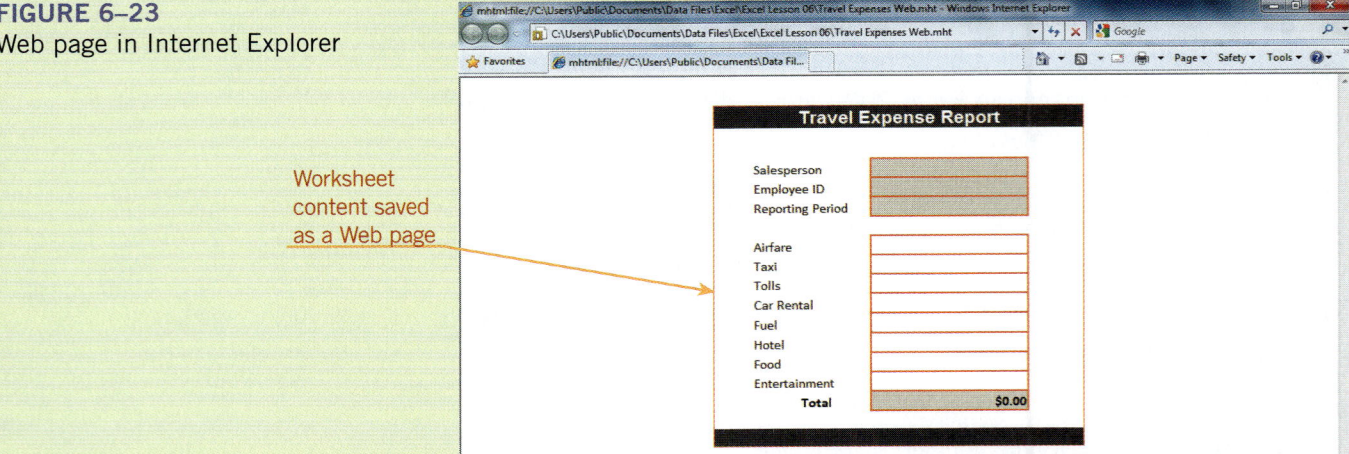

14. Close the browser. Save the workbook as **Travel Expenses** followed by your initials, and leave it open for the next Step-by-Step.

Working with Comments

A *comment* is a note attached to a cell that you can use to explain or identify information contained in the cell. For example, you might use comments to provide the full text of abbreviations entered in cells. You might also use comments to explain the calculations in cells that contain formulas, or to provide feedback to others without altering the worksheet structure. For example, a supervisor might use comments to offer suggestions to an employee on how to improve the worksheet format.

Inserting a Comment

All of the comments tools are located on the Review tab of the Ribbon in the Comments group. The New Comment button inserts a comment in the active cell. A comment box appears to the right of the selected cell with the user name followed by a colon at the top of the box. Type the comment, and then click outside the comment box to close it. A red triangle appears in the upper-right corner of the cell to indicate that it contains a comment. The comment box appears whenever you point to the cell that contains it. It disappears when you move the pointer to another cell.

Editing and Deleting a Comment

To edit a comment, click the cell that contains the comment. Then click the Edit Comment button in the Comments group on the Review tab. Edit the text as usual. To delete a comment, click the cell that contains the comment. Then click the Delete button in the Comments group on the Review tab. The comment is removed from the cell.

▶ **VOCABULARY**
comment

TIP

You can show or hide all the comments in a worksheet by toggling the Show All Comments button in the Comments group. Use the Previous and Next buttons to move between comments in the worksheet.

Step-by-Step 6.12

1. Click cell **A4**. You want to add a comment to this cell.

2. Click the **Review** tab on the Ribbon. In the Comments group, click the **New Comment** button. The comment box appears to the right of the active cell. Your name (or another user's name, depending on your settings in Excel) appears in the comment box.

3. In the comment box, type the following comment: **Please change to Employee Number**.

4. Click cell **A13**. The comment box for cell A4 disappears, and a small red triangle appears in the upper-right corner of cell A4 to indicate that the cell contains a comment.

5. On the Review tab, in the Comments group, click the **New Comment** button.

EXTRA FOR EXPERTS

The user name in the comment box matches the user name entered for that copy of Excel. To change the user name, click the File tab, and then click Options in the navigation bar. The Excel Options dialog box appears with the General options displayed. In the Personalize your copy of Microsoft Office section, in the User name box, type the name you want to appear in comments. Click OK.

6. In the comment box, type the following comment: **The per diem maximum is $50.**

7. Click cell **A16**. The comment box for cell A13 disappears, and a small red triangle appears in the upper-right corner of cell A13, indicating that the cell contains a comment.

8. Point to cell **A13**. The cell comment appears, as shown in **Figure 6–24**.

FIGURE 6–24
Comments added to the worksheet

Button to insert a new comment in the active cell

Red triangle indicates the cell has a comment

Comments group contains all the tools for working with comments

Comment box appears when you point to its cell

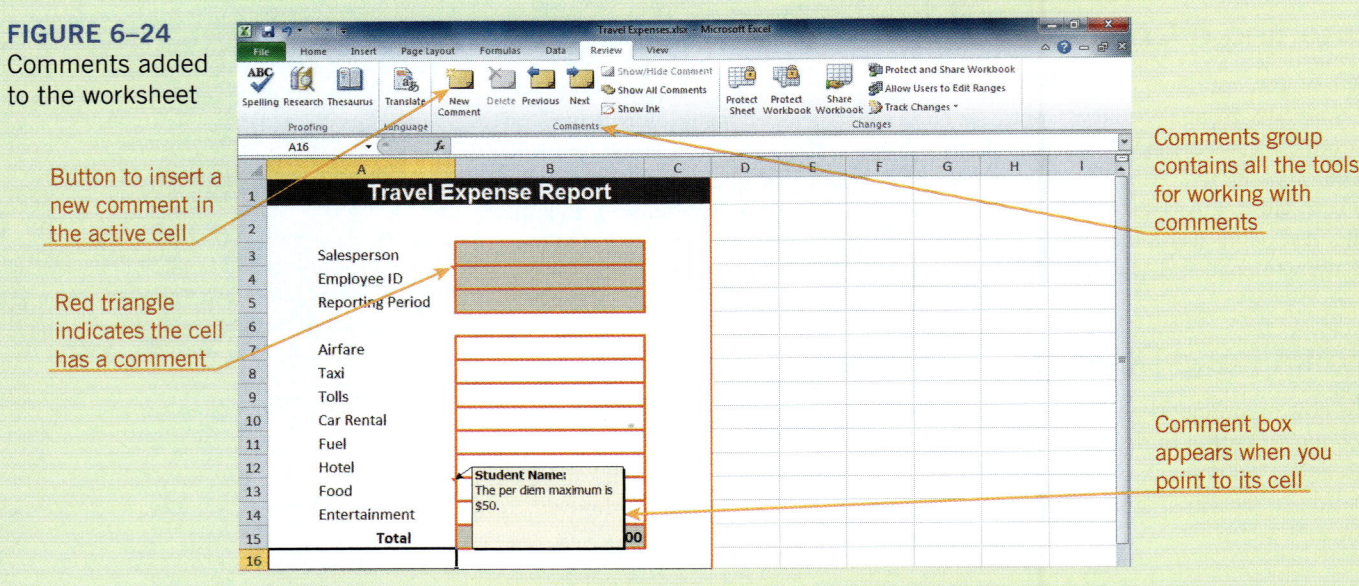

9. Click cell **B3**, and then enter your name.

10. Save, print, and close the workbook. Leave Excel open for the next Step-by-Step.

Using the Research Task Pane

▶ **VOCABULARY**
Research task pane

The *Research task pane* provides access to information typically found in references such as dictionaries, thesauruses, and encyclopedias. In Excel, the Research task pane also provides numerical data typically used in a worksheet, such as statistics or corporate financial data.

To open the Research task pane, click the Review tab on the Ribbon, and then, in the Proofing group, click the Research button. The Research task pane appears along the right side of the program window. In the task pane, select a reference book, a research site, or a business and financial site, and then search for a subject or topic. Your computer must be connected to the Internet to use the Research task pane.

Step-by-Step 6.13

1. Open the **Stock.xlsx** workbook from the drive and folder where your Data Files are stored.

2. Save the workbook as **Stock Quotes** followed by your initials.

3. In cell A2, enter the current date.

4. Click the **Review** tab on the Ribbon. In the Proofing group, click the **Research** button. The Research task pane appears on the right side of the program window.

5. In the Search for box, type **AMZN**.

6. Click the **All Reference Books** arrow, and then click **MSN Money Stock Quotes**. The search results appear in the task pane. The Last amount is the most recent price for that stock.

7. Click cell **C5**, and then enter the amount that appears for *Last*. The current price is entered in cell C5. Excel returns the total value in cell E5 by multiplying the value in cell C5 by the value in cell D5.

8. On the Research task pane, in the Search for box, type **HD**. Click the **Start searching** button ⮞. The most recent price for The Home Depot stock appears in the search results box.

9. Click cell **C6**, and then enter the Last amount. The current price is entered in cell C6, and the value amounts are calculated.

⌐— WARNING

If your computer is not connected to the Internet, you can read but not complete Steps 5 through 10. Enter the values shown in Figure 6–25 in the range C5:C9 in your worksheet. Then, continue with Step 11.

◗ TIP

You can change which reference books and research sites are available from the Research task pane. Click the Research options link at the bottom of the task pane, check and uncheck services as needed, and then click OK.

10. Repeat the process in Steps 7 and 8 to find the current prices for the ticker symbols INTC, JNJ, and MSFT, and enter the Last amounts in the range C7:C9. Your worksheet should be similar to **Figure 6–25**. The actual amounts in the Price and Value columns will differ because they are based on the most recent stock prices.

FIGURE 6–25
Research
task pane

Button to toggle the
Research task pane
open and closed

Ticker symbol

Reference to search

Current stock price
appears in the
search results (the
stock price you see
may differ)

Link to change
the research and
reference services
available from the
Research task pane

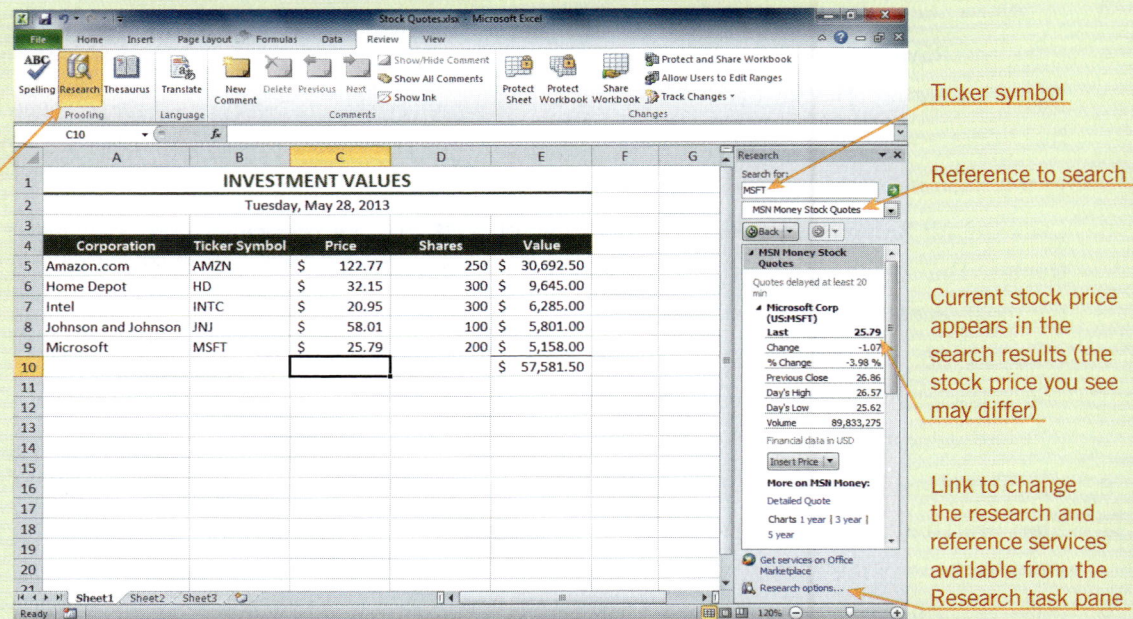

11. On the Review tab, in the Proofing group, click the **Research** button. The Research task pane closes.

12. Insert a header with your name and the current date. Save, print, and close the workbook, and then close Excel.

SUMMARY

In this lesson, you learned:

■ Sorting rearranges worksheet data in ascending or descending alphabetical, numerical, or chronological order. Filtering displays a subset of data in a worksheet that meets specific criteria.

■ Conditional formatting formats worksheet data by changing the appearance of cells that meet a specified condition, such as a comparison or rank.

■ Hiding rows and/or columns lets you use the same worksheet to view different data. You can unhide the hidden rows and columns at any time.

■ Shapes, such as rectangles, circles, arrows, lines, flowchart symbols, and callouts, can help make a worksheet more informative. Excel has a gallery of shapes you can insert.

■ SmartArt graphics enhance worksheets by providing visual representations of information and ideas. Excel has a variety of SmartArt graphics you can use and customize.

- Pictures can make a worksheet's appearance more attractive. You can insert a picture from a file or use the Clip Art task pane to search for pictures. You can also use the Screenshot tool to insert a picture of an entire program window or a screen clipping of a part of a window's contents.

- Templates are predesigned workbook files that can be used as the basis or model when creating a new workbook. A template includes all parts of the workbook that will not change, such as labels, formulas, and formatting.

- You can use a cell or an object to create hyperlinks to another Web page, another file, a specific location in the current workbook, a new document, or an e-mail address.

- You can save a workbook in a different file format, so it can be opened in other programs or in an earlier version of Excel.

- Comments are notes that are added to cells to provide additional information or feedback about that cell's contents. The Research task pane provides access to information typically found in references such as dictionaries, thesauruses, and encyclopedias. In Excel, it also provides numerical data, such as current stock prices.

VOCABULARY REVIEW

Define the following terms:

ascending sort	hyperlink	screenshot
comment	object	shape
conditional formatting	picture	SmartArt graphic
descending sort	Research task pane	sort
filter	screen clipping	template
filter arrow		

REVIEW QUESTIONS

TRUE / FALSE

Circle T if the statement is true or F if the statement is false.

T   F   **1.**   Sorting always arranges data in a worksheet with the smallest values listed first.

T   F   **2.**   Filtering reorganizes data so it appears in a different order.

T   F   **3.**   Hiding deletes a row or column from a worksheet.

T   F   **4.**   Inserting a comment in a cell does not affect the results of a formula contained in that cell.

T   F   **5.**   Excel workbooks can be saved in other file formats.

MATCHING

Match the correct term in Column 2 to its description in Column 1.

Column 1

_____ 1. Workbook used as a model to create other workbooks

_____ 2. Changes the look of cells that meet a specific condition

_____ 3. Organizes data in a more meaningful order

_____ 4. A cell or picture that opens another location or file, an e-mail address, a new document, or a Web page when clicked

_____ 5. Displays a subset of data that meet certain criteria

_____ 6. A message that explains or identifies information in a cell

Column 2

A.   Filter

B.   Comment

C.   Conditional formatting

D.   Hyperlink

E.   Sorting

F.   Template

FILL IN THE BLANK

Complete the following sentences by writing the correct word or words in the blanks provided.

1. A(n) _____ sort arranges data with numbers from highest to lowest.

2. Highlighting cells based on their rank, such as the top 10 items, is an example of _____ formatting.

3. A(n) _____ is anything that appears on the screen that you can select and work with as a whole, such as a shape, picture, or chart.

4. A(n) _____ is an area of a program window that you can insert in a workbook as object.

5. The _____ task pane provides access to information typically found in dictionaries, thesauruses, and encyclopedias.

■ PROJECTS

If you have a SAM 2010 user profile, your instructor may have assigned an autogradable version of the indicated project. If so, log into the SAM 2010 Web site at *www.cengage.com/sam2010* to download the instruction and start files.

PROJECT 6–1

1. Open the **Zoom.xlsx** workbook from the drive and folder where your Data Files are stored. Save the workbook as **Zoom Salaries** followed by your initials. The worksheet contains the annual salaries and ratings of Level 10 employees.

2. Sort the data in the range A6:E20 by the Performance Rating in descending numerical order (largest to smallest).

3. In cell F5, enter **Salary Category** as the label.

4. In cell F6, enter the following formula to indicate the employee's salary category (low or high) based on his or her annual salary: **=IF(D6<36001,"Low","High")**.

5. Copy the formula in cell F6 to the range F7:F20.

   The Level 10 management is concerned that employee salaries do not reflect the annual performance ratings. If salaries are allocated based on annual ratings, employees with higher performance ratings should appear near the top of the worksheet and have *High* in the Salary Category column. Employees with lower ratings should appear near the bottom of the worksheet and have *Low* in the Salary Category column. When a salary does not reflect the employee's annual rating, the salary category in column F might appear to be out of place.

6. Insert a comment in the Employee ID column for each employee you think is underpaid explaining why you believe that employee is underpaid based on the data in the worksheet.

7. Apply conditional formatting to the Annual Salary column to highlight the top five annual salaries with light red fill with dark red text.

8. Insert a header with your name and the current date. Save, print, and close the workbook.

SAM PROJECT 6–2

1. Open the **Top.xlsx** workbook from the drive and folder where your Data Files are stored. Save the workbook as **Top Films** followed by your initials.

2. Conditionally format the data to highlight the top 10 highest grossing films using a green fill with dark green text. Column D contains the number of dollars that the film grossed.

3. Conditionally format the data to highlight the bottom 10 lowest grossing films using a yellow fill with dark yellow text.

4. Sort the data by Gross in descending order (largest to smallest). Make a note of which movie has the largest gross.

5. Sort the data by Release Date in ascending order (oldest to newest) and then by Film in ascending order (A to Z).

6. Add a left arrow callout in columns E and F pointing to the highest grossing film. Enter the text **Top grossing movie of all time!** in the callout.

7. Insert a header with your name and the current date. Make sure the callout will print on the same page as the file data. Save, print, and close the workbook.

PROJECT 6–3

1. Open the **City.xlsx** workbook from the drive and folder where your Data Files are stored. Save the workbook as **City Facts** followed by your initials.

2. Click cell B2 and turn on the filter arrows.

3. Run the following AutoFilters to answer the following questions. Remember to restore the records after each filter by clearing the filter.

Column	AutoFilter	Criterion
B	Top 10	4 items
C	Top 10	Bottom 4 items
D	Top 10	10 percent
G	Equals	0

   A. What are the four largest cities in the United States?
   B. What are the four cities in the United States with the coldest average January temperatures?
   C. What cities are in the top 10% of the average highest July temperatures?
   D. How many of the 30 largest cities are at sea level (have altitudes of 0)?

4. Save and close the workbook.

PROJECT 6–5

1. Start Excel. In Backstage view, on the New tab, display the Sample templates installed on your computer. Create a new workbook based on the **Billing Statement** template.

2. Save the workbook as **Roberts Statement** followed by your initials.

3. Zoom the worksheet so you can see the entire statement, if it is not already in view.

4. Enter the following data in the worksheet.

Cell	Data
B1	(your name)
C8	15679
C10	EX6-5
F2	(504) 555-8796
F3	(504) 555-8797
F8	**Anita Roberts**
F9	**4509 Lumpton Road**
F10	**New Orleans, LA 70135**
F11, F12	(delete cell contents)
B15	**10/8/13**
C15	**Event Planning**
D15	**013**
E15	**Graduation Party**
F15	**325**
G15	**50**

5. Save, print, and close the workbook.

PROJECT 6–4

1. Open the **Eco.xlsx** workbook from the drive and folder where your Data Files are stored. Save the workbook as **Eco Container** followed by your initials.

2. Hide columns B through E to remove the quarterly data from view.

3. Unhide columns B through E to restore the quarterly data.

4. Hide rows 7 through 14 to remove the regional data from view.

5. Insert a header with your name and the current date. Print the worksheet.

6. Unhide rows 7 through 14 to restore the regional data.

7. Insert the **Bamboo.png** picture from the drive and folder where your Data Files are stored.

8. Using the sizing handles, resize the bamboo picture to an appropriate size and then drag the picture to an attractive position on the worksheet.

9. Format the picture using the color, artistic effect, picture style, or picture effects of your choice.

10. Preview the workbook and change the page orientation if needed so that the worksheet prints on one page.

11. Save, print, and close the workbook.

PROJECT 6–6

1. Open the **Bus.xlsx** workbook from the drive and folder where your Data Files are stored. Save the workbook as **Bus Records** followed by your initials.

2. On the Insert tab, in the Illustrations group, click the Picture button. The Insert Picture dialog box appears.

3. Insert the **Bus.bmp** picture from the drive and folder where your Data Files are stored.

4. Use the Dialog Box Launcher in the Size group on the Picture Tools Format tab to open the Format Picture dialog box.

5. In the Scale section, in the Height box, type **41%**. Click Close.

6. Drag the picture so that it fits within the range E1:E3.

7. Remove the picture background so that only the bus remains in the picture. You need to drag the sizing handles so that the entire bus is visible, leaving only the background marked to delete.

8. Add a Glow picture effect, using Orange, 18 pt glow, Accent color 6.

9. Insert a header with your name and the current date. Save, print, and close the workbook.

PROJECT 6–7

1. Open the **Creative.xlsx** workbook from the drive and folder where your Data Files are stored. Save the workbook as **Creative Cubicle** followed by your initials.

2. In cell D8, insert the following comment: **Shut down for two hours for maintenance**.

3. In cell D9, insert the following comment: **Production time increased by two hours to make up for maintenance on Machine 102**.

4. In cell G9, insert the following comment: **Shut down for major repairs**.

5. Insert a cube shape in the upper-left corner of the workbook.

6. On the Drawing Tools Format tab, in the Size group, enter **0.5"** in the Shape Height box and the Shape Width box.

7. Change the shape fill color to Orange, Accent 6.

8. Change the shape effect so the 3-D Rotation is Off Axis 1 Right.

9. Copy and paste the cube shape, and then drag the copy so it overlaps the lower-right corner of the first cube.

10. Insert a header with your name and the current date. Save, print, and close the workbook.

 # CRITICAL THINKING

ACTIVITY 6–1

Additional clip art is available on Office.com. You can access the site by clicking *Find more on Office.com content* in the Clip Art task pane. If you have Internet access, search for the following clip art items:

- Lion
- Valentine heart
- Doctor
- Cactus

Copy each clip art item to a blank worksheet. Resize and format each item using effect and options that you choose.

ACTIVITY 6–2

SmartArt graphics are a simple way to present hierarchical information or relationships, such as for a team, club, school, family, or organization. For example, your school probably has a principal, teachers, and students. In a worksheet, insert a SmartArt graphic to illustrate at least three levels of that hierarchy. Format the SmartArt graphic appropriately.

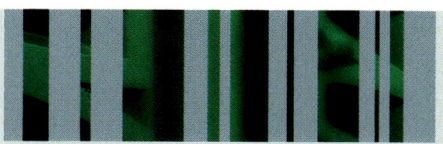
LESSON 7

Working with Multiple Worksheets and Workbooks

■ OBJECTIVES

Upon completion of this lesson, you should be able to:

- Move between worksheets in a workbook.
- Rename worksheets and change the sheet tab color.
- Reposition, hide and unhide, and insert and delete worksheets.
- Create cell references to other worksheets.
- Create 3-D references.
- Print all or part of a workbook.
- Arrange multiple workbooks in the program window.
- Move and copy worksheets between workbooks.

■ VOCABULARY

3-D reference

destination

source

worksheet range

When you have a lot of data to manage, you can organize that data in multiple worksheets or even in multiple workbooks. To work effectively, you need to know how to move between worksheets, rename worksheets, and change their sheet tab colors. You will find it helpful to reorder, hide, and insert or delete worksheets. You can also create cell references to other worksheets or to other workbooks, which means you can share data between worksheets and workbooks. You can print all or part of a workbook, and display more than one workbook at the same time. You can also move or copy worksheets from one workbook to another. You'll learn all these skills in this lesson.

Moving Between Worksheets

A workbook is a collection of worksheets. Each worksheet within the workbook is identified with a sheet tab that appears at the bottom of the workbook window. The name of the worksheet appears on the sheet tab. Unless you rename the worksheets, they are identified with the default names *Sheet1*, *Sheet2*, and so on, as shown in **Figure 7–1**.

Sheet tabs for the inactive worksheets

Sheet tab for the active worksheet

Tab scrolling buttons

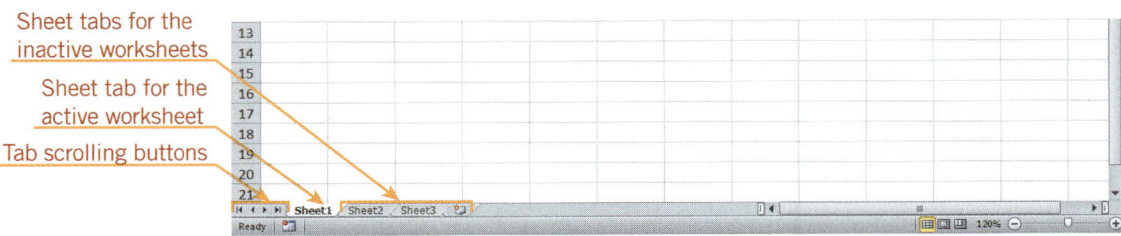

FIGURE 7–1   Default sheet tabs in a workbook

To view a specific worksheet, simply click its sheet tab. The worksheet that appears in the workbook window is called the active worksheet (or active sheet). The active sheet has a white sheet tab. If you don't see the sheet tab for the worksheet you want to display, use the tab scrolling buttons to display the sheet tab.

Identifying Worksheets

To better identify worksheets and their contents, you can give them more descriptive names. You can also change the color of each sheet tab.

Renaming a Worksheet

Although you can use the default worksheet names (*Sheet1*, *Sheet2*, and so on), a good practice is to use descriptive names to help identify the contents of each worksheet. For example, the worksheet name *Quarter 1 Budget* is a better reminder of a worksheet's contents than *Sheet1*. To rename a worksheet, double-click its sheet tab. The worksheet name in the sheet tab is selected. Type a new name for the worksheet, and then press the Enter key.

TIP

To rename a worksheet, you can also right-click its sheet tab, and then click Rename on the shortcut menu. Type a new name, and then press the Enter key.

Changing the Color of a Sheet Tab

Another way to categorize worksheets is by changing the color of the sheet tabs. For example, a sales manager might use different colors to identify each sales region. To change the sheet tab color, right-click the sheet tab you want to change, point to Tab Color on the shortcut menu, and then click the color you want for that sheet tab.

Step-by-Step 7.1

1. Open the **Crystal.xlsx** workbook from the drive and folder where your Data Files are stored. Save the workbook as **Crystal Sales** followed by your initials.

2. Click the **Sheet3** sheet tab. The Sheet3 worksheet appears as the active sheet. This worksheet summarizes the sales data stored in the other worksheets.

3. Double-click the **Sheet3** sheet tab. The worksheet name is highlighted.

4. Type **Corporate**, and then press the **Enter** key. The name *Corporate* appears on the third sheet tab.

5. Double-click the **Sheet1** sheet tab to make Sheet1 the active sheet and to highlight the worksheet name, type **Western**, and then press the **Enter** key. The Sheet1 worksheet is renamed as *Western*.

6. Rename the Sheet2 worksheet as **Eastern**. Rename the Sheet4 worksheet as **Northern**.

7. Right-click the **Corporate** sheet tab, and then point to **Tab Color**. A palette of colors appears, as shown in **Figure 7–2**.

Command to rename the selected sheet tab

Command to change the tab color for the selected sheet tab

Command to remove color from the selected sheet tab

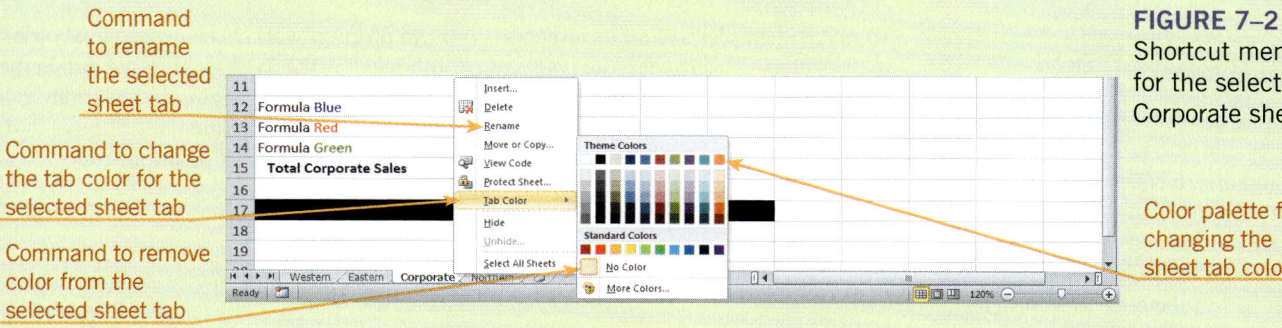

FIGURE 7–2
Shortcut menu for the selected Corporate sheet tab

Color palette for changing the sheet tab color

8. In the Theme Colors section, click **Black, Text 1** (the second color in the first row). A black line appears at the bottom of the Corporate sheet tab.

9. Click the **Northern** sheet tab. The Northern worksheet becomes the active sheet, and you can see the black sheet tab for the Corporate worksheet.

10. Right-click the **Northern** sheet tab, point to **Tab Color** to open the color palette, and then, in the Theme Colors section, click **Orange, Accent 6** (the last color in the first row).

11. Right-click the **Western** sheet tab, point to **Tab Color**, and then click **Aqua, Accent 5** (the ninth color in the first row).

12. Right-click the **Eastern** sheet tab, point to **Tab Color**, and then, in the Theme Colors section, click **Purple, Accent 4** (the eighth color in the first row).

13. Click the **Corporate** sheet tab. The Corporate worksheet is active, and the colored sheet tabs are visible for the regional worksheets, as shown in **Figure 7–3**.

FIGURE 7–3
Renamed and colored sheet tabs

Color is a shaded line when the sheet tab is selected

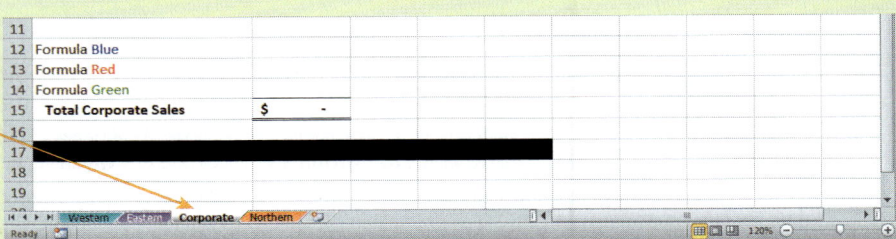

14. Save the workbook, and leave it open for the next Step-by-Step.

Managing Worksheets Within a Workbook

Often, data and analysis are best organized on multiple worksheets. For example, you can enter financial data for each quarter of the year in four different worksheets, and then summarize the annual data in a fifth worksheet. Another common workbook organization is to place sales data for each sales territory or region in its own worksheet, and then summarize the total sales in another worksheet.

Repositioning a Worksheet

To make it simpler to find information, you can position worksheets in a logical order, such as placing a summary worksheet first, followed by the worksheets that contain the data being summarized. You can reposition a worksheet by dragging its sheet tab to a new location. A placement arrow indicates the new location, as shown in **Figure 7–4**. When you release the mouse button, the worksheet moves to that position.

EXTRA FOR EXPERTS

You can create a copy of a worksheet by pressing the Ctrl key as you drag and drop a sheet tab. When you release the mouse button, a copy of the selected worksheet is added in the location indicated by the arrow and the original worksheet remains in its same location. The sheet tab has the same name as the original worksheet, followed by a number in parentheses.

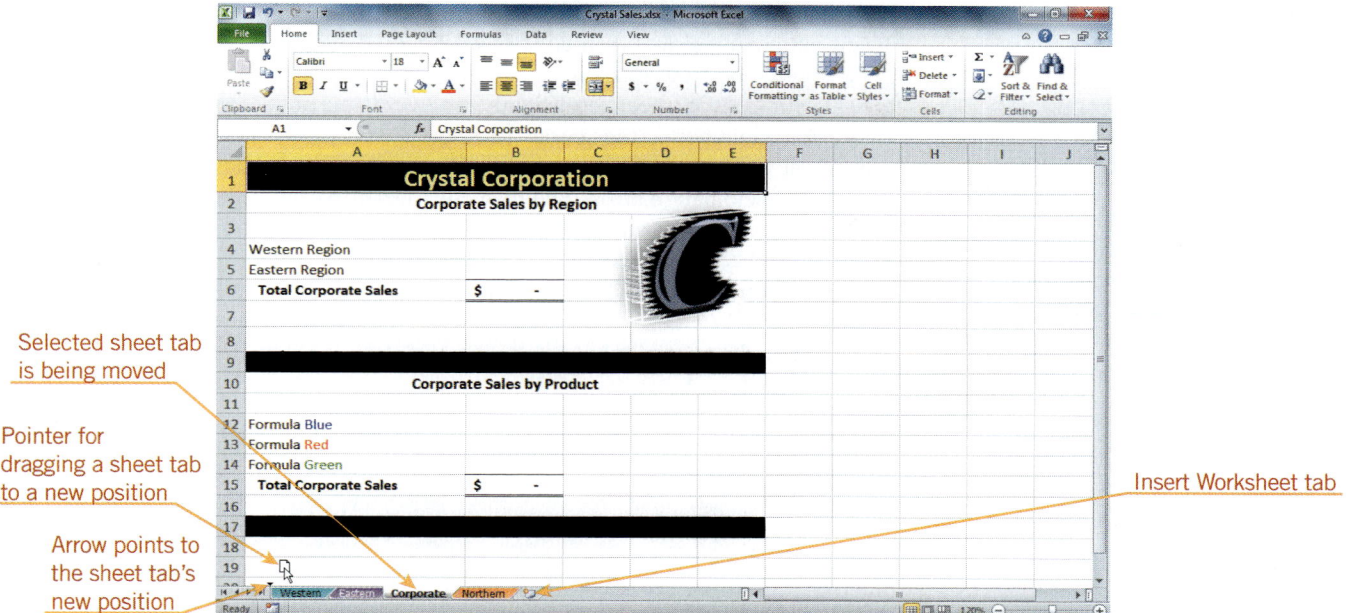

FIGURE 7–4   Sheet tab being repositioned

Hiding and Unhiding a Worksheet

Some workbooks include many worksheets. Some workbooks might contain data you do not need to see, but still want to save, such as a list of employee names or data from past months. You can keep the sheet tabs organized by hiding the worksheets you do not need to view. Right-click the worksheet you want to hide, and then click Hide on the shortcut menu. To unhide a worksheet, right-click any sheet tab, and then click Unhide on the shortcut menu. The Unhide dialog box appears, as shown in **Figure 7–5**. Click the worksheet you want to unhide, and then click OK.

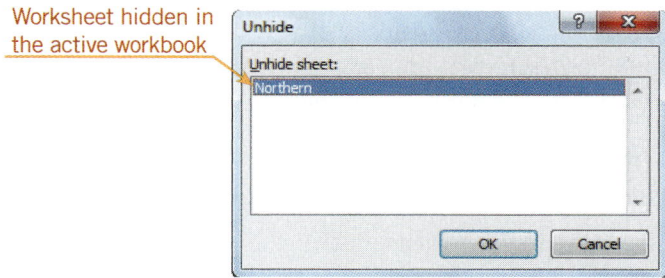

FIGURE 7–5   Unhide dialog box

Inserting and Deleting Worksheets

By default, each workbook contains three worksheets. You can always add or delete worksheets as needed to accommodate your data. To insert a blank worksheet, click the Insert Worksheet tab next to the existing sheet tabs. A new worksheet is added to the right of the last worksheet. After adding it, you can drag the new worksheet to the position you want. Another option is to click the sheet tab of the worksheet that will *follow* the new sheet. On the Home tab of the Ribbon, in the Cells group, click the Insert button arrow, and then click Insert Sheet. A new worksheet is inserted to the right of the sheet you selected.

Deleting a worksheet permanently removes it and all its contents from the workbook. You cannot undo the action. To delete a worksheet, click the sheet tab for the worksheet you want to remove. On the Home tab of the Ribbon, in the Cells group, click the Delete button arrow, and then click Delete Sheet. If the worksheet is blank, the worksheet is permanently removed from the workbook without confirmation. If the worksheet contains data, a dialog box appears to confirm that you want to delete the worksheet, as shown in **Figure 7–6**. Click Delete to continue the action, or click Cancel to leave the worksheet in the workbook. After clicking Delete, you cannot undo the action.

> **TIP**
>
> You can also right-click a sheet tab, click Delete on the shortcut menu, and then click Delete in the message box to delete a worksheet.

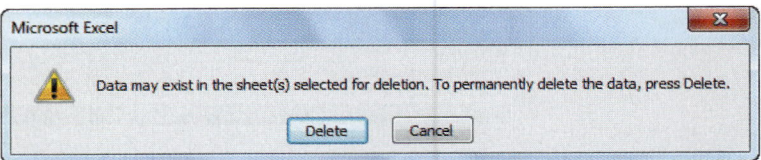

FIGURE 7–6   Message that appears when deleting a worksheet

Step-by-Step 7.2

1. Click and drag the **Corporate** sheet tab to the left until the arrow points to the left of the Western sheet tab, as shown in Figure 7–4.

2. Release the mouse button. The sheet tab for the Corporate worksheet is first.

3. Right-click the **Northern** sheet tab, and then click **Hide** on the shortcut menu. The Northern worksheet and its sheet tab are hidden.

4. Right-click any sheet tab, and then click **Unhide** on the shortcut menu. The Unhide dialog box appears, as shown in Figure 7–5, listing the name of the hidden worksheet in the workbook.

5. Click **Northern**, if it is not already selected, and then click **OK**. The Northern worksheet and its sheet tab reappear.

6. Make sure the Northern worksheet is the active sheet.

7. On the Home tab of the Ribbon, in the Cells group, click the **Delete button arrow**, and then click **Delete Sheet**. A dialog box appears warning that data may exist in the worksheet selected for deletion, as shown in Figure 7–6.

8. Click **Delete**. The Northern worksheet is deleted, and its sheet tab no longer appears at the bottom of the worksheet.

9. Save the workbook, and leave it open for the next Step-by-Step.

Consolidating Workbook Data

In some cases, you might need several worksheets to solve one numerical problem. For example, a business that has several divisions might keep the financial results of each division in a separate worksheet. Then another worksheet might combine those results to show summary results for all divisions.

Creating Cell References to Other Worksheets

Rather than retyping data and formulas on multiple worksheets, you can create a reference to existing data and formulas in other places. For example, you could use this type of reference to display regional sales totals on a summary sheet. The location of the data being referenced is the *source*. The location where the data will be used is the *destination*.

To display data or formula results from one worksheet in another worksheet in the same workbook, you use a formula in the format shown in **Figure 7–7**. First, click the destination cell where you want to display the data or formula results from another worksheet. Type an equal sign to begin the formula. Click the sheet tab for the worksheet that contains the source cell or source range you want to reference, and then click the source cell or select the source range to include it in the formula. Finally, press the Enter key to complete the formula. For example, the reference *Sheet2!B3* refers to the value contained in cell B3 on Sheet2 and the reference *Sheet2!A1:C3* refers to the values contained in the range A1:C3 on Sheet2.

> ▶ **VOCABULARY**
> **source**
> **destination**
> **3-D reference**

> **TIP**
>
> The contents of a source cell appear in the destination cell. Any change you make to the source cell also changes the value in the destination cell.

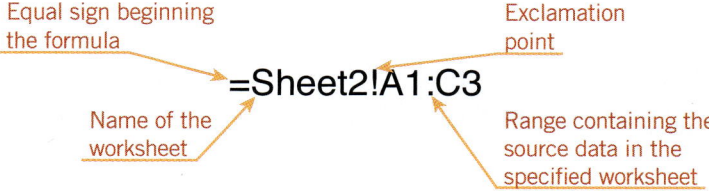

Equal sign beginning the formula — Exclamation point — =Sheet2!A1:C3 — Name of the worksheet — Range containing the source data in the specified worksheet

FIGURE 7–7   Formula with a reference to another worksheet

Creating 3-D References

A *3-D reference* is a reference to the same cell or range in multiple worksheets that you use in a formula. You can use 3-D references to incorporate data from other worksheets into the active worksheet. You can use a 3-D reference with 18 different functions, including SUM, AVERAGE, COUNT, MIN, MAX, and PRODUCT. For example, you might want to enter the SUM function in a summary worksheet to add several numbers contained in other worksheets, such as with quarterly or regional sales data. In general, to use 3-D references, worksheets should have the same organization and structure.

▶ **VOCABULARY**
worksheet range

A 3-D reference includes the worksheet range, an exclamation point, and a cell or range, as shown in the formula in **Figure 7–8**. A *worksheet range* is a group of adjacent worksheets. In a worksheet range, as in a cell range, a colon separates the names of the first worksheet and the last worksheet in the group. An exclamation mark separates the worksheet range from its cell or range reference. For example, the reference *Sheet2:Sheet4!B3* refers to the values contained in cell B3 on Sheet2, Sheet3, and Sheet4 and the reference *Sheet2:Sheet4!A1:C3* refers to the values contained in the range A1:C3 on Sheet2, Sheet3, and Sheet4.

Equal sign beginning the formula

Exclamation point

Worksheet range

Range containing the source data in the specified worksheet

=Sheet2:Sheet4!A1:C3

FIGURE 7–8   Formula with a 3-D reference

Because a worksheet range is a group of adjacent worksheets, moving a worksheet into the range or removing a worksheet from the range affects the formula results. In the 3-D reference *Sheet2:Sheet4!B3*, if you move Sheet1 so it is positioned between Sheet3 and Sheet4, the value in cell B3 of Sheet1 is also included in the 3-D reference.

Table 7–1 gives other examples of formulas with worksheet and 3-D references.

TABLE 7–1   Formulas that reference other worksheets

FORMULA	DESCRIPTION
=Sheet4!D9	Displays the value from cell D9 in the Sheet4 worksheet
=Sheet1!D10+Sheet2!D11	Adds the value from cell D10 in the Sheet1 worksheet and the value from cell D11 in the Sheet2 worksheet
=SUM(Sheet2!D10:D11)	Adds the values from cells D10 and D11 in the Sheet2 worksheet
=SUM(Sheet2:Sheet4!D12)	Adds the value from cell D12 in the Sheet2, Sheet3, and Sheet4 worksheets

TECHNOLOGY CAREERS

Excel workbooks are extremely useful in areas of business that have a quantitative orientation, such as accounting and finance. In accounting, formulas are used to build financial statements. Financial officers in corporations use worksheets to project sales and control costs.

Step-by-Step 7.3

1. Click the **Corporate** sheet tab. You will enter formulas in this worksheet that reference cells in the Western and Eastern worksheets.

2. Click cell **B4**, and then type = to begin the formula.

3. Click the **Western** sheet tab. The worksheet name and an exclamation mark are added to the formula in the Formula Bar, which is *=Western!*. The Western worksheet appears in the workbook window so you can select a cell or range.

4. Click cell **B6**. The cell address is added to the reference in the Formula Bar, which is *=Western!B6*. The Western worksheet remains visible so you can select additional cells.

5. Press the **Enter** key. The formula is entered, and the Corporate worksheet is active again. The formula result $525,367 appears in cell B4.

6. In the Corporate worksheet, click cell **B5**, if it is not the active cell. Type = to begin the formula. Click the **Eastern** sheet tab, and then click cell **B6**. The formula *=Eastern!B6* appears in the Formula Bar. Press the **Enter** key. The formula is entered in cell B5 of the Corporate worksheet, displaying the result $521,001.

7. In the Corporate worksheet, click cell **B12**. Type = to begin the formula. Click the **Western** sheet tab, and then click cell **B3**. The formula *=Western!B3* appears in the Formula Bar.

8. Type + to enter the operator, click the **Eastern** sheet tab, and then click cell **B3**. The formula *=Western!B3+Eastern!B3* appears in the Formula Bar.

9. Press the **Enter** key. The formula is entered in cell B12 of the Corporate worksheet, which shows the formula result $306,744.

10. In the Corporate worksheet, click cell **B13**, if it is not already selected, and then type **=SUM(** to begin the formula.

11. Click the **Western** sheet tab, press and hold the **Shift** key, and then click the **Eastern** sheet tab. Release the **Shift** key. The formula with the worksheet range reference *=SUM('Western:Eastern'!* appears in the Formula Bar.

12. Click cell **B4**, and then press the **Enter** key. The cell reference is added to the 3-D reference in the formula, which is *=SUM('Western:Eastern'!B4)*. The formula result $551,399, which adds the values in cell B4 in the Eastern and Western worksheets, appears in cell B13.

13. Copy the formula in cell B13, and then paste the formula into cell B14. The value in cell B15 is the same as the value in cell B6, as shown in **Figure 7–9**.

FIGURE 7–9
Data summarized on one worksheet

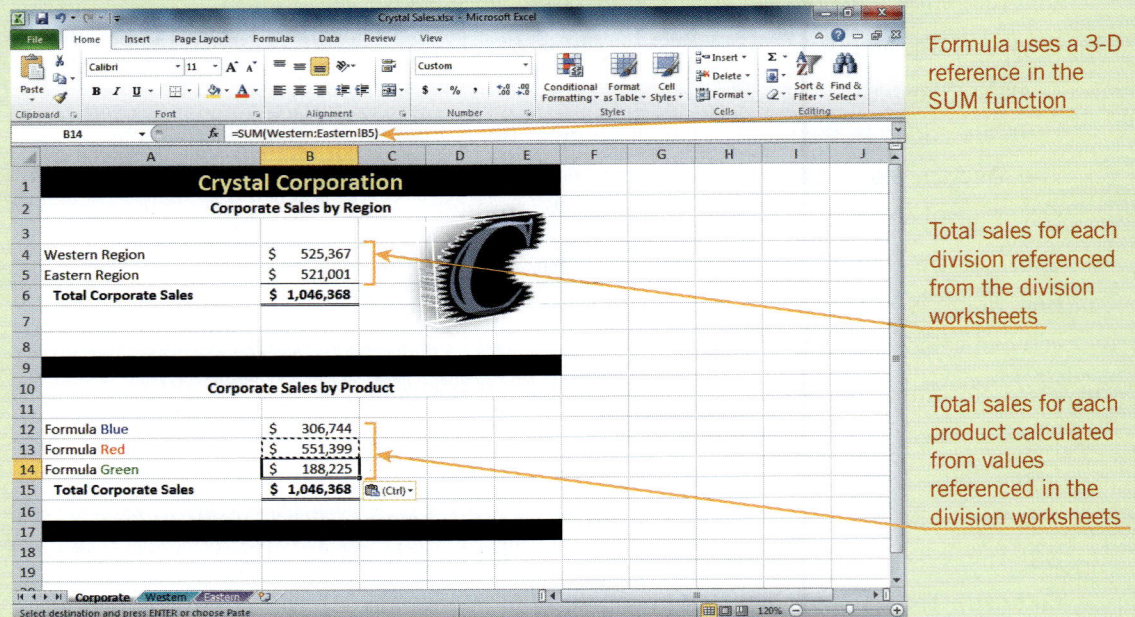

Formula uses a 3-D reference in the SUM function

Total sales for each division referenced from the division worksheets

Total sales for each product calculated from values referenced in the division worksheets

14. Save the workbook, and leave it open for the next Step-by-Step.

Printing a Workbook

So far, you have printed an active worksheet or selected areas of an active worksheet. You can also print an entire workbook, selected worksheets, or selected areas of a workbook. You designate the portion of the workbook to print on the Print tab in Backstage view, as shown in **Figure 7–10**. These options are described in **Table 7–2**.

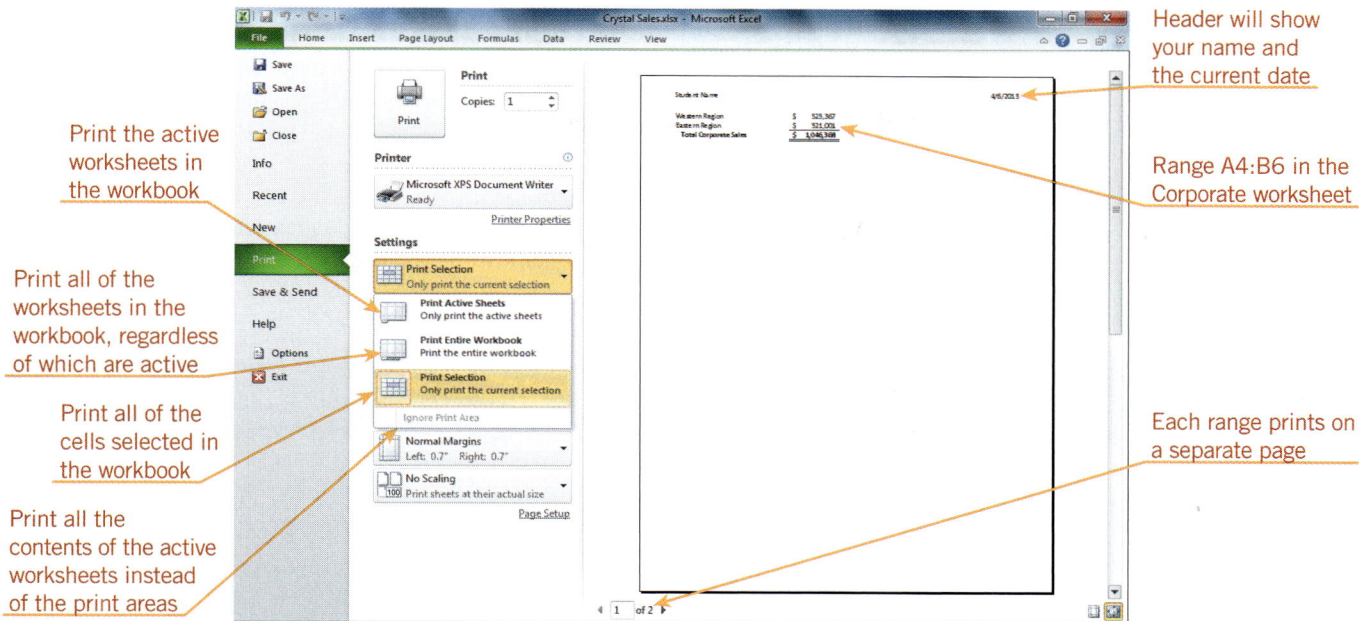

Print the active worksheets in the workbook

Print all of the worksheets in the workbook, regardless of which are active

Print all of the cells selected in the workbook

Print all the contents of the active worksheets instead of the print areas

Header will show your name and the current date

Range A4:B6 in the Corporate worksheet

Each range prints on a separate page

FIGURE 7–10   Print tab in Backstage view

TABLE 7–2   Print options

OPTION	DESCRIPTION
Print Active Sheets	Prints worksheet displayed in the workbook window, or a group of selected worksheets (Ctrl key +click sheet tabs to select multiple worksheets)
Print Entire Workbook	Prints all of the worksheets in the workbook
Print Selection	Prints the adjacent or nonadjacent ranges selected within a single worksheet
Ignore Print Area	Prints the entire worksheet, regardless of what print area is set for that worksheet

Printing Nonadjacent Selections of a Worksheet

You have already learned how to set a print area for a specific range in a worksheet. However, at times you might want to print more than one part of a worksheet on a page. For example, you might want to print the top and bottom sections of a work-sheet, but not the middle section. To do this, you need to select multiple ranges in the worksheet.

To select more than one cell or range in a worksheet, select the first cell or range, hold down the Ctrl key, select each additional cell or range, and then release the Ctrl key. You can set the print area to include the nonadjacent range, and then print the active sheet as usual. Another alternative is to click Print Selection in the Settings sec-tion on the Print tab.

Printing More Than One Worksheet

When a workbook includes multiple worksheets, you will often want to print more than one worksheet at a time. To print all of the worksheets in the workbook, click Print Entire Workbook in the Settings section on the Print tab. To print specific worksheets in a workbook, you must first select the worksheets. To select multiple worksheets in a workbook, hold down the Ctrl key as you click the sheet tab of each worksheet you want to include in the group, and then release the Ctrl key (this method is referred to as Ctrl+click). In the Settings section on the Print tab, click Print Active Sheets.

Step-by-Step 7.4

1. Insert a header with your name and the current date.

2. In the Corporate worksheet, select the range **A4:B6**.

3. Hold down the **Ctrl** key, select the range **A12:B15**, and then release the **Ctrl** key. A nonadjacent range is selected in the Corporate worksheet.

4. Click the **File** tab on the Ribbon. In the navigation bar, click **Print**. The Print tab appears.

5. In the Settings section, click the top button. Point to **Print Selection** in printing options, as shown in Figure 7–10.

6. Click **Print Selection**. The range A4:B6 will print on page 1 and the range A12:B15 will print on page 2, as shown in the preview.

7. Click the **Print** button. The selected areas are printed.

8. Click the **Western** sheet tab, hold down the **Ctrl** key, click the **Eastern** sheet tab, and then release the **Ctrl** key. The two sheet tabs are selected.

9. Click the **File** tab on the Ribbon. In the navigation bar, click **Print**. The Print tab appears.

10. In the Settings section, click the top button, and then click **Print Active Sheets**. The Print tab shows a preview the selected worksheets.

11. Click the **Print** button. The worksheets with the data for each region are printed on separate pages.

12. Save and close the workbook. Leave Excel open for the next Step-by-Step.

Working with Multiple Workbooks

So far, you have worked with worksheets in the same workbook. Sometimes you might want to use data from worksheets in different workbooks. You can view these worksheets on the screen by arranging the workbooks. If you want to use the data from a worksheet in one workbook in another workbook, you can move or copy the worksheet to the new workbook.

Arranging Workbooks

Arranging lets you view more than one workbook on the screen at the same time. To arrange all the open workbooks, click the View tab on the Ribbon. In the Window group, click the Arrange All button. The Arrange Windows dialog box appears, as shown in **Figure 7–11**. Click the arrangement that you want to use to view the workbooks: Tiled, Horizontal, Vertical, or Cascade.

Layouts for arranging the open workbooks in the workbook window

Check to arrange all the windows in the active workbook

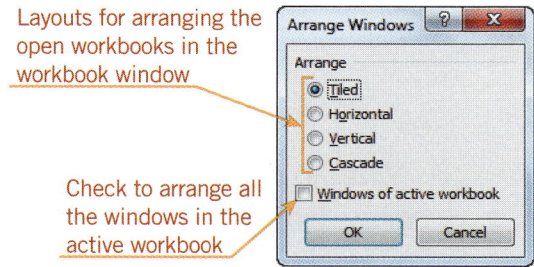

FIGURE 7–11   Arrange Windows dialog box

You can tell which workbook is active by looking at its title bar. The active workbook has a gray title bar, an Excel program icon in the upper-left corner, sizing buttons, and scroll bars. To make a workbook active, click its title bar or click anywhere in the worksheet. All of the buttons and commands on the Ribbon are available as usual.

Moving and Copying Worksheets Between Workbooks

When you need to include a worksheet from one workbook in another workbook, you can copy or move the worksheet. Right-click the sheet tab of the worksheet you want to move or copy, and then click Move or Copy on the shortcut menu. The Move or Copy dialog box appears. Click the To book arrow and click the workbook where you want to move or copy the selected worksheet. After you select the destination workbook, the names of all of its worksheets appear in the Before sheet box. Click the worksheet that you want to appear after the copied or moved worksheet. If you want to move the worksheet, click OK. If you want to copy the worksheet, click the Create a copy check box, and then click OK.

> **TIP**
>
> To move or copy multiple worksheets, first select the worksheets you want to move or copy, and then move or copy the worksheets as usual.

Step-by-Step 7.5

1. Open the **Annual.xlsx** workbook from the drive and folder where your Data Files are stored. Save the workbook as **Annual Income** followed by your initials.

2. Open the **March.xlsx** workbook from the drive and folder where your Data Files are stored. Save the workbook as **March Income** followed by your initials.

3. Click the **View** tab on the Ribbon. In the Window group, click the **Arrange All** button. The Arrange Windows dialog box appears, as shown in Figure 7–11.

4. Click the **Horizontal** option button, and then click **OK**. Both workbooks appear in the workbook window, as shown in **Figure 7–12**.

FIGURE 7–12
Workbooks arranged horizontally

Active workbook has an icon, a gray title bar, sizing buttons, and scroll bars

Inactive workbook has a white title bar and no scroll bars

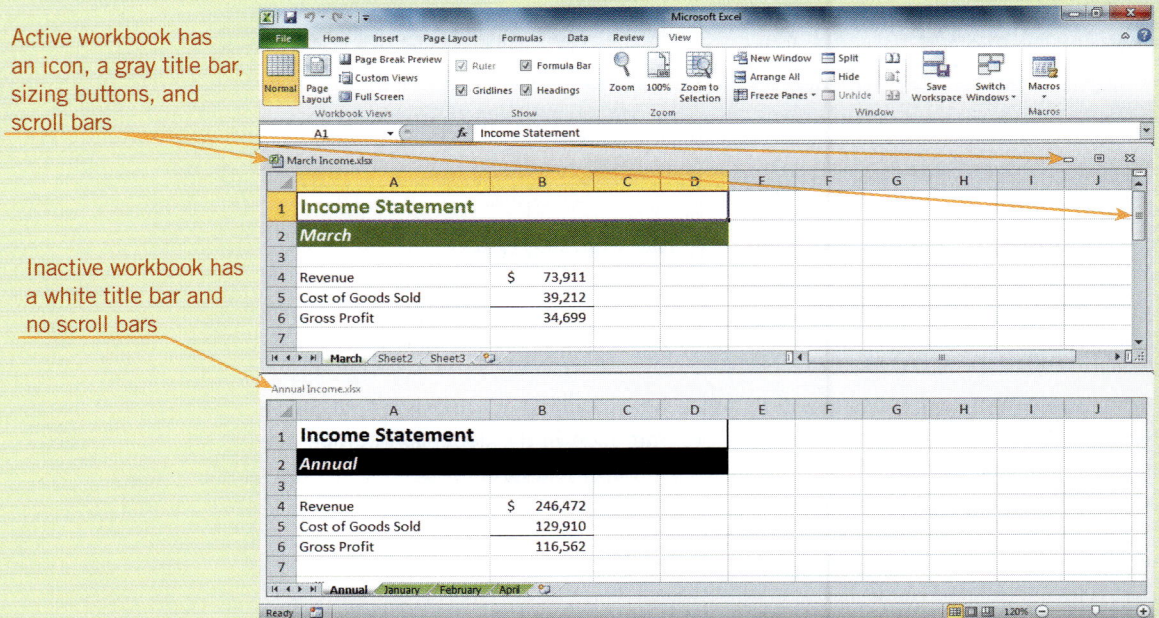

5. In the March Income workbook, right-click the **March** sheet tab, and then click **Move or Copy** on the shortcut menu. The Move or Copy dialog box appears.

6. Click the **To book** arrow, and then click **Annual Income.xlsx**. The worksheets in the Annual Income workbook appear in the Before sheet box.

7. In the Before sheet box, click **April** so the March worksheet will follow the February worksheet.

8. Click the **Create a copy** check box. The dialog box settings should appear similar to those in **Figure 7–13**.

FIGURE 7–13
Move or Copy dialog box

Workbook you want to copy a worksheet to

Worksheet you want to appear after the copied workbook

Check to copy rather than move the worksheet

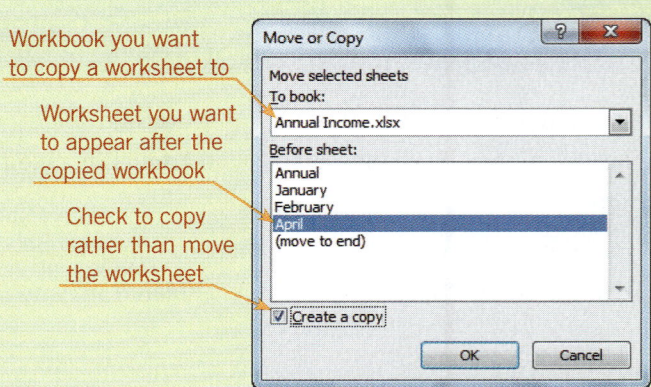

9. Click **OK**. A copy of the March worksheet appears in the Annual Income workbook before the April worksheet.

10. Click in the **March Income** workbook to make it the active workbook, and then on the title bar of the March Income workbook, click the **Close Window** button 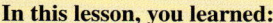 to close the workbook.

11. Click the **Maximize** button on the title bar of the Annual Income workbook. The workbook expands to fill the window.

12. Click the **Annual** tab. Notice that the totals that were updated include the values from the March worksheet because of the 3-D references in the formulas.

13. Click the **Annual** sheet tab, hold down the **Shift** key, click the **April** sheet tab, and then release the **Shift** key to select all the worksheets in the workbook. Insert a header with your name and the current date. The header appears on all the worksheets.

14. Click the **File** tab to open Backstage view. On the navigation bar, click **Print**. On the Print tab, in the Settings section, click the top button, and then click the **Print Entire Workbook**. Click the **Print** button. Save and close the workbook.

SUMMARY

In this lesson, you learned:

- Sheet tabs identify the names of worksheets. You click a sheet tab to make a worksheet the active sheet.

- You can rename worksheets with more descriptive names to better identify them. You can also change the color of the sheet tabs.

- Data is often best organized in multiple worksheets. You can drag a sheet tab to a new position to organize the worksheets in a more logical order. You can hide worksheets from view and then unhide them when needed. You can also insert and delete worksheets to accommodate the data.

- Rather than retyping data, you can create references to cells or ranges in another worksheet. You can also create formulas with 3-D references to the same cell or range in multiple worksheets.

- You can print entire workbooks, active worksheets, or selections in one or more worksheets.

- Arranging multiple workbooks in the workbook window lets you view their contents at the same time. Worksheets can be moved or copied from one workbook to the location you specify in the same or another workbook.

■ VOCABULARY REVIEW

Define the following terms:

3-D reference
destination

source

worksheet range

REVIEW QUESTIONS

TRUE / FALSE

Circle T if the statement is true or F if the statement is false.

T   F   **1.**   Hiding a worksheet permanently removes it from the workbook.

T   F   **2.**   You can insert a worksheet in a workbook as needed to accommodate your data.

T   F   **3.**   When you create a reference to a cell in another worksheet, the location where the data will be used is the source.

T   F   **4.**   A worksheet range is a group of adjacent worksheets.

T   F   **5.**   In addition to printing an active worksheet or selected areas of an active worksheet, you can also print an entire workbook, selected worksheets, or selected areas of a workbook.

MATCHING

Match the correct formula result in Column 2 to its formula in Column 1.

Column 1

1. =Sheet2!D10

2. =Sheet2!D10+Sheet3!D11

3. =SUM(Sheet2:Sheet4!D10)

4. =SUM(Sheet2!D10:D11)

5. =Sheet3!D10+Sheet3!D11

Column 2

A. Inserts the value in cell D10 of the Sheet2 worksheet

B. Adds the values in cells D10 and D11 of the Sheet3 worksheet

C. Adds the values in cells D10 and D11 of the Sheet2 worksheet

D. Adds the values in cell D10 of the Sheet2 worksheet and cell D11 of the Sheet3 worksheet

E. Adds the values in cell D10 in the Sheet2, Sheet3, and Sheet4 worksheets

FILL IN THE BLANK

Complete the following sentences by writing the correct word or words in the blanks provided.

1. A(n) _____ is a collection of worksheets.

2. The worksheet that appears in the workbook window is the _____.

3. _____ identify worksheets within a workbook and appear at the bottom of the workbook window.

4. You can create formulas with _____ to the same cell or range in multiple worksheets.

5. _____ multiple workbooks in the workbook window lets you view their contents at the same time.

■ PROJECTS

If you have a SAM 2010 user profile, your instructor may have assigned an autogradable version of the indicated project. If so, log into the SAM 2010 Web site at *www.cengage.com/sam2010* to download the instruction and start files.

PROJECT 7–1

1. Open the **Rain.xlsx** workbook from the drive and folder where your Data Files are stored. Save the workbook as **Rain Records** followed by your initials.

2. Move the Sheet2 worksheet to the left of the Sheet3 worksheet.

3. Rename the worksheets and change the sheet tab colors as listed below:

Worksheet	New Name	Tab Color
Sheet1	**Annual**	Aqua, Accent 5
Sheet2	**January**	Aqua, Accent 5, Lighter 80%
Sheet3	**February**	Aqua, Accent 5, Lighter 60%
Sheet4	**March**	Aqua, Accent 5, Lighter 40%

4. Delete the Sheet5 worksheet.

5. In the Annual worksheet, in cell B3, display the total rainfall recorded in the January worksheet in cell B34.

6. In the Annual worksheet, in cell B4, display the total rainfall recorded in the February worksheet in cell B31.

7. In the Annual worksheet, in cell B5, display the total rainfall recorded in the March worksheet in cell B34.

8. Insert a header with your name and the current date in the Annual worksheet, and then save the workbook.

9. Print the Annual worksheet, and then close the workbook.

 PROJECT 7–2

1. Open the **Vote.xlsx** workbook from the drive and folder where your Data Files are stored. Save the workbook as **Vote Tally** followed by your initials.

2. Rename the worksheets and change the sheet tab colors as listed below:

Worksheet	New Name	Tab Color
Sheet1	**District 5**	Red
Sheet2	**P107**	Yellow
Sheet3	**P106**	Purple
Sheet4	**P105**	Green

3. Delete the Sheet5 worksheet.

4. Reposition the worksheets so they appear in the following order from left to right: District 5, P105, P106, and P107.

5. In the District 5 worksheet, in cell D7, enter a formula that adds the values in cell C5 of each of the precinct worksheets.

6. In the District 5 worksheet, in cell D9, enter a formula that adds the values in cell C7 of each of the precinct worksheets.

7. In the District 5 worksheet, in cell D11, enter a formula that adds the values in cell C9 of each of the precinct worksheets.

8. In the District 5 worksheet, in cell D13, enter a formula that adds the values in cell C11 of each of the precinct worksheets.

9. Insert a header with your name and the current date in the District 5 worksheet, and then save the workbook.

10. Print the District 5 worksheet, and then close the workbook.

PROJECT 7–3

1. Open the **Alamo.xlsx** workbook from the drive and folder where your Data Files are stored. Save the workbook as **Alamo Industries** followed by your initials.

2. Change the sheet tab colors as listed below:

Worksheet	Tab Color
Consolidated	Green
Alamogordo	Orange
Artesia	Light Blue

3. In the Consolidated worksheet, in cell D6, enter a formula that adds the values in cell B6 of the Alamogordo and Artesia worksheets.

4. In the Consolidated worksheet, in cell D7, enter a formula that adds the values in cell B7 of the Alamogordo and Artesia worksheets.

5. In the Consolidated worksheet, in cell D9, enter a formula that adds the values in cell B9 of the Alamogordo and Artesia worksheets.

6. In the Consolidated worksheet, in cell D10, enter a formula that adds the values in cell B10 of the Alamogordo and Artesia worksheets.

7. Insert a header with your name and the current date in the Consolidated worksheet, and then save the workbook.

8. Print all of the worksheets in the workbook, and then close the workbook.

PROJECT 7–4

1. Open the **Delta.xlsx** workbook from the drive and folder where your Data Files are stored. Save the workbook as **Delta Circuitry** followed by your initials.

2. Reposition the worksheets so they appear in the following order from left to right: Year, January, February, and March.

3. Change the worksheet tab colors as listed below:

Worksheet	Tab Color
Year	Red
January	Purple, Accent 4
February	Orange, Accent 6
March	Blue, Accent 1

4. In the Year worksheet, in cells B5, B6, and B7, display the total January monthly production for Circuits 370, 380, and 390. These values are recorded in the January worksheet in the range F4:F6.

5. In the Year worksheet, in cells C5, C6, and C7, display the total February monthly production for each circuit. These values are recorded in the February worksheet in the range F4:F6.

6. In the Year worksheet, in cells D5, D6, and D7, display the total March monthly production for each circuit. These values are recorded in the March worksheet in the range F4:F6.

7. Insert a header with your name and the current date in the Year worksheet, and then save the workbook.

8. Print the Year worksheet, and then close the workbook.

■ CRITICAL THINKING

ACTIVITY 7–1

Suppose you manage a local clothing store chain. Each of the chain's three stores has sent you a workbook in the same format that contains inventory data. You want to use the data you received to create a summary workbook with totals from all three stores. Use Excel Help to find out how you can create an external reference to a cell or range in another workbook. Write a brief description of your findings.

LESSON 8

Working with Charts

**Estimated Time:
2.5 hours**

■ OBJECTIVES

Upon completion of this lesson, you should be able to:

- Identify the types of charts you can create in Excel.
- Create an embedded chart in a worksheet and move a chart to a chart sheet.
- Update a data source.
- Choose a chart layout and style.
- Create a 3-D chart.
- Display and hide chart elements.
- Format and modify a chart.
- Create sparklines.

■ VOCABULARY

axis

chart

chart area

chart layout

chart sheet

chart style

column chart

data label

data marker

data series

data source

data table

embedded chart

exploded pie chart

legend

line chart

pie chart

plot area

scatter chart

sparkline

▶ **VOCABULARY**
chart

A *chart* is a graphical representation of data. Charts make the data in a worksheet easier to understand by providing a visual picture of the data. For example, the left side of the worksheet shown in Figure 8–1 shows the populations of three major American cities over a 25-year time period. You might be able to detect the population changes by carefully examining the table. However, the population changes in each city are easier to see when the data is illustrated in a chart, such as the one shown on the right side of the worksheet in **Figure 8–1**. In this lesson, you will learn how to create, edit, and format charts.

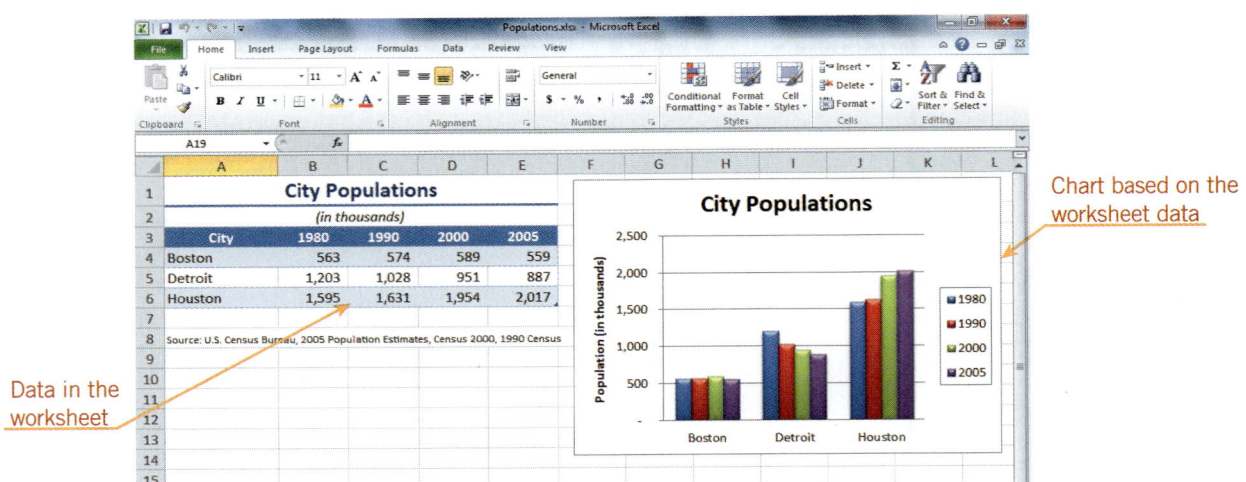

FIGURE 8–1 Worksheet data and chart

Comparing Chart Types

You can create a variety of charts in Excel. Each chart type works best for certain types of data. In this lesson, you will create four of the most commonly used charts: a column chart, a line chart, a pie chart, and a scatter chart. These charts as well as several other types of charts are available in the Charts group on the Insert tab on the Ribbon, as shown in **Figure 8–2**.

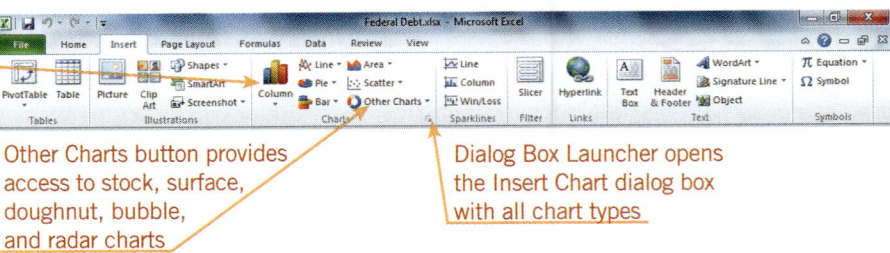

FIGURE 8–2 Charts group on the Insert tab

Column Chart

A *column chart* uses bars of varying heights to illustrate data in a worksheet. It is useful for showing relationships among categories of data. For example, the column chart in Figure 8–1 has one vertical bar to represent the population of each city in four different years. The bars show how the population of one city compares to populations of other cities.

Line Chart

A *line chart* is similar to a column chart, but it uses points connected by a line instead of bars. A line chart is ideal for illustrating trends over time. For example, the line chart shown in **Figure 8–3** illustrates the federal budget debt from 1995 to 2009. The vertical *axis* represents the federal budget debt in billions of dollars, and the horizontal axis shows the years. The line chart makes it easy to see that the federal budget debt has increased over time. A line chart can include multiple lines to compare two or more sets of data. For example, you could use a second line to chart the tax revenue received during the same time period.

▶ **VOCABULARY**

column chart

line chart

axis

TIP

Businesses often use column, bar, and line charts to illustrate growth over several periods. For example, a column chart can illustrate the changes in yearly production or income over a 10-year period.

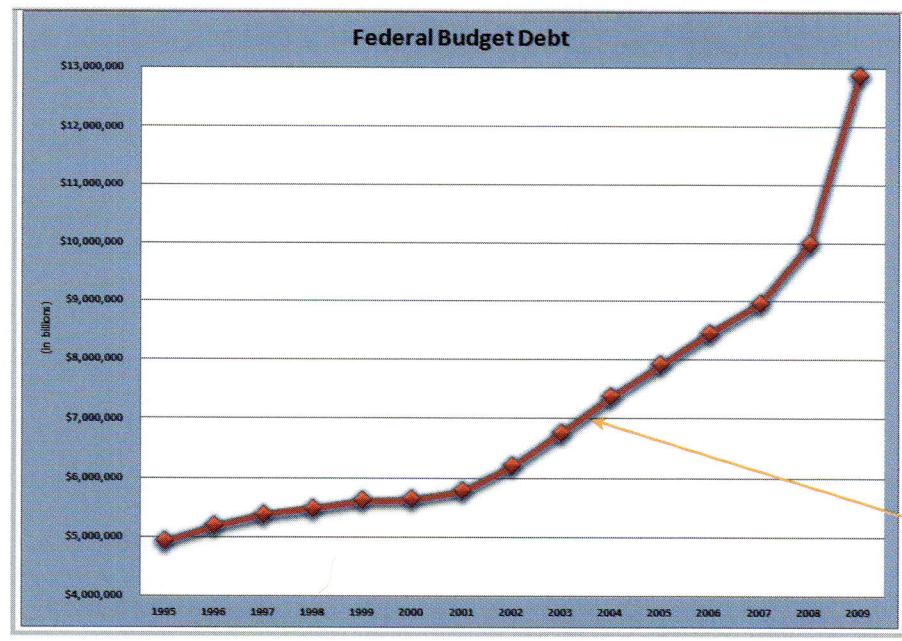

Ideal for illustrating trends of data over time

FIGURE 8–3   Line chart

Pie Chart

A *pie chart* shows the relationship of parts to a whole. Each part is shown as a "slice" of the pie. For example, **Figure 8–4** shows a pie chart that illustrates the grades earned by students in a class. Each slice represents one letter grade, and its size corresponds to the number of students who earned that grade.

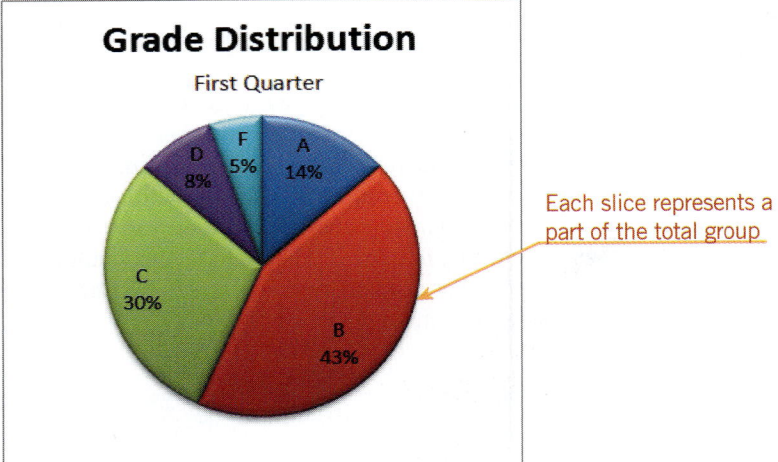

Each slice represents a part of the total group

FIGURE 8–4   Pie chart

You can pull one slice or multiple slices away from the pie to distinguish them, creating an *exploded pie chart*. This is helpful when you want to emphasize a specific part of the pie.

Scatter Chart

A *scatter chart*, sometimes called an XY chart, shows the relationship between two categories of data, such as a person's height and weight. One category is represented on the vertical axis, and the other category is represented on the horizontal axis. Because the data points on a scatter chart are not related to each other, they are usually not connected to each other with a line, like they are in a line chart. For example, **Figure 8–5** shows a scatter chart with one data point for each of 12 individuals, based on the person's height and weight. In most cases, a taller person tends to weigh more than a shorter person. However, because some people are underweight and others are overweight, you cannot use a line to represent the relationship between height and weight.

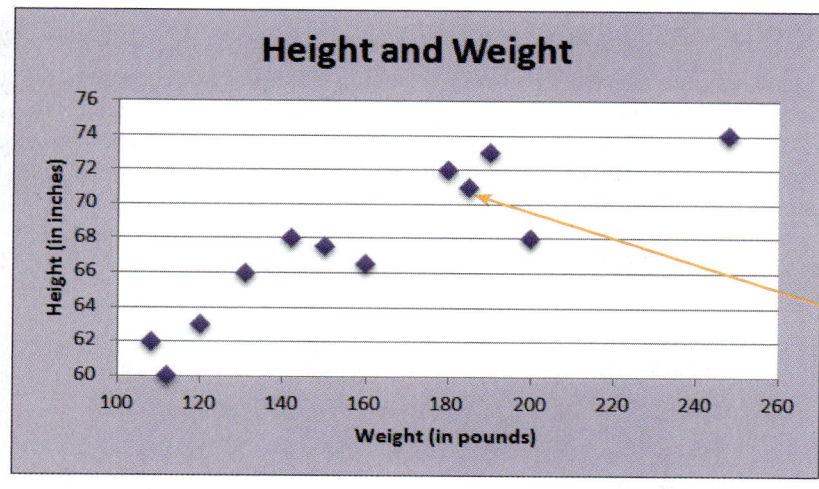

FIGURE 8–5   Scatter chart

Creating a Chart

The process for creating a chart is similar no matter which chart type you want to create. First, you select the data you want to use for the chart. Second, you select a chart type. Finally, you select the chart location. In this section, you will create a column chart.

Selecting the Data to Chart

Charts are based on data. In Excel, the chart data, called the ***data source***, is stored in a range of cells in the worksheet. When you select the data source for a chart, you should also include the text you want to use as labels in the chart. You can also choose whether to chart more than one series of data. A ***data series*** is a group of related information in a column or row of a worksheet that is plotted on the chart.

▶ **VOCABULARY**
data source

data series

Selecting a Chart Type

The next step is to select the type of chart you want to create, such as a column, pie, or line chart. Each chart type has a variety of subtypes you can choose from. The chart types are available on the Insert tab in the Charts group. You can click the button for a specific chart type and then select the subtype you want. The Insert Chart dialog box, shown in **Figure 8–6**, provides access to all of the chart types and subtypes. You open the Insert Chart dialog box by clicking the Dialog Box Launcher in the Charts group on the Insert tab.

Chart types you can create in Excel

Chart types organized by chart subtypes

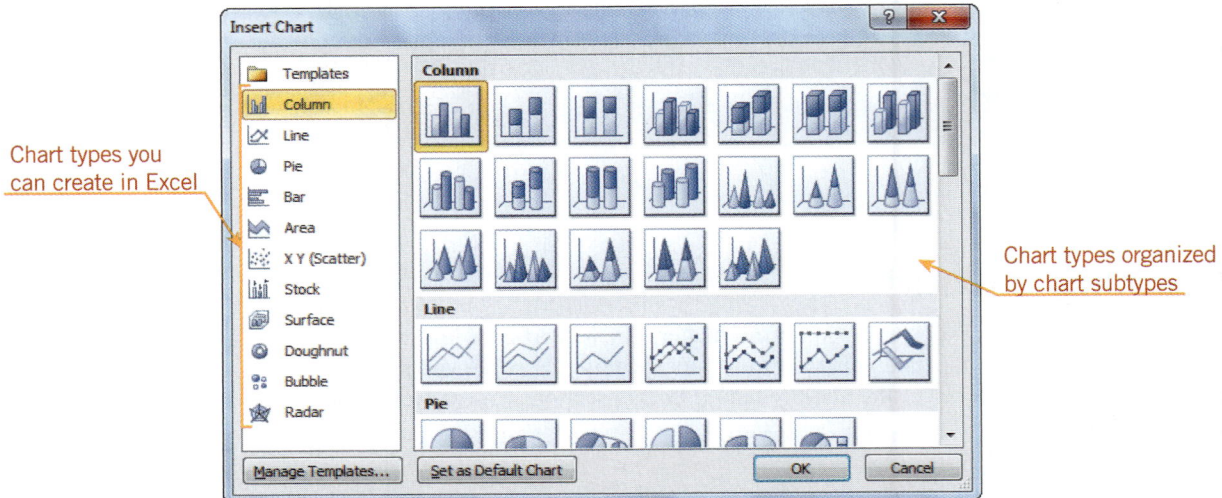

FIGURE 8–6   Insert Chart dialog box

Choosing the Chart Location

▶ **VOCABULARY**
embedded chart

After you select a chart type and subtype, the chart is inserted in the center of the worksheet, as shown in **Figure 8-7**. This is called an *embedded chart*. When a chart is selected, the Chart Tools appear on the Ribbon with three tabs: Design, Layout, and Format. Also, a selection box with sizing handles appears around the chart. The embedded chart can be viewed at the same time as the data from which it is created. When you print the worksheet, the chart is also printed.

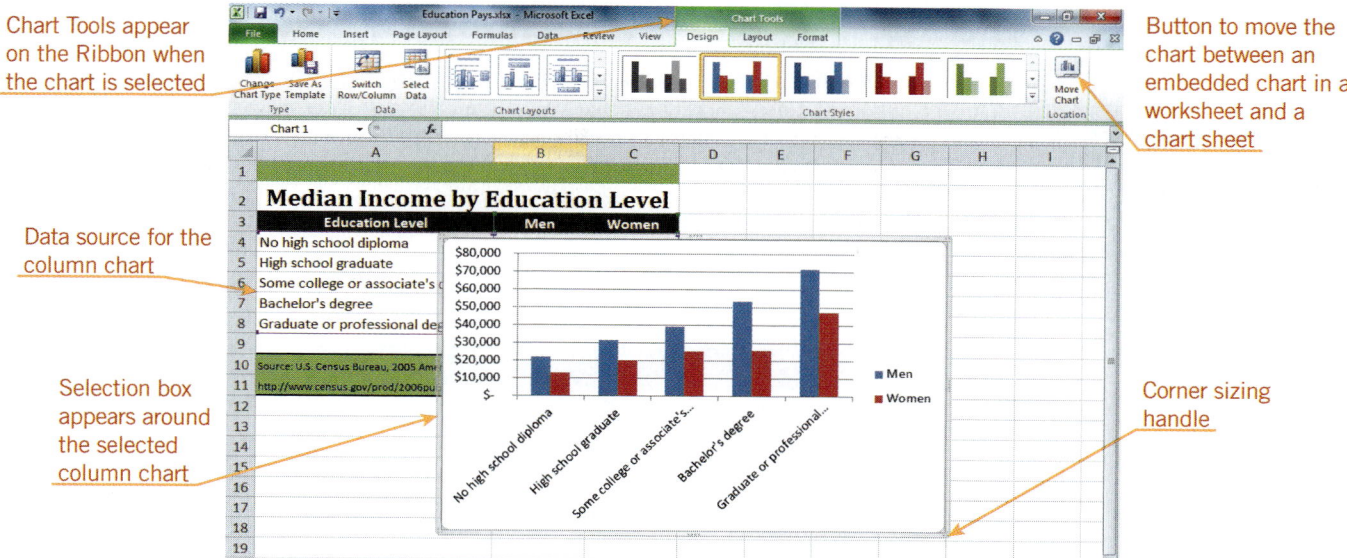

Chart Tools appear on the Ribbon when the chart is selected

Button to move the chart between an embedded chart in a worksheet and a chart sheet

Data source for the column chart

Selection box appears around the selected column chart

Corner sizing handle

FIGURE 8–7   Embedded chart

An embedded chart might cover the data source or other information in the worksheet. You can quickly move and resize the embedded chart so it fits better within the worksheet. You move an embedded chart by dragging the selected chart by its selection box to a different part of the worksheet. You resize an embedded chart by dragging one of the sizing handles, which are indicated by the dots at the corners and sides of the selected chart.

You can move an embedded chart to a *chart sheet*, which is a separate sheet in a workbook that stores a chart. A chart sheet does not contain worksheet cells, data, or formulas. A chart sheet displays the chart without its data source, and is convenient when you plan to create more than one chart from the same data or want to focus on the chart rather than its underlying data.

EXTRA FOR EXPERTS

You can keep a chart's height and width in the same proportion as you resize it by pressing Shift as you drag a corner sizing handle.

▶ **VOCABULARY**
chart sheet

TIP

You can rename a chart sheet like any other worksheet. Right-click its sheet tab, and then click Rename on the shortcut menu. Type a descriptive name for the chart sheet, and then press the Enter key.

TIP

Embedded charts are useful when you want to print a chart next to the data the chart illustrates. When a chart will be displayed or printed without the data used to create the chart, a separate chart sheet is usually more appropriate.

To move an embedded chart to a chart sheet, click the Chart Tools Design tab on the Ribbon. Then, in the Location group, click the Move Chart button. The Move Chart dialog box appears, as shown in **Figure 8–8**. You can choose to move the chart to a new chart sheet that you name or to any worksheet in the workbook as an embedded chart. You can use the same process to move a chart from a chart sheet to any worksheet as an embedded chart.

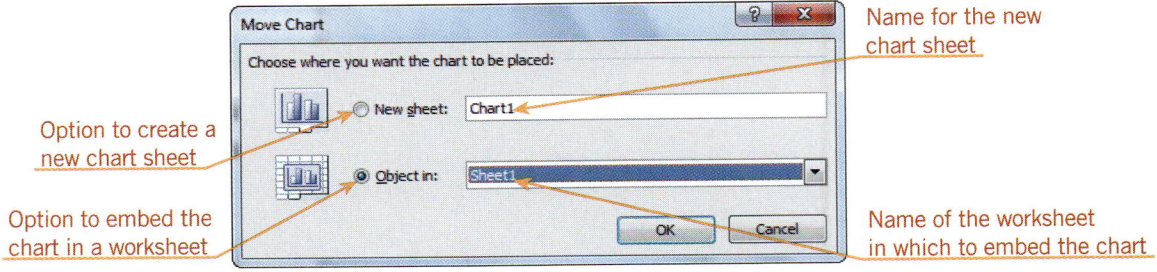

Name for the new chart sheet

Option to create a new chart sheet

Option to embed the chart in a worksheet

Name of the worksheet in which to embed the chart

FIGURE 8–8 Move Chart dialog box

Step-by-Step 8.1

1. Open the **Education.xlsx** workbook from the drive and folder where your Data Files are stored. Save the workbook as **Education Pays** followed by your initials. Column A contains education levels, and columns B and C contain the median incomes of men and women for each corresponding education level.

2. Select the range **A3:C8**. This is the data you want to chart.

3. Click the **Insert** tab on the Ribbon. In the Charts group, click the **Column** button. A gallery of available column chart subtypes appears.

4. In the 2-D Column section, point to **Clustered Column** (the first chart in the first row). A ScreenTip appears with a description of the selected chart: *Clustered Column. Compare values across categories by using vertical rectangles.*

5. Click the **Clustered Column** button. The 2-D clustered column chart is embedded in the worksheet. A selection box with sizing handles appears around the chart, as shown in Figure 8–7.

6. Point to the selection box. The pointer changes to the move pointer. Drag the selected chart so that the upper-left corner of the chart is in cell A13. The chart is repositioned in the worksheet.

7. Drag the lower-right sizing handle to cell **D26**. The chart is sized to cover the range A13:D26.

8. On the Ribbon, click the **Design** tab, if it is not already selected.

9. In the Location group, click the **Move Chart** button. The Move Chart dialog box appears, as shown in Figure 8–8.

10. Click the **New sheet** option button. The text in the New sheet box is selected so you can type a descriptive name for the chart sheet.

11. In the New sheet box, type **Column**.

12. Click **OK**. The embedded chart moves to a chart sheet named *Column*, as shown in **Figure 8–9**. The chart illustrates the value of education in attaining higher income. The columns get higher on the right side of the chart, indicating that those who stay in school are rewarded with higher incomes.

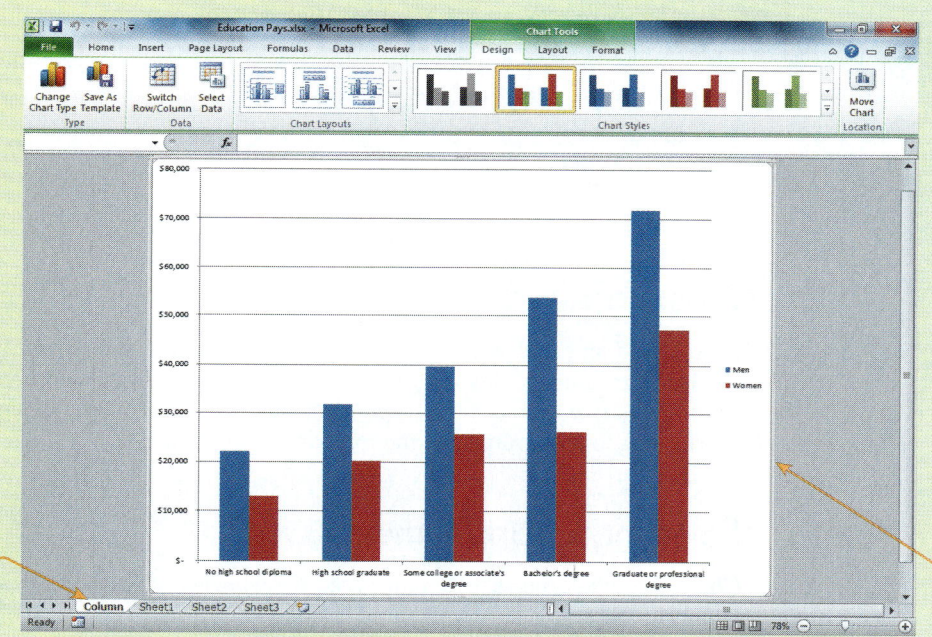

FIGURE 8–9
Column chart sheet added to workbook

Sheet tab for the chart sheet

Selected chart in the chart sheet

13. Save the workbook, and leave it open for the next Step-by-Step.

TECHNOLOGY CAREERS

Excel worksheets are used in education to evaluate and instruct students. Instructors use worksheets to track student grades and to organize the number of hours spent on certain topics. Charts help illustrate these numerical relationships.

Updating a Data Source

Charts are based on the data stored in a worksheet. If you need to change the data in the worksheet, the chart is automatically updated to reflect the new data. You switch between a chart sheet and a worksheet by clicking the appropriate sheet tabs.

Step-by-Step 8.2

1. Click the **Sheet1** sheet tab. This worksheet with the data source appears.

2. Click cell **A5**, and then enter **High school diploma**.

3. Click the **Column** sheet tab to display the chart sheet. The label for the second column reflects the edit you made to the data source.

4. Save the workbook, and leave it open for the next Step-by-Step.

Designing a Chart

▶ **VOCABULARY**
legend

Most charts include some basic elements, such as a title and *legend*, which you can choose to include or hide. You can also choose a chart style and layout to give the chart a cohesive design. Finally, you can add labels and other elements to make the chart easier to understand and interpret and more attractive.

Selecting Chart Elements

Charts are made up of different parts, or elements. **Figure 8–10** identifies some common chart elements, which are described in **Table 8–1**. Not all elements appear in every type of chart. For example, a pie chart does not have axes. Also, you can choose which chart elements to use in a chart.

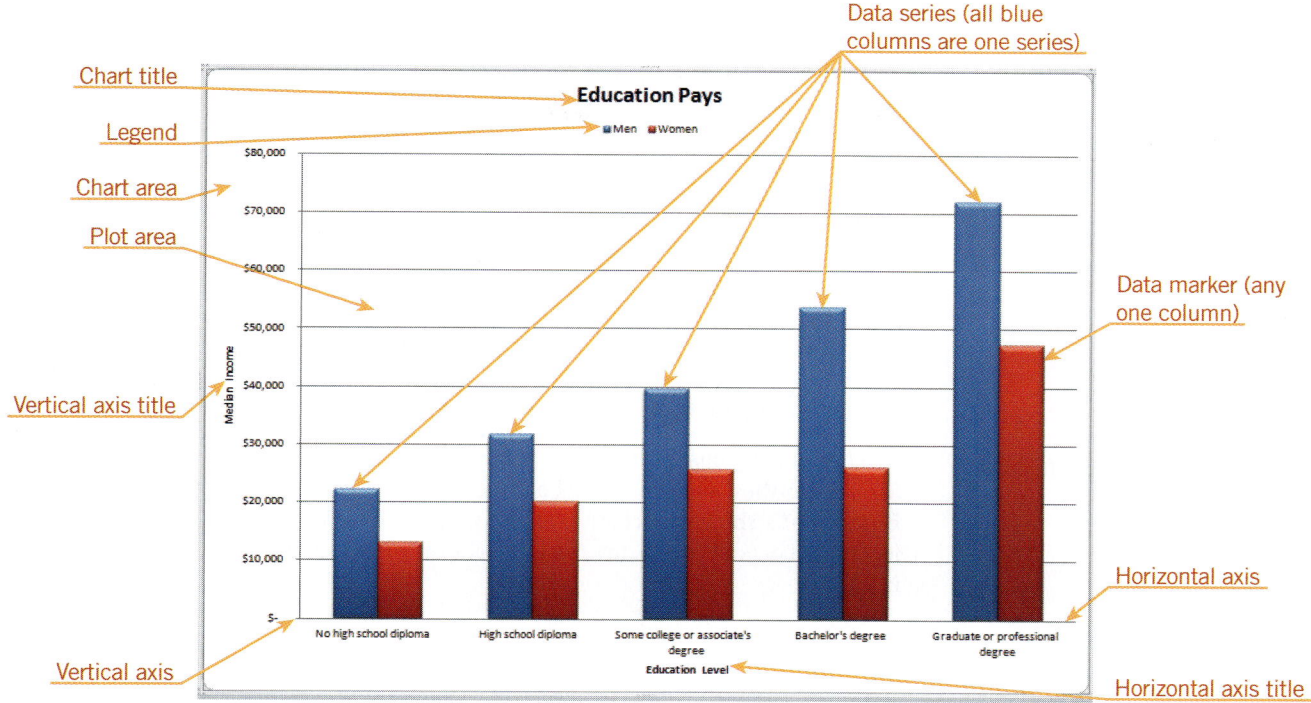

FIGURE 8–10   Chart elements

TABLE 8–1   Chart elements

ELEMENT	DESCRIPTION
Chart area	The entire chart and all other chart elements
Plot area	The area that displays the graphical representation of data
Data series	Related information in a worksheet column or row that is plotted on a chart; many charts can include more than one data series
Data marker	A symbol (such as a bar, line, dot, slice, and so forth) that represents a single data point or value from the corresponding worksheet cell
Data label	Text or numbers that provide additional information about a data marker, such as the value from the worksheet cell (not shown in Figure 8–10)
Axes	Lines that establish a relationship between data in a chart; most charts have a horizontal x-axis and a vertical y-axis
Titles	Descriptive labels that identify the contents of the chart and the axes
Legend	A list that identifies the patterns, symbols, or colors used in a chart
Data table	A grid that displays the data plotted in the chart (not shown in Figure 8–10)

The quickest way to select a chart element is to click it. You can tell that you are clicking the correct element by first pointing to the element to display a ScreenTip with its name. A selected chart element is surrounded by a selection box. You can also use the Ribbon to select chart elements. When the chart is selected, click the Format tab or the Layout tab on the Ribbon. In the Current Selection group, click the arrow next to the Chart Elements box. A menu of chart elements for the selected chart appears. Click the name of the element you want to select.

After you select a chart element, you can modify it. For example, you can select the chart title or an axis title, and then enter new text for the title. You can also use the standard text formatting tools to change the font, font size, font color, and so forth of the selected title.

Choosing a Chart Layout and Style

You can quickly change a chart's appearance by applying a layout and style. A *chart layout* specifies which elements are included in a chart and where they are placed. **Figure 8–11** shows the chart layouts available for column charts. For example, the legend appears above, below, to the right of, or to the left of the chart in different layouts.

Layouts include different elements and placements

FIGURE 8–11   Chart Layouts gallery for column charts

A *chart style* formats the chart based on the colors, fonts, and effects associated with the workbook's theme. **Figure 8–12** shows the chart styles available for column charts.

Styles include different colors and effects

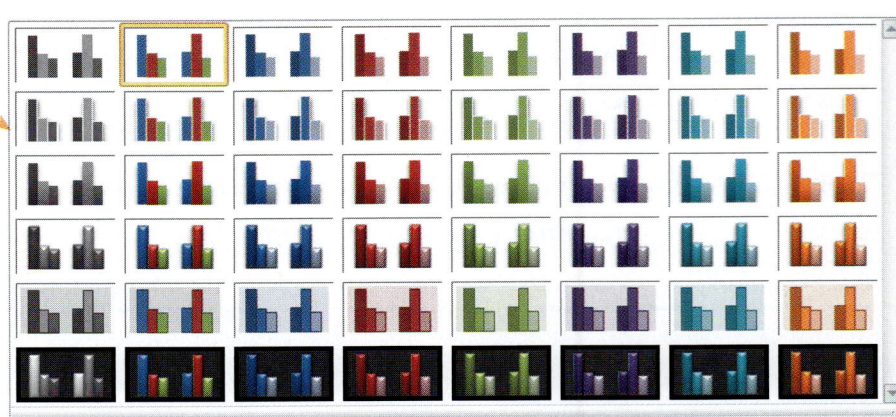

FIGURE 8–12   Chart Styles gallery for column charts

You can quickly choose a layout and style for a selected chart from the Ribbon. Click the Design tab on the Ribbon. In the Chart Layouts group, click the chart layout you want to use. In the Chart Styles group, click the chart style you want to use.

Arranging Chart Elements

You can modify a chart's appearance by displaying and hiding specific chart elements and rearranging where they are positioned. For example, you can choose when and where to display the chart title, axis titles, legend, *data labels*, *data table*, axes, gridlines, and the *plot area*. First, select the chart. Then click the Layout tab on the Ribbon. The Labels, Axes, and Background groups on the Layout tab contain buttons for each chart element. Finally, use the commands on the appropriate button to display that element in a particular location in the *chart area* or hide it.

▶ **VOCABULARY**

data label

data table

plot area

chart area

Step-by-Step 8.3

1. On the Ribbon, click the **Design** tab, if it is not already selected.

2. In the Chart Layouts group, click the **More** button ▾. The Chart Layouts gallery appears, as shown in Figure 8–11.

3. Click **Layout 9** (the third layout in the third row). Placeholders for the chart title and axes titles are added to the chart.

4. Click the **Chart Title** to select it. Type **Education Pays**, and then press the **Enter** key. The chart title is updated.

5. Click the vertical **Axis Title** to select it, type **Median Income**, and then press the **Enter** key.

6. Click the horizontal **Axis Title** to select it, type **Education Level**, and then press the **Enter** key.

7. On the Design tab, in the Chart Styles group, click the **More** button ▾. The Chart Styles gallery appears, as shown in Figure 8–12.

8. Click **Style 26** (the second style in the fourth row). The chart changes to match the selected style.

9. On the Ribbon, click the **Layout** tab.

10. On the Layout tab, in the Labels group, click the **Legend** button. A gallery appears with different placement options for the legend.

11. Click **Show Legend at Top**. The legend moves to below the chart title, as shown in Figure 8–10.

12. On the Ribbon, click the **Insert** tab. In the Text group, click the **Header & Footer** button. The Page Setup dialog box appears with the Header/Footer tab active. Click the **Custom Header** button. The Header dialog box opens.

▶ **TIP**

You can delete a selected chart by pressing Delete. You can delete chart sheets by right-clicking the sheet tab for the chart sheet, and then clicking Delete on the shortcut menu.

13. In the Left section box, type your name. Click in the **Right section** box, and then click the **Insert Date** button 🗓. Click the **OK** button in each dialog box. The header is added to the chart sheet.

14. Save the workbook, print the chart sheet, and close the workbook. Leave Excel open for the next Step-by-Step.

Creating a 3-D Chart

A pie chart shows the relationship of a part to a whole. Each part is shown as a "slice" of the pie. The slices are different colors to distinguish each *data marker*. Pie charts, as with many chart types, can be two-dimensional (2-D) or three-dimensional (3-D). When you select the chart style, click a 3-D chart subtype to create a 3-D chart.

Step-by-Step 8.4

1. Open the **Great.xlsx** workbook from the drive and folder where your Data Files are stored. Save the workbook as **Great Plains** followed by your initials.

2. Select the range **A5:B8**. This range contains the data that shows the sales for each product segment.

3. Click the **Insert** tab on the Ribbon. In the Charts group, click the **Pie** button.

4. In the 3-D Pie section, click **Pie in 3-D** (the first chart in the row). A 3-D pie chart is embedded in the worksheet.

5. On the Ribbon, click the **Design** tab, if the tab is not already selected. In the Chart Layouts group, click the **More** button 🔽. The Chart Layouts gallery appears.

6. Click **Layout 1** (the first layout in the first row). The legend disappears, and each slice of the pie shows the label and the percentage of the whole it comprises.

7. In the chart, click the **Chart Title**, type **Annual Sales by Segment**, and then press the **Enter** key. The new chart title is entered above the chart.

8. Move and resize the chart to fit within the range **D1:H9**. The 3-D pie chart, shown in **Figure 8–13**, illustrates that soybeans account for the largest percentage of annual sales.

⊡ EXTRA FOR EXPERTS

To create an exploded pie chart, select one of the 2-D or 3-D exploded pie chart subtypes. Or, you can click the data markers in an existing pie chart to select the series, click the slice you want to explode, and then drag the selected slice away from the pie.

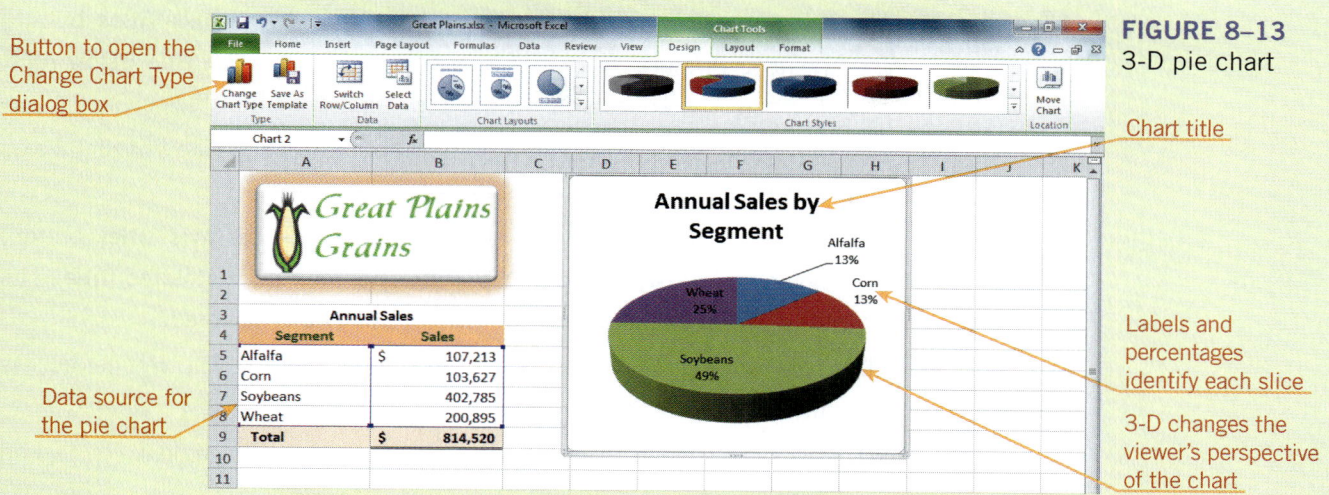

Button to open the Change Chart Type dialog box

Data source for the pie chart

Chart title

Labels and percentages identify each slice

3-D changes the viewer's perspective of the chart

FIGURE 8–13
3-D pie chart

9. Click cell **A11** to deselect the pie chart.

10. Insert a header with your name and the current date, and then print the worksheet.

11. Save and close the workbook. Leave Excel open for the next Step-by-Step.

Formatting and Modifying a Chart

Scatter charts are sometimes called XY charts because they place data points between the x-axis and the y-axis. Scatter charts can be harder to design because you must designate which data should be used on each axis.

Step-by-Step 8.5

1. Open the **Coronado.xlsx** workbook from the drive and folder where your Data Files are stored. Save the workbook as **Coronado Foundries** followed by your initials.

2. Select the range **B5:B15**. Press and hold the **Ctrl** key, select the range **D5:D15**, and then release the **Ctrl** key. This nonadjacent range contains the data you want to chart.

3. Click the **Insert** tab on the Ribbon. In the Charts group, click the **Scatter** button. In the Scatter section, click **Scatter with only Markers** (the first chart in the first row). The scatter chart is embedded in the worksheet.

4. On the Ribbon, click the **Layout** tab. In the Labels group, click the **Chart Title** button, and then click **Above Chart**. The chart title appears above the scatter chart and is selected.

5. Type **June Production and Scrap Report**, and then press the **Enter** key.

6. On the Layout tab, in the Labels group, click the **Axis Titles** button, point to **Primary Horizontal Axis Title**, and then click **Title Below Axis**. The axis title appears below the horizontal axis and is selected.

7. Type **Units Produced**, and then press the **Enter** key. The horizontal axis title is updated.

8. On the Layout tab, in the Labels group, click the **Axis Titles** button, point to **Primary Vertical Axis Title**, and then click **Rotated Title**. The axis title is rotated along the vertical axis and is selected.

9. Type **Units of Scrap**, and then press the **Enter** key. The vertical access title is updated.

10. Click the **Legend** to select it, and then press the **Delete** key. The legend is removed from the chart.

11. Right-click the **chart area** of the selected chart, and then click **Move Chart** on the shortcut menu. The Move Chart dialog box appears.

12. Click the **New sheet** option button. In the New sheet box, type **Scatter Chart**.

13. Click **OK**. The scatter chart appears on a new chart sheet. The chart illustrates that factories with larger production tend to generate more scrap.

14. Save the workbook, and leave it open for the next Step-by-Step.

Formatting a Chart

The Chart Tools provide a simple way to create professional-looking charts. However, you might want to fine-tune a chart's appearance to better suit your purposes. For example, you might want to change the color of a data marker or the scale used for the axis. To make changes to an element's fill, border color, border style, shadow, 3-D format, alignment, and so forth, you need to open its Format dialog box. The Format dialog box for each chart element contains options for editing specific characteristics of that element.

To access the Format dialog box for a chart element, select the chart element you want to edit. Then, on the Format tab on the Ribbon, in the Current Selection group, click the Format Selection button. The Format dialog box for the selected element appears. You can also right-click the element you want to edit, and then click the corresponding Format command on the shortcut menu.

Step-by-Step 8.6

1. On the Ribbon, click the **Format** tab.

2. In the Current Selection group, click the **Chart Elements arrow** to open a menu of elements on the selected chart, and then click **Horizontal (Value) Axis**.

3. In the Current Selection group, click the **Format Selection** button. The Format Axis dialog box appears with the Axis Options active, as shown in **Figure 8–14**.

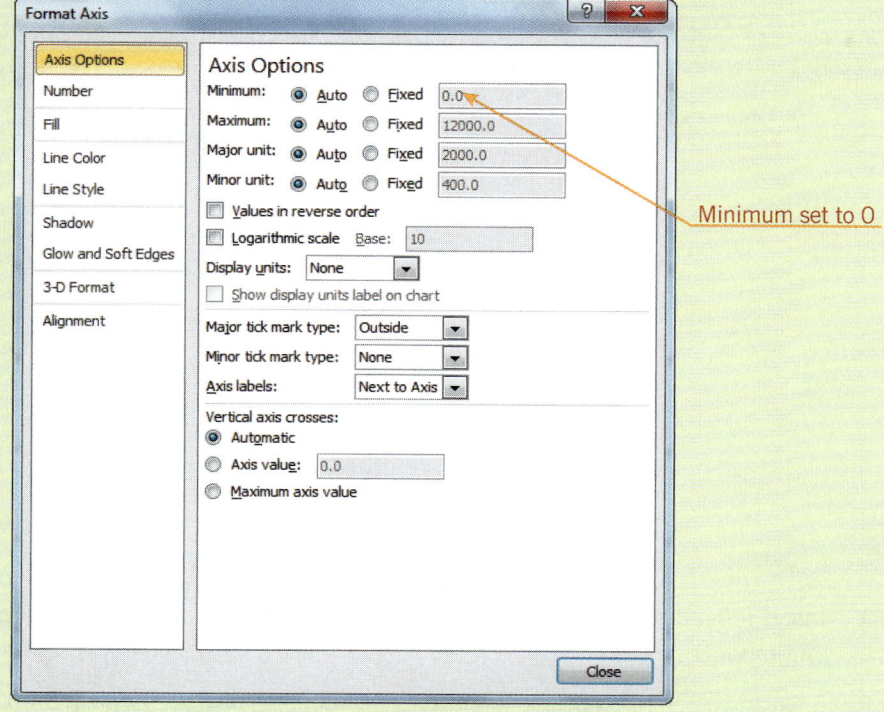

FIGURE 8–14
Format Axis dialog box for the horizontal (value) axis

4. Next to Minimum, click the **Fixed** option button. In the Minimum Fixed box, select the current value, and then type **4000**. The x-axis ranges from 4,000 to 12,000 units produced.

5. Click **Close**. The section of the chart to the left of 4,000 on the x-axis, which did not have any data points, disappears.

6. Point to the **Vertical (Value) Axis** on the chart. The ScreenTip appears, confirming that the correct element will be selected.

7. Click the **Vertical (Value) Axis** on the chart, right-click the selected axis, and then click **Format Axis** on the shortcut menu. The Format Axis dialog box appears with the Axis Options active.

8. Next to Maximum, click the **Fixed** option button. In the Maximum Fixed box, select the current value, and then type **250**.

9. Click **Close**. The section of the chart above 250 on the y-axis, which did not have any data points, disappears.

10. Point to the **Chart Area**. Verify that the ScreenTip reads *Chart Area*. Click the **Chart Area** to select it. See **Figure 8–15**.

FIGURE 8–15
Scatter chart

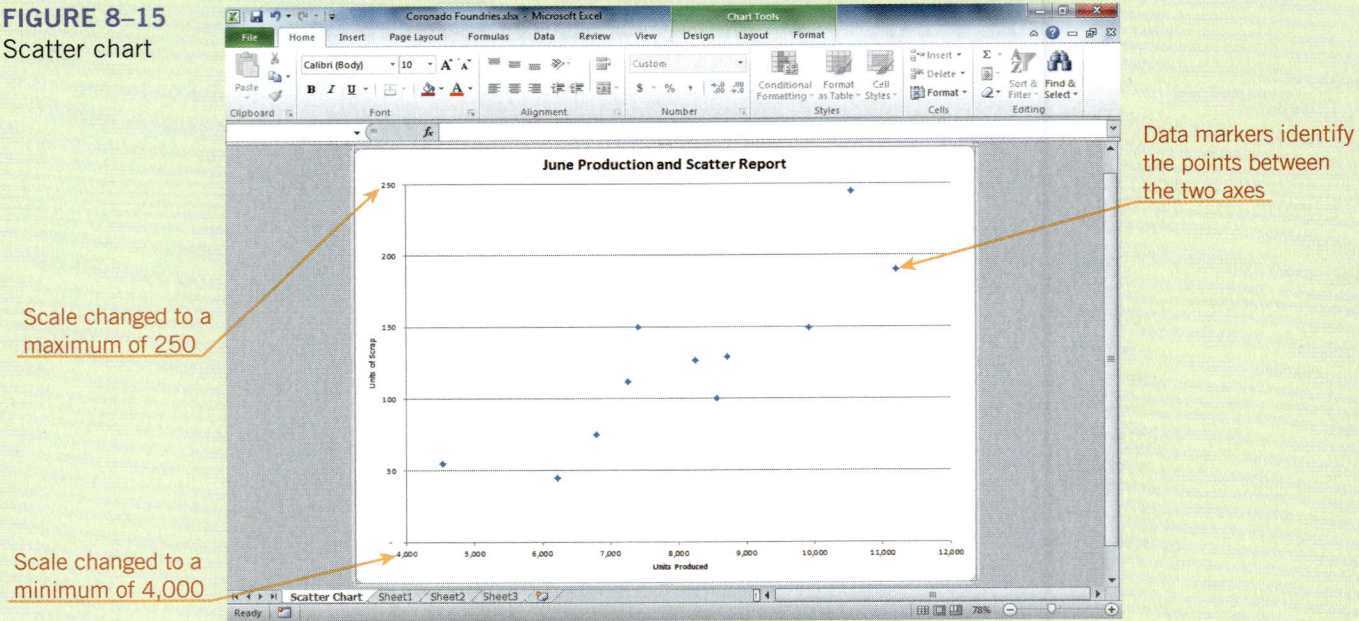

Data markers identify the points between the two axes

Scale changed to a maximum of 250

Scale changed to a minimum of 4,000

11. Insert a header with your name and the current date, and then print the chart sheet.

12. Save and close the workbook. Leave Excel open for the next Step-by-Step.

Editing and Formatting Chart Text

You might want to change a chart title's font or color to make a chart more attractive and interesting. You use the standard text formatting tools to make changes to the fonts used in the chart.

Step-by-Step 8.7

1. Open the **Red.xlsx** workbook from the drive and folder where your Data Files are stored. Save the workbook as **Red Cross** followed by your initials.

2. Click the **Bar Chart** sheet tab. The bar chart illustrates the operating expenses for each year.

3. Click **American Red Cross** to select the chart title.

4. Click to the right of the last **s** in the title. The insertion point appears at the end of the title.

5. Press the **Enter** key. The insertion point is centered under the first line of the title.

6. Type **Operating Expenses**, and then click the **Chart Area**. The chart resizes to accommodate the second line of the title.

7. Click the **Horizontal (Value) Axis** to select it.

8. Click the **Home** tab on the Ribbon. In the Font group, click the **Font Size arrow**, and then click **10**. The font size of the horizontal axis labels changes to 10 points.

9. Click the **Vertical (Category) Axis** to select it.

10. On the Home tab, in the Font group, click the **Font Size arrow**, and then click **10**. The font size of the vertical axis labels changes to 10 points.

11. Save the workbook, and leave it open for the next Step-by-Step.

Changing the Chart Type

You can change the chart type or subtype at any time. Select the chart, and then on the Design tab, in the Type group, click the Change Chart Type button. The Change Chart Type dialog box appears, and includes the same options as the Insert Chart Type dialog box. The only difference is that the chart type and subtype you select update the selected chart instead of creating a new chart.

> **TIP**
>
> Not all charts are interchangeable. For example, data suitable for a pie chart is often not logical in a scatter chart. However, most line charts are easily converted into column or bar charts.

Step-by-Step 8.8

1. On the Ribbon, click the **Design** tab.

2. In the Type group, click the **Change Chart Type** button. The Change Chart Type dialog box appears with the Bar chart type selected.

3. In the Line section, click **Line with Markers** (the fourth line chart subtype).

4. Click **OK**. The bar chart changes to a line chart with markers.

5. Rename the chart sheet as **Line Chart**. **Figure 8–16** shows the chart with the new chart type and style.

FIGURE 8–16
Line chart

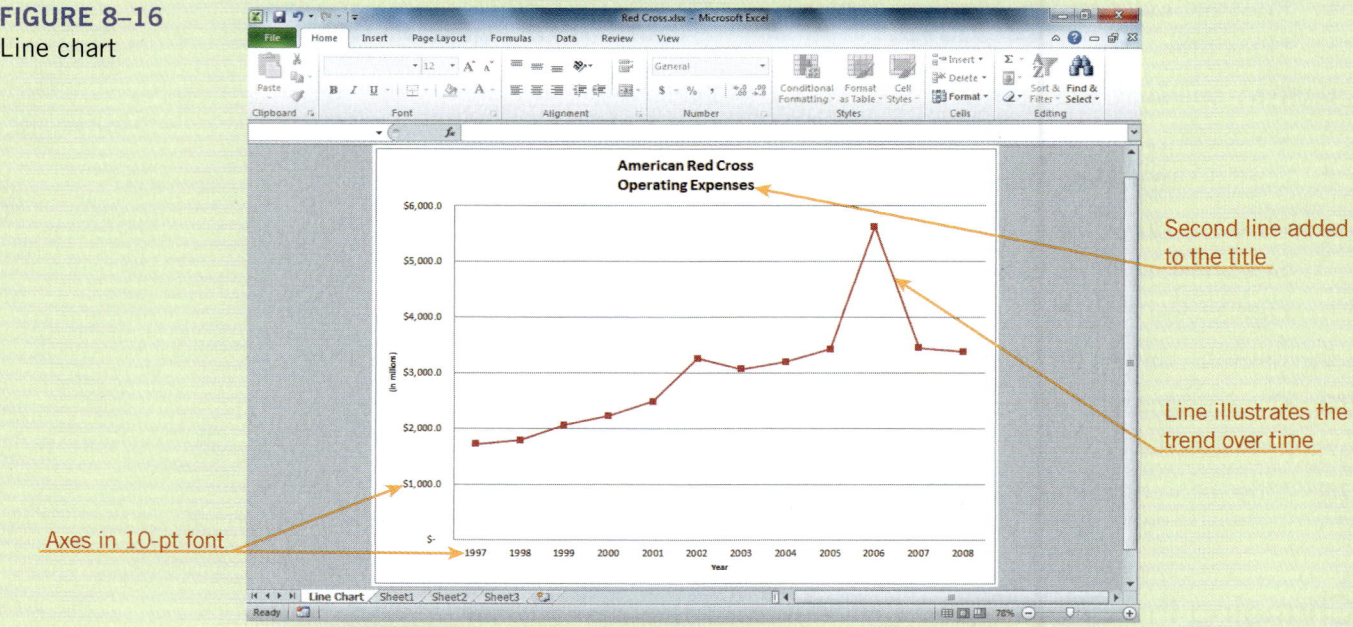

6. Insert a header with your name and the current date, and then print the chart sheet.

7. Save the workbook, and leave it open for the next Step-by-Step.

Inserting Sparklines

Sparklines are mini charts that you can insert into a cell. They are useful for highlighting patterns or trends in data. **Figure 8–17** shows examples of the three types of sparklines you can create: line, column, and win/loss. A line sparkline is a line chart that appears within one cell. A column sparkline is a column chart that appears within one cell. A win/loss sparkline inserts a win/loss chart, which tracks gains and losses, within one cell.

▦ EXTRA FOR EXPERTS

You can format a sparkline by changing its style and line and marker color using tools on the Design tab that appears on the Ribbon when you select a sparkline.

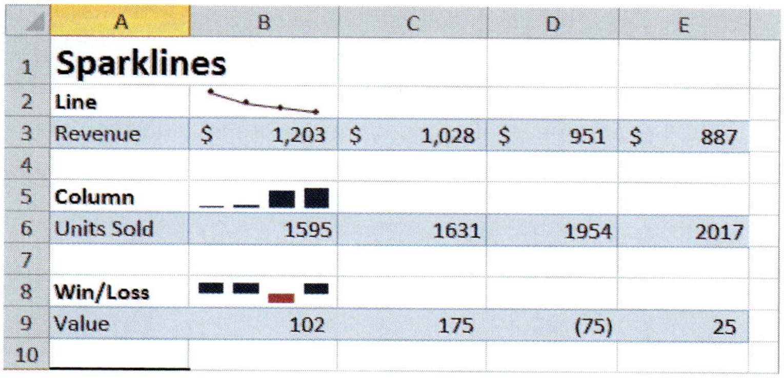

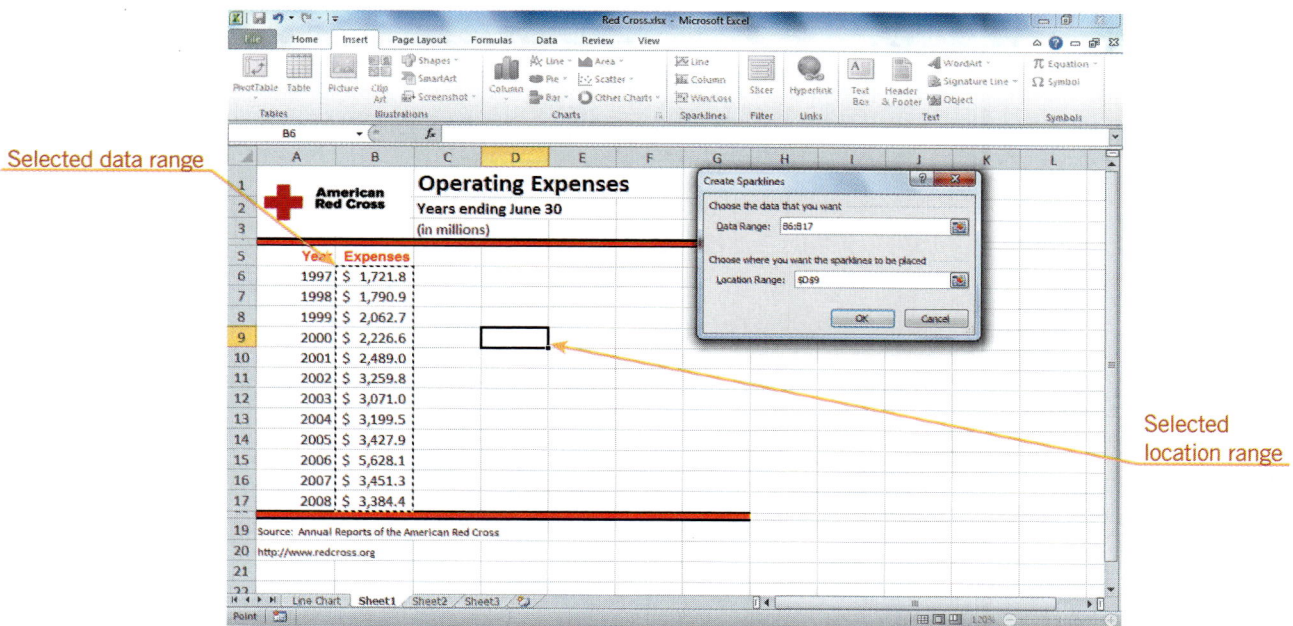

FIGURE 8–17   Examples of line, column, and win/loss sparklines

To create a sparkline, first select the range where you want to insert the sparkline. In the Sparklines group on the Insert tab, click the button corresponding to the type of sparkline you want to create. The Create Sparklines dialog box appears, as shown in **Figure 8–18**. You select the cells that contain the data you want to chart with the sparkline. Click Create. A sparkline for each data series appears in a separate worksheet cell in the location range you selected.

FIGURE 8–18   Create Sparklines dialog box

After you create sparklines, you can modify them, using tools on the Design tab. You can show a variety of data markers on the sparklines, including the high and low points, negative point, first and last points, and all data points. These options are available in the Show group. You can change the appearance of a sparkline by selecting a style from the Style gallery, or using the Sparkline Color button or the Marker Color button to choose new colors for the sparkline or data markers, respectively. You can also change the sparkline type from one type to another using the buttons in the Type group.

Step-by-Step 8.9

1. Click the **Sheet1** sheet tab. This is the worksheet with the data.

2. Click cell **D9**. This cell is where you want the sparkline to appear.

3. Click the **Insert** tab on the Ribbon.

4. In the Sparklines group, click the **Line** button. The Create Sparklines dialog box appears.

5. Make sure the insertion point is in the Data Range box, and then select the range **B6:B17** in the worksheet. This range contains the data you want to chart in the sparkline. The Create Sparklines dialog box should look like Figure 8–18.

6. Click **OK**. The line sparkline inserted in cell D9 shows how expenses have continually increased, with a sharp spike in a recent year.

7. Select the range **D9:G11**.

8. Click the **Home** tab on the Ribbon. In the Alignment group, click the **Merge and Center** button 🔲. The line sparkline increases to fill the merged cell, making it easier to see.

9. On the Ribbon, click the **Design** tab. The Design tab appears on the Ribbon when a sparkline is selected, and contains options for formatting the sparkline.

10. In the Show group, click the **High Point** check box, the **Low Point** check box, and the **Markers** check box. Data markers are added to each data point. The markers for the high and low points are a different color than the rest of the data points. See **Figure 8–19**.

FIGURE 8–19
Line sparkline

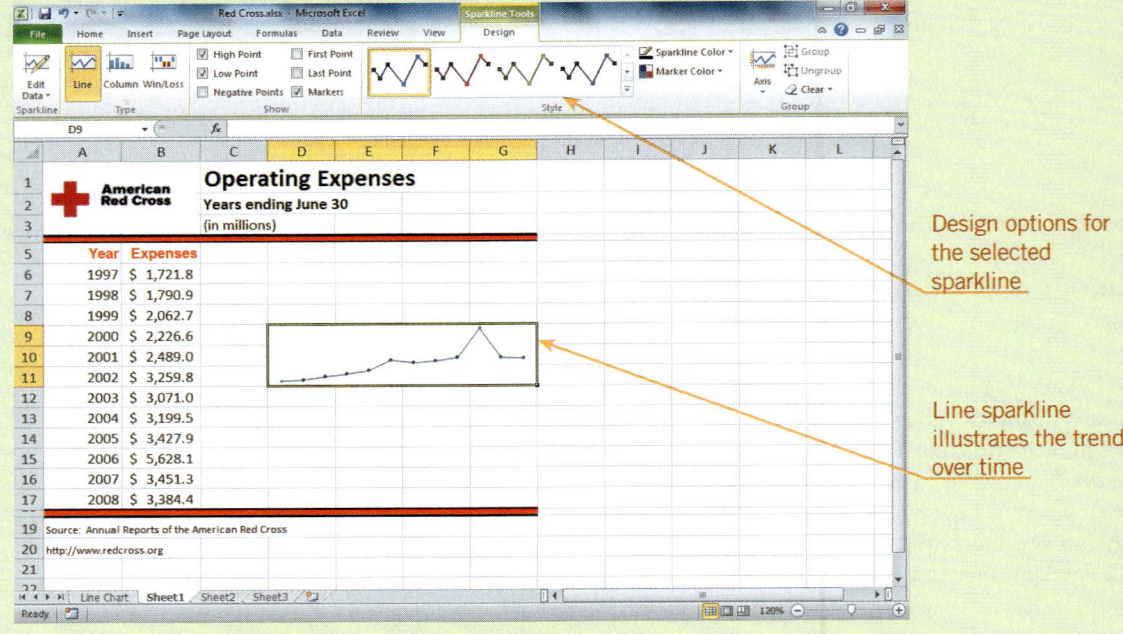

Design options for the selected sparkline

Line sparkline illustrates the trend over time

11. On the Design tab, in the Type group, click the **Column** button. The line sparkline changes to a column sparkline. The bars for the high and low points have different colors. Because a column sparkline doesn't have data points, it doesn't have any markers on it. See **Figure 8–20**.

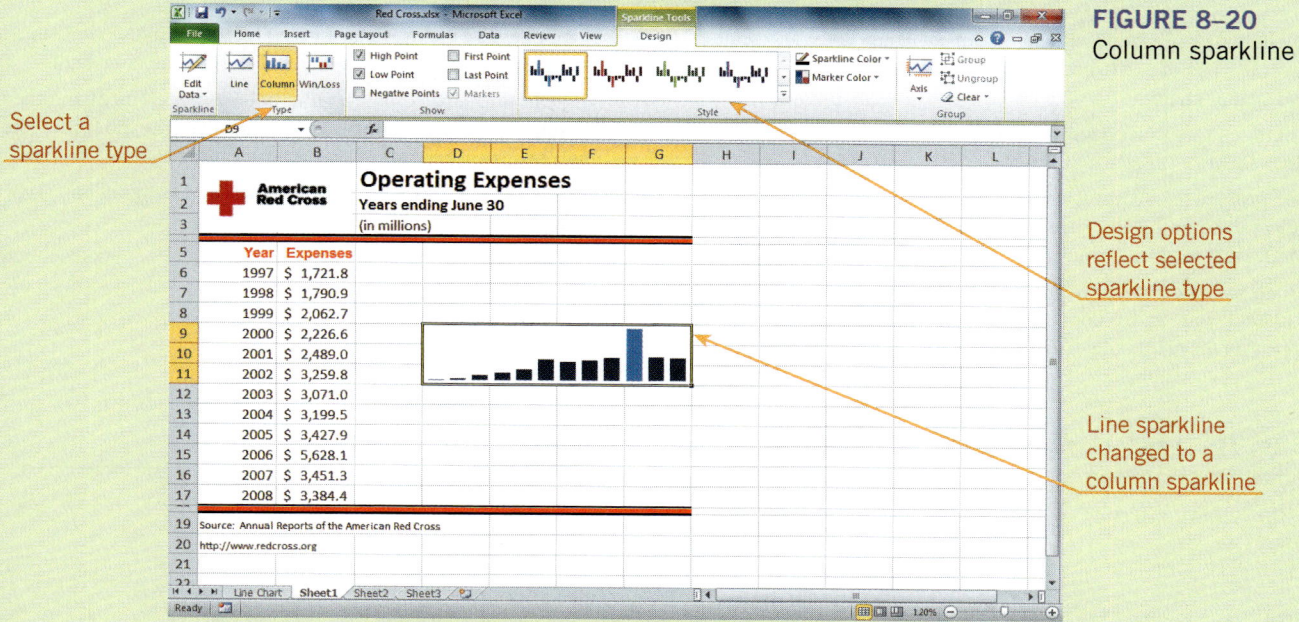

Select a sparkline type

Design options reflect selected sparkline type

Line sparkline changed to a column sparkline

FIGURE 8–20
Column sparkline

12. On the Design tab, in the Style group, click the **More** button ▼. In the Style gallery, click **Sparkline Style Dark #3** (the third style in the fifth row). The bar colors in the sparkline are updated with colors from Sparkline Style Dark #3.

13. Insert a header with your name and the current date, and then print the worksheet.

14. Save and close the workbook.

SUMMARY

In this lesson, you learned:

- A chart is a graphical representation of data. You can create several types of worksheet charts, including column, line, pie, and scatter charts.

- Charts can be embedded within a worksheet or created on a chart sheet.

- The process for creating a chart is the same for all chart types. Select the data for the chart. Select a chart type. Move, resize, and format the chart as needed.

- Charts are made up of different parts, or elements. You can apply a chart layout and a chart style to determine which elements appear in the chart, where they appear, and how they look.

- If the data in a chart's data source is changed in the worksheet, the chart is automatically updated to reflect the new data.

- You can fine-tune a chart by clicking a chart element and then opening its Format dialog box. You can also edit and format the chart text, using the standard text formatting tools.

- You can change the type of chart in the Change Chart Type dialog box.

- Sparklines are mini charts you can insert into a worksheet cell to show a pattern or trend. The three types of sparklines are line, column, and win/loss.

■ VOCABULARY REVIEW

Define the following terms:

axis	data label	legend
chart	data marker	line chart
chart area	data series	pie chart
chart layout	data source	plot area
chart sheet	data table	scatter chart
chart style	embedded chart	sparkline
column chart	exploded pie chart	

■ REVIEW QUESTIONS

TRUE / FALSE

Circle T if the statement is true or F if the statement is false.

T   F   **1.**   Charts are a graphical representation of data.

T   F   **2.**   An embedded chart can be moved and resized.

T   F   **3.**   A sparkline is a mini chart that is inserted within a cell.

T   F   **4.**   When the data source changes, charts created from that data do not change.

T   F   **5.**   After you create a chart, you can change the chart type or subtype.

FILL IN THE BLANK

Complete the following sentences by writing the correct word or words in the blanks provided.

1. A(n) _____ chart is represented by a circle divided into portions.

2. A group of related information in a column or row of a worksheet that is plotted on a chart is a(n) _____.

3. A(n) _____ chart is inserted on the same sheet as the data being charted.

4. In a chart, the _____ shows the patterns or symbols that identify the different types of data.

5. A(n) _____ specifies which elements are included in a chart and their locations.

MATCHING

Match the correct chart type in Column 2 to its description in Column 1.

Column 1

1. Shows the relationship of parts to a whole.

2. Shows the relationship between two categories of data, creating data points that are unrelated to each other

3. Illustrates trends over time

4. Shows relationships among categories of data

5. Tracks gains or losses

Column 2

A. Column chart

B. Line chart

C. Pie chart

D. Scatter chart

E. Win/loss sparkline

◼ PROJECTS

If you have a SAM 2010 user profile, your instructor may have assigned an autogradable version of the indicated project. If so, log into the SAM 2010 Web site at *www.cengage.com/sam2010* to download the instruction and start files.

PROJECT 8–1

1. Open the **Largest.xlsx** workbook from the drive and folder where your Data Files are stored. Save the workbook as **Largest Cities** followed by your initials.

2. Select the data in the range A5:B14, and then insert an embedded column chart using the 2-D clustered column style.

3. Move the chart to a chart sheet named **Column Chart**.

4. Apply Layout 6 and Style 29 to the chart. Delete the Series 1 Data Labels from the chart if it appears over the Jakarta column.

5. Enter the chart title as **10 Largest Cities in the World**.

6. Enter the vertical axis title as **Population in Millions**.

7. Insert a header with your name and the current date, and then print the chart sheet. Save and close the workbook.

SAM PROJECT 8–2

1. Open the **Concession.xlsx** workbook from the drive and folder where your Data Files are stored. Save the workbook as **Concession Sales** followed by your initials.

2. Select the range H5:H10, and then create line sparklines for the data range B5:E10.

3. Show high point markers on the line sparklines, and format them with Sparkline Style Dark #3.

4. Insert a header with your name and the current date. Print the worksheet.

5. Using the data in the range A4:E10, create an embedded 2-D clustered column chart.

6. Move the chart to a chart sheet named **Column Chart**.

7. Apply the Layout 1 chart layout to the chart. Apply the Style 34 chart style to the chart.

8. Change the chart title to **Concession Sales**. Change the font size of the chart title to 24 points.

9. Add the following rotated vertical axis title: **Sales in Dollars**. Change the font size of the axis title to 14 points.

10. Change the font size of the horizontal and vertical axis labels to 12 points and make them bold.

11. Move the legend to above the chart. Change the font size of the legend to 12 points.

12. Right-click the plot area of the chart, and then click Format Plot Area on the shortcut menu. In the Format Plot Area dialog box that appears, click the Solid fill option button. Click the Color button, and then click White, Background 1, Darker 15% (the first color in the third row). Click Close.

13. Which product(s) has decreased in sales over the last four games? Which product(s) has increased in sales over the last four games?

14. Insert a header with your name and the current date. Print the chart sheet. Save and close the workbook.

PROJECT 8–3

1. Open the **Run.xlsx** workbook from the drive and folder where your Data Files are stored. Save the workbook as **Run Times** followed by your initials.

2. Using the data in the range A5:B14, insert an embedded line chart with markers in the worksheet.

3. Apply chart Style 39.

4. In the range A5:A14, delete the word **Week**, leaving only the week number.

5. Add a horizontal axis title below the axis with the text **Week**.

6. Add a rotated vertical axis with the text **Time in Minutes**.

7. Do not include a chart title or legend in the chart.

8. Resize and move the chart to fill the range C4:K19.

9. Insert a header with your name and the current date. Print the worksheet with the embedded chart, and then save and close the workbook.

PROJECT 8–5

1. Open the **Cash.xlsx** workbook from the drive and folder where your Data Files are stored. Save the workbook as **Cash Surplus** followed by your initials.

2. Using the data in the range A6:B13, create an embedded pie chart using the Pie in 3-D style.

3. Move the chart to a chart sheet named **3-D Pie Chart**.

4. Choose the chart layout that includes a chart title and data labels with percentages, but does not include a legend.

5. Change the chart title to **Where We Spend Our Money**.

6. Apply the Style 26 chart style.

7. Change the font size of the chart title to 24 points.

8. Change the font size of the data labels to 14 points.

9. Based on the chart, in which area(s) does the family spend the most?

10. Insert a header with your name and the current date. Print the chart sheet. Save and close the workbook.

PROJECT 8–4

1. Open the **McDonalds** workbook from the drive and folder where your Data Files are stored. Save the workbook as **McDonalds Report** followed by your initials.

2. Using the data in the range A3:B6, create an embedded pie chart using the Pie in 3-D style.

3. Apply the Layout 6 chart layout and the Style 18 chart style.

4. Enter the chart title **Total Restaurants**.

5. Show the legend at the top of the chart.

6. Move the chart to a chart sheet named **Pie Chart**.

7. Format the font sizes of the chart title to 28 points, the data labels (showing the slice percentages) to 18 points, and the legend to 14 points.

8. Insert a header with your name and the current date. Print the chart sheet. Save and close the workbook.

PROJECT 8–6

1. Open the **Study.xlsx** workbook from the drive and folder where your Data Files are stored. Save the workbook as **Study and Grades** followed by your initials.

2. Using the data in the range B4:C21, create an embedded scatter chart with only markers.

3. Move the chart to a chart sheet named **Scatter Chart**.

4. Apply the Layout 4 chart layout to the chart.

5. Add the following chart title above the chart: **Relationship Between Study Time and Test Grades**.

6. Add the following horizontal axis title below the axis: **Hours of Study**.

7. Add the following rotated vertical axis title: **Test Grades**.

8. Change the font size of the chart title to 20 points.

9. Change the font size of the axis titles to 14 points.

10. Delete the legend.

11. Format the vertical axis so its minimum value is fixed at 50.

12. What relationship, if any, does the chart show between test grades and study time?

13. Insert a header with your name and the current date. Print the chart sheet. Save and close the workbook.

PROJECT 8–7

1. Open the **Starburst.xlsx** workbook from the drive and folder where your Data Files are stored. Save the workbook as **Starburst Growth** followed by your initials.

2. Using the data in the range A5:F7, create an embedded 2-D line chart with markers.

3. Move the chart to a chart sheet named **Line Chart**.

4. Apply the Layout 1 chart layout to the chart. Apply the Style 32 chart style to the chart.

5. Change the chart title to **Starburst Software Net Revenues and Net Income**.

6. Change the vertical axis title to **(Dollars in Millions)**.

7. Show the legend at the top of the chart.

8. Have the company's net revenues decreased, increased, or remained stable?

9. Insert a header with your name and the current date. Print the chart sheet.

10. Press and hold the Ctrl key as you drag and drop the sheet tab for the Line Chart chart sheet directly to the right of the Line Chart sheet tab to make a copy. Rename the copied chart sheet **Clustered Column Chart**.

11. Change the chart type to a clustered column chart.

12. Print the chart sheet. Save and close the workbook.

PROJECT 8–8

1. Open the **Chico.xlsx** workbook from the drive and folder where your Data Files are stored. Save the workbook as **Chico Temperatures** followed by your initials.

2. Using the data in the range A3:M5, create an embedded 2-D line chart with markers.

3. Move the chart to a chart sheet named **Line Chart**.

4. Apply the Layout 5 chart layout to the chart. Apply the Style 28 chart style to the chart.

5. Change the chart title to **Average Temperatures in Chico, California**.

6. Change the vertical axis title to **Temperatures in Fahrenheit**.

7. On the Ribbon, click the Layout tab. In the Current Selection group, use the Chart Elements arrow to select Series "High" in the chart.

8. Click the Format Selection button to open the Format Data Series dialog box. Make the following changes:
   a. Click Marker Fill to display the options. Click the Solid fill option button. Click the Color button, and then click Dark Red in the Standard Colors section.
   b. Click Line Color to display the options. Click the Solid line option button. Click the Color button, and then click Dark Red in the Standard Colors section.
   c. Click Marker Line Color to display the options. Click the Solid line option button. Click the Color button, and then click Dark Red in the Standard Colors section if necessary.

9. Click Close to close the Format Data Series dialog box.

10. On the Layout tab, in the Current Selection group, use the Chart Elements arrow to select Series "Low" in the chart.

11. Click the Format Selection button to open the Format Data Series dialog box. Make the following changes:
   a. Click Marker Fill to display the options. Click the Solid fill option button. Click the Color button, and then click Blue in the Standard Colors section.
   b. Click Line Color to display the options. Click the Solid line option button. Click the Color button, and then click Blue in the Standard Colors section.
   c. Click Marker Line Color to display the options. Click the Solid line option button. Click the Color button, and then click Blue in the Standard Colors section if necessary.

12. Click Close to close the Format Data Series dialog box.

13. Insert a header with your name and the current date. Print the chart sheet. Save and close the workbook.

CRITICAL THINKING

ACTIVITY 8–1

For each scenario, which chart type would be the most appropriate to illustrate the data? Justify your answer.

Scenario 1. A scientist has given varying amounts of water to 200 potted plants. Over 35 days, the height of the plant and the amount of water given to the plant are recorded in a worksheet. What is the best chart type to illustrate the connection between water and plant growth?

Scenario 2. A corporation developed a new product last year. A manager in the corporation recorded the number of units sold each month. He noticed that sales in summer months were much higher than sales in winter months. What chart type can he use to illustrate this trend to other sales managers?

Scenario 3. Students entering a high school come from five middle schools. The principal has recorded the name of the middle school and the number of students from each middle school. What chart type can she use to show which middle schools supply significantly more students than other middle schools?

ACTIVITY 8–2

You recently opened Sounds Good CDs, a store that buys and sells used CDs and DVDs. As a small business owner, you are responsible for budgets and inventory. Initially, you manually tracked the inventory and budget data in a notebook. Now that the business is growing, this method has become too cumbersome. You decide to transfer the data into an electronic format.

In a new workbook, create and format one worksheet to track inventory and one worksheet to track the budget. Both worksheets should contain the name of your store—Sounds Good CDs—and a title describing the data.

For the inventory worksheet, include (a) the title of the CD or DVD, (b) the artist, (c) the quantity of each, and (d) the cost per item. Enter the data shown in **Figure 8–21** in the worksheet. Rename the worksheet as **Inventory**.

Title	Artist	Quantity	Cost
Nerve Net	Brian Eno	4	$ 6.95
Thursday Afternoon	Brian Eno	2	$ 7.95
Geometry	Robert Rich	3	$ 5.95
On This Planet	Steve Roach	3	$ 8.95
Possible Planet	Steve Roach	5	$ 6.95

FIGURE 8–21

The budget worksheet records the expected income and expenses for the month. Include rows for (a) sales revenue, (b) purchases of CDs, (c) rent expense, (d) utilities expense, (e) tax expense, and (f) net income. Include columns for (a) actual amounts and (b) budgeted amounts. Then, enter the data shown in **Figure 8–22**.

	Actual	Budgeted
Sales Revenue	$ 14,875	$ 12,950
Purchases of CDs	6,500	5,800
Rent	975	975
Utilities	425	425
Taxes	817	667
Net Income		

FIGURE 8–22

For the Actual Net Income, enter a formula that subtracts the purchases and expenses from revenue. For the Budgeted Net Income, enter a formula that subtracts the purchases and expenses from revenue. Rename the worksheet as **Budget**.

Insert column sparklines in the range D6:D10 based on the data in the range B6:C10. Change the last point marker color to a different color than the first point marker color.

Using the data you entered in the Budget worksheet, create an embedded chart that compares the actual and budgeted values in each category. Use an appropriate chart type. Choose which chart elements to display, where they should be located, and how the chart is formatted.

For both worksheets, insert a header with your name and the current date, and then print the worksheets.

EXCEL UNIT REVIEW

Introductory Microsoft Excel

 ## REVIEW QUESTIONS

TRUE / FALSE

Circle T if the statement is true or F if the statement is false.

T   F   **1.**   The active cell reference appears in the Formula Bar.

T   F   **2.**   To select a group of cells, you must click each cell individually until all cells in the range are selected.

T   F   **3.**   The Save As dialog box appears every time you save a worksheet.

T   F   **4.**   The formula =$B$4+C9 contains an absolute cell reference.

T   F   **5.**   After you edit the data source in the worksheet, the chart is also updated to reflect the changes.

MATCHING

Match the description in Column 2 with the text position function in Column 1.

Column 1		Column 2
_____ 1. Wrapping	A.	Displays cell contents on multiple lines
_____ 2. Orientation	B.	Aligns the text to the right, left, or center
_____ 3. Indenting	C.	Combines several cells into one and places the contents in the middle of the cell
_____ 4. Alignment	D.	Moves the text several spaces to the right or left
_____ 5. Merge and Center	E.	Displays text at an angle, vertically, up, or down

FILL IN THE BLANK

Complete the following sentences by writing the correct word or words in the blanks provided.

1. A(n) _____ cell reference changes when copied or moved.

2. _____ formatting is used to highlight cells that meet specific criteria.

3. The _____ function adds a range of numbers in a worksheet.

4. A(n) _____ chart uses wedges in a circle to represent values in a worksheet.

5. The _____ contains information that is printed at the top of every page.

MATCHING

Match the correct result in Column 2 to the formula in Column 1. Assume the following values appear in the worksheet:

Cell	Value
B2	5
B3	6
B4	4
B5	7

Column 1

_____ 1. =10+B5

_____ 2. =B2*B4

_____ 3. =(B3+B4)/B2

_____ 4. =AVERAGE(B3:B4)

_____ 5. =SUM(B2:B5)

Column 2

A. 22

B. 20

C. 17

D. 5

E. 2

PROJECTS

PROJECT 1

1. Open the **Gas.xlsx** workbook from the drive and folder where your Data Files are stored. Save the workbook as **Gas Sales** followed by your initials.

2. Format cell A1 with the Title cell style. Format the range A2:A3 with bold.

3. Change the width of column A to 15. Change each of the widths of columns B through D to 12.

4. Merge and center the range A1:D1.

5. In cell B2, enter the current date, and then apply the Long Date format.

6. Merge and center the range B2:D2.

7. In cell B3, enter **3:55 PM** for time, and then apply the Time format.

8. Merge and center the range B3:D3.

9. Format the text in the range A2:D3 in 12-point Cambria.

10. Wrap the text in cell C5.

11. Format range A5:D5 with the Accent 1 cell style, and then bold and center the text in the cells.

12. Format the range B6:B9 in the Number format with a comma separator and no decimal places.

13. Format the range C6:D9 in the Currency format.

14. In cell B10, use the SUM function to add the total number of gallons sold, and then format the cell with the Total cell style.

15. In cell D10, use the SUM function to add the total sales, and then format the cell with the Total cell style. Click cell A12. **Figure UR–1** shows the completed worksheet.

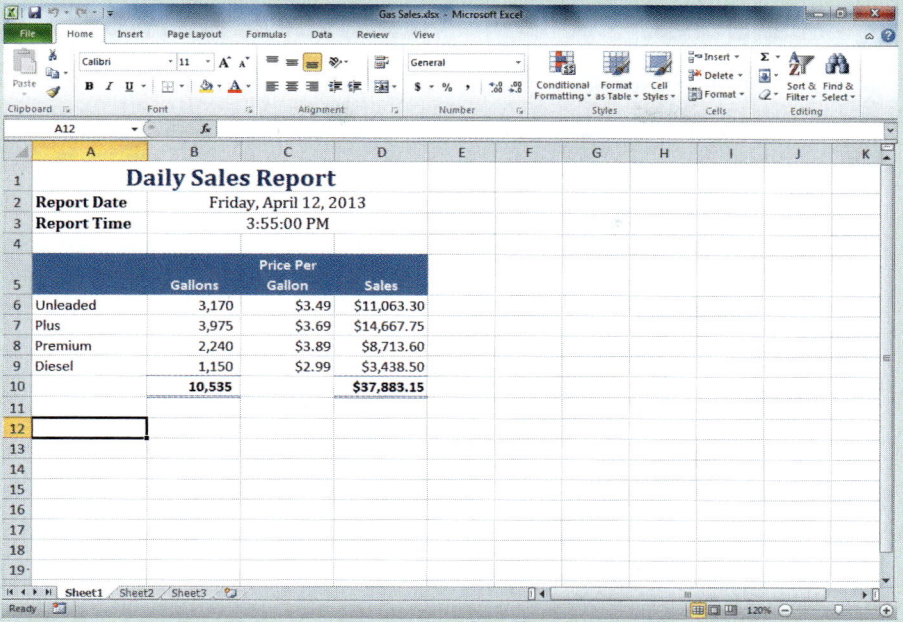

FIGURE UR–1

16. Insert a header with your name and the current date. Save, print, and close the workbook.

PROJECT 2

1. Open the **Organic.xlsx** workbook from the drive and folder where your Data Files are stored. Save the workbook as **Organic Financials** followed by your initials.

2. Format the company name and other headings in bold. Format the company name in a larger font than the rest of the text in the financial statement.

3. Merge and center each of the first four rows across columns A and B.

4. Separate the headings from the body of the financial statement by one row.

5. Resize the columns so you can view all of their contents.

6. Format the first (Revenue) and last (Net income) numbers in the financial statement to display dollar signs and thousands separators, but no decimal places.

7. Format all the other numbers to include a thousands separator but no dollar sign and no decimal places. Compare your worksheet to **Figure UR–2**.

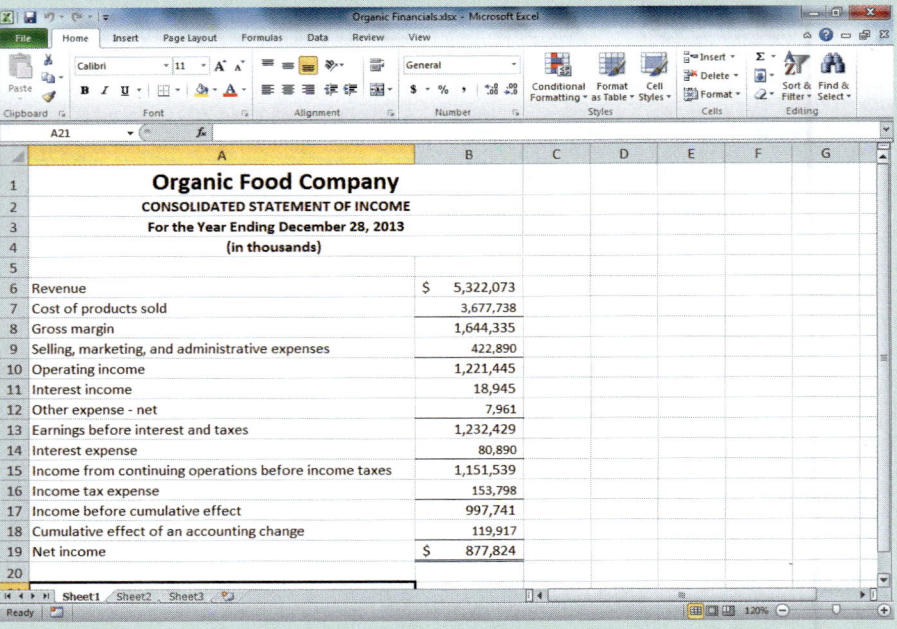

FIGURE UR–2

8. Format the worksheet to make it visually attractive and appealing, such as by adding borders, font colors, fill colors, alignments, cell styles, and so forth as appropriate.

9. Insert a header with your name and the current date. Save, print, and close the workbook.

PROJECT 3

1. Open the **Club.xlsx** workbook from the drive and folder where your Data Files are stored. Save the workbook as **Club Members** followed by your initials.

2. Sort the range A2:B16 by the values in column B in order from largest to smallest.

3. Resize the columns as needed to so that all the content is displayed.

4. Format the worksheet title with the Title cell style to distinguish it from the other text in the workbook.

5. Enter the text **Exceptional and Outstanding Members** in a new row above the row for Susan Estes, and then format the text in bold and italic.

6. Enter the text **Exceptional Members** in a new row above the row for Susan Estes, and then format the text in bold.

7. Enter the text **Outstanding Members** in a new row above the row for Jose Santos, and then format the text in bold.

8. Enter the text **Other Active Members** in a new row above the row for Mohamed Abdul, and then format the text in bold and italic.

9. Delete the row with Allen Tse.

10. Format the numbers in column B using the Number format with a thousands separator and no decimal places. Your worksheet should look similar to **Figure UR–3**.

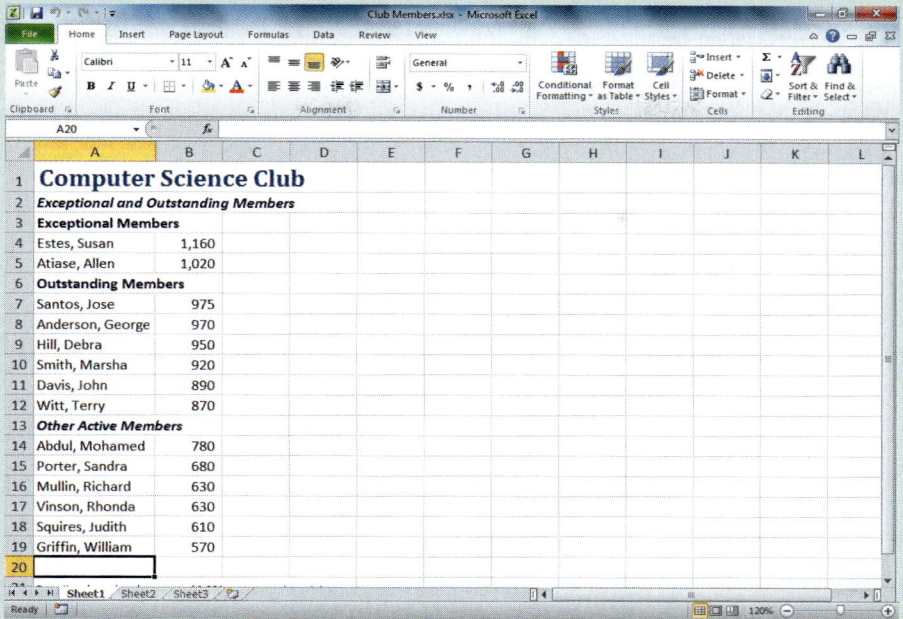

FIGURE UR–3

11. Format the worksheet using cell styles, alignments, font styles, colors, and so forth to make the worksheet visually appealing.

12. Insert a header with your name and the current date. Save, print, and close the workbook.

PROJECT 4

1. Open the **CompNet.xlsx** workbook from the drive and folder where your Data Files are stored. Save the workbook as **CompNet Expenses** followed by your initials.

2. Create an embedded Pie in 3-D chart based on the data in the range A12:B17. Move the chart to chart sheet named **Expenses Chart**.

3. Apply the chart layout that includes a chart title above the chart and labels and percentages on the slices.

4. Apply the Style 10 chart style.

5. Enter **Expenses for 2013** as the chart title, and then change the font size to 24 points.

6. Change the font size of the data labels to 11 points. Compare your worksheet with **Figure UR–4**.

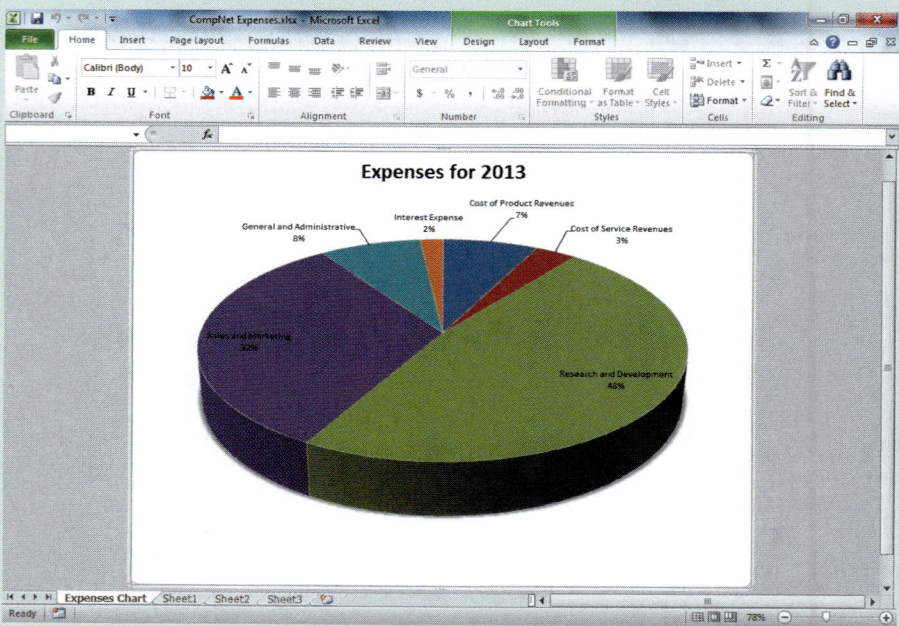

FIGURE UR–4

7. Based on the chart, what is the largest expense category? What is the smallest expense category?

8. Insert a header with your name and the current date. Save, print, and close the workbook.

■ SIMULATION

You work at the Java Internet Café, which has been open only a few months. The café serves coffee, other beverages, and pastries, and offers Internet access. Seven computers are set up on tables along the north side of the store. Customers can come in, have a cup of coffee and a pastry, and browse the Web.

Your manager asks you to create a menu of coffee prices and computer prices. You will do this by integrating Microsoft Excel and Microsoft Word.

JOB 1

1. Create a new workbook. Save the workbook as **Coffee Prices** followed by your initials.

2. Enter the data shown in **Figure UR–5** in the worksheet.

	A	B	C	D	E
1	Coffee Prices				
2					
3	House coffee	2		Café latte	3.5
4	Refills	0.5		Cappucino	3.5
5	Espresso	2.75		Café breve	3.25
6	Extra shot	0.55		Café con panna	3.75
7					

FIGURE UR–5

3. Change the widths of columns A and D to 20. Change the widths of columns B and E to 10. Change the width of column C to 4.

4. Left-align the data in columns B and E.

5. Indent and italicize the text in cells A4 and A6.

6. Change the font of all data to Arial, 12 points.

7. Format the data in columns B and E as Currency.

8. Merge and center the range A1:E1. Change the font of the text in the merged cell A1 to Arial, 14 points. Format the merged cell A1 with a bottom border.

9. Hide the gridlines from view. Save the workbook. Copy the data in the range A1:E6.

10. Start Word and open the **Java.docx** document from the drive and folder where your Data Files are stored. Save the document as **Java Menu** followed by your initials.

11. On a blank line below the *Menu* heading, center the blank line, and then paste a link to the worksheet data you copied. On the Home tab, in the Clipboard group, click the Paste button arrow to open the Paste menu, and then click Paste Special. The Paste Special dialog box appears. In the Paste Special dialog box, click the Paste link option button, and then click Microsoft Excel Worksheet Object, as shown in **Figure UR–6**. Click OK.

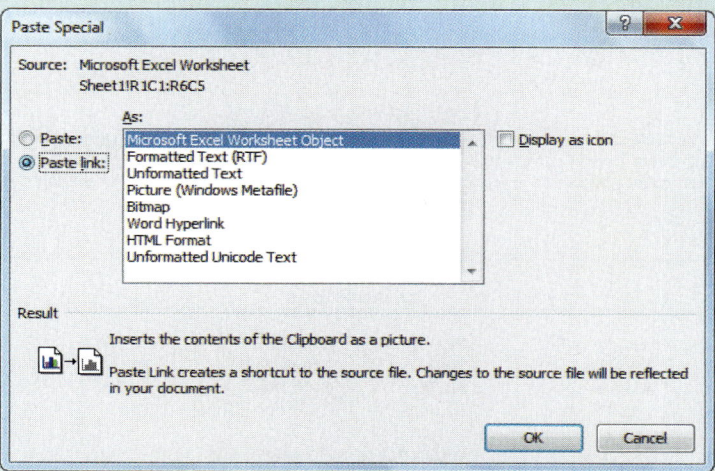

FIGURE UR–6

12. Switch to Excel, and then open the **Computer.xlsx** workbook from the drive and folder where your Data Files are stored. Save the workbook as **Computer Prices** followed by your initials.

13. Copy the data in the range A1:C13.

14. Switch to the **Java Menu** document.

15. On a blank line after the Coffee Prices menu items, center the line if it is not already centered, and then paste a link to the worksheet data you copied. On the Home tab, in the Clipboard group, click the Paste button arrow to open the Paste menu, and then click Paste Special. In the Paste Special dialog box, click the Paste link option button, click Microsoft Excel Worksheet Object, and then click OK.

16. Insert your name and the current date in the blank line of the footer.

17. Preview the document. Adjust the placement of data if necessary so that all data fits on one page.

18. Save, print, and close the **Java Menu** document.

19. Close the **Coffee Prices** and **Computer Prices** workbooks without saving changes.

JOB 2

The menu you created has been very successful. However, your manager asks you to make a few changes.

1. Open the **Coffee Prices** and **Computer Prices** workbooks you saved in Job 1.

2. Edit the **Coffee Prices** and **Computer Prices** workbooks as shown in **Figure UR–7**.

Java Internet Café

2001 Joliet Avenue
Boulder, CO 80302-2001
303.555.JAVA
JavaCafe@cybershop.com

Java Internet Café offers customers high-speed Internet access as well as free Wi-Fi. Bring your own computer or use one of ours. Each of our computers has a special interface to help new users get started. Enjoy one of our specialty coffees as you check your email or surf the Web! Ask your server to help you get started.

Menu

Coffee Prices

House coffee	$2.00	Café latte	$3.50
Refills	$0.~~50~~ .75	Cappucino	$3.50
Espresso	$~~2.75~~ 3.00	Café breve	$3.25
Extra shot	$0.55	Café con panna	$3.75

Computer Prices

Workstation with Internet/Email	$8.00/hour
After the first hour, charges accrue by the minute only.	
Use of Webcam	~~$2.00/session~~ Free
Print (black and white)	$0.25/page
Print (color)	$0.50/page
Print color photo paper (4x6)	$1.00/page
High resolution scanning	$2.00/page
Photocopy (black and white)	$0.25/page
Photocopy (color)	$0.50/page
Fax ∧ (domestic only)	$2.00/first page
	$0.50/each additional page

Sit back, sip your coffee, and surf the web.

FIGURE UR–7

3. Save and close the **Coffee Prices** and **Computer Prices** workbooks.

4. Open the **Java Menu** document you created in Job 1.

5. Update the document when prompted because you revised the linked files since you saved and closed the Java Menu document.

6. Make the correction in the footer, as shown in Figure UR–7.

7. Save the document as **Java Menu Revised** followed by your initials.

8. Print and close the document.

INTRODUCTORY UNIT

MICROSOFT ACCESS 2010

LESSON 1

Microsoft Access Basics

■ OBJECTIVES

Upon completion of this lesson, you should be able to:

- Understand databases and database terminology.
- Start Access, open a database, and open an object.
- Navigate a datasheet, edit a record, and undo a change.
- Select records and fields, and delete a record.
- Cut, copy, and paste data.
- Change the appearance of a datasheet.
- Preview and print a table.
- Close an object and exit Access.

■ VOCABULARY

best fit

compacting

database

database management system (DBMS)

datasheet

datasheet selector

Datasheet view

field

field name

field selector

field value

Navigation Pane

record

record selector

Each day, people rely on the information in databases for a variety of reasons. A database can store information about the books in a library, the medicines available at a pharmacy, or the customers at a DVD rental store. Whether you use a database to get the information you need, or a professional such as a doctor uses a database to retrieve information about you, databases are an important part of organizing your life.

Database Basics

▶ **VOCABULARY**
database management system (DBMS)

Access is a program known as a ***database management system (DBMS)***. A DBMS allows you to store, retrieve, analyze, and print information. You do not, however, need a computer to have a DBMS. A set of file folders or any system for managing data can be a DBMS. There are distinct advantages, however, to using a computerized DBMS.

A computerized DBMS is much faster, more flexible, and more accurate than using file folders. A computerized DBMS is also efficient and cost effective. A DBMS such as Access can store thousands of pieces of data that users can quickly search and sort, helping them to save time otherwise spent digging through file folders. For example, a computerized DBMS can find all the people with a certain zip code faster and more accurately than you could by searching through a large list or through folders.

Starting Access

To start Access, click the Start button on the taskbar, click All Programs, click Microsoft Office, and then click Microsoft Access 2010. After a few seconds, Access starts and opens Backstage view, as shown in **Figure 1–1**. The New tab contains options for creating a new database, opening an existing database, and getting Help while using Access.

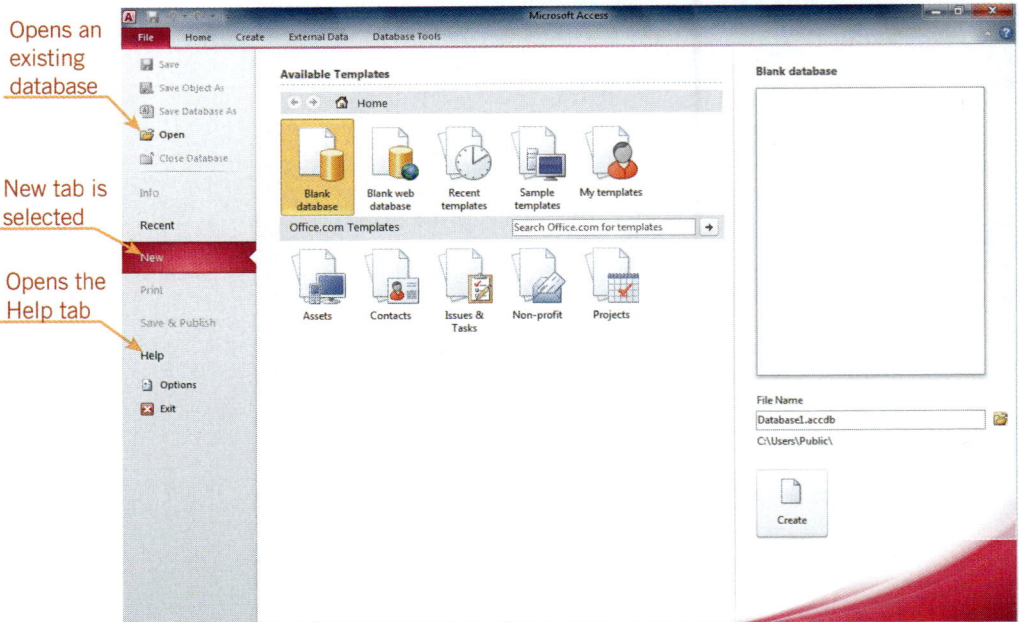

FIGURE 1–1   New tab in Access Backstage view

Step-by-Step 1.1

1. With Windows running, click the **Start** button 🪟 on the taskbar.
2. Click **All Programs**, click **Microsoft Office**, and then click **Microsoft Access 2010**. Access opens the File tab and displays the New tab in Backstage view as shown in Figure 1–1. Leave this tab open for the next Step-by-Step.

Opening a Database

A *database* is a collection of objects. The objects work together to store, retrieve, display, and summarize data and also to automate tasks. The object types are tables, queries, forms, reports, macros, and modules. You can open an existing database by clicking Open in the navigation bar on the File tab, which displays the Open dialog box so you can browse to and open the desired database, or by clicking Recent in the navigation bar on the File tab, which displays a list of databases you have recently opened on the Recent tab. To open a database using the Recent tab, click the database name in the list.

After opening a database, the *Navigation Pane* opens on the left side of the screen, as shown in **Figure 1–2**. The Navigation Pane lists the objects in the database.

▶ **VOCABULARY**
database
Navigation Pane

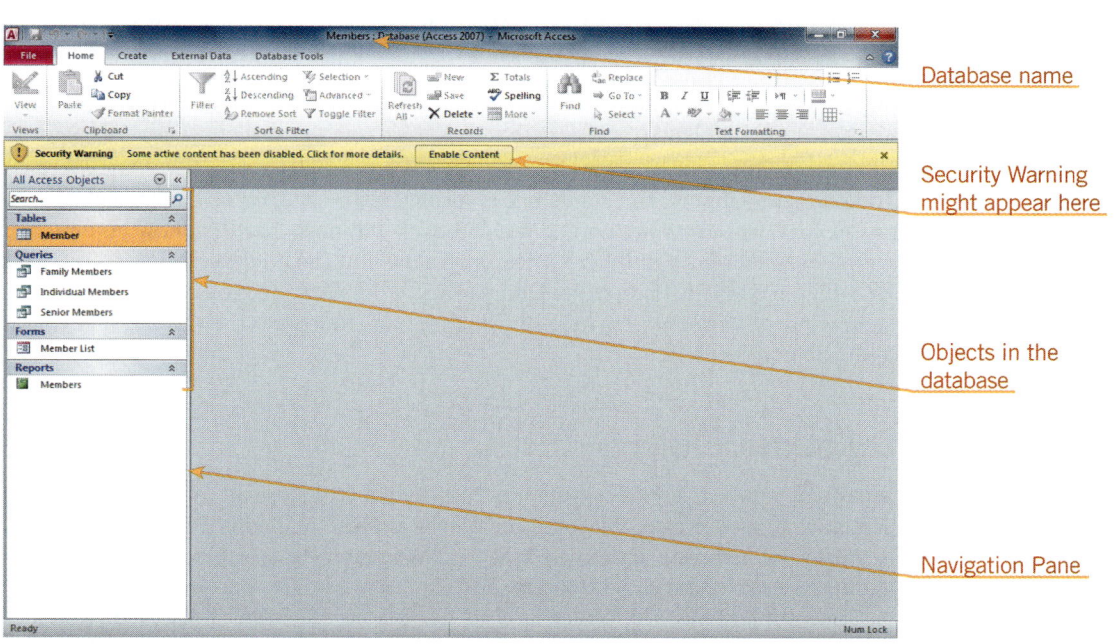

Database name

Security Warning might appear here

Objects in the database

Navigation Pane

FIGURE 1–2   Navigation Pane

Step-by-Step 1.2

1. On the File tab, click **Open** in the navigation bar. The Open dialog box appears.

2. Navigate to the drive and folder where your Data Files are stored, open the **Access** folder, and then open the **Access Lesson 01** folder.

3. Double-click **Members.accdb** (or **Members** if your file extensions are not displayed) in the folder. Access opens the Members database. The Navigation Pane displays the objects in the database, as shown in Figure 1–2.

4. If the Security Warning opens, as shown in Figure 1–2, click the **Enable Content** button in the Security Warning to close it. Leave the database open for the next Step-by-Step.

When you open a database, Access assumes that the database might contain something that could damage your computer. This is why you might see the Security Warning. The files in this book do not contain anything that might damage your computer. You can choose to close the Security Warning or just leave it open. In this book, when you open a database, you should click the Enable Content button in the Security Warning so your screens will match the ones shown in the book.

The Access Screen

Like other Office 2010 programs, the Access screen has a title bar, Quick Access Toolbar, and Ribbon. The status bar is located at the bottom of the screen. As you use Access, various windows and dialog boxes will open based on how you interact with the database. As in other Office programs, you can click the Microsoft Access Help button on the Ribbon to get help while you are working. You can use the Access Help window to browse for help by clicking links to topics or by typing a key term in the Search text box.

Database Objects

When you create a database, you create a file that will store all of the objects in the database. As you create objects in the database, the Navigation Pane displays them in a list. You can change the way that the Navigation Pane displays objects, so you might see them organized differently.

Each object has a different icon to identify its function. **Table 1–1** describes each type of object that you can create in a database and shows the icon used to identify the object in the Navigation Pane.

TABLE 1–1   Database objects

OBJECT	ICON	DESCRIPTION
Table		Stores all the data in the database in a format called a datasheet. A datasheet is similar in appearance to a worksheet. A database usually contains many tables.
Query		Used to search for and retrieve data from tables using conditions. A query is a question you ask the database.
Form		Displays data from one or more tables or queries in a format that might be similar in appearance to a paper form.
Report		Displays data from one or more tables or queries in a format that is usually customized for on-screen viewing or printing. A report is commonly used to summarize data and to calculate totals.
Macro		Automates database operations by allowing you to issue a single command to perform a task, such as opening a form or closing a database.
Module		Similar to a macro, but allows more complex programming of database operations. Creating a module requires the use of a programming language.

The Navigation Pane

When you open a database, the Navigation Pane displays the objects contained in the database. The database might contain any or all of the database objects described in Table 1–1 or just a single table. When you double-click a table, query, form, or report object in the Navigation Pane, the object opens in the main part of the Access window so you can view its contents. The object name appears on a tab at the top of the window to identify its name and object type, as shown in **Figure 1–3**. When many objects are open, clicking a tab displays the object. When you want to display more of the open object, you can close the Navigation Pane by clicking the Shutter Bar Open/Close Button at the top of the Navigation Pane. To open it again, click the Shutter Bar Open/Close Button on the left side of the screen.

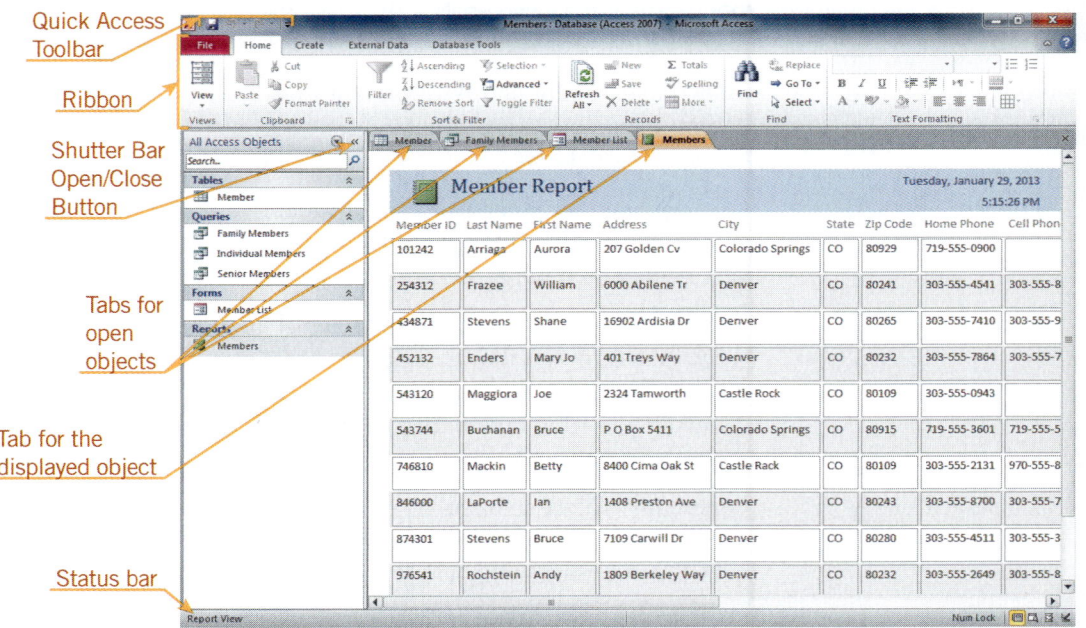

FIGURE 1–3   Open database objects

Step-by-Step 1.3

1. In the Navigation Pane, double-click **Member**. The Member table opens in Datasheet view.

2. In the Navigation Pane, double-click **Family Members**. The Family Members query opens in Query Datasheet view.

3. In the Navigation Pane, double-click **Member List**. The Member List form opens in Form view.

4. In the Navigation Pane, double-click **Members**. The Members report opens in Report view, as shown in Figure 1–3.

5. Click the **Member** tab to display the Member table datasheet.

6. Click the **Shutter Bar Open/Close Button** ⟨⟨ at the top of the Navigation Pane. The Navigation Pane closes. Leave the objects open for the next Step-by-Step.

Working with Records

Some terms are essential to know when working with databases. These terms relate to the way data is organized in a table. A **record** is a complete set of data. In the Member table, the data about each member is stored as a record. In a table, a record appears as a row, as shown in **Figure 1–4**.

▶ VOCABULARY

record

fields

field name

field value

Datasheet view

datasheet

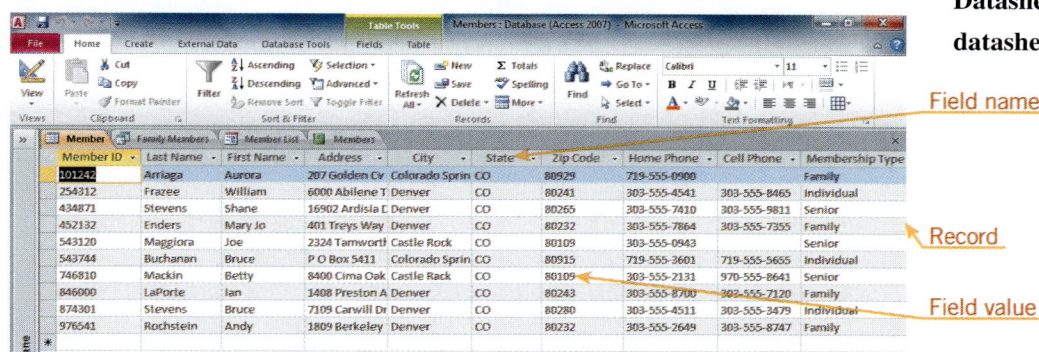

FIGURE 1–4   Records and fields in a table

Each record is made up of one or more **fields**. For example, the first name of each member is placed in a field that stores first names. In a table, fields appear as columns. To identify the fields, each field has a **field name**. The data entered into a field is called a **field value**. In the Member table, for example, the first record has *Aurora* as the field value in the First Name field.

You can enter records directly into the table using Datasheet view. In **Datasheet view**, the table displays its data in rows and columns in a **datasheet**.

The techniques used to enter records in the table should be familiar to you. Press Enter or Tab to move to the next field as you enter data. The field names describe the data that you enter in each field. For example, a Zip Code field might be designed to accept only numbers, or a State field might only accept entries consisting of two letters. When you enter an improper field value, an error message appears and tells you what to do to correct your mistake.

After entering records in a table, you do not need to save the changes as you do in other Office programs. Access automatically saves the changes you make to records.

Navigating Records in Datasheet View

You can use the pointer to move the insertion point to any field in a table by clicking in the desired field. You can also use the keys shown in **Table 1–2** to navigate a table.

TABLE 1–2   Using the keyboard to navigate in Datasheet view

KEY	DESCRIPTION
Enter, Tab, or right arrow	Moves to the next field in the current record
Left arrow or Shift+Tab	Moves to the previous field in the current record
End	Moves to the "Click to Add" column in the current record
Home	Moves to the first field in the current record
Up arrow	Moves up one record and stays in the same field
Down arrow	Moves down one record and stays in the same field
Page Up	Moves up one screen for the current field
Page Down	Moves down one screen for the current field
Ctrl+Home	Moves to the first field in the first record
Ctrl+End	Moves to the last field in the last record

Step-by-Step 1.4

1. Click the **Member ID** field for the second record, which contains the field value 254312. The insertion point appears in the field value, the Member ID field has an orange outline that identifies it as the current field, and the fields in the rest of the record appear with a blue background to indicate that the record is selected.

2. Press **Tab**. The Last Name field for the second record is selected.

3. Press the **down** key twice. The insertion point moves to the Last Name field for the fourth record, as shown in **Figure 1–5**.

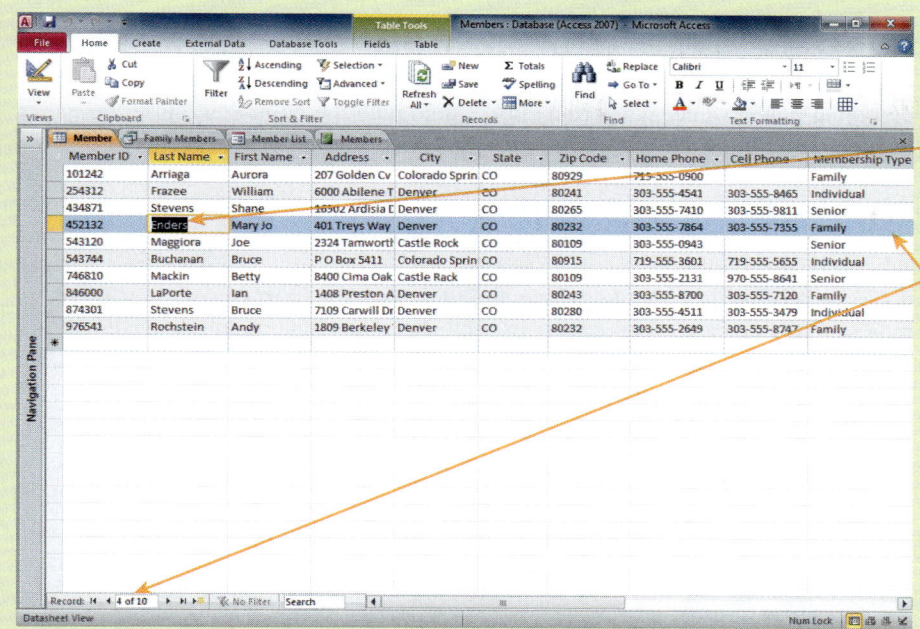

FIGURE 1–5
Navigating a table
datasheet

4. Press **Home**. The Member ID field for the fourth record is selected.

5. Press **Page Down**. The first field in the blank row at the bottom of the datasheet is selected.

6. Press **Ctrl+Home**. The first field value in the first record is selected. Leave the Member table open for the next Step-by-Step.

Editing Records

To make editing records easier, Access includes navigation buttons on the record navigation bar at the bottom of the datasheet. These buttons let you select records. They are very helpful when a table contains hundreds or thousands of records because they make it easy to move to the record you need. **Figure 1–6** shows the navigation buttons.

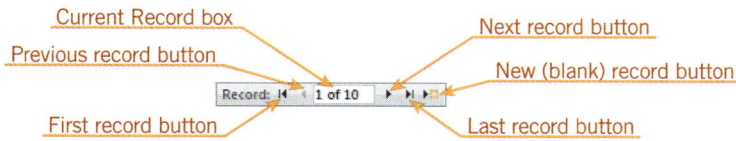

FIGURE 1–6   Record navigation bar in Datasheet view

Clicking the First record button selects the first record in the table, and clicking the Last record button selects the last record in the table. The Next record and Previous record buttons select the next and previous record in the table. To select a specific record in a table, click in the Current Record box, select the value it contains, and then type the number of the record you want to select. Press Enter to move to the specified record. To add a new record to the table, click the New (blank) record button on the record navigation bar.

When you press Enter or Tab to move to a field, Access selects the contents of the field. When a field value is selected, you can replace the contents of the field by typing a new value. When you click a field with the pointer, the insertion point appears in the field. When the insertion point appears in a field, you can use the arrow keys to move the insertion point through the field value. Press Backspace to delete characters to the left of the insertion point, or press Delete to delete characters to the right of the insertion point. When an entire record is selected, the record selector changes color from gray to orange, and the background color of the fields in the record change from white to blue. In Figure 1–5, the fourth record is selected, as indicated by the orange record selector for that row, the blue background color of the fields in the row (except for the Last Name field, which is the active field), and the "4 of 10" that appears in the Current Record box.

Undoing Changes to a Field

If you make a mistake when typing a field value, you can click the Undo button on the Quick Access Toolbar to undo your typing and restore the field value to its original state. You can also press Esc to restore the contents of the entire field.

Step-by-Step 1.5

1. Click the **Last record** button ▶| on the record navigation bar to select the last record in the table.

2. Press **Tab** to move to the Last Name field.

3. Type **Richman**, and then press **Tab**. The First Name field is the current field.

4. Click the **First record** button |◀ on the record navigation bar to move to the First Name field in the first record. Click the **Next record** button ▶ on the record navigation bar to move to the next record.

5. Click in the **Current Record** box on the navigation bar, select the **2**, type **7**, and then press **Enter**. Record 7 is the current record.

6. Click the **Address** field value (*8400 Cima Oak*) for the seventh record. Press **Tab** to move to the City field. The field value *Castle Rack* is selected.

7. Click the insertion point to the right of the letter "R" in *Rack*. Press **Delete**, type **o**, and then press **Tab** twice.

8. Press the **down** key, type **11111**, and then press **Enter**.

9. Click the **Undo** button ↺ on the Quick Access Toolbar. The Zip Code field value *11111* returns to its original state (*80243*).

10. Press **Ctrl+Home**. Leave the Member table open for the next Step-by-Step.

Selecting Records and Fields

You can quickly select entire records and fields by clicking a record or field selector. A *field selector* appears at the top of each column in a table and contains the field name. Clicking a field selector selects the entire column. A *record selector* appears to the left of the first field for each record. Clicking a record selector selects the entire record. You can also select all of the records and fields in a table by clicking the *datasheet selector*, which is the box in the upper-left corner of a datasheet.

   You can select more than one field by clicking the field selector in one column, holding down Shift, clicking the field selector in another column, and then releasing Shift. The two fields, and all the fields between them, will be selected. **Figure 1–7** shows five selected fields. You can use the same method to select multiple records. You can also select multiple fields or records by clicking and dragging across the field or record selectors.

▶ **VOCABULARY**
field selector
record selector
datasheet selector

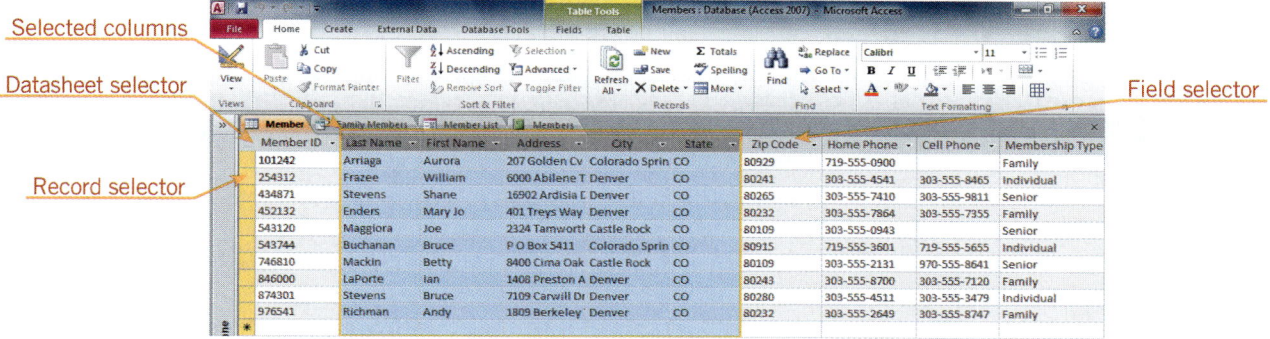

FIGURE 1–7   Selected columns in a datasheet

Step-by-Step 1.6

1. Click the **Last Name** field selector to select the entire column.

2. Press and hold down **Shift**, click the **State** field selector, and then release **Shift**. Five columns are selected, as shown in Figure 1–7.

3. Click the **Member ID** field selector. The Member ID field is selected, and the five columns are deselected.

4. Click the **Member ID** field value for the first record (*101242*) to deselect the column.

5. Click the **record selector** for the third record, with the Member ID field value *434871*. The entire record for Shane Stevens is selected.

6. Click the **datasheet selector** in the upper-left corner of the datasheet. All fields and records in the table are selected.

7. Click the **Member ID** field value for the first record (*101242*) to deselect the datasheet. Leave the table open for the next Step-by-Step.

Deleting Records

To delete a record from a table, select the record and then press Delete. A message box opens, as shown in **Figure 1–8**, warning you that you are about to delete a record. Click Yes to permanently delete the record or click No to cancel the deletion. After deleting a record, you cannot use the Undo button or press Esc to restore it. Deleting a record is permanent.

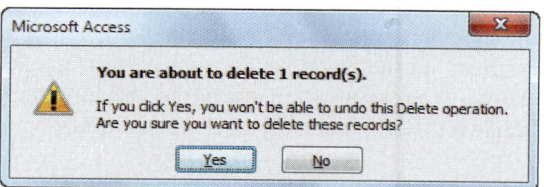

FIGURE 1–8   Message warning that you are about to delete a record

Step-by-Step 1.7

1. Click the **row selector** for the record with the Member ID *846000*.

2. Press **Delete**. A dialog box opens, as shown in Figure 1–8, warning that you are about to delete one record.

3. Click **Yes**. Leave the table open for the next Step-by-Step.

Cutting, Copying, and Pasting Data

The Cut, Copy, and Paste commands in Access work the same way as they do in other Office programs. You can use the commands to copy and move data within a table or into other tables. The Cut, Copy, and Paste commands are available as buttons on the Ribbon, as options on the shortcut menu, and as keyboard shortcuts. To cut or copy an entire record, select the record and click the Cut or Copy button in the Clipboard group on the Home tab.

Using the Cut, Copy, and Paste commands can sometimes be tricky, because data pasted in a table might overwrite the existing data. When you cut or copy an entire record and want to paste it into a table as a new record, click the arrow at the bottom of the Paste button in the Clipboard group on the Home tab, and then click Paste Append. When you select a record and click the Cut button, you will see the same warning message as when you press Delete. However, using the Cut button copies the record to the Clipboard, so you can paste it back into the table or into another table.

Step-by-Step 1.8

1. Click the **record selector** for the record for Shane Stevens (with the Member ID *434871*).

2. In the Clipboard group on the Home tab, click the **Copy** button.

3. In the Clipboard group on the Home tab, click the **Paste button arrow**. Click **Paste Append**. A copy of the record for Shane Stevens is pasted at the bottom of the datasheet.

4. In the Member ID field for the pasted record for Shane Stevens, change the Member ID field value to **457900**, and then press the **up** key.

5. Click the **record selector** for the original record for Shane Stevens (with the Member ID *434871*).

6. In the Clipboard group on the Home tab, click the **Cut** button. A dialog box opens and warns that you are about to delete one record.

7. Click **Yes**. The record is deleted.

8. On the record navigation bar, click the **New (blank) record** button. A new record is added to the table. The first field in the new record contains the insertion point.

9. In the Clipboard group on the Home tab, click the **Paste button arrow**, and then click **Paste Append**. The original record for Shane Stevens is pasted at the bottom of the datasheet.

10. Click the **record selector** for the record for Shane Stevens (with the Member ID *457900*), and then press **Delete**. Click **Yes**.

11. Press **Page Up**. Leave the Member table open for the next Step-by-Step.

Changing Datasheet Layout

You can make many changes to the datasheet layout, including changing row height and column width, rearranging columns, freezing columns, and changing the background color of rows in the datasheet.

Changing the Row Height

When you change the row height in a datasheet, the change affects every row in the datasheet. To change the row height, point to the bottom of any record selector. The pointer changes shape to a double arrow, as shown in **Figure 1–9**. Click and drag the row border up or down to adjust the row height.

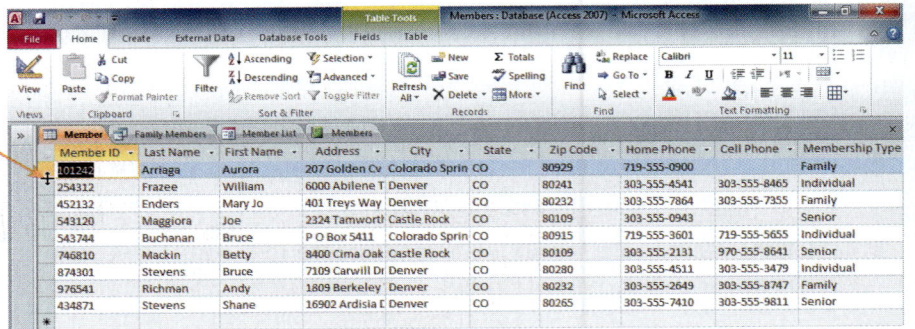

FIGURE 1–9   Changing the row height

You can also specify an exact row height. In the Records group on the Home tab, click the More button, and then click Row Height. The Row Height dialog box opens, as shown in **Figure 1–10**. The standard (default) row height is 14.25. To change the row height to another value, select the value in the Row Height text box, type a new value, and then click OK.

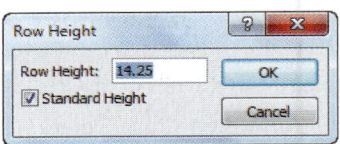

FIGURE 1–10   Row Height dialog box

Step-by-Step 1.9

1. Point to the bottom border of the record selector for the first record in the table (with the Member ID *101242*). The pointer is positioned correctly when it changes to a double-arrow shape ✛.

2. Click and drag the row border down until it appears on top of the bottom of the record selector for the second record, and then release the mouse button. The change affects every row in the table, as shown in **Figure 1–11**.

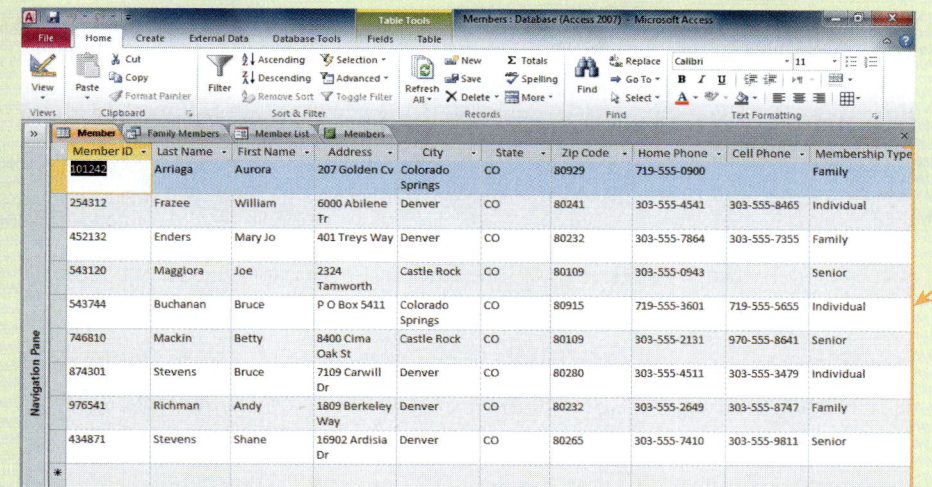

FIGURE 1–11
Datasheet after
increasing the row
height

New row height
applied to all rows

3. In the Records group on the Home tab, click the **More** button, and then click **Row Height**. The Row Height dialog box opens.

4. In the Row Height dialog box, click the **Standard Height** check box to add a check mark to it. The value in the Row Height text box changes to 14.25.

5. Click **OK**. The row height returns to the default setting. Leave the table open for the next Step-by-Step.

TIP

Another way to change the row height is to right-click any record selector, and then click Row Height on the shortcut menu.

Changing Column Width

Often, the default column widths are too wide or too narrow to display the data in the field. Adjusting the column width is similar to adjusting the row height. To change the column width, point to the right edge of the field selector for the column that you want to resize. The pointer changes to a double arrow, as shown in **Figure 1–12**. Click and drag the border to the right to make the column wider or drag the border to the left to make the column narrower. Unlike rows, which must all have the same height, each column can have a different width.

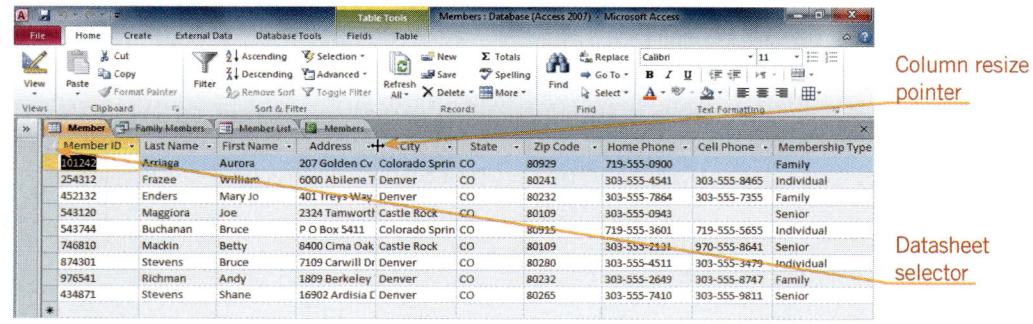

Column resize
pointer

Datasheet
selector

FIGURE 1–12   Changing the column width

Another way of resizing a column is to change it to ***best fit***, which automatically resizes the column to the best width for the data contained in the column. To resize a column to best fit, point to the right border of the field selector for the column that you want to resize, and then double-click the border.

Step-by-Step 1.10

1. Point to the right border of the **Address** field selector so the pointer changes to a double-arrow shape ✛, as shown in Figure 1–12.

2. Click and drag the right border of the **Address** field selector to the right about one-half inch (to the "t" in the word "City" in the field selector to the right of the Address field selector), and then release the mouse button. All of the data in the Address field should be visible.

3. Point to the right border of the **City** field selector so the pointer changes to a double-arrow shape ✛, and then double-click. The City field is resized to best fit the data it contains.

4. Click the **datasheet selector** to select all columns in the datasheet.

5. Point to the right border of the **Member ID** field selector so the pointer changes to a double-arrow shape ✛, and then double-click. All visible columns in the datasheet are resized to best fit.

6. Click the **Member ID** field value for the first record (*101242*) to deselect the columns. Leave the table open for the next Step-by-Step.

EXTRA FOR EXPERTS

When a datasheet is selected and you use a field selector border to resize all columns, only the columns that are visible on the screen are resized to best fit. To resize columns that aren't visible, scroll the datasheet and resize them individually.

Rearranging Columns in a Datasheet

In Datasheet view, you can rearrange the order of the columns in a datasheet by dragging them to a new location. First, click the field selector for the column you want to move. Then, click and hold down the mouse button on the field selector and drag the column to the new location. A black vertical line follows the pointer to show where the column will be inserted. Release the mouse button to insert the column in its new location.

Step-by-Step 1.11

1. Click the **First Name** field selector.

2. Click and drag the **First Name** field selector to the left until the black vertical line appears between the Member ID and Last Name columns.

3. Release the mouse button. The First Name column appears between the Member ID and Last Name columns, as shown in **Figure 1–13**. Leave the table open for the next Step-by-Step.

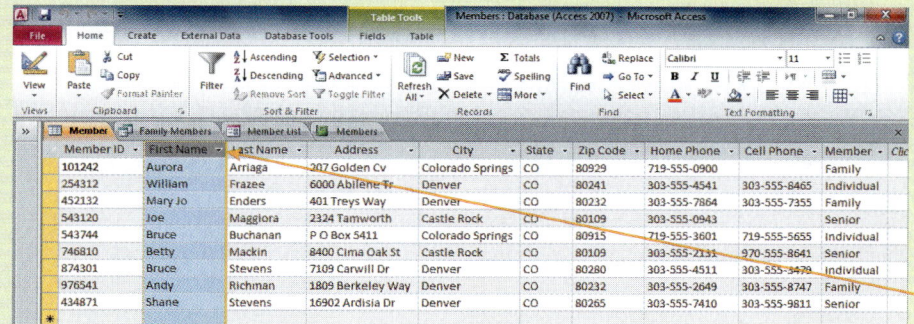

FIGURE 1–13
Moving a column in a datasheet

New position of the First Name column

Freezing Columns

When a table has many columns, you might want to freeze one or more columns so you can still see them on the screen as you scroll the datasheet.

To freeze columns, select the field selectors for the columns that you want to freeze, click the More button in the Records group on the Home tab, and then click Freeze Fields. To unfreeze columns, click the More button in the Records group on the Home tab, and then click Unfreeze All Fields.

Step-by-Step 1.12

1. Click the **field selector** for the Member ID column.

2. In the Records group on the Home tab, click the **More** button, and then click **Freeze Fields**. Press **Home** to deselect the Member ID column.

3. Slowly drag the horizontal scroll bar at the bottom of the window to the right and notice that the Member ID column remains visible as you scroll the other columns. (Note: If you do not see a horizontal scroll bar, your screen is wide enough to display all of the columns. Continue to Step 4.)

4. Click the **More** button in the Records group on the Home tab, and then click **Unfreeze All Fields**. Leave the table open for the next Step-by-Step.

Changing the Background Row Color

By default, the rows in a datasheet are displayed with alternating light and dark background colors to make the data in the records easier to read. You can change the colors used by clicking the arrow on the Alternate Row Color button in the Text Formatting group on the Home tab. As shown in **Figure 1–14**, a gallery of colors opens and displays different themes and color selections. Pointing to a color in the gallery displays its name in a ScreenTip. Clicking a color in the gallery applies it to the datasheet.

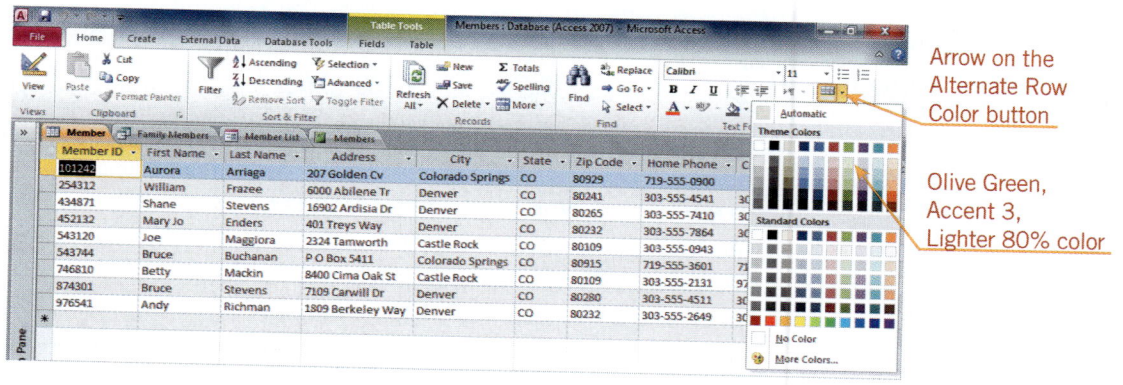

FIGURE 1–14 Gallery with color choices for the background row color

Step-by-Step 1.13

1. In the Text Formatting group on the Home tab, click the **Alternate Row Color button arrow**.

2. In the Theme Colors section, click the **Olive Green, Accent 3, Lighter 80%** color (the seventh color in the second row). The gallery closes and the new background color appears in every other row in the datasheet. Leave the table open for the next Step-by-Step.

Previewing and Printing a Table

Before printing a datasheet or any other database object, you should view it in Print Preview so you can check the print settings. To view an object in Print Preview, click the File tab, click Print in the navigation bar, and then click Print Preview. **Figure 1–15** shows Print Preview for the Member table datasheet. You can use the options on the Ribbon to change the printer, to change the page layout (portrait or landscape and the page margins), or to change the zoom setting on the report so you can view the entire page or a close-up of its contents. You can use the page navigation bar at the bottom of Print Preview to display additional pages when the object contains them. After previewing the object and making any adjustments, click the Close Print Preview button in the Close Preview group on the Print Preview tab to return to Datasheet view.

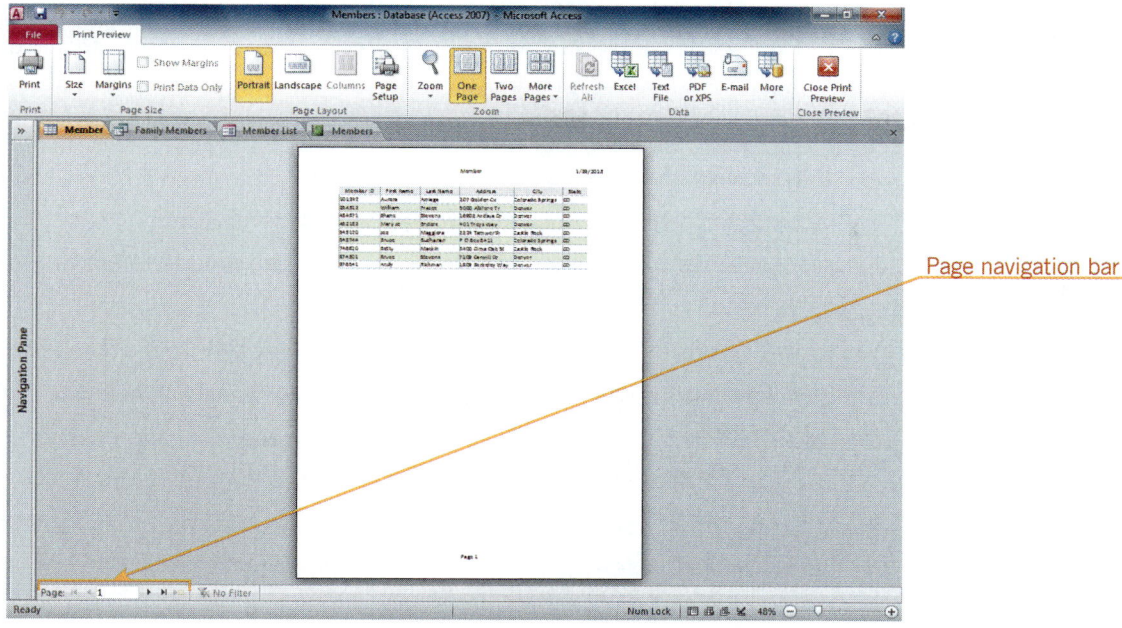

FIGURE 1–15   Print Preview for the Member table datasheet

You can print a datasheet by clicking the File tab, clicking Print in the navigation bar, and then clicking Quick Print to print the datasheet using the default printer and the default print, or clicking Print to select a printer and adjust the print settings. As shown in **Figure 1–16**, you can choose to print all the records, only the selected records, or certain pages.

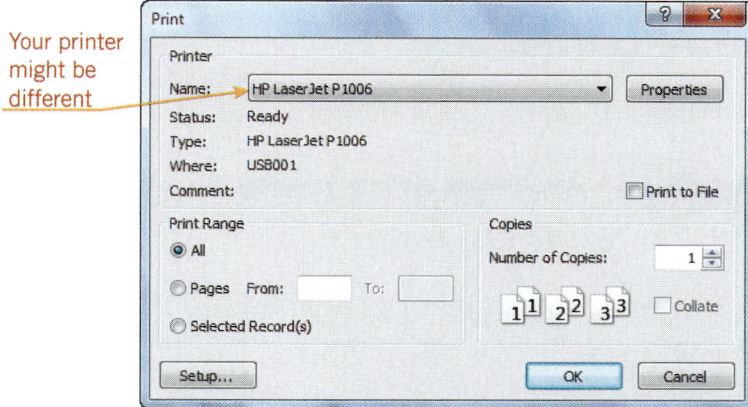

FIGURE 1–16   Print dialog box

Step-by-Step 1.14

1. Click the **File** tab, click **Print** in the navigation bar, and then click **Print Preview**. The Member table datasheet appears in Print Preview, as shown in Figure 1–15.

2. In the Page Layout group on the Print Preview tab, click the **Landscape** button.

3. On the page navigation bar, click the **Next Page** button 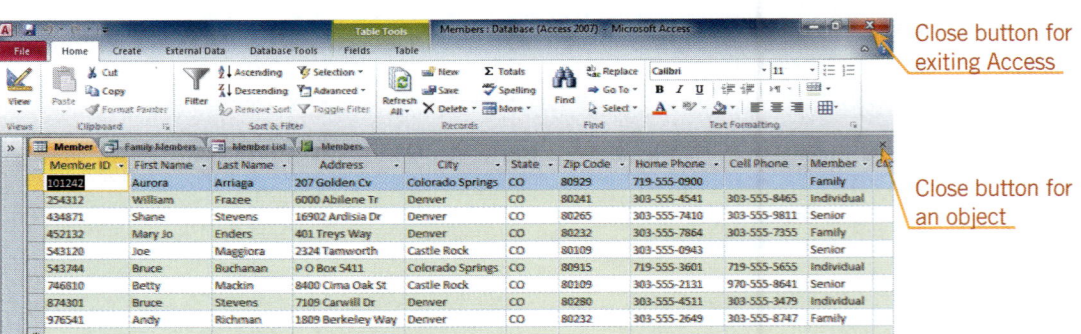 to view the second page of the datasheet.

4. In the Zoom group on the Print Preview tab, click the **Zoom** button. The zoom settings for the page change so that you can read the data in the datasheet.

5. In the Close Preview group on the Print Preview tab, click the **Close Print Preview** button. The datasheet is displayed in Datasheet view.

6. Click the **File** tab on the Ribbon, click **Print** in the navigation bar, and then click **Print**. The Print dialog box opens, as shown in Figure 1–16.

7. Make sure that your printer appears in the Name box and that the **All** option button is selected in the Print Range section. Click **OK**. Leave the table open for the next Step-by-Step.

Saving and Closing Objects

As you are entering and changing data in a table, Access saves your changes to the data automatically. When you make changes to the layout or appearance of a datasheet, such as changing row height or column widths or changing the background row colors, you must save your changes by clicking the Save button on the Quick Access Toolbar. If your table already has a name, Access saves the table when you click the Save button. If you haven't given your table a name, the Save As dialog box opens first and requests a name.

You can close an object by clicking the Close button on the object's tab, as shown in **Figure 1–17**.

> **TIP**
>
> When you make changes to the layout of a datasheet and try to close the table, Access will prompt you to save your changes.

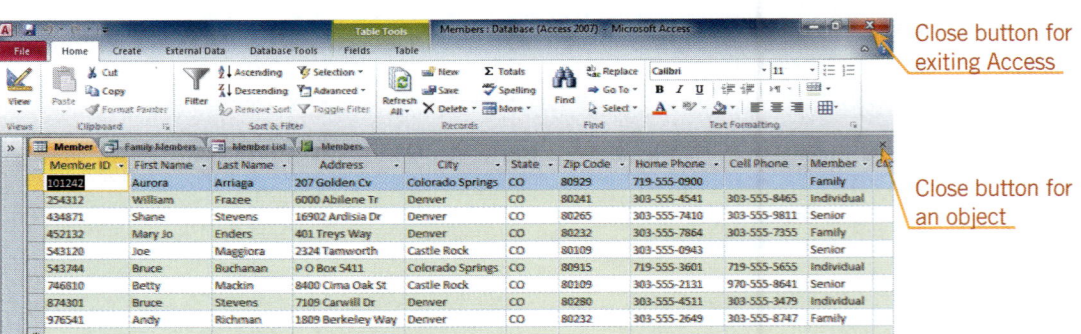

FIGURE 1–17 Closing a database object

Step-by-Step 1.15

1. On the Quick Access Toolbar, click the **Save** button 🔲. Access saves the layout changes you made in the table.

2. Click the **Close 'Member'** button ☒ on the table window. The table closes.

3. Click the **Close 'Members'** button ☒ on the report window. The report closes.

4. Click the **Close 'Member List'** button ☒ on the form window. The form closes.

5. Click the **Close 'Family Members'** button ☒ on the query window. The query closes. Leave the database open for the next Step-by-Step.

Compacting and Repairing a Database

As you add and delete data or objects in a database, the database can become fragmented and use disk space inefficiently. *Compacting* a database rearranges how the database is stored on the disk and optimizes the performance of the database. Access combines compacting and repairing into one step. Depending on the size of the database and your computer's settings, it might take only a second or up to a minute to compact and repair a database. When the database you are compacting is small in size, like the Members database, you might not even notice that Access is compacting it because it will happen quickly.

▶ **VOCABULARY**
compacting

Step-by-Step 1.16

1. Click the **File** tab on the Ribbon. The Info tab displays information about the current database.

2. Click the **Compact & Repair Database** button. Access compacts and repairs the database, and displays the Home tab.

3. Leave the database open for the next Step-by-Step.

Closing a Database and Exiting Access

When you are finished working in a database, you can close it by clicking the File tab on the Ribbon, and then clicking Close Database in the navigation bar. After Access closes the database, the File tab opens.

As in other Office 2010 programs, you exit Access by clicking the File tab on the Ribbon, and then clicking Exit. You can also close Access by clicking the Close button on the title bar. Exiting Access takes you back to the Windows desktop.

Step-by-Step 1.17

1. Click the **File** tab on the Ribbon, and then click **Close Database** in the navigation bar. The database closes. Backstage view displays the New tab.
2. In the navigation bar, click **Exit**. Access closes.

SUMMARY

In this lesson, you learned:

- Access is a program known as a database management system (DBMS). A DBMS allows you to store, retrieve, analyze, and print information.

- A database is a collection of objects. The objects work together to store, retrieve, display, and summarize data and also to automate tasks. The object types are tables, queries, forms, reports, macros, and modules. You can open an object by double-clicking it in the Navigation Pane.

- You can open an existing database by clicking the File tab on the Ribbon, clicking Open in the navigation bar, and then browsing to and double-clicking the database you want to open. You can also click the File tab on the Ribbon, and then click Recent in the navigation bar to select the database from a list of recently opened files.

- You can use the keys on the keyboard to move through the records and fields in a datasheet. You can also use the buttons on the record navigation bar in Datasheet view to move around the datasheet. The record navigation bar buttons allow you to select the first record, the last record, the previous record, or the next record. You can also use a button to add a new record or use the Current Record box to select a specific record.

- A record is a complete set of data. Each record is made up of one or more fields. Each field is identified by a field name. The data entered into a field is called a field value. To select an entire row in a datasheet, click the record selector for the row. To select an entire field in a datasheet, click the field selector at the top of the column. To select multiple columns, click the field selector for the first column, press and hold down Shift, click a field selector in another column, and then release Shift. To select all fields and rows in a datasheet, click the datasheet selector.

- To delete a record from a table, select the record and then press Delete. Use the Cut, Copy, and Paste buttons in the Clipboard group on the Home tab to move and copy data. Clicking the arrow at the bottom of the Paste button and then clicking Paste Append appends a copied or cut record to the bottom of the datasheet.

- You can make many layout changes to a datasheet, such as changing the row height or column width, freezing columns, and changing the background row color of every other row.

- Before printing a database object, use Print Preview to check the print settings and to adjust the way the object is printed.

- You can close an object by clicking its Close button. To exit Access, click the Close button on the title bar.

◼ VOCABULARY REVIEW

Define the following terms:

best fit	datasheet selector	field value
compacting	Datasheet view	Navigation Pane
database	field	record
database management system (DBMS)	field name	record selector
datasheet	field selector	

■ REVIEW QUESTIONS

TRUE / FALSE

Circle T if the statement is true or F if the statement is false.

T   F   **1.**   Microsoft Access allows you to store, retrieve, analyze, and print information.

T   F   **2.**   The object that stores data in the database is a form.

T   F   **3.**   Clicking a record selector in a datasheet selects an entire row.

T   F   **4.**   Pressing and holding down Alt allows you to select more than one column in a datasheet.

T   F   **5.**   Changing the height of one row in a datasheet changes the height of all rows.

WRITTEN QUESTIONS

Write a brief answer to each of the following questions.

1. How do you delete a record in Datasheet view?

2. What does the Paste Append command do?

3. When should you freeze columns in a datasheet?

4. Why should you preview an object before printing it?

5. Which database object allows you to search for and retrieve data?

FILL IN THE BLANK

Complete the following sentences by writing the correct word or words in the blanks provided.

1. Access is a program known as a(n) _____.

2. The _____ lists the objects in the current database.

3. To move to the first field in the current record, press _____.

4. You can select all of the records and fields in a table datasheet by clicking the _____.

5. _____ a database rearranges how the database is stored on the disk and optimizes the performance of the database.

■ PROJECTS

If you have a SAM 2010 user profile, your instructor may have assigned an autogradable version of the indicated project. If so, log into the SAM 2010 Web site at *www.cengage.com/sam2010* to download the instruction and start files.

PROJECT 1–1

1. Start Access.

2. Open the **Restaurants.accdb** database from the Access Lesson 01 folder where your Data Files are stored.

3. Open the **Favorites** table in Datasheet view.

4. Enter the records shown in **Figure 1–18**. (The first record was added for you.)

5. Resize the columns in the datasheet to best fit.

6. Preview the datasheet in Print Preview. Change the page layout to landscape.

7. Print the datasheet. Close Print Preview.

8. Save the table, and then close it.

9. Close the database, and then exit Access.

⊞ Favorites				
Name	Address	Phone	Specialty	Favorite Dish
Rosie's	8722 University Ave	817-555-6798	Mexican	Chicken fajitas
Health Hut	3440 Slide Rd	817-555-8971	Healthy foods	Fruit salad
Tony's BBQ	2310 S Lamar	817-555-7410	BBQ	Pulled pork sandwich
Stella's	7822 Broadway	817-555-7144	Italian	Lasagna
Westside Inn	5845 S 1st St	817-555-8200	American	Curry chicken salad
Alamo Diner	451 San Jacinto	817-555-0120	American	Chili cheese fries
*				

FIGURE 1–18

 PROJECT 1–2

1. Open the **Employees.accdb** database from the Access Lesson 01 folder where your Data Files are stored.

2. Open the **Department** table in Datasheet view.

3. Go to record 7 and change the first name to **Natalie**.

4. Go to record 11 and change the title to **Account Executive**.

5. Go to record 14 and change the department to **Marketing**.

6. Go to record 1 and change the last name to **Abraham**.

7. Undo your last change.

8. Select record 5. Delete record 5.

9. Select the datasheet (all rows and all columns). Change all columns to best fit.

10. Change the row height to **15**.

11. Move the First Name column so it appears between the Employee ID and Last Name columns.

12. Change the alternate row color in the datasheet to Dark Blue 1 (in the Standard Colors section, second row, fourth column).

13. Preview the datasheet in Print Preview. Change the page layout to landscape.

14. Print the datasheet, and then close Print Preview.

15. Save the Department table, and then close it.

16. Compact and repair the database.

17. Close the database, and then exit Access.

PROJECT 1–3

1. Open the **Stores.accdb** database from the Access Lesson 01 folder where your Data Files are stored.

2. Open the **Manager** table in Datasheet view.

3. Copy record 4 and paste it at the bottom of the datasheet.

4. In the pasted record, change the Name to **Vision Eyewear**, the Address to **7500 Hwy 15 West**, the Zip Code to **43601**, the Phone to **419-555-0122**, the Specialty to **Contemporary eyewear**, and the Manager to **Trent Rodriguez**. Press the Tab key.

5. Move the Phone column so it appears between the Name and Address columns.

6. Resize all columns to best fit.

7. Freeze the Name column.

8. Scroll to the right until the Specialty column appears to the right of the Name column.

9. Unfreeze all columns.

10. Change the alternate row color of the datasheet to Maroon 1 (in the Standard Colors section, the sixth color in the second row).

11. Preview the datasheet in Print Preview. Change the page layout to landscape.

12. Print the datasheet, and then close Print Preview.

13. Save the Manager table, and then close it.

14. Compact and repair the database.

15. Close the database, and then exit Access.

◼ CRITICAL THINKING

ACTIVITY 1–1

When you are working in Access and need help completing a task, the Access Help window can help you find an answer. Start Access and click Help in the navigation bar on the File tab. Click Microsoft Office Help to open the Access Help window. In the Search text box, type **Navigation Pane**, and then click the Search button. Review the links that you find and click ones that you believe will give you more information about viewing and managing objects using the Navigation Pane. Read the information that appears. After following several links and reading their contents, write a brief summary of two new things that you learned about the Navigation Pane. When you are finished with your report, close the Access Help window and exit Access.

ACTIVITY 1–2

In this lesson, you learned how to compact and repair a database to reduce the size of a database and repair any errors. Another utility that you might use is one that creates a backup copy of the database. When you back up a database, you create a copy of everything in the database at the time of the backup. If the database ever becomes damaged or destroyed, you can restore the backup copy to minimize the amount of work you'll need to do to replace the damaged copy of the database.

Start Access, and click Help in the navigation bar on the File tab. Click Microsoft Office Help to open the Access Help window. In the Search text box, type **Back up a database**, and then click the Search button. Review the information that you find, and then answer the following questions on a sheet of paper

1. What steps do you follow to back up a database?

2. What happens when you restore a whole database?

3. What steps do you follow to restore a database?

LESSON 2

Creating a Database

■ OBJECTIVES

Upon completion of this lesson, you should be able to:

- Create a database.
- Design, create, and save a table in Datasheet view.
- Set a field's data type and name in Datasheet view.
- Add, delete, rename, and move fields in Design view.
- Change field properties in Design view.
- Set field properties in Design view.

■ VOCABULARY

alphanumeric data

AutoNumber

Blank database template

data type

Default Value property

Description property

design grid

Design view

Field Properties pane

field property

Field Size property

Format property

primary key

Required property

template

Access provides you with many options when creating databases and the tables that will store your data. In this lesson, you will learn about the different options you can use to create a database and a table. You will also create a table, add fields to a table, change a field's data type and properties, and add records to a table.

Creating a Database

The first step in creating a database is to create the file that will store the database objects. You can choose to create a database using one of the many templates that are installed with Access. These templates contain objects that you can use to organize data about events, projects, tasks, and other categories of data. When you use a ***template*** to create a database, the template creates the database and one or more table, query, form, and report objects that you use to enter and view data. Another option is to use the ***Blank database template***, which creates a database with an empty table in it.

To create a database, start Access. On the New tab in Backstage view, click the template you want to use or click the Blank database template to create a database that contains an empty table. Access asks you to specify a file name to use and a location in which to store the database, as shown in **Figure 2–1**.

▶ **VOCABULARY**

template

Blank database template

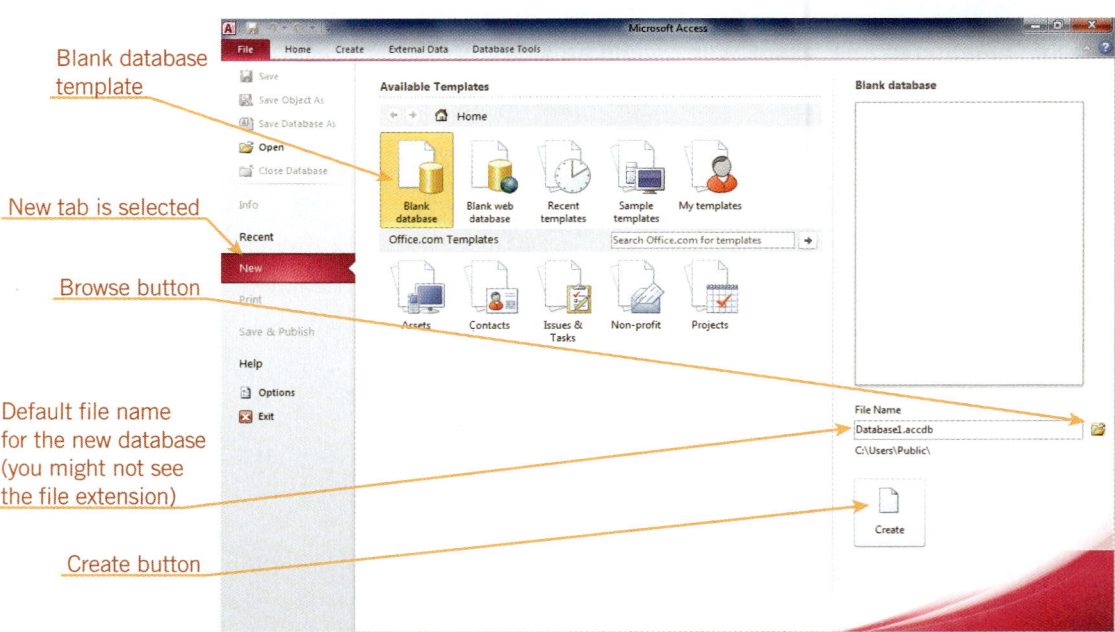

Blank database template

New tab is selected

Browse button

Default file name for the new database (you might not see the file extension)

Create button

FIGURE 2–1   Creating a new, blank database

After specifying the file name and the location in which to store the database, click the Create button to create the new database and open it in Access. When you create a blank database, Access opens an empty table in Datasheet view so that you can start entering data, as shown in **Figure 2–2**.

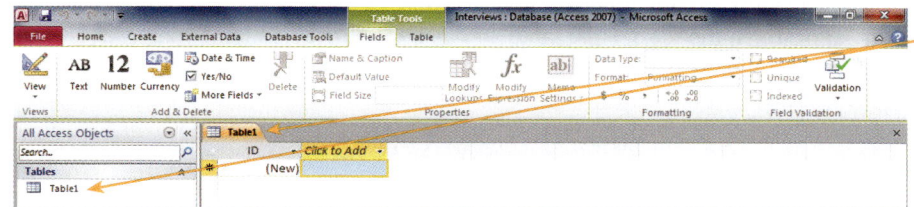
Default table name

FIGURE 2–2   New, empty table created

Step-by-Step 2.1

1. With Windows running, click the **Start** button 🪟 on the taskbar. Click **All Programs**, click **Microsoft Office**, and then click **Microsoft Access 2010**.

2. On the New tab, click the **Blank database** template, if necessary. See Figure 2–1.

3. In the Blank database pane, click the **Browse** button 📂. The File New Database dialog box opens.

4. Navigate to the drive and folder where your Data Files are stored, and then open the **Access Lesson 02** folder. Click **OK**.

5. In the Blank database pane, click in the File Name text box to select the default database name (Database1.accdb), and then type **Interviews** followed by your initials.

6. Click the **Create** button. Access creates the Interviews database and opens it. Access also opens a new, empty table, as shown in Figure 2–2. Leave the table open for the next Step-by-Step.

> **TIP**
>
> Access might add the file name extension "accdb" to your file name automatically. You do not need to type it.

EXTRA FOR EXPERTS

You can also create a new table in a database by clicking the Create tab on the Ribbon, and then clicking the Table button in the Tables group.

Creating and Saving a Table

When you create a blank database, Access creates the first table in the database for you and names it *Table1*. You can change this name when you save the table for the first time. To save a table, click the Save button on the Quick Access Toolbar. In the Save As dialog box, type the name of the table, and then click OK. The new table name appears on the tab for the table and also in the Navigation Pane, as shown in **Figure 2–3**. In many databases, data is stored in more than one table.

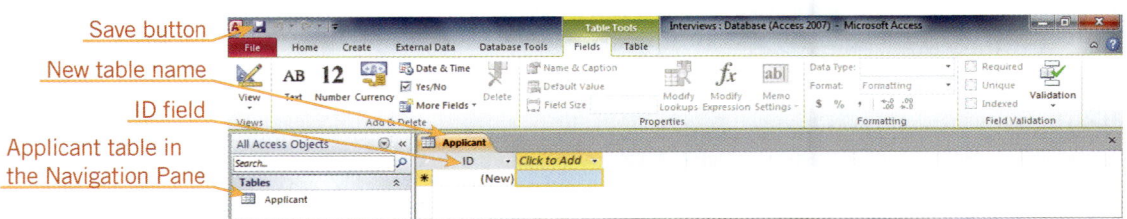

Save button
New table name
ID field
Applicant table in the Navigation Pane

FIGURE 2–3   Table after saving it

Step-by-Step 2.2

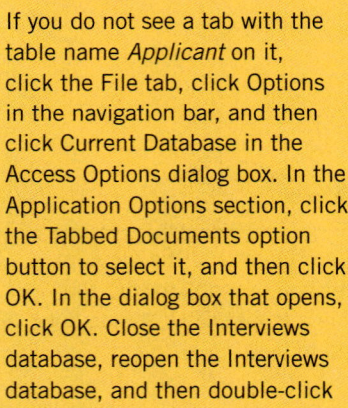

WARNING

If you do not see a tab with the table name *Applicant* on it, click the File tab, click Options in the navigation bar, and then click Current Database in the Access Options dialog box. In the Application Options section, click the Tabbed Documents option button to select it, and then click OK. In the dialog box that opens, click OK. Close the Interviews database, reopen the Interviews database, and then double-click the Applicant table to open it.

1. On the Quick Access Toolbar, click the **Save** button 🔲. The Save As dialog box opens. The default name *Table1* is selected.

2. In the Table Name text box, type **Applicant**.

3. Click **OK**. The tab for the table now displays the table name *Applicant*. The Applicant table appears in the Navigation Pane, as shown in Figure 2–3. Leave the table open for the next Step-by-Step.

Designing a Table

After creating a table in a database, you need to tell Access which fields to include in the table. When you create a blank database, the table that Access creates for you contains one field named *ID*. Access sets the ID field as the table's primary key. In a table, the **primary key** is the field that contains a unique field value for each record in the table. In some tables, this field is called an **AutoNumber** because it automatically adds a unique number to the primary key field for each record in the table. You can tell that Access created an AutoNumber for the ID field because of the word *(New)* in the first record's field. When you add the first record to the table, Access will change *(New)* to a unique number.

VOCABULARY
primary key
AutoNumber

In some tables, your data might already have a field that stores unique numbers for each record. This unique field might store student identification numbers, employee numbers, or Social Security numbers. These types of values are also good candidates to use as a table's primary key field. The advantage of setting a primary key is that Access does not let you enter duplicate values for this field in different records. In other words, if you enter the student ID 1001 in the record for a student named John Hooper, Access does not let you enter the same student ID number in a record for another student. You learn more about primary key fields later in this lesson.

Understanding Data Types

Before creating all the fields for your table, you must decide which data type to assign to the field based on the field values you will enter. A field's *data type* determines the kind of data that you can enter in the field, such as numbers or text, or a combination of numbers and text (also called *alphanumeric data*). **Table 2–1** describes some common data types that you can use when you create a table.

▶ **VOCABULARY**
data type
alphanumeric data

TABLE 2–1   Common data types in Access

DATA TYPE	DESCRIPTION
Text	Accepts field values containing letters, numbers, spaces, and certain symbols such as an underscore (_). A Text field can store up to 255 characters and is used to store data such as names and addresses.
Number	Stores numbers. Number fields are usually values that will be used in calculations, such as multiplying the cost of an item by the number of items ordered to get a total. Number fields are sometimes used to restrict the entered field values to numbers.
Currency	Accepts monetary values and displays them with a dollar sign and decimal point.
Date/Time	Stores dates, times, or a combination of both.
Yes/No	Stores Yes/No, True/False, or On/Off values.
Lookup	Creates a field that lets you "look up" a value from another table or from a list of values entered by the user.
Memo	Accepts field values containing alphanumeric data, but can store field values containing up to 65,535 characters. Memo fields usually store long passages of text, such as detailed notes about a person or product.
Attachment	Stores graphics, sound, and other types of files as attachments.
Hyperlink	Stores a value that contains a hyperlink. Clicking the value activates the link and opens a Web page or other location, or addresses a message to an e-mail address.
Calculated	Opens the Expression Builder dialog box, which lets you specify fields and operators to use in calculations. The result of the calculation appears as the field's value, and determines the field's actual data type.
AutoNumber	Adds a unique numeric field value to each record in a table. AutoNumber fields are often used for primary key fields.

Setting a Field's Data Type and Name in Datasheet View

When you create a table in Datasheet view, clicking the Click to Add field selector opens the list of data types show in **Figure 2–4** and described in Table 2–1. After clicking the desired data type in the list, the list closes and the default field name is selected, so you can type the field name used in your table design. The field name is added to the field selector after you press Tab or Enter. After you have added all of the fields to your table, the last column in the table contains the Click to Add field selector in case you need to add another field later.

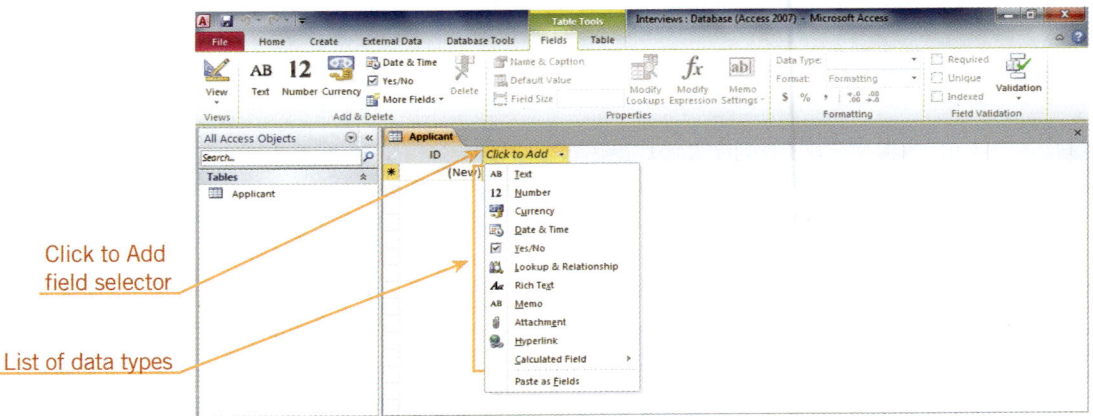

Click to Add field selector

List of data types

FIGURE 2–4   Creating a new field

Step-by-Step 2.3

1. In the datasheet, click the **Click to Add** field selector. Figure 2–4 shows the list that opens.

2. In the list, click **Text**. The list closes, the field's data type is set to Text, and the default field name *Field1* is selected in the field selector.

3. Type **First Name**.

4. Press **Tab**. The field name changes to *First Name*. The Click to Add list opens for the next field in the table.

5. In the list, click **Text**, type **Last Name**, and then press **Tab**. The third field's name and data type are set and the Click to Add list opens for the fourth field.

6. In the list, click **Text**, type **Phone**, and then press **Tab**.

7. In the list for the fifth field, click **Date & Time**, type **Appointment Date**, and then press **Tab**.

8. In the list for the sixth field, click **Number**, type **Job Number**, and then press **Tab**.

9. In the list for the seventh field, click **Text**, type **Notes**, and then press the **down** key. Leave the table open for the next Step-by-Step.

Entering Records in Datasheet View

The First Name, Last Name, Phone, and Notes fields are Text fields that will contain alphanumeric data with less than 255 characters. The Appointment Date field is a Date/Time field that will store dates. To make sure that all job numbers contain only digits, the Job Numbers field has the Number data type. **Figure 2–5** shows the table after creating all the fields.

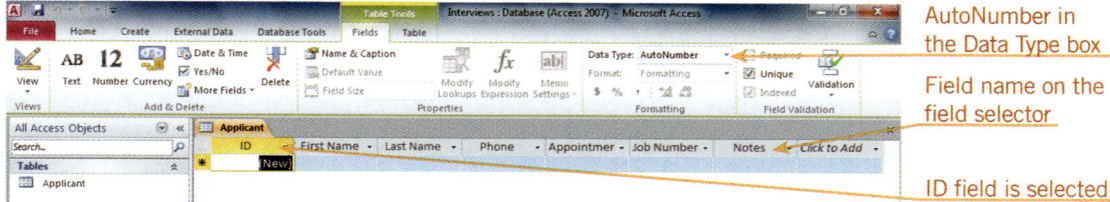

AutoNumber in the Data Type box

Field name on the field selector

ID field is selected

FIGURE 2–5   Table after creating all the fields

When Access created the table, it created the ID field and assigned it the AutoNumber data type. When you enter a new record in the table, you do not need to type a value in this field. The value *(New)* appears in the ID field. After you enter a field value in the record, Access changes the value *(New)* to a unique value in the ID field automatically.

Step-by-Step 2.4

1. With the ID field for the first record active, press **Tab**.

2. In the First Name field, type **Adam**. Press **Tab**.

3. In the Last Name field, type **Hoover**. Press **Tab**.

4. In the Phone field, type **505-555-7844**. Press **Tab**.

5. In the Appointment Date field, type **9/22/2013**. Press **Tab**.

6. In the Job Number field, type **5492**. Press **Tab**. The insertion point is in the Notes field. Leave the table open for the next Step-by-Step.

Changing a Field's Data Type in Datasheet View

When you need to change the data type for a selected field, you can do so by clicking the Data Type arrow in the Formatting group on the Fields tab. The Notes field has the Text data type, but it needs to use the Memo data type. You can click the Data Type arrow in the Formatting group to display a list of data types for fields, as shown in **Figure 2–6**. Clicking a data type in the list changes the data type for the current field and also closes the list.

The AutoNumber value in your table might be different

Data Type arrow

Notes field is selected

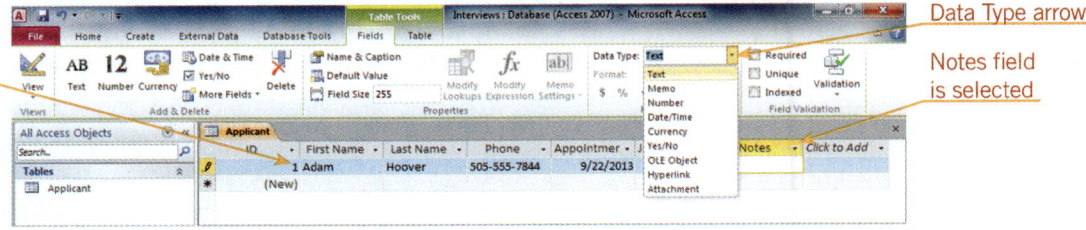

FIGURE 2–6   Data Type list with the Notes field selected

Step-by-Step 2.5

1. With the Notes field for the first record active, click the **Data Type** arrow in the Formatting group on the Fields tab. Figure 2–6 shows the list that opens.

2. In the Data Type list, click **Memo**. The Notes field now uses the Memo data type.

3. Press **Tab**. The first record is complete, and the ID field for the second record is selected. The value "(New)" indicates that this field uses the AutoNumber data type.

4. Use **Figure 2–7** to enter the remaining records in the table. Leave the table open for the next Step-by-Step.

FIGURE 2–7
Records added to the Applicant table

Your numbers in the ID field might be different

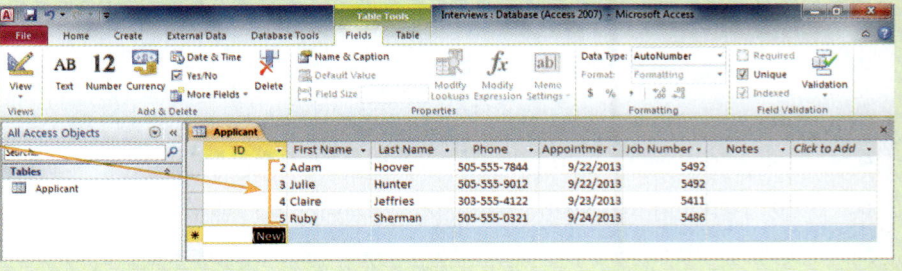

Working in Design View

When you are working on a table in Datasheet view, you can change the data type of a field. However, sometimes you need to make certain types of changes to a field that you cannot make in Datasheet view. In *Design view*, you can add, delete, and make changes to the way that fields store data. To change to Design view, click the View button in the Views group on the Fields tab. **Figure 2–8** shows the Applicant table in Design view. Notice that the field names and data types appear in the *design grid* in the top half of the Table window. The bottom half of the Table window is called the *Field Properties pane*. The properties for a field depend on the field's data type. For example, if the selected field in the design grid has the AutoNumber data type, the Field Properties pane displays the properties for an AutoNumber field. If the selected field has another data type, the Field Properties pane displays only those properties for that field's data type.

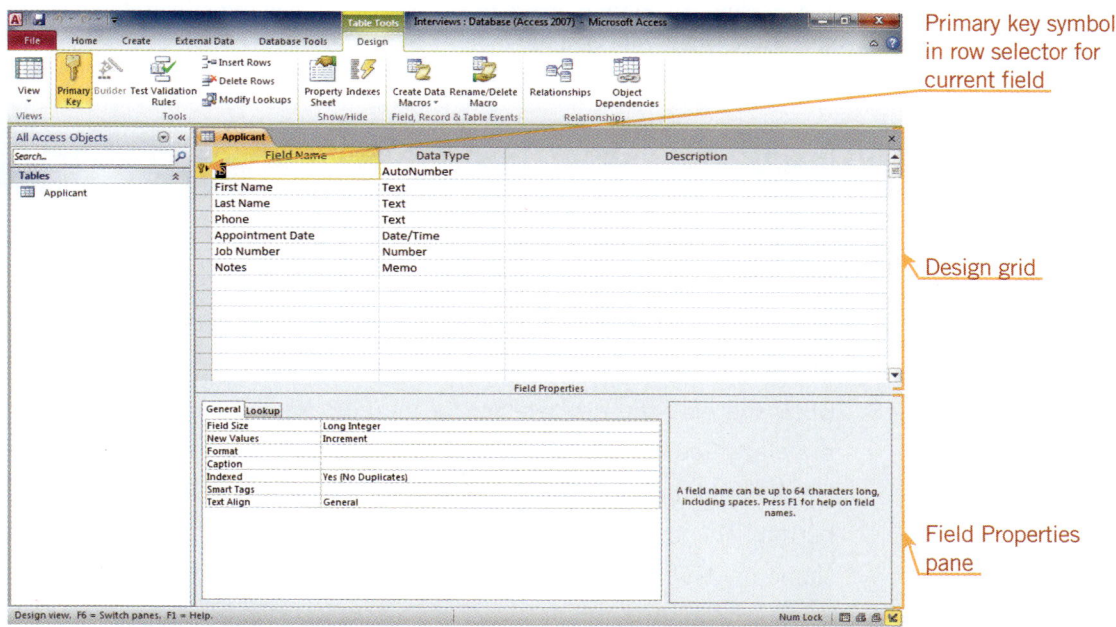

Primary key symbol
in row selector for
current field

Design grid

Field Properties
pane

FIGURE 2–8   Applicant table in Design view

Notice that the row selector for the ID field in Figure 2–8 has a key symbol in it. This key indicates that the field is the table's primary key. To set a table's primary key, click the Primary Key button in the Tools group on the Design tab. This button is a toggle button. For a primary key field, clicking the Primary Key button removes the key symbol from the field. For a field that is not the table's primary key, clicking the Primary Key button adds the key symbol to the field. The row selector for the ID field is also orange. Just like when you select a record selector in a datasheet, the row selector for a selected field in the design grid changes color when the field is selected.

Adding, Deleting, Renaming, and Rearranging Fields in Design View

You can use the options in the Tools group on the Design tab to add and delete fields. You can also drag selected fields to new locations in the design grid. To insert a new field between two existing rows in a table, click the row selector for the row *below* where you want the new field to appear. Then click the Insert Rows button in the Tools group on the Design tab. If you want to add a new field at the end of the table, click in the first empty row in the design grid, and then type the field's name. You can delete a field by clicking the row selector for the field you want to delete, and then clicking the Delete Rows button in the Tools group on the Design tab. To rename a field, edit the field name in the design grid and press Tab. To change a field's data type, click the Data Type box for the field in the design grid. An arrow appears on the right side of the box. Clicking the arrow displays a list of data types so you can click the data type you want from the list. Any changes that you make in Design view are automatically updated in Datasheet view when you save the table.

Step-by-Step 2.6

1. In the Views group on the Fields tab, click the **View** button. The Applicant table opens in Design view, as shown in Figure 2–8.

2. Click the **row selector** for the Last Name field. The field is selected, as indicated by the orange border that surrounds the row.

3. Click and drag the **row selector** for the Last Name field up one row, so the black line appears between the First Name and ID fields. When the black line is between the First Name and ID fields, release the mouse button. The Last Name field now appears between the ID and First Name fields.

4. In the design grid, double-click the word **Appointment** in the Appointment Date field.

5. Type **Appt** and then press the **down** key. The field name changes to *Appt Date*. The Job Number field is selected.

6. With the Job Number field selected, click the **Insert Rows** button in the Tools group on the Design tab. A new row is inserted above the Job Number field.

7. Type **Confirmed** and then press **Tab**.

8. Click the **Data Type** arrow for the Confirmed field. **Figure 2–9** shows the list of data types.

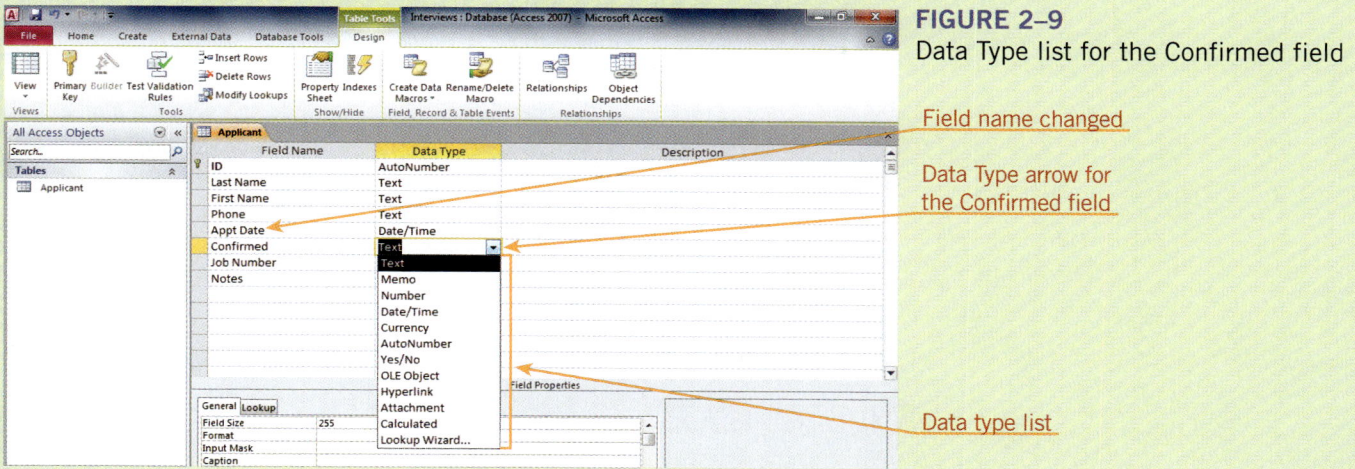

FIGURE 2–9
Data Type list for the Confirmed field

Field name changed

Data Type arrow for the Confirmed field

Data type list

9. In the list, click **Yes/No**.

10. On the Quick Access Toolbar, click the **Save** button 🖫. Leave the table open for the next Step-by-Step.

Description

The ***Description property*** in the design grid is an optional field property that you can use to describe what to enter in the field. When you give your fields descriptive names, it helps you remember the field values to enter in the fields. For example, the Last Name field name easily communicates what field values to enter in the field. When you are entering data in the field, the Description property can remind you what field value to enter, because it appears on the status bar in Datasheet view. For example, **Figure 2–10** shows that the Description property for the Confirmed field in the Applicant table was set to *Has the interview been confirmed?* In this case, the Description property makes it easier to enter the field value. Because this field uses the Yes/No data type, the field value is *Yes* (the check box contains a check mark) if you confirmed the interview; otherwise, the field value is *No* (the check box is empty).

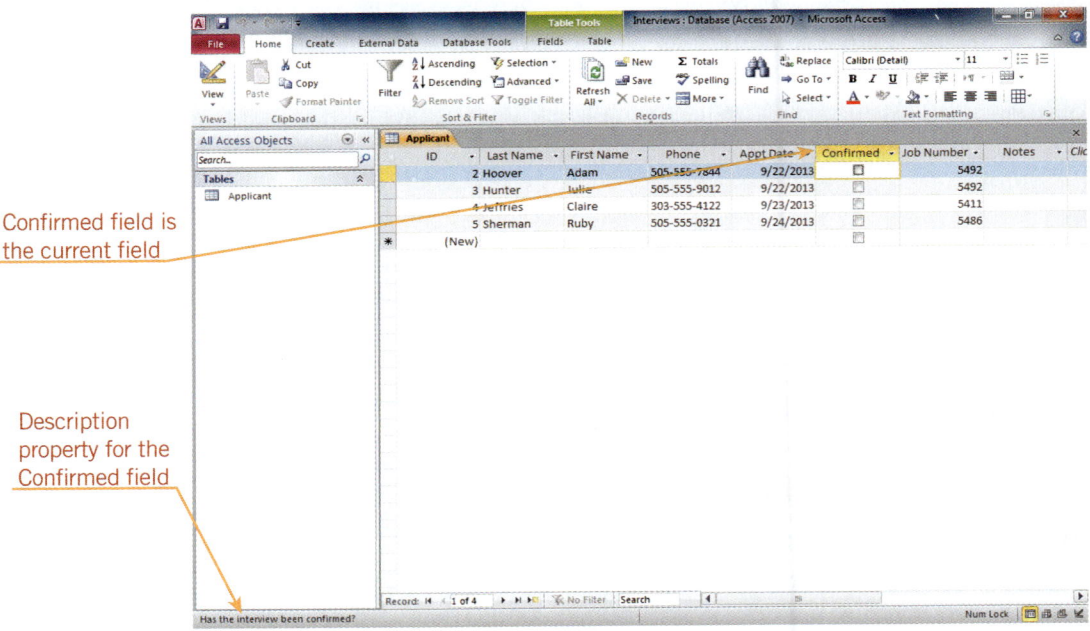

Confirmed field is the current field

Description property for the Confirmed field

FIGURE 2–10   Description property for the Confirmed field

Step-by-Step 2.7

1. Press **Tab**. The insertion point moves to the Description property for the Confirmed field.

2. Type **Has the interview been confirmed?**

3. Press **Enter**. The Description property for the Confirmed field is set, as shown in **Figure 2–11**. When you update certain field properties, the Property Update Options button might appear. If you click this button and then click the update option in the list, you can also update the field property in other database objects that use it. Leave the table open for the next Step-by-Step.

FIGURE 2–11
Confirmed field
Description
property

Description property

Property Update
Options button

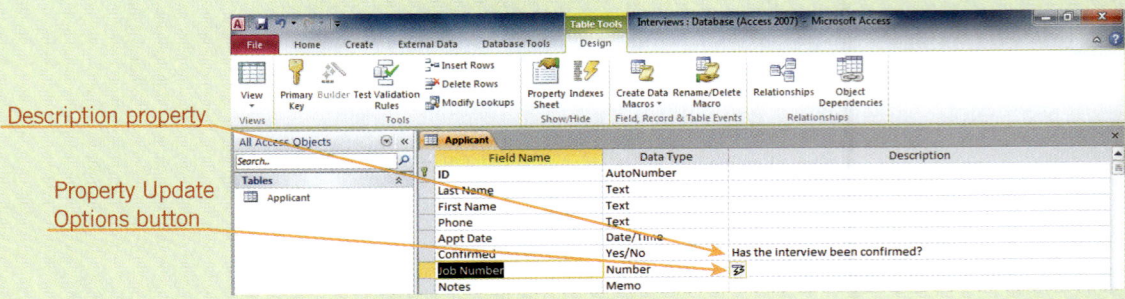

Changing Field Properties in Design View

When you created the fields in the Applicant table in Datasheet view, you assigned each field a name and a data type. When you set a field's data type, the field is given certain properties that help you to define and maintain the data you enter in the field. A *field property* describes a field's contents beyond the field's basic data type, such as the number of characters the field can store or the allowable values that you can enter in the field. For example, **Figure 2–12** shows the field properties for a Text field. Sometimes you won't need to change a field's properties at all. You can view and change field properties in Design view. Remember that the field properties for a field will vary depending on the field's data type.

▶ **VOCABULARY**
field property
Field Size property

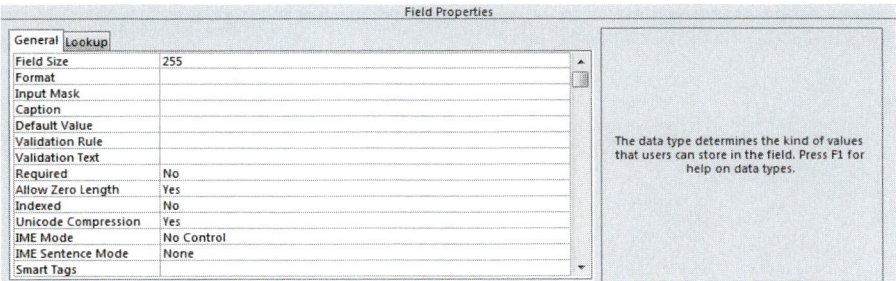

FIGURE 2–12   Field properties for a Text field

Changing the Field Size

The *Field Size property* sets the number of characters you can store in a Text, Number, or AutoNumber field. For Text fields, the default value is 255 characters. This means that every field value must contain 255 or fewer characters. You can change the Field Size property for a Text field to store fewer characters. For example, if you create a field that stores state abbreviations, you might set the Field Size property to two characters, because all state abbreviations contain two characters. This change will ensure that no one can enter a three-character state abbreviation, which would be an incorrect field value. Also, when you decrease the Field Size property, the field requires less disk space to store the field values. All fields are given the default field properties for the data type assigned to them, unless you change the default field properties.

For Number fields, the Field Size property uses a different way of expressing the length. The default Field Size property for a Number field is Long Integer, which stores very large positive and negative whole numbers. Other field sizes for Number fields store numbers with decimals (such as 101.24), positive whole numbers only, and numbers that are less than or equal to 255. You select the field size by evaluating the numbers that you plan to store in the field and choosing the one that takes the smallest amount of disk space. The field size options for Number fields are Byte, Integer, Long Integer, Single, Double, Replication ID, and Decimal.

EXTRA FOR EXPERTS

Always be careful when changing a Field Size property to make sure that you will not lose any data in your fields. If a field value is 30 characters, and you reduce the field size to 20 characters, Access will delete the last 10 characters in the field value for all existing records.

If you have computer programming experience, the available field sizes might be familiar to you. If the options mean nothing to you, don't worry. There is an easy way to select the appropriate field size. If your field stores whole numbers only, use the Integer or Long Integer field size. If your field stores numbers with decimal places, choose the Single or Double field size. To change the Field Size property for a Number field, click in the Field Size box in the Field Properties pane. Click the arrow that appears to display the field size options for a Number field, as shown in **Figure 2-13**, and then click the one you want to use.

The Job Number field is selected and has the Number data type

Arrow on the Field Size box

Field size options in the list that opens

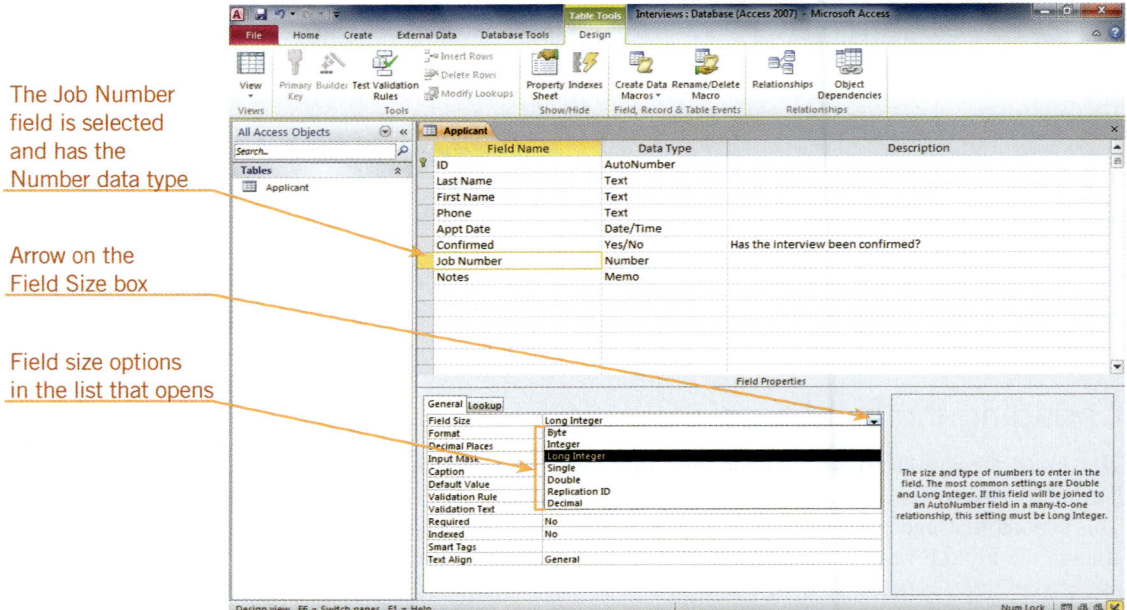

FIGURE 2–13   Setting the Field Size property for a Number field

After you change the Field Size property, Access might open the dialog box shown in **Figure 2–14** to warn you that your changes might affect the data that is already stored in your table. For example, when you change the Field Size property for a Text field from 255 characters to 20 characters, Access decreases the number of characters in the field from 255 to 20. This means that any field values in the table that have 21 or more characters will be changed to 20 characters, resulting in a loss of data. After you change the Field Size property and save the table, you cannot undo your changes.

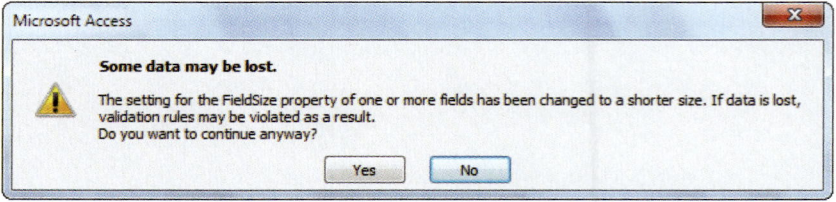

FIGURE 2–14   Dialog box that opens when you save a table after making changes to a field's size

Step-by-Step 2.8

1. In the design grid, click the **Last Name** field.

2. In the Field Properties pane, double-click the value **255** in the Field Size box to select it. Type **20**.

3. In the design grid, click the **First Name** field.

4. In the Field Properties pane, double-click the value **255** in the Field Size box to select it. Type **20**.

5. In the design grid, click the **Phone** field. Double-click the value **255** in the Field Size box in the Field Properties pane. Type **15**.

6. In the design grid, click the **Job Number** field.

7. In the Field Properties pane, click in the **Field Size** box. An arrow appears on the right side of the box.

8. On the Field Size box, click the **arrow**. The list of field size options for Number fields opens.

9. In the Field Size list, click **Integer**. Leave the table open for the next Step-by-Step.

Setting a Field's Format

Use the *Format property* to specify how you want Access to display numbers, dates, times, and text. For example, the default format for dates is *10/28/2013*. Using the Format property, you can change the format to *28-Oct-2013* or *Monday, October 28, 2013*. When you set a field's Format property, Access displays the field value using the format you specify, even if it is not stored that way in the table. So, if you enter a date in the table as *10-28-13* but the Format property is set to display the date as *Monday, October 28, 2013*, that's how the date will be displayed.

▶ **VOCABULARY**
Format property

EXTRA FOR EXPERTS

The Format property displays Currency field values with a dollar sign and decimal point. If you enter 10 in a Currency field, Access formats it as $10.00.

Step-by-Step 2.9

1. In the design grid, click the **Appt Date** field.

2. In the Field Properties pane, click in the **Format** box. An arrow appears on the right side of the box.

3. On the Format box, click the **arrow**. In the Format list, click **Short Date**.

4. On the Quick Access Toolbar, click the **Save** button 🖫. The dialog box shown in Figure 2–14 opens.

5. Click **Yes**.

6. In the Views group on the Design tab, click the **View** button. The table is displayed in Datasheet view.

7. Click the **check box** in the Confirmed field for the first record (Adam Hoover). A check mark appears in the check box, indicating a "Yes" response. Notice the Description value on the status bar in the lower-left corner of the screen. (The other changes that you made to the fields in the table aren't readily visible in Datasheet view.)

8. In the Views group on the Home tab, click the **View** button. The table is displayed in Design view. Leave the table open for the next Step-by-Step.

Setting a Field's Default Value

The **Default Value property** enters the same field value in a field every time a new record is added to the table. For example, if most of the customers in a database of names and addresses live in California, you can enter *CA* as the Default Value property for the State field. When you add a new record, the State field will automatically contain the field value *CA*. If you need to change the default value when you enter a new record, select the default value and type a new value.

Using the Required Property

The **Required property** specifies whether you must enter a field value in a record. For example, in an employee database, you might set the Required property for a Phone field to *Yes* so that you must enter a phone number for each employee. If you try to enter a record for a new employee without entering a phone number, Access will open a dialog box similar to the one shown in **Figure 2–15** with an error message that describes why Access will not add the record to the table.

EXTRA FOR EXPERTS

When you enter a default value for a Text field, Access adds quotation marks around the field value. When you enter a default value for a Number field, Access does not add the quotation marks.

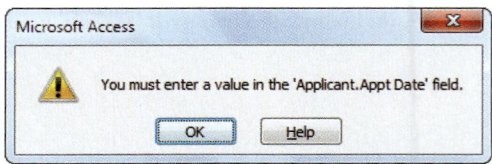

FIGURE 2–15 Dialog box that opens when you don't enter a required field value

When you click in the Required box for a field, an arrow appears on the right side of the box. Clicking the arrow displays the values *Yes* and *No* in a list. The default Required property for most fields is No.

After you change a field's Required property to Yes, the dialog box shown in **Figure 2–16** opens when you save the table. This dialog box opens when you change the Required property because Access will test all of the existing field values in the field to make sure that they contain a field value. When you click Yes, Access will close the dialog box if there are no problems. If problems do exist, Access will help you decide what to do.

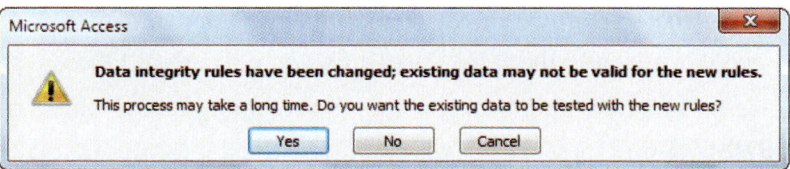

FIGURE 2–16   Dialog box that opens when saving a table after setting a required value

Step-by-Step 2.10

1. In the design grid, click the **Notes** field.

2. In the Field Properties pane, click in the **Default Value** box.

3. In the Default Value box, type **Elise McDonnell will be the interviewer.** (Be sure to type the period.)

4. In the design grid, click the **Appt Date** field.

5. In the Field Properties pane, click in the **Required** box. An arrow appears on the right side of the box.

6. In the Required box, click the **arrow**. In the list that opens, click **Yes**.

7. On the Quick Access Toolbar, click the **Save** button 💾. The dialog box shown in Figure 2–16 opens.

8. Click **Yes**.

9. In the Views group on the Design tab, click the **View** button. Leave the table open for the next Step-by-Step.

After setting the properties for the fields in your table, you can use Datasheet view to enter records in the table.

Step-by-Step 2.11

1. At the top of the Navigation Pane, click the **Shutter Bar Open/Close Button** ⟪. The Navigation Pane closes.

2. In the upper-left corner of the datasheet, click the **datasheet selector**. Double-click the right edge of the **ID** field selector. All columns in the datasheet are resized to best fit.

3. In the Records group on the Home tab, click the **New** button. A new record is added to the table. The ID field is the current field.

4. Press **Tab**, type **Peters**, press **Tab**, type **James**, press **Tab**, and type **970-555-6721**.

5. Press **Tab** five times to skip entering a field value in the Appt Date field and go to the next record. The dialog box shown in Figure 2–15 opens. Because the Required property for the Appt Date field is set to Yes, you must enter a field value in this field.

6. Click **OK**. Click in the Appt Date field, and then type **09/24/13**. Press **Tab**. Notice that the Format property for the Appt Date field changed the field value you entered to the Short Date format, 9/24/2013, even though you entered the field value as 09/24/13.

7. In the Confirmed field, press **spacebar**. Access adds a check mark to the field, which indicates a Yes value.

8. Press **Tab**, and then type **5486** in the Job Number field.

9. Press **Tab**. The Default Value property entered the value in the Notes field automatically.

10. Save the table. On the Access title bar, click the **Close** button ▇. Access closes the Applicant table and the Interviews database, and then exits.

SUMMARY

In this lesson, you learned:

- Creating a database creates a file that stores database objects. You can create a database using a template that creates one or more table, query, form, and report objects. You can also create a database using the Blank database template, which creates a database with an empty table.

- A field's data type determines the kind of data that you can enter in the field, such as numbers or text, or a combination of numbers and text (also called alphanumeric data).

- You can create a table in Datasheet view by selecting the data type and typing the field name for each field you plan to use in your table. After entering the fields, you can enter the first record. Access also creates an ID field to serve as the table's primary key. The primary key is the field that contains unique field values for each record in the table.

- To save a table, click the Save button on the Quick Access Toolbar. Type the table name in the Table Name text box in the Save As dialog box, and then click OK. The table name appears on the tab for the table and also in the Navigation Pane.

- When you are working in Design view, you can add new fields to a table by clicking the Insert Rows button in the Tools group on the Design tab. After adding a field, type its name and set its data type. You can delete a field from a table by selecting it in the design grid, and then clicking the Delete Rows button in the Tools group. To rename a field, click its name in the Field Name box, and then type the new name. To move a field, click its row selector in the design grid, and then drag it to the new position.

- A field property describes a field's contents beyond the field's basic data type. The properties you can set for a field depend on the field's data type. You can add an optional Description property to identify the data to enter in a field. You can also change the Field Size property to set the number of characters in a Text field or to select the type of numbers to store in a Number field. The Format property lets you specify how to display numbers, dates, times, and text. When a field uses a commonly entered value, you can set the Default Value property to enter that value in new records automatically. Use the Required property when a field must contain a value.

VOCABULARY REVIEW

Define the following terms:

alphanumeric data	Description property	Field Size property
AutoNumber	design grid	Format property
Blank database template	Design view	primary key
data type	Field Properties pane	Required property
Default Value property	field property	template

REVIEW QUESTIONS

TRUE / FALSE

Circle T if the statement is true or F if the statement is false.

T F **1.** When you use the Blank database template to create a new database, Access opens a table named *Table1* for you.

T F **2.** A table's primary key might be an AutoNumber field.

T F **3.** A field with the Text data type can store up to 65,535 characters.

T F **4.** To insert a new field in a table in Design view, first click the row above where you want the new field to appear in the design grid.

T F **5.** The Description property is an optional field property that helps users understand what data to enter in a field.

WRITTEN QUESTIONS

Write a brief answer to each of the following questions.

1. What steps do you take to create a new database?

2. How do you create a new field in a table in Datasheet view?

3. How do you change a field's data type in Datasheet view?

4. What is the Field Size property?

5. What is the Format property?

FILL IN THE BLANK

Complete the following sentences by writing the correct word or words in the blanks provided.

1. A table's _____ is the field that contains a unique field value for each record in the table.

2. The _____ data type stores field values with 255 or fewer characters with letters, numbers, spaces, and certain symbols such as an underscore (_).

3. The _____ data type stores numbers that might be used in calculations.

4. The _____ data type adds a unique numeric field value to each record in a table.

5. The bottom half of the Table window in Design view is called the _____ pane.

PROJECTS

If you have a SAM 2010 user profile, your instructor may have assigned an autogradable version of the indicated project. If so, log into the SAM 2010 Web site at *www.cengage.com/sam2010* to download the instruction and start files.

PROJECT 2–1

1. Start Access. Use the Blank database template to create a new database. Store the database in the Access Lesson 02 folder with your Data Files. Use the file name **Music** followed by your initials.

2. Save the table that Access opens using the name **1980s Albums**.

3. In Datasheet view, create three fields in columns 2 through 4. In column 2, create an **Artist** field with the Text data type. In column 3, create a **Title** field with the Text data type. In column 4, create a **Release Year** field with the Number data type.

4. Use **Figure 2–17** to enter three records in the table. (Remember, the ID field value is added automatically. Do not type it. Your ID field values might differ from the ones shown in Figure 2–17.)

9. Change the Field Size property for the Title field to **50**.

10. In Design view, add a new field named **Publisher** to the table so it appears between the Title and Release Year fields. Use the Text data type and change the Field Size property to **30**. Set the Description property to **Label that released the album**.

11. Set the Required property for the Artist field to Yes.

12. Save the table. When the dialog box opens and warns about data loss, click Yes. When the dialog box opens and warns about testing the data with the new rules, click Yes.

13. Change to Datasheet view. Print the datasheet in landscape orientation.

14. Close the table and database, and then exit Access.

FIGURE 2–17

5. Resize all columns in the datasheet to best fit.

6. Save the table. Change to Design view.

7. Change the data type for the Release Year field to Text. Set the Field Size property to **4**.

8. Change the Field Size property for the Artist field to **25**.

 **PROJECT 2–2**

1. Start Access. Use the Blank database template to create a new database. Store the database in the Access Lesson 02 folder with your Data Files. Use the file name **Retail Stores** followed by your initials.

2. Save the table that Access opens using the name **Retailers**.

3. In Datasheet view, create the following fields in columns 2 through 7, being sure to assign the correct data type to each field: **Store Name** (Text), **Address** (Text), **Phone Number** (Text), **Credit Card** (Text), **Date Opened** (Date & Time), and **Outlet Number** (Number).

4. Resize all columns in the datasheet to best fit.

5. Use **Figure 2–18** to enter the first record in the table. (Remember, the ID field value is added automatically. Do not type it. Your ID field value might differ from the one shown in Figure 2–18.)

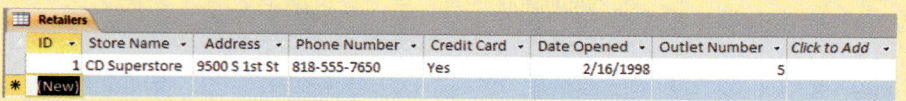

ID	Store Name	Address	Phone Number	Credit Card	Date Opened	Outlet Number	Click to Add
1	CD Superstore	9500 S 1st St	818-555-7650	Yes	2/16/1998	5	
(New)							

FIGURE 2–18

6. Click the Credit Card field for the first record. Use the Data Type arrow in the Formatting group on the Fields tab to change the data type to Yes/No. When the dialog box opens and warns about data loss, click Yes.

7. Save the table. Change to Design view.

8. Enter the Description property **Does the store accept credit cards?** for the Credit Card field.

9. Change the Field Size property for the Store Name field to **30**.

10. Change the Field Size property for the Address field to **30**.

11. Change the Field Size property for the Phone Number field to **15**.

12. Move the Outlet Number field so it appears between the Store Name and Address fields.

13. Save the table. When the dialog box opens and warns about data loss, click Yes.

14. Change to Datasheet view. Print the datasheet in landscape orientation.

15. Close the table and database, and then exit Access.

PROJECT 2–3

1. Open the **Company.accdb** database from the Access Lesson 02 folder with your Data Files.

2. Open the **Staff** table in Datasheet view. Change to Design view.

3. Move the Last Name field so it appears between the Employee ID and Title fields.

4. Move the First Name field so it appears below the Last Name field.

5. Change the name of the SS Number field to **SSN**.

6. Delete the Department field from the table. When asked if you want to permanently delete the field, click Yes.

7. Change the data type of the Salary field to Currency.

8. Set the Format property for the Birth Date field to Short Date.

9. Set the Default Value property for the Title field to **Sales Representative**.

10. Change the Employee ID field so it is the table's primary key.

11. Change the Required property for the SSN field to Yes.

12. Set the Description property for the Salary field to **Employee's monthly salary**.

13. Save the table. When asked if you want to test the data with the new rules, click Yes.

14. Change to Datasheet view. In a new record, enter the following field values: Employee ID: **2746**, Last Name: **Wells**, First Name: **Wendy**, Title: **Sales Representative**, SSN: **657-57-1600**, Address: **2610 21st St**, Zip Code: **79832-2610**, Birth Date: **2-15-72**, Salary: **2150**.

15. Print the datasheet in portrait orientation.

16. Close the table and database, and then exit Access.

CRITICAL THINKING

ACTIVITY 2–1

Organize a group of contact information that you might have, such as people in your family or in your class. Use the Blank database template to create a database to organize your data. Give the database a name that accurately reflects the data, and add your initials to the end of the file name. Store the database in the Access Lesson 02 folder with your Data Files.

Create and design a table for your data using a table template. To use a table template, close the Table1 table that Access created by clicking its Close button. On the Ribbon, click the Create tab. In the Templates group on the Create tab, click the Application Parts button. In the list that opens, click Contacts.

Open the Contacts table created by the template, click the Home tab on the Ribbon, and then change to Design view. Use Design view to edit, move, add, and delete the fields you want to use to store your data. Save the table.

In Datasheet view, enter at least two records in the table. Print the table. Close the table and exit Access.

ACTIVITY 2–2

In this lesson, you created a new database. When you open a database for the first time, you might see the Security Warning below the Ribbon. Use Access Help to search for information about trusting a database and creating a trusted location. On a sheet of paper, describe a trusted location and how to create a trusted location using Access.

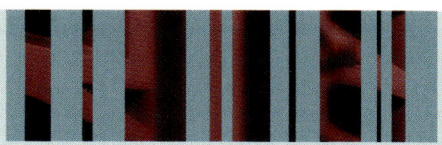
LESSON 3

Creating Queries

■ OBJECTIVES

Upon completion of this lesson, you should be able to:

- Create a query using a Wizard.
- Sort and filter data in a datasheet.
- Create a query in Design view.
- Create relationships in a database.
- Create a query based on more than one table.
- Use operators in a condition in a query.
- Calculate data using a query.

■ VOCABULARY

And operator

AutoFilter

calculated field

common field

condition

expression

filter

Filter By Form

Filter By Selection

foreign key

multitable query

one-to-many relationship

Or operator

query

referential integrity

relationship

Simple Query Wizard

sort

subdatasheet

Total row

The most important feature of a database that you will use is to ask it questions about the data it stores in tables. Extracting information from a database is essential for many businesses to function. In Access, you use a query to extract information from a database. In this lesson, you will learn how to create queries.

Creating a Query with the Simple Query Wizard

▶ **VOCABULARY**

query

condition

Simple Query Wizard

A *query* is a database object that lets you ask the database about the data it contains. The result of a query is a datasheet that includes the records you asked to see. You can use a query to see all orders placed after a certain date or all customers who live in a certain zip code. When you specify a certain date or zip code in a query, these specifications are called conditions. A *condition* (also called a *criterion*) is a way of telling the query which data you are interested in seeing. For example, when you ask to see customers living in a certain zip code, the zip code *78001* is a condition. When the condition has two or more parts to it, such as customers who have ordered a specific part and who live in a certain zip code, the two conditions are called *criteria*. You can also create a query that doesn't contain any conditions, but still displays any or all of the fields that you want to see.

A query is based on a table (or on another query), and some queries are based on more than one table (or query). When you say that a query is *based on* a table, it means that the data in the query datasheet is really data that is stored in a table. When you open a query object, you *run* the query. Running a query displays a datasheet that is similar in appearance to the datasheet you see when you open a table. However, the query uses the conditions to display only the records and fields that you asked to see. When you run a query, the data in the table on which the query is based still exists in the table. A query is just another way of viewing the table's data.

An easy way to create a query is to use the *Simple Query Wizard*, which asks you what data you want to see by letting you select options in dialog boxes. To start the Simple Query Wizard, click the Create tab on the Ribbon. The Create tab contains options for creating different database objects. In the Queries group on the Create tab, click the Query Wizard button. The New Query dialog box opens, as shown in **Figure 3–1**.

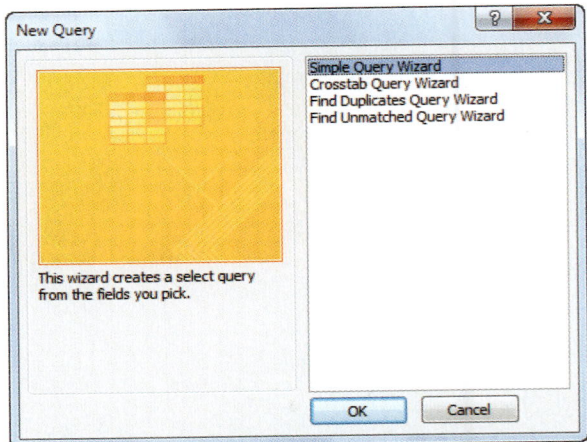

FIGURE 3–1   New Query dialog box

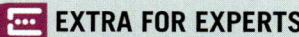
Make sure that the Simple Query Wizard option is selected, and then click OK. The first Simple Query Wizard dialog box opens, as shown in **Figure 3–2**. You use the Tables/Queries arrow in this dialog box to select the table (or query) that contains the data you want your new query to display. After selecting the table (or query) on which to base your new query, you click a field in the Available Fields list box, and then click the Select Single Field button to add one field at a time to the new query. To add all fields to the new query, click the Select All Fields button. When you add a field to a query, the field moves from the Available Fields list box to the Selected Fields list box.

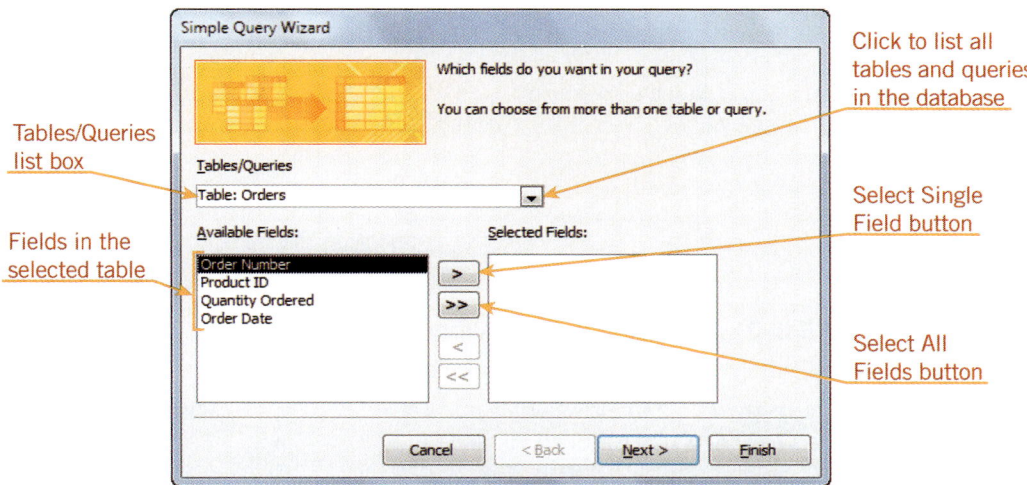

FIGURE 3–2   First Simple Query Wizard dialog box

When you click Next, the second Simple Query Wizard dialog box gives you the option of creating a detail query or a summary query. A *detail query* shows every field in each record. A *summary query* lets you summarize relevant data, such as adding the field values in a column that stores price data. Access gives you the choice of creating a summary query only when the data you selected could be used in calculations.

In the last Simple Query Wizard dialog box, Access suggests a title for your query by using the object name on which the query is based, plus the word "Query," as shown in **Figure 3–3.** You can change the default query title or use the one Access suggests. When you click Finish, the query datasheet is displayed.

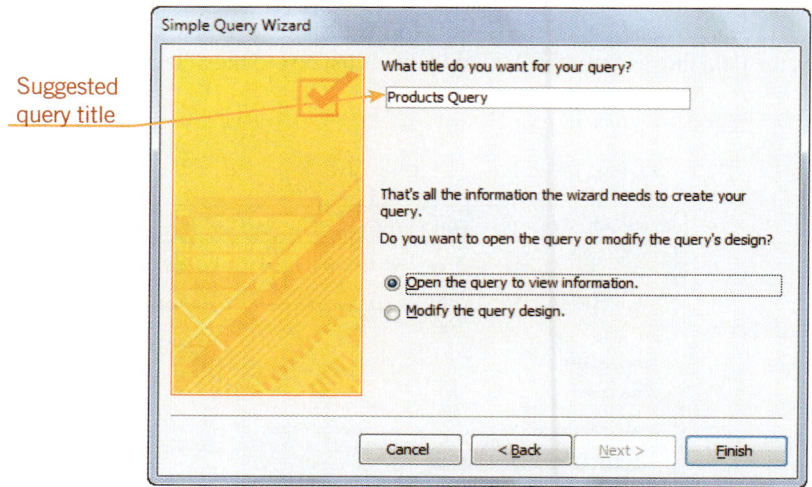

FIGURE 3–3   Final Simple Query Wizard dialog box

Step-by-Step 3.1

1. Start Access. Open the **Product.accdb** database from the Access Lesson 03 folder where your Data Files are stored.

2. If the Security Warning appears below the Ribbon, click the **Enable Content** button.

3. On the Ribbon, click the **Create** tab.

4. In the Queries group on the Create tab, click the **Query Wizard** button. The New Query dialog box opens, as shown in Figure 3–1.

5. Make sure **Simple Query Wizard** is selected, and then click **OK**. The first Simple Query Wizard dialog box opens, as shown in Figure 3–2. *Table: Orders* is selected in the Tables/Queries list box because it is the first table in the alphabetical list of tables in the database.

6. Click the **Tables/Queries arrow**, and then click **Table: Products**. The fields in the Products table appear in the Available Fields list box.

7. In the Available Fields list box, click **Product Name**, and then click the **Select Single Field** button `>` . The Product Name field moves to the Selected Fields list box, which adds this field to the query.

8. In the Available Fields list box, click **Retail Price**, and then click the **Select Single Field** button . The Retail Price field moves to the Selected Fields list box. The Retail Price field is the second field added to the query.

9. Click **Next**. The second Simple Query Wizard dialog box asks if you want to create a detail query or summary query. Make sure the **Detail** option button is selected.

10. Click **Next**. The final Simple Query Wizard dialog box asks you for a title, as shown in Figure 3–3. The default query title is *Products Query*, which is the name of the table on which the query is based, plus the word *Query*.

11. Select **Products Query** in the text box, and then type **Price List** as the new query title.

12. Make sure that the **Open the query to view information** option button is selected.

13. Click **Finish**. The query datasheet opens, as shown in **Figure 3–4**. The datasheet contains the Product Name and Retail Price fields for 48 records from the Products table. Leave the query open for the next Step-by-Step.

TIP

The title you give to a query is also used as the query object name.

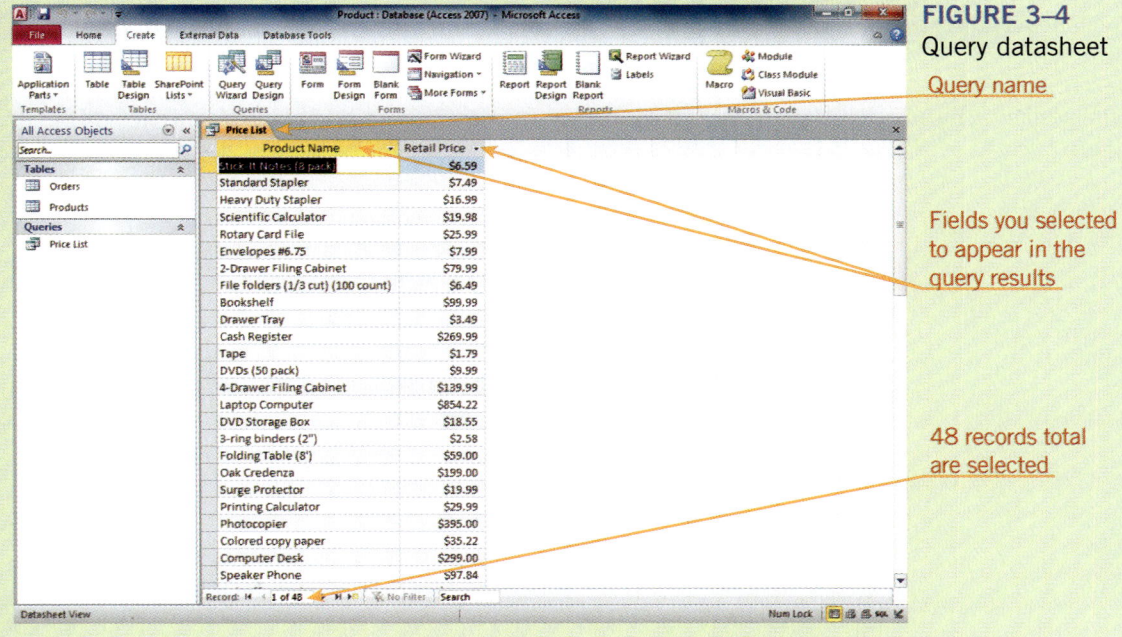

FIGURE 3–4
Query datasheet

Query name

Fields you selected to appear in the query results

48 records total are selected

Sorting Data

When you view a table or query datasheet, the records might not appear in the order that you would like to see them listed. For example, you might want to list customers in alphabetical order or list prices in order from least expensive to most expensive. When you view field values in ascending or descending order from A to Z or from smallest to largest, you apply a *sort* to the field. Sorting a field in *ascending* order arranges records from A to Z, or from smallest to largest. Sorting a field in *descending* order arranges records from Z to A, or from largest to smallest. An easy method to change the way data is sorted is to click any field value in the field you want to sort, and then click the Ascending or Descending buttons in the Sort & Filter group on the Home tab.

▶ **VOCABULARY**

sort

Step-by-Step 3.2

1. In the Retail Price column, click the value in the first row (*$6.59*). The Retail Price field is selected.

2. On the Ribbon, click the **Home** tab.

3. In the Sort & Filter group, click the **Ascending** button. The records are sorted in ascending order by retail price, with the record for the least expensive item, a clipboard priced at $1.29, at the top of the datasheet.

4. In the Sort & Filter group, click the **Descending** button. The records are sorted in descending order by retail price, as shown in **Figure 3–5**, with the record for the most expensive item, a laptop computer priced at $854.22, at the top of the datasheet. Leave the query open for the next Step-by-Step.

EXTRA FOR EXPERTS

When a field is sorted, an arrow appears on the field selector to indicate the way records are sorted. In Figure 3–5, the Retail Price field selector has a small down arrow to indicate a descending sort order. An ascending sort order displays a small up arrow on the field selector.

FIGURE 3–5
Records sorted in descending order by retail price

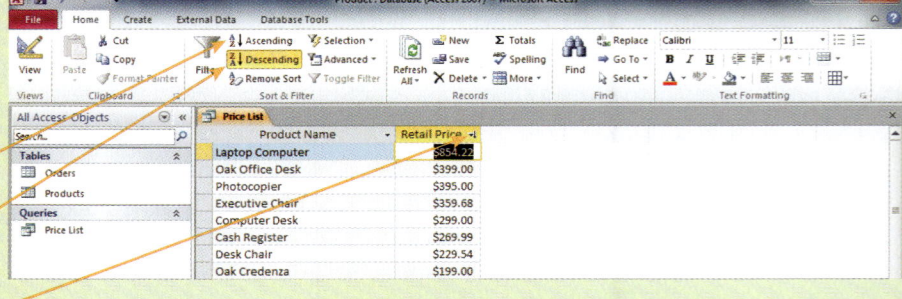

Ascending button

Descending button

Indicates a descending sort order for this field

Filtering Data

When you are viewing a table or query datasheet, you might want to display records that contain a certain value, such as products that have a retail price of $9.99. You can use a filter to view the data in this way. A *filter* temporarily displays records in a datasheet based on the condition that you specify. You can think of a filter as "filtering out" the records that do not match the condition.

You can use different types of filters to display the data you need. When you use *Filter By Selection*, you select a field value (such as *Oak Office Desk*), or part of a field value (such as the just letter *D*) in a datasheet, and then click the Selection button in the Sort & Filter group on the Home tab. A menu opens with a list of options for filtering the field. For numerical data, the options let you filter records that have the same field value as the one you selected, field values that do not equal the selected field value, field values that are less than or equal to or greater than or equal to the selected field value, and in other ways. For fields defined with the Text data type, the options let you filter records that have the same field value, have different field values, contain the field value, or do not contain the field value. Clicking an option in the menu displays only those records in the datasheet that match the filter condition.

You can use *Filter By Form* when you need to display records that contain one or more values based on the values stored in one or more fields. To use Filter By Form, click the Advanced button in the Sort & Filter group on the Home tab. In the menu that opens, click Filter By Form. The datasheet temporarily hides all the records it contains and displays a list box for a selected field, as shown in **Figure 3–6**. Clicking an arrow in a field displays the field's values in a list. When you click a value in the list, you set the filter. Click the Toggle Filter button in the Sort & Filter group on the Home tab to display only the records in the datasheet that match the filter. You can set the filter for one or more fields in the datasheet.

▶ **VOCABULARY**
filter
Filter By Selection
Filter By Form

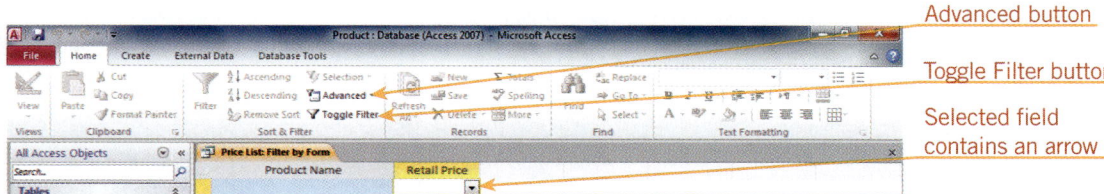

Advanced button

Toggle Filter button

Selected field contains an arrow

FIGURE 3–6   Price List datasheet after selecting Filter By Form

VOCABULARY
AutoFilter

An easy way to sort and filter data using the same options available in the Sort & Filter group is to use an AutoFilter. An ***AutoFilter*** is a menu that opens when you click the arrow on the right side of a field selector. The menu contains options for sorting data and clearing any filters that you have already applied. It also contains options for using Filter By Selection and Filter By Form. **Figure 3–7** shows the AutoFilter that opens when you click the arrow on the Product Name field selector and then point to Text Filters. This menu shows the Filter By Selection options for the Product Name field, which has the Text data type.

Click the arrow on the field selector to open the AutoFilter

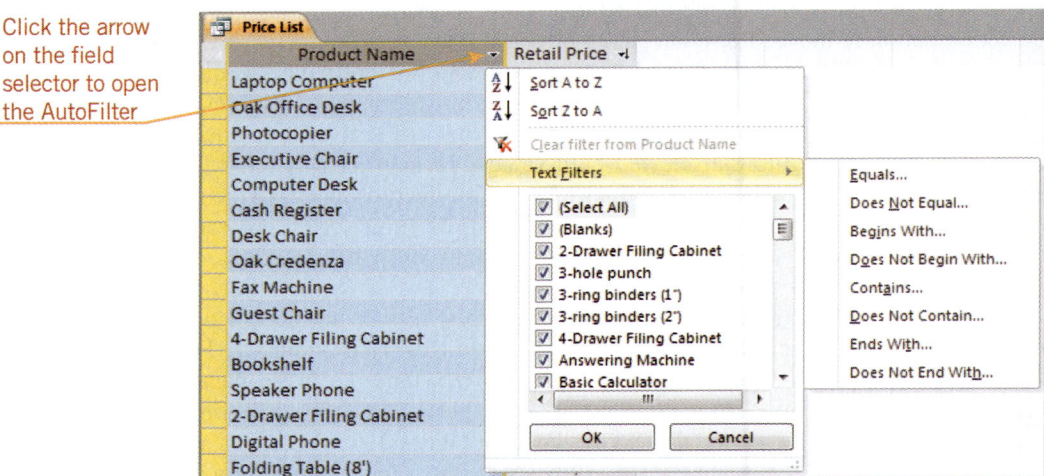

FIGURE 3–7 AutoFilter for the Product Name field (a Text field)

Figure 3–8 shows the AutoFilter that opens when you click the arrow on the Retail Price field selector, and then point to Number Filters. This menu shows the Filter By Selection options for the Retail Price field, which has the Number data type.

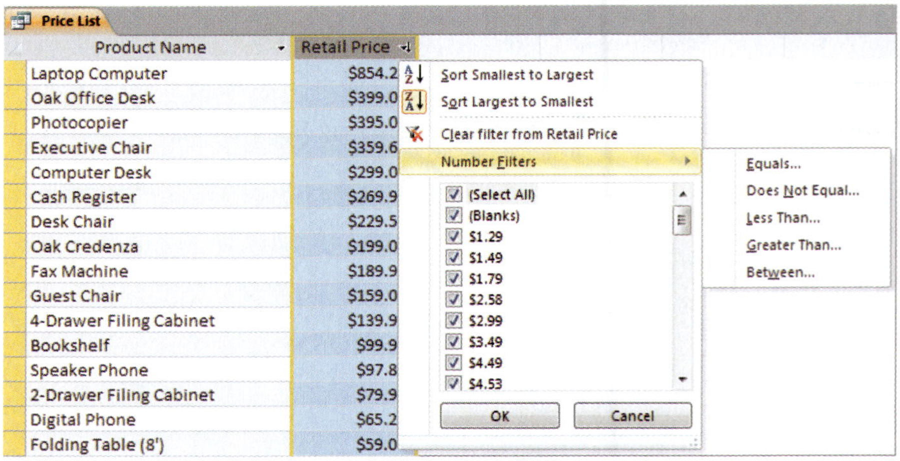

FIGURE 3–8 AutoFilter for the Retail Price field (a Number field)

After applying a filter to a field, clicking the Toggle Filter button in the Sort & Filter group on the Home tab removes the filter and displays all records in the datasheet again. To delete a filter from a query, click the Advanced button, and then click Clear All Filters.

Step-by-Step 3.3

1. Make sure the Retail Price field in the datasheet is sorted in descending order (see Figure 3–5). In the datasheet, click the second value in the Product Name field (*Oak Office Desk*).

2. In the Sort & Filter group on the Home tab, click the **Selection** button, and then click **Contains "Oak Office Desk"**. The filter is applied and one record is displayed in the datasheet.

3. In the Sort & Filter group, point to the **Toggle Filter** button. The Toggle Filter button has a "Remove Filter" ScreenTip because clicking it will remove the filter. Click the **Toggle Filter** button. The filter is removed and all records are displayed.

4. In the Product Name field in the second row in the datasheet, double-click **Desk** to select the word *Desk*.

5. Click the **Selection** button, and then click **Contains "Desk"**. Four records that contain the word *Desk* anywhere in the Product Name field are displayed, as shown in **Figure 3–9**.

FIGURE 3–9
Using Filter By Selection to display records that contain the word "Desk"

Orange Toggle Filter button indicates a filter has been applied

Filter icon on the field selector

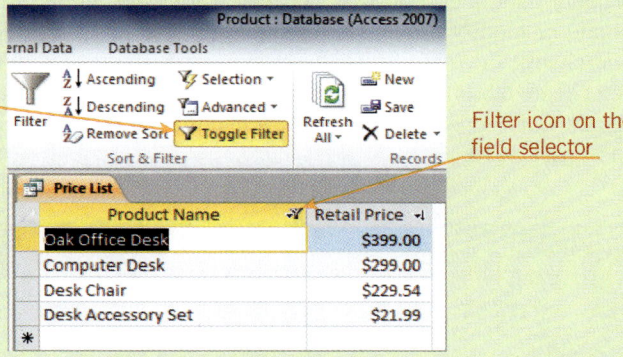

6. Click the **Toggle Filter** button. The filter is removed, the filter icon is removed from the Product Name field selector, and the datasheet displays all 48 records. Even though you removed the filter from the records, you need to clear the filter to delete it from the query.

7. In the Sort & Filter group on the Home tab, click the **Advanced** button, and then click **Clear All Filters**.

8. In the Sort & Filter group on the Home tab, click the **Advanced** button, and then click **Filter By Form**. The data in the datasheet is hidden and an arrow appears in the first row in the Product Name field.

9. Click in the first row in the Retail Price field. An arrow appears in the first row for the Retail Price field. (See Figure 3–6.)

10. Click the **arrow** on the Retail Price field. The list that opens displays all of the field values in the Retail Price field. In the list, click **9.99**.

11. Point to the **Toggle Filter** button. The Toggle Filter button has an "Apply Filter" ScreenTip because clicking the button will apply the filter. Click the **Toggle Filter** button. Two records are displayed in the datasheet, both containing the value $9.99 in the Retail Price field.

12. Click the **Toggle Filter** button. The filter is removed and all 48 records appear in the datasheet.

13. Click the **arrow** on the Retail Price field selector. The AutoFilter opens. In the AutoFilter, click **Sort Smallest to Largest**. The values in the Retail Price field are sorted in order from smallest to largest.

14. Click the **Close 'Price List'** button ▣ to close the query. Click **Yes** to save the query. Leave the database open for the next Step-by-Step.

Creating a Query in Design View

Sorting and filtering changes the way that data is displayed in a table or query datasheet. For a table datasheet, using the commands in the Sort & Filter group on the Home tab and the AutoFilter are your only options for applying a sort or filter. For a query datasheet, however, you have more sorting and filtering options when you create or modify a query in Design view. In the Query Design window, you build and change the query using the design grid. To create a query in Design view, click the Create tab on the Ribbon. In the Queries group, click the Query Design button. A new query opens in Design view and the Show Table dialog box opens, as shown in **Figure 3–10**.

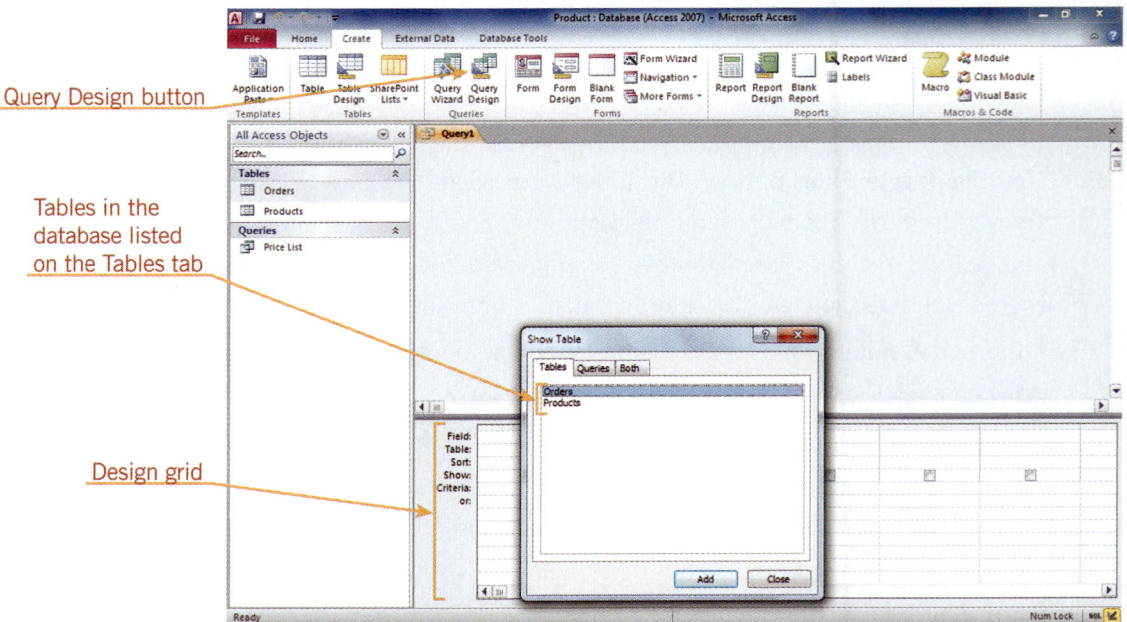

Query Design button

Tables in the database listed on the Tables tab

Design grid

FIGURE 3–10 Show Table dialog box in Query Design view

Because databases often include more than one table, you can select the table in the Show Table dialog box that contains the data you want to see in the query datasheet, and then click Add. After adding a table to the query design, click Close to close the Show Table dialog box. After adding the Orders table to the query design, the fields in the Orders table appear in a field list, as shown in **Figure 3–11**.

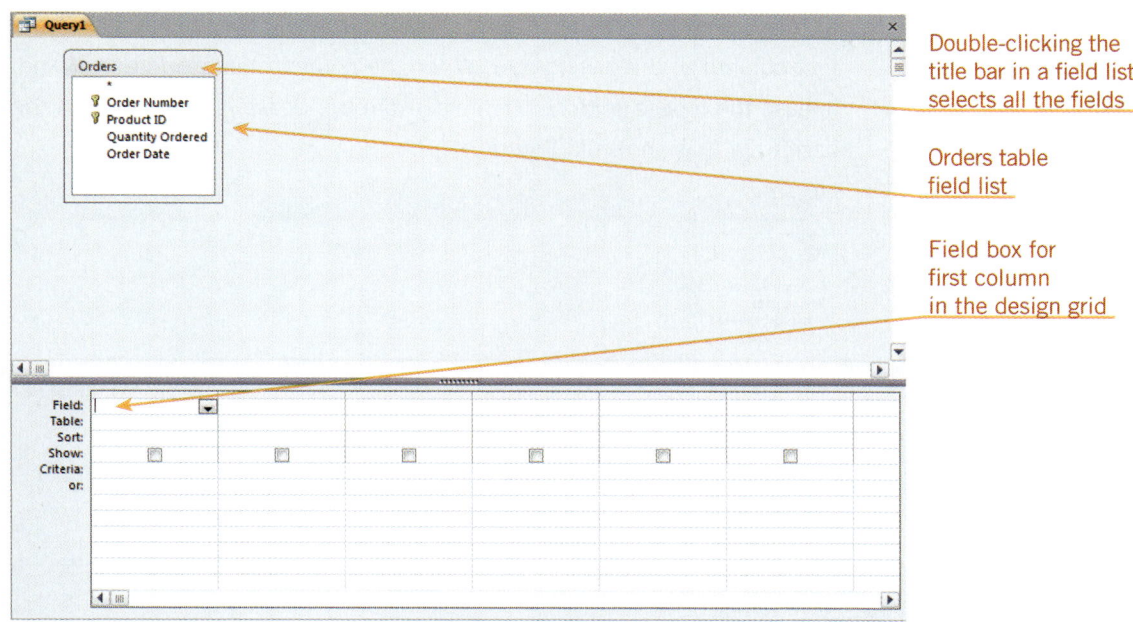

Double-clicking the title bar in a field list selects all the fields

Orders table field list

Field box for first column in the design grid

FIGURE 3–11   Orders table field list added to the query design

The Query window in Design view is divided into two parts. The top part of the window shows the field list for the table you included in the query design. The bottom part of the window contains a design grid that allows you to specify the fields to include in the query datasheet, any conditions that you want to use to filter data, and any sort orders you want to use in the query datasheet. Double-click the fields in the table's field list to add them to a query. A query can contain one, some, or all of the fields in the table. You can add the fields in any order to the design grid. To add all of the fields to a query in one step, double-click the table name at the top of the field list to select all the fields, and then drag any field into the first Field box in the design grid.

After creating a query, you can save it by clicking the Save button on the Quick Access Toolbar.

Step-by-Step 3.4

1. On the Ribbon, click the **Create** tab. In the Queries group on the Create tab, click the **Query Design** button. The Query window opens in Design view, and the Show Table dialog box opens on top of the Query window. See Figure 3–10.

2. In the Show Table dialog box, make sure **Orders** is selected. Click **Add**. The Orders table field list is added to the Query window.

3. In the Show Table dialog box, click **Close**. The Show Table dialog box closes. See Figure 3–11.

4. At the top of the Orders table field list, double-click **Orders**. All the fields in the Orders table are selected.

5. In the Orders table field list, drag any selected field to the Field box in the first column of the design grid. When the pointer changes to a ⬚ shape, release the mouse button. The fields from the Orders table appear in the design grid, as shown in **Figure 3–12**.

FIGURE 3–12
Fields added to the design grid

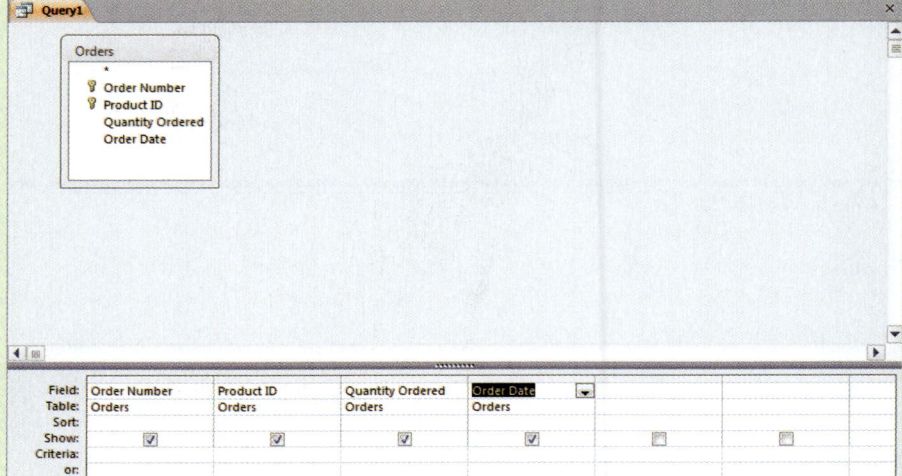

6. On the Quick Access Toolbar, click the **Save** button 🖫. The Save As dialog box opens. The default query name, Query1, is selected.

7. In the Query Name text box, type **Orders List**. Click **OK**. Leave the query open for the next Step-by-Step.

Moving and Sorting Fields in Design View

TIP

Clicking the right side of the Sort box in the design grid selects the box, displays the arrow, and opens the list in one step.

You can set a sort order for a field using the field's Sort box in the design grid. When you click in a field's Sort box, an arrow appears on the right side of the box. Clicking the arrow displays the Ascending, Descending, and (not sorted) options in a list. Click the Ascending or Descending option to set the sort order. To remove a sort from a field, click the (not sorted) option.

When you need to sort data first based on the values in one field, and then by the values in a second field, you need to set the sort orders for the two fields using the Sort boxes in the design grid. For example, you might sort customer names first by last name and then by first name. To sort on two or more fields, the field that you want to sort first (for example, Last Name) must be to the *left* of the field that you want to sort next (for example, First Name). Sorts on more than one field are applied in left-to-right order, so this is why the first sort field must be to the left of the second sort field in the design grid. You can move a field in the design grid by clicking the bar above the field (see **Figure 3–13**), and then dragging the field to the new location. As you drag the field, a black vertical line shows you where the field will appear when you release the mouse button.

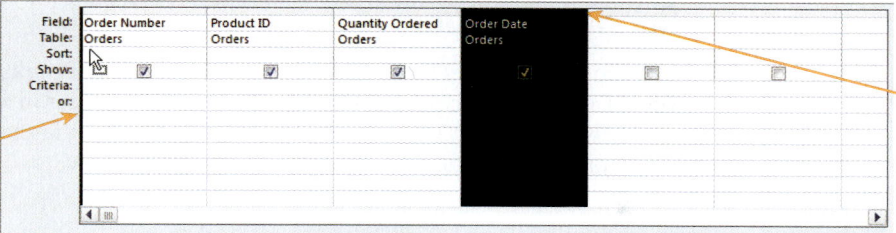

Black vertical bar indicates where the field will be moved while you are dragging the field

Click the bar at the top of the column to select it

FIGURE 3–13   Moving the Order Date field

Step-by-Step 3.5

1. In the design grid, point to the **bar** at the top of the Order Date column so the pointer changes to a ⬇ shape, and then click the **bar**. The field is selected, as shown in Figure 3–13.

2. Point to the **bar** so the pointer changes to a ⬉ shape, and then click and drag the **bar** at the top of the Order Date column to the left. When the black vertical line appears to the left of the Order Number column (see Figure 3–13), release the mouse button. The Order Date field now appears first in the design grid, so it will now appear first in the query datasheet.

3. Click in the **Sort** box for the Order Date field. The Order Date field is deselected, and an arrow appears on the right side of the field's Sort box.

4. Click the **arrow**. A list opens, as shown in **Figure 3–14**.

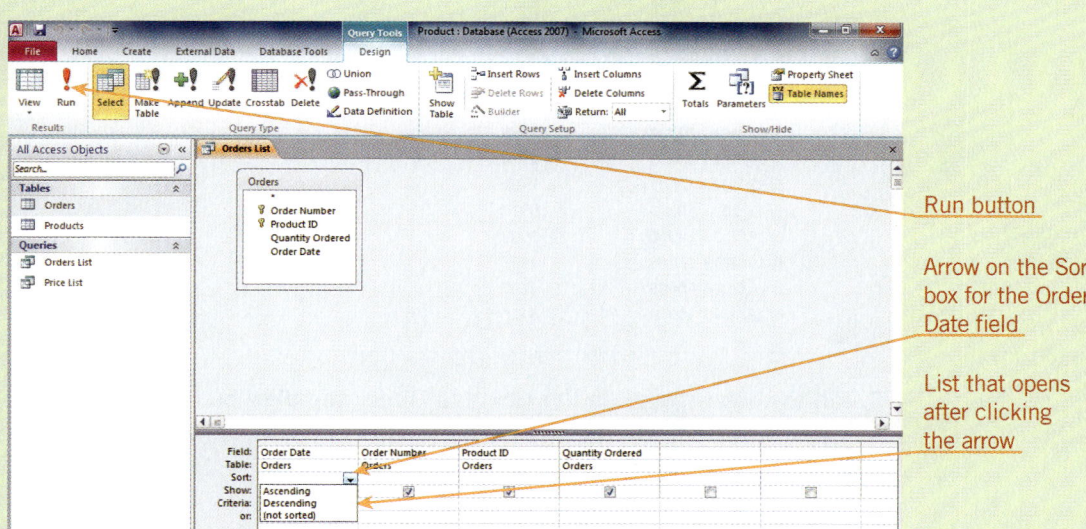

FIGURE 3–14
Sort options for the Order Date field

Run button

Arrow on the Sort box for the Order Date field

List that opens after clicking the arrow

5. Click **Ascending** in the list.

6. Click the right side of the **Sort** box for the Order Number field to display the arrow and the list in one step. Click **Descending**. Leave the query open for the next Step-by-Step.

Running a Query

You can run the query by clicking the Run button in the Results group on the Query Tools Design tab. When you run a query, the results appear in a query datasheet. To return to the query in Design view, click the View button in the Views group on the Home tab. Before running a query, it is a good idea to save it.

Step-by-Step 3.6

1. On the Quick Access Toolbar, click the **Save** button 📄.

2. In the Results group on the Design tab, click the **Run** button. The query datasheet displays 24 records from the Orders table, with the Order Date field listed first. The records are sorted first in ascending order by the values in the Order Date field, and then in descending order by the values in the Order Number field. See **Figure 3–15**.

FIGURE 3–15
Orders List query datasheet

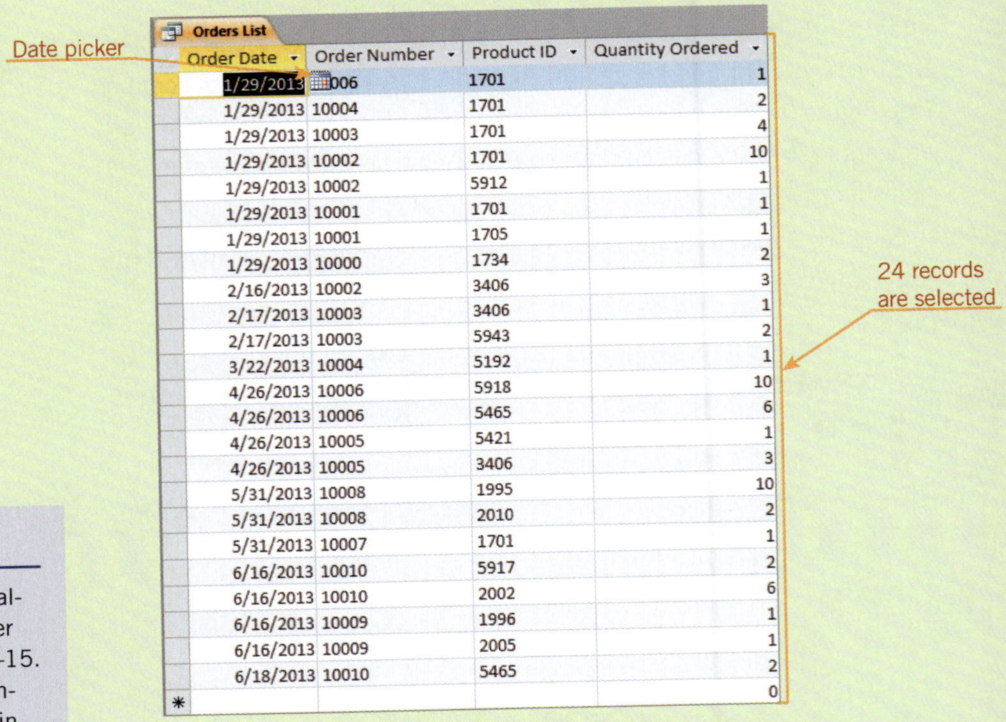

Date picker

24 records are selected

Order Date	Order Number	Product ID	Quantity Ordered
1/29/2013	10006	1701	1
1/29/2013	10004	1701	2
1/29/2013	10003	1701	4
1/29/2013	10002	1701	10
1/29/2013	10002	5912	1
1/29/2013	10001	1701	1
1/29/2013	10001	1705	1
1/29/2013	10000	1734	2
2/16/2013	10002	3406	3
2/17/2013	10003	3406	1
2/17/2013	10003	5943	2
3/22/2013	10004	5192	1
4/26/2013	10006	5918	10
4/26/2013	10006	5465	6
4/26/2013	10005	5421	1
4/26/2013	10005	3406	3
5/31/2013	10008	1995	10
5/31/2013	10008	2010	2
5/31/2013	10007	1701	1
6/16/2013	10010	5917	2
6/16/2013	10010	2002	6
6/16/2013	10009	1996	1
6/16/2013	10009	2005	1
6/18/2013	10010	5465	2
*			0

Orders List

TIP

When working with date field values, you might see a date picker like the one shown in Figure 3–15. Clicking this icon opens a calendar. You can enter date values in the field by clicking them on the calendar.

3. In the Views group on the Home tab, click the **View** button. The query is displayed in Design view. Leave the query open for the next Step-by-Step.

Adding a Condition to a Field

You already learned that queries usually contain conditions that help to answer a question about the data in the table. If the question is "Which orders contain an order for Product ID 1701?" then you need to add a condition to the query design before you run it. To add a condition to a field, click in the field's Criteria box, and then type the condition. If the field has the Text or Memo data type, Access will add quotation marks around the condition after you type it and go to another field or run the query. You can type the quotation marks if you like, but it's not necessary to do so.

Step-by-Step 3.7

1. In the design grid, click in the **Criteria** box for the Product ID field.

2. Type **1701**.

3. Press **Tab**. The condition for the Product ID field is set. Because the Product ID field has the Text data type, Access adds quotation marks around the condition.

4. On the Quick Access Toolbar, click the **Save** button 🖫.

5. In the Results group on the Design tab, click the **Run** button. The query datasheet displays six records containing orders for Product ID 1701. The records are still sorted first in ascending order by Order Date, and then in descending order by Order Number. See **Figure 3–16**.

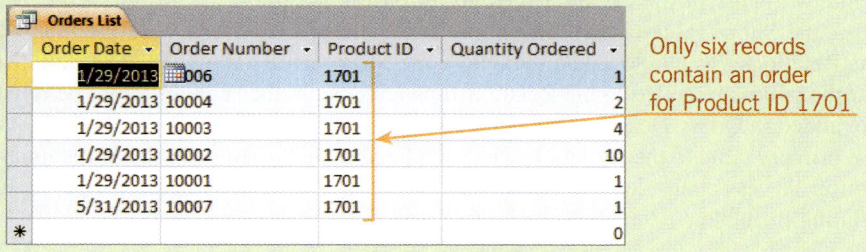

Only six records contain an order for Product ID 1701

FIGURE 3–16
Orders List query datasheet

6. Click the **Close 'Orders List'** button ✕ to close the query. Leave the database open for the next Step-by-Step.

Creating Table Relationships

When a database contains more than one table, as most databases do, the feature of the database management system that lets you connect the data in the tables is a relationship. To create a ***relationship*** between two tables, you must design the tables so they contain a common field. A ***common field*** is a field that appears in both tables, has the same data type, and contains the same values. A common field is also called a *matching field* because its values must match in the common field in both tables involved in the relationship. The common field usually has the same field name in the related table, but this is not a requirement. When the common field has the same name in both tables, it makes it easier to identify the common field in a relationship.

▶ VOCABULARY
relationship
common field

When you relate the tables in a database, you can create queries and other objects that display information from more than one table at once. For example, suppose you relate a table containing information about students (student ID number, name, address, and phone number) to a table containing information about classes (class ID number, class name, and room). As designed, these two tables do not have a common field. However, if you add the field from the Student table that contains the student ID number to the Class table, the Student ID field becomes a common field in both tables. After relating the tables, you can use the Student ID field in the Class table to identify the students enrolled in the class. Without this common field, you wouldn't have a way to use a query to display a query that lists the students in each class.

You can create different types of relationships depending on the data used in the tables you are relating. The most common relationship is a one-to-many relationship. (The other types of relationships are one-to-one and many-to-many.) In a ***one-to-many relationship***, *one* record in the first table (called the *primary table*) can match *many* (actually, zero, one, or many) records in the second table (called the *related table*). The common field in the related table is called a ***foreign key*** when it is used in a relationship. In the primary table, the common field is usually the table's primary key.

When you relate tables, Access uses a set of rules to ensure that there are matching values in the common field used to form the relationship, both at the time you create the relationship and as you enter data in the tables after you create the relationship. This set of rules is called referential integrity. ***Referential integrity*** protects the data in the tables to make sure that data is not accidentally deleted or changed, resulting in inconsistent data. To enforce referential integrity between tables, click the Enforce Referential Integrity check box when creating the relationship. If you break one of the rules when relating tables or entering data into related tables, Access displays a message telling you about the problem and doesn't update the database.

To create a relationship between tables, click the Database Tools tab on the Ribbon. In the Relationships group, click the Relationships button. The Relationships window opens. In the Relationships group on the Relationships Tools Design tab, click the Show Table button. The Show Table dialog box opens. Add the tables to the Relationships window, and then close the Show Table dialog box. The field lists for the tables are added to the Relationships window, in the same way that field lists are added in Query Design view. After adding the field lists, drag the primary key in the primary table to the foreign key in the related table. When you release the mouse button, Access opens the Edit Relationships dialog box, where you select options for relating the tables.

▶ **VOCABULARY**

one-to-many relationship

foreign key

referential integrity

Step-by-Step 3.8

1. On the Ribbon, click the **Database Tools** tab.

2. In the Relationships group, click the **Relationships** button. The Show Table dialog box opens on top of the Relationships window.

3. In the Show Table dialog box, make sure **Orders** is selected, and then click **Add**. Click **Products**, click **Add**, and then click **Close**. The field lists for the Orders and Products tables are added to the Relationships window, and the Show Table dialog box closes.

4. Click and drag the **Product ID** field from the Products field list to the Product ID field in the Orders field list, and then release the mouse button. The Edit Relationships dialog box opens, as shown in **Figure 3–17**.

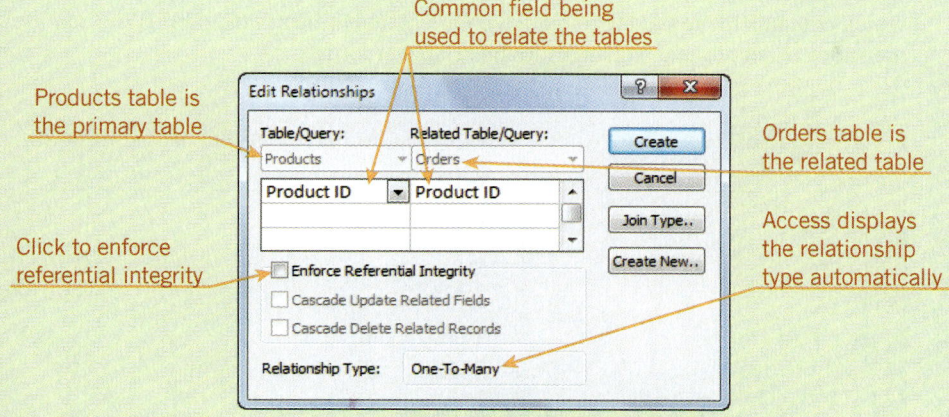

FIGURE 3–17
Edit Relationships dialog box

5. Click the **Enforce Referential Integrity** check box.

6. Click **Create**. **Figure 3–18** shows the relationship between the tables. A one-to-many relationship has a "1" on the side of the primary table and an infinity symbol on the side of the related table. The key symbol next to a field name in a field list indicates the table's primary key. When you see two keys in a single table, the primary key is the combination of those fields.

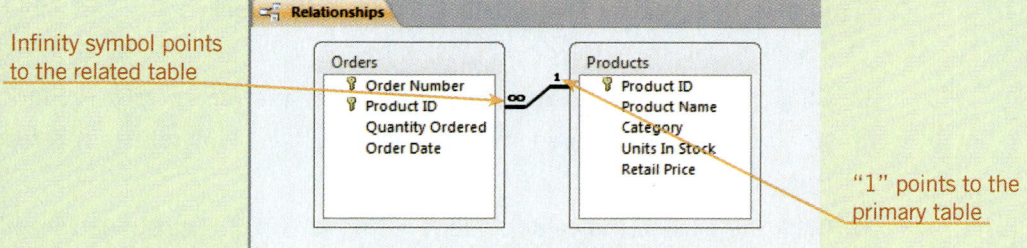

FIGURE 3–18
Relationships window after creating a one-to-many relationship

7. In the Relationships group on the Design tab, click the **Close** button. In the dialog box, click **Yes** to save the changes you made. Leave the database open for the next Step-by-Step.

Viewing Related Records

After creating a one-to-many relationship between two tables, you can view the data in the related table by opening the datasheet for the primary table. In the relationship you just created, the Products table is the primary table. **Figure 3–19** shows a column with indicators in each row. Clicking the expand indicator opens a *subdatasheet*, which contains the related records in the Orders table (the related table). You can use the subdatasheet to make changes to the related records.

▶ **VOCABULARY**
subdatasheet

Collapse indicator

Subdatasheet
displays orders for
Product ID 1701

Expand indicator

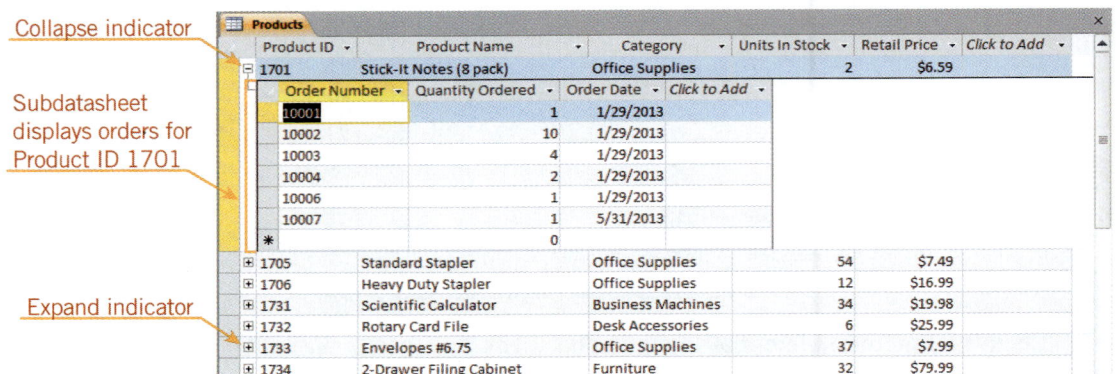

FIGURE 3–19   Subdatasheet in the Products table

Step-by-Step 3.9

1. In the Navigation Pane, double-click the **Products** table. The table opens in Datasheet view.

2. Click the **expand indicator** ⊞ to the left of the record with Product ID 1701. Figure 3–19 shows that there are *many* (six) related records from the Orders table for Product ID 1701.

3. Click the **expand indicator** ⊞ for Product ID 1733. The subdatasheet is empty, which means that there are *zero* related records in the Orders table for Product ID 173 3.

4. Click the **expand indicator** ⊞ for Product ID 1705. The subdatasheet shows that there is *one* related record from the Orders table for Product ID 1705.

5. Click the **collapse indicator** ⊟ to the left of the record with Product ID 1701. The subdatasheet closes.

6. Click the **Close 'Products'** button ☒ to close the Products table. Leave the database open for the next Step-by-Step.

Creating a Multitable Query

After defining relationships in a database, you can create a query that is based on more than one table. Queries that are based on more than one table are sometimes called **multitable queries**. For example, you might want to view customer information with the orders placed by the customers. To do this, you need data from the table that stores customer information and the table that stores order information.

Creating a query based on more than one table simply requires you to add each table's field list to the query design. After you add two related tables to the query design, a join line shows the relationship between the tables, as shown in **Figure 3–20**. The join line connects the common field used to relate the tables. It also defines the type of relationship by using the "1" to represent the "one" side of the relationship and the infinity symbol to represent the "many" side of the relationship. Keep in mind that you can add the common field to the design grid from either table—after all, the common field contains *matching* values, so it doesn't matter which one you choose.

▶ **VOCABULARY**
multitable queries

⊞ EXTRA FOR EXPERTS

When you add a table's field list to the query design, you might not see all the fields in the field list initially if the table contains a lot of fields. You can view the other fields by using the scroll bar that appears on the field list. You can also use the pointer to resize the field list so you can see more fields at once.

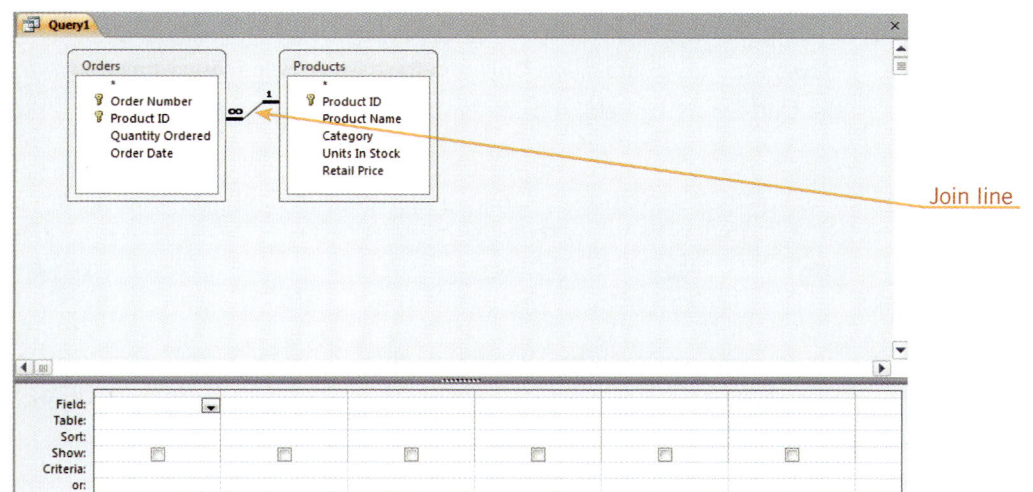

FIGURE 3–20   Joined tables in Query Design view

The skills for adding a table's field list, adding fields to the design grid, sorting fields, and specifying conditions are the same for a multitable query as they are for a query based on a single table.

Step-by-Step 3.10

1. On the Ribbon, click the **Create** tab. In the Queries group on the Create tab, click the **Query Design** button.

2. In the Show Table dialog box, make sure **Orders** is selected, click **Add**, click **Products**, click **Add**, and then click **Close**. The Query window displays the field lists for the Orders and Products tables. The join line connects the tables using the common field, Product ID. See Figure 3–20.

3. In the Orders field list, double-click **Order Number**. The Order Number field is added to the first column in the design grid.

4. In the Products field list, double-click the following fields in the order shown to add them to the second, third, fourth, and fifth columns in the design grid: **Product ID**, **Product Name**, **Units In Stock**, and **Retail Price**.

5. Click the right side of the **Sort** box for the Product Name field, and then click **Ascending** in the list. (If you don't see the list right away, click the arrow to display it.)

6. Click in the **Criteria** box for the Units In Stock field. Type **0** (a zero, not the capital letter O), and then press **Tab**.

7. On the Quick Access Toolbar, click the **Save** button 🖫. In the Save As dialog box, type **Product Prices**, and then click **OK**.

8. In the Results group on the Design tab, click the **Run** button. **Figure 3–21** shows the query datasheet. Only one item (Oak Office Desk) has a zero in the Units In Stock field, indicating that this product is out of stock.

FIGURE 3–21
Datasheet for a query based on two tables

Field from the Orders table   Fields from the Products table

One record selected with zero units

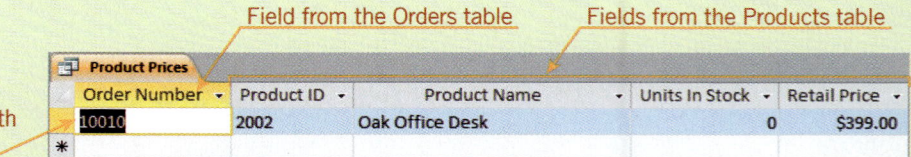

Product Prices				
Order Number ▾	Product ID ▾	Product Name ▾	Units In Stock ▾	Retail Price ▾
10010	2002	Oak Office Desk	0	$399.00
*				

9. In the Views group on the Home tab, click the **View** button. The query is displayed in Design view. Leave the query open for the next Step-by-Step.

Using Operators in a Condition

The Product Prices query selects records for products that are out of stock (the Units In Stock field value is zero). This is called an *exact match condition* because the records must contain the value 0 in the Units In Stock field to be displayed in the query datasheet. Based on the data in the database, the query selects only one record, for an Oak Office Desk.

Another type of condition that you can create displays a record in the query datasheet when the record matches a range of values. This is called a *range-of-values condition*. For example, you might use a condition to find orders with a Units In Stock value of 2 (an exact match condition) or a Units In Stock value of 5 or more (a range-of-values condition).

To create a range-of-values condition, you need to include a relational operator in the condition. You can use the relational operators listed in **Table 3–1** in a condition.

TABLE 3–1   Relational operators

OPERATOR	DESCRIPTION
>	Greater than
<	Less than
=	Equal to
>=	Greater than or equal to
<=	Less than or equal to
<>	Not equal

You can also use the And or Or operators in a query. The *And operator* selects records that match *all* of two or more conditions in a query. For example, if you want to find records that meet more than one condition, such as employees who earn more than $30,000 a year *and* who have been with the company for less than two years, you can use the And operator. To create a query with the And operator, enter the condition for the first field and the condition for the second field on the *same* Criteria row in the design grid.

The *Or operator* selects records that match *at least* one of two or more conditions in a query. For example, if you want to find records for employees who earn more than $30,000 a year *or* who have been with the company for less than two years, you can use the Or operator. To create a query with the Or operator, enter the condition for the first field in the Criteria row in the design grid and the condition for the second field in the "or" row—a *different* row—in the design grid.

▶ **VOCABULARY**

And operator

Or operator

Step-by-Step 3.11

1. Select the **0** in the Criteria box for the Units In Stock field, and then press **Delete**.

2. Type **>5** in the Units In Stock Criteria box.

3. Run the query. The datasheet displays 15 records for products that have more than five units in stock.

4. In the Views group on the Home tab, click the **View** button.

5. Click in the **Criteria** box for the Retail Price field, and then type **<20**. Adding this criterion to the query creates an And condition that will select records for products that have a value of less than $20.00 in the Retail Price field and have more than five units in stock. See **Figure 3–22**.

FIGURE 3–22
Query design that uses an And condition

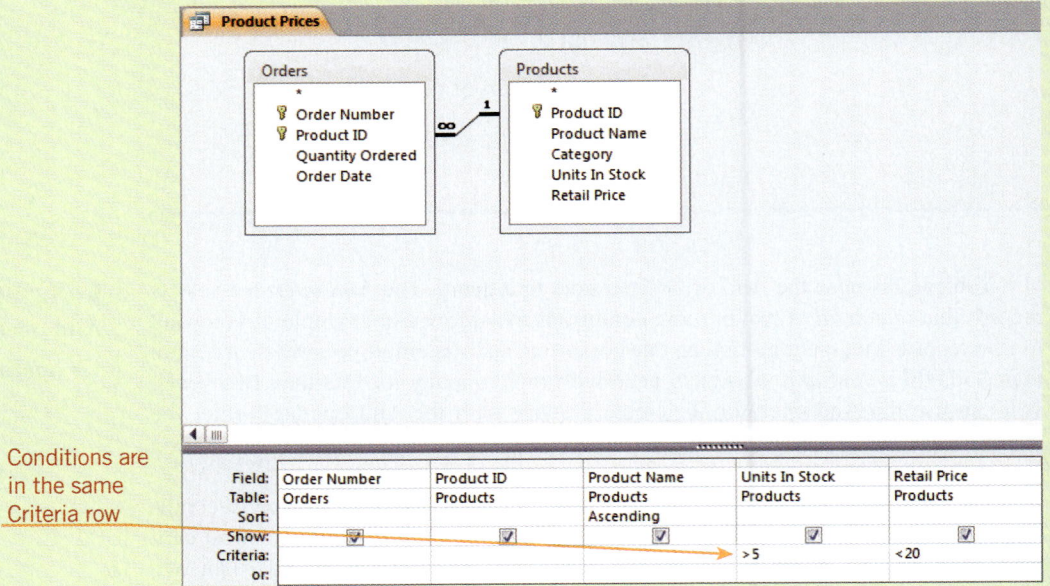

Conditions are in the same Criteria row

6. Run the query. **Figure 3–23** shows the results of the query with the And condition. Only 8 records match both conditions of having more than five units in stock and a retail price of less than $20.00.

FIGURE 3–23
Datasheet for a query with an And condition

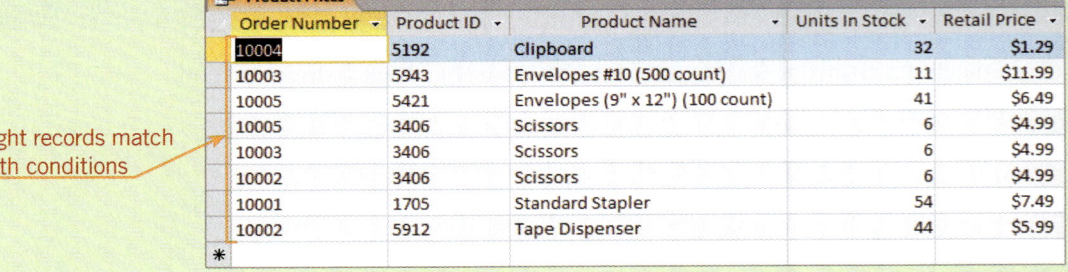

Eight records match both conditions

7. Change to Design view. Select the condition **<20** in the Criteria row for the Retail Price field, and then press **Delete**.

8. Press the **down** key. The insertion point moves to the "or" row for the Retail Price field.

9. Type **<20**. Adding this criterion to the query creates an Or condition that will select records for products that have a value of less than $20.00 in the Retail Price field or have more than five units in stock. **Figure 3–24** shows the query design.

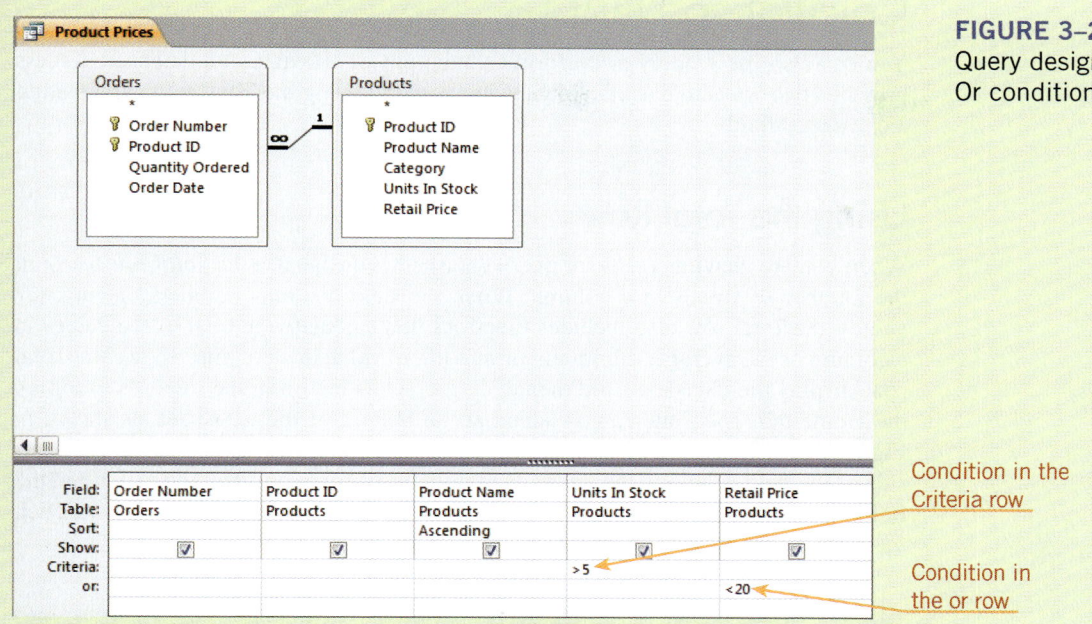

FIGURE 3–24
Query design that uses an
Or condition

Condition in the
Criteria row

Condition in
the or row

10. Run the query. **Figure 3–25** shows the results of the query with the Or
     condition. Only 22 records match either condition of having more than
     five units in stock or a retail price of less than $20.00. Leave the query
     open for the next Step-by-Step.

Order Number	Product ID	Product Name	Units In Stock	Retail Price
10000	1734	2-Drawer Filing Cabinet	32	$79.99
10010	5917	Answering Machine	53	$49.99
10004	5192	Clipboard	32	$1.29
10010	5465	Desk Accessory Set	8	$21.99
10006	5465	Desk Accessory Set	8	$21.99
10006	5918	Digital Phone	57	$65.29
10003	5943	Envelopes #10 (500 count)	11	$11.99
10005	5421	Envelopes (9" x 12") (100 count)	41	$6.49
10008	2010	Fax Machine	15	$189.95
10009	1996	Printing Calculator	221	$29.99
10003	3406	Scissors	6	$4.99
10005	3406	Scissors	6	$4.99
10002	3406	Scissors	6	$4.99
10001	1705	Standard Stapler	54	$7.49
10001	1701	Stick-It Notes (8 pack)	2	$6.59
10007	1701	Stick-It Notes (8 pack)	2	$6.59
10006	1701	Stick-It Notes (8 pack)	2	$6.59
10004	1701	Stick-It Notes (8 pack)	2	$6.59
10003	1701	Stick-It Notes (8 pack)	2	$6.59
10002	1701	Stick-It Notes (8 pack)	2	$6.59
10008	1995	Surge Protector	5	$19.99
10002	5912	Tape Dispenser	44	$5.99

FIGURE 3–25
Datasheet for a query with an
Or condition

22 records match
either condition

Calculating Data

You can also use a query to perform calculations on the data in a database. Access provides two ways to calculate data using a query: using the Total row and creating a calculated field.

Using the Total Row

When you are viewing a table or query datasheet, you can use the ***Total row*** to count the number of values in a column. When the field contains numbers or currency values, the Total row also includes functions that calculate the total of the values in a column or the average, minimum, or maximum value in a column. To use the Total row, display the datasheet, and then click the Totals button in the Records group on the Home tab. The Total row is added at the bottom of the datasheet, as shown in **Figure 3–26**. When you click in the Total row for a field, an arrow appears on the left side of the field. Clicking the arrow displays a list of functions that you can use in the field. The functions vary based on the field's data type. To hide the Total row, click the Totals button a second time.

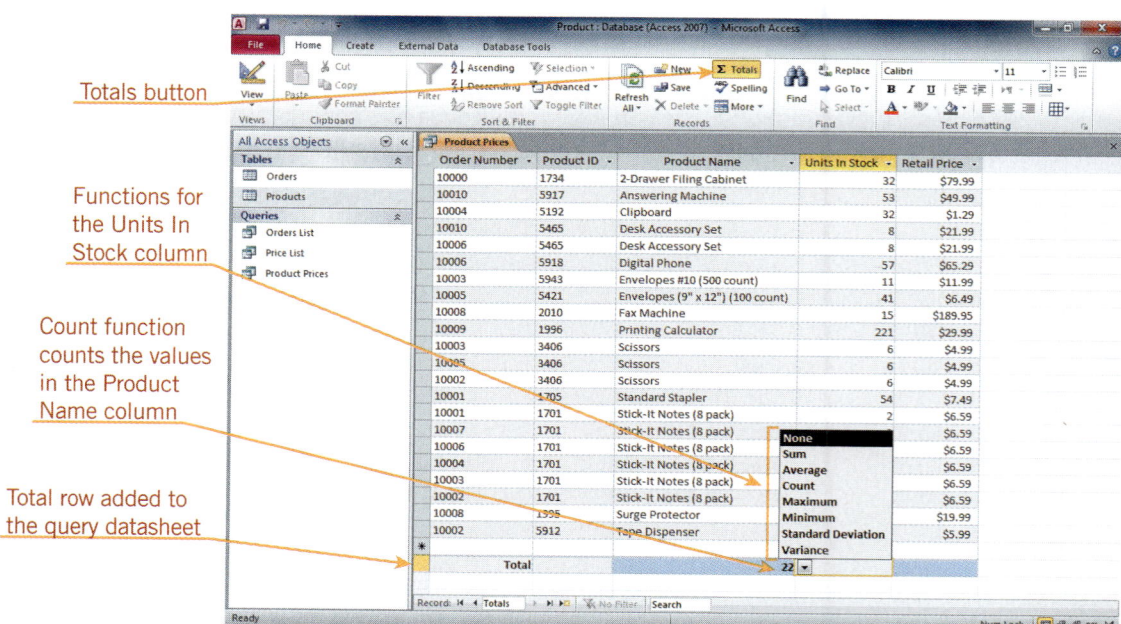

FIGURE 3–26   Total row added to the query datasheet

Step-by-Step 3.12

1. In the Records group on the Home tab, click the **Totals** button. The Total row is added to the datasheet.

2. Click in the **Total** row for the Product Name field. An arrow appears on the left side of the field.

3. Click the **arrow**, and then click **Count**. The Count function counts the number of values in the Product Name column. The value 22 in the Total row indicates that there are 22 products.

4. Click in the **Total** row for the Units In Stock field, and then click the **arrow**. The functions available for the Units In Stock field, which uses the Number data type, appear in the list. See Figure 3–26.

5. In the list, click **Sum**. The Sum function adds the values in the field. The value 611 in the Total row indicates the total number of units in stock.

6. Click in the **Total** row for the Retail Price field, click the **arrow**, and then click **Average**. The Average function calculates the average value and displays $25.77 in the Total row.

7. In the Records group on the Home tab, click the **Totals** button. The Totals row is hidden.

8. Click the **Close 'Product Prices'** button 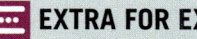 to close the query, and then click **Yes** to save it. Leave the database open for the next Step-by-Step.

Creating a Calculated Field in a Query

Because Access can use mathematical operators (+, -, *, and /) to perform calculations on numeric and date data, you do not need to include fields in your tables that store the *result* of a calculation. For example, creating a table with a field that stores a person's age would be considered poor table design because this value changes once a year on a person's birthday. A better table design includes a field that stores a person's birth date. If you need to display a person's age, you can subtract the person's birth date from the current date. The result will always produce the person's age.

To perform a calculation in a query, you add a new field to the query and enter the calculation you need to perform. When a field displays a value that is calculated using other fields in the query, it is called a *calculated field*. The calculation is called an *expression*. In an expression, field names are enclosed in square brackets, which is required when a field name containing spaces is used in an expression. Access uses the expression in the calculated field to display the result in the datasheet. For example, if today's date is June 16, 2013, and your birth date is May 31, 1996, the result of the expression (your age) is 17.

How do you create a calculated field? You can type it directly into an empty column in the design grid for the query in Design view. This method works fine, but it is difficult to read the expression because the default column width in the design grid only displays about 20 characters. For this reason, it's worth the extra step to right-click the empty Field box in the design grid, and then click Zoom on the shortcut menu. The Zoom dialog box provides plenty of space to see your expression as you type it. When you have entered the expression, click OK to close the Zoom dialog box. Then you can run the query as usual.

Step-by-Step 3.13

1. On the Ribbon, click the **Create** tab. In the Queries group on the Create tab, click the **Query Design** button.

2. In the Show Table dialog box, add the **Orders** and **Products** tables to the query design, and then click **Close**.

3. In the Products table field list, double-click the **Product ID** field to add it to the first column in the design grid.

4. In the Products table field list, double-click the **Product Name** field to add it to the second column in the design grid.

5. Add the **Quantity Ordered** field from the Orders table to the third column in the design grid, and then add the **Retail Price** field from the Products table to the fourth column in the design grid.

6. On the Quick Access Toolbar, click the **Save** button 💾. In the Save As dialog box, type **Order Line Totals**, and then click **OK**. The query design is shown in **Figure 3–27**.

FIGURE 3–27
Order Line Totals
query design

Field that you
will enter the
expression into

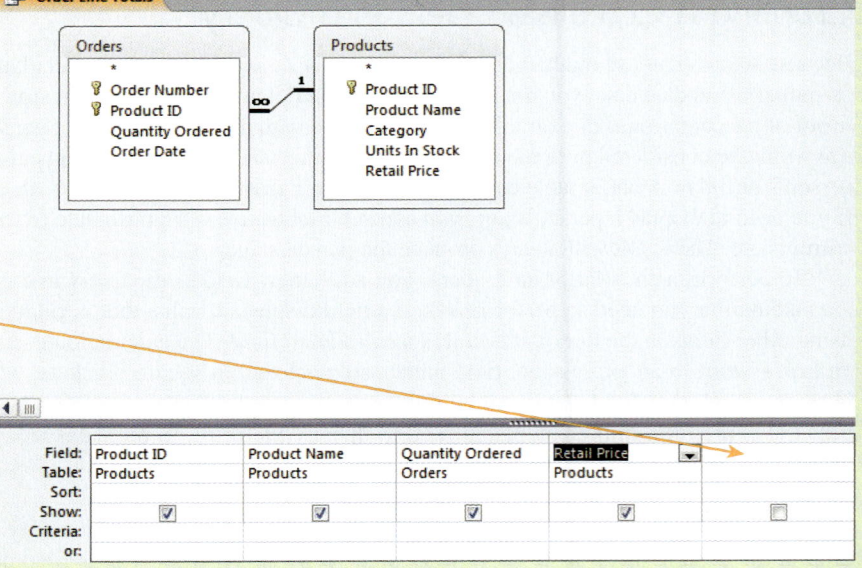

7. Right-click the empty **Field** box to the right of the Retail Price field in the design grid to open the shortcut menu.

8. On the shortcut menu, click **Zoom**. The Zoom dialog box opens.

9. Type **[Quantity Ordered] * [Retail Price]** in the Zoom dialog box, as shown in **Figure 3–28**.

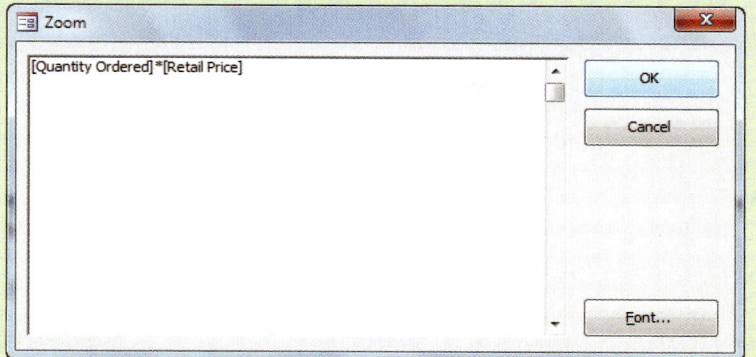

FIGURE 3–28
Expression in the Zoom dialog box

10. Click **OK**. The Zoom dialog box closes. The expression appears in the design grid in the column to the right of the Retail Price field.

11. Save the query. In the Results group on the Design tab, click the **Run** button. The datasheet includes the calculated field, as shown in **Figure 3–29**. Leave the query open for the next Step-by-Step.

FIGURE 3–29
Order Line Totals query datasheet

Product ID	Product Name	Quantity Ordered	Retail Price	Expr1
1701	Stick-It Notes (8 pack)	1	$6.59	$6.59
1701	Stick-It Notes (8 pack)	10	$6.59	$65.90
1701	Stick-It Notes (8 pack)	4	$6.59	$26.36
1701	Stick-It Notes (8 pack)	2	$6.59	$13.18
1701	Stick-It Notes (8 pack)	1	$6.59	$6.59
1701	Stick-It Notes (8 pack)	1	$6.59	$6.59
1705	Standard Stapler	1	$7.49	$7.49
1734	2-Drawer Filing Cabinet	2	$79.99	$159.98
1995	Surge Protector	10	$19.99	$199.90
1996	Printing Calculator	1	$29.99	$29.99
2002	Oak Office Desk	6	$399.00	$2,394.00
2005	Desk Chair	1	$229.54	$229.54
2010	Fax Machine	2	$189.95	$379.90
3406	Scissors	3	$4.99	$14.97
3406	Scissors	1	$4.99	$4.99
3406	Scissors	3	$4.99	$14.97
5192	Clipboard	1	$1.29	$1.29
5421	Envelopes (9" x 12") (100 count)	1	$6.49	$6.49
5465	Desk Accessory Set	6	$21.99	$131.94
5465	Desk Accessory Set	2	$21.99	$43.98
5912	Tape Dispenser	1	$5.99	$5.99
5917	Answering Machine	2	$49.99	$99.98
5918	Digital Phone	10	$65.29	$652.90
5943	Envelopes #10 (500 count)	2	$11.99	$23.98

Calculated field displays the result of multiplying the Quantity Ordered by the Retail Price for each row

When you create a calculated field in a query, Access gives it a name using the letters "Expr" and a number (in this case, 1) to indicate the first expression in the query. The field name Expr1 isn't meaningful. You can change the name of a calculated field by preceding the expression with the column name you want to use and a colon (such as Order Line Total: [Quantity Ordered] * [Retail Price]). Because you already created the expression, you can edit the field name to replace the default *Expr1* column name with *Order Line Total*.

Step-by-Step 3.14

1. In the Views group on the Home tab, click the **View** button.

2. In the calculated field, double-click **Expr1**. Do not select the colon or any other text in the Field box.

3. Type **Order Line Total** and press **Tab**. **Figure 3–30** shows the revised expression in the last column of the design grid.

FIGURE 3–30
Renaming the calculated field

"Order Line Total" will be the new column heading

Field:	Product ID	Product Name	Quantity Ordered	Retail Price	Order Line Total: [Qua
Table:	Products	Products	Orders	Products	
Sort:					
Show:	✓	✓	✓	✓	✓
Criteria:					
or:					

4. Save and run the query. Double-click the right side of the field selector for the Order Line Total column to resize it to best fit. **Figure 3–31** shows the datasheet with the new calculated field name.

FIGURE 3–31
Query datasheet with the revised calculated field name

New column heading in the resized column

Order Line Totals

Product ID	Product Name	Quantity Ordered	Retail Price	Order Line Total
1701	Stick-It Notes (8 pack)	1	$6.59	$6.59
1701	Stick-It Notes (8 pack)	10	$6.59	$65.90
1701	Stick-It Notes (8 pack)	4	$6.59	$26.36
1701	Stick-It Notes (8 pack)	2	$6.59	$13.18
1701	Stick-It Notes (8 pack)	1	$6.59	$6.59
1701	Stick-It Notes (8 pack)	1	$6.59	$6.59
1705	Standard Stapler	1	$7.49	$7.49
1734	2-Drawer Filing Cabinet	2	$79.99	$159.98
1995	Surge Protector	10	$19.99	$199.90
1996	Printing Calculator	1	$29.99	$29.99
2002	Oak Office Desk	6	$399.00	$2,394.00
2005	Desk Chair	1	$229.54	$229.54
2010	Fax Machine	2	$189.95	$379.90
3406	Scissors	3	$4.99	$14.97
3406	Scissors	1	$4.99	$4.99
3406	Scissors	3	$4.99	$14.97
5192	Clipboard	1	$1.29	$1.29
5421	Envelopes (9" x 12") (100 count)	1	$6.49	$6.49
5465	Desk Accessory Set	6	$21.99	$131.94
5465	Desk Accessory Set	2	$21.99	$43.98
5912	Tape Dispenser	1	$5.99	$5.99
5917	Answering Machine	2	$49.99	$99.98
5918	Digital Phone	10	$65.29	$652.90
5943	Envelopes #10 (500 count)	2	$11.99	$23.98

EXTRA FOR EXPERTS

To change the way values are formatted in a calculated field, select the field in the design grid in Query Design view, and then click the Property Sheet button in Show/Hide group on the Design tab. Click the right side of the field's Format box on the General tab, and then click the desired format. Click the Property Sheet button again to close the Property Sheet.

5. Save the query, and then close it.

6. Click the **Close** button [X] on the Access title bar to close the database and to exit Access.

SUMMARY

In this lesson, you learned:

- A query is a database object that lets you ask the database a question about the data it contains. You can create a query quickly and easily using the Simple Query Wizard, which asks you about the data you want to see and lets you select options in dialog boxes.

- You can change the way data is sorted in a datasheet by applying an ascending or a descending sort order to one of the fields.

- You can use a filter in a datasheet to temporarily display records in a datasheet based on a condition that you specify. Filter By Selection lets you select a field value or part of a field value in a datasheet and then filter out all records that do not match the filter. Filter By Form lets you display records that match a value you select in a field. An AutoFilter opens when you click the arrow on a field selector. You can use an AutoFilter to sort and filter data. You can also move and sort fields in Design view. To run a query, click the Run button in the Results group on the Query Tools Design tab.

- When you need to create a query that uses conditions to select records, create the query in Query Design view.

- Use the Relationships window to create relationships between tables in a database by joining tables with a field that contains matching field values. A one-to-many relationship exists when one record in the primary table matches zero, one, or many records in the related table. Referential integrity is the set of rules that Access uses to protect data in the tables and to make sure that data is not accidentally deleted or changed.

- A multitable query is a query that is based on more than one table.

- When you need to use a query to search for records that match a range of values, use a relational operator in the query design. When you need to select records that match all of two or more conditions in a query, use the And operator by placing the criteria in the same Criteria row in the design grid. When you need to select records that match at least one of two or more conditions in a query, use the Or operator by placing the first condition in the Criteria row and the second condition in the or row in the design grid.

- In Access, you can perform calculations by using the Total row in a datasheet, or by creating a calculated field in the design grid in Query Design view.

 ## VOCABULARY REVIEW

Define the following terms:

And operator	Filter By Form	referential integrity
AutoFilter	Filter By Selection	relationship
calculated field	foreign key	Simple Query Wizard
common field	multitable query	sort
condition	one-to-many relationship	subdatasheet
expression	Or operator	Total row
filter	query	

REVIEW QUESTIONS

TRUE / FALSE

Circle T if the statement is true or F if the statement is false.

T F **1.** When you sort a field that contains text values in ascending order, data is arranged from A to Z.

T F **2.** Applying a filter is a temporary way of selecting records in a datasheet.

T F **3.** To remove a filter from a datasheet, click the Cancel Filter button.

T F **4.** A common field used to relate tables must have the same field name in the related table.

T F **5.** The >= relational operator selects records that are greater than or equal to the value in the condition.

WRITTEN QUESTIONS

Write a brief answer to each of the following questions.

1. What information do you specify when you run the Simple Query Wizard?

2. What steps do you follow to use Filter By Form in a datasheet?

3. How do you add all fields from a table to the design grid in Query Design view in one step?

4. When a relationship exists between two tables in a database, what name is given to the matching field in the related table?

5. What is a subdatasheet?

FILL IN THE BLANK

Complete the following sentences by writing the correct word or words in the blanks provided.

1. A(n) _____ is a database object that you can use to find answers to questions about the data in a database.

2. When you view field values in ascending or descending order from A to Z or from smallest to largest, you apply a(n) _____ to the field.

3. Applying a(n) _____ to a datasheet temporarily displays records based on the condition that you specify.

4. To display all records in a datasheet after you applied a filter, click the _____ button.

5. To create a relationship between two tables, you must design the tables so they contain a(n) _____ field.

■ PROJECTS

If you have a SAM 2010 user profile, your instructor may have assigned an autogradable version of the indicated project. If so, log into the SAM 2010 Web site at *www.cengage.com/sam2010* to download the instruction and start files.

PROJECT 3–1

1. Open the **Agents.accdb** database from the Access Lesson 03 folder where your Data Files are stored.

2. Use the Simple Query Wizard to create a query that includes all fields from the Agents table. Name the query **Agents Listing**.

3. Use a button in the Sort & Filter group on the Home tab to sort the records in alphabetical order by Last Name.

4. Use the Affiliation field and Filter By Selection to apply a filter that selects records for agents who do *not* work for Keller McCormack.

5. Remove the filter, and then clear all filters.

6. Use Filter By Form to select records for agents who work for Keller McCormack. Apply the filter, and then change the First Name and Last Name field values in the first row to your first and last names. Print the datasheet in landscape orientation.

7. Remove the filter.

8. Save the query, close the query, and then exit Access.

 PROJECT 3–2

1. Open the **Listings.accdb** database from the Access Lesson 03 folder where your Data Files are stored.

2. Create a new query in Query Design view. Add the Agents table field list to the query design.

3. Add all fields from the Agents table to the query design in the order that they appear in the field list.

4. In the design grid, move the Last Name field so it appears between the Agent ID and First Name fields.

5. Sort the records in ascending order first by Last Name, and then in ascending order by First Name.

6. Add a condition to the query design so that only those agents who work for Montglow Real Estate appear in the query datasheet. (The Affiliation field stores the agent's employer.)

7. Save the query as **Montglow Realtors**.

8. Run the query. In the first row, change the Last Name and First Name field values to your last and first names. Print the datasheet in landscape orientation.

9. Close the Montglow Realtors query, and then exit Access.

PROJECT 3–3

1. Open the **Realtors.accdb** database from the Access Lesson 03 folder where your Data Files are stored.

2. In the Relationships window, create a relationship between the Agents and Houses tables. Use the Agent ID field in the primary Agents table and the Agent ID field in the related Houses table as the common field. (Use the scroll bar on the Houses table field list to see the Agent ID field in the list.)

3. Enforce referential integrity in the relationship. Close the Relationships window and save your changes.

4. Create a new query in Query Design view. Add the Agents and Houses field lists to the query design.

5. Add the following fields from the Agents table field list to the design grid in the order listed: Agent ID, Affiliation, and Last Name.

6. Add the following fields from the Houses table field list to the design grid in the order listed: Listing ID, Date Listed, and Price.

7. Save the query as **Listings By Agent**, and then run the query.

8. Change to Design view. Add a condition to the Date Listed field to select properties that were listed after 9/16/2013. Save and run the query.

9. Change to Design view. Change the query design to select records for properties that were listed after 9/16/2013 *and* that have a price that is less than $100,000. Save and run the query.

10. Change to Design view. Change the query design to select records that were listed after 9/16/2013 *or* that have a price that is less than $100,000. Save and run the query. In the first row in the datasheet, change the value in the Last Name field to your last name. Print the datasheet in landscape orientation.

11. Close the Listings By Agent query, and then exit Access.

PROJECT 3–4

1. Open the **Properties.accdb** database from the Access Lesson 03 folder where your Data Files are stored. Close the Navigation Pane.

2. In the Relationships window, create a relationship between the Agents and Houses tables. Use the Agent ID field in the primary Agents table and the Agent ID field in the related Houses table as the common field. (Use the scroll bar on the Houses table field list to see the Agent ID field in the list.)

3. Enforce referential integrity in the relationship. Close the Relationships window and save your changes.

4. Create a new query in Query Design view. Add the Agents and Houses field lists to the query design.

5. Add the following fields from the Agents table field list to the design grid in the order listed: Agent ID, Last Name, and Affiliation.

6. Add the following fields from the Houses table field list to the design grid in the order listed: Listing ID, Bedrooms, Bathrooms, Garages, and Price.

7. Save the query as **Detailed Listings**, and then run the query.

8. Change to Design view. Click in the Field box to the right of the Price field in the design grid. (You might need to scroll the design grid to see the new field.) Open the Zoom dialog box. In the Zoom dialog box, enter the following expression to calculate the estimated real estate commission for each listing: **Price * 0.06**. Save and run the query.

9. In Design view, change the default field name *Expr1* for the calculated field to **Estimated Commission**. Save and run the query. Resize the Estimated Commission field to best fit.

10. Change to Design view. Click the Field box for the Estimated Commission field, and then click the Property Sheet button in the Show/Hide group on the Query Tools Design tab. On the General tab in the Property Sheet, change the Format property to Currency. Click the Property Sheet button again to close the Property Sheet. Save and run the query.

11. Use the Total row in the datasheet to calculate the average price of all properties and the total (sum) of all estimated commissions.

12. In the first row in the datasheet, change the Last Name field value to your first and last names. Print the datasheet in portrait orientation.

13. Save and close the query, and then exit Access.

■ CRITICAL THINKING

ACTIVITY 3–1

You are a realtor with three new clients who are ready to buy homes. List on paper each client's requirements for purchasing a home. For example, Buyer #1 might want a three-bedroom house with a brick exterior and have a budget of $90,000.

Using the **Realtors.accdb** database in the Access Lesson 03 folder where your Data Files are stored, create a query to locate the Listing ID, Address, and other pertinent information for each client. Save the queries using the names **Buyer 1**, **Buyer 2**, and **Buyer 3**. After running each query, print the results in landscape orientation.

ACTIVITY 3–3

In addition to the Simple Query Wizard, Access includes other wizards that can help you create queries. One is the Find Unmatched Query Wizard, which finds records in one table that have no matching records in a second table. For example, this type of query is useful when you need to find students who are not enrolled in any classes, or realtors who have no listings.

Open the **Realtors.accdb** database from the Access Lesson 03 folder where your Data Files are stored. On the Create tab, click the Query Wizard button. In the New Query dialog box, click Find Unmatched Query Wizard, and then click OK. The Find Unmatched Query Wizard starts and opens the first dialog box, in which you select the table that you want to search for unmatched records. Make sure that Table: Agents is selected, and then click Next.

In the second dialog box, choose the table that contains the matching (related) records. Make sure that Table: Houses is selected, and then click Next.

ACTIVITY 3–2

Referential integrity is the set of rules that Access uses to check for valid relationships between tables. It also ensures that related data is not accidentally deleted or changed. Start Access and use Access Help to search for topics about **referential integrity**. In the list of links that opens, click "Guide to table relationships" and read the information in the section entitled "Understanding referential integrity." Determine which conditions must be met before you can enforce referential integrity in a relationship. Write a brief essay that explains the importance of referential integrity in a relational database and identifies some of the problems that referential integrity is designed to prevent and control.

In the third dialog box, choose the fields that contain matching records. (If you also completed Project 3–3 and already created the relationship between the tables, click Next, and then skip to the next paragraph in this activity.) Scroll the Houses field list until you see Agent ID at the bottom of the list, and then click Agent ID. Click the Match Fields button between the field lists. The text *Agent ID < = > Agent ID* appears in the Matching fields box to indicate the matching fields. Click Next.

In the fourth dialog box, click the Select All Fields button to add all fields from the Agents table to the query datasheet. Click Next.

In the final dialog box, click Finish to accept the default query name and display the datasheet. Change the Last Name field value for the first row to your first and last names, print the datasheet, and then close the Agents Without Matching Houses query and the database. Which realtor in the database has no listings?

LESSON 4

Creating and Modifying Forms

■ OBJECTIVES

Upon completion of this lesson, you should be able to:

■ Create a form using different form tools.

■ Create a form using the Form Wizard.

■ Navigate records using a form.

■ Use a form to find, replace, update, and delete data.

■ Create and modify a form in Layout view.

■ Resize and move controls in a form.

■ Add an unbound control to a form in Design view.

■ Preview and print a form.

■ VOCABULARY

bound control

control

control layout

Datasheet tool

Detail section

Field List pane

Find

form

Form Footer section

Form Header section

Form tool

Form view

Form Wizard

Layout view

Multiple Items tool

record source

Split Form tool

theme

unbound control

In this lesson, you will learn about the different features you can use to create a form to display the data in your database. You will also learn how to navigate and edit records displayed in a form, and use a form to add and delete records.

Creating a Form

A *form* is a database object that displays data from one or more tables or queries in a format that has a similar appearance to a paper form. The tables or queries that provide the data to be displayed in a form are called the *record source*. Most database experts agree that users should make all database updates using a form, instead of using table datasheets, because forms provide more control over the way data is displayed, updated, and entered. In addition, most users find that working in a form is easier than working in a table datasheet. The form can contain messages about how to enter data, format data in different ways to call attention to it, and include features that prevent users from updating data that should not be changed.

Creating a Form with the Form Tool

Access includes tools that you can use to create different kinds of forms. After selecting the table or query in the Navigation Pane on which to base the form, click the Create tab on the Ribbon. The different options for creating forms are located in the Forms group on the Create tab. Click the Form button to use the *Form tool*, which creates a simple form that includes all the fields in the selected table or query, uses a simple format, and includes a title with the same name as the table or query on which it is based. **Figure 4–1** shows a form created using the Form tool. Each field in the record source appears in the form. In Figure 4–1, the "Listing ID" text appears in a label, and the field value for the first record (2042) appears in a text box. When fields appear in a form, they appear in *controls*. In this form, the Listing ID label and the Listing ID text box are controls. You can click the buttons on the record navigation bar at the bottom of the Form window to navigate the records in the record source and display them in the form.

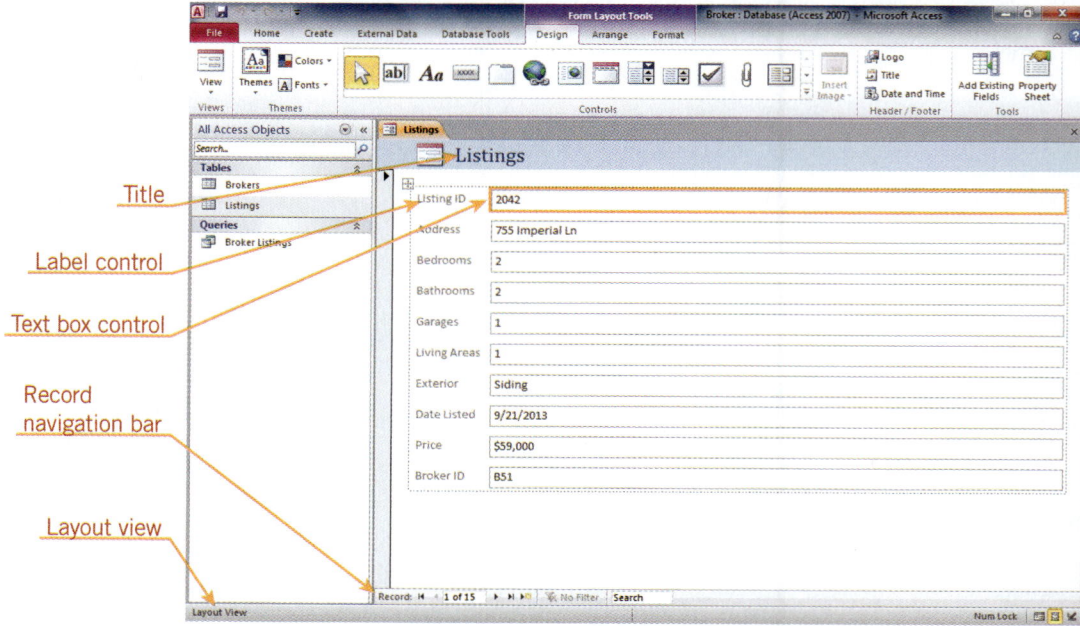

FIGURE 4–1   Form created by the Form tool

When you use a tool to create a form, the form opens in Layout view. In *Layout view*, you can view the controls in the form and data from the record source at the same time. You can also make certain changes to the form's format and appearance, such as resizing a control. When you click a control in Layout view, an orange border appears around the control to indicate that it is selected.

Creating a Form with the Split Form Tool

The *Split Form tool* creates a form using all the fields in the selected table or query and splits the window into two panes, as shown in **Figure 4–2**. To create a split form, click the More Forms button in the Forms group on the Create tab, and then click Split Form. In the top pane, you see a form that is similar to the one created by the Form tool. In the bottom pane, you see a datasheet that contains the form data. The two views are synchronized—when you select a field in the top pane, it is also selected in the bottom pane.

▶ VOCABULARY
Layout view
Split Form tool
Multiple Items tool
Datasheet tool

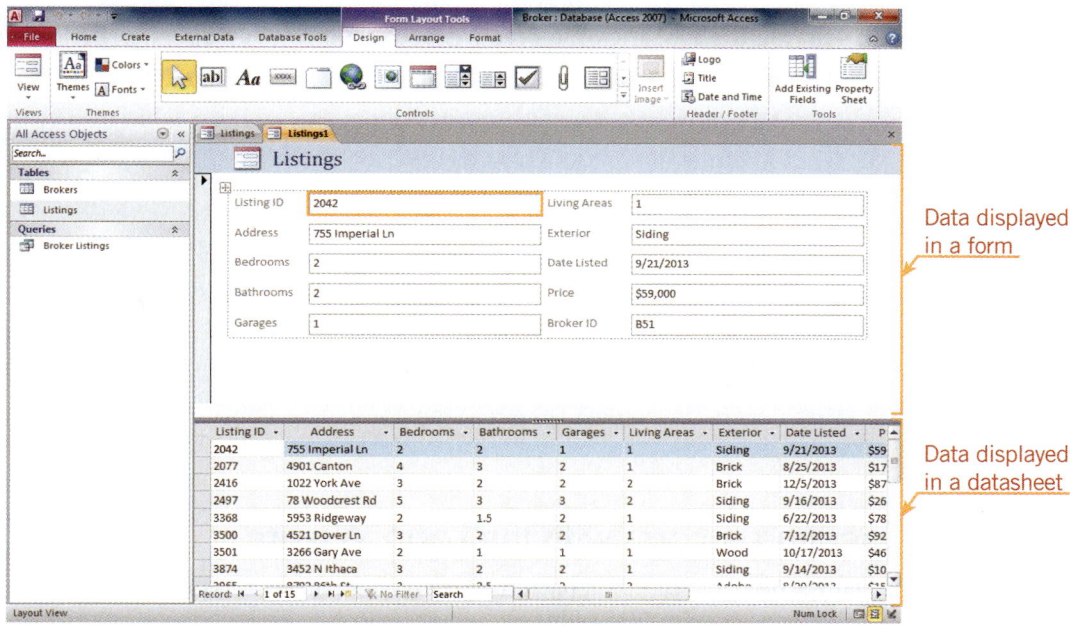

Data displayed in a form

Data displayed in a datasheet

FIGURE 4–2   Form created by the Split Form tool

Creating a Form with the Multiple Items and Datasheet Tools

The *Multiple Items tool* creates a form that lists all the fields in a datasheet format, but using a style that is similar to the form created by the Form tool. The *Datasheet tool* creates a form that looks just like a datasheet. All of these tools create forms quickly and easily. To use the Multiple Items tool or the Datasheet tool, click the More Forms button in the Forms group on the Create tab, and then click Multiple Items or Datasheet in the list.

Step-by-Step 4.1

1. Open the **Broker.accdb** database from the Access Lesson 04 folder where your Data Files are stored.

2. If the Security Warning opens, click the **Enable Content** button.

3. In the Navigation Pane, click the **Listings** table to select it.

4. On the Ribbon, click the **Create** tab. In the Forms group, click the **Form** button. The Form tool creates a form using all the fields in the Listings table and displays the first record in the Listings table. See Figure 4–1.

5. On the Ribbon, click the **Create** tab. In the Forms group, click the **More Forms** button, and then click **Split Form**. Access creates a split form based on the Listings table, as shown in Figure 4–2.

6. On the Ribbon, click the **Create** tab. In the Forms group, click the **More Forms** button, and then click **Multiple Items**. Access creates a multiple items form, which displays the data from the Listings table in a form with a format similar to a datasheet.

7. On the Ribbon, click the **Create** tab. In the Forms group, click the **More Forms** button, and then click **Datasheet**. Access creates a form based on the Listings table that looks like a table or query datasheet.

8. Click the **Close** button ☒ to close each form that you created. Save each form using the form name that Access suggests. Leave the database open for the next Step-by-Step.

▤ EXTRA FOR EXPERTS

Table, form, and report objects in the database can have the same name. For example, the Broker database can contain a Listings table and a Listings form. However, you cannot give the same name to a table and a query object in the same database.

▶ **VOCABULARY**
Form Wizard

theme

Creating a Form with the Form Wizard

When you need to create a simple form quickly, you can use the *Form Wizard*, which helps you create a form by letting you select options in dialog boxes to specify the form's record source and layout. To start the Form Wizard, click the Create tab, and then click the Form Wizard button in the Forms group. The Form Wizard provides four form layouts from which to choose. The Columnar layout displays fields in a stacked column format, with labels to the left of their controls. The Tabular layout displays fields with the labels at the top of a column that contains the field values. The Datasheet layout displays fields in a datasheet format. The Justified layout displays fields across the screen in the order in which they occur. A form's style, also called a *theme*, formats the form and its controls using a predefined color, font, and design scheme. After creating a form with any Form tool, you can use the tools and features in Access to customize the form.

Step-by-Step 4.2

1. On the Ribbon, click the **Create** tab. In the Forms group, click the **Form Wizard** button. The first dialog box of the Form Wizard opens.

2. Click the **Tables/Queries** arrow, and then click **Table: Brokers** in the list. The fields in the Brokers table appear in the Available Fields list box.

3. Click the **Select All** button to move all fields to the Selected Fields list box, as shown in **Figure 4–3**.

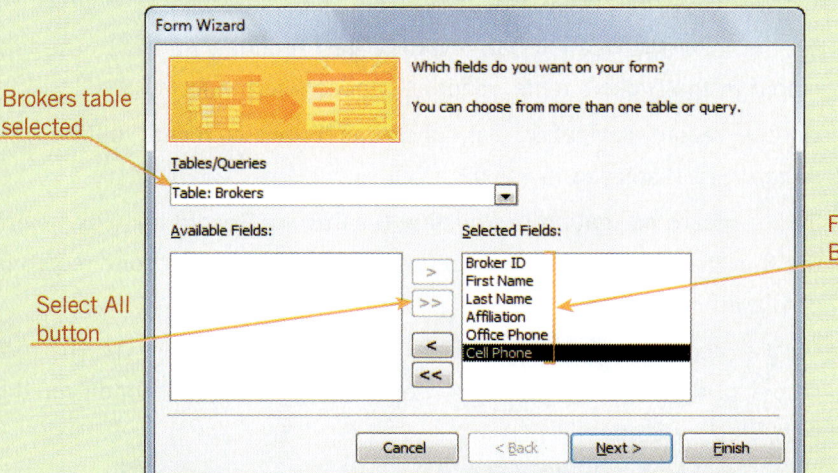

FIGURE 4–3
Form Wizard dialog box after selecting the table and fields to include

4. Click **Next**. The second Form Wizard dialog box opens.

5. Make sure that the **Columnar** option button is selected, and then click **Next**. In the final dialog box, you enter a title for the form or accept the default name. You'll accept the default name, Brokers.

6. Click **Finish**. The Brokers form appears in Form view, as shown in **Figure 4–4**. The default Office theme is applied to the form. The theme formats the form's colors and fonts. Leave the form open for the next Step-by-Step.

TIP

The default form name is the name of the table or query object on which the form is based.

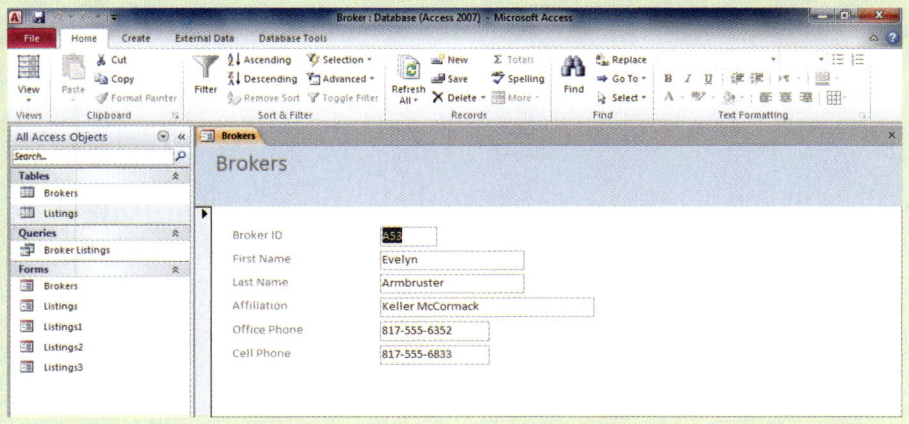

FIGURE 4–4
Brokers form in Form view

Navigating a Form

▶ **VOCABULARY**
Form view
Find

When you create a form using the Form Wizard, the form opens in Form view. When a form is displayed in *Form view*, you will see each record in the record source, one at a time, in the form. Form view includes a record navigation bar at the bottom of the Form view window that you can use to navigate the records. This record navigation bar has the same buttons with the same functions as the record navigation bar you used to navigate records in a table or query datasheet.

Step-by-Step 4.3

1. On the record navigation bar, click the **Last record** button ▶|. The last record in the Brokers table, record 9, appears in the form.

2. On the record navigation bar, click the **Previous record** button ◀. Record 8 is displayed in the form.

3. On the record navigation bar, click in the **Current Record** text box, select the **8** in the text box, type **2**, and then press **Enter**. The second record is displayed in the form.

4. On the record navigation bar, click the **First record** button |◀. The first record is displayed in the form. Leave the Brokers form open for the next Step-by-Step.

Using a Form to Find and Replace Data

You have used filters and queries to find data in a database. Another option for finding data in a database quickly is to use the *Find* command, which is available when you are using a table or query datasheet, form, or report. When you click the Find button in the Find group on the Home tab, the Find and Replace dialog box shown in **Figure 4–5** opens.

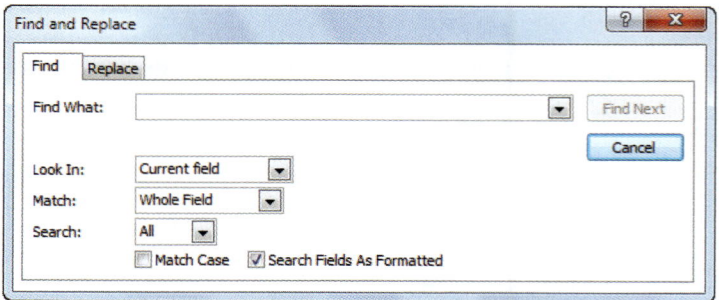

FIGURE 4–5   Find and Replace dialog box

You have several options for finding data, including finding and replacing data. If you select part of a field value in the form (one or more characters or a single word) before clicking the Find button, the selected text appears in the Find What list box automatically. If nothing is selected or more than one word is selected before clicking the Find button, the Find What list box is empty, in which case you type the value you want to find in the list box.

When a field is selected in the form, "Current field" appears in the Look In list box when you open the Find and Replace dialog box. If you want to search the entire table for a matching field value, click the Look In arrow, and then click "Current document." You can use the options in the Match menu to search any part of the field, the whole field, or the start of the field as follows:

- If you type *S* in the Find What list box, and then select the Any Part of Field option in the Match menu, you'll find values that contain the letter *S* anywhere in the value.

- If you select the Whole Field option, you'll find values that contain *only* the letter *S*.

- If you select the Start of Field option, you'll find values that *begin* with the letter *S*.

The Search option lets you search the entire form, or up and down from the location of the insertion point. The two check boxes—Match Case and Search Fields As Formatted—let you search for a matching value that has the same case as the entry in the Find What list box and search for formatted values, respectively. When the Match Case check box is selected, typing *Stars* in the Find What list box will find a record that contains the word *Stars* but will not select a record that contains the word *stars*. To start searching the form for matching records, click Find Next.

If you click the Replace tab in the Find and Replace dialog box, you will see additional options for finding text and replacing it with different text. The only difference is that you type the value that you want to find in the Find What list box and type the value that you want to replace it with in the Replace With list box. **Figure 4–6** shows the Replace tab. Notice the Replace and Replace All buttons. When you start searching the form for matching values by clicking Find Next, you'll find the first matching value. Clicking Replace replaces that instance and resumes searching for the Find What value; clicking Replace All replaces that instance and all others that match.

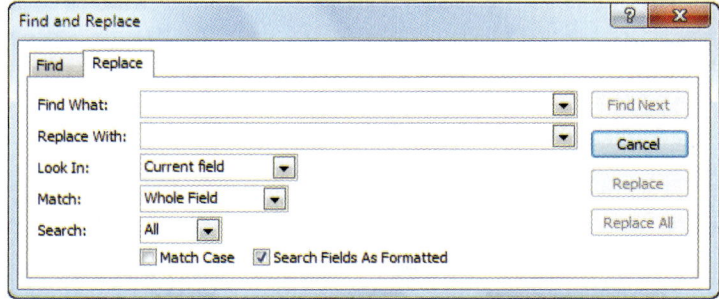

FIGURE 4–6   Replace tab in the Find and Replace dialog box

Step-by-Step 4.4

1. Double-click the word **McCormack** in the Affiliation field in the first record to select it.

2. In the Find group on the Home tab, click the **Find** button. The Find and Replace dialog box opens. Notice that the selected field value *McCormack* in the Affiliation field appears in the Find What list box. See **Figure 4–7**.

FIGURE 4–7
Find and Replace dialog box with selected Find What value

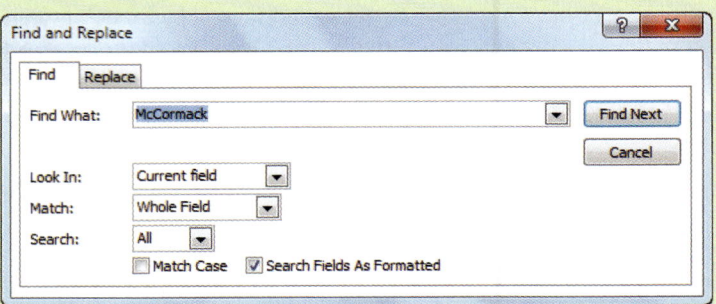

> **TIP**
>
> If necessary, drag the Find and Replace dialog box to below the Cell Phone field in the form so you can see all the fields in the form.

3. Make sure that the options in your dialog box match the ones shown in Figure 4–7. Click **Find Next**. Because the Match option is set to Whole Field, and there is no field value in the Affiliation field that contains only the word *McCormack*, Access opens a dialog box indicating that it found no matching items.

4. Click **OK** to close the dialog box.

5. Click the **Match** arrow in the Find and Replace dialog box, and then click **Any Part of Field**. Click **Find Next**. The Find command locates the word *McCormack* in the fourth record and selects it.

6. Click **Find Next**. The Find command locates a match in the first record. It displays the first record and selects the word *McCormack* in the record.

7. In the Find and Replace dialog box, click the **Replace** tab.

8. In the Replace With list box, type **Greene**.

> **EXTRA FOR EXPERTS**
>
> When you need to find and replace data, click the Replace button in the Find group on the Home tab. The Find and Replace dialog box opens with the Replace tab activated.

9. Click the Look In arrow, click **Current document**, and then make sure the Match value is **Any Part of Field**. Click **Replace**. The word *McCormack* in the first record is replaced with the word *Greene*. The next record containing the Find What value is selected (record 4).

10. Click **Replace**. The word *McCormack* is replaced with the word *Greene* in the fourth record. Click **Replace**. Because record 4 contains the last occurrence of the word *McCormack* in the Affiliation field, a dialog box opens and indicates that Access cannot find any more matches.

11. Click **OK** to close the dialog box.

12. Click **Cancel** to close the Find and Replace dialog box. Leave the Brokers form open for the next Step-by-Step.

You need to be careful when replacing text because you might accidentally replace text that you didn't intend to change. For example, if you want to replace the word *Green* with the word *Red*, your Find What value is *Green* and your Replace With value is *Red*. When you replace the text, you'll replace the word *Green* with the word *Red* as you intended. However, you'll also change the word *Greenfield* or *Greenley* to *Redfield* and *Redley*, which are changes that you might not intend to make. This is a good reason to use Replace rather than Replace All. With Replace All you do not have the option to choose to replace a specific word. By using Replace, if you find a word that you don't want to replace, click Cancel to skip it.

Using a Form to Update Data

You can also use a form to update the record source, add new records, or delete existing records. Because you can customize a form to display data in different ways, most database experts recommend using a form instead of a table datasheet to make changes. To change a field value, select it and type the new value. To add a new record, click the New button in the Records group on the Home tab to open a blank form, into which you can type the field values for the new record. When you are finished adding the new record, press Tab to move to a new record or close the form.

Step-by-Step 4.5

1. On the record navigation bar, click the **First record** button ⏮ to display the first record.

2. In the form, double-click **Armbruster** in the Last Name field to select it.

3. Type **Arlington** and then press **Tab**. The record is updated.

4. In the Records group on the Home tab, click the **New** button. A blank form is displayed. The insertion point is blinking in the Broker ID text box, ready for you to type the field value.

5. Type **E99** and then press **Tab**. The insertion point moves to First Name field, which is the next text box.

6. Type **Hector** in the First Name text box, and then press **Tab**.

7. Complete the record by typing the values shown in **Figure 4–8**. Remember to press Tab to move to the next field. Do not press Tab after typing the field value in the Cell Phone text box.

FIGURE 4–8
Adding a record in Form view

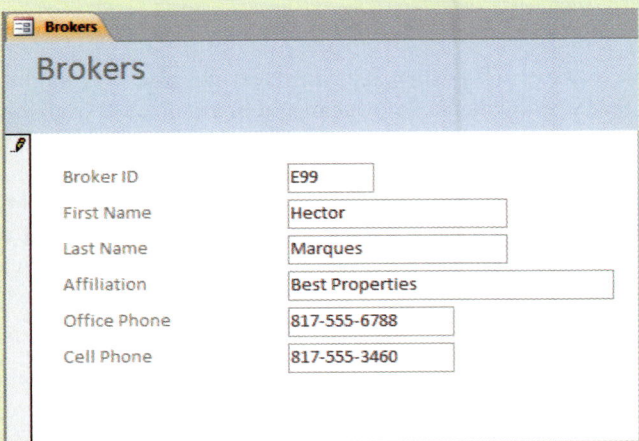

8. Press **Tab**. Record 10 is added to the Brokers table and a blank form for Record 11 appears.

9. On the Navigation Pane, double-click **Brokers** in the Tables group. The Brokers table opens in Datasheet view. Notice that the record you added, with the Broker ID E99, appears in the datasheet. Leave the Brokers table and the Brokers form open for the next Step-by-Step.

You might be wondering why the record for Hector Marques appears in record 4 in the table, instead of in record 10 as shown in the form. When you use a form to add a record, it is added in a blank form at the end of the record source. However, when you display the datasheet for the table or query on which the form is based, the new record appears in order based on the values in the primary key field. In the Brokers table, the Broker ID field is the table's primary key, and values in this column are alphabetical. That's why record E99 is listed fourth. Hector's record will be record 10 in the form until you close it and then reopen it, and then it will also appear as record 4 in the form.

Using a Form to Delete Data

Access provides two important options when using a form to delete a field value or record. When you click the Delete button in the Records group on the Home tab, you'll delete the selected field value. If you click the Delete button arrow, and then click Delete Record, you'll delete the record that is currently displayed in the form. Be careful when deleting data. You can use the Undo button on the Quick Access Toolbar to restore a deleted field value, but deleting a record permanently deletes it from the record source.

Step-by-Step 4.6

1. Click the **Close 'Brokers'** button ⊠ to close the Brokers table.

2. On the record navigation bar for the Brokers form, click the **Previous record** button ◀. Hector's record is still record 10 in the form.

3. Close the Brokers form.

4. Double-click **Brokers** in the Forms group in the Navigation Pane to reopen the form.

5. Navigate to record **4**, which contains Hector's record.

6. Press **Tab** to select the value *Hector* in the First Name text box.

7. In the Records group on the Home tab, click the **Delete** button. The field value in the First Name field is deleted.

8. On the record navigation bar, click the **Previous record** button ◀.

9. On the record navigation bar, click the **Next record** button ▶. The First Name field contains no value.

10. On the Quick Access Toolbar, click the **Undo** button ↺. The field value *Hector* is added back to the First Name text box.

11. In the Records group on the Home tab, click the **Delete button arrow**. In the list, click **Delete Record**. The dialog box shown in **Figure 4–9** opens.

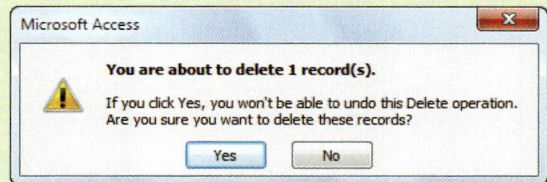

12. In the dialog box, click **Yes**. Hector's record is deleted from the Brokers table and is no longer displayed in the form. Notice that the Undo button on the Quick Access Toolbar is not available; you cannot restore a deleted record.

13. Close the Brokers form. Leave the database open for the next Step-by-Step.

> **TIP**
>
> Similar to changing records in a table datasheet, you do not need to save your changes when adding or updating records using a form. You only need to save a form when you change its design.

FIGURE 4–9
Dialog box that opens when you delete a record

Creating and Modifying a Form in Layout View

When you need to create a form to match an existing paper form—or when you need to create a form different from the forms you can create with a form tool or wizard—you can create a form from scratch. To create a new form, click the Create tab on the Ribbon, and then click the Blank Form button in the Forms group. A blank form opens in Layout view, and the Field List pane opens on the right side of the

▶ **VOCABULARY**
Field List pane
control layout

screen. The *Field List pane* contains the tables in the database and displays the fields they contain. When you double-click a field in the Field List pane, Access adds the field to the form. As you add fields to a form in Layout view, Access adds them to a control layout. A *control layout* is a "container" that groups together the controls in a form so that you can change them as a group. You can change the way the controls are arranged by changing the control layout, or you can remove controls from the layout to work with them individually.

The first task is to create a blank form in Layout view, and then to use the Field List pane to add fields to the form.

Step-by-Step 4.7

1. On the Ribbon, click the **Create** tab. In the Forms group, click the **Blank Form** button. A blank form opens in Layout view. The Field List pane opens on the right side of the screen. See **Figure 4–10**.

FIGURE 4–10
Blank form in
Layout view

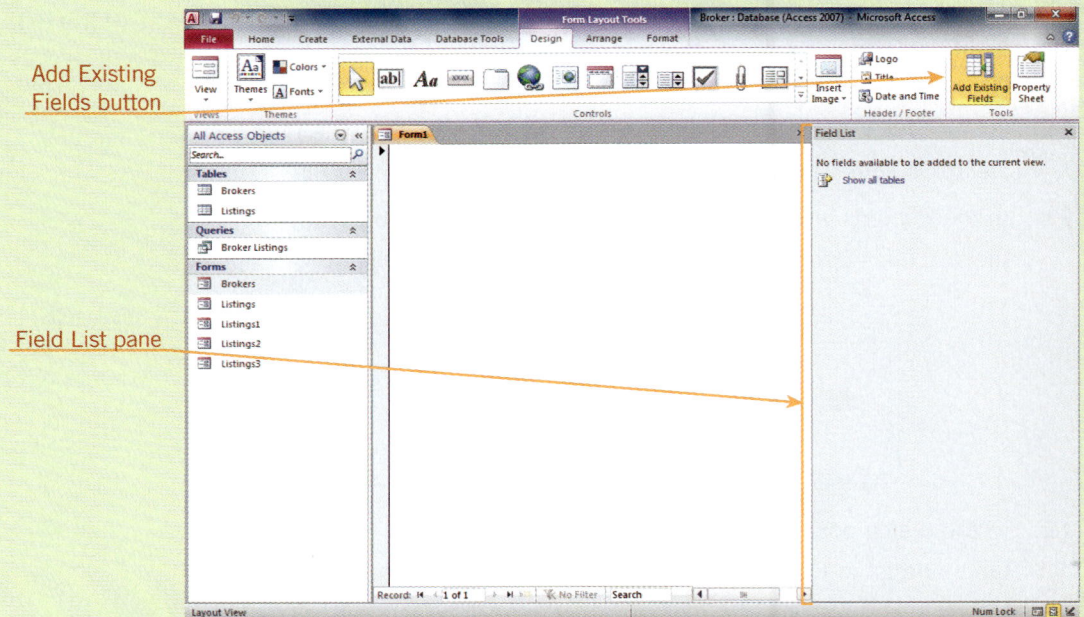

2. If necessary, click **Show all tables** in the Field List pane, and then click the **expand indicator** ⊞ to the left of the Listings table in the Field List pane to see the fields in the table.

3. In the Listings field list, double-click **Listing ID**. The label and text box controls for the Listing ID field are added to the upper-left corner of the form. When you add a field from one table, its related table—in this case, the Brokers table—moves to the "Fields available in related tables" section of the Field List pane. See **Figure 4–11**.

⚠ WARNING

If you do not see the Field List pane, click the Add Existing Fields button in the Tools group on the Design tab. If you do not see "Show all tables" in the Field List pane as shown in Figure 4–10, you won't need to click Show all tables in Step 2.

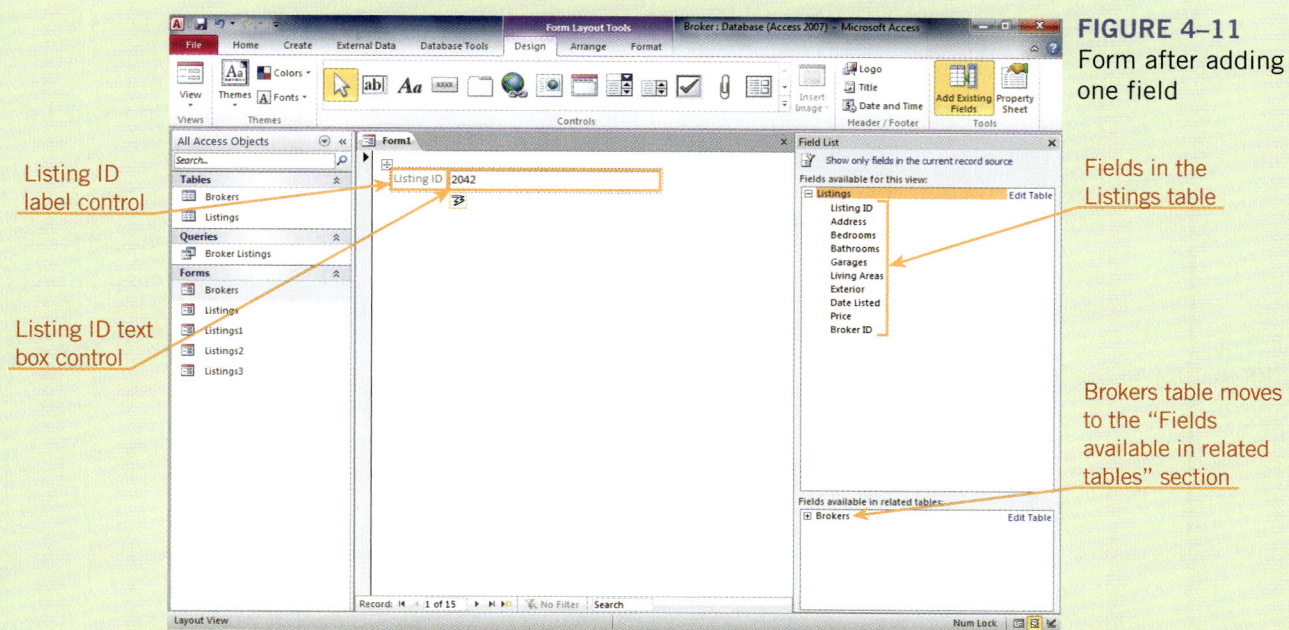

FIGURE 4–11
Form after adding one field

Listing ID label control

Listing ID text box control

Fields in the Listings table

Brokers table moves to the "Fields available in related tables" section

4. In the Field List pane, in the Listings table, double-click **Address**. The label and text box controls for the Address field are added to the form in the control layout. See **Figure 4–12**.

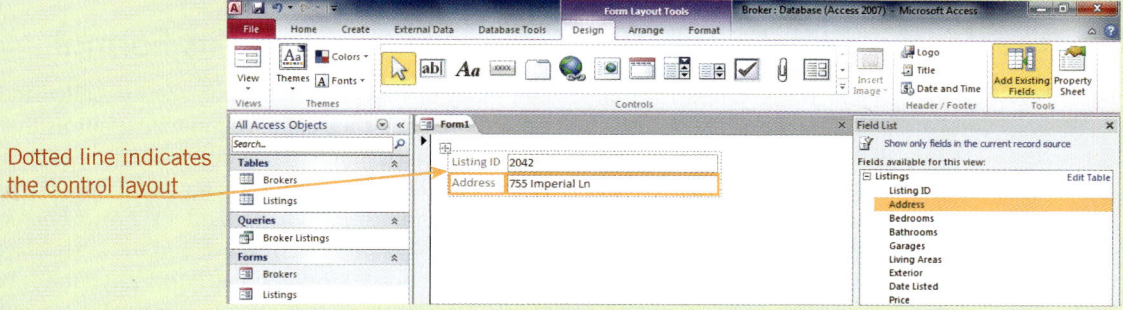

FIGURE 4–12
Form after adding two fields

Dotted line indicates the control layout

5. Double-click the following fields in the Listings table in order listed: **Bedrooms**, **Bathrooms**, **Garages**, **Living Areas**, **Date Listed**, and **Price**.

6. In the Fields available in related tables pane, click the **expand indicator** ⊞ to the left of the Brokers table to display the fields.

7. In the Brokers table in the Fields available in related tables section, double-click the **First Name** field. The Brokers table and its fields move to the top of the Field List pane. The First Name field is added to the form as a combo box control and not as a text box control because this field is in a related table. You can use the Property Update Options button to change it to a text box control.

8. Below the selected First Name control, click the **Property Update Options** button , and then click **Change to Text Box** in the menu that opens. The First Name control changes to a text box control.

TIP

If you accidentally add the wrong field to the control layout, click the field in the form to select it, and then press Delete.

9. In the Brokers table field list, double-click the following fields in the order listed: **Last Name** and **Cell Phone**.

10. In the Tools group on the Design tab, click the **Add Existing Fields** button to close the Field List pane.

11. On the Quick Access Toolbar, click the **Save** button 🖫 to open the Save As dialog box, type **Listings And Agents** in the Form Name text box, and then click **OK**. See **Figure 4–13**. Leave the form open for the next Step-by-Step.

FIGURE 4–13
Form after adding all fields

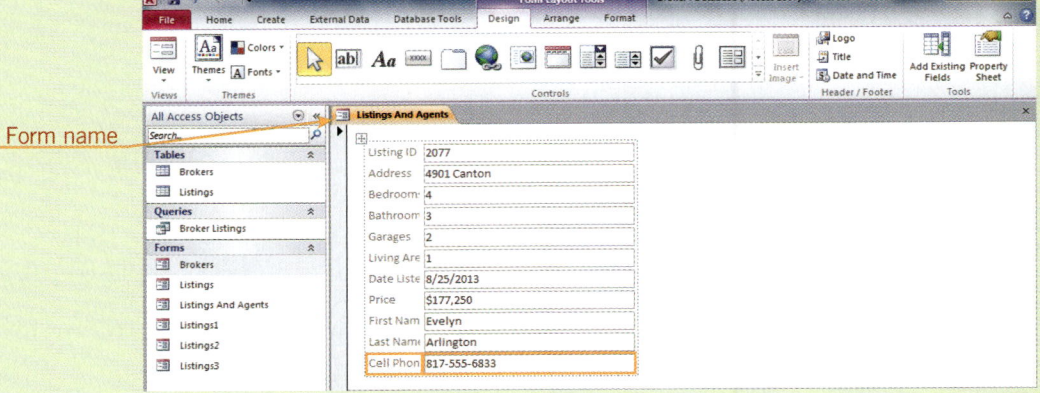

Form name

Adding a Title to a Form and Changing its Format

When you create a form in Layout view, at first it contains one section called the *Detail section*. The form you just created contains a Detail section with controls that display one record at a time. When your form design requires other features, such as a title or a page number, you can add two additional sections to the form. The *Form Header section* displays information at the top of each form, and the *Form Footer section* displays information at the bottom of each form. You can add these sections to a form by clicking a tool in the Header/Footer group on the Form Layout Tools Design tab. When you add a control to one of these sections, the Form Header and Form Footer sections are added to the form as a pair, even when you add a control to the form that appears in only one of the two sections.

You can add two types of controls to a form. A *bound control* is connected to a field in the record source and is used to display, enter, and update data. An *unbound control* is not connected to a record source and is used to display information, lines, rectangles, and pictures.

Figure 4–13 shows the Header/Footer group on the Design tab in Layout view, which includes buttons that add different types of controls to a form. For example, clicking the Logo button adds a picture to a form, and clicking the Title button adds a title control in the Form Header section.

To add a title to a form, which adds an unbound control to the form, click the Title button in the Header/Footer group on the Design tab. Access will add the Form Header and Form Footer sections to the form and add a title control to the Form Header section. The default form title is the form's name. Because you already saved the form as "Listings And Agents," this is the form title that will be added when you add a title control to the form. You can edit the title by clicking and editing text just like you would in a document. You can also change the default font size, color, and style of the title text using the buttons in the Font group on the Format tab.

▶ **VOCABULARY**

Detail section

Form Header section

Form Footer section

bound control

unbound control

🔳 **EXTRA FOR EXPERTS**

When working in Layout view, adding a control to the Form Header section adds the Form Header and Form Footer sections to the form, but you won't see the Form Footer section until you change to Design view because it is empty.

Step-by-Step 4.8

1. In the Header/Footer group on the Design tab, click the **Title** button. Access adds the Form Header and Form Footer sections to the form, and adds a title control to the Form Header section. (You won't see the Form Footer section until you change to Design view because it's empty.) The text in the title control is "Listings And Agents," which is the same as the form's name.

2. Click the **Format** tab, and then in the Font group, click the **Bold** button **B**. The title is formatted in bold. The text is deselected, and the title control is selected, as indicated by its orange border shown in **Figure 4–14**.

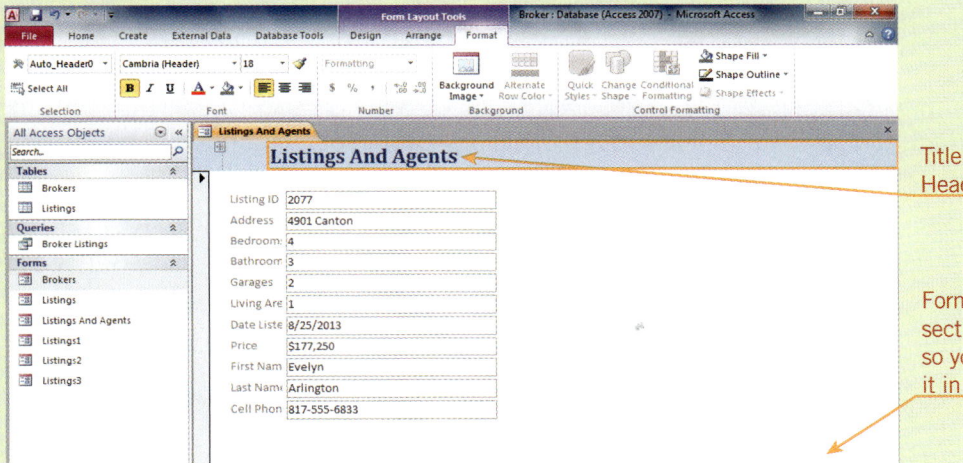

FIGURE 4–14
Title control added to form

Title added to Form Header section

Form Footer section is empty, so you can't see it in Layout view

3. With the title control still selected, click the **Font Color arrow** in the Font group. A gallery of colors opens.

4. In the gallery, click the **Dark Red** color (the first color in the last row of the Standard Colors section). The gallery closes and the text in the title control is formatted as dark red.

5. Click to the left of the letter "A" in the word "And" in the title to position the insertion point, press **Delete**, and then type **a**. The title changes to "Listings and Agents." Leave the form open for the next Step-by-Step.

> **TIP**
>
> A form can have a different name and title. The form's name is "Listings And Agents," and the form's title is "Listings and Agents."

Resizing a Control in a Form

When you add controls to a form, you might need to adjust their widths to display the values they contain correctly. For the Listings And Agents form, the text box controls are much wider than the data they contain. When you resize controls in a control layout in Layout view, reducing the width of *one* control reduces all the widths of all *other* controls in the control layout at the same time. When resizing the controls, be sure to resize them with the longest data value displayed in the form, so you don't accidentally resize a control too narrowly and limit what users can see. You can resize a control by dragging its edge to a new location. You can also resize a control precisely. As you resize a control, the status bar displays the width of the control in characters and lines. By watching the lower-left corner of the status bar as you resize a control, you can specify the width of the control using an exact number of characters.

Step-by-Step 4.9

1. Use the record navigation bar to display record **11** in the form. This record contains the longest Address field value in the record source.

2. Click the **Address** text box to select it. An orange border appears around the text box. A dotted outline surrounds all the controls in the control layout.

3. Point to the right edge of the Address text box control. When the pointer changes to a ↔ shape, press and hold the mouse button and slowly drag the right edge of the Address text box control to the left. When the Characters value on the left side of the status bar is 16, as shown in **Figure 4–15**, release the mouse button. Because all of the text boxes in the form are part of a control layout, they are all resized to the same size.

FIGURE 4–15
Resizing the text box controls in a control layout

Pointer on Address text box control

Record 11 contains the longest Address field value

Status bar indicates number of lines and characters while resizing

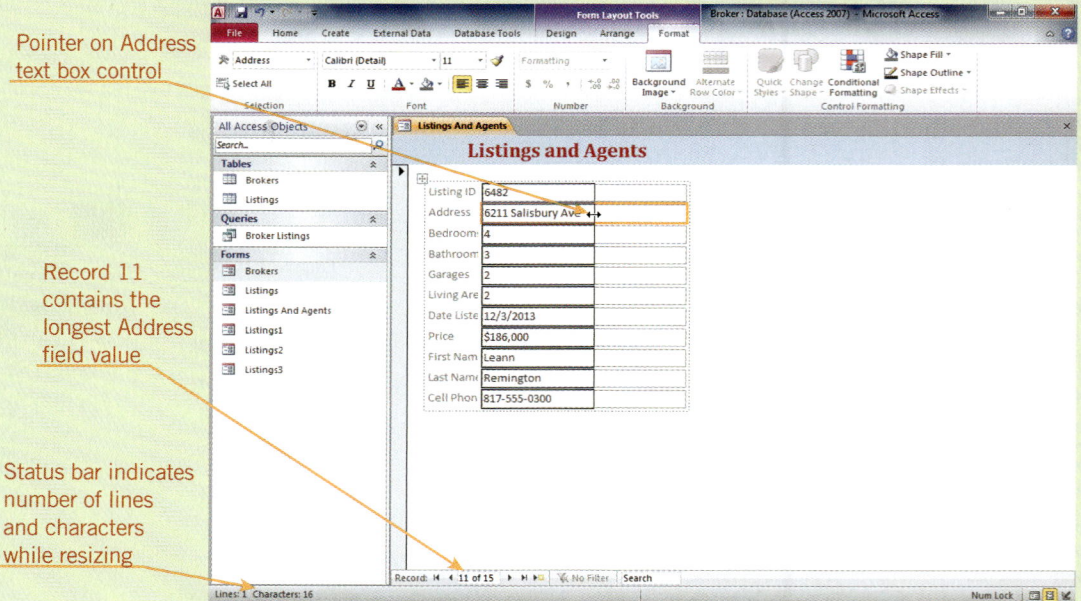

4. Save the form. Leave the form open for the next Step-by-Step.

Moving a Control in a Form

When controls are grouped in a control layout, moving one control moves all the selected controls in the group. When you need to move one or more controls in a form, you'll need to select and then remove them from the control layout first. To select one control, you click it. To select a group of controls, click the first control, press and hold down Shift, click the other controls, and then release Shift. Some people call this "Shift-Click" because you hold down Shift while clicking the other controls. To remove one or more selected controls from a control layout, right-click the control to open the shortcut menu, point to Layout, and then click Remove Layout.

Step-by-Step 4.10

1. Click the **First Name** text box (which contains the value *Leann*) to select it. An orange border appears around the text box.

2. Press and hold down **Shift**.

3. Click the **Last Name** text box, click the **Cell Phone** text box, and then release **Shift**. **Figure 4–16** shows the three selected controls.

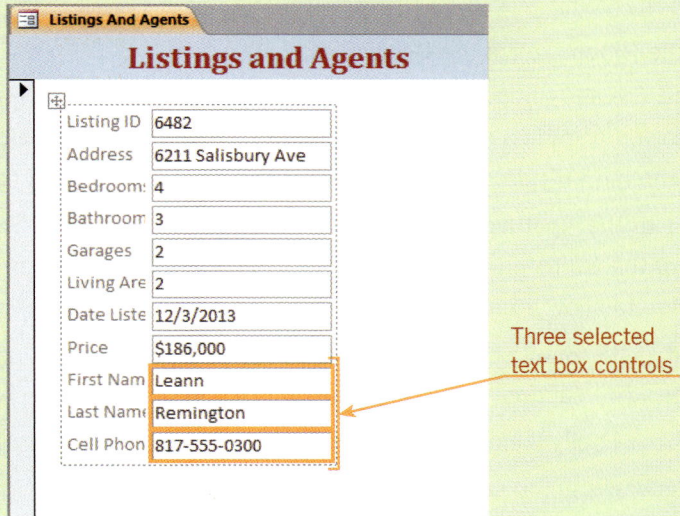

FIGURE 4–16
Selected controls in a form

Three selected
text box controls

4. Right-click one of the selected controls to open the shortcut menu, point to **Layout**, and then click **Remove Layout**. The selected controls are removed from the control layout. An orange border appears around the three text box controls for the First Name, Last Name, and Cell Phone fields, and the dotted border is removed from the fields on the form.

5. Press and hold **Shift**, click the **First Name**, **Last Name**, and **Cell Phone** labels, and then release **Shift**. The three label controls and text box controls are selected, with an orange border around each control.

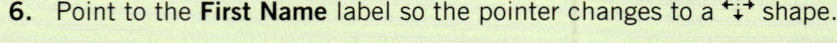

TIP

If you move the controls to the wrong location, click the Undo button on the Quick Access Toolbar, and then repeat Steps 6 and 7.

6. Point to the **First Name** label so the pointer changes to a ✛ shape.

7. Click and drag the selected controls to the top of the form, so the top left corner of the outline of the controls is to the right of and aligned with the top of the Listing ID controls, as shown in **Figure 4–17**, and then release the mouse button to move the selected controls.

FIGURE 4–17
Controls removed from control layout and moved to new position

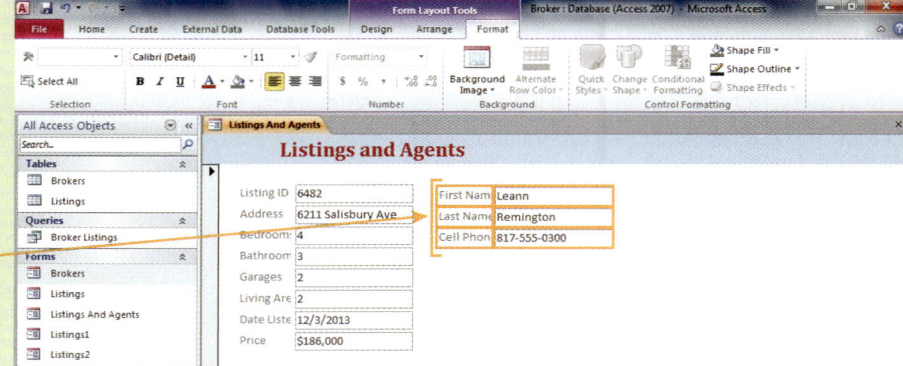

Controls in new position

8. Save the form.

9. On the Ribbon, click the **Design** tab.

10. In the Themes group, click the **Themes** button. A gallery of themes opens. When you point to a theme in the gallery, its name appears in a ScreenTip and the form displays a Live Preview of the theme's fonts and colors.

11. Point to the **Apothecary** theme, which is the first theme in the second row of the Built-In section. Notice that the colors and fonts in the form change to show a Live Preview of this theme.

12. Point to the **Equity** theme, which is the third theme in the fourth row in the Built-In section, and notice the changes in the form.

13. Click the **Equity** theme to apply it to the form and close the Themes gallery.

14. In the Views group on the Design tab, click the **View** button. The form is displayed in Form view. See **Figure 4–18**. Leave the form open for the next Step-by-Step.

FIGURE 4–18
Form with Equity theme applied to it

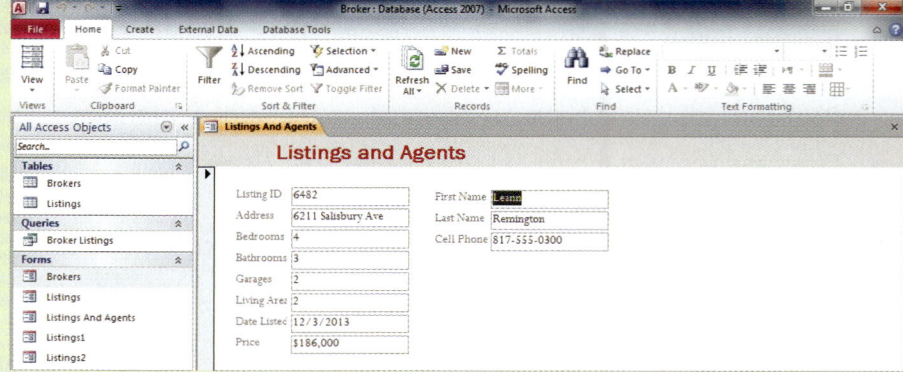

Adding an Unbound Control to a Form in Design View

Some changes that you need to make to a form require you to work in the third form view, Design view. In Design view, you see the controls that you added to the form on a grid, as shown in **Figure 4–19**. Unlike when working in Layout view, the controls do not display data from the record source. You must be in Design view to add controls such as lines, rectangles, and labels to a form. You add controls to the form by clicking the button for the desired control in the Controls group on the Design tab, and then clicking to position the control in the form. Another difference when working in Design view is that you see the Form Header, Detail, and Form Footer sections in the form. Each section contains a section bar at the top that you can click and select. You adjust the size of a section by clicking the bottom edge of the section and dragging it up or down to change its height. When you do not see a grid below a section, like the Form Footer section shown in Figure 4–19, the section height is set to zero. To expand a section, click the bottom edge of the section bar and then drag the border down to the desired height. You can see the position of objects in Design view as you are moving them, and you can position controls precisely by looking at the horizontal and vertical rulers that appear on the top and left sides of the form.

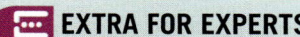 **EXTRA FOR EXPERTS**

To delete a control from a form, click the control to select it, and then press Delete.

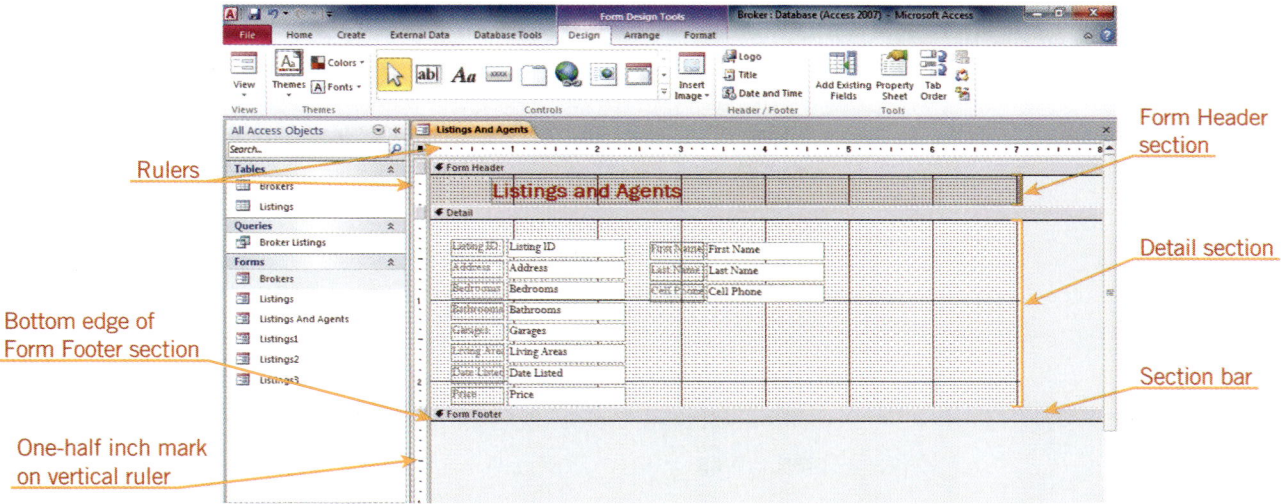

FIGURE 4–19 Form in Design view

Step-by-Step 4.11

1. Right-click the **Listings And Agents** object tab, and then click **Design View** on the shortcut menu. The form is displayed in Design view, as shown in Figure 4–19.

2. Point to the bottom edge of the Form Footer section so the pointer changes to a ✛ shape, and then drag the section bar down until the outline of the bottom edge of the section bar is at the one-half inch mark on the vertical ruler. Release the mouse button. The height of the Form Footer section increases, as shown in **Figure 4–20**.

FIGURE 4–20
Form Footer section with increased height

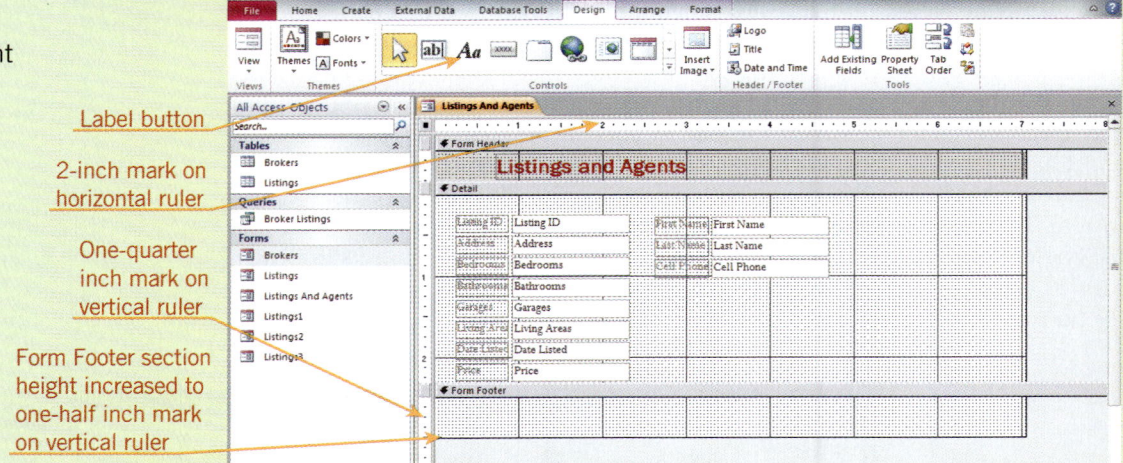

3. In the Controls group on the Design tab, click the **Label** button. The Label tool is selected. When you move the pointer over the form, it changes to a ⁺A shape.

4. Move the ⁺A pointer into the Form Footer section so the plus sign in the pointer is at the 2-inch mark on the horizontal ruler and the one-quarter-inch mark on the vertical ruler, and then click. **Figure 4–21** shows the label control added to the Form Footer section. The insertion point is blinking inside the control, which will expand in size when you start typing.

FIGURE 4–21
Form Footer section with label control added

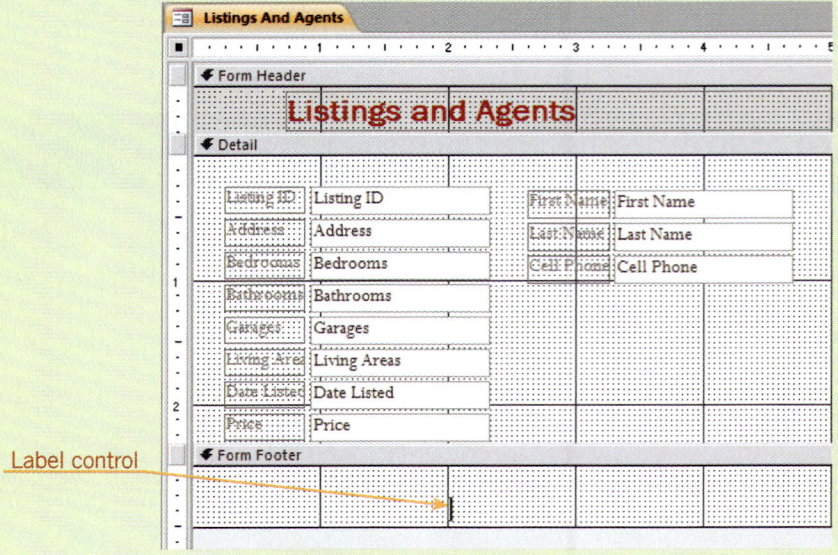

5. Type your first and last names, and then press **Enter**.

6. Save the form.

7. In the Views group on the Design tab, click the **View** button. The form is displayed in Form view, and the label control in the Form Footer section displays your name. Leave the form open for the next Step-by-Step.

Previewing and Printing a Form

You can preview and print a form. To preview a form, click the File tab to display Backstage view, click Print on the navigation bar, and then click Print Preview. Each record in the record source appears in a miniature version of the form, one after the other, on the page. To print all records in the form, click the File tab, click Print on the navigation bar, and then click Print to open the Print dialog box. Make sure the All option button is selected, and then click OK.

To print the form with the current record displayed, you must be in Form view and navigate to the desired record. Click the File tab, click Print on the navigation bar, and then click Print. The Print dialog box opens. Click the Selected Record(s) option button, and then click OK.

Step-by-Step 4.12

1. Click the **File** tab to display Backstage view, click **Print** on the navigation bar, and then click **Print Preview**. The form is displayed in Print Preview.

2. Use the buttons on the page navigation bar to display each page of the form. Notice that each record appears in a form, and the forms for each record are stacked on top of each other. The form's title, "Listings and Agents," appears once at the top of the first page, and your name appears once after the last form on the last page.

3. In the Close Preview group on the Print Preview tab, click the **Close Print Preview** button.

4. Navigate to record **3** in the form.

5. Click the **File** tab, click **Print** on the navigation bar, and then click **Print**. In the Print dialog box, make sure your printer is selected in the Name box, click the **Selected Record(s)** option button, and then click **OK**. The current record in the form is printed.

6. Close the **Listings And Agents** form.

7. Close the database, and then exit Access.

SUMMARY

In this lesson, you learned:

- A form is a database object that displays data from a record source. You can create a form using a form tool or wizard, or you can create a blank form from scratch.

- You can use the record navigation bar in Form view to navigate the records displayed in a form.

- The Find command is used to locate records in a table or query datasheet, form, or report. When finding data in a form, you need to identify the text to find, the field in which to search (or to search the entire form), the type of search to conduct (whole field, any part of field, or start of field), the desired case of the search text, and the direction to search or to search the entire form. You can also find and replace data using the Replace tab in the Find and Replace dialog box.

- You can use a form to update records or to add and delete records. When you make changes to data in a form, the changes are made in the record source on which the form is based.

- You can create a blank form and add fields to it by double-clicking the fields in the Field List pane in Layout view. When

you add fields to a form, they are added to the form as controls in a control layout. You can resize and change the controls in a control layout as a group. You can also remove controls from a control layout so you can work with them individually.

- When you create a form in Layout view, the form has one default section, called the Detail section, that contains the controls that display the data in a form. Two other sections, which are added when the form's design uses controls that appear in these sections, are the Form Header section and the Form Footer section. The Form Header section usually contains the form's title, and the Form Footer section might contain labels that describe the form.

- You can add two types of controls to a form. A bound control is connected to a field in the record source and is used to display, enter, and update data. An unbound control is not connected to a record source and is used to display information, lines, rectangles, and pictures.

- You can preview and print all the records in a form, or you can use the Print dialog box to print only selected records in a form.

VOCABULARY REVIEW

Define the following terms:

bound control	form	Layout view
control	Form Footer section	Multiple Items tool
control layout	Form Header section	record source
Datasheet tool	Form tool	Split Form tool
Detail section	Form view	theme
Field List pane	Form Wizard	unbound control
Find		

REVIEW QUESTIONS

TRUE / FALSE

Circle T if the statement is true or F if the statement is false.

T   F   **1.**   The table or query on which a form is based is called a record source.

T   F   **2.**   The Multiple Items tool creates a form that displays a form and a datasheet in separate panes.

T   F   **3.**   Many database experts agree that updates to the data in a database should be made using forms.

T   F   **4.**   When you click the Delete button in the Records group on the Home tab, the record displayed in Form view is deleted.

T   F   **5.**   When you add fields to a form in Layout view, the fields are added to a control layout.

WRITTEN QUESTIONS

Write a brief answer to each of the following questions.

1. The Find and Replace dialog box offers three options to help you match data in a form when searching the database. What are these three options and what do they do?

2. If you delete a record using a form, is it possible to undo the action? Why or why not?

3. How do you add fields to a blank form in Layout view?

4. When working in Layout view, how do you remove a field from a control layout in a form?

5. What is the difference between a bound control and an unbound control?

FILL IN THE BLANK

Complete the following sentences by writing the correct word or words in the blanks provided.

1. The _____ creates a simple form that includes all the fields in the selected table or query, uses a simple format, and includes a title with the same name as the record source.

2. When you add a field to a form in Layout view, the field's label and text box are added to the form in an object called a(n) _____.

3. When a form is displayed in _____ view, you can view the controls in the form and data from the record source at the same time.

4. The _____ creates a form using all the fields in the selected table or query and splits the window into two panes.

5. The _____ creates a form that looks just like a datasheet.

■ PROJECTS

If you have a SAM 2010 user profile, your instructor may have assigned an autogradable version of the indicated project. If so, log into the SAM 2010 Web site at *www.cengage.com/sam2010* to download the instruction and start files.

PROJECT 4–1

1. Open the **Recreation.accdb** database from the Access Lesson 04 folder with your Data Files.

2. Use the Form tool to create a form based on the Class table. Save the form as **Class Listing**.

3. Apply the Angles theme to the form.

4. Navigate the records in the record source until you find the record that has the longest field value in the Class Name text box.

5. Resize the width of the text boxes so the longest Class Name field value is displayed correctly.

6. Select the text box control for the Teacher ID field and then remove it from the control layout.

7. Select the Teacher ID label and text box controls, and then move them to the right of the Class ID text box, so the bottom edges of the Class ID and Teacher ID controls are aligned.

8. Change the text in the title control to **Class Listing**. Press Enter.

9. Change to Form view, and then navigate to record 8. Change the field value in the Location text field to your first and last names.

10. Print record 8.

11. Use the Class Listing form to add a new record using the following information: Class ID: **201**, Class Name: **Masters Swimming**, Location: **Swim Center**, Start Date: **6/1/2013**, End Date: **6/30/2013**, Fee: **100.00**, and Teacher ID: **12910**.

12. Save and close the form, close the Recreation database, and then exit Access.

SAM PROJECT 4–2

1. Open the **Teacher.accdb** database from the Access Lesson 04 folder with your Data Files.

2. Use the Split Form tool to create a form based on the Teacher table. Save the form as **Teacher Split Form**.

3. In the datasheet, select the First Name column value for the second record. Type your first name. Press Tab, and then type your last name in the Last Name column for record 2.

4. Change the text in the title control to **Teacher Information**, and then change the font style to italic. Save and close the form.

5. Use the Multiple Items tool to create a form based on the Class table. Save the form as **Class Information**.

6. In Layout view, resize the columns in the Class Information form so that each column is just wide enough to display the widest field value it contains.

7. Change the text in the title control to **Class Information**. Then change the font style to bold and the font color to Dark Blue (last row, column 9 in the Standard Colors gallery).

8. Change to Design view. Click below the Form Footer section to deselect any selected controls. Increase the height of the Form Footer section so it is one-half inch. Add a label to the Form Footer section at the 3-inch mark on the horizontal ruler and the one-quarter-inch mark on the vertical ruler. Type your first and last names in the label control.

9. Save the Class Information form, and then change to Form view.

10. Preview the Class Information form. Print the page in landscape orientation.

11. Close the Class Information form, close the Teacher database, and then exit Access.

PROJECT 4–3

1. Open the **Class.accdb** database from the Access Lesson 04 folder with your Data Files.

2. Create a blank form and save it as **Teachers And Classes**.

3. Add the following fields from the Class table to the form in the order listed: Class ID, Class Name, Location, Start Date, End Date, and Fee.

4. Use the Teacher table field list to add the Teacher ID field to the form, use the Property Update Options button to change the Teacher ID control to a text box control, and then add the following fields from the Teacher table to the form in the order listed: First Name, Last Name, and Phone. Close the Field List pane.

5. Select the Class ID label control, and then drag its right edge to the *right*, so that the text in all of the label controls in the control layout is fully visible.

6. Select the Teacher ID, First Name, Last Name, and Phone text box controls, and then remove them from the control layout.

7. Select the label and text box controls for the Teacher ID, First Name, Last Name, and Phone fields, and then move them to the right of the Class ID, Class Name, Location, and Start Date fields so the top of the Teacher ID text box is aligned with the top of the Class ID text box.

8. Add a title control to the form and use the default title.

9. Apply the Essential theme to the form.

10. Save the form and change to Design view.

11. Increase the height of the Form Footer section to one-half inch. Then add a label to the Form Footer section at the 2-inch mark on the horizontal ruler and the one-quarter-inch mark on the vertical ruler that contains your first and last names.

12. Save the form and change to Form view.

13. Navigate to record 9 in the form (Class ID 123). Change the End Date field value to **6/30/2013**. Print record 9.

14. Close the Teachers And Classes form, close the Class database, and then exit Access.

■ CRITICAL THINKING

ACTIVITY 4–1

Open the **Broker.accdb** database from the Access Lesson 04 folder with your Data Files. Use the Form Wizard to create a form based on the Broker Listings query. Include all fields from the Broker Listings query in the form, view the data by broker in a form with a subform, use a Tabular layout, and use the name **Brokers Form** for the main form and **Listings Subform** for the subform. Click Finish. The form opens in Form view. Use the buttons on the record navigation bar at the bottom of the Form window to scroll through the records. How is the data in the subform related to the data in the main form? Explain your answer.

Display record 5 in the main form, change the field values in the Last Name and First Name fields to your last and first names, and then print record 5. Close the form, close the Broker database, and then exit Access.

ACTIVITY 4–2

Open the **Broker.accdb** database from the Access Lesson 04 folder with your Data Files. Open the **Listings** form in Layout view, examine the form's contents, and then change to Design view. Drag the bottom edge of the Detail section down approximately one inch to increase the height of this section. In the Controls group on the Design tab, click the Text Box button. Move the pointer to the Detail section, and click the plus sign in the pointer at the 4-inch mark on the horizontal ruler, approximately two rows of grid dots below the Broker ID text box control. A text box control and attached label are added to the form. Click in the text box control (which contains the word *Unbound*), and then type **=[Price]*0.06** and press Enter. Click the label control (which contains the word *Text* and a number) to select it, double-click the text in the label control to select it, and then type **Commission**. Click the text box control (which contains the expression you entered), click the Property Sheet button in the Tools group on the Design tab to open the Property Sheet, click the All tab (if necessary), and then set the Format property to Currency. Close the Property Sheet, save the form, and then change to Form view. What kind of text box control did you create? What value is displayed in the Commission text box? Close the Listings form, close the Broker database, and then exit Access.

LESSON 5

Creating and Modifying Reports

■ OBJECTIVES

Upon completion of this lesson, you should be able to:

- Create a report using the Report tool, the Label Wizard, and the Report Wizard.
- Modify a report in Layout view.
- Modify a report in Design view.
- Add a line, label, and picture to a report.
- Move a control in a report.
- Resize a report.

■ VOCABULARY

grouping level

Label Wizard

Line tool

Print Preview

read-only

report

report selector

Report tool

Report Wizard

In this lesson, you will learn how to create and modify reports that display the data from the tables in your database in a format that you can print.

Creating a Report Using the Report Tool

A **report** is a database object that displays data from one or more tables or queries in a format that has an appearance similar to a printed report. Just as with forms, the tables or queries that contain the data used in a report are called the record source. You can use a report to create a formatted list of information or to summarize information in different ways. You can even use reports to print form letters and mailing labels.

Access includes tools that you can use to create different kinds of reports. After selecting the table or query in the Navigation Pane on which to base the report, click the Create tab on the Ribbon. The different options for creating reports are located in the Reports group on the Create tab. The **Report tool** quickly creates a simple report that includes all the fields in the selected table or query, uses a columnar format, formats the report using a theme, and includes a title with the same name as the record source. A report's theme formats the report and its controls using a predefined color, font, and design scheme. In addition, Access adds the current date and time at the top of the report and a page number at the bottom of the report. **Figure 5–1** shows a report created using the Report tool. The record source for the report is the Teacher table. Each field in the Teacher table appears in the report. When fields appear in a report, they appear in controls. For example, in this report, the Teacher ID label and the records shown below the labels appear in controls.

▶ **VOCABULARY**
report
Report tool

EXTRA FOR EXPERTS

The themes for forms and reports are the same. Most developers use the same theme for all forms and reports in a database so these objects will have a consistent and familiar appearance to users.

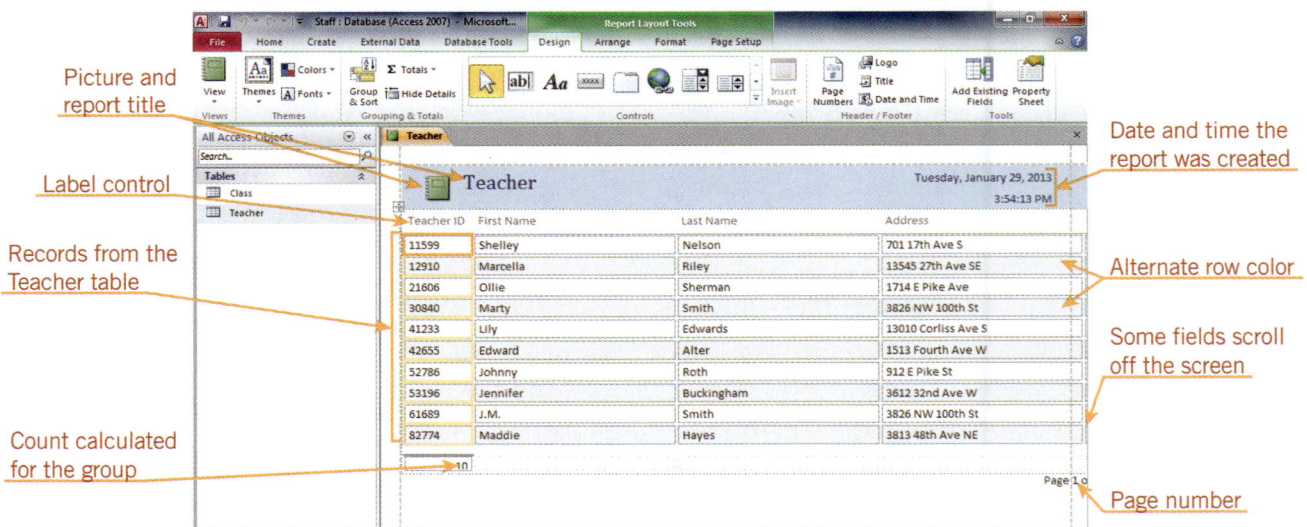

FIGURE 5–1   Report created using the Report tool

When you use the Report tool to create a report, the report opens initially in Layout view. In Layout view, you can view the controls in the report and data from the record source at the same time. In Layout view, you can make certain types of changes to the report's format and appearance, such as resizing a control. When you click a control in Layout view, an orange border appears around it to indicate that the control is selected.

Step-by-Step 5.1

1. Open the **Staff.accdb** database from the Access Lesson 05 folder where your Data Files are stored.

2. If the Security Warning opens, click the **Enable Content** button.

3. In the Navigation Pane, click the **Teacher** table to select it.

4. On the Ribbon, click the **Create** tab.

5. In the Reports group, click the **Report** button. Access creates a report using all the fields in the Teacher table, and formats it using the default Office theme. See Figure 5–1.

6. On the Quick Access Toolbar, click the **Save** button 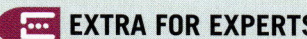. Save the report as **Teacher List**.

7. Click the **Close 'Teacher List'** button ⊠ to close the report. Leave the database open for the next Step-by-Step.

> **EXTRA FOR EXPERTS**
>
> Click the Themes button in the Themes group on the Design tab, and then point to a theme in the gallery to preview the theme, or click a theme to apply it.

The data in a report is *read-only*, which means that you can view it but you cannot change it. If you need to make changes to the data in a report, close the report, and then open the record source on which the report is based. After making changes in the record source, the new data will be updated automatically when you open the report again.

> ▶ **VOCABULARY**
> **read-only**
> **Label Wizard**

Creating a Report Using the Label Wizard

The *Label Wizard* lets you create a report that you can use to print standard or custom labels. To create labels, select the record source in the Navigation Pane, click the Create tab on the Ribbon, and then click the Labels button in the Reports group. Then use the Label Wizard dialog boxes to select the label you are using; to choose the font name, style, size, and color to use when printing the labels; to select the fields to include from the record source and their arrangement when printed on the labels; to select an optional sort order; and to choose a name for the report. **Figure 5–2** shows a report of mailing labels, printed three labels across the page and sorted in alphabetical order by the values in the Last Name field.

TIP

You can use the buttons in the Data group on the Print Preview tab to save the data in the report in another file format, such as a Microsoft Word document.

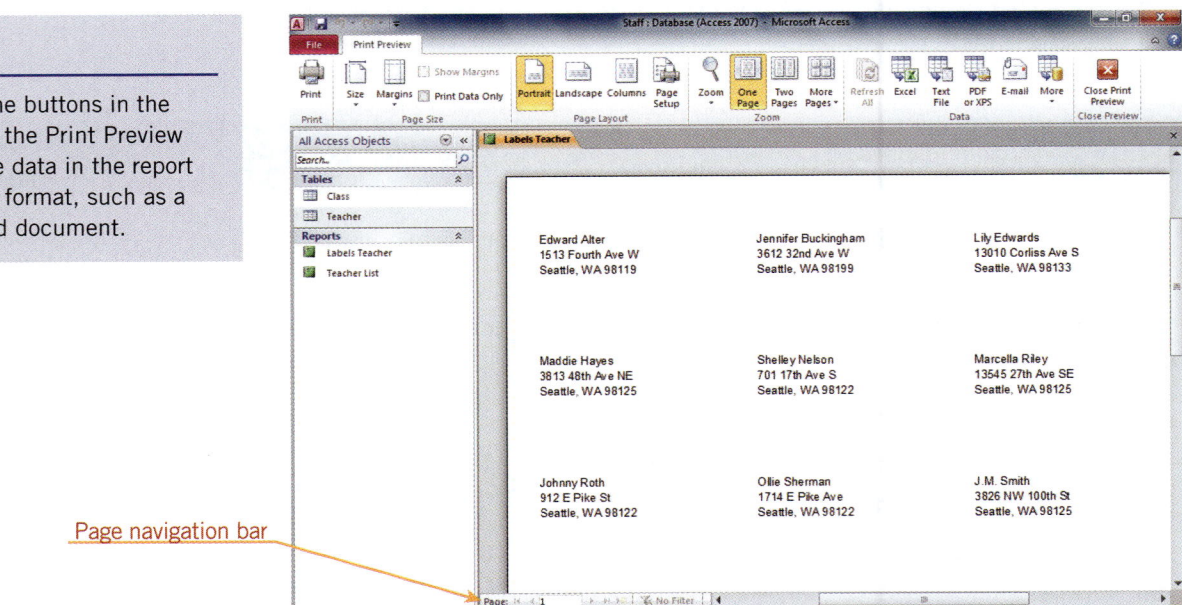

Page navigation bar

FIGURE 5–2   Report created using the Label Wizard

VOCABULARY
Print Preview

When you use a wizard to create a report, the report opens in *Print Preview*. When a report contains more than one page, you can click the buttons on the page navigation bar at the bottom of the Print Preview window to view additional pages in the report. You can also use the options on the Print Preview tab to change the page layout or zoom settings for the report.

Step-by-Step 5.2

1. In the Navigation Pane, make sure the **Teacher** table is selected.

2. On the Ribbon, click the **Create** tab. In the Reports group, click the **Labels** button. The Label Wizard starts and opens the first dialog box, in which you choose the type of label. See **Figure 5–3**.

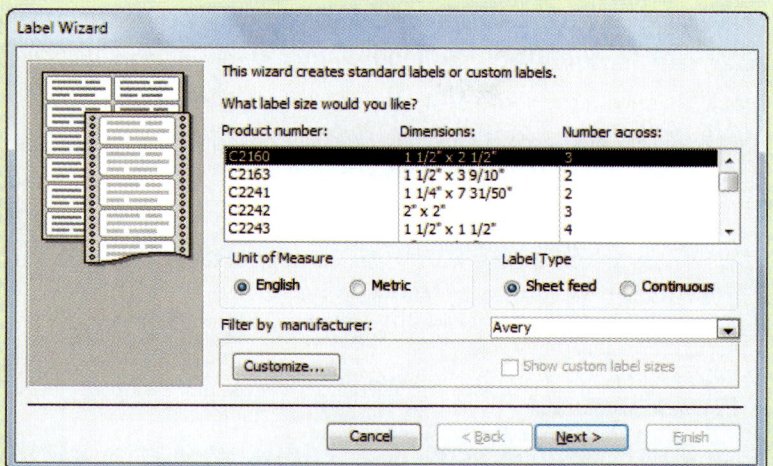

FIGURE 5–3
Using the Label Wizard to choose
a label

3. Make sure that **Avery** is selected in the Filter by manufacturer list box and
    that **C2160** is selected in the Product number column, and then click
    Next. **Figure 5–4** shows the second Label Wizard dialog box, in which you
    specify the font name, size, weight, and color that you want to use.

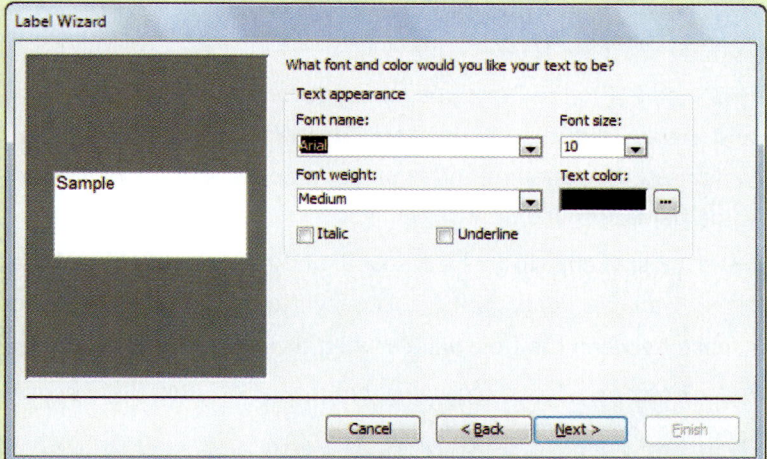

FIGURE 5–4
Using the Label Wizard to choose
the font

4. Make sure that the settings in your dialog box specify the Font name **Arial**, the Font size **10**, the Font weight **Medium**, and the Text color **black**, as shown in Figure 5–4, and then click **Next**. The third dialog box contains the Available fields list box, which contains the fields in the record source you selected. See **Figure 5–5**.

FIGURE 5–5
Using the Label Wizard to add fields to the label

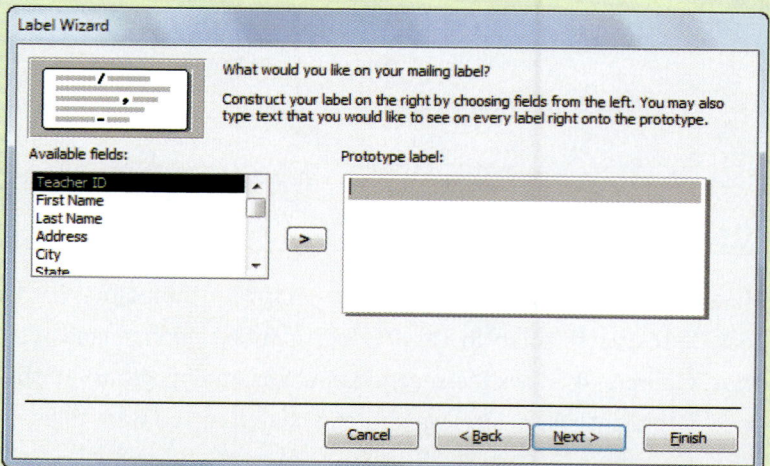

5. Double-click **First Name** in the Available fields list box. The First Name field is added to the Prototype label section. Notice that the First Name field is enclosed in curly brackets. This is how Access indicates a field name used in a label. An insertion point appears to the right of the First Name field.

6. Press the **spacebar** to insert a space, and then double-click **Last Name** in the Available fields list box. You need to press the spacebar to insert a space between the field values when they are printed on the label.

7. Press **Enter** to start a new line on the label, and then double-click **Address**.

8. Press **Enter**, double-click **City**, type a **comma**, press the **spacebar**, double-click **State**, press the **spacebar**, and then double-click **Zip**. **Figure 5–6** shows the completed prototype of the label.

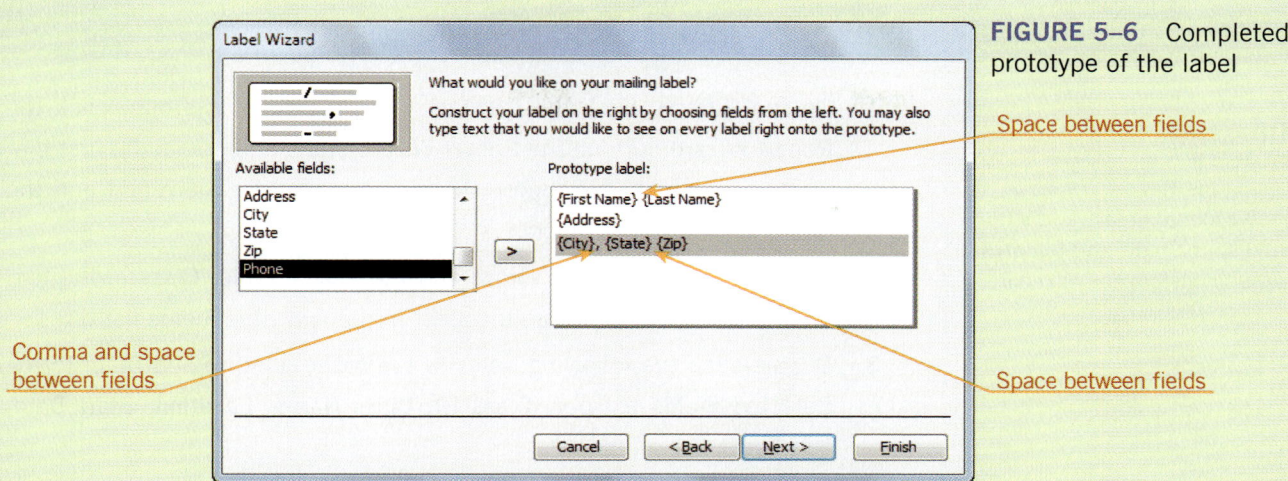

9. Make sure that your prototype label matches the one shown in Figure 5–6, and then click **Next**.

10. In the Available fields list box in the fourth dialog box, double-click **Last Name** to add it to the Sort by list box. The labels will be printed in alphabetical order based on the values in the Last Name field.

11. Click **Next**. In the final dialog box, make sure **Labels Teacher** appears in the text box and that the **See the labels as they will look printed** option button is selected, and then click **Finish**. Refer back to Figure 5–2, which shows the report in Print Preview.

12. Click the **Close 'Labels Teacher'** button ☒ to close the Labels Teacher report.

13. Close the Navigation Pane. Leave the database open for the next Step-by-Step.

Creating a Report Using the Report Wizard

When you need to create a customized report quickly, you can use the *Report Wizard*, which asks you about the report you want to create and lets you select options in dialog boxes to specify the report's record source and layout. Another option for a report is to select a grouping level. A *grouping level* organizes data based on one or more fields. For example, in a customer report, you might choose to group records using the State field so the records will be listed by the state in which customers live. You can also choose an optional sort order for the report, so records in one or more fields are sorted in ascending or descending order. The layout options for reports are Stepped, Block, and Outline, which arrange data in different ways. You can also choose the page orientation for the report (portrait or landscape). When you use the Report Wizard to create a report, Access applies the default theme for the database to the report.

▶ **VOCABULARY**
Report Wizard

grouping level

Step-by-Step 5.3

TIP

After using the Report Wizard or the Report tool to create a report, you can use the tools and features in Access to customize the report.

1. On the Ribbon, click the **Create** tab. In the Reports group, click the **Report Wizard** button. The Report Wizard starts and opens the first dialog box, in which you choose the record source for the report and the fields to print in the report.

2. Click the **Tables/Queries** arrow, and then click **Table: Class** in the list. The fields for the Class table appear in the Available Fields list box.

3. Double-click the following fields in the order listed to add them to the Selected Fields list box: **Class ID**, **Class Name**, **Location**, **Start Date**, and **Fee**.

4. Click the **Tables/Queries** arrow, and then click **Table: Teacher** in the list. The fields for the Teacher table appear in the Available Fields list box.

5. Double-click the following fields in the order listed to add them to the Selected Fields list box below the selected Fee field from the Class table: **Teacher ID**, **First Name**, and **Last Name**.

6. Click **Next**. The dialog box shown in **Figure 5–7** asks how you want to view your data. Leave the Report Wizard open for the next Step-by-Step.

FIGURE 5–7
Report Wizard dialog box that asks how you want to view your data

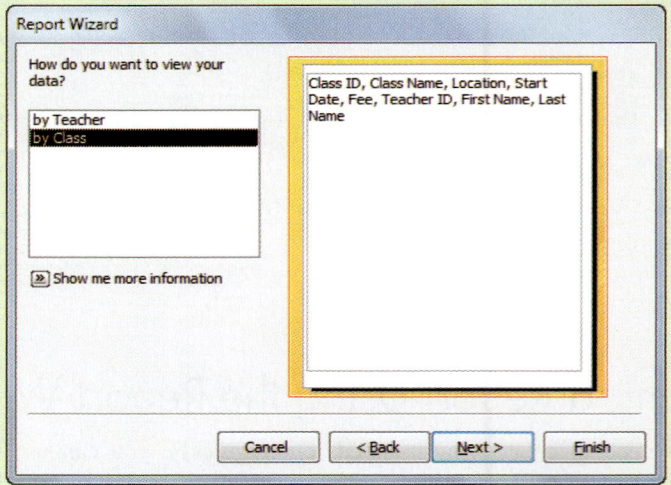

The dialog box shown in Figure 5–7 opens because you added fields from two related tables to the report's design. The sample page on the right of the dialog box illustrates how the data will be grouped in the report if it is grouped by the selected option (in this case, data is grouped by the Class table). You can also choose to group data by the Teacher table. In this case, you'll see the teacher's ID, first name, and last name and the classes each teacher has in a group. After selecting a grouping option based on a table, you can use the next dialog box to add an additional grouping level to the report by choosing a field.

Step-by-Step 5.4

1. In the dialog box, click **by Teacher**. The sample page changes to show the data grouped by teacher. See **Figure 5–8**.

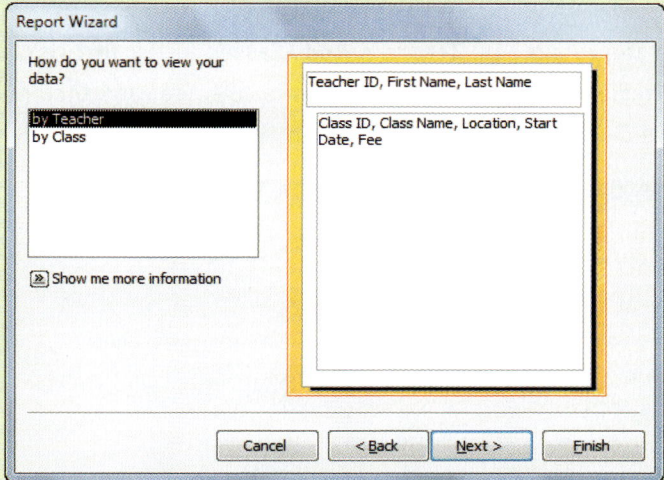

FIGURE 5–8
Report Wizard dialog box that shows data grouped by teacher

2. Click **Next**. You won't add an additional grouping level field to the report.

3. Click **Next**. A dialog box opens and asks if you want to add a sort order to the report. The default sort order, Ascending, is already set. To change to descending sort order, click the Ascending button to change it to Descending.

4. Click the **arrow** on the first text box, click **Class Name** in the list, and then click **Next**. The next dialog box requests information about the layout and page orientation that you would like to use in the report. A preview of the selected Stepped layout appears on the left side of the dialog box, as shown in **Figure 5–9**.

> **TIP**
>
> You cannot sort data in a report using a field that is already used to group records.

Sample report layout using the selected options

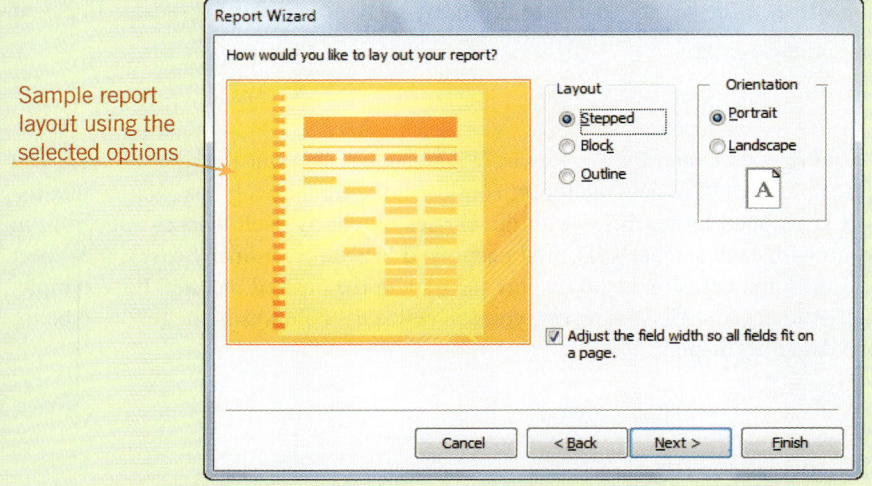

FIGURE 5–9
Report Wizard dialog box that requests page layout information

5. Click the **Block** option button to view a sample of this layout.

6. Click the **Outline** option button to view a sample of this layout.

7. Click the **Landscape** option button, click the **Block** option button, and then click **Next**. The final dialog box lets you accept the default report title or enter a new one. The report title you enter will also be the report object's name.

8. Enter the report title **Teachers And Classes** in the text box, make sure the **Preview the report** option button is selected, and then click **Finish**. **Figure 5–10** shows the report in Print Preview.

FIGURE 5–10
Report created using
the Report Wizard

Report pages
use landscape
orientation

Teacher with
four classes

Teacher with
one class

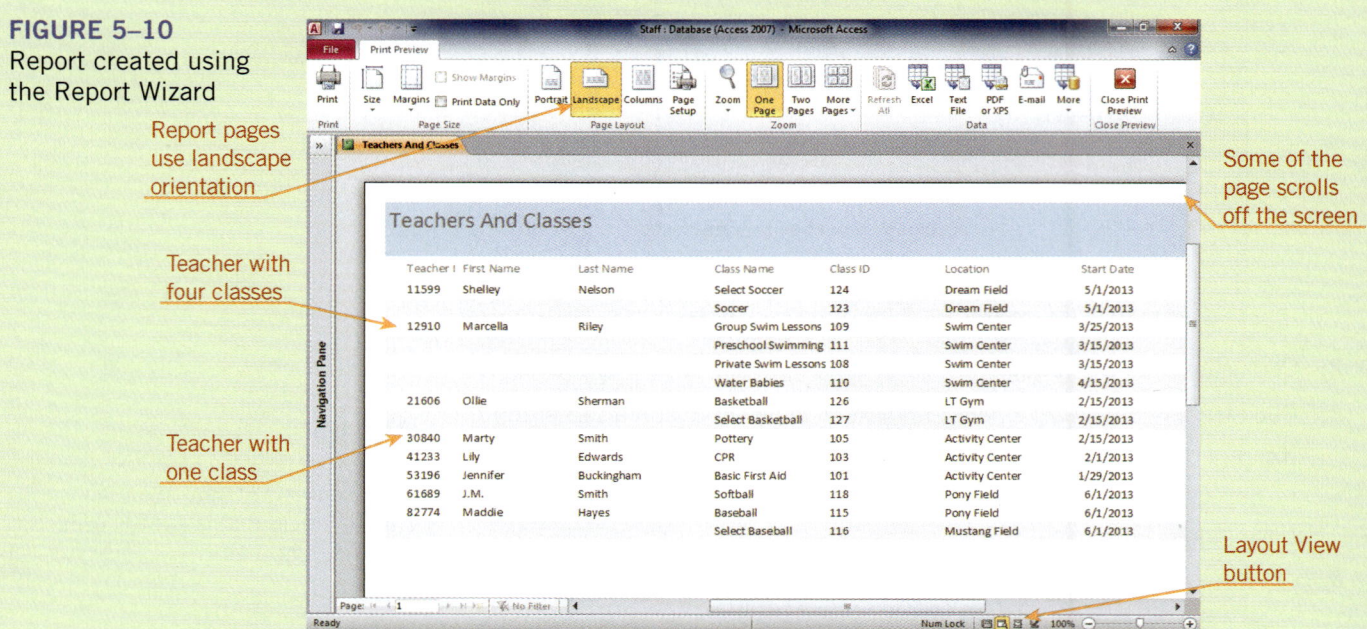

Some of the
page scrolls
off the screen

Layout View
button

9. Use the horizontal scroll bar to scroll the report so you can see the right side of the page.

10. In the Zoom group on the Print Preview tab, click the **Zoom button arrow**, and then click **Fit to Window**. Leave the report open for the next Step-by-Step.

The report created by the Report Wizard opens in Print Preview because you chose the default "Preview the report" option in the final dialog box. Notice that the report is grouped by teachers, with the classes taught by each teacher appearing in a group with each teacher's ID, first name, and last name. In many cases, the report will need some adjustments to display the data in the desired manner. For example, in the Teachers And Classes report, you can resize the columns in the report to better fit the data they display.

Modifying a Report in Layout View

Most developers use reports to provide on-screen displays or paper printouts of data in the database. An easy way to create a report is to use the Report Wizard to specify the report's record source, fields, grouping and sorting levels, layout, and name. However, if you find that the Report Wizard doesn't create the *exact* report that you need, you can use Layout view to make adjustments. When you close the report in Print Preview, Access displays the report in Design view. To change directly to Layout view, click the Layout View button on the status bar.

When the controls in a report exceed the page width that you selected for the report, you can usually resize the fields to make them fit on the page. Controls in reports are grouped in control layouts, just like they are in forms. When resizing a control in Layout view, you can use the outline of the control as you drag it with the pointer to see the actual width of the control. You can also look at the status bar to see the control's width in characters and size a control exactly.

> **EXTRA FOR EXPERTS**
>
> You can remove a control from a control layout in a report just like you can for a form. Display the report in Layout view, click the control to select it, right-click the control to open the shortcut menu, point to Layout, and then click Remove Layout.

Step-by-Step 5.5

1. On the status bar, click the **Layout View** button ⊞. The report is displayed in Layout view, as shown in **Figure 5–11**. (If the Field List pane opens when you change to Layout view, click the Add Existing Fields button in the Tools group on the Design tab to close it.)

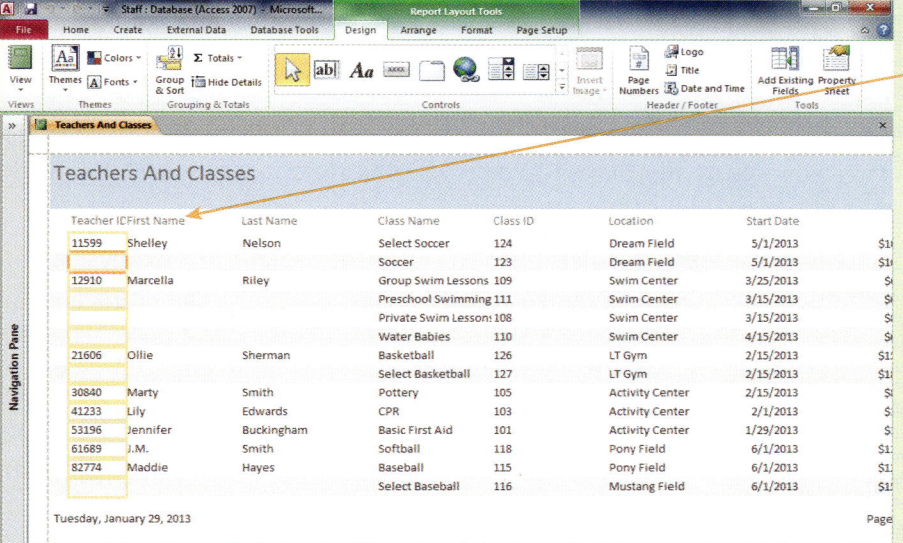

First Name label control

FIGURE 5–11
Teachers And Classes report in Layout view

2. Click the **First Name** label control (at the top of the column) to select the control, press and hold **Shift**, click the first text box control in the First Name column (which contains the field value *Shelley*) to select it, and then release **Shift**. The entire First Name column is selected, with an orange border around the label control and each text box control in the column. You'll resize this column from the left side, so the column size decreases. This will also add some space between the Teacher ID and First Name columns, so you can resize the Teacher ID column later.

3. Point to the left edge of the **First Name** label control. When the pointer changes to a ↔ shape, click and slowly drag the left edge of the **First Name** label control to the right, which decreases the size of the First Name column from the left side. When the lower-left corner of the status bar shows the width as 10 characters, release the mouse button. **Figure 5–12** shows the resized First Name column. Because the label and all of the text boxes in the column are part of a control layout, they are all resized to 10 characters wide.

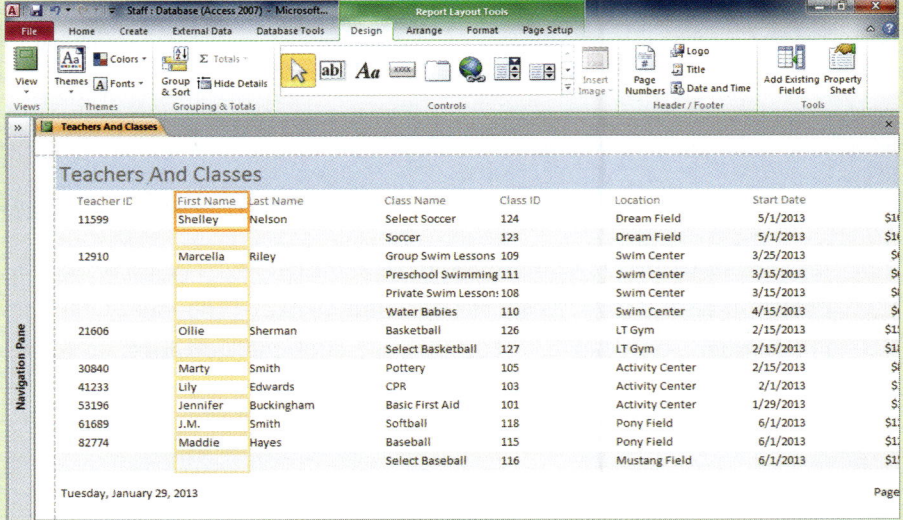

4. Use the technique described in Steps 2 and 3 to select and resize the left side of the **Class ID** column to the right to decrease its width to 8 characters.

5. Use the technique described in Step 2 to select the **Class Name** column, and then use the ↔ pointer to drag the right edge of the column to the right to increase the column width to 20 characters.

6. Use the technique described in Step 2 to select the **Teacher ID** column (the first column in the report), and then use the pointer to resize the right side of the **Teacher ID** column to the right to increase its width to 10 characters.

7. Use the horizontal scroll bar on the Report window to scroll the report to the right so you can see the Fee column, use the technique described in Step 2 to select the **Fee** column, and then use the pointer to resize the right side of the **Fee** column to the left to decrease its width to 10 characters. **Figure 5-13** shows the report with the resized columns. Leave the report open for the next Step-by-Step.

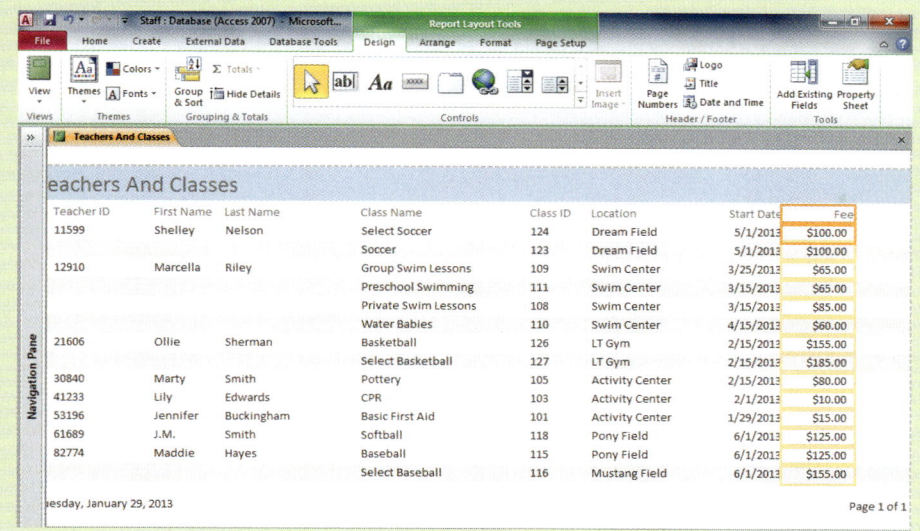

FIGURE 5–13
Report with resized columns

EXTRA FOR EXPERTS

In Layout view, you can change the font, size, style, and other attributes of the text in controls. Click a control to select it, and then use the options in the Text Formatting group on the Home tab to change the text's font, size, and style.

Modifying a Report in Design View

Similar to working with forms, there are certain types of changes for reports that you must make in Design view. When you view a report in Design view, you see the different sections of the report.

Step-by-Step 5.6

1. On the Quick Access Toolbar, click the **Save** button 🖫 to save the changes to the report.

2. On the status bar, click the **Design View** button 🖉. The report is displayed in Design view, as shown in **Figure 5–14**. Leave the report open for the next Step-by-Step.

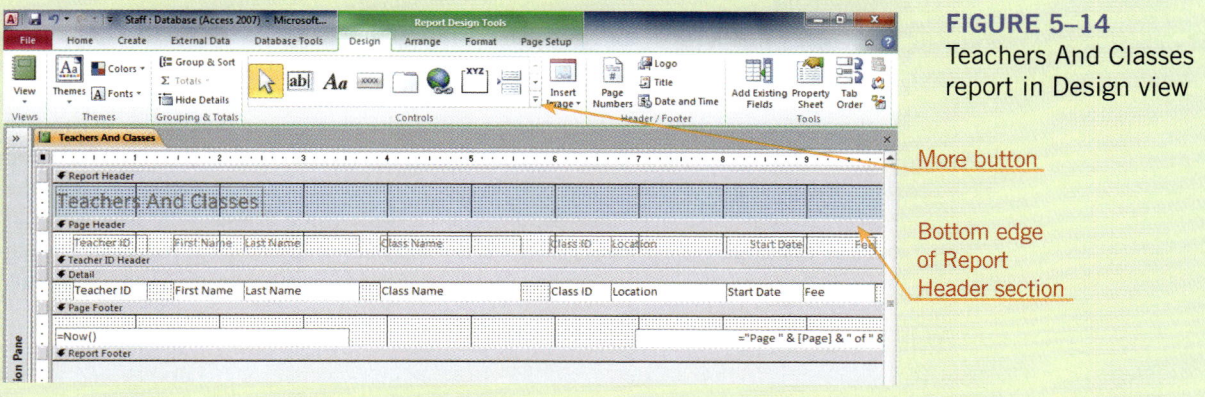

FIGURE 5–14
Teachers And Classes report in Design view

More button

Bottom edge of Report Header section

Table 5–1 identifies and describes the sections in a report. Just like in Design view for forms, you can adjust the height of a section by dragging its bottom edge up or down, and you can select a section in a report by clicking its section bar.

TABLE 5–1   Report sections

SECTION	DESCRIPTION
Report Header	This section is printed once at the top of the first page of the report, and usually includes the report title.
Page Header	Because this section is printed at the top of every page of the report, you can use it to print a title or other information that is required on every page.
Group Header	This section is printed at the beginning of each new group of records. The section name includes the field name that is used to group records.
Detail	This section is printed once for each row in the record source and contains the main body of the report.
Group Footer	This section is printed at the end of each group of records and usually includes summary options, such as totals. The section name includes the field name that is used to group records.
Page Footer	Because this section is printed at the bottom of every page of the report, you can use it to include page numbers or other information that you want to print at the bottom of every page.
Report Footer	This section is printed once at the bottom of the last page of the report, and usually includes summary information for the entire report, such as grand totals.

The Controls group on the Design tab for a report looks similar to the Controls group that you see in Design view for a form. To add a control to a report, click the button in the Controls group (or click the More button in the Controls group to display buttons not shown on the Ribbon), and then click the desired location in which to add the control in the report.

Adding a Line to a Report

The *Line tool* lets you draw a line in a report. Adding lines to a report makes it easier for users to identify the report sections and also adds visual interest. To insert a line, click the More button in the Controls group on the Design tab, and then click the Line button. Move the pointer to the report, position the plus sign in the pointer where you want the line to begin, and then click and drag the pointer to the location where you want the line to end. When you release the mouse button, the line will appear in the report. To draw a straight line, press and hold Shift while drawing the line. You can use the horizontal and vertical rulers at the top and left side of the report in Design view to help you draw a line on the report, or to position other controls on the report.

Step-by-Step 5.7

1. Point to the bottom edge of the **Report Header** section. When the pointer changes to a ✚ shape, click and drag the **Report Header** section down to the ¾-inch mark on the vertical ruler.

2. In the Controls group on the Design tab, click the **More** button ⬇ to open the Controls gallery, and then click the **Line** button (second row, third button).

3. Move the pointer to the **Report Header** section. Position the plus sign in the ⁺⤵ pointer at the ½-inch mark on the vertical ruler and in the first column of grid dots (just below the "T" in the Teachers And Classes title).

4. Press and hold **Shift**. Hold down the left mouse button, and then drag the pointer to the 9.5-inch mark on the horizontal ruler. Release the mouse button, and then release **Shift**. A line appears in the Report Header section, as shown in **Figure 5–15**.

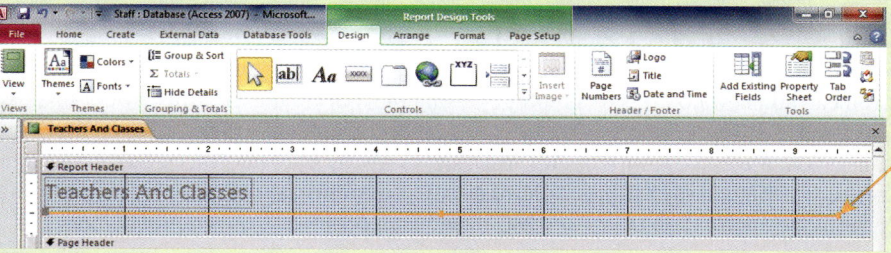

FIGURE 5–15
Line in Report Header section

Selected line control

5. On the Ribbon, click the **Format** tab.

6. In the Control Formatting group, click the **Shape Outline** button, point to **Line Thickness**, and then point to the fourth line style in the list. Notice that the ScreenTip identifies the line thickness as "3 pt," which indicates a line thickness of three points.

7. Click the line with the ScreenTip "3 pt."

TIP

To change the style of a selected line, click the Shape Outline button, point to Line Type, and then click one of the line styles.

8. Click the **Report Header** section bar to deselect the line control. **Figure 5–16** shows the line with the thickness you selected.

FIGURE 5–16
Report Header section
with line added

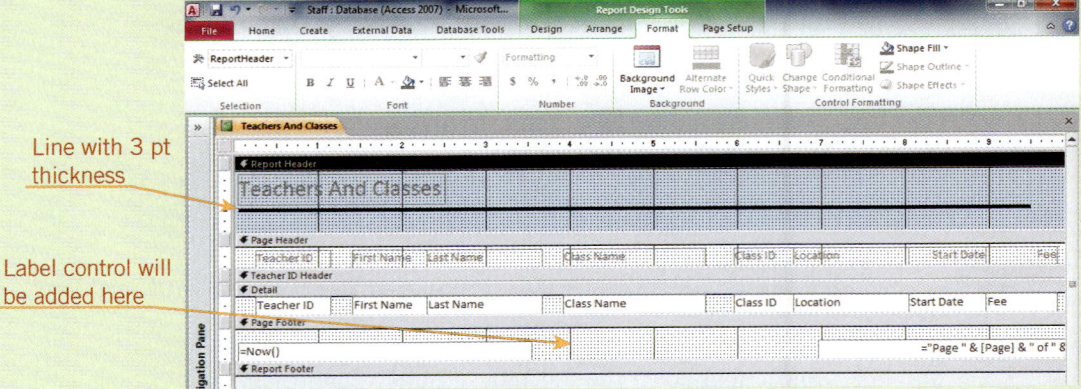

Line with 3 pt thickness

Label control will be added here

9. On the Quick Access Toolbar, click the **Save** button to save the report. Leave the report open for the next Step-by-Step.

Adding a Label Control to a Report

You can add new controls to a report by using the tools in the Controls group. Just like when used in forms, you can add text to a report by adding it in the label control. You can delete a control from a report in Design view by clicking it to select it and then pressing Delete. If the selected control is part of a control layout, you'll need to remove it from the control layout first, or you'll delete all controls in the control layout.

Step-by-Step 5.8

1. On the Ribbon, click the **Design** tab.

2. In the Controls group, click the **Label** button (third button from the left).

3. Move the pointer to the Page Footer section. Move the plus sign in the $^+$A pointer to the 4-inch mark on the horizontal ruler, in the fourth row of grid dots from the top of the Page Footer section. (Refer to Figure 5–16 for this location, if necessary.) Click to insert the label control, which is a very narrow box that contains the insertion point.

4. Type your first and last names, and then press **Enter**. The insertion point is removed from the label control, which now has an orange border to show that it's still selected.

5. On the Quick Access Toolbar, click the **Save** button to save the report.

> **TIP**
>
> Point to a button in the Controls group to display its name in a ScreenTip.

6. On the status bar, click the **Print Preview** button 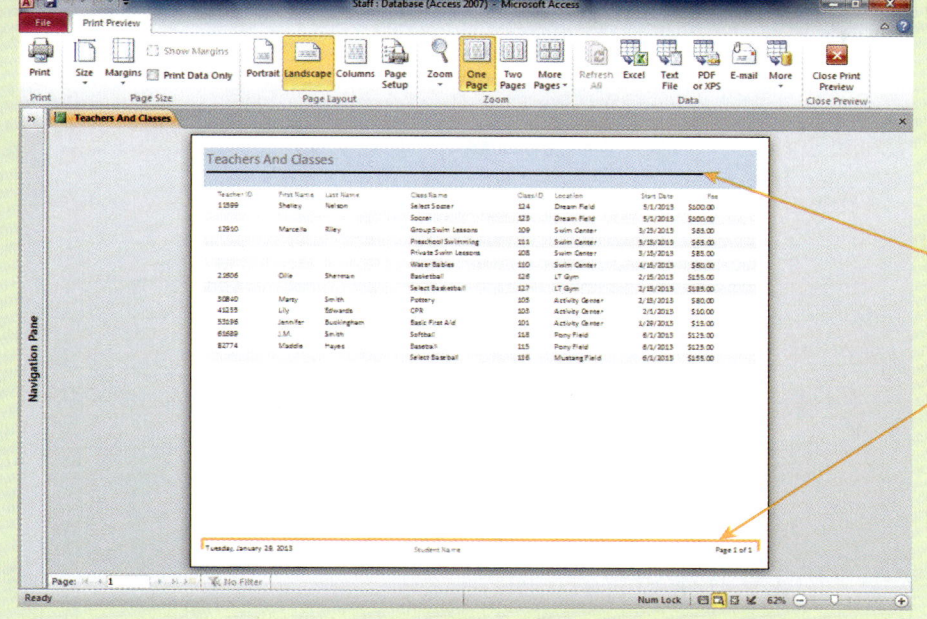. **Figure 5–17** shows the report with the line and label controls added to it. Leave the report open for the next Step-by-Step.

FIGURE 5–17
Teachers And Classes report in Print Preview

Line in Report Header section

Today's date, label with your name, and page number in Page Footer section

Moving a Control in Design View

The report's controls all fit on the page, but the control in the Page Footer section, which was added by the Report Wizard and contains the page number, is not aligned with the data on the report. You can drag a control to position it better on the page.

Step-by-Step 5.9

1. On the status bar, click the **Design View** button.
2. In the Page Footer section, click the control on the right, which contains the text that begins *="Page " &*. The control is selected when it has an orange border.
3. Point to the top edge of the selected control so the pointer changes to a ⁜ shape.

4. Drag the selected control to the left, so the left edge of the control is at the 6.25-inch mark on the horizontal ruler and the bottom edge of the control is at the bottom of the Page Footer section. **Figure 5–18** shows the new position of the control. Leave the report open for the next Step-by-Step.

FIGURE 5–18
Control in new position

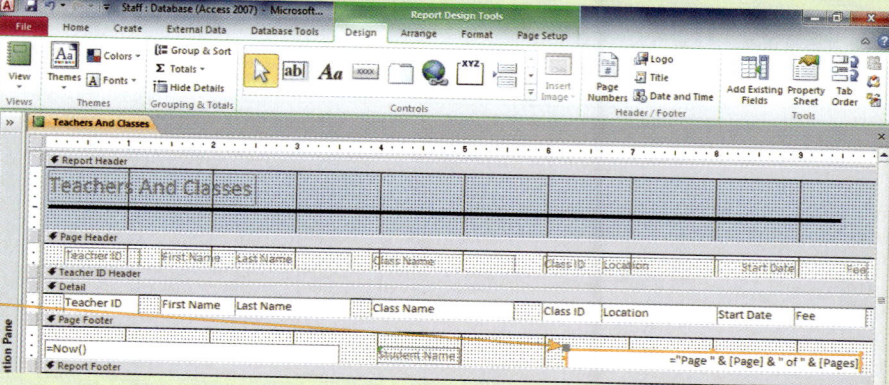

Drag control's left edge to here

Resizing a Report

When you create a report using the Report Wizard, you might need to adjust the report's width to eliminate blank pages. You know that you need to make this change when you switch to Print Preview and get an error message that tells you that your report contains blank pages or when you see blank pages in the report.

To resize a report, you can position the pointer on the report's right edge in Design view so it changes to a ✛ shape, and then click and drag the report's right edge to the left to reduce the report's width. Another way to resize a report is to use the **report selector**, which appears in the upper-left corner of the report, where the horizontal and vertical rulers intersect. When you see a small, green triangle on the report selector, clicking the report selector displays the Error Checking Options button, which you can click to open a shortcut menu with options for correcting the error. When the report contains blank pages, the shortcut menu contains options to edit the report margins, or remove extra report space. To resize the report to fit its controls, click the Remove Extra Report Space option.

The controls for the Fee field are just past the 9.5-inch mark on the horizontal ruler. To practice resizing the report, you'll use the pointer to increase the report's width, and then you'll use the report selector and the Error Checking Options button to resize the report to fit the controls it contains.

▶ **VOCABULARY**
report selector

Step-by-Step 5.10

1. Use the horizontal scroll bar to scroll the report to the right, so you can see the right edge of the report and the 13-inch mark on the horizontal ruler.

2. Point to the right edge of the report so the pointer changes to a ✛ shape, and then click and drag the report's right edge to the right. When the report's edge is at the 13-inch mark on the horizontal ruler, release

the mouse button. The report is resized to 13 inches wide. Notice that the report selector now displays a small, green triangle, indicating that the report contains an error. See **Figure 5-19**. (If you do not see the green triangle, follow the instructions in the Tip box on this page.)

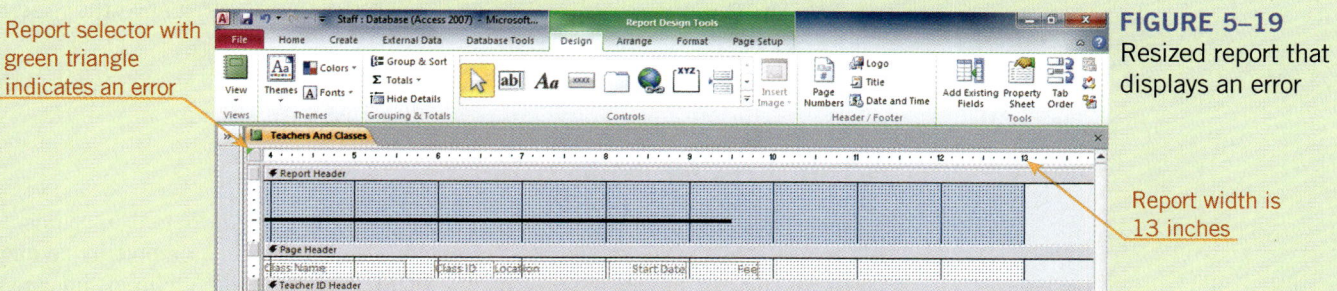

Report selector with green triangle indicates an error

FIGURE 5–19
Resized report that displays an error

Report width is 13 inches

3. On the status bar, click the **Print Preview** button 🔍. A dialog box opens and indicates that some pages may be blank.

4. Click **OK**. The dialog box closes, and the report appears in Print Preview. Notice that the Next Page button on the page navigation bar is active, indicating that the report contains one or more additional pages.

5. On the page navigation bar, click the **Next Page** button ▶. The second page of the report is blank, except for the default colors used in the report.

6. On the status bar, click the **Design View** button 📐 to display the report in Design view.

7. Click the **report selector**. The Error Checking Options button ◈ appears below the report selector.

8. Click the **Error Checking Options** button ◈. **Figure 5–20** shows the shortcut menu that opens after you click the button.

TIP

If you do not see the green triangle shown in Figure 5-19, save and close the report, click the File tab on the Ribbon, click Options in the navigation bar, click Object Designers, scroll down the page, click the Enable error checking check box, click OK, open the report in Design view, and close the Navigation Pane.

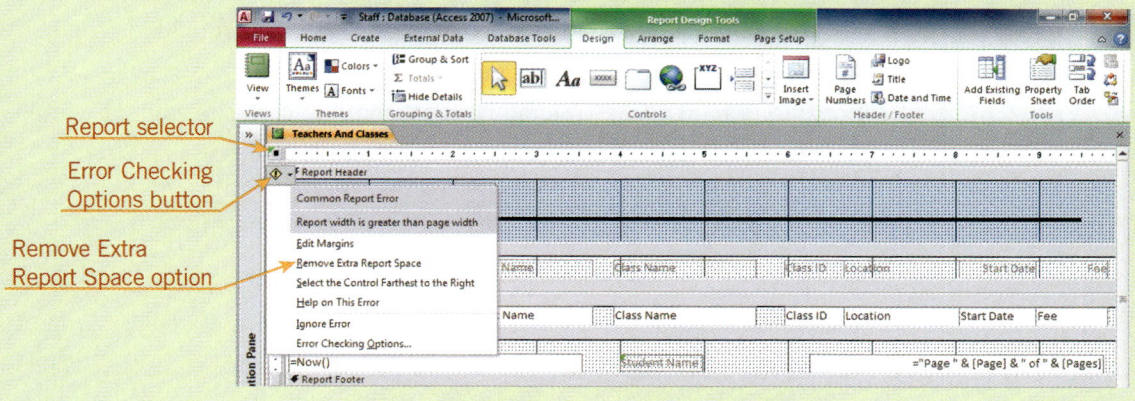

Report selector

Error Checking Options button

Remove Extra Report Space option

FIGURE 5–20
Error Checking Options shortcut menu

9. On the shortcut menu, click **Remove Extra Report Space**. The report's width is reduced to fit the controls it contains. You can see the right edge of the report now, just to the right of the controls at or around the 9.75-inch mark on the horizontal ruler.

10. On the Quick Access Toolbar, click the **Save** button 💾. Leave the report open for the next Step-by-Step.

Adding a Picture to a Report

Reports are usually printed or viewed on the screen. Although the default appearance of a report is adequate, sometimes you might want to enhance a report by adding a picture. You can add any type of picture to a report, including a clip-art image, a graphic that you create using another program, or a digital image. To add a picture to a report, click the Insert Image button in the Controls group on the Design tab, and then click Browse. In the Insert Picture dialog box, browse to and select the file that contains the picture you want to insert in the report. After selecting the file, click OK. The pointer changes shape when you move it over the report. Click the plus sign in the pointer in the upper-left corner where you want to insert the picture. An image control is added to the report. You can use the sizing handles on the selected image control to resize the picture to the desired size and shape. You can also drag the selected image control to reposition it in the report.

Step-by-Step 5.11

1. In the Controls group on the Design tab, click the **Insert Image** button, and then click **Browse**. The Insert Picture dialog box opens.

2. Browse to the **Access Lesson 05** folder with your Data Files.

3. Click the **Teacher.gif** file to select it, and then click **OK**. The Insert Picture dialog box closes.

4. Position the plus sign in the ⁺🖼 pointer at the 4-inch mark on the horizontal ruler and one row of grid dots below the Report Header section bar, and then click. An image control containing the Teacher.gif picture is inserted in the report, as shown in **Figure 5–21**.

FIGURE 5–21
Image control
added to report

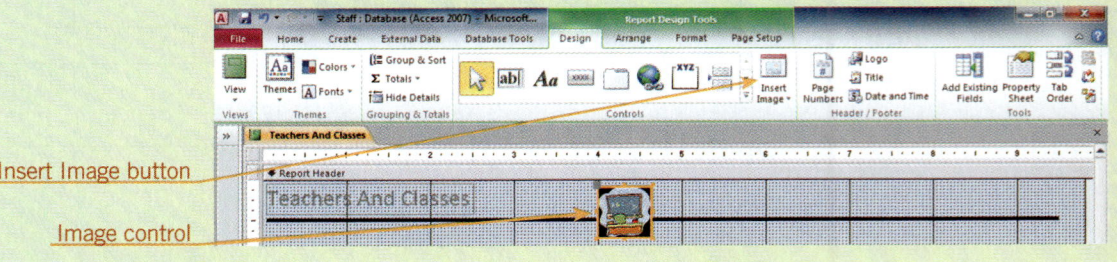

Insert Image button

Image control

5. Drag the selected image control to the right in the Report Header section so that the right edge of the image control is at the right edge of the report. There should be one row of grid dots above the picture. **Figure 5–22** shows the image control in the new location.

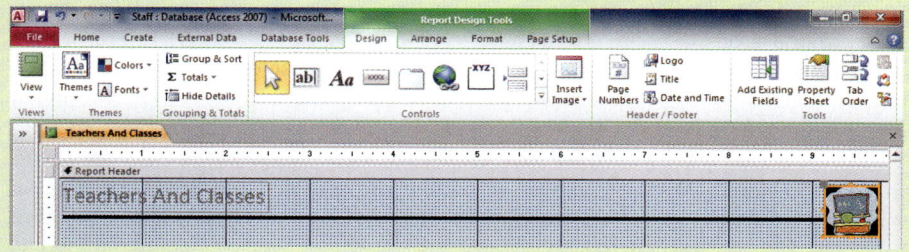

FIGURE 5–22
Image control moved to new location

6. On the Quick Access Toolbar, click the **Save** button.

7. On the status bar, click the **Print Preview** button. **Figure 5–23** shows the completed report.

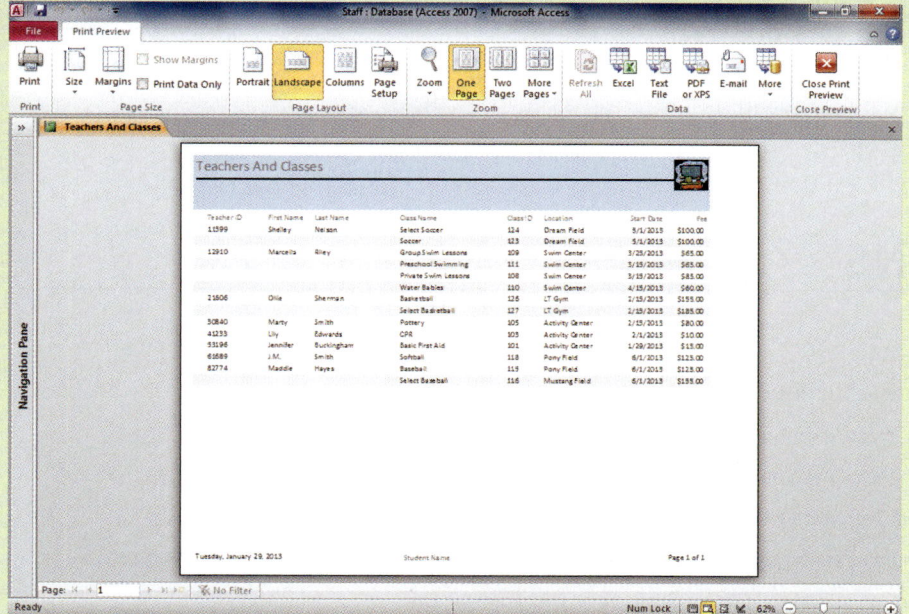

FIGURE 5–23
Completed report in Print Preview

8. In the Close Preview group on the Print Preview tab, click the **Close Print Preview** button.

9. Close the Teachers And Classes report.

10. Click the **Close** button on the Access title bar to exit Access.

SUMMARY

In this lesson, you learned:

- A report is a database object that displays data from one or more tables or queries in a format that has an appearance similar to a printed report. You can use the Report tool or the Report Wizard to create a report. You can also use the Label Wizard to create a report that is used to print labels.

- When used in a report, a field that is used as a grouping level organizes data into groups. You can also choose to sort data within the groups based on a field.

- When working in Layout view, you can resize the controls in a control layout by selecting the control and dragging its edge to increase or decrease its width.

- You can use Design view to change the height of a report section. You can also add a line, label, or picture to a report. You can change the location of a control in a report by dragging it to a new location.

- When a report contains blank pages, drag the right edge of the report to resize the report, or click the report selector to select the report, click the Error Checking Options button, and then click the Remove Extra Report Space option on the shortcut menu to resize the report.

VOCABULARY REVIEW

Define the following terms:

grouping level	Print Preview	report selector
Label Wizard	read-only	Report tool
Line tool	report	Report Wizard

REVIEW QUESTIONS

TRUE / FALSE

Circle T if the statement is true or F if the statement is false.

T   F   1.   When you use the Report tool to create a report, you can base it on two or more tables.

T   F   2.   When a report is displayed in Layout view, you can use it to change the data the report contains.

T   F   3.   When you use the Report Wizard to create a report, you can base it on one or more tables.

T   F   4.   If you want to print something only at the bottom of the last page of a report, add the content in the Page Footer section.

T   F   5.   To draw a straight line in a report, press and hold down Shift while you draw the line.

WRITTEN QUESTIONS

Write a brief answer to each of the following questions.

1. List the steps for using the Report tool to create a report based on a table.

2. List the steps for using the Label Wizard to create a report based on a table.

3. What information might you include in the Report Header section of a report?

4. How do you use the report selector to resize a report that contains one or more blank pages when the report selector contains a small, green triangle on it?

5. Which button in the Controls group on the Design tab do you use to add a picture to a report?

FILL IN THE BLANK

Complete the following sentences by writing the correct word or words in the blanks provided.

1. The _____ creates a simple report that includes all the fields in the selected table or query, uses a simple columnar format, formats every other row in the report with a gray color, and includes a title with the same name as the record source.

2. The _____ creates a report that you can use to print standard or custom labels.

3. The data in a report is _____, which means that you can view it but you cannot change it.

4. A(n) _____ organizes data in a report based on one or more fields.

5. The _____ section is printed once at the bottom of the last page of the report, and usually includes summary information for the entire report, such as grand totals.

■ PROJECTS

If you have a SAM 2010 user profile, your instructor may have assigned an autogradable version of the indicated project. If so, log into the SAM 2010 Web site at *www.cengage.com/sam2010* to download the instruction and start files.

PROJECT 5–1

1. Open the **Sales.accdb** database from the Access Lesson 05 folder with your Data Files.

2. Use the Report tool to create a report based on the Brokers table.

3. In Layout view, resize each column so that it is just wide enough to display the longest value in the column.

4. In Design view, add a label control at the top of the Report Footer section and at the 4-inch mark on the horizontal ruler. Type your first and last names in the label control.

5. Use the report selector and the Error Checking Options button to resize the report to remove extra report space.

6. Save the report using the name **Brokers**.

7. Display the report in Print Preview. Change the page orientation to landscape. Make sure that the report is displayed on a single page. If necessary, display the report in Layout view or Design view and make any required adjustments. Save the report, and then close it.

8. Use the Report tool to create a report based on the Listings table.

9. In Layout view, resize each column so that each column is just wide enough to display the longest value in the column.

10. In Design view, add a label control at the top of the Report Footer section and at the 1-inch mark on the horizontal ruler. Type your first and last names in the label control.

11. Use the report selector and the Error Checking Options button to resize the report to remove extra report space.

12. Save the report using the name **Listings**.

13. Display the report in Print Preview, change to landscape orientation, and make sure that it is displayed on a single page. If necessary, display the report in Layout view or Design view and make any required adjustments. Save the report if you make any changes, and then close it.

14. Close the database and exit Access.

SAM PROJECT 5–2

1. Open the **Supplies.accdb** database from the Access Lesson 05 folder with your Data Files.

2. Use the Report tool to create a report based on the Products table.

3. In Layout view, resize each column so that each column is just wide enough to display the longest value in the column. Scroll down the page and check to be sure that all values in each column are displayed.

4. In Design view, add a label control at the top of the Report Footer section and at the 1-inch mark on the horizontal ruler. Type your first and last names in the label control.

5. Click the control in the Report Footer section that displays a sum of the values in the Retail Price field and remove it from the control layout.

6. Press Delete to delete the control in the Report Footer section that displays a sum of the values in the Retail Price field.

7. Delete the image control to the left of the Products title.

8. Insert the **Office.gif** file as a picture in the Report Footer section of the report, so the upper-left corner of the picture is at the 6-inch mark on the horizontal ruler and at the top of the Report Footer section.

9. Use the pointer to resize the report so its right edge is aligned with the controls that display the date and time in the Report Header section.

10. Save the report using the name **Products**.

11. Preview the report. If necessary, display the report in Layout view or Design view and make any required adjustments. Save the report, and then print it.

12. Close the database, and then exit Access.

PROJECT 5–3

1. Open the **Agencies.accdb** database from the Access Lesson 05 folder with your Data Files.

2. Use the Report Wizard to create a new report based on the Brokers and Listings tables.

3. Add the following fields from the Brokers table to the report in the order listed: Affiliation, Broker ID, First Name, Last Name, Office Phone, and Cell Phone.

4. Add the following fields from the Listings table to the report in the order listed: Price, Address, and Date Listed.

5. View the data by brokers.

6. Use the Affiliation field as a grouping level. (Click the Affiliation field, and then click the ⟩ button.)

7. Sort the data in ascending order by Price.

8. Choose the Stepped layout and the Landscape orientation.

9. Use the report title **Brokers And Listings** and choose the option to preview it.

10. In Layout view, resize each column so that the column is just wide enough to display the longest value in the column. (*Hint*: You might need to resize some columns from the left and others from the right. Resize the columns so they are closer together by first resizing columns that are far apart from the left, and then from the right.)

11. Change to Print Preview and make sure that all the data in the main body of the report fits on one page. If necessary, return to Layout view and continue resizing the columns.

12. Add a label control anywhere in the Report Header section that contains your first and last names. Press Enter after typing your name, and then move the label control so its right edge is aligned at the 10-inch mark on the horizontal ruler and at the top of the Report Header section.

13. Save and preview the report.

14. Close the report, close the database, and exit Access.

■ CRITICAL THINKING

ACTIVITY 5–1

Open the **Sales.accdb** database from the Access Lesson 05 folder with your Data Files. Open the Brokers report that you created in Project 5-1 in Print Preview. Why does the label control that contains your name print above the page number? What change would you need to make to print your name below the page number? Write your answer on a sheet of paper. Your answer should be specific to the Brokers report. Close the report, close the database, and exit Access.

ACTIVITY 5–2

Open the **Sales.accdb** database from the Access Lesson 05 folder with your Data Files. Open the Listings report that you created in Project 5-1 in Print Preview. A line and a number appear at the bottom of the Price column. What does the number represent? What do you call this? What was used to create this number? You used the Report tool to create the Listings report. Why do you think that the Report tool added this number to the report? Write your answer on a sheet of paper. Your answer should be specific to the Listings report. Close the report, close the database, and exit Access.

ACTIVITY 5–3

In this lesson, you learned how to use the Label Wizard to create labels that you might use to address envelopes or packages. What other uses can you think of for creating labels from a database? On a sheet of paper, give one example of the kind of labels that you might need and how you would use Access to create a record source and print the labels.

LESSON 6

Integrating Access

■ OBJECTIVES

Upon completion of this lesson, you should be able to:

- Import data from other programs into an Access database.
- Export data from an Access database to other programs.
- Prepare a form letter for merging with a data source.
- Merge a form letter with a data source.
- Edit a data source to print specific form letters.

■ VOCABULARY

comma-separated values (CSV)

data source

delimited data

delimiter

export

form letter

import

main document

merge field

In this lesson, you will learn how to use Access to import and export data from other programs and to create form letters.

Importing and Exporting Data

Sometimes you might find that you need to use the data stored in an Access database in another program. For example, a friend or coworker who does not have Access might request information from you. You can share the information with them by saving it in another file format. When you save data in another file format, you *export* the data from the database. You can export data to many other formats, including a Word document, an Excel workbook, or a text file. Access also exports data to another Access database, another database format, or an HTML document (which creates a Web page).

> **VOCABULARY**
>
> **export**
>
> **import**

You might also find yourself in a situation where you need to add data stored in a different format to an Access database. Instead of entering the records one at a time, you can *import* the data into the database. When you import data, you copy it from another Access database, an Excel workbook, a text file, or another compatible file format into an existing or new table in the current database. Importing saves you time and effort by adding records to a new or existing table automatically. Fortunately, Access includes features that make it easy to import and export data to and from a database.

Importing and Exporting Documents

When you need to export data from a database table to a Word document, select the table in the Navigation Pane, click the External Data tab on the Ribbon, click the More button in the Export group, and then click Word. When you export the data, it will be saved as an RTF file, which stands for Rich Text Format. Most word processors, including Word, can open files with the .rtf file extension.

Step-by-Step 6.1

1. Open the **School.accdb** database from the Access Lesson 06 folder where your Data Files are stored.

2. If the Security Warning opens, click the **Enable Content** button.

3. Click the **Student** table in the Navigation Pane to select it. On the Ribbon, click the **External Data** tab.

4. In the Export group, click the **More** button, and then click **Word**. The Export – RTF File dialog box opens, as shown in **Figure 6–1**.

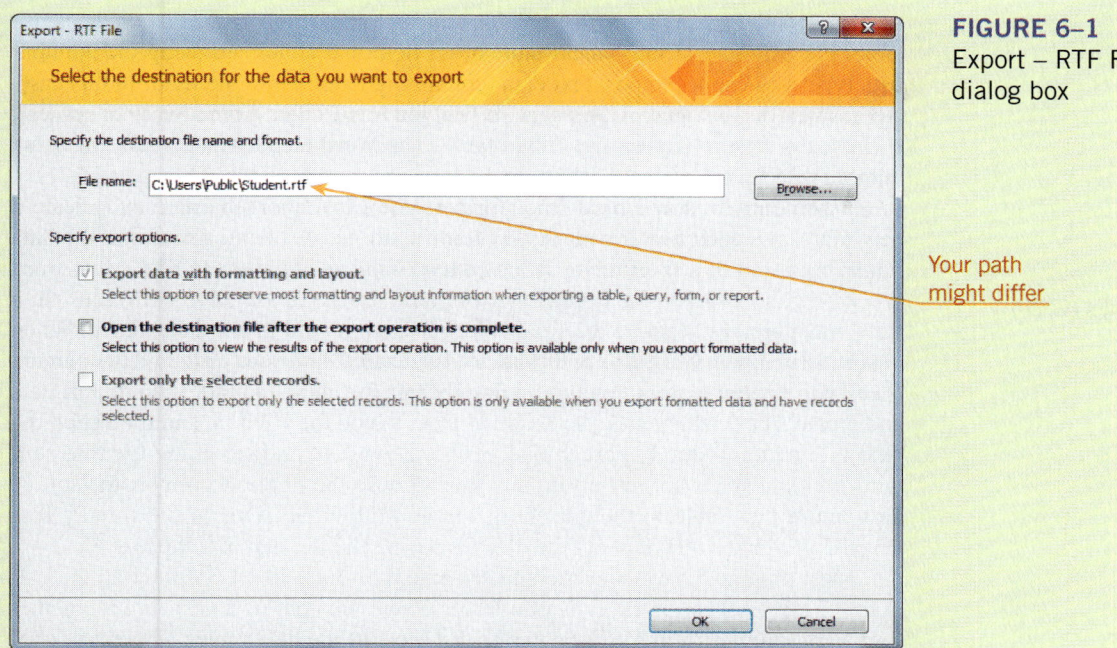

FIGURE 6–1
Export – RTF File
dialog box

Your path
might differ

5. Click **Browse** and navigate to the drive and folder where your Data Files are stored, open the **Access Lesson 06** folder, and then click **Save** in the File Save dialog box to close it.

6. Click the **Open the destination file after the export operation is complete** check box to add a check mark to it.

7. Click **OK** to export the data. Word starts and opens the Student.rtf file that you created. The data appears in a table format when viewed in Word. See **Figure 6–2**.

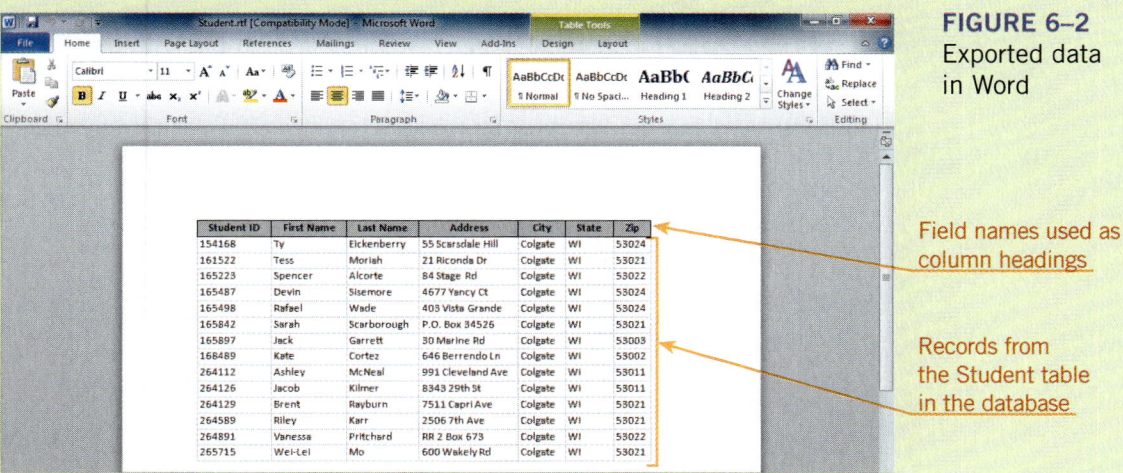

FIGURE 6–2
Exported data
in Word

Field names used as
column headings

Records from
the Student table
in the database

8. Click the **Close** button [X] on the Word title bar to close Word.

9. Click **Close** to close the Export – RTF File dialog box. (You do not need to save the export steps.) Leave the database open for the next Step-by-Step.

You can import data from a Word document into an existing database table when the data has the same number of columns and the same *type* of data as the database table. For example, if the Access table has a field that is defined using the Number data type, you cannot import text data (containing letters) into the field. In this case, Access will display an error message. When you import data from a Word document, it is usually best to store it in a Word table. The Word table must contain the same number of columns as the database table.

When data is stored in another format, you can import the data and create a new table in a database in one step. When importing data from a text file, the data might be stored in a file format called ***comma-separated values (CSV)***. Most word processing, spreadsheet, and database programs can read and save CSV files. In a CSV file, commas separate the field values in each record in the data source. When data is formatted using comma separators, it is called ***delimited data*** and the comma is called a ***delimiter***. A paragraph mark indicates the end of a record. To import data and create a new table, click the External Data tab on the Ribbon, and then click the Text File button in the Import & Link group. Browse to and select the file that contains the data you want to import, and then choose the option to import the source data into a new table in the current database. Follow the steps in the Import Text Wizard to create a new table in the database using the file name of the text file.

Most programs have converters to separate the values in a CSV file into the columns of a worksheet or the cells of a table. When you convert a CSV file to another format, the program removes the commas that separate the field values. If there are quotation marks around text values in a text file, the conversion process also removes them.

▶ **VOCABULARY**
comma-separated values (CSV)
delimited data
delimiter

Step-by-Step 6.2

1. In the Import & Link group on the External Data tab, click the **Text File** button. The Get External Data – Text File dialog box opens, as shown in **Figure 6–3**.

FIGURE 6–3
Get External Data – Text File dialog box

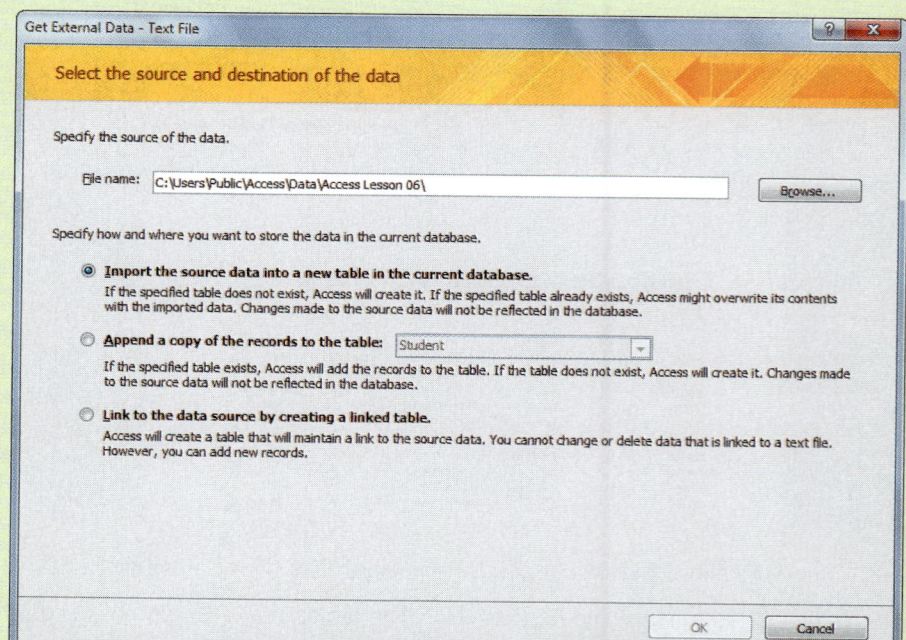

2. Click **Browse**. If necessary, navigate to and open the **Access Lesson 06** folder, click **Student.txt** to select it in the File Open dialog box, and then click **Open**.

3. Make sure that the **Import the source data into a new table in the current database** option button is selected, and then click **OK**. The Import Text Wizard starts and opens the first dialog box, as shown in **Figure 6–4**.

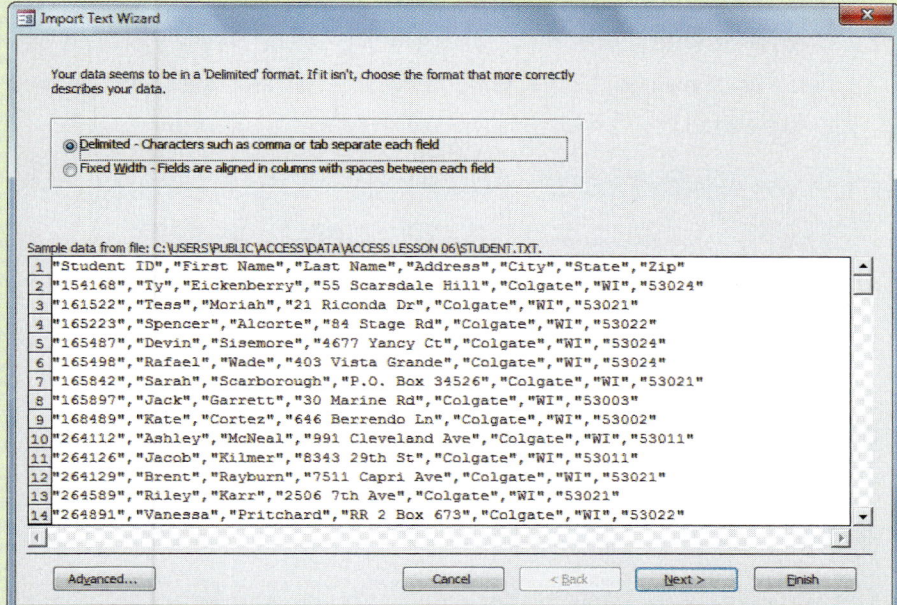

FIGURE 6–4
First Import Text Wizard
dialog box

4. Make sure that the **Delimited** option button is selected, and then click **Next**. The second dialog box requests information about the delimiter that separates the fields in the data source, as shown in **Figure 6–5**.

Click this check box to use the values in the first row as field names

First row of text file contains field names

Each row will become one record

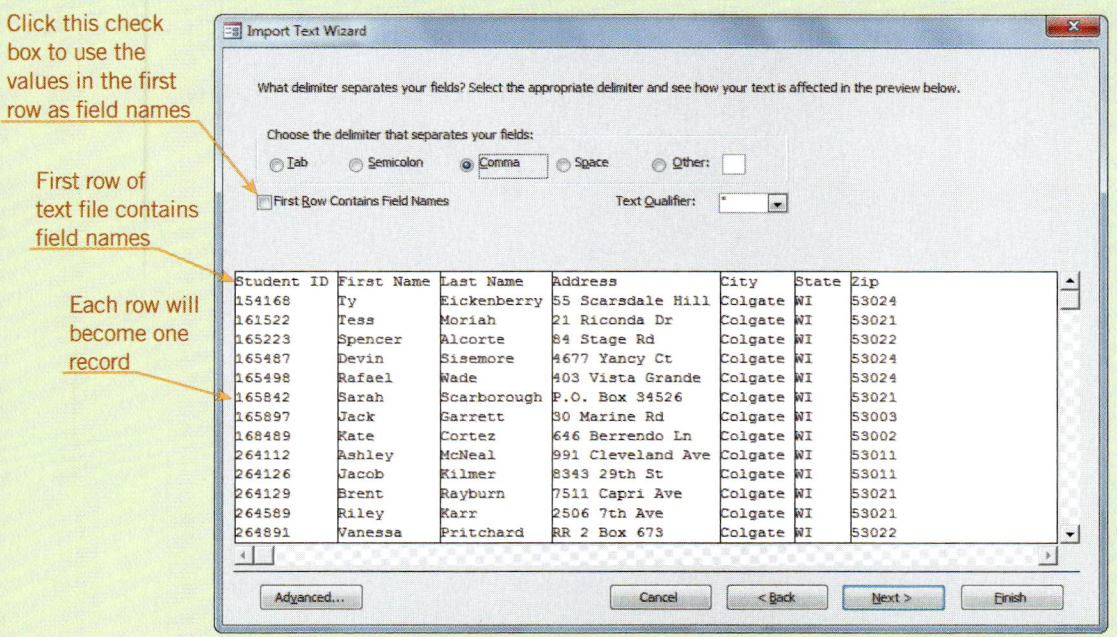

FIGURE 6–5
Second Import
Text Wizard
dialog box

5. Make sure that the **Comma** option button is selected, and then click the **First Row Contains Field Names** check box to add a check mark to it. If you don't identify the first row as containing field names, the field names will be added in a record, instead of as field names.

6. Click **Next**. The third dialog box asks you about the data types you want to use for each field. If you do not choose any data types for the fields, Access assigns the Text data type to each field.

7. Click **Next**. The fourth dialog box lets you set or create a primary key field, as shown in **Figure 6–6**. Leave the Wizard open for the next Step-by-Step.

FIGURE 6–6
Fourth Import Text Wizard dialog box

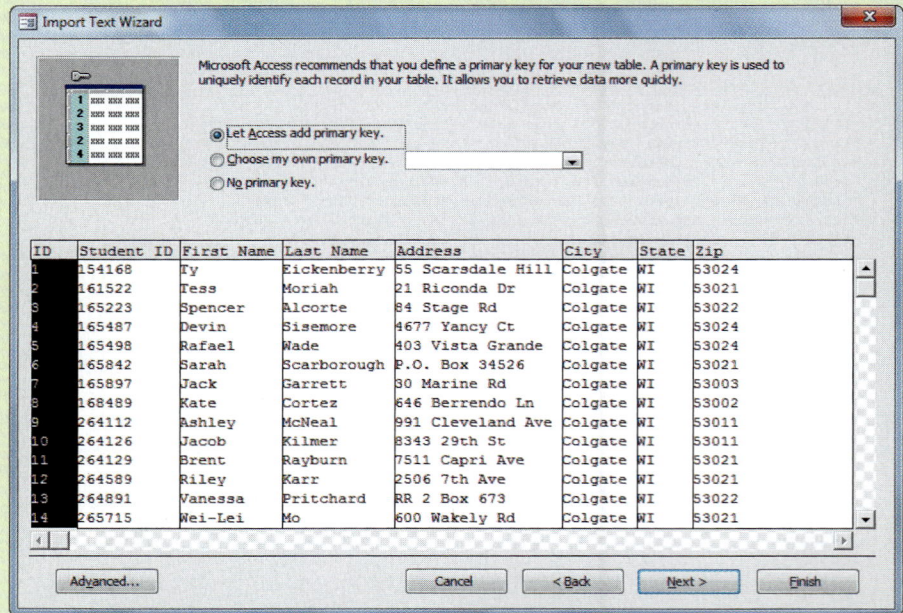

Recall that the primary key field stores unique values for each record in a table. The Student ID field already contains unique field values, so you can use the arrow on the list box to the right of the "Choose my own primary key" option button to select the Student ID field as the table's primary key. You can also choose not to set a primary key, or you can let Access create a primary key. If you select the option for Access to create a primary key, Access creates a field named ID at the beginning of the table and assigns it the AutoNumber data type.

Step-by-Step 6.3

1. Click the **Choose my own primary key** option button. Because the Student ID field is the first field in the table, it is selected automatically in the list box.

2. Click **Next**. The final dialog box asks you for a table name.

3. In the Import to Table text box, type **Student Word**, and then click **Finish**.

4. Click **Close** in the Get External Data – Text File dialog box to close it. (Do not save the import steps.)

5. In the Navigation Pane, double-click **Student Word** to open the table. Leave the Student Word table open for the next Step-by-Step.

The table contains the imported data. The field names are from the first row of the text file because you chose the option to use the values in the first row as the field names. All the fields in the table have the Text data type because you didn't set them to other data types using the Import Text Wizard. The Text fields have the default properties as well, which includes a default Field Size property of 255 characters. If you need to customize this table, you could change to Design view and reevaluate the data types and field properties for each field so they use the settings you need.

Importing and Exporting Workbooks

When you need to export data from a database table to an Excel workbook, click the External Data tab on the Ribbon, and then click the Excel button in the Export group. When you export the data, it will be saved in Excel format, with each field in the table stored in a worksheet column and each record in the table stored as a row in the worksheet.

 EXTRA FOR EXPERTS

You can export data from a database to a specific version of Excel by selecting a different file format in the Export – Excel Spreadsheet dialog box. The default file format is Excel Workbook (*.xlsx).

Step-by-Step 6.4

1. In the Export group on the External Data tab, click the **Excel** button. The Export – Excel Spreadsheet dialog box opens, as shown in **Figure 6–7**.

FIGURE 6–7
Export – Excel Spreadsheet
dialog box

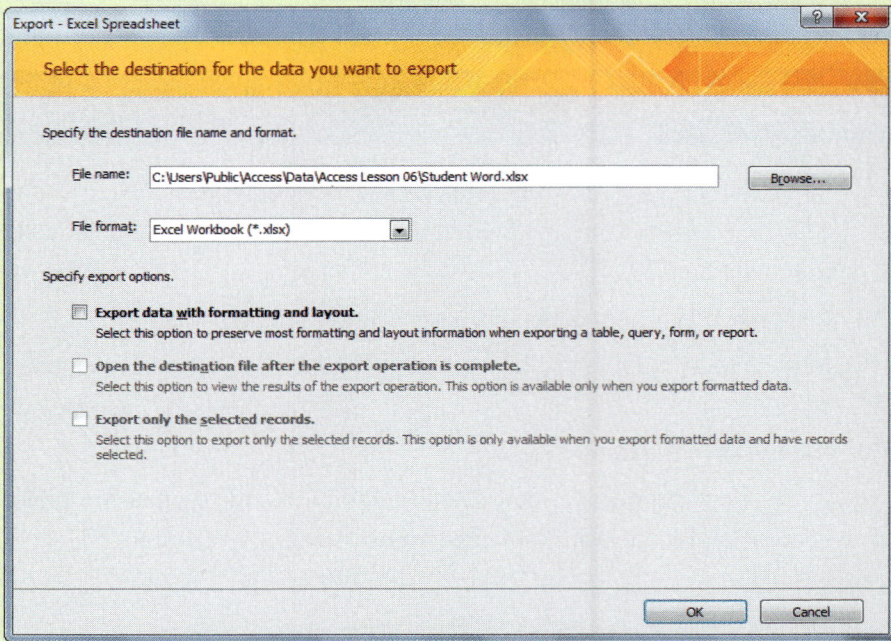

2. If the path to the Access Lesson 06 folder with your Data Files does not appear in the File name text box, click **Browse**, navigate to and open the **Access Lesson 06** folder, and then click **Save** in the File Save dialog box.

3. Click the **Export data with formatting and layout** check box to add a check mark to it.

4. Click the **Open the destination file after the export operation is complete** check box to add a check mark to it.

5. Click **OK**. Excel starts and opens the file that contains the data you exported. See **Figure 6–8**.

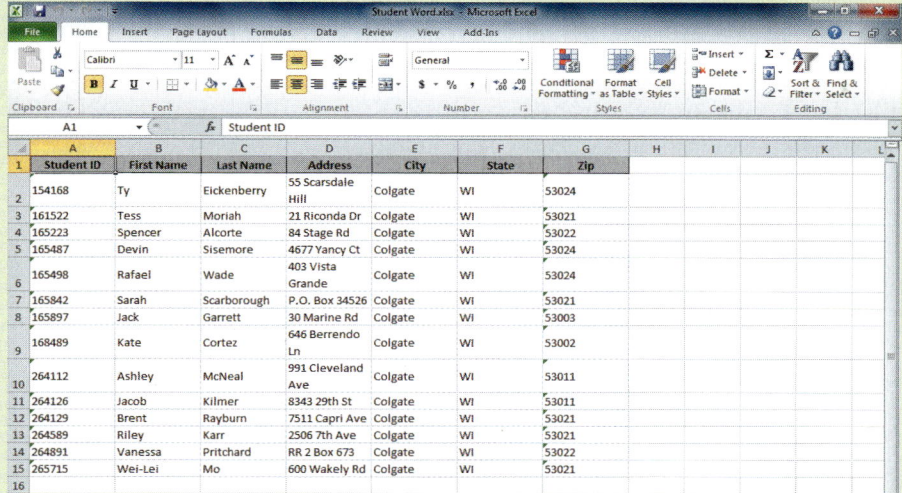

FIGURE 6–8
Excel worksheet with the exported data

6. Click the **Close** button ![X] on the Excel title bar to close Excel.

7. Click **Close** to close the Export – Excel Spreadsheet dialog box. (Do not save the export steps.)

8. Click the **Close 'Student Word'** button ![X] to close the Student Word table. Leave the database open for the next Step-by-Step.

You can also import data stored in a workbook into a new or existing database table. When you use the data in a workbook to add records to a database table, the columns in the worksheet must be the same as the fields in the database and contain the same type of data. When you need to create a new table using the data in a workbook, the Import Spreadsheet Wizard guides you through the process.

Step-by-Step 6.5

1. In the Import & Link group on the External Data tab, click the **Excel** button. The Get External Data – Excel Spreadsheet dialog box opens.

2. Click **Browse**, if necessary navigate to and open the **Access Lesson 06** folder, click **Student Excel.xlsx**, and then click **Open**.

3. Make sure that the **Import the source data into a new table in the current database** option button is selected. See **Figure 6–9**.

FIGURE 6–9
Get External Data – Excel
Spreadsheet dialog box

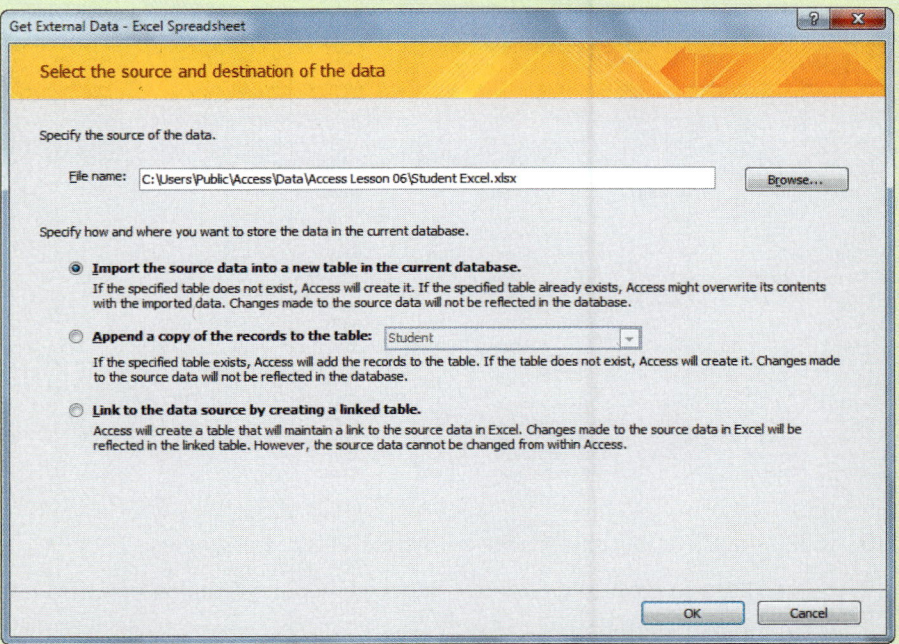

4. Click **OK**. The Import Spreadsheet Wizard dialog box opens, as shown in **Figure 6–10**.

FIGURE 6–10
First Import
Spreadsheet Wizard
dialog box

Click this check box to use the values in the first row as field names

First row of worksheet contains field names

Each row will become one record

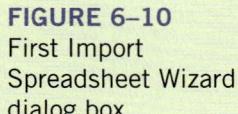

5. Click the **First Row Contains Column Headings** check box to add a check mark to it, and then click **Next**. The second dialog box lets you set data types for fields. As when importing a text file, you can set the data types now or do so after creating the table. If you choose not to change the data types, Access will assign the Text data type and the default property settings for Text fields to all fields in the table.

6. Click **Next**. The third dialog box asks you about the table's primary key.

7. Click the **Choose my own primary key** option button. Make sure that **Student ID** appears in the list box to the right of the Choose my own primary key option button, and then click **Next**. The final dialog box asks you for the table name.

8. In the Import to Table text box, type **Student Excel**, and then click **Finish**.

9. In the Get External Data – Excel Spreadsheet dialog box, click **Close**. (Do not save the import steps.)

10. In the Navigation Pane, double-click **Student Excel** to open the table in Datasheet view. The table contains the data that was stored in the columns and rows in the Excel workbook.

11. Click the **Close 'Student Excel'** button ☒ to close the Student Excel table. Leave the database open for the next Step-by-Step.

TECHNOLOGY CAREERS

Databases are helpful in the sales business. Salespersons can create a database to store detailed information about their customers. They can then create queries and filters to search the database for specific information. They can also use the database to create reports, form letters, and mailing labels.

Creating Form Letters

▶ **VOCABULARY**

form letter

data source

main document

merge fields

Another way to integrate Access and Word is to create form letters. A *form letter* is a document that includes codes that insert information from a data source. The *data source* might be information stored in a Word document, an Excel workbook, an Access database, or another file format. When you merge the data source with the form letter, one letter is created for each record in the data source. In this case, the form letter is also called the *main document*. Form letters are used to customize letters and other documents. When used with a data source, Word does the work of addressing letters or customizing forms, so you don't need to type the information directly and create each letter individually.

For example, suppose a fourth grade teacher wants to send a letter to the parents of students in her class to welcome them to the new school year. Instead of typing each recipient's name, mailing address, salutation (such as Dear Mr. and Mrs. Peterson), and child's name in each letter and printing it, the teacher can create a form letter with the basic information she wants to include in the letter. Then the teacher can create a data source that stores the mailing address and student information for each child in her class. When she merges the main document with the data source, Word creates letters using the specific address and student information from each record in the data source. All the teacher needs to do is set up the process and load the printer with paper.

Creating a Form Letter

A form letter is a document that you create using Microsoft Word and that contains codes to tell Word where to insert the fields in records in the data source. The codes are the same as the field names used in the data source. When you insert the codes in a main document, they are called *merge fields*. When you insert a merge field in a Word document, the field name is enclosed in double angle brackets. For example, the merge field for a First Name field is displayed as <<First_Name>> in the Word document. When you merge the main document and the data source, Word replaces <<First_Name>> with the First Name field value in the first record of the data source, and inserts the first name.

You can use any document as a form letter, including documents that you create from scratch or a template. You can start a mail merge from Word or from Access. To start a mail merge using Access, open the database that contains the data source for the form letters, and then click the data source (table or query) in the Navigation Pane to select it. Click the External Data tab on the Ribbon. In the Export group, click the Word Merge button. The Microsoft Word Mail Merge Wizard starts and

> **TIP**
>
> When a field name in the data source contains a space, the merge field in Word replaces the space with an underscore character. For example, the field name First Name becomes <<First_Name>>.

asks if you want to link your data to an existing document or create a new document. If you click the option to use an existing document, and then click OK, the Select Microsoft Word Document dialog box opens. Use the options to browse to and select the document, and then click Open. Word starts and opens the document you selected, and sets the data source to the object you selected in the database. If you choose the option to create a new document, and then click OK, Word starts and opens a new document. In either case, after Word starts, the Mailings tab is selected on the Ribbon and the Mail Merge task pane opens on the right side of the window, as shown in **Figure 6–11**.

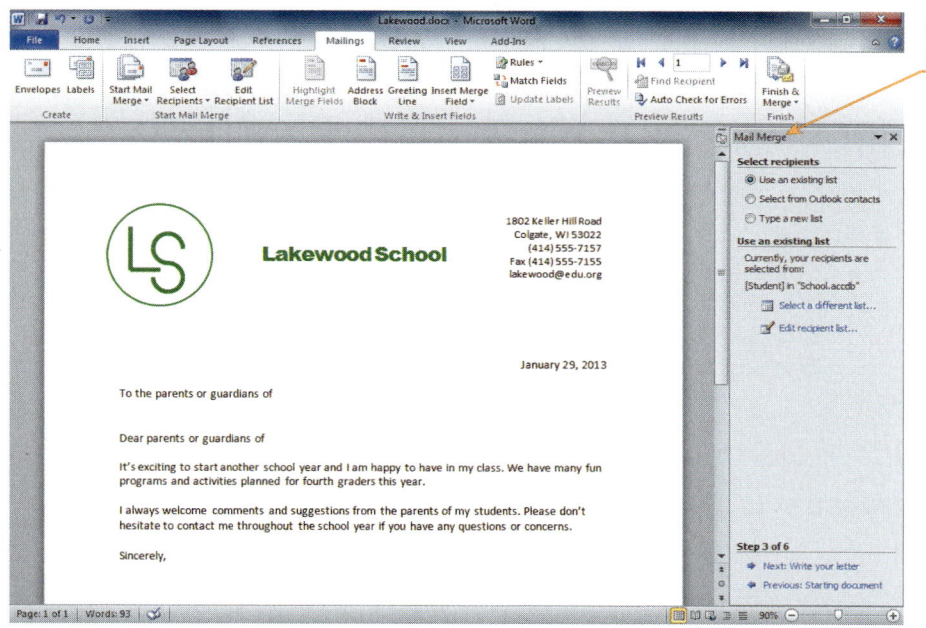

FIGURE 6–11   Existing document selected for mail merge

You can type or edit content in the document and use the tools in Word to make any changes to the letter, such as changing the font style or adding pictures. If you are creating a document from scratch, the first step is to select the type of document you are creating (letter, e-mail message, envelope, label, or a directory). For a form letter, choose the Letters option button. The second step asks you to select the document you want to use or to create a new document. After making your selection, click the Next: Select recipients link at the bottom of the Mail Merge task pane to select the data source.

In the third step, shown in Figure 6–11, you select the data source that contains the records for the recipients. This data source might be an existing list, an Outlook contact, or data that you type. When you start the mail merge from Access, Word sets the data source for you automatically.

If you want to merge all the records in the data source, you don't need to do anything else. If you want to merge selected records in the data source, click the Edit recipient list link in the Mail Merge task pane to open the Mail Merge Recipients dialog box, shown in **Figure 6–12**. The name of the data source appears in the first column, and the fields in the data source appear in columns to the left of the Data Source column. In Figure 6–12, the data source is an Access database.

Data source for each record

Fields in the data source

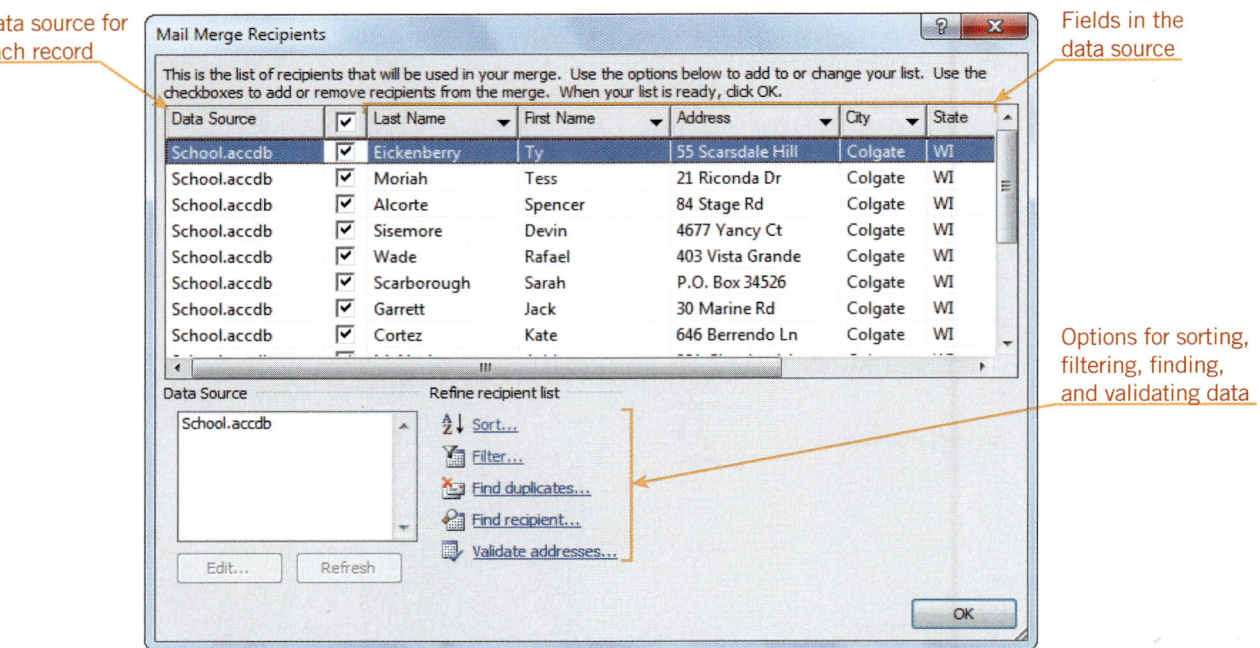

Options for sorting, filtering, finding, and validating data

FIGURE 6–12   Mail Merge Recipients dialog box

A check box is shown to the left of the first field for each record; a check mark indicates that the record will be merged. If you want to remove a record from the mail merge, clear its check box. Also notice the "Refine recipient list" section, which provides options for sorting and filtering data, finding duplicate records, locating a specific recipient, and validating addresses. You can use these options when you need to change how letters are merged when you complete the mail merge. For example, if you want to print form letters in alphabetical order based on a specific field, you can click the Sort link to open the Filter and Sort dialog box with the Sort Records tab selected, as shown in **Figure 6–13**. To sort on a specific field, click the Sort by list arrow, and then select the field that you want to sort. Figure 6–13 shows that the mail merge will be sorted in ascending order based on the values in the Last Name field.

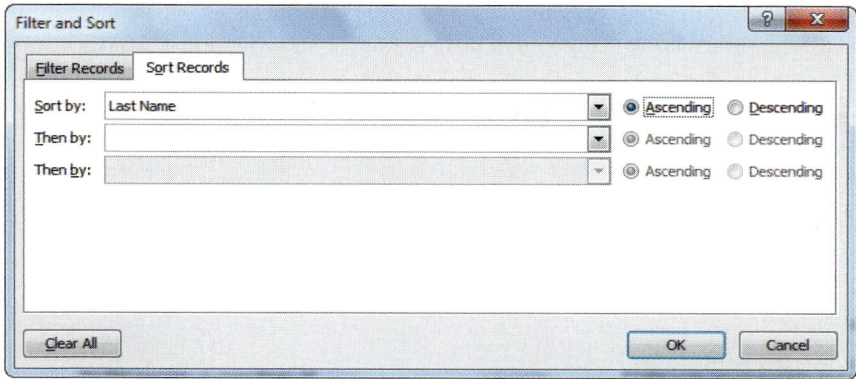

FIGURE 6–13   Sort Records tab in the Filter and Sort dialog box

You can also filter records by clicking the Filter link in the Refine recipient list section in the Mail Merge Recipients dialog box, which opens the Filter and Sort dialog box with the Filter Records tab selected. To create a filter, use the Field list arrow to select the field to filter, use the Comparison list arrow to choose the filter operator, and then type a value in the Compare to text box. **Figure 6–14** shows a filter to select records with the last name *Cortez*.

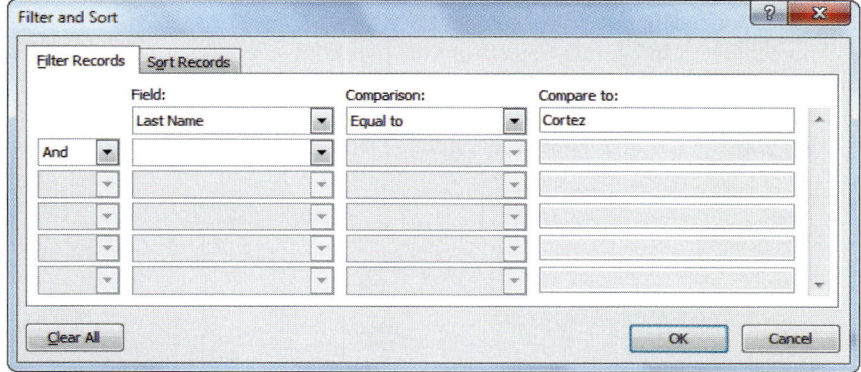

FIGURE 6–14   Filter Records tab in the Filter and Sort dialog box

When you click OK to close the Filter and Sort dialog box, you'll apply the new settings to the form letters. However, the changes you make are not reflected in the data source. Click OK to close the Mail Merge Recipients dialog box, and then click the Next: Write your letter link at the bottom of the Mail Merge task pane. If necessary, make any changes to the content of the letter, just like you would in any other document.

Word provides several options for adding merge fields to a document. You can use the Address block link in the Mail Merge task pane to add an address to the letter in the location of the insertion point. You can also add merge fields individually at the location of the insertion point by clicking the Insert Merge Field button in the Write & Insert Fields group on the Mailings tab. If you click the Address block link in the Mail

Merge task pane, the Insert Address Block dialog box opens and shows a preview of the address information that you will be inserting, as shown in **Figure 6–15**.

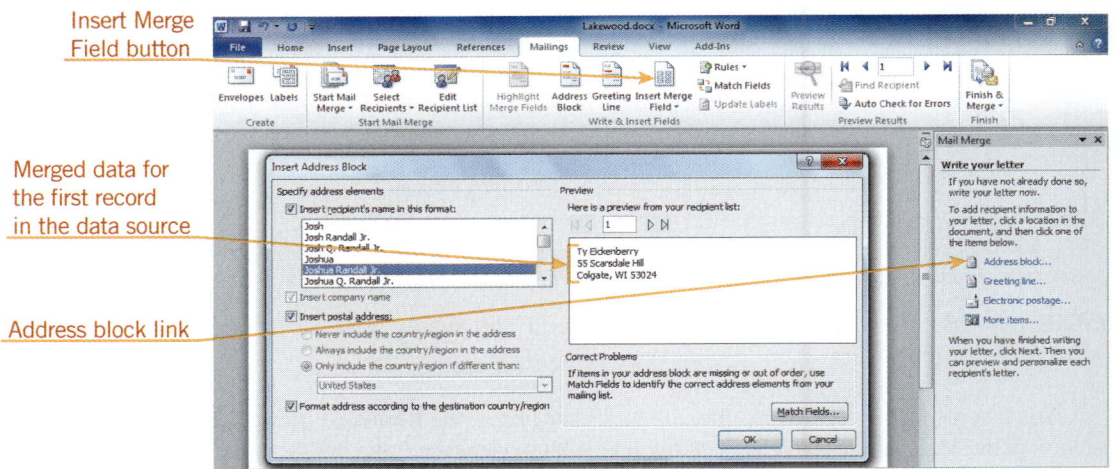

FIGURE 6–15   Insert Address Block dialog box

If the preview of the address block is correct, click OK. (If it is incorrect, click Match Fields to make adjustments.) After inserting the address block, it appears as <<AddressBlock>> in the main document.

You can insert individual fields from the data source wherever necessary in the main document. For example, you can include a first name in the middle of a sentence to customize the content. **Figure 6–16** shows the first and last names added to the salutation and the first name inserted in the first sentence of the first paragraph.

FIGURE 6–16   Document with merge fields inserted

Be careful when inserting fields individually—you will need to type any surrounding punctuation, such as inserting a space between field names so the first and last names print as "Riley Karr" instead of as "RileyKarr" and typing a comma or colon after the salutation.

After adding the merge fields to the letter, click the Next: Preview your letters link at the bottom of the Mail Merge task pane. The main document displays one letter for each record in the data source. **Figure 6–17** shows the first letter. Notice that the <<AddressBlock>> merge field was replaced by the address information for Ty Eickenberry. Ty's first and last names replaced the <<First_Name>> and <<Last_Name>> fields in the salutation. Ty's first name replaced the <<First_Name>> field in the first sentence of the first paragraph. If you click the next and previous buttons in the Preview your letters section of the Mail Merge task pane, you'll see the next and previous records as they will appear in the final letter.

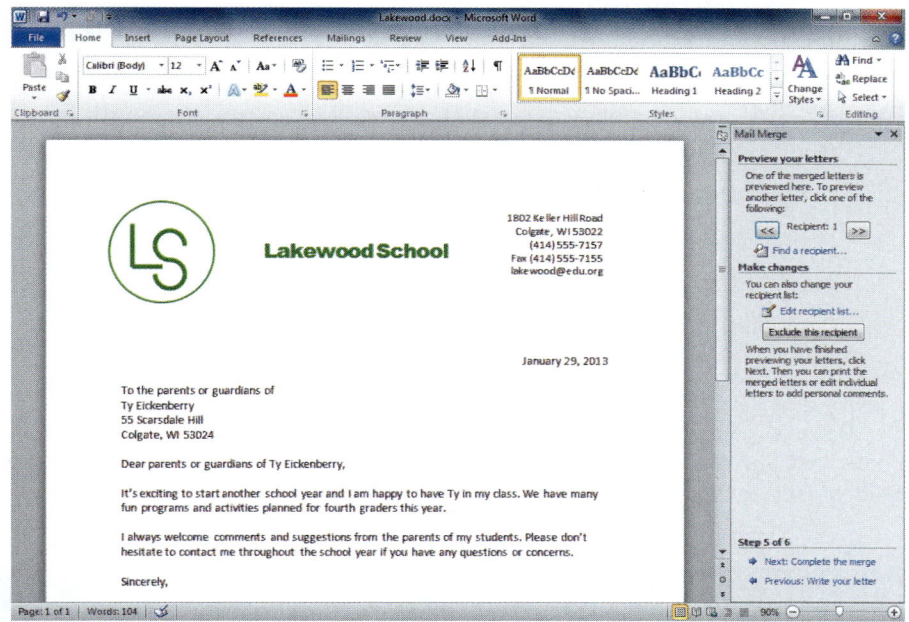

FIGURE 6–17   Merged letter for the first record

After verifying that your form letters are correct, click the Next: Complete the merge link at the bottom of the Mail Merge task pane. Click the Print link in the Merge section of the Mail Merge task pane to print the letters.

Step-by-Step 6.6

1. In the Navigation Pane, click the **Student** table to select it as the data source.

2. In the Export group on the External Data tab, click the **Word Merge** button. The Microsoft Word Mail Merge Wizard dialog box opens.

3. If necessary, click the **Link your data to an existing Microsoft Word document** option button, and then click **OK**. The Select Microsoft Word Document dialog box opens.

4. If necessary, navigate to and open the **Access Lesson 06** folder, click **Lakewood.docx**, and then click **Open**. The Select Microsoft Word Document dialog box closes. Word starts and opens the document you selected.

5. If necessary, click the **Lakewood.docx** program button on the taskbar to switch to Word.

6. If necessary, click the **Maximize** button 🔲 on the Word title bar to maximize the program window. (See Figure 6–11.) Leave Word open for the next Step-by-Step.

Because you started the mail merge from Access, the Mail Merge task pane opens with the Step 3 of 6 task displayed. The data source is already set to the Student table in the School database because you selected the data source in Access.

Step-by-Step 6.7

1. At the bottom of the Mail Merge task pane, click the **Next: Write your letter** link. The Step 4 of 6 Mail Merge task pane is displayed.

2. In the document, click the blank line below the paragraph that contains the text *To the parents or guardians of*.

3. In the Mail Merge task pane, click the **Address block** link. The Insert Address Block dialog box opens. (See Figure 6–15.) Make sure the settings in your dialog box match the ones shown in Figure 6–15, and then click **OK**. The <<AddressBlock>> field is added to the document.

4. In the document, click to the right of the line that contains the text *Dear parents or guardians of*. In the Write & Insert Fields group on the Mailings tab, click the **Insert Merge Field button arrow**. In the list, click **First_Name**.

5. Press the **spacebar**.

6. In the Write & Insert Fields group on the Mailings tab, click the **Insert Merge Field button arrow**. In the list, click **Last_Name**.

7. Type a comma.

8. In the first paragraph of the document, click after the space following the word *have* in the first sentence. Click the Insert Merge Field button arrow, and then click **First_Name** to insert the First Name field in the sentence.

9. Press the **spacebar** and make sure that the <<First_Name>> field that you just inserted has a space on each side of it, so the text will be merged correctly.

10. At the bottom of the Mail Merge task pane, click the **Next: Preview your letters** link. The data source is merged with the letter. (See Figure 6–17.)

11. In the Mail Merge task pane, click the [>>] button to display the next merged letter.

12. In the Mail Merge task pane, click the [<<] button to display the previous merged letter.

13. At the bottom of the Mail Merge task pane, click the **Next: Complete the merge** link. The Mail Merge task pane displays options to merge the letters or to edit individual letters.

14. On the Quick Access Toolbar, click the **Save** button [💾]. Leave Word open for the next Step-by-Step.

Editing the Recipient List

The default setting for a mail merge is to merge all the records in the data source. If you only need to merge certain records, you can set a filter or choose specific records individually.

Step-by-Step 6.8

1. At the bottom of the Mail Merge task pane, click the **Previous: Preview your letters** link. The Step 5 of 6 Mail Merge task pane is displayed. (See Figure 6–17.)

2. In the Mail Merge task pane, click the **Edit recipient list** link. The Mail Merge Recipients dialog box opens. (See Figure 6–12.)

3. Click the **check box** next to the Data Source column heading at the top of the column of check boxes. The check marks are removed from all check boxes.

4. Click the **check box** to the left of the record for Rafael Wade to add a check mark to it.

5. Click **OK** to close the Mail Merge Recipients dialog box.

6. In the Preview your letters section of the Step 5 of 6 Mail Merge task pane, click the `>>` button to display the next record. Because you set the mail merge to merge only one record, there are no "next" letters.

7. On the Quick Access Toolbar, click the **Save** button 🖫.

8. Click the **Close** button ❌ on the Word title bar to close Word.

9. Click the **Close** button ❌ on the Access title bar to close the Student database and Access.

SUMMARY

In this lesson, you learned:

- You can import and export data from a database and use it in other programs. When importing data, you can append records to an existing table or create a new table. When appending records to an existing table, the data source must have the same number of fields and contain the same type of data as the existing table.

- Delimited data contains commas or other separators to separate the fields in a data source. When the delimiter is a comma, the data is called comma-separated values (CSV). Access, Excel, and other programs can read and process CSV files.

- A form letter is a document that includes codes that merge information from a data source. The data source might be information stored in a Word document, an Excel workbook, an Access database, or another file format. When you merge the data source with the form letter, one letter is merged for each record in the data source.

- A merge field tells Word where to insert data from the data source.

- To merge certain records from a data source in a form letter, edit the recipient list by applying a filter or by selecting individual records.

VOCABULARY REVIEW

Define the following terms:

comma-separated values (CSV)
data source
delimited data

delimiter
export
form letter

import
main document
merge field

REVIEW QUESTIONS

TRUE / FALSE

Circle T if the statement is true or F if the statement is false.

T   F   **1.**   When importing data from a Word document into an existing Access database table, the Word document data must contain the same number of columns and type of data as the database table.

T   F   **2.**   When importing data into a database using the Import Text Wizard, you cannot specify a primary key for a new table.

T   F   **3.**   When importing data into a new database table, the fields will have the default property settings for a Text field unless you choose new data types for the fields.

T   F   **4.**   When creating a mail merge in Word, the data source must be a table in an Access database.

T   F   **5.**   You can insert a merge field anywhere in a form letter.

WRITTEN QUESTIONS

Write a brief answer to each of the following questions.

1. List three file formats that you can use to import data into a database.

2. List three file formats that you can use to export data from a database.

3. In a comma-separated values file, what is the delimiter that separates fields? What is the delimiter that separates records?

4. How do you insert a merge field into a Word document?

5. Describe the steps to insert the city, state, and zip code fields from a data source in a letter. Use the field names City, State, and Zip in your answer. The data should be printed on a single line in the format *City, State Zip*.

FILL IN THE BLANK

Complete the following sentences by writing the correct word or words in the blanks provided.

1. When you save database data in another file format, you _____ the data from the database.

2. When you _____ data into a database, you copy it from another Access database, an Excel workbook, a text file, or another compatible file format into an existing or new table in the current database.

3. A paragraph mark, comma, or space character are examples of _____ that might be used in a text file that you are importing into Access.

4. When you insert a merge field into a Word document, the field name is enclosed in _____.

5. To insert a merge field into a Word document, click the _____ button in the Write & Insert Fields group on the Mailings tab.

PROJECTS

If you have a SAM 2010 user profile, your instructor may have assigned an autogradable version of the indicated project. If so, log into the SAM 2010 Web site at *www.cengage.com/sam2010* to download the instruction and start files.

PROJECT 6–1

1. Open the **Inventory.accdb** database from the Access Lesson 06 folder where your Data Files are stored.

2. Choose the option to import data from an Excel workbook.

3. Choose the Products.xlsx file in the Access Lesson 06 folder as the data source.

4. Choose the option to import the source data into a new table in the current database.

5. Complete the steps in the Import Spreadsheet Wizard and accept the default settings. The first row in the data source contains column headings. Choose the Product ID field as the table's primary key. In the last dialog box, enter **Products** in the Import to Table text box.

6. If necessary, close the Get External Data – Excel Spreadsheet dialog box without saving the import steps.

7. Close the database and exit Access.

 PROJECT 6–2

1. Open the **Items.accdb** database from the Access Lesson 06 folder where your Data Files are stored.

2. Select the Products table, and then choose the option to export data from the Products table to a text file.

3. Click Browse and set the destination for the exported text file to the Access Lesson 06 folder. Click OK in the Export – Text File dialog box. The delimiter is a comma and the first row contains field names. Do not save the export steps.

4. Import the data in the Products.txt file in the Access Lesson 06 folder into a new table in the Items database. The delimiter is a comma and the first row contains field names. Do not set the data types for any of the fields. Choose the Product ID field as the table's primary key. Change the default table name to **Products Import**.

5. If necessary, close the Get External Data – Text File dialog box without saving the import steps.

6. Close the database and exit Access.

PROJECT 6–3

1. Open the **InfoTech.accdb** database from the Access Lesson 06 folder where your Data Files are stored.

2. Select the Employee table in the Navigation Pane, and then start a mail merge using the Abbott.docx document in the Access Lesson 06 folder.

3. In the main document, on the second line below the date, insert an address block.

4. On the line that contains the word *Dear*, type a space, insert the First_Name field, and then type a comma.

5. Preview the letters.

6. Exclude Donna Abbott from the mail merge by displaying her record and using a button in the Mail Merge task pane.

7. Save the document and close Word.

8. Close the database and exit Access.

PROJECT 6–4

1. Open the **InfoTech.accdb** database from the Access Lesson 06 folder where your Data Files are stored.

2. Select the Employee table in the Navigation Pane, and then start a mail merge using the Sales.docx document in the Access Lesson 06 folder.

3. In Word, set a filter to select only those records that have the field value *Sales* in the Department field in the data source.

4. Sort the records in alphabetical (ascending) order by Last Name.

5. On the second line below the date, insert an address block.

6. On the line that contains the word *Dear*, type a space, insert the First_Name field, and then type a comma.

7. Preview the letters.

8. Save the document and close Word.

9. Close the database and exit Access.

■ CRITICAL THINKING

ACTIVITY 6–1

One of the data types you can use in an Access table is the Attachment data type, which lets you store a file created in another program as part of a record in a table. You can save files in many different file formats, including files created with Office 2010 programs and files created by graphics programs.

Start Access, and then use Access Help to learn more about the Attachment data type by searching using the text "Attach files to records." Click the "Attach files and graphics to the records in your database" link, and then read the page that opens. On a sheet of paper, answer the following questions.

1. When a Word document is attached to a record in a database table, which program displays the document when you open it from Access?

2. Are there any rules for naming attachments stored in a database table? If so, what are the rules?

3. Can you attach a file with any filename extension using the Attachment data type? Explain your answer.

ACTIVITY 6–2

Start Access and use the Blank database template in the Available Templates section to create a new database named **Swimming.accdb** in the Access Lesson 06 folder with your Data Files. Close the default table that opens (Table1). Import the data in the Clubs.txt text file in the Access Lesson 06 folder into a new table in the Swimming database. The delimiter is a comma and the first row contains field names. Do not change the data types of any fields. Choose the Club Code field as the table's primary key. Import the data into a new table named **Clubs**. Do not save the import steps.

Import the data in the Officials.xlsx Excel workbook in the Access Lesson 06 folder into a new table in the Swimming database. The first row contains column headings. Do not change the data types of any fields. Choose the Official ID field as the table's primary key. Import the data into a new table named **Officials**. Do not save the import steps.

Create a relationship between the primary Clubs table and the related Officials table, using the Club Code field. Choose the option to enforce referential integrity. Save and close the Relationships window.

Use the Simple Query Wizard to create a query that includes the Club Code and Club Name fields from the Clubs table and the First Name, Last Name, and Position fields from the Officials table. Use the query name **Club Officials**.

Export the data in the Club Officials query to an Excel workbook named **Club Officials.xlsx** in the Access Lesson 06 folder.

You created a new database and imported data from a text file and a workbook into the database to create two new tables. You related the tables using a common field, and then created a query that includes data from both tables. Finally, you exported the data in the query to an Excel workbook.

How could you continue improving the database that you created? (*Hint:* Think about the fields in the tables and their data types and field properties.) When other swim teams need to add officials to the database, what advice would you give them about sending their data to you? (*Hint:* Consider the rules you learned about importing data into existing tables.)

Close the database and exit Access.

ACCESS UNIT REVIEW

Introductory Microsoft Access

 ## REVIEW QUESTIONS

TRUE / FALSE

Circle T if the statement is true or F if the statement is false.

T   F   **1.**   A database is a collection of objects that store, retrieve, display, and summarize data.

T   F   **2.**   A field's data type stores the field's name.

T   F   **3.**   A query always contains a condition.

T   F   **4.**   Forms are always based on queries.

T   F   **5.**   You cannot edit the data displayed in a report.

WRITTEN QUESTIONS

Write a brief answer to each of the following questions.

1. What data type would you choose for a field that stores numeric data that you will use in calculations?

2. What field property do you use to change the number of characters that a Text field can store?

3. What is a filter?

4. Describe how to delete a record using a table datasheet.

5. Define the term *comma-separated values* and explain how a CSV file is used when importing data into an Access database.

FILL IN THE BLANK

Complete the following sentences by writing the correct word or words in the blanks provided.

1. A(n) _____ allows you to store, retrieve, analyze, and print information stored in a database.

2. Use the _____ data type to automatically add a unique value to a field in a table as you enter new records.

3. A(n) _____ is a menu that opens when you click the arrow on the right side of a field selector, and contains options for sorting data in the field.

4. The "container" that groups together the controls in a form so that you can change them as a group is called a(n) _____.

5. To create a simple report using all of the fields in a table or query, first select the table or query in the Navigation Pane, and then click the _____ button in the Reports group on the Create tab.

■ PROJECTS

PROJECT AC 1

1. Open the **Favorites.accdb** database from the Access Unit Review folder where your Data Files are stored.

2. Open the **Stores** table in Design view.

3. Move the Hours field so it appears between the Specialty and Credit Cards fields.

4. Insert a new field between the Hours and Credit Cards fields. Use the field name **Last Visit** and assign the field the Date/Time data type. Change the field's Format property to Short Date.

5. Change the Field Size property for the Specialty field to 30.

6. Change the data type of the Credit Cards field to Yes/No, and then change the Format property to Yes/No.

7. Change the Required field property for the Name field to Yes.

8. Set the Store ID field so it is the table's primary key.

9. Save the table, click Yes twice in the dialog boxes warning about data loss and data integrity rules, change to Datasheet view, and then resize the columns in the datasheet to best fit.

10. Enter today's date in the Last Visit field for the Electronics Plus record.

11. Change the Specialty field value for the Electronics Plus record to your first and last names.

12. Preview the datasheet, and then print it in landscape orientation. Save and close the Stores table.

13. Compact and repair the database.

14. Close the database, and then exit Access.

PROJECT AC 2

1. Open the **Dining.accdb** database from the Access Unit Review folder where your Data Files are stored.

2. Open the **Restaurants** table in Design view.

3. Change the Restaurant ID field so it is the table's primary key.

4. Change the Field Size property for the Name field to **30**, and change its Required property to Yes.

5. Change the Format property of the Last Visit field to Short Date.

6. Change the data type of the Reservations field to Yes/No, and then change the Format property to Yes/No.

7. Change the data type of the Meal Cost field to Currency.

8. Save the table, click Yes twice in the dialog boxes warning about data loss and data integrity rules, and then change to Datasheet view.

9. In Datasheet view, change the Format property for the Last Visit field to Long Date. Resize the Last Visit column to best fit.

10. Preview the datasheet, print it in landscape orientation, and then save and close the table.

11. Close the database, and then exit Access.

PROJECT AC 3

1. Open the **Personnel.accdb** database from the Access Unit Review folder where your Data Files are stored.

2. In the Relationships window, create a relationship using the Employee ID field in the primary Employees table and the Employee ID field in the related Personal Data table. Choose the option to enforce referential integrity. Save your changes, and then close the Relationships window.

3. Use the Simple Query Wizard to create a query based on the Employees and Personal Data tables. Include the following fields in the order listed from the Employees table in the query: Employee ID, First Name, and Last Name. Include the following fields in the order listed from the Personal Data table in the query: Title, Department, Date of Birth, and Salary.

4. Choose the option to create a detail query and use the query title **Employee Data**.

5. In the query datasheet, sort the records from smallest to largest using the Salary field.

6. Filter the records so that only those employees working in the Marketing department are displayed.

7. Use the Total row to calculate the average salary for employees working in the Marketing department.

8. In the record with Employee ID 1007, change the First Name and Last Name field values to your first and last names.

9. Preview and print the Employee Data query in landscape orientation, and then save and close the Employee Data query.

10. In Query Design view, create a new query using the Employees and Personal Data tables. Add the Employee ID, First Name, and Last Name fields from the Employees table to the query design. Then add the Salary field from the Personal Data table to the query design.

11. Use a condition to select the records for only those employees with salaries greater than $2,000.

12. Save the query as **High Salaries**, and then run the query.

13. In the record with Employee ID 1099, change the First Name and Last Name field values to your first and last names.

14. Preview and print the High Salaries query, and then close the High Salaries query.

15. Close the database, and then exit Access.

PROJECT AC 4

1. Open the **Meals.accdb** database from the Access Unit Review folder where your Data Files are stored.

2. Use the Form tool to create a form based on the Restaurants table.

3. Resize the width of the text boxes in the control layout in the form to 23 characters.

4. Apply the Angles theme to the form.

5. Change the form title to **My Favorite Restaurants**.

6. Change to Form view and delete the record with the Restaurant ID SAL2.

7. Display the record with the Restaurant ID TON1 in the form. Change the Name field value to your first and last names. Print the form for this record only.

8. Save the form using the name **My Favorite Restaurants**.

9. Close the form, close the database, and then exit Access.

PROJECT AC 5

1. Open the **Price.accdb** database from the Access Unit Review folder where your Data Files are stored.

2. Use the Report Wizard to create a report based on the Products table. Include all fields in the report.

3. Group the report by Category and sort the records in ascending order based on the Retail Price field.

4. Choose the Block layout and Landscape orientation.

5. Change the report title to **Products By Category**, and then choose the option to preview the report.

6. Change to Layout view. Resize each column so that it is just wide enough to display the longest value in the column. Scroll down the page to check and make sure that the field values in each column are completely visible.

7. Change to Design view and move the text box control that contains the page number to the left, so its right edge is at the 9.75-inch mark on the horizontal ruler.

8. Save the report, preview the report, and then print it.

9. Close the report, close the database, and then exit Access.

■ SIMULATION

You work at the newly renovated Java Internet Café. The café serves coffee and pastries and offers clients the opportunity to use the café's computers and Wi-Fi to gain Internet access. In addition to free wireless access, seven computers are set up on tables in quiet areas of the café. The café has many regular early morning customers who grab a cup of coffee and a pastry and then use one of the computers to check e-mail and browse the Internet before going to work or school.

The café charges a $10 monthly fee for Internet service. All membership fees for March were due on March 1. A few members have not paid their monthly fees. Your manager asks you to send out a reminder letter to customers with outstanding balances.

JOB AC 1

1. Open the **Java.accdb** database from the Access Unit Review folder where your Data Files are stored.

2. Open the **Members** table in Datasheet view.

3. Scott Payton just paid his membership fee for March. Update his record to show his $10 payment.

4. The café has a new member who paid her $10 dues for April. Use the following information to add the record for Halie Shook to the Members table:
   Member ID: **hsht**
   Title: **Ms.**
   First: **Halie**
   Last: **Shook**
   Address: **1290 Wood Crest Ln**
   City: **Boulder**
   State: **CO**
   Zip: **80302**

5. Close the Members table.

6. Merge the records in the Members table with the **Reminder.docx** letter in the Access Unit Review folder where your Data Files are stored.

7. Edit the recipient list so letters are merged only for those clients who have not paid their dues for March. (*Hint:* Use a filter to select records for members who have March field values equal to 0 (zero). Use the Mail Merge Recipients dialog box to remove Halie Shook from the recipient list (she was not a member in March and should not receive a letter).

8. On the second line below the date field, add an address block.

9. On the second line below the address block you just inserted, add a greeting line in the format *Dear Mr. Stanley* followed by a comma.

10. Preview the merged letters.

11. Change the manager's name (Trace Green) in the closing to your first and last names. Exclude the first and second recipients and print the third recipient's letter only.

12. Save the document and close Word.

13. Close the database, and then exit Access.

JOB AC 2

You need to create mailing labels so you can mail the member statements for April.

1. Open the **Java.accdb** database from the Access Unit Review folder where your Data Files are stored.

2. Use the Label Wizard to create mailing labels for the Members table.

3. Use the Avery C2160 label and accept the default font settings. Add the Title, First, and Last fields on the first line of the label, separated by spaces; add the Address field on the second line of the label; and the City, State, and Zip fields on the last line of the label. There should be a comma and space between the City and State fields and a space between the State and Zip fields.

4. Save the report as **Labels Members**, and then preview it.

5. Close the report, close the database, and exit Access.

INTRODUCTORY UNIT

MICROSOFT POWERPOINT 2010

LESSON 1   **1.5 HRS.**
Microsoft PowerPoint Basics

LESSON 2   **2.0 HRS.**
Creating and Enhancing PowerPoint Presentations

LESSON 3   **1.5 HRS.**
Working with Visual Elements

LESSON 4   **2.0 HRS.**
Expanding on PowerPoint Basics

Estimated Time:
1.5 hours

LESSON 1

Microsoft PowerPoint Basics

■ OBJECTIVES

Upon completion of this lesson, you should be able to:

- Start PowerPoint, and understand the elements of the PowerPoint window.
- Open an existing presentation, and save it with a new name.
- Navigate a presentation and change views.
- Use the Slides and Outline tabs and the Slide and Notes panes.
- Change the layout on a slide.
- Delete a slide.
- Print a presentation.
- Exit PowerPoint.

■ VOCABULARY

animation

broadcasting

handouts

layout

Live Preview

Normal view

Notes Page view

Notes pane

Outline tab

PowerPoint presentation

Reading view

Slide pane

Slide Show view

Slide Sorter view

Slides tab

thumbnails

transition

Introduction to PowerPoint

▶ **VOCABULARY**
PowerPoint presentation

Microsoft PowerPoint 2010 is a Microsoft Office program that can help you create a professional, computerized slide show to use as part of a presentation. A ***PowerPoint presentation*** is an electronic slide show that allows you to present and deliver your message by using slides, outlines, speaker's notes, and audience handouts. PowerPoint presentations are viewed using a computer and monitor. Presentations are usually shown to an audience using a projector on a screen. A presentation can include text, drawn graphics, clip art, photographs, tables, charts, narration, and even video. Presentations can also include links to Web sites, so if you are connected to the Internet as you run the slide show, you can further enhance your presentation.

This lesson introduces you to some of the features available in PowerPoint 2010. You'll learn how to open and save a presentation, view the slide show, and switch views. You'll also learn how to delete a slide and print the presentation in a variety of ways.

Starting PowerPoint

Like other Office applications, you start PowerPoint by clicking the Start button, clicking All Programs, clicking Microsoft Office, and then clicking Microsoft PowerPoint 2010. If the Microsoft PowerPoint icon is on the desktop, you can double-click it to start PowerPoint rather than locating the command on the All Programs menu. The PowerPoint program opens, as shown in **Figure 1–1**.

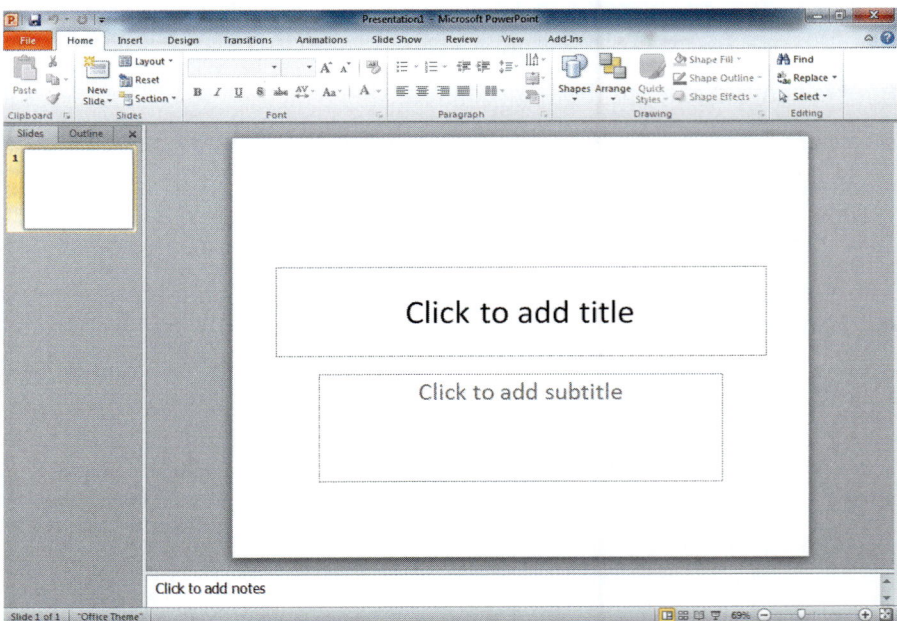

FIGURE 1–1   The PowerPoint window

Step-by-Step 1.1

1. On the taskbar, click the **Start** button 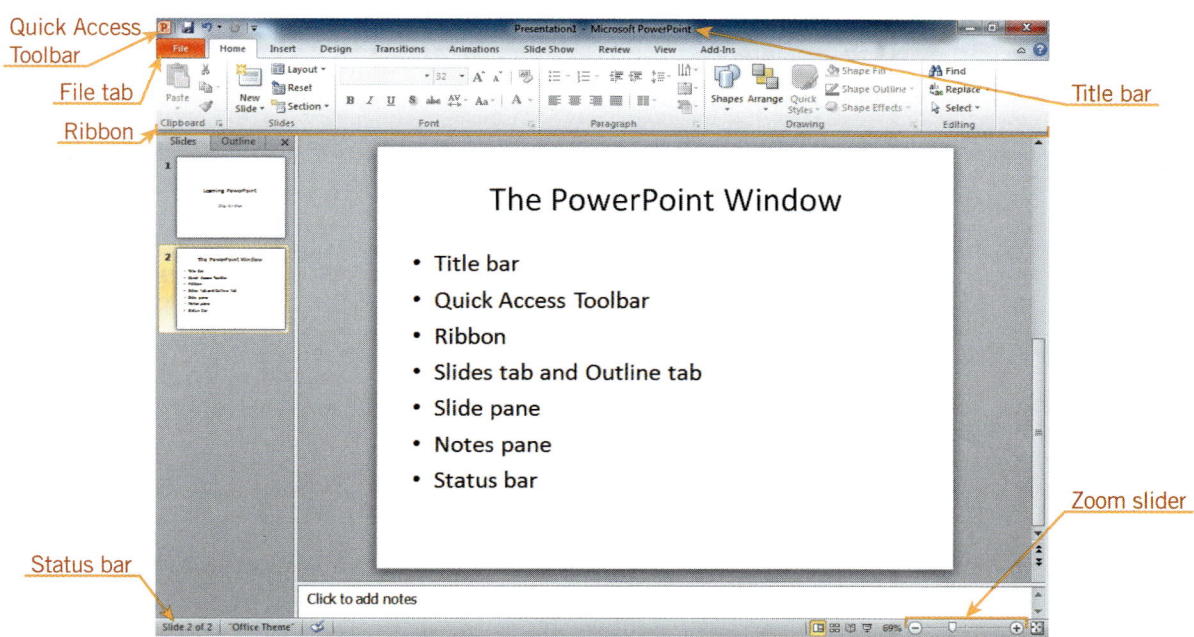 to open the Start menu.

2. Click **All Programs**, click **Microsoft Office**, and then click **Microsoft PowerPoint 2010**. The PowerPoint window opens with a new blank slide in the PowerPoint window. The new blank slide is a blank title slide. You will review the program window that is on the screen in the next Step-by-Step.

3. Leave the blank presentation open for the next Step-by-Step.

> **TIP**
>
> The first slide in a presentation is the title slide. The title slide provides a purpose similar to a title page in a report. The title slide introduces the presentation to your audience.

Reviewing the PowerPoint Window

The PowerPoint window shares several common elements and tools with other Office programs, such as Word, Excel, and Access. PowerPoint has several views that you will learn about. You work with these elements and tools in the different views to create presentations. Refer to **Figure 1–2**, which shows a simple presentation with two slides and identifies the elements in *Normal view*, which is a view of the presentation that allows you to add and delete slides, and add text and elements to slides.

> ▶ **VOCABULARY**
> **Normal view**

FIGURE 1–2   PowerPoint window in Normal view

The title bar, at the top of the window, identifies the window as a PowerPoint window and lists the name of the open presentation. For a new presentation, the name is simply Presentation followed by a number until you give it a name when you save the file.

The Quick Access Toolbar is on the left side of the title bar. You can add or remove buttons on the Quick Access Toolbar to meet your working style. For example, you might want to add the New, Open, or Spelling command.

Like other Office programs, the Ribbon contains the graphic collection of command buttons that are organized by tabs and in groups. The Home tab is the default tab on the Ribbon and includes many of the commands you will use most often when creating the slides. The File tab, which opens Backstage view, includes file management commands such as the Save, Save As, Open, Close, and Print commands.

The status bar appears at the bottom of your screen and provides information about the current presentation and slide. The area on the left side of the status bar shows which slide is displayed in the Slide pane and tells you the total number of slides in the presentation. On the right end of the status bar, you can click the View buttons to switch views, the way you view the presentation. As in other programs, the *Zoom slider* adjusts the zoom percentage of the window. To the right of the Zoom slider, the Fit slide to current window button is useful for quickly adjusting the selected slide to best fit in the current window.

> **TIP**
>
> Read more about Backstage view in the Microsoft Office 2010 Basics and the Internet lesson at the beginning of this book.

▶ **VOCABULARY**
Zoom slider

Step-by-Step 1.2

1. On the Ribbon, click the **Insert** tab to view the different commands. You can see that the buttons have images to show what each button does. The buttons are organized into the Tables, Images, Illustrations, Links, Text, Symbols, and Media groups.

2. On the Ribbon, click the **View** tab to view the different commands. PowerPoint has several views that you will learn about as you learn to create presentations.

3. On the Ribbon, click the **Design** tab to view the different commands. You can use buttons on this tab to add color and designs to your presentations.

4. On the status bar, click the **Zoom In** button ⊕ two times, and then click the **Zoom Out** button ⊖ four times so the Zoom percentage is 40%. Refer to **Figure 1–3**.

> **EXTRA FOR EXPERTS**
>
> The Zoom In and Zoom Out buttons increase or decrease the zoom level by values of 10. Drag the Zoom slider to change the zoom percentage as a sliding scale.

FIGURE 1–3
Zoom controls

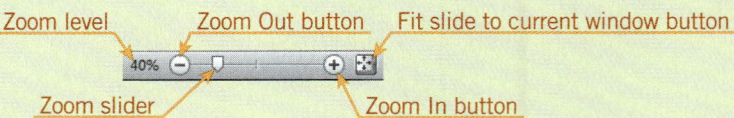

5. On the status bar, click the **Fit slide to current window** button 🖾.

6. Leave the presentation open for the next Step-by-Step.

Opening an Existing Presentation and Viewing a Slide Show

When you want to open an existing presentation that you have recently viewed, you can choose the presentation from the Recent Presentations list in Backstage view. To view the Recent Presentations list, click the File tab on the Ribbon, and then click Recent on the navigation bar. If the presentation you want to work on or view is not on that list, click Open on the navigation bar, and then browse in the Open dialog box to locate the presentation file name. The Open dialog box is shown in **Figure 1–4**. The files and folders will differ for each computer system.

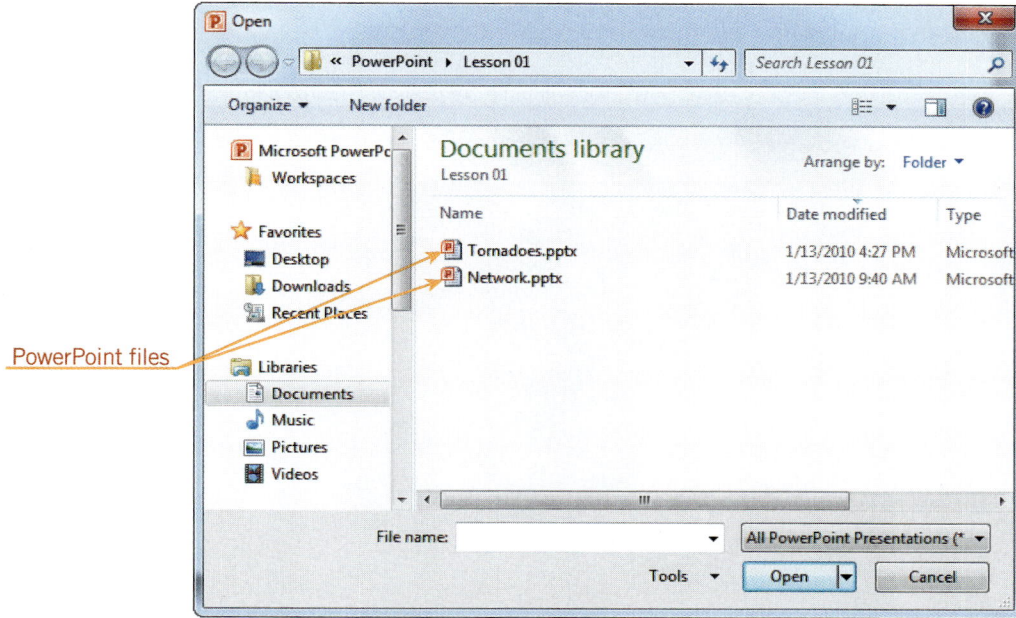

FIGURE 1–4 Open dialog box

Click the presentation you want to open, and then click Open. The presentation you selected appears on the screen in the PowerPoint window.

To view the presentation as a slide show, click the Slide Show button on the status bar. You can also click the Slide Show tab on the Ribbon, and then, in the Start Slide Show group, click the From Beginning or From Current Slide button. The slide show opens on the screen, and you can view it as it would appear if you were presenting it. You can press the right arrow key or the spacebar on the keyboard to advance the slides and the left arrow key to review a previous slide. You can also click the mouse button to advance a slide.

A slide show is a series of slides. *Transition* refers to the way each new slide appears on the screen. You can select from many exciting transition effects, such as checkerboards, swirls, dissolves, wipes, and cuts, to make your slide show fun to watch.

You can animate objects on a slide. An *animation* is an effect you can apply to text, objects, graphics, or pictures to make those objects move during a slide show. You can set up a slide to advance automatically through the animation or to pause and allow users to start the animation effect manually when it is most convenient.

As you view the presentation in Step-by-Step 1.3, press the right arrow key, Enter, or the spacebar, or click to advance to the next animation or slide.

▶ **VOCABULARY**
transition

animation

Step-by-Step 1.3

TIP

You can press the left arrow key or Page Up on the keyboard to view the previous slide or animation in the presentation.

1. On the Ribbon, click the **File** tab, and then on the navigation bar, click **Open**.

2. In the Open dialog box, navigate to the drive and folder where your Data Files are stored.

3. Click **Tornadoes.pptx**, and then click **Open**. The presentation file appears, as shown in **Figure 1–5**. The title slide is in the Slide pane.

FIGURE 1–5
Title slide for Tornadoes presentation

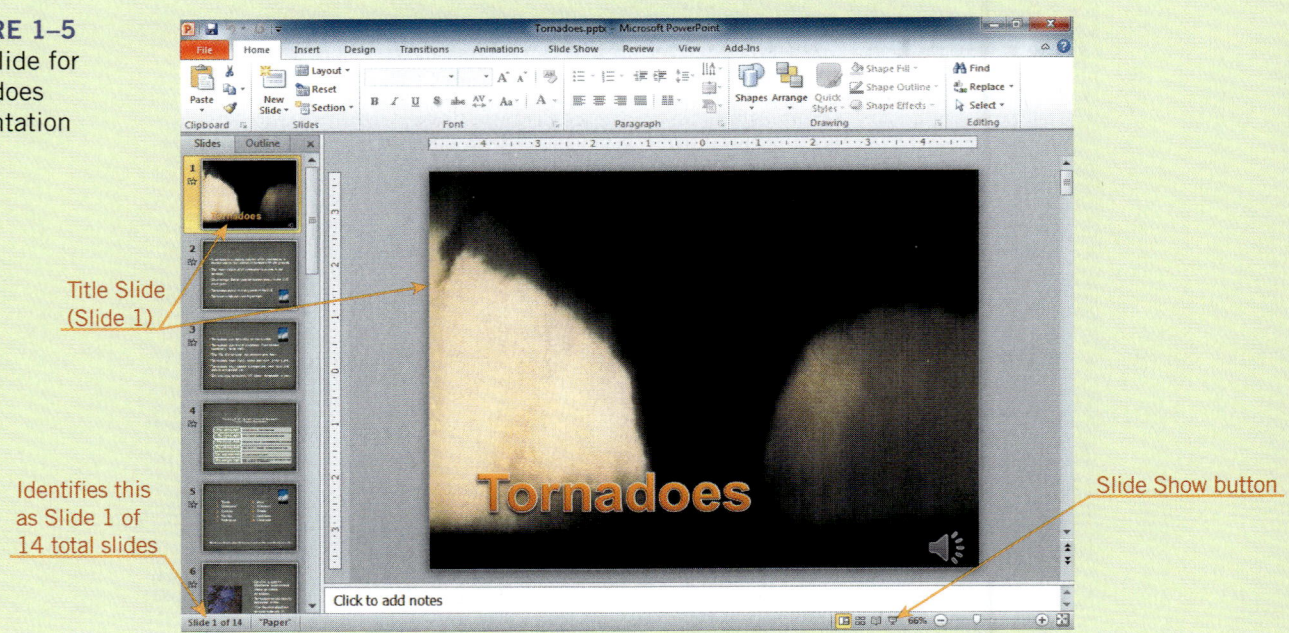

Title Slide (Slide 1)

Identifies this as Slide 1 of 14 total slides

Slide Show button

4. On the status bar, click the **Slide Show** button ⬚. The title slide fills the screen , as shown in **Figure 1-6**, and you see the word *Tornadoes* in the lower-left. Then, the background image flies onto the screen, and the word *Tornadoes* becomes animated. If your computer has a sound card and speakers, you also hear a thunderstorm.

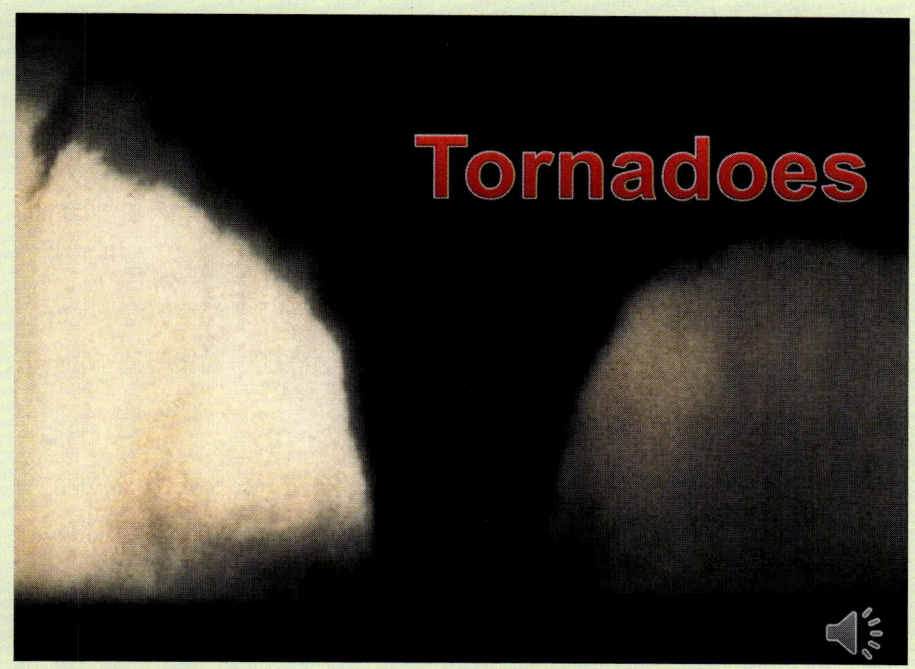

FIGURE 1–6
The slide fills the screen

5. Click the mouse to advance to the next slide. The transition makes Slide 1 look like it is shredding into pieces, and then Slide 2 is assembled from these pieces. The text animation on the slide advances automatically until five bulleted items appear.

6. Click the mouse again to advance to the next slide. Click the mouse as many times as necessary to display each bullet. The title of this slide appeared automatically. This slide show is set up so some text appears automatically, and some when you click the mouse.

7. Click the mouse as many times as necessary to advance the slides. As each slide in the presentation continues, notice the examples of animation. Some slides include pictures, and some of the pictures are animated. One of the slides includes an animated movie of a tornado. Slide 12, titled "Web Resources," contains several hyperlinks. If your computer is connected to the Internet, you can click one of those links to open the Web site in your browser. After you click the last slide, the Thank You on the last slide spins away.

8. Click the mouse again. The presentation ends with a black slide. The black slide lets you know the slide show is over.

9. Click the mouse one more time to end the slide show and return to Normal view.

10. Leave the presentation open for the next Step-by-Step.

TIP

There are many ways to advance through a slide show. Try pressing the right arrow key, the spacebar, the page up key, or using the scroll wheel on your mouse.

Saving a Presentation

To save a new presentation the first time, you use the Save As command. You can also use the Save As command to give an existing presentation a new name. If the presentation does not have a name, click the Save button on the Quick Access Toolbar to open the Save As dialog box, as shown in **Figure 1–7**. You can open the Save As dialog box by clicking the File tab on the Ribbon, and then clicking Save As. In the Save As dialog box, use the navigation pane to find the drive and folder where you will save your presentation. Click in the File name box to select the default name, such as Presentation1, type a new file name, and then click Save.

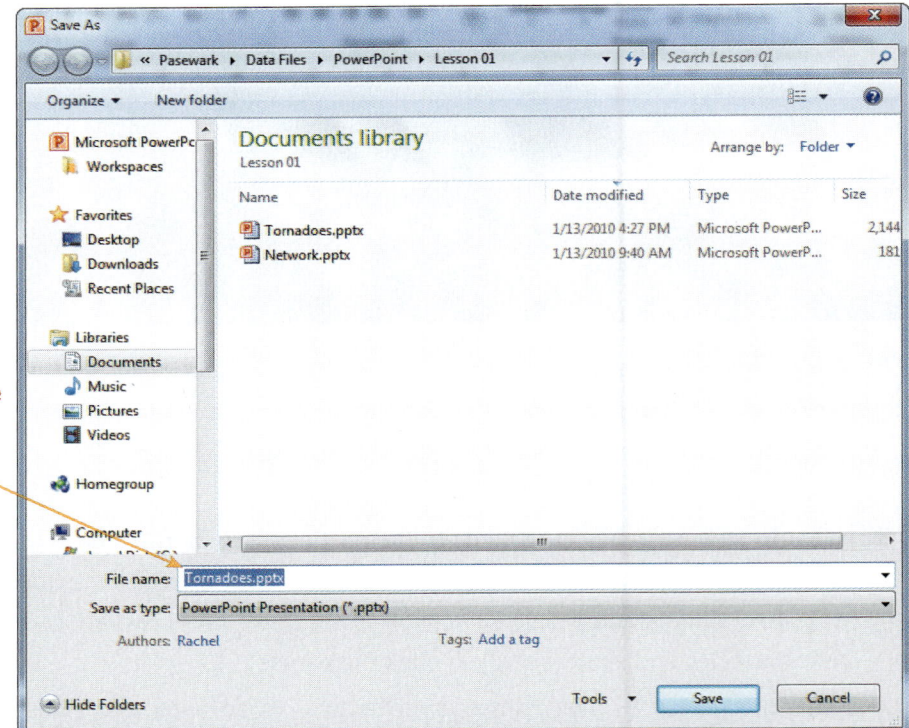

Presentation will be saved with a pptx file extension

FIGURE 1–7   Save As dialog box

INTERNET

To save a presentation to a folder on the Web that you can allow other people to access, click the File tab. In Backstage view, click Save and Send, click Save to Web, click Sign In, and then follow the directions to SkyDrive to save the presentation to a special folder on the Web making it available for viewing or editing from any computer.

The next time you want to save changes to your presentation, click the Save button on the Quick Access Toolbar or press Ctrl+S. These commands save the file without opening the dialog box.

Step-by-Step 1.4

1. Click the **File** tab, and then on the navigation bar, click **Save As**. The Save As dialog box opens.

2. Navigate to the drive and folder where your Data Files are stored.

3. Click in the **File name** box, and then type **Tornado Report** followed by your initials.

4. Click **Save**. Leave the presentation open for the next Step-by-Step.

Changing Views

You can view a presentation four different ways using buttons found in the Presentation Views group of the View tab on the Ribbon: Normal, Slide Sorter, Notes Page, and Reading view. (See **Figure 1–8**.) You can also change to Normal view, Slide Sorter view, Reading view or start a slide show quickly by clicking one of the View Shortcut buttons on the status bar, shown in **Figure 1–9**.

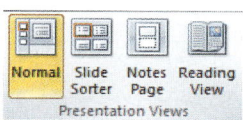

FIGURE 1–8   Presentation Views group on the View tab

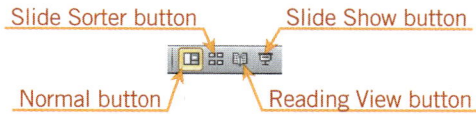

FIGURE 1–9   View shortcuts on the status bar

Normal View

You do most work creating slides in Normal view. This view can have up to four panes: the Slides tab and Outline tab, the Slide pane, the Notes pane, and the Task pane.

Using the Slides Tab and Outline Tab

When you are working with the slides in a presentation, PowerPoint displays all the slides in a pane on the left side of your screen. This pane has two tabs at the top, the Slides tab and the Outline tab. The **Slides tab** displays your slides as small pictures or **thumbnails**. The **Outline tab** displays all the text on your slides in outline

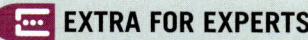

EXTRA FOR EXPERTS

Click and drag the pane borders to adjust the size of the different panes.

▶ **VOCABULARY**

Slides tab

thumbnails

Outline tab

form. The Outline tab does not show you any graphics on a slide. See **Figure 1–10**. This pane lets you see the order of your slides and gives you a quick overview of the slides. It's a good way to see which slides come before and after other slides. Depending on the Zoom factor, you will see more slides (with smaller thumbnails) or less slides (with larger thumbnails). To switch between these modes, click the Slides tab or the Outline tab.

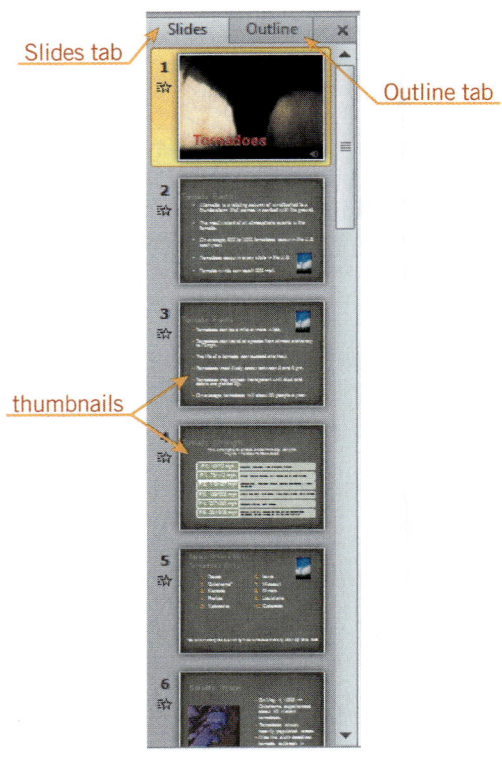

FIGURE 1–10   Slides tab

TIP

While the Slides tab can show you several slides as thumbnails at one time, Slide Sorter view gives you an overview of all the slides in a presentation.

To select any slide in a presentation, click the thumbnail on the Slides tab or click the text on the Outline tab. You can use the Outline tab to add or edit text on the slide. You can reorder slides by dragging the thumbnail on the Slides or Outline tab. You can close the pane by clicking the Close button in the upper-right corner of the pane. Click the Normal button on the status bar to restore this pane.

Step-by-Step 1.5

EXTRA FOR EXPERTS

You can also press Page Down to view the next slide or press Page Up to view the previous slide in any view.

1. Click the **Outline** tab. The slide number appears to the left of the text on the Outline tab.

2. On the Outline tab, drag the **scroll box** down in the scroll bar until you can see slide 8, and then click the **slide 8** slide icon ▣. Slide 8 appears in the Slide pane.

3. On the **Outline** tab, click anywhere on the selected text to deselect it.

4. On the Outline tab, in the second bullet point in Slide 8, double-click **75,000** to select the number, type **93,000**, and then press **spacebar**. Notice the number also changes on the slide in the Slide pane.

5. Click the **Slides** tab, and then click the **Save** button 💾 on the Quick Access toolbar.

6. Leave the presentation on the screen for the next Step-by-Step.

Using the Ribbon

The Ribbon on the top of the screen contains commands for the various tasks you will use when creating presentations. For example, on the Ribbon, you can click the Design tab to view themes, which are slide designs. You can then click the More button in the Themes group to open a gallery of themes and see all the thumbnails, as shown in **Figure 1–11**. The *Live Preview* feature lets you see the effect the theme will have on your slides before you apply it in your presentation. If you select a slide, you can see how the theme will change the background and text on the slide as you move the mouse pointer over each thumbnail.

▶ **VOCABULARY**
Live Preview

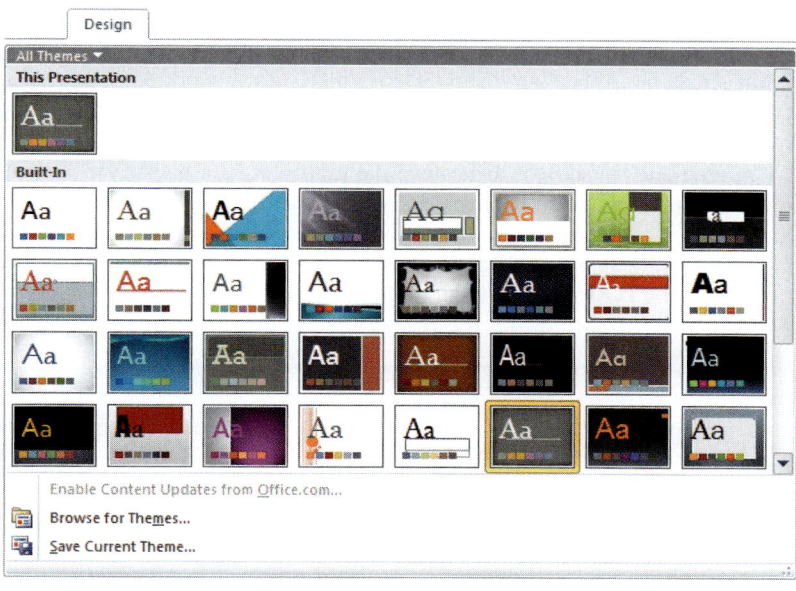

FIGURE 1–11   Themes gallery on the Design tab

Step-by-Step 1.6

1. On the Ribbon, click the **Design** tab.

2. On the Slides tab, drag the **scroll box** up to the top of the scroll bar, and then click the **slide 3** thumbnail. The slide number appears to the left of the slide thumbnail on the Slides tab.

■ EXTRA FOR EXPERTS

On the Ribbon, on the Design tab, in the Themes group, click the More button to open the Themes gallery and try out more themes for the slides.

3. On the Design tab, in the Themes group, move the pointer over each of the theme thumbnails to preview the different theme effects on the slide (but do not click the mouse button).

4. In the Themes group, click the **Colors** button to open the Built-in Theme Colors gallery, and then slowly move the pointer over each of the **Color Themes** thumbnails to preview the different color theme effects on the slide.

5. Press **Esc** to close the Colors menu without selecting anything.

6. In the Themes group, click the **Fonts** button to open the Built-in Fonts gallery, and then slowly move the pointer over each of the Font Themes thumbnails to preview the different font effects on the slide.

7. On the Ribbon, click the **Home** tab.

8. Leave the presentation on the screen for the next Step-by-Step.

Using the Slide Pane

▶ VOCABULARY
Slide pane

The **Slide pane** is the workbench for PowerPoint presentations. It displays one slide at a time and is useful for adding and editing text, inserting and formatting illustrations or objects, or generally modifying a slide's appearance. The Slide pane displays your slides in an area large enough for you to easily work on a slide. You can select the slide to view in the Slide pane by clicking the thumbnail on the Slides tab, by scrolling the Slide pane, or by pressing Page Up or Page Down on the keyboard.

If you drag and select text, then move the mouse pointer back over the selected text, the Mini toolbar appears. The Mini toolbar has buttons for common formatting commands, such as font color, font style, font size, text alignment, and styling. Although buttons for these commands also appear in the Font group on the Ribbon, it is sometimes quicker to use the Mini toolbar. See **Figure 1–12**.

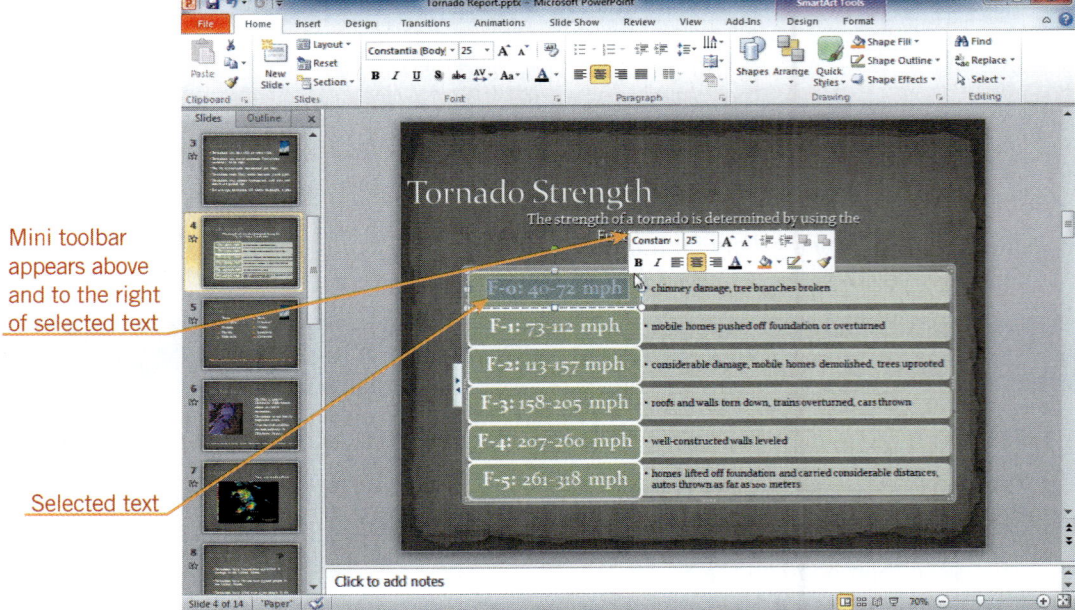

FIGURE 1–12   The Mini toolbar

Step-by-Step 1.7

1. On the Slides tab, click the **slide 5** thumbnail.

2. In the Slide pane, drag to select the text **Oklahoma City has been hit by more tornadoes than any other city since 1890** at the bottom of the slide.

3. In the Font group on the Home tab, click the **Font Color** button arrow 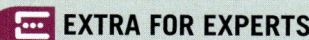. A palette of colors opens.

4. In the first row of the palette in the Theme Colors section, click the sixth color box **Orange, Accent 2** (when you position the pointer on top of the box, a ScreenTip appears identifying the color). The text is formatted for the new color.

5. Save your work. Leave the presentation on the screen for the next Step-by-Step.

> **EXTRA FOR EXPERTS**
>
> When you drag to select text, the Mini toolbar appears, and you can use the buttons on it instead of the buttons on the Ribbon, if you wish.

Inserting a New Slide with a New Slide Layout

The slide *layout* is how objects are placed on a slide. Objects include text, images, illustrations, tables, media, and charts. When you create a slide, you determine the layout. The default layout includes placeholders for different objects on a slide. There are placeholders for slide titles, text, and content. When you insert a new slide, you can select the layout. You can also change the layout for a slide that already has content. On the Home tab, in the Slides group, click the Layout button to view the different default layouts. See **Figure 1–13**.

▶ **VOCABULARY**
layout

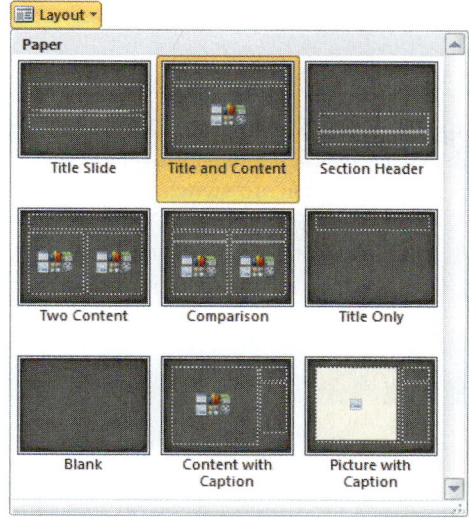

FIGURE 1–13   Default layouts

The Title and Content layout provides two placeholders, one for a title and one for content. Content can be text or any object. You click the placeholder and begin to type text, or you can click any one of the content icons to add an object. You will learn how to add text and content to slides in the next lesson.

Step-by-Step 1.8

1. On the Slides tab, scroll down until you can see slide 7, and then click the **slide 7** thumbnail.

2. On the Home tab, in the Slides group, click the lower part of the **New Slide** button. A gallery of layouts that you can choose for the new slide opens.

3. Click the **Title and Content** thumbnail on the Layout gallery. You added a new slide 8 with the Title and Content layout to the presentation.

4. Leave the presentation on the screen for the next Step-by-Step.

Notes Page View

▶ **VOCABULARY**

Notes Page view

Notes pane

Slide Sorter view

The *Notes Page view* displays your slides on the top portion of the page, with any speaker notes that have been entered for each slide appearing in the *Notes pane* on the bottom of the page. You can use these notes to help you as you make a presentation. Notes are also helpful if you print a handout for your audience to guide them through your presentation. To add speaker notes, click in the Notes pane and begin typing. You can also enter notes in Notes Page view. To switch to Notes Page view, on the Ribbon, click the View tab, and then in the Presentation Views group, click the Notes Page button. To enter a note, click in the Click to add text placeholder below the image of the slide. You will learn more about the Notes pane and how to use it effectively in Lesson 2.

Using Slide Sorter View

Slide Sorter view displays thumbnails of the slides on the screen so that you can move and arrange slides easily by clicking and dragging. Slide Sorter view gives you an overview of the entire presentation. To switch to Slide Sorter view, on the status bar, click the View Shortcuts Slide Sorter button. You can also click the Slide Sorter button on the View tab in the Presentation Views group.

Step-by-Step 1.9

1. On the status bar, click the **Slide Sorter** button ⊞. The screen appears, as shown in **Figure 1–14**.

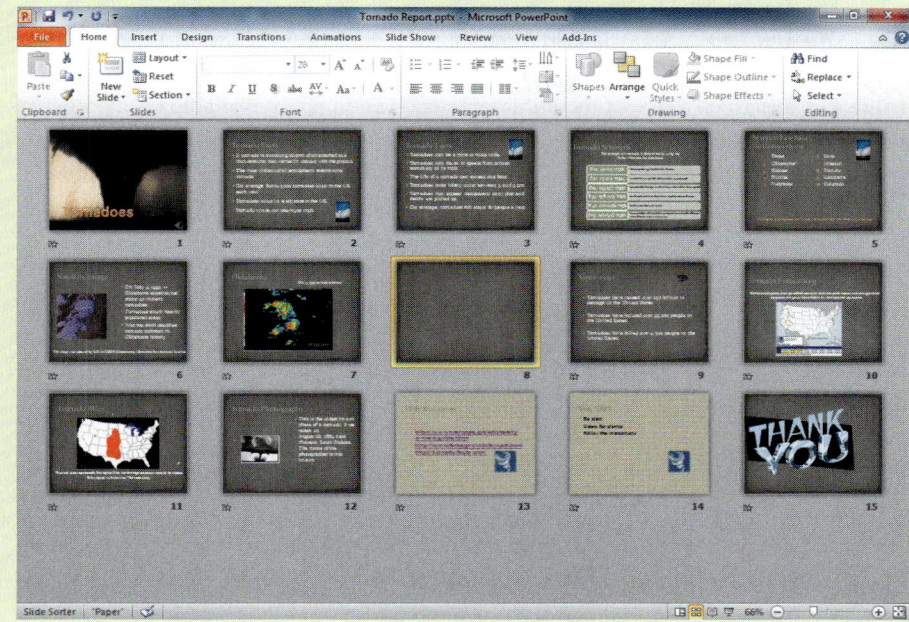

FIGURE 1–14
Slide Sorter view

2. Click the **slide 11** thumbnail so that it is selected and outlined in gold. The slide number appears below and to the right of the thumbnail.

3. Drag the **slide 11** thumbnail to the left of slide 6. A line appears between the two slides. Release the mouse button. Slide 11 moves to become slide 6, and all other slides are moved forward and renumbered.

4. Click the **slide 1** thumbnail and then save your work.

5. Leave the presentation on the screen for the next Step-by-Step.

Using Slide Show View

In *Slide Show view*, you run your presentation on the computer as if it were a slide projector to preview how it will look to your audience. When you run the slide show, each slide fills the screen. Any animations, sounds, and videos will play in Slide Show view. To switch to this view, click the View tab on the Ribbon and then click the Slide Show button in the Presentation Views group, or click the Slide Show button on the status bar, or press F5.

▶ **VOCABULARY**
Slide Show view

INTERNET

Broadcasting a PowerPoint presentation to the Web allows others to watch your presentation as you give it from a remote location through a Web browser. Your audience does not have to have PowerPoint installed on their computer to view your broadcast presentation. To broadcast a presentation, click the File tab, click Save & Send, click the Broadcast Slide Show command, and sign in to your Windows Live account or to a SharePoint Server.

If you move the mouse pointer to the lower-left corner of the screen as the slide show runs, a Slide Show toolbar appears. This menu, which has four buttons, helps you control the slide show. You can also right-click (click the right mouse button) any slide to open the shortcut menu, which includes additional commands. See **Figure 1–15**. **Table 1–1** describes a few of the commonly used commands available on the toolbar and on the shortcut menu.

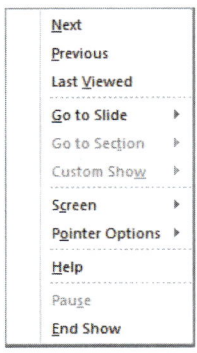

FIGURE 1–15   Slide Show shortcut menu

TABLE 1–1   Commonly used commands in Slide Show view

BUTTON	COMMAND ON SHORTCUT MENU	DESCRIPTION	NOTES
➡	Next	Advances to the next slide	
⬅	Previous	Displays the previous slide	
	Last Viewed	Displays the slide viewed immediately before the current slide	
✏	Pointer Options	Allow you to annotate a slide	Options include Arrow, Pen, Highlighter, Arrow options for Automatic, Hidden, Visible, and Ink Color options
	Screen	Changes the screen	Can display a black or white screen or switch to another open program
	Go to Slide	Displays a list of all slides in the presentation	Click to advance to any specific slide in the presentation
	End Show	Ends the slide show	

Step-by-Step 1.10

1. On the status bar, click the **Slide Show** button . Slide 1 appears on the screen and you watch the animations on the slide.

2. Click the mouse to advance to slide 2.

3. Right-click anywhere on the slide. On the shortcut menu, point to **Go to Slide**, and then click **14 Stay SAFE**. Slide 14 appears on the screen.

4. Right-click anywhere on the slide, and then click **End Show** on the shortcut menu. The slide show ends and appears in Slide Sorter view again.

5. Leave the presentation open for the next Step-by-Step.

> **TIP**
>
> You can press Esc anytime during a presentation to return to the view displayed prior to viewing the show.

Using Reading View

In *Reading view*, you run your presentation very much like Slide Show view. The slide does not quite fill the screen and you can use navigation buttons on the status bar beneath the slide. **Figure 1–16** shows Slide 10 in Reading view.

▶ **VOCABULARY**
Reading view

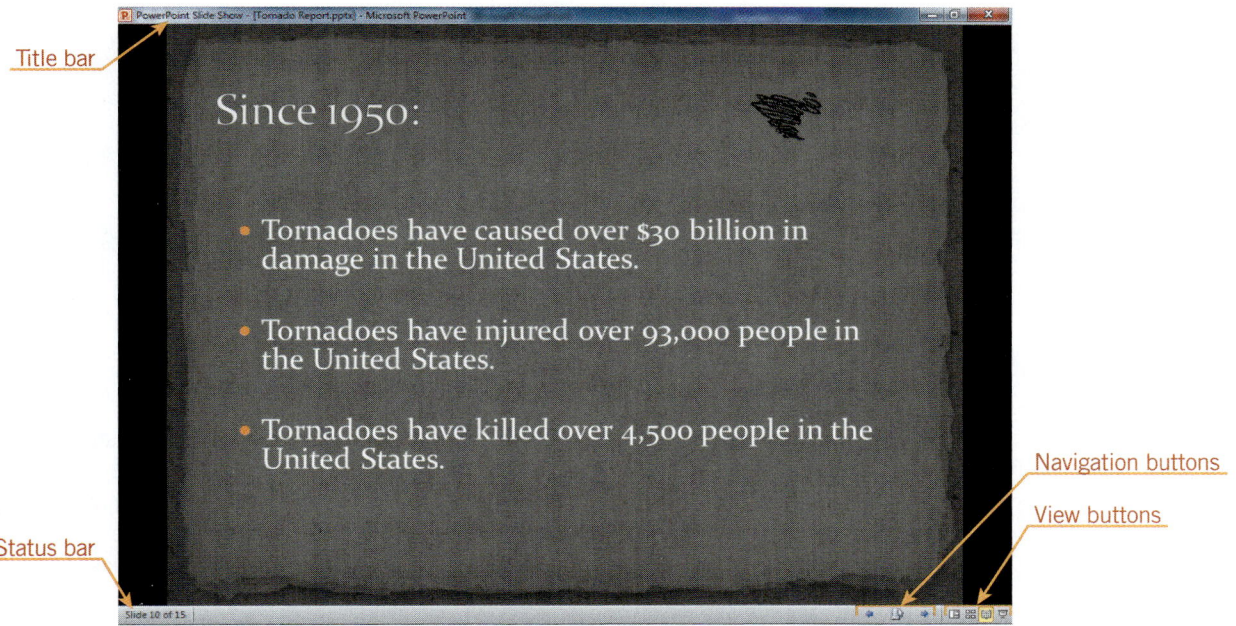

FIGURE 1–16   Slide in Reading view

Deleting Slides

If you decide that a slide does not fit your presentation, you can easily delete it. In Normal view, with the particular slide displayed, press Delete on the keyboard. You can also delete a slide, by right-clicking the slide, then cick Delete Slide on the shortcut menu. If you accidentally delete the wrong slide, immediately click the Undo Delete Slide button on the Quick Access Toolbar to restore the slide.

EXTRA FOR EXPERTS

If you make a mistake while using an Office program, you can press Ctrl+Z to undo the last entry. By default, you can undo up to 20 entries in PowerPoint. You can change the number of actions you can undo by changing the PowerPoint Options. Click the File tab, click Options, click Advanced in the left pane, and then change the number in the Maximum number of undos box as needed. Note, more undos requires more memory on your computer.

Step-by-Step 1.11

1. In Slide Sorter view, right-click the **slide 9** thumbnail, the new blank slide you inserted in a previous Step-by-Step. A shortcut menu opens.

2. On the shortcut menu, click **Delete Slide**. The slides renumber, and now there are 14 slides in the presentation.

3. Click the **slide 13** thumbnail.

4. Save the presentation and leave it open for the next Step-by-Step.

Printing a Presentation

VOCABULARY
handouts

PowerPoint offers several print options that can enhance your presentation for an audience. You can print all the slides in the presentation, you can print *handouts* that contain small pictures or thumbnails of your slides, along with an area for taking notes. You can also print a text outline of the presentation. Click the File tab on the Ribbon, then click Print to view the Print options in Backstage view, as shown in **Figure 1–17**. You can choose to print your presentation using the various settings in the center pane. Using the Handouts option, you can print handouts with two, three, four, six, or nine slides per page and choose whether they are ordered horizontally or vertically. If you are printing multiple copies of your presentation, you can choose how you want the pages collated.

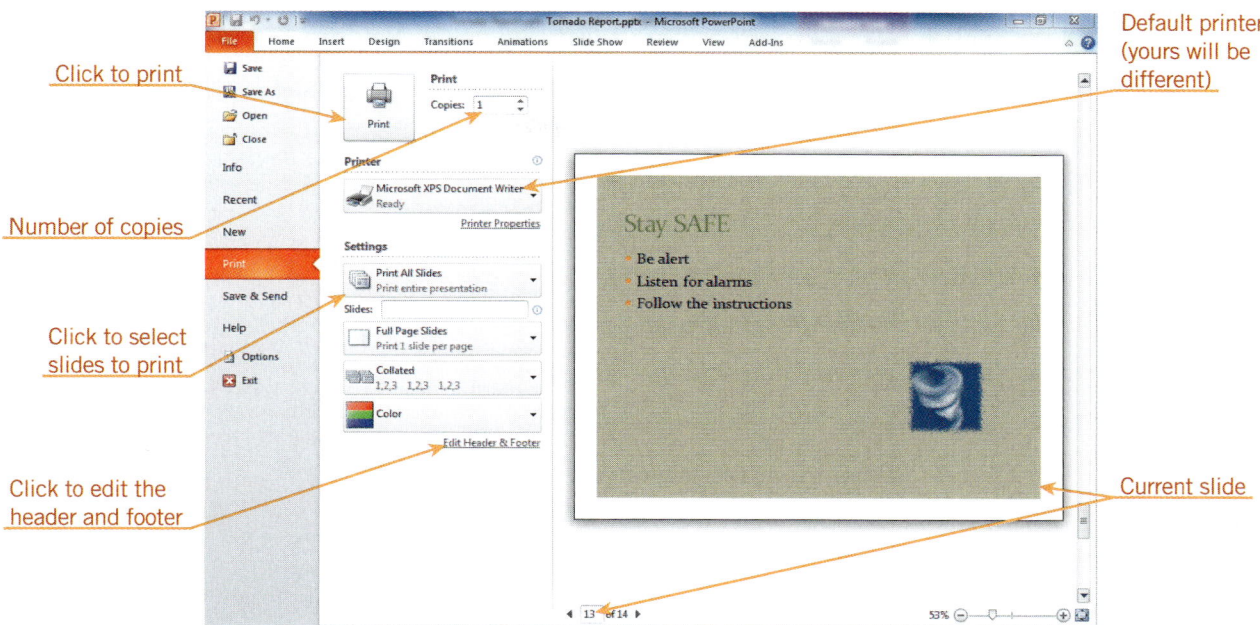

FIGURE 1–17   Print options

You can choose to print all the slides, only the current slide, or any combination of slides in your presentation. If you aren't printing your presentation in color, you can choose either the Grayscale or Pure black-and-white option. To make sure the slides print on the page correctly, there is a Scale to fit paper option. With the Frame slides option, you can choose whether the border of the slides appears when printed.

Step-by-Step 1.12

1. Click the **File** tab, and then on the navigation bar, click **Print**. The Print tab appears in Backstage View. (Refer again to Figure 1–17.)

2. In the first section, click the **Print All Slides** button, and then click **Print Current Slide**.

3. Make sure **1** appears in the Copies box. The selected slide, **slide 13**, appears in the right pane of Backstage view, as it would if you printed it.

4. To help distinguish your work from your classmates, enter your name in the presentation. At the bottom of the first section, click the **Edit Header and Footer** link to open the Header and Footer dialog box. Click the **Footer** check box, type your name in the Footer box, click the **Notes and Handouts** tab, click the **Footer** check box again, type your name in the Footer box, and then click **Apply to All**. Notice that your name appears at the bottom of slide 13 in the preview.

5. At the top of the first section, click the **Print** button, and then click **OK** in the Print dialog box to print the current slide.

> **TIP**
>
> You can preview what your presentation will look like when printed in black and white. On the Print tab in Backstage view, click the Color button, and then click Grayscale or Pure Black and White. You can also click the Grayscale or Black and White button in the Color/Grayscale group on the View tab on the Ribbon.

6. Click the **File** tab again, and then on the navigation bar, click **Print**. In the Settings section, click the **Print Current Slide** button, click **Print All Slides**, click the **Full Page Slides** button, and then click **Outline**.

7. Click the **Outline** button to open that menu again. See **Figure 1–18**.

FIGURE 1–18
Print Layout options

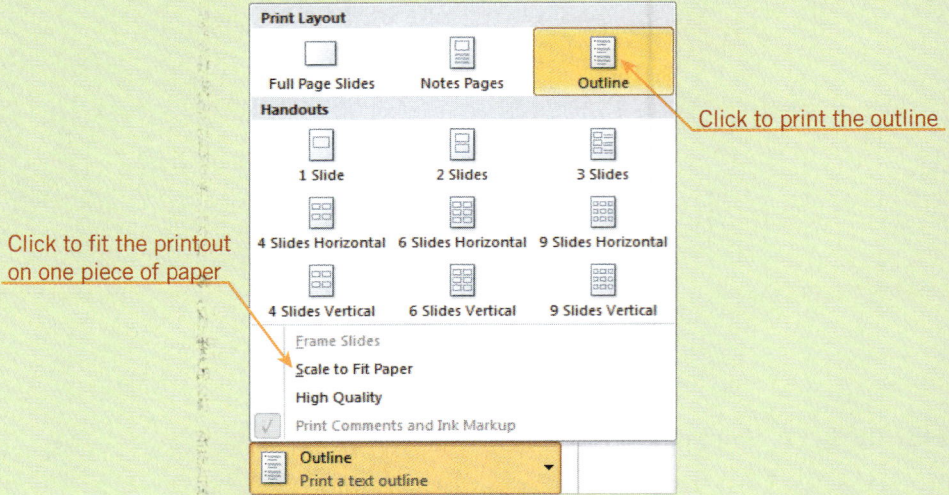

8. Click **Scale to Fit Paper**. Now the printout of the outline will fit on one piece of paper. The slide appears in the Print Preview tab window as an outline.

9. At the top of the first section, click the **Print** button, and then click **OK**. The presentation prints as an outline on one page.

10. Click the **File** tab, and then on the navigation bar, click **Print** again. In the center section, click the **Full Page Slides** button, and then in the Handouts section, click **9 Slides Horizontal**. This will print the first nine slides on one piece of paper, arranged horizontally, and the remaining five slides on another piece. Notice the right side of the Print tab changes to show this.

11. Click the **Print** button at the top of the center section. The presentation prints as a handout.

12. Click the **Home** tab on the Ribbon to leave Backstage view. Leave the presentation open for the next Step-by-Step.

Closing a Presentation and Exiting PowerPoint

When you want to close a presentation, click the File tab, and then on the navigation bar, click Exit, or click the presentation window Close button. If there are any unsaved changes to a presentation you have been working on, you will be asked if you want to save them before exiting.

Step-by-Step 1.13

1. Click the **File** tab, and then on the navigation bar, click **Exit** to close the presentation and exit PowerPoint.

2. Click **Yes** if prompted to save your changes.

SUMMARY

In this lesson, you learned:

- PowerPoint is an Office application that can help you create a professional presentation. When you start PowerPoint, you have the choice of opening an existing presentation or creating a new one.

- You can view your presentation in five different ways: Normal view, Slide Sorter view, Slide Show view, Reading view, and Notes Page view. Each view has its own advantages.

- You can insert slides, add text and objects to slides, and delete slides as you work to create the presentation.

- To view the presentation with animations and transitions, you use Slide Show or Reading view. A slide show can advance automatically or by clicking or pressing specific keys on the keyboard.

- You can print your presentation as slides using the Slides option, with notes using the Notes Pages option, or as an outline using the Outline View option. You can also choose to print handouts with two, three, four, six, or nine slides per page.

- To exit PowerPoint, click the File tab on the Ribbon, and then on the navigation bar, click Exit.

VOCABULARY REVIEW

Define the following terms:

animation	Notes Page view	Slide Show view
broadcasting	Notes pane	Slide Sorter view
handouts	Outline tab	Slides tab
layout	PowerPoint presentation	thumbnail
Live Preview	Reading view	transition
Normal view	Slide pane	Zoom slider

REVIEW QUESTIONS

MULTIPLE CHOICE

Select the best response for the following statements.

1. When you start PowerPoint, the first slide you see is the _____ slide.

   A. main

   B. Slide Sorter

   C. title

   D. animation

2. In which pane do you do most of the work creating and building slides?

   A. Outline

   B. Slide

   C. Notes

   D. Standard

3. Which of the following describes how objects are placed on a slide?

   A. Content   C. Animation

   B. Layout   D. Panes

4. How do you delete a selected slide?

   A. Click Delete Slide on the shortcut menu.

   B. Click the Erase Slide button.

   C. Click the New Slide button.

   D. Click the Zoom Out button.

5. Which of the following shows thumbnails of the slides?

   A. Notes pane   C. Outline tab

   B. Slide Show view   D. Slides tab

FILL IN THE BLANK

Complete the following sentences by writing the correct word or words in the blanks provided.

1. When you click the Title and Content thumbnail, you create a new slide from the _____ gallery.

2. The _____ tab in Normal view displays all of the text on your slides in the tab thumbnail.

3. The _____ shows only the text or words on the slides.

4. _____ are small images of the slides.

5. You can print _____ that contain small pictures or thumbnails of your slides.

MATCHING

Match the correct View in column 1 with the Description in column 2.

View   **Description**

_____ 1. Slide Sorter   A. Shows overview of all slides in the presentation

_____ 2. Normal   B. Displays each slide so that it fills the entire screen and so that you can see animations and transitions

_____ 3. Reading   C. Displays slides on the top portion of the page, with speaker notes on the bottom of the page

_____ 4. Slide Show   D. Full screen view of slides but with the title and status bar with navigation buttons

_____ 5. Notes Page   E. Use to add content to slides

PROJECTS

If you have a SAM 2010 user profile, your instructor may have assigned an autogradable version of the indicated project. If so, log into the SAM 2010 Web site at *www.cengage.com/sam2010* to download the instruction and start files.

PROJECT 1–1

1. Open the **Network.pptx** Data File.

2. Save the presentation as **Network Summary** followed by your initials.

3. Run the presentation as a slide show. Click to advance each slide, see the transitions and animations, and to display the bulleted items on each slide.

4. Leave the presentation open for the next project.

 ## PROJECT 1–2

1. View the **Network Summary** presentation in Slide Sorter view.

2. Select and move slide number 6 so that it is the second slide in the presentation.

3. Use the Font Color button in the Font group on the Home tab to change the color of any text on any slide.

4. Print the presentation as audience handouts with 9 Slides Vertical per page.

5. Switch to Reading view, and then run the presentation as a slide show.

6. Save and close the presentation. Exit PowerPoint.

PROJECT 1–3

1. Search the Internet for a PowerPoint project about a subject that interests you.

2. Create a presentation with the list of your ideas on two slides.

3. Save the project to your computer.

4. Run the presentation as a slide show.

5. Print the presentation as audience handouts on one piece of paper.

6. Save and close the presentation. Exit PowerPoint.

 CRITICAL THINKING

ACTIVITY 1–1

You can change the way that PowerPoint displays when you initially open the program. Open the PowerPoint Options dialog box by clicking the File tab, and then on the navigation bar, clicking Options. Review the General, Proofing, Save, and Advanced options that are available. Click Cancel to not save any changes.

ACTIVITY 1–2

It is helpful to plan a presentation before you actually create it on the computer. Sketch out ideas on paper for a presentation on one of the topics below, or make up your own. The presentation should have at least four slides. Include a title slide and indicate where you would put clip art, a video, and animation.

- Help start a community campaign to keep your city clean.
- Encourage people to donate blood in the blood drive campaign next week.
- Explain the procedure for some safety technique (performing CPR, fire prevention, how to baby-proof a house, performing first-aid).
- Offer the opportunity to be involved in a community project or volunteer organization.
- Explain the advantages of adopting an animal from the local shelter.
- Provide information about a new class that will be available in the fall.

LESSON 2

Creating and Enhancing PowerPoint Presentations

■ OBJECTIVES

Upon completion of this lesson, you should be able to:

- Create presentations and add slides.
- Insert headers and footers.
- Use the Slide Master and the Notes and Handout Master.
- Format slides, change layouts, and apply themes.
- Insert and edit text, then change alignment, spacing, case, and tabs.
- Check spelling, style, and usage.
- Add hyperlinks, clip art, and sounds.
- Apply custom animation and transitions.

■ VOCABULARY

align

animation

blank presentation

effect options

handout master

hyperlink

layout master

live preview

motion paths

notes master

placeholder

slide master

slide transitions

template

themes

Creating Presentations

▶ **VOCABULARY**

blank presentation

template

When you start PowerPoint, a new ***blank presentation*** appears on the screen. You can begin a new presentation from a blank presentation, or you can use any of the built-in features to help you start a new presentation. There are different methods you can use to create a presentation. In this lesson, you will learn how to create a presentation from a template and how to enhance a presentation and make it your own. You will learn how to add different elements and features to create a presentation that communicates your ideas and interests your audience.

Starting to Create a Presentation

To create your presentation, you can start with a blank presentation, you can use slides from an existing presentation, you can use a template, or you can create a presentation from an existing theme. A ***template*** is simply a presentation that includes theme elements, text, and graphics predesigned for a presentation. Templates are often very useful to help you get started on your presentation. The templates that come with PowerPoint are already formatted with certain themes, graphics, colors, fonts, and layouts. Templates often include some text to help you get started.

Start PowerPoint, click the File tab, and then click New to view the Available Templates and Themes in Backstage view, as shown in **Figure 2–1**. Blank Presentation is the first option; however, you can select from Recent templates, Sample templates, Themes, My templates, and New from existing. The list of Recent Templates contains the template files that were last opened.

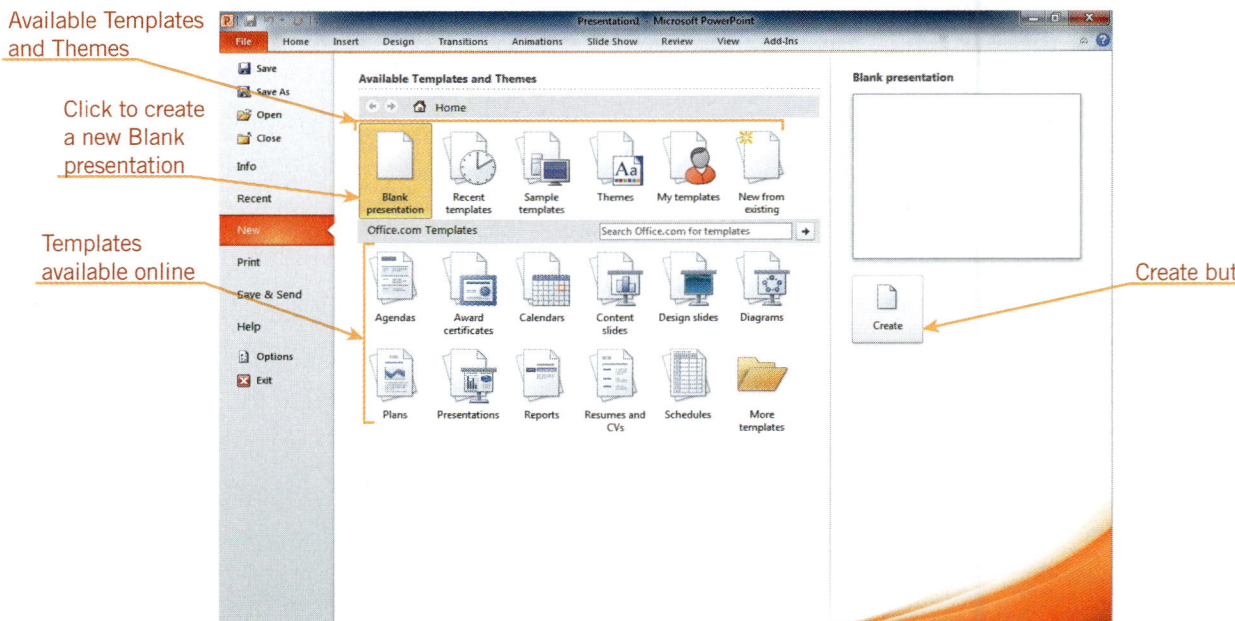

FIGURE 2–1   The New tab in Backstage view

The Blank Presentation option on the New tab in Backstage view lets you create a presentation from scratch, using the layout, format, colors, and graphics you prefer. If you decide to create a presentation using a template, you can choose a template that is right for the presentation you have planned. The Sample templates are shown in **Figure 2–2**.

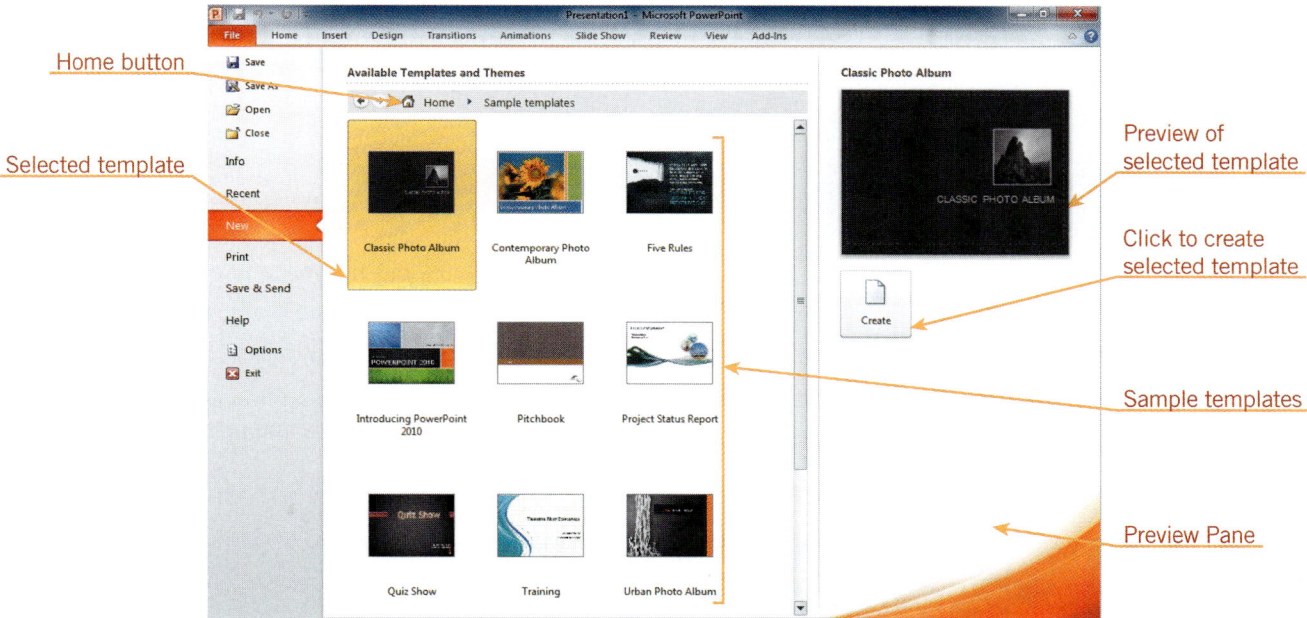

Home button

Selected template

Preview of selected template

Click to create selected template

Sample templates

Preview Pane

FIGURE 2–2   Sample templates on the New tab

When you select templates in Backstage view, you navigate through folders to find the template that you want. A navigation bar that works just like the Address bar in Windows Explorer appears above the list of templates in the center pane. Click the previous folder to back up a level, click Home to go to the first level showing all the templates, or click the Forward and Back buttons as needed to find the template to download.

If your computer is connected to the Internet, you can select from professional templates that are posted on Microsoft Office Online Web site at www.office.com. To choose a template from Microsoft's Web site, click the type of template you would like in the Office.com Online section, open a folder to display templates in that category, and then click any thumbnail. In Backstage view, the right pane is the *Preview pane* as it shows a preview of the selected template. Once you find the template you want, click Download, as shown in **Figure 2–3**.

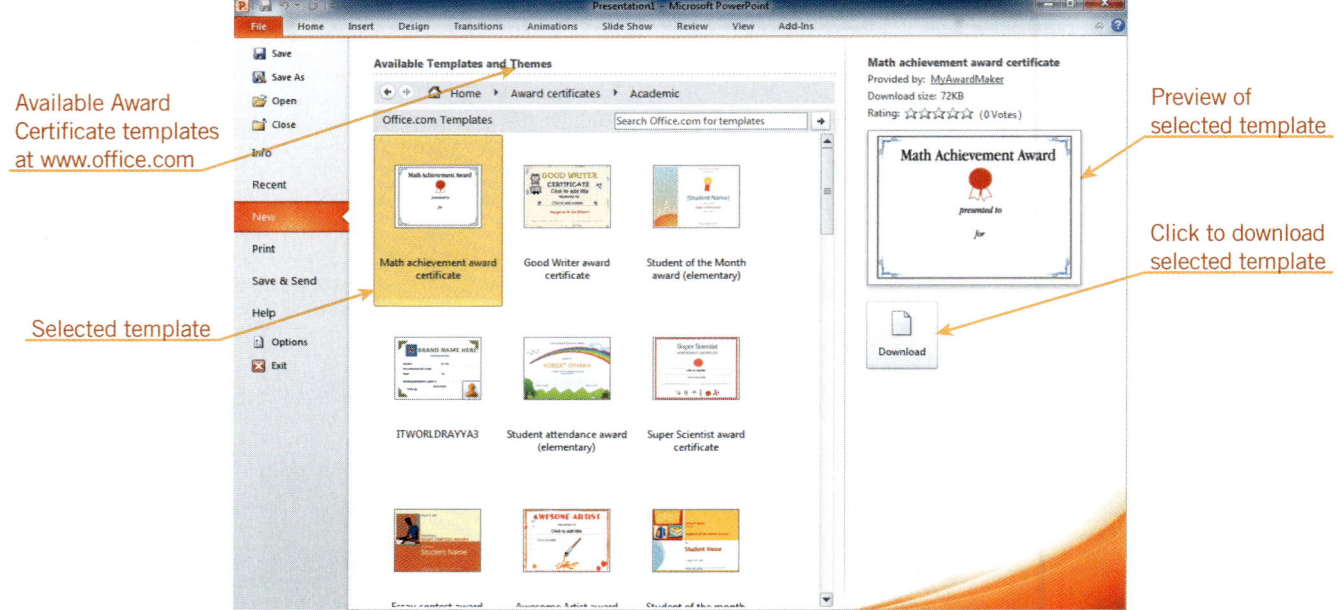

FIGURE 2–3   Award certificates category in the Available Templates and Themes section

Unless you have a particular reason for creating a presentation from a blank document, it is easier and less time consuming to use a template. You can always modify the presentation as you go along.

Step-by-Step 2.1

If the Introducing PowerPoint 2010 template is not available on your system, select any other template to complete these steps.

1. Start PowerPoint. Click the **File** tab, and then click **New**. Backstage view opens with options for templates, themes, or a new blank presentation.

2. In the top row, click **Sample templates**, scroll to view the available templates, and then click the **Introducing PowerPoint 2010** thumbnail.

3. Click the **Create** button in the Preview pane.

   A presentation that includes 20 slides, complete with sample content, is created, as shown in **Figure 2–4**. The text is formatted, and many of the slides include graphics. You can view, edit, and modify this presentation just as you would any presentation. You can add and delete slides as necessary for your purposes.

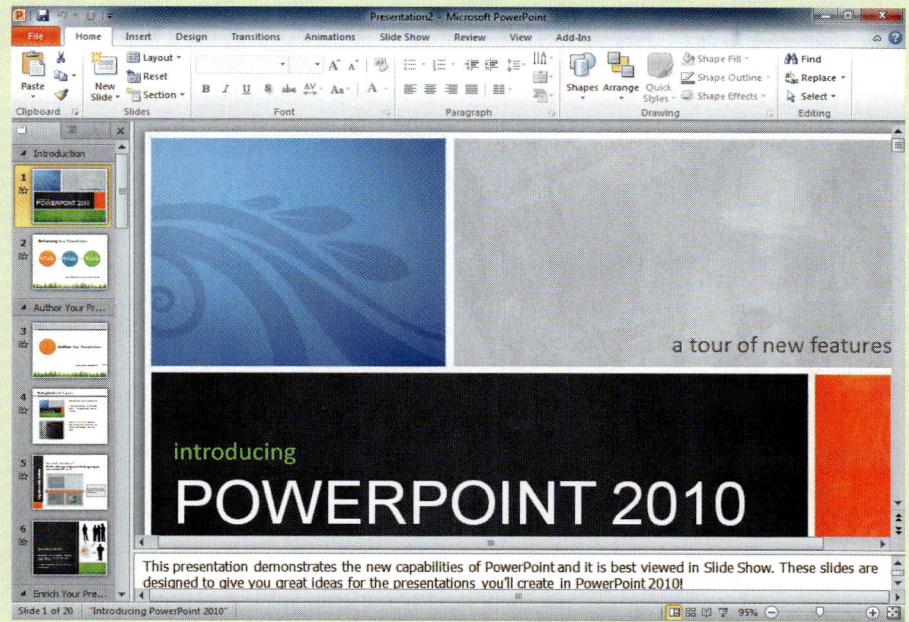

FIGURE 2–4
Presentation from template

4. On the Quick Access Toolbar, click the **Save** button 🖫, navigate to the drive and folder where your Data Files are stored, and then save the presentation as **PowerPoint2010 Tour**, followed by your initials.

5. On the status bar, click the **Slide Show** button 🖳 and then press **spacebar** to advance through all of the slides in the presentation.

6. Click the **File** tab, and then click **Close** to close the presentation.

7. Leave PowerPoint open for the next Step-by-Step.

TIP

The Introducing PowerPoint 2010 presentation has useful information about PowerPoint 2010 and the new features in the program. At any point if you want to stop the show, press Esc.

Creating Presentations from Existing Templates

If you cannot find a template that you like on Office.com or that came with PowerPoint, you can use one created by yourself or a colleague.

EXTRA FOR EXPERTS

PowerPoint templates have a .potx file extension. PowerPoint presentations have a .pptx file extension.

Step-by-Step 2.2

1. Click the **File** tab, and then click **New**.

2. In the top row in the Available Templates and Themes section, click **New from existing**. The New from Existing Presentation dialog box opens.

3. Navigate to the drive and folder where your Data Files are stored, click **EMT.potx**, and then click **Create New**. EMT.potx is a template that was created for you. You created a new presentation from that template.

4. On the Quick Access Toolbar, click the **Save** button 🖫.

TIP

Be sure the file extension for the selected file is .potx.

5. Navigate to the drive and folder where your Data Files are stored, and then save the presentation as **EMT Rosewood**, followed by your initials.

6. On the vertical scroll bar, click the **Next Slide** button ⬇ as many times as needed to view the slides, and then press **Home** to return to the first slide. There are several slides in the presentation, but they do not have color, graphics, or any enhancements that would make a presentation fun and interesting to watch.

7. Leave the presentation open for the next Step-by-Step.

Inserting Headers and Footers

You can add text to every slide using the Header and Footer dialog box. You can also add the slide number, date, or time in a header or footer. Click the Insert tab on the Ribbon, and then in the Text group, click the Header & Footer button. This opens the Header and Footer dialog box, which has two tabs. You can add headers and footers to the slides or the notes and handouts.

Step-by-Step 2.3

1. On the Ribbon, click the **Insert** tab, and then in the Text group, click the **Header & Footer** button to open the Header and Footer dialog box. The **Slide** tab should be selected, as shown in **Figure 2–5**.

FIGURE 2–5
Header and Footer dialog box

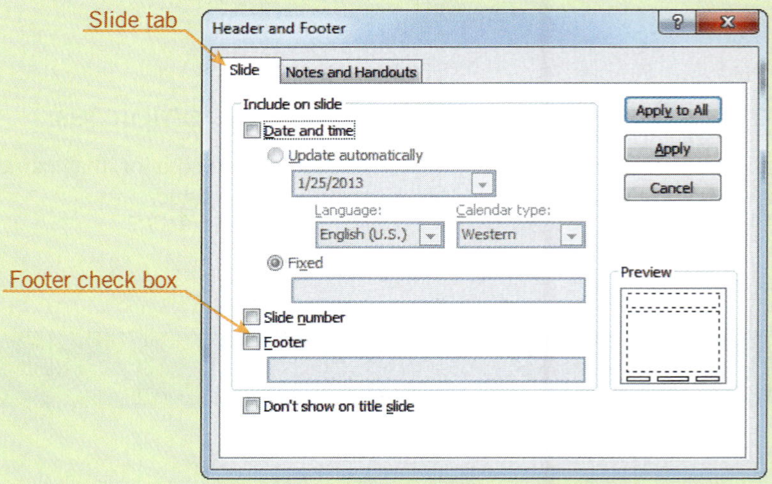

2. Click the **Footer** check box, and then, in the Footer box, type **This presentation is not intended as a substitute for professional medical training.**

3. Click **Apply to All**. The footer appears on all the slides in the presentation. See **Figure 2–6**.

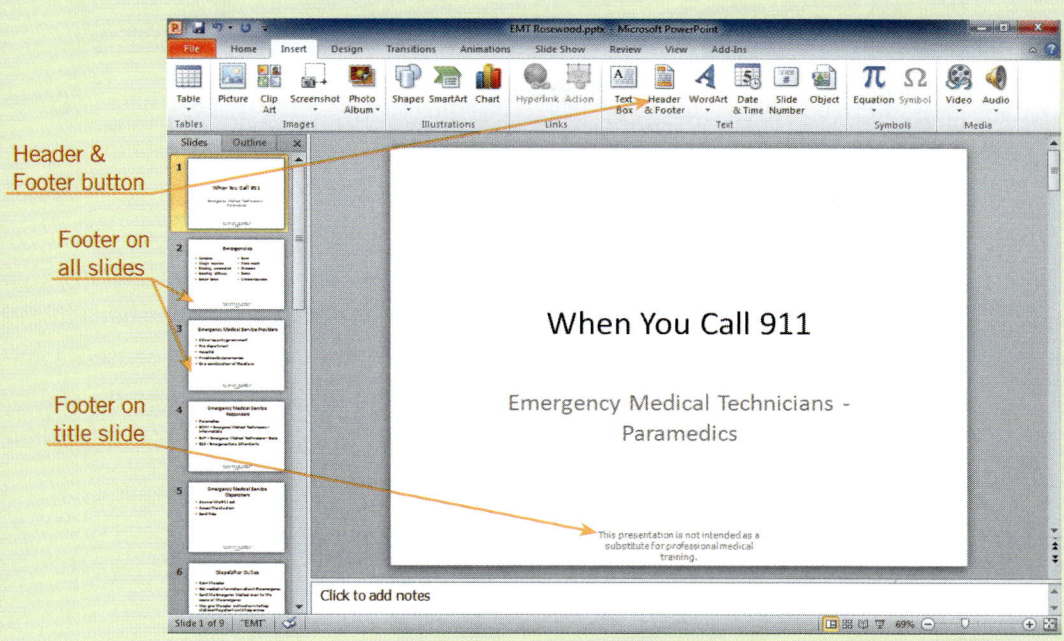

FIGURE 2–6
Footer added to all slides

4. On the vertical scroll bar, click the **Next Slide** button ⬇ three times to view the next three slides, and then press **Home** to return to the first slide.

5. Leave the presentation open for the next Step-by-Step.

Applying Themes

You can use a theme to change the appearance of your slides without changing the content. *Themes* are predesigned graphic styles that you can apply to existing slides. Themes include fonts, colors, graphics and effects. After you apply a theme, you can change the color theme, font, formatting, and layout of your slides to create a different look.

Applying Themes to the Entire Presentation

To apply a theme to a presentation, first click the Design tab on the Ribbon. The Themes group on the Design tab displays all the available themes. Click the More button in the Themes group to open the Themes gallery. When you position the pointer over a theme, the name of the theme appears in a ScreenTip and the selected slide shows a Live Preview of the effect of the theme on the slide. Click the theme thumbnail to apply the theme to all the slides in the presentation.

▶ **VOCABULARY**
themes

⊟ **EXTRA FOR EXPERTS**

To create a new presentation with a theme different from the default theme, click the File tab to open Backstage view, and then on the navigation bar, click New. In the top row in the Available Templates and Themes section, click Themes. Click the theme you want to use, and then click the Create button.

Step-by-Step 2.4

1. On the Ribbon, click the **Design** tab, and then in the Themes group click the **More** button [▾] to open the Themes gallery.

2. Move the mouse pointer over several of the themes to use Live Preview to see the effect on the slides.

3. Click the **Austin** theme (use the ScreenTips to help you identify this theme). PowerPoint applies the Austin theme to all of the slides in the presentation, as shown in **Figure 2–7**. The new theme caused some changes to be made to the format of some of the elements on the slides. The fonts changed, the footer moved to the right side of the title slide, and new graphics appear on the slides.

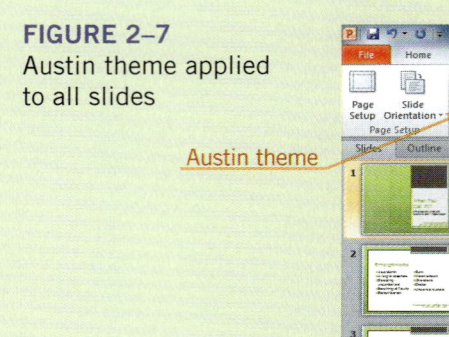

> **TIP**
>
> The themes in the gallery are organized in alphabetical order.

FIGURE 2–7
Austin theme applied to all slides

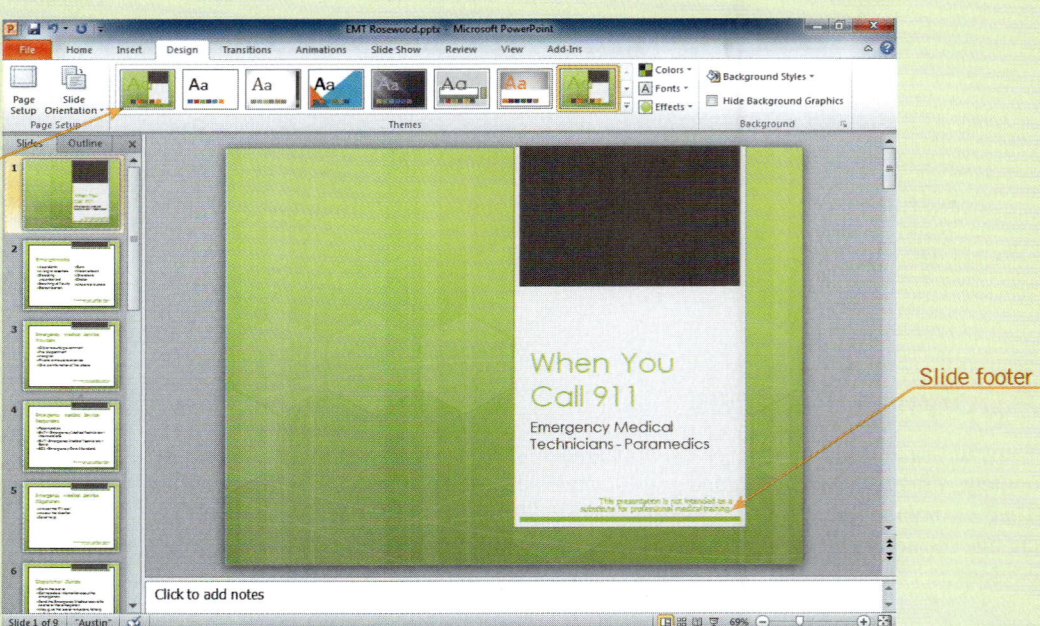

4. Save the presentation and leave it open for the next Step-by-Step.

Changing Theme Colors

All themes come with default theme fonts and theme colors. The styles of the fonts and the palette of colors help define the theme. You can change the theme fonts and colors at any time. Colors are assigned to specific elements in a presentation such as title or body text, background and accents. Themes create a unified look because the same colors are used for the same elements throughout a presentation. To apply different colors to your presentation, on the Ribbon, click the Design tab, and then in the Themes group, click the Colors button. A menu showing the list of the colors for each theme, as shown in **Figure 2–8**. You can use Live Preview with this menu. To apply a different set of theme colors to all of the slides without changing the theme, click the color scheme you want to use.

FIGURE 2–8   Colors gallery

You can apply a different color theme to all the slides by clicking the theme on the menu. You can also apply a color theme to selected slides. To select more than one slide, hold down Ctrl while you click the slides on the Slides tab. To apply color themes to only the selected slides, click the Colors button, right-click the Theme colors in the gallery, and then click Apply to Selected Slides on the shortcut menu.

Changing Theme Fonts

To apply a different set of theme fonts to your presentation, on the Ribbon, click the Design tab, and then in the Themes group, click the Fonts button. A menu opens listing the font sets for each theme. You can again use Live Preview to see the effect of applying each set of fonts. To apply a different set of fonts to the slides, simply click the set of fonts in the menu.

Applying a Theme to Individual Slides

You can use a theme to change the appearance of a single slide or several slides without changing the rest of the slides in the presentation. To select more than one slide, hold down Ctrl while you click the slides on the Slides tab. To view the themes, click the Design tab. If you right-click the theme thumbnail in the Themes group, the shortcut menu options let you apply the theme to all of the slides in your presentation or to only the select slides. To apply the new theme to these selected slides, click Apply to Selected Slide on the shortcut menu to apply the new theme to the selected slide rather than all the slides in the presentation.

TIP

You can use different colors to show a change of topics in your presentation.

TIP

Right-click the theme thumbnail to view options that you can use to set the default theme or add the Gallery to the Quick Access Toolbar.

Step-by-Step 2.5

1. On the Slides tab, click the **slide 6** thumbnail, *Dispatcher Duties*.

2. On the Design tab, click the **More** button ⊡ in the Themes group to open the Themes gallery.

3. In the Themes gallery, point to the **Apothecary** theme, see the effect on the slide, right-click the **Apothecary** theme, and then click **Apply to Selected Slides**. The theme of the current slide changes to the new theme.

4. In the Themes group, click the **Colors** button to open the Colors gallery, right-click **Flow**, and then click **Apply to Selected Slides**. The color of the text in the title as well as the color of the text in the body of the slide changed to dark teal. The bullets also changed from gray to blue to match the new theme colors.

5. Save the presentation and leave it open for the next Step-by-Step.

📼 EXTRA FOR EXPERTS

The Apply to Matching Slides option applies the selected theme to all slides in the presentation that have the same layout as the selected slide.

▶ VOCABULARY

slide master

placeholder

layout masters

📼 EXTRA FOR EXPERTS

Layouts also include placeholders for slide objects such as tables, charts, SmartArt graphics, movies, sounds, pictures, and clip art.

Using the Slide Master

The *slide master* controls the formatting for all the slides in the presentation. For each presentation the slide master stores information about the theme and slide layouts, including the background, color, fonts, effects, placeholder sizes and placement on the slides. *Placeholders* are the boxes in layouts that hold the content or slide objects such as body text and titles. Each slide master has several *layout masters*. There is a slide master and associated layouts for each theme in the presentation. You can use the slide master to change such items as the font, size, color, style, alignment, spacing, and background. Changing the slide master affects the appearance of all of the slides in a presentation associated with that master slide or layout, and gives all slides associated with the master a consistent look. You can add headers and footers to slides in the slide master. You can also place an object, such as a logo or graphic, on every slide by placing the object on the slide master.

To view the slide master and layouts, as shown in **Figure 2–9**, you need to switch to Slide Master view. Click the View tab on the Ribbon, and then in the Master Views group, click the Slide Master button. When you are in Slide Master view, the pane on the left displays the slide master as the first thumbnail and the layouts as thumbnails underneath it. The layouts are nested beneath each slide master. When you point to the slide master or to a layout, a ScreenTip displays the name of the master and the slide numbers of the slides in the presentation to which that layout is applied. To make changes to the slide master or a layout, click the master in the pane on the left to display it in the Slide pane.

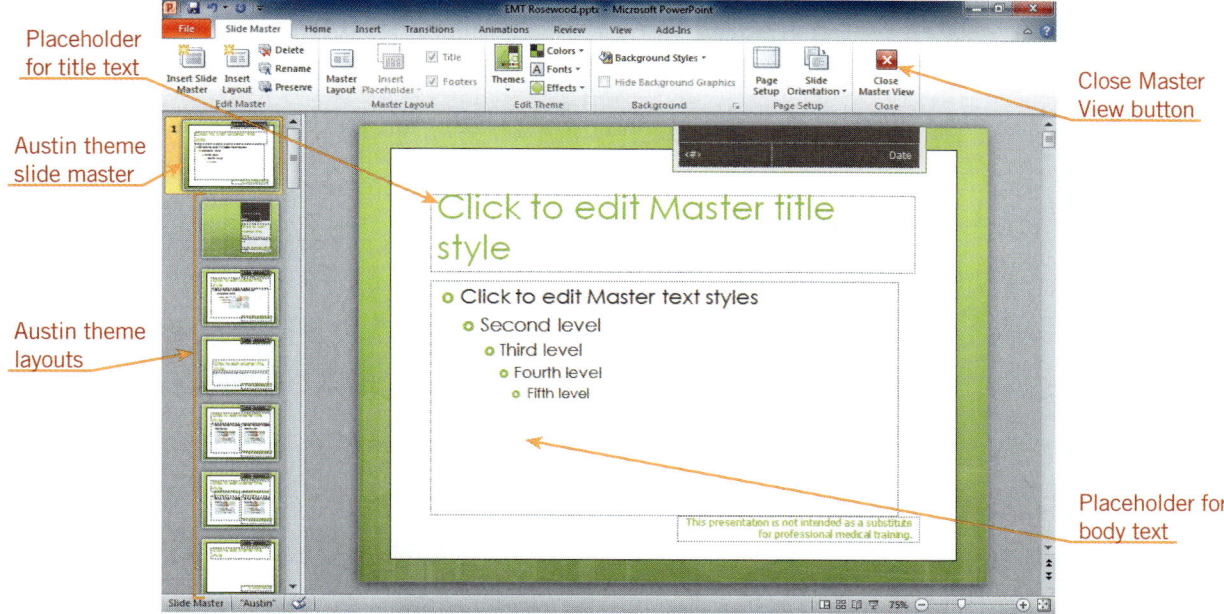

Placeholder for title text

Close Master View button

Austin theme slide master

Austin theme layouts

Placeholder for body text

Click to edit Master title style

o Click to edit Master text styles
   o Second level
      o Third level
         o Fourth level
            o Fifth level

This presentation is not intended as a substitute for professional medical training.

FIGURE 2–9   Slide Master view

In Slide Master view, the Slide Master tab appears on the Ribbon. Use the buttons in the Edit Master group to insert a new layout master or insert a new slide master. The Master Layout group buttons help you change the master layout, including headers and footers. The Edit Theme buttons change the theme characteristics for the entire slide show. The Background group buttons work to change the graphics behind the objects, and open the Format Background dialog box to change the Fill or Picture on the background of the selected layouts. The Page Setup group changes the slide orientation from Portrait to Landscape and changes margins for the entire slide show. Click the Close Master View button to return to Normal view.

TIP

You can override the formats applied to the presentation by the slide master by making changes directly to individual slides.

Step-by-Step 2.6

1. On the Ribbon, click the **View** tab, and then click the **Slide Master** button in the Presentation Views group to open Slide Master view. You see the Apothecary slide master.

2. Scroll to the top of the slide layout thumbnails, and then click the first thumbnail, the **Austin Slide Master**. Refer back to Figure 2–9.

EXTRA FOR EXPERTS

Display the slide master by pressing Shift and clicking the Normal button on the status bar in the lower-right corner of your screen. Press Shift and click the Slide Sorter button on the status bar in the lower-right corner of your screen to display the handout master.

3. In the pane on the left, click the **second thumbnail** to view the Title
    Slide Layout for the Austin master. Refer to **Figure 2–10**.

    The Hide Background Graphics check box is selected for this layout. This
    is set by the theme. Later in these steps you will add a graphic to the slide
    master that will not appear on the title slide because this box is checked.

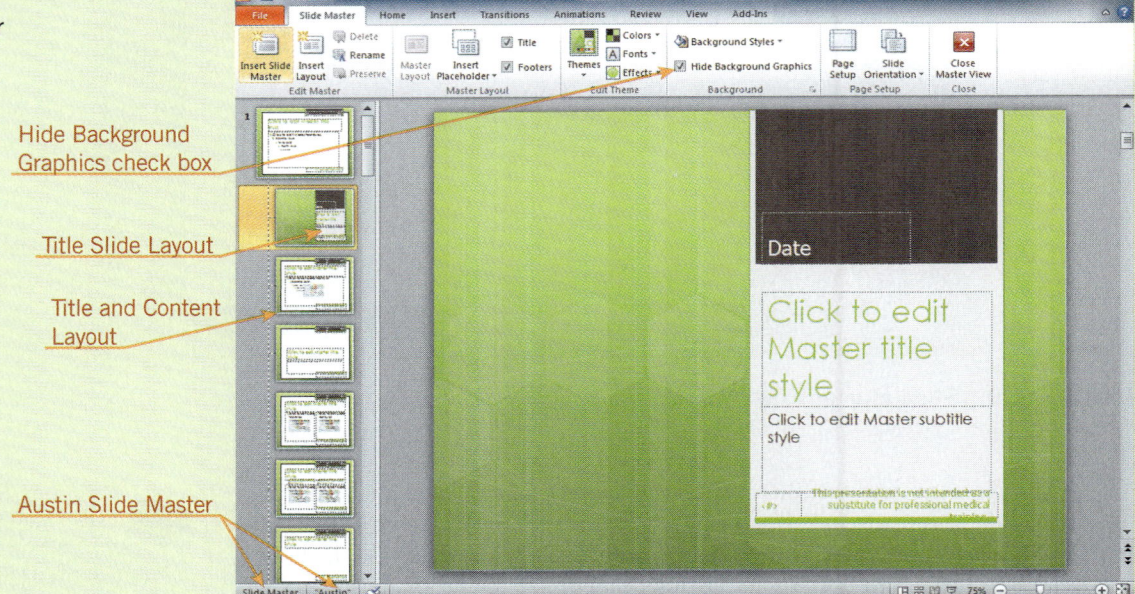

FIGURE 2–10
Austin Slide Master

Hide Background
Graphics check box

Title Slide Layout

Title and Content
Layout

Austin Slide Master

4. Point to the **third thumbnail**, the Title and Content Layout. The ScreenTip
    tells you which slides are used by the Title and Content Layout.

5. Click the **first thumbnail** to view the Austin Slide Master. On the Ribbon,
    click the **Insert** tab, and then in the Images group, click the **Picture** but-
    ton to open the Insert Picture dialog box.

6. Navigate to the drive and folder where your Data Files are stored, click
    FirstAid.jpg, and then click **Insert**. The image of a red cross on a black
    background appears on the center of the slide master.

7. Click and drag the picture to the lower-left corner of the slide.

8. Position the pointer on top of the **upper-right sizing handle** so that it
    changes to ⤢, and then drag down and to the left to resize the picture
    smaller until the sizing handle is on top of the lower-left corner of the
    content placeholder. See **Figure 2–11**.

Picture Tools
Format tab

Content placeholder

Background graphics
hidden

Sizing handle

Inserted and
resized image

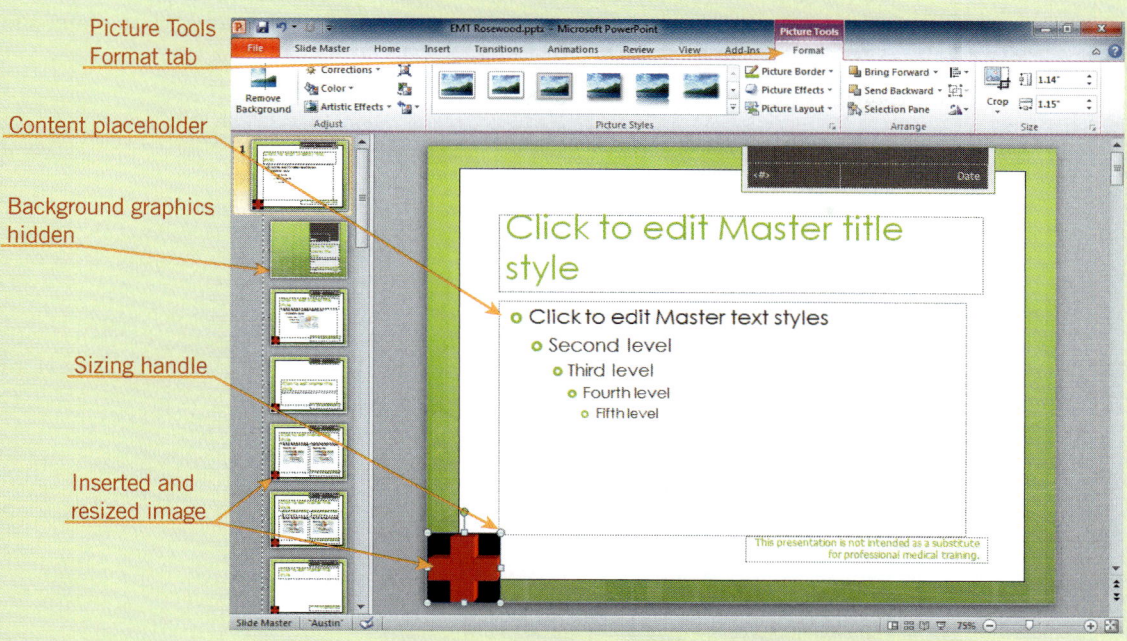

FIGURE 2–11
Inserting a picture
on the slide master

9.   On the Ribbon, click the **Slide Master** tab, and then in the Close group, click the **Close Master View** button. Slide Master view closes and you see the presentation in Normal view again.

10. View the slides in the presentation. Slides 2–5 and 7–9, use the Austin theme, so they show the image of the red cross in the lower-left corner of the slide. Slide 6, which uses the Apothecary theme, does not show the image because it has its own slide master which does not include the image. The title slide does not show the image because the Hide Background Graphics check box is selected for the Title Slide Layout for this theme.

11. Save the presentation and leave it open for the next Step-by-Step.

Using the Notes Master and Handout Master

PowerPoint has other masters that are similar to the slide master. The *handout master* lets you add items that you want to appear on all your handouts, such as a logo, the date, the time, and page numbers. On the *notes master*, you include any text or formatting that you want to appear on all your speaker notes. Click the View tab on

▶ **VOCABULARY**
handout master

notes master

the Ribbon, and then in the Master Views group, click the Handout Master button to view the handout master, as shown in **Figure 2–12**. Click the Notes Master button to view the notes master, as shown in **Figure 2–13**.

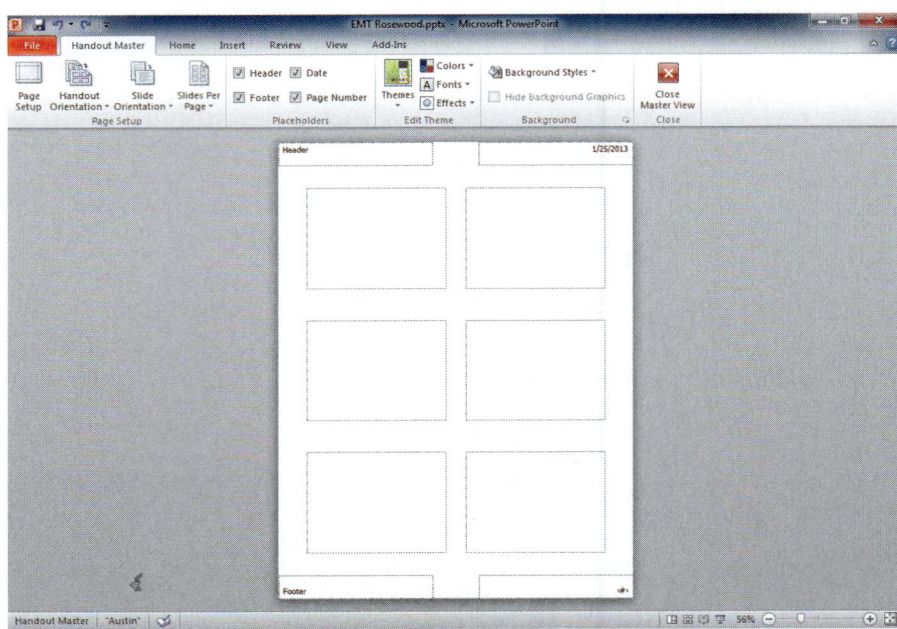

FIGURE 2–12   Handout master

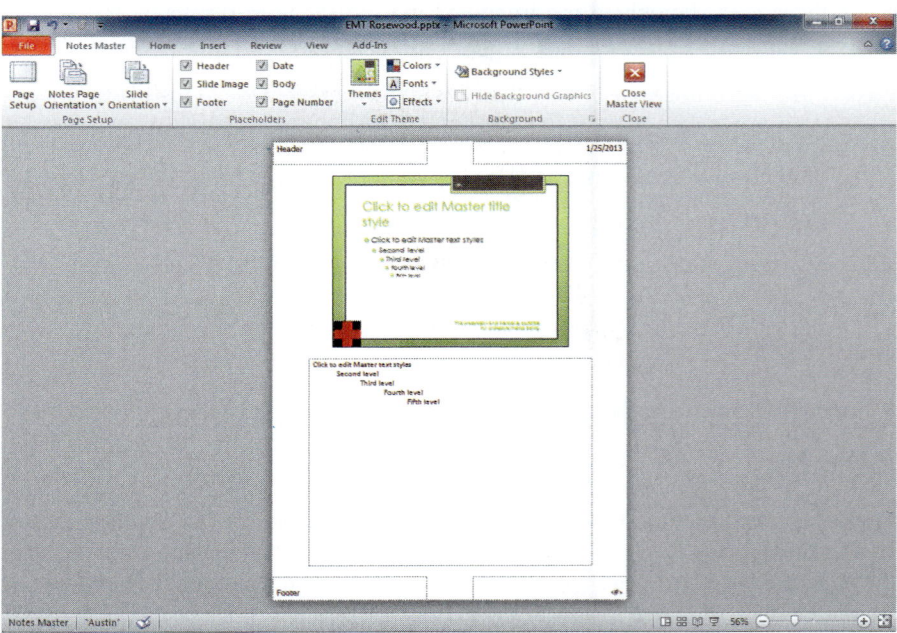

FIGURE 2–13   Notes master

Editing Pictures in PowerPoint

PowerPoint contains tools that allow you to edit, format, and stylize a picture to get the exact effect you need for a slide. Select the picture you want to edit to make the Picture Tools Format tab appear on the Ribbon. The Picture Tools Format tab includes buttons that allow you to adjust the picture's contrast, color and brightness, set a transparent color, or compress the picture. You can also apply a picture style and add a border. Use the Background Removal tool to remove the background of a picture so it blends in with the background of the slide. The picture editing tools include the ability to apply artistic effects. These are similar to effects you might find in picture editing programs, such as making the picture look like glass, appear cartoon-like, or seem to be painted using watercolors. You can arrange the picture to line up or **align** with the other objects on the slide. There are several align commands that place your object relative to other objects on the slide. Align commands include Left, Center, Right, Top, Middle, and Bottom. You can also crop, rotate, resize, or reposition the picture as needed to best fit the slide. The Reset Picture feature will undo all changes you made and display the picture as it originally appeared.

▶ **VOCABULARY**
align

Step-by-Step 2.7

1. On the Slides tab, click the **slide 1** thumbnail. On the Ribbon, click the **Insert** tab, and then in the Images group, click the **Picture** button to open the Insert Picture dialog box.

2. In the drive and folder where your Data Files are stored, click **Rose.jpg**, and then click **Insert**. A picture of a red rose appears in the center of the slide and fills the slide.

3. On the Picture Tools Format tab on the Ribbon, in the Size group, click in the **Shape Height** text box, type **2** and then press **Enter**. You don't need to change the width because it adjusted proportionally to 3" when you changed the shape height.

4. Drag the image of the rose to the center of the green panel so that it is positioned in a way that you find appropriate for the slide.

5. On the Format tab, in the Arrange group, click the **Align** button [icon] to open the menu, and then click **Align Middle**. The photo is now in the middle of the green panel.

6. In the Picture Styles group, click the **More** button [icon] to open the Picture Styles gallery, and then slowly point to several picture styles to see the effect on the picture and read the ScreenTips identifying the name of each style.

7. In the Picture Styles gallery, click the **Metal Rounded Rectangle** style in the last row, second to last style.

8. In the Adjust group, click the **Artistic Effects** button. Move the mouse pointer over several of the thumbnails to see the effect on the photo and read the ScreenTips, and then click the **Glass** effect, the last effect in the third row.

9. In the Adjust group, click the **Color** button, and then in the Recolor section, click the **Green**, **Accent color 1 Dark** color box.

10. In the Adjust group, click the **Compress Pictures** button, make sure the **Apply only to this picture** check box is selected, and the **Use document resolution** option button is selected, and then click **OK**.

11. Click to deselect the picture and compare your slide to **Figure 2–14**.

FIGURE 2–14
Formatted picture
on the title slide

Formatted picture

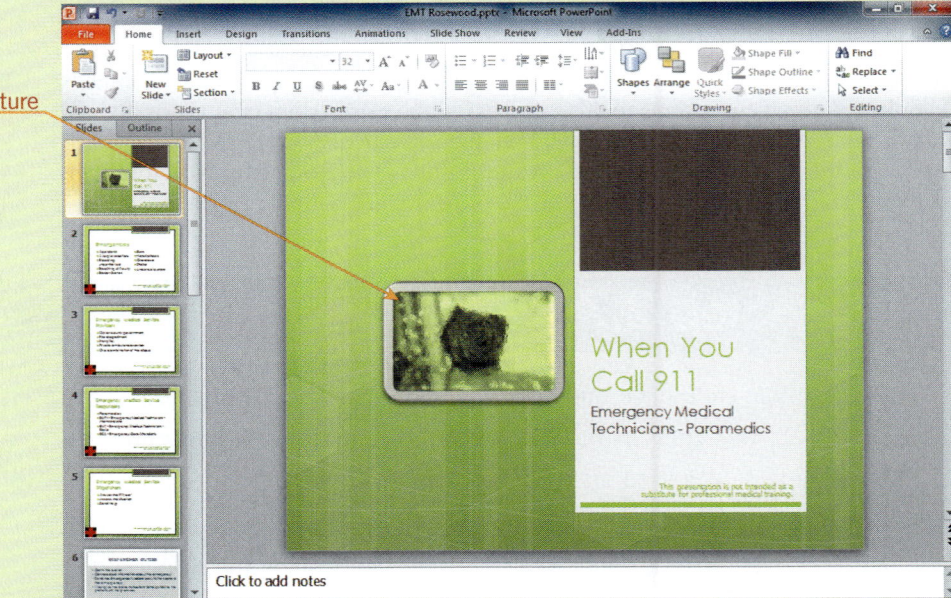

12. Save the presentation and leave it open for the next Step-by-Step.

Understanding Layouts

When you want to change the arrangement of text or graphics on slides easily, you can use the theme's layouts. PowerPoint includes nine layouts that you can choose from to create a new slide or change the layout of an existing slide. The layouts include placeholders for text and content. Text includes paragraphs and bulleted lists. Content can be clip art, tables, organization charts, SmartArt graphics, objects, graphs, video, and media clips. Just click a placeholder icon and replace it with your own file or object. You can choose the layout that best fits the need of a particular slide.

Adding Slides

As you continue to create your presentation, you will want to add slides. On the Ribbon, on the Home tab, in the Slides group, click the New Slide button or right-click the slide thumbnail on the Slides tab or in Slide Sorter view, and click New Slide on the shortcut menu. You can also click the New Slide button arrow, then click Duplicate Selected Slides to insert a new slide that is the same as the selected slide or slides. In Normal view, PowerPoint places the new slide after the selected slide, using the same layout as the selected slide. Clicking the New Slide button arrow

EXTRA FOR EXPERTS

You can reuse slides from other presentations. In the Slides group, click the New Slide button arrow, click the Reuse Slides command to open the Reuse Slides task pane, select the presentation that has the slides, and then select each slide you want to reuse.

opens the Slide Layout gallery, which allows you to choose a layout for the new slide. The Slide Layout gallery has the nine standard layouts based on the theme that has been applied. Click a layout to insert a new slide with that layout.

Step-by-Step 2.8

1. On the Slides tab, click the **slide 9** thumbnail, *Features of Emergency Departments*.

2. In the Slides group, click the **New Slide** button arrow to open the Slide Layout gallery. Because you applied a second theme to one of the slides in this presentation, there are two sets of layouts in the gallery labeled with the theme names: Austin and Apothecary.

3. In the Austin section, click the **Two Content** layout to insert a new slide with the Austin theme. The new slide 10 has a title placeholder and two content placeholders. Your slide should look similar to **Figure 2–15**.

TIP

The status bar tells you the slide number of the selected slide, total number of slides, and theme of the slide.

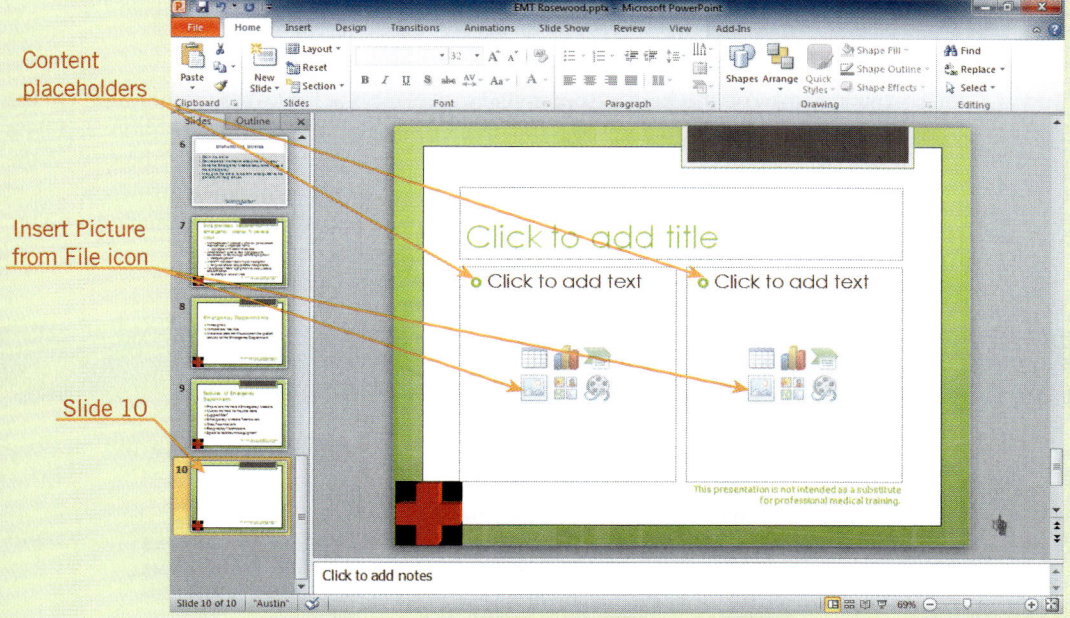

FIGURE 2–15
New slide with Two Content layout

Content placeholders

Insert Picture from File icon

Slide 10

4. In the right content placeholder, click the **Insert Picture from File** icon to open the Insert Picture dialog box. In the drive and folder where your Data Files are stored, click **FirstAid.jpg**, and then click **Insert**.

5. Use the buttons on the Picture Tools Format tab to apply your choice of picture effects to format the picture.

6. Save the presentation and leave it open for the next Step-by-Step.

Finding and Replacing Text on Slides

To find and replace text, on the Home tab of the Ribbon, in the Editing group, use the Find and Replace buttons. The Find what box is in the Find dialog box as well as the Replace dialog box. The Find command locates the word or phrase you type in the Find what box. The Replace command locates the word or phrase you type in the Find what box and replaces it as directed with the word or phrase you have typed in the Replace with box in the Replace dialog box. See **Figure 2–16**. Click Find Next to find the next occurrence, Replace to replace the next occurrence, and Replace All to replace all occurrences.

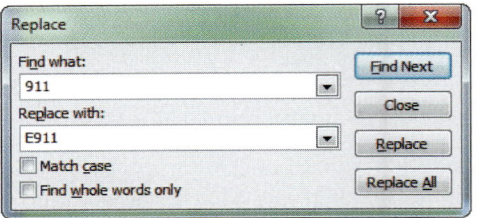

FIGURE 2–16   Replace dialog box

Finding and Replacing Fonts on Slides

You can also use the Replace command to replace one font with another font. On the Home tab in the Editing group, click the arrow next to the Replace button, and then click Replace Fonts. The Replace Font dialog box opens. You select the font in the presentation that you want to replace, and then you click the With arrow and select the font you want to replace it with. Click Replace and all the text formatted with the original font will be reformatted with the replacement font.

Step-by-Step 2.9

1. On the Home tab, in the Editing group, click the **Replace** button. The Replace dialog box opens at the bottom of the screen.

2. In the Find what box, type **Staff**, and then press **Tab**. The insertion point moves to the Replace with box.

3. In the Replace with text box, type **Personnel**, and then click **Find Next**. PowerPoint finds the word "Staff" on slide 9.

4. Click **Replace**. The word "Staff" is replaced on slide 9 with the word "Personnel" and PowerPoint searches for the next instance of the word "Staff." A dialog box opens telling you that PowerPoint has finished searching the presentation.

5. Click **OK** to close that dialog box, and then in the Replace dialog box, click **Close**.

6. Save the presentation and leave it open for the next Step-by-Step.

Adding Text to Slides

As you continue to work on your presentation, you may find that you need to add text to help explain a concept or introduce a new idea. Words should be used sparingly on a slide. However, you can always add text to existing slides to improve the presentation.

Working with Placeholders

The slide layouts create placeholders on the slides that reserve a space in the presentation for the type of information you want to insert. To replace a text placeholder, click the placeholder text. A box with a hashed-line border appears around the text. You can then type whatever you like. One way to enter text on a slide is to work in the Slide pane; this way you can see the text you enter, the formatting, and the placement on the slide.

TIP

You can also add a text box to a slide. A text box is created by clicking the Insert tab on the Ribbon, and then, in the Text group, clicking the Text box button.

Step-by-Step 2.10

1. On the Slides tab, click the **slide 10** thumbnail.

2. In the Slide pane, click the **Click to add title** placeholder, and then type **CPR**.

3. In the left content placeholder, click the **Click to add text** placeholder, type **Begin rescue breathing**, then press **Enter**. A new bullet appears for the second line in the content placeholder.

4. Type **Begin chest compressions**, press **Enter**, and then type **Call 911**. The slide has a slide title and a bulleted list with 3 lines of text in the left placeholder. The image you entered is in the right placeholder.

5. On the Ribbon, on the Home tab, click the **New Slide** button arrow in the Slides group, and then click the **Title and Content** layout to create a new slide 11.

6. In the Slide pane, click the **Click to add title** placeholder, and then type **Why Study First Aid?**.

7. Click the **Click to add text** placeholder, type **Injury and illness occur daily**, press **Enter**, type **Knowledge can help**, press **Enter**, and then type **Proper reaction may improve recovery**.

8. In the Slides group, click the **New Slide** button to insert a new slide 12 with a Title and Content layout.

9. In the Slide pane, click the **Click to add title** placeholder, and then type **Emergencies**.

10. Click the **Click to add text** placeholder. Type the following and press **Enter** after each line, and then click a blank area of the slide to deselect the placeholder. Compare your screen to **Figure 2–17** when you are finished.

- ■ **Bleeding**
- ■ **Shock**
- ■ **Fractures**
- ■ **Poisoning**
- ■ **CPR**

FIGURE 2–17
New slides on Slides tab

Slide 12

Slide title

Bullet list

New slides

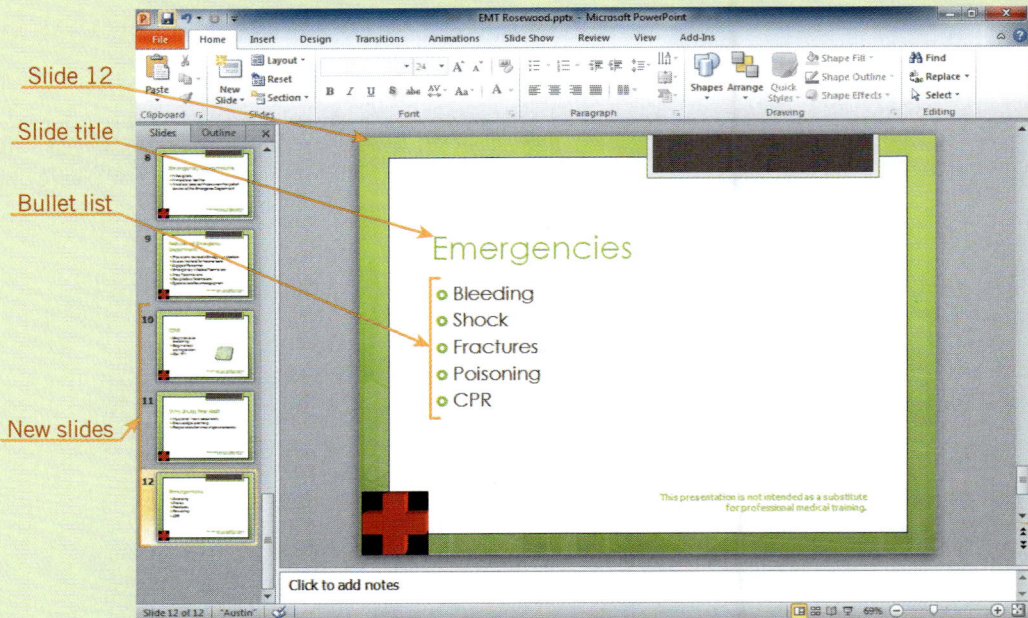

11. Save the presentation and leave it open for the next Step-by-Step.

Using the Outline Tab to Enter Text

You have learned how to enter text by typing it directly on the slide in the Slide pane. You can enter the rest of the presentation using the Outline tab. When you enter text using the Outline tab, pressing the Tab and Enter keys doesn't work the same way as when you work in the Slide pane.

Step-by-Step 2.11

1. In the left pane, click the **Outline** tab.

2. On the Ribbon, on the Home tab, click the **New Slide** button in the Slides group to insert a new slide 13 with a Title and Content layout.

3. On the Outline tab, type **Bleeding** as the title of the new slide 13. You did not have to click the title placeholder as you type on the Outline tab. The text appears in the placeholder on the Slide pane.

4. Press **Enter** and then press **Tab**. The insertion point is now after a new bullet that was created on the Bleeding slide.

5. Type the following as the content on the slide, pressing **Enter** after each line:

   - **Apply pressure**
   - **Use a clean bandage**
   - **Elevate injury**
   - **Slow bleeding**
   - **Call 911**

6. Press and hold **Ctrl**, and then press **Enter** to insert a new slide with a Title and content layout. Type **Shock** as the title for this slide.

7. Press **Enter** and then press **Tab** to move the insertion point the first bullet for this slide.

8. Type the following as the content on the slide, pressing **Enter** after each line:

   - **Lie down**
   - **Elevate legs**
   - **Maintain body temp**
   - **Monitor breathing**
   - **Provide air**
   - **Call 911**

9. Insert another new slide with the **Title and Content** layout using any method. Using either the Outline tab or the Slides tab, type **CPR ABC** as the title of this slide.

10. Type the following as the content on the slide:

    - **Airway**
    - **Breathing**
    - **Circulation**

TIP

If you press Tab, the text will become a bullet on the previous slide.

TIP

When the insertion point is in the slide title, you can also press and hold Ctrl, and then press Enter to move the insertion point into the content placeholder.

11. Compare your Outline tab and your slides with **Figure 2–18**. Save the presentation and leave it open for the next Step-by-Step.

FIGURE 2–18
New slides on the Outline tab

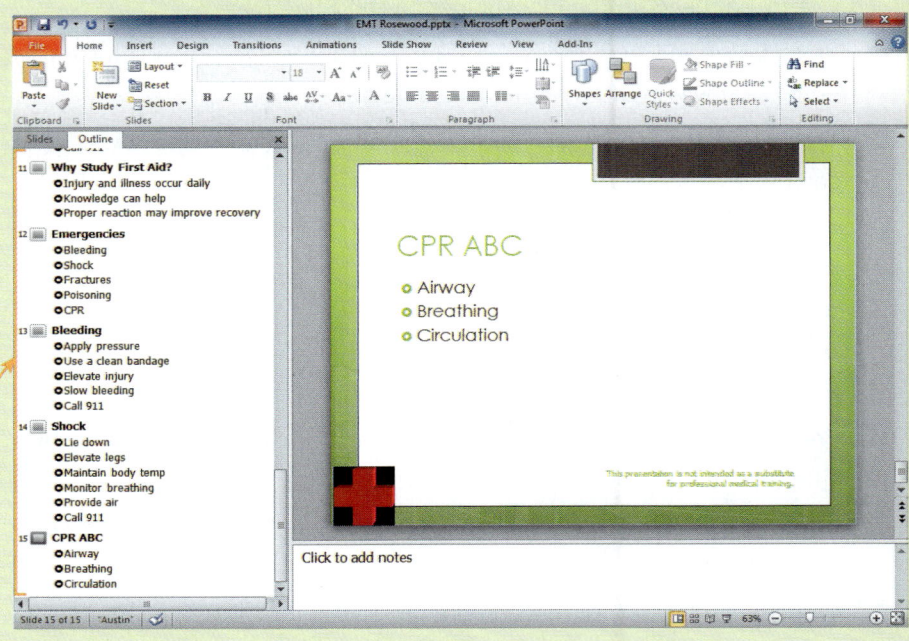

Entering Text in Text Boxes and Shapes

TIP

To move a text box, click the border to select it then use the move pointer to drag. To resize a text box, drag the sizing handles.

You have learned how to enter text by typing it directly on the slide in the Slide pane. You also learned that you can enter text using the Outline tab. These methods enter text into placeholders. There are times when you want to enter text on a slide where there is no placeholder. In this case, the text box or shape provides the perfect solution. You can use the Text Box tool to add text to a slide without using a content or text placeholder. On the Ribbon, on the Insert tab, in the Text group, click the Text Box button. To add a shape, on the Home tab click the Shapes button to open the Shapes gallery. The Shapes button is also on the Insert tab in the Illustrations group. Once you open the Shapes gallery, click to select a shape, then use the pointer to draw the shape on the slide. To add text to a shape, select the shape, then type the text in the shape.

Step-by-Step 2.12

1. In the pane on the left, click the **Slides** tab. **Slide 15**, *CPR ABC*, is selected and appears in the Slide pane.

2. On the Ribbon, click the **Insert** tab, and then in the Text group, click the **Text Box** button.

3. In the Slide pane, click in the middle of the slide. You created a text box on the slide.

4. Type **If the patient does not respond, call 911.**, and then click a blank area of the slide. Compare your screen to **Figure 2–19**. If your text box is in a different position than in the figure, click it, and then click drag the border of the text box (not a sizing handle) to move the text box to a new position on the slide.

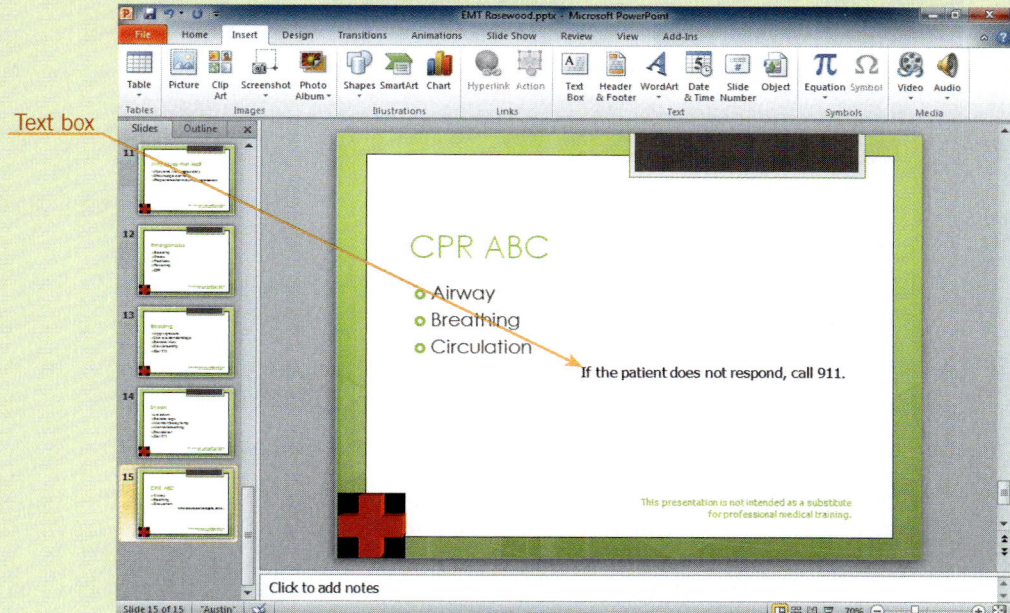

FIGURE 2–19
Text box on slide

5. On the Slides tab, click the **slide 3**, *Emergency Medical Service Providers* thumbnail.

6. On the Home tab on the Ribbon, in the Drawing group, click the **Shapes** button. The Shapes gallery opens. Use the Screen Tips in the Shapes gallery to identify the shapes you want.

7. In the Rectangles section, click the **Rounded Rectangle** shape 🔲.

8. Click in the area of the slide just below and to the right of the word "above". A rectangle with rounded corners appears on the slide.

TIP

At higher resolutions, the Shapes button appears as a gallery on the Ribbon.

9. Type **EMS saves lives** as shown in **Figure 2–20**.

FIGURE 2–20
Text in a shape

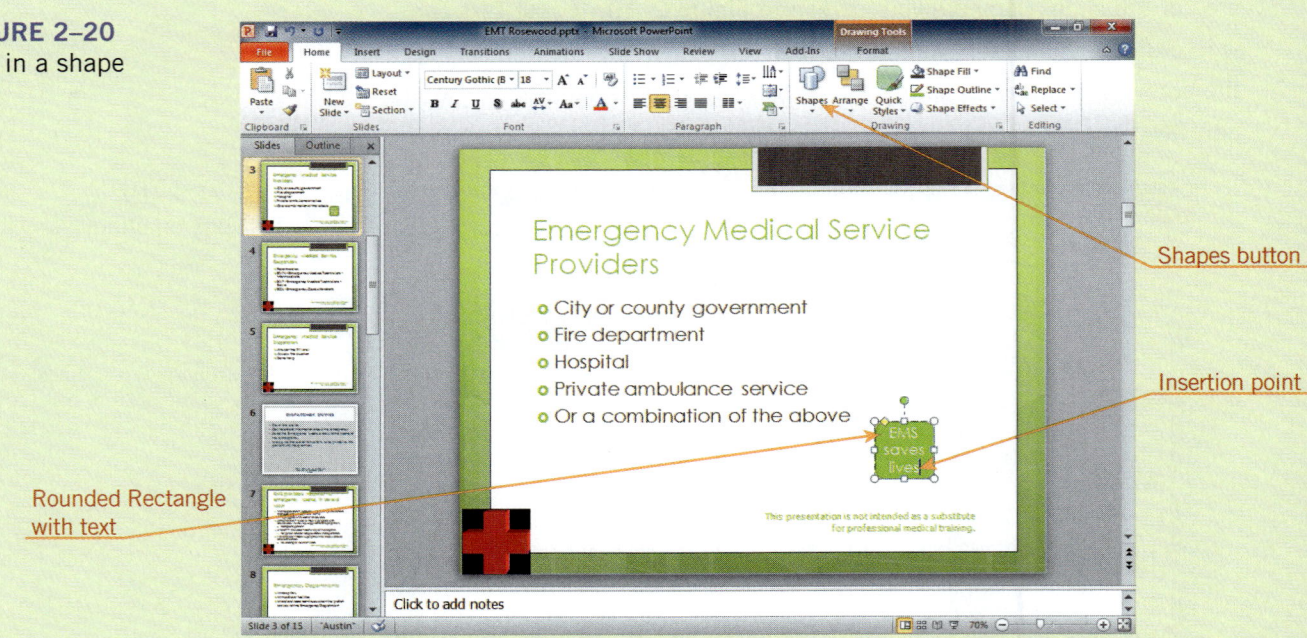

Shapes button

Insertion point

Rounded Rectangle
with text

10. Click the **Outline** tab. The outline for slide 3 does not include the shape with the text.

11. Scroll the Outline tab to view the outline for slide 15. The text box text does not appear on the Outline tab.

12. Save the presentation and leave it open for the next Step-by-Step.

Adding Notes to Slides

A good PowerPoint presentation generally contains brief, main points about the subject. You want your audience listening to you rather than reading large amounts of text on slides. Use the speaker notes to remind yourself of any additional information you need to include in your speech. To add speaker notes, click in the Notes pane below the Slide pane and begin typing, or switch to Notes Page view. If the text is too small to read in Notes Page view, you can increase the size by using the Zoom slider on the status bar.

Step-by-Step 2.13

1. In the pane on the left, click the **Slides** tab, and then click the **slide 10** thumbnail, *CPR*.

2. In the Notes pane, click the **Click to add notes** placeholder, and then type **Remember the ABCs of CPR: Airway, Breathing, Circulation**. See **Figure 2–21**.

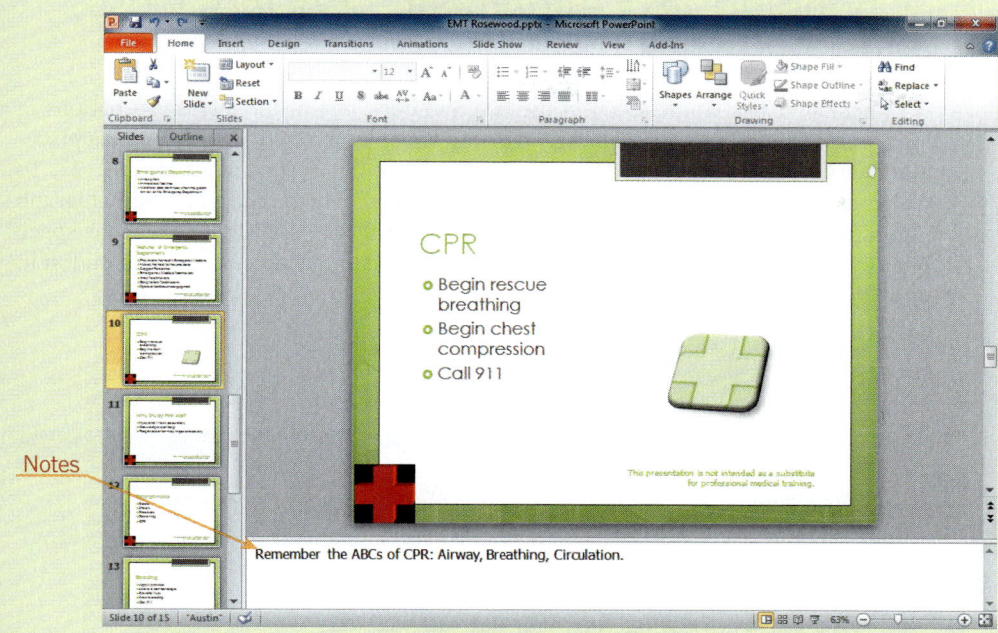

FIGURE 2–21
Note in Notes pane in
Normal view

3. On the Ribbon, click the **View** tab, and then in the Presentation Views group, click the **Notes Page** button to see the Notes Page for slide 10. See **Figure 2–22**.

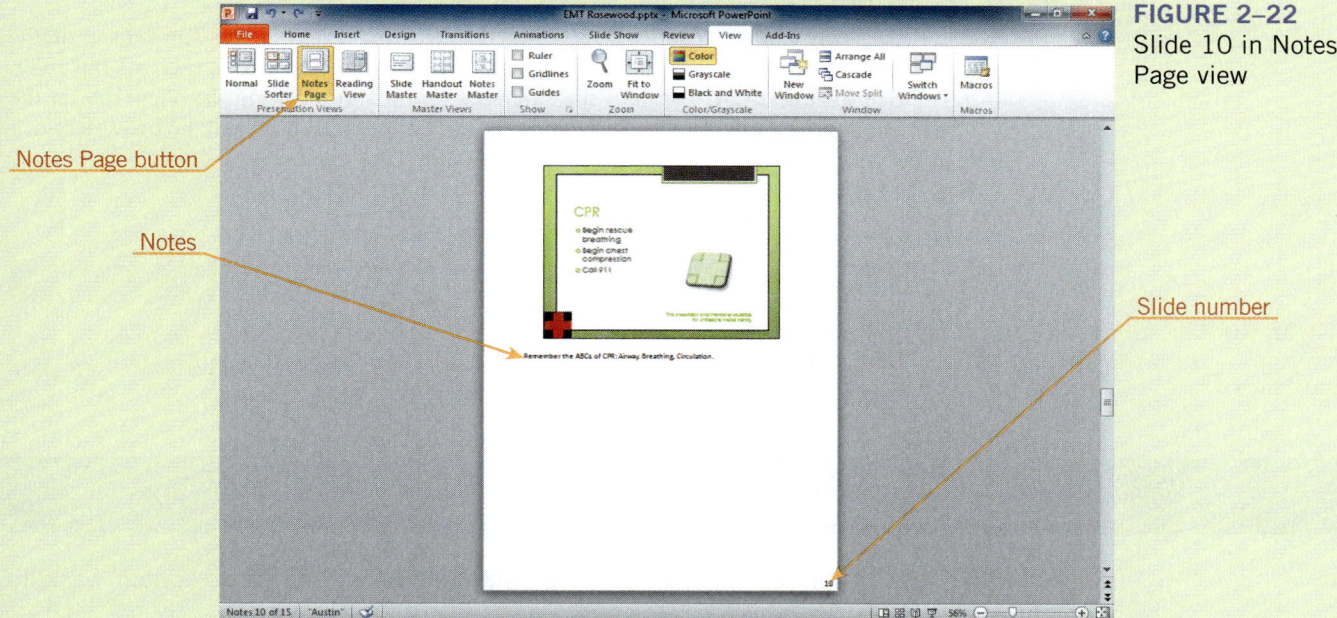

FIGURE 2–22
Slide 10 in Notes
Page view

4. Save the presentation and leave it open for the next Step-by-Step.

Changing Text Alignment, Spacing, Case, and Tabs

To change text alignment, select the text and click one of the alignment buttons in the Paragraph group on the Home tab on the Ribbon. Selected text in a content place-holder will also display the Drawing Tools Format tab as shown in **Figure 2–23**. To change line spacing, select the text, click the Line Spacing button in the Paragraph group, and then select the line spacing you want to use. To change the space between the characters or letters in your slide, use the Character Spacing button in the Font group.

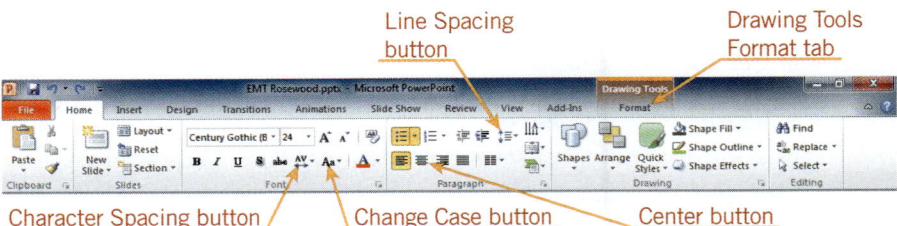

FIGURE 2–23   Drawing Tools Format tab

To change the case of text, first select the text. On the Ribbon, on the Home tab, in the Font group, click the Change Case button, and then choose one of the five options: Sentence case, lowercase, UPPERCASE, Capitalize Each Word, or tOGGLE cASE.

You can set a tab by selecting the text and clicking the Tab button at the left of the horizontal ruler. Clear a tab by dragging the tab marker off the ruler. See **Figure 2–24**. You turn the rulers on and off by clicking the View tab on the Ribbon, and then in the Show/Hide group, click the Ruler check box to select it.

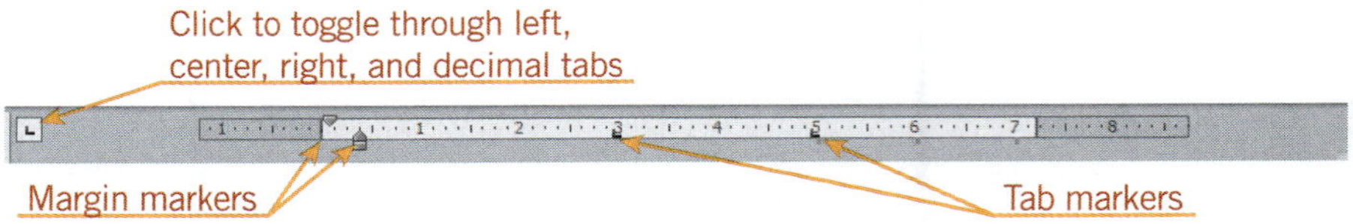

FIGURE 2–24   Tabs and margins on the ruler

Step-by-Step 2.14

1. On the status bar, click the **Normal** button ⊞ to switch back to Normal view.

2. On the Slides tab, click the **slide 15** thumbnail, *CPR*. Click the **Home** tab, and then in the Slides group, click the **New Slide** button. In the Slide pane, click the **Click to add title** placeholder, and then type **Web Resources** as the slide title.

3. Click in the content placeholder, type **American Red Cross** as the first bullet, press **Enter**, type **American Heart Association** as the second bullet, press **Enter**, and then type **KidsHealth** as the third bullet.

4. On the Home tab on the Ribbon, in the Paragraph group, click the **Center** button . Because the insertion point was positioned in the third bullet, "KidsHealth," it is now centered on the slide.

5. Click directly on the **content placeholder border** so it becomes a solid line. Any formatting changes will now apply to all the text in the placeholder.

6. In the Paragraph group, click the **Line Spacing** button to display the Line Spacing options, and then click **2.0**. All of the bulleted text is now double-spaced.

7. Drag to select the text **American Red Cross**. In the Font group, click the **Change Case** button , and then click **UPPERCASE**.

8. Click anywhere in the **American Heart Association** bullet, and then in the Paragraph group, click the **Align Text Right** button . The text is right-aligned with the right margin of the content placeholder. Your slide should look similar to **Figure 2–25**.

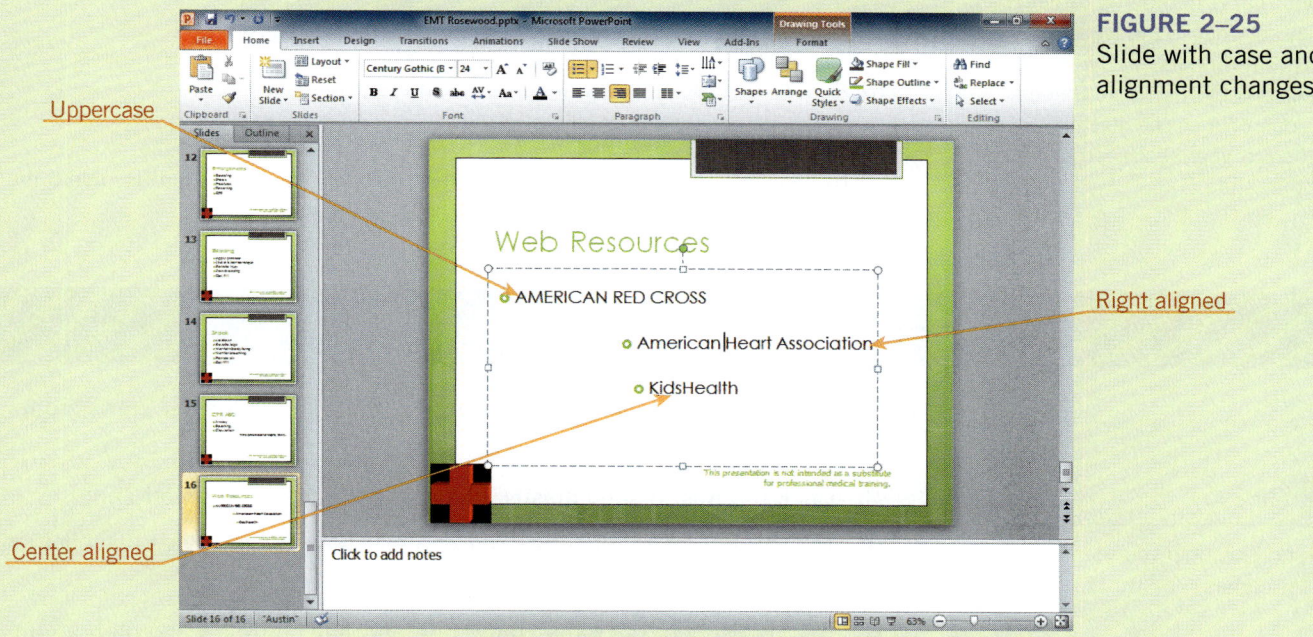

FIGURE 2–25
Slide with case and alignment changes

9. Save the presentation and leave it open for the next Step-by-Step.

Working with Bullets

Bullets define each new idea in the Content placeholder on a slide. Default bullets are determined by the theme. To change the formatting of bullets, selecting the text or placeholder, and then click the arrow next to the Bullets button in the Paragraph group on the Home tab to display the Bullets gallery. You cannot select a bullet to make changes; you must select the associated text. For more choices, click Bullets and Numbering to open the Bullets and Numbering dialog box, shown in **Figure 2–26**. On the Bulleted tab, you can select a bullet style or you can add a graphical bullet by clicking the Picture button. You can also change the bullet color or its size in relation to the text.

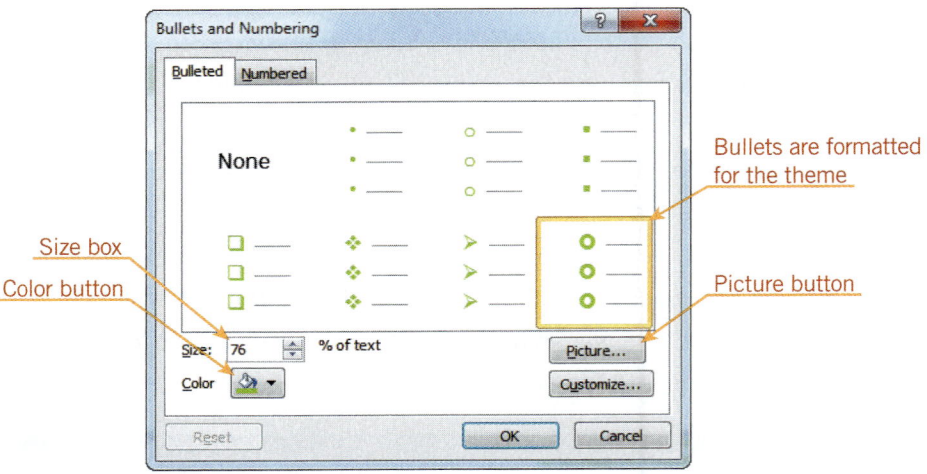

FIGURE 2–26   Bullets and Numbering dialog box

To change the appearance of the bullets throughout a presentation, make the changes on the slide master.

Step-by-Step 2.15

1. On the Ribbon, click the **View** tab, and then in the Master Views group, click the **Slide Master** button.

2. Click the **Austin slide master** (the first thumbnail in the left pane).

3. In the Slide pane, click the **Click to edit Master text styles** placeholder in the Content placeholder.

4. On the Ribbon, click the **Home** tab, and then, in the Paragraph group, click the **Bullets button arrow** ⬚▾ to open the Bullets gallery and menu. Click **Bullets and Numbering**. The Bullets and Numbering dialog box opens with the Bulleted tab selected. (Refer back to Figure 2–26.)

5. Click the **Star Bullets** icon. In the Size box, double-click **76**, and then type **125**. Click **OK**. The dialog box closes and the bullet style and size changes for the first level bullet on the slide master, as shown in **Figure 2–27**.

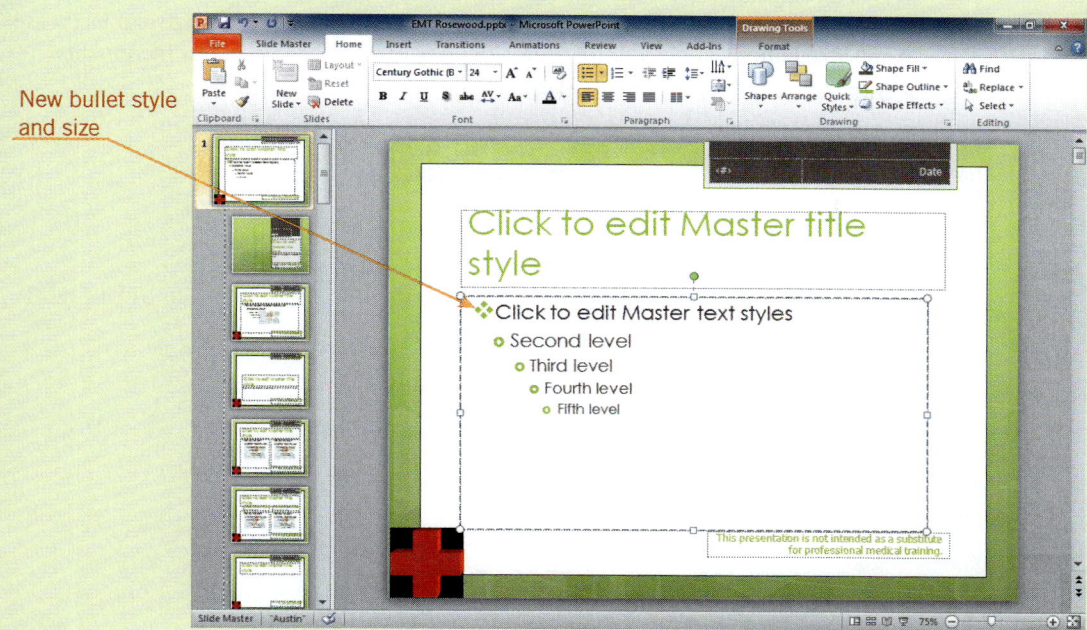

New bullet style and size

FIGURE 2–27
New bullet in the
Slide Master

6. On the status bar, click the **Normal** button to close Slide Master view. In the Slide pane, press **Home** to view slide 1, and then press **Page Down** to view slide 2 and see the changes to the first level bullets on the slide.

7. Save your work and leave the presentation open for the next Step-by-Step.

Changing Font Attributes

In a theme, the format of the text for body text, titles, and bullets on your slides is predetermined so that the layout, color theme, font, size, and style are consistent throughout the presentation. You can alter the format by making changes to individual slides. You change the font, style, size, effects, and color using the buttons on the Home tab in the Font group.

To make changes to words, first select the text. When you select text in a placeholder, the border of the placeholder is a dashed line. If you want to format all of the text in one placeholder, you can select the entire placeholder by clicking the border of the placeholder so it becomes a solid line. Any formatting to a selected placeholder will affect all of the text in the placeholder.

You can also use the Mini toolbar, shown in **Figure 2–28**, as a shortcut to changing the font, font size, font style, and font color. The Increase Font Size and Decrease Font Size buttons allow you to change the font size quickly in preset increments.

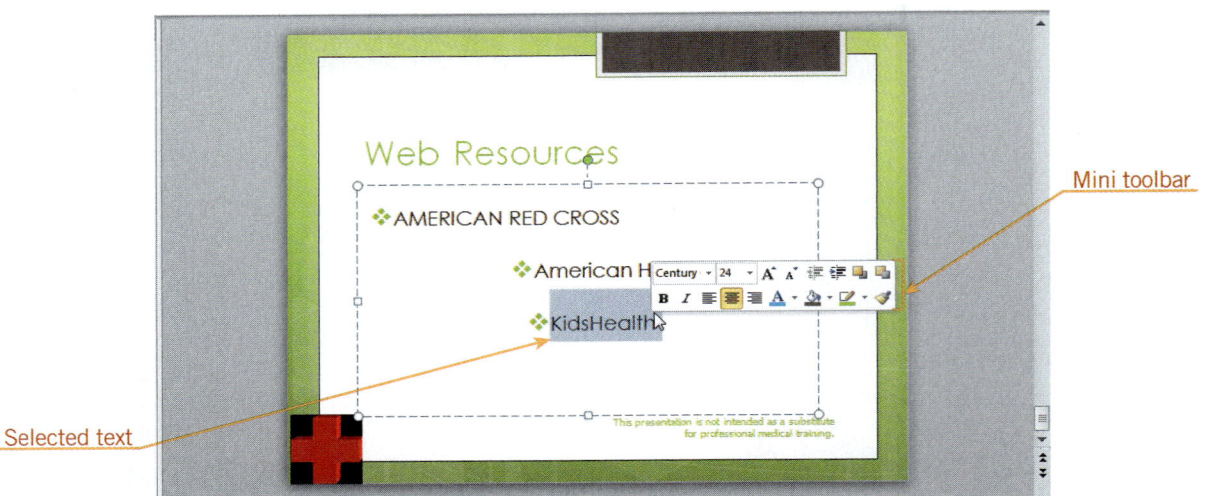

FIGURE 2–28   Mini toolbar appears for selected text

Step-by-Step 2.16

1. On the Slides tab, click the **slide 13** thumbnail, *Bleeding*, and then in the Slide pane, drag to select the text **clean**.

2. On the Ribbon, on the Home tab, in the Font group, click the **Font Color** button arrow . A palette of colors opens, organized into Theme colors and Standard colors.

TIP

You can also click More colors to open the Colors palette.

3. Point to several colors and watch how the Live Preview shows the effect on the selected text, and then click any color.

4. In the Slide pane, double-click **injury**. In the Font group, click the **Font** button arrow Calibri (Body) ▼ to display a list of installed fonts.

5. Point to several of the fonts in the list and watch how the Live Preview shows the effect on the selected text, and then click any font.

6. In the Slide pane, double-click **911**. In the Font group, click **Font Size** button arrow 40 ▼ to display a list of font sizes.

7. Point to several of the sizes in the list and watch how the Live Preview shows you the effect on the selected text, and then click **36**. Click a blank area of the slide, and then compare your slide to **Figure 2–29**.

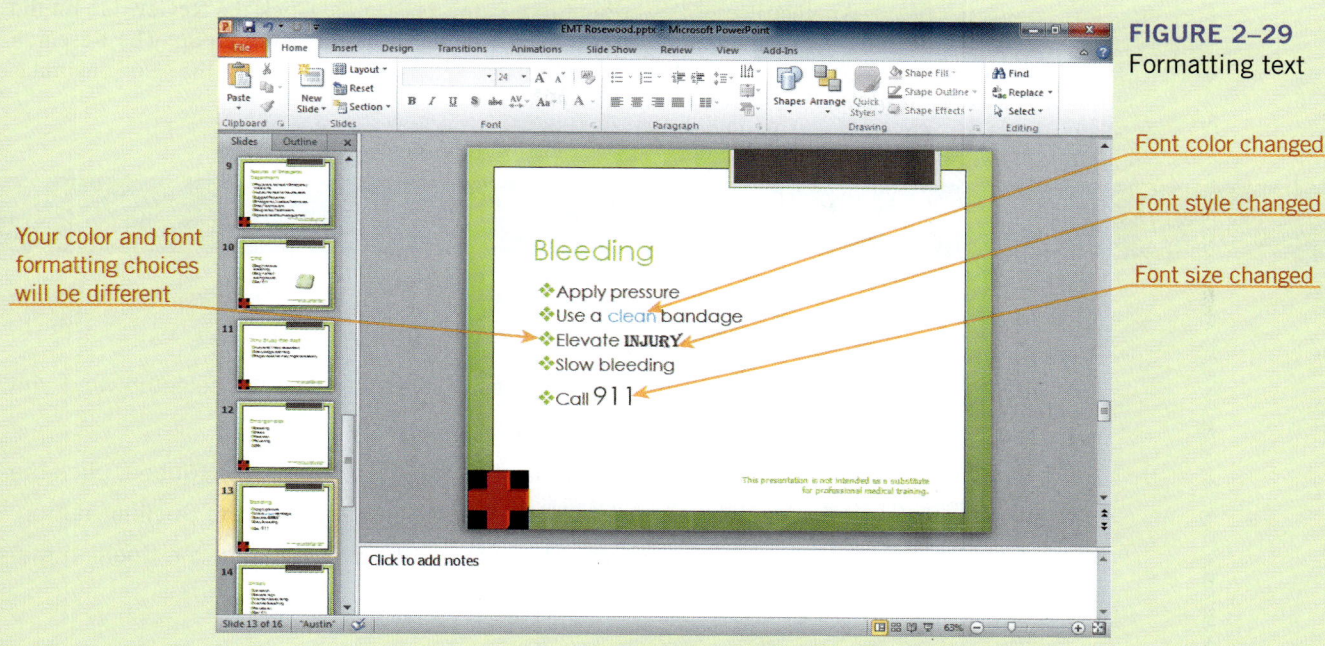

FIGURE 2–29
Formatting text

Font color changed

Font style changed

Font size changed

Your color and font formatting choices will be different

8. Save your work, and leave the presentation open for the next Step-by-Step.

Checking Spelling, Style, and Usage

Automatic spell checking identifies misspellings and words that are not in PowerPoint's dictionary by underlining them with a wavy red line immediately after you type them. To correct a misspelled word, right-click the underlined word. A shortcut menu appears with a list of suggested correctly spelled words. Click the suggestion that you want, and PowerPoint replaces the misspelled word. You can turn the automatic spell checker on or off, or change the way that it checks your document by clicking the File tab, clicking Options, and then clicking Proofing.

You can also check the spelling in a presentation after it is complete. Click the Review tab on the Ribbon, then, in the Proofing group, click the Spelling button. The Spelling dialog box contains options for ignoring words, making changes, or adding words to your own custom dictionary. When all spelling has been checked, a dialog box opens with the message "The Spelling Check is complete."

TECHNOLOGY CAREERS

An effective presentation should be consistent, error-free, and visually appealing. PowerPoint helps you determine if your presentation conforms to the standards of good style. For instance, title text size should be at least 36 points and the number of bullets on a slide should not exceed six. You should try to limit the number of words in each bullet to six. This is called the 6 by 6 rule, although sometimes you have to make exceptions.

Another useful PowerPoint tool is the Thesaurus. Click the Review tab on the Ribbon, and then click the Thesaurus button in the Proofing group. The Research task pane appears and offers a selection of alternative words with the same or similar meanings.

Step-by-Step 2.17

1. On the Slides tab, click the **slide 2** thumbnail, *Emergencies*, and then in the Slide pane double-click **Allergic**. The word is selected.

2. Type **Allrgic**, and then press **spacebar** to replace the selected word and enter a misspelled word in your presentation.

3. On the Slides tab, click the **slide 1** thumbnail. On the Ribbon, click the **Review** tab, and then in the Proofing group, click the **Spelling** button. Because there are spelling errors in the presentation, the Spelling dialog box opens, as shown in **Figure 2–30**.

FIGURE 2–30
Checking spelling

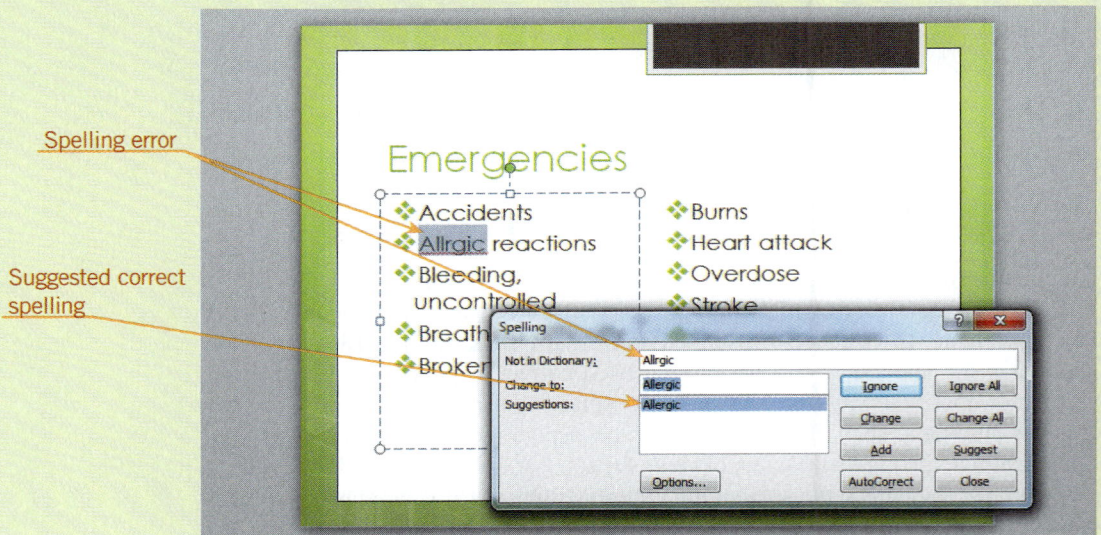

NOTE: Depending on how accurately you typed the text during these steps, you might have different words shown in the dialog box. You can choose to click Ignore to skip the words that are correct.

4. Review the suggestions in the dialog box. If the word in the Not in Dictionary box is "Allrgic" and the word in the Change to box is "Allergic," click **Change** to insert the correct spelling of Allergic. If another word appears as a misspelled word, select the correct spelling in the Suggestions list, and then click **Change**.

5. When the spell checker is finished, click **OK** in the spelling check is complete message box.

6. On the Slides tab, click the **slide 6** thumbnail, *Dispatcher Duties*, and then in the first bullet in the Slide pane, drag to select the word **Calm.**

7. On the Ribbon, click the **Review** tab, and then in the Proofing group, click the **Thesaurus** button.

8. Scroll down in the Research task pane to see the list of synonyms and antonyms under pacify (v.), point to the word **Soothe** until it is outlined with a box, click the **down arrow** next to the word, and then click **Insert**. The word *Soothe* replaces the word *Calm*.

9. In the upper-right corner of the Research task pane, click the **Close** button ☒.

10. Save the presentation and leave it open for the next Step-by-Step.

Deleting Placeholders and Text from Slides

To change or delete text on an existing slide, scroll to display the slide you want to change. Then, select the text you want to change so that it is highlighted. Press Delete, Backspace, or type the new text to replace the selected text.

To delete a placeholder, click the placeholder box so that it is a solid line, and then press Delete. The text within the placeholder is replaced with the default placeholder text "Click to add text." Select the placeholder, then press Delete again to remove the placeholder from the slide.

Changing Slide Layouts

To change the layout for an existing slide, select the slide or slides. You can change more than one slide at a time by pressing and holding Ctrl, and then clicking slides on the Slides tab. On the Home tab, in the Slides group, click the Layout button, and then scroll to view the available layouts.

NET BUSINESS

Many businesses take place on the world stage. Being able to communicate in more than one language is essential if you want to conduct business among non-English speaking people. Sometimes, you might find you just need to include a word in a language other than English on a slide to make a point or reach an audience. PowerPoint provides a translation tool that gives you that power. You can use the Mini Translator to translate a word or a selected phrase when you point to it. Click the Review tab on the Ribbon, and then in the Language group, click the Translate button. To select the language you want to translate to, click Choose Translation Language, click the Translate to arrow, select the language, and then click OK. Next, click the Translate button again, and then click Mini Translator to turn it on. Now when you point to a word or select a phrase and then point to it, the Mini Translator appears displaying the translation of the word. The Mini Translator first appears faintly, and then darkens, similar to the Mini toolbar, when you move the mouse pointer onto it. Click the Translate button menu again, and then click Mini Translator to turn this feature off.

Step-by-Step 2.18

1. On the Slides tab, click the **slide 8** thumbnail, *Emergency Departments*. On the Ribbon, click the **Home** tab, and then in the Slides group, click the **Layout** button. The Layout gallery appears.

2. In the Slides group, click the **Layout** button, and then in the Austin section, click the **Picture with Caption** layout. The slide changes to the Picture with Caption layout. Click the **Undo** button.

3. In the Slides group, click the **Layout** button again, and then in the Austin section, click the **Comparison** layout to apply it to the slide. See **Figure 2–31**.

FIGURE 2–31
Comparison layout applied to slide 8

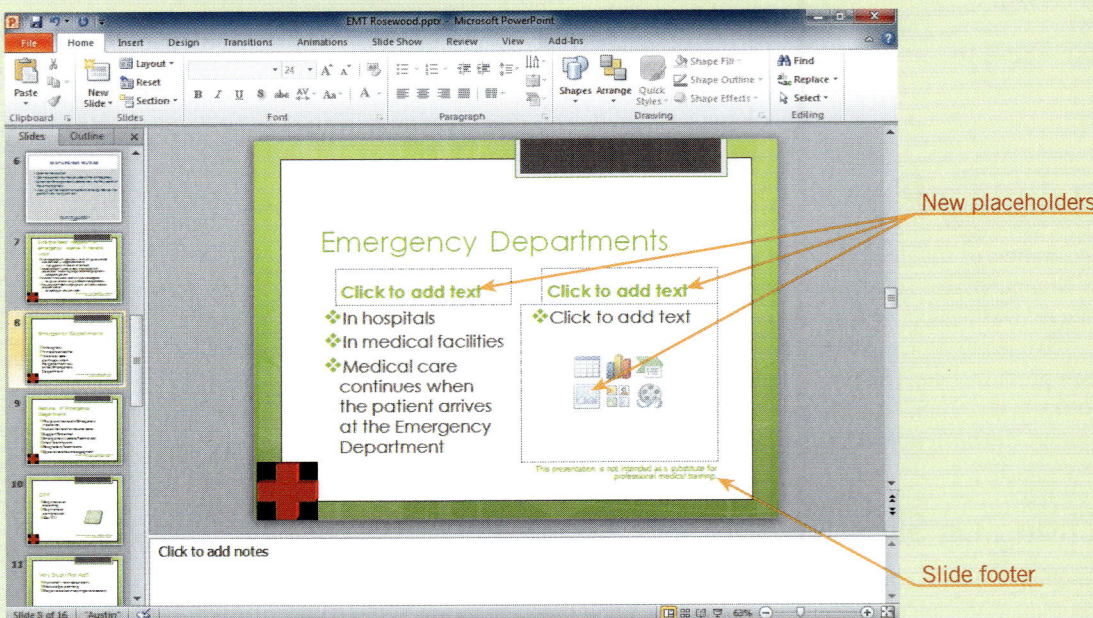

4. Save the presentation and leave it open for the next Step-by-Step.

Adding Clip Art and Sounds to Slides

If a content placeholder appears on a slide, you can choose from six objects: a table, a chart, a SmartArt graphic, a picture from file, clip art, and a media clip. You will work with tables, charts, media clips, and SmartArt graphic objects in Lesson 3.

Working with Clip Art

When you click the Insert Clip Art icon, the Clip Art task pane opens. See **Figure 2–32**. You find clips based on a keyword search. You can also import clips from other sources into the Clip Art Gallery and connect to the Web to access more clips. A keyword is a phrase or a word that describes the item you want in the Search text box. Click the Go button to show the results.

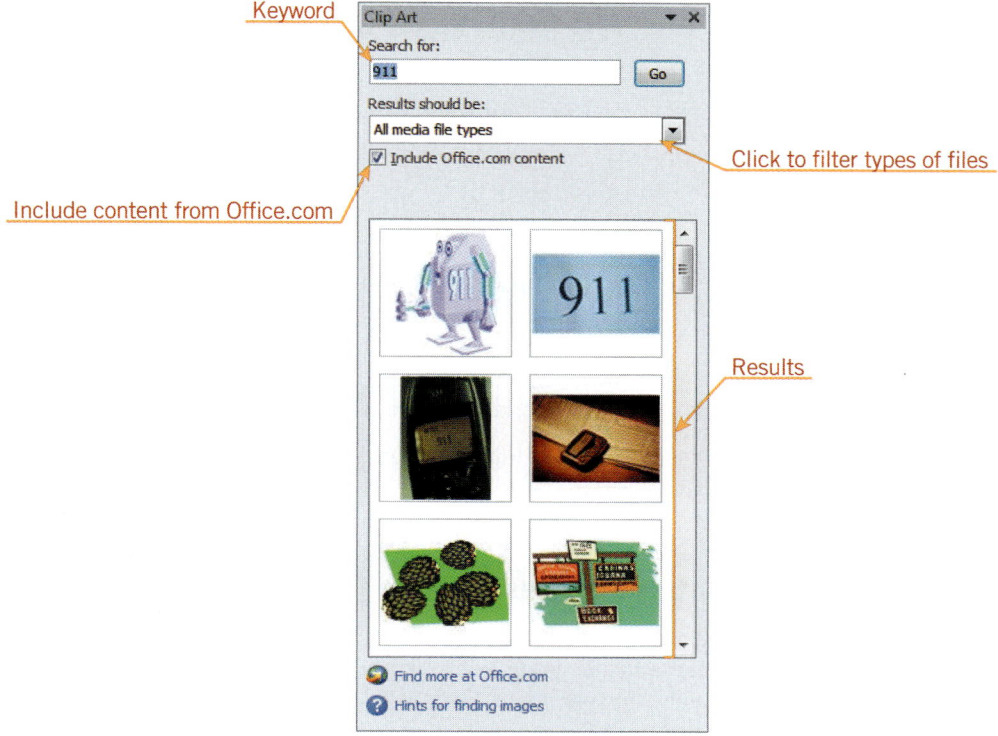

FIGURE 2–32   Results from search in the Clip Art task pane

If there is no content placeholder, you can still insert clip art on a slide. On the Ribbon, on the Insert tab, click the Clip Art button in the Images group. The Clip Art task pane opens. This task pane offers several options for finding the item you want to insert. To find an item, type one or more words into the Search for text box that might help identify the item. You can narrow your search by selecting from the Results should be options. In the Results should be box, you specify the media types you want to search for: Illustrations, Photographs, Video, and Audio. When the Include Office.com content check box is selected, the search includes clips on the Microsoft Office.com Web site as well as clip art that is on your computer.

The results appear in the task pane. You can click the clip thumbnail to insert the image or you can select from a menu of options. When you point to an icon in the task pane, an arrow for a drop-down menu appears to the right of the item. Click Insert to insert the image in the slide at the location of your insertion point. Click Preview/Properties to view the image and its properties without adding it to your document.

Step-by-Step 2.19

TIP

You will get more results if you include Office.com content and are connected to the Internet during the search.

1. In the Slide pane on slide 8, in the Content placeholder, click the **Clip Art** icon ▦ to open the Clip Art task pane. Click the **Results should be** arrow, and then click the check boxes next to **Photographs**, **Videos**, and **Audio** to remove the check marks so that only the **Illustrations** check box is selected.

2. Click in the **Search for** box, type **Emergency 911**, and then click **Go.** Clip art that is associated with the phrase "Emergency 911" appears in the task pane. If you do not get results, try different keywords, such as "emergency", "rescue", or "911".

3. Review the results, and then click a thumbnail of the clip to insert the clip of your choice. The clip art you chose is inserted on the slide in the placeholder.

TIP

To move clip art, click the object and drag. To resize, click the handles and drag.

4. In the upper-right corner of the Clip Art task pane, click the **Close** button ✖ to close the task pane.

5. Save the presentation and leave it open for the next Step-by-Step.

Adding Sound to Slides

You can add sound effects to any slide by inserting a sound. Click the Insert tab on the Ribbon, then, in the Media group, click the Audio button. You can insert a sound from a file that is stored on your computer or a disk, you can insert a sound using the Clip Art task pane or from a file stored on your computer, or you can record a sound for the presentation. Recorded sound is good for narration or you can create your own soundtrack. When a sound is on a slide, you will see the sound icon on the slide.

Step-by-Step 2.20

1. Display **slide 10**, *CPR*, in the Slide pane.

2. On the Ribbon, click the **Insert** tab, and then in the Media group, click the **Audio** button. The Insert Audio dialog box opens.

3. In the drive and folder where your Data Files are stored, click **911.wav**, and then click **Insert**. The dialog box closes and a sound icon and playback controls appear in the Slide pane as shown in **Figure 2–33**.

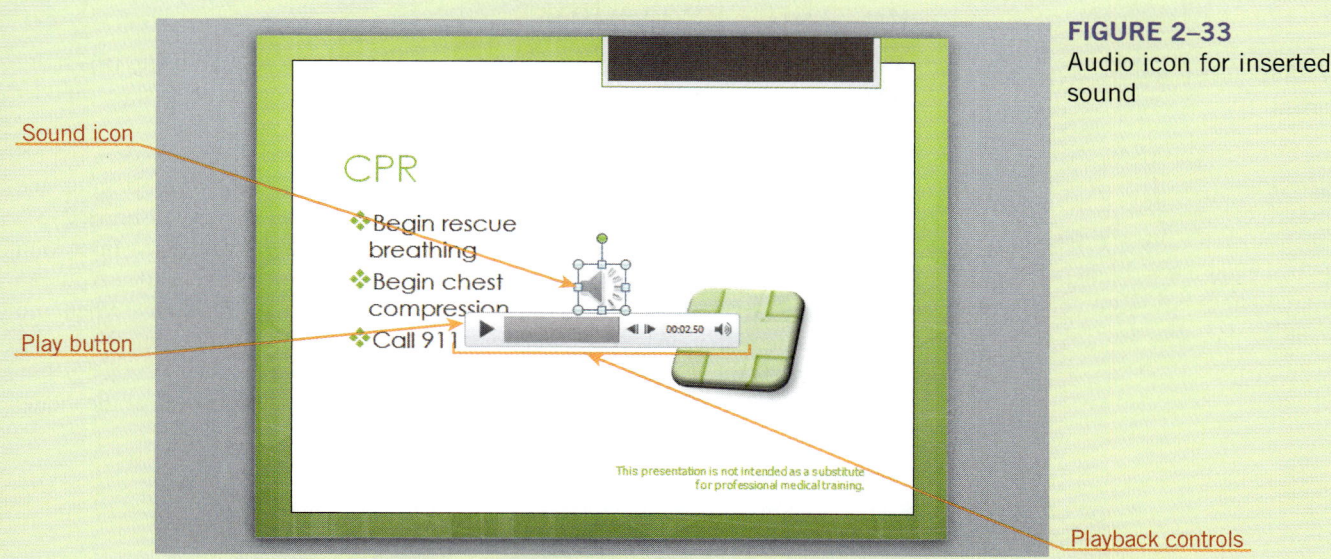

FIGURE 2–33
Audio icon for inserted sound

4. Click the **Play** button ▶ to hear the sound. (You will not hear the sound if your computer does not have speakers.) You can choose to have the sound play automatically or only when the sound icon is clicked during the slide show.

5. On the Ribbon, click the **Audio Tools Playback** tab. In the Audio Options group, click the **Start** arrow, click **Automatically** and then click the **Hide During Show** check box. See **Figure 2–34**. Now the sound will play automatically during the slide show and the sound icon will not be visible.

FIGURE 2–34
Audio Tools Playback tab on the Ribbon

6. On the status bar, click the **Reading View** button 📖. You hear the 911 sound file.

7. On the status bar, click the **Normal** button.

8. Save the presentation and leave it open for the next Step-by-Step.

Inserting Hyperlinks

► **VOCABULARY**

hyperlink

TIP

You can also link to an Internet site by typing the Web address in the Address box in the Insert Hyperlink dialog box.

A *hyperlink* allows you to jump to another slide, a file, or to a Web site if you are connected to the Internet. You can also add a hyperlink that opens a message window for an e-mail address.

To insert a hyperlink in a presentation, select the text you want to make a hyperlink. On the Ribbon, click the Insert tab, and then in the Links group, click the Hyperlink button. The Insert Hyperlink dialog box opens, as shown in **Figure 2–35**. In the Link to section, choose where you want the link to go. The Look in section allows you to specify the Current Folder, Browsed Pages, or Recent files. You can also add the text for a ScreenTip to help the person using the slide show. When you click OK, the dialog box closes and the text you selected before opening the dialog box changes to a hyperlink is inserted in the document. The text you selected is formatted with a different color and underlined. The hyperlink color is one of the theme colors. Click it to go to the linked location.

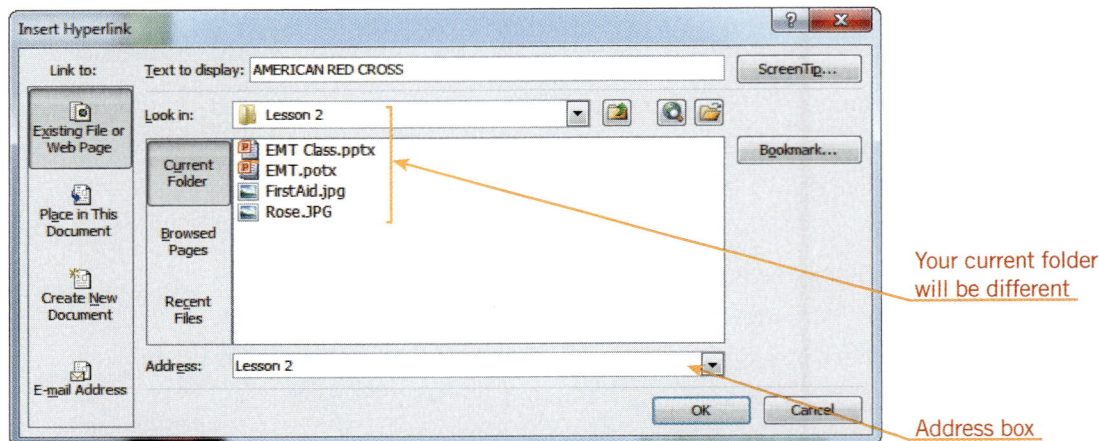

FIGURE 2–35   Insert Hyperlink dialog box

Step-by-Step 2.21

1. On the Slides tab, click the **slide 16** thumbnail, *Web Resources*.

2. In the Slide pane, select the **AMERICAN RED CROSS**. On the Ribbon, click the **Insert** tab, and then in the Links group, click the **Hyperlink** button. The Insert Hyperlink dialog box opens.

3. In the Address box, type **www.redcross.org**, and then click **OK**. The text is underlined in the slide and colored orange, indicating that it is a hyperlink. The program inserts http:// before www automatically.

4. Select the **American Heart Association**. In the Links group, click the **Hyperlink** button, type **www.americanheart.org** in the Address box, and then click **OK**.

5. Select **KidsHealth**, and then create a hyperlink to www.kidshealth.org.

6. On the status bar, click the **Reading View** button 📖. On the slide, point to the **American Heart Association** link, so that the pointer changes to 🖑 indicating it is a hyperlink. See **Figure 2–36**.

FIGURE 2–36
Pointing to a hyperlink on a slide in Reading view

7. If you are connected to the Internet, click the **American Heart Association** hyperlink to open your Web browser and display the home page of the American Heart Association. Close the browser window.

8. On the status bar, click the **Normal view** button 🔲 and then click the **Slide Show** button. The Web Resources slide fills the screen in Slide Show view.

9. Close your Web browser, and then press **Esc** to exit the slide show.

10. Save the presentation and leave it open for the next Step-by-Step.

> **EXTRA FOR EXPERTS**
>
> When you type an e-mail address on a slide, such as myaddress@ mailbox.com PowerPoint automatically creates a hyperlink that opens a new message window addressed to that e-mail address.

Using Animation

You can add select animation effects to any of the objects on a slide. *Animation* is what makes slide shows fun and interesting to watch. You can have a lot of fun creating animations on slides. When you animate an object, text, or slide, you add a visual effect. Animation enhances your presentation and increases audience interest.

On the Ribbon, click the Animations tab. You add Animations by clicking the Animation in the Animation group, or you can click the Add Animation button in the

▶ **VOCABULARY**
animation

▶ **VOCABULARY**

Motion Paths

Live Preview

Advanced Animation group. See **Figure 2–37**. For more control over the way animations are displayed and played, you can click the Animation Pane button to open the Animation pane. Animations are organized into Entrance, Emphasis, Exit, and Motion Paths categories. Entrance and Exit animations define the animation for the entry and exit of an object. Emphasis defines the animation of an object that is showing on the slide. *Motion Paths* allow you to make an object move on the slide. As you point to each animation in the Animation gallery, a *Live Preview* will show you the effect on your object. You can click the More Effects option to display a dialog box containing all the animation features. Click the Start arrow to determine how the animation begins. Animations can start On Click, With Previous, or After Previous.

FIGURE 2–37   Animations gallery

Using the Animation Pane

On the Animations tab in the Advance Animation group, click the Animation pane button to open the Animation pane. This pane helps you track and organize the animations you set for each object. Each animated object is assigned a number on the slide, and the corresponding number is listed in the Animation pane. You can select how an object is animated, arrange animation order, determine whether to display the animation manually or automatically, and adjust the speed of the animation.

In the Animation pane, to the right of each animated object, an arrow opens the animation drop-down menu, which contains the commands that determine several animation settings for the object including the Start options, *Effect options*, and Timing options. To make adjustments to the effects, click the Effect Options button to open the Effect dialog box. In this dialog box, you can select enhancements for the animation. You can also choose a sound to accompany it. You have the option of dimming the object after it has been animated. If you are animating a text object, the text can appear all at once, by the word, or by the letter, and you can increase or decrease the delay percentage. The Timing tab allows you to adjust the timing of the animation and determine the trigger for the animation. When animating text, the Text Animation tab allows you to animate the text as a group or by individual levels.

Adding or Changing Slide Animation

You can apply an animation to the current (displayed) slide. Select the placeholder to apply animation to all text items on the placeholder. You can also individually animate text boxes, pictures, and transitions into the slide. After you apply an animation, the Preview button on the Animation tab allows you to preview the animation. Animations play in Slide Show and Reading view.

To copy an animation from one object to another, select the object with the animation you want to duplicate, click the Animation Painter button in the Advanced Animation group on the Animation tab, and then click the object you want to copy the animation to.

> **VOCABULARY**
> **Effect options**

 EXTRA FOR EXPERTS

The Show Advanced Timeline feature displays the time of the animation as a horizontal line graph. This allows you to easily see the timing of each object all at once.

Step-by-Step 2.22

1. On the Slides tab, click the **slide 8** thumbnail, *Emergency Departments*.

2. Select the **clip art** you inserted in a previous Step-by-Step.

3. On the Ribbon, click the **Animations** tab, and then in the Advanced Animations group, click the **Add Animation** button to open the Animation gallery. In the Entrance section, click the **Bounce** animation.

4. In the Advanced Animation group, click the **Animation Pane** button to open the Animation Pane. The object is listed in the task pane as Picture 2.

5. In the Advanced Animation group, click the **Add Animation** button to open the Animation gallery again. Click **More Entrance Effects** to open the Add Entrance Effect dialog box, and then scroll down the list of Entrance effects to the Exciting section. Click **Boomerang** in the Exciting section, and then click **OK**. A second animation has been added to the picture. See **Figure 2–38**.

FIGURE 2–38
Animation Pane

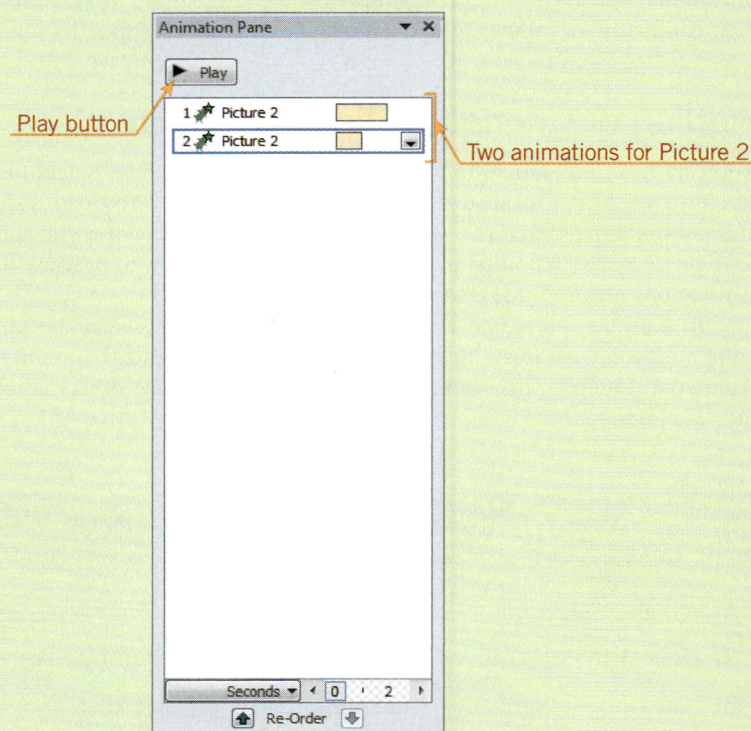

6. In the Animation Pane, click **Play** to view the sequence of animations.

7. On the Animations tab on the Ribbon, click the **Animation Pane** button to close the Animation Pane.

8. Save the presentation and leave it open for the next Step-by-Step.

TIP

Notice the animation icon in the Slide pane for the slide. This icon identifies the slide as having an animation. You will see later that this is the same icon used to identify transitions.

 VOCABULARY

slide transitions

Using Slide Transitions

When you run a presentation, *slide transitions* determine how one slide is removed from the screen and how the next one appears. You can set the transitions between slides. On the Ribbon, click the Transitions tab, then, in the Transition to This Slide group, click any of the transitions. You can click the More button to view additional transitions, as shown in **Figure 2–39**.

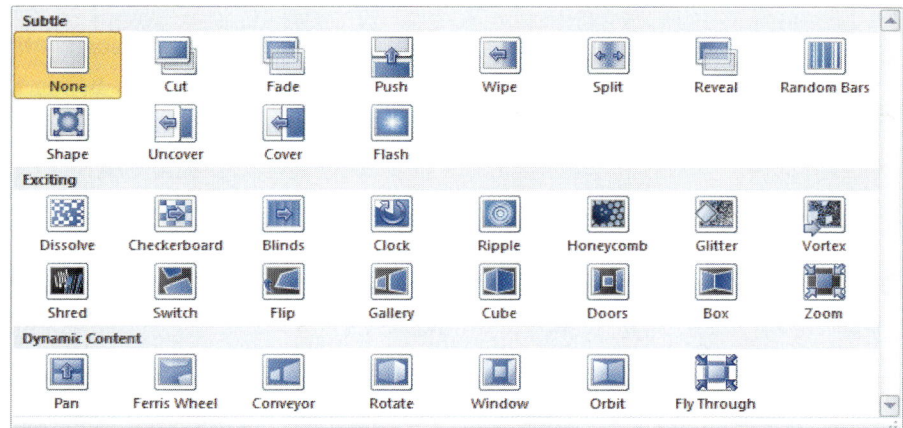

FIGURE 2-39   Transitions gallery

The Ribbon includes commands for a list of effects. The best view to use when you work on the transitions is Slide Sorter view. In the Timing slide section, you determine various aspects of speed and duration for the transition. You can set the duration of the transition—how long you actually view the transition. You can select the speed at which a slide displays before the next slide appears. You also determine whether to advance the slides manually or set the timing to advance slides automatically after a specified time. Click After and enter the number of seconds you want the slide to be displayed on the screen. If you click Apply to All, the selections you made affect all slides in the presentation. You can apply a transition to several slides by holding Ctrl down, and then clicking the slides on the Slides or Outline tab or in Slide Sorter view.

EXTRA FOR EXPERTS

If you choose Random Transition, PowerPoint randomly chooses a transition effect for each slide when you run the presentation.

Step-by-Step 2.23

1. On the status bar, click the **Slide Sorter** button 🔡, and then drag the Zoom slider to display 70% so that you can see all the slides.

2. Click the **slide 1** thumbnail. On the Ribbon, click the **Transitions** tab, and then in the Transition to this Slide group, click several of the **transitions** to see the transition on slide 1.

3. Click the transition that you like best. An icon beneath the slide thumbnail indicates that a transition is applied to the slide. On the Transitions tab, in the Timing group, notice that **On Mouse Click** has a check mark in the check box, and **No Sound** appears in the Sound box.

4. Click the **slide 2** thumbnail, *Emergencies*, press and hold **Shift**, scroll as needed, and then click the **slide 16** thumbnail, *Web Resources*. You selected slides 2–16.

TIP

Select the best zoom percentage for your screen so you can see all the slides in the window.

5. Click a transition of your choice for these slides. Watch the screen as the transition is applied to each slide. The ⊞☆ icon appears beneath each slide thumbnail. This transition icon is the same icon you saw when you added animations to the slide. Your screen should look similar to **Figure 2–40**.

FIGURE 2–40
Transitions in Slide Sorter view

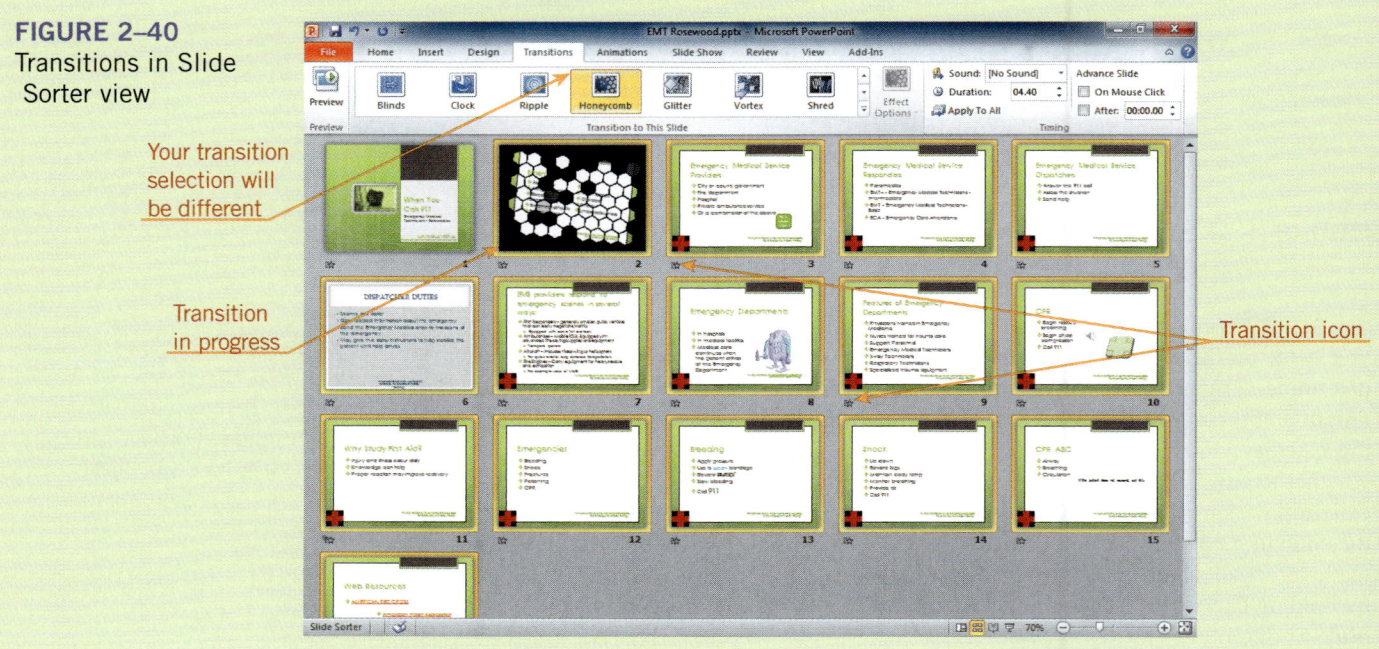

Your transition selection will be different

Transition in progress

Transition icon

Preparing the Notes and Handouts

You want to be able to identify your presentation from among the others in your class. To personalize your presentation in a classroom or lab setting, add your name as a footer to the Notes and or Handouts pages. If you want to print the whole presentation, but don't want to use a lot of paper, you can print handouts or notes.

Step-by-Step 2.24

1. Click the **Insert** tab on the Ribbon, and then in the Text group, click the **Header & Footer** button to open the Header and Footer dialog box. Add your name as a footer to the Notes and Handouts, and then apply the footer to all slides.

2. Save the presentation, and then view the presentation in Slide Show or Reading view to see the final presentation.

3. Switch to Normal view when you are finished.

4. If your instructor wants a printout, click the **File** tab, and then on the navigation bar, click **Print** to open Backstage view.

5. In the Settings section, click the **Print All Slides** button to print the entire presentation, in the Slides section, click the **Full Page Slides** button to open the Print Layout gallery, in the Handouts section, click **9 Slides Horizontal**, and then click the **Print** button to print the handouts on two pages with nine slides per page.

6. Close the presentation, and then exit PowerPoint.

SUMMARY

In this lesson, you learned how to:

- Use PowerPoint to create new presentations using blank presentations or templates.
- Insert headers and footers in a presentation.
- Use the slide, notes, and handout masters.
- Enhance presentations in PowerPoint by applying slide layouts, themes, and color.

- Add slides to an existing PowerPoint presentation.
- Add text to slides and find and replace text.
- Change the appearance of text and bullets in PowerPoint.
- Check spelling, style, usage, and translate text.
- Add clip art, sounds, and hyperlinks.
- Apply animations and transitions to slides.

■ VOCABULARY REVIEW

Define the following terms:

align	hyperlink	placeholder
animation	layout master	slide master
blank presentation	Live Preview	slide transitions
effect options	motion paths	template
handout master	notes master	themes

■ REVIEW QUESTIONS

FILL IN THE BLANK

Fill in the best answer:

1. The _____ controls formatting for all the slides in a presentation.

2. Click the _____ button so that pictures in the presentation take up less disk space.

3. The slide _____ determines where content and objects are placed on a slide.

4. A(n) _____ is how one slide is removed from the screen and the next one appears.

5. Predesigned graphic styles that can be applied to your slides are called _____.

TRUE / FALSE

Circle T if the statement is true or F if the statement is false.

T   F   **1.**   You can change the appearance of the bullets—such as their shape, size, or color.

T   F   **2.**   The sound icon never appears during Slide Show.

T   F   **3.**   Graphics do not appear on the Outline tab.

T   F   **4.**   Automatic spell checking identifies misspellings and words not in PowerPoint's dictionary by highlighting them in yellow.

T   F   **5.**   You can select more than one slide by holding down the spacebar while clicking the slides.

WRITTEN QUESTIONS

Write a brief answer to each of the following questions.

1. How can you easily create a new presentation using the format, colors, and style you prefer without starting with a new, blank presentation? Explain why.

2. What types of content can you add to a Content placeholder using the icons?

3. How do you change colors and fonts on a slide?

4. How do you animate text or an object on a slide?

5. How do you insert a hyperlink?

PROJECTS

If you have a SAM 2010 user profile, your instructor may have assigned an autogradable version of the indicated project. If so, log into the SAM 2010 Web site at *www.cengage.com/sam2010* to download the instruction and start files.

PROJECT 2–1

1. Start PowerPoint.

2. Open the presentation **EMT Class.pptx** from the drive and folder where you store your Data Files.

3. Save the presentation as **EMT Class Spring Session**, followed by your initials.

4. View the presentation.

5. In Normal view on slide 2, change the slide layout to Two Content. Add relevant clip art or a photograph to the slide, using the Clip Art icon in the content placeholder.

6. Apply a new theme to all the slides in the presentation.

7. Apply a second theme only to the World Wide Web slide.

8. Using the Notes pane, enter the note **Be sure to connect to the Internet.** on slide 7. Enter notes on at least other two slides.

9. On slide 8 Cardiopulmonary Resuscitation, use the Outline tab to add two lines: **Saves lives** and **Improves recovery**.

10. Insert one new slide at the end of the presentation using the Comparison Layout. Add any text to the placeholders.

11. Add a hyperlink on slide 7 to the Web page address **www.cdc.gov**. Create the text CDC as the text that appears on the slide. Add two other links of your choice to the slide.

12. Add clip art, photographs, or any sounds that you find in the Clip Art task pane to several of the slides. Use image effects on the images you added.

13. Create at least two animations in the slide show; animate any objects or text.

14. Switch to Slide Sorter view and add at least two different transitions to the slide show.

15. Use the Thesaurus to replace at least one word with a synonym. Run the spelling checker.

16. Switch to Slide Show view and run the presentation.

17. Add your name as a footer to the Notes and Handouts pages, and then print the handouts as 6 slides per page.

18. Save the presentation, then exit PowerPoint.

 PROJECT 2–2

1. Start PowerPoint. Use the New from Existing Presentation command to create a new presentation from the EMT Class-Spring Session.pptx file you created in Project 2–1.

2. Save the presentation as **EMT Class-Spring Session – Copy** followed by your initials.

3. Open the Outline tab.

4. Insert a new slide after the last slide using the Title and Content layout.

5. On the last slide type **Prices** as the title of the slide.

6. Add the following in the content placeholder on the new slide:

   Beginning Class — $200

   Intermediate Class — $225

   Advanced Class — $350

7. Format the text on slide 17 Circulation so that each line has a different font color, font style, and font size.

8. View the Slide Master and change the first level bullet to Hollow Square bullets using a Standard Red color.

9. Save your changes, print the slides as Handouts 9 slides per page. Exit PowerPoint.

PROJECT 2–3

1. Use the New from Existing Presentation feature to open the **EMT Class-Spring Session – Copy.pptx** presentation and save it as **EMT Class-Spring Session – Copy2** followed by your initials.

2. In Normal view, go to slide 1 and type the following in the Notes pane: **Be sure everyone has a handout.**

3. Print slide 1 using the Notes Pages print options.

4. Enhance the slide show, adding any additional objects or animations that you want. Check spelling. Save and print the entire presentation as handouts with 9 slides on a page.

5. Close the presentation and then exit PowerPoint.

CRITICAL THINKING

ACTIVITY 2–1

Use a template, either installed or from the Microsoft Office Web site, and the skills you learned in this lesson to create a presentation for an organization to which you belong. Be sure to check your presentation for correct spelling, punctuation, and grammar usage. Include clip art, at least one image from a file, and add animations and transitions to the slide show. Include one hyperlink to a favorite Web site. Save and print the entire presentation as handouts with six slides on a page.

ACTIVITY 2–2

Create a presentation using the ideas you organized in Critical Thinking Activity 1–2 in Lesson 1. Choose a theme. Add sound and clip art. Include slide transitions and animation. Run the presentation for your class.

LESSON 3

Working with Visual Elements

■ OBJECTIVES

Upon completion of this lesson, you will be able to:

- Insert, convert, and edit SmartArt graphics.
- Create and format WordArt.
- Build and format charts.
- Create and modify a table.
- Draw, edit, and format an object.
- Copy, move, order, and group objects.
- Create a text box on a shape.
- Animate shapes.
- Add a header or footer.

■ VOCABULARY

adjustment handle

category axis

cell

chart

column

datasheet

grouping

handle

organization chart

rotate handle

row

SmartArt graphic

table

value axis

WordArt

PowerPoint presentations provide a visual representation of your ideas and the concepts you want to present to your audience. With limited text on the slides, you can enhance your presentation with the many different graphic elements available within PowerPoint. Most people understand abstract ideas better if given visual clues and images. PowerPoint is an excellent teaching tool. Learning new skills is easy if graphics show you what you are supposed to do. In this lesson, you will learn how to create exciting and artistic presentations by using SmartArt graphics, WordArt, shapes, tables, and charts.

Working with SmartArt Graphics

When you have to present information to an audience, text is not always the best way to present content. Graphics are a more powerful way to visually convey information about flow, sequence, process, and organization. Graphics can simplify ideas. *SmartArt graphics*, which are dynamic diagrams and graphics, are available for you to use on your slides in PowerPoint.

> ▶ **VOCABULARY**
> **SmartArt graphics**

You can insert a SmartArt graphic on a slide by clicking the SmartArt icon on a content placeholder. To create a SmartArt graphic on a slide that does not have the SmartArt icon, click the Insert tab on the Ribbon. In the Illustrations group, click the SmartArt button to open the Choose a SmartArt Graphic dialog box gallery. You can also convert existing text into a SmartArt graphic by selecting the text object or text you want to convert, and then on the Home tab in the Paragraph group, click the Convert to SmartArt Graphic button and then select a SmartArt graphic from the gallery. PowerPoint includes over 80 basic styles of SmartArt graphics that are organized into eight categories: List, Process, Cycle, Hierarchy, Relationship, Matrix, Pyramid, and Picture. See **Figure 3–1**.

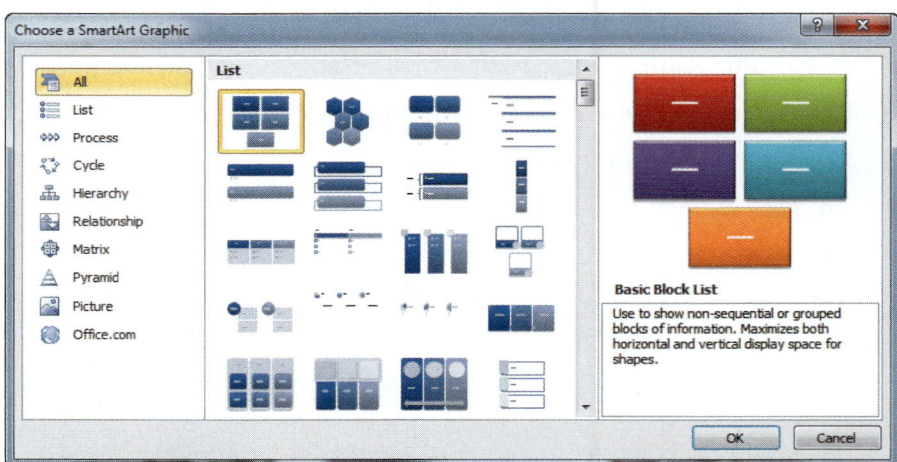

FIGURE 3–1   Choose a SmartArt graphic dialog box

Step-by-Step 3.1

1. Open the presentation file **History of Cotton.pptx** from the drive and folder where you store the Data Files for this lesson.

2. Save the presentation as **History of Cotton Report**, followed by your initials.

3. Click the **Home tab** on the Ribbon if it is not already selected, on the Slides tab click **slide 4**, *Types of Cotton*, to select the slide, click anywhere in the bullet list, and then in the Paragraph group, click the **Convert to SmartArt Graphic** button [icon] to open the SmartArt gallery.

4. Move the pointer slowly over the different **SmartArt thumbnails** in the gallery, view the Live Preview effect on the text, and then click the **Pyramid List SmartArt** style. See **Figure 3–2**.

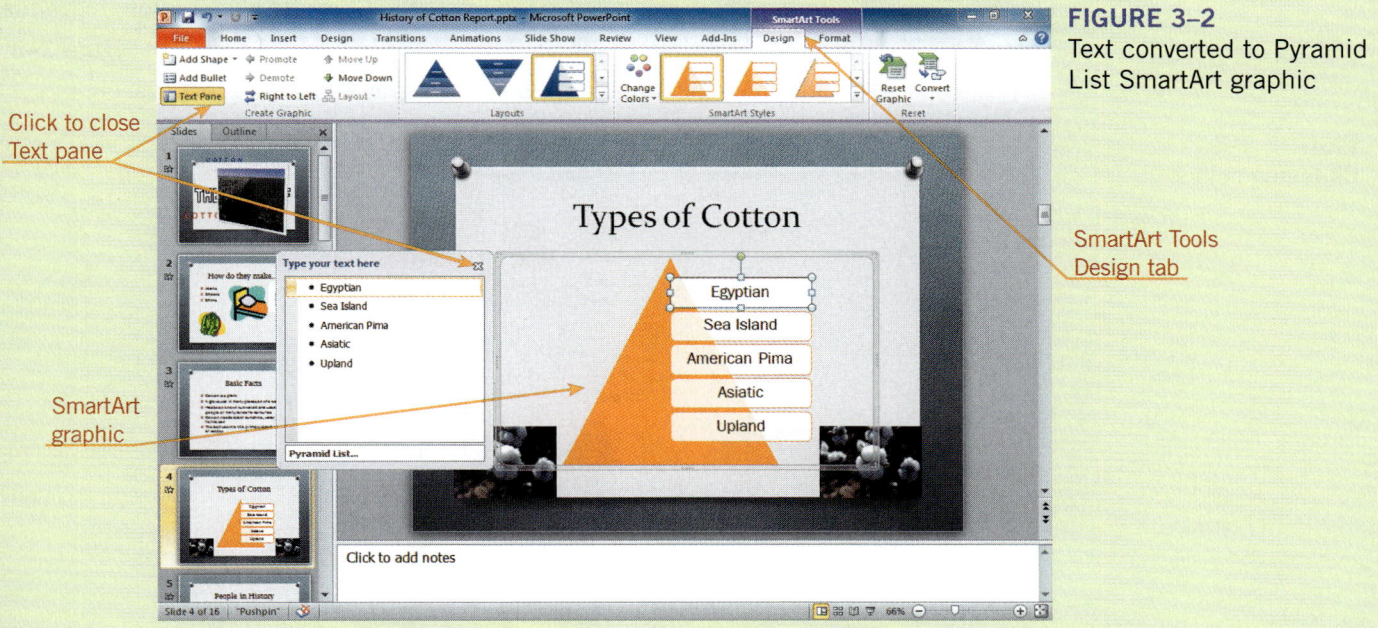

FIGURE 3–2
Text converted to Pyramid List SmartArt graphic

5. Save the presentation and then leave the presentation open for the next Step-by-Step.

Designing SmartArt Graphics

Each SmartArt graphic style can be altered in countless ways to give you artistic control over how the graphic looks on the slide. Work with the SmartArt Tools tab on the Ribbon to change layouts, styles, and colors. You can add additional shapes or bullets. Some SmartArt graphics include icons that you click to insert graphics and photographs. You can work using the features available through the buttons on the SmartArt Tools Format tab to change the way the text looks on each shape. You can use the Text pane to add text or edit and delete existing text. The Text pane provides an easy way to enter text in a SmartArt graphic. You can enter text either in the Text pane or directly in the SmartArt graphic.

Step-by-Step 3.2

1. Click the **Text pane close** button to close the Text pane.

2. Click the **SmartArt Tools Design** tab. In the SmartArt Styles group, click the **More** button ⬇ to open the gallery, move the pointer over the different SmartArt styles to see the Live Preview effect, and then in the 3-D group, click the **Bird's Eye Scene** icon.

3. In the SmartArt Styles group, click the **Change Colors** button, move the pointer over the different styles in the gallery, as shown in **Figure 3–3**, and then click **Gradient Range – Accent 2** in the Accent 2 section.

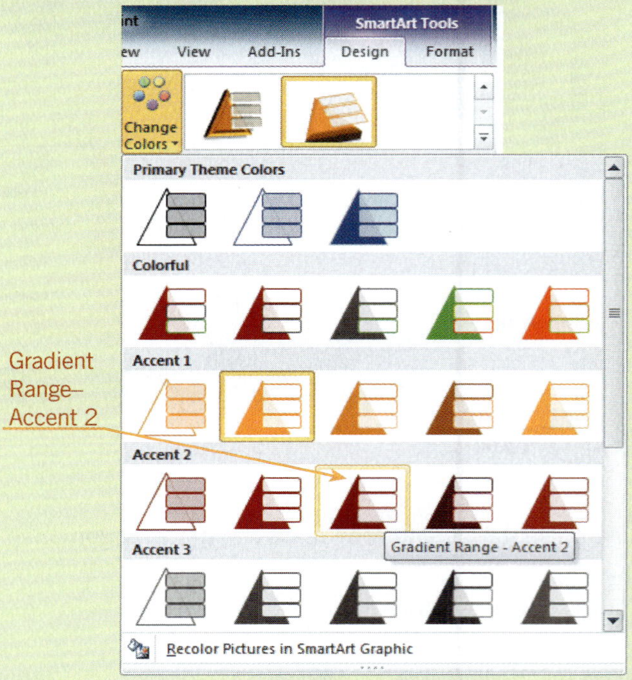

FIGURE 3–3
Changing colors

4. Click the **triangle shape** in the SmartArt graphic, click the **SmartArt Tools Format** tab on the Ribbon, and then in the Shape Styles group click the **Shape Fill** button arrow. The Shape Fill colors palette opens.

5. In the Theme Colors section, click **Indigo, Text 2**. You have formatted the SmartArt graphic to present the different types of cotton in a very dramatic way.

6. Save the presentation and leave it open for the next Step-by-Step.

Working with Organization Charts

Organization charts are useful for showing the hierarchical structure and relationships within an organization. An organization chart is a way to graphically explain the structure of an organization in terms of rank. You can also use an organization chart to show relationships among objects, animals, or things that are related in a structured way. For a company or organization, the chart usually shows the managers and subordinates who make up its workforce. The graphics, such as boxes or ovals, contain the name of a person, position, or object. Vertical lines drawn between the graphics show the direct relationships among superior and subordinate items in the chart. A horizontal line shows a lateral or equal relationship on the same level.

To add an organization chart to a slide, you can apply a Content layout to a slide and then click the SmartArt Graphic icon in the content placeholder. The Hierarchy category of SmartArt Graphics provides many different layouts for you to use as you create the organization chart on the slide.

To fill in the chart, click in a text box and type the text. Use the SmartArt tools on the Ribbon to add more boxes to the organization chart. Graphic elements are grouped with the text boxes to enhance the chart. Graphics can include shapes as well as pictures or clip art.

▶ **VOCABULARY**
organization chart

Step-by-Step 3.3

1. Scroll down the Slides pane, click **slide 14**, *Products and Byproducts of Cotton*, click the **Home** tab on the Ribbon. The slide displays a content placeholder with the six icons. An organization chart is a SmartArt graphic.

2. Click the **Insert SmartArt Graphic** icon in the content placeholder. The Choose a SmartArt Graphic dialog box opens.

3. In the left pane, click **Hierarchy**, click the **Hierarchy** icon in the center pane, as shown in **Figure 3–4**, and then click **OK**. The Hierarchy chart appears on the slide with text placeholders, and the SmartArt Tools Design tab appears on the Ribbon. You can change the layout and style of the hierarchy chart at any time.

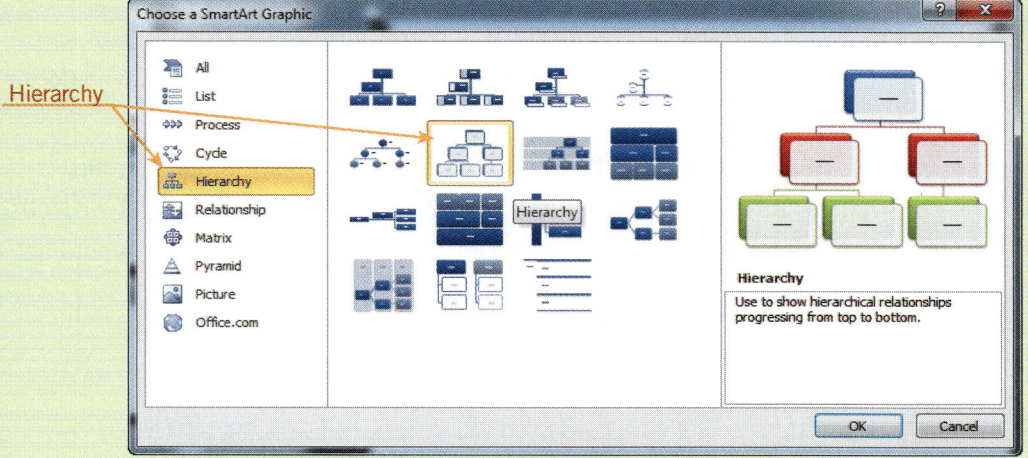

FIGURE 3–4
Choose a SmartArt Graphic dialog box

4. Save the presentation and leave it open for the next Step-by-Step.

NET BUSINESS

In many large companies the organization chart can be large and complicated, so companies often break the chart into several smaller charts for different departments. Using the tools available in PowerPoint, a manager can create a useful org chart (short for organization chart) to help explain the hierarchy of the business to all staff members and employees in the company.

Entering Text in a SmartArt Graphic

You can type text directly in the graphic or you can open the Text pane to the left of the SmartArt graphic to enter the text. Click the Text Pane button to open and close the Text pane. Each text box in a SmartArt graphic can be formatted to meet your needs for the slide. SmartArt graphics consist of text boxes and graphic elements that are grouped together. You can add and delete shapes and text boxes. You can promote and demote shapes and text boxes. As you enter text in the text box, the font size will adjust so the text is visible in the graphic. If at any time you want to go back to the original graphic, on the SmartArt Tools Design tab, click the Reset Graphic button. If at any time you want to change the SmartArt graphic to text, click the Convert button, then click Convert to text.

Step-by-Step 3.4

1. Click the top box **Text placeholder** if it is not already selected, and then type **Cotton**.

2. Click the left **Text placeholder** on the second level, and then type **Lint**.

3. On the second level, click in the right **Text placeholder**, and then type **Cotton Seed**.

4. On the third level, click the left **Text placeholder**, and then type **Fabric**.

5. On the third level, click the middle **Text placeholder** border so the shape has a solid line, and then press **Delete**. The third level now has two shapes.

6. On the third level, click the right **Text placeholder**, and then type **Cotton Seed Oil**.

7. Click the **SmartArt Tools Design** tab. In the Create Graphic group, click the **Add Shape** button arrow, click **Add Shape After**, and then type **Hulls**. There are two subordinate shapes for Cotton Seed and one subordinate shape for Lint. Refer to **Figure 3–5**.

> **TIP**
>
> If you make a mistake, you can press Ctrl+Z to undo your previous actions.

> **TIP**
>
> You can move boxes or shapes in a SmartArt Graphic once you create them if you find that categories or levels change. Use the Promote and Demote buttons in the Create Graphic group to move shapes in the SmartArt graphic to different levels.

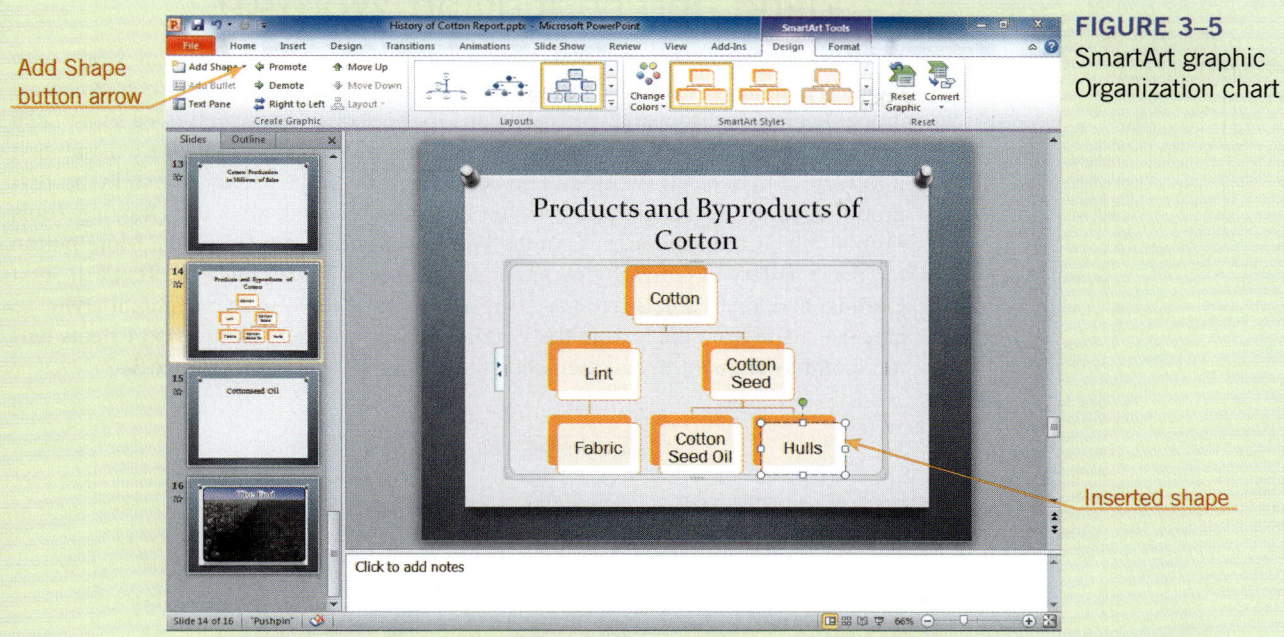

Add Shape
button arrow

Inserted shape

FIGURE 3–5
SmartArt graphic
Organization chart

8. Save the presentation and leave it open for the next Step-by-Step.

You can animate a SmartArt graphic just as you do other slide objects. Click the Animations tab on the Ribbon, click the Custom Animation button, and then in the Custom Animation task pane, click the Add Effect button. Choose how you want to introduce the elements of the SmartArt graphic. You can select entry or exit animations, or have a segment animated for emphasis. If you want to add sound, click the Animation list arrow in the Custom Animation task pane, and then click Effect Options.

Creating and Formatting WordArt

WordArt is decorative text that you can insert on a slide. You can work with QuickStyles, predetermined combinations of color, fills, fonts, and effects, to create dramatic graphics from text. WordArt can also be shaped so the text fits a shape such as an arc, arrow, or oval. You can create new text as WordArt or change existing text into WordArt. To insert WordArt, click the Insert tab on the Ribbon. Next, in the Text group, click the WordArt button. If you have text selected, click the Drawing Tools Format tab on the Ribbon, and, in the WordArt Styles group, click the More button to open a gallery of QuickStyles, as shown in **Figure 3–6**, or click the Text Fill, Text Outline, and Text Effects buttons to create WordArt in your own personal style. To create a shape from the text, in the WordArt Styles group, click the Text Effects button, point to Transform, and then click the shape you want. See **Figure 3–7**.

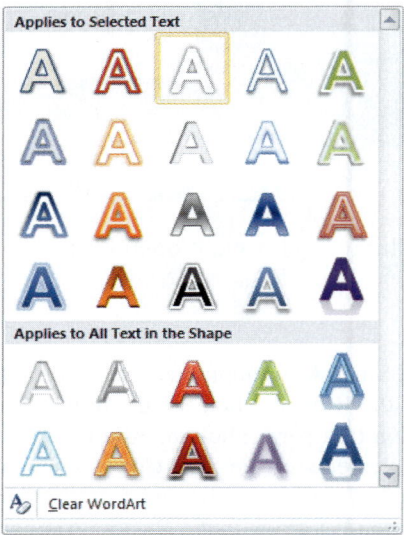

FIGURE 3–6   WordArt Gallery

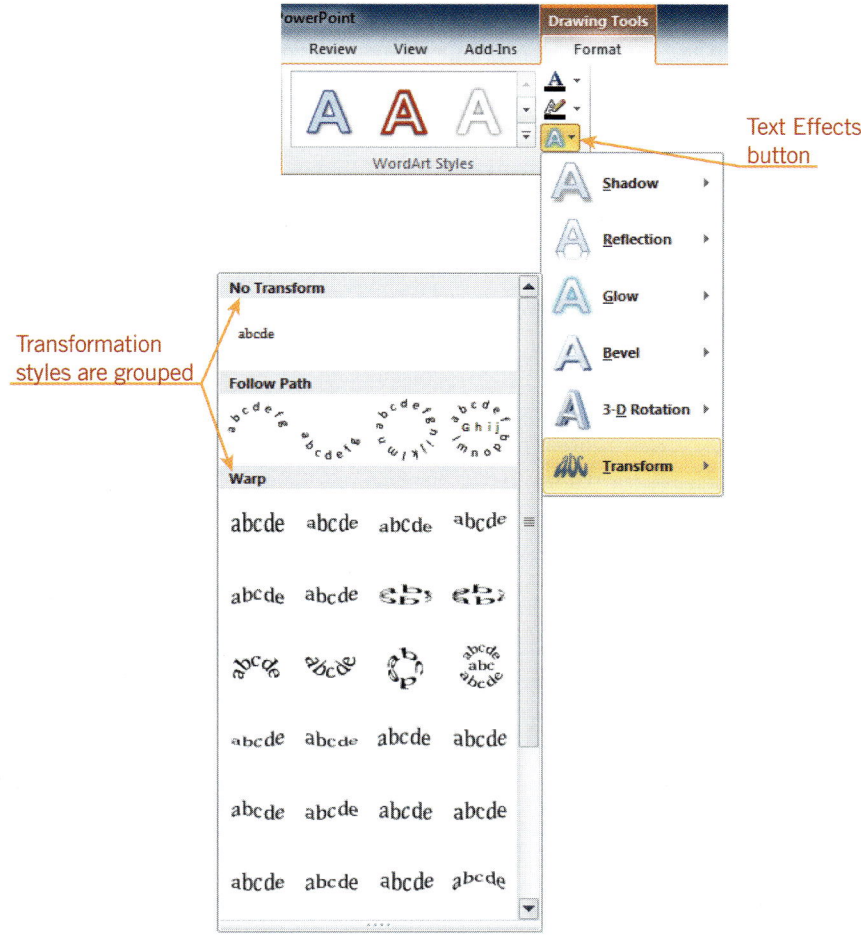

FIGURE 3–7   Word Art Transformation options

Step-by-Step 3.5

1. On the Slides tab, click **slide 11** (photograph of bales of cotton), and then click the **Insert** tab on the Ribbon.

2. In the Text group, click the **WordArt** button, click the **Fill – Red, Accent 2, Double Outline – Accent 2** icon (third row, last column), and then type **Wrapped for Protection.** The text you typed "Wrapped for Protection" replaces the default text and is styled in the text box.

3. On the **Drawing Tools Format** tab, click the **More** button ⬇ in the WordArt Styles group to open the WordArt Styles gallery, move the pointer over the styles to see the effect on the text, and then in the Applies to All Text in the Shape section, in the next to last row, click **Fill – Orange Accent 1, Plastic Bevel, Reflection**.

4. In the WordArt Styles group, click the **Text Effects** button , point to **Transform**, move the pointer over the styles to see the effect on the text, and then in the Warp section, click **Ring Outside**. If the text is a little difficult to read, you can resize it.

5. Using the **Resize Pointer**, drag the **lower-right sizing handle** to the left to shrink the box so you can read the words, and then use the **Move Pointer** ✛ to drag the WordArt shape to the sky part of the photograph so that the WordArt on the slide looks like **Figure 3–8**.

FIGURE 3–8
WordArt formatted on a slide

WordArt

6. Save your work and then leave the presentation open for the next Step-by-Step.

Working with Charts

Charts, also called ***graphs***, provide a visual way to display numerical data in a presentation. When you create a chart in PowerPoint, you are working in a program called Microsoft Excel. If you do not have Microsoft Excel installed, PowerPoint opens a program called Microsoft Graph to create and edit the chart. Microsoft Graph is much less powerful than Excel, but for simple graphing it does the job just fine. When you are building and modifying a chart, Microsoft Excel (or Graph) features, commands, and buttons become available to help you.

If you have an existing chart in an Excel worksheet, you can include that chart on a slide by linking or embedding the worksheet as an object in the slide. You will learn about linking and embedding objects in Lesson 4.

TECHNOLOGY CAREERS

Working in technology, you often have to work with more than one application or program. The files you create with different programs can be integrated to help you present different aspects of an idea, project, or job. When you link or embed files, you work with more than one file. When you are working in PowerPoint to create presentations, the presentation file is the destination file. The file—a Microsoft Excel file, for example—that has a chart that you want to link or embed is called the source file. A linked object, such as an Excel chart, is created in a source file and inserted into a destination file, such as a PowerPoint slide, while maintaining a connection between the two files. You need to save the source file in a folder with the destination file. The linked object in the destination file can be updated when the source file is updated.

The main difference between linking and embedding is where you store the data and how you update the data after you place it in the destination file. An embedded object can also be created in another application, such as Excel. An embedded object is inserted into a destination file. Once embedded, the object becomes part of the destination file. You do not need to save the source file or have the source file in the folder with the destination file. Changes you make to the embedded object are reflected in the destination file. The source file contains the information that is used to create the object. When you change information in a destination file, the information is not updated in the source file.

Building a Chart

To create a chart in a presentation, choose a slide layout that contains a content placeholder for a chart. Click the content placeholder Insert Chart icon to open the Insert Chart dialog box, as shown in **Figure 3–9**. To create a chart on a slide that does not have the Insert Chart icon on the Content Layout placeholder, on the Ribbon click the Insert tab, and in the Illustrations group click the Chart button. Once you select a chart type, the chart appears on the slide with default data. The screen splits in two, with PowerPoint and Excel windows open side by side. The data for the chart is in the Excel window. This is the *datasheet*, a worksheet that appears with the chart and has the numbers for the chart. You replace the sample data with your own. The chart changes to reflect the new data. When you are ready to return to the presentation, click the Close button to close the Excel window and you will see the chart on the PowerPoint slide.

 **VOCABULARY**
datasheet

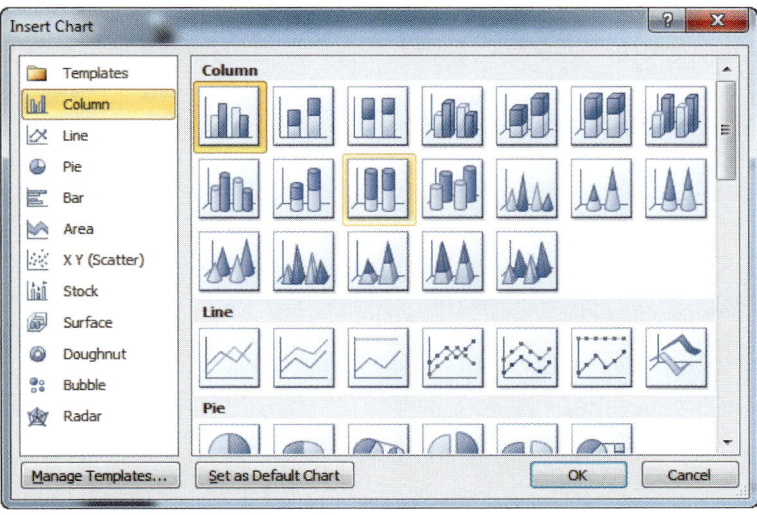

FIGURE 3–9 Insert Chart dialog box

A worksheet is made up of columns and rows. The intersection of each column and row is a cell. Cells are identified by their column letter and row number. The cell that is at the intersection of column C and row 3 would be cell C3.

Step-by-Step 3.6

1. Click **slide 7**, *Where Does Cotton Grow?* This slide has a Title and Content slide layout.

2. Click the **Insert Chart** icon on the content placeholder.

3. In the Insert Chart dialog box, **Column** is selected in the left pane, click the **Clustered Column** icon (first icon, first row), and then click **OK**.

The window splits so that you have PowerPoint open in a window on the left side of the screen and Excel open in a window on the right side of the screen. See **Figure 3–10**. The sample data in the Excel window is shown as a sample chart in the PowerPoint window. Excel displays the data in a worksheet. To enter data in an Excel worksheet, you click the cell and then type the numbers or text. You press Enter after you type the data in each cell. You can also press Tab to move from cell to cell. You have to replace the data with meaningful numbers for your chart. For this lesson, you can leave the numbers alone and simply enter the labels (the text) for the chart, to learn how charts work.

> **TIP**
>
> Press Enter to enter the text in cell A2 and move the insertion point to cell A3 and begin typing the next entry.

FIGURE 3–10
Creating a chart

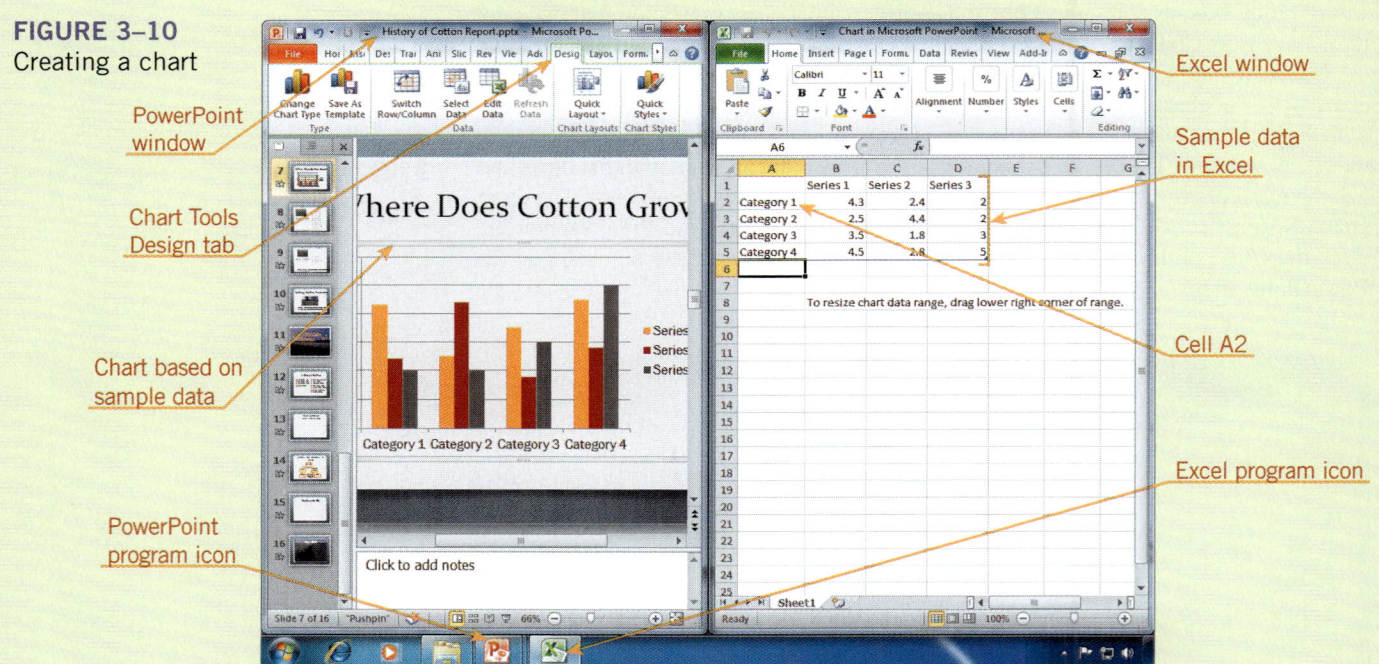

4. In the Excel window, click cell **A2**, and then type **Texas**.

5. Click cell **A3**, and then type **Missouri**.

6. Click cell **A4**, and then type **Virginia**.

7. Click cell **A5**, and then type **Alabama**.

8. Click cell **B1**, type **2010**, press **Tab**, type **2011**, press **Tab**, type **2012**, and then press **Enter**. The data is entered in the worksheet, as shown in **Figure 3–11**.

	A	B	C	D
1		2010	2011	2012
2	Texas	4.3	2.4	2
3	Missouri	2.5	4.4	2
4	Virginia	3.5	1.8	3
5	Alabama	4.5	2.8	5
6				

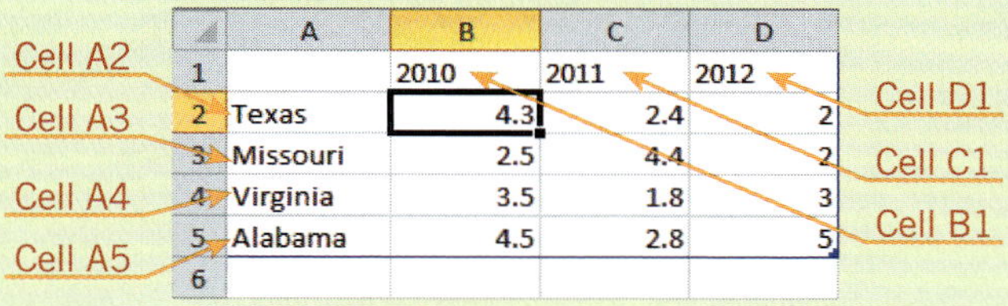

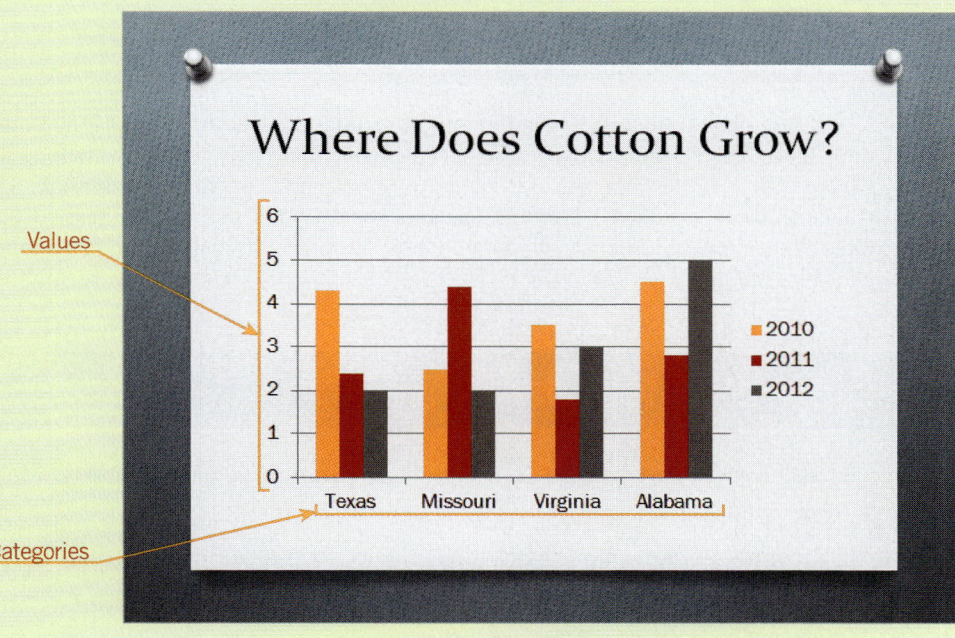

FIGURE 3–11
Data in Excel

The chart changes to reflect the new data. The states are listed on the horizontal axis. This is called the ***category axis*** or the x axis. The values in the worksheet are the numbers on the vertical axis. This is called the ***value axis*** or the y axis. and the legend shows each year in a different color for each column in the chart.

9. Click the Microsoft Excel **Close** button and return to the presentation, and then maximize the PowerPoint window if necessary. The chart looks like **Figure 3–12**.

FIGURE 3–12
Final Chart

10. Save the presentation and leave it open for the next Step-by-Step.

VOCABULARY
category axis
value axis

Formatting a Chart

The chart gives a visual representation of numeric data. Any text you add to the chart helps your audience understand the data by identifying what each number refers to. A legend identifies the data series or bars in a column chart. A title gives the chart a name. To format and edit the chart, you can use the Ribbon commands on the Chart

Tools Design tab, the Chart Tools Layout tab, and the Chart Tools Format tab, as shown in **Figure 3–13**.

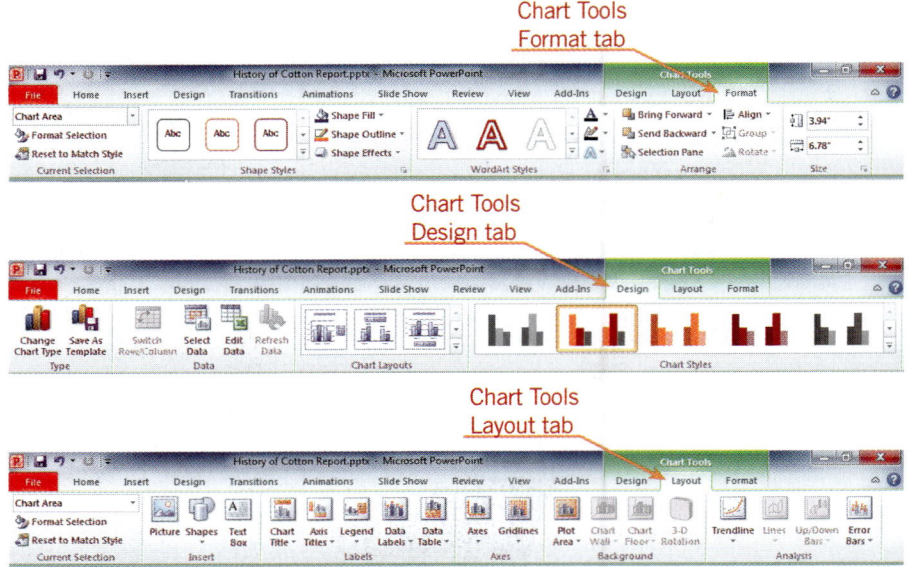

FIGURE 3–13   Chart Tools

If you need to modify a chart at any time, click the chart to select it and open the Chart Tools tab on the Ribbon. You can change the type of chart by clicking the Change Chart Type button in the Type group on the Chart Tools Design tab. The Change Chart Type dialog box that opens is basically the same as the Insert Chart dialog box shown in Figure 3–9. All you have to do is choose a chart type and then choose a subtype.

Step-by-Step 3.7

1. Click the **chart** to activate it and display the Chart Tools contextual tabs on the Ribbon.

2. Click the **Chart Tools Layout** tab on the Ribbon, in the Labels group click the **Chart Title** button, on the menu click **Centered Overlay Title**, and then type **Top Cotton Producing States**.

3. On the Chart Tools Layout tab on the Ribbon, in the Labels group, click the **Data Labels** button to open the menu, and then click **Inside End**.

4. Click the **Chart Tools Design** tab on the Ribbon, click the **More** button ▾ in the Chart Styles group, and then click the **Style 45** icon. Your chart should look similar to **Figure 3–14**.

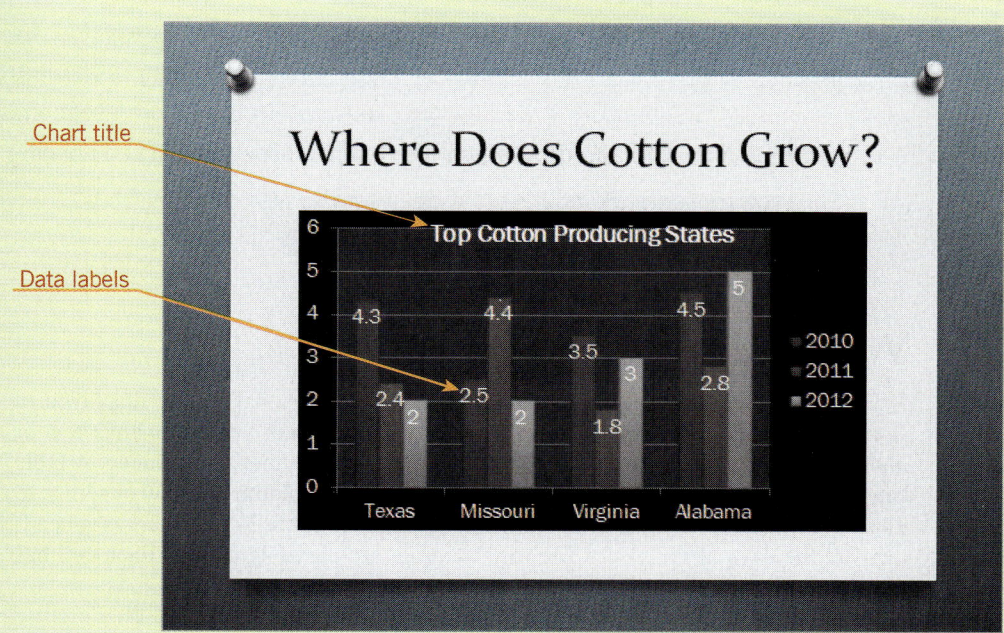

FIGURE 3–14
Formatted column chart

5. On the Chart Tools Design tab in the Type group, click the **Change Chart Type** button. In the Change Chart Type dialog box, in the left pane, click **Pie**. In the Pie section, click the **Pie in 3-D** icon (second pie icon), and then click **OK**. The chart is now a 3-D pie chart. See **Figure 3–15**.

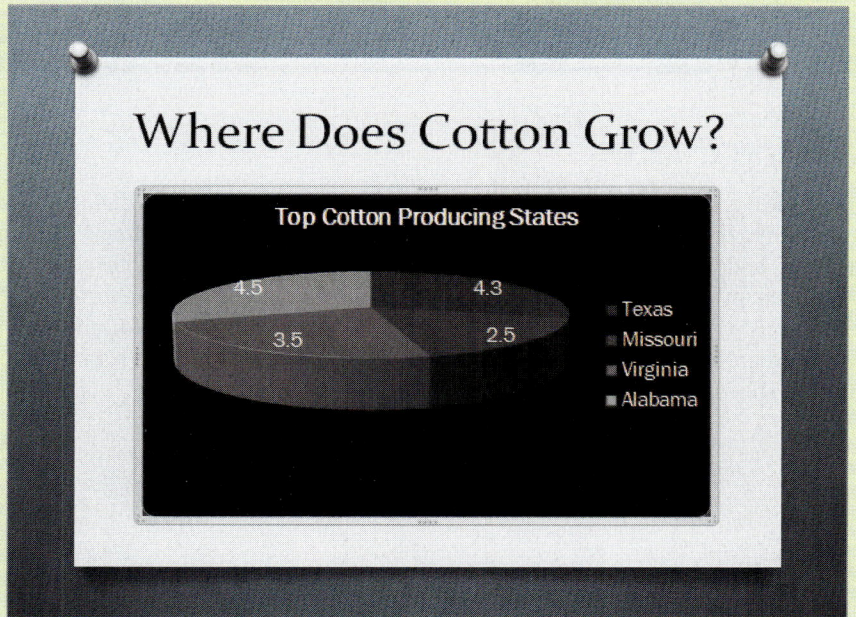

FIGURE 3–15
3-D Pie chart

6. Click the **Chart Tools Design** tab on the Ribbon, if not already selected. In the Type group, click the **Change Chart Type** button, and then in the left pane, click **Column**. Click the **Stacked Cone** icon in the Column section, and then click **OK**. The data is now charted in a series of stacked cones.

7. Save the presentation and leave it open for the next Step-by-Step.

Working with Tables

Tables are useful when you need to organize information that can be displayed in *rows* and *columns*. Each intersection of a row and column is a *cell*. You enter text or numbers in each cell. Tables can be formatted to enhance their appearance. A table can have column headings to identify each item in each column and row headings to identify the rows. A sample table for a club appears in **Table 3–1**. The column headings are the days of the week. The row headings are the assignments. Each cell has the name of a club member.

TABLE 3–1   A sample table

	MONDAY	TUESDAY	WEDNESDAY	THURSDAY	FRIDAY
Breakfast	Jennifer	Emily	Michael	David	Simon
Lunch	Emily	Michael	David	Simon	Jennifer
Dinner	Michael	David	Simon	Jennifer	Emily

Creating a Table

To include a table on a slide, you can use the Content slide layout and click the Insert Table icon to open the Insert Table dialog box. Type the number of columns and rows you want, and then click OK, and a table is inserted on the slide. Type the text in the table; you can move between cells by pressing the Tab key. If you prefer to use the Ribbon and you want to drag a table, click the Insert tab on the Ribbon, and then in the Tables group, click the Table icon. Drag to specify the number of rows and columns, as shown in **Figure 3–16**.

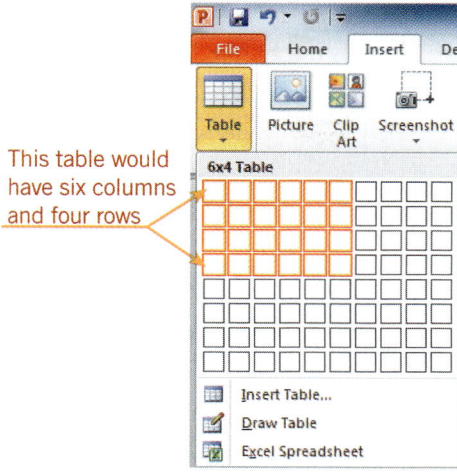

This table would have six columns and four rows

FIGURE 3–16   Dragging to create a table

Step-by-Step 3.8

1. Click **slide 13**, *Cotton Production in Millions of Bales*, in the Slides pane. Slide 13 is selected. The slide layout is Title and Content.

2. On the content placeholder, click the **Insert Table** icon to open the Insert Table dialog box.

3. In the Number of columns text box, type **4**, and then press **Tab**.

4. In the Number of rows text box, type **9**, as shown in **Figure 3–17**, and then click **OK**.

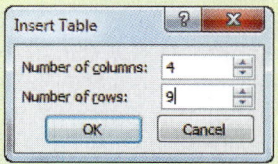

FIGURE 3–17
Insert Table Dialog Box

PowerPoint inserts a table with four columns and nine rows on the slide. The table is formatted according to the Pushpin theme. You can change the formatting at any time. The Table Tools contextual tabs appear on the Ribbon. The insertion point is in the first cell, ready for you to type the data. The table style applied by the theme on the slide includes a different style for column headings. You do not want column headings.

5. Click the **Table Tools Design** tab, if not already selected. In the Table Styles Options group, click the **Header Row** check box to remove the check mark.

6. Type the data as shown in **Figure 3–18**. Click each cell or press **Tab** to move from cell to cell. Do not worry if the text does not seem to fit or is not centered. You will format, align, and adjust the table data later.

FIGURE 3–18
Completed table

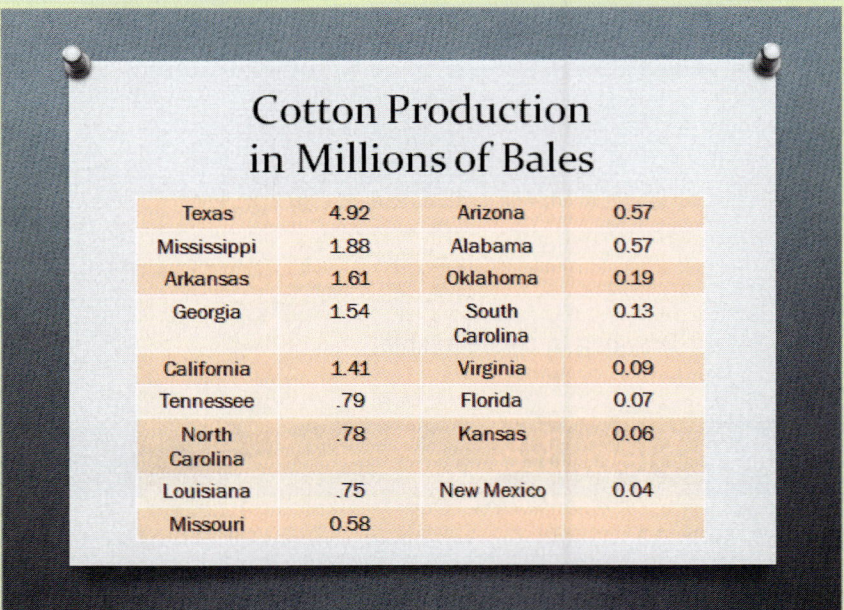

7. Save the presentation and leave it open for the next Step-by-Step.

Modifying Table Styles

To modify a table's borders, fill, or text boxes, select the table to open the Table Tools Design tab on the Ribbon, shown in **Figure 3–19**. You can apply a table style to format the table elements at once. If you want to work on individual elements, click the different buttons to change the shading, borders, and effects to give the table a unique look.

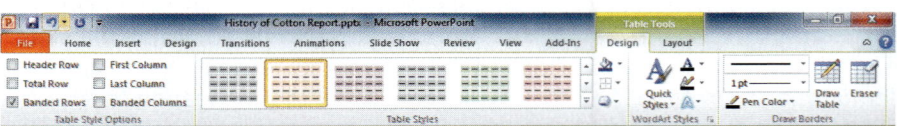

FIGURE 3–19   Table Tools Design Tab

Step-by-Step 3.9

1. Click the table to select it.

2. Click the **Table Tools Design** tab on the Ribbon, and then click the **More** button 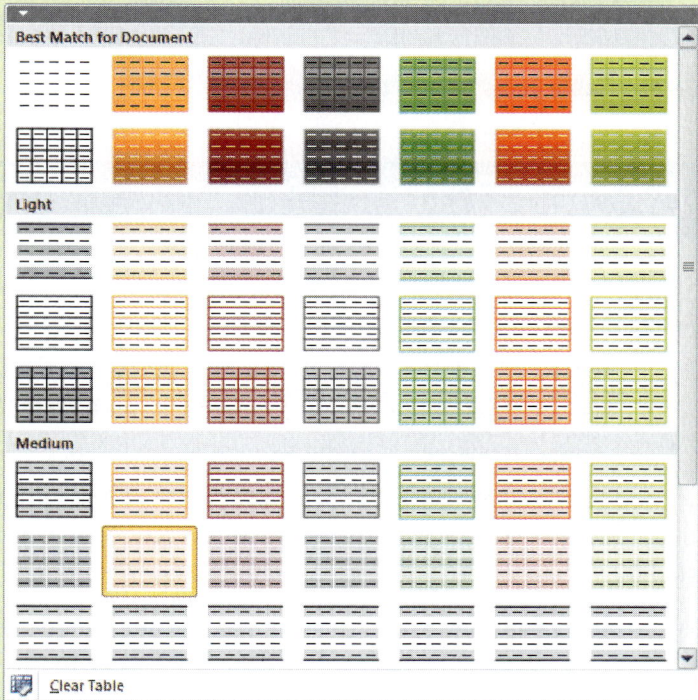 in the Table Styles group to open the gallery, as shown in **Figure 3–20**. The Table Styles gallery is organized into sections: Best Match for Document, Light, Medium, and Dark.

FIGURE 3–20
Table Styles gallery

3. Move the pointer over the different table styles in the gallery and watch as Live Preview shows the effect on the table.

4. Scroll down the gallery. In the Dark section, click **Dark Style 1 – Accent 5**.

5. Save the presentation and leave it open for the next Step-by-Step.

Modifying Table Layout

You can insert or delete columns and rows, merge or split cells, and change the alignment. You can add gridlines, distribute content among cells, rows, and columns, and even change the direction of text in a cell. You work using the Table Tools Layout tab on the Ribbon. See **Figure 3–21**. To change the width of a column or row, you can also click and drag a border.

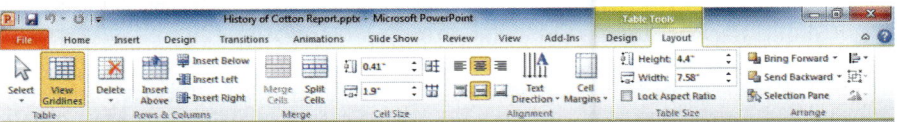

FIGURE 3–21   Table Tools Layout tab

Step-by-Step 3.10

1. On the Table Tools Layout tab, in the Alignment group, click the **Center Vertically** button ▤.

2. Click the **Texas** cell. In the Rows & Columns group, click the **Insert Above** button, and then in the Merge group, click the **Merge Cells** button. A new row with one cell is in the top row of the table.

3. In the new top row, type **Data from US Department of Agriculture**, in the Cell Size group, click the **Table Row Height** text box, type **.75** and then press **Enter**.

4. Click the **Table Tools Design** tab on the Ribbon, and then in the Table Styles Options group, click the **Header Row** check box. The new row is now a header row and has header row formatting.

5. Place the pointer on the right middle sizing handle of the table border, drag ⬌ to the right to make the table slightly wider so that both North and South Carolina fit on one line in their cells and the table fits on the slide. Reposition the table as shown in **Figure 3–22**.

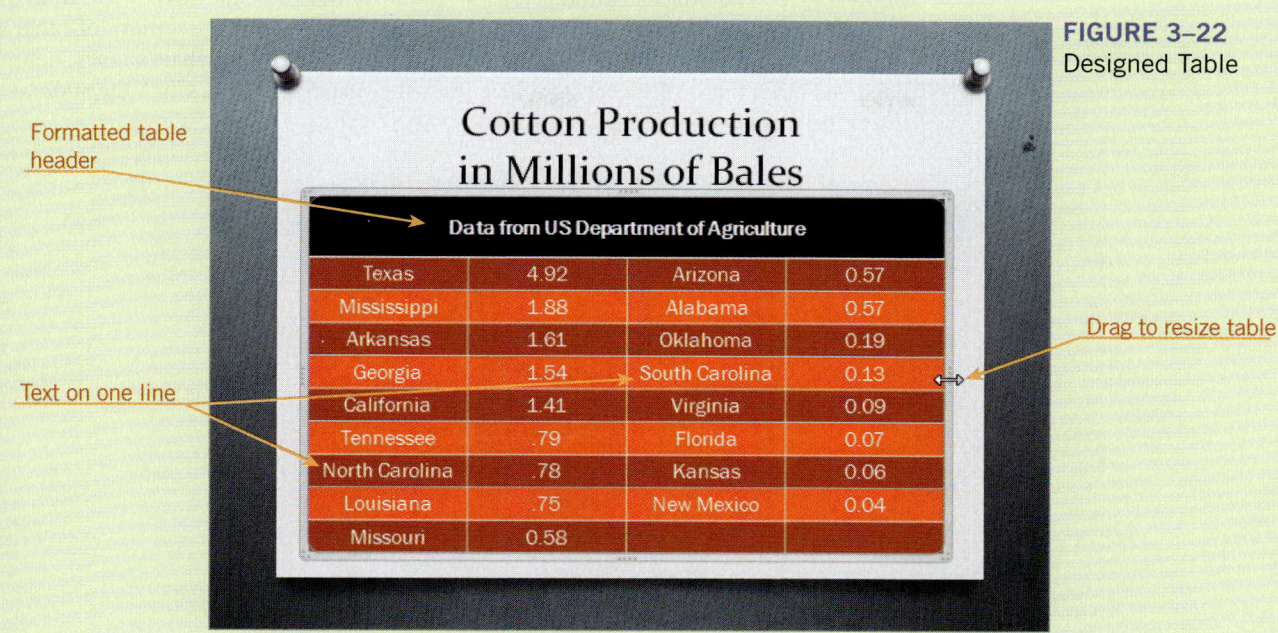

Formatted table header

Text on one line

Drag to resize table

FIGURE 3–22
Designed Table

6. Save the presentation and leave it open for the next Step-by-Step.

Creating Shapes and Objects

You can add shapes and other drawing objects to your presentation to make it more interesting. Shapes include arrows, circles, cones, and stars. On the Insert tab, you can click the Shapes button to display a gallery of available shapes, as shown in

Figure 3–23. The Shapes button is also available by means of the shapes and drawing tools on the Home tab in the Drawing group. There are also a variety of other shapes you can add, including equation shapes, connectors, flow chart shapes, banners, and other kinds of objects that help draw the shape you want. Click the slide to insert the shape with a predefined size.

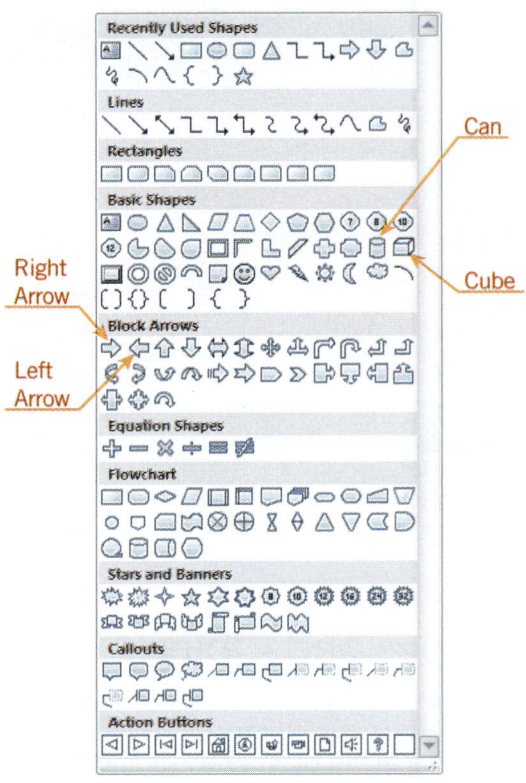

FIGURE 3–23   Shapes gallery

Drawing an Object

The Shapes gallery contains buttons for drawing objects such as lines, circles, arrows, and squares. Click the corresponding button to activate the tool. The Rectangle tools draw rectangles and squares. The Oval tool draws ovals and circles. To use a tool, click and hold the mouse button, and then drag to draw. To create a perfect circle or square, hold down the Shift key as you drag.

Selecting an Object

When you click an inserted object to select it, little squares appear at the edges of the graphic. These small squares are called *handles*. They indicate that the object is selected, and they allow you to manipulate the object. Drag these handles to resize the object. The yellow boxes are *adjustment handles*. The green circle is the *rotate handle*. You will learn more about selecting and manipulating objects later in the lesson.

▶ **VOCABULARY**

handle

adjustment handle

rotate handle

Step-by-Step 3.11

1. Click **slide 15**, *Cottonseed Oil*.

2. On the Home tab, in the Drawing group, click the **Shapes** button to open the Shapes gallery.

3. In the Basic Shapes section, click the **Cube** icon, as shown in Figure 3–23.

4. Click in the left side of the slide below the title text. A cube is drawn and handles appear on the object.

5. In the Drawing group, click the **Shapes** button to open the Shapes gallery. In the Recently Used Shapes section, click the **Cube** icon, and then click the right side of the slide below the title text to create another cube.

6. Create one more cube near the bottom of the slide, below the cube on the right side of the slide. Refer to **Figure 3–24** for placement.

> **TIP**
>
> The Shapes button appears on the Home tab in the Drawing group on the Ribbon. It also appears on the Insert tab in the Illustrations group.

FIGURE 3–24
Six drawn objects

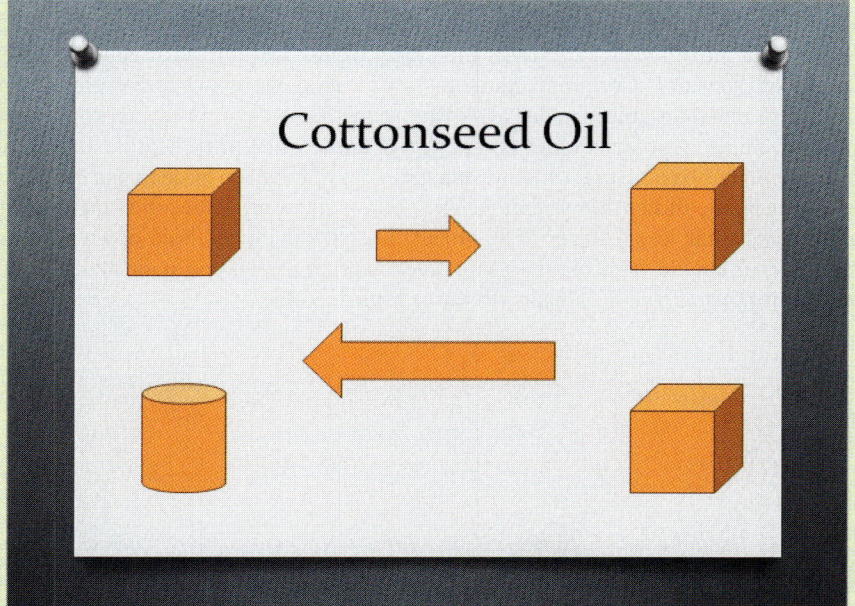

7. In the Drawing group, click the **Shapes** button to open the Shapes gallery. In the **Basic Shapes** section, click the **Can** icon, and then click near the bottom of the slide, below the left cube, to create a can similar to the one in Figure 3–24.

8. In the Drawing group, click the **Shapes** button to open the Shapes gallery. In the **Block Arrows** section, click the **Right Arrow** icon.

9. Click to the right of the left cube, and then drag to the right to draw an arrow to the right of the first cube you created.

10. In the Drawing group, click the **Shapes** button to open the Shapes gallery, in the Block Arrows section, click the **Left Arrow** icon, and then draw a left arrow in the middle of the screen, about twice as long as the arrow you drew in Step 9. Your slide should look similar to Figure 3–24.

11. Save the presentation and leave it open for the next Step-by-Step.

Manipulating Objects

Once you have created an object, there are many ways of manipulating it to achieve the final effect you want. You can rotate, fill, scale, or size an object, as well as change its color and position.

As you learned earlier in the lesson, to select an object, simply click it. To deselect an object, click another object or click any blank area on the slide. Handles do more than indicate that an object is selected. When you select an object, sizing handles surround it allowing you to manipulate it. They make it easy to resize an object that is too large or too small. Select the object to make the handles appear, and then drag one of the handles inward or outward to make the object smaller or larger.

You can move the object, resize the object, rotate the object, or change the key features of the shape. Corner sizing handles are round circles. Drag a corner handle outward to make an object wider and taller at the same time. Drag a corner handle inward to make an object shorter and narrower at the same time. Middle sizing handles are square boxes. Drag a square sizing handle to increase or decrease the size of the object in one dimension at a time. The yellow diamond is the adjustment handle and it changes the key features of an object. To scale an object, hold down Shift and drag a corner handle. This maintains an object's proportions. You scale and size clip-art graphics just as you do objects. Refer to **Figure 3–25**.

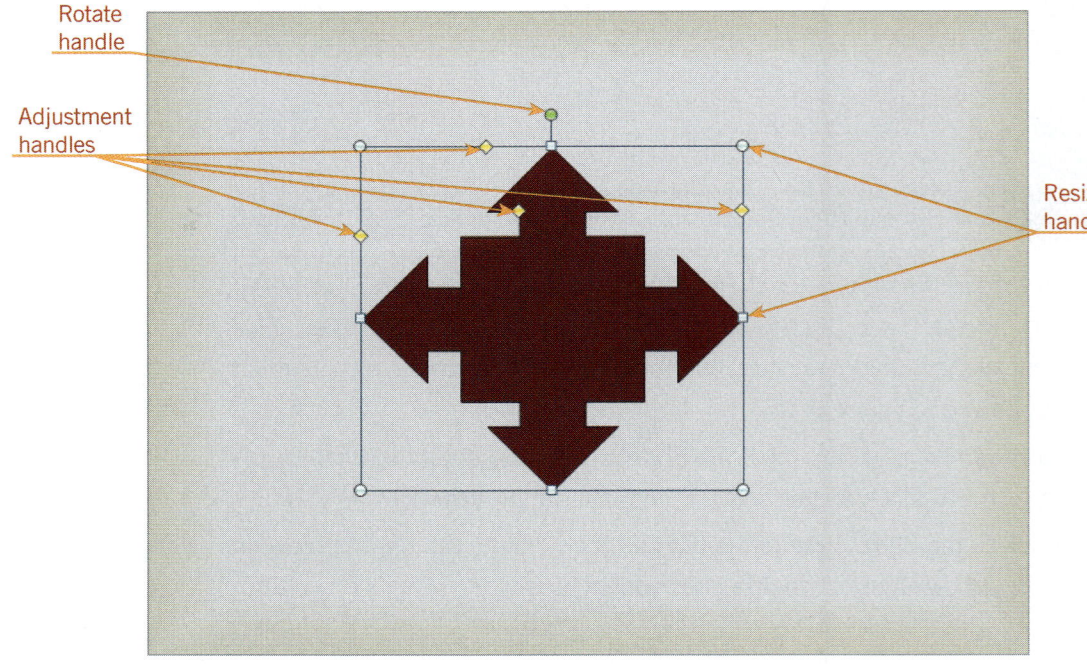

Rotate handle

Adjustment handles

Resize handles

FIGURE 3–25   Selected object

Selecting More Than One Object

Sometimes you will want to select more than one object. PowerPoint gives you several ways to select more than one object using the mouse. One method is to shift-click; another is to draw a selection box around a group of objects. You can also click the Select button in the Editing group on the Home tab on the Ribbon to select all objects, or open the Selection and Visibility task pane.

Shift-Clicking

To shift-click, hold down the Shift key and click each of the objects you want to select. Use this method when you need to select objects that are not close to each other, or when the objects you need to select are near other objects you do not want to select. If you select an object by accident, click it again to deselect it, while still holding down the Shift key.

Drawing a Selection Box

Using the Select Objects tool, you can drag a selection box around a group of objects. On the Home tab on the Ribbon, in the Editing group, click the Select button and then click Select Objects. Use a selection box when all of the objects you want selected are near each other and can be surrounded with a box. Be sure your selection box is large enough to enclose all the selection handles of the various objects. If you miss a handle, the corresponding item will not be selected.

Combining Methods

You can also combine these two methods. First, use the selection box, and then shift-click to include objects that the selection box might have missed.

Rotating an Object

One way of modifying an object is to rotate it. When an object is selected, the Arrange commands appears in the Arrange group of the Drawing Tools Format tab. The Arrange button which opens a menu of commands including the Rotate commands, appears on the Home tab in the Drawing group. The rotate commands on the Arrange menu are Rotate Right 90°, Rotate Left 90°, Flip Vertical, Flip Horizontal, and More Rotation Options. The Rotate Right command moves a graphic in 90-degree increments to the right. The Rotate Left command rotates the graphic in

90-degree increments to the left. You can also drag the rotate handle, the green circle on a selected object, to rotate a graphic to any angle. You can flip an object by choosing the Flip Horizontal or Flip Vertical command. Refer to **Figure 3–26**.

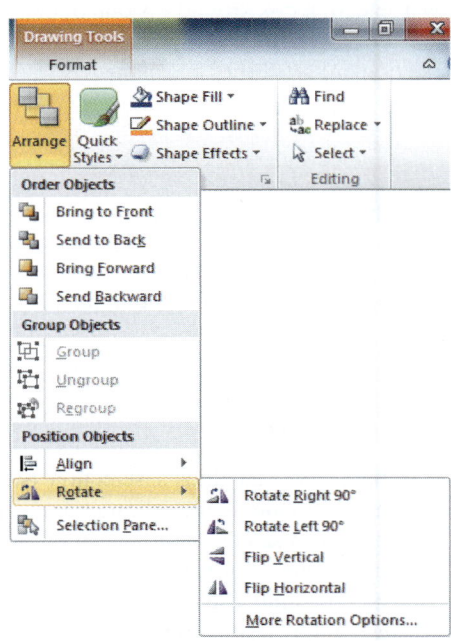

FIGURE 3–26   Rotate commands

Using Guides and Gridlines

When you move objects on a slide, sometimes you want to be able to align and organize the objects along a grid. PowerPoint offers gridlines and guides to help you place objects exactly where you want them on the slide. Click the View tab on the Ribbon, then in the Show group, click the Guides check box to display a vertical and a horizontal guide on the slide. When you drag the guides, a measurement box appears to help you identify the exact location on the slide. Click the Grids check box to display a grid. When you move an object, it will snap to the nearest grid point. You can turn off the Snap to Grid feature. Right-click the slide and then click Grid and Guides or on the View tab, click the Show group launcher to open the Grid and Guides dialog box for other options. See **Figure 3–27**. The grid and guidelines help you place objects on the slide.

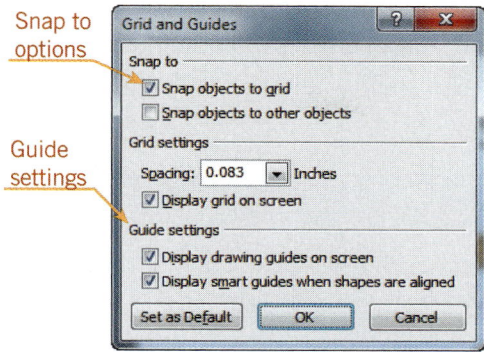

Snap to options

Guide settings

FIGURE 3–27   Grid and Guidelines dialog box

Step-by-Step 3.12

1. On the Ribbon, click the **View** tab. In the Show group, click the **Guides** check box, and then click the **Gridlines** check box. The grid and guidelines appear on the slide.

2. Drag the **horizontal guide** up until the measurement box displays 1.00.

3. Click the **left arrow** in the middle of the screen. Sizing handles appear around the perimeter of the shape, two adjustment handles appear at the prominent features—the arrow head and the arrow body—and a rotate handle appears near the top of the shape.

4. Drag the green **rotate handle** in a counterclockwise direction until the arrow is pointing from the upper-right cube to the can.

5. Click the **right arrow** you created on the slide, then drag it up so the point of the arrow is on the horizontal guide and the guide goes through the middle of the arrow.

6. On the Drawing Tools Format tab in the Arrange group, click the **Rotate** button, and then click **Rotate Left 90°**. The arrow is now pointing up. See **Figure 3–28**.

FIGURE 3–28
Positioning objects

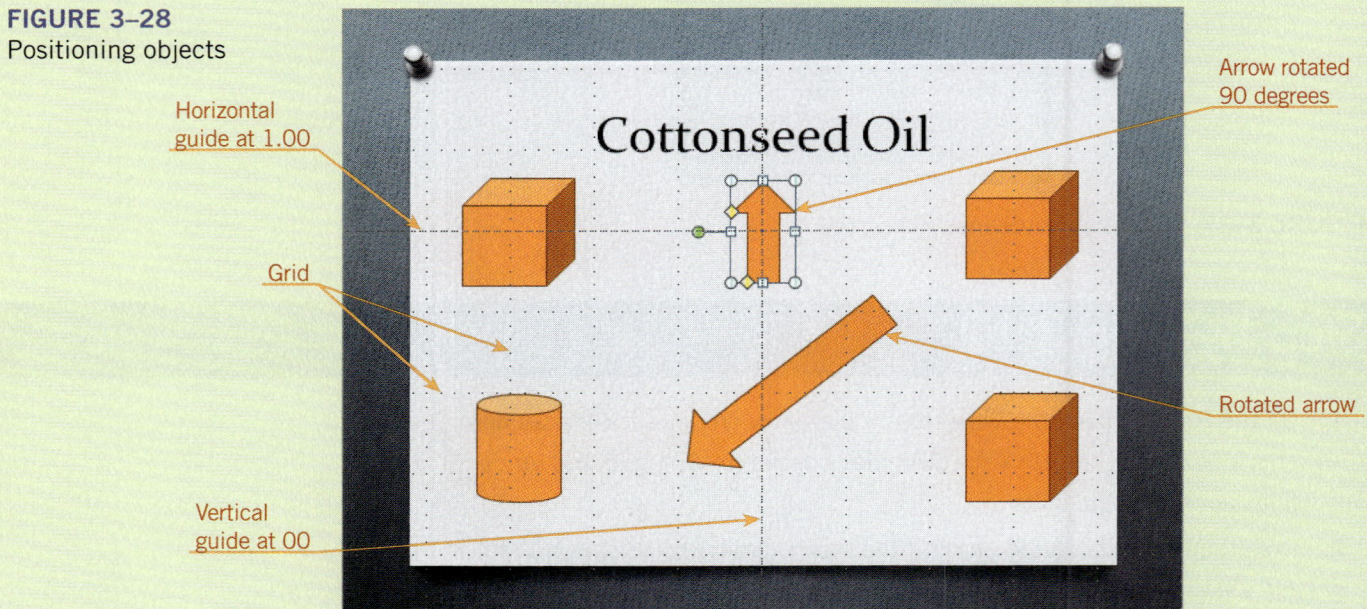

Horizontal guide at 1.00

Arrow rotated 90 degrees

Grid

Rotated arrow

Vertical guide at 00

TIP

As you rotate an object, the pointer will appear as a **rotate pointer**.

7. On the Ribbon, click the **View** tab. In the Show group, click the **Guides** check box, and then click the **Gridlines** check box to remove the check marks. The grid and guidelines no longer appear on the slide.

8. Save the presentation and leave it open for the next Step-by-Step.

Applying Formatting

The Drawing Tools Format tab on the Ribbon contains tools you can use to apply formatting to visual elements in a presentation. You can change the fill, line, or font color. You can apply Shape Styles or WordArt Styles, or arrange objects for added effects.

Filling a Shape and Changing Shape Effects

Filling an object can help add interest to your drawing objects. Select the object you want to fill and click the Shape Fill button in the Shape Styles group on the Drawing Tools Format tab. See **Figure 3–29**. You can fill a shape with theme or standard colors, or click More Fill Colors to open a full color palette in the Colors dialog box. You can also use a picture, gradient, or texture to fill a shape.

FIGURE 3–29   Shape Fill options

Changing Line Color

Another way to apply formatting to a drawing object is to change the line color. Click the Shape Outline button in the Shape Styles group on the Drawing Tools Format tab. See **Figure 3–30**. Click to select a theme or standard color in the palette, or click More Outline Colors to open a full color palette in the Colors dialog box. Other Outline options include changing the weight or thickness of the outline or creating dashes or a designed line.

FIGURE 3–30   Shape Outline options

Changing Shape Effects

Another way to apply formatting to a drawing object is to change the shape effects. Click the Shape Effects button in the Shape Styles group on the Drawing Tools Format tab. Shape effects include Shadow, Reflection, Glow, Soft Edges, Bevel, and 3-D Rotation.

To work on the shape, or design your shape, you can use the Format Shape dialog box, shown in **Figure 3–31**. To open the Format Shape dialog box, click the Shape Styles dialog box launcher in the Shape Styles group.

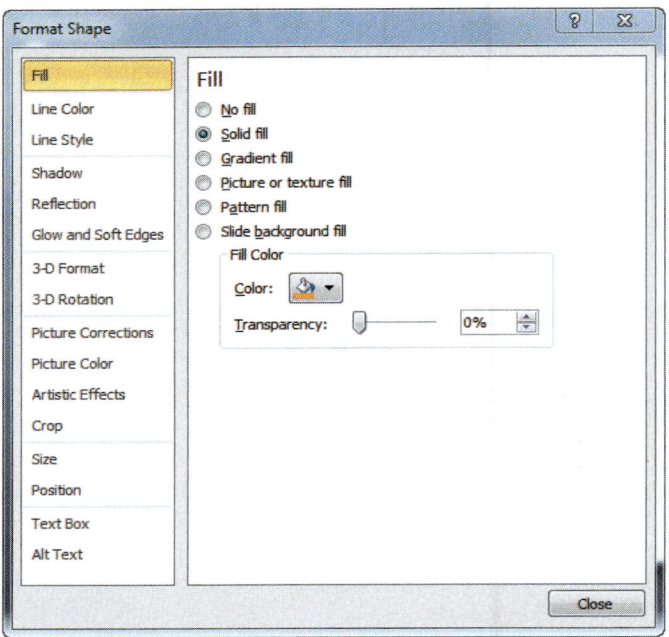

FIGURE 3–31   Format Shape dialog box

Step-by-Step 3.13

1. Click the **upper-left cube object**. On the Drawing Tools Format tab, in the Shape Styles group, click the **Shape Fill** button arrow, and then click **Picture**. The Insert Picture dialog box opens.

2. Locate the folder that contains the Data Files for this lesson, click the **Cotton Gin.jpg** picture file, and then click **Insert**. The picture of the cotton gin appears on the cube.

3. Click the **lower-right cube object**. On the Drawing Tools Format tab, in the Shape Styles group, click the **Shape Fill** button arrow, and then click **Picture**. The Insert Picture dialog box opens.

4. Click **Potato Chip Plant.jpg**, and then click **Insert**. The picture of the potato chip plant appears on the face of the cube.

5. Click the **can object**. On the Drawing Tools Format tab, in the Shape Styles group, click the **Shape Fill** button arrow, and then click **Green Accent 4** in the Theme Colors section.

6. Click the **upper-right cube object**. On the Drawing Tools Format tab, in the Shape Styles group, click the **Shape Effects** button, point to **Glow**, and then in the Glow Variations section, click **Red**, **18 pt glow Accent color 2**, in the last row.

7. The **upper-right cube** should still be selected. On the Drawing Tools Format tab, in the Shape Styles group, click the **Shape Outline** button. In the Theme Colors section, click **Orange Accent 5**, click the **Shape Outline** button arrow, point to **Dashes**, and then click **Long Dash**. Click a blank area on the slide. Your shapes should look similar to **Figure 3–32**.

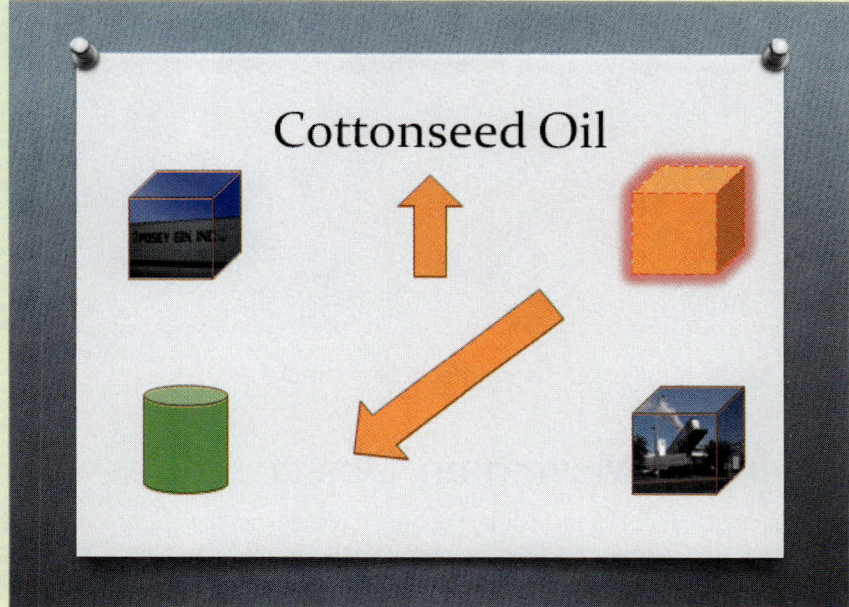

FIGURE 3–32
Formatted shapes

8. Save the presentation and leave it open for the next Step-by-Step.

Applying Artistic Effects

Formatting images or photographs can be fun and provide professional appeal to your slides. PowerPoint includes a collection of artistic effects that can be applied to pictures. Use the artistic effects to make an image look as though it is a watercolor painting, broken glass, wrapped in plastic, or even cast in cement! You should use these effects sparingly as they can overwhelm the slide and take the focus away from your message. To open the Artistic Effects gallery, select the picture to display the Picture Tools Format tab. In the Adjust group, click Artistic Effects. You can see the effect on the picture using Live Preview. See **Figure 3–33**.

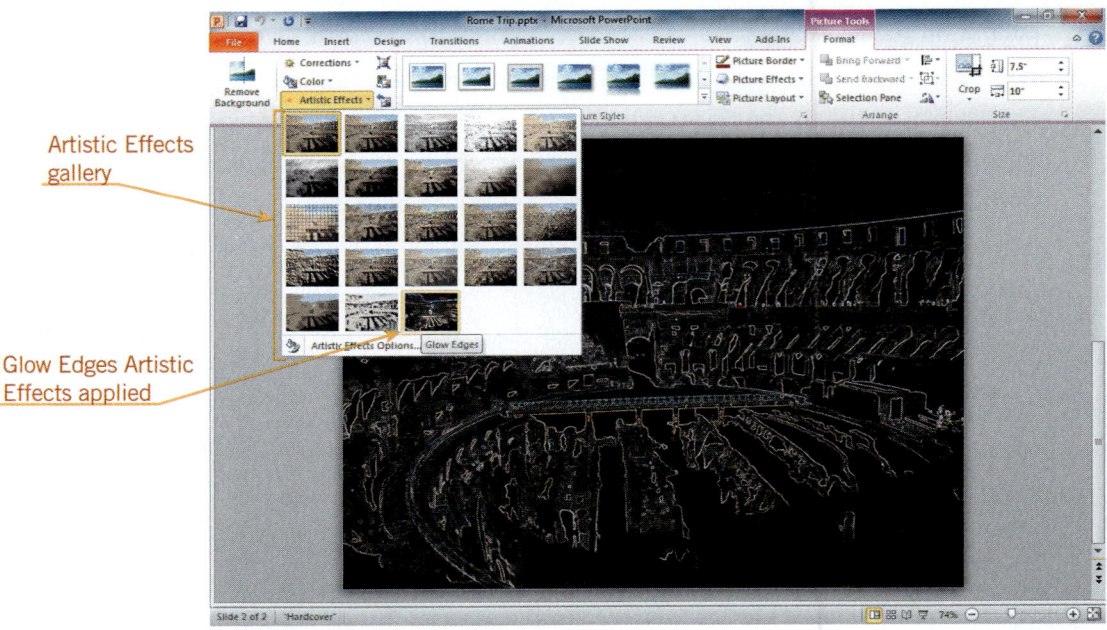

Artistic Effects gallery

Glow Edges Artistic Effects applied

FIGURE 3–33   Applying Artistic Effects to a picture

Copying or Moving an Object

When you create an object on a slide, you might decide that the object is not in the correct place. You can move text or graphic objects. To move an object, first select it and then drag it into place. You can cut, copy, and paste objects the same way you do text. The Cut and Copy commands place a copy of the selected image on the Office Clipboard. Pasting an object from the Office Clipboard places the object in your drawing. Paste Options include being able to retain the objects formatting based on the original theme. You can also paste an object as a picture. Once you paste an object, you can then move it into position.

Grouping Objects

As your drawing becomes more complex, you might find it necessary to "glue" objects together into groups. *Grouping* allows you to work with several items as if they were one object. To group objects, select the objects you want to group, and then on the Home tab on the Ribbon, in the Drawing group, click the Arrange button to open the menu shown in **Figure 3–34**, and then click Group. You can ungroup objects using the Ungroup command.

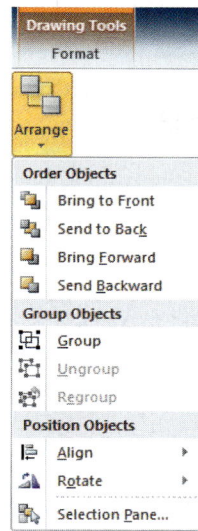

FIGURE 3–34   Arrange commands

Step-by-Step 3.14

1. Click the **upper-left cube**, press and hold **Ctrl**, click the **upper-right cube,** click the **lower-right cube**, and then release **Ctrl**. The three cube objects are selected.

2. On the Drawing Tools Format tab, in the Arrange group, click the **Group** button, and then click **Group**. The three cubes are now grouped into one object. Sizing handles and the rotate handle affect all three objects at once. Any formatting changes or resizing will affect all objects in the group.

3. Move the pointer over the **upper-left sizing handle** until it becomes a diagonal double arrow pointer .

4. Click and drag the **pointer** up and to the left so that the slide title is inside the group frame and you enlarge the three cubes.

5. Click the **Drawing Tools Format** tab. In the Arrange group, click the **Align** button and then click **Align Center**. The objects are larger and centered on the slide, as shown in **Figure 3–35**.

FIGURE 3–35
Grouping objects

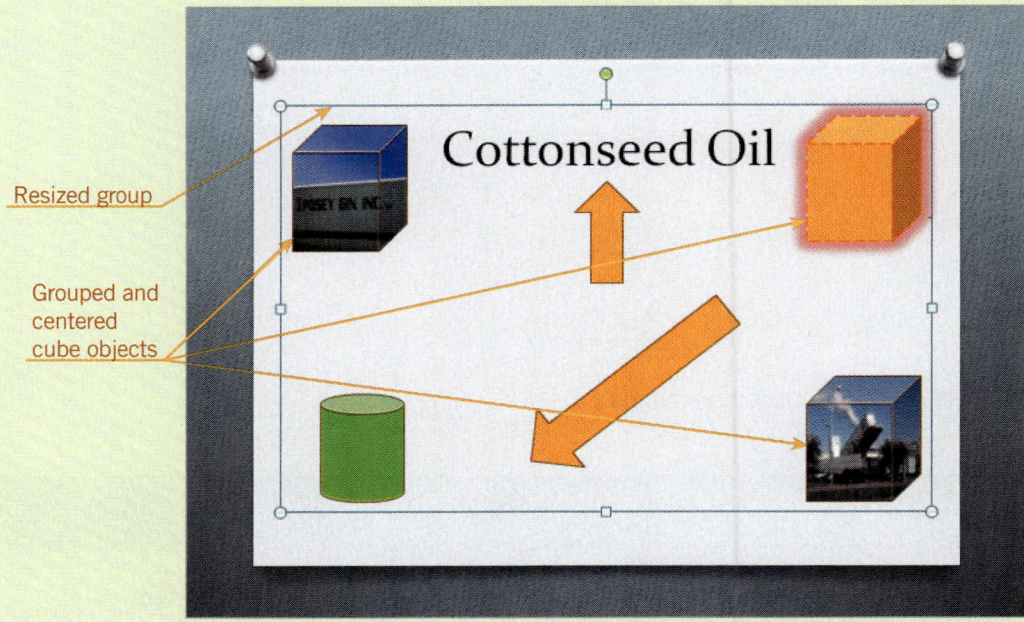

Resized group

Grouped and centered cube objects

6. Click the **can object**, and then drag the yellow **adjustment handle** down slightly so it is even with the two middle sizing handles. You changed a feature of the object by dragging the yellow adjustment handle.

7. Click the **top arrow object** between the two top cubes, use the **rotate handle** pointer ↻ to rotate the arrow to the right 90 degrees so the arrow faces the orange cube. Right-click the border of the arrow. Drag the arrow slightly down and to the right, release the right mouse button, and then click **Copy Here**. A copy of the arrow is pasted below the original arrow, offset from the original arrow.

8. Use the Move pointer ✛ to drag the **arrow object** to a new position between the can and the lower-right cube, to the right of the longer arrow.

9. Click the **can object**. On the Home tab, in the Clipboard group, click the **Copy** button 📋, and then right-click a blank area of the slide, in the Paste Options section. Click the **Use Destination Theme** Paste button 📋, right-click a blank area of the slide, and then click the **Use Destination Theme** Paste button 📋 again to add two new cans to the slide.

10. Move the **arrows** as needed, and then arrange the **cans** as shown in **Figure 3–36**.

> **TIP**
>
> Paste Options include the option of pasting the object as a picture. If the object was copied using another theme, you can paste with the original theme.

> **TIP**
>
> If any of the cans appears to go behind another and you want to bring it forward, click the Arrange button, and then click Bring to Front.

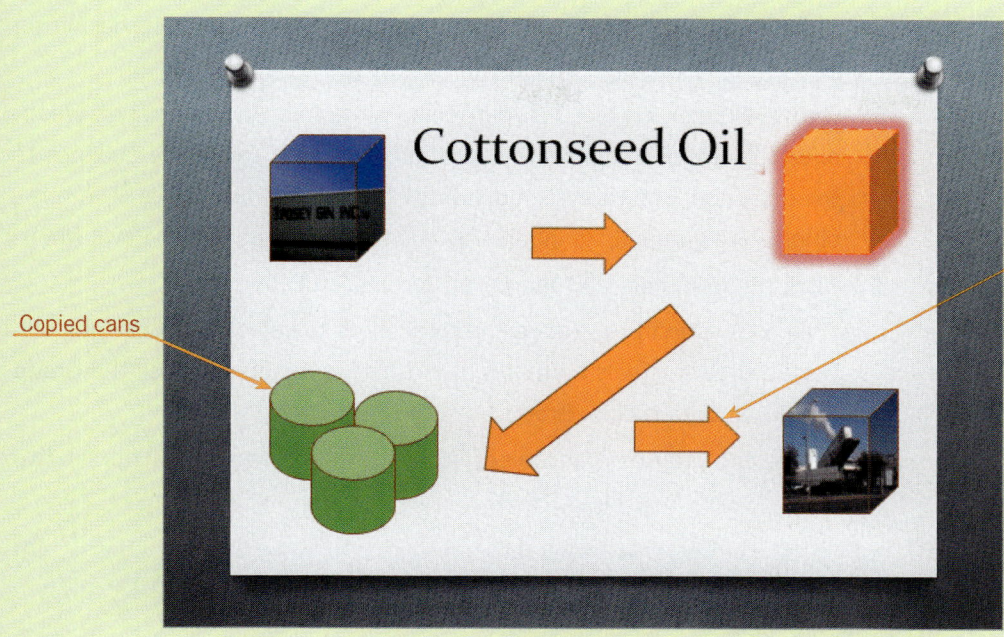

FIGURE 3–36
Shapes copied and moved

Copied and
moved arrow

Copied cans

Cottonseed Oil

11. Save the presentation and leave it open for the next Step-by-Step.

Create a Text Box on a Shape

To place text inside a shape, simply click the shape and then begin to type. A text box will appear on the shape. You can wrap text or change the alignment of text in a shape by working in the Format Shape dialog box. Right-click any shape, and then click Format Shape to open the Format Shape dialog box. You cannot type text on an object that is part of a group. You can ungroup the object to add special formatting or text, and then regroup it to make it part of the original group again.

Step-by-Step 3.15

1. Click any **cube** to select the cube group. On the Home tab on the Ribbon, in the Drawing group, click the **Arrange** button, and then click **Ungroup**. The three cubes are no longer grouped.

2. Click a blank area of the slide to deselect the three cubes, and then click the **upper-right cube** that does not have a picture.

3. Type **Cottonseed Oil Mill** inside the text box. The text wraps in the shape.

4. Drag to select the text **Cottonseed Oil Mill** you just typed in the cube. On the Ribbon, click the **Drawing Tools Format** tab, click the **More** button ⬇ in the WordArt Styles group, move the pointer over the different WordArt styles to see the effects, and then click **Gradient Fill – Gray, Outline - Gray** in the third row.

5. If the shape is not big enough to fit the text, drag the corner sizing handles to resize the cube so all the text fits on two lines.

6. On the Ribbon, on the Drawing Tools Format tab, in the Arrange group, click the **Group** button, and then click **Regroup**. You made changes to the one cube, and then regrouped it with the other two cubes. The three objects are grouped again, and are treated as one object by PowerPoint.

7. Click the front **can**, and then type **Cottonseed Oil**.

8. Drag a **selection box** around the three cans to select the three objects. On the Drawing Tools Format tab, in the Arrange group, click the **Group** button, and then click **Group.**

9. Resize the grouped can object so the text Cottonseed Oil fits on two lines, as shown in **Figure 3–37**.

FIGURE 3–37
Text added to objects

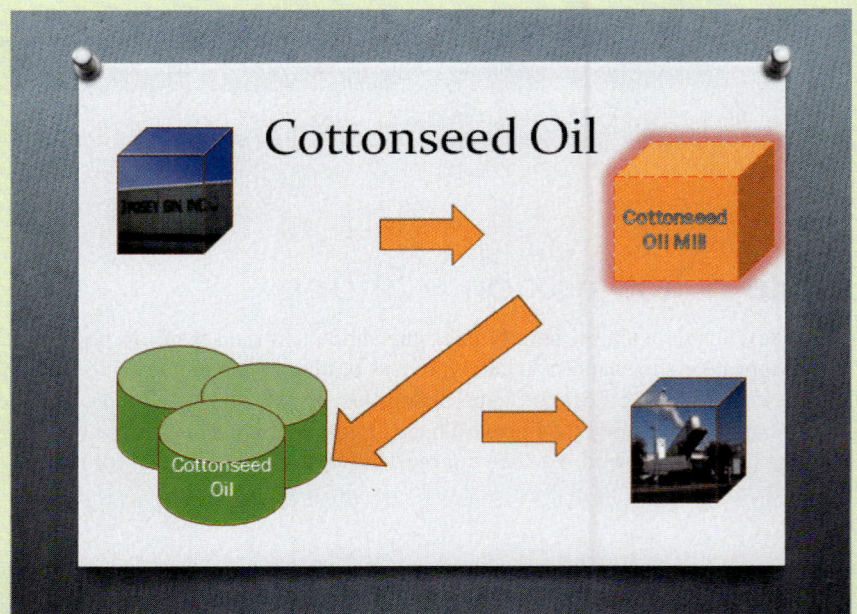

10. Save the presentation and leave it open for the next Step-by-Step.

Animating Shapes

When you create shapes on a slide, often you want to add animation to the shapes to help the slide to tell a story. Grouped objects will animate as a single object. If you want the individual objects in a group to animate separately, you have to ungroup them. If you take the time to create an animation that includes several effects and you want that same sequence of effects applied to another object, you can use the Animation Painter. Select the object with the animation effects you want to copy, click the Animation tab on the Ribbon, then in the Advanced Animation group, click the Animation Painter. To apply the same animation to more than one object, double-click the Animation Painter button. The Animation Pointer ⌖ is 'sticky' and any objects you click will have that animation applied to it.

Step-by-Step 3.16

1. Click any **cube** on the slide, and then click the **Drawing Tools Format** tab. In the Arrange group, click **Group**, click **Ungroup**, and then click a blank area on the slide.

2. Click the **upper-right cube**, click the **Animations** tab on the Ribbon, click the **Add Animation** button to open the Animation gallery, and then in the Entrance section, click **Swivel**. The effect is set to start On Click.

3. Click the **upper-right cube**, click the **Animations** tab on the Ribbon, click the **Add Animation** button to open the Animation gallery, and then in the Emphasis section, click **Color Pulse**. The cube has two animation tags.

4. Click the **upper-right cube**, in the Advanced Animation group, click the **Animation Painter button**, and then use the Animation Pointer ⌖ to click the **upper-left cube** with the picture on it. The same animations are applied to the second cube and animation tags 3 and 4 appear next to that cube.

TIP

Click the Preview button on the Animations tab at any time to test your animations.

5. Click the **upper-right cube**, in the Advanced Animation group, click the **Animation Painter button**, and then use the Animation Pointer ⌖ to click the **lower-right cube** with the picture on it. The same animations are applied to the third cube and animation tags 5 and 6 appear next to that cube. See **Figure 3–38**.

FIGURE 3–38
Using the Animation Painter

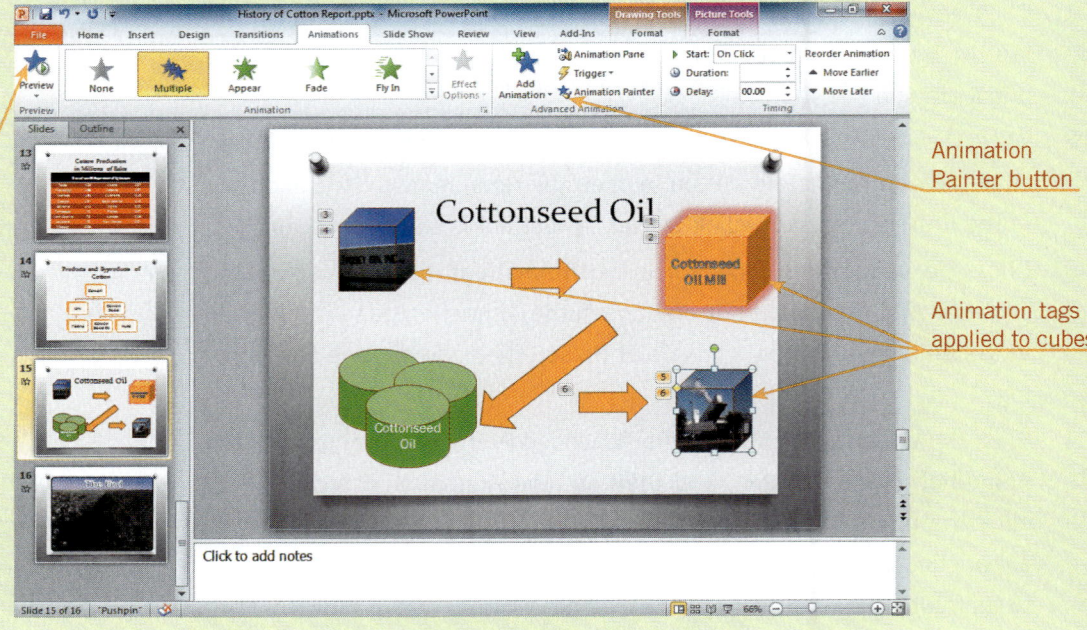

Preview button

Animation Painter button

Animation tags applied to cubes

Using the Animation Pane

As you build the animations in a slide, it is often helpful to get an overall picture of the sequence and timings of the animations. The Animation Pane provides that feature. Click the Animations tab on the Ribbon, then in the Advance Animation group, click the Animation Pane button. Use the Animation Pane in the next step-by-step to finish animating this slide. If you use the Add Animation button, animations build upon each other. If you use the Animations gallery that is what is applied to the object.

Step-by-Step 3.17

1. On the Animations tab, in the Advanced Animation group, click the **Animation Pane** button. The Animation Pane opens. You see the six animations currently applied to the cubes on the slide.

2. Click the **top arrow** between the two cubes, click the **Add Animation** button, click **More Entrance Effects**, in the Add Entrance Effect dialog box, scroll to the Exciting group, click **Boomerang**, and then click **OK**. This effect is currently set to start On Click.

3. In the Timing Group, click the **Start** list arrow, and then click **After Previous**. The animation for the arrow will begin after the cube animations.

4. Select the **left arrow** that points to the cans in the middle of the slide, click the **More** button ⊡ in the Animation group to open the Animations gallery, and then in the Emphasis section, click **Object Color**.

5. Click **left arrow** again, in the Animation group click the **Effect Options** button, on the palette in the Theme Colors section, click the **blue box** in the first row, fourth column. In the Timing group, click the **Duration** box, type **.75**, and then set the animation to start **After Previous**.

6. Click the **cans group**, click the **More** button ⊡ in the Animation group to open the Animations gallery, scroll to the Exit section, click **Shrink & Turn**, click the **Start** list arrow in the Timing section, and then click **After Previous**.

7. Click the **bottom arrow**, click the **More** button ⊡ in the Animation group to open the Animations gallery, scroll to the Exit section, click Zoom, click the **Start** list arrow, and then click **After Previous**.

   The slide should look similar to **Figure 3–39**, although the numbers for your objects may be different.

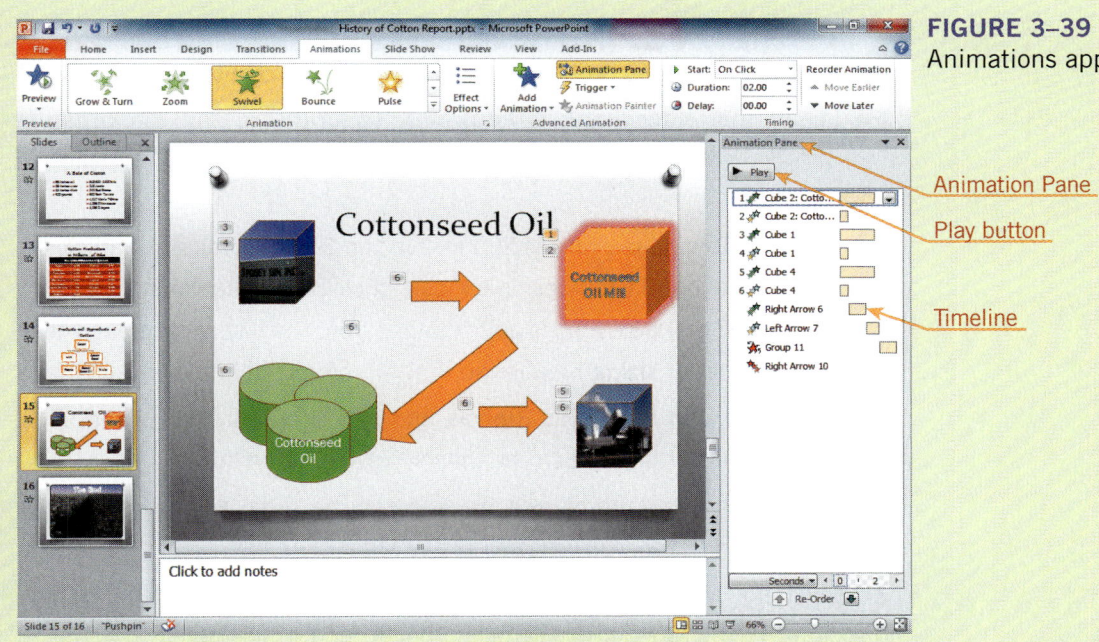

FIGURE 3–39
Animations applied to objects

8. Click **Cube 2:Cotton..** in the first animation in the Animation Pane, click the **Play** button in the Animation Pane, and then watch the timeline and animations for the slide.

9. Close the Animation Pane, save the presentation, and then leave it open for the next Step-by-Step.

Ordering Visual Elements

If you add an object to a slide that already contains other objects, the last object is stacked on top of the other objects. To bring an object forward or send it backward, select the object you want to move, and click the Bring to Front, Send to Back, Bring Forward, or Send Backward command in the Arrange group on the Drawing Tools Format tab. These commands are also available on the Picture Tools Format tab on the Ribbon. You can also access this feature by right-clicking the object, then making a selection from the shortcut menu. When you insert a picture, you might find that the picture has a background color. Often you can remove the background color, so the picture looks integrated with the total image you are trying to create. PowerPoint has powerful image editing tools that help you edit pictures to achieve these visual effects. To remove background color, click the picture, then on the Picture Tools Format tab, click the Remove Background button.

Step-by-Step 3.18

1. Click **slide 15**, *Cottonseed Oil*, click the **Home** tab on the Ribbon, in the Slides group click the **New Slide** button arrow, and then click the **Blank** layout.

2. Click the **Insert** tab on the Ribbon, and then, in the Images group, click the **Picture** button to open the Insert Picture dialog box.

3. Locate the folder that has the Data Files for this lesson, click the file **Sky.jpg**, and then click **Insert**. The picture of a blue sky appears on the slide.

4. Click the **Design** tab on the Ribbon, in the Background group click the **Hide Background Graphics** check box, click the **Background Styles** button, click **Style 1** to remove any graphics from the background, and then drag the **corner sizing handles** so that the picture fills the entire slide.

5. Click the **Insert** tab on the Ribbon, and then, in the Images group, click the **Picture** button to open the Insert Picture dialog box.

6. Locate and insert the picture **Truck.jpg** on the slide, and then move the truck down to the lower portion of the slide.

7. Click the **Insert** tab on the Ribbon, and then, in the Images group, click the **Picture** button to open the Insert Picture dialog box, insert the picture **Highway.jpg** on the slide, and then resize and position the **Highway.jpg** picture so that it covers the bottom half of the slide and covers the Truck.jpg picture.

8. On the Picture Tools Format tab, in the Arrange group, click **Send Backward**. The truck appears again. The stacking order of the pictures should be sky, highway, and then truck. You should see all three images.

9. Click the **Truck.jpg** picture on the slide and resize the picture so that it is proportional to the cars in the Highway.jpg picture, and then move the **Truck.jpg** picture so that it is positioned on the left side of the overpass, slightly off the slide (see **Figure 3–40**).

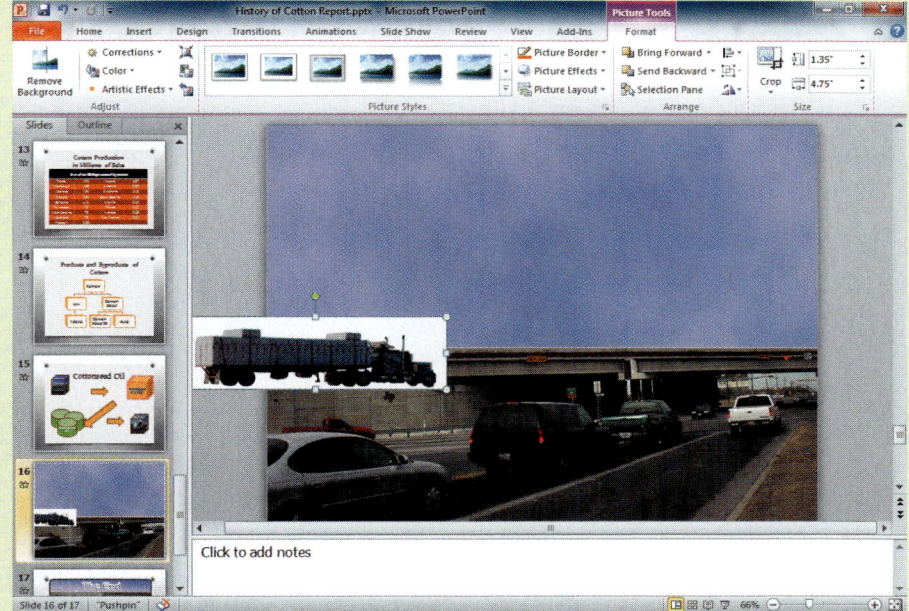

FIGURE 3–40
Pictures inserted on a slide

10. Click the **Truck.jpg** picture so it is selected. On the Picture Tools Format tab on the Ribbon, in the Adjust group, click the **Remove Background** button. The Background Removal tab appears and the image is marked for changes. The purple areas will be discarded. See **Figure 3–41**.

TIP

If you make a mistake coloring a picture, click the Reset Picture button.

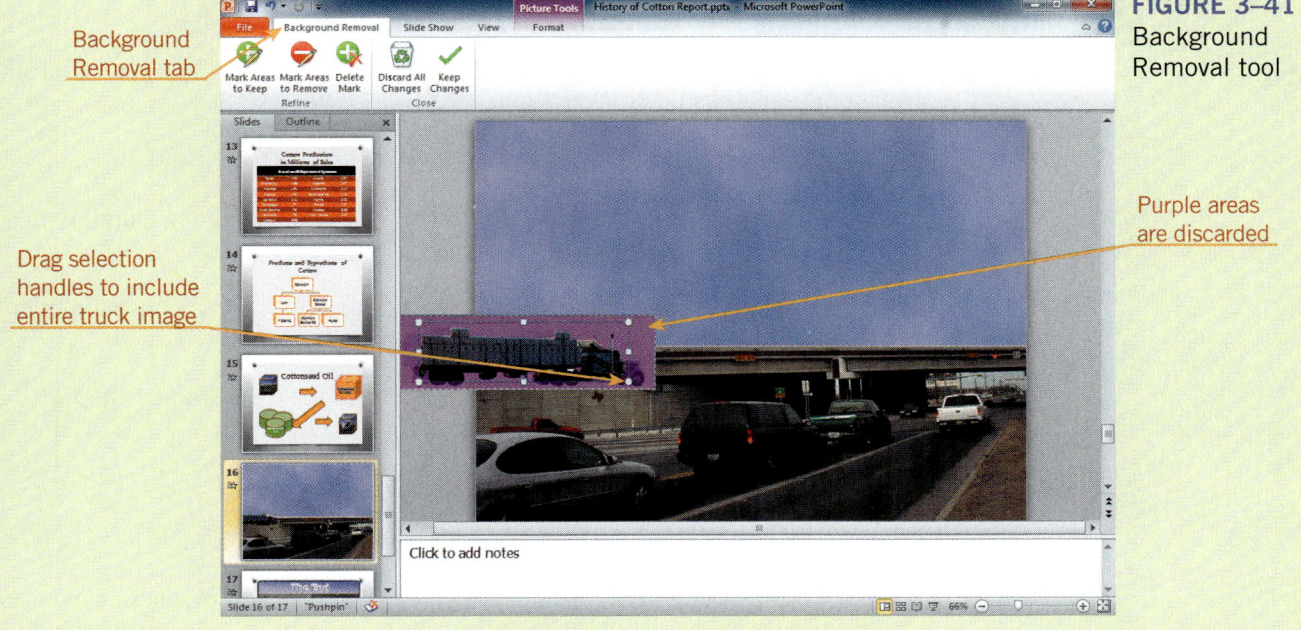

FIGURE 3–41
Background Removal tool

Background Removal tab

Drag selection handles to include entire truck image

Purple areas are discarded

11. Carefully drag the selection handles as needed to include the entire truck image inside the dashed lines, and then click the **Keep Changes** button on the Background Removal tab. The white background is gone and the truck should blend in with the sky above it and the overpass below it. See **Figure 3–42**.

FIGURE 3–42
Background removed

12. Drag the truck image so the truck appears to be on the overpass but is still off the slide to the left.

13. With the **Truck.jpg** picture selected, click the **Animations** tab on the Ribbon, click the **More Animations** button ⌅ to open the gallery, scroll to Motion Paths, click **Lines**, click the **Effect Options** button in the Animation group, and then click **Right**. The truck should move to the right along the overpass in the picture.

14. Click the **Motion Path** on the slide, drag the red side of the path to extend it off the slide on the right side of the overpass. See **Figure 3–43**.

FIGURE 3–43
Motion path extended

Motion path starts here

Motion path ends here

15. Verify that the animation is set to start On Click, click the **Duration** text box, and then type **5.00**.

16. Click the **Preview** button. The truck appears to travel along the motion path on the slide for five seconds.

17. Save the presentation and leave it open for the next Step-by-Step.

Inserting Objects on a Slide

Objects can include Excel charts, media clips, video, bitmaps, or almost any other media file that can be embedded into a PowerPoint presentation. To insert an object on a slide, click the Insert tab on the Ribbon. To insert a picture of any program that is not minimized on the taskbar, click the Screenshot button in the Images group. A menu of available images appears and you can click to insert on a slide. See **Figure 3–44**.

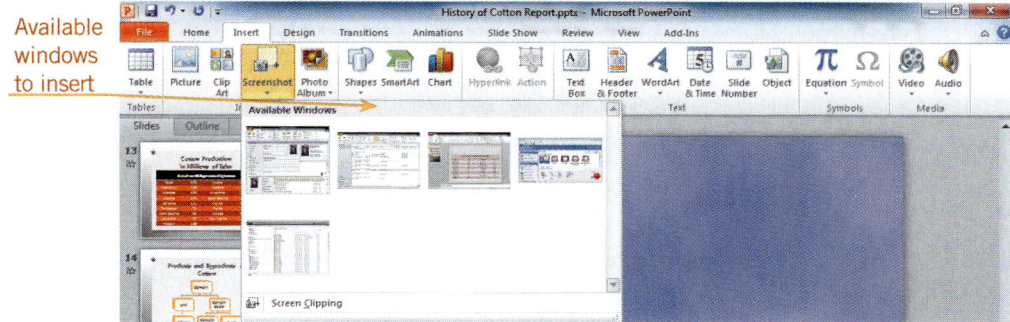

FIGURE 3–44   Inserting a screenshot

To insert an object, click the Object button in the Text group. The Insert Object dialog box opens, as shown in **Figure 3–45**. Scroll through the list of objects that are compatible with PowerPoint, and click the type of object you want to insert. If you are inserting an object that has already been created, click Create from file. The dialog box changes to allow you to locate the file you want to insert. Click OK to close the Browse dialog box, and click OK again to embed the file. You will learn more about embedding files in the next lesson.

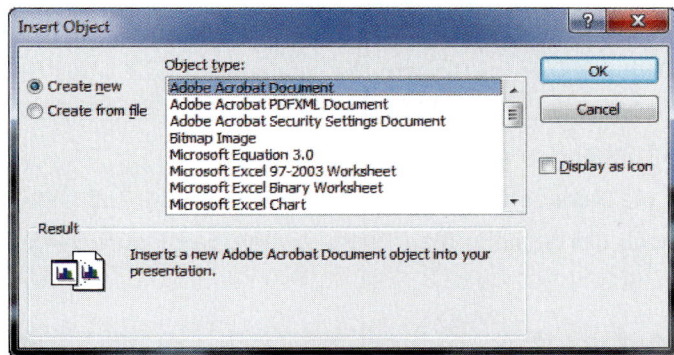

FIGURE 3–45   Insert Object dialog box

Inserting a video helps bring concepts to life. Video is an excellent medium to transmit ideas. PowerPoint video editing tools make it possible for you to create the perfect video for your presentation. To insert a video, click the Video button in the Media group. To insert a sound, click the Audio button in the Media group.

Video can be formatted just as a picture can. The Video Tools Format tab is shown in **Figure 3–46**. Video can be edited to play in any way that best suits your presentation. See **Figure 3–47**.

FIGURE 3–46   Video Tools Format tab

FIGURE 3–47   Video Tools Playback tab

Step-by-Step 3.19

1. Select **slide 2**, *How do they make...?*, click the **clipart** of a bed, then press **Delete**. Click the **Insert** tab on the Ribbon, in the Media group, click the **Video button arrow** and then click **Video from File**.

2. In the Insert Video dialog box, locate and click **cribbedding.mpg** from the Data Files for this lesson, then click **Insert**. The video is inserted in the center of the slide with video editing controls selected and the Video Tools Format tab selected.

3. Click the **More** button ⏷ in the Video Styles group, and then click **Metal Rounded Rectangle** in the Intense section. See **Figure 3–48**.

FIGURE 3–48
Video formatted

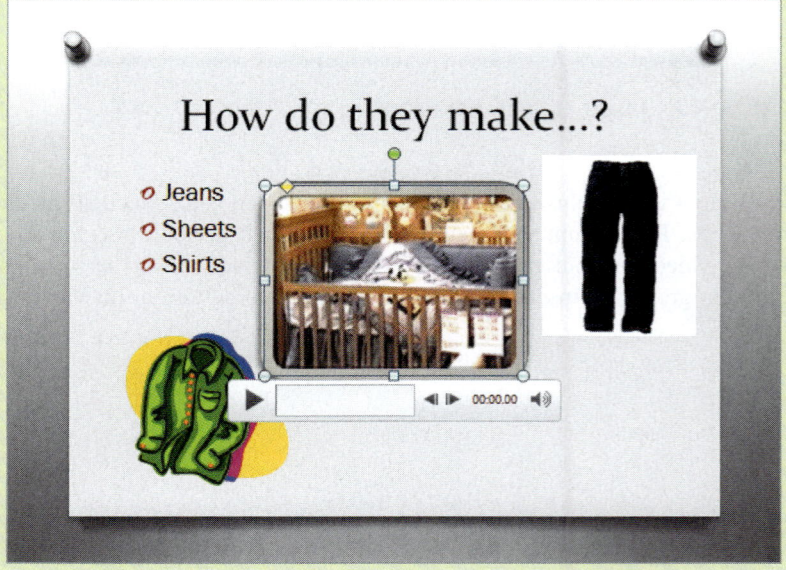

4. Click the **Video Tools Playback** tab, if not already selected, in the Video Options group, click the **Start** list arrow, and then click **Automatically**.

5. Click the **Play button** in the Preview section, and then view the short video.

6. Save the presentation and leave it open for the next Step-by-Step.

 TIP

In the Preview section, the Play button is a Pause button while the video is playing. Click it to stop the video.

Adding a Header or Footer

You add a header or footer to the slides or notes pages by using the Header and Footer dialog box. Click the Insert tab on the Ribbon; in the Text group, click the Header & Footer button. The Header and Footer dialog box opens on the screen, as shown in **Figure 3–49**. Slides have footers. You can add the date and time, slide number, and any text you want to the footer of the slide. Although a footer is often defined as text that appears on the bottom of a page or slide, some themes place the footer in different places on the slide. When you click the Notes and Handouts tab, you have the option of creating a header as well as a footer. The header appears at the top of the notes page, the footer at the bottom of the page. Some items that you might include in a header or footer are the presenter's name, e-mail address, Web site address, or phone number.

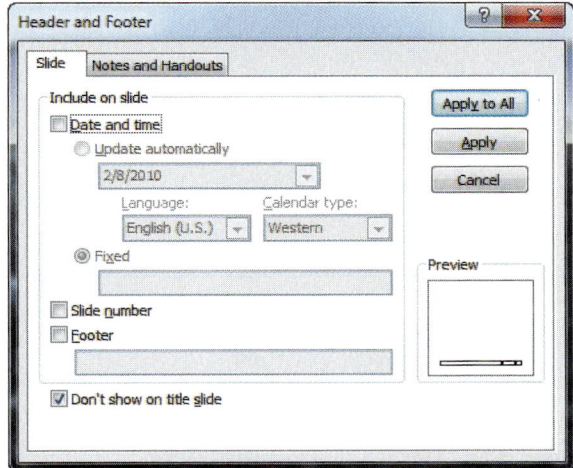

FIGURE 3–49   Header and Footer dialog box

Step-by-Step 3.20

1. Click the **Insert** tab on the Ribbon, and then, in the Text group, click the **Header & Footer** button. The Header and Footer dialog box opens.

2. Click the **Notes and Handouts** tab in the Header and Footer dialog box.

3. Click the **Footer** check box, and then type **The Story of Cotton**.

4. Click the **Date and time** check box, if it is not already selected. It is set to Update automatically.

5. Click the **Header** check box. In the Header text box, type your name.

6. Click **Apply to All**.

7. Click the **File tab**, review the Print options, and then print the slide show as directed by your teacher.

8. Save and close the presentation, and then exit PowerPoint.

SUMMARY

In this lesson, you learned:

- How to insert and modify SmartArt graphics to give special effects to text and graphics on a slide.

- How to create and format WordArt.

- How to build and format charts in a presentation using Microsoft Excel.

- How to create, format, and modify a table.

- How to add shapes and objects to your presentation to add effects to the text.

- How to rotate, fill, scale, or size an object as well as change its fill or line color.

- How to copy, move, order, and group objects on a slide.

- How to animate shapes and use the animation painter to copy animation.

- How to order visual elements, create a motion path, and make and remove a background from a picture.

- How to insert objects on slides, including worksheets, sounds, and videos.

- How to add a header or a footer to slides in a presentation.

 ## VOCABULARY REVIEW

Define the following terms:

adjustment handle	datasheet	row
category axis	grouping	SmartArt graphic
cell	handle	table
chart	organization chart	value axis
column	rotate handle	WordArt

REVIEW QUESTIONS

TRUE / FALSE

Circle T if the statement is true or F if the statement is false.

T   F   **1.**   Organization charts are useful for showing the hierarchical structure and relationships within an organization.

T   F   **2.**   After you insert a table on a slide, you can convert it to a pie chart to better understand the data.

T   F   **3.**   When an object is selected, the yellow boxes are adjustment handles.

T F   **4.**   Grouping allows you to work with several items as if they were one object.

T F   **5.**   Video cannot be formatted using the same styles as Pictures.

MULTIPLE CHOICE

Select the best response for the following statements.

1. To apply the same animation to more than one object, it is suggested that you use the _____.

   A. Animation Painter   **C.** Format Painter

   B. SmartArt Graphics   **D.** Animation Pane

2. Use the _____ feature to make an image look as though it is a watercolor painting, broken glass, wrapped in plastic, or even cast in cement!

   A. Animation Painter   **C.** Artistic Effects

   B. SmartArt Graphics   **D.** Picture Styles

3. Which command do you use to turn a graphic, such as an arrow, from facing right to facing down?

   A. Rotate Left 90°   **C.** Flip Vertical

   B. Rotate Right 90°   **D.** Flip Horizontal

4. Which feature makes it possible for you to delete unwanted portions of a picture to make it look as though it is part of another image on the slide?

   A. Motion Paths   **C.** Swipe Animation

   B. Insert Texture   **D.** Background Removal

5. If you want to create a SmartArt graphic from a bullet list on a slide, you click the _____ button.

   A. Insert SmartArt   **C.** Convert to WordArt

   B. Convert to SmartArt   **D.** Insert WordArt

FILL IN THE BLANK

Complete the following sentences by writing the correct word or words in the blanks provided.

1. On the View tab, in the Show group, click the _____ check box to display a vertical and a horizontal line on the slide to help you place objects.

2. The _____ is a worksheet that appears with the chart and has the numbers for the chart.

3. You can type text directly in the graphic or you can open the _____ to the left of the SmartArt graphic to enter text.

4. An object will follow a(n) _____ on a slide; the green side is the starting and the red side is the ending position.

5. _____ are useful when you need to organize information that can be displayed in rows and columns.

PROJECTS

If you have a SAM 2010 user profile, your instructor may have assigned an autogradable version of the indicated project. If so, log into the SAM 2010 Web site at *www.cengage.com/sam2010* to download the instruction and start files.

PROJECT 3–1

1. Start PowerPoint, open the **Shelter.pptx** presentation from the drive and folder where you store your Data Files, and then save it as **Animal Shelter**, followed by your initials.

2. Display slide 4, and then convert the text to a SmartArt graphic of your choice.

3. Insert a new slide after slide 4 with the blank layout, draw five different objects on the slide, and then enter text on at least three of the objects. Group two of the objects. Format the objects using fills and styles.

4. Display the gridlines and guides. Move the horizontal guide to a new position. Add an object to the slide you created in Step 4 using the guide. Remove the gridlines and guides from view.

5. Create a table on a slide. Create a header row. Enter the text of your choice. Format text in the table. Format the table using a style.

6. Create a chart on a slide with the title **Funds Raised This Year**. Enter data for at least four rows and four columns in the data sheet.

7. Add your name to the handouts as a footer on all slides, print the presentation handouts, and then save the presentation.

SAM PROJECT 3–2

1. Open the **DogsAndCats.pptx** presentation from the drive and folder where you store your Data Files, and then save it as **DogsAndCats Palace**, followed by your initials.

2. Display the slide with the chart. On the Chart Tools Design tab, in the Type group, click the Change Chart Type button and then choose a Chart Type. Apply a new chart type to the chart. Add data labels to the chart.

3. Change two of the data points. Add a chart title to the chart.

4. Insert a new slide after slide 8, and then add two pictures of your choice, from your own files or search the Internet for images you like. You can also use Clip Art.

5. Use the Background Removal tool on one of the pictures.

6. Order the photos on the slide in a way that makes sense to you, and then animate one of the photos using a motion path.

7. Animate the SmartArt graphic. Use the Animation Painter to copy an animation from one object to another object in the presentation.

8. Open another window and any program you choose on your computer. Use the ScreenShot tool to add that screen to a new slide in the presentation after slide 9.

9. Add your name as a footer on the notes page. Save the presentation. View the presentation and then note any changes you want to make.

10. Save the presentation, print the handouts with four slides per page, and then exit PowerPoint.

CRITICAL THINKING

ACTIVITY 3–1

Use the Internet to research a company. Use the information you find to create a presentation about the company that includes an organization chart, a SmartArt graphic, a chart, a table, and at least one other SmartArt object. Be sure to include an animated object.

- Apply a theme to the presentation.
- Include your name in the header of the handouts.
- Use the spelling checker to make sure you have no spelling errors in the presentation.
- Save the presentation using the name of the company.

ACTIVITY 3–3

Think about a company that you want to start. Use a template from Microsoft Office Online to create several slides in a new presentation to let people know about your company. The presentation should include at least four slides:

- A title slide with the name of your company
- A slide with a chart
- A slide with two drawn objects
- A slide with a SmartArt graphic
- A slide with a formatted table
- Include your name in the slides footer
- Save the presentation as MyCompany followed by your initials

ACTIVITY 3–2

You want to make some changes to some graphics on several slides. Use the Microsoft Office PowerPoint Help system to find out how to do the following:

- Change the shape of any drawn object, such as a star or arrow, on a slide.
- Display text vertically instead of horizontally in a table cell.
- Change the various features in a chart.

LESSON 4

Expanding on PowerPoint Basics

■ OBJECTIVES

Upon completion of this lesson, you should be able to:

- Integrate PowerPoint with other Office programs.
- Create new slide masters.
- Create Action buttons.
- Insert comments and work collaboratively with others.
- Create custom slide shows, organize slides into sections, and hide slides for specific audiences.
- Rehearse timings, set up a slide show, and use on-screen annotation tools.
- Send a presentation using email, package a presentation for CD, and broadcast a presentation option.
- Save a presentation as a video.

■ VOCABULARY

Action button

comment

custom show

destination file

Document Inspector

document properties

embed

Format Painter

grid

guidelines

import

link

linked object

Package for CD

Presenter view

Snap to

source file

A presentation is meant to be shared with other people as a tool for teaching or viewed by audiences to share ideas and concepts. Often a presentation includes information from other programs. Rather than recreating the chart, document, graphic, or video created in another program, you can easily include this information in a slide show. Once you have completed a presentation, you have several options for preparing it so it can be viewed by others. Slide shows do not always have to follow the same order of slides. You can create action buttons to create a show that displays specific slides in any order as needed. You can create custom shows, sections, and hide slides to use the same series of slides in different ways for different audiences. You can add comments and collaborate with others about the slides to help you create the perfect presentation. During a slide show, you can use pens and highlighters to make notes and then save the notes in the presentation for later use. PowerPoint provides many different ways for you to deliver a presentation including broadcasting it on the Web for people who are not in the same room as you, saving the presentation as a video, and e-mailing it in different formats to meet the needs of your audience. In this lesson, you will learn how all these features work together to help you create and deliver quality slide shows to your audience.

Integrating PowerPoint with Other Office Programs

As you learn to work with the different computer programs, you will develop preferences for using certain programs for various tasks. You may find that you created a chart or have data in Microsoft Excel, for example, that you want to include as part of your PowerPoint presentation. You may also have a document that you created in Microsoft Word, and you want to include that text in the presentation. You do not have to recreate that work to use it in a presentation. You can easily insert objects and link or embed text or data from other programs into slides.

Inserting Text from a Word Outline

If you have a lot of text that you want to use in a presentation, you may find it easier to type the text using Microsoft Word. You can then import text from Word to create a new presentation or add slides to an existing presentation. *Import* means to bring a file or part of a file into the presentation. A Word outline is the easiest kind of document to import because it is formatted with styles, and each heading level is translated into a corresponding level of text in PowerPoint. For example, Heading 1 text is converted to slide titles. If the Word document does not have heading styles applied, PowerPoint uses the Tabs that create paragraph indentations to create the slides. If a paragraph begins at the margin without a tab, the paragraph becomes the slide title. Each tab creates a new level text in bulleted lists on the slide.

▶ **VOCABULARY**
import

Step-by-Step 4.1

1. Click the Start button ⊕ on the taskbar, type **Microsoft Word** in the Search box, and then click **Microsoft Word 2010** on the Programs menu to start Microsoft Word.

2. Click the **File** tab on the Ribbon, click **Open**, locate the drive and folder where you store your Data files, click **Planet Facts.docx** and then click **Open** to open the document file. Notice that the Planet Facts document is formatted as an outline. Each planet name is a Level 1 head.

3. Click the **File** tab on the Ribbon, and then click **Exit** to close the file and exit Word.

4. Start PowerPoint to open a new blank presentation.

5. In the new presentation title slide, click the **Click to add title** place-holder, type **Our Solar System**, click the **Click to add subtitle** place-holder, and then type **Planet Facts**.

6. On the Home tab, in the Slides group, click the **New Slide** button arrow, and then click **Slides from Outline** at the bottom of the Layout gallery. The Insert Outline dialog box opens.

7. In the Insert Outline dialog box, navigate to the Data Files for this lesson, click the document file **Planet Facts.docx**, and then click **Insert**.

PowerPoint imports the Word document text into the presentation and formats it as slides. Nine new slides appear. There is one slide for each Level 1 head. The way the outline was created set up the slide show so that the planet name is the title of each slide. See **Figure 4–1**.

Slide title from Level 1 head text

Bullet text from Level 2 head text

New slides

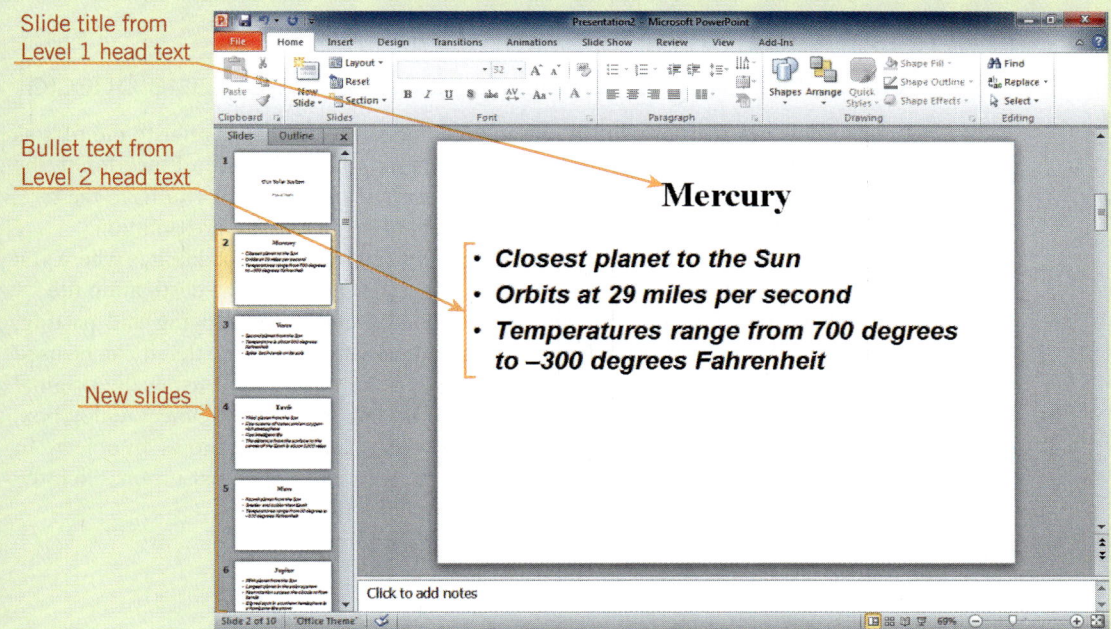

FIGURE 4–1
Slides inserted from a Word outline

8. Click the **Save** button 🖫 on the Quick Access toolbar, locate the folder where you store the Data Files for this lesson, and then save the presentation as **Our Solar System**, followed by your initials. Leave the presentation open for the next Step-by-Step.

Applying a Theme

The outline was inserted into a new blank presentation. The Office theme is applied to the slides in the presentation by default. Now that you have the text in the slides, you can begin to work on the design and graphics to enhance the presentation.

Step-by-Step 4.2

> **TIP**
>
> Themes are in alphabetical order in the Themes gallery.

1. Click the **Design** tab on the Ribbon. In the Themes group, click the **More** button ⤓ to open the Themes gallery, and then in the gallery click the **Newsprint** theme. This theme adds a gray background to the slides, puts a red bar at the top of the slides, and places the slide title at the bottom of the slide above a thin red line.

2. Click **slide 1** on the Slides tab, click the **Slide Show** button 🖵 on the status bar, and then click to advance the slides and view the slide show. The presentation includes 10 slides.

3. Press **Esc** after you view the last slide, to return to Normal view.

4. Save the presentation and leave it open for the next Step-by-Step.

Understanding Embedding, Linking, and Paste Special

> ▶ **VOCABULARY**
> **destination file**
> **source file**
> **embed**

When you work with more than one file, it is often convenient to refer to the files as source or destination files. Since you are creating a presentation in PowerPoint, the presentation file is the *destination file*. The *source file* is where you have the text, chart, numbers, or whatever data it is you want to bring into the presentation.

Remember that the main difference between linking and embedding is where you store the data and how you update the data after you place it in the destination file.

When you move data among applications by cutting or copying and pasting, Microsoft Office changes the format of the data you are moving so that it can be used in the destination file. When it is easier to edit the information using the original application, you can *embed* the data as an object using the Insert Object dialog box. You have two options: create a new object or insert an existing file as an object. To create a new object, click the Insert tab on the Ribbon, in the Text group, click the Object button to open the Insert Object dialog box. See **Figure 4–2**.

Create new option button

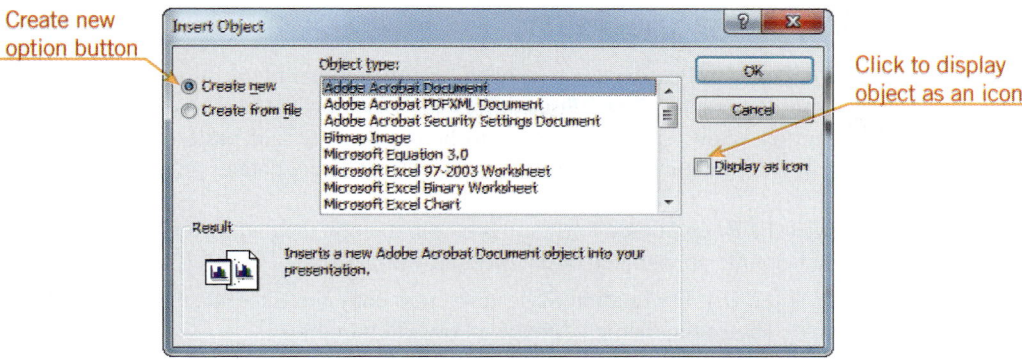

Click to display object as an icon

FIGURE 4–2   Insert Object dialog box—Create new option

If you have already created the object and saved it as a file, you can insert an object from an existing file. Click the Insert tab on the Ribbon, in the Text group click the Object button to open the Insert Object dialog box, and then click the Create from file option button. See **Figure 4–3**.

Create from file option button

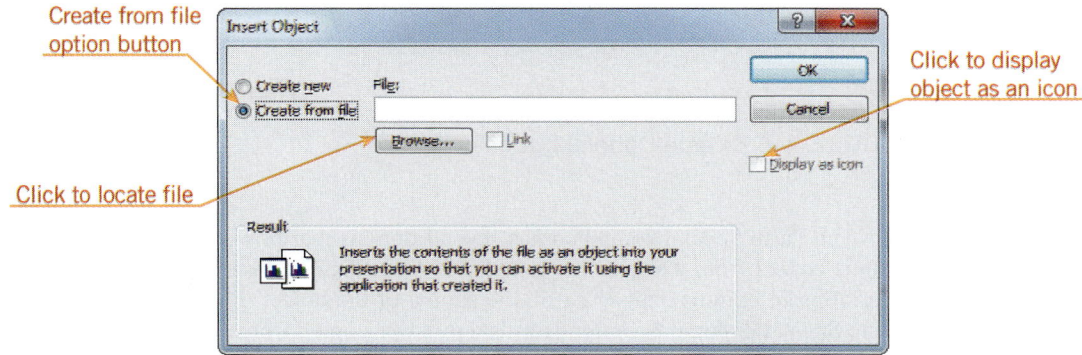

Click to display object as an icon

Click to locate file

FIGURE 4–3   Insert Object dialog box—Create from file option

The embedded information becomes part of the new file, but as a separate object that can be edited using the application that created it. For example, if a table from a Word document is embedded into a PowerPoint presentation, PowerPoint enables the table to be edited using Word. If you insert an object from a file, you can choose to link the object. If you *link* the object, a connection is retained between the source and destination files. With a linked object, if you update the source file, the data in the destination file is also updated. It is a way to always have the most recent data on the slides.

▶ **VOCABULARY**
link

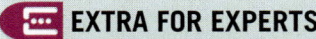 **EXTRA FOR EXPERTS**

If you click the Display as icon check box in the Insert Object dialog box, the program's icon will be displayed in the slide. The icon is a clue as to the originating program.

Using Paste Special

Data from one application can be embedded into another application, using the copy and paste commands. PowerPoint offers Paste option buttons when you click the Paste button arrow, see **Figure 4–4**, to help you copy and paste data either from within the presentation or among programs. Using Excel data as an example:

- Click the Keep Source Formatting button to copy the data as a PowerPoint table but keep the appearance of the original worksheet.
- Click the Use Destination Styles button to copy the Excel data as a PowerPoint table and use the theme to create a PowerPoint table.
- Click the Embed button to copy the Excel data as a worksheet that can be edited in Excel.
- Click the Picture button to copy the Excel data as a graphic or picture that cannot be edited.
- Click the Keep Text Only button to copy the Excel data text in a text box.

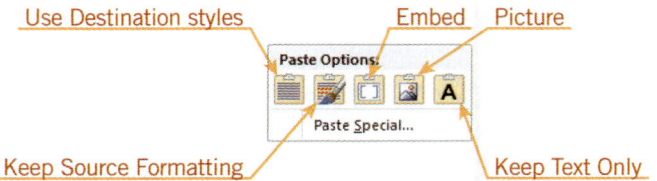

FIGURE 4–4   Paste Options buttons

The Paste Special command has several options that provide flexibility in how data is copied from a source file to a destination file. The Paste Special dialog box has different options depending on the source of the object. **Figure 4–5** shows the Paste Special dialog box options for data that was copied from an Excel worksheet.

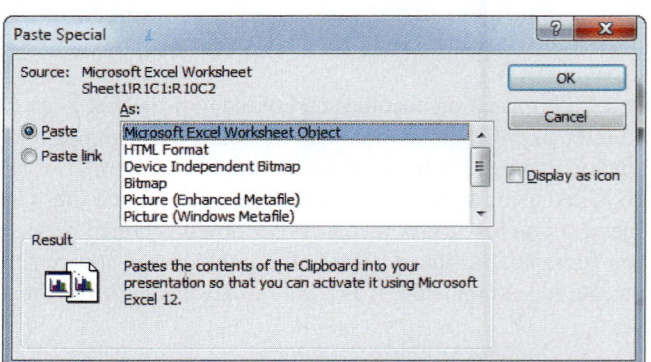

FIGURE 4–5   Paste Special options for Excel data

Figure 4–6 shows the Paste Special dialog box for text that was copied from a Word document. If you choose to paste a link, you will link rather than embed the data, so you will retain the connection between the source and destination files.

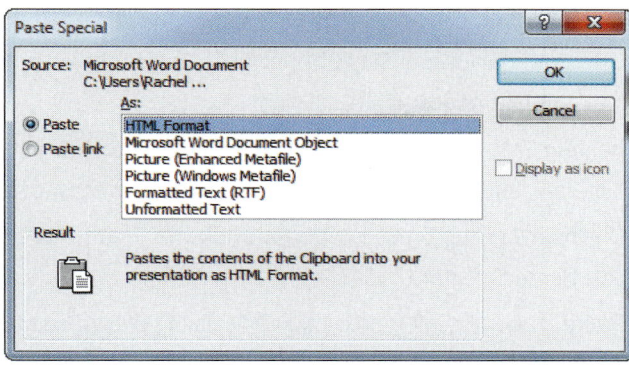

FIGURE 4–6   Paste Special options for Word text

Table 4–1 explains the different Paste Special options.

TABLE 4–1   Paste Special options

OPTION	PASTES THE CONTENTS OF THE CLIPBOARD INTO THE PRESENTATION AS
HTML Format	HTML format; HTML is the format that can be read by a browser, the format of Web pages
Microsoft Office Word	A document that can be edited using Microsoft Word Document Object
Picture (Enhanced Metafile)	An enhanced metafile picture, to edit the contents using Picture Tools
Picture (Windows Metafile)	A metafile picture, to edit the contents using Picture Tools
Formatted Text (RTF)	Formatted text in Rich Text Format, retaining coding and formatting
Unformatted Text	Unformatted text, with all coding removed

Step-by-Step 4.3

1. Click **slide 6**, *Jupiter*, on the Slides tab. Click the **Home** tab on the Ribbon, in the Slides group, click the **New Slide** button arrow, and then click the **Blank** slide layout.

2. Click the **Start** button on the taskbar, click **Microsoft Word 2010** to start Word. Click the **File tab**, click **Open**, locate the drive and folder where you store the Data Files for this lesson, and then open the document file **The Moons of Jupiter.docx**. Notice that the document is one page.

3. Click the **Enable Editing** button, if necessary. In the Editing group on the Ribbon, click the **Select** button, and then click **Select All**. All of the text in the Word document is selected.

4. In the Clipboard group on the Ribbon, click the **Copy** button 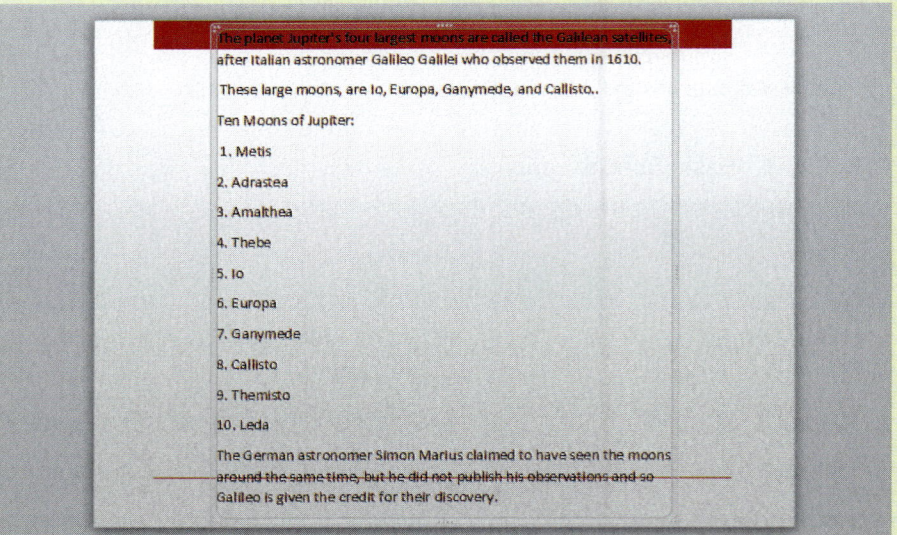 to copy the text to the Clipboard.

5. Click the **File** tab, and then click **Exit** to close the file and exit Word. Slide 7, a blank slide, should be in the PowerPoint window on your screen.

6. In the Clipboard group on the Ribbon, click the **Paste** button arrow, and then click **Paste Special**.

7. In the Paste Special dialog box, click **Microsoft Word Document Object**, and then click **OK**. Your slide should look similar to **Figure 4–7**.

FIGURE 4–7
Word text pasted as an object on a slide

The planet Jupiter's four largest moons are called the Galilean satellites, after Italian astronomer Galileo Galilei who observed them in 1610.

These large moons, are Io, Europa, Ganymede, and Callisto..

Ten Moons of Jupiter:

1. Metis

2. Adrastea

3. Amalthea

4. Thebe

5. Io

6. Europa

7. Ganymede

8. Callisto

9. Themisto

10. Leda

The German astronomer Simon Marius claimed to have seen the moons around the same time, but he did not publish his observations and so Galileo is given the credit for their discovery.

8. Save the presentation and leave it open for the next Step-by-Step.

Editing Embedded Data

To make changes to the Word file embedded in the PowerPoint presentation, double-click the text you want to edit. Word, the program in which the file was created, opens so that you can edit the text. When you finish and return to PowerPoint, the presentation includes the changes you made to the text. You can also resize and reposition the borders of the object box to place the pasted object as you want on a slide.

Step-by-Step 4.4

1. Display **slide 7**, if it is not already displayed in the Slide pane.

2. Double-click inside the **Word object box** anywhere on the text, to activate Word for editing the text. The Word Home tab on the Ribbon appears above the slide. You have full access to all the Word editing features. See **Figure 4–8**.

Word Home tab

Word text object on PowerPoint slide

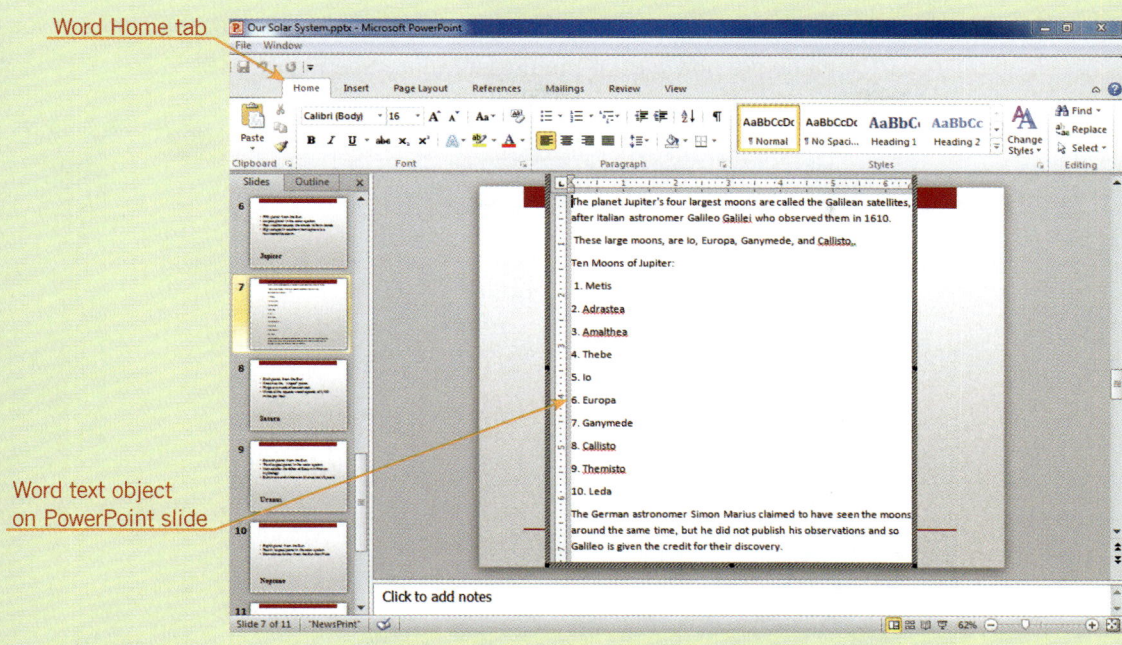

FIGURE 4–8
Editing the Word text in Word

3. In the first paragraph, add a comma after "Galileo Galilei". In the second paragraph, click to the right of the second period after the word Callisto, press **Backspace** to delete the extra period, and then delete the **comma** after "large moons".

4. Click to the right of the word **Ten** just above the list of moons, and then type **of the**.

5. In the list of moons double-click **Io**, press and hold **Ctrl**, double-click **Europa**, double-click **Ganymede**, and then release **Ctrl** so that all three moons are selected.

6. On the Home tab, in the Font group, click the **Font Color** list arrow ![A icon], and then click **Dark Blue, Text 2** in the Theme Colors palette.

7. Drag to select from **1. Metis** to **10. Leda** to select the entire list of moons. On the Ribbon, click the **Page Layout** tab, in the Page Setup group, click the **Columns** button, and then click **Three**.

8. Click outside the Word object to exit Word. Notice that the changes you made are now part of the presentation. See **Figure 4–9**.

FIGURE 4–9
Formatted Word object

Text edited

Font color changed

List in three columns

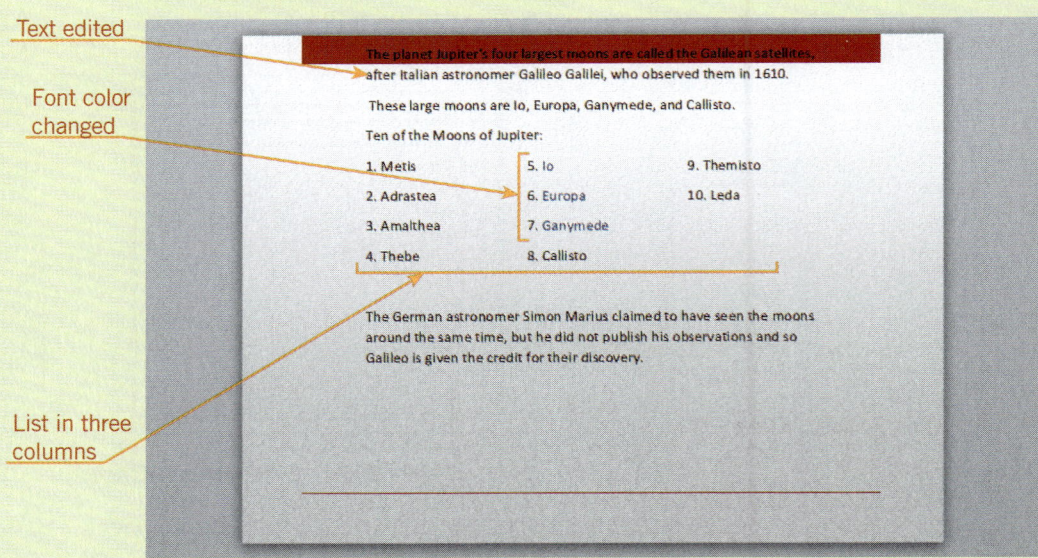

9. Save the presentation and leave it open for the next Step-by-Step.

Importing an Excel Worksheet into a Presentation

You learned how to build and modify a chart on a slide and use Excel to edit and change the chart and data on the slide. Excel offers powerful tools for creating worksheets and charts. Therefore, you may want to create the worksheet in Excel and then import data from the existing Excel worksheet.

Step-by-Step 4.5

1. Click **slide 11**, *Pluto*, on the Slides tab. In the Slides group, click the **New Slide** button arrow, and then click the **Blank** slide layout to insert a new slide with a blank layout. The new slide 12 is selected.

2. On the Ribbon, click the **Insert** tab, and then in the Text group, click **Object** to open the Insert Object dialog box.

3. Click the **Create from file** option button, click **Browse**, locate the folder where you store the Data Files for this lesson, click the Excel file **Planets.xlsx**, click **OK**, and then click **OK** to close the Insert Object dialog box and insert the Planets.xlsx worksheet file.

4. Use the diagonal resize pointers ⬊ and ⬈ to drag the corners of the Excel worksheet object so the object is as wide as the red bar and fits between the red bar and the red line on the slide. Use the move pointer ✛ to position the object in the center of the slide. Your screen should look similar to **Figure 4–10**.

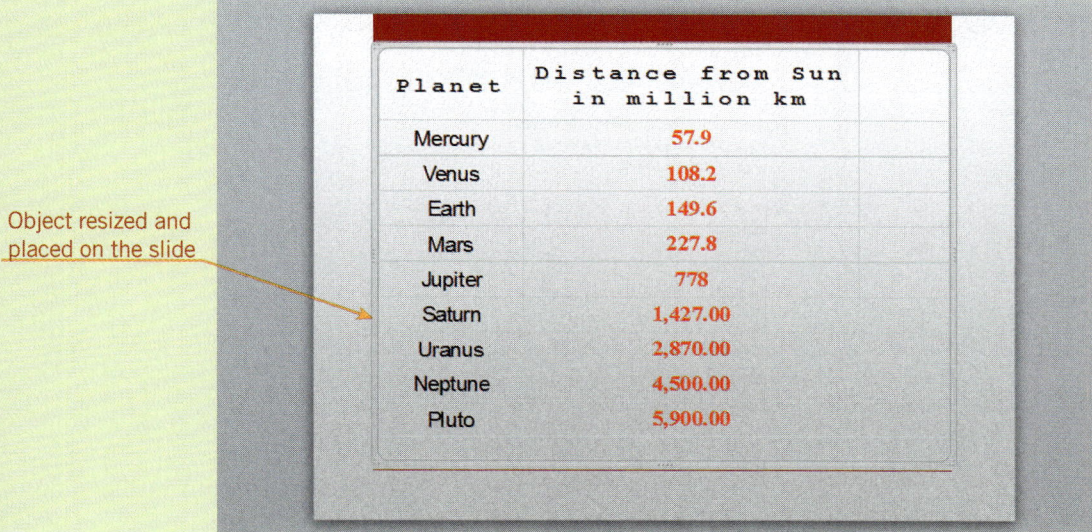

FIGURE 4–10
Excel worksheet inserted in PowerPoint slide

Object resized and placed on the slide

5. Double-click the **Excel worksheet object** to open it for editing in Microsoft Excel. The Excel Home tab appears on the Ribbon.

6. Click **cell A1** and drag to **cell B10**. You selected the cells from A1 to B10.

7. Click the **Insert** tab on the Excel Ribbon. In the Charts group, click the **Bar** button, and then click the **Clustered Bar in 3-D** chart type button. A chart is created in Excel. See **Figure 4–11**. You can continue to use the Excel chart-formatting features to enhance and resize the chart, or you can change the data in the worksheet using the Excel features.

FIGURE 4–11
Chart created in Excel on a PowerPoint slide

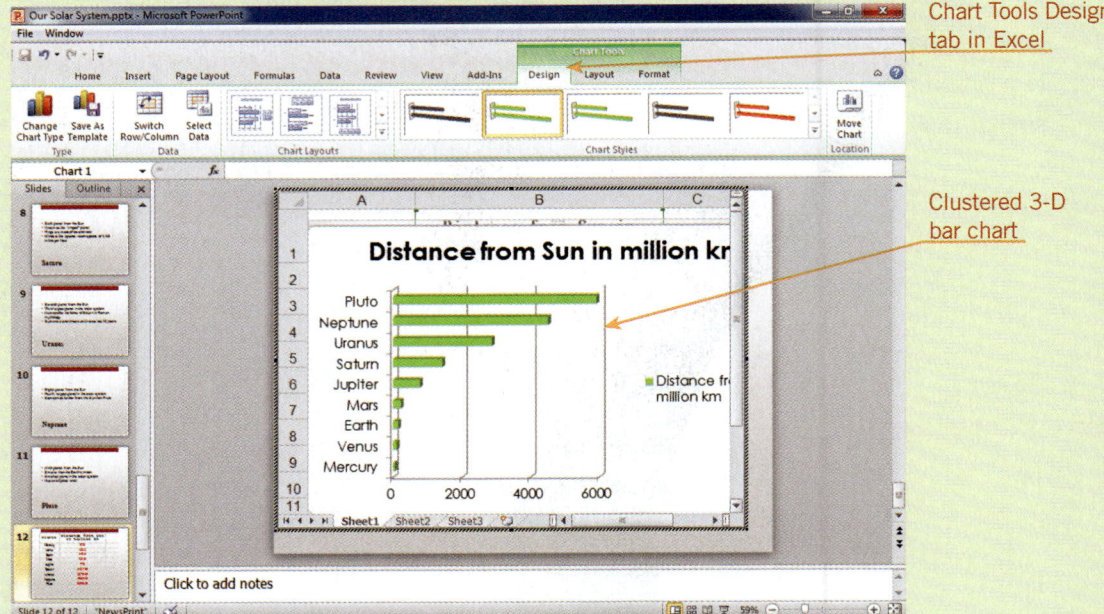

8. Click a blank area of the slide to exit Excel and return to the slide in PowerPoint.
9. Save the presentation and leave it open for the next Step-by-Step.

Reusing Slides from Other Presentations

Slides often take time to create. If you have presentations with slides that work well, you can certainly use them in more than one presentation. There are different methods for reusing slides. You can copy and paste slides from one presentation to another. Open the presentation that has the slides you want to copy. Switch to Slide Sorter view. Click to select the slides you want to reuse, and then on the Home tab on the Ribbon, in the Clipboard group, click the Copy button. Open the new presentation or the presentation in which you want to paste the slides, switch to Slide Sorter view, and then click after the slide that you want the new slides to follow. On the Ribbon, in the Clipboard group, click Paste.

You can also use a Slide Library to store favorite slides that you want to reuse again and again. To use the Reuse Slides task pane, click the New Slide button, and then click Reuse Slides. You browse to find the PowerPoint file that has the slides or the Slide Library.

EXTRA FOR EXPERTS

To duplicate one or more slides, click to select the slides you want to duplicate, click the Copy button arrow, and then click Duplicate. Or, click the New Slide button arrow and then click Duplicate Selected slides.

Step-by-Step 4.6

1. Click **slide 12**, the last slide in the presentation, if it is not already selected, and then click the **Slide Sorter** button on the status bar.

2. Click the **Home** tab on the Ribbon. In the Slides group, click the **New Slide** button arrow, and then click **Reuse Slides** at the bottom of the gallery. The Reuse Slides task pane opens.

3. In the Reuse Slides task pane, click **Browse**, and then click **Browse File** to open the Browse dialog box.

4. Locate the folder where your Data Files are stored for this lesson, click the presentation file **Sun Facts.pptx**, and then click **Open**. Five slides appear in the Reuse Slides task pane.

5. In the Reuse Slides task pane, point to each slide to see an enlarged version of each of the slides from the Sun Facts presentation. See **Figure 4–12**.

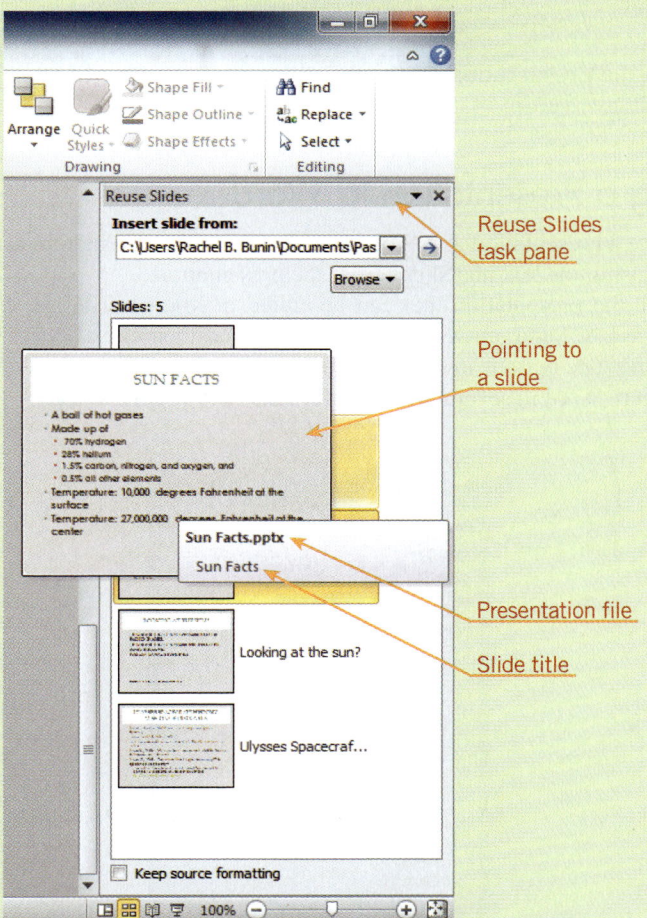

FIGURE 4–12
Reusing slides from another presentation

6. In the Reuse Slides task pane, click each of the five slides, and then click the Reuse Slides task pane **Close** button to close the task pane. Each slide is inserted into the current presentation. The slides have taken on the NewsPrint theme of the current presentation. See **Figure 4–13**.

FIGURE 4–13
Slides inserted
in current
presentation

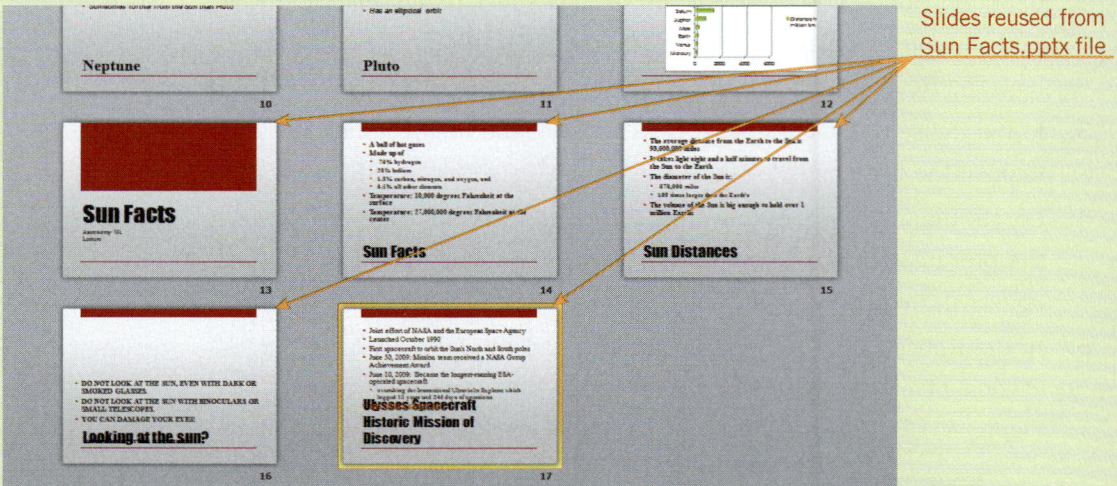

Slides reused from
Sun Facts.pptx file

7. Save the presentation and leave it open for the next Step-by-Step.

Sending a Presentation to Word

You can save a presentation as a Word document to use as a handout, or create other documents using the text and slides from the presentation.

To save the presentation that can be edited in Microsoft Word, click the File tab, click Save & Send, click Create Handouts, and then click Create Handouts in the right pane. The options in the Send To Microsoft Word dialog box can send your presentation to Word in several different formats. See **Figure 4–14**.

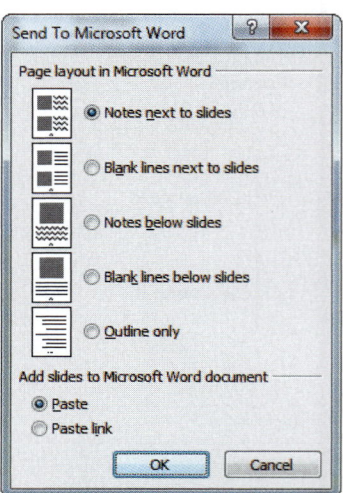

FIGURE 4–14   Send To Microsoft Word

Step-by-Step 4.7

1. Click the **File** tab, click **Save & Send**, in the center pane click **Create Handouts,** and then in the right pane click **Create Handouts**. The Send To Microsoft Word dialog box opens.

2. Click the **Blank lines next to slides** option button in the dialog box.

3. Click **OK**. The presentation is exported into Word and formatted as a document.

4. Click the **Document1 Word** button on the taskbar, close the Navigation pane if it is open, and then scroll through the document to view all the pages. See **Figure 4–15**.

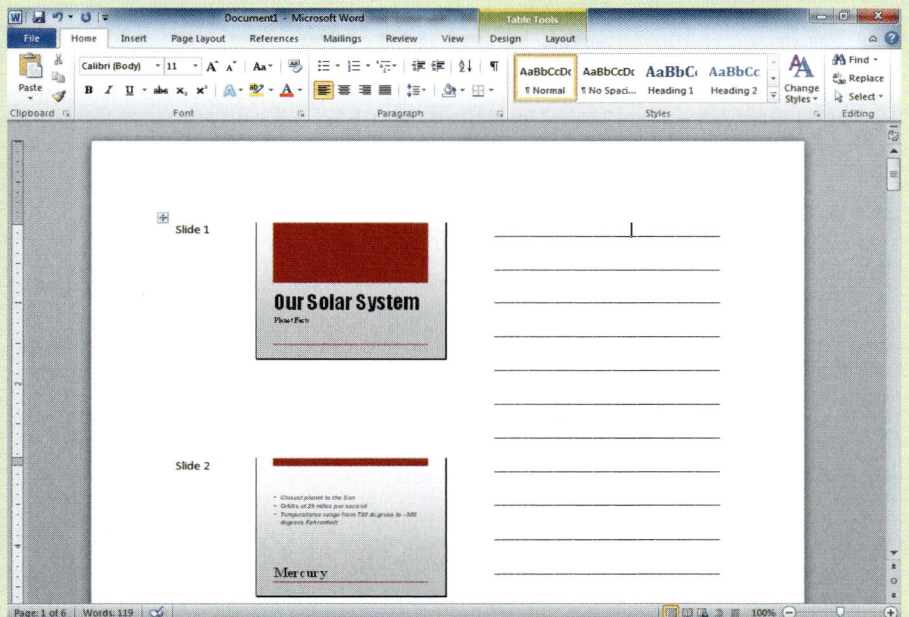

FIGURE 4–15
Presentation handouts saved as a Word file

5. Type your name on the first page of the document on the lines next to slide 1, Our Solar System, click the **Save** button on the Quick Access toolbar, and then save the document as **Solar System Handouts**, followed by your initials.

6. Click the **File** tab, click **Print**, click **the Print All Pages** button, click **Print Current Page**, and then click **Print** to print the first page of the document.

7. Click the **File** tab, and then click **Exit** to close the document and exit Word. The presentation file is on the screen in a PowerPoint window in Slide Sorter view.

WARNING

You have to delete same number of underlines as characters in your name so the document does not create a new page.

Creating New Masters

PowerPoint allows you to apply more than one slide master to a presentation. This is useful if your presentation contains slides with more than one theme or any other features that are controlled by the slide master. This saves time as you are creating presentations, because you can choose which master to apply to each slide.

There are several ways that you can create a new master. Display the slide masters by clicking the View tab on the Ribbon, and then clicking the Slide Master button. In the Edit Master group, click the Insert Slide Master button. See **Figure 4–16**.

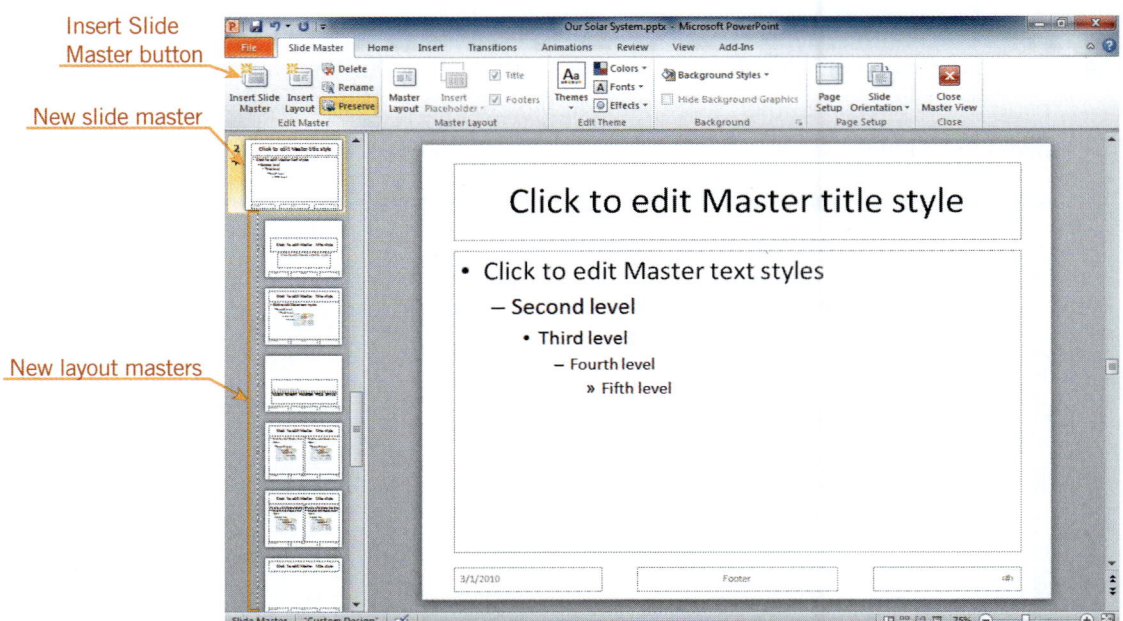

FIGURE 4–16   Inserting a new slide master

Another way to create a slide master is to apply a new theme. Each theme will generate a new slide master and the corresponding layout masters.

Creating New Layout Masters

PowerPoint allows you to create a new layout master for any slide master. When you click the New Slide button, you are presented with a series of layouts for that slide master. There may be times when you want to place objects and text on a slide and the existing masters do not quite work for you. PowerPoint allows you to create a custom slide layout and then add the placeholders as needed. The placeholders available on the Insert Placeholder menu are: Content, Text, Picture, Chart, table, SmartArt, Media, and Clip Art.

Step-by-Step 4.8

1. Click **slide 1**, *Our Solar System*, in Slide Sorter view to select the first slide.

2. Click the **View** tab on the Ribbon. In the Master Views group, click the **Slide Master** button to switch to Slide Master view.

3. Point to the **Slide Master** thumbnail in the left pane. The ScreenTip tells you that the NewsPrint slide master is used by all 17 slides in the presentation.

4. On the Slide Master tab on the Ribbon, in the Edit Master group, click the **Insert Layout** button. A new layout is added to the bottom of the left pane as part of the NewsPrint slide master. It has a Title placeholder, a Date, Footer, and Slide number placeholder.

5. On the Slide Master tab on the Ribbon, in the Master Layout group, click the **Insert Placeholder** button arrow. You can select from a list of placeholders and place them anywhere on the layout master.

6. Click **SmartArt**, point to the upper-left corner of the slide below the lower-left corner of the red bar, press and hold the left mouse button, and then drag to draw a box in the center of the slide to just above the Master title style placeholder as shown in **Figure 4–17**.

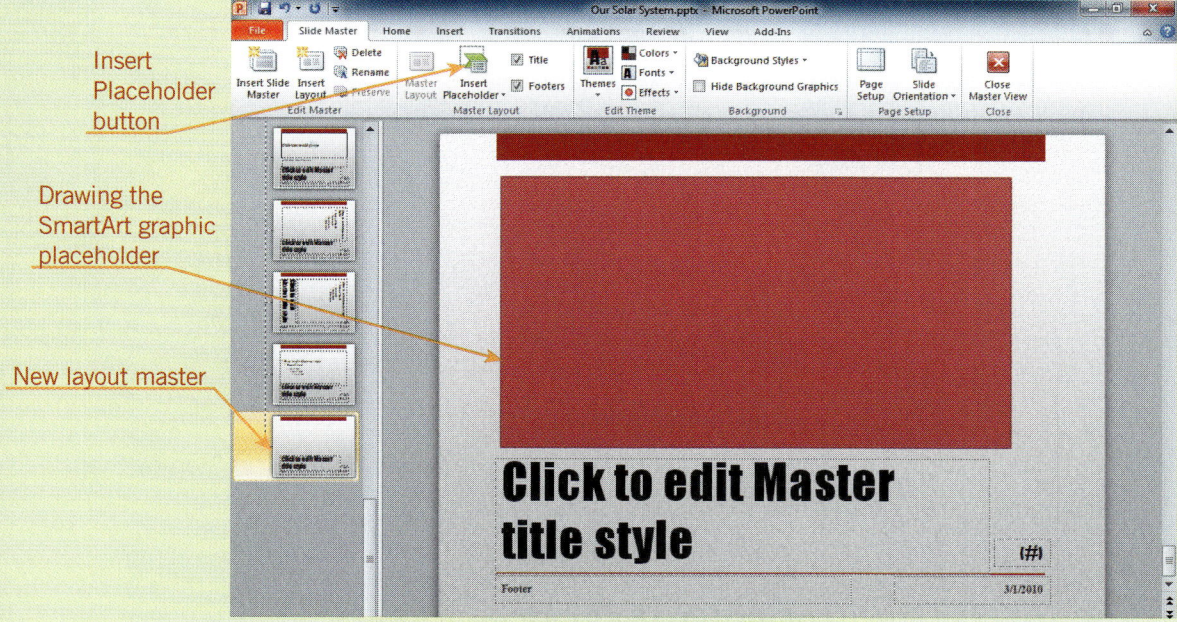

FIGURE 4–17
Inserting a new layout master

7. Release the mouse button. A SmartArt graphic placeholder appears centered on the slide.

TIP

You can name custom layouts with descriptive titles.

8. Click the **Close Master View** button in the Close group to return to Slide Sorter view with the **Home** tab selected on the Ribbon. In the Slides group, click the **New Slide** button arrow to open the Layout gallery, and then click the **Custom Layout thumbnail**. A new slide is inserted with the new custom layout that you just created.

9. Double-click the new **slide 2** to open it in Normal view, and then click the **Click icon to add SmartArt Graphic** icon in the new slide to open the Choose a SmartArt Graphic dialog box.

10. Click **List** in the left pane, click the **Vertical Box List** icon, and then click **OK**. You added a Vertical Box List SmartArt graphic.

11. Type **The Sun** to add the text to the first **Text** placeholder, click the second **Text** placeholder, type **The Planets**, click the third **Text** placeholder, and then type **The Moons**.

12. Click **Click to add title**, and then type **Overview** as the title for the slide. Your completed slide should look like **Figure 4–18**.

FIGURE 4–18
New slide using custom layout

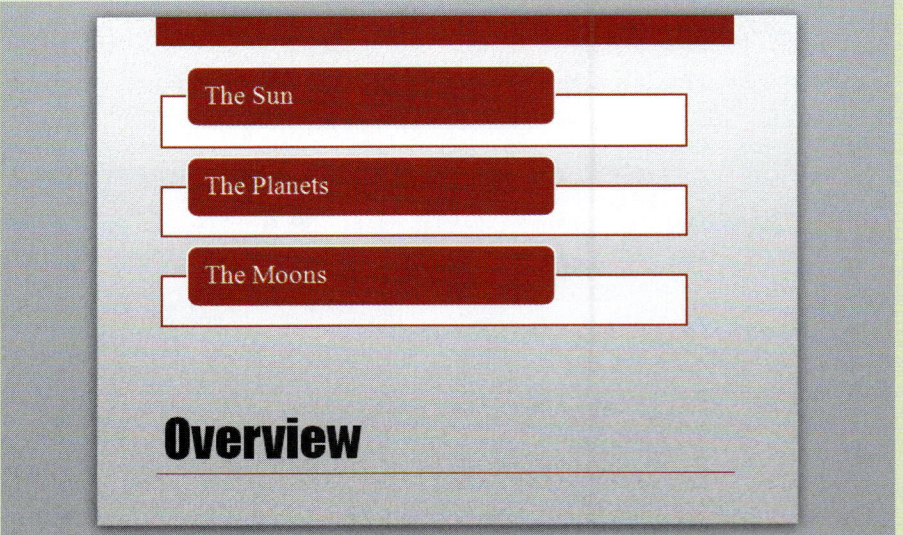

13. View the presentation as a slide show.

14. Save the presentation and leave it open for the next Step-by-Step.

Formatting Text and Objects

You have learned the basics of formatting text and objects. Formatting enhances the presentation giving you the freedom to change colors, fonts, and effects in both text and objects. PowerPoint has several helpful features to make formatting easier.

Replacing Text Fonts

You can replace a font throughout your presentation to another font. On the Home tab on the Ribbon, in the Editing group, click the Replace list arrow, and then click Replace Fonts. The Replace Font dialog box opens, as shown in **Figure 4–19**. In the Replace box, choose the font you want to replace. In the With box, choose the font you want to use as a replacement, and then click Replace. Any text in the presentation that has the Replace font will now have the font you designated in the With box.

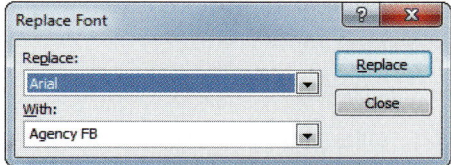

FIGURE 4–19   Replace Fonts dialog box

Step-by-Step 4.9

1. Click **slide 3**, *Mercury*, and then click **miles** in the body text.

2. On the Home tab on the Ribbon, in the Editing group, click the **Replace** list arrow, and then click **Replace Fonts**.

   The Replace Font dialog box opens. The body text on the slides is in the Arial font. In the Replace box, Arial is selected.

3. Click the **With** list arrow, scroll the font list, click **Cambria**, and then click **Replace**. All the text in Arial font throughout the presentation is replaced with the Cambria font.

4. Click **Close** to close the Replace Fonts dialog box. Save the presentation. Leave the presentation open for the next Step-By-Step.

Using the Format Painter

If you format an object with certain attributes, such as fill color and line color, and then want to format another object the same way, use the *Format Painter*. Select the object whose attributes you want to copy, click the Format Painter button, and then click the object you want to format. You can use the same process to copy text attributes, such as font, size, color, or style, to other text. To copy attributes to more than one object or section of text, select the object whose attributes you want to copy, double-click the Format Painter button, and then click each of the objects or sections of text you want to format. When you are finished, click the Format Painter button. The Format Painter button is located on the Mini toolbar, as well as on the Home tab on the Ribbon in the Clipboard group.

▶ **VOCABULARY**
Format Painter

Step-by-Step 4.10

1. Click **slide 4**, *Venus*, and then click and drag to select the words **900 degrees Fahrenheit** in the second bullet.

2. In the Font group, click the **Font Color** list arrow , and then click the **Orange** color swatch in the Standard Colors palette.

3. With **900 degrees Fahrenheit** still selected, in the Clipboard group, click the **Format Painter** button .

4. The pointer changes to .

5. On the Slides tab, click **slide 3**, *Mercury*, and then click and drag the pointer over the words **700 degrees to –300 degrees Fahrenheit**.

   You have painted the formatting. The format of the text changed so it is the same as 900 degrees Fahrenheit in the second bullet point on the Venus slide.

6. Save the presentation and leave it open for the next Step-by-Step.

> **TIP**
>
> Format painting can be used to copy several formats such as text that is a specific font, style, size, and color at one time.

Using the Grid, Guides, and Rulers to Align Objects

A good presentation uses short phrases, pictures, and graphs to convey its point. Out-of-alignment text or pictures can distract from the point of a presentation. Use the *grid*, *guidelines*, and ruler in concert to place objects on a slide. To align a text box or picture, you can display the grid and guidelines on the slide pane; the ruler identifies the exact placement on the slide. As you learned in Lesson 3, to turn on the grid and to display the guidelines, click the View tab on the Ribbon, and then, in the Show group, click the Guide or Gridlines check boxes. Alternatively, to turn on Grids and Guide lines, you can right-click any blank area of a slide (do not click inside a placeholder) and click Grid and Guides to open the Grid and Guides dialog box. The *Snap to* option "Snap objects to grid" moves an object to the closest inter-section of the grid on a slide. The grid appears to be "magnetic," which is very useful when you want to place objects exactly in position. The Grid settings section sets the spacing between the intersections of the gridlines. You can also choose to display the grid by clicking the check box. The Guide settings area displays a set of crosshairs on the screen to help you align an object in the center, left, right, top, or bottom of the slide. The Ruler option displays a vertical and horizontal ruler on the slide pane to identify the exact placement of objects. Click the Ruler check box in the Show group to display the ruler.

> **TIP**
>
> If you click a guide and begin to drag it, a ScreenTip appears with the location of the guide on the ruler so you can place the guide exactly where you want it on the slide.

> ▶ **VOCABULARY**
>
> **Snap to**
>
> **grid**
>
> **guidelines**

Step-by-Step 4.11

1. Click **slide 5**, *Earth*, on the Slides tab to select the slide, right-click any blank area of the slide, and then, on the shortcut menu, click **Grid and Guides**. The Grid and Guides dialog box opens.

2. Click the **Display grid on screen** check box to insert a check mark, click the **Display drawing guides on screen** check box to insert a check mark, verify that the **Snap objects to grid** check box has a checkmark, and then click **OK**.

3. Click the **View** tab on the Ribbon, notice the check marks in the **Gridlines** and **Guides** check boxes, then click the **Ruler** check box to insert a check mark and display the vertical and horizontal rulers.

4. Click the **Insert** tab on the Ribbon, and then, in the Text group, click the **Text Box** button. To the right of the vertical guide and below the horizontal guide, click in a blank area of the slide, and then type **Our home planet**.

5. Use the Move pointer to drag the **Our home planet** text box so that the top sizing handles are at the **–1"** position on the vertical ruler and the green rotation handle and the middle sizing handles are on the vertical guide at the **0"** position on the horizontal ruler. See **Figure 4–20**.

> **TIP**
>
> To temporarily disable the snap to feature, press and hold ALT while dragging the object.

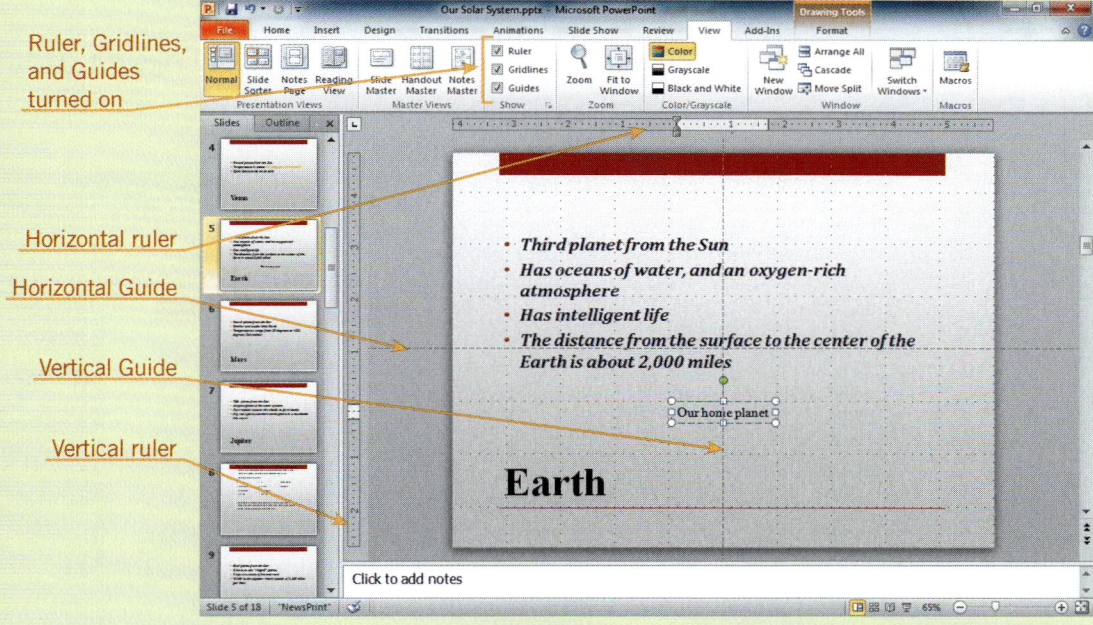

FIGURE 4–20
Using the gridlines, guides, and ruler

6. Click the **View** tab, if it is not already selected, in the Show group, click the **Ruler** check box to remove the check mark, click the **Gridlines** check box to remove the check mark, and then click the **Guides** check box to remove the check mark.

7. Save the presentation and leave it open for the next Step-by-Step.

Inserting Comments

Working with friends or coworkers to collaborate on a project is sometimes the way to get the best presentation. You may have a question about the content or design of a particular slide, or you may have a comment about the entire presentation. You do not have to be present with the slide show to pass along comments. You can insert *comments* in the slide for others to see. You can use the Comment features on the Review tab on the Ribbon, in the Comments group. You can insert, review, and edit comments. Each user's comment will have a different color or initial, so you can identify who originated each comment.

▶ **VOCABULARY**
comment

📟 **EXTRA FOR EXPERTS**

Click the Show Markup button to display comments and changes in the presentation.

Step-by-Step 4.12

▶ **TIP**

The letters or name identifying the source of the note will vary, depending on whom the computer is registered to.

1. Click **slide 6**, *Mars*, click the **Review** tab on the Ribbon, and then, in the Comments group, click the **New Comment** button. A new comment opens.

2. Type **This slide needs clip art.** in the comment box. See **Figure 4–21**.

FIGURE 4–21
Inserting a comment

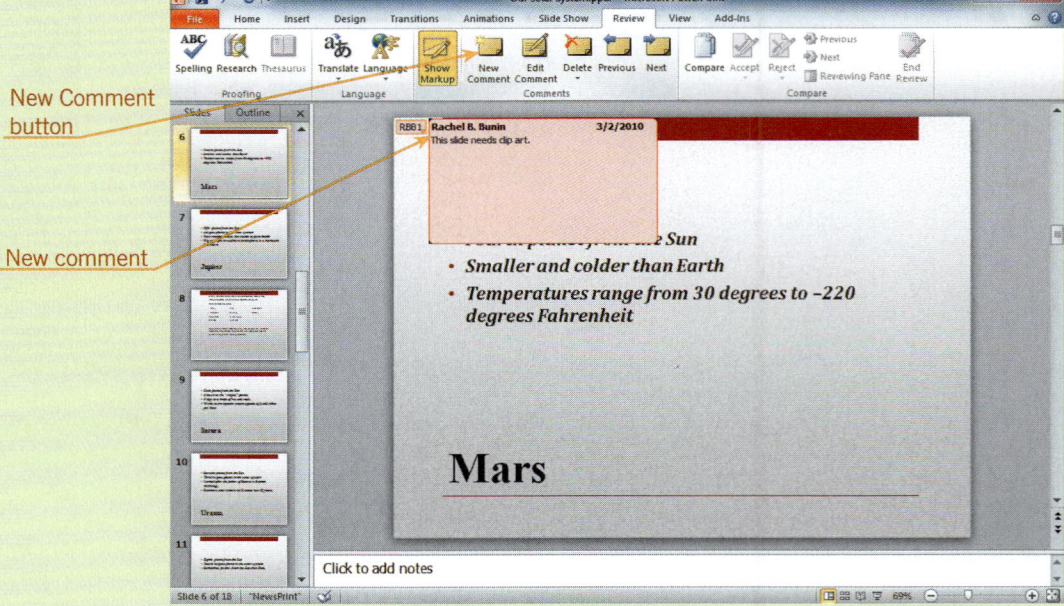

New Comment button

New comment

3. Click **slide 8**, *Jupiter Moons*. In the Comments group, click the **New Comment** button, and then type **This slide needs a title and a new layout.** in the comment box.

4. In the Comments group, click the **Previous** button to review the last comment, click the **Next** button to review the next comment, and then click the **Next** button to review the last comment. You can click the Previous and Next buttons to review all the comments in a presentation.

5. Save the presentation and leave it open for the next Step-by-Step.

 TIP

In the Comments group, click the Delete button arrow to open a menu to delete the current comment, Delete all Markup on the Current Slide, or Delete All Markup in this Presentation.

Using the Compare Tool

Rather than just commenting on each other's work, sometimes group members working on a presentation will make changes to the presentation. Being able to compare ideas and see the changes that each member contributes is possible by using the Compare tool. The Compare tool makes it possible to see which changes have been made by each contributor and create one presentation file that includes all the changes. By merging all versions of a presentation, you are able to work with the latest version of the shared file. The compared view shows the changes made among the versions. You can use the Revisions panel to see the changes that were made. To use the Compare tool, click the Review tab on the Ribbon, in the Compare group, click the Compare button. In the Choose File to Merge with Current Presentation dialog box, select the file you wish to merge, and then click Open. The Reviewing pane displays the changes to the Presentation and a popup box identifies all changes that you can accept or reject. See **Figure 4–22**.

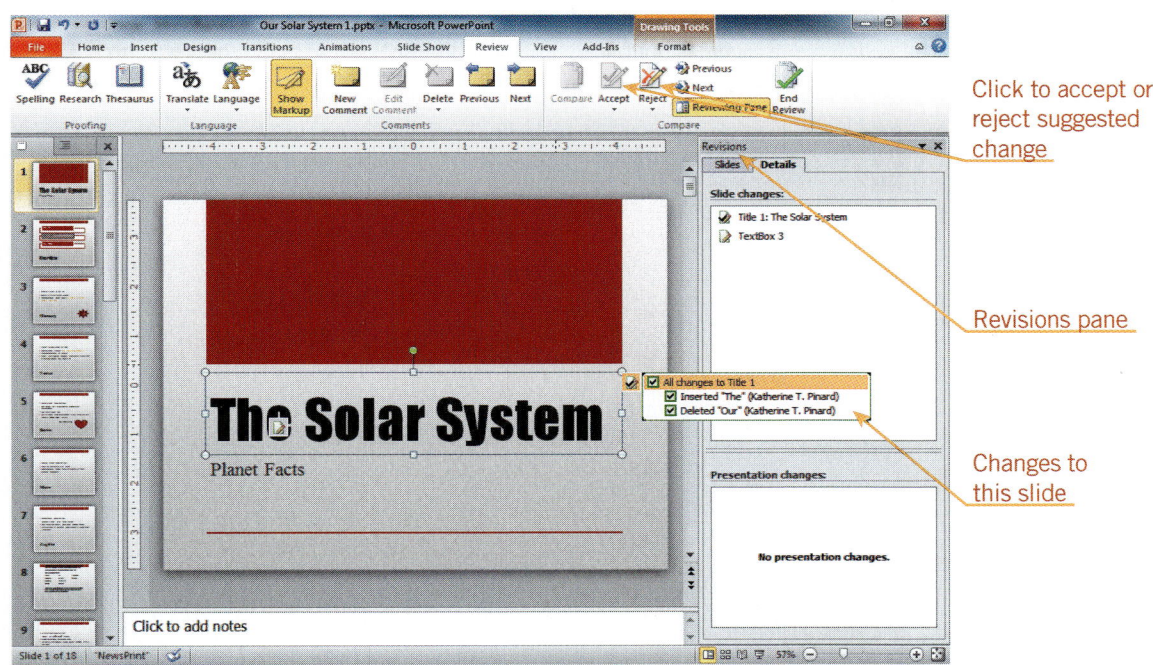

FIGURE 4–22   Comparing two presentations

Delivering a Presentation

To start a slide show, click the Slide Show button on the status bar. You can start the slide show at any slide by displaying or selecting the slide you want to begin with before clicking the Slide Show button. You can also set up and then begin to view the slide show by clicking the buttons using the Slide Show tab on the Ribbon. See **Figure 4–23**.

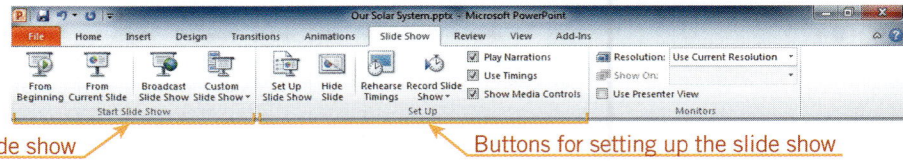

Buttons for starting the slide show   Buttons for setting up the slide show

FIGURE 4–23   Slide Show tab

Adding Sections to Your Presentation

A well-organized document is always better than a disorganized one. If your presentation has a lot of slides, you might find it helpful to break the presentation into sections. Working with sections helps you organize long presentations making it easier to work with them as you create and edit the slides. Sections are also helpful when you deliver a presentation. How you organize your presentation is up to you. You can create sections based on content, on type of slide, or on some other presentation feature. For example, a presentation on teaching a skill may include background information on the skill, hands-on activities, video presentations, and then a recap. If you have organized your presentation in sections, you can easily jump to the relevant section of the presentation as needed. To add a section, click the first slide in the section you want to create, on the Home tab, in the Slides group, click Section, and then click Add Section. A section marker appears on the Slides tab. Sections have the "untitled" name by default. The Section menu includes options to rename, collapse, expand, and remove sections easily. Sections are easily viewed in both Normal view and Slide Sorter view, see **Figure 4–24**.

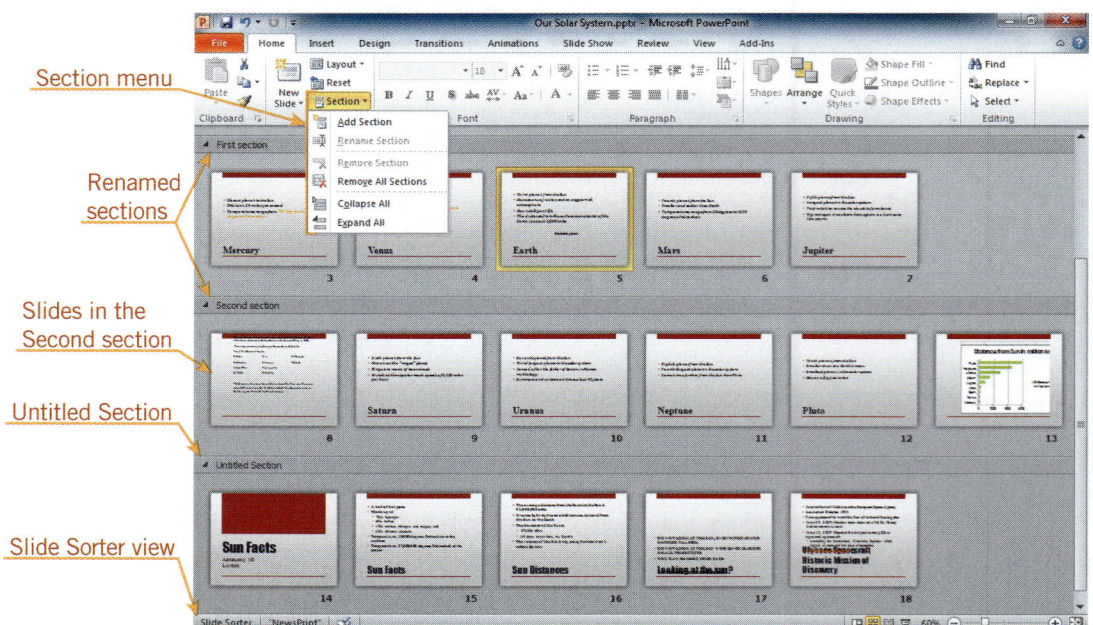

FIGURE 4–24   Adding sections

Creating Custom Shows

A *custom show* is a way to limit the slides in any slide show for a particular audience. Click the Slide Show tab on the Ribbon, click the Custom Slide Show button in the Start Slide Show group, and then click Custom Shows. The Custom Shows dialog box allows you to select an existing custom show or create a new one. Click New to open the Define Custom Show dialog box in which you select the slides you want in a show and then name the show. See **Figure 4–25**.

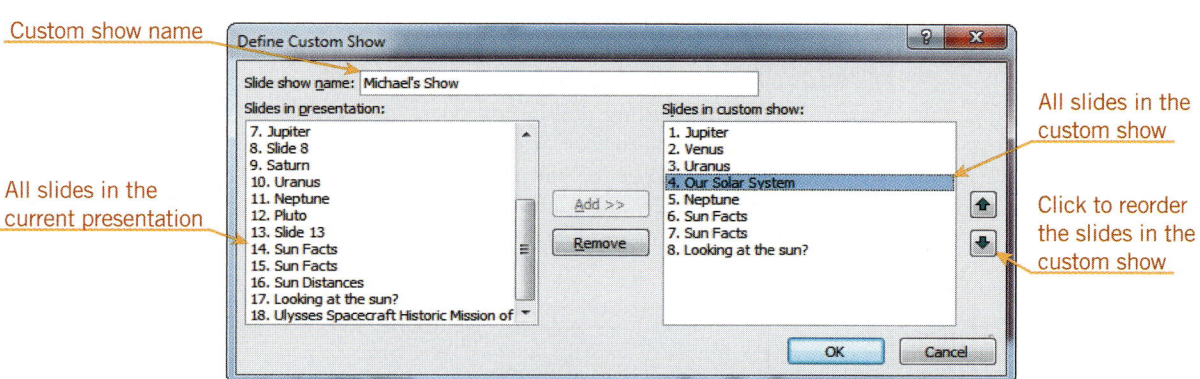

FIGURE 4–25   Define Custom Show dialog box

Using On-Screen Tools

There are on-screen navigation tools you can use to control a presentation while presenting it. When you run the presentation, buttons appear in the lower-left corner of the screen. Click the Menu button and a Slide show menu is displayed, as shown in **Figure 4–26**.

FIGURE 4–26   Slide show menu

When you click the mouse, the slides advance in order. You can choose the Previous or Next button to display the slide before or after the current one. To go to another slide, choose Go to Slide from the menu that is displayed and Slide Navigator from the submenu. Click the slide you want to display. To exit the slide show, choose End Show from the menu.

The Slide show menu (also available if you right-click the screen in Slide Show view) has many useful features. To make the screen appear blank, point to Screen, and then click Black Screen or White Screen. Switch Programs displays the Windows toolbar to give you access to other programs that you may want to display during a presentation.

Creating Action Buttons

▶ **VOCABULARY**
Action button

Another on-screen tool is the Action button. *Action buttons* are buttons that are inserted on a slide. They enable you to jump from slide to slide, even to slides in another slide show, or to other documents. Action buttons are assigned hyperlinks to direct the actions. You can insert an Action button using one of two methods. Click the Shapes button, and then click the Action button you want in the Action Buttons group. The Action Setting dialog box opens automatically. You can also insert an Action button using a custom shape. Open the Shapes gallery, and then draw the shape that you want to be the button. With the shape selected, click the Insert tab on the Ribbon, and then, in the Links group, click the Action button. Create the Action button using the Action Settings dialog box, as shown in **Figure 4–27**.

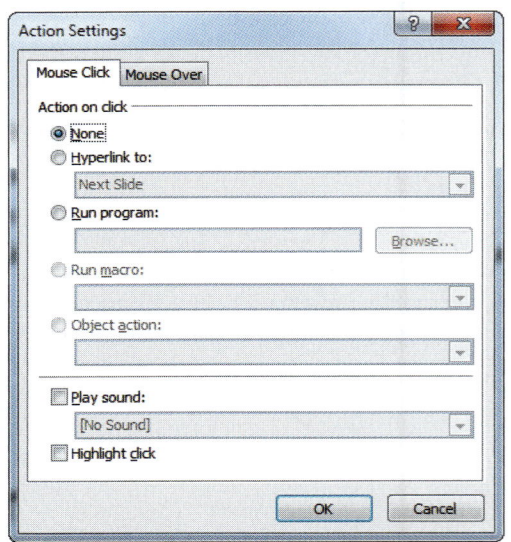

FIGURE 4–27   Action Settings dialog box

Step-by-Step 4.13

⚠ **WARNING**

If the Shapes button is expanded, you don't have to click the Shapes button. Just click the Sun icon in the Basic Shapes section.

1. Click **slide 3**, *Mercury*, on the Slides tab to display it in the Slide pane.

2. On the Home tab in the Drawing group, click the **Shapes** button. In the Basic Shapes section, click the **Sun** icon, and then drag to draw a sun shape on the lower-right corner of the slide.

3. Click the **Insert** tab on the Ribbon, and then click the **Action** button in the Links group. The Action Settings dialog box opens. The Sun shape is selected. You will apply an action to this drawn shape.

4. Click the **Hyperlink to** option button, and then click the **Hyperlink to** list arrow, scroll down, and then click **Slide**. The Hyperlink to Slide dialog box opens.

5. Click **slide 14**, *Sun Facts*, click **OK**, and then click **OK** again. The Action button on slide 3 is hyperlinked to slide 14.

6. Click **slide 14**, *Sun Facts*, on the Slides tab to display it, click the **Insert** tab, click the **Shapes** button in the Illustrations group, click the **Action Button: Back or Previous** icon in the Action Buttons section (the first icon, last row), and then drag to draw a **box** on the lower-right corner of the slide below the red line. The Action Settings dialog box opens, the Hyperlink to option button is selected, and Previous Slide is selected.

7. Click the **Hyperlink to** list arrow, scroll down, click **Last Slide Viewed**, refer to **Figure 4–28**, and then click **OK**.

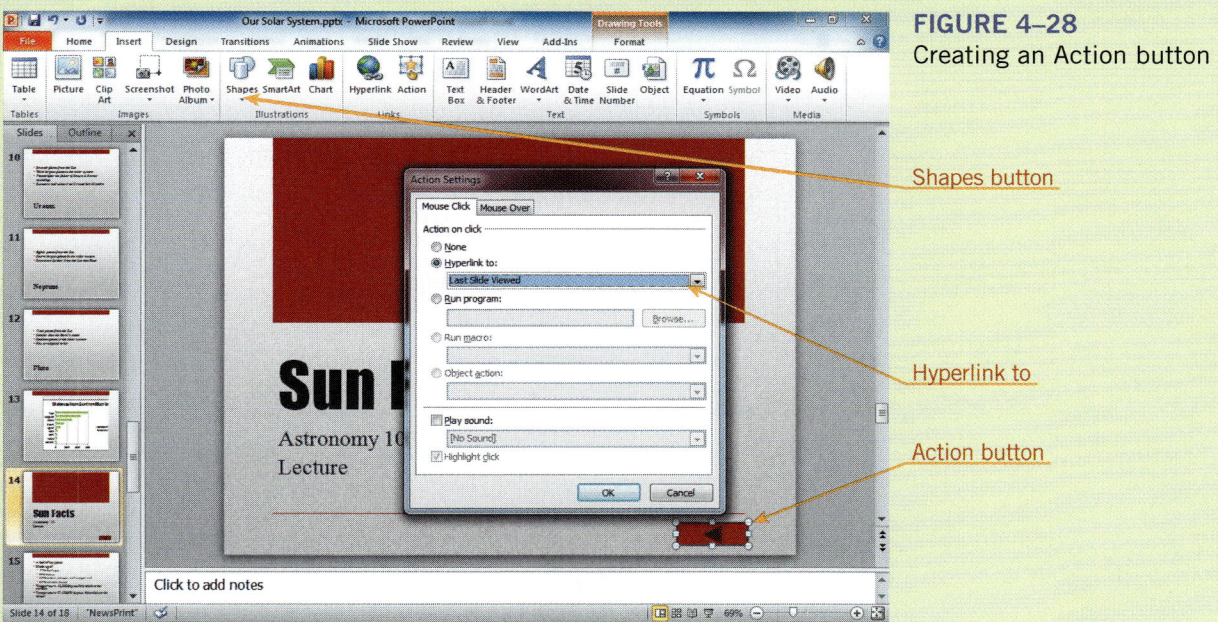

FIGURE 4–28
Creating an Action button

Shapes button

Hyperlink to

Action button

You have created a return button in the lower-right corner of the slide that hyperlinks back to the last viewed slide. If you view slide 14 by clicking the hyperlink on slide 3, and then click the Action button on slide 14, you will return to slide 3.

8. Click the **Slide Show** tab on the Ribbon, click the **From Beginning** button in the Start Slide Show group, and then press the **spacebar** two times. View slide 1 and slide 2.

9. When you get to slide 3, click the **sun** action button. The presentation jumps to slide 14, *Sun Facts*.

10. Click the **return** Action button that you drew to return to **slide 3**, *Mercury*.

11. Finish viewing the presentation.

12. Save the presentation and leave it open for the next Step-by-Step.

Hiding Slides

If you need to limit the number of slides you are showing to a particular audience, you can quickly hide slides. You can hide a slide and then quickly unhide a slide by clicking the Hide Slide button in the Set Up group on the Slide Show tab. If you just need to hide a slide for one show, using this feature is faster than creating a custom show.

Step-by-Step 4.14

1. Click the **Slide Sorter** button 🔲 on the status bar to switch to Slide Sorter view, and then click **slide 13**, *Distance from Sun in Million km* chart.

2. On the Ribbon, click the **Slide Show** tab, and then, in the Set Up group, click the **Hide Slide** button.

3. Click **slide 18**, the last slide, and then, in the Set Up group, click the **Hide Slide** button.

   Notice that the slide number in the lower-right corner of the hidden slides has a box and a slash through it, showing that it is a hidden slide.

4. Click **slide 11**, *Neptune*, on the Slide Show tab on the Ribbon, and then, in the Start Slide Show group, click the **From Current Slide** button. The presentation begins on slide 11.

5. Click to advance through the slide show. Notice that you did not see slide 13 or slide 18 during the show.

6. Click **slide 13**, *Distance from Sun in Million km* chart. In the Set Up group, click the **Hide Slide** button, click **slide 18**, *the last slide*, and then, in the Set Up group, click the **Hide Slide** button. These slides are no longer hidden.

7. Save the presentation and leave it open for the next Step-by-Step.

Annotating a Show

As you are presenting the slide show to the audience, you can use the on-screen annotation tools to emphasize specific text or graphics on a slide. You have several pointer options. When you move your mouse during the slide show, an arrow appears so that you can point out parts of the slide. Right-click the screen, point to Pointer Options, point to Arrow Options, and then select from: Automatic, Visible, and Hidden. Automatic displays the arrow as you move it around a slide, but hides it if you do not move the mouse for a short period of time. Visible displays the arrow all of the time during a presentation, and Hidden hides the arrow during a presentation. The Pen and Highlighter are tools that allow you to write or highlight features on the screen. You can choose the colors from the Ink Color menu. The Eraser tool erases any ink it touches, and Erase All Ink on Slide deletes all ink marks.

Step-by-Step 4.15

1. Click **slide 1**, *Our Solar System*. On the Slide Show tab on the Ribbon in the Start Slide Show group, click the **From Current Slide** button. The presentation begins on slide 1. Press the **spacebar** to advance the show to slide 2, *Overview*.

2. Right-click the **slide** on the screen, point to **Pointer Options** on the on-screen navigation tools menu, and then click **Highlighter**.

3. Right-click the **slide** on the screen again, point to **Pointer Options**, point to **Ink Color**, and then click the **Light Blue** color swatch in the Standard Colors section of the palette.

4. Press the **spacebar** to advance the show to **slide 2**, *Overview*, and then drag the pointer to highlight the words The Sun. See **Figure 4–29**.

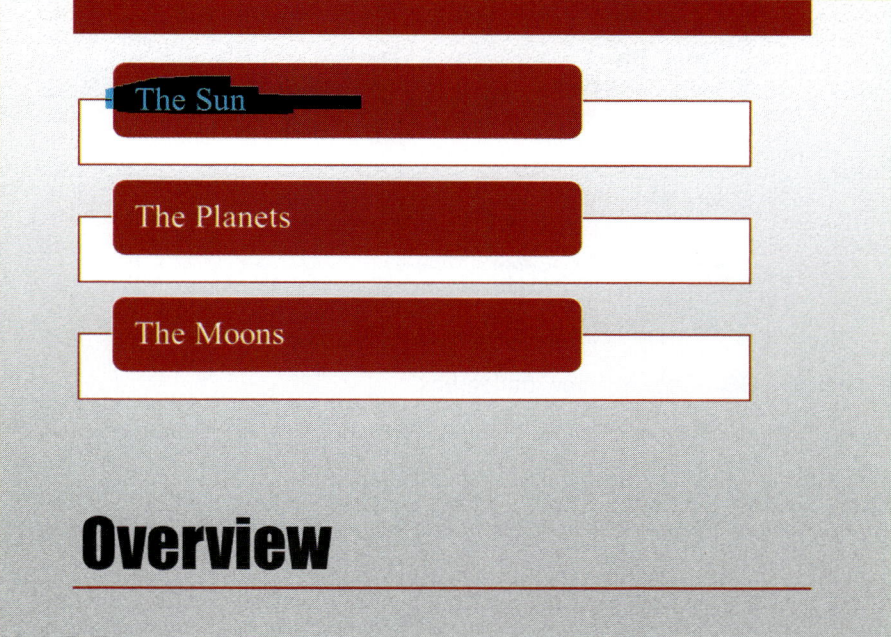

FIGURE 4–29
Annotating a slide show

5. Right-click the **slide** on the screen, point to **Pointer Options** on the on-screen navigation tools menu, and then click **Arrow**. The pen changes to a pointer.

6. Right-click the **slide** on the screen, and then click **End Show** from the menu to exit the slide show. You will be prompted by a message box asking if you want to keep or discard your ink annotations.

7. Click **Discard**.

8. Save your work and then leave the presentation on the screen for the next Step-by-Step.

Setting Up a Slide Show

PowerPoint has many features to help you make a presentation interesting and effective. There are several options for delivering a presentation. A presentation can be set up to be self-running, for viewing at a trade show booth, for example. You can also broadcast a presentation for remote viewers who view the show using a browser over the Internet. However, the most common method is to run a presentation with a speaker who directs the show.

To set up the slide show, on the Slide Show tab on the Ribbon, click the Set Up Slide Show button. The Set Up Show dialog box opens (**Figure 4–30**). It has six sections. See **Table 4–2**.

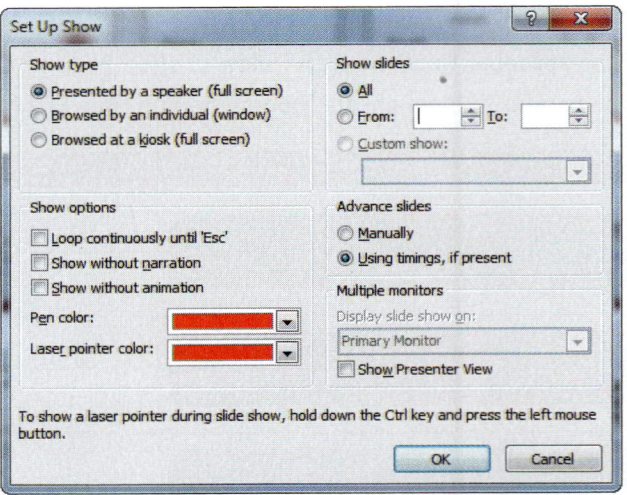

FIGURE 4–30   Set Up Show dialog box

TABLE 4–2   Understanding Set Up Show

OPTION	DESCRIPTION
Show type	Determines how the show will be viewed
Show slides	Allows you to choose which slides you are showing
Show options	Allows you to choose features that you want to include when making your presentation
Advance slides	Determines whether you advance the slides manually or automatically
Multiple monitors	Sets up your computer when you are using a secondary monitor or projector. Allow you to select Presenter View
Pen Color	Lets you determine pen and laser pointer colors

Presenter View

If you create numerous notes for your presentation using the Notes pane, ***Presenter view*** offers a way for you to view your presentation with the speaker notes showing on one computer screen, while an audience views the presentation without viewing the speaker notes on another computer screen. This feature is useful if you are presenting to an audience and want to be able to track your presentation and use your notes as a script. It offers you a way to deliver a professional presentation. When you work in Presenter view you can use thumbnails to select slides to show your audience without them seeing you actually select specific slides. Presenter view only works if your computer is set up with two or more monitors.

▶ **VOCABULARY**
Presenter view

Step-by-Step 4.16

1. Click the **Slide Show** tab on the Ribbon, and then click the **Set Up Slide Show** button. The Set Up Show dialog box opens.

2. In the Show type section, click the **Presented by a speaker option** button, if it is not already selected.

3. In the Show slides section, click **From**. The first box should be 1. Press **Tab**, and then type **18** in the To text box.

4. In the Advance slides section, click **Using timings**, **if present**, if it is not already selected.

5. Click **OK**.

6. Save your work and then leave the presentation on the screen for the next Step-by-Step.

Rehearsing Timing

PowerPoint can automatically advance the slides in your presentation at preset time intervals. This is helpful in the case of an unattended presentation at a kiosk or sales booth, or if you must make a presentation within a specific time limit.

To rehearse timing for a presentation, on the Slide Show tab in the Set Up group, click the Rehearse Timings button. The slide show automatically starts, and the Rehearsal toolbar (See **Figure 4–31**), with a timer for the slide and a timer for the presentation, appears on the screen. When you think enough time has passed for a slide to appear on the screen, click the Next button. The presentation advances to the next slide, and the slide timer starts over. You can pause the timer by clicking the Pause button. The Repeat button resets the slide timer back to zero and the presentation timer back to the time that has elapsed, through the previous slide. When you get to the end of the show, a dialog box appears, asking if you want to keep the slide timings for the presentation.

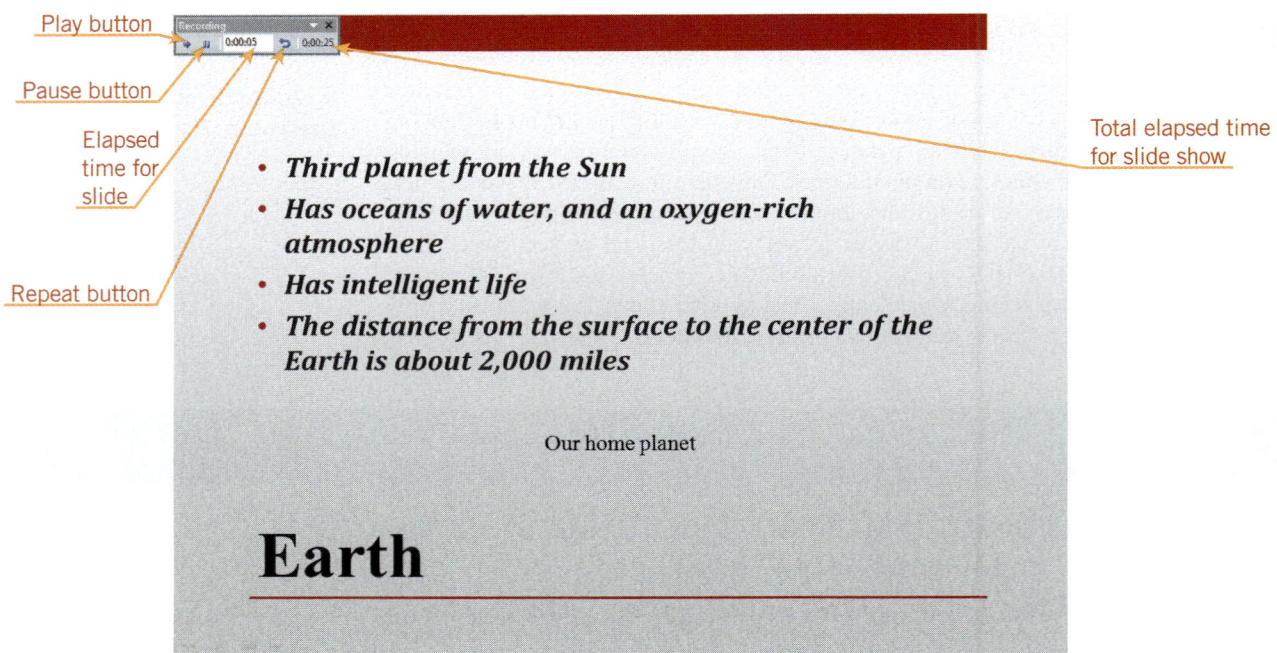

FIGURE 4–31   Rehearsing timings

To view rehearsal times for each slide, view the presentation in Slide Sorter view. The time allotted to each slide is listed at the lower-left corner of each slide. You can further edit the timing of each slide by opening the Slide Transition dialog box and changing the time below the Advance slide area of the dialog box.

Step-by-Step 4.17

1. Switch to **Slide Sorter view** if it is not the current view.

2. Click the **Slide Show** tab on the Ribbon, and then, in the Set Up group, click the **Rehearse Timings** button. The slide show starts, and the timers for the slide and the slide show begin.

3. Click the **Next** button every three to four seconds. Don't worry if you click in slightly less or more time.

   When you reach the end of the slide show, a message box opens, shows you the total time for the slide show, and asks if you want to keep the timings.

4. Click **Yes**. The presentation returns to Slide Sorter view.

5. Click the **Transitions** tab on the Ribbon. In the Timing group, in the Advance Slide section, click the **After up arrow** to add 2 seconds to the first slide.

   You can continue to adjust the time for each slide using the Advance slide section in the Timing group.

6. Click the **Slide Show button** on the status bar. The slides will automatically advance at the rate you set for each slide.

7. Save the changes to the presentation and then leave the presentation open on the screen for the next Step-by-Step.

TIP

Use the Transitions tab to apply different transition effects to each slide.

NET BUSINESS

Not everyone has PowerPoint installed on their computers nor will everyone be able to attend your presentation. In a world where many people work remotely from home or different offices around the world, PowerPoint 2010 lets you broadcast a presentation to others at remote locations whether or not they have PowerPoint installed on their computers. The Broadcast Slide Show feature works with SharePoint Server 2010 or Windows Live. To broadcast your presentation, click the Slide Show tab, in the Start Slide Show group, click the Broadcast Slide Show button, and then click Start Broadcast. In order for the people you want to view the broadcast to have access to the link to the show, they have to create a Windows Live ID and then log into Windows Live ID. To do so, go to www.login.live.com. The broadcast service will e-mail the link to your presentation to the people you designate, so that they can log in using their Windows Live account and be a part of the presentation. The broadcast displays the PowerPoint slide show; it will not transmit the audio from your presentation. If you want the remote audience to hear your presentation, you can set up a conference call using the phone system or voice over IP so that participants can hear your narration, ask questions, and participate in the presentation.

Inspecting a Document and Viewing Document Properties

Before you send a presentation out for review, or even submit it as final, it is a good idea to inspect the document for personal information or anything that you might not want to "travel" with the presentation file. The *Document Inspector* is a feature that can get this job done easily. To use the Document Inspector, click the File tab, click Info, click Check for Issues, and then click Inspect Document. The Document Inspector dialog box gives you choices as to what you want to look for. See **Figure 4–32**.

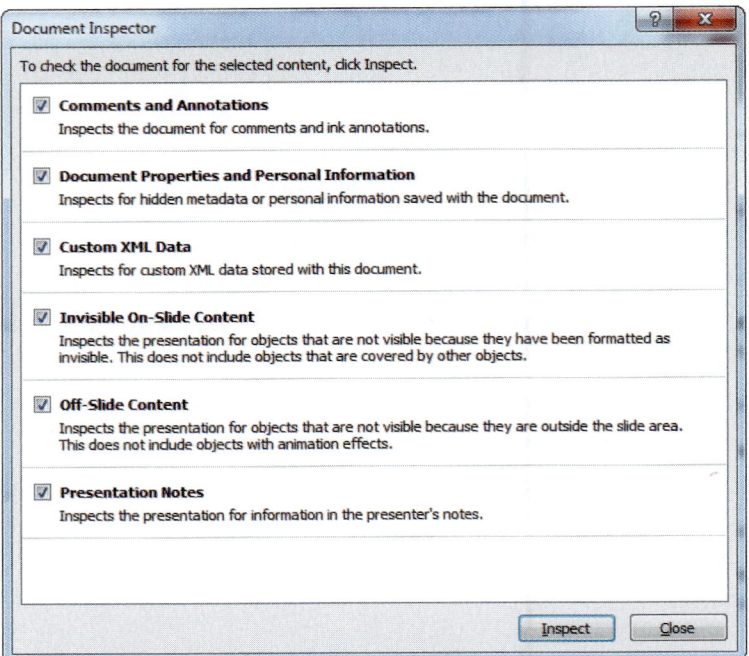

FIGURE 4–32   Document Inspector

The Document Properties Panel stores information about the document, the *document properties*, that can be helpful as you develop the presentation. Document properties include the author name, document title, subject, keywords, category, and status. You may choose to remove this information before you pass a file along. You may also choose to modify the default information that is added when you create a document. To view the Document Properties pane, click the File tab, click Info, click Properties, and then click Show Document Panel. See **Figure 4–33**.

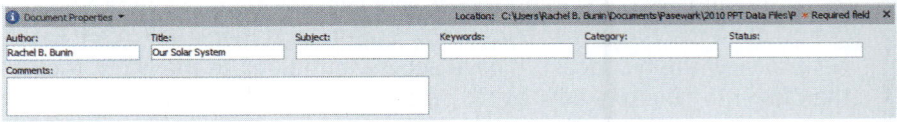

FIGURE 4–33   Document Properties Panel

Step-by-Step 4.18

1. Click the **File** tab, click **Info**, click **Check for Issues**, and then click **Inspect Document**.

   The Document Inspector dialog box opens.

2. Verify that all the boxes have check marks, and then click **Inspect**.

   Review the inspection results. The document should have comments and personal information.

3. Click **Remove All** to remove the Comments and Annotations.

4. Click **Remove All** to remove the Document Properties and Personal Information.

5. Click **Reinspect**, click **Inspect**, and then click **Close** to close the Document Inspector.

Embedding Fonts

Not all computers have every font style installed on them. If you are giving your presentation on a computer other than your own, your presentation text might not look exactly as it did when you created it. PowerPoint can embed fonts into your presentation so that your text appears exactly as you originally created it.

 TIP

You do not have to embed common fonts, such as Times New Roman, Arial, or Courier New, that are installed with Windows.

To embed fonts in your presentation, click the File tab, and then click Options to open the PowerPoint Options dialog box. Click Save in the left pane. The Customize how documents are saved pane appears, as shown in **Figure 4–34**. Click the Embed fonts in the file option button, and then click Embed only the characters used in the presentation option button. Click OK to close the PowerPoint options dialog box.

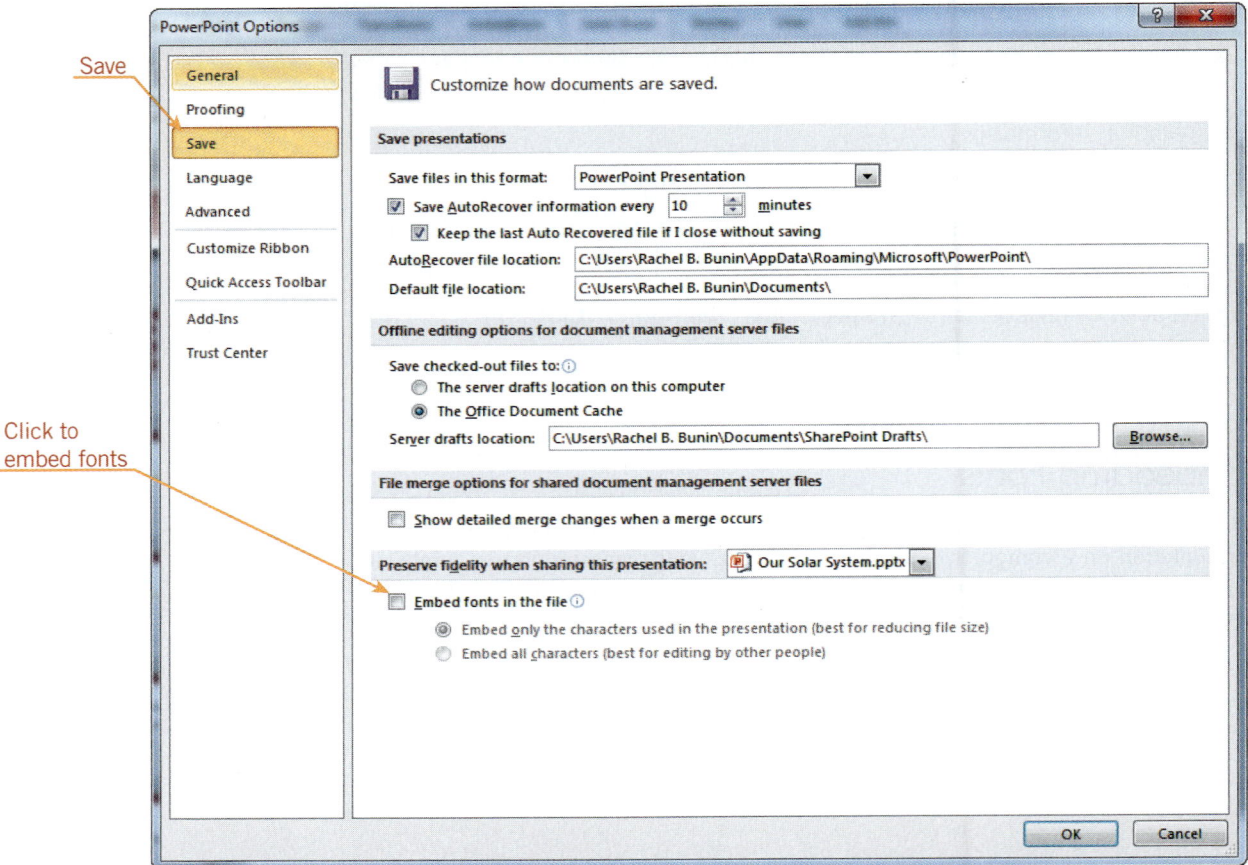

FIGURE 4–34   PowerPoint Save options

Step-by-Step 4.19

1. Click the **File** tab, and then click **Options** to open the PowerPoint Options dialog box.

2. Click **Save** in the left pane. The Customize how documents are saved pane opens.

3. Click the **Embed fonts in the file** option button, and then click **Embed only the characters used in the presentation (best for reducing file size)** option button.

4. Click **OK** to close the PowerPoint Options dialog box.

5. Click the **Save** button on the Quick Access toolbar to save the file. Notice the green progress bar on the status bar indicating that the fonts are being embedded in the file.

6. Leave the presentation open on the screen for the next Step-by-Step.

Using Package Presentation for CD and Copying Presentations to Folders

Some presentations can be quite large. Once you add images, video, and photographs, the files can exceed the limits of a disc or small flash drive. If you are giving your presentation on another computer, you can use *Package for CD* to compact all your presentation files into a single, compressed file that fits on a CD. You can then unpack the files when you reach your destination computer.

To use this feature, click the File tab, click Save & Send, click Package Presentation for CD and then click Package for CD. The Package for CD dialog box is shown in **Figure 4–35**. The dialog box gives several options for preparing your presentation. The Add button selects the presentation you want to package. The Copy to Folder button allows you to choose the destination folder for your files. The Options button opens another dialog box where you can choose the linked files and fonts you want to package. If the computer on which you are giving your presentation does not have PowerPoint installed, you can download a PowerPoint Viewer. This dialog box will also allow you to include a password on your PowerPoint file.

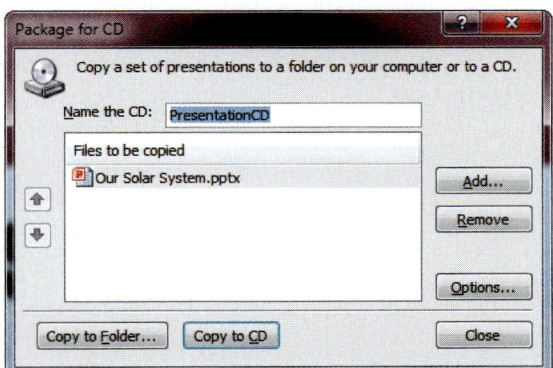

FIGURE 4–35 Package for CD dialog box

Step-by-Step 4.20

1. Click the **File** tab, click **Save & Send**, click **Package Presentation for CD** and then click **Package for CD**.

2. In the Package for CD dialog box, in the Name the CD box, type **Solar System** followed by **your initials**, and then click the **Copy to Folder** button. The Copy to Folder dialog box opens.

3. Click the **Browse** button, locate the folder where you store your Data Files, click **New Folder** in the Choose Location dialog box, type **Package Solar System – Your Name**, and then click **Select** twice. The folder location appears in the Location section of the Copy to Folder dialog box.

4. Click **OK**, and then click **Yes** to copy the linked files to the package. The files are copied to the folder. Close any open dialog boxes.

5. Click the **Options** button. The Options dialog box opens. This presentation does not include any linked files, and you embedded the fonts and checked for private information in the previous Step-by-Step.

6. Deselect both the **Linked files** and **Embedded TrueType fonts** check boxes.

7. Click **Viewer Package** in the Package type section, if it is not already selected, and then click **OK**.

8. Insert a blank CD in the CD burner of your computer.

9. Click **Copy to CD**, and the files are copied to the destination CD burner.

10. Save the presentation and leave it on the screen for the next Step-by-Step.

Sending a Presentation via E-mail

There are several ways you can use e-mail in conjunction with PowerPoint. You can send a presentation as an e-mail attachment or e-mail it to a recipient for review.

Open the presentation you want to send, click the File tab, click Save & Send, and then click Send Using E-mail. The Send Using E-Mail options in Backstage view are shown in **Figure 4–36**.

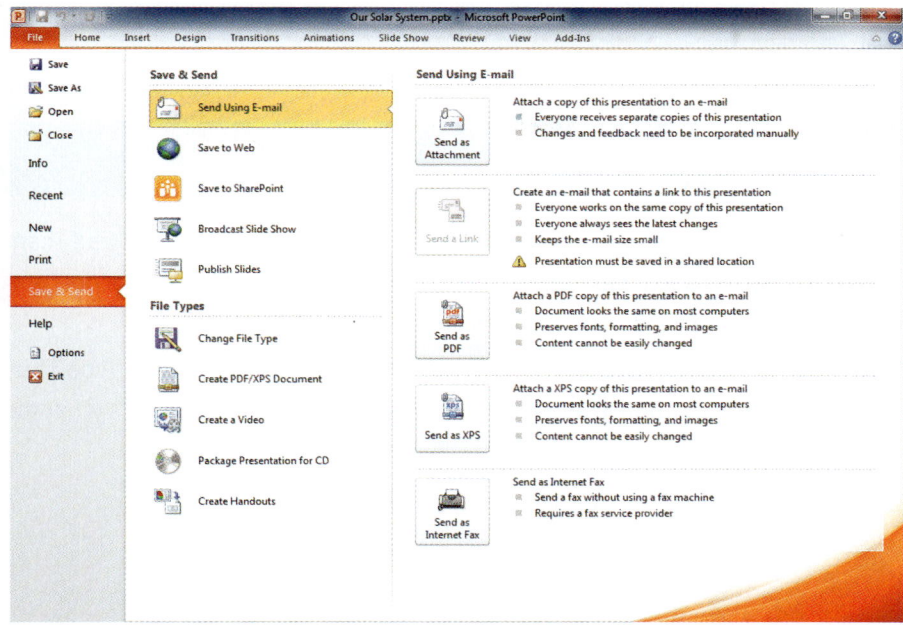

FIGURE 4–36   Send Using E-mail options

If you click Send as Attachment, if you have the Outlook e-mail program installed on your computer, a new blank message will open with the presentation attached. See **Figure 4–37**. Fill in the recipient information, type a message, and click Send. A copy of the presentation is e-mailed, but the original stays open so you can continue working on it.

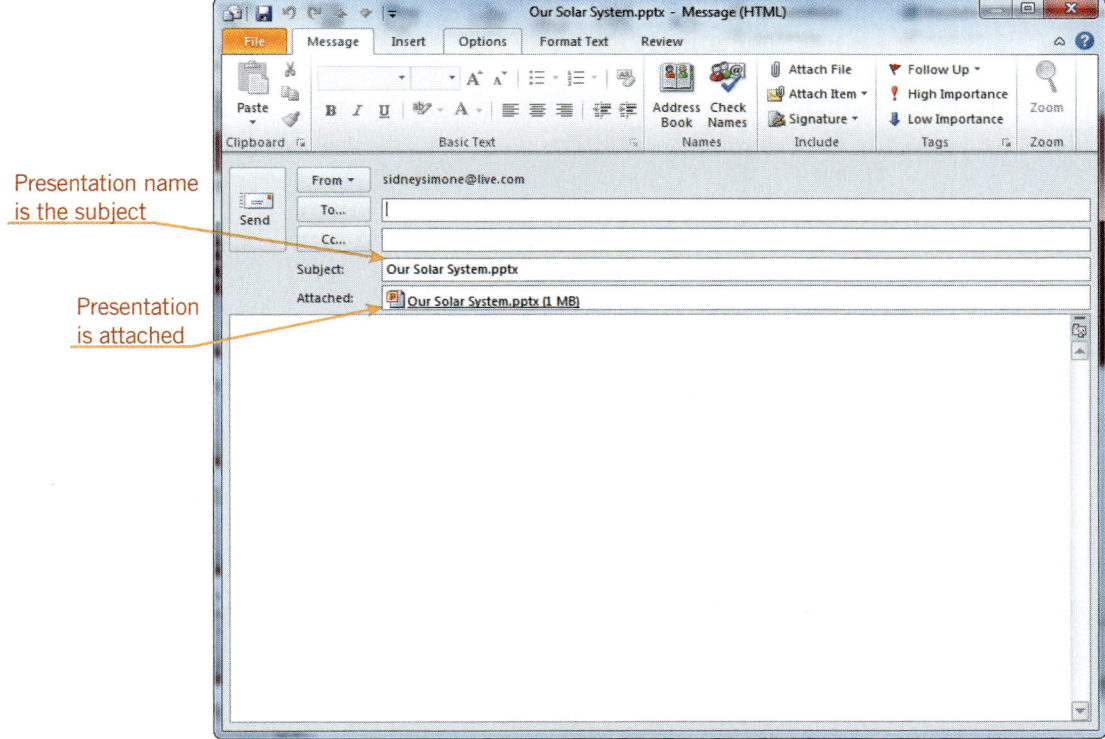

FIGURE 4–37   New e-mail message

To complete this next Step-by-Step, arrange with a friend to exchange presentations via e-mail.

Step-by-Step 4.21

— WARNING

If you do not have Microsoft Outlook installed on your computer, you will not be able to complete this Step-by-Step.

 EXTRA FOR EXPERTS

You can mark a presentation as final so other people can look at the presentation but cannot make any changes to it. Click the File tab, click Info, click Protect Presentation, and then click Mark as Final. You can also password-protect your presentation file if you want to safeguard who can and cannot look at the slide show. Click the File tab, click Info, click Protect Presentation, and then click Encrypt with Password. You will be asked to create a password and then confirm the password. Be sure you remember the password or write it down in a safe place. If you forget the password, you will not be able to open the presentation again.

1. Click the **File** tab, click **Save & Send**, click **Send Using E-mail** and then click **Send as Attachment.** The Microsoft Outlook e-mail program opens a new message window with the presentation as an attachment.

2. Enter the e-mail address of a friend, click in the **message body**, type **This is the presentation I told you about**, and then click **Send** to exchange your presentations.

3. Close the Microsoft Outlook e-mail program if it is open.

Setting Up the Pages

You can alter the output format of your presentation by working in the Page Setup dialog box. You can change the orientation of your slides or notes, handouts, and outline. Before you print or share a presentation, you should check spelling, review the design of each slide, and run the show to check timings.

Step-by-Step 4.22

1. Click the **Design** tab, and then in the Page Setup group, click the **Page Setup** button. See **Figure 4–38**.

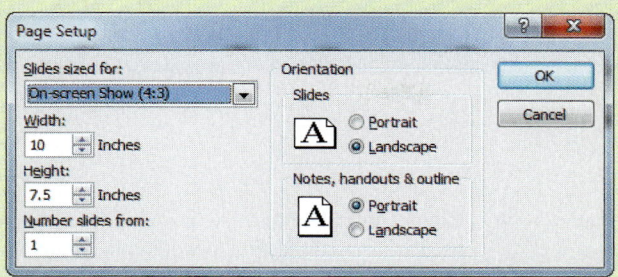

FIGURE 4–38
Page Setup dialog box

2. Click the **Slides sized for** list arrow, review the options, click **On-screen Show 4:3** and then click **OK**.

3. Click the **Insert** tab, in the Text group, click **Header & Footer**, click the **Notes and Handouts** tab, click the **Header** check box, type **your name** in the Notes and Handouts Header text box, and then click **Apply to All**.

4. Click the **Review** tab, and then in the Proofing group, click the **Spelling** button, and check for any spelling errors.

5. If your teacher wants a printout, click the **File** tab, click **Print**, and then print your presentation as **Handouts (6 Slides Per Page)**.

6. Save and close the presentation.

7. Exit PowerPoint.

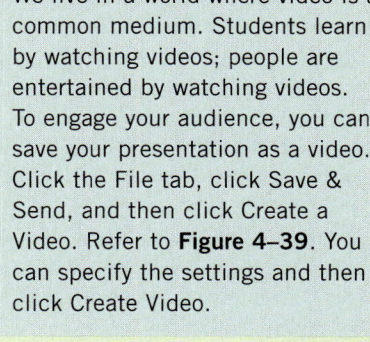

EXTRA FOR EXPERTS

We live in a world where video is a common medium. Students learn by watching videos; people are entertained by watching videos. To engage your audience, you can save your presentation as a video. Click the File tab, click Save & Send, and then click Create a Video. Refer to **Figure 4–39**. You can specify the settings and then click Create Video.

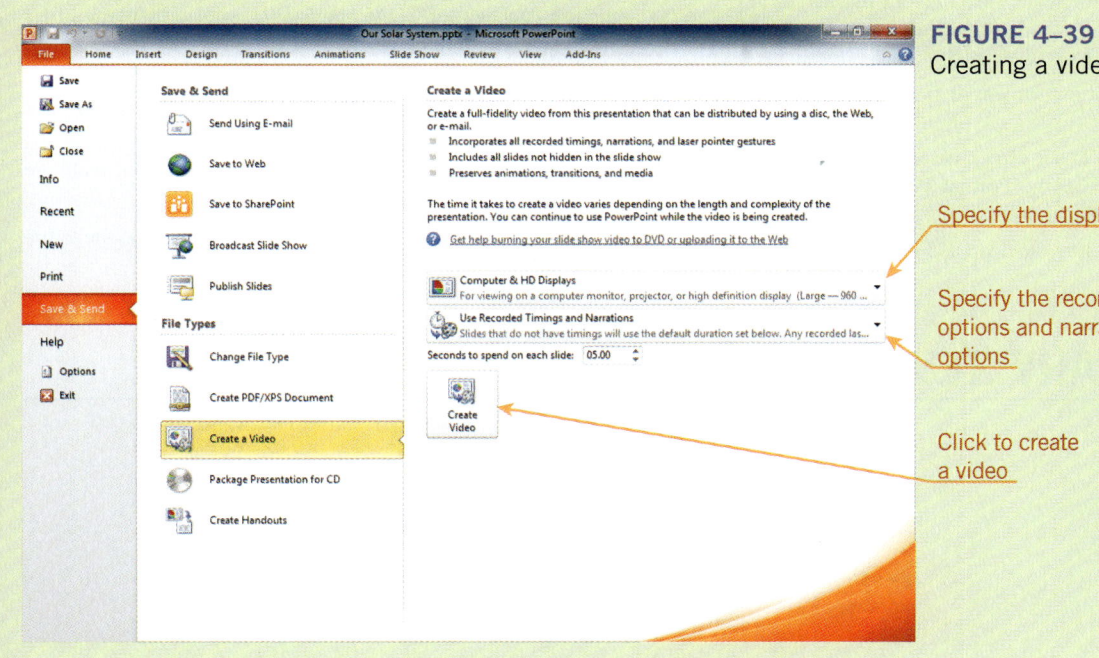

FIGURE 4–39
Creating a video

Specify the display

Specify the recorded options and narration options

Click to create a video

SUMMARY

In this lesson, you learned:

- To embed or link data from other applications such as Microsoft Excel and Microsoft Word into PowerPoint presentations. Embedded information can be edited using the original application. To make changes to an embedded object, double-click on it to open the application that created it. Changes made when editing are reflected in the destination file.

- Text can be imported from Word to create a new presentation or add slides. It is easiest for PowerPoint to convert the text to slides when the Word document is in outline form.

- Slides can be copied and pasted from one presentation to another. You can also use a Slide Library to store favorite slides that you want to reuse again and again. You can also save a presentation as a Word document to use as a handout, or create other documents using the text and slides from the presentation.

- To apply multiple slide masters to a presentation. This can help you save time if you are creating a presentation containing slides with more than one theme or any other features that are controlled by the slide master.

- PowerPoint allows you to create a new layout master for any theme or slide master. You can also create custom slide layouts and then add the placeholders as needed.

- To replace fonts throughout an entire presentation, use the Replace Font dialog box.

- To copy the formatting of an object or text by clicking the Format Painter button. Use the Format Painter to apply the same format to another object or text.

- To align a text box or picture, you can add grid lines, the ruler, and guides to slides.

- Comments can be inserted in a slide for others to see. You can use the Compare feature to work collaboratively with others.

- A custom show can be created to limit the slides displayed in any slide show for particular audiences. You can hide slides for certain audiences.

- Action buttons are the buttons inserted on a slide that enable you to jump from slide to slide, even to slides in another slide show, or to other documents.

- When presenting a slide show, you can use on-screen annotation tools to emphasize specific text or graphics on a slide. The Pen, and Highlighter tools allow you to write or highlight features on the screen. The Eraser tool erases any ink it touches, and Erase All Ink on Slide deletes all ink marks.

- A presentation can be set up to be self-running, so that it automatically advances the slides at preset time intervals.

- To inspect a presentation for personal information or anything that you might not want to "travel" with the presentation file, using the Document Inspector.

- If you are giving your presentation on another computer, you can use Package for CD to compact all your presentation files into a single, compressed file that fits on a CD. You can then unpack the files when you reach your destination computer.

- PowerPoint helps you easily broadcast a presentation for remote users to view on the Internet.

- To send a presentation as an e-mail attachment to a recipient for review.

- To alter a presentation's output format depending on the target audience.

■ VOCABULARY REVIEW

Define the following terms:

Action button	embed	linked object
comment	Format Painter	Package for CD
custom show	grid	Presenter view
destination file	guidelines	Snap to
Document Inspector	import	source file
document properties	link	

REVIEW QUESTIONS

FILL IN THE BLANK

Complete the following sentences by writing the correct word or words in the blanks provided.

1. A Word _____ is the easiest kind of document to import because it is formatted with styles, and each heading level is translated into a corresponding level of text in PowerPoint.

2. If you format an object with certain attributes, such as fill color and line color, and then want to format another object the same way, use the Format _____ .

3. The Paste _____ command has several options that provide you with flexibility in how you copy data from a source file to a destination file.

4. In order to be sure the Excel chart in the slide always has the most up-to-date numbers, you should link it rather than _____ it in the presentation.

5. The placeholders available on the Insert Placeholder menu are: Content, Text, Picture, Chart, table, _____, Media, and Clip Art.

TRUE / FALSE

Circle T if the statement is true or F if the statement is false.

T   F   **1.**   Being able to compare ideas and see the changes that each member contributes to the presentation is possible by using the Compare tool.

T   F   **2.**   A broadcast show is a way to limit the slides in any slide show for a particular audience.

T   F   **3.**   Action buttons enable you to jump from slide to slide, even to slides in another slide show, or to other documents.

T   F   **4.**   The Document Inspector is a feature that checks to see if all slides have correct spelling and grammar and the transitions and timings are appropriate for the show.

T   F   **5.**   If you are giving your presentation over the Internet, you can use Package for CD to compact all your presentation files into a single, compressed file that can be posted on a Web site.

MATCHING

Write the letter of the term or phrase from Column 2 that best matches the description in Column 1.

Column 1

_____ 1. Helps you organize long presentations so that you can work with them when creating and editing your work.

_____ 2. A way for you to view your presentation with the speaker's notes showing on one computer screen, while an audience views the presentation without viewing the speaker notes on another computer screen.

_____ 3. Where you have the text, chart, numbers, or whatever data it is you want to bring into the presentation.

_____ 4. Used when you want a presentation to contain only certain slides.

_____ 5. Moves an object to the closest intersection of the grid on a slide.

Column 2

A. Presenter View

B. Custom Show

C. Snap to

D. source file

E. sections

F. Slide Navigator

G. Exit show

PROJECTS

If you have a SAM 2010 user profile, your instructor may have assigned an autogradable version of the indicated project. If so, log into the SAM 2010 Web site at *www.cengage.com/sam2010* to download the instruction and start files.

PROJECT 4–1

For an astronomy club meeting, you need to create a custom slide show presentation about the solar system. After the presentation, the club members ask you for a file so that they can post the presentation to their Web site.

1. Start PowerPoint and open the The Solar System presentation file you worked on earlier in this lesson. Save the presentation as **Astronomy Club**, followed by your initials.

2. Change the theme to a new theme of your choice.

3. Replace the current font for the slide titles throughout the presentation with a font of your choice.

4. Select the title Our Solar System on slide 1, change the font to 60-point Aharoni.

5. Add a comment to the second slide.

6. Insert a text box on slide 7 with a new fact about Jupiter, format the text box using a new font, fill, and color. You can also apply a shape effect. Use grids and guidelines to place the box on the slide.

7. Insert a new text box on slide 9, Saturn, with a new fact about Saturn. Use the Format Painter to apply the same format as the text box on slide 7 to the text box on slide 9.

8. Add an action button on a slide, the action button can link to any other slide in the presentation.

9. Inspect the document, and then view the document properties.

10. Add your name to the notes and handout footer. Save, print the presentation as handouts with four slides per page, and then close the presentation.

 PROJECT 4–2

You decide to create another presentation about the moons around each planet.

1. Open a new blank presentation. Enter the title on the title Slide as **Many Moons**, and then type **By Your name** as the subtitle.

2. Save the presentation as **Many Moons.pptx**.

3. Insert a new slide with a blank layout.

4. Start Word and view the Planet Number of Moons.docx Data File that has a Word table containing the following information:

Planet	Number of Moons
Mercury	0
Venus	0
Earth	1
Mars	2
Jupiter	16
Saturn	18
Uranus	15
Neptune	8
Pluto	1

5. Embed the Word table in the Many Moons presentation file that is open.

6. Center the text box on the slide. Open the file in Word and format the text as you see fit.

7. View the presentation.

8. Create a custom layout using a SmartArt graphic and a clip art placeholder.

9. Create a slide using the new custom layout.

10. Add another slide using this text, and format the text:

Planet	Time to Rotate Around Sun
Mercury	88 Earth days
Venus	224.7 Earth days
Earth	365.3 days
Mars	687 Earth days
Jupiter	12 Earth years
Saturn	29.5 Earth years
Uranus	84 Earth years
Neptune	165 Earth years
Pluto	248 Earth years

11. Add as many slides as you want to create the presentation. Apply a theme and use graphics and design elements to enhance the presentation.

12. Inspect the file, and then check the document properties.

13. Save, print the presentation as handouts with two slides per page, and then close the presentation.

CRITICAL THINKING

ACTIVITY 4–1

Your supervisor wants you to insert a chart into the presentation you are editing for him. You decide to use a Microsoft Excel chart that you will create on your own. Use the Excel Help system to find out how to enter data in a worksheet, and then create a chart using Excel. Use the features on the Chart Tools Layout tab to add titles, gridlines, and data labels. Embed the chart in a new presentation.

ACTIVITY 4–2

Create an outline in Word using heading styles. Use at least three Heading 1 styles so your presentation has at least three slides. Import the text into PowerPoint to create a new presentation. Email the presentation to a friend. If you have access to a LiveID, broadcast the presentation, and send a link to a friend to view the presentation.

Introduction to Microsoft PowerPoint

◤ REVIEW QUESTIONS

TRUE / FALSE

Circle T if the statement is true or F if the statement is false.

T   F   1.   To add text and graphics to a slide, it is best to work in Normal view.

T   F   2.   A transition is an effect you can apply to text, objects, graphics, or pictures to make those objects move during a slide show.

T   F   3.   The Zoom Slider adjusts the font size on the slide.

T   F   4.   There are many ways to advance slides in a slide show; you can click, press Enter, press the arrow keys, press Page Down or Page Up, or press Spacebar.

T   F   5.   You cannot change colors or fonts in a theme.

MULTIPLE CHOICE

Select the best response for the following statements.

1. In Normal view, you can:

    A.   View each slide on a full screen.

    B.   See an overview of all the slides in the presentation.

    C.   Add text, graphics, charts, sounds, and other objects to a slide.

    D.   View each slide as a thumbnail with notes next to the slide.

2. What reserves space on a slide for text, graphics, or an object?

    A.   Master   C.   Placeholder

    B.   Template   D.   Object box

3. An organization chart is an example of _____ .

    A.   SmartArt   C.   animation

    B.   text box   D.   theme

4. Which PowerPoint feature should you use to organize data in rows and columns on a slide?

   A. Text box   C. Placeholder

   B. SmartArt   D. Table

5. You can apply formatting or design changes to all the slides in the presentation using the _____.

   A. Notes master   C. Header and Footer dialog box

   B. Slide master   D. Handout master

FILL IN THE BLANK

Complete the following sentences by writing the correct word or words in the blanks provided.

1. Title and Content, Comparison, and Two Content are examples of slide _____.

2. Create _____ if you want to show some slides to one audience and other slides to another audience, and reorder slides for yet another audience from the same presentation.

3. Use the _____ to copy the Fly In and Swivel effects from one object to another.

4. Apply a(n) _____ such as Austin to change the overall design of all the slides in the presentation.

5. The _____ includes information about the presentation such as Author, Title, Subject, Keywords, Category, and Status.

■ PROJECTS

PROJECT PPT 1

1. Use the Angles installed theme to create a new presentation.

2. Type **My Favorite States** as the slide title, then type by your name as the subtitle.

3. Save the presentation as **States Project 1.pptx**, followed by your initials.

4. Insert a new slide with a Title and Content layout.

5. Type the name of the state you live in as the title of the slide. (*Note*: If you do not live in the United States, type the name of a state you want to learn more about.)

6. Type four facts about your state in the content placeholder.

7. Insert a third slide with a Title and Content layout.

8. Type the name of a state you want to visit as the title of the third slide. Enter three facts about that state in the content placeholder.

9. Use the Outline tab to add two more slides to the presentation. Enter state names as the title and three facts for each state.

10. Change the font color for the facts on slides 3, 4, and 5 to different colors of your choice.

11. View the presentation in Slide Sorter view.

12. Add transitions and timings to the title slide in the presentation.

13. Add clip art to the title slide.

Figure UR–1 shows an example of what your presentation might look like.

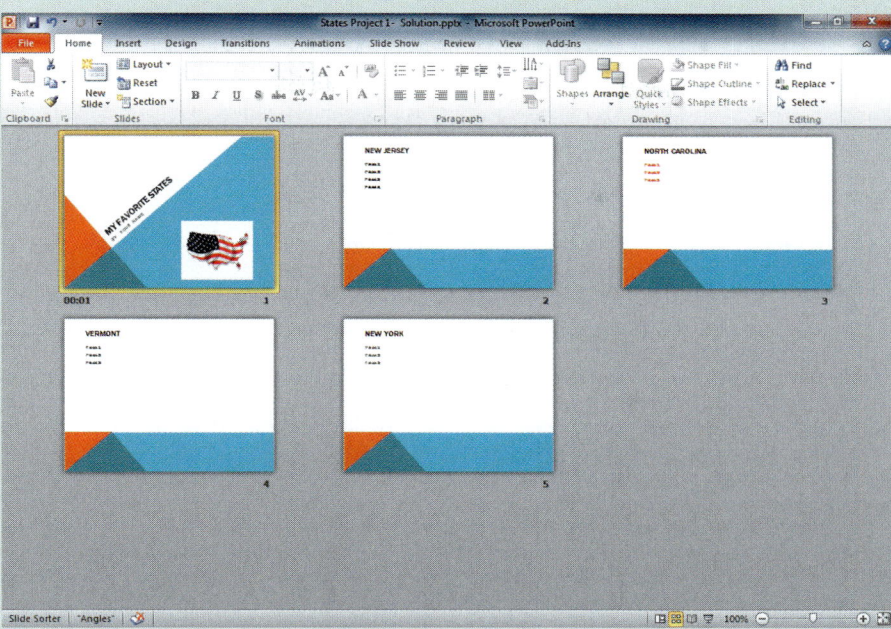

FIGURE UR–1

14. Add your name to the handouts header. Print the presentation as handouts with four slides per page.

15. View the presentation as a slide show. Save and close the presentation.

PROJECT PPT 2

1. Open the **States Project 1.pptx** presentation file you created in Project 1, and then save the presentation as **States Project 2.pptx**, followed by your initials.

2. Add at least two more slides, choose two more states, adding content for each of them.

3. Change the theme of the presentation.

4. Change the clip art on the title slide and then apply an effect to the clip art on the title slide. Add another clip to the slide and remove the background color if necessary to make the clip blend in with the slide.

5. Change the layout of the third slide to Two Content.

6. Replace the right placeholder with a picture that is relevant to the state you chose.

7. Add a speaker's note to slide 4: **Remember to show the flags for all states.**

8. Change the style of the bullets for all slides in the presentation to a different color and style.

9. Add a small graphic object to the slide master so it appears on all slides.

10. Change the font attributes for the Title and Content slide layout to a different color and font style.

11. Draw a different shape on at least three slides of your choice. Add effects to the shapes.

12. Insert a last slide with hyperlinks to www.usa.gov and www.whitehouse.gov. Give the slide a meaningful title. Format and design the slide as necessary.

13. Apply animation effects to at least two slides. Use the Animation Painter to copy the animation to another object in the presentation.

14. Apply slide transitions to all the slides.

15. Check the spelling. Refer to **Figure UR–2** for a sample of what the final presentation might look like.

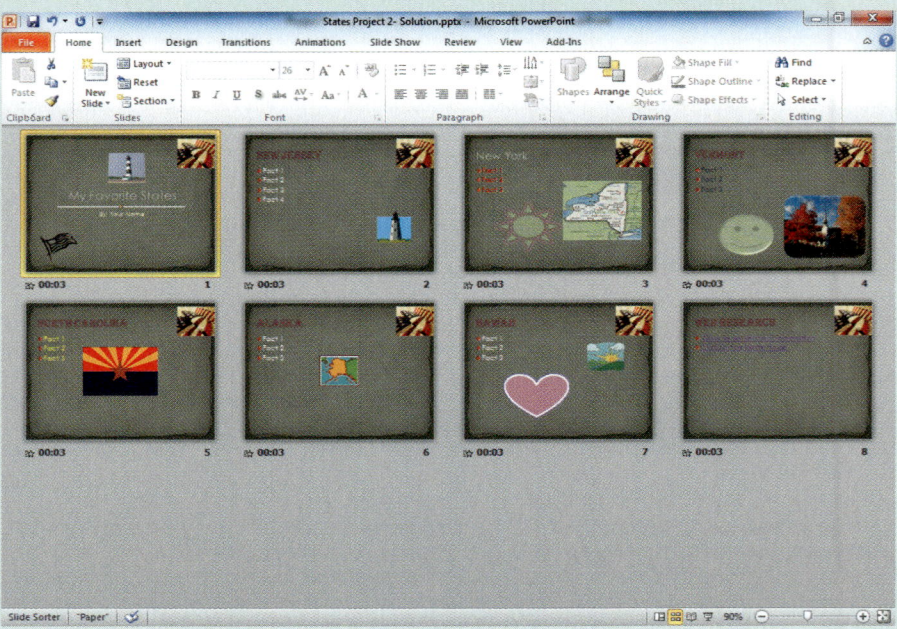

FIGURE UR–2

16. Print the presentation as audience handouts with six slides per page.

17. Save and close the presentation.

PROJECT PPT 3

1. Create a new presentation file from a template (you can use an installed template or one from Microsoft Office Online). Templates include content, so you can select a template with a topic that is of interest to you. Save the presentation as **Project 3 Template Presentation.pptx**, followed by your initials.

2. Insert a SmartArt graphic on one slide, and then convert any existing text on another slide to a SmartArt graphic. If the template does not have enough slides to complete the following steps, add additional slides.

3. Create and format WordArt on two slides.

4. Create a line chart on a slide, then format the chart. Add an appropriate slide title.

5. Create a table with three columns and three rows. Enter text in all the cells. You can enter any text that is relevant to the presentation topic.

6. Use a Table Style to modify the table's style and layout.

7. Insert a new slide, give the slide a meaningful title, draw and format a star and an arrow shape, then scale and size the shapes. Group the shapes into one object.

8. On a new slide, draw five shapes. Format the shapes with colors and fills. Enter a descriptive title on the slide.

9. Insert an oval object on the slide with five shapes, then type **This is an oval.** to create a text box on the oval shape.

10. Animate the drawn objects.

11. Add a footer with your name and the current date to all slides.

12. Apply transition effects and timings to the slides.

13. Create and save one custom show in the presentation. Add your name to the Document Properties Panel.

14. Save your work. View the slide show, and then print the presentation in any view.

15. Refer to **Figure UR–3** for a sample of what the presentation might look like in Slide Sorter view.

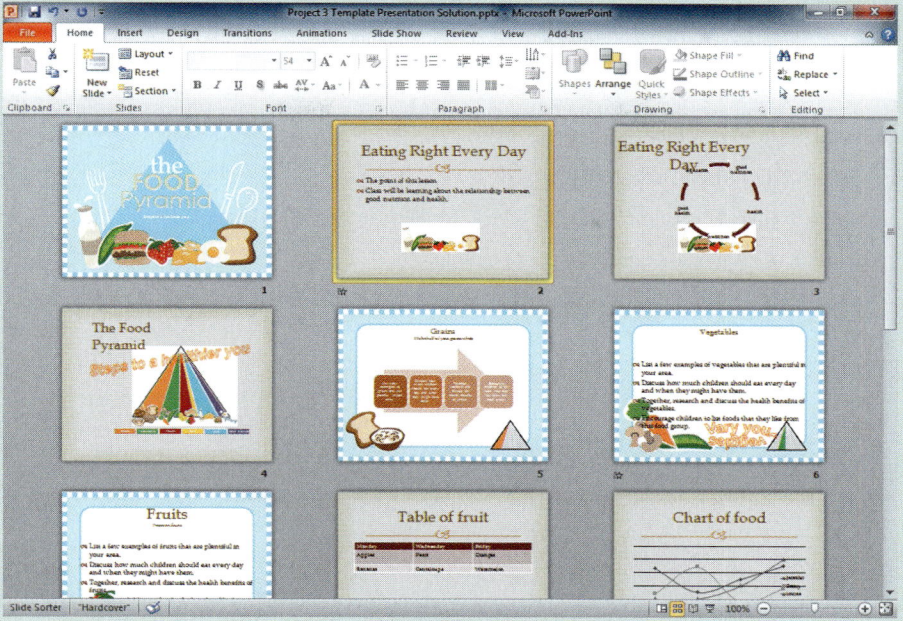

FIGURE UR–3

16. Save and close the presentation.

PROJECT PPT 4

1. Open the **Project 3 Template Presentation.pptx** presentation that you created in Project 3, and then save the presentation as **Project 4 Template Presentation.pptx**, followed by your initials.

2. Switch to Slide Master view, then create a new layout master that includes a picture placeholder, a media placeholder, and text placeholder. Refer to **Figure UR–4** for a sample of what the new layout might look like. You can format the text or change the bullets. Create one slide that uses the new custom layout.

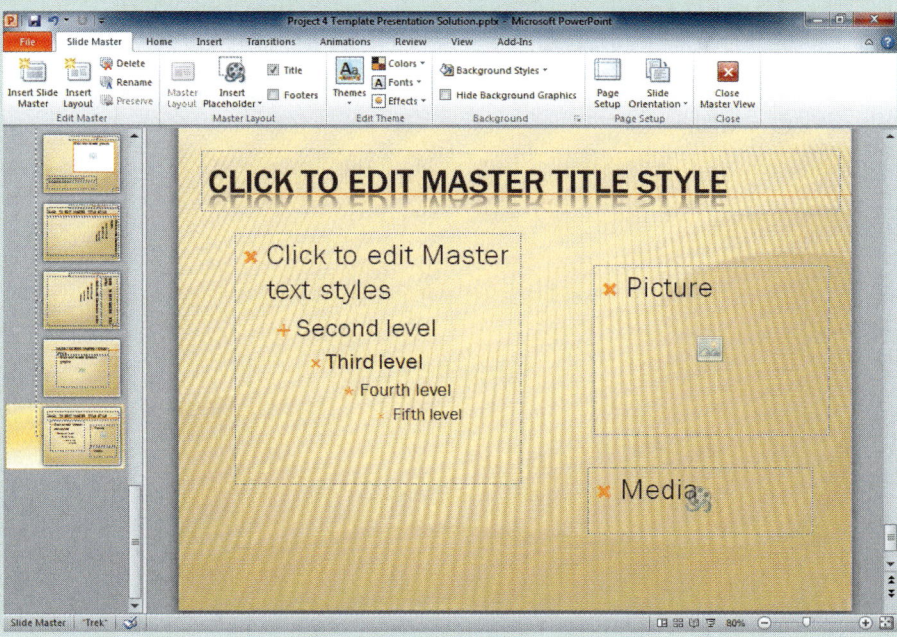

FIGURE UR–4

3. Change the theme of the presentation. Work the design and objects until you are happy with the design of the presentation.

4. Align text and pictures on any of the slides using the Arrange commands.

5. Insert comments on three of the slides.

6. Use the Rehearsal toolbar to set up the timing for the slide show.

7. Send the presentation via e-mail to a friend or colleague.

8. View the presentation, return to Slide Sorter view, hide a slide, then view the presentation again.

9. Save and print the presentation as handouts with four slides per page.

10. Save the presentation as a Video, preview it in Media Player or whatever the default video player is on your computer.

11. Save and close the presentation.

12. Exit PowerPoint.

SIMULATION

JOB PPT 1

The Java Internet café is working to increase the number of members who visit the café. They also want to find a way to ensure that customers stay longer and order more food and drinks once they come to the café. The manager asks you to create a presentation to show to all new members so they can learn about all the benefits of coming to the Java Internet cafe.

1. Start PowerPoint and open the **Java Cafe.pptx** presentation from the drive and folder where you store your Data Files. Save the presentation as **Java Cafe Info.pptx**, followed by your initials.

2. Apply a theme to the presentation.

3. Convert the text on slide 2: *Welcome* into a SmartArt graphic. You can change the formatting as you see fit.

4. Change the layout of slide 3: *Introduction* to Two Content layout and insert a clip art picture relevant to the slide.

5. Create WordArt on slide 4: *Agenda* using the text **Have Fun!**

6. On slide 5: *Overview*, draw and format three shapes, then insert the text **Good for you!** onto one shape. Animate the shapes.

7. Insert a new slide after slide 2 with a Title Only layout. Type **Sample Coffee Pricing** as the title. Insert the Microsoft Excel worksheet Data File, **Coffee Prices.xlsx**, as an embedded object. Search for two clip art objects using the keyword **coffee**. Insert both appropriate clips on the slide and then group the two clips.

8. On slide 8: *Vocabulary*, add a hyperlink on the text **Google** to www.google.com. Preview the page and test the hyperlink.

9. Add clip art images as needed to other slides.

10. Insert a sound file for clapping from the Clip Organizer to the last slide. It should play automatically and loop until stopped.

11. Add transitions and timings to all the slides.

12. Add your name as a footer to the handout master.

13. View the slide show. Save and print the presentation as handouts with nine slides per page.

14. Close the presentation and then exit PowerPoint.

🕐 **Estimated Time for Unit:**
3.5 hours

INTRODUCTORY UNIT

MICROSOFT OUTLOOK 2010

LESSON 1   **1 HR.**
Outlook Basics and E-Mail

LESSON 2   **1.5 HRS.**
Calendar

LESSON 3   **1 HR.**
Working with Other Outlook Tools

LESSON 1

Outlook Basics and E-Mail

■ OBJECTIVES

Upon completion of this lesson, you will be able to:

- Start Outlook.
- Create a list of contacts.
- View, sort, and print the Contacts list.
- Send, receive, and print e-mail messages.
- Create and use an Address Book.
- Create a contact group.
- Create a signature.
- Attach files to e-mail messages.
- Create, move, and archive folders.
- Search, save, and delete e-mail messages.

■ VOCABULARY

Address Book

archive

contact

e-mail

Navigation Pane

Quick Steps

Reading Pane

Ribbon

signature

Spam

Introducing Outlook

Outlook is a desktop information manager that helps you organize information, communicate with others, and manage your time efficiently. You can use the various features of Outlook to send and receive e-mail, schedule events and meetings, store information about business and personal contacts, including your friends' status updates from social networks; create to-do lists that integrate with your appointments; view interactions such as e-mail, instant messaging, and *Voice over Internet Protocol (VoIP)* phone calls; create reminders; and subscribe to online content feeds. You can use these tools to group together information for easy access and maximum productivity. For example, you may want to create a category named Key Customers for your most important clients. You can also arrange Outlook to show your activities, appointments, and messages for the day.

Outlook is integrated with other Office 2010 programs, which makes it easy to share information for different tasks. For example, you can open an Outlook e-mail Message window from other Office applications, use an Outlook Contacts list to create a mail merge in Word, or share any file from Excel, Word, or PowerPoint.

Starting Outlook

To start Outlook, click the Start button on the taskbar. Click All Programs on the Start menu, click Microsoft Office on the submenu, and then click Microsoft Office Outlook 2010. The Outlook window opens, ready to display e-mail messages, as shown in **Figure 1–1**.

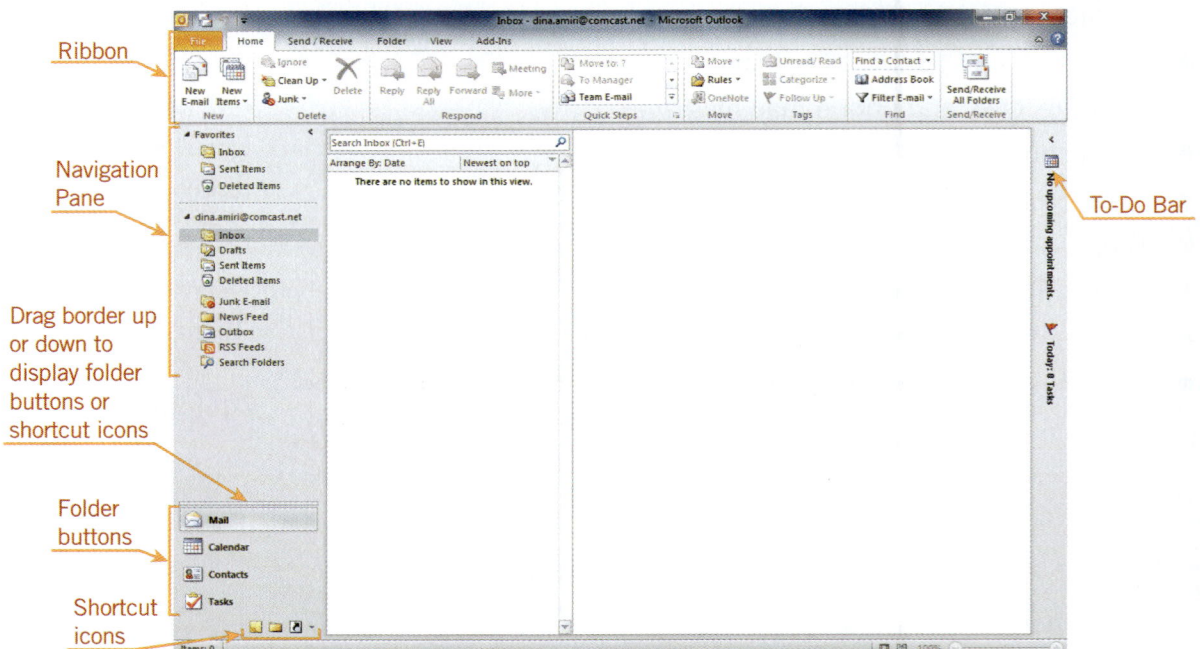

FIGURE 1–1   Outlook window

By default, Outlook separates sections of the window so you can quickly do what you want to accomplish. You can select an action or command on the Ribbon, find the folder you want to view in the Navigation Pane, view and track messages in the Reading Pane, read additional contact information in the People Pane, and view a summary of your appointments and tasks in the To-Do Bar.

In Outlook, the ***Ribbon*** places the basic commands you use the most on the Home, Send/Receive, Folder, View, and Add-Ins tabs.

The ***Navigation Pane*** is located on the left side of the Outlook window and provides centralized navigation to all parts of Outlook. It includes view buttons and shortcut icons you can use to quickly access the information you need. From the Navigation Pane you can access the main Outlook components: Mail, Calendar, Contacts, Tasks, Notes, Folder List, Shortcuts, and Journal, or create a new shortcut. **Table 1–1** describes each of these elements. You can drag the top of the view buttons pane up or down to adjust the number of buttons or icons that are visible. The content available in the Navigation Pane varies depending on the selected view.

TABLE 1–1   Navigation Pane options

ICON	NAME	DESCRIPTION
	Mail	Contains e-mail messages that you have sent and received.
	Calendar	Schedules your appointments, meetings, and events.
	Contacts	Lists information about those with whom you communicate.
	Tasks	Creates and manages your to-do lists.
	Notes	Keeps track of anything you need to remember.
	Folder List	Lists all of your folders.
	Shortcuts	Provides quick access to folders in any Outlook view.
	Journal	Records entries to document your work.

Outlook organizes messages by subject in the message list; you can read the entire message in the ***Reading Pane***. You can view a specific component by clicking its icon at the bottom of the Navigation Pane. Once open, you can rearrange your view of any component, such as Mail, Calendar, or Tasks, by clicking the View tab on the Ribbon, and then clicking the options and views relevant to that component.

VOCABULARY
Ribbon
Navigation Pane
Reading Pane

TIP

You can hide, show, or customize options in any section of Outlook. To customize the Navigation Pane, right-click a component, click Navigation Pane Options, and then select or move options as desired.

TIP

To minimize or expand the Navigation Pane and the To-Do Bar, click the Expand arrow or Minimize arrow, for each pane, respectively.

Step-by-Step 1.1

1. Click the **Start** button  on the taskbar.
2. Click **All Programs** on the Start menu and then click **Microsoft Office** on the submenu. Click **Microsoft Outlook 2010**. (*Note*: You may be prompted to set up a personal account.)
3. The Outlook window opens with the Navigation Pane open, as shown in Figure 1–1. Leave this pane open for the next Step-by-Step.

Creating a Contacts List

► VOCABULARY
contact

You can store information about the people or organizations with whom you communicate by creating a Contacts list. A *contact* is any person or company in your Address Book. Your Contacts list can contain e-mail, address, phone, a picture, video, and other information and activity. You can create contacts in several ways. Using the Navigation Pane, click the Contacts button to display the Contacts Pane, as shown in **Figure 1–2**. You can also create a contact from an e-mail message that you open or preview, or from an electronic business card you receive.

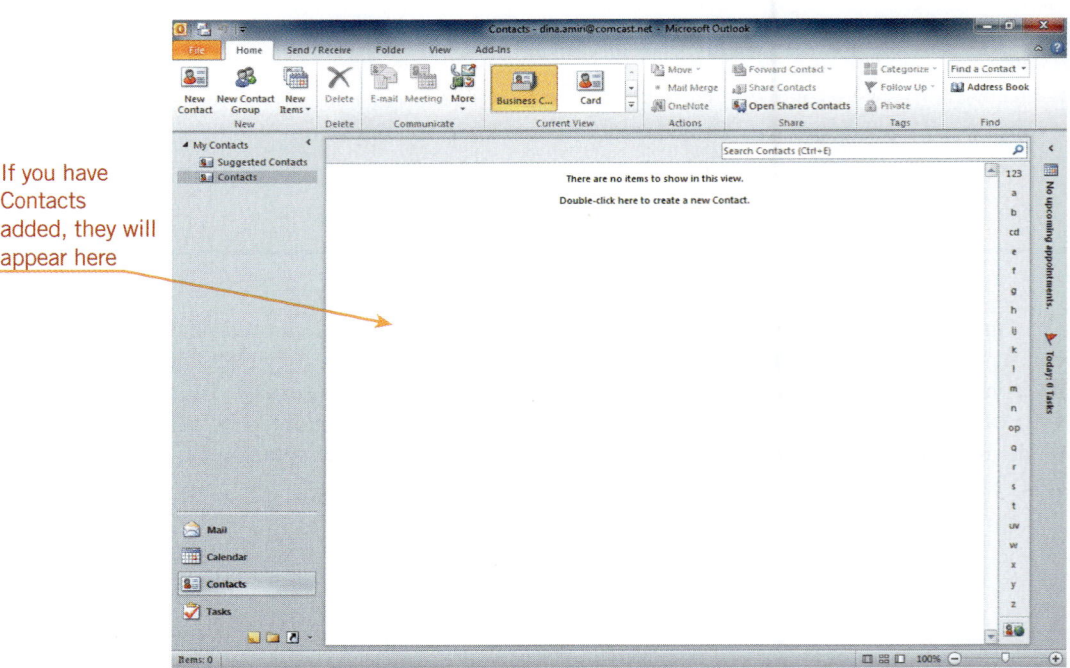

If you have Contacts added, they will appear here

FIGURE 1–2   Contacts Pane

Adding a Contact

To add a contact, click the Contacts view button in the Navigation Pane. On the Ribbon, click the Home tab, and then in the New group, click the New Contact button. A new Contact window opens with the title Untitled – Contact, as shown in **Figure 1–3**. When you finish adding information about the contact, on the Contact tab, in the Actions group, click the Save & Close button to return to the Contacts Pane, or click the Save & New button to add another contact.

The Contact tab contains tools for customizing your contact's information and for communicating with your contact. Once you've entered some information about the contact, you can add display details, set up a meeting with or e-mail the contact, add a photograph, categorize the contact, even find a map to their address. Commands on the Insert tab allow you to attach files or e-mail messages to the entry, or insert illustrations, tables, different media, links, or text in the Notes section of the Contact window. The Format Text tab allows you to modify the font layout and style attributes, including Quick Styles, of the contact information as it appears in the Contact window. The Review tab contains proofing options, such as spell check and thesaurus, and language options, such as translation and language preferences. Office add-ins appear on the Add-Ins tab.

> **TIP**
>
> You can store information for both individuals and companies by manually entering the data or by grabbing information from an open e-mail message. Right-click the sender's or any recipient's e-mail address on the From or CC lines, and then click Add to Outlook Contacts.

> **TIP**
>
> To update information about a contact, double-click the contact's name in the Contacts list. Make your changes and then, on the Contact tab, in the Actions group, click the Save & Close button.

Step-by-Step 1.2

1. In the Navigation Pane, click the **Contacts** view button. The Contacts Pane appears, similar to Figure 1–2.

2. On the Ribbon, on the Home tab, in the New group, click the **New Contact** button. A new Contact window opens, as shown in Figure 1–3.

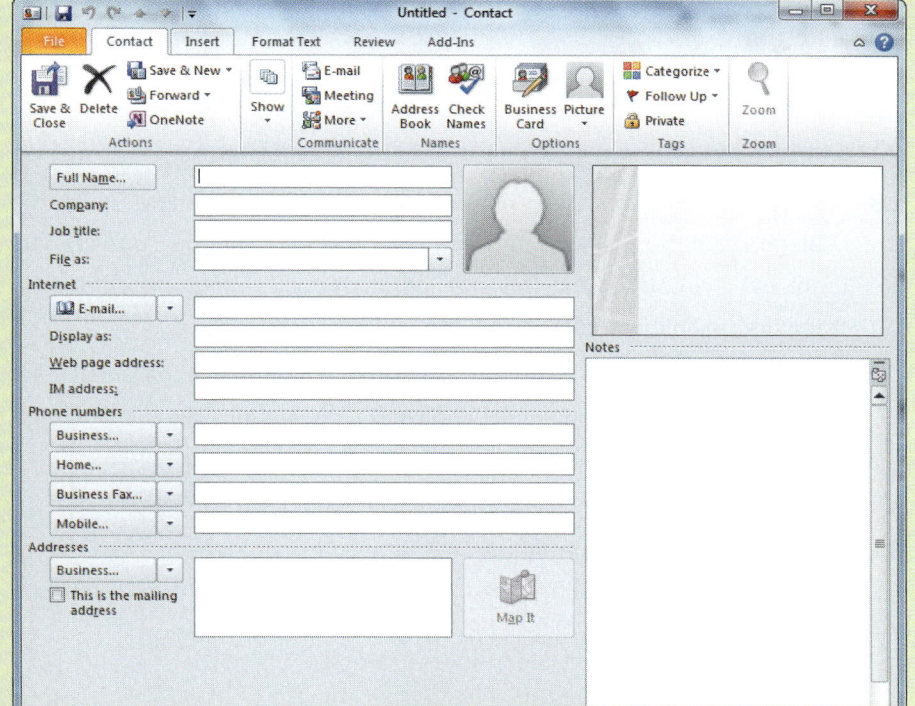

FIGURE 1–3
New Contact window

3. In the Full Name box, type **Sofia Acosta**.

4. Press **Tab** or **Enter**. The title of the Contact window automatically changes to Sofia Acosta – Contact, and the surname is automatically placed first in the File as box.

5. In the Company box, type **Flamenco Media** and then press **Tab** or **Enter**.

6. In the Job title box, type **Owner** and then press **Tab** or **Enter**.

7. For the remaining boxes, type the information shown in **Figure 1–4**.

FIGURE 1–4
Completed contact information

Category color

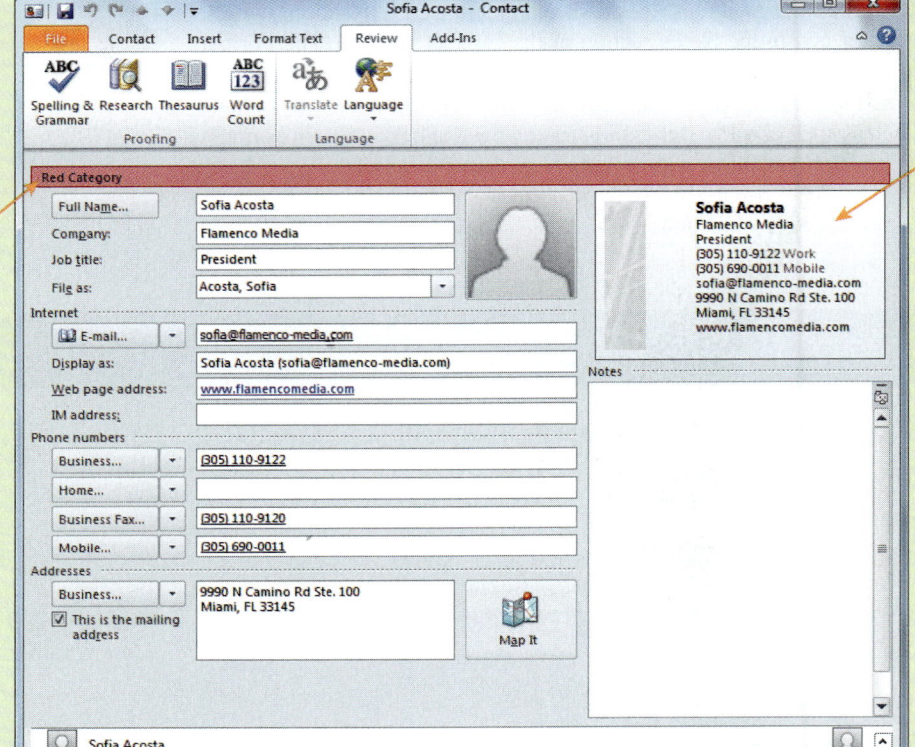

Virtual electronic business card created automatically

8. On the Ribbon, on the Contact tab, in the Tags group, click the **Categorize** button, and then click **Red Category** for the contact. The contacts are color-coded for easy identification. (*Note*: If prompted to rename the color category, click **No**.)

9. When you have completed entering the contact information, on the Contact tab, in the Actions group, click the **Save & Close** button. The contact information is saved, and a Business Card appears in the Contacts Pane.

10. Add two more contacts using the information shown in **Figure 1–5**.

11. After entering the information for the second contact, on the Contact tab, in the Actions group, click the **Save & Close** button to return to the Contacts Pane.

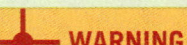 **WARNING**

Notice that after you type the e-mail address, the contact's full name and e-mail address automatically appear in the Display As box, and a virtual business card showing the contact information is visible.

Carlisle, Paul		Morris, Jaidan	
Full Name:	Paul Carlisle	Full Name:	Jaidan Morris
Job Title:	Director of Marketing	Job Title:	Regional Director
Company:	Minmark Company	Company:	McGinnis Enterprises
Business:	11178 Sixth Street West St. Petersburg, FL 33703	Business:	24452 Oakland Ave. Austin, TX 78746
Business:	(727) 999-3333	Business:	(512) 144-7824
Mobile:	(727) 277-7622	Mobile:	(512) 440-0001
Business Fax:	(727) 999-3334	Business Fax:	(512) 147-7825
E-mail:	pcarlisle@minmark.com	E-mail:	j.morris@mcent.com
Business Home Page:	www.minmark.com	Business Home Page:	www.mcginenterprises.com
Categories:	Green Category	Categories:	Green Category

FIGURE 1–5
Two more contacts

12. In the Contacts list, double-click **Sofia Acosta**. The Contact window for Sofia Acosta opens.

13. In the Job title box, delete **Owner** and then type **President**. On the Ribbon, on the Contact tab, in the Actions group, click the **Save & Close** button to save your changes. Leave the Contacts list open for the next Step-by-Step.

Viewing, Sorting, and Printing Contacts

When you receive an e-mail message, you can quickly view contact information and interact with a sender or anyone included in an e-mail distribution. To do so, move the mouse pointer over a name in the Reading Pane to reveal a collapsed Contact Card. You can use icons at the bottom of the card to send a new e-mail or instant message, place a VoIP call, and schedule meetings and other tasks. To view full contact information, click the Expand Contact Card arrow. Collapsed and expanded views of the Contact Card are shown in **Figure 1–6**.

Collapsed card

Move mouse pointer over sender's name

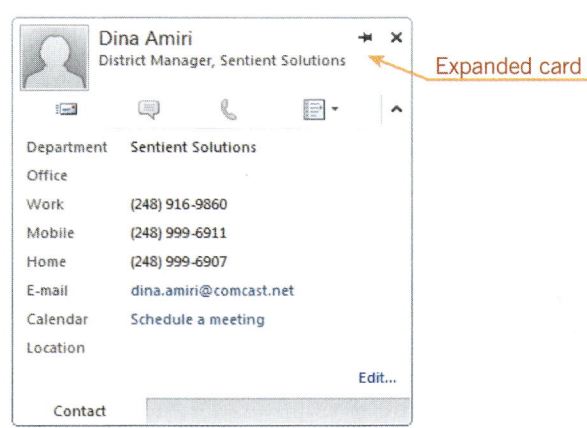

Expanded card

FIGURE 1–6 View a collapsed and expanded Contact Card

EXTRA FOR EXPERTS

In addition to viewing the information supplied by a contact, you can connect to them through the **Outlook Social Connector (OSC)**. You can use the OSC to view your communication history with them. You can also connect to different social networks and download the posts of your contacts. For example, when you open an e-mail message, you can expand the People Pane at the bottom of the message window, and then click the Toggle People Pane button to read your e-mail history or upcoming appointments with the contact and their status updates from a social networking site.

To change how you view all your contacts, on the Home tab, in the Current View group, click a view option. To select additional views, click the More button in the Current View group. You can select Business Card, Card, Phone, and List views, which are described in **Table 1–2**. When you click the Contacts view button in the Navigation Pane, Business Card is the default view in the Contacts Pane.

TABLE 1–2 View options for Contacts

VIEW	DESCRIPTION
Business Card	Displays company logos, layouts, designs, photos, links, or other images.
Card	Includes field names with general information.
Phone	Lists contacts in a table with all phone numbers included.
List	Lists contacts in a table alphabetically by company.

If you select Phone or List view for your contacts, you can arrange them further in the Arrangement group of the View tab. Here you can arrange the Contacts list by Date (or date of last conversation if in Phone view), Company, Categories, or Location.

To change the order of a column as it appears in Phone or List view, click and hold the column label, and then drag it to a new position. If you want to change the order of multiple columns, the sort order, filters, and other settings for any view, click the View tab. In the Current View group, click the View Settings button. In the Advanced View Setting dialog box, click the description you'd like to change, adjust settings, and then click OK.

To print your Contacts list in the current view, on the Ribbon, click the File tab and then in Backstage view, click Print. Depending on the view, you can select a style in the Print What section. A preview of the style appears on the right. For example, from Business Card and Card views, you can print your contacts as cards, booklets, memo, or a phone list. From Phone or List views, you can only print in a table format.

TIP

To sort or filter contacts in Business Card or Card view, right-click a blank part of the main Contacts window, and then click Reverse Sort or Filter. Reverse Sort switches the alphabetical listing from A–Z to Z–A. When you click Filter, the Filter dialog box opens, where on the Contacts tab you can search for specific words, e-mail addresses, or the time the card was created or modified. Additional options are available on the More Choices and Advanced tabs.

Step-by-Step 1.3

1. With the Contacts Pane open, on the Home tab, in the Current View group, click the **More** button ⬇, and then click **Phone**. Your screen should look similar to **Figure 1–7**.

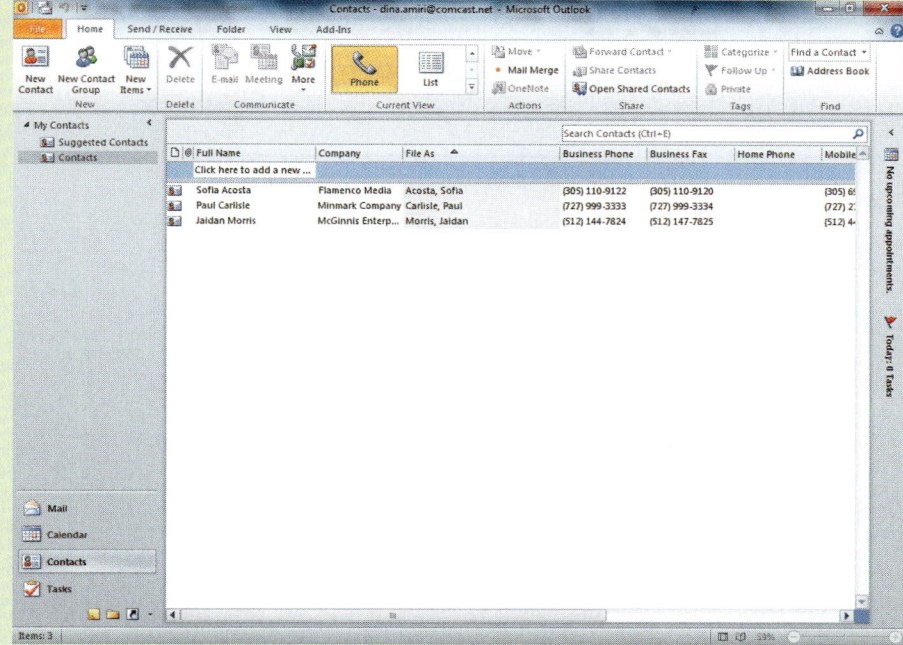

FIGURE 1–7
View Contacts in Phone view

> **TIP**
>
> To adjust the width of columns, position the mouse pointer over a column divider, and then drag to widen or narrow it. To view all data fields in the Contacts Pane, you may need to shorten the columns that do not have data.

2. Click the **View** tab, and then in the Arrangement group, click **Categories**. Notice that the names are separated by color category.

3. Click the **File** tab, click **Print** in Backstage view, and then click the **Print** button. The Contacts will print as a phone list in Table Style.

TIP

To adjust properties for the selected printer, click the Print Options button, click Properties in the Print dialog box, and then adjust the settings you want.

5. Click the **Actual Size** button 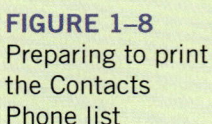 in the Preview Pane, and then compare your screen to **Figure 1–8**. The magnification of the preview is increased. Notice that the list is two pages because all the contact fields are included.

FIGURE 1–8
Preparing to print the Contacts Phone list

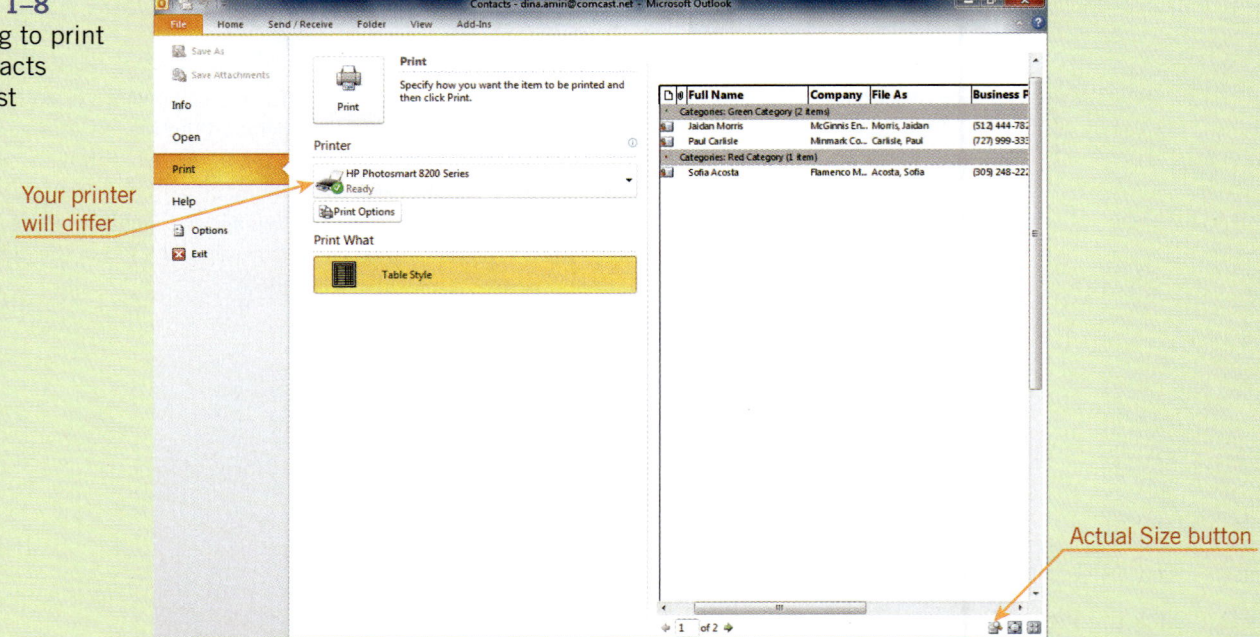

6. Click the **Home** tab. Leave Outlook open for the next Step-by-Step.

NET BUSINESS

Contact lists in Outlook are helpful in any project in which you have many colleagues and associates. For example, salespeople can create a Contact list to store detailed information on each of their clients. They can organize this information by assigning a category to each client. A Contact list can also make it easy to communicate with clients. To quickly send an e-mail message to a contact from any view, simply drag the contact onto the Mail view button or to the Mail shortcut icon in the Navigation Pane. A new Message window opens with the contact's name in the To box. Type your message and then click the Send button. You will learn more about sending e-mail messages later in this lesson.

Using E-Mail

One of the most common and useful Internet services is *e-mail* (electronic mail), which uses a computer network to send and receive messages. E-mail is an essential global communications tool. It is fast, paperless, and accessible from many different devices. In addition to your computer, you can use e-mail from Internet-connected mobile devices, such as pocket PCs that can also play games, or smartphones, such as Blackberries and iPhones.

To use electronic mail, you need an e-mail address that includes your name; your host, server, or domain name; and an extension that tells whether the account is at a school, business, government location, or in another country. No one else has your unique e-mail address. E-mail addresses are composed of a user name to the left of the @ symbol, and a domain name, which is the text equivalent of an Internet address. Examples include:

yourteacher@yourschool.edu

tickets@comedycentral.com

president@whitehouse.gov

Using Outlook, you can send e-mail messages to others connected by your intranet. If you have an Internet connection, you can send messages to anyone who also has an Internet connection. Your software needs to be configured with the appropriate profile and service settings to send and receive e-mail. Remember that even though you may communicate primarily with friends and family using social networking or text messaging, e-mail remains the most effective way to communicate in business and many other environments.

Setting E-Mail Options for Messages

Make sure that Mail is selected in the Navigation Pane. On the Home tab, in the New group, click the New E-mail button. A new Message window opens, as shown in **Figure 1–9**. To help you manage your e-mail messages, on the Home tab, you can use commands in the Respond group to perform common tasks, such as replying to or forwarding a message. You can use shortcuts in the *Quick Steps* group to streamline common workflow tasks, such as moving a message to a particular folder, marking the message as Done, or replying to and deleting a message automatically. The Insert tab contains commands for inserting tables, shapes and images, and you also insert links and other objects. You can select a theme, fields, and other message choices on the Options tab, format text on the Format Text tab, and check spelling and other editorial functions on the Review tab.

Outlook provides several settings that you can modify when sending and receiving messages. For example, you can set a message's importance. On the Message tab, in the Tags group, you can modify the default importance setting, Normal, by

INTERNET

E-mail was used on the Internet many years before Web pages even existed. Since 1971, billions and billions of e-mail messages have been sent. Some estimate the percentage of *spam*, electronic junk mail, to be up to 50 percent of all e-mail.

EXTRA FOR EXPERTS

You can also create a custom Quick Step that combines one or more actions, such as categorizing a message and then moving it to a particular folder. On the Home tab, in the Quick Steps group, click Create New, and in the Name box, type a name for the new Quick Step. Select an action from the Choose an action list, select the details for that action, and then click Add Action. You can add multiple actions to a custom Quick Step. In the Optional section at the bottom of the dialog box, you can select a keyboard shortcut for the action and a tooltip that will appear when you move the mouse over the quick step.

clicking the High Importance button or the Low Importance button. Click the Options tab to modify additional settings, such as requesting a receipt in the Tracking group, or delivery options in the More Options group.

You can modify the basic formatting features of your message, such as the font, size, color, and text alignment. On the Message tab, click the attribute you want to change in the Basic Text group. To modify the Theme, Theme Fonts, Theme Colors, Theme Effects, and Page Color, on the Ribbon, click the Options tab, and then in the Themes group, click the feature you want to change.

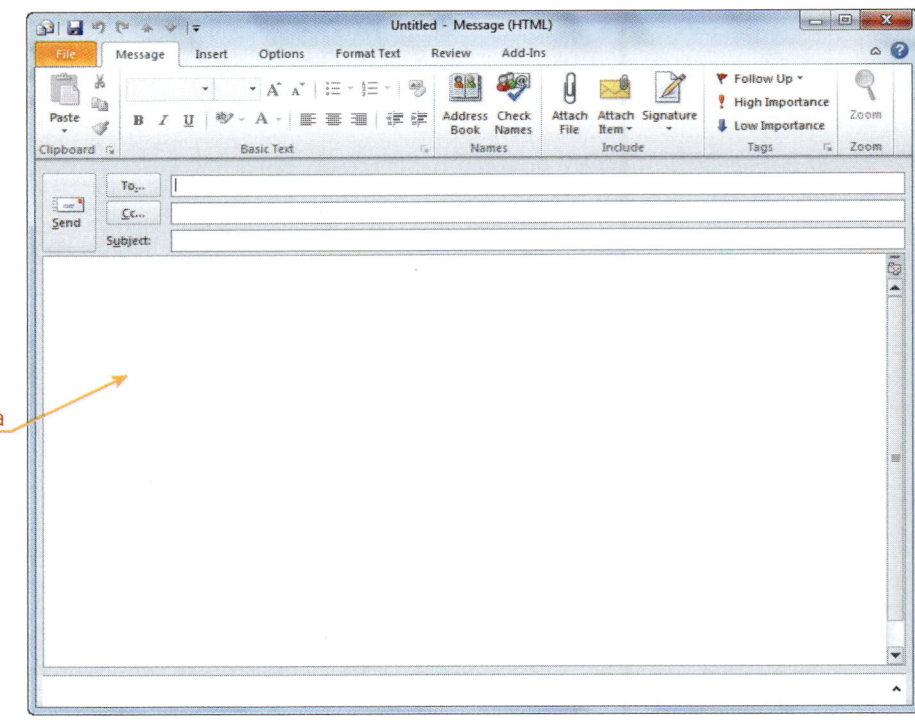

Message area

FIGURE 1–9   New Message window

Step-by-Step 1.4

1. In the Navigation Pane, click the **Mail** view button. If necessary, click the **Inbox** folder in the Mail section of the Navigation Pane to display the Inbox, and then make sure the **Home** tab is selected.

2. Click the welcome **message** from Microsoft or another message if you have one in your Inbox. You can read the message in the Reading Pane.

3. On the Ribbon, on the Home tab, in the New group, click the **New E-Mail** button. The new Message window opens, similar to Figure 1–9.

4. In the Message window, on the Message tab, in the Tags group, click **High Importance**. When the recipient receives the message, a red exclamation mark will appear next to the message in the Inbox, indicating that it is of high importance.

5. Click in the **message area**, then on the Message tab, in the Basic Text group, click the **Font** list arrow, scroll down, and then click **Arial**.

6. Click the **Insert** tab, in the Illustrations group, click **Picture**, open the Sample Pictures folder, or navigate to a location where you store your pictures, click a **photo**, and then click **Insert**. Options for editing the image appear on the Picture Tools Format tab.

7. Click the **Options** tab, and then in the Tracking group, click the **Request a Delivery Receipt** check box. A check mark appears in the box, indicating that it is selected.

8. Click the **Close** button in the Message window. A message box will open asking you to save changes. Click **No** and then leave Outlook open for the next Step-by-Step.

Sending, Receiving, and Printing E-Mail Messages

The Mail section of the Navigation Pane contains mail folders, such as the Inbox folder for incoming mail, and the Outbox folder, which stores outgoing mail. The Drafts folder stores unsent items, and the Junk E-mail folder stores items identified as spam. The Sent Items folder stores the e-mail messages you've sent, and Deleted Items stores the messages you've deleted.

To create and send an e-mail message, open a new Message window, as shown in Figure 1–9. In the To box, type the e-mail address of the person to whom you are sending the message. You can send a copy of the message to someone by typing his or her e-mail address in the Cc box. You can also send a *Bcc* (blind carbon copy) of the message to someone, which means that person's name will not be visible to the other recipients when they open the message. In the Subject box, type the subject of your message and then in the message body area, type your message, and if you want, you can insert images, tables, charts, and other elements.

You can also spell check a message (which you should always do), print, attach a file to it, and save it to your hard drive or flash drive. When you're finished writing your message, you can send it by clicking the Send button.

You can view a message by clicking it in the Inbox. To open an e-mail message fully, which might be necessary to view a complete conversation thread or graphics, double-click the message in the Inbox. After reading a message, you can reply to it or forward it to someone else. To reply to it, on the Message tab, in the Respond group, click the Reply button. To forward it, on the Message tab, in the Respond group, click the Forward button. You can also print the message, or go on to read the next message.

 VOCABULARY
Bcc

TIP

To add the Bcc field to a Message window, on the Ribbon, click the Options tab, and then click the Bcc button in the Show Fields group.

Step-by-Step 1.5

1. On the Ribbon, on the Home tab, click the **New E-mail** button. A blank Message window opens, as shown in **Figure 1–9**.

2. In the To box, type your **e-mail address** or one provided by your instructor.

3. In the Subject box, type **Test e-mail**.

4. In the message area, type **This is my sample**.

5. Click the **Send** button. Your mail is sent, and if Outlook is set up correctly for intranet e-mail, you should receive the message in a few moments. (*Note*: If you do not receive the message shortly, click the **Send/Receive All Folders** button 🖼 on the Quick Access toolbar.)

6. Double-click the **e-mail message** with the subject "Test e-mail" to open the message.

7. Click the **File** tab, click **Print** in Backstage view, and then click the **Print** button to print the message. Press and hold **Alt+Tab** to view the message, and then close the message.

8. Click the **Home** tab, and then click the **Sent Items** folder in the Mail section of the Navigation Pane to display the list of sent messages. The message you sent to yourself appears at the top.

9. Click the **Outbox** folder in the Mail section of the Navigation Pane. The view is blank. If the message is still waiting to be sent, it appears in this folder. (*Note*: You may need to scroll down in the All Mail Items section to find the Outbox folder.) Leave Outlook open for the next Step-by-Step.

TIP

To reply to the sender in an open message, on the Message tab, in the Respond group, click the Reply button. To respond to all the recipients listed in the message, click the Reply All button. To forward a message to another recipient, click the Forward button, insert the person's address, and then click the Send button.

TIP

You can also press the F9 key to send and receive messages.

Creating an Address Book

Most of the time, you will be sending e-mail messages to the same people. To make sending an e-mail message easier, you can access names and addresses from the *Address Book*, a collection of personal and professional contact information. Outlook creates Address Book information automatically when you add a new contact with an e-mail address to your Contacts list. The Address Book contains the contact's name and e-mail address.

To display the Address Book, make sure the Mail Pane is open and then on the Ribbon, on the Home tab, in the Find group, click the Address Book button. The Address Book window opens, as shown in **Figure 1–10**. To add a new contact from the open Address Book, click File on the menu bar, and then click New Entry. The New Entry dialog box opens, as shown in **Figure 1–11**. Make sure that New Contact is selected and then click OK. The new Contact window opens, where you can add information about the contact. When you save and close the Contact window, the new contact appears in the Address Book.

To display more detailed information about a contact listed in the Address Book, double-click the contact's name to open the Contact window.

▶ **VOCABULARY**
Address Book

TIP

Because you can also send a fax from your computer if it set up to do so, Outlook creates a separate contact for fax numbers so you can access them with one click.

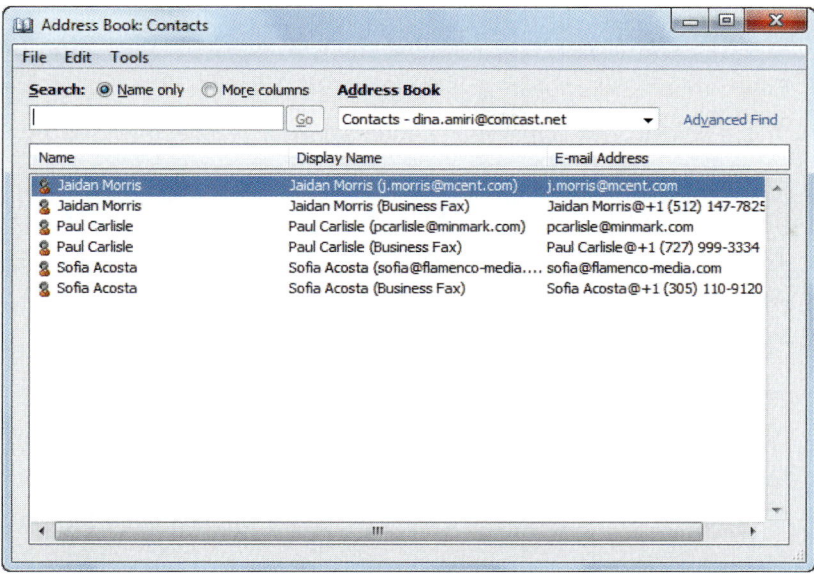

FIGURE 1–10   View contacts in the Address Book window

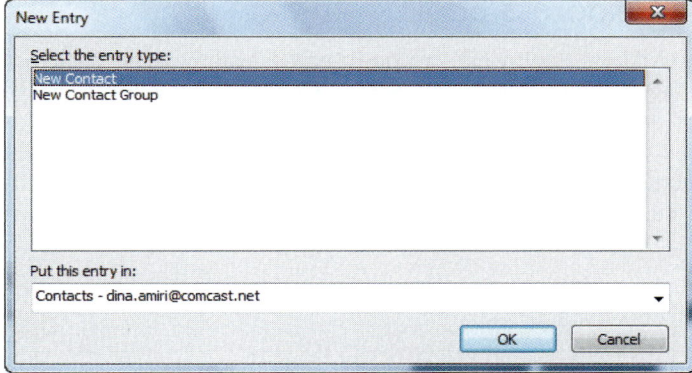

FIGURE 1–11   New Entry dialog box

Step-by-Step 1.6

1. Click the **Inbox** folder in the Mail section of the Navigation Pane to display the Inbox.

2. To display the Address Book, on the Home tab, in the Find group, click **Address Book**. The Address Book dialog box opens, as shown in Figure 1–10.

3. On the menu bar, click **File**, and then click **New Entry**. The New Entry dialog box opens, as shown in Figure 1–11.

4. In the New Entry dialog box, if not already selected, click **New Contact**, and then click **OK**. The new Contact window opens.

5. In the Full Name box, type your **first** and **last name**, and then press **Tab** or **Enter**. Your name appears as Last name, First name in the File as box.

6. In the E-mail box, type your **e-mail address** or one provided by your instructor.

7. On the Ribbon, on the Contact tab, click the **Save & Close** button in the Actions group. The Address Book dialog box reappears with your name added to the list.

8. Double-click the listing for **Paul Carlisle**. The Contact window opens, showing detailed information about Paul Carlisle.

9. When finished viewing, on the Ribbon, in the Actions group, click the **Save & Close** button to close the Contact window. Close the Address Book dialog box to return to the Inbox. Leave Outlook open for the next Step-by-Step.

Using an Address Book

To open the Address Book while creating a new e-mail message, click the To button in the Message window. The Select Names: Contacts dialog box opens with names from your Contacts list, as shown in **Figure 1–12**. Select the contact to whom you want to send the message, and then click the To button at the bottom of the dialog box. The contact's name appears in the To box. Click OK and the contact's name appears in the To box in the Message window as the recipient of the e-mail message. When you finish your e-mail message, click the Send button.

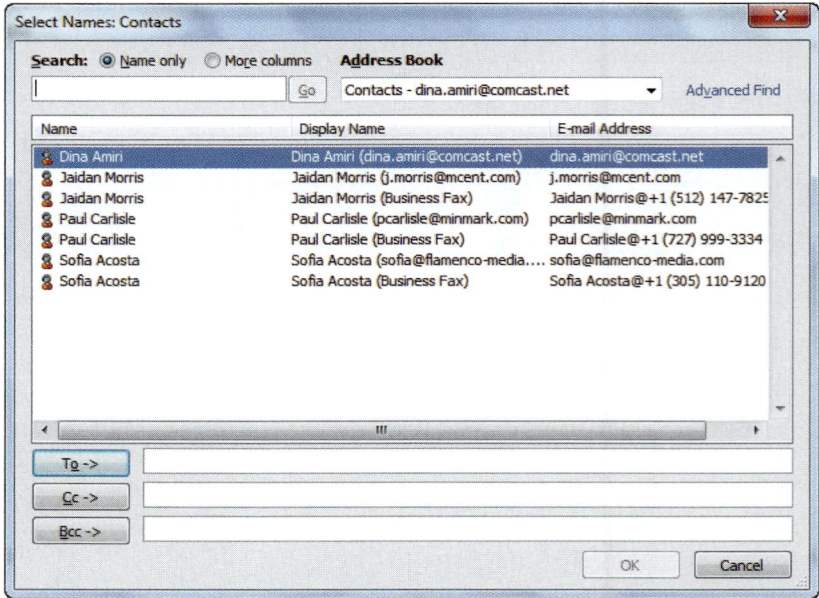

FIGURE 1–12   Select Names: Contacts dialog box

Step-by-Step 1.7

1. On the Ribbon, on the Home tab, in the New group, click the **New E-mail** button. A blank e-mail Message window opens.

2. Click the **To** box. The Select Names: Contacts dialog box opens, as shown in Figure 1–12.

3. Select **your name** from the list of contacts and then click the **To** button. Your name appears in the To box.

4. Click **OK**. The new Message window reappears, and your name appears in the To box as the recipient of the e-mail message.

5. In the Subject box, type **Tomorrow's meeting**.

6. In the Message area, type **Late starting time: 1:30 pm**.

7. Click the **Send** button.

8. Click the **Sent Items** folder in the Mail Folder section of the Navigation Pane to see the sent message. (*Note:* If you do not receive the message shortly, click the Send/Receive All Folders button on the toolbar.) Leave Outlook open for the next Step-by-Step.

Creating a Contact Group

You can use your time more efficiently by creating contact groups. *Contact groups* are collections of contacts that provide an easy way to send messages to everyone within a group or department. They eliminate the need to individually select e-mail recipients.

To create a contact group, click the Contacts view button in the Navigation Pane. On the Home tab, in the New group, click the New Contact Group button. A new Contact Group window opens with the title Untitled – Contact Group. In the Name box, type a unique name for the contact group. On the Ribbon, on the Contact Group tab, in the Members group, click Add Members, and then select where you want to add members for your contact group: From Outlook Contacts, From Address Book, or from New E-mail Contact. Select the names you want to include in your contact group by typing them in the Search box or by selecting them in the list, and then click the Members button. When you are finished, click OK, and then on the Contact Group tab, in the Actions group, click Save & Close. The new contact group appears in the current view selected in the Reading Pane.

▶ **VOCABULARY**
Contact groups

Step-by-Step 1.8

1. In the Navigation Pane, click the **Contact** view button, then on the Ribbon, on the Home tab, in the New group, click the **New Contact Group** button. A blank Contact group window opens.

2. In the Contact Group window, in the Name box, type **Web 2.0 Marketing Blitz**.

3. On the Contact Group tab, in the Members group, click the **Add Members** button, and then click **From Outlook Contacts**. The Select Members window opens.

4. In the Search box, type **Sofia**, and then click the **Members** button at the bottom of the window.

5. Double-click **Jaidan Morris**. (*Note*: Click the entry that has his e-mail address, not the Business Fax number.)

6. When finished adding names, click **OK**. The Web 2.0 Marketing Blitz–Contact Group window has Sofia Acosta and Jaidan Morris listed as members.

7. On the Contact Group tab, in the Actions group, click **Save & Close**.

8. In the Reading Pane, right-click the **Web 2.0 Marketing Blitz** contact group, and then click **Quick Print** in the list.

9. In the Navigation Pane, click the **Mail** view button. Leave Outlook open for the next Step-by-Step.

TIP

To edit a contact group, view Contacts in the Reading Pane, and then double-click the contact group name to open it. You can edit a contact by double-clicking their name, and add or remove a contact by clicking an entry on the Contact Group tab, in the Members group.

Creating a Signature

You can change the appearance of your e-mail message by adding a background, color or image, or graphics, themes, even your digital business card. An easy way to add a professional or unique look and feel to your messages is to create a *signature* to add to the end of each of your messages.

To create a signature, open a new Message window, then, on the Ribbon, on the Message tab, in the Include group, click Signature, and then click Signatures. In the Signatures and Stationery dialog box, on the E-mail Signature tab, click New. In the New Signature dialog box, type a name for the signature and then click OK. In the Edit Signature box, type the text for your signature. Format the text, add images, electronic business cards, or hyperlinks as desired. In the Choose default signature section, click the New messages or Replies/forwards list arrows to select the signature so Outlook automatically includes it in new messages you send, or when you reply or forward message. Click OK to close the Signatures and Stationery dialog box.

▶ **VOCABULARY**
signature

TIP

While it may be tempting to add lots of graphics or a digital business card with your photo to your messages, be aware that many companies and individuals view e-mail messages in plain text. Plain text does not support graphics of any kind, but helps prevent viruses and obviously reduces the file size of the message.

Step-by-Step 1.9

1. On the Ribbon, on the Home tab, in the New group, click the **New E-mail** button. On the Message tab, in the Include group, click the **Signature** button, and then click **Signatures**. The Signatures and Stationery dialog box opens.

2. In the Signatures and Stationery dialog box, on the E-mail Signature tab, in the Select signature to edit section, click **New**. In the New Signature dialog box, type **your name** and then click **OK**. A new signature is added to the list, and the Signatures and Stationery dialog box looks similar to **Figure 1–13**.

Your name will differ

Your e-mail account will differ

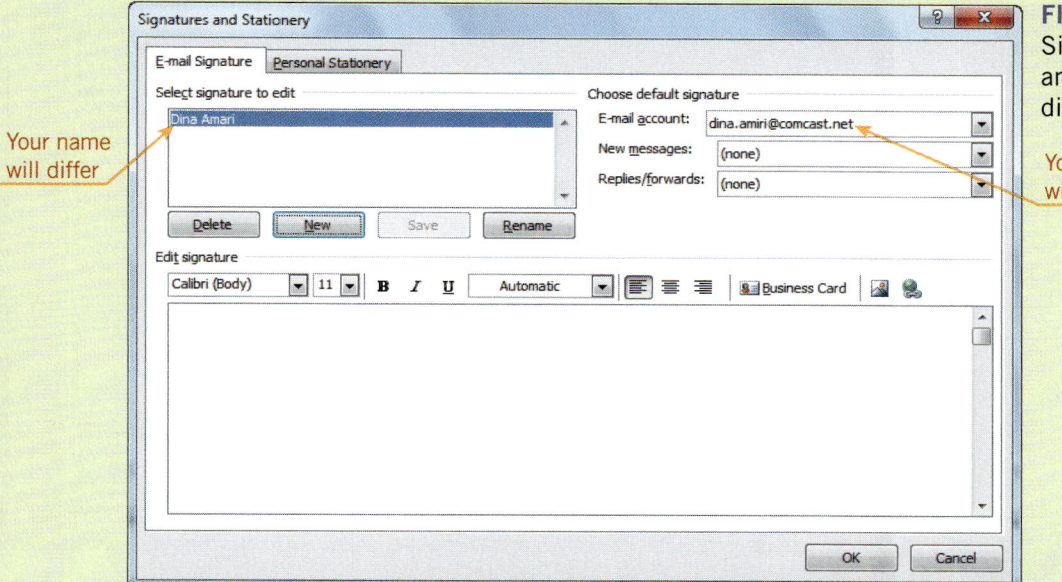

FIGURE 1–13
Signatures and Stationery dialog box

3. In the Edit signature section, click the **Italic** button *I*. Click the **Font arrow**, scroll down, and then click **Candara**. Click the **Font Size** arrow and then click **12**.

4. In the Edit signature box, type **your name**. In the Select signature to edit section, click the **Save** button.

5. In the Choose default signature section, make sure that your name appears in the New messages box. If necessary click the **New Messages** arrow, and then select your name. Click **OK** to close the Signatures and Stationery dialog box. Your signature is saved for new messages.

6. Close the new **Message window**, and then on the Home tab, in the New group, click the **New E-mail** button. Your signature appears in the message area. Leave Outlook open for the next Step-by-Step.

TIP

To manually insert a signature into a single message, on the Ribbon, in the Include group, click Signature. In the Signatures and Stationery dialog box, in the Choose default signature section, click the New messages list arrow, and then click the signature name you want to include.

Attaching Files to E-Mail Messages

TIP

To attach an e-mail message, business card, or calendar to a message, on the Message tab, in the Include group, click the Attach Item button, and then select an option.

Outlook enables you to attach a variety of files to e-mail messages and send them to others. After you have created and addressed a new message, on the Ribbon, on the Message tab, in the Include group, click the Attach File button. The Insert File dialog box opens, showing the folders and files in the Documents folder, similar to **Figure 1–14**. Browse to the location where the file is located, then click the file to select it. At the bottom of the dialog box, click the Insert button. In the Message window, the attached file appears in the Attached box.

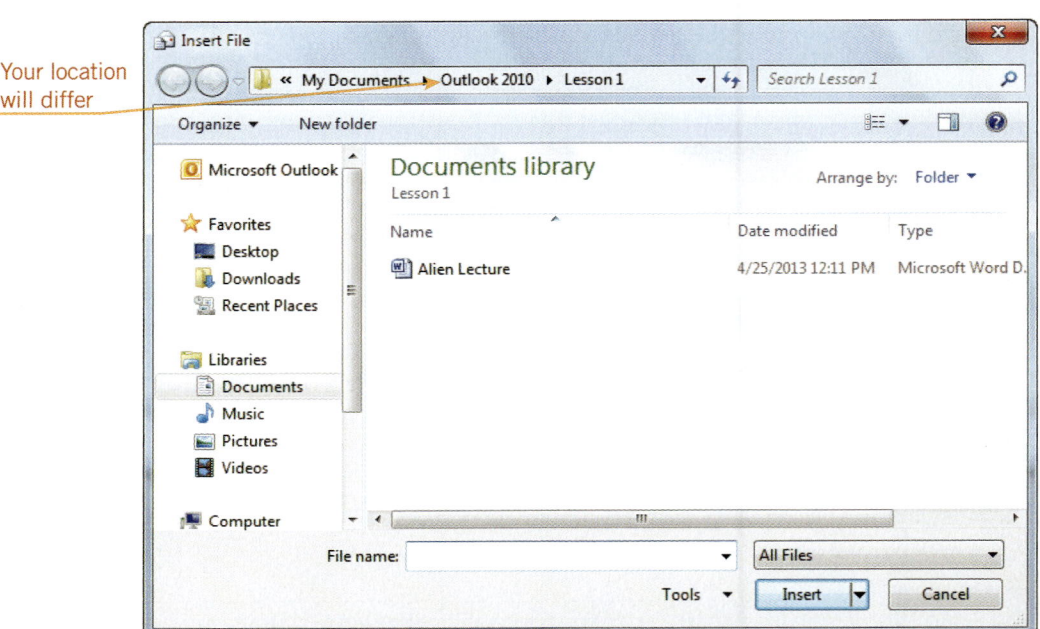

Your location will differ

FIGURE 1–14   Insert File dialog box

Step-by-Step 1.10

TIP

You can also double-click a name to add it to the To box.

1. On the Ribbon, on the Home tab, in the New group, click the **New E-mail** button.

2. Click the **To** button. The Select Names window opens.

3. In the Select Names window, click your **name** from the list of contacts and then click the **To** button. Your name appears in the To box.

4. Click **OK**. Your name appears as the recipient in the new e-mail.

5. In the Subject box, type **Planetarium announcement**.

6. On the Message tab, in the Include group, click the **Attach File** button. The Insert File dialog box opens, as shown in Figure 1–14.

7. In the Insert File dialog box, locate the folder where your Data Files are stored, click the **Alien Lecture** Word document, and then click the **Insert** button at the bottom of the dialog box. The document name appears in the Attached box in the Message window.

8. Click the **Send** button. You are the recipient of the e-mail and the attachment. Leave Outlook open for the next Step-by-Step.

TIP

You can attach many different file types to your messages, including photographs, illustrations, sound, video, text, and spreadsheet files. Note, however, that the maximum attachment size you can mail depends on what your Internet Service Provider (ISP), allows and what your recipient's ISP allows, which can range from 1MB to over 50MB.

Creating, Moving, and Archiving Folders

At times it is necessary to clean off your desk, file some papers, and discard accumulated documents. There will be times when your Outlook mailbox also needs to be reorganized and cleaned out. The process of organizing, storing, and saving old documents is called *archiving*. Outlook can archive all items, including attachments, which manages space in your Inbox.

▶ **VOCABULARY**
archiving

You can create new folders to organize documents from the Inbox. On the Ribbon, on the Folder tab, in the New group, click the New Folder button. The Create New Folder dialog box opens, as shown in **Figure 1–15**. In the Name box, type the name of the folder you want to create. In the Folder contains box, select what you want to store in the folder, such as the default selection, Mail and Post Items. In the Select where to place the folder box, click the location where you want to place the new folder. Click OK, and the new folder appears in the list of folders in the Navigation Pane.

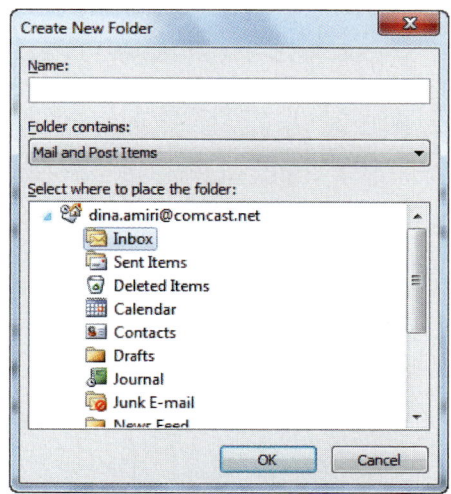

FIGURE 1–15   Create New Folder dialog box

TIP

To view items in an archived folder, in the Navigation Pane, click Archives.

You can transfer old files to a storage file by clicking the File tab, and then click Info in Backstage view. Click Cleanup Tools, and then click Archive, as shown in **Figure 1–16**. The Archive dialog box opens, as shown in **Figure 1–17**. Select the option to Archive this folder and all subfolders and then select the folder to be archived. In the Archive items older than box, click the arrow and select a date from the calendar. Click OK, and all of the files in your folder with dates prior to the date you selected are archived.

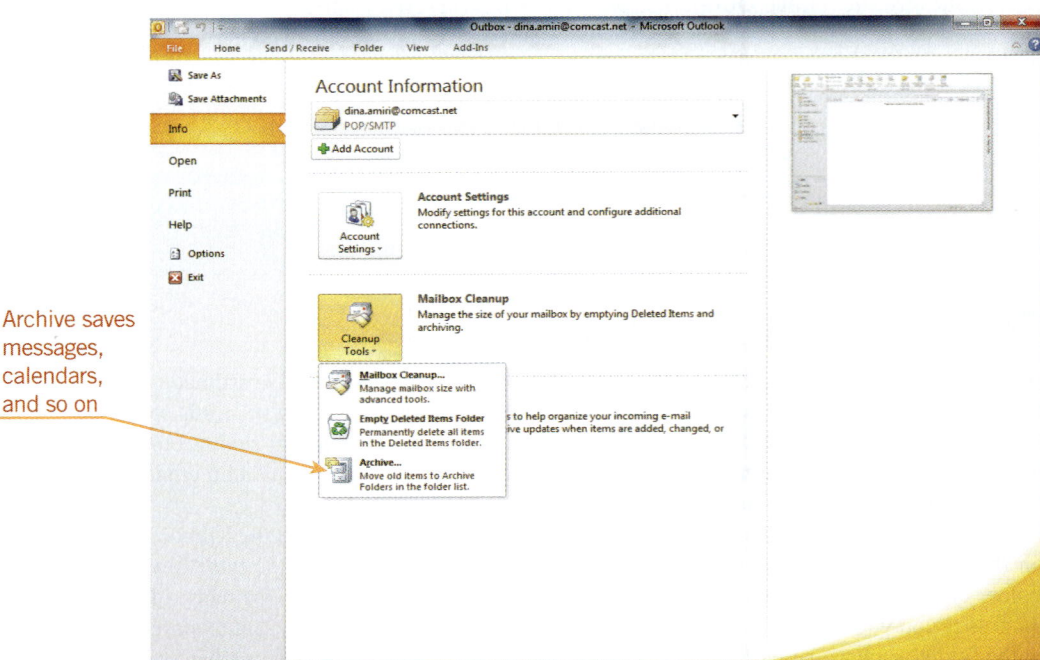

Archive saves messages, calendars, and so on

FIGURE 1–16   View Cleanup Tools in Backstage view

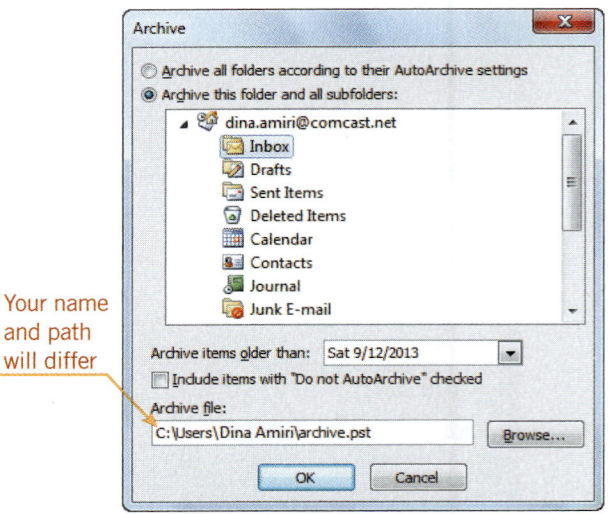

Your name and path will differ

FIGURE 1–17   Archive dialog box

Step-by-Step 1.11

1. On the Ribbon on the Folder tab, click **New Folder**. The Create New Folder dialog box opens.

2. In the Create New Folder dialog box, in the *Name* box, type **Outlook Lesson 1**. In the Folder contains box, make sure that **Mail and Post Items** is selected.

3. In the Select where to place the folder box, click **Inbox**, and then click **OK**. The new folder appears as a subfolder under Inbox folder in the Navigation Pane.

4. In the Inbox, select the message named **Planetarium announcement**. Place the pointer on the selected message and then drag the message to the Outlook Lesson 1 folder in the Navigation Pane. When finished, click the **Outlook Lesson 1** folder to view its contents; the message appears in the folder.

5. Click the **Sent Items** folder in the Navigation Pane. Select the **Planetarium announcement** message you previously sent to yourself.

6. Click the **File** tab, and then in Backstage view, click **Info**, click **Cleanup Tools**, and then click **Archive**, as shown in Figure 1–16. Click the menu bar and then click **Archive**. The Archive dialog box opens.

7. In the Archive dialog box, click the **Sent Items** folder in the Archive this folder and all subfolders section, and then the **Archive items older than arrow**. A calendar opens. Choose a date approximately three months prior to today's date and then click **OK**. Your messages with dates prior to the date you selected are archived.

8. Click the **Home** tab, then click the **Inbox** folder in the Navigation Pane. Leave Outlook open for the next Step-by-Step.

> **TIP**
>
> To specify when AutoArchive runs or to turn it off, on the Ribbon, on the Folder tab, in the Properties group, click the AutoArchive Settings button, and then adjust settings as desired.

Saving, Searching, and Deleting E-Mail Messages

There are many occasions when you might need to e-mail messages in a different file type to your hard drive or flash drive. To save a message as a text, HTML (Web page) file, or in an Outlook message format, click the File tab, and then in Backstage view, click Save As. Click the Address bar arrow and navigate to the location where you want to save the message. By default, the file name is the message's subject line and the default file type is an Outlook message format. You can use the Search Inbox box to find e-mail messages matching specific criteria, such as those containing keywords. Note that if you type more than one word, Outlook will search for messages that contain each individual word in any part of the message. If you want to search for a particular phrase, such as "surprise party," you must type the words in quotation marks. When you click the Search Inbox box, the Search Tools Search tab appears, as shown in **Figure 1–18**. Here you can select where you want to look for messages and the attributes of the messages, such as who sent them, and category, and whether the messages have attachments.

Click Search text box to open Search tab

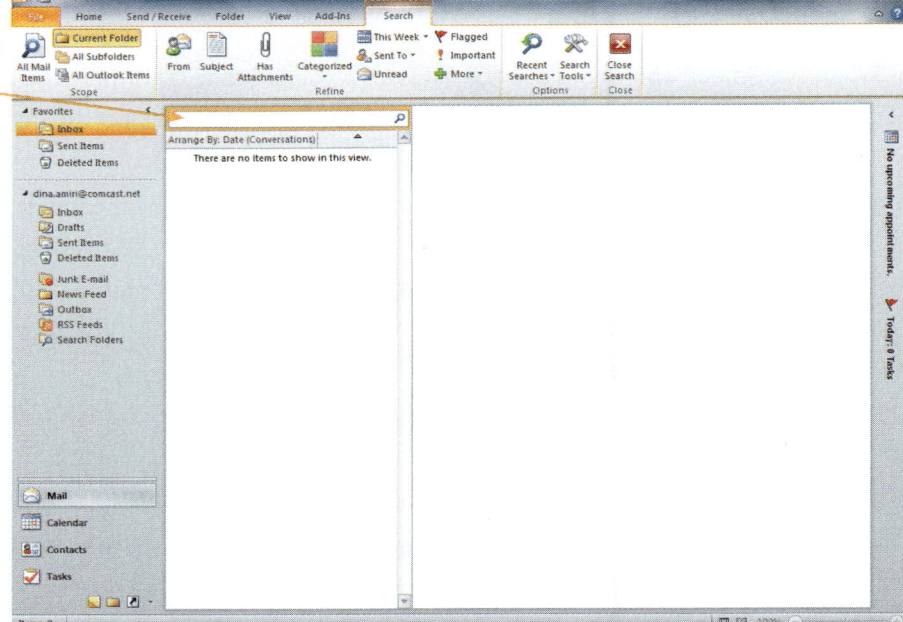

FIGURE 1–18   Search tools for finding messages

TIP

By default, Outlook groups messages with the same subject into a single folder, known as a **conversation**. This makes it easy to track the discussion on a topic. To clean up the redundant messages and keep only the ones that contain unique content, select a conversation in the Inbox, and then on the Home tab, in the Delete group, click the Clean Up button, and then select whether to clean up by conversation, folder, or folder and subfolders. You can change how Outlook cleans up messages by clicking the Settings button in a cleanup dialog box, or by clicking the File tab, and then clicking Options in Backstage view.

To delete a message, select the message to be deleted in the Inbox and then on the Home tab, in the Delete group, click the Delete button. You can also press Delete on the keyboard or click and drag the message to the Deleted Item folder in the Navigation Pane. The message is moved to the Deleted Items folder, where you can later retrieve or permanently delete it.

Step-by-Step 1.12

1. On the Ribbon, on the Home tab, in the New group, click the **New E-mail** button. A new Message window opens.

2. In the To box, type **your e-mail address** or one provided by your instructor.

3. In the Subject box, type **To Be Deleted**.

4. In the Message area, type **Delete this message**.

5. Click the **Send** button. After receiving the e-mail, double-click the **message** to open it.

6. Click the **File** tab, and then click **Save As** in Backstage view. The Save As dialog box opens.

7. Navigate to the folder where you save files for this course. The title of the e-mail message appears in the File name box.

8. Click **Save**, and the message is saved as an HTML document in the folder you selected.

9. Close the message, then, on the Navigation Pane, click **Inbox**.

10. In the Reading Pane, click the **Search Inbox** box, type **Delete this message**. Notice that as soon as you begin typing, Outlook highlights the words in messages that match the search criteria and displays the first message in the Reading Pane.

11. Click the **message** to select it, if necessary, and then press **Delete** on the keyboard. The message is sent to the Deleted Items folder.

12. Click the **Close** button in the upper-right corner of the window to close Outlook. The Outlook window closes and the Microsoft Windows desktop appears.

TIP

By default, Outlook searches the current folder for messages that contain the keywords. To expand the search into other folders, after you perform the first search, on the Search Tools' Search tab, in the Scope group, click the Current Folder button, or click Try searching again in All Mail Items in the message list.

SUMMARY

In this lesson, you learned:

- Outlook is a desktop information manager that helps you organize information, communicate with others, and manage your time. You can use the various features of Outlook to send and receive e-mail, schedule events and meetings, store information about business and personal contacts, create to-do lists that integrate with your appointments, record information about interactions, create reminders, and subscribe to online content feeds.

- The Contacts list is a useful tool where you can store mail, phone, and other information about people and companies. You can view or print your contacts in several ways, including as address cards or as a phone list.

- E-mail has is an essential global communications tool, accessible from many different devices. In addition to your computer, you can use e-mail from pocket PCs that can also play games, or smartphones, such as Blackberries and iPhones.

- Most of the time you will be sending e-mail messages to the same people. To make sending an e-mail message easier, you can use an Address Book, listing the addresses that you use most often.

- Using contact groups to send the same message to several people is efficient and allows you to use or modify the list however you need.

- Adding an electronic signature to your e-mail messages helps set the right tone for your contacts and correspondence. Outlook allows you to attach background color, photos, and graphics for a distinctive touch.

- Using Outlook, you can send e-mail messages to others connected to your network or to anyone around the world with an Internet connection. Outlook enables you to attach a variety of files to e-mail messages and send these files to others. You can view and organize your messages in a variety of ways, as well as archive them and save them to your computer.

◼ VOCABULARY REVIEW

Define the following terms:

Address Book	Contact groups	Reading Pane
archive	e-mail	Ribbon
Bcc	Navigation Pane	signature
contact	Quick Steps	Spam

◼ REVIEW QUESTIONS

TRUE / FALSE

Circle T if the statement is true or F if the statement is false.

T   F   **1.**   The Navigation Pane contains a calendar.

T   F   **2.**   The default view for Contacts is Phone list.

T   F   **3.**   In the Contact window, you can add a photograph or a nickname to the contact's listing.

T   F   **4.**   You can create multiple contact groups, but you cannot edit one after you create it.

T   F   **5.**   You can create multiple signatures for your messages.

FILL IN THE BLANK

Complete the following sentences by writing the correct word or words in the blanks provided.

1. When you delete an e-mail message, Outlook automatically moves it to the _____ folder.

2. To include an e-mail recipient, but hide his or her name, you use the _____ field in the Message window.

3. If you want to add a color bar to a contact or e-mail message, you click the _____ button in the Tags group.

4. The feature that includes one or more actions with a one-click button is known as a _____ _____.

5. When you work with messages in folders such as Inbox, Deleted Items, and Sent Mail, you are working in the _____ _____.

WRITTEN QUESTIONS

Write a brief answer to the following questions.

1. What is a contact?

2. Name two different devices on which you can use e-mail.

3. Name three types of contact information included in the Contact window.

4. Explain the importance of creating contact groups.

5. Explain what an e-mail signature is and how it is useful.

◼ PROJECTS

PROJECT 1–1

You recently met two people you want to add to your Contacts list.

1. Display your current contacts.

2. Add the two contacts using this information. Save and close when you finish.

Name: **Austin Trujillo**

Job Title: **Associate Professor**

Company: **Clark Junior College**

Address: **1880 Orchard Road**

Berkshire, VT 53217

Business Phone: **(420)115-7642**

Mobile: **(420)115-7666**

Business Fax: **(420)115-7644**

E-mail: **a_trujillo@cjc.edu**

Category: **Purple** (name it **School**)

Name: **Allie Hunter**

Job Title: **Head Pro**

Company: **Litchfield Tennis Club**

Address: **34 Segalla Lane**

Litchfield, PA 60211

Home Phone: **(709)555-0901**

Mobile: **(709)919-3779**

E-mail: **hunter@spoloc.org**

Category: **Blue** (name it **Friends**)

3. View the Contacts list as Cards.

4. View the Contacts list as a Phone List.

5. Print a copy of your Contacts list as a Phone List.

6. Delete one of the contacts you typed.

7. Leave Outlook open for the next project.

PROJECT 1–2

Create and send an e-mail message to your staff concerning the monthly staff meeting.

1. Display messages in the Inbox.

2. Create a new mail message and type your **e-mail address** or the e-mail address of a classmate in the To box.

3. Type **Monthly Staff Meeting** as the subject.

4. In the message area, type **Meeting held in Conference Room A from 2:00 to 3:30 p.m. Be prepared to give an update on projects.**

5. Click the High Importance button to identify the message as high priority.

6. Send the message.

7. Open the Sent Items folder to see the sent message. (*Note*: It might take a few minutes for your message to arrive.)

8. Open the message and then print it.

9. Delete the e-mail message.

10. Leave Outlook open for the next project.

PROJECT 1–3

Create and send an e-mail message to yourself about the promotion of a staff member.

1. Open a new message, and then create or edit your signature by changing its font style and color and another attribute of your choice.

2. Create a new e-mail message and send it to yourself. Access your e-mail address from the Address Book.

3. Type **Congratulations to Larissa Jenkins** as the subject.

4. In the message area, type: **Please join me in congratulating Larissa Jenkins, who has been promoted to Creative Director. This promotion is well deserved!**

5. Send the message.

6. Open the Sent Items folder to view the sent message.

7. Print this e-mail message.

8. Delete this e-mail message.

9. Close Outlook.

■ CRITICAL THINKING

ACTIVITY 1–1

Streamline your workflow in Outlook by setting the options to use a Quick Step. Create a new folder in the Inbox. Select a message in the Inbox, and then on the Home tab, in the Quick Steps group, click the Move to: button. Rename the Quick Step to Move to: *the name of the new folder*. Next, in the Action s section, select the folder from the Choose folder list, and then save the Quick Step. Test the Quick Step with another message.

LESSON 2

Calendar

■ OBJECTIVES

Upon completion of this lesson, you should be able to:

- View Calendar.
- Schedule and change appointments.
- Schedule, change, and delete events.
- Schedule a meeting and respond to a meeting request.
- Customize the Calendar.
- Print a calendar.

■ VOCABULARY

appointment

Date Navigator

event

meeting

resources

task

Introducing Calendar

Outlook Calendar is designed to help you stay organized and coordinate your activities with others. Calendar lets you enter your activities, such as appointments, meetings, events, and tasks. You can create these actions quickly using buttons in the New group on the Home tab. An *appointment* is an activity that involves only you at a set date and time (although you have the option to invite or involve other people if you wish). A *meeting* is similar to an appointment, in that it has a scheduled date and time, but includes other people and a place, even if it is a virtual location, such as a conference call. An *event*, such as a conference or school orientation, can last over the course of one or more days. Since it doesn't fit in a single time slot, it appears at the top of the Calendar beneath the affected days. The last item, *task*, also involves only you and appears in the Tasks area when you select Work Week or Week views. You'll learn more about tasks in the next lesson.

The Calendar can help you stay organized by allowing you to schedule your activities on a daily, weekly, monthly, or yearly basis. To help you anticipate and prepare for your upcoming appointments, meetings, events, and tasks, Calendar can create reminders and categorize your activities so you can view them quickly and easily. You can schedule meetings using Calendar and, because Outlook is an integrated program, you can receive responses to planned meetings through e-mail.

Viewing the Calendar

The Calendar, shown in **Figure 2–1**, allows you to enter your appointments, meetings, events, and tasks. You can display the Calendar by clicking the Calendar folder button or the Calendar icon on the Navigation Pane, or by clicking a date in the Date Navigator.

You can view the Calendar in various time periods or by type of action. In Figure 2–1, the Calendar is displayed in Week view, where you can view appointments, meetings, events, and tasks for a full week. To change the view option, on the Ribbon, on the Home tab, click a view in the Arrange group. You can change the Calendar to Day, Work Week (typically Monday–Friday), Week, Month, or Schedule View (where you can view the calendar appointments and meeting for one or more people). Cells in the Calendar display the scheduled activities for the time frame you choose.

Use the *Date Navigator*, the monthly Calendar at the top of the Navigation Pane, to change dates by clicking the date you want to view. You can change months by clicking the Back or Forward arrows next to the month.

VOCABULARY

appointment

meeting

event

task

Date Navigator

WARNING

If the To-Do Bar is visible, the Date Navigator appears on the right side of the Outlook window. To turn off the To-Do Bar, click the View tab, in the Layout group, click the To-Do Bar button, and then click Off.

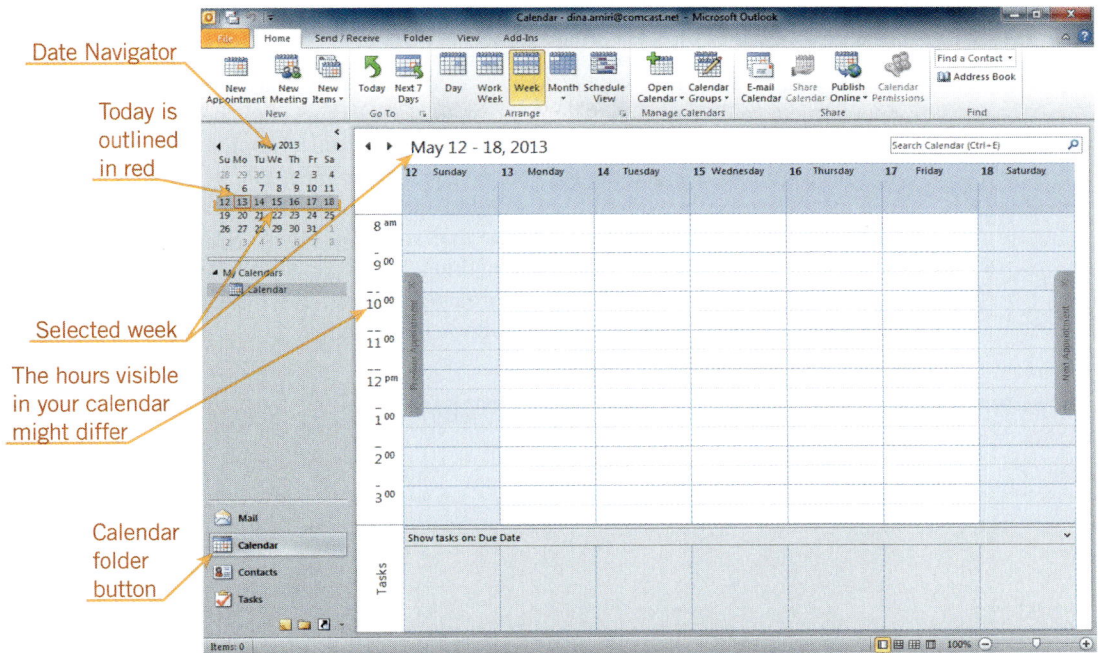

Date Navigator

Today is outlined in red

Selected week

The hours visible in your calendar might differ

Calendar folder button

FIGURE 2–1   Viewing the Calendar

Step-by-Step 2.1

1. Start Outlook, then on the Navigation Pane, click the **Calendar** button and then on the Home tab, in the Arrange group, click the **Week** button, if necessary. The Calendar opens, similar to Figure 2–1.

2. In the Arrange group, click the **Day** button. In the Date Navigator, click **tomorrow's date**. Notice that the date changes automatically in the Calendar. If you have appointments scheduled, they appear in the appropriate time cell.

3. In the Arrange group, click the **Month** button to display the month. Notice that today's date is outlined in red in the Date Navigator and is highlighted in yellow on the calendar.

4. In the Arrange group, click the **Week** button to return to Week view.

5. Click the **Forward** button 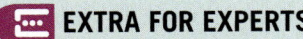 next to the date to display next week's schedule. Notice that the highlighted week in the Date Navigator changes as you scroll to the next week. Leave the Calendar open for the next Step-by-Step.

EXTRA FOR EXPERTS

You can move a few months at a time in the Calendar by pressing and holding the name of the month in the Date Navigator and then clicking a month in the list. To quickly move to a date several months or years away, press and hold a Back or Forward arrow button.

Scheduling an Appointment

To add an appointment to your Calendar, select the day for which you want to set up the appointment, and then on the Home tab, in the New group, click the New Appointment button. A new Appointment window opens, with the title Untitled – Appointment, as shown in **Figure 2–2**. On the Ribbon, on the Appointment tab, in the Actions group, you can determine how to proceed with the appointment. In the Show group, you can click the Scheduling button to view the free and busy times of optional participants, which is helpful for determining meeting times. The Insert tab allows you to insert files, signatures, images, media, and other formatted objects. The Format Text and Review, and tabs operate the same across the Outlook interface.

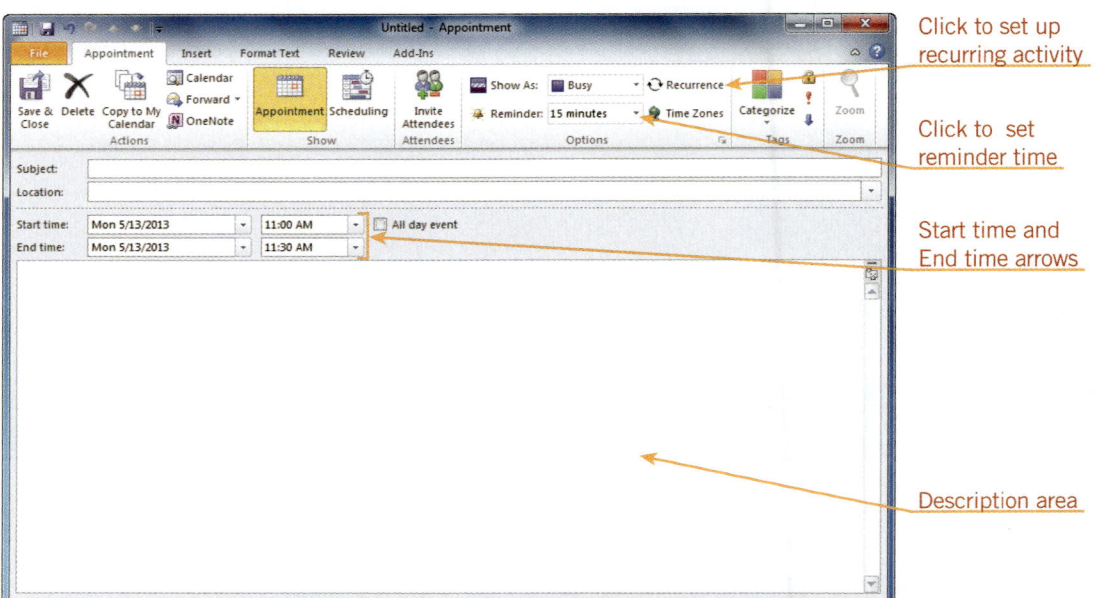

FIGURE 2–2   New Appointment window

On the Appointment tab, in the Options group, in the Show As box, you can designate how an appointment is marked in the Calendar. You can show an appointment as free, tentative, busy, or out of office. In the Reminder box, you can set up a reminder of how often Outlook notifies you of an appointment. You can choose not to be reminded, or to be reminded any time from when the appointment actually starts to two weeks ahead of time. You can also select a custom reminder sound if you wish. When it is time for the reminder, the sound plays, and a dialog box opens, where you can dismiss the reminder, click the Snooze button to be reminded again later, or open the appointment to review the details. You can click the Recurrence button to set up an appointment to occur repeatedly, which is an effective tool to make sure you never miss an activity, no matter how busy you are. In the Tags group, you can click the Categorize button to color-code your appointments. The Private button prevents other users on an intranet or sharing an online calendar from viewing your appointment information. When Private is selected, a lock icon appears next to the appointment on the Calendar. You can also rank an appointment's importance as High or Low.

To create an appointment, type the subject and location of the appointment in the appropriate boxes. Click the up and down arrows to change the Start time or End time, if necessary. Select the All day event check box if the appointment is scheduled for the entire day.

When you have entered all the necessary information about the appointment, on the Ribbon, in the Actions group, click the Save & Close button to return to the Calendar. You'll see the appointment in the designated time.

TIP

When you invite participants to an appointment, Outlook automatically converts it to a meeting.

Step-by-Step 2.2

1. At the top of the Calendar, click the **Week** button, and then in the Date Navigator, click tomorrow's date, if necessary. The date is selected in the Calendar.

2. Click the **New Appointment** button on the toolbar. The Appointment window opens, as shown in Figure 2–2.

3. In the Subject box, type **Lunch with Zach Anderson**.

4. In the Location box, type **Tortilla Flats**.

5. In the Description area, type **Bring latest Web site prototypes**.

6. Click the **hour arrow** next to Start time and then click **11:30 AM**.

7. Click the **hour arrow** next to End time and then click **1:00 PM**. Notice that the end time options also tell you how long the appointment is scheduled to last, in this case, 1.5 hours.

8. On the Ribbon, in the Options group, click the **arrow** next to Show As, and then click **Out of Office**.

9. Click the **arrow** next to Reminder and then click **30 minutes**.

10. In the Tags group, click the **Private** button 🔒.

EXTRA FOR EXPERTS

You can quickly enter an appointment in Day or Week view by positioning the pointer over a time, clicking the cell when prompted, and then typing the details. Or, you can pre-select the appointment time by clicking a time cell to select it in the Calendar, and then clicking the New Appointment button on the Standard toolbar.

11. In the Actions group, click the **Save & Close** button. The appointment information and key icon appear in the appointment, as shown in **Figure 2–3**. The lock icon indicates that the appointment is private. Leave the Calendar open for the next Step-by-Step.

FIGURE 2–3
Viewing an appointment

Appointment time slots are blocked out

Default time slots are half hours

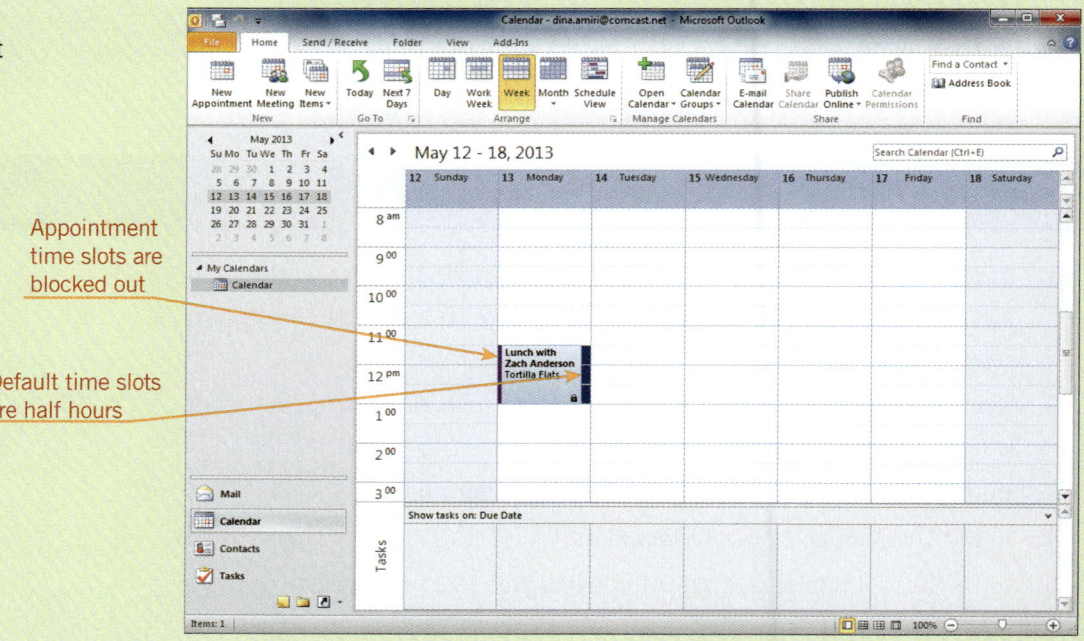

Changing an Appointment

EXTRA FOR EXPERTS

You can set the date and time for an appointment by typing the way you speak, such as "next Friday" or "midnight" in the date and time fields of the Appointment window; Outlook automatically converts the words into the correct date and time.

To simply move the start or end times of an appointment, view the appointment in Week or Day view, click the top or bottom border and drag to a new time. To move an appointment to an entirely new time, drag it to a new time or day. To edit an appointment, you select the appointment, and then use functions on the Appointment, Calendar Tools tab. To delete an appointment, click to select it, and then press Delete on the keyboard, or on the Calendar Tools tab, in the Actions group, click the Delete button. You can also edit an appointment by double-clicking it in any view. The Appointment window opens, where you can make changes.

Step-by-Step 2.3

1. On the Home tab, in the Arrange group, click the **Day** button, and then double-click the **Lunch with Zach Anderson** appointment. The Appointment window opens.

2. Change the Location to **The Deli Minsk**.

3. In the Description area, press **Enter** after the word *prototypes*, and then type the following:

Have Brad make reservations, see if Sofia can join us, and call Zach about changes.

4. In the Tags group, click the **Private** button to turn it off.

5. In the Actions group, click the **Save & Close** button. The appointment no longer contains the lock icon. Notice on the Ribbon that the Calendar Tools Appointment tab is active because you edited an existing appointment.

6. Press and hold the **Lunch with Zach Anderson** appointment, drag it down so the top border aligns with 12 pm, and then release the mouse button. The appointment times are now 12:00 pm to 1:30 pm.

7. Click the **Lunch with Zach Anderson** appointment to select it, position the pointer over the bottom appointment handle, and then when the pointer changes to a sizing pointer ↕, drag the border to **2 pm**. The appointment times are now 12:00 pm to 2:00 pm. See **Figure 2–4**.

> **TIP**
>
> You can press Tab to move around the fields in a dialog box.

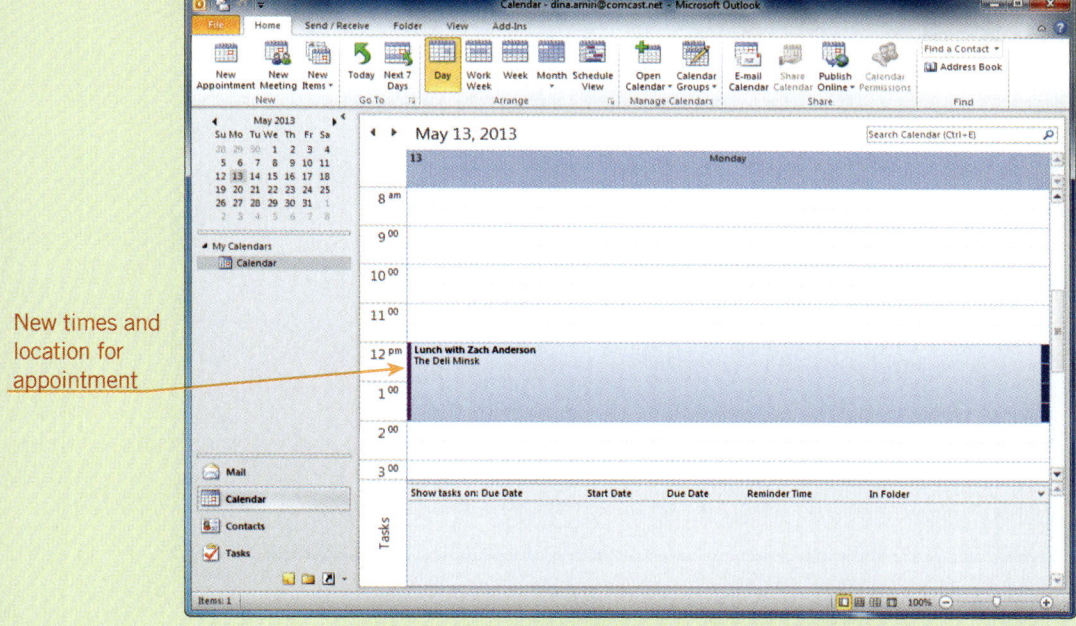

New times and location for appointment

FIGURE 2–4
Modified appointment

8. Position the pointer over the appointment until the subject, location, and times appear, similar to a ScreenTip. Notice that you can easily see the important details about the appointment. Leave the Calendar open for the next Step-by-Step.

Scheduling an Event

An event is an activity that usually lasts an entire day or more. Because it does not have an assigned time, it appears in the Calendar, but does not by default block out time in it. Instead, an event appears as a banner message at the top of the day or days affected. Other scheduled activities on those days appear normally. An annual event occurs every year on the same date, such as a birthday, or every year at a different time, such as a vacation or some holidays. A recurring event occurs at the same time every day, week, or month, such as a day-long managers' meeting that is scheduled every quarter (every three months). You can use your Calendar to schedule any type of event.

Use the Date Navigator to create the event. Next, on the Home tab, in the New group, click the New Appointment button, and then in the Appointment window, click the All day event check box next to the Start time. A new Event window opens with the title Untitled – Event, as shown in **Figure 2–5**. Tabs on the Ribbon are the same as for appointments, although events have different default settings, such as showing the event as free instead of busy. Fill in basic information about the event, such as subject, location, and description. Choose the Reminder option if you would like to be reminded of the event. For example, you could be reminded two days ahead of time to buy a birthday card for someone. The left side of the status bar shows how many reminders you have. On the Ribbon, in the Actions group, click the Save & Close button. The event appears as the top entry in any Calendar view.

> **TIP**
>
> You can also create a new event on the Home tab in the New group by clicking the New Items button, and then clicking All Day Event.

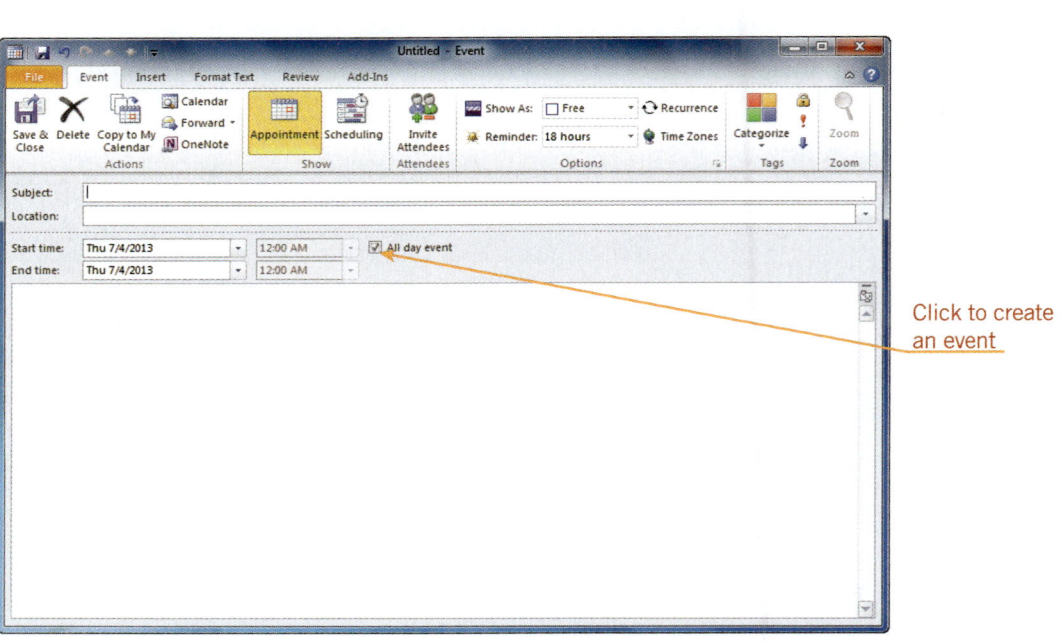

Click to create an event

FIGURE 2–5   Event window

If an event repeats at the same time, you can change it to a recurring event. In the Calendar, click the event, and then on the Ribbon, on the Calendar Tools, Appointment tab, in the Options group, click the Recurrence button to open the Appointment Recurrence dialog box. Or, if you have an Event window open, on the Ribbon in the Options group, click the Recurrence button to open the Appointment Recurrence dialog box. You can choose a recurrence pattern and your event will appear on the Calendar every day, week, month, or year. Type a range of recurrence or a beginning and end date for how long the event should appear in the Calendar. Choose OK to return to the Event window or Calendar, and notice that the title bar now contains the recurrence icon, which resembles a circular arrow.

> **EXTRA FOR EXPERTS**
>
> To remove a recurring event, double-click an event, click the Open the series option button, click OK, then in the Appointment Recurrence dialog box, click the Remove Recurrence button, and then click OK.

Step-by-Step 2.4

1. In the Date Navigator, find and click **July 4**.

2. If necessary, on the Home tab, in the Arrange group, click the **Month** button. In the New group, click the **New Appointment** button, and then click the **All day event** check box to select it.

3. Type the event information shown in **Figure 2–6**. On the Ribbon, in the Options group, click the **Show As** list arrow, click **Tentative**, click the **Reminder** list arrow, and then click **1 day**.

> **EXTRA FOR EXPERTS**
>
> If you deselect the All day event check box in the Event window, the event automatically becomes an appointment.

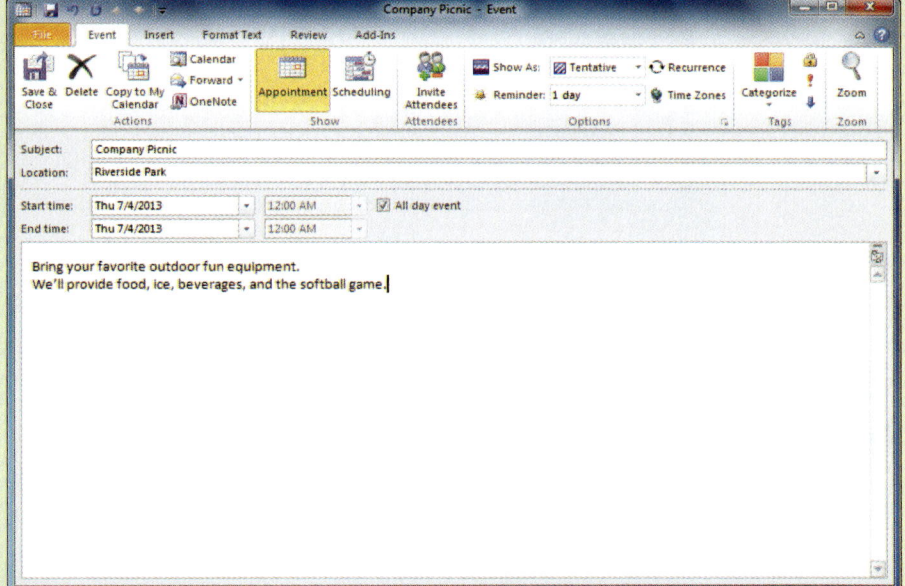

FIGURE 2–6
Add day event settings

4. When finished, in the Actions group, click the **Save & Close** button. The event appears with the Tentative striped pattern. In the Arrange group, click **Week**, and view the event in the Calendar.

5. In the Date Navigator, click the **back arrow**, and then click **June 10**.

6. On the Home tab, in the New group, click the **New Items** button, and then click **All Day Event**. A new Event window opens.

7. In the Subject box, type **Anthony's Birthday**.

8. On the Ribbon, in the Options group, click the **Recurrence** button. The Appointment Recurrence dialog box opens, similar to that shown in **Figure 2–7**.

FIGURE 2–7
Appointment Recurrence dialog box

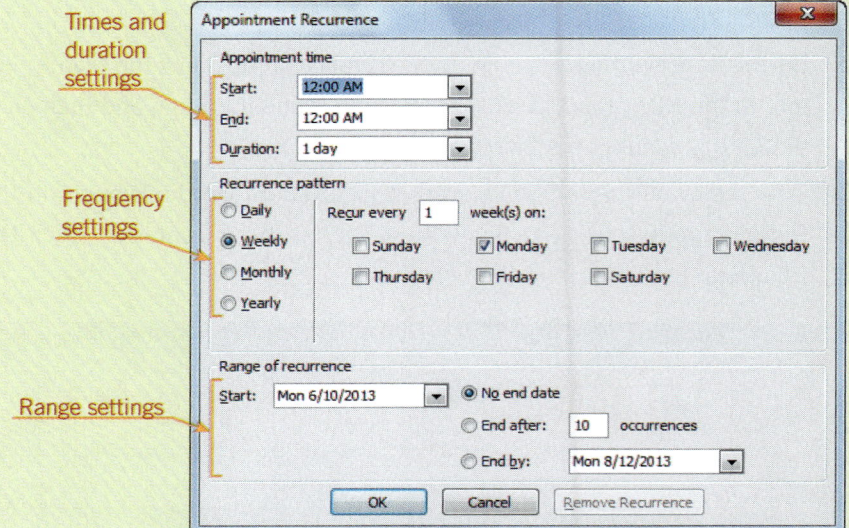

9. In the Recurrence pattern section, click the **Yearly** option button, and then click **OK**. In the Recurring Event window, the recurrence information appears beneath the Location text box.

10. In the Options group, click the **Reminder** arrow, and then click **1 day**.

11. In the Actions group, click the **Save & Close** button. Click the **Week** button at the top of the Calendar, if necessary. The event appears at the top of the day's actions, as shown in **Figure 2–8**. Leave the Calendar open for the next Step-by-Step.

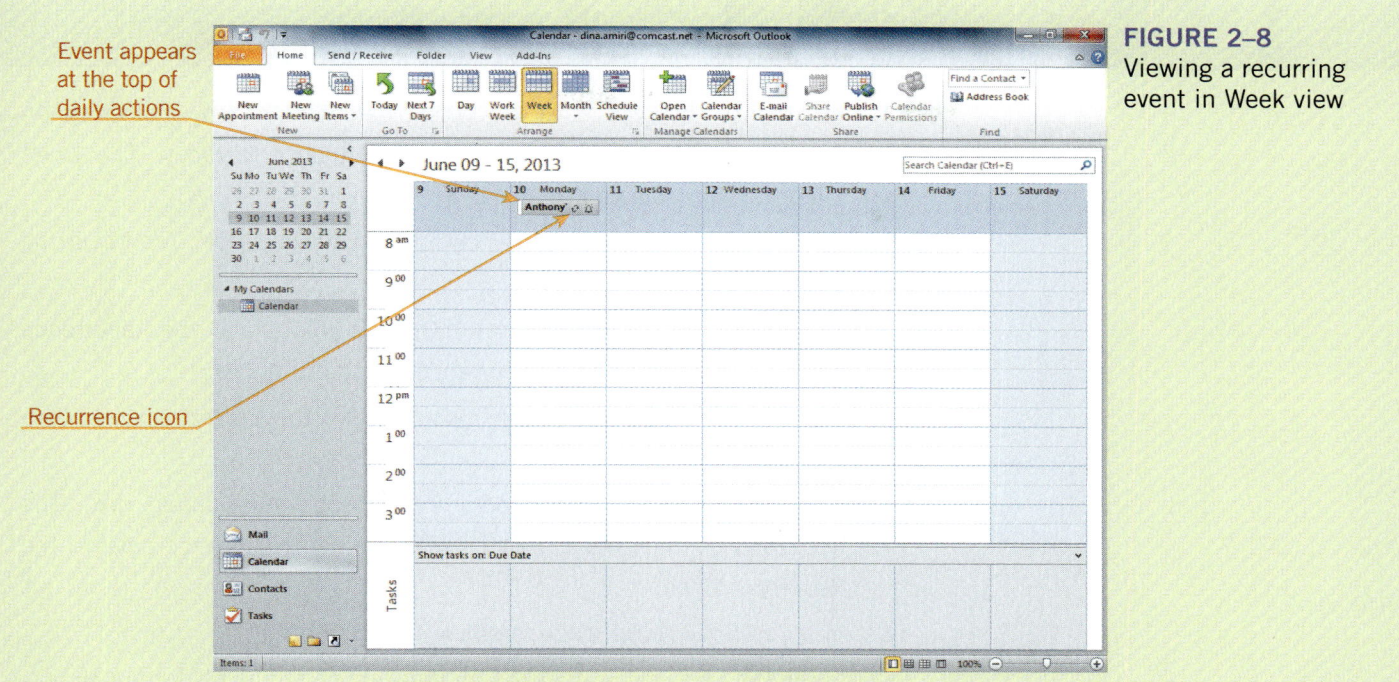

Event appears at the top of daily actions

Recurrence icon

FIGURE 2–8
Viewing a recurring event in Week view

Changing and Deleting an Event

To edit an event, double-click the event in the Calendar. If the event is nonrecurring, the Event window opens. If the event is marked as one that recurs, the Open Recurring Item dialog box opens, where you can choose whether to modify the single occurrence of the event or every occurrence of the event, as shown in **Figure 2–9**. When you select the Open this occurrence option button and then click OK, the Event window opens. Here you can edit specific settings that affect that individual event, such as start and end times or location. When you select the Open the series option button and then click OK, the Recurring Event window opens, where you can edit settings that affect the series of recurring actions, such as when it recurs. To do so, on the Recurrent Event tab, in the Options group, click the Recurrence button. You can then adjust options in the Appointment Recurrence dialog box. To delete an event, in the Actions group, click the Delete button, or right-click the event in the Calendar and then click Delete.

Modifies a single occurrence of the event

Modifies every occurrence of the event

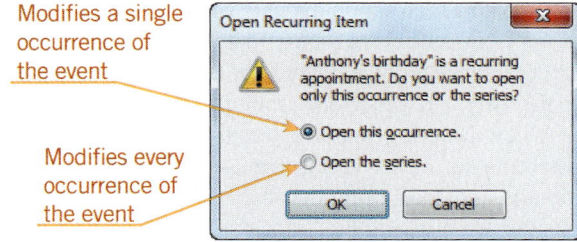

FIGURE 2–9 Open Recurring Item dialog box

Step-by-Step 2.5

1. You realize that you have the wrong date for Anthony's birthday. In the Calendar, double-click the event **Anthony's Birthday**. The Open Recurring Item dialog box opens, as shown in Figure 2–9.

2. Click the **Open the series** option button and then click **OK**. The Recurring Event window opens.

3. On the Recurring Event tab, in the Options group, click the **Recurrence** button. The Appointment Recurrence dialog box opens.

4. In the Recurrence pattern section, double-click the **day** text box, and then type **22**.

5. Click **OK** to close the Appointment Recurrence dialog box. The Recurring Event window appears with the new recurrence date on the Recurrence line.

6. In the Actions group, click the **Save & Close** button.

7. In the Date Navigator, click **22**. In the Arrange group, click the **Day** button. Anthony's Birthday event appears at the top of the Calendar.

8. Click **Anthony's Birthday** to select it and then on the Calendar Tools, Appointment Series tab, in the Actions group, click the **Delete** button, then click **Delete Series**. Anthony's Birthday event for June this year and all its occurrences are removed from the Calendar.

9. In the Go To group, click the **Today** button to go back to today's date. Leave the Calendar open for the next Step-by-Step.

TIP

You can change the date of a single occurrence in the Calendar by dragging the event to a different day, and then clicking Yes when prompted.

VOCABULARY
resources

Scheduling a Meeting and Responding to a Meeting Request

If you and your co-workers use Outlook, you can use your Calendar to schedule meetings and resources. Outlook places meetings in your Calendar just as it does for appointments and events. A meeting is an appointment to which you invite people and for which you schedule resources. *Resources* are rooms, materials, and/or equipment needed for a meeting, such as a conference room, computer, or large plasma screen.

To create a meeting, on the Home tab, in the New group, click the New Meeting button. A new Meeting window opens with the selection times and the title Untitled – Meeting, as shown in **Figure 2–10**. The Meeting window lets you select meeting details and send a notice of the meeting to attendees. If you first select the date in the Date Navigator, that day is selected in the Meeting window. On the Ribbon, on the Meeting tab, in the Actions group, you can determine how to proceed with the meeting request, such as by clicking the Calendar button to check for conflicts. The Show group function is the same as for events and appointments. Specific to meetings is the Attendees group. You can access the Address Book and the Check Names feature, and select the type of response to receive from attendees. Click the To button and select contacts to add as attendees, and then type a subject, location, description, and start and end times.

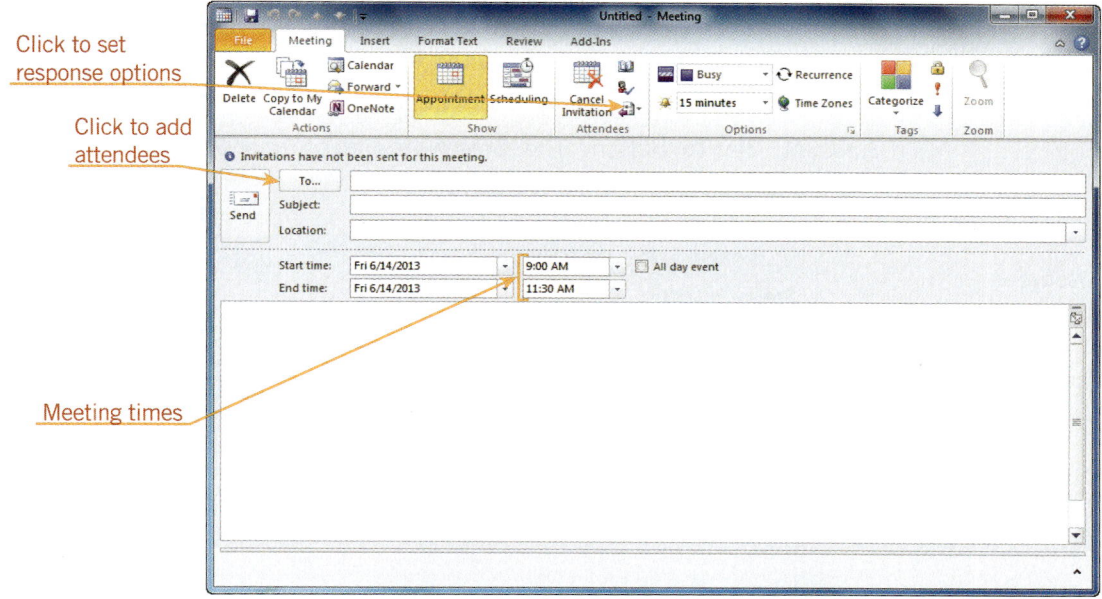

FIGURE 2–10 New Meeting window

You and your attendees can adjust for any meeting conflicts and find the best time for everyone to meet. Once attendees open a meeting invitation, they can perform several actions specific to the meeting. The new proposed meeting appears in a slice of the day's calendar alongside other appointments and meetings, making it easy to see if there is a conflict with another action. On the Ribbon, in the Respond group, attendees can accept, accept tentatively, or decline the invitation, and propose a new time. They can also delete, reply, reply to all, or forward the meeting message. The responses to the meeting requests appear in your Inbox.

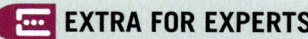 **EXTRA FOR EXPERTS**

If you have an existing e-mail message whose distribution list includes the same people you want to invite to a meeting, you can easily create a meeting request from the message. Open the message, and then in the Respond group, click the Reply with a Meeting button.

Step-by-Step 2.6

1. In the Date Navigator, choose a date, and then make sure you are in Day view. Click and hold the **9 am** time slot, and then drag to **11:30 am**. Five half-hour time slots are selected.

2. On the Home tab, in the New group, click the **New Meeting** button. The Meeting window opens with 9:00 AM selected as the Start time and 11:30 AM selected as the End time, as shown in Figure 2–10.

3. Click the **To** button. The Select Attendees and Resources window appears, as shown in **Figure 2–11**.

FIGURE 2–11
Select Attendees and Resources window

Your list of names will differ

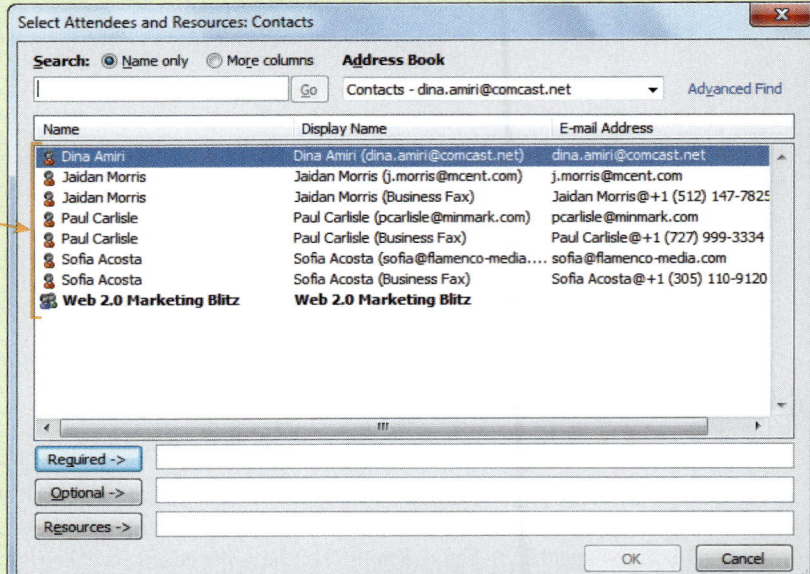

4. Press and hold **Ctrl** and then click each individual name in the list. (If the same name appears more than once, select the first instance.) Be sure to click your name, as well. When finished, click **Required**. Click the beginning of the Required box, type the e-mail address of a class-mate or an address given to you by your instructor, and then click **OK**.

5. In the Subject box, type **Contract Negotiations**. The subject text appears as the Meeting window title.

6. In the Location box, type **Algonquin Conference Room**.

7. On the Ribbon, in the Attendees group, click the **Response Options** button, and then make sure that both **Request Responses** and **Allow New Time Proposals** have check marks next to them.

8. In the Description area, type **Sorry for the late notification.** Compare your Meeting window to **Figure 2–12**.

FIGURE 2–12
Completed Meeting window

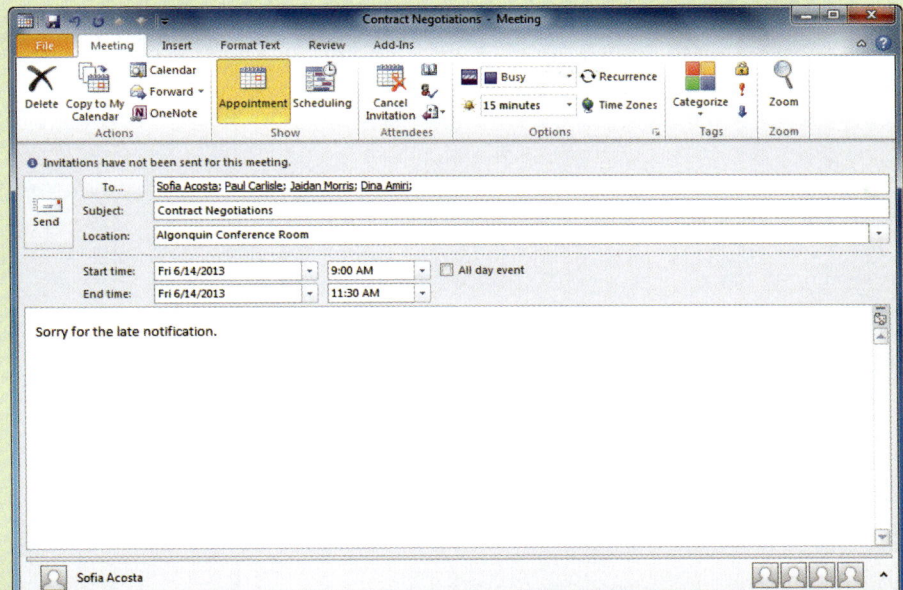

9. Click the **Send** button. Outlook sends the e-mail message to you and the attendees. The meeting appears in your Calendar at 9:00 am.

10. Click the **Mail** folder button on the Navigation Pane to see the meeting e-mail message you received. If necessary, click the Inbox folder in the Mail section of the Navigation Pane to display the Inbox view.

11. A meeting e-mail message has a calendar icon next to it, indicating that it is a meeting message. Double-click the meeting e-mail message you sent to yourself to open it. As the organizer, you do not need to respond to the request, and you can cancel the meeting and contact attendees. The meeting time appears in the message as it appears in Day view on your Calendar.

12. If possible, open the meeting e-mail message you sent to a classmate or other e-mail address on another computer. An attendee will receive a message that resembles **Figure 2–13**.

FIGURE 2–13
Attendee meeting e-mail message

Attendees select a meeting response option

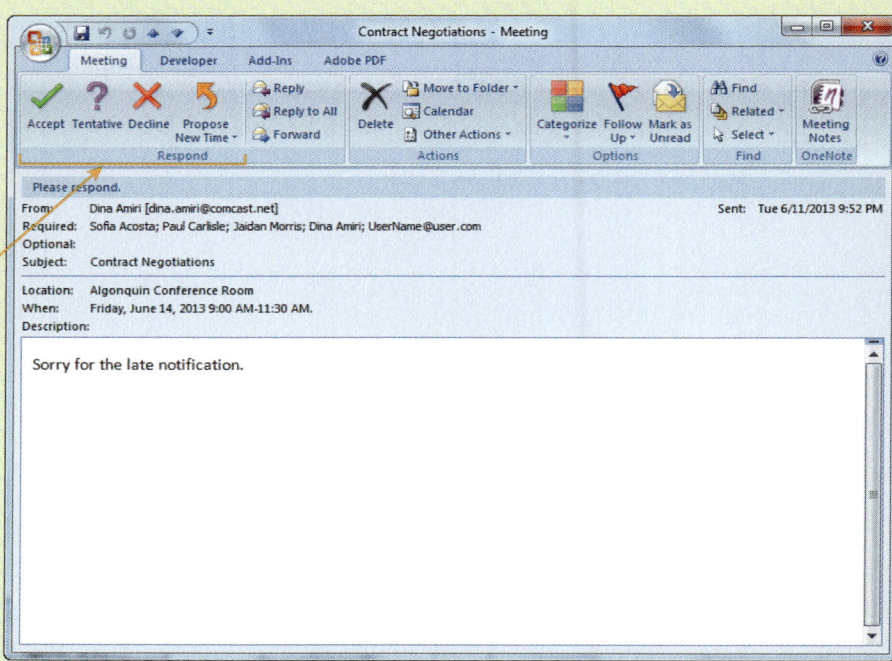

EXTRA FOR EXPERTS

To save a Meeting invitation without sending it, click the File tab, and then click Close. In the Microsoft Office Outlook dialog box, click the Save changes but don't send option button, and then click OK.

13. On the attendee's computer, on the Meeting tab, in the Respond group, click the **Accept** button ✓, and then click **OK** to send the response now. Outlook sends the acceptance back to the organizer.

14. On your computer, on the Navigation Pane, click the **Calendar** folder button to return to today's date in Calendar view. Leave the Calendar open for the next Step-by-Step.

Customizing the Calendar

You can modify many settings in the Calendar to adjust its appearance and how it displays time. For example, in Month view, you can adjust the amount of detail that is visible by clicking the launcher in the Arrange group to open the Outlook Options dialog box. The Calendar tab is selected, where you can adjust settings such as time, reminders, holidays, display colors and font, scheduling preferences. See **Figure 2–14**.

You can use keyboard commands to quickly switch between features in Outlook. **Table 2–1** shows common keyboard commands.

TIP

You can also open the Outlook Options dialog box by clicking the File tab, and then clicking Options, or by right-clicking a time cell and then clicking Calendar Options.

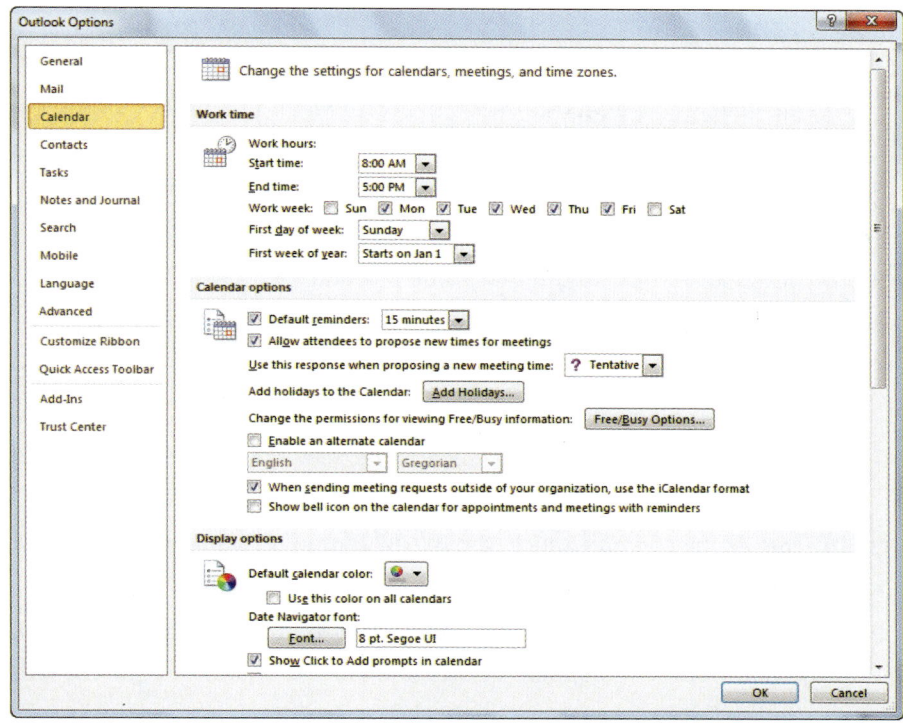

FIGURE 2–14   Calendar options in the Outlook Options dialog box

TABLE 2–1   Keyboard shortcuts for Outlook features

SHORTCUT	DESCRIPTION
CTRL KEY+1	Switch to Mail.
CTRL KEY+2	Switch to Calendar.
CTRL KEY+3	Switch to Contacts.
CTRL KEY+4	Switch to Tasks.
CTRL KEY+5	Switch to Notes.
CTRL KEY+6	Switch to Folder List in Navigation Pane.
CTRL KEY+7	Switch to Shortcuts.

Step-by-Step 2.7

1. In the Date Navigator, click the **date** that you scheduled the contract negotiations meeting. On the Home tab, in the Arrange group, click and hold the **Month** button, and then alternately click the **Low**, **Medium**, and **High** options. Notice changes in the level of detail as you click each option button.

2. In the Arrange group, click the **launcher** ⬚. The Outlook Options dialog box opens, where you can adjust settings for all of Outlook's features. Make sure the Calendar tab is active. See Figure 2–14.

3. In the Work time section, click the **Monday** box to deselect it. The work week is now Tuesday–Friday.

4. Click the **arrow** next to the Start time box and then click **7:30 AM**.

5. Click the **arrow** next to the End time box and then click **3:30 PM**.

6. In the Display options section, click the **arrow** next to the Default calendar color box and then click the **yellow** color in the list.

7. Click **OK** to return to the Calendar. The new color is applied to the Calendar.

8. In the Arrange group, click the **Week** button to view the new week format.

9. In the Arrange group, click the **Work Week** button. The adjusted work days and work hours appear in the Calendar, as shown in **Figure 2–15**. Leave the Calendar open for the next Step-by-Step.

FIGURE 2–15
Modified Calendar

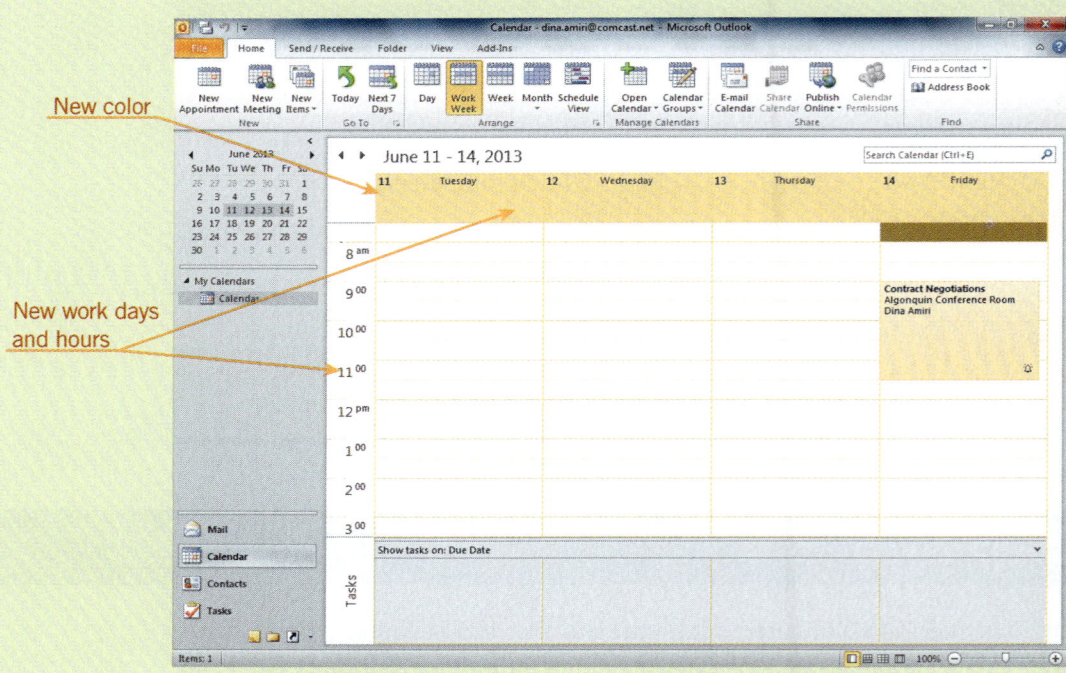

ETHICS IN TECHNOLOGY

You can share your calendars with friends, family, fellow students, or work colleagues in different ways. To access a share option, on the Home tab, select an option in the Share group, or in the Navigation Pane, right-click a Calendar in the My Calendars section, point to Share, and then select an option. The E-mail Calendar allows you to select a date range and level of detail that will appear in the message. Outlook inserts calendar information directly into an open Message window. Outlook provides an online publishing feature that allows you to share one or more calendars. Share Calendar requires that you and the people with whom you want to share your calendar first sign up for a free account at Office Online. Outlook notifies your calendar-sharing recipients with an e-mail to subscribe to your published online calendar. You can publish a calendar to Office.com or to a WebDAV server, which often includes your local Internet Service Provider.

You can also publish a calendar at Windows Live, another free online service to which you must first create a profile. You create and share calendars using the Calendar feature, located on the More menu. To synchronize a Windows Live Calendar with an Outlook Calendar, you must download and install the Outlook Hotmail Connector.

Printing a Calendar

Outlook provides several options for printing your Calendar. You can select from the following styles: Daily, Weekly Agenda, Weekly Calendar, Monthly, Tri-fold (which separates the daily Calendar, tasks list, and weekly Calendar), and Calendar Details (which includes the description area). To print your Calendar in the current view, on the Ribbon, click the File tab and then in Backstage view, click Print. Depending on the view, you can select a style in the Print What section. A preview of the style appears on the right, as shown in **Figure 2–16**. You can use the view buttons in the bottom-right corner of the window to zoom in or out and view a full page or multiple pages.

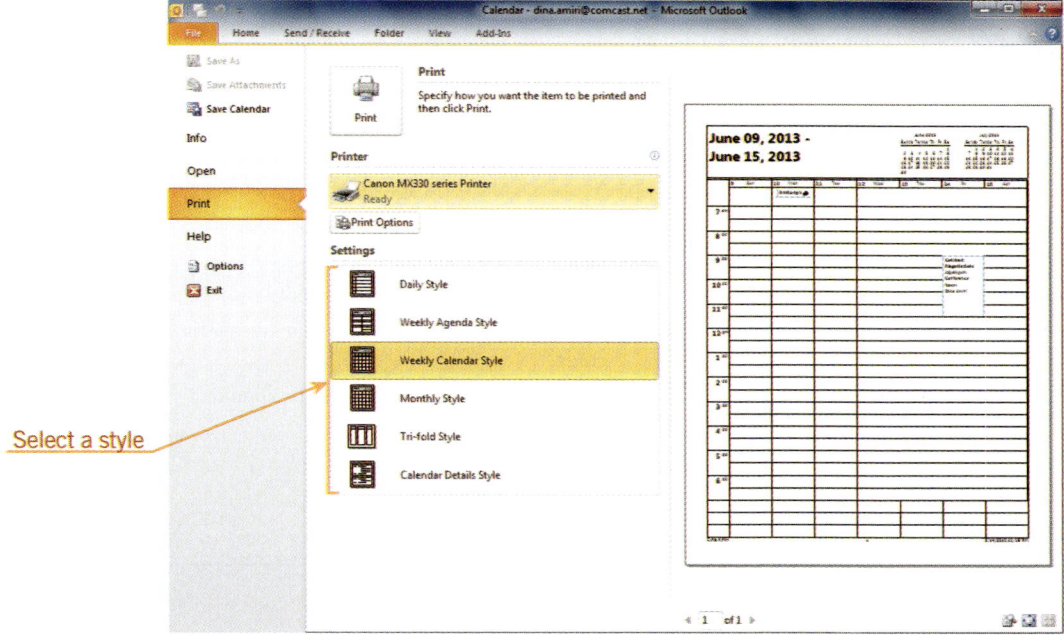

Select a style

FIGURE 2–16 Print options in Backstage view

Once you've selected a style, click the Print Options button to open the Print dialog box. You can change the style last-minute from the options in the Print style section. Click OK to print. You can print a more specific range of dates by selecting Start and End dates in the Print range section.

Step-by-Step 2.8

1. On the Home tab, in the Arrange group, click the **Week** button, if necessary, and then in the Date Navigator, click the date where you scheduled the contract negotiations meeting.

2. Click the **File** tab, and then click **Print**. Print styles appear in the Print What section, as shown in Figure 2–16.

3. Click each **style** to preview it, click **Weekly Agenda Style**, and then click the **Print** button.

4. When you finish printing, click the **Home** tab, click the **Contract Negotiations** appointment to select it, and then press **Delete**. The Meeting window opens. Because you already sent out invitations for the meeting, Outlook requires that you send a cancellation message. Click **Send Cancellation**. The appointment is deleted from the Calendar.

5. Click the **Close** button in the upper-right corner of the window to close Outlook. The Outlook window closes and the Microsoft Windows desktop appears.

SUMMARY

In this lesson, you learned that:

- The Calendar is used to schedule appointments, events, meetings, and tasks. You can view the Calendar in daily, weekly, or monthly format. If you use the Reminder option, Outlook notifies you before each activity.

- Using Calendar, you can schedule a meeting and invite other people to the meeting. You can also use Calendar to respond to meeting requests.

- The Appointment Recurrence dialog box makes it easy to schedule events that occur annually.

- You can customize the Calendar by altering days, time, and color.

- You can print the Calendar information in a variety of styles.

◼ VOCABULARY REVIEW

Define the following terms:

appointment	event	resources
Date Navigator	meeting	task

◼ REVIEW QUESTIONS

TRUE / FALSE

Circle T if the statement is true or F if the statement is false.

T   F   **1.**   It is possible to set a work week to begin on a Thursday.

T   F   **2.**   You can set a reminder option to notify you months before an appointment.

T   F   **3.**   It is impossible to make changes to an annual event once it is placed into the Calendar.

T   F   **4.**   You can modify a single instance of a recurring event.

T   F   **5.**   An event is always an activity that has a set start and end time.

FILL IN THE BLANK

Complete the following sentences by writing the correct word or words in the blanks provided.

1. To set up a monthly appointment, you open the _____ _____ dialog box.

2. When you open a meeting invitation message, your response options are Accept, Decline, Propose New Time, or _____.

3. The presence of a(n) _____ icon tells you that an activity is private.

4. The _____ _____ is a small monthly calendar that appears in the Navigation Pane.

5. Assigning a conference room, projector, and other equipment to a meeting is known as adding a _____.

WRITTEN QUESTIONS

Write a brief answer to the following questions.

1. Which view would you select to view just your job-related activities? Name one place where it is located.

2. Where do events appear in Week view?

3. What is the difference between an appointment and an event?

4. What icon appears with an appointment on the Calendar to indicate that it is recurrent?

5. Describe the difference between deleting an event or an appointment and deleting a meeting that has been sent to attendees.

◼ PROJECTS

PROJECT 2–1

1. Open Outlook, select tomorrow's date in the Date Navigator, and then display the Calendar in Day view.

2. Open a New Appointment window.

3. Select the appointment time from 9:00 to 11:00 am.

4. Add an appointment with **Long-Term Goals Training** as the subject.

5. Add the location of the appointment as **Atrium Training Room**.

6. Add description of the appointment as **Training with staff and management**.

7. Set a reminder for one hour before the appointment.

8. Set the Show As option as Busy. Save and close the Appointment window.

9. Add another appointment from 8:00 to 8:30 am with **Coffee with Dylan** as the subject and **Daily Grind Coffee Shop** as the location.

10. Do not set a reminder. Show the time as Out of Office, and use the Private option.

11. Add a description of the appointment: **Ask to borrow his kayak this weekend.** Save and close the Appointment window.

12. Leave the Calendar open for the next project.

PROJECT 2–2

1. Move the time of the Long-Term Goals Training appointment to 10:00 am to noon.

2. Change the location to **Conference Room 4**.

3. Add a new line to the end of the description: **Make copies of new office policy for tuition reimbursement.**

4. In the Date Navigator, select this Sunday for an event.

5. Add **My Best Friend's Birthday** as an annual event.

6. Set a reminder for one day before the event date. Save and close the Event window.

7. Leave the Calendar open for the next project.

PROJECT 2–3

1. Display the Calendar with today's date.

2. Create a new meeting for a week from today from 2:00 pm to 4:30 pm. Do not add any attendees to the To box.

3. Type **Computer Upgrade** as the subject and **Conference Room A** as the location.

4. Label the meeting with the High Importance option.

5. Set a reminder for 18 hours before the meeting.

6. Add a description to the meeting: **Take extra copies of agenda and handouts.**

7. Close the Meeting window and save changes. Move to next week and notice the meeting in the Calendar.

8. Close Outlook.

◼ CRITICAL THINKING

ACTIVITY 2–1

Create your personal Calendar for this month. Be sure to include class and social activities, recurring events such as sports or exercise, and single events, such as concerts, movies, or plays. You can also schedule medical or dental appointments and your work or classroom hours. When you are finished, print your Calendar in the style of your choice, and then delete all the entries for this activity.

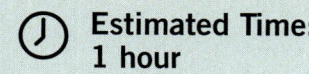

LESSON 3

Working with Other Outlook Tools

■ OBJECTIVES

Upon completion of this lesson, you should be able to:

- Use the To-Do Bar.
- Create a Tasks list.
- Manage tasks.
- Assign tasks.
- View and print a Tasks list.
- Use the Journal.
- Use Notes.
- Exit Outlook.

■ VOCABULARY

Daily Task List

Journal

Notes

task

To-Do List

Using the To-Do Bar

The To-Do Bar gathers and summarizes information about the day's activities in different ways. You can display the To-Do Bar in any view, depending on your personal preference. It appears by default in every view except Calendar view.

The To-Do Bar includes the Date Navigator, a summary of your meetings, appointments and events, a text box where you can create new tasks, and at the bottom, a ***To-Do List*** of upcoming tasks. By default, you view the To-Do List when you click the Tasks folder button on the Navigation Pane. **Figure 3–1** shows items in the To-Do Bar in Task view.

▶ **VOCABULARY**
To-Do List

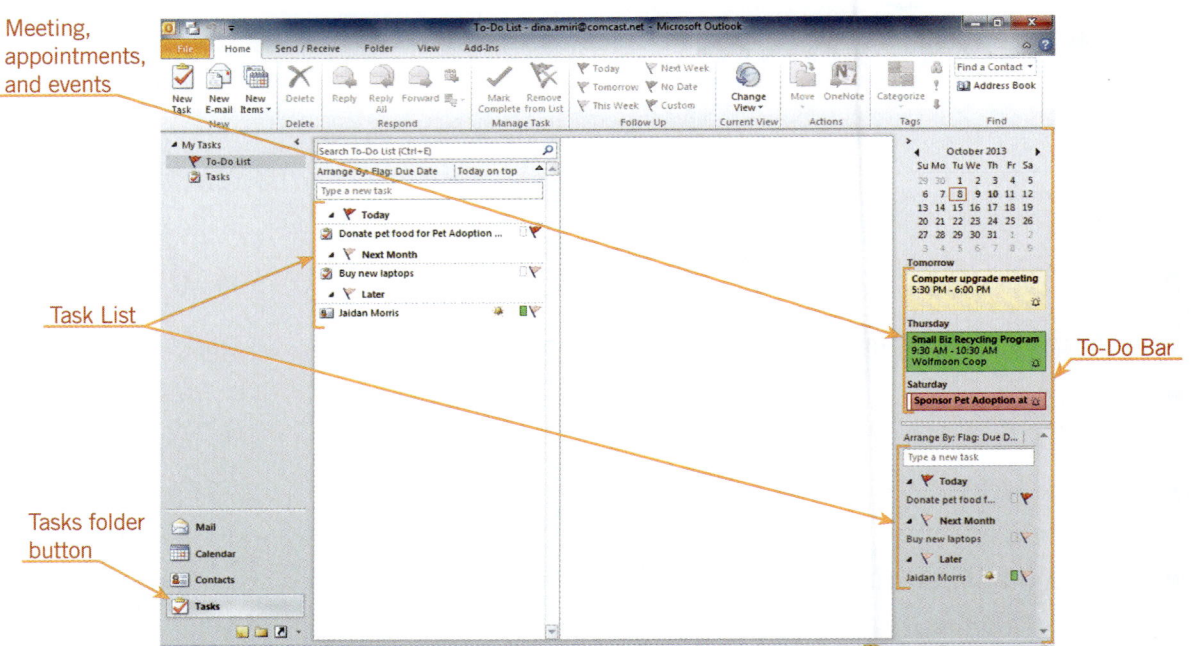

FIGURE 3–1   View the To-Do List in Task view

In the To-Do Bar, you can show the current and next month calendars by dragging the left border of the To-Do Bar. To customize the To-Do Bar, on the Ribbon, click the View tab, then, in the Layout group, click the To-Do Bar button, and then click Options in the list. The To-Do Bar Options dialog box opens, as shown in **Figure 3–2**. You can click check boxes to show or hide the Date Navigator, appointments, events, details, and the Task List. To show multiple months vertically, click the box next to Number of month rows, and then type a number from 1 to 9.

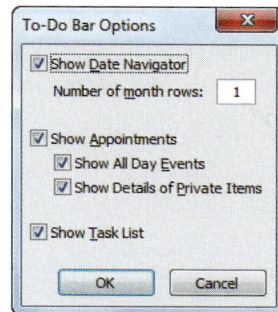

FIGURE 3–2   To-Do Bar Options dialog box

Step-by-Step 3.1

1. On the Navigation Pane, click the **Tasks folder** button. The Tasks window is visible, as shown in **Figure 3–3**.

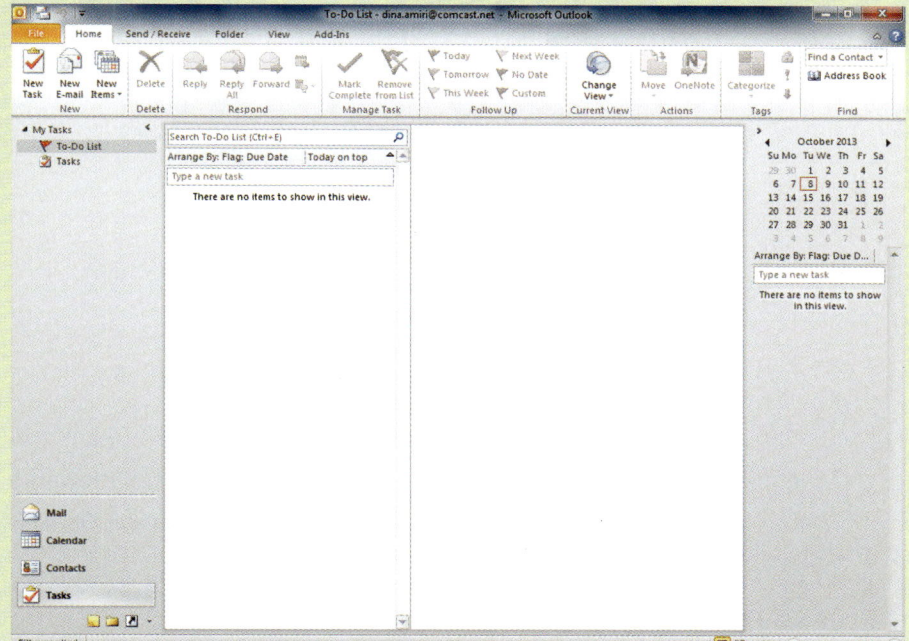

FIGURE 3–3
Tasks view

2. Click the **View** tab, then in the Layout group, click the **To-Do Bar** button, and then click **Options**. The To-Do Bar Options dialog box opens.

3. Make sure that check marks appear in every check box. In the *Show Date Navigator* section, click the **value** in the Number of month rows, type **2**, and then click **OK**. The next month appears in the Date Navigator, as shown in **Figure 3–4**.

FIGURE 3–4
Modified To-Do Bar

4. On the View tab, in the Layout group, click the **To-Do Bar** button, and then click **Options**. In the *Show Date Navigator* section, click the **value** in the Number of month rows, type **1**, and then click **OK**. Leave Outlook open for the next Step-by-Step.

Creating a Tasks List

Meetings, appointments, and events are activities you can monitor in the To-Do-Bar. You can use Tasks view in Outlook to create and manage your tasks. A *task* is any activity you want to perform and monitor to completion. You can create specific tasks, or flag a contact or e-mail message for follow-up. You can assign tasks to color categories, specify start and due dates, check the status of and prioritize tasks, and set reminders. The To-Do List lists tasks similar to an Inbox for e-mail messages. To view the specifics of a task, you select a task in the Tasks window, and then view details in the Reading Pane.

A simple way to create a task in the To-Do Bar is to type a subject in the Type a new task text box. Or, on the Home tab, in the New group, click the New

 VOCABULARY
task

TIP

You can quickly create a task from the Mail window by dragging an e-mail message from the Inbox to the Task List section of the To-Do Bar.

Task button. A new Task window opens with the title Untitled – Task, as shown in **Figure 3–5**. You can choose a subject, specify start and due dates, priority, and set a percentage that represents how much of the task is completed. On the Task tab, in the Show group, you can click the Details button to record and view specific information for invoicing a client. In the Manage Task group, you can mark the task as complete, assign it to one or more people, and send a status report about the task. As with other Outlook activities, in the other groups, you can mark a task as recurring, categorize or mark it for follow-up, or identify it as private. When you are done creating the task, in the Actions group, click the Save & Close button.

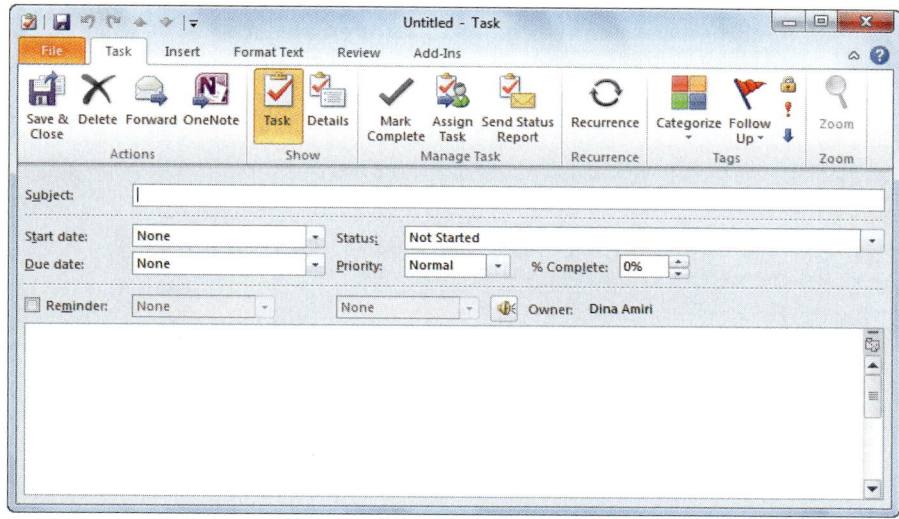

FIGURE 3–5   New Task window

You can view tasks no matter what other activities you are managing in Outlook. Tasks are visible on the To-Do Bar in the To-Do List. They are visible when you select Tasks in the Navigation Pane, and in the *Daily Task List*, located at the bottom of the Calendar in Day, Work Week, or Week view. To view and sort the complete list of active and completed tasks, on the Navigation Pane, click the Tasks icon in the My Tasks section.

VOCABULARY
Daily Task List

Step-by-Step 3.2

1. On the Home tab, in the New group, click the **New Task** button. The Untitled - Task window opens, as shown in Figure 3–5.

2. In the *Subject* box, type **Donate pet food for Pet Adoption day**.

3. In the *Start date* box, click the **arrow** next to the box, and then click the second Tuesday in the Calendar.

4. In the *Due date* section, click the **arrow** next to the box, and then click the third Friday in the Calendar.

5. In the *Status* box, click the **arrow** next to the box, and then click **In Progress**.

FIGURE 3–6
New Donate pet food task

6. In the *Priority* box, click the **arrow** next to the box, and then click **High**.

7. In the *% Complete* box, click the **up arrow** next to the box until **50%** appears.

8. In the *Reminder* section, click the **check box** to select it, click the **arrow** next to the time box, and then click **8:00 A.M.**, if necessary.

9. In the Description area, type **Collect kibble for dogs/puppies and cats/kittens.**

10. On the Ribbon, in the Tags group, click the **Categorize** button, and then click the **Orange Category**. Your Task dialog box should appear similar to **Figure 3–6**. (*Note*: If prompted to rename the color category, click No.)

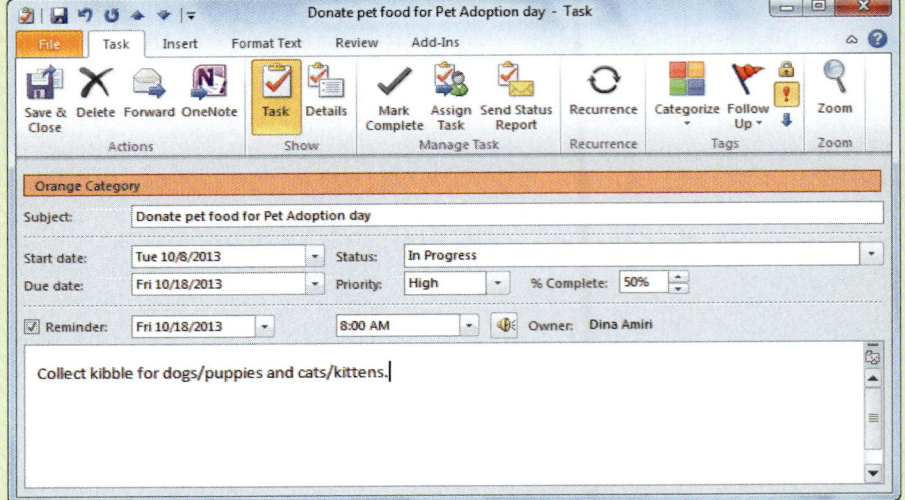

11. In the Actions group, click the **Save & Close** button.

12. On the Home tab, in the Current View group, click the **Change View** button, and then click **To-Do List**, if necessary.

13. Create two more tasks using the information shown in **Figure 3–7** and **Figure 3–8**, respectively. (*Note*: Enter your own dates.) Leave Outlook and the Tasks List open for the next Step-by-Step.

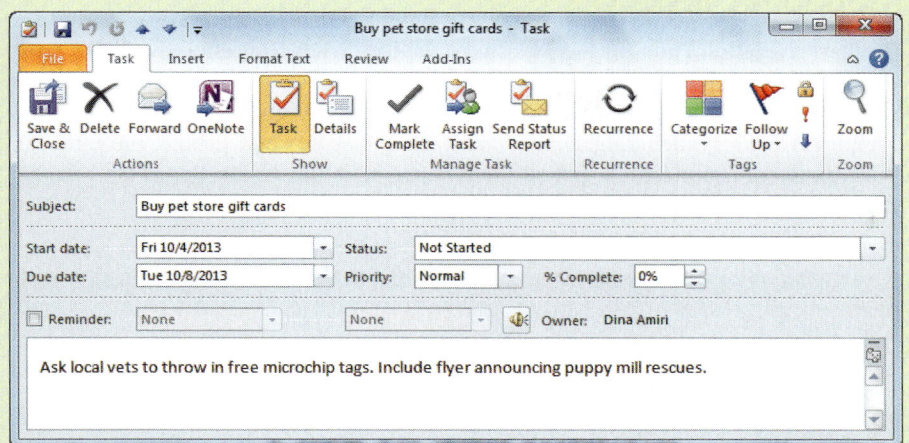

FIGURE 3–7
New Buy pet store gifts
cards task

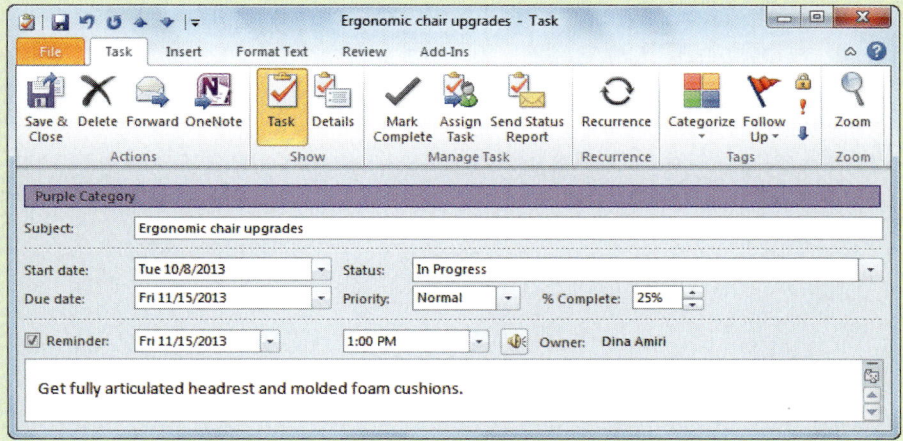

FIGURE 3–8
New Ergonomic chair
upgrades task

TIP

You can easily create a task from an e-mail message (including attachments) or a contact by using the Move command. For example, to create a task from an e-mail message, select the message, click the Move button in the Move group on the Home tab, click Other Folder, click Tasks in the Move Items dialog box, and then click OK. A new Task window opens with the e-mail message shown as an icon in the description area. The subject line of the e-mail message appears as the subject line of the new task. The next time you want to move an e-mail message to the Task folder, the Task icon will appear in the list under the Move command.

Managing Tasks

On the Navigation Pane, in the My Tasks section, when you click the Tasks icon, you sort and group tasks, move tasks up and down the list, add and delete tasks, edit a task, or mark a task off when you complete it. See **Figure 3–9**. Outlook shows completed tasks by including a check mark in the task box and striking through text. When marked Completed, a task no longer appears in the To-Do Bar Tasks List, but you can still view it in the Tasks window.

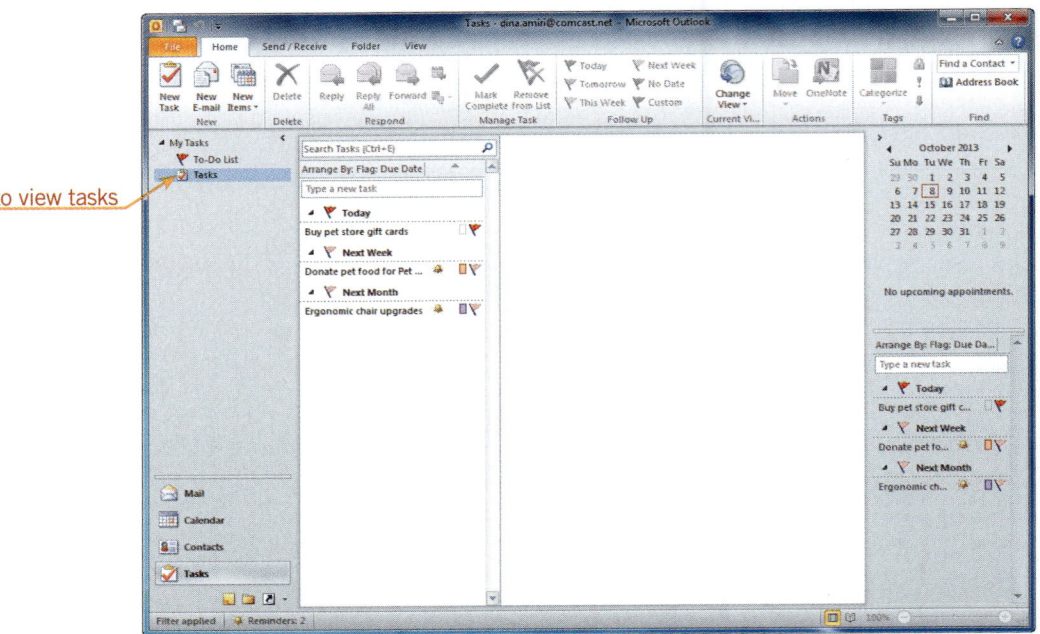

FIGURE 3–9   Tasks List

To sort or group task details, on the Home tab, in the Current View group, click the Change View button, and then select an option. You can view a variety of attributes, as shown in **Table 3–1**.

TABLE 3–1   View options for the Tasks list

VIEW	DESCRIPTION
Detailed	Lists subject, status, due date, modified date, date completed, in folder, categories, and follow up status.
Simple List	Lists subject, due date, categories, and follow up status.
To-Do List	Lists the active tasks in the To-Do List by due date.
Prioritized	Separates tasks by priority.
Active	Includes the active tasks, lists subject status, due date, % complete, and categories.
Completed	Lists only completed tasks.
Today	Lists tasks due today.
Next Seven Days	Lists tasks due in the next seven days.
Overdue	Lists only overdue tasks.
Assigned	Lists tasks assigned to others.
Server Tasks	Lists tasks assigned from a SharePoint site.

To mark a task complete, double-click the task to open it, and then click the up arrow next to the % Complete box until 100% appears in the box. When a task is complete, it is no longer visible in the To-Do Bar. However, in the To-Do List and in the Daily Task List in Day or Week view in the Calendar, a line appears through the task and a check mark appears in the corresponding box. To delete a task, right-click the task and then click Delete. To edit a task, double-click it, make your changes, and then on the Task tab, in the Actions group, click the Save & Close button.

TIP

You can also mark a task as complete by right-clicking it the Task window or To-Do Bar, and then clicking Mark Complete in the list, or on the Home tab, in the Manage Task group, by clicking the Mark Complete button.

Step-by-Step 3.3

1. On the Navigation Pane, in the My Tasks section, click the **Tasks** icon. The tasks appear in the To-Do List, as shown in Figure 3–9. In Simple List view, basic task information such as Subject, Due Date, and Categories is visible.

2. On the Home tab, in the Current View group, click the **Change View** button, and then click the **Detailed** button. Additional task information, including the task's status and its folder are visible. The tasks are arranged by Due Date. (*Note*: If necessary, adjust the columns so you can read your entries in the Subject, Status, Due Date, and Categories columns.)

3. In the To-Do Bar, click the **Arrange By** text above the Type a new task text box, as shown in **Figure 3–10**, and then click **Importance**. The tasks are arranged by importance, from High to Normal. Notice that rearranging tasks in the To-Do Bar does not affect their arrangement in the To-Do List.

FIGURE 3–10
Task arrangement options in the To-Do Bar

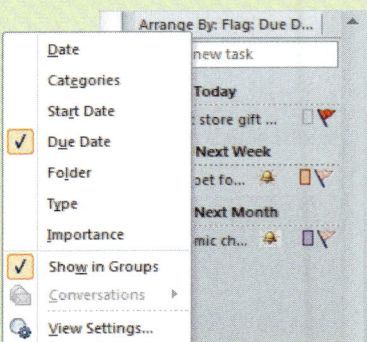

4. In the Tasks List, double-click the **Buy pet store gift cards** task. In the % Complete section, click the **up** arrow until **100%** appears in the box, and then on the Task tab, in the Actions group, click the **Save & Close** button. In the To-Do List, the Complete check box is selected, the subject is grayed out, and the task has a strikeout line running through it. In the To-Do Bar, the task no longer appears in the list, as shown in **Figure 3–11**.

FIGURE 3–11
Completed task

Completed task has a strikeout line

Task removed from To-Do Bar

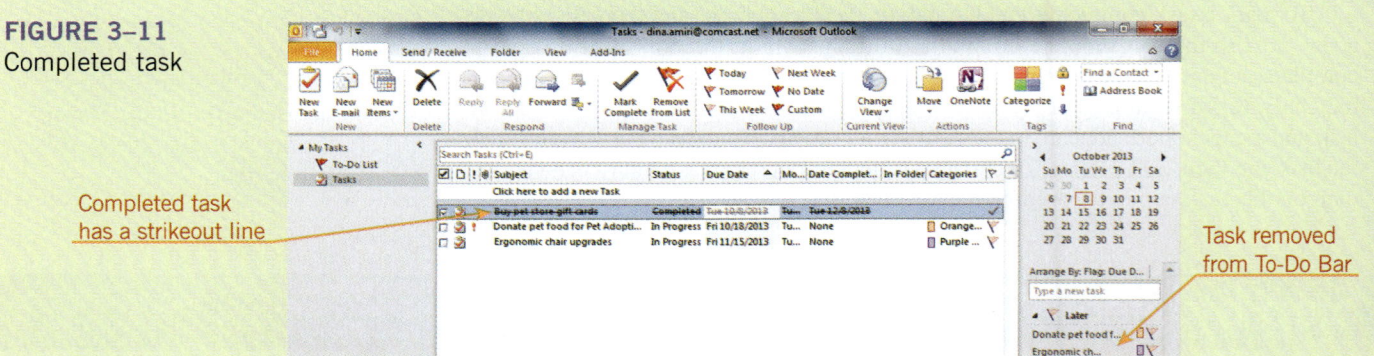

5. Make sure the **Buy pet store gift cards** task is selected in the To-Do List, and then on the Home tab, in the Delete group, click the **Delete** button. The task is deleted from the Tasks List. Leave Outlook and the Tasks List open for the next Step-by-Step.

ETHICS IN TECHNOLOGY

Managers can use the Tasks list to keep track of their employees' workloads. A manager can assign and delegate tasks to each employee, which also creates an evidence trail of who gets assigned which tasks. To do this, the manager creates a Task Request and sends it to the employee. The employee responds to the Task Request by either accepting or declining the request. When finished with the task, the employee marks the task as complete, thus providing documentation of their accomplishments.

Assigning Tasks

At times, you need to delegate tasks to others. You can create a new task and assign it to someone, or you can assign an existing task to someone. To assign a task to someone else, double-click an existing task or create a new task. In the Task window, on the Task tab, in the Manage Task group, click the Assign Task button. The To section appears, just as in a new e-mail Message window, where you can enter e-mail addresses for one or more recipients. Click the Send button to deliver the task to the recipient or recipients.

Step-by-Step 3.4

1. On the Home tab, in the New group, click the **New Task** button. A new Task window opens.

2. In the *Subject* box, type **Task Assignment**.

3. In the *Start date* section, click the **arrow** next to the box, and then click next Wednesday in the Calendar.

4. In the *Due date* section, click the **arrow** next to the box, and then click next Friday in the Calendar.

5. On the Task tab, in the Manage Task group, click the **Assign Task** button.

6. Click the **To** button and the Select Task Recipient dialog box opens. Click a classmate's name or one assigned by your instructor from the list of contacts, click the **To** box at the bottom of the dialog box, and then click **OK** to close the dialog box.

7. Click the **Send** button to send the message to your classmate.

8. For this lesson, assume another classmate is sending you a task request at the same time. If a dialog box opens reminding you that you are no longer the owner of the task, click **OK**.

EXTRA FOR EXPERTS

To cancel an assigned task, open the task, and then on the Task bar, in the Manage Task group, click the Cancel Assignment button.

TIP

You cannot assign or send a task to yourself.

9. On the Navigation Pane, click the **Mail folder** button and then click the **Inbox** folder, if necessary. On the Quick Access toolbar, click the **Send/Receive All Folders** button 🖳. When the task request arrives from your classmate who is assigning you a task, double-click the **message** to open it. The Assigned task window opens, similar to **Figure 3–12**.

FIGURE 3–12
Assigned task window

Person who assigned task

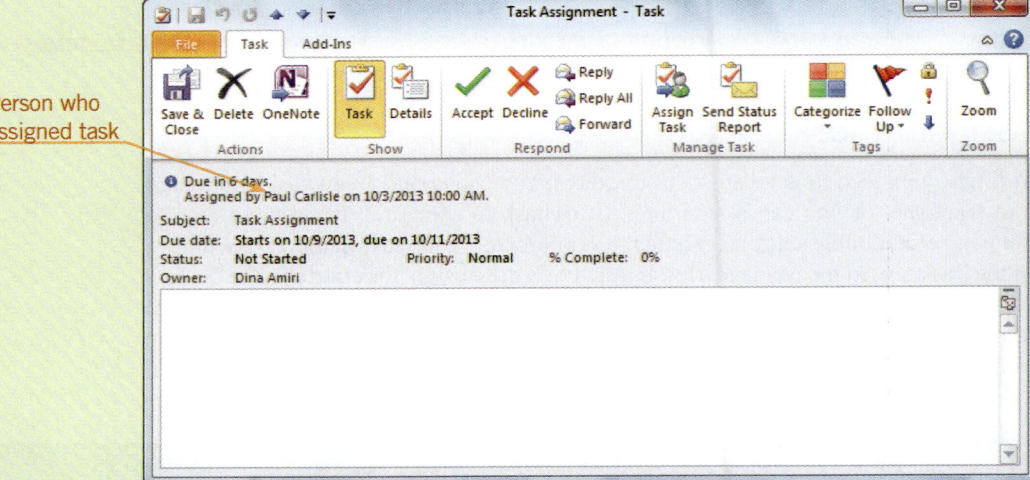

10. On the Task tab, in the Respond group, click the **Decline** button. The Declining Task dialog box opens.

11. Make sure the **Send the response now** option button is selected, and then click **OK**. The message is sent to your classmate.

12. On the Navigation Pane, click the **Tasks folder** button at the bottom of the pane and leave the Tasks List open for the next Step-by-Step.

Viewing and Printing the Tasks List

You can print your Tasks list in the current view of the To-Do List. Depending on the current view, you can print your tasks in a table style, which looks similar to the To-Do List, or in a memo style, which places each task on its own page.

To print your Tasks in the current view, on the Ribbon, click the File tab and then in Backstage view, click Print. Depending on the view, you can select a style in the Print What section. A preview of the style appears on the right. You can use the view buttons in the bottom-right corner of the window to zoom in or out and view a full page or multiple pages.

Once you've selected a style, click the Print button. To change the style last-minute from the options in the Print style section, click the Print Options button to open the Print dialog box, make your changes, and then click Print.

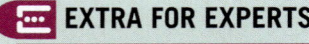 **EXTRA FOR EXPERTS**

To quickly assign a task to someone, on the Home tab, in the New group, click the New Items button, and then click Task Request in the list.

Step-by-Step 3.5

1. On the Home tab, in the Current View group, click the **Change View** button, and then click **Detailed**, if necessary.

2. Click the **File** tab, and then click **Print**. The Table Style appears in the Print What section.

3. Click the **Print** button. Leave Outlook open for the next Step-by-Step.

Using the Journal

You can use the *Journal* to record entries and document your interactions with contacts. You can create journal entries manually to keep track of phone calls and other activities, or you can choose to record e-mail, meetings, and tasks automatically. You can view journal entries in a timeline,

To also use the Journal to track documents and messages associated with a contact, you must first turn it on. On the View tab, in the Layout group, click the Navigation Pane button, and then click Options. On the Navigation Pane Options dialog box, click the check box next to Journal to select it, and then click OK. Click Yes in the Microsoft Outlook dialog box to open the Journal Options dialog box, where you can select the items, files, and people you want to track automatically, shown in **Figure 3–13**.

▶ **VOCABULARY**
Journal

Select items, files, and people to track automatically

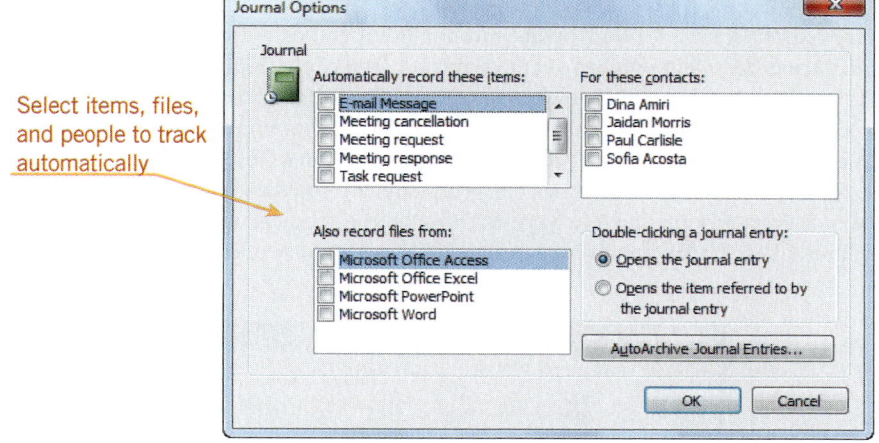

FIGURE 3–13   Journal Options dialog box

Click OK in the Microsoft Outlook dialog box, then view the Journal timeline. This is where you can add entries manually, as shown in **Figure 3–14**.

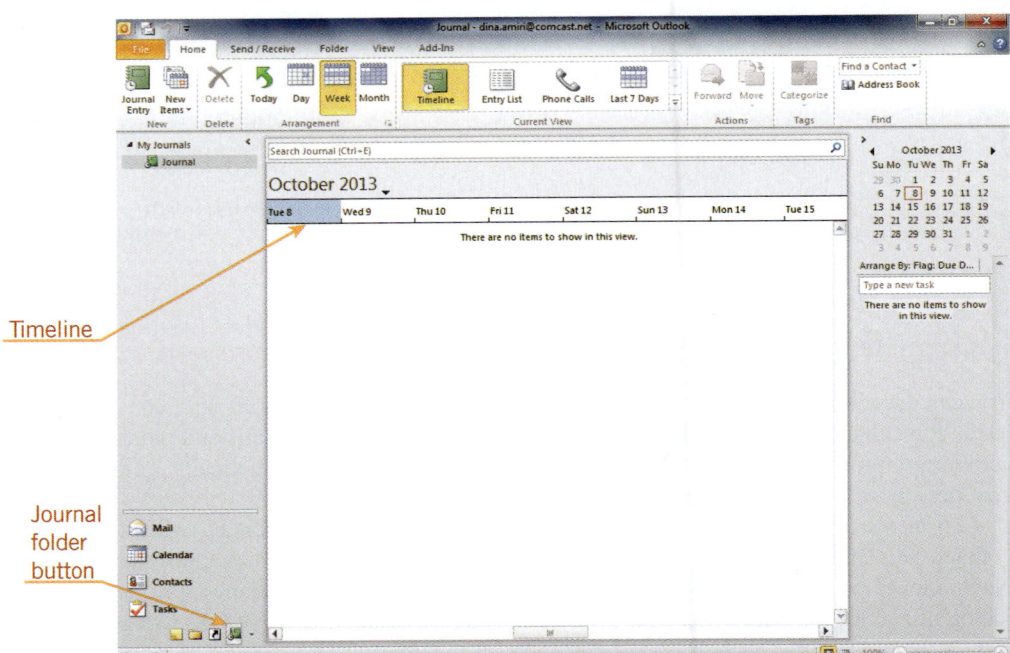

FIGURE 3–14   Viewing the Journal window in timeline view

To add a new Journal entry, on the Home tab, in the New group, click the Journal Entry button. A new window opens with the title Untitled – Journal Entry, as shown in **Figure 3–15**. Here you can set the type and time of the Journal entry. You can set the duration by selecting a preset time or by recording the actual time you spend on the interaction. On the Journal Entry tab, in the Timer group, you can click the Start Timer button and the Pause Timer button to capture the time you spend on an activity, as if you were using a stopwatch. When you are finished with the Journal entry, in the Actions group, click the Save & Close button. You can rearrange your view of the Journal on the Home tab in the Current View group by clicking a view option.

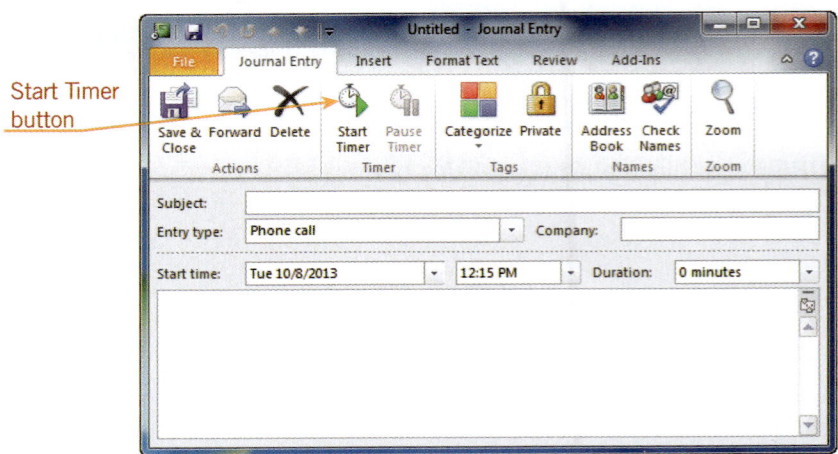

FIGURE 3–15   New Journal Entry window

Step-by-Step 3.6

1. On the bottom of the Navigation Pane, click the **Configure buttons** button ▼, point to **Add or Remove Buttons**, and then click **Journal**. The Journal folder button appears on the Navigation Pane.

2. Click the **Journal folder** button 📖, and then click **No** to turn on the Journal. The Journal window opens with a view of the Timeline, as shown in Figure 3–14.

3. On the Home tab, in the New group, click the **Journal Entry** button. The Untitled - Journal Entry window opens, as shown in Figure 3–15.

4. In the *Subject* box, type **Interview keynote speaker for conference**.

5. In the *Entry type* box, make sure that **Phone call** is selected.

6. In the *Duration* box, choose **15 minutes**.

7. In the *Description* area, type **Remind her that the presentations need to be less than 45 minutes.**

8. On the Journal Entry tab, in the Actions group, click the **Save & Close** button. The journal entry appears in timeline view, as shown in **Figure 3–16**. Leave Outlook open for the next Step-by-Step.

> **TIP**
>
> You can also use the Activities page in a Contact window to track e-mail messages without having to turn on the Journal.

FIGURE 3–16
View a Journal entry

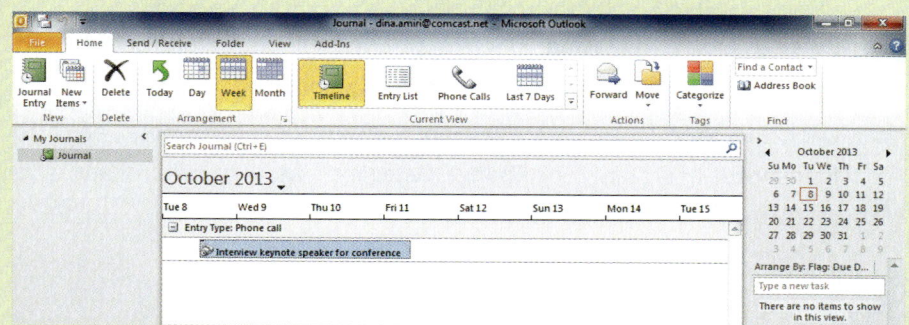

Using Notes

The *Notes* feature is the electronic equivalent of using paper sticky notes as reminders. You can use notes to type anything you need to remember, such as an errand, a great idea, or a question to ask a coworker. You can assign contacts from your Address Book to your notes, and, just as you can with e-mail and Calendar, you can also assign categories to notes.

> ▶ **VOCABULARY**
> **Notes**

At the bottom of the Navigation Pane, click the Notes folder button to display Notes. To add a note, on the Home tab, click the New Note button on the Standard toolbar. A blank note opens, as shown in **Figure 3–17**. Outlook automatically adds the date and time. Click the Close button on the note to save and close it.

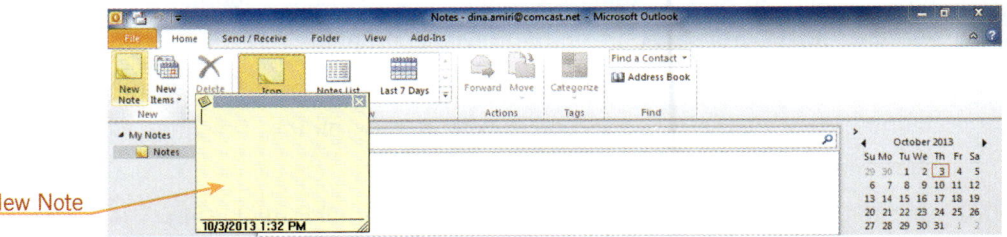

New Note

FIGURE 3–17   View a Note

Step-by-Step 3.7

EXTRA FOR EXPERTS

To change size and view of the Notes icons, click the View tab, and then in the Arrangement group, click Large Icon, Small Icons, or List.

EXTRA FOR EXPERTS

You can change a note's default color, size, and font by clicking the File tab and then clicking Outlook Options. In the Outlook Options dialog box, in the Notes and Journal tab, and then change settings in the Notes Options dialog box.

1. At the bottom of the Navigation Pane, click the **Notes folder** button.

2. On the Home tab, in the New group, click the **New Note** button. A note window opens, as shown in Figure 3–17.

3. Type **Fax lunch order to Gourmet in a Box** and then click the **Close** button ⊠ at the top of the note. The note appears in Notes.

4. On the Home tab, in the New group, click the **New Note** button, and then type **Download ringtones for company phones**.

5. Click the **Note** icon ▤ in the upper-left corner of the note, point to **Categorize**, and then click **Orange Category**. The note color changes to orange. (*Note*: If prompted to rename the color category, click No. Click another color if orange is already renamed.)

6. Click the **Close** button to close the note.

7. On the Home tab, in the New group, click the **New Note** button, and then type **Fax direct deposit form to bank**.

8. Click the **Note** icon ▤ in the upper-left corner of the note, and then click **Contacts** to open the Contacts for Note dialog box.

9. In the Contacts for Note dialog box, click **Contacts** to open the Select Contacts dialog box.

10. In the Select Contacts dialog box, in the Items section, click **Acosta, Sofia** (or another contact) and then click **OK**. In the Contacts for Note dialog box, click **Close**.

11. Click the **Note** icon ▤ in the upper-left corner of the note, point to **Categorize**, and then click **Blue Category**. The note color changes to blue. (*Note*: If prompted to rename the color category, click No. Click another color if blue is already renamed.)

12. Click the **Close** button to close the note.

13. Click the **View** tab, and then in the Arrangement group, click the **List** button. The notes appear in a list view, as shown in **Figure 3–18**.

WARNING

When you delete a note, Outlook does not prompt you confirm the action; it just deletes the note.

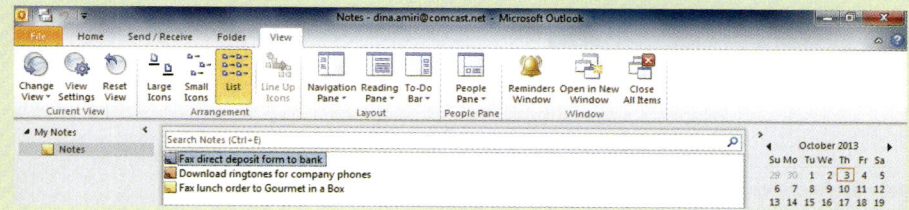

FIGURE 3–18
View Notes in a list

Exiting Outlook

You can exit Outlook by clicking the File tab and then clicking Exit.

Step-by-Step 3.8

1. On the Ribbon, click the **File** tab, and then make sure that Info is selected.

2. Click the **Cleanup Tools** button, click **Empty Deleted Items Folder**, and then click **Yes** to delete the items.

3. Click **Exit**. The Outlook window closes.

EXTRA FOR EXPERTS

You can also click the Close button on the Outlook title bar to exit Outlook.

SUMMARY

In this lesson, you learned:

■ The To-Do Bar gathers information about activities from Calendar, Tasks, and Mail and summarizes the information in one window.

■ You can create tasks from several views, including the To-Do Bar. You can assign categories, specify start and end dates, check the status of tasks, prioritize, and set reminders. You can also move tasks up and down the list, sort by subject or due date, add or delete tasks, edit a task, assign or delegate a task, or mark a task off when you complete it. In addition, you can view a Tasks list from different views and print a Tasks list in different styles.

■ The Journal is used to record entries and document your work. You can set Outlook to record entries automatically or use the Journal Entry dialog box to record entries manually.

■ The Notes feature is similar to using paper sticky notes as reminders. The date and time are automatically added. You can change the color of a note and view notes according to color.

■ When you've completed your work in Outlook, you can exit the program.

◼ VOCABULARY REVIEW

Define the following terms:

Daily Task List   Notes   To-Do List
Journal   task

◼ REVIEW QUESTIONS

TRUE / FALSE

Circle T if the statement is true or F if the statement is false.

T   F   **1.**   Making Journal entries in Outlook is similar to using paper sticky notes.

T   F   **2.**   You can view tasks in the Calendar in the Daily Task List.

T   F   **3.**   You can view multiple calendars in the Date Navigator.

T   F   **4.**   You can view both active and completed tasks in Outlook.

T   F   **5.**   A note is usually an activity you want to perform and monitor to completion.

FILL IN THE BLANK

Complete the following sentences by writing the correct word or words in the blanks provided.

1. Tasks in the To-Do Bar appear at the _____.

2. To log a short reminder, you should use a _____.

3. To keep track of the number of hours you spend on a project, you should create a _____ entry.

4. If you see a checkmark next to a task, that tells you that the task is _____.

5. Before a task gets reassigned, a recipient must _____ it and then send it back.

WRITTEN QUESTIONS

Write a brief answer to the following questions.

1. What does a completed task look like?

2. How do you create a task in the To-Do Bar?

3. What is the default appearance of a note in Notes?

4. In what window can you time your activity as if you had a stopwatch? What other items can you track?

5. What happens to a completed task in the To-Do Bar?

■ PROJECTS

PROJECT 3–1

1. Open Outlook and then display Tasks view.

2. Mark all existing tasks as complete.

3. Add a new task with **Paint living room** as the subject and a due date of this Saturday.

4. Set a reminder at 3 P.M. on Friday.

5. In the text box, type **Get another drop cloth**. Save and close the Task window.

6. Add another new task with **Pick up carpet samples** as the subject and a due date of this Thursday.

7. Set a reminder at 10 A.M. on Wednesday. Set the priority as High. Save and close the Task window.

8. View the tasks in Detailed view.

9. Sort the tasks by Due Date.

10. Print the Tasks list in Table view. Leave Outlook open for the next project.

PROJECT 3–3

1. Display Notes.

2. Add a red note that says **Order flowers for Aunt Kate's birthday**.

3. Add a green note that says **Send an e-card**.

4. Add a yellow note that says **Call Tracey (168-3113) about white water rafting**.

5. View the notes by Category.

6. Exit Outlook.

PROJECT 3–2

1. Display the Journal.

2. Create a new journal entry with **Phone interview** as the subject.

3. Use Phone call as the Entry type.

4. Type **Rocky Mountain Press** as the Company.

5. Choose a duration of 30 minutes.

6. In the text box, type **Will send photographer Monday**.

7. Categorize the entry as purple. Save and close the Journal Entry window. Leave Outlook open for the next project.

◼ CRITICAL THINKING

ACTIVITY 3–1

Pick a type of small business that you would like to own. Describe in paragraph form how you would use the Calendar, Tasks, and Journal features of Outlook to organize information, communicate with others, and manage time. Make a list of four or more categories for grouping all of the information.

ACTIVITY 3–2

Your supervisor asks you to change the default settings for Journal tracking or the automatic recording of Outlook activities. Use the Help system and Backstage view to search for the steps to change the defaults. Write down the steps.

INTRODUCTORY UNIT

MICROSOFT PUBLISHER 2010

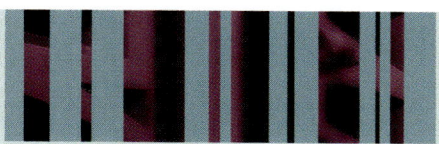

LESSON 1

Microsoft Publisher Basics

■ OBJECTIVES

Upon completion of this lesson, you should be able to:

- Start Publisher.
- Choose a template.
- Understand the Publisher window.
- Create a business information set.
- Save a publication.
- Modify a publication.
- Change the font and color scheme.
- Insert a building block.
- Print a publication.
- Close a publication.

■ VOCABULARY

building block

business information set

color scheme

Design Checker

font scheme

logo

Page Navigation Pane

Quick Access toolbar

Ribbon

status bar

tab

template

title bar

Introduction to Publisher

▶ **VOCABULARY**
templates

Publisher is a desktop publishing program that you can use to create a wide assortment of publications, such as newsletters, brochures, business cards, and restaurant menus. Publisher contains hundreds of predesigned layouts called *templates* that you can use as the basis for professional-looking projects. All you have to do is add your own custom touches.

Starting Publisher

▨ **EXTRA FOR EXPERTS**

Templates are both installed and online. You can choose to view both installed and online templates or just one or the other by clicking the list arrow in the top-left corner of the Available Templates window.

To start Microsoft Office Publisher 2010, click the Start button, point to All Programs, click Microsoft Office, and then click Microsoft Publisher 2010. Microsoft Publisher opens showing the Available Templates window, as shown in **Figure 1–1**. Templates are grouped by category, such as Calendars and Greeting Cards, and can be found in the middle pane of the window. Each category can be further divided by subcategories. You may need to scroll to see all of them. The left pane of the window displays the File menu commands. Notice that the New command is selected by default. If you do not need to create a new document but instead need to open an existing document, you can click Open on the File menu instead. Notice also that you can click Recent on the File menu to gain easy access to recently opened Publisher documents.

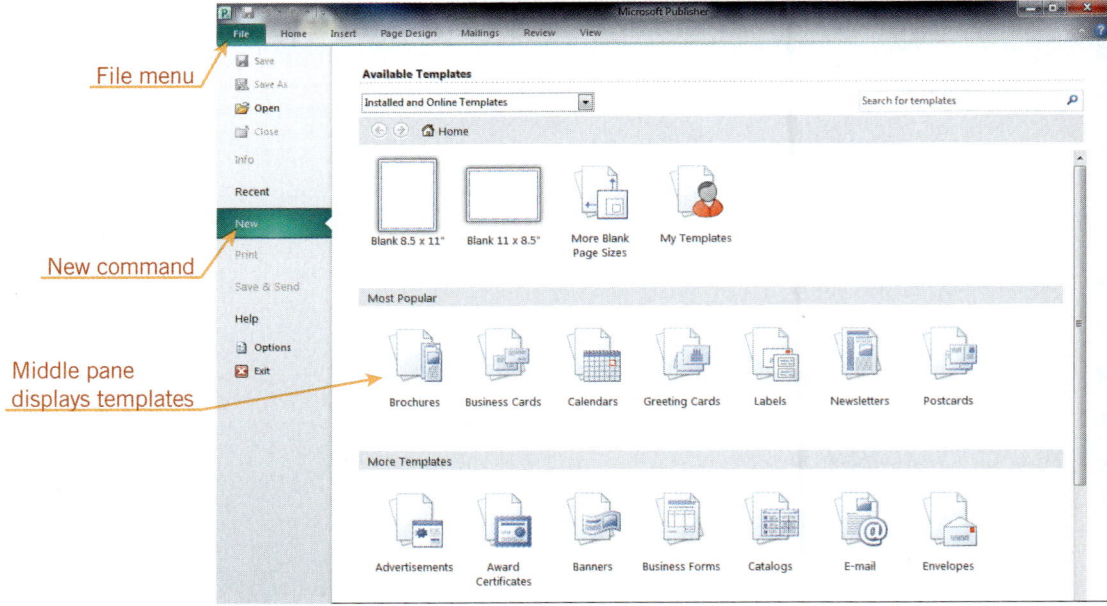

FIGURE 1–1   Available Templates window

Step-by-Step 1.1

1. Click the **Start** button 🔵 to open the Start menu.
2. Point to **All Programs** to open the All Programs menu.
3. Click **Microsoft Office**.
4. Click **Microsoft Publisher 2010** to start the program, and then leave the program open for the next Step-by-Step.

Choosing a Template

Publisher makes it easy for you to get started on a project right away. If you know the type of publication you want to create, simply click a category in the Available Templates window, and then click a template in the middle pane. Once you click a category, the right pane appears in the window. This pane shows a thumbnail image of the selected template at the top of the pane and options to customize the template below. **Figure 1–2** shows the Banded newsletter template selected from the Newsletters category. Notice the options below the thumbnail preview for customizing the template. For example, you can change the color scheme or the font scheme. Keep in mind; you do not have to use a template. There are several blank templates available at the top of the window for you to design your own publications. When you are ready, click the Create button to close the Available Templates window and open the new publication.

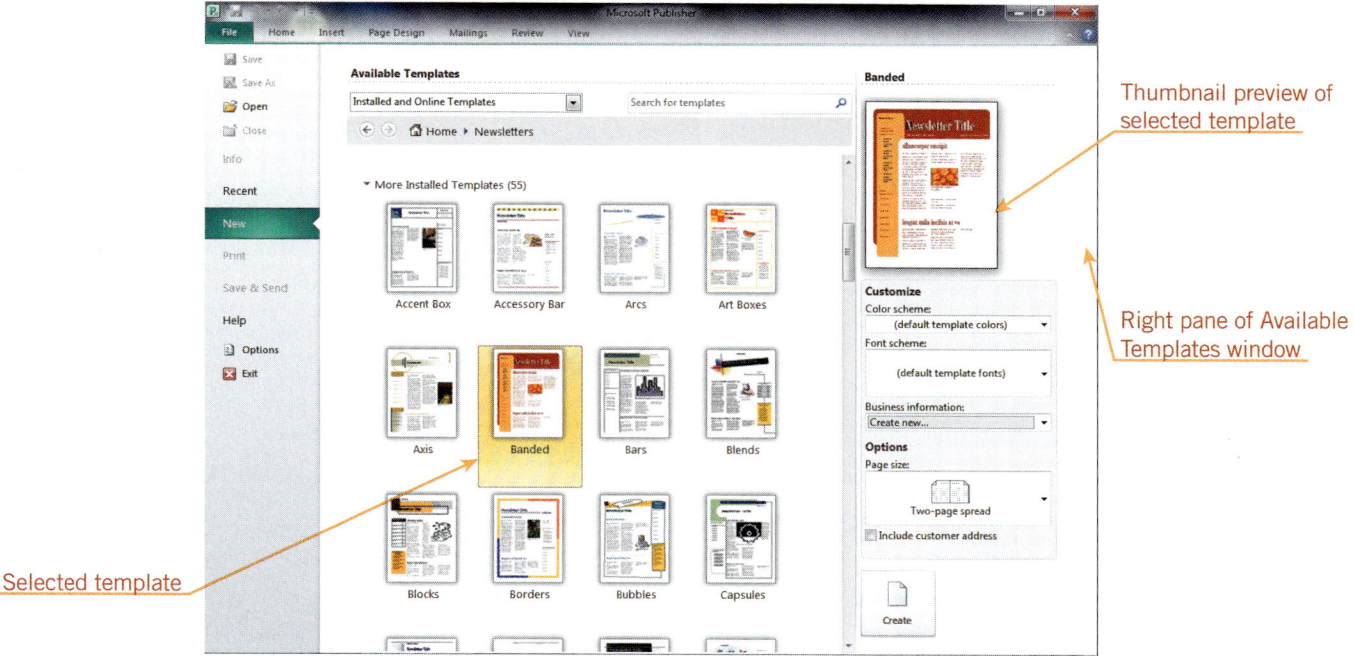

FIGURE 1–2   Banded newsletter template preview

Understanding the Publisher Window

Once you click the Create button in the Available Templates window, the template opens in the document window as a new publication. As shown in **Figure 1–3**, the document window includes the *title bar* at the top of the window. The title bar displays the document name and the control buttons for restoring, maximizing, minimizing, or closing the window.

The *Quick Access Toolbar* is directly to the left of the title bar. It includes buttons for frequently used commands, such as Save and Undo. Below the title bar is the *Ribbon*. The Ribbon includes all of the buttons and options available for working in Publisher. Buttons are categorically arranged by *tabs*. For example, the Insert tab includes all of the available options for inserting objects into your publication. Buttons are placed in **groups** within each tab. To the left of the publication is the *Page Navigation Pane*. It includes thumbnail images of each page in the publication. Notice in the figure, there are four pages to the Banded newsletter and the first page is selected in the Page Navigation Pane. You can view another page in the publication by clicking the corresponding thumbnail image in the Page Navigation Pane. The *status bar* is at the bottom of the document window. It displays the number of pages in the document, a zoom slider for changing the page magnification and buttons for changing the view to a single page view or a two-page spread view.

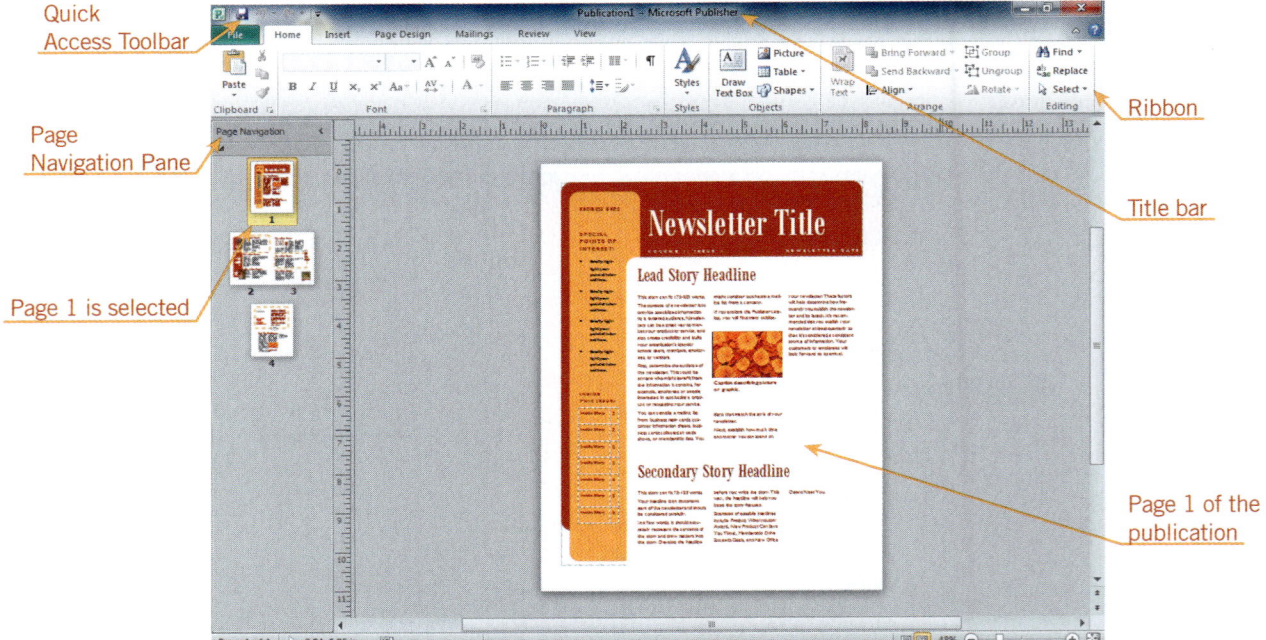

FIGURE 1–3   Microsoft Publisher window

Creating Business Information Sets

A *business information set* is a collection of information about an individual, such as name, company name, address, telephone number, e-mail address, and so on. Business information sets are stored in Publisher and are associated with templates; the information in the set is automatically plugged into templates that call for them. For example, imagine you are creating a brochure that requires your return address. The required information for your return address is pulled from the business information set and plugged into the template, saving you time and effort. You can create business information sets using the Edit Business Information command on the Business Information menu in the Text group of the Insert tab. **Figure 1–4** shows the Business Information dialog box. From this window, you can edit the existing business information set, create a new business information set or delete a business information set. If you create more than one business information set, it is a good idea to assign a descriptive name to each, such as "Personal" or "Work." When you choose a new template, you can pick from a list of business information sets (if you have created more than one) in the Available Templates window before clicking Create.

▶ **VOCABULARY**
business information set

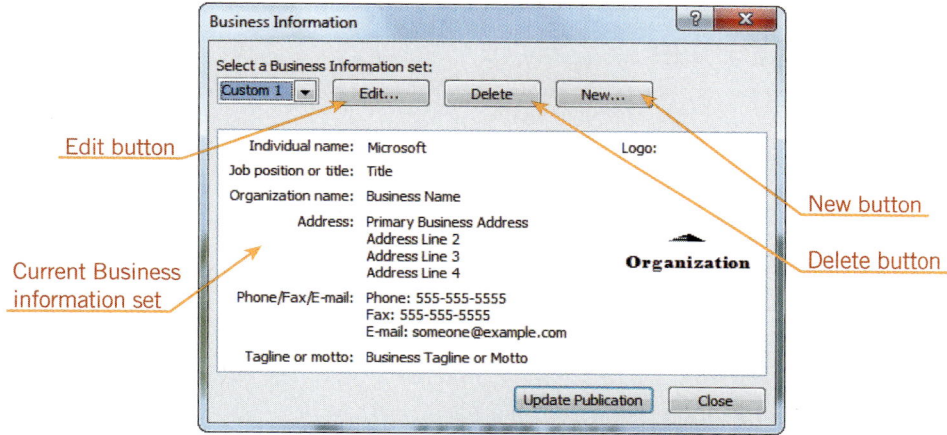

FIGURE 1-4   Business Information dialog box

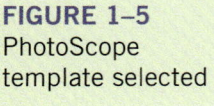

Step-by-Step 1.2

1. Select the **Business Cards** category in the Available Templates window, and then click **PhotoScope** in the Installed Templates subcategory, as shown in **Figure 1–5**.

FIGURE 1–5
PhotoScope template selected

Installed Templates subcategory

PhotoScope template

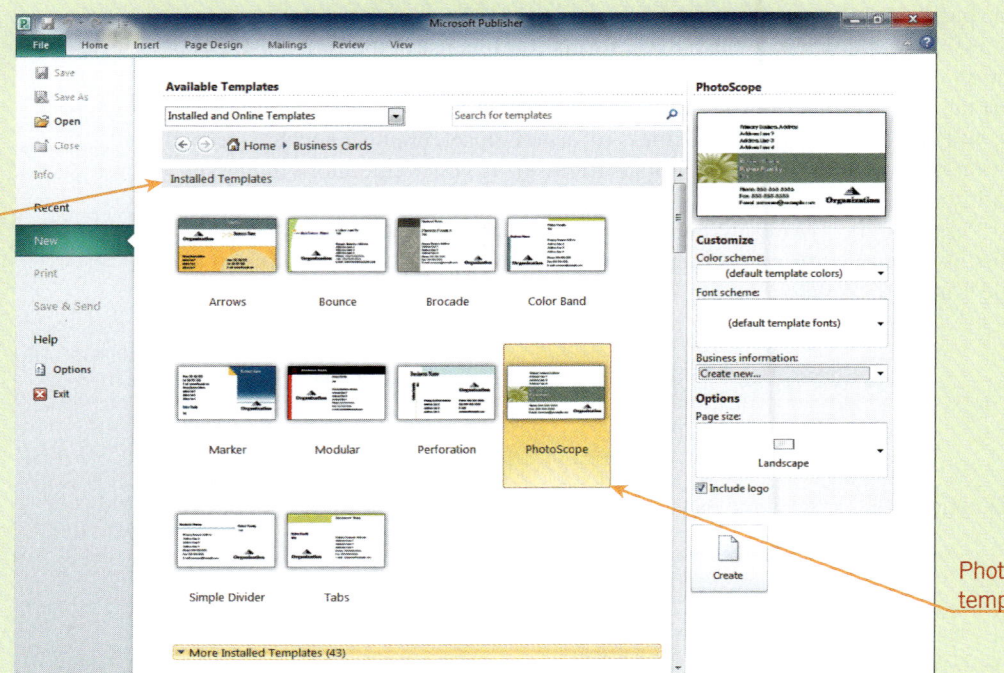

2. Click **Create**.

3. On the Ribbon, click the **Insert** tab.

4. In the Text group, click **Business Information**, and then click **Edit Business Information**, as shown in **Figure 1–6**.

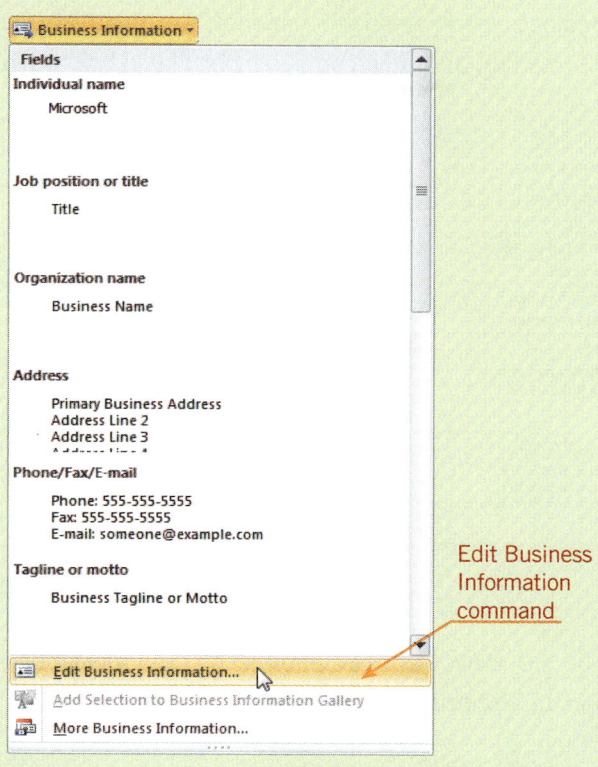

FIGURE 1–6
Creating a business information set

5. In the Individual name text box of the Create New Business Information
    Set dialog box, type **Maryann Lockhart**.

6. In the Job position or title text box, type **Technician**.

7. In the Organization name text box, type **Lawson Electronics**.

8. In the Address text box, type

    1218 Albany Street

    Anderson, IN 46011

9. In the Phone, fax, and e-mail text box, type

    Phone: 812-555-9213

    Fax: 812-555-9211

    E-mail: mlockhart@lawson.com

10. In the Business Information set name text box, highlight Custom 1, type **Work Information**, and then compare your dialog box to **Figure 1–7**.

FIGURE 1–7
Create New Business Information
Set dialog box

11. In the Create New Business Information Set dialog box, click **Save**, click **Update Publication**, and then leave the file open for the next Step-by-Step.

Saving a Publication

When you create a new publication, you'll want to name it and save it to your hard drive. To save a new publication you can simply click the Save button on the Quick Access toolbar or use the Save command on the File menu. The Save As dialog box will appear prompting you to name your publication and save it to a specific location. If you do not assign a descriptive name to your publication, it will retain its default name "Publication1". Each successive publication that you create will be assigned the next successive number, such as "Publication2", "Publication3", and so on. As you work on the publication, you should continue to save your work often. Once a publication has been named and saved, the Save command will update the latest version.

 EXTRA FOR EXPERTS

You can customize the Quick Access toolbar by adding more buttons to it. Click the Customize Quick Access Toolbar list arrow, then select a command from the menu.

TIP

You can also use the Save As command to save an existing publication with a new name. This allows you to duplicate your publication, apply a new name to it, and make any necessary modifications to the copy.

Step-by-Step 1.3

1. On the Ribbon, click **File**, and then click **Save As**. The Save As dialog box appears.

2. Type **New Card solution**, in the File name text box.

3. Click **Save**, then compare your screen to **Figure 1–8**.

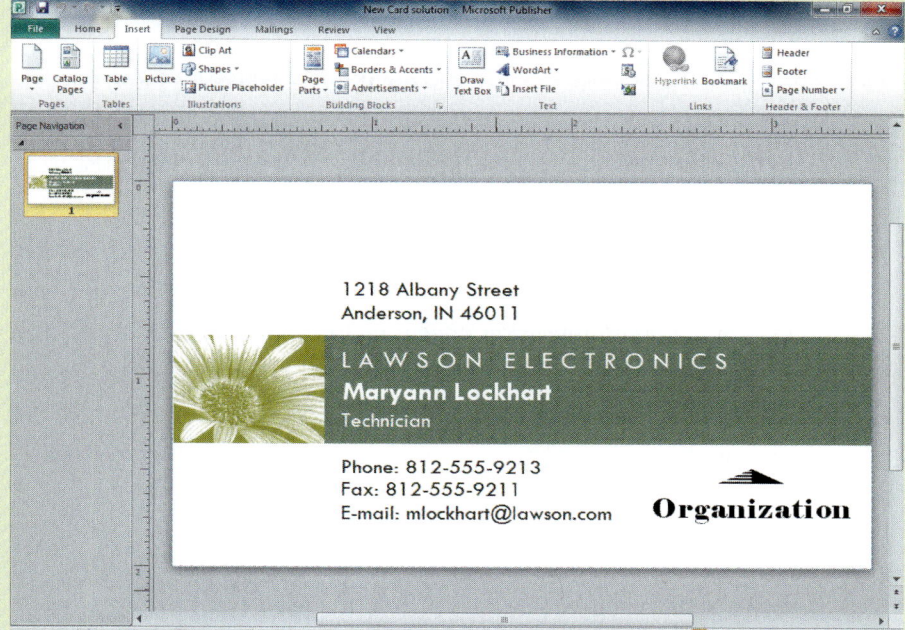

FIGURE 1–8
Saved publication

4. Leave the file open for the next Step-by-Step.

Modifying a Publication

Choosing a template is often a good place to start when creating a publication. Publisher offers numerous ways to modify a publication and to customize it to meet your needs. You can add, delete, move, rotate, and scale text boxes and graphics. Publisher supplies you with basic shape tools and clip art so that you can create simple graphics from scratch. You can also add your own graphics and photographs to a publication. Modifications are made using options on the Ribbon. Most companies use their logo on all business publications for consistency and brand recognition. A *logo* is a symbol that is designed to help customers remember a business and its products. In Publisher, you can create your own logo from scratch, from clip art, or use one created in another software program.

▶ **VOCABULARY**
logo

Step-by-Step 1.4

1. Right-click the logo in the bottom-right corner of the business card, and then click **Delete Object**.

2. On the Ribbon, click the **Insert** tab, if necessary, and then click **Clip Art**.

3. In the Clip Art task pane on the right, click the **Results should be** list arrow, and then make sure that the **All media types** check box is checked.

4. In the Clip Art task pane, click the **Include Office.com content** check box, if necessary.

5. In the Clip Art task pane, type **Electronics** in the Search for text box, and then click **Go**.

6. Scroll down in the task pane until you see the green television image, as shown in **Figure 1–9**, and then click the **green television** image. If you do not see the green television image, feel free to choose another similar image that you like. The clip art image is centered horizontally and vertically on the business card and remains selected. The Format tab appears on the Ribbon with another tab above it named Picture Tools.

FIGURE 1–9
Green clip art of television

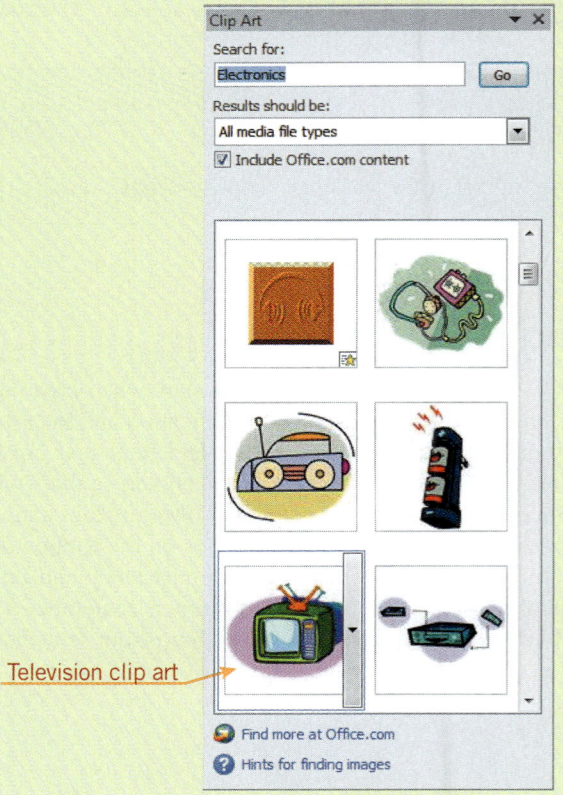

Television clip art

7. Close the Clip Art task pane.

8. On the Ribbon, click the **Format** tab to activate all of the options available for formatting a picture.

9. In the Size group, click the **small arrow** in the lower-right corner of the Size group to open the Format Picture dialog box.

10. In the Format Picture dialog box, click the **Lock aspect ratio** check box if it is not already checked.

11. In the Scale section, type **25** in the Height text box, and then press **Tab** to move the cursor to the Width text box. Note that when you select the Lock aspect ratio box, the Width value will automatically change to match any adjustments made to the Height value, as shown in **Figure 1–10**.

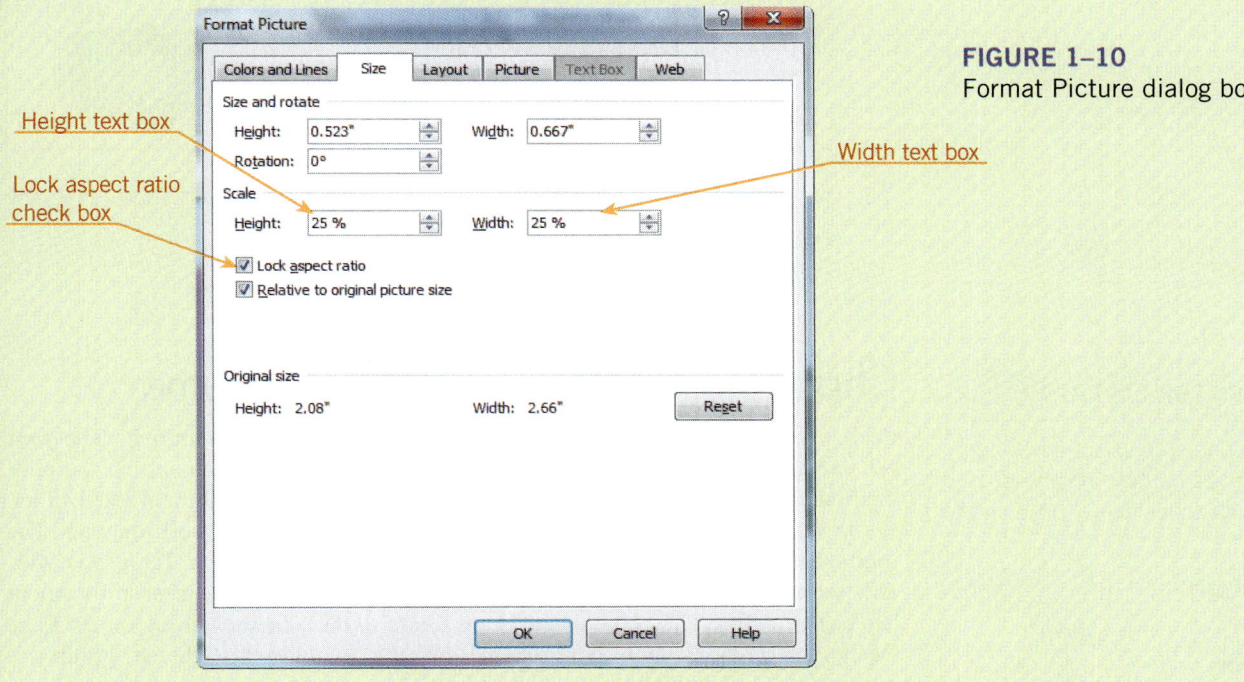

FIGURE 1–10
Format Picture dialog box

12. Click **OK**, drag the image to the lower-right corner of the business card, and then click anywhere on the screen to deselect the image so that your business card resembles **Figure 1–11**.

FIGURE 1–11
Formatted clip art

1218 Albany Street
Anderson, IN 46011

L A W S O N   E L E C T R O N I C S
Maryann Lockhart
Technician

Phone: 812-555-9213
Fax: 812-555-9211
E-mail: mlockhart@lawson.com

13. On the Quick Access toolbar, click the **Save** button, and then leave the file open for the next Step-by-Step.

Changing the Font and Color Scheme

Each publication has a color scheme and font scheme built into it. The *font scheme* is a named set of two fonts used for all of the text elements in the publication. Typically, these fonts work well together and compliment each other. *Color schemes* are named sets of four colors that also work well together. The font scheme and color scheme can be changed in the Available Templates window when you choose a template and in the Publisher window after a document has been created. The color schemes are found in the Schemes group on the Page Design tab on the Ribbon. Font schemes are also found in the Schemes group and are accessed by clicking the Fonts button.

Step-by-Step 1.5

1. On the Ribbon, click the **Page Design** tab.

2. In the Schemes group, click the **Mulberry color scheme**.

3. In the Schemes group, click the **Fonts** button.

4. In the list of font schemes, click the **Metro font scheme**, or another font scheme of your choice if Metro is not available.

5. Compare your screen to **Figure 1–12**.

FIGURE 1–12   Business card with new color and font schemes

6. On the Quick Access toolbar, click the **Save** button. Leave the file open for the next Step-by-Step.

Inserting a Building Block

Just as Publisher provides a collection of templates for creating publications, it also provides *building blocks*: a collection of designs and text placeholders that can be used to further enhance a publication's appearance and functionality. As shown in **Figure 1–13**, the Building Blocks group on the Insert tab includes Page Parts, Calendars, Borders & Accents, and Advertisements. Clicking one of these four buttons displays all of the options in that category.

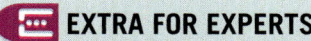
VOCABULARY
building blocks

EXTRA FOR EXPERTS

Building blocks have the same color scheme as the current publication.

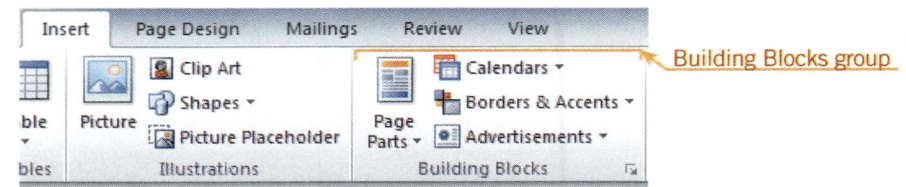

FIGURE 1–13   Building Blocks group on the Insert tab

Step-by-Step 1.6

1. Right-click the **flower** image on the left side of the business card, and then click **Delete Object**.

2. On the Ribbon, click the **Insert** tab, if necessary, and then click the **Borders & Accents** button in the Building Blocks group.

3. Click **More Borders and Accents** in the list, and then scroll down to the bottom of the Building Block Library.

4. Click **Pixel Pattern**, as shown in **Figure 1–14**, and then click **Insert**.

FIGURE 1–14

The Pixel Pattern building block in the Building Block Library

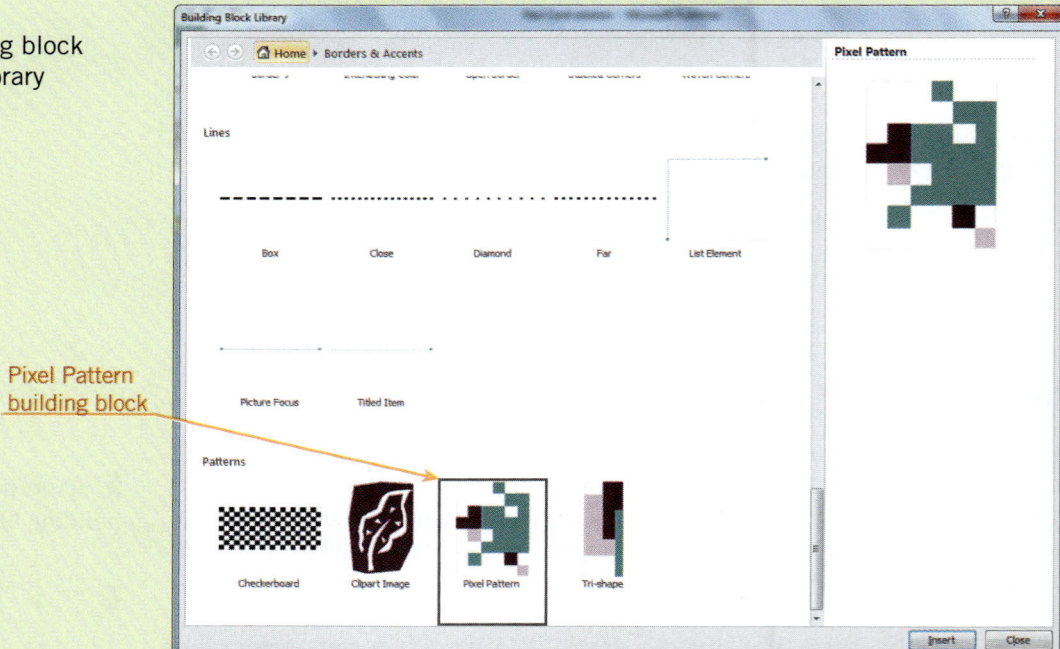

5. Drag the Pixel Pattern building block to the approximate location shown in **Figure 1–15**. Resize the building block, if necessary.

Pixel Pattern
building block

FIGURE 1–15
The Pixel Pattern
building block in the
business card

6. Click another area of the publication to deselect the object.

7. On the Quick Access toolbar, click the **Save** button. Leave the file open for the next Step-by-Step.

Using Design Checker

When you are working long and hard on a publication, especially a multipage one, you might not catch all of your errors. For example, your publication may have overflow text or an object that is not positioned properly on the page. The *Design Checker* feature finds and lists potential design problems associated with your publication. To check your publication, click File, then click the Run Design Checker button. Using the Design Checker pane on the right side of your publication, you can select from four different check types: general design, commercial printing, Website, and e-mail. Publisher creates a list of errors that you can opt to fix or leave as is. Some errors can be fixed automatically, while others must be fixed manually.

▶ **VOCABULARY**
Design Checker

Printing a Publication

You may print your publication by clicking the File menu, then clicking Print, which opens the Print window. As shown in **Figure 1–16**, many options are provided in the Print window. You can choose the number of copies and the page range to print. For some types of publications, such as business cards, you have the option to print one copy or multiple copies per page. The Preview window allows you to see how your publication will print before you click the Print button. If you are working in a classroom or lab setting, you may need to click the Printer name arrow to choose a specific printer.

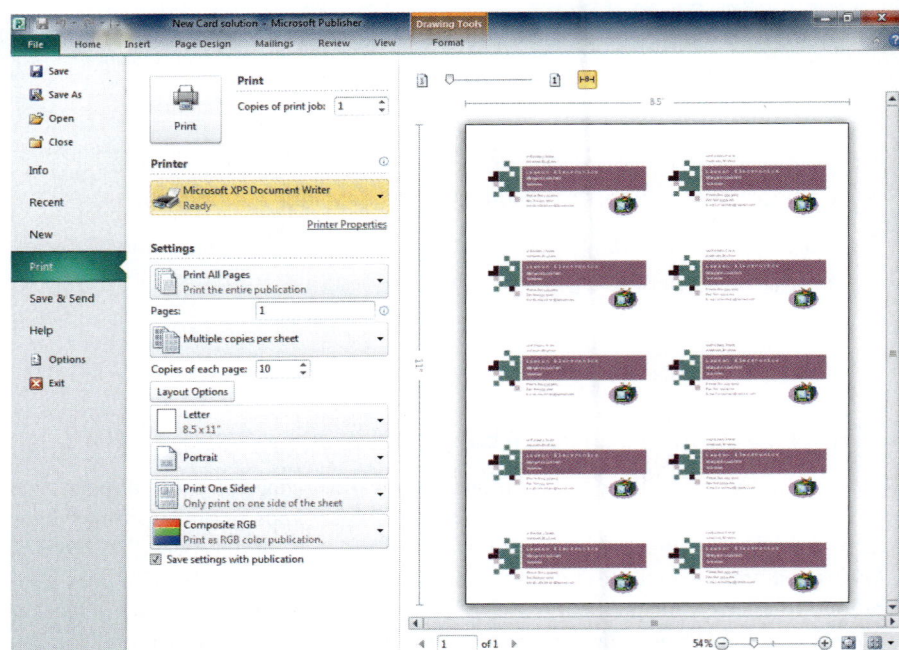

FIGURE 1–16   The Print window

Closing a Publication

Unlike other Microsoft Office 2010 programs, the Publisher program does not have a Close Window button in the top-right corner, only a Close button, which will close the entire Publisher program. To close your publication, but not the entire Publisher program, click File on the menu bar, then click Close.

Step-by-Step 1.7

1. On the Quick Access toolbar, click the **Save** button to save the publication. Your business card should look similar to the one shown in **Figure 1–17**.

2. On the Ribbon, click **File**, and then click **Print**.

3. In the Print window, keep the current settings, and then click **Print**.

4. On the Ribbon, click **File**, and then click **Close**.

FIGURE 1–17
Final business card

SUMMARY

In this lesson, you learned:

- Microsoft Publisher is a program that allows you to produce professional-looking publications in almost any format imaginable. Publisher makes this process even easier with the use of templates and building blocks.

- You can modify a template using options on the Ribbon. You can change the color scheme and the font scheme of a publication as well as the page size. Templates can also be modified by moving, adding, deleting, and resizing graphics and text boxes.

- A building block is a design or text placeholder that can be added to a publication. Building blocks are found in the Building Blocks group on the Insert tab.

- Business information sets are collections of information about individuals. They are stored in Publisher and used with templates.

- It is important to save your work often. The first time you save a publication, the Save As dialog box opens so that you can name and save your file.

- When you are finished with your publication, you can print the publication using the Print window and then close Publisher.

 ## VOCABULARY REVIEW

Define the following terms:

building block	logo	status bar
business information set	Page Navigation Pane	tab
color scheme	Quick Access toolbar	template
Design Checker	Ribbon	title bar
font scheme		

REVIEW QUESTIONS

FILL IN THE BLANK

1. _____ information sets are collections of information about individuals.

2. The Page _____ pane includes thumbnail images of each page in a publication.

3. When a picture is selected the Format tab appears on the Ribbon with another tab above it called _____.

4. The _____ toolbar includes buttons for frequently used commands, such as Save and Undo.

5. Color schemes are named sets of _____ colors that work well together and complement each other.

TRUE / FALSE

Circle T if the statement is true or F if the statement is false.

T F **1.** The best way to create a blank publication is to choose a template, and then remove any items on it.

T F **2.** The Design Checker is used to add building blocks to your publication.

T F **3.** In the Print window, you can print a range of pages instead of the entire publication.

T F **4.** You can change the color scheme of a publication in the Available Templates window.

T F **5.** Page Parts is one of the many template categories in the Available Templates window.

WRITTEN QUESTIONS

Write a brief answer to each of the following questions.

1. List two ways to change the color scheme.

2. List at least one change that you can make to a template before you click the Create button.

3. Which Publisher feature allows you to create a collection of information about an individual?

4. Once a publication is created, what are at least three ways that you can modify it?

5. What happens the first time you save a new publication?

■ PROJECTS

PROJECT 1–1

1. Start Publisher, if necessary.

2. On the Ribbon, click File, and then click Open.

3. Navigate to the location of the data files for this lesson, click Yoga, and then click Open.

4. Save the file as **Yoga solution**.

5. Change the color scheme to Solstice in the Schemes group on the Page Design tab, or another color scheme of your choice if Solstice is not available.

6. Change the font scheme to Flow, or another font scheme of your choice if Flow is not available.

7. Right-click the Organization logo, and then click Delete Object.

8. Right-click the Number text box, and then click Delete Object.

9. Type your name after "Authorized by" in the text box. (Depending on the setup of your classroom, your publication may or may not show a business information set. Leave all other text boxes as they are.)

10. Type **January 1, 2014** after Expires in the text box.

11. Change the business name to **Yoga World**.

12. Save and print your publication, and then close the file.

PROJECT 1–2

1. Start Publisher, if necessary.

2. On the Ribbon, click File, and then click Open.

3. Navigate to the location of the data files for this lesson, click Coupon, and then click Open.

4. Save the file as **Coupon solution**.

5. On the Ribbon, click the Insert tab, and then click Advertisements.

6. Click the Top Oval coupon.

7. On the Ribbon, click the Page Design tab, and then change the font scheme to Apex, or another font scheme of your choice if Apex is not available.

8. Replace "Name of Item or Service" with Yoga Classes.

9. Replace the Organization Name with **Yoga World** and location or landmark with **All locations**. Do not change the telephone number.

10. Change the expiration date to one of your choice.

11. Save and print your publication, and then close the file.

■ CRITICAL THINKING

ACTIVITY 1–1

Use a Business Card template to create a business card for yourself that you can use for babysitting services or dog-walking services. Use any of the skills that you have learned in this lesson to customize your business card. As you design your card, think about colors, fonts, and graphics that will work well to represent your image. Enter your own information or use an existing business information set. Feel free to remove any unnecessary business information, such as the fax number. Save the business card as **My Card solution**, print one copy, and then close the file.

ACTIVITY 1–3

Use a template from the Available Templates window to create a birthday card. (*Hint*: Look under Greeting Cards.) Add a personalized message to the inside of the card. (*Hint*: To display the inside page of your card, use the Page Navigation Pane.) Save your card as **Birthday Card solution**, print your card, and then close Publisher.

ACTIVITY 1–2

Use the PhotoScope letterhead template to create a letter. Save the publication as **My Letter solution**. Insert a new page so that your publication has two pages. Remove the Organization logo from page 1 and then insert a piece of clip art that suggests PhotoScope is a photography company. Position the clip art in the lower right corner where the Organization logo was. Change the color scheme to any one that you like. Save and close the file.

LESSON 2

Enhancing Publisher Documents

■ OBJECTIVES

Upon completion of this lesson, you should be able to:

- Understand guides.
- Enter text.
- Insert pictures.
- Work with objects.
- Create a building block.
- Insert text from a Word document.
- Use Find and Replace.
- Check the spelling in a publication.

■ VOCABULARY

building blocks

layout guides

master page

object

panel heading

Enhancing Your Publisher Documents

The use of business information sets, templates, and building blocks helps you get a jump start on creating publications. Enhancing Publisher projects with your own pictures and text is fun, easy, and provides a way for you to create attractive and professional-looking publications tailored to meet your school, business, and personal needs.

Beginning a Brochure

Step-by-Step 2.1

1. Start **Microsoft Publisher 2010**, if necessary, and then click **Brochures** in the Available Templates window.

2. In the middle pane, scroll down to the More Installed Templates, Informational section, and then click **Accent Box**, as shown in **Figure 2–1**.

3. In the Customize section, click the **Business Information** list arrow, click **Work Information**, if necessary, and then click **Create**.

   Work Information is the name of the business information set that you created in Lesson 1. If you did not create a business information set in Lesson 1, feel free to create a new set with your own information.

4. Save the file as **Brochure solution**, and then leave the document open for the next Step-by-Step.

FIGURE 2–1
Choosing the Accent Box template

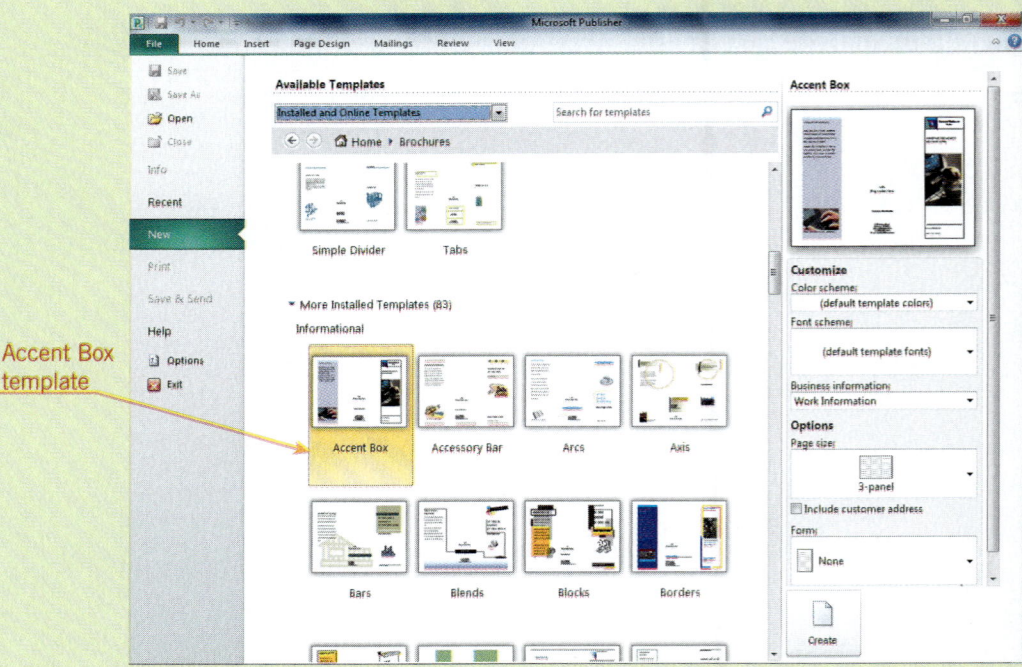

Accent Box template

Understanding Guides

Publisher has many types of *layout guides* to help you position objects in a publication. Each template has guides already in place, depending on the type of template you are using, including margin guides, grid guides, column guides, row guides, and baseline guides. When viewing publication pages, you'll quickly realize that the default guides cannot be moved manually. However, you can add new layout guides by clicking the Guides button in the Guides group on the Page Design tab. As shown in **Figure 2–2**, there are many layout guide combinations that you can add to your pages for aligning text and objects. The layout guides that you add to a publication can be moved manually with the mouse pointer.

Finally, you can create your own ruler guides by simply placing the pointer over the horizontal or vertical ruler. The pointer becomes a double arrow pointer. To create a guide, drag the pointer from the ruler onto the page and release the pointer wherever you want to position the new guide. Once positioned, ruler guides can be moved freely on the page.

To temporarily hide guides, click the View tab on the Ribbon, then click the Guides check box to remove the checkmark.

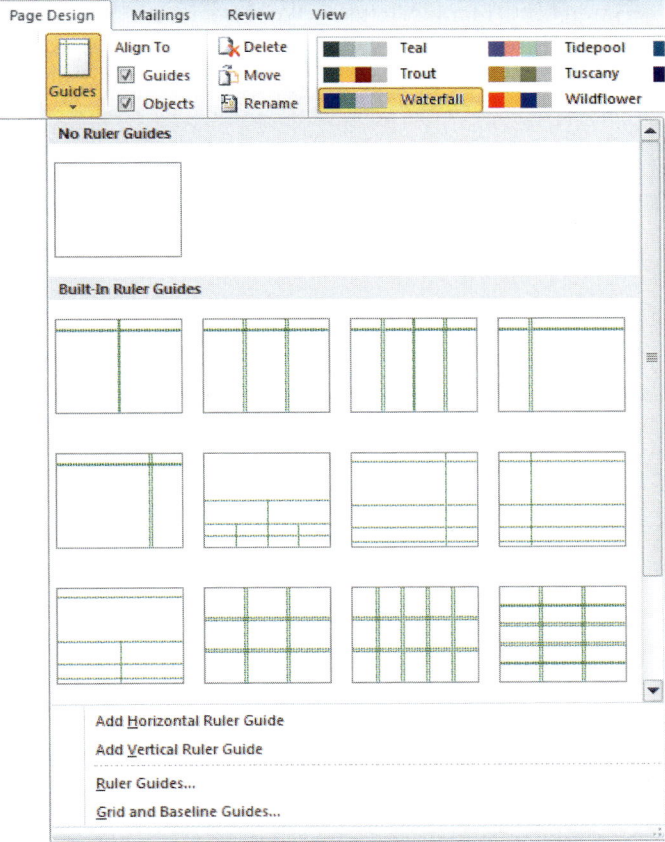

FIGURE 2–2   Viewing layout guides

Understanding Master Pages

If you want to move the locked layout guides that appear on templates, you must switch to the master page for the current publication. The *master page* is a background page that includes placeholders for text and graphics as well as layout guides. Simply press the Master Pages button in the Page Background group on the Page Design tab, and then click Edit Master Pages. The master page opens in the document window. On the master page, you can drag guides to new locations with ease. To return to the publication pages, click the Close Master Page button in the Close group on the Master Page tab.

Entering Text

When developing newsletters, brochures, flyers, or postcards, you will need to add your own information to your project. Using Publisher templates, you can add text directly into text boxes or panel headings. A *panel heading* is the area provided for the title or heading of a project or section of a project. Once an area for adding text has been selected, you can zoom in for better viewing and editing and, with Microsoft Publisher, you always have the option to resize and reposition text boxes. You can also insert text from a Microsoft Word document, something that you'll learn about later in this lesson.

▶ **VOCABULARY**

master page

panel heading

 EXTRA FOR EXPERTS

To view your document without guides, click the View tab on the Ribbon, then click the Guides checkbox in the Show group to remove the checkmark.

 EXTRA FOR EXPERTS

It is best to use master pages for multi-page documents for consistency in your layout.

Step-by-Step 2.2

1. The Brochure solution file should be open from the previous Step-by-Step.

2. Display page **1** by using the Page Navigation Pane, if necessary, and then click the **Zoom In** button ⊕ on the status bar to zoom to **90%**.

3. Click inside the text box that reads **Back Panel Heading,** and then type **Our Mission**.

4. Click three times anywhere in **Our Mission** to highlight the phrase.

5. On the Ribbon, click the **Center** button ▤ in the Paragraph group on the Home tab, to center the text in the text box.

6. Click in the text box below **Our Mission** to select it, and then type:

   It is our mission to provide students with a quality computer education in a timely manner. Students will be better prepared for their future and obtain knowledge that will help them further their careers and personal lives.

7. In the same panel, click the caption below the photograph of the keyboard, type **A Happy Student**, and then center the text.

8. On the Page Design tab, apply the **Vineyard** color scheme and the **Median** font scheme to the publication.

9. Save your work, compare your first panel of the brochure to **Figure 2–3**, and then leave the document open for the next Step-by-Step.

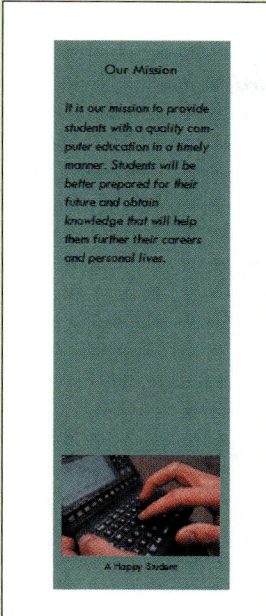

FIGURE 2–3
First pane of brochure

Inserting Pictures

One of the best ways to personalize a flyer or brochure (and to make it look more professional) is to add artwork and photographs. This can be done easily by adding clip art or your own photographs and illustrations. You can insert pictures as new objects in Publisher, or you can replace existing pictures with newly inserted pictures in the same location. To insert a picture, simply click the Insert tab on the Ribbon, and then click the Picture button in the Illustrations group. You'll be prompted to navigate to the place where you have stored your pictures, select the picture, and then click Insert. Pictures are automatically centered horizontally and vertically on the page, unless they are replacing an existing picture. To replace an existing picture, click the picture, then click Change Picture in the Adjust group on the Format tab. The new picture appears in the same location as the original picture. If the picture is larger than the placeholder, the placeholder crops the picture. If the picture is smaller than the frame, the background elements will appear inside the picture placeholder. Once a picture is inserted into a publication, it can be resized, rotated, or flipped to fit your needs. You can also crop a picture, adjust its brightness and contrast, and even create transparent areas in the picture. To format a picture, you must first select it. When you select a picture, the Format tab is automatically selected and displays Picture Tools, which includes groups of buttons for formatting pictures. If a button is not available, it may be that the picture you are trying to format is grouped to something else.

 EXTRA FOR EXPERTS

If you want to remove a picture but not its placeholder, select the picture, click Change Picture, and then click Remove Picture.

Step-by-Step 2.3

1. Click the image in the first pane of page 1 (hands at the keyboard), and then click the **Ungroup** button ⊞ in the Arrange group on the Home tab. The picture and the caption were grouped together.

2. Click another point on the page to deselect all, right-click the **keyboard picture**, click **Change Picture**, and then click **Change Picture** again.

3. Navigate to the location where you store your Data Files, click **William.tif**, and then click **Insert**.

   The new picture replaces the keyboard picture. The picture is centered within the placeholder and crop marks appear around the image, as shown in **Figure 2–4**.

FIGURE 2–4
New picture inserted into placeholder

Crop marks

4. Drag the top crop mark up until you see all of the child's face, as shown in **Figure 2–5**, and then drag the bottom crop mark down until you see some of the child's sweater.

FIGURE 2–5
Dragging the crop mark to reveal more of the picture

Drag crop mark up to reveal top of child's head

5. Remove the "A Happy Student" text box.

6. Click outside the picture to deselect it.

7. Save your work, compare your first page to **Figure 2–6**, and then keep the document open for the next Step-by-Step.

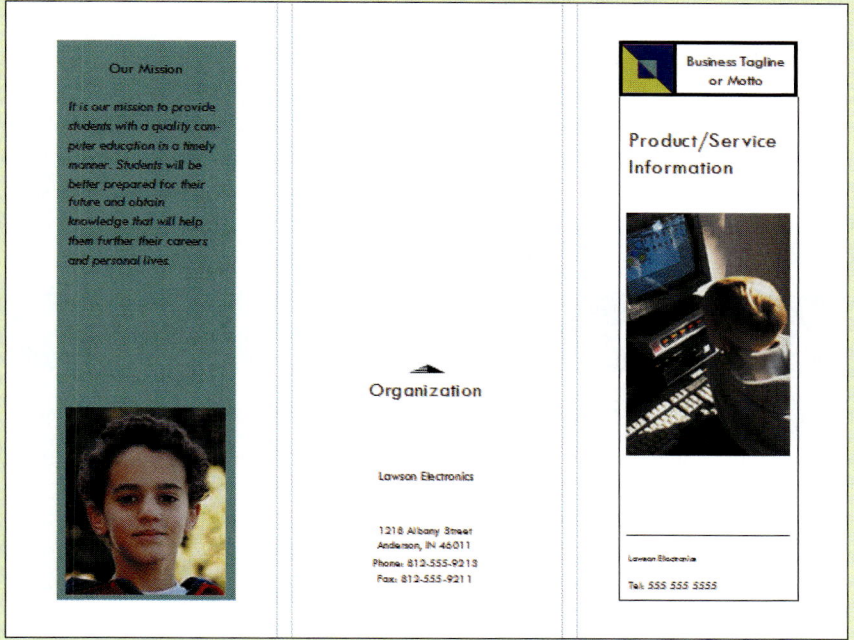

FIGURE 2–6
The first pane completed

▶ **VOCABULARY**
objects

Working with Objects

Text boxes, shapes, clip art, and pictures are all *objects*. Objects are any items that can be modified in Publisher using the provided tools and features. When you select an object, the Ribbon changes appearance showing additional tabs above the Format tab, depending on what type of object you have selected. These include Picture Tools, Text Box Tools, and Drawing Tools. Clicking the Format tab when you see one of these additional tabs displays all of the formatting buttons available for the selected object. For example, you can enter specific values for an object's height and width using the Height and Width text boxes in the Size group. This is much easier than trying to draw a shape with a specific width or height from scratch.

Arranging Objects

The Arrange group has many important features for manipulating objects, all of which add to making your publication look professional. For example, using the Align and Distribute buttons, you can align objects by their tops, bottoms, centers, and left or right sides. Distributing objects means to place the same distance horizontally or vertically between objects. Once you have aligned or distributed the objects to your liking, it's a good idea to group them together to ensure that they are not moved or deleted by accident. You'll find the Group and Ungroup buttons in the Arrange group. Rotate or Flip is another helpful set of commands found in the Arrange group. You can rotate an object left or right 90° or use the Free Rotate tool. You can also flip an object horizontally or vertically.

Layering Objects

In Publisher, you also have the ability to stack or layer items using the Order commands. Imagine that you want to create an illustration of a dartboard using circles, each one smaller than the last and of a different color. You could "stack" the circles perfectly using any combination of the four Order commands in the Arrange group. The Send to Back command sends the selected object to the back of the stack, and the Bring to Front command brings the selected object to the top of the stack. The Send Backward and Bring Forward commands send the selected object back or forward one level at a time.

Step-by-Step 2.4

1. In the Brochure solution file we are working on, the rulers may or may not be showing. If you do not see the rulers, click the **View** tab on the Ribbon, and then click the **Rulers** check box.

2. Position the pointer on the horizontal ruler, drag the double arrow pointer down to the 2-inch mark on the vertical ruler, and then release the pointer. Your screen should resemble **Figure 2–7**.

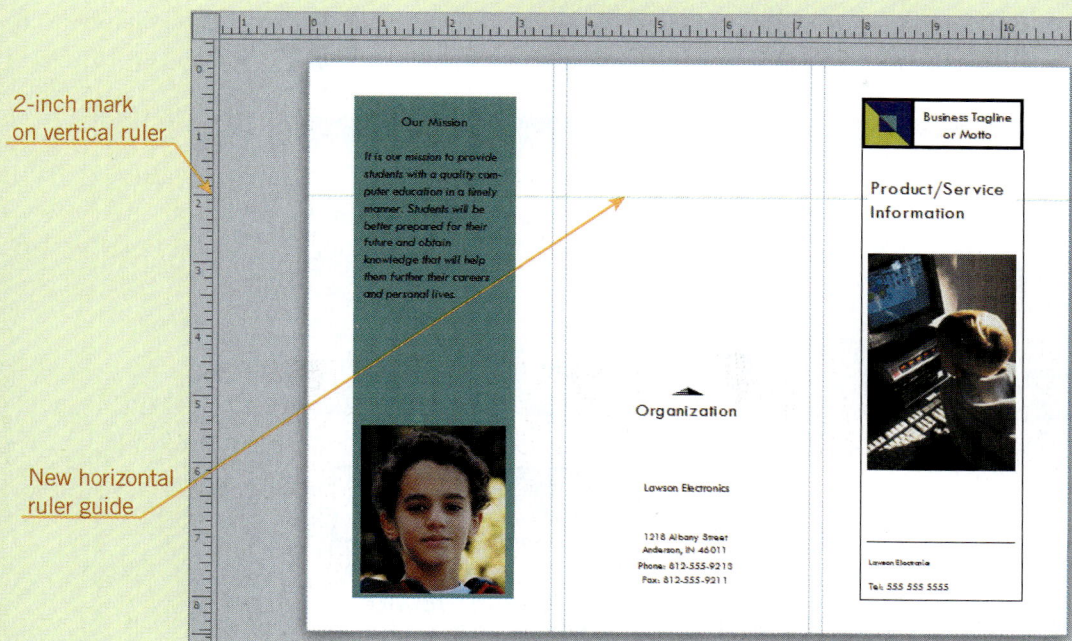

FIGURE 2–7
Creating a ruler guide

2-inch mark on vertical ruler

New horizontal ruler guide

3. On the Ribbon, click the **Insert** tab, click the **Shapes** button, and then click **Rectangle** in the Basic Shapes section.

4. Drag the mouse pointer anywhere in the middle pane of the brochure to create a rectangle of any size. Notice the Drawing Tools tab appears above the Format tab on the Ribbon.

5. Click the **Format** tab, if necessary, and then highlight the value in the Shape Height text box in the Size group.

6. Type **.5**, highlight the value in the Shape Width text box, then type **.5**, as shown in **Figure 2–8**. The rectangle is now a small square.

FIGURE 2–8
Resizing a shape

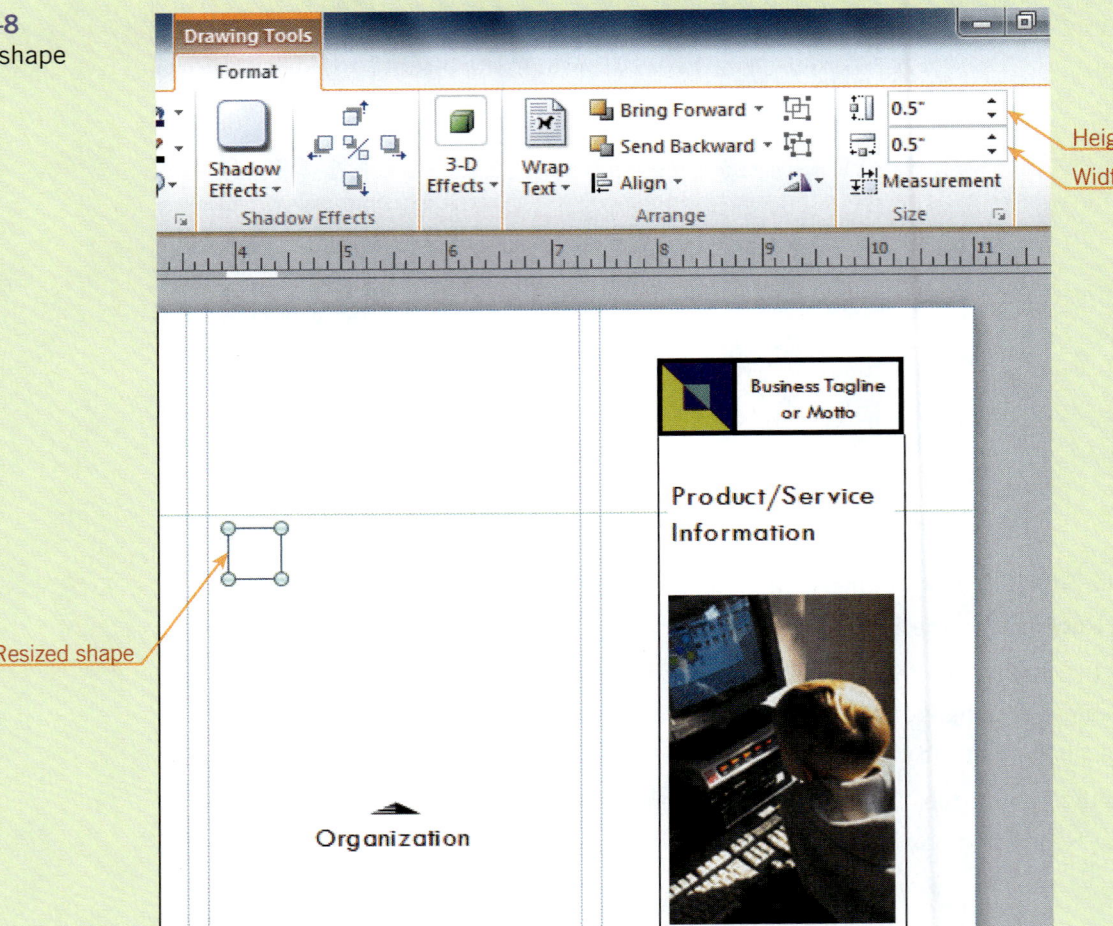

7. Press and hold **Ctrl**, drag the square to the right, release the pointer, and then release Ctrl to make a duplicate of the square.

8. Repeat Step 7 to create a third square.

   You have three squares in the middle pane, as shown in **Figure 2–9**. Do not worry about their exact location in the pane at this time.

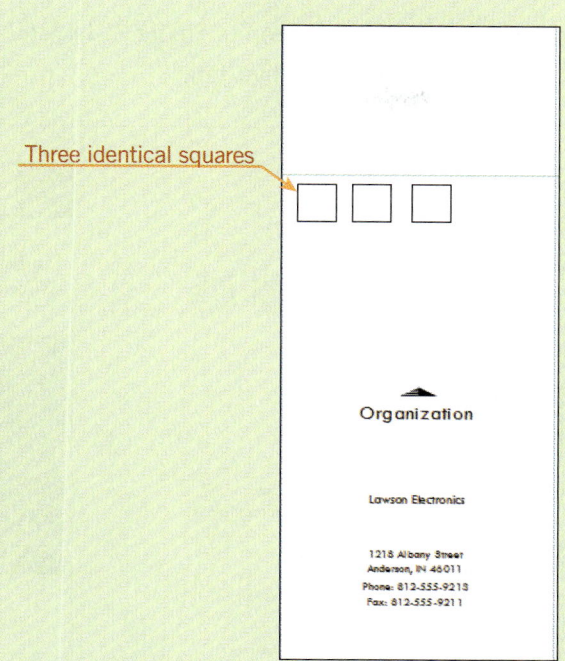

FIGURE 2–9
Creating duplicates of the square

9. Click the **first square**, press and hold **Shift**, click the next **two squares**, and then release Shift to select all three squares.

10. In the **Arrange** group, click the **Align** button, and then click **Distribute Horizontally**, click the **Align** button, and then click **Align Top**.

11. With the three squares still selected, click the **Group** button.

12. Drag the group toward the green guide, and snap the top of the group to the guide. Use the arrow keys to center the group in the middle pane, if necessary.

13. With the group still selected, click the **Format** tab, if necessary, click the **Shape Fill** button arrow, and then click **Accent 3 (RGB (102, 153, 153)), Lighter 40%**.

14. Save your work, compare your screen to **Figure 2–10**, and then keep the document open for the next Step-by-Step.

FIGURE 2–10
New artwork added
to the middle pane

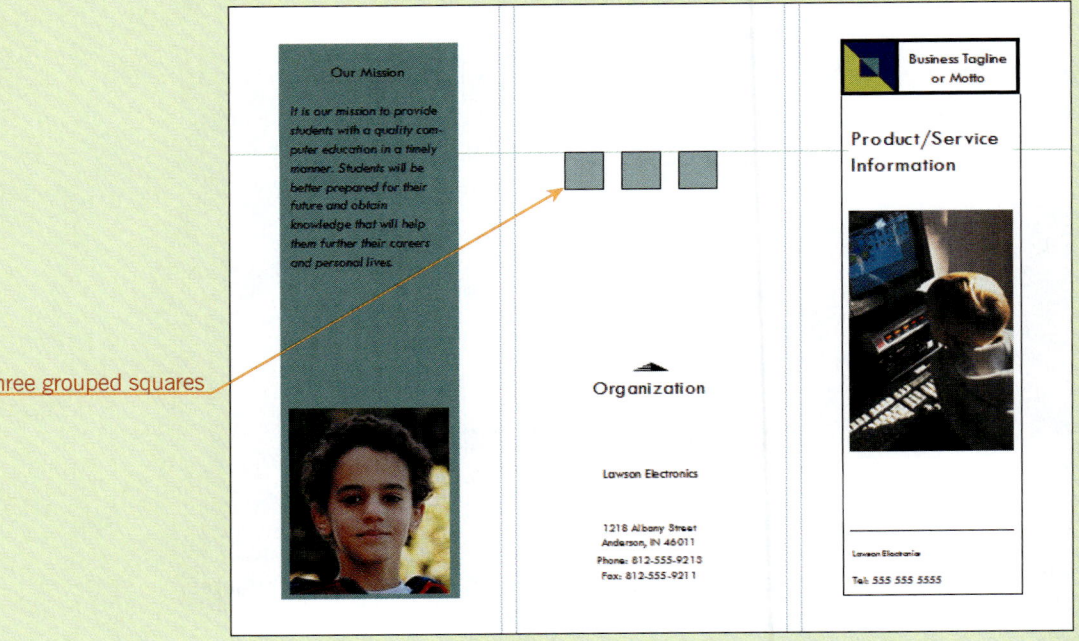

Three grouped squares

Creating Building Blocks

Building blocks are a collection of designs and text placeholders that can be used to further enhance a publication's appearance and functionality. In Lesson 1, you inserted building blocks that are installed with Publisher. You can create your own building blocks for storing text and graphics for future use. Imagine that you design brochures for a summer camp. Each year you use the same camp logo as well as specific information, such as vaccine requirements. The elements that will be reused each year can be stored as building blocks. Creating building blocks saves lots of time and energy and, more importantly, ensures that the brochures have a consistent look and feel to them each year. You can also be certain that important text is intact. This is very important for any information, such as legal requirements, that must be perfect. Once a building block is created, it can be used in any publication. To get started, simply right-click an object, then click Save as Building Block. The Create New Building Block dialog box opens. Here you can assign a descriptive name to your building block and choose which gallery it should go in: Page Parts, Borders & Accents, Calendars, Business Information, or Advertisements. You can then choose a category within the gallery. For example, if you choose Page Parts as the gallery, you can place the building block in any one of the Page Parts categories, such as Headings or Stories.

Step-by-Step 2.5

1. In the middle pane of the brochure, right-click the **bottom text box** that contains the Telephone and Fax information, and then click **Save as Building Block**.

2. In the Create New Building Block dialog box, select the contents of the Title text box, and then type **Telephone Numbers**.

3. Click the **Gallery** list arrow, and then click **Business Information**.

4. Click the **Category** list arrow, and then click **Contact Information**.

5. Click **OK**.

6. Click the **Show Building Block Library** icon in the corner of the Building Blocks group on the Insert tab. The Building Block Library opens.

7. Click the **Business Information folder**, and then locate the **Telephone Numbers** building block, as shown in **Figure 2–11**.

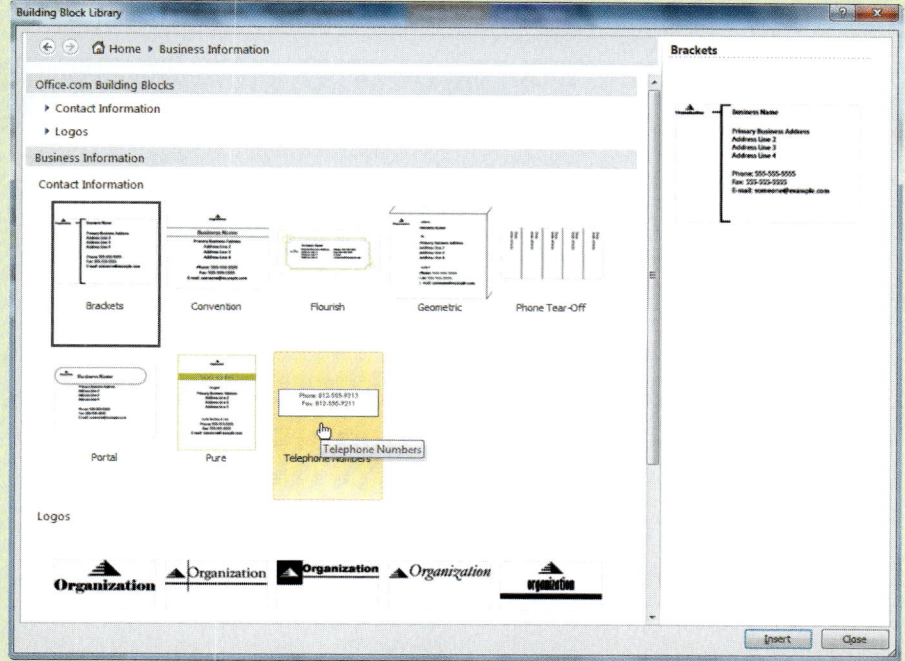

FIGURE 2–11
Viewing the Telephone Numbers building block in the Building Block Library

8. Click **Close**, save your work, and then leave the document open for the next Step-by-Step.

Inserting Text from a Word Document

When a publication calls for a large amount of text, it is sometimes easier to create it in Microsoft Word and then insert it into Publisher. Once in Publisher, the text can still be edited and formatted to your liking. It's easy to insert text from a Word document. First, create a text box as a placeholder to put your text into. Click the Insert tab on the Ribbon, and then click the Insert File button in the Text group. Once you find the text file you want, click OK, and the text falls right into place. If there is too much text to fit the text box, a small box with three dots appears on the text box. You can click this box to move the extra text to another text box in the publication. Or you can resize the text box to accommodate the text.

Step-by-Step 2.6

1. In the middle pane, right-click the Organization object directly below the group of squares and above the Lawson Electronics text box, and then click **Delete Object**.

2. On the Ribbon, click the **Insert** tab, and then click the **Draw Text Box** button in the Text group.

3. Drag to create a text box in the middle pane that is approximately the same size of the text box shown in **Figure 2–12**. Notice the Text Box Tools tab appears on the Ribbon. All of the buttons on the Ribbon are for formatting text.

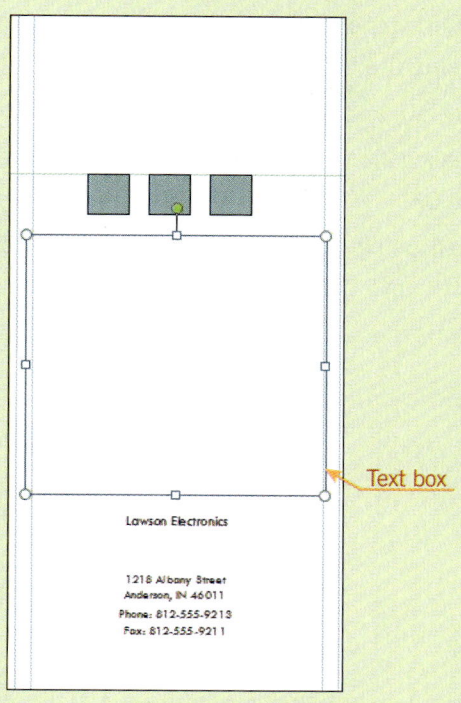

FIGURE 2–12
Text box in middle pane

4. Click the **Insert** tab, and then click the **Insert File** button in the Text group.

5. Navigate to the location where you store your Data Files, click **New Classes.doc**, and then click **OK**.

6. Format the text using fonts and sizes that you like using the buttons in the Font group on the Format tab. **Figure 2–13** shows an example.

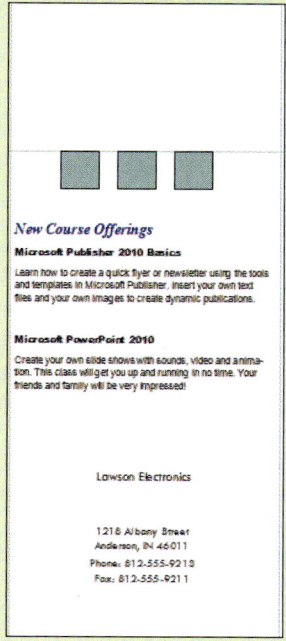

FIGURE 2–13
Formatted text

7. Click the **page 2 thumbnail** on the Page Navigation Pane, and then delete the large text box in the middle pane.

8. Create a text box in the middle pane that fills approximately the top half of the pane using the Draw Text Box button.

9. Click the **Insert** tab, and then click the **Insert File** button in the Text group.

10. Navigate to the location where you store your Data Files, click **Prices.doc**, and then click **OK**.

11. Format the text using the fonts, sizes, and colors of your choice, and then resize and move the text box, as necessary.

12. Save your work, deselect, and then compare your middle pane to **Figure 2–14**.

FIGURE 2–14
Formatted text in the middle pane

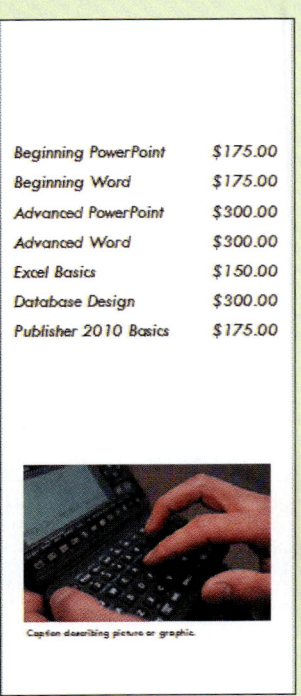

13. Keep the document open for the next Step-by-Step.

Using Find and Replace

One of the most powerful features in Publisher is the Find and Replace feature. This feature searches your publication for a specific word or phrase and replaces it with a new one. We want to change the name of the camp in a brochure. Instead of searching each paragraph of your brochure for the camp name in order to change it, you could simply type Camp Arrowhead in the Find what text box and type Campers' Dream in the Replace with text box of the Find and Replace pane, as shown in **Figure 2–15**. You can find and replace a word or phrase one at a time using the Find Next and Replace buttons or replace them all at once using the Replace All button. Using Find and Replace not only saves time but it also eliminates the possibility of misspellings and inconsistencies in your publication.

Publisher will search for every instance of Camp Arrowhead

Every instance of Camp Arrowhead will be replaced with Campers' Dream

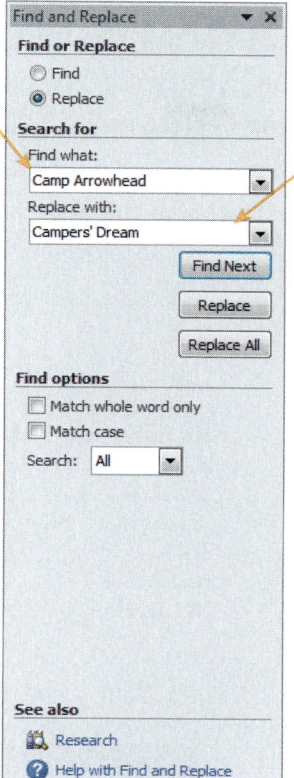

FIGURE 2–15   Find and Replace pane

Checking the Spelling in a Publication

Spelling checkers have become standard features in most software applications. You are probably familiar with using spelling checkers in your work and rely on them each time you finish an assignment. However, you should not solely rely on spelling checkers alone to proof your work. Sometimes you may use the wrong word by mistake, such as "their" instead of "they're" or "there." Since "their" is spelled correctly, the spelling checker won't flag it as a problem. Therefore, make sure you always read your work carefully after you check the spelling to increase the likelihood of finding content errors. To check the spelling in Publisher documents, click the Spelling button on the Review tab. For each misspelled word, Publisher offers a list of suggestions to replace the misspelled word. Since proper names are not stored in Publisher's electronic dictionary, they are often flagged as misspellings. In this case, simply click Ignore in the Check Spelling dialog box.

Step-by-Step 2.7

1. Click the **Home** tab, and then click the **Replace** button in the Editing group.

2. On the Find and Replace pane, click the **Replace** option button, if necessary.

3. On the Find and Replace pane, in the Find what text box, type **Lawson Electronics**.

4. In the Replace with text box, type **Lawson Computers**, click **Replace All**, and then click **OK** in the dialog box stating that the search is complete. Close the **Find and Replace** pane.

5. Click the page two thumbnail in the Page Navigation Pane, and then delete all of the objects in the first pane and the text box in the third pane so that your second page resembles **Figure 2–16**.

FIGURE 2–16
Page two of the brochure

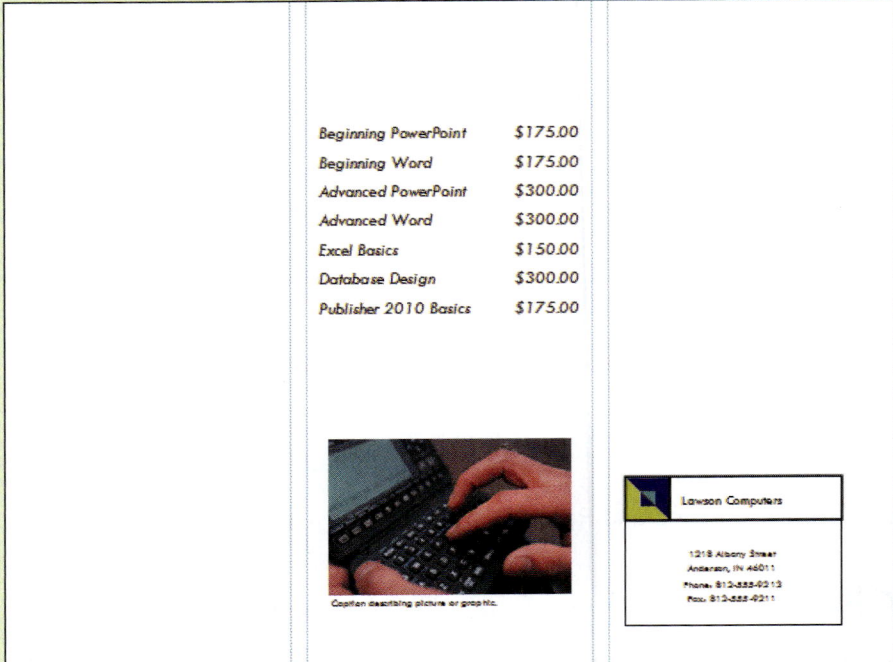

6. Select the first page of the brochure, and then replace "Business Tagline or Motto" with **New Classes** in the third pane.

7. Select the phone number text box on the first pane of the brochure. Highlight the telephone number and then type: **Phone: 812-555-9213**.

8. Replace "Product/Service Information" with **Winter/Spring 2014**, and then center the text.

9. Deselect, and then compare your first page of the brochure with **Figure 2–17**.

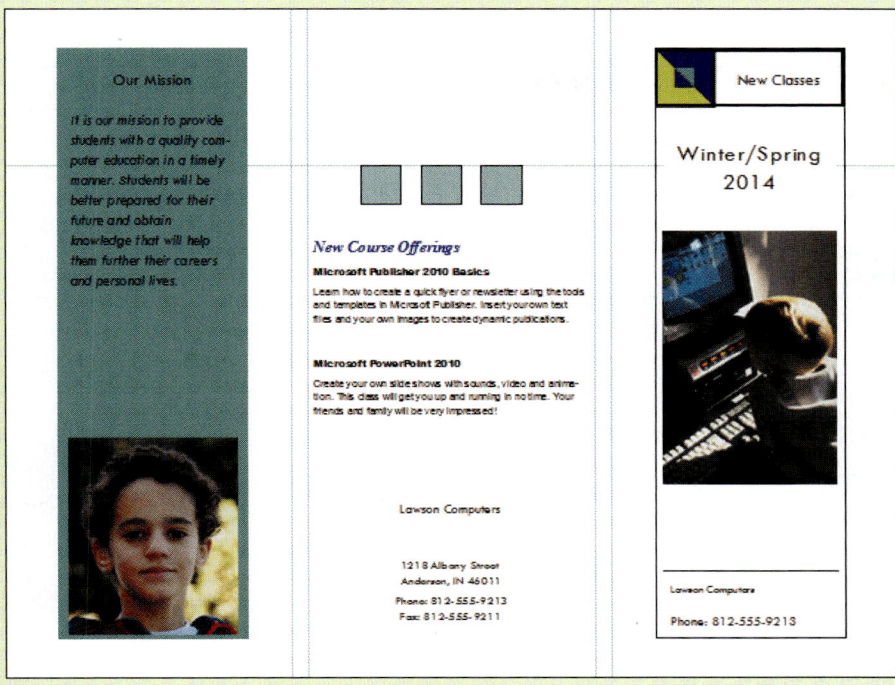

FIGURE 2–17
Page one of the brochure

10. Save your work, close the publication, and then exit Publisher.

SUMMARY

In this lesson, you learned:

- Layout guides include column, row, baseline, and margin guides. All guides help you to align objects on the publication page. Layout guides on each template are locked but can be moved on the master page. There are many layout guide combinations that you can add to your publication using the Guides button in the Layout group on the Page Design tab. Ruler guides are dragged from the horizontal or vertical rulers.

- Publisher templates come with text box placeholders that you can customize by entering your own text. You can add text directly into text boxes or panel headings. When you have entered text, it's best to zoom in on the text so that you can easily modify it.

- In addition to using the provided clip art in Publisher, you can insert your own photographs and illustrations using the Picture button in the Illustrations group on the Insert tab. Pictures can be modified using the many formatting options on the Ribbon. When a picture is selected, the Ribbon displays the Picture Tools tab above the Format tab.

- Publisher provides many ways to work with objects. The Arrange group offers a collection of commands for manipulating objects—all of which help create a professional-looking page. You can align and distribute objects, layer objects, rotate and flip objects, and group them together. Grouping allows you to treat a batch of objects as one object.

- You can convert your own text and graphics to building blocks so that they can be used over and over. You can name new building blocks as well as categorize them. Then, when you need to use a building block, you can access it from the Building Blocks group on the Insert tab.

- Inserting text from a Word document is easy and saves time. To insert text, simply create a text box, then, using the Insert File button, navigate to the location of the text file on your hard drive. Once the text is inserted, you can format it in Publisher.

- The Find and Replace pane is used for replacing specific characters, words, or phrases. This is a powerful feature that ensures accuracy within a publication and saves time.

- Publisher offers a standard spelling checker that examines a publication for any misspelled words, offers a list of suggested replacements, and lets you fix a misspelling by choosing one of the suggestions. If a word is not misspelled, you can ignore the entry. In addition to using the spelling checker, it is always best to proofread a document for content and accuracy.

VOCABULARY REVIEW

Define the following terms:

building blocks   master page   panel heading
layout guides   object

REVIEW QUESTIONS

FILL IN THE BLANK

1. Text boxes, shapes, clip art, and pictures are all _____.

2. To place the same distance horizontally or vertically between objects is to _____ them.

3. The _____ page is a background page that includes placeholders for text and graphics as well as layout guides.

4. _____ help you position objects in a publication.

5. _____ allows you to treat a batch of objects as one object.

TRUE / FALSE

Circle T if the statement is true or F if the statement is false.

T   F   **1.**   The Send Backward command sends the selected object to the backmost layer of the page.

T   F   **2.**   If you cannot access a button for formatting an object, the object may be grouped to something else.

T   F   **3.**   The Change Picture command centers the picture horizontally and vertically on the publication page.

T   F   **4.**   You should not rely on the spelling checker alone to proof a document.

T   F   **5.**   The Find and Replace pane is an example of a Publisher object.

WRITTEN QUESTIONS

Write a brief answer to each of the following questions.

1. Why is it sometimes important to group items?

2. What would be a good reason for creating your own building blocks?

3. What types of objects can be converted to building blocks?

4. Imagine you have a Publisher document with four picture objects: a bed, a blanket, a pillow, and a stuffed animal. Then imagine that you try and overlap the objects so that the blanket is on top of the bed, the pillow is on top of the blanket and the stuffed animal is on top of the pillow but you do not get these results. How would you go about arranging the four pictures so that they were stacked in the following order from bottom to top: bed, blanket, pillow, stuffed bear?

5. Which type of guide can be moved freely?

■ PROJECTS

PROJECT 2–1

1. Start Publisher, if necessary.

2. On the Ribbon, click File, and then click Open.

3. Navigate to your Lesson 2 folder, click Ballet Classes, and then click Open.

4. Save the file as **Ballet Classes solution**.

5. Right-click the cloud image. Then, click Delete Object.

6. Change the color scheme to **Burgundy**.

7. Display the Clip Art pane, and then search for an image of a ballerina.

8. Place the ballerina image on top of the dark gray rectangle (which is on top of the larger pink rectangle), then resize it, if necessary, so that the dark gray rectangle frames the image.

9. Click the image, press and hold [Shift], and then click the dark gray rectangle.

10. On the Ribbon, click the Format tab under the Picture Tools tab, click the Align button in the Arrange group, and then click Align Center.

11. Click the Align button in the Arrange group, and then click Align Middle.

12. Click the Group button in the Arrange group.

13. Type an appropriate caption under your ballerina image, and format the text to your liking.

14. Position the cursor after "9" in the Monday column of the April calendar, press [Enter], and then type **Ballet class**.

15. Repeat Step 14 to place "Ballet class" on the next three Mondays (16th, 23rd, and 30th).

16. Save and print your document, and then close the document.

PROJECT 2–2

1. Start Publisher, if necessary.

2. On the Ribbon, click File, and then click Open.

3. Navigate to your Lesson 2 folder, click Flyer, and then click Open.

4. Save the file as **Flyer solution**.

5. Click the text box that is on top of the light blue rectangle.

6. On the Ribbon, click the Insert tab, click the Insert File button in the Text group, and then insert **Publisher.doc** from the drive and folder where you store your Data Files.

7. Zoom in on the text, using the zoom controls on the status bar.

8. On the Ribbon, click the Review tab, and then click Spelling.

9. Change the first misspelled word "brochurs" to "brochures".

10. Change the second misspelled word "informasion" to "information".

11. Click Yes to search the rest of the document, and then click OK.

12. Click the Home tab, and then click the Replace button in the Editing group.

13. In the Find and Replace pane, type **requirements** in the Find what text box.

14. Type **prerequisites** in the Replace with text box, and then click Find Next.

15. In the Find and Replace pane, click Replace, and then click OK in the dialog box stating that the search is complete.

16. Format the text to your liking.

17. Right-click the text, and then click Save as Building Block.

18. In the Create New Building Block dialog box, change the title to **Publisher description**, save it in the Page Parts gallery, and in the General category, and then click OK.

19. Replace the cloud image with a photograph from the Clip Art task pane. (Try to find a picture of a student or students at a computer.) Type **school**, **computer**, or **learning** in the Search for text box of the Clip Art pane.

20. Position the new image wherever you like on the page.

21. Save your work.

22. Print one copy of the document, and then exit Publisher.

CRITICAL THINKING

ACTIVITY 2–1

Start Publisher, click the Blank 8.5" × 11" template. Save the publication as **Guides solution**. Create three vertical ruler guides at the 3", 4", and 5" marks. Create four horizontal ruler guides at the 4", 5", 6", and 7" marks. Create a text box in the top-left corner that snaps to the inside of the top and left margin guides. Type **Guide Template** in the text box, and then change the font size to 16 pt. Using the Format tab under the Drawing Tools tab on the Ribbon, change the height of the text box to 1" and the width to 2.5". Save your work, and then exit Publisher.

ACTIVITY 2–2

Open Layers from your Lesson 2 Data Files folder, and then save it as **Layers solution**. Using the Format tab under the Drawing Tools tab on the Ribbon, change the widths and heights of the four squares to 1" × 1", 2" × 2", 3" × 3", and 4" × 4". Use commands in the Arrange group on the Home tab to stack the four squares on top of each other, with the largest at the bottom of the stack and the smallest at the top. Place the star on top of the smallest square. Select all five objects, and then align their centers and their middles. Group the five objects together, and then convert the grouped item to a building block. Name it **Star Logo** and assign it to the Page Parts gallery and the General category. Position the grouped item in the approximate center of the page, save your work, print one copy, and then exit Publisher.

ACTIVITY 2–3

Did you know that there are bookmark templates in Publisher? Start Publisher, and from the Available Templates window, click the More Categories folder, click the All Bookmarks folder, then click the Bookmarks (birds) template in the Bookmarks section and then click Download. Save the publication as **Bookmarks solution**. Print the bookmarks, cut them out and give them to friends. Exit Publisher.

CAPSTONE SIMULATION

Green Way Lawn Care Service

Introduction

In this book, you learned to use Word, Excel, Access, PowerPoint, Outlook, and Publisher. In this business simulation, you will apply the skills you learned in each Office 2010 program, following a realistic schedule for the month of May.

First, you will modify a PowerPoint presentation, and then you will use Word to create a form letter to advertise the services of Green Way Lawn Care Service. You will use Publisher to create an advertising flyer. You will create a calendar using Outlook. You will use Access to maintain customer address and billing information and Excel to calculate and maintain earnings and expenses data. You will use Access and Word to integrate data to create a customer invoice that will be delivered to customers.

Background

You started Green Way Lawn Care Service last spring. Over the spring and summer you cared for ten lawns in the neighborhood using environmentally friendly methods and products. You offered the following services:

- Mowing
- Edging
- Hedge trimming
- Fertilization and weed control

Your current tasks are preparing for the upcoming spring season and contacting current customers. You are also thinking of ways to attract new customers.

As you increase the number of lawns you maintain, you will need some extra help to finish each job more quickly. Because you own two lawn mowers, an edger, a weed eater, and a hedge trimmer, you realize that the potential exists to have several machines operating at the same time. You also realize that if you hire additional workers, you could complete each job faster than you could by working alone.

May 1

You are thinking of asking two friends, Marcus and Julia, to help you with Green Way Lawn Care Service. You created a PowerPoint presentation to give them an overview of the business. You decide to make a few modifications to the presentation.

1. Start PowerPoint and open the **Presentation.pptx** file from the Capstone folder where your Data Files are stored.

2. Save the file as **Presentation** followed by your initials.

3. After slide 6, insert a new slide with the Title and Content layout. Enter the title and text on the slide, as shown in **Figure CS-1**.

Option #2

▸ I can ask Marcus and Julia to join the business
  ◦ Advantages
    • Together we can complete jobs faster
    • We would share the profits and work
  ◦ Disadvantages
    • Are there enough lawns to mow?
    • Who would keep accurate customer records?

FIGURE CS–1

4. Change the title of slide 8 to **Option #3**.

5. Change the title of slide 6 to **Option #1**.

6. Use Slide Show view to view the presentation from the beginning.

7. Print the presentation as handouts with nine horizontal slides per page.

8. Save and close the presentation, and then close PowerPoint.

Marcus and Julia agree to join your business. The three of you plan to work together and share the profits. You will earn a greater share of the profit because everyone will be using your equipment. You brainstorm to solve the anticipated problems of the new business and decide that you can use Microsoft Office for advertising the business, creating bills for customers, and calculating profits.

May 3

The three of you compile addresses for potential customers and estimated weekly fees into a file named Potential Customers.txt. Names are available for some of the addresses because they were your customers from the previous year. Other contacts are from referrals, people you have met, and the addresses of your clients' neighbors. When names are unavailable, the word "Resident" is used. All addresses are in the city of Chesapeake, VA 23322. The weekly fee is an estimate based on the size of the potential customer's yard.

You will import this information into a database that will supply addresses and fees for an advertising letter and an invoice, should these contacts become customers.

1. Start Access and use the Blank database template to create a new database in the Capstone folder where your Data Files are stored and named **Neighbors.accdb**. Close the Table1 table that opens.

2. In the Import & Link group on the External Data tab, click the Text File button. Import the **Potential Customers.txt** file from the Capstone folder into a new table in the current database. The first row contains field names. You should not set the data types for fields. Let Access add the table's primary key, and make sure that the table name is Potential Customers. Do not save the import steps.

3. Open the **Potential Customers** table in Design view. Move the First Name field so it appears below the Title field. Then use the information in **Table CS-1** to change the field names and set the field properties, as necessary, for the Potential Customers table.

TABLE CS–1

FIELD NAME	DATA TYPE	FIELD PROPERTIES
Customer ID	AutoNumber	Primary key
Title	Text	Field Size: 10
First Name	Text	Field Size: 20
Last Name	Text	Field Size: 20
Address	Text	Field Size: 40
City	Text	Field Size: 50
Fee	Currency	

4. Save the table. Click Yes in the dialog box that warns about data loss.

5. Switch to Datasheet view, and then resize all columns to best fit.

6. Save and close the table. Leave Access open.

May 4

Marcus wrote the form letter shown in **Figure CS-2** to advertise the services available through Green Way Lawn Care Service. First, you will design a letterhead template. You will also personalize the letter by merging the names and addresses of potential customers in the Potential Customers table with the form letter.

May 4, 2013

Dear

Green Way Lawn Care Service would like to add you to our growing list of clients who rely on us to provide environmentally-friendly lawn services. We can create a custom plan to suit your individual needs, or you can sign up for our standard weekly package that includes:

- Mowing
- Edging and weeding
- Trimming hedges
- Fertilization and weed control

The estimated fee for our weekly standard package is based on the size of your lawn, and you will be billed monthly. We guarantee all of our work, and can provide references in your neighborhood.

If you would like to consider using our services, or if you have any questions, please contact us at 757-555-3894.

Sincerely,

Student's name   Marcus Reider   Julia Perez

FIGURE CS–2

1. Start Word.

2. Design a letterhead template for Green Way Lawn Care Service that you can use with the letter shown in Figure CS-2. Include the company's name and the following address and telephone number in the letterhead template:

   221 Kentwick Avenue

   Chesapeake, VA 23322

   757-555-3894

   Add an appropriate logo to the letterhead template using a clip art image or picture. Save the document as a template in the Capstone folder where your Data Files are stored using the name **Letterhead Template.dotx**. Close the file.

3. Create a new Word document based on the Letterhead Template. Save the new document as **Form Letter.docx** followed by your initials. Type the form letter shown in Figure CS-2. (You will add the merge fields later.)

4. Save the document and leave it open.

May 5

You plan to visit potential customers next week. You will print the form letters for potential customers with the word "Resident" in the Title field of the Potential Customers table.

1. Save the Form Letter document as **Resident Letters.docx**, followed by your initials, in the Capstone folder where your Data Files are stored.

2. Close the Resident Letters document, and then close Word.

3. In Access, choose the option on the External Data tab to begin a merge with Word. Link your data to the Resident Letters document.

4. In Word, edit the recipient list by applying a filter to merge records that contain (equal) the word *Resident* in the Title field. (There should be four records.)

5. Add an address block to the letter, below the date, with a blank line between the date and the address block, and a blank line between the address block and the salutation.

6. On the line that includes the word *Dear*, type a space, and then insert the Title field. Type a comma after the merge field you just inserted.

7. Merge the letter with recipient 1, and then print the first page.

8. Save and close the document. Leave Word open.

May 6

Anticipating a response to the letters, Julia suggests creating the billing information file for May.

You will create a workbook that you can use to calculate and track billing. Create columns to show the weekly amount due for each customer, starting with the third week in May. For example, the Week 3 column will contain the amount due for the third week in May. The May Bill column will contain the total amount due for each customer for the month of May. The May Paid column will contain the amount paid by each customer for the month of May.

1. Start Excel.

2. Save the new workbook that opens as **Billing.xlsx** followed by your initials, in the Capstone folder where your Data Files are stored.

3. In cell A1, type **Week 3**.

4. In cell B1, type **Week 4**.

5. In cell C1, type **May Bill**.

6. In cell D1, type **May Paid**.

7. Enter a formula in cell C2 to calculate a total for the bills for the third and fourth weeks in May. (*Hint*: The total is the sum of the amounts in the Week 3 and Week 4 columns.)

8. Copy the formula you added in cell C2 down to cells C3 through C31.

9. Save and close the workbook. Leave Excel open.

May 7

The three of you decide to create a flyer that will advertise your services. Use Publisher to create the flyer using a template. You can use the logo and some of the information from the previously created form letter in your flyer. Save the publication as **GWFlyer.pub** followed by your initials in the Capstone folder where your Data Files are stored. Put your name somewhere on the flyer. Print and close the publication.

May 8

The following people (mostly former customers) have notified you that they would like to hire Green Way Lawn Care Service:

Carver, Alton	Levine, Heather
Cash, H. J.	Phillipston, Paul
Guy, D. P.	Rigby, Eddy
Harper, G. H.	Strayer, L. T.

In addition, based on the flyer you created, the residents at 209 Kentwick (Mr. Tom Alfreds) and 213 Fordham (Ms. Lillian Spears) have decided to hire Green Way Lawn Care Service.

1. Switch to Access.

2. Open the **Potential Customers** table in Design view. Add two new fields to the table using the information provided in **Table CS-2**.

TABLE CS–2

FIELD NAME	DATA TYPE
Current Customer	Yes/No
Amount Due	Currency

3. The names of the residents at 209 Kentwick and 213 Fordham were unknown when the database was created. Edit the Title, Last Name, and First Name fields to update these records. Resize each column in the datasheet to best fit.

4. Add a check mark to the Current Customer field for people who have hired Green Way Lawn Care Service. You might want to use the Find command or sort the records alphabetically by last name to help you find customer records.

5. Save the table and leave the table and Access open.

May 9

In anticipation of billing new customers, Julia writes a draft of the invoice shown in **Figure CS-3**. She will create the invoice using Word.

June 2, 2013

Charges for the month of May

We have calculated your May invoice based on our contract amount of $ per week. The amount due for May is $.

Please make your check payable to "Green Way Lawn Care Service." Payment is due by June 30.

Thank you for your business.

FIGURE CS–3

1. Switch to Word.

2. Use the Letterhead Template file to create a new document. Save the document as **Invoice.docx** followed by your initials in the Capstone folder where your Data Files are stored.

3. Create the invoice shown in Figure CS-3. (You will insert the merge fields later.)

4. Save and close the document. Leave Word open.

May 10

In response to your advertising, the following people have notified you that they would like to hire Green Way Lawn Care Service for the summer:

Mata, Ricardo	Goldberg, Richard
Novack, D. K.	Torres, Raul
Lake, Jasmine	Sanchez, Mercedes
Mueller, Anne	Aslam, Ritu
Keung, Yi	Johnson, Virginia
Robinson, T. R.	Roberts, Chad
Lauer, Corey	Page, Misha

Switch to the **Potential Customers** table in Access and edit the records for the new customers to show that they are current customers. Leave the table open.

May 11

For planning purposes, you decide to create a calendar showing the May schedule.

1. Start Outlook and change to Calendar view.

2. Display the month of May 2013 in Month view.

3. Insert the information shown in **Figure CS-4** into the calendar by clicking the day and entering each task as an all-day event.

FIGURE CS–4

4. Print the monthly calendar. Be sure to choose the dates **5/1/13** to **5/31/13** in the print range.

5. Close Outlook.

May 12

Julia prepares a monthly income statement to report the profits of Green Way Lawn Care Service. **Figure CS-5** shows a draft of the income statement for May. All three partners agree that this income statement will provide information to evaluate the progress of their business venture.

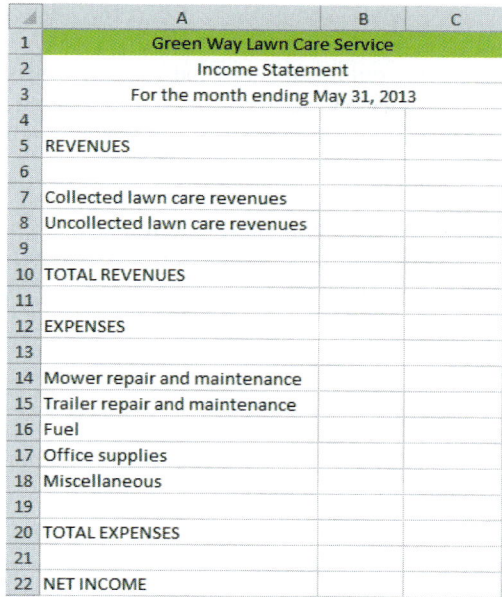

FIGURE CS–5

1. Switch to Excel. Create a new workbook and set up an income statement, as shown in Figure CS-5, for May.

2. Save the workbook as **Income Statement.xlsx** followed by your initials in the Capstone folder where your Data Files are stored. (You will add the values and formulas later.) Leave the workbook open.

May 14

The following people have notified you that they want to hire Green Way Lawn Care Service for the summer:

Dye, Allen	Liu, Lin-Ji
Richardson, Delia	Gibb, H. R.

The residents at 208 Picnic (Ms. Regina Hinkle) and 213 Picnic (Ms. Jeanne Garland) have also decided to hire Green Way Lawn Care Service.

1. Switch to Access.

2. The title and names of the residents at 208 Picnic and 213 Picnic were unknown when the database was created. Edit these records to update the information.

3. Add a check mark to the Current Customer field for people who have hired Green Way Lawn Care Service.

4. Leave the table open.

May 16

You want to make sure your equipment is in good working order before the summer begins, so you take it to the local mower repair shop for servicing. The cost of servicing is $211.37. You also buy new tires and replace a brake light for your trailer. The total cost for these items is $382.53.

1. Switch to the **Income Statement** workbook in Excel. Record the expenses for mower repair and maintenance and for the trailer repair and maintenance in the appropriate cells in column C.

2. Format the cells in column C using the Accounting format. Display a dollar sign as the symbol.

3. Save the workbook. Leave the workbook open.

May 21

Green Way Lawn Care Service serviced the lawns of the following customers:

Aslam	Mueller
Dye	Novack
Goldberg	Page
Johnson	Roberts
Keung	Robinson
Lake	Sanchez
Mata	Torres

1. Switch to the **Potential Customers** table in Access.

2. Use the AutoFilter option to create a filter to display current customers. (*Hint*: Current customers have a check mark—a "True" value—in the Current Customer field.)

3. Sort the records in ascending order using the Last Name field. Save the table.

4. Switch to Excel and open the **Billing.xlxs** workbook you created on May 6. Insert three new columns to the left of column A.

5. Switch to the **Potential Customers** table in Access. Move the Fee column in the datasheet to the right of the Address field. Use the mouse to select the Last Name, Address, and Fee columns, and then copy the data in these three columns to the Clipboard.

6. Click cell A1 in the **Billing** workbook, and then paste the data you copied from the Access table.

7. Adjust the row height and column widths in the Billing workbook to display the data.

8. In the Billing workbook, format the cells in columns D, E, F, and G with the Accounting format and a dollar sign as the symbol.

9. Enter the amount due (listed in the Fee column) in the Week 3 column for the customers whose lawns have been serviced.

10. Change the column headings in row 1 to bold and centered, remove the fill color, and remove the cell borders. Resize all columns in the worksheet to display the complete data.

11. Save the Billing workbook.

12. Switch to the **Income Statement** workbook and enter the following expenses: **$28.55** for fuel and **$15.85** for miscellaneous.

13. Save the Income Statement workbook and leave it open.

May 24

Green Way Lawn Care Service has serviced the lawns of the following customers:

Alfreds	Lauer
Carver	Levine
Cash	Liu
Garland	Phillipston
Gibb	Richardson
Guy	Rigby
Harper	Spears
Hinkle	Strayer

1. Switch to the **Billing** workbook and enter the amount due for each customer in the Week 4 column.

2. Save the workbook and leave it open.

3. Switch to the **Income Statement** workbook and add the following expenses to the worksheet: **$17.39** for fuel and **$6.56** for miscellaneous. (*Hint*: Replace the value $28.55 in the Fuel row with the formula **=28.55+17.39**, and replace the value in the Miscellaneous row with a formula that adds the two values.)

4. Save the workbook and leave it open.

May 28

Green Way Lawn Care Service has serviced the lawns of the following customers:

Aslam	Mueller
Dye	Novack
Goldberg	Page
Johnson	Roberts
Keung	Robinson
Lake	Sanchez
Mata	Torres

1. Switch to the **Billing** workbook and enter the amount due for each customer in the Week 4 column.

2. Save the workbook and leave it open.

3. Switch to the **Income Statement** workbook and modify formulas as necessary to add the following additional expenses to the worksheet: **$10.18** for fuel and **$6.78** for office supplies.

4. Save the workbook and leave it open.

May 30

During the month of May, Green Way Lawn Care Service spent $32.79 on paper and $21.56 on miscellaneous expenses.

1. Record the amounts for office supplies and miscellaneous expenses in the Income Statement workbook in the appropriate cells.

2. Save the workbook and leave it open.

May 31

Julia is preparing the monthly bills for May. She will print the bills and distribute them in person.

1. Switch to Access and the **Potential Customers** datasheet.

2. With the filter still applied to display current customers, sort the records in alphabetical order by last name, if necessary.

3. Switch to the **Billing** workbook. Copy the amounts in the May Bill column (cells F2 through F31) to the Clipboard.

4. Switch to the **Potential Customers** datasheet Access. Click the Amount Due field selector in the Potential Customers table to select the entire field, and then paste the values into the column. When the message box opens and asks if you want to paste the records, click Yes.

5. In Word, open the **Invoice** document you created, and then save it as **May Invoice.docx** followed by your initials in the Capstone folder where your Data Files are stored. Close the document and leave Word open.

6. Switch to the **Potential Customers** datasheet in Access, and then save and close the table. Use the External Data tab to merge the May Invoice document with data from the Potential Customers table. Edit the recipient list to select the records for the customers with the last names Spears and Lauer.

7. Use the Insert Merge Field button in the Write & Insert Fields group on the Mailings tab to insert the merge fields shown in **Figure CS-6** in the document. Make sure to insert the proper spacing between merge fields.

Green Way Lawn Care Service

221 Kentwick Avenue ♣ Chesapeake, VA 23322 ♣ 757-555-3894

June 2, 2013

Charges for the month of May

«Title» «First_Name» «Last_Name»

«Address»

«City»

We have calculated your May invoice based on our contract amount of $«Fee» per week. The amount due for May is $«Amount_Due».

Please make your check payable to "Green Way Lawn Care Service." Payment is due by June 30.

Thank you for your business.

FIGURE CS–6

8. Merge the document, and print the letter to Mr. Corey Lauer.

9. Save and close the document, and then close Word.

June 3

When Julia delivers the invoices, the following customers are at home and promptly pay the amount due in full:

Alfreds	Lauer
Aslam	Levine
Cash	Mata
Dye	Novack
Garland	Page
Goldberg	Rigby
Guy	Roberts
Hinkle	Robinson
Lake	Sanchez

Switch to the **Billing** workbook and record the amount collected in the May Paid column. Save the workbook and leave it open.

June 8

The following customers sent payments to Green Way Lawn Care Service to pay the amount due in full:

Gibb	Phillipston
Harper	Spears
Johnson	Strayer
Liu	

1. Record the collection of these amounts in the May Paid column of the Billing workbook.

2. Save the workbook and leave it open.

June 9

Julia wonders about the unpaid bills. She wants to calculate the amounts billed to the customers and the amounts paid.

1. In cell A33 of the Billing workbook, type **TOTALS** and change the text to bold.

2. Enter a formula in cell F33 to calculate a total for the May Bill column. Make sure that the cell's format uses the Accounting format and a dollar sign as the symbol.

3. Copy the formula in cell F33 to cell G33.

4. In cell A34, type **Uncollected**.

5. In cell B34, enter a formula to subtract the total in the May Paid column from the total in the May Bill column. Make sure that the cell's format uses the Accounting format and a dollar sign as the symbol.

6. Sort the records using the May Paid column so the records for the five customers with unpaid invoices appear at the bottom of the list.

7. In cell A35, type your first and last names. Save, print, and close the workbook.

Green Way Lawn Care Service

June 10

Green Way Lawn Care Service has now compiled the data for the first month of operations. The partners want to know if they made a profit in May. They need print-outs of the May income statement to assess their progress.

1. Switch to the **Income Statement** workbook. This file already contains updated expenses for May.

2. In cell C7, enter **1074** and in cell C8, enter **266**.

3. In cell C10, enter a formula to calculate the total revenues (collected revenues plus uncollected revenues).

4. In cell C20, enter a formula to calculate the total amount for all expenses.

5. In cell C22, enter a formula to calculate the net income for the month (total revenues minus total expenses).

6. Make sure that column C uses the Accounting format and a dollar sign as the symbol.

7. Enter your name in cell A24. Save, print, and close the workbook. Close Excel.

8. Close all other Office programs.

APPENDIX A

Computer Concepts

The Computer: An Overview

A computer is a machine that is used to store, retrieve, and manipulate data. A computer takes **input**, uses instructions to **process** and **store** that data, and then produces **output**. You enter the data into the computer through a variety of input devices, such as a keyboard or mouse. The processor processes the data to produce information. Information is output presented in many ways such as an image on a monitor, printed pages from a printer, or sound through speakers. Computer **software** is stored instructions or programming that runs the computer. **Memory** inside the computer stores the programs or instructions that run the computer as well as the data and information. Various **storage devices** are used to transfer or safely store the data and information on **storage media**.

A **computer system** is made up of components that include the computer, input, and output devices. Computer systems come in many shapes, sizes, and configurations. The computer you use at home or in school is often called a **personal computer**. **Desktop computers** often have a 'computer case' or a **system unit**, which contains processing devices, memory, and some storage devices. **Figure A–1** shows a typical desktop computer. Input devices such as the mouse or pointing device, and keyboard are attached to the system unit by cables or wires. Output devices, such as the monitor (display device), speakers, and printer are also attached to the system unit by cables or wires. ***Wireless technology*** makes it possible to eliminate wires and use the airwaves to connect devices. ***Laptop*** or ***notebook*** computers have all the essential parts: the keyboard, pointing device, and display device all in one unit. See **Figure A–2** for a typical notebook computer.

FIGURE A–1   A desktop computer system

FIGURE A–2   A laptop computer

When learning about computers, it is helpful to organize the topics into a discussion about the hardware and the software, and then how the computer processes the data.

Computer Hardware

The physical components, devices, or parts of the computer are called ***hardware***. Computer hardware includes the essential components found on all computers such as the central processing unit (CPU), the monitor, the keyboard, and the mouse. Hardware can be divided into categories: Input devices, processors, storage devices, and output devices. *Peripheral devices* are additional components, such as printers, speakers, and scanners that enhance the computing experience. Peripherals are not essential to the computer, but provide additional functions for the computer.

Input Devices

There are many different types of input devices. You enter information into a computer by typing on a keyboard or by pointing, clicking, or dragging a mouse. A *mouse* is a handheld device used to move a pointer on the computer screen. Similar to a mouse, a *trackball* has a roller ball that turns to control a pointer on the screen. Tracking devices, such as a *touchpad*, are an alternative to the trackball or mouse. Situated on the keyboard of a laptop computer, they allow you to simply move and tap your finger on a small electronic pad to control the pointer on the screen.

Tablet PCs allow you to input data by writing directly on the computer screen. Handwriting recognition technology converts handwritten writing to text. Many computers have a microphone or other *sound input device* which accepts speech or sounds as input and converts the speech to text or data. For example, when you telephone a company or bank for customer service, you often have the option to say your requests or account number. That is *speech recognition technology* at work!

Other input devices include scanners and bar code readers. You can use a *scanner* to convert text or graphics from a printed page into code that a computer can process. You have probably seen *bar code readers* being used in stores. These are used to read bar codes, such as the UPC (Universal Product Code), to track merchandise or other inventory in a store. See **Figure A–3**.

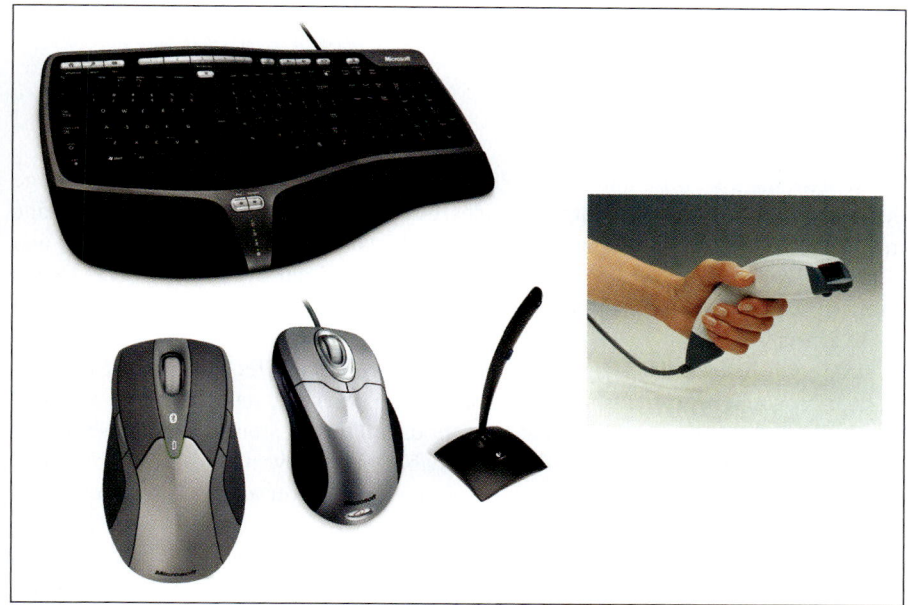

FIGURE A–3 Examples of input devices

Processing Devices

Processing devices are mounted inside the system unit of the computer. The *motherboard* is where the computer memory and other vital electronic parts are stored. See **Figure A–4**. The *central processing unit* (**CPU**) is a silicon chip that processes data and carries out instructions given to the computer. The CPU is stored on the motherboard of the computer. The *data bus* includes the wiring and pathways by which the CPU communicates with the peripherals and components of the computer.

FIGURE A–4 A motherboard

Storage Devices

Computers have to store and retrieve data for them to be of any use at all. Storage devices are both input and output devices. A *storage medium* holds data. Storage media include hard drives, tape, memory cards, solid state flash drives, CDs, and DVDs. A *storage device* is the hardware that stores and retrieves data from a storage medium. Storage devices include hard drives, card readers, tape drives, and CD and DVD drives.

Storage devices use magnetic, optical, or solid state technologies. Magnetic storage uses magnetic fields to store data and can be erased and used over and over again. Optical technology uses light to store data. Optical storage media use one of three technologies: read-only (ROM), recordable (R), or rewritable (RW). Solid state storage uses no moving parts and can be used over and over again. There are advantages and disadvantages to each technology.

Most computers have more than one type of storage device. The main storage device for a computer is the *hard drive* that is usually inside the system unit. Hard drives use magnetic storage. The hard drive reads and writes data to and from a round magnetic platter, or disk. **Figure A–5** shows a fixed storage unit. It is not removable from the computer.

FIGURE A–5 An internal hard drive

External and removable hard drives that can plug into the USB port on the system unit are also available. External drives offer flexibility; allowing you to transfer data between computers easily. See **Figure A–6**. At the time this book was written, typical hard drives for a computer system that you might buy for your personal home use range from 500 gigabytes (GB) to 2 terabytes.

FIGURE A–6 An external hard drive

APPENDIX A

The *floppy disk drive* is older technology that is no longer available on new computers. Some older computers still have a floppy disk drive which is mounted in the system unit with access to the outside. A floppy disk is the medium that stores the data. You put the floppy disk into the floppy disk drive so the computer can read and write the data. The floppy disk's main advantage was portability. You can store data on a floppy disk and transport it for use on another computer. A floppy disk can hold up to 1.4MB (megabytes) of information. A Zip disk is similar to a floppy disk. A *Zip disk* is also an older portable disk technology that was contained in a plastic sleeve. Each disk held 100MB or 250MB of information. A special disk drive called a *Zip drive* is required to read and write data to a Zip disk.

Optical storage devices include the *CD drive* or *DVD drive* or *Blu-ray drive*. CDs, DVDs, and *Blu-ray drive (BD)* use optical storage technology. See **Figure A–7**.

FIGURE A–7   A CD/DVD/Blu-ray drive

These drives are typically mounted inside the system unit, although external versions of these devices are also available. Most new computers are equipped with CD/DVD burners. That means they have read and write capabilities. You use a CD/DVD drive to read and write CDs and DVDs. A *CD* is a compact disc, which is a form of optical storage. Compact discs can store 700 MB of data. These discs have a great advantage over other forms of removable storage as they can hold vast quantities of information—the entire contents of a small library, for instance. They are also fairly durable. Another advantage of CDs is their ability to hold graphic information, including moving pictures, with the highest quality stereo sound. A *DVD* is also an optical disc that looks like a CD. It is a high-capacity storage device that can contain up to 4.7GB of data, which is a seven-fold increase over a CD. There are two variations of DVDs that offer even more storage—a 2-layer version with 9.4GB capacity and double-sided discs with 17GB capacity. A DVD holds 133 minutes of data on each side, which means that two two-hour full-length feature movies can be stored on one disc. Information is encoded on the disk by a laser and read by a CD/DVD drive in the computer. ***Blu-ray discs (BD)*** offer even more storage capacity. These highest-capacity discs are designed to record full-length high-definition feature films. As of this writing, a BD can store upwards of 35GB of data. Special Blu-ray hardware, including disc players available in gaming systems and Blu-ray burners, are needed to read Blu-ray discs.

A CD drive only reads CDs, a DVD drive can read CDs and DVDs, a Blu-ray drive reads BDs, CDs, and DVDs. CD/DVD/BD drives look quite similar, as do the discs. See **Figure A–8**.

FIGURE A–8   CDs, DVDs, and Blu-rays look alike

APPENDIX A

Solid state storage is another popular storage technology. A ***USB flash drive*** is a very portable small store device that works both as a drive and medium. It plugs directly into a USB port on the computer system unit. You read and write data to the flash drive. See **Figure A–9**.

FIGURE A–9   A flash drive

Solid state card readers are devices that can read solid state cards. Solid state storage is often used in cameras. See **Figure A–10**.

FIGURE A–10   Solid state card and card reader

Magnetic tape is a medium most commonly used for backing up a computer system, which means making a copy of files from a hard drive. Although it is relatively rare for data on a hard drive to be completely lost in a crash (that is, for the data or pointers to the data to be partially or totally destroyed), it can and does happen. Therefore, most businesses and some individuals routinely back up files on tape. If you have a small hard drive, you can use DVDs or CD-ROMs or solid state storage such as a flash drive or memory card to back up your system. **Figure A–11** shows a tape storage system.

FIGURE A–11   Tape storage system

Output Devices

The *monitor* on which you view your computer work is an output device. It provides a visual representation of the information stored in or produced by your computer. The typical monitor for today's system is a flat-screen monitor similar to a television. Computer monitors typically use *LCD technology*. LCD stands for Liquid Crystal Display. See **Figure A–12**. LCD monitors provide a very sharp picture because of the large number of tiny dots, called *pixels*, which make up the display as well as its ability to present the full spectrum of colors. *Resolution* is the term that tells you how clear an image will be on the screen. Resolution is measured in pixels. A typical resolution is 1024 × 768. A high-quality monitor may have a resolution of 1920 × 1080, or 2560 × 1440 or higher. Monitors come in different sizes. The size of a monitor is determined by measuring the diagonal of the screen. Laptops have smaller monitors than desktop computers. A laptop monitor may be 13", 15", or 17". Desktop monitors can be as large as 19"–27" or even larger.

FIGURE A–12   An LCD monitor

APPENDIX A

Printers are a type of output device. They let you produce a paper printout of information contained in the computer. Today, most printers use either inkjet or laser technology to produce high-quality print. Like a copy machine, a *laser printer* uses heat to fuse a powdery substance called *toner* to the page. *Ink-jet printers* use a spray of ink to print. Laser printers give the sharpest image and often print more pages per minute (ppm) than ink-jet printers. Ink-jet printers provide nearly as sharp an image, but the wet printouts can smear when they first are printed. Most color printers, or photo printers for printing photographs, are ink-jet printers. Color laser printers are more costly. These printers allow you to print information in a full array of colors, just as you see it on your monitor. See **Figure A–13**.

FIGURE A–13   Printers

Laptop or Notebook Computer

A *laptop computer*, also called a *notebook computer*, is a small folding computer that can literally fit in a person's lap or in a backpack. Within the fold-up case of a laptop is the CPU, data bus, monitor (built into the lid), hard drive (sometimes removable), USB ports, CD/DVD drive, and trackball or digital tracking device. The advantage of the laptop is its portability—you can work anywhere because you can use power either from an outlet or from the computer's internal, rechargeable batteries. Almost all laptops have wireless Internet access built into the system. The drawbacks are the smaller keyboard, smaller monitor, smaller capacity, and higher price, though some laptops offer full-sized keyboards and higher quality monitors. As technology allows, storage capacity on smaller devices is making it possible to offer laptops with as much power and storage as a full-sized computer. See **Figure A–14**.

FIGURE A–14   Laptop computers

Personal Digital Assistants (PDA) and Smartphones

A *Personal Digital Assistant (PDA)* is a pocket-sized electronic organizer that helps you to manage addresses, appointments, expenses, tasks, and memos. If you own a cell phone, chances are it is a *Smartphone* and it can do more than just make and receive phone calls. Today, many handheld devices, such as cell phones and Personal Digital Assistants include features such as a full keypad for text messaging and writing notes, e-mail, a browser for Web access, a calendar and address book to manage contacts and appointments, a digital camera, radio, and digital music player. Most handheld devices also include software for games, financial management, personal organizer, GPS, and maps. See **Figure A–15**.

FIGURE A–15 Smartphones

The common input devices for PDAs and some Smartphones include touch-sensitive screens that accept input through a stylus pen or small keyboards that are either built in to the device or available as software on the screen. Data and information can be shared with a Windows-based or Macintosh computer through a process called synchronization. By placing your handheld in a cradle or through a USB port attached to your computer, you can transfer data from your PDA's calendar, address book, or memo program into your computer's information manager program and vice versa. The information is updated on both sides, making your handheld device a portable extension of your computer.

How Computers Work

All input, processing, storage, and output devices function together to make the manipulation, storage, and distribution of data and information possible. Data is information entered into and manipulated or processed within a computer. Processing includes computation, such as adding, subtracting, multiplying, and dividing; analysis planning, such as sorting data; and reporting, such as presenting data for others in a chart or graph. This next section explains how computers work.

Memory

Computers have two types of memory—RAM and ROM. **RAM**, or **random access memory**, is the silicon chips in the system unit that temporarily store information when the computer is turned on. RAM is what keeps the software programs up and running and provides visuals that appear on your screen. You work with data in RAM up until you save it to a storage media such as a hard disk, CD, DVD, or solid state storage such as flash drive.

Computers have sophisticated application programs that include a lot of graphics, video, and data. In order to run these programs, computers require a lot of memory. Therefore, computers have a minimum of 512MB of RAM. Typical computers include between 2GB and 4GB of RAM to be able to run most programs. Most computer systems are expandable and you can add on RAM after you buy the computer. The more RAM available for the programs, the faster and more efficiently the machine will be able to operate. RAM chips are shown in **Figure A–16**.

FIGURE A–16   RAM chips

ROM, or *read-only memory*, is the memory that stays in the computer when it is turned off. It is ROM that stores the programs that run the computer as it starts or "boots up." ROM holds the instructions that tell the computer how to begin to load its operating system software programs.

Speed

The speed of a computer is measured by how fast the computer processes each instruction. There are several factors that affect the performance of a computer: the speed of the processor, or the *clock speed*, the *front side bus speed*—the speed of the bus that connects the processor to main memory—the speed in which data is written and retrieved from the hard drive or other storage media, and the speed of the graphics card if you are working on programs that use a lot of graphic images. These all factor into a computer's performance.

The speed of a computer is measured in *megahertz (MHz)* and *gigahertz (GHz)*. Processor speed is part of the specifications when you buy a computer. For example, to run Windows 7 on a computer, you need a processor that has 1 gigahertz (GHz) or faster 32-bit (x86) or 64-bit (x64) processor. Processors are sold by name and each brand or series has its own specifications. Processor manufacturers include AMD, Intel, and Motorola.

Networks

Computers have expanded the world of communications. A ***network*** is defined as two or more computers connected to share data. ***LANs (local area networks)*** connect computers within a small area such as a home, office, school, or building. Networks can be wired or wireless. The ***Internet*** is the largest network in the world connecting millions of computers across the globe. Using the Internet, people can communicate across the world instantly.

Networks require various communication devices and software. ***Modems*** allow computers to communicate with each other by telephone lines. Modem is an acronym that stands for "MOdulator/DEModulator." Modems convert data in bytes to sound media in order to send data over the phone lines and then convert it back to bytes after receiving data. Modems operate at various rates or speeds. ***Network cards*** in the system unit allow computers to access networks. A ***router*** is an electronic device that joins two or more networks. For example, a home network can use a router and a modem to connect the home's LAN to the Internet. A ***server*** is the computer hardware and software that "serves" the computers on a network. Network technology is sometimes called "client-server." A personal computer that requests data from a server is referred to as a ***client***. The computer that stores the data is the ***server***. On the Internet, the computer that stores Web pages is the ***Web server***. **Figure A–17** shows a network diagram.

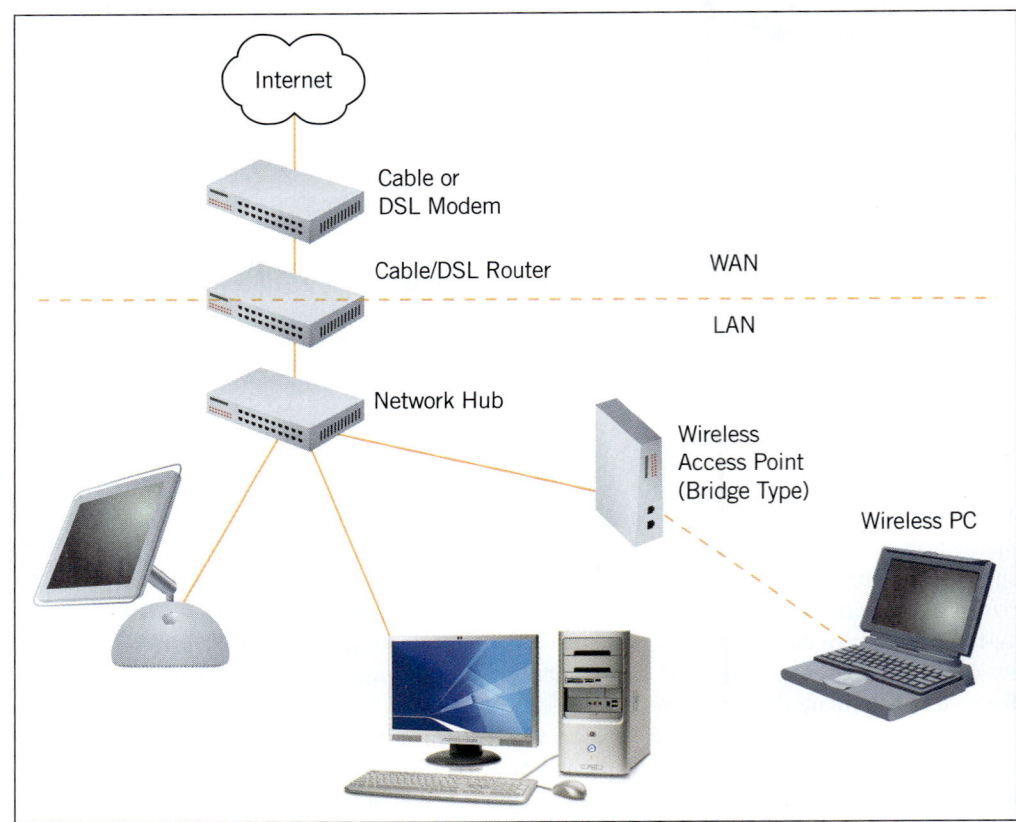

FIGURE A–17   Diagram of a network

Networks have certain advantages over stand-alone computers: they allow communication among the computers; they allow smaller capacity computers to access the larger capacity of the server computers on the network; they allow several computers to share peripherals, such as one printer; and they can make it possible for all computers on the network to have access to the Internet.

Connect to the Internet

To connect to the Internet you need to subscribe to an ***Internet Service Provider (ISP)***. There are several technologies available. Connection speeds are measured in bits per second. Upload speeds are slower than download speeds. ***Dial-up*** is the oldest, and the slowest Internet access technology that is offered by local telephone companies. To get access to the Internet, your computer has to dial out through a phone line. Many people have moved to ***always-on connection technologies***. The computer is always connected to the Internet if you turn the computer on, so you don't have to dial out. These always-on faster technologies, known as a ***Digital Subscriber Line (DSL)***, include cable connections, satellites, and fiber optic. They are offered by telephone and cable television companies, as well as satellite service providers. It can be noted that satellite Internet access is the most expensive and dialup is the cheapest. DSL is through phone lines. **Table A–1** shows a brief comparison of these technologies based on the time this book was written and average speed assessments.

TABLE A–1   Comparing average Internet access options

FEATURE	SATELLITE	DSL	CABLE	FIBER OPTIC
Max. High Speed	Download speeds ranging anywhere from 768 Kbps up to 5.0 Mbps	Download speed 10 Mbps/ upload speed 5 Mbps	Download speed 30 Mbps/ upload speed 10 Mbps	Download speed 50 Mbps/ upload speed 20 Mbps
Access is through	Satellite dish	Existing phone line	Existing TV cable	Fiber-optic phone lines
Availability	Available in all areas; note that satellite service is sensitive to weather conditions	Generally available in populated areas	Might not be available in rural areas	Might not be available in all areas as fiber-optic lines are still being installed in many areas

Software

A ***program*** is a set of instructions that the computer uses to operate. ***Software*** is the collection of programs and other data input that tells the computer how to run its devices, how to manipulate, store, and output information, and how to accept the input you give it. Software fits into two basic categories: systems software and applications software. A third category, network software, is really a type of application.

Systems Software

The ***operating system*** is the main software or ***system software*** that runs a computer and often defines the type of computer. There are two main types or platforms for personal computers. The Macintosh computer, or Mac, is produced by Apple Computer, Inc. and runs the Mac operating system. The PC is a Windows-based

APPENDIX A

computer produced by many different companies, but which runs the Microsoft Windows operating system.

Systems software refers to the operating system of the computer. The operating system is a group of programs that is automatically copied in from the time the computer is turned on until the computer is turned off. Operating systems serve two functions: they control data flow among computer parts, and they provide the platform on which application and network software work—in effect, they allow the "space" for software and translate its commands to the computer. The most popular operating systems in use today are the Macintosh operating system, MAC OS X and several different versions of Microsoft Windows, such as Windows XP, Windows Vista, or Windows 7. See **Figure A–18** and **Figure A–19**.

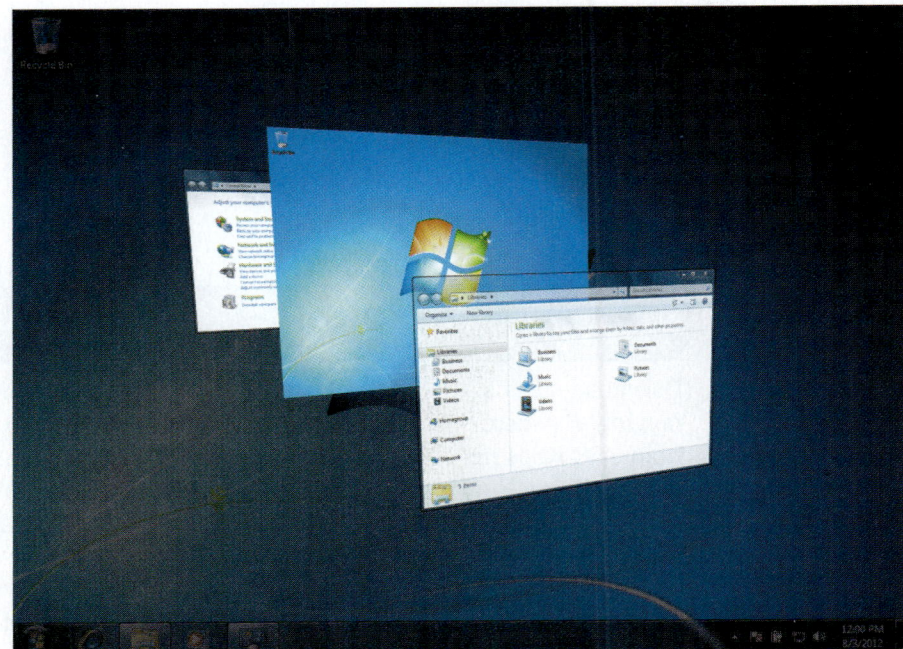

FIGURE A–18   Windows 7 operating system

FIGURE A–19   Mac OS

Since its introduction in the mid-1970s, Macintosh has used its own operating system, a graphical user interface (GUI) system that has evolved over the years. The OS is designed so users "click" with a mouse on pictures, called icons, or on text to give commands to the system. Data is available to you in the WYSIWYG (what-you-see-is-what-you-get) format; that is, you can see on-screen what a document will look like when it is printed. Graphics and other kinds of data, such as spreadsheets, can be placed into text documents. However, GUIs take a great deal of RAM to keep all of the graphics and programs operating.

The original OS for IBM and IBM-compatible computers (machines made by other companies that operate similarly) was DOS (disk operating system). It did not have a graphical interface. The GUI system, Windows™, was developed to make using the IBM/IBM-compatible computer more "friendly." Today's Windows applications are the logical evolution of GUI for IBM and IBM-compatible machines. Windows is a point-and-click system that automatically configures hardware to work together. You should note, however, that with all of its abilities comes the need for more RAM, or a system running Windows will operate slowly.

Applications Software

When you use a computer program to perform a data manipulation or processing task, you are using applications software. Word processors, databases, spreadsheets, graphics programs, desktop publishers, fax systems, and Internet browsers are all applications software.

Network Software

A traditional network is a group of computers that are hardwired (connected together with cables) to communicate and operate together. Today, some computer networks use RF (radio frequency) wireless technology to communicate with each other. This is called a *wireless network*, because you do not need to physically hook the network together with cables. In a typical network, one computer acts as the server, controlling the flow of data among the other computers, called nodes, or clients on the network. Network software manages this flow of information.

History of the Computer

Though various types of calculating machines were developed in the nineteenth century, the history of the modern computer begins about the middle of the last century. The strides made in developing today's personal computer have been truly astounding.

Early Development

The ENIAC, or Electronic Numerical Integrator and Computer, (see **Figure A–20**) was designed for military use in calculating ballistic trajectories and was the first electronic, digital computer to be developed in the United States. For its day, 1946, it was quite a marvel because it was able to accomplish a task in 20 seconds that normally would take a human three days to complete. However, it was an enormous machine that weighed more than 20 tons and contained thousands of vacuum tubes, which often failed. The tasks that it could accomplish were limited, as well.

FIGURE A–20   The ENIAC

From this awkward beginning, however, the seeds of an information revolution grew. The invention of the silicon chip in 1971, and the release of the first personal computer in 1974, launched the fast-paced information revolution in which we now all live and participate.

Significant dates in the history of computer development are listed in **Table A–2**.

TABLE A–2 Milestones in the development of computers

YEAR	DEVELOPMENT
1948	First electronically stored program
1951	First junction transistor
1953	Replacement of tubes with magnetic cores
1957	First high-level computer language
1961	First integrated circuit
1965	First minicomputer
1971	Invention of the microprocessor (the silicon chip) and floppy disk
1974	First personal computer (made possible by the microprocessor)

The Personal Computer

The PC, or personal computer, was mass marketed by Apple beginning in 1977, and by IBM in 1981. It is this desktop device with which people are so familiar and which, today, contains much more power and ability than did the original computer that took up an entire room. The PC is a small computer (desktop size or less) that uses a microprocessor to manipulate data. PCs may stand alone, be linked together in a network, or be attached to a large mainframe computer. See **Figure A–21**.

FIGURE A–21 An early IBM PC

APPENDIX A

Computer Utilities and System Maintenance

Computer operating systems let you run certain utilities and perform system maintenance to keep your computer running well. When you add hardware or software, you make changes in the way the system operates. With Plug and Play, most configuration changes are done automatically. The *drivers*, software that runs the peripherals, are installed automatically when your computer identifies the new hardware. When you install new software, many changes are made to the system automatically that determine how the software starts and runs.

In addition, you might want to customize the way the new software or hardware works with your system. You use *utility software* to make changes to the way hardware and software works. For example, you can change the speed at which your mouse clicks, how quickly or slowly keys repeat on the keyboard, and the resolution of the screen display. Utilities are included with your operating system. If you are running Windows XP, Windows Vista, or Windows 7, the Windows Control Panel provides access to the many Windows operating system utilities. **Figure A–22** shows the System and Security utilities in the Control Panel for Windows 7.

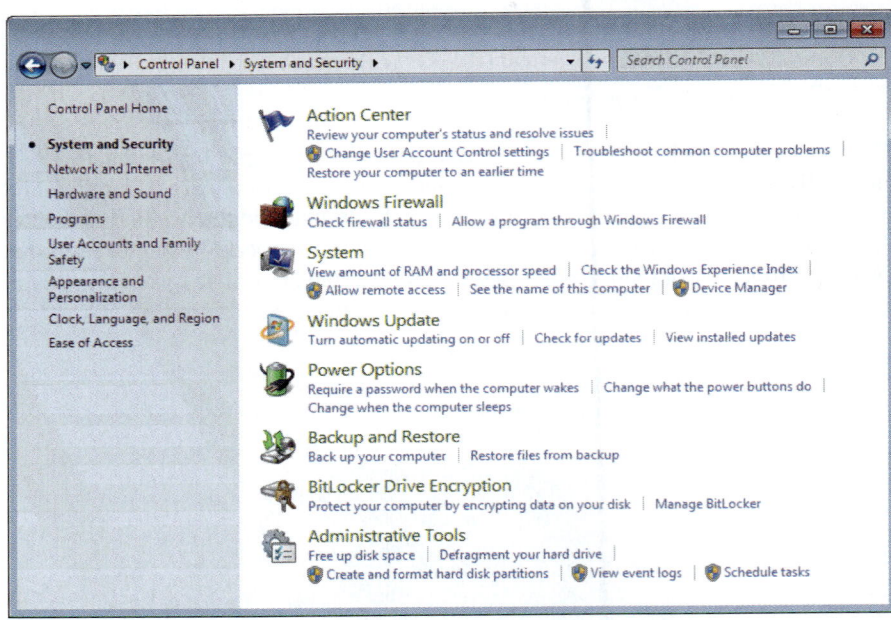

FIGURE A–22 Control Panel for Windows 7

Virus and Spyware Protection

Certain maintenance should be performed regularly on computers. *Viruses* are malicious software programs that can damage the programs on your computer causing the computer to either stop working or run slowly. These programs are created by people, called *hackers*, who send the programs out solely to do harm to computers. Viruses are loaded onto your computer without your knowledge and run against your wishes. *Spyware* is also a form of a program that can harm your computer. There are utilities and programs called *antispyware* and *antivirus* programs that protect your computer from spyware and viruses.

You should install and update your antivirus and spyware protection software regularly, and scan all new disks and any incoming information from online sources for viruses. Some systems do this automatically; others require you to install software to do it.

Disk Maintenance

From time to time, you should run a program that scans or checks the hard drive to see that there are not bad sectors (areas) and look for corrupted files. Optimizing or defragmenting the hard disk is another way to keep your computer running at its best. Scanning and checking programs often offers the option of "fixing" the bad areas or problems, although you should be aware that this could result in data loss.

Society and Computers

The electronic information era has had global effects and influenced global change in all areas of people's lives including education, government, society, and commerce. With the changes of this era have come many new questions and responsibilities. There are issues of ethics, security, and privacy.

Ethics

When you access information—whether online, in the workplace, or via purchased software—you have a responsibility to respect the rights of the person or people who created that information. Digital information, text, images, and sound are very easy to copy and share, however, that does not make it right to do so. You have to treat electronic information with respect. Often images, text, and sound are copyrighted. *Copyright* is the legal method for protecting the intellectual property of the author— the same way as you would a book, article, or painting. For instance, you must give credit when you copy information from the Web or another person's document.

If you come across another person's personal information, you must treat it with respect. Do not share personal information unless you have that person's permission. For example, if you happen to pass a computer where a person left personal banking information software open on the computer or a personal calendar available, you should not share that information. If e-mail comes to you erroneously, you should delete it before reading it.

When you use equipment that belongs to your school, a company for which you work, or others, here are some rules you should follow:

1. Do not damage computer hardware.

2. Do not add or remove equipment without permission.

3. Do not use an access code or equipment without permission.

4. Do not read others' e-mail.

5. Do not alter data belonging to someone else without permission.

6. Do not use the computer for play during work hours or use it for personal profit.

7. Do not access the Internet for nonbusiness related activities during work hours.

8. Do not install or uninstall software without permission.

9. Do not make unauthorized copies of data or software or copy company files or procedures for personal use.

10. Do not copy software programs to use at home or at another site in the company without permission.

APPENDIX A

Security and Privacy

The Internet provides access to business and life-enhancing resources, such as distance learning, remote medical diagnostics, and the ability to work from home more effectively. Businesses, colleges and universities, and governments throughout the world depend on the Internet every day to get work done. Disruptions in the Internet can create havoc and dramatically decrease productivity.

With more and more financial transactions taking place online, *identity theft* is a growing problem, proving a person's online identity relies heavily upon their usernames and passwords. If you do online banking, there are several levels of security that you must pass through, verifying that you are who you claim to be, before gaining access to your accounts. If you divulge your usernames and passwords, someone can easily access your accounts online with devastating effects to your credit rating and to your accounts.

Phishing is a criminal activity that is used by people to fraudulently obtain your personal information, such as usernames, passwords, credit card details, and your Social Security information. Your Social Security number should never be given out online. Phishers send e-mails that look legitimate, but in fact are not. Phishing e-mails will often include fake information saying that your account needs your immediate attention because of unusual or suspected fraudulent activity. You are asked to click a link in the e-mail to access a Web site where you are then instructed to enter personal information. See **Figure A–23** and **Figure A–24**. Phishing e-mail might also come with a promise of winning some money or gifts. When you get mail from people you don't know, the rules to remember are "you never get something for nothing," and "if it looks too good to be true, it's most likely not true."

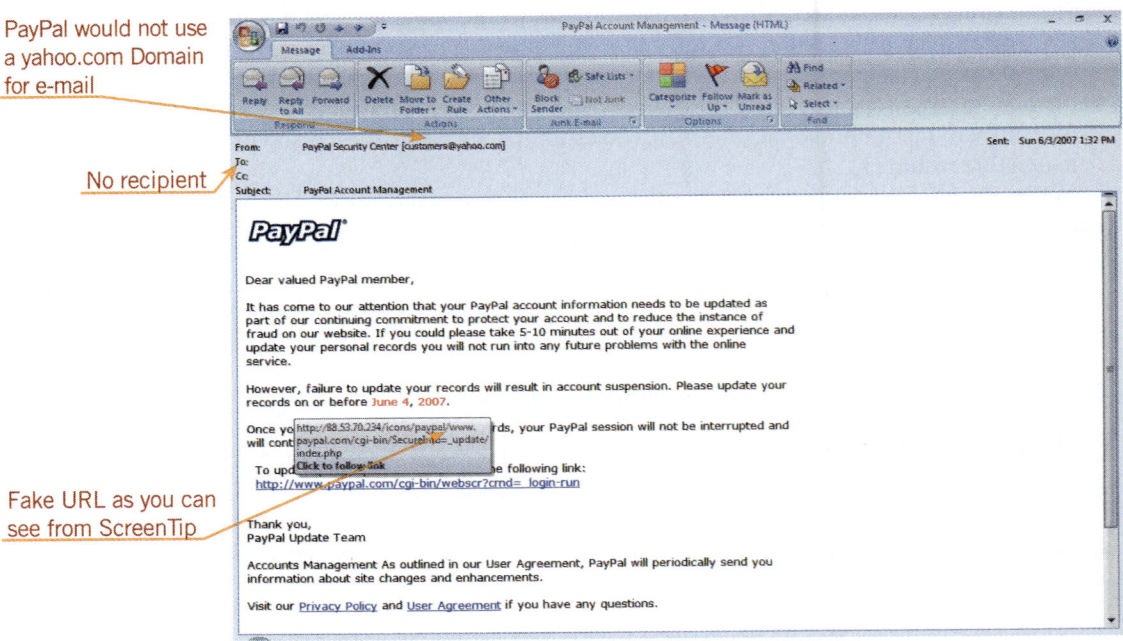

PayPal would not use a yahoo.com Domain for e-mail

No recipient

Fake URL as you can see from ScreenTip

FIGURE A–23   Fake PayPal e-mail for phishing

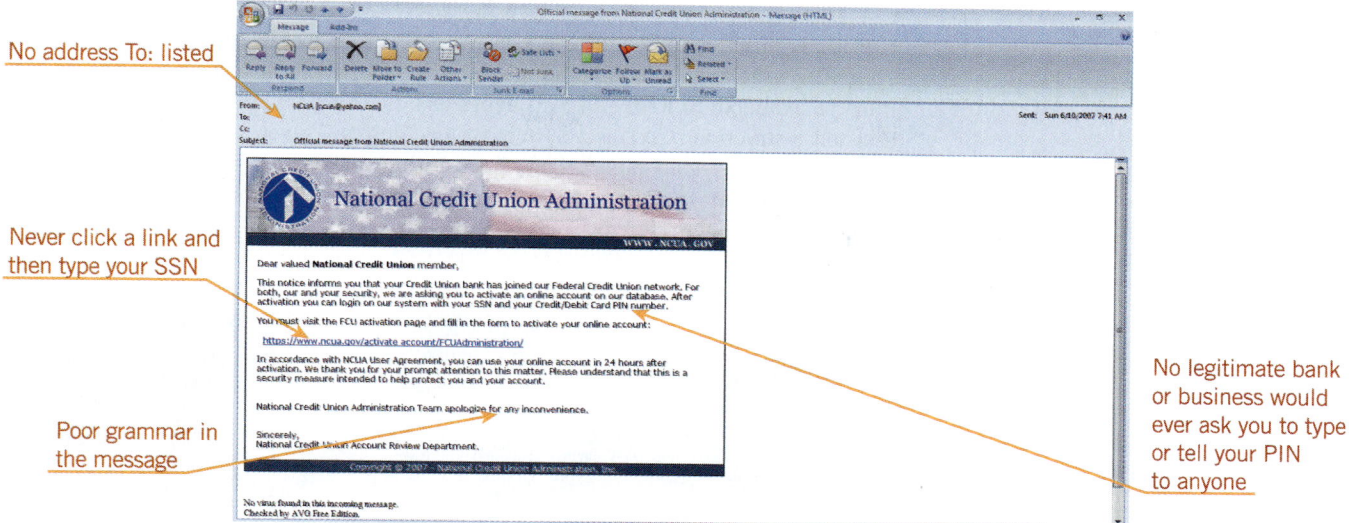

FIGURE A–24 Fake Credit Union e-mail for phishing

Whatever the ruse, when you click the link provided in the phishing e-mail, your browser will open a Web site that looks real, perhaps like your bank's site, eBay, or PayPal. But, in fact, this is a fake site set up to get you to give up your personal information. Phishing sites are growing. You should never click a link provided in an e-mail to get to sites such as your bank, eBay, or PayPal. Your bank or any other legitimate Web site will never ask you to type personal information on a page linked from an e-mail message. Always type the Web page address directly in the browser. Banks and Web sites have been trying to stop phishing sites through technology. Other attempts to reduce the growing number of reported phishing incidents include legislation and simply educating users about the practice.

Just as you would not open someone else's mail, you must respect the privacy of e-mail sent to others. When interacting with others online, you must keep confidential information confidential. Do not endanger your privacy, safety, or financial security by giving out personal information to someone you do not know.

EXTRA FOR EXPERTS

Ebay is an online auction Web site that provides people a way to buy and sell merchandise through the Internet. PayPal is a financial services Web site that provides a way to transfer funds between people who perform financial transactions on the Internet.

Career Opportunities

In one way or another, all careers involve the computer. Whether you are a grocery store clerk using a scanner to read the prices, a busy executive writing a report that includes charts, graphics, and detailed analysis on a laptop on an airplane, or a programmer writing new software—almost everyone uses computers in their jobs. Farmers use computers to optimize crops and order seeds and feed. Most scientific research is done using computers.

There are specific careers available if you want to work with computers in the computer industry. Schools offer degrees in computer programming, computer repair, computer engineering, and software design. The most popular jobs are systems analysts, computer operators, database managers, database specialists, and programmers. Analysts figure out ways to make computers work (or work better) for a particular business or type of business. Computer operators use the programs and devices to conduct business with computers. Programmers write the software for applications or new systems. There are degrees and jobs for people who want to create and maintain Web sites. Working for a company maintaining their Web site can be a very exciting career.

APPENDIX A

There are courses of study in using CAD (computer-aided design) and CAM (computer-aided manufacturing). There are positions available to instruct others in computer software use within companies and schools. Technical writers and editors must be available to write manuals about using computers and software. Computer-assisted instruction (CAI) is a system of teaching any given subject using the computer. Designing video games is another exciting and ever-growing field of computer work. And these are just a few of the possible career opportunities in an ever-changing work environment. See **Figure A–25**.

FIGURE A–25   Working in the computer field

What Does the Future Hold?

The possibilities for computer development and application are endless. Things that were dreams or science fiction only 10 or 20 years ago are now reality. New technologies are emerging constantly. Some new technologies are replacing old ways of doing things; others are merging with those older methods and devices. Some new technologies are creating new markets. The Internet (more specifically, the Web), cell phones, and DVD videos are just a few inventions of the past decades that did not have counterparts prior to their inventions. We are learning new ways to work and play because of the computer. It is definitely a device that has become part of our offices, our homes, and our lives.

Social networking has moved from the streets and onto the Web. People meet and greet through the Internet using sites such as MySpace, Facebook, and Twitter.

Emerging Technologies

Today the various technologies and systems are coming together to operate more efficiently. Convergence is the merging of these technologies. Telephone communication is being combined with computer e-mail and Web browsing so users can set a time to meet online and, with the addition of voice technology, actually speak to each other using one small portable device.

The Web, now an important part of commerce and education, began as a one-way vehicle where users visited to view Web pages and get information. It has evolved into sites where shopping and commerce takes place and is now evolving into a technology where users create the content. Web 2.0 and sites such as Facebook.com, flickr.com, LinkedIn.com, twitter.com, wikipedia.com, and youtube.com have content generated by the people that visit the Web sites. See **Figure A–26**.

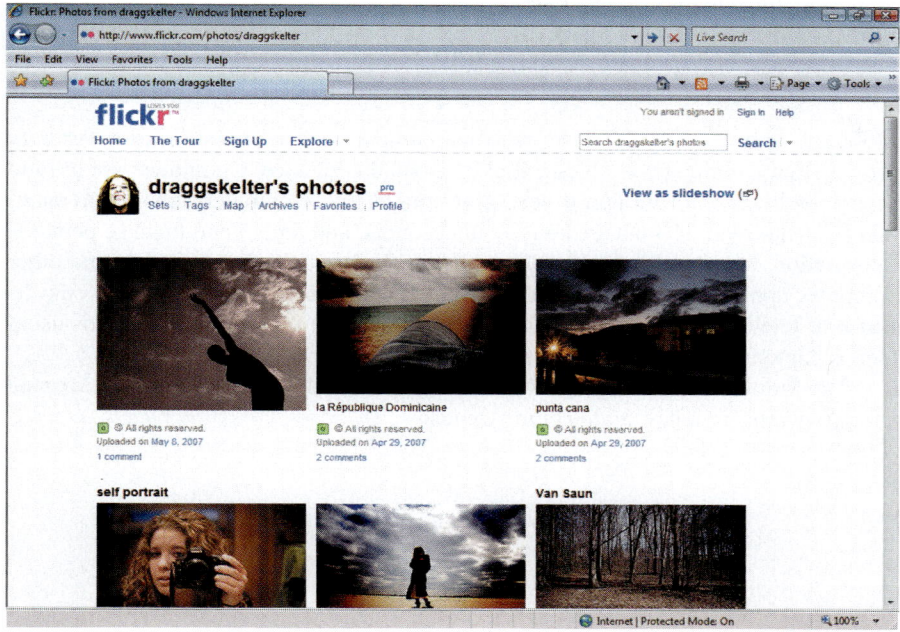

FIGURE A–26   User generated content

Computers have radically changed the way the medical profession delivers health care. Through the medical community, computers have enhanced medicine and healthcare throughout the world.

Trends

There are many trends that drive the computer industry. One trend is for larger and faster storage. From megabytes, to gigabytes, to terabytes, storage is becoming less an issue as the cost of storage is also dropping. RAM today is increasing exponentially. The trend is to sell larger blocks of RAM with every new personal computer. Newer processors also operate at speeds that are faster than the previous generation processors.

The actual size of computers is decreasing. Technology is allowing more powerful components to fit into smaller devices—laptops are lighter, monitors take up less space on the desktop, and flash drives can fit in your pocket and store gigabytes of data.

Home Offices

More and more frequently, people are working out of their homes—whether they are employees who are linked to their office in another location or individuals running their own businesses. *Telecommuting* meets the needs of many industries. Many companies allow workers to have a computer at home that is linked to their office and employees can use laptop computers to work both from home and on the road as they travel. A laptop computer, in combination with a wireless network, allows an employee to work from virtually anywhere and still keep in constant contact with her or his employer and customers.

Business communication is primarily by e-mail and telephone. It is very common for serious business transactions and communications to occur via e-mail rather than through the regular mail. Such an arrangement saves companies time and workspace and, thus, money.

Home Use

More and more households have personal computers. The statistics are constantly proving that a computer is an essential household appliance. Computers are used to access the Internet for shopping, education, and leisure. Computers are used to maintain financial records, manage household accounts, and record and manage personal information. More and more people are using electronic banking. Games and other computer applications offer another way to spend leisure dollars, and the convergence of television, the Internet, and the computer will find more households using their computers for media such as movies and music.

The future is computing. It's clear that this technology will continue to expand and provide us with new and exciting trends.

APPENDIX B

Keyboarding Touch System Improvement

Introduction

- *Your Goal—Improve your keyboarding skills using the touch system so you are able to type without looking at the keyboard.*

Why Improve Your Keyboarding Skills?

- To type faster and more accurately every time you use the computer
- To increase your enjoyment while using the computer

Instead of looking back and forth from the page to see the text you have to type and then turning back to the keyboard and pressing keys with one or two fingers, using the touch system you will type faster and more accurately.

⊢— WARNING

Using two fingers to type while looking at the keyboard is called the "hunt and peck" system and is not efficient when typing large documents.

Getting Ready to Build Skills

In order to get ready you should:

1. **Prepare your desk and computer area.**
   a. Clear your desk of all clutter, except your book, a pencil or pen, the keyboard, the mouse, and the monitor.
   b. Position your keyboard and book so that you are comfortable and able to move your hands and fingers freely on the keyboard and read the book at the same time.
   c. Keep your feet flat on the floor, sit with your back straight, and rest your arms slightly bent with your finger tips on the keyboard.
   d. Start a word-processing program, such as Microsoft Word, or any other text editor. You can also use any simple program such as the Microsoft Works word processor or WordPad that is part of the Windows operating system. Ask your teacher for assistance.

EXTRA FOR EXPERTS

There are two forms that you will complete as you work through this appendix to improve your typing skills: the **Timed Typing Progress Chart** and the **Keyboarding Technique Checklist**. Both forms are printed as the last two pages at the end of this Appendix.

2. Take a two-minute timed typing test according to your teacher's directions.

3. Calculate your words a minute (WAM) and errors a minute (EAM) using the instructions on the timed typing progress chart. This will be the base score you will compare to future timed typing.

4. Record today's Date, WAM, and EAM on the Base Score line of the writing progress chart.

5. Repeat the timed typing test many times to see improvements in your score.

6. Record each attempt on the Introduction line of the chart.

Getting Started

Keyboarding is an essential skill in today's workplace. No matter what your job, most likely you have to learn to be an effective typist. Follow the hints below to help you achieve this goal:

- Ignore errors.
- To complete the following exercises, you will type text that is bold and is not italicized and looks **like this**.
- If you have difficulty reaching for any key, for example the y key, practice by looking at the reach your fingertips make from the j key to the y key until the reach is visualized in your mind. The reach will become natural with very little practice.
- To start on a new line, press Enter.

Skill Builder 1

Your Goal—Use the touch system to type the letters j u y h n m and to learn to press the spacebar.

Keys

What to Do

1. Place your fingertips on the home row keys as shown in **Figure B–1**.

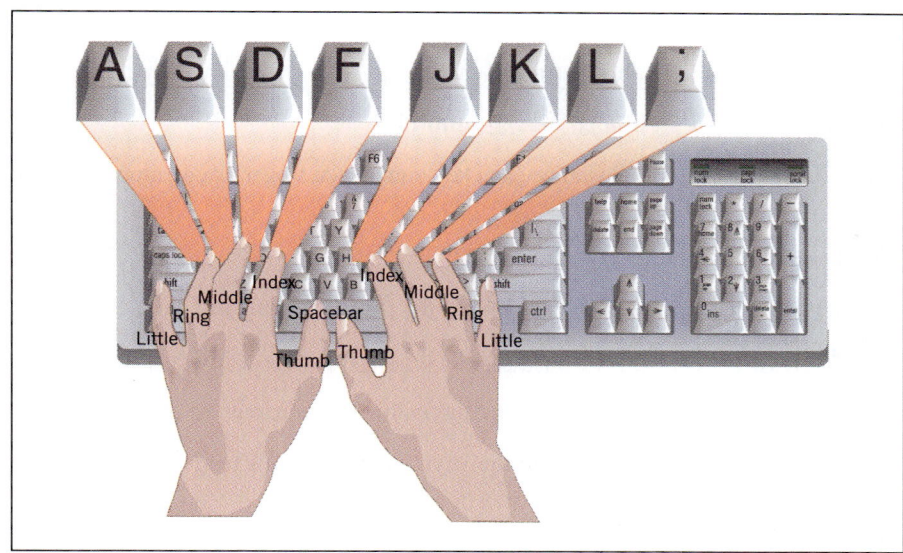

FIGURE B–1   Place your fingertips on the Home Row keys

2. Look at **Figure B–2**. In step 3, you will press the letter keys j u y h n m. To press these keys, you use your right index finger. You will press the spacebar after typing each letter three times. The spacebar is the long bar beneath the bottom row of letter keys. You will press the spacebar with your right thumb.

TIP

The home row keys are where you rest your fingertips when they are not typing. The index finger of your right hand rests on the J key. The index finger of your left hand rests on the F key. Feel the slight bump on these keys to help find the home row keys without looking at the keyboard.

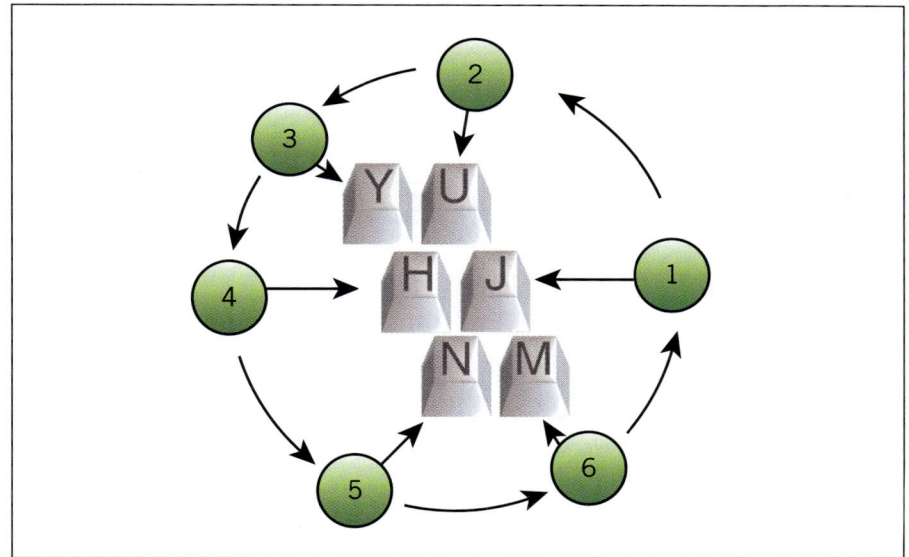

FIGURE B–2   Pressing the J U Y H N M keys

3. Look at your keyboard. Repeat the letters silently to yourself as you move your right index finger from the j key to press each key three times, and then press the spacebar. Start typing:

jjj uuu jjj yyy jjj hhh jjj nnn jjj mmm

jjj uuu jjj yyy jjj hhh jjj nnn jjj mmm jjj

4. Repeat the same drill as many times as it takes for you to reach your comfort level.

    jjj uuu jjj yyy jjj hhh jjj nnn jjj mmm

    jjj uuu jjj yyy jjj hhh jjj nnn jjj mmm jjj

5. Close your eyes and visualize each key under each finger as you repeat the drill in step 4.

6. Look at the following two lines and type:

    jjj jjj jjj juj juj juj jyj jyj jyj jhj jhj jhj jnj jnj jnj jmj jmj jmj

    jjj jjj jjj juj juj juj jyj jyj jyj jhj jhj jhj jnj jnj jnj jmj jmj jmj

7. Repeat step 6, this time concentrating on the rhythmic pattern of the keys.

8. Close your eyes and visualize the keys under your fingertips as you type the drill in step 4 from memory.

9. Look at the following two lines and type these groups of letters:

    j ju juj j jy jyj j jh jhj j jn jnj j jm jmj j ju juj j jy jyj j jh jhj j jn jnj j jm jmj

    jjj ju jhj jn jm ju jm jh jnj jm ju jmj jy ju jh j u ju juj jy jh jnj ju jm jmj jy

10. You may want to repeat Skill Builder 1, striving to improve typing letters that are most difficult for you.

Skill Builder 2

The left index finger is used to type the letters f r t g b v. Always return your left index finger to the f key on the home row after pressing the other keys.

Your Goal—Use the touch system to type f r t g b v .

Keys

What to Do

1. Place your fingertips on the home row keys as you did in Skill Builder 1, Figure B–1.

2. Look at **Figure B–3**. Notice how you will type the letters f r t g b v and then press the spacebar with your right thumb.

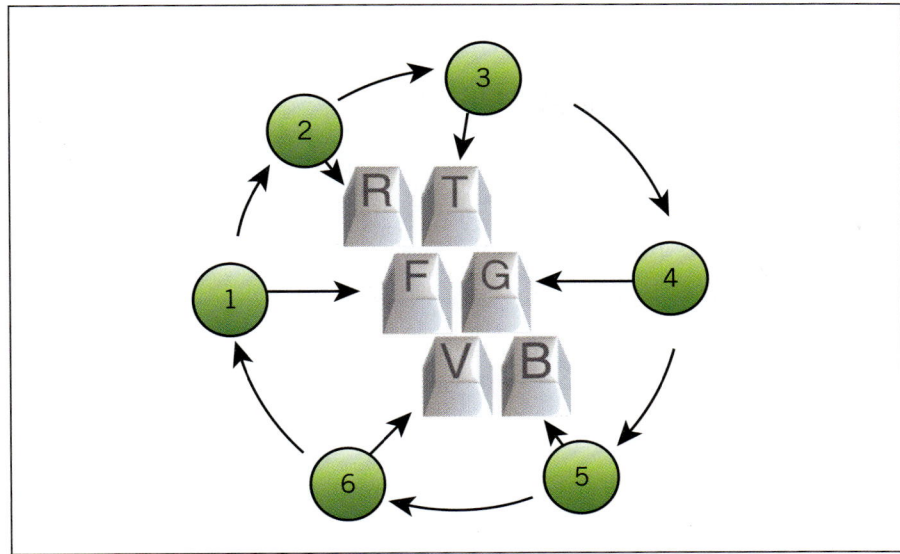

FIGURE B–3   Pressing the F R T G B V keys

3. Look at your keyboard. To press these keys, you use your left index finger. You will press the spacebar after typing each letter three times. The spacebar is the long bar beneath the bottom row of letter keys. You will press the spacebar with your right thumb.

   After pressing each letter in the circle, press the home key f three times as shown. Don't worry about errors. Ignore them.

   fff rrr fff ttt fff ggg fff bbb fff vvv

   fff rrr fff ttt fff ggg fff bbb fff vvv fff

4. Repeat the same drill two more times using a quicker, sharper stroke.

   fff rrr fff ttt fff ggg fff bbb fff vvv

   fff rrr fff ttt fff ggg fff bbb fff vvv fff

5. Close your eyes and visualize each key under each finger as you repeat the drill in step 4.

6. Look at the following two lines and key these groups of letters:

   fff fff fff frf frf frf ftf ftf ftf fgf fgf fgf fbf fbf fbf fvf fvf fvf

   fff fff fff frf frf frf ftf ftf ftf fgf fgf fgf fbf fbf fbf fvf fvf fvf

7. Repeat step 6, this time concentrating on a rhythmic pattern of the keys.

8. Close your eyes and visualize the keys under your fingertips as you type the drill in step 4 from memory.

9. Look at the following two lines and type these groups of letters:

   fr frf ft ftf fg fgf fb fbf fv fvf

   ft fgf fv frf ft fbf fv frf ft fgf

10. You are about ready to type your first words. Look at the following lines and type these groups of letters (remember to press the spacebar after each group):

jjj juj jug jug jug rrr rur rug rug rug

ttt tut tug tug tug rrr rur rub rub rub

ggg gug gum gum gum mmm mum

mug mug mug hhh huh hum hum hum

11. Complete the Keyboarding Technique Checklist.

Skill Builder 3

Your Goal—Use the touch system to type k i , d e c.

Keys (K) (I) (,) (comma)

What to Do

1. Place your fingertips on the home row keys. The home row key for the left middle finger is d. The home row key for the right middle finger is k. You use your left middle finger to type d, e, c. You use your right middle finger to type k, i, , as shown in **Figure B–4**.

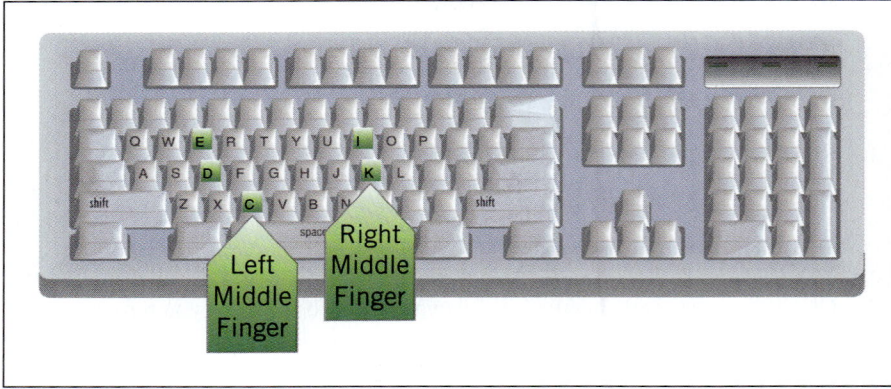

FIGURE B–4 Pressing the K I , D E C keys

2. Look at your keyboard and locate these keys: k i , (the letter k key, the letter i key, and the comma key).

3. Look at your keyboard. Repeat the letters silently to yourself as you press each key three times and put a space between each set of letters and the comma to type:

kkk iii kkk ,,, kkk iii kkk ,,, kkk iii kkk ,,, kkk iii kkk ,,, kkk iii kkk ,,, kkk

4. Look at the characters in step 3 and repeat the drill two more times using a quicker, sharper stroke.

5. Close your eyes and repeat the drill in step 3 as you visualize each key under each finger.

6. Repeat step 3, do not look at the keyboard, and concentrate on the rhythmic pattern of the keys.

Keys   C

What to Do

1. Place your fingertips on the home row keys.

2. Look at your keyboard and locate these keys: d e c (the letter d key, the letter e key, and the letter c key).

3. Look at your keyboard. Repeat the letters silently to yourself as you press each key three times and put a space between each set of letters to type:

   ddd eee ddd ccc ddd eee ddd ccc ddd eee ddd ccc ddd eee ddd ccc ddd

4. Look at the letters in step 3 and repeat the drill two more times using a quicker, sharper stroke.

5. Close your eyes and repeat the drill in step 3 as you visualize each key under each finger.

6. Repeat step 3, do not look at the keyboard, and concentrate on the rhythmic pattern of the keys.

7. Look at the following lines of letters and type these groups of letters and words:

   fff fuf fun fun fun ddd ded den den den

   ccc cuc cub cub cub vvv vev vet

   fff fuf fun fun fun ddd ded den den den

   ccc cuc cub cub cub vvv vev vet

8. Complete the Keyboarding Technique Checklist.

Skill Builder 4

Your Goal—Use the touch system to type l o . s w x and to press the left Shift key.

Keys   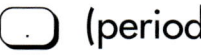 (period)

What to Do

1. Place your fingertips on the home row keys. The home row key for the left ring finger is s. The home row key for the right ring finger is l. You use your left ring finger to type s w x. You use your right ring finger to type l o . as shown in **Figure B–5**.

FIGURE B–5   Pressing the L O . S W X keys

2. Look at your keyboard and locate the following keys: l o . (the letter l key, the letter o key, and the period key).

3. Look at your keyboard. Repeat the letters silently to yourself as you press each key three times and put a space between each set of letters and the periods to type:

   lll ooo lll ... lll ooo lll ... lll ooo lll ... lll ooo lll ... lll ooo lll ... lll ooo lll ... lll

4. Look at the line in step 3 and repeat the drill two more times using a quicker, sharper stroke.

5. Close your eyes and repeat the drill in step 3 as you visualize each key under each finger.

6. Repeat step 3, do not look at the keyboard, and concentrate on the rhythmic pattern of the keys.

Keys

1. Place your fingertips on the home row keys.

2. Look at your keyboard and locate the following letter keys: s w x

3. Look at your keyboard. Repeat the letters silently to yourself as you press each key three times and put a space between each set of letters to type:

   sss www sss xxx sss www sss xxx sss www sss xxx sss www sss xxx sss

4. Look at the line in step 3 and repeat the same drill two more times using a quicker, sharper stroke.

5. Close your eyes and repeat the drill in step 3 as you visualize each key under each finger.

6. Repeat step 3, do not look at the keyboard, and concentrate on the rhythmic pattern of the keys.

Key Shift (SHIFT) (Left Shift Key)

You press and hold the Shift key as you press a letter key to type a capital letter. You press and hold the Shift key to type the character that appears above the numbers in the top row of the keyboard and on a few other keys that show two characters.

Press and hold down the left Shift key with the little finger on your left hand while you press each letter to type capital letters for keys that are typed with the fingertips on your right hand. See **Figure B–6**.

FIGURE B–6   Using the Shift keys

1. Type the following groups of letters and the sentence that follows.

   jjj JJJ jjj JJJ yyy YYY yyy YYY nnn NNN nnn NNN mmm MMM

   Just look in the book. You can see well.

2. Complete a column in the Keyboarding Technique Checklist.

Skill Builder 5

Your Goal—Use the touch system to type a q z ; p / and to press the right Shift key.

Keys (;) (Semi-Colon) (P) (/)

APPENDIX B

What to Do

1. Place your fingertips on the home row keys. The home row key for the left little finger is a. The home row key for the right little finger is ;. You use your left little finger to type a q z. You use your right little finger to type ; p / as shown in **Figure B–7**.

FIGURE B–7 Pressing the A Q Z ; P / and the right Shift key

2. Look at your keyboard and locate the following keys: ; p / (the semi-colon, the letter p, and the forward slash).

3. Repeat the letters silently to yourself as you press each key three times and put a space between each set of characters to type:

   ;;; ppp ;;; /// ;;; ppp ;;; /// ;;; ppp ;;; ///

   ;;; ppp ;;; /// ;;; ppp ;;; /// ;;; ppp ;;; /// ;;;

4. Look at the lines in step 3 and repeat the drill two more times using a quicker, sharper stroke.

5. Close your eyes and repeat the drill in step 3 as you visualize each key under each finger.

6. Repeat step 3, do not look at the keyboard, and concentrate on a rhythmic pattern of the keys.

Keys (A) (Q) (Z)

1. Place your fingertips on the home row keys.

2. Look at your keyboard and locate the following keys: a q z (the letter a, the letter q, and the letter z).

3. Look at your keyboard. Repeat the letters silently to yourself as you press each key three times and put a space between each set of letters and type:

   aaa qqq aaa zzz aaa qqq aaa zzz aaa qqq aaa zzz aaa qqq aaa zzz aaa

4. Look at the line in step 3 and repeat the same drill two more times using a quicker, sharper stroke.

5. Close your eyes and repeat the drill in step 3 as you visualize each key under each finger.

6. Repeat step 3, do not look at the keyboard, and concentrate on the rhythmic pattern of the keys.

Key Shift (SHIFT) (Right Shift Key)

Press and hold down the right Shift key with the little finger on your right hand while you press each letter to type capital letters for keys that are typed with the fingertips on your left hand.

1. Type the following lines. Press and hold down the right Shift key with the little finger of your right hand to make capitals of letters you type with the fingertips on your left hand.

    sss SSS rrr RRR

    Press each key quickly. Relax when you type.

2. Complete another column in the Keyboarding Technique Checklist.

Skill Builder 6

You will probably have to type slowly at first, but with practice you will learn to type faster and accurately.

Your Goal—Use the touch system to type all letters of the alphabet.

What to Do

1. Close your eyes. Do not look at the keyboard and type all letters of the alphabet in groups of three with a space between each set as shown:

    aaa bbb ccc ddd eee fff ggg hhh iii jjj

    kkk lll mmm nnn ooo ppp qqq rrr sss

    ttt uuu vvv www xxx yyy zzz

2. Repeat step 1, concentrating on a rhythmic pattern of the keys.

3. Repeat step 1, but faster than you did for step 2.

4. Type the following sets of letters, all letters of the alphabet in groups of two with a space between each set as shown:

    aa bb cc dd ee ff gg hh ii jj kk ll mm nn oo pp qq rr ss tt uu vv ww xx yy zz

5. Type the following letters, all letters of the alphabet with a space between each letter as shown:

    a b c d e f g h i j k l m n o p q r s t u v w x y z

APPENDIX B

6. Continue to look at this book. Do not look at the keyboard, and type all letters of the alphabet backwards in groups of three with a space between each set as shown:

zzz yyy xxx www vvv uuu ttt sss rrr

qqq ppp ooo nnn mmm lll kkk jjj iii

hhh ggg fff eee ddd ccc bbb aaa

7. Repeat step 6, but faster than the last time.

8. Type each letter of the alphabet once backwards:

z y x w v u t s r q p o n m l k j i h g f e d c b a

9. Think about the letters that took you the most amount of time to find the key on the keyboard. Go back to the Skill Builder for those letters, and repeat the drills until you are confident about their locations.

Timed Typing

Prepare to take the timed typing test, according to your teacher's directions.

1. **Prepare your desk and computer area.**
   a. Clear your desk of all clutter except your book, a pencil or pen, the keyboard, the mouse, the monitor, and the computer if it is located on the desk.
   b. Position your keyboard and book so that you are comfortable and able to move your hands and fingertips freely.
   c. Keep your feet flat on the floor, sitting with your back straight, resting your arms slightly bent with your fingertips on the keyboard.

2. Take a two-minute timed typing test according to your teacher's directions.

3. Calculate your words a minute (WAM) and errors a minute (EAM) scores using the instructions on the Timed Typing Progress Chart in this book.

4. Record the date, WAM, and EAM on the Skill Builder 6 line in the Timed Typing Progress Chart printed at the end of this appendix.

5. Repeat the timed typing test as many times as you can and record each attempt in the Timed Typing Progress Chart.

Skill Builder 7

Your Goal—Improve your typing techniques—which is the secret for improving your speed and accuracy.

What to Do

1. Rate yourself for each item on the Keyboarding Technique Checklist printed at the end of this appendix.

2. Do not time yourself as you concentrate on a single technique you marked with a "0." Type only the first paragraph of the timed typing.

3. Repeat step 2 as many times as possible for each of the items marked with an "0" that need improvement.

4. Take a two-minute timed typing test. Record your WAM and EAM on the Timed Typing Progress Chart as 1st Attempt on the Skill Builder 7 line. Compare this score with your base score.

5. Looking only at the book and using your best techniques, type the following technique sentence for one minute:

    .   2   .   4   .   6   .   8   .   10   .   12   .   14   .   16

    Now is the time for all good men and women to come to the aid of their country.

6. Record your WAM and EAM in the Timed Typing Progress Chart on the 7 Technique Sentence line.

7. Repeat steps 5 and 6 as many times as you can and record your scores in the Timed Typing Progress Chart.

Skill Builder 8

Your Goal—Increase your words a minute (WAM) score.

What to Do

You can now type letters in the speed line very well and with confidence. Practicing all of the other letters of the alphabet will further increase your skill and confidence in keyboarding.

1. Take a two-minute timed typing test.

2. Record your WAM and EAM scores as the 1st Attempt in the Timed Typing Progress Chart.

3. Type only the first paragraph only one time as fast as you can. Ignore errors.

4. Type only the first and second paragraphs only one time as fast as you can. Ignore errors.

5. Take a two-minute timed typing test again. Ignore errors.

6. Record only your WAM score as the 2nd Attempt in the Timed Typing Progress Chart. Compare only this WAM with your 1st Attempt WAM and your base score WAM.

Get Your Best WAM

1. To get your best WAM on easy text for 15 seconds, type the following speed line as fast as you can, as many times as you can. Ignore errors.

    .   2   .   4   .   6   .   8   .   10

    Now is the time, now is the time, now is the time,

APPENDIX B

2. Multiply the number of words typed by four to get your WAM (15 seconds × 4 = 1 minute). For example, if you type 12 words for 15 seconds, 12 × 4 = 48 WAM.

3. Record only your WAM in the 8 Speed Line box in the Timed Typing Progress Chart.

4. Repeat steps 1–3 as many times as you can to get your very best WAM. Ignore errors.

5. Record only your WAM for each attempt in the Timed Typing Progress Chart.

Skill Builder 9

Your Goal—Decrease errors a minute (EAM) score.

What to Do

> **TIP**
>
> How much you improve depends upon how much you want to improve.

1. Take a two-minute timed typing test.

2. Record your WAM and EAM as the 1st Attempt in the Timed Typing Progress Chart.

3. Type only the first paragraph only one time at a controlled rate of speed so you reduce errors. Ignore speed.

4. Type only the first and second paragraphs only one time at a controlled rate of speed so you reduce errors. Ignore speed.

5. Take a two-minute timed typing test again. Ignore speed.

6. Record only your EAM score as the 2nd Attempt in the Timed Typing Progress Chart. Compare only the EAM with your 1st Attempt EAM and your base score EAM.

Get Your Best EAM

1. To get your best EAM, type the following accuracy sentence (same as the technique sentence) for one minute. Ignore speed.

   Now is the time for all good men and women to come to the aid of their country.

2. Record only your EAM score on the Accuracy Sentence 9 line in the Timed Typing Progress Chart.

3. Repeat step 1 as many times as you can to get your best EAM. Ignore speed.

4. Record only your EAM score for each attempt in the Timed Typing Progress Chart.

Skill Builder 10

Your Goal—Use the touch system and your best techniques to type faster and more accurately than you have ever typed before.

What to Do

1. Take a one-minute timed typing test.

2. Record your WAM and EAM as the 1st Attempt on the Skill Builder 10 line in the Timed Typing Progress Chart.

3. Repeat the timed typing test for two minutes as many times as necessary to get your best ever WAM with no more than one EAM. Record your scores as 2nd, 3rd, and 4th Attempts.

 TIP

You may want to get advice regarding which techniques you need to improve from a classmate or your instructor.

Assessing Your Improvement

1. Circle your best timed typing test for Skill Builders 6-10 in the Timed Typing Progress Chart.

2. Record your best score and your base score. Compare the two scores. Did you improve?

	WAM	EAM
Best Score	_____	_____
Base Score	_____	_____

3. Use the Keyboarding Technique Checklist to identify techniques you still need to improve. You may want to practice these techniques now to increase your WAM or decrease your EAM.

Timed Typing

Every five strokes in a timed typing test is a word, including punctuation marks and spaces. Use the scale above each line to tell you how many words you typed.

```
           .         2      .        4      .        6      .
If you learn how to key well now, it
     8      .      10     .      12     .      14     .      16
is a skill that will help you for the rest
          .      18     .      20     .      22     .      24
of your life. How you sit will help you key
     .      26     .      28     .      30     .      32     .      34
with more speed and less errors.  Sit with your
          .      36     .      38     .      40     .      42
feet flat on the floor and your back erect.
        44     .      46     .      48     .      50
To key fast by touch, try to keep your
     .      52     .      54     .      56     .      58     .
eyes on the copy and not on your hands or
     60     .      62     .      64     .      66     .      68
the screen.  Curve your fingers and make sharp,
          .      70     .
quick strokes.
   72     .      74     .      76     .      78     .
Work for speed first.  If you make more
     80     .      82     .      84     .      86     .      88
than two errors a minute, you are keying too
     .      90     .      92     .      94     .      96     .
fast. Slow down to get fewer errors. If you
        98     .     100     .     102     .     104     .
get fewer than two errors a minute, go for
   106     .
speed.
```

Timed Typing Progress Chart

Timed Writing Progress Chart

Last Name: _____   *First Name:* _____

Instructions

Calculate your scores as shown in the following sample. Repeat timed writings as many times as you can and record your scores for each attempt.

Base Score	Date	WAM	EAM	Time

To calculate WAM: Divide words keyed by number of minutes to get WAM. For example: 44 words keyed in 2 minutes = 22 WAM [44/2=22]

To calculate EAM: Divide errors made by minutes of typing to get EAM

For example: 7 errors made in 2 minutes of typing = 3.5 EAM [7/2=3.5]

Skill Builder	Date	1st Attempt (a) WAM	1st Attempt (b) EAM	2nd Attempt WAM	2nd Attempt EAM	3rd Attempt WAM	3rd Attempt EAM	4th Attempt WAM	4th Attempt EAM
Sample	9/2	22	3.5	23	2.0	25	1.0	29	2.0
Introduction									
6									
7									
8					-----				
9				-----					
10									
7 Technique Sentence									
8 Speed Line			-----		-----		-----		-----
9 Accuracy Sentence		-----		-----		-----		-----	

APPENDIX B

Keyboarding Technique Checklist

Last Name: _____   *First Name:* _____

Instructions

1. Write the Skill Builder number, the date, and the initials of the evaluator in the proper spaces.

2. Place a check mark (✓) after a technique that is performed satisfactorily.

3. Place a large zero (0) after a technique that needs improvement.

Skill Builder Number:	Sample									
Date:	9/1									
Evaluator:	SL									
Technique										
Attitude										
1. Enthusiastic about learning	✓									
2. Optimistic about improving	✓									
3. Alert but relaxed	✓									
4. Sticks to the task; not distracted	✓									
Getting Ready	✓									
1. Desk uncluttered										
2. Properly positions keyboard and book	✓									
3. Feet flat on the floor	✓									
4. Body erect, but relaxed	0									
Keyboarding										
1. Curves fingers	0									
2. Keeps eyes on the book	✓									
3. Taps the keys lightly; does not "pound" them	0									
4. Makes quick, "bouncy," strokes	0									
5. Smooth rhythm	0									
6. Minimum pauses between strokes	✓									

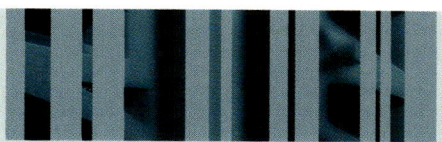

APPENDIX C

Differences between Windows 7, Windows Vista, and Windows XP

The Windows Experience

- Microsoft offers many new features in Windows 7 that are not available in Windows XP and Windows Vista.

- The overall Windows experience has been vastly improved from Windows XP to Windows 7. If you make the jump from XP to Windows 7, you will discover a great number of changes that are for the better. In addition, many of the new features introduced in Windows Vista were retained in this latest version of the popular operating system. Upgrading to Windows 7 is also an easier, more streamlined transition.

- With Windows 7, Microsoft has simplified everyday tasks and works more efficiently. This is all in response to issues users had with the Windows XP and Windows Vista experience. The major differences between Windows XP, Windows Vista, and Windows 7 are in the Start menu, dynamic navigation, desktop gadgets, improved security, search options, parental controls, and firewall, as well as improvements to the Windows Aero feature, see **Figure C–1**.

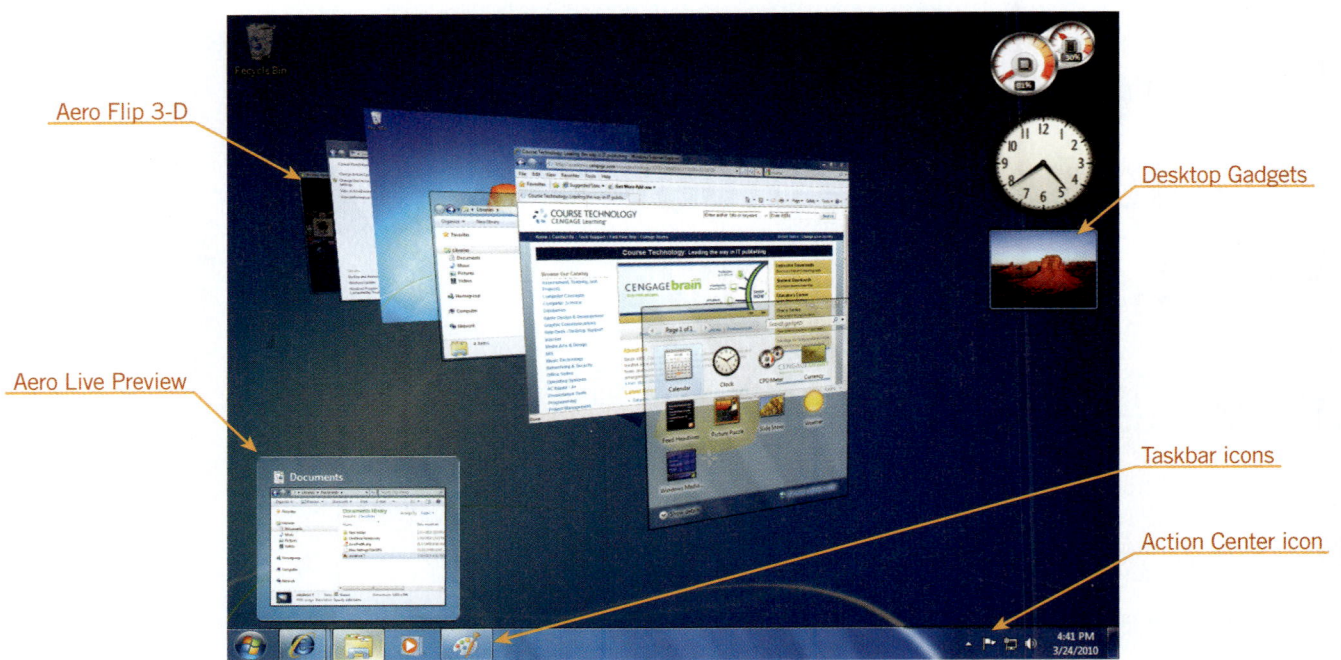

Aero Flip 3-D

Aero Live Preview

Desktop Gadgets

Taskbar icons

Action Center icon

FIGURE C–1   Windows 7 Features

Windows Aero

- Windows Aero is a new graphic interface feature which gives a "transparent" quality to windows, dialog boxes, and other items in the Windows Vista and Windows 7 environment.

- Flip 3-D, or simply Flip, shows mini versions of windows and thumbnails in the Windows 7 environment when turned on.

Windows XP users had to download Windows Desktop Enhancements and PowerTools from the Microsoft Web site to change their Windows experience. Windows Vista and Windows 7 now have many different themes and options built into the operating system, making it easy to modify the Windows experience. One theme, introduced in Windows Vista is Aero.

Windows Aero is a feature which was first introduced in Windows Vista and is not available in the Windows XP operating system. Windows Aero, enabled by default in Windows 7, is a more aesthetically pleasing user interface to Windows Vista and Windows 7 systems. For example, Windows XP utilizes ScreenTips only when pointing to items on the Taskbar, Desktop, and Menus. The basic ScreenTips found in Windows XP have been enhanced to show live "sneak-previews" of windows with a simple point to the icon on the taskbar , as shown in **Figure C–2**.

Windows 7 made major improvements to the function of Aero. These new features include Aero Peek, Aero Shake, Aero Snap, Touch UI, and many other visual effects covered in this section. Compare the evolution of the Taskbar ScreenTip in Windows XP to Windows Vista and finally in Windows 7 in the figures below.

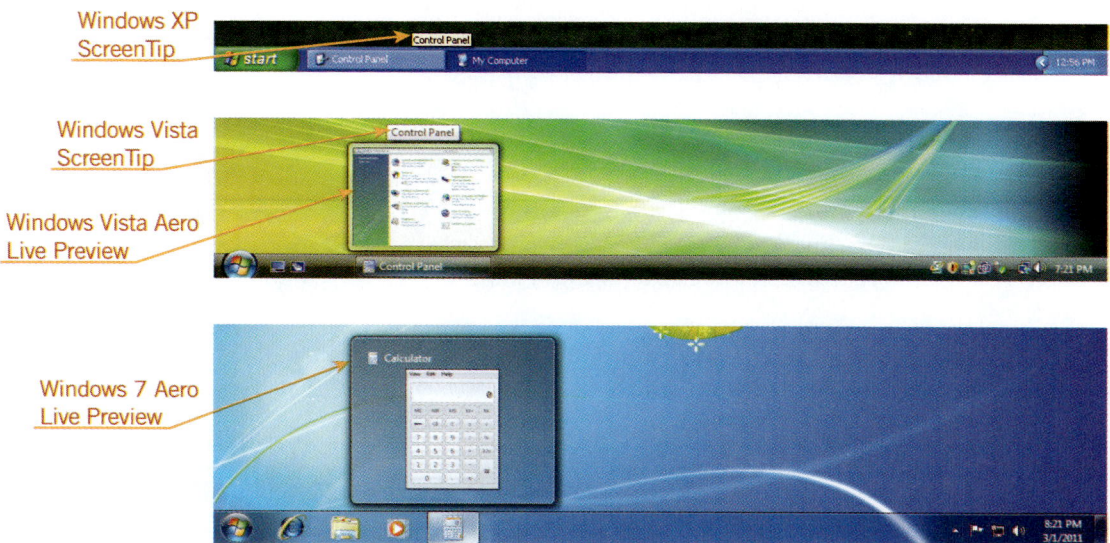

FIGURE C–2   Comparing Windows XP taskbar with Windows Vista and Windows 7

Understanding the Desktop

- Gadgets, introduced in Windows Vista, and Jump Lists, introduced in Windows 7, are two new desktop features.
- Windows 7 also includes multiple Aero themes to customize your desktop including the Desktop Background Slideshow.

APPENDIX C

At first glance, the Windows XP desktop only appears to differ slightly from that of Windows Vista, but the new features available with Windows 7 are substantial. The icons, shortcuts, folders, and files are generally the same; however, there are major aesthetic visual differences in this version. The most obvious addition from XP to Vista is the desktop gadget. Gadgets were not available in Windows XP. In **Figure C–4**, notice the appearance of three gadgets on the sidebar. Desktop gadgets are also available in Windows 7; however the sidebar function has been abandoned. Users simply add the gadget to the desktop.

The Taskbar in Windows XP includes the notification area, quick launch (when enabled), Start button, and icon(s) representing open programs. Beginning with Windows 7, you can now easily pin items to the Taskbar instead of using a quick launch feature. Jump lists, Aero themes and the Desktop Background Slideshow, explained in this chapter, are also new features to Windows 7.

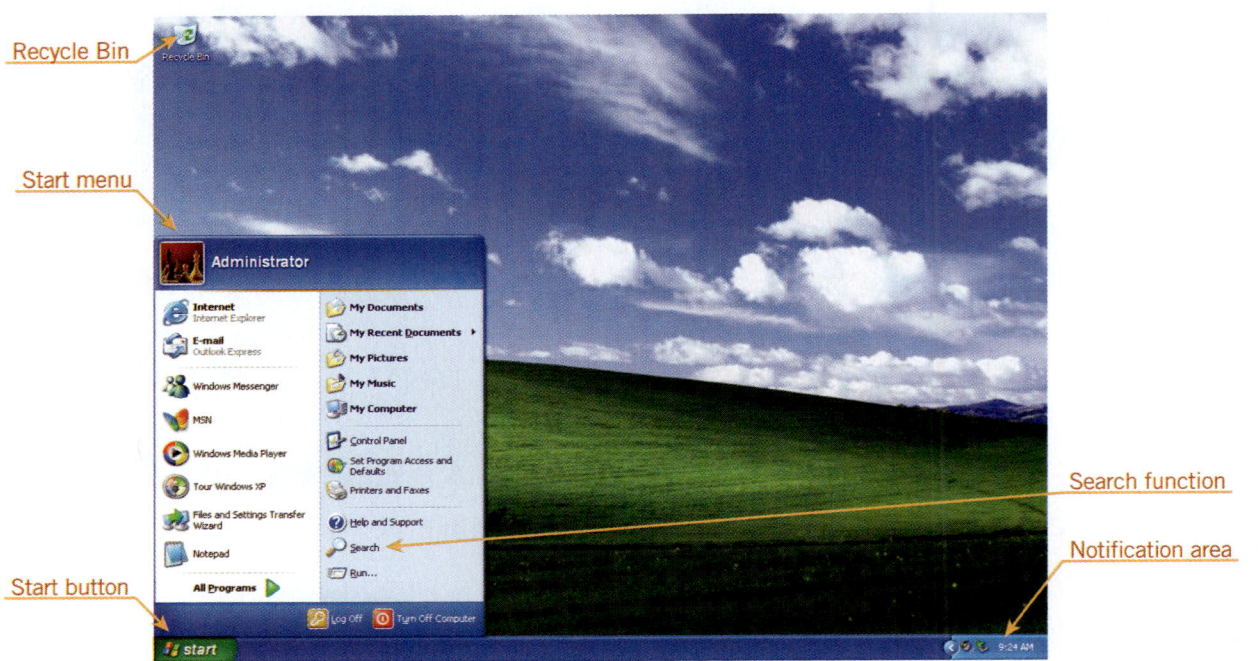

FIGURE C–3   Windows XP Start menu and Desktop

The Start menu has been slightly enhanced from Windows XP to Windows 7. All Programs no longer appears on an additional menu, it has been merged with the Start menu. Windows Vista introduced a search function built into the Start menu, which allows users to search the computer easily for documents, applications, and help. Compare the evolution in desktops from Windows XP to Windows 7 in **Figures C–3, C–4,** and **C–5**.

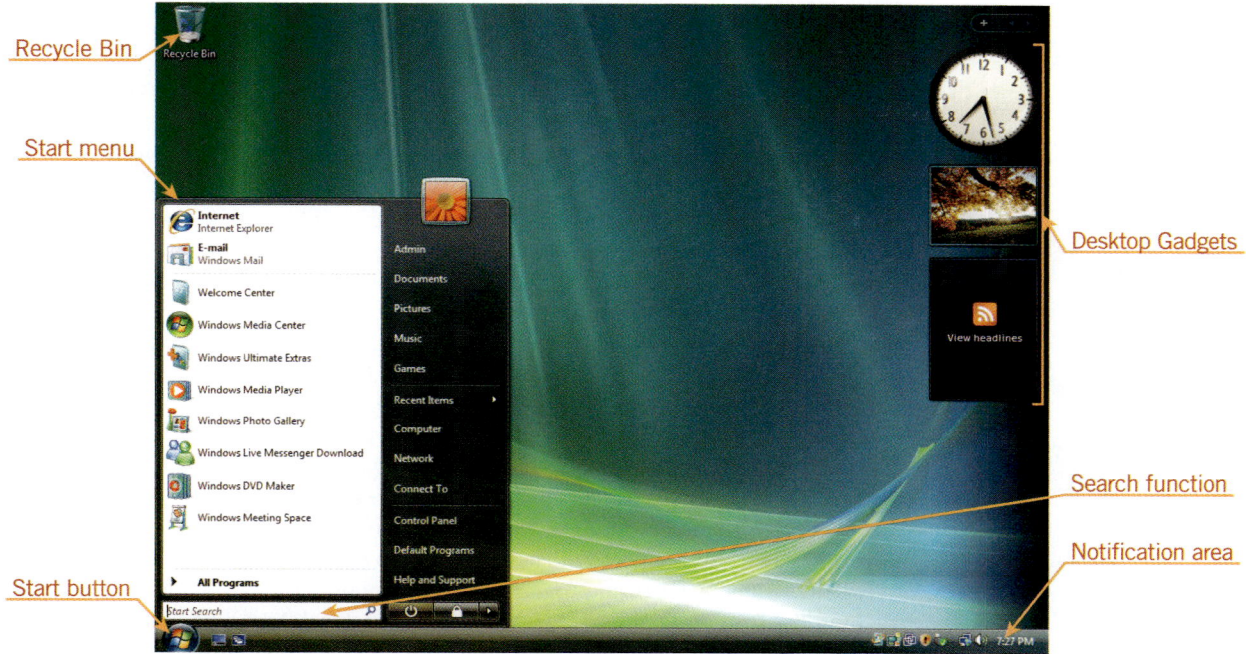

FIGURE C–4 Windows Vista Start menu and Desktop

FIGURE C–5 Windows 7 Start menu and Desktop

Navigating in Windows

- The Address bar in Windows 7 now functions differently, with more direct navigation functions.
- Windows 7 now includes a comprehensive Navigation pane in Windows Explorer.

Windows Explorer provides the tools to navigate and locate items on your computer. The Address bar has been upgraded from Windows XP to allow for easier movement between folders. In Windows XP, the only available methods were the Back button and drop-down arrow. See **Figure C–6**. A big difference is in the function of the path. You may now click the folder in your path to move back. You may also begin a search directly from the Address bar, which is a new Windows 7 feature. Windows XP users' only option to search was to utilize the Search Companion.

The Navigation pane, which provides links to common or recently used folders, is dramatically different in Windows 7, compared to Windows XP, which only featured Favorites. "My Documents", the default user folder in Windows XP, is now a collection of folders grouped in Libraries in Windows 7. These folders, as well as Favorites, are easily found on the new Navigation pane and are easily customizable.

To switch between open programs easily, Windows XP's only option aside from clicking the icon on the Taskbar, was to tab through available programs, in a basic method with no preview of the program state. Windows Flip, introduced in Windows Vista, allows you to move to an open file, window or program by pressing the Alt+Tab keys, while showing a preview of the program's current state in Aero. The Windows Vista version of Flip was enhanced for Windows 7 users, although the function remains the same. See **Figures C–8** and **C-9** on the following pages.

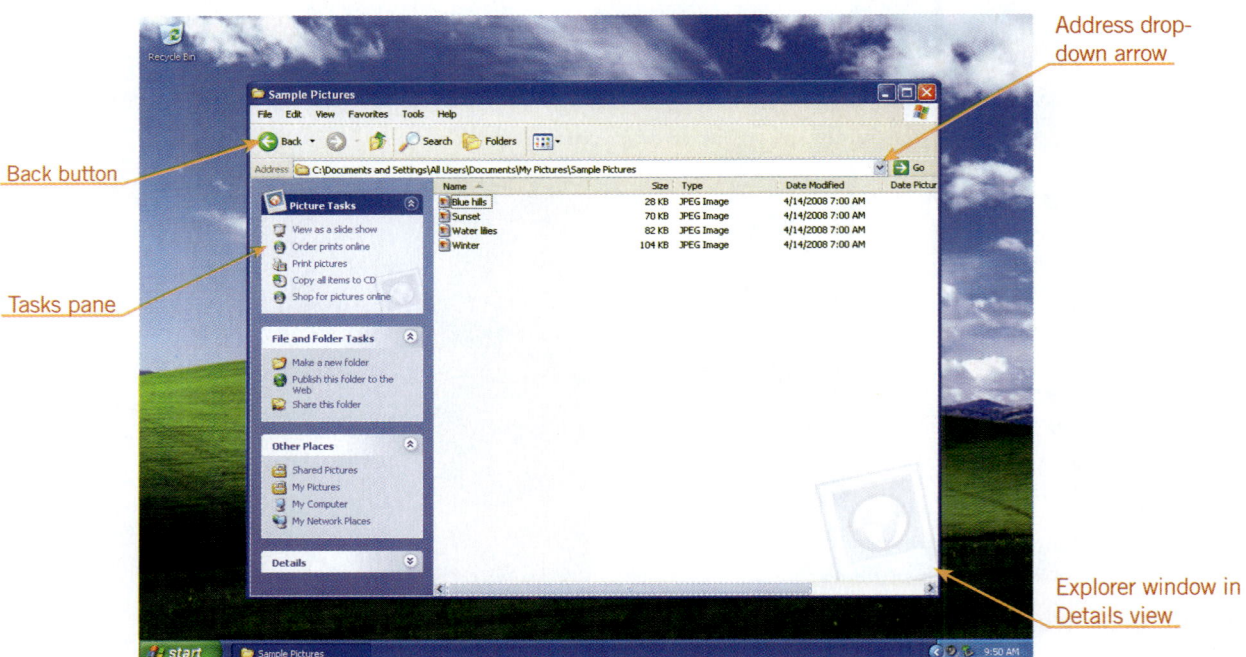

FIGURE C–6   Windows Explorer as seen in Windows XP

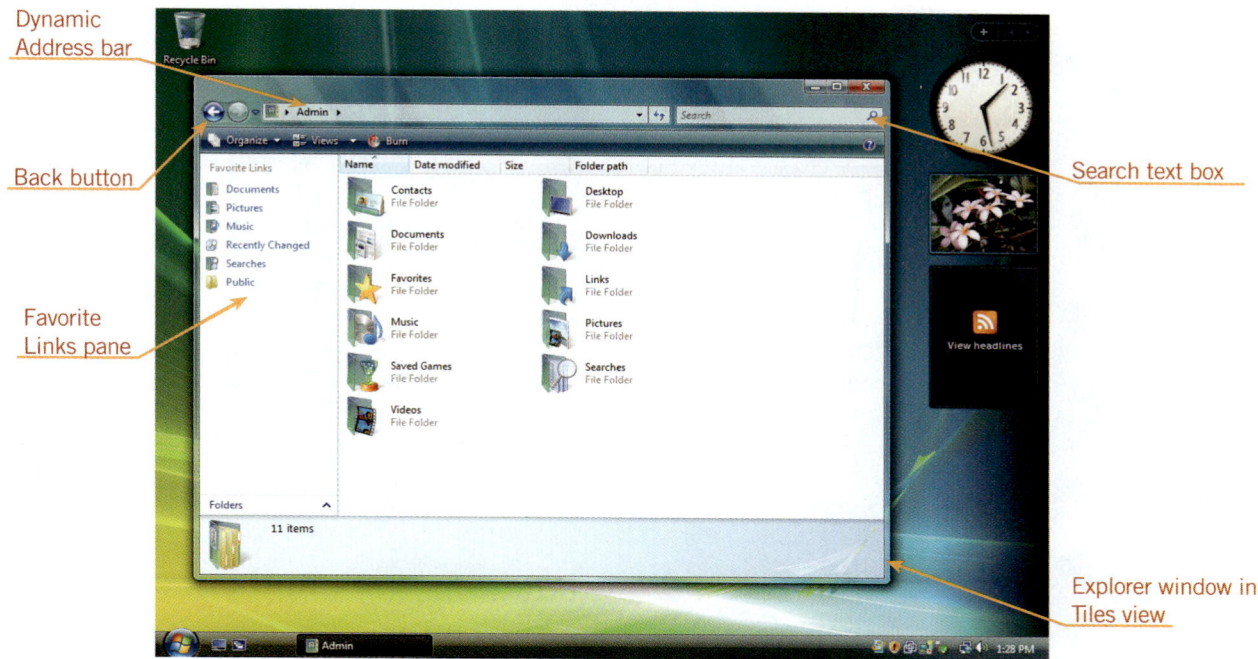

Dynamic Address bar

Back button

Favorite Links pane

Search text box

Explorer window in Tiles view

FIGURE C–7   Windows Explorer as seen in Windows Vista

Aero Flip tabs through open programs

Taskbar buttons for open programs

FIGURE C–8   Flip in Windows Vista

Aero Flip 3-D tabs through open programs

Taskbar buttons for open programs

FIGURE C–9   Flip 3-D in Windows 7

Using Windows

- The new Aero Shake and Aero Snap allow you to easily move, resize, minimize and maximize open windows.

- The Control Panel now includes additional descriptive links, making it easy to find the item you are looking to modify.

Moving and resizing windows in Windows 7 provides the same essential functions as it did in previous Windows versions, with a few additions. In Windows XP and Vista, you had to manipulate each window individually, by clicking and dragging. You can still click and drag to resize and move windows; however this function has been upgraded and revamped in Windows 7. Aero Shake allows you to "shake" all open windows except that particular window to a minimized state. Aero Snap is a new way to easily resize open windows to expand vertically, or side-by-side.

The Control Panel, revamped in Windows Vista, has a new look in Windows 7, compared to that in Windows XP. The Search text box allows you to search for the Control Panel task you wish to perform. There are also descriptive linked items now replacing the "classic" icon format. **Figures C–10**, **C–11**, and **C–12**, which are shown on the following pages, illustrate the differences in the Control Panel from Windows XP to Windows 7.

Switch to Classic View for basic icon arrangement

Control Panel

Grouped categories

FIGURE C–10 Windows XP Control Panel

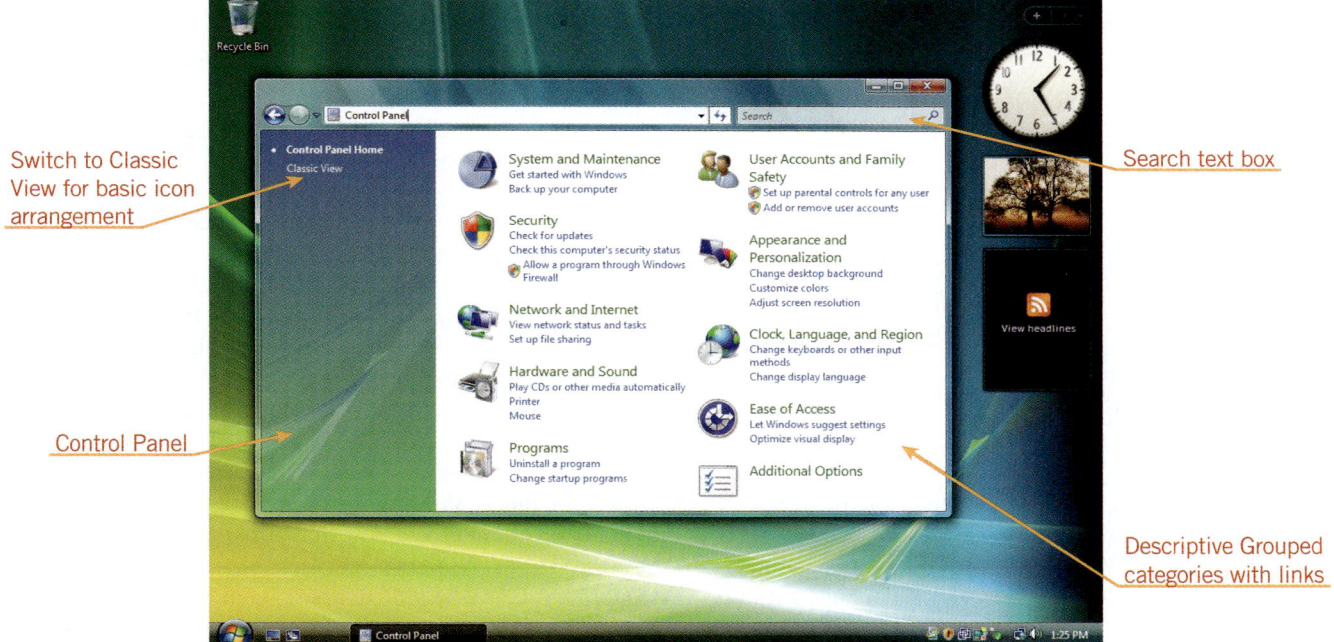

Switch to Classic View for basic icon arrangement

Control Panel

Search text box

Descriptive Grouped categories with links

FIGURE C–11 Windows Vista Control Panel

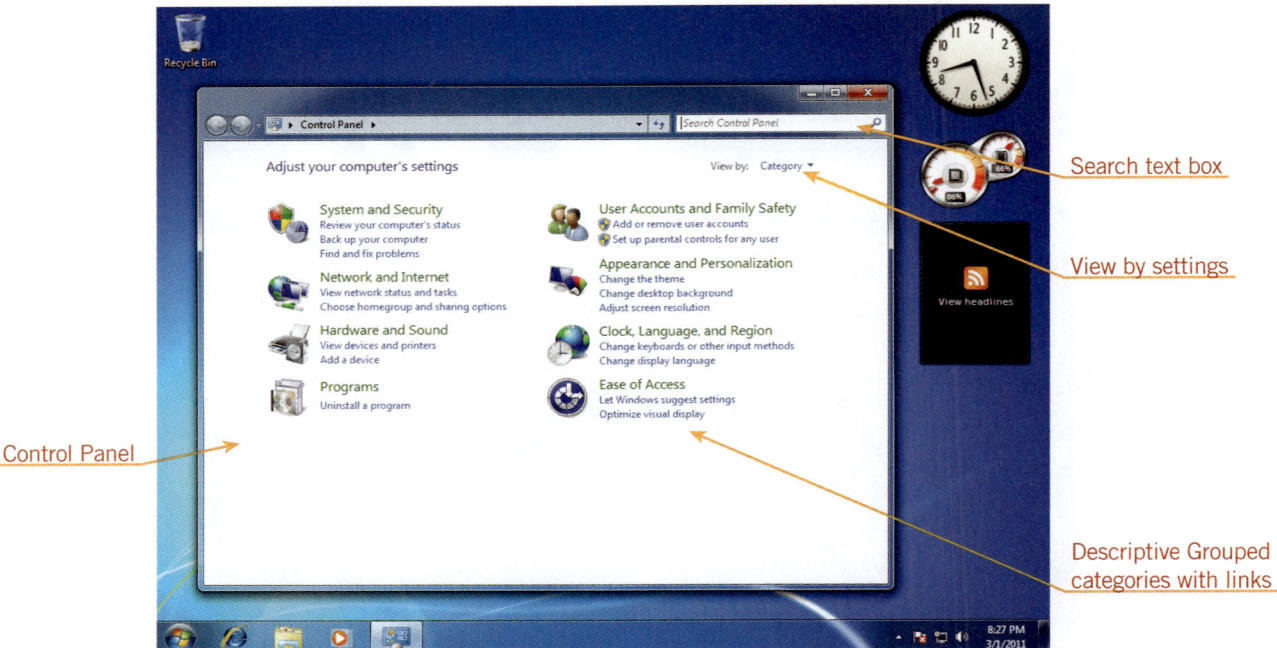

Search text box

View by settings

Control Panel

Descriptive Grouped categories with links

FIGURE C–12   Windows 7 Control Panel

Managing Your Computer

- The Action Center is a new feature in Windows 7 which consolidates message traffic from Windows maintenance and security features.
- Basic system utilities, such as Disk Cleanup and Disk Defragmenter, remain essentially the same from Windows XP to Windows 7.

Windows XP and Windows Vista's only method of receiving information on security and maintenance was the Security Center, available from the Control Panel. Windows 7 has improved this function, by creating a new Action Center, which communicates with the firewall, spyware protection, and antivirus software. Windows 7 users can now navigate to the Action Center by visiting the System and Security section of the Control Panel to view computer status and resolve issues. The Action Center is also pre-configured in Windows 7 to send important alerts to the Notification area of the taskbar.

One of the major upgrades in Windows 7 is in performance. Windows 7 was designed to run on less memory, shutting down services when not in use. In the Control Panel of Windows 7, there is a new Performance and Information Tools section. If you are a previous Windows XP user, you should familiarize yourself with this new feature. You will be able to assess your computer's performance, adjust settings, run disk cleanup, and launch advanced tools to manage your computer.

Windows Defender, introduced in Windows Vista is Microsoft's answer to spyware protection. This was not available for Windows XP users, pre Windows XP Service Pack 2. Windows XP Service Pack 2 users could download it from the Microsoft Web site and install it manually. Windows 7 also includes Windows Defender by default.

Windows Update, introduced in Windows XP has remained the same throughout the transitions through Windows Vista and Windows 7. Windows Update, which automatically downloads and installs important updates, was one of the only ways

Microsoft offered to maintain a secure PC with Windows XP. Now, in Windows 7, the Action Center, Performance Information and Tools, Windows Defender, and Windows Update work together to keep your computer secure. **Figures C–13**, **C–14**, and **C–15**, which are shown on the next few pages, compare Windows XP and Vista's Security Centers with Windows 7 Security Center and Action Center.

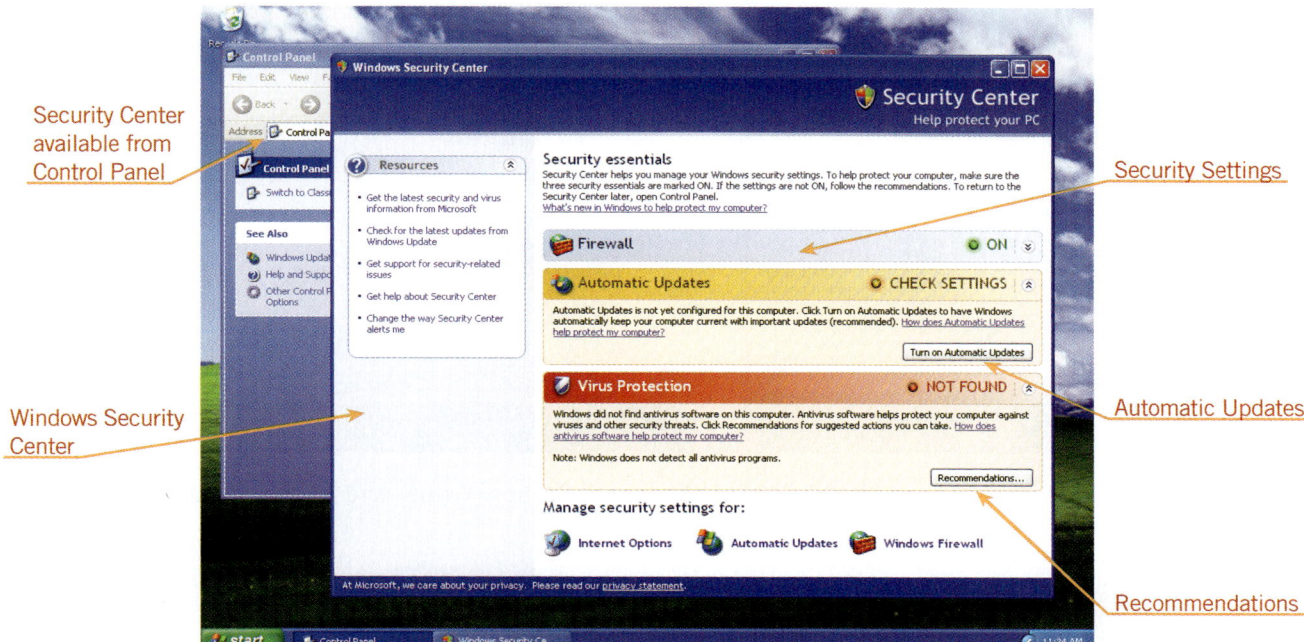

FIGURE C–13   Windows XP Security Center

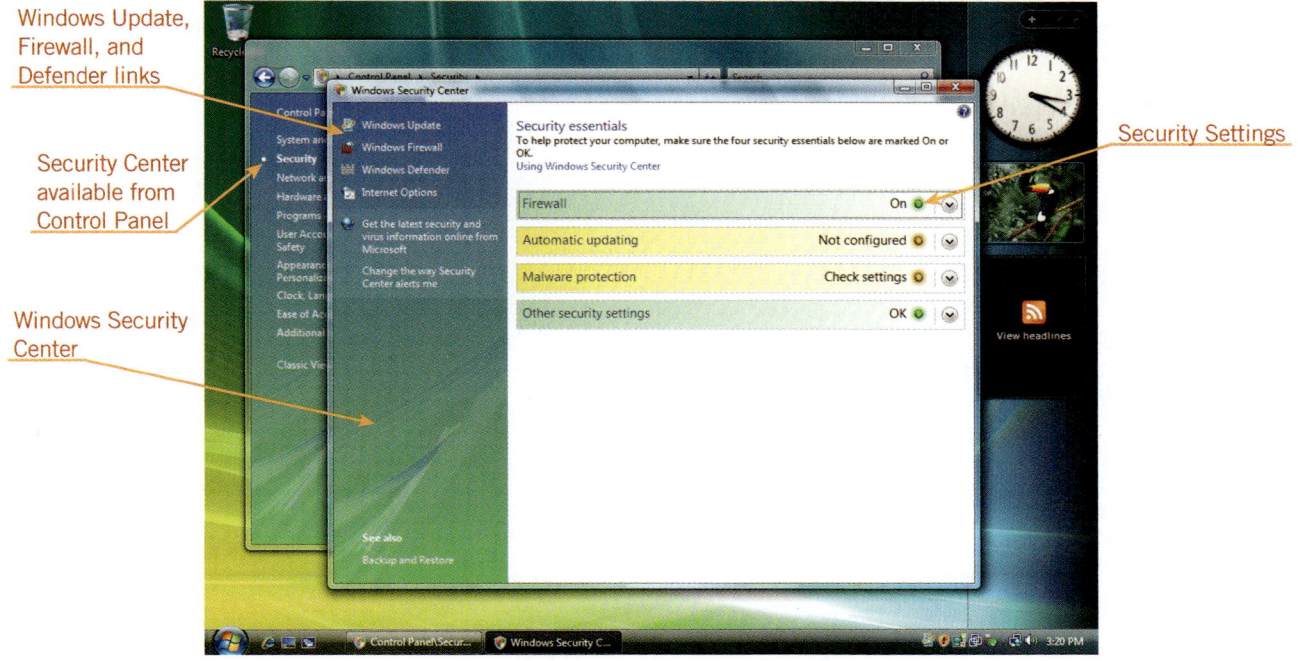

FIGURE C–14   Windows Vista Security Center

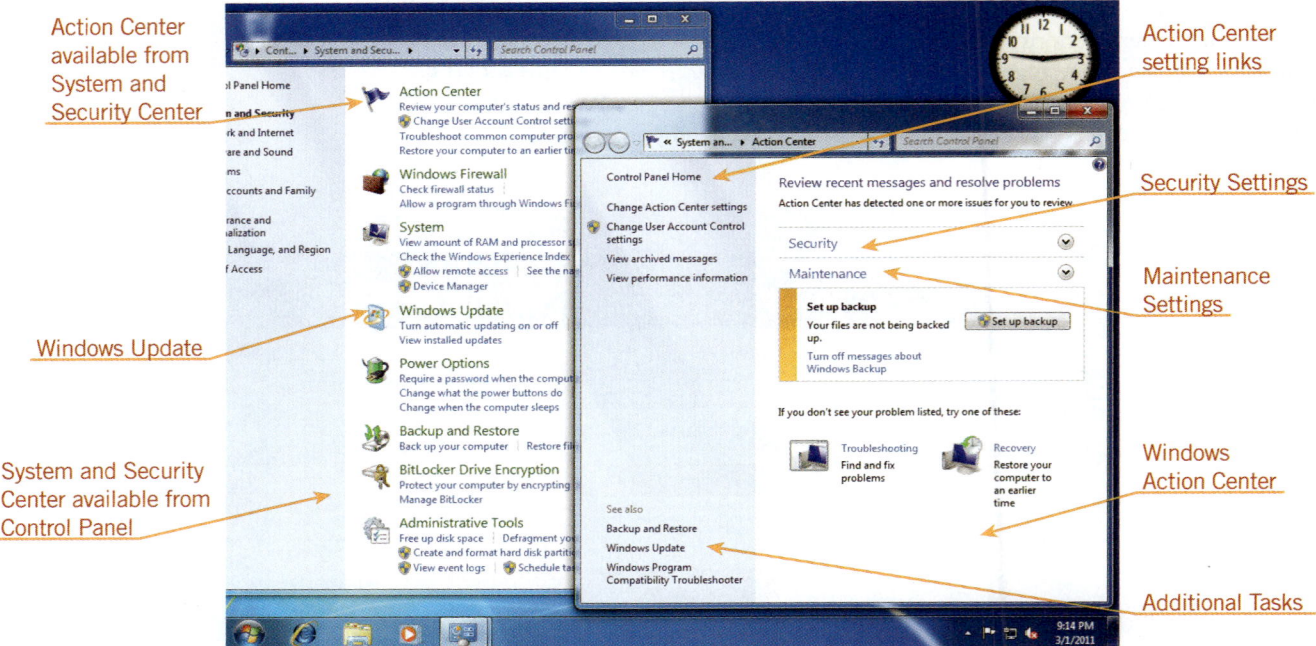

FIGURE C–15   Windows 7 Security Center and Action Center

APPENDIX D

Using SkyDrive and Office Web Apps

■ OBJECTIVES

Upon completion of this lesson, you should be able to:

- Explore cloud computing and Windows Live.
- Obtain a Windows Live ID and sign in to Windows Live.
- Upload files to SkyDrive.
- Use Office Web Apps View and Edit modes.
- Create folders on SkyDrive.
- Organize files on SkyDrive.
- Give permission for access to a folder on your SkyDrive.
- Co-author using the Excel Web App.

■ VOCABULARY

cloud computing

co-author

Office Web Apps

OneNote

SkyDrive

Windows Live

If the computer you are using has an active Internet connection, you can go to the Microsoft Windows Live Web site and use SkyDrive to store and share files. From SkyDrive, you can also use Office Web Apps to create and edit Word, PowerPoint, Excel, and OneNote files, even when you are using a computer that does not have Office 2010 installed. In this Appendix, you will learn how to obtain a Windows Live ID, how to share files with others on SkyDrive, and how to use the Word, Excel, and PowerPoint Web Apps, including co-authoring in the Excel Web App.

Understanding Cloud Computing and Windows Live

> **VOCABULARY**
> **cloud computing**
> **Windows Live**

Cloud computing refers to data, applications, and even resources that are stored on servers that you access over the Internet rather than on your own computer. With cloud computing, you access only what you need when you need it. Many individuals and companies are moving towards "the cloud" for at least some of their needs. For example, some companies provide space and computing power to developers for a fee. Individuals might subscribe to an online backup service so that data is automatically backed up on a computer at the physical location of the companies that provide that service.

Windows Live is a collection of services and Web applications that you can use to help you be more productive both personally and professionally. For example, you can use Windows Live to send and receive email, chat with friends via instant messaging, share photos, create a blog, and store and edit files. Windows Live is a free service that you sign up for. When you sign up, you receive a Windows Live ID, which you use to sign into your Windows Live account. **Table D–1** describes the services available on Windows Live.

TABLE D–1   Services available via Windows Live

SERVICE	DESCRIPTION
Email	Send and receive e-mail using a Hotmail account
Instant Messaging	Use Messenger to chat with friends, share photos, and play games
SkyDrive	Store files, work on files using Web Apps, and share files with people in your network
Photos	Upload and share photos with friends
People	Develop a network of friends and coworkers and use it to distribute information and stay in touch
Downloads	Access a variety of free programs available for download to a PC
Mobile Device	Access applications for a mobile device: text messaging, using Hotmail, networking, and sharing photos

SkyDrive is an online storage and file sharing service. With a Windows Live account, you receive access to your own SkyDrive, which is your personal storage area on the Internet. You upload files to your SkyDrive so you can share the files with other people, access the files from another computer, or use SkyDrive's additional storage. On your SkyDrive, you are given space to store up to 25 GB of data online. Each file can be a maximum size of 50 MB. You can also use your SkyDrive to share files with friends and coworkers. After you upload a file to your SkyDrive, you can choose to make the file visible to the public, to anyone you invite to share your files, or only to yourself. You can also use SkyDrive to access Office Web Apps. When you save files to SkyDrive on Windows Live, you are saving your files to an online location. SkyDrive is like having a personal hard drive "in the cloud."

Office Web Apps are versions of Microsoft Word, Excel, PowerPoint, and *OneNote*, an electronic notebook program included with Microsoft Office, that you can access online from your SkyDrive. Office Web Apps offer basic functionality, allowing you to create and edit files created in Word, PowerPoint, and Excel online in your Web browser. An Office Web App does not include all of the features and functions included with the full Office version of its associated application. However, you can use the Office Web Apps from any computer that is connected to the Internet, even if Microsoft Office 2010 is not installed on that computer.

Obtaining a Windows Live ID

To save files to SkyDrive or to use Office Web Apps, you need a Windows Live ID. You obtain a Windows Live ID by going to the Windows Live Web site and creating a new account.

> *Note*: If you already have a Windows Live ID, you can skip Step-by-Step D.1.

> **VOCABULARY**
> **SkyDrive**
> **Office Web Apps**
> **OneNote**

Step-by-Step D.1

1. Start Internet Explorer. Click in the Address bar, type **www.windowslive.com**, and then press **Enter**. The page where you can sign into Windows Live opens.

2. Click the **Sign up** button. The Create your Windows Live ID page opens.

3. Follow the instructions on the screen to create an ID with a new, live.com email address or create an ID using an existing email address.

4. After completing the process, if you signed up with an existing email address, open your email program or go to your Web-based email home page, and open the email message automatically sent to you from the Windows Live site. Click the link to open the Sign In page again, sign in with your user name and password if necessary, and then click the **OK** button in the page that appears telling you that your email address is verified.

5. Exit Internet Explorer.

WARNING

If the URL doesn't bring you to the page where you can sign into Windows Live, use a search engine to search for *Windows Live*.

Uploading Files to SkyDrive

You can access your SkyDrive from the Windows Live page in your browser after you signed in with your Windows Live ID, or from Word, Excel, PowerPoint, or OneNote. Then you can upload a file to a private or public folder on your SkyDrive.

Uploading a File to SkyDrive from Backstage View

If you are working in a file in Word, Excel, or PowerPoint, you can save the file to your SkyDrive from Backstage view. To do this, you click the File tab, click Save & Send in the navigation bar, and then click Save to Web. After you do this, the right pane changes to display a Sign In button that you can use to sign in to your Windows Live account. See **Figure D–1**.

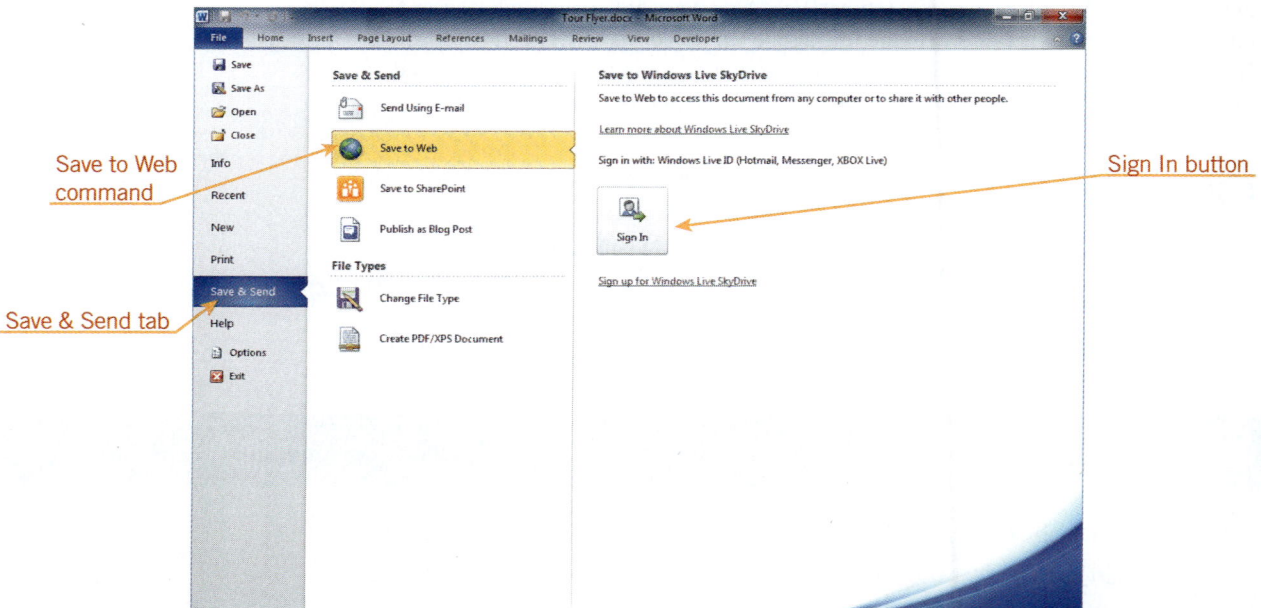

FIGURE D–1   Save & Send tab in Backstage view in Word after clicking Save to Web

Click the Sign In button to sign into Windows Live. After you enter your user name and password, the right pane in Backstage view changes to list the folders on your SkyDrive and a Save As button now appears in the right pane. See **Figure D–2**.

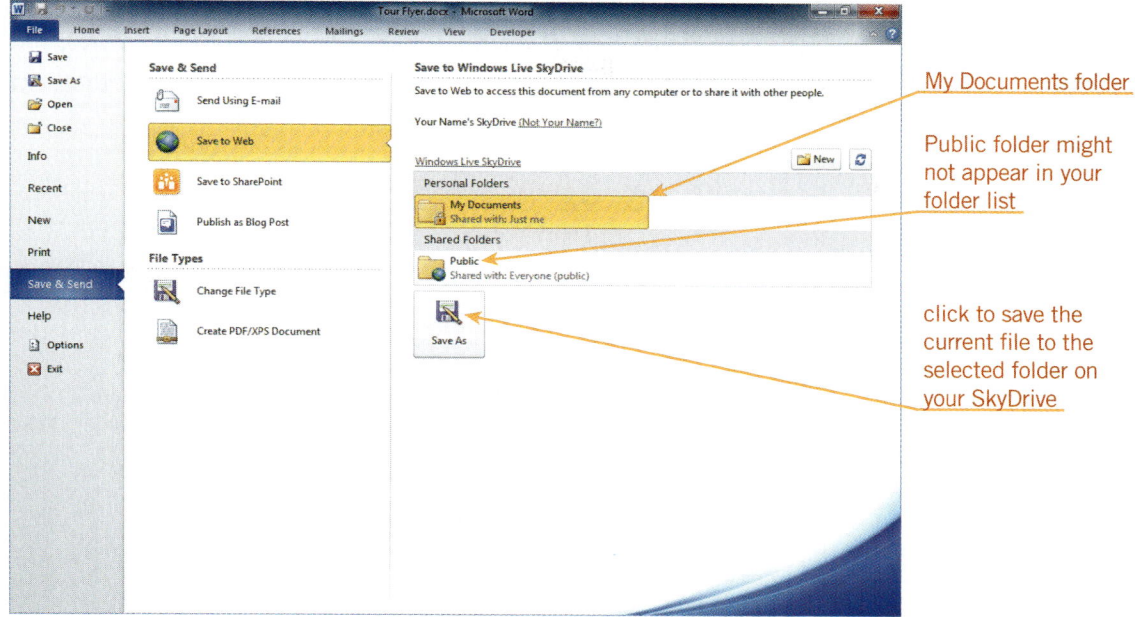

FIGURE D–2 Save & Send tab after connecting to Windows Live

To save the file, click the correct folder, and then click the Save As button.

Step-by-Step D.2

1. Start Word. Open the file named **Tour Flyer.docx** document from the drive and folder where your Data Files are stored.

2. Click the **File** tab, and then click **Save & Send** on the navigation bar. The Save & Send options appear in Backstage view as shown in Figure D–1.

3. Under Save & Send, click **Save to Web**.

4. Click the **Sign In** button. The Connecting to docs.live.net dialog box opens. See **Figure D–3**. If you are already signed into Windows Live, you will see the folders in your SkyDrive account listed instead of the Sign In button. Skip this step (Step 4) and Step 5.

FIGURE D–3
Connecting to docs.live.net
dialog box

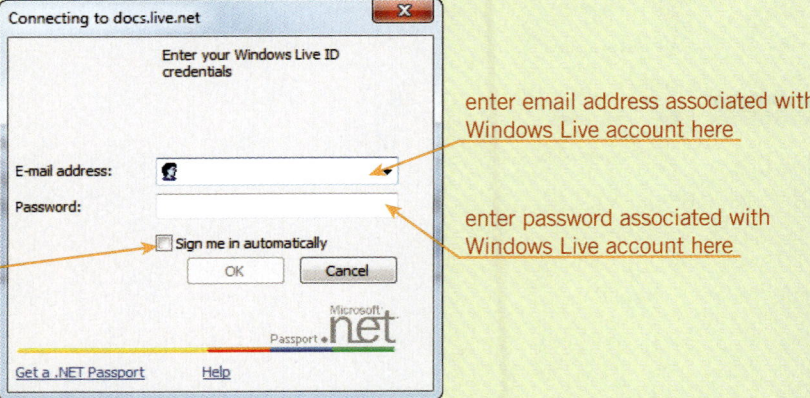

5. In the E-mail address box, type the email address associated with your Windows Live ID account. Press **Tab**, and then type the password associated with your Windows Live account in the Password box. Click the **OK** button. The dialog box closes, and another dialog box appears briefly while you connect to the Windows Live server. After you are connected, the folders on your SkyDrive appear in the right pane in Backstage view, as shown in Figure D–2.

6. In the right pane, click the **My Documents** folder, and then click the **Save As** button. Backstage view closes, and then after a few moments, the Save As dialog box opens. The path in the Address bar identifies the Public folder location on your SkyDrive.

7. Click the **Save** button. The dialog box closes and the Tour Flyer file is saved to the My Documents folder on your SkyDrive.

8. Exit Word.

Uploading a File to SkyDrive in a Browser

You can also add files to SkyDrive by starting from an Internet Explorer window. To do this, go to www.windowslive.com, and then log in to your Windows Live account. See **Figure D–4**.

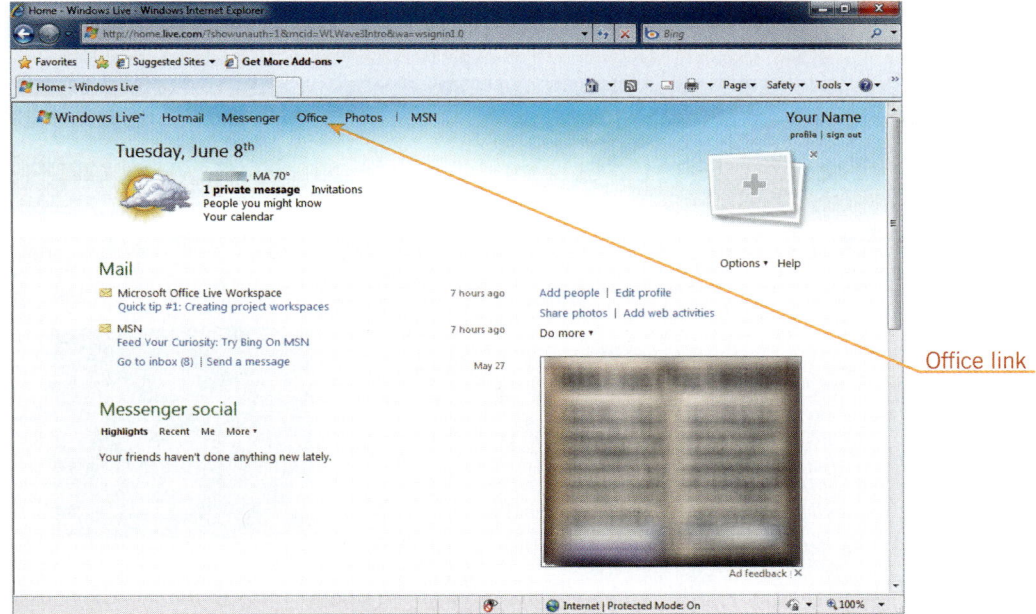

FIGURE D–4   Windows Live home page

To get to your SkyDrive, you click the Office link in the list of navigation links at the top of the window. To see all the folders on your SkyDrive, click View all in the Folders list on the left. See **Figure D–5**.

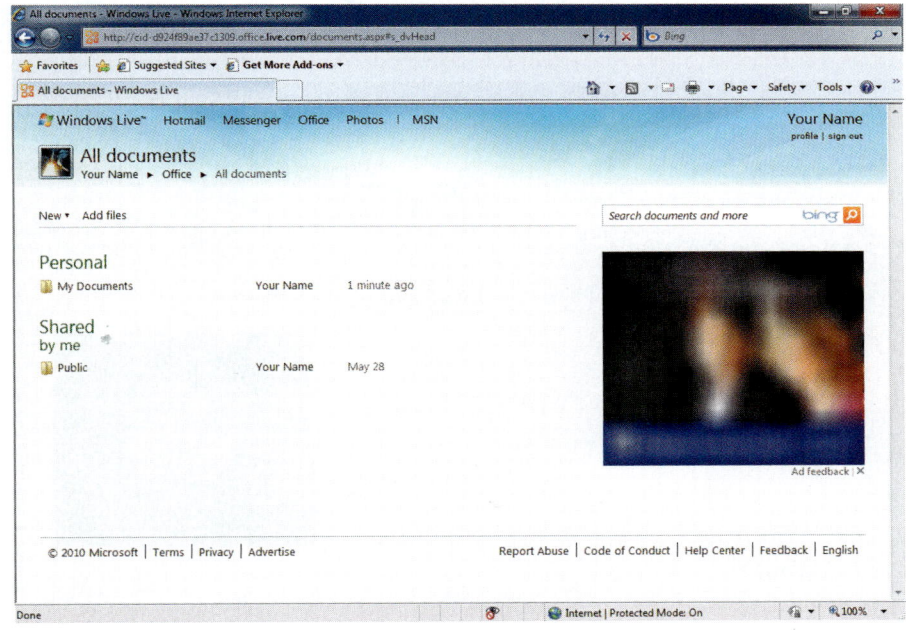

FIGURE D–5   Folders list on SkyDrive

Click the folder to which you want to add the file to open it. See **Figure D–6**.

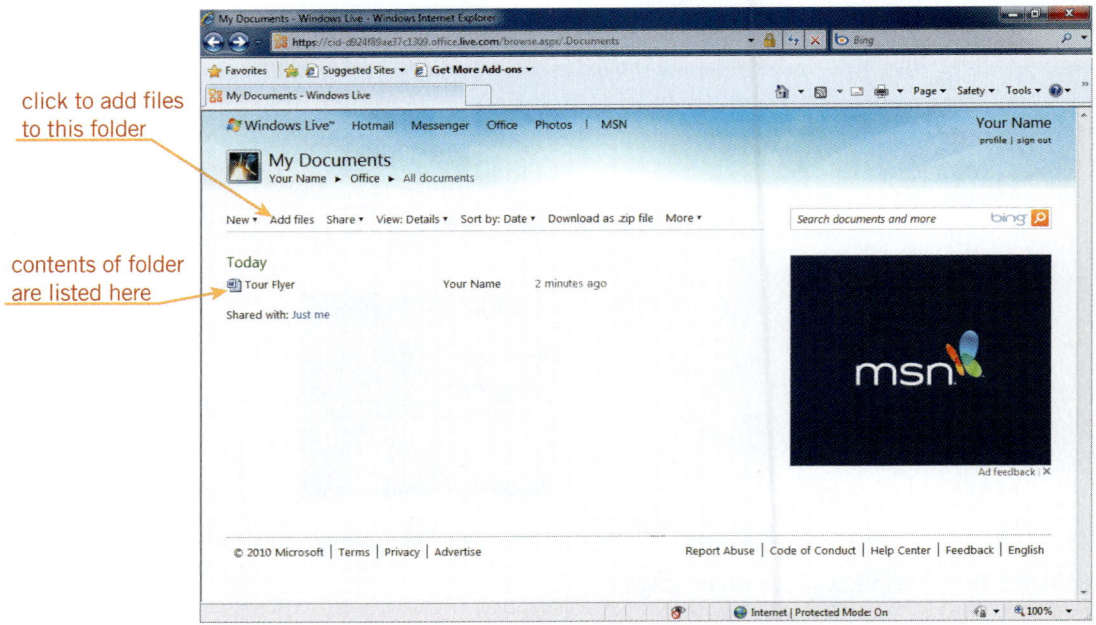

click to add files to this folder

contents of folder are listed here

FIGURE D–6 My Documents folder page on SkyDrive

Click the Add files link to open the Add documents to *Folder Name* page; for example, if you click the Add files link in the My Documents folder, the Add documents to My Documents page appears. See **Figure D–7**.

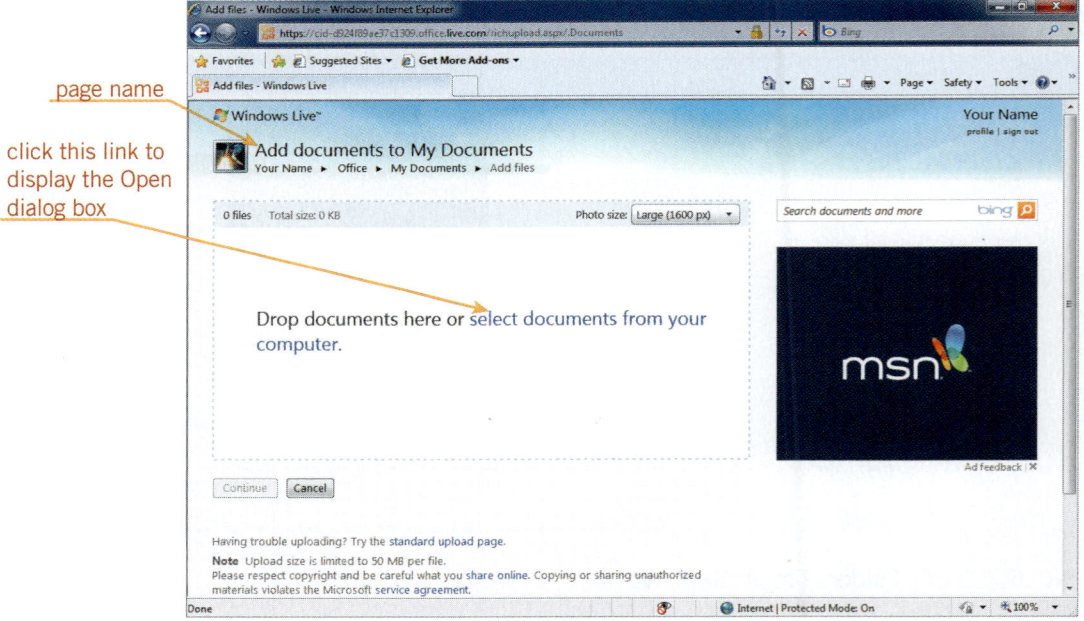

page name

click this link to display the Open dialog box

FIGURE D–7 Add documents to My Documents page on SkyDrive

Click the "select documents from your computer" link to display the Open dialog box. Locate the drive and folder where the file is stored, click it, and then click Open. The file uploads and is listed in the box. Click Continue to display the folder containing the files you uploaded to your SkyDrive.

Step-by-Step D.3

1. Start Internet Explorer. Click in the Address bar, type **www.windowslive. com**, and then press **Enter**.

2. If the Sign In page appears, type your Windows Live ID user name and password in the appropriate boxes, and then click **Sign in**. Your Windows Live home page appears similar to the one shown in Figure D–4.

3. In the list of command links at the top of the window, click **Office**. Your SkyDrive page appears.

4. In the list under Folders on the left, click **View all**. All the folders on your SkyDrive appear, similar to Figure D–5.

5. Click the **My Documents** folder. The My Documents page appears, similar to Figure D–6.

6. In the list of command links, click the **Add files** link. The Add documents to My Documents page appears, as shown in Figure D–7.

7. Click the **select documents from your computer** link, navigate to the drive and folder where your Data Files are stored, click **Tour Sales.pptx**, and then click the **Open** button. The file uploads and appears in the box on the Add documents to My Documents page.

8. At the bottom of the box, click the **select more documents from your computer** link. In the Open dialog box, click **Tour Data.xlsx**, and then click **Open**. The Excel file is listed in the box along with the PowerPoint file.

9. Below the box, click **Continue**. The My Documents folder page appears listing the files in that folder.

10. Keep the My Documents folder page displayed in Internet Explorer for the next Step-by-Step.

Using Office Web Apps

There are two ways to work with files using the Office Web Apps. You can view a file or you can edit it using its corresponding Office Web App. From your SkyDrive, you can also open the document directly in the full Office 2010 application if the application is installed on the computer you are using. You do not need to have Microsoft Office 2010 programs installed on the computer you use to access Office Web Apps.

Using a Web App in View Mode

To use a Web App in View mode, simply click its filename in the folder. This opens the file in View mode in the Web App. **Figure D–8** shows the Tour Flyer Word file open in the Word Web App in View mode.

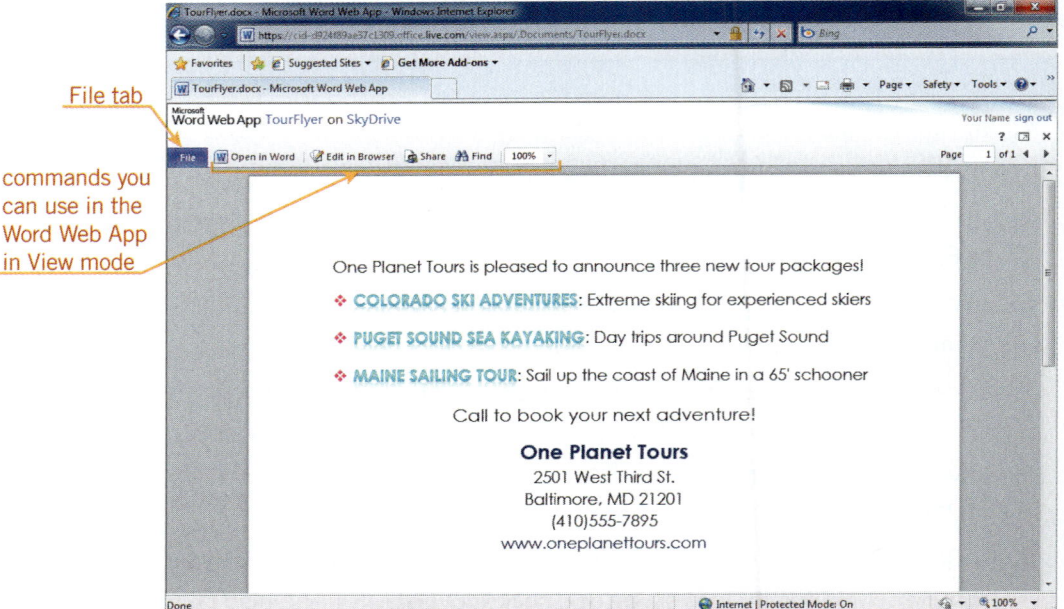

FIGURE D–8 Tour Flyer document open in View mode in Word Web App

Step-by-Step D.4

1. Click **Tour Flyer**. The Tour Flyer document opens in the Word Web App in View mode, as shown in Figure D–8.

2. Click anywhere in the document window, and then type any character. Nothing happens because you are allowed only to view the document in View mode.

3. Click the **File** tab. A list of commands opens. Note that you can print the document using the Print command on this menu.

4. Click **Close**. The document closes and the My Documents folder page appears again.

5. Leave the My Documents folder page open for the next Step-by-Step.

TIP

Position the mouse over a file icon to see the full filename and other details about the file.

Using a Web App in Edit Mode

You can also edit documents in the Office Web Apps. Although the interface for each Office Web App is similar to the interface of the full-featured program on your computer, a limited number of commands are available for editing documents using the Office Web App for each program. To edit a file in a Web App, point to the file in the folder page, and then click the Edit in browser link. You will see a Ribbon with a limited number of tabs and commands on the tabs. **Figure D–9** shows the file Tour Sales open in the PowerPoint Web App in Edit mode.

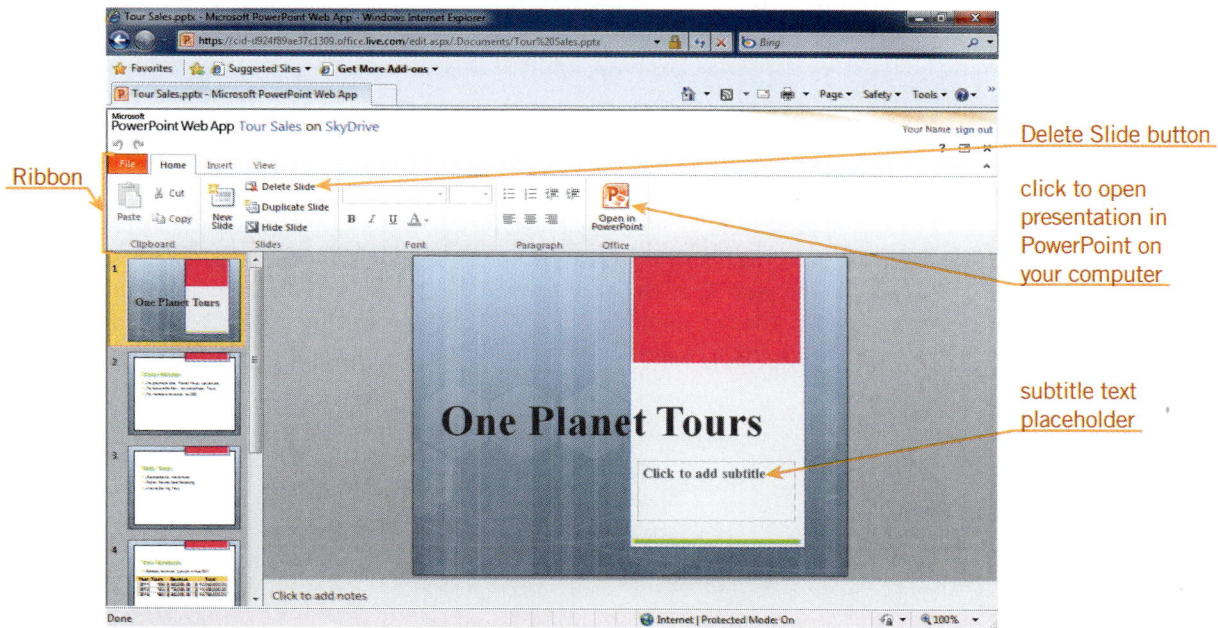

FIGURE D–9 Tour Sales presentation open in Edit mode in PowerPoint Web App

Step-by-Step D.5

TIP

To create a new file on SkyDrive using an Office Web App, open a folder, click the New link, and then select the appropriate Office Web App.

TIP

When you make changes to a file using a Web App, you do not need to save your changes before you close it because changes are saved automatically.

1. In the list of files in the My Documents folder, point to **Tour Sales**. A list of commands for working with the file appears.

2. In the list of commands, click the **Edit in browser** link. The Tour Sales presentation appears in the PowerPoint Web App in Edit mode, as shown in Figure D–9. In Edit mode, you see a version of the familiar Ribbon.

3. In the Slide pane, click in the subtitle text placeholder, and then type your name.

4. In the Slides tab, click **Slide 3** to display it in the Slide pane. The slide title is *New Tours*.

5. On the Home tab, in the Slides group, click the **Delete Slide** button. The *New Tours* slide is deleted from the presentation and the new Slide 3 (*Tour Revenue*) appears in the Slide pane. Now you will examine the other two tabs available to you in the PowerPoint Web App.

6. Click the **Insert** tab on the Ribbon. The only objects you can insert in a slide using the PowerPoint Web App in Edit mode are pictures and SmartArt. You can also create a hyperlink.

7. Click the View tab. Note that you cannot switch to Slide Master view in the PowerPoint Web App.

8. Leave the Tour Sales file open in the PowerPoint Web App for the next Step-by-Step.

Editing a File Stored on SkyDrive in the Program on Your Computer

If you are working with a file stored on your SkyDrive and you want to use a command that is available in the full-featured program on your computer but is not available in the Web App, you need to open the file in the full-featured program on your computer. You can do this from the corresponding Office Web App by clicking the Open in *Program Name* button on the Home tab on the Web App Ribbon.

Step-by-Step D.6

1. Click the **Home** tab. In the Office group, click the **Open in PowerPoint** button. The Open Document dialog box appears warning you that some files can harm your computer. This dialog box opens when you try to open a document stored on a Web site.

2. Click the **OK** button. PowerPoint starts on your computer and the revised version of the Tour Sales presentation opens on your computer. The presentation is in Protected view because it is not stored on the local computer you are using.

3. In the yellow Protected View bar, click the **Enable Editing** button. Now you can insert a footer on the slides.

4. Click the **Insert** tab, and then click the **Header & Footer** button in the Text group.

5. Click the **Footer** check box, type **2013 Sales Projections** in the Footer box, and then click the **Apply to All** button. When you use the full-featured version of a program, you do need to save the changes you made, even when it is stored in a folder on your SkyDrive.

6. On the Quick Access Toolbar, click the **Save** button 🖫. The modified file is saved to your SkyDrive.

7. In the PowerPoint window title bar, click the **Close** button ❌. The PowerPoint program closes and you see your browser window listing the contents of the My Documents folder.

8. Click the **Tour Sales** file. Slide 1 of the Tour Sales file appears in the PowerPoint Web app in View mode.

9. At the bottom of the window, click the **Next Slide** button ▶ twice. Slide 3 (*Tour Revenue*) appears in the window. Remember that you deleted the original Slide 3, *New Tours*. Also note that the footer you added is on the slide.

10. Click the **File** tab, and then click **Close**. The PowerPoint Web App closes and the My Documents page appears.

11. Leave the My Documents page open for the next Step-by-Step.

WARNING

You can also open a document stored on your SkyDrive in the program stored on your computer from View mode in the corresponding Office Web App.

WARNING

If the Connecting to dialog box opens asking for your Windows Live ID credentials, type the email address associated with your Windows Live ID in the E-mail address box, type your password in the Password box, and then click the OK button.

Creating Folders on Your SkyDrive

You can keep your SkyDrive organized by using file management techniques, similar to the way you organize files on your computer's hard drive. You can create a folder in your SkyDrive in the Internet Explorer window or from Backstage view in the program on your computer.

To create a folder on your SkyDrive in Internet Explorer, click the New link in the list of commands, and then click Folder to open the Create a new folder page on your SkyDrive. See **Figure D–10**.

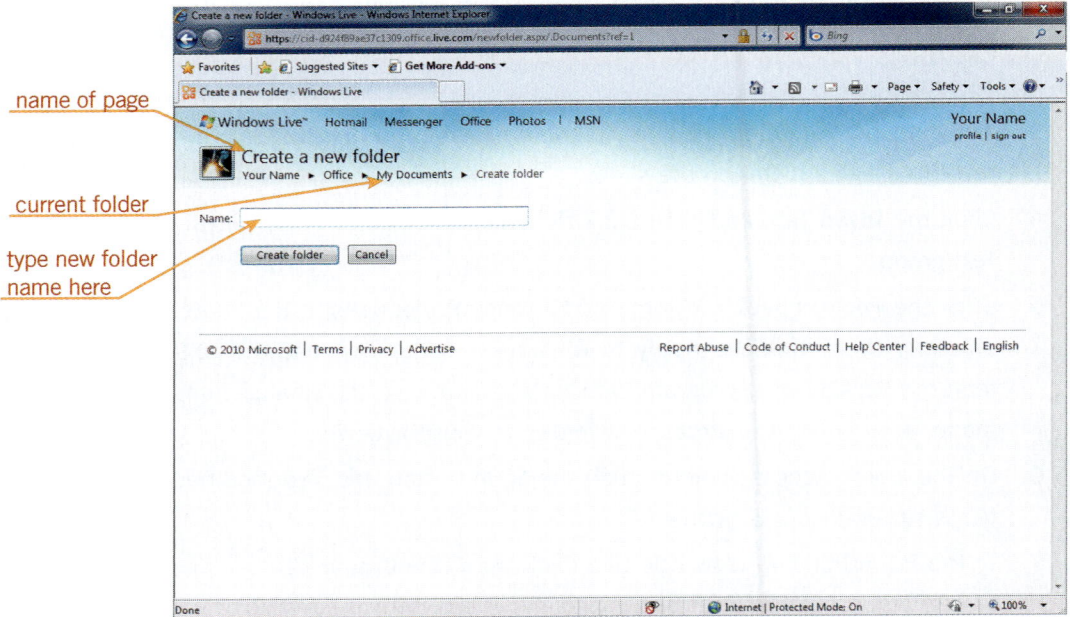

FIGURE D–10   Create a new folder page on SkyDrive

To create a new folder on your SkyDrive from the Save & Send tab in Backstage view in an application, click the New button in the upper-right. This opens the same Create a new folder page shown in Figure D–10.

Type the name for the new folder in the Name box, and then click Next. The Add files to *Folder Name* page that you saw earlier appears. If you want to upload a file to the new folder, you can do so at this point. If you don't, you can click the link for the new folder or click the SkyDrive link to return to your SkyDrive home page.

Step-by-Step D.7

1. In the list of command links, click the **New** link, and then click **Folder**. The Create a new folder page appears with the insertion point in the Name box.

2. In the Name box, type **Sales**, and then click **Create folder**. The new empty folder is displayed in the browser window. You can see that you are looking at the contents of the new folder by looking at the navigation links. See **Figure D–11**.

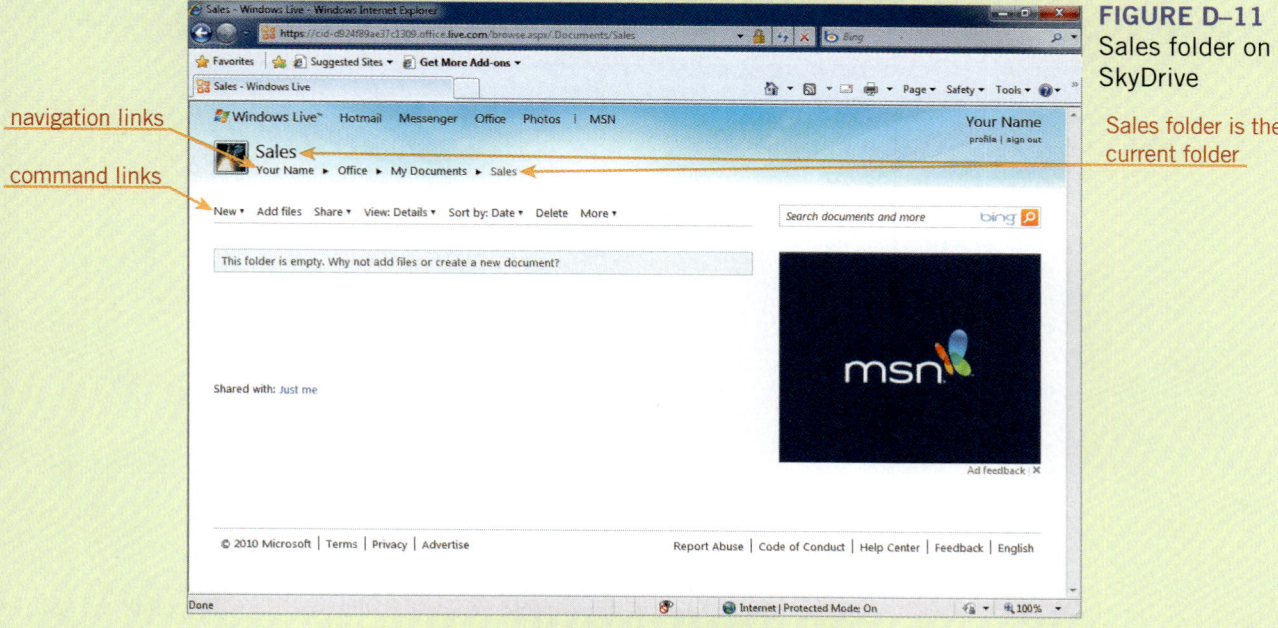

FIGURE D–11
Sales folder on SkyDrive

navigation links

command links

Sales folder is the current folder

3. Leave the Sales folder page open for the next Step-by-Step.

Organizing Files on Your SkyDrive

As on your hard drive, you can move and delete files on your SkyDrive. To move or delete a file, first display the commands for working with the file by pointing to its name in the file list in the folder. To move a file, click the More link, and then click Move to open the "Where would you like to move *File Name*?" page. See **Figure D–12**.

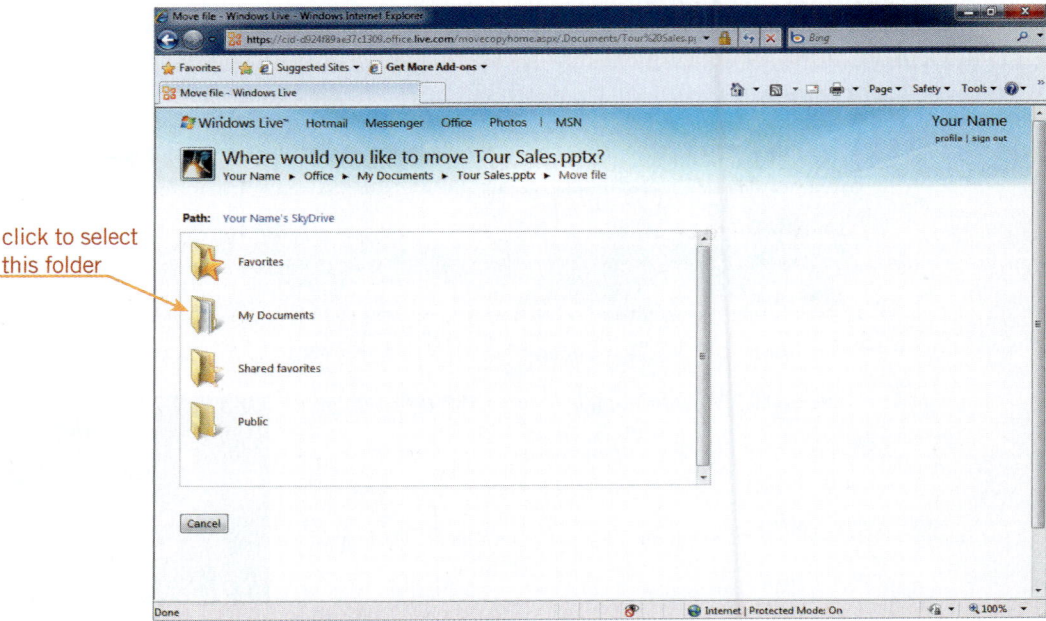

FIGURE D–12   Folder list that appears when moving a file

In the list of folders, click a folder. Then, at the top of the list, click the "Move this file into *Folder Name*" command. The folder into which you moved the file appears, along with a message telling you that the file was moved.

To delete a file, point to it to display the commands for working with the file, and then click the Delete button in the list of command links.

Step-by-Step D.8

1. In the list of navigation links, click the **My Documents** link. Point to **Tour Sales**. The commands for working with this file appear.

2. In the list of command links, click the **More** link, and then click **Move**. The "Where would you like to move Tour Sales.pptx?" page appears, and a list of folders on your SkyDrive appears.

3. In the list of folders, click the **My Documents** folder to display the list of folders located inside that folder. Click the **Sales** folder. The contents of the Sales folder appear in the list of folders. Because this folder does not contain any additional folders, you see only a command to create a New folder and the command to move the file.

4. In the list of folders, click **Move this file into Sales**. After a moment, the contents of the Sales folder appear, along with a message telling you that you have moved the Tour Sales file from the My Documents folder.

5. In the list of navigation links, click the **My Documents** link. The contents of the My Documents folder appear.

6. Point to **Tour Flyer**. In the list of command links, click the **Delete** button . A dialog box opens warning you that you are about to permanently delete the file.

7. Click **OK**. The dialog box closes, the file is deleted from the My Documents folder on your SkyDrive.

8. Leave the My Documents folder page open for the next Step-by-Step.

WARNING

Depending on the resolution of your computer, you might not need to click the More link to access the Move command.

Giving Permission for Access to a Folder on Your SkyDrive

If you upload a file to a private folder, you can grant permission to access the file to anyone else with a Windows Live ID. You can grant permission to folders located at the same level as the My Documents folder. You cannot grant permission to individual files or to folders located inside a locked folder. If you grant permission to someone to access a folder, that person will have access to all the files in that folder.

To grant permission to someone, click the folder to display its contents, click the Share link in the list of navigation links, and then click Edit permissions. The Edit permissions for *Folder Name* page appears. You can use the slider bar to make the contents of the new folder public by sharing it with everyone, your friends as listed on your Windows Live ID account and their friends, just your friends, or only some friends. You can also share it only with specific people that you list in the box in the Add Specific People section. When you type someone's name or email address associated with the person's Windows Live ID account in the box in the Add specific people section, and then press Enter, the person's name appears in a box below with a check box next to the name or email address. The box to the right of the person's name or email address indicates that the person can view files in the shared folder. You can then click the arrow to change this so that the person can view, edit, or delete files. See **Figure D–13**. Click Save at the bottom of the window to save the permissions you set.

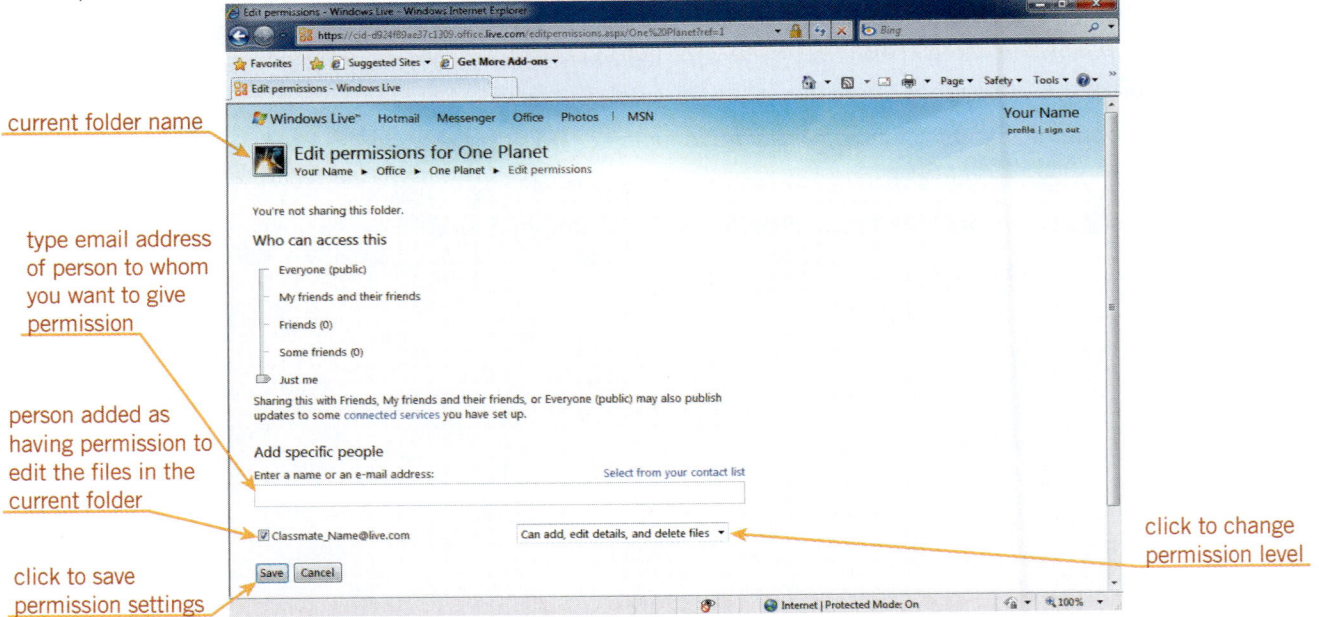

FIGURE D–13   Edit permissions for One Planet page on SkyDrive

To complete the next Step-by-Step, you need to work with a partner who also has a Windows Live ID account.

Step-by-Step D.9

1. In the list of navigation links, click the **Office** link, and then in the list of links on the left, click **View all**. The All documents page appears.

2. In the list of command links, click the **New** link, and the click **Folder**. The Create a folder page appears with a temporary folder name in the Name box. The temporary name is selected, so you can just type the new name.

3. In the Name box, type **One Planet**. Click **Next**. The One Planet folder page appears.

4. In the list of navigation links, click the **Office** link. In the list of folders on the left, click the **My Documents** link. The My Documents folder page appears.

5. In the file list, point to **Tour Data**, click the **More** link, and then click **Move**. The Where would you like to move Tour Data.xlsx? page appears.

6. In the list of folders, click **One Planet**. In the new list that appears, click the **Move this file into One Planet**. The One Planet page appears with the Tour Data file listed.

7. In the list of command links, click the **Share** link. Click **Edit permissions**. The Edit permissions for One Planet page appears.

8. Under Add specific people, click in the **Enter a name or an e-mail address** box, type the email address of your partner, and then press **Enter**. The email address you typed appears below the box. A check box next to the email address is selected, and a list box to the right identifies the level of access for this person. The default is Can add, edit details, and delete files, similar to Figure D–13. You want your partner to be able to edit the file, so you don't need to change this.

9. At the bottom of the window, click **Save**. The Send a notification for One Planet page appears. You can send a notification to each individual when you grant permission to access your files. This is a good idea so that each person will have the URL of your folder. Your partner's email address appears in the To box.

> **TIP**
>
> Because you are creating a folder at the same level as the My Documents folder, there is a Share with box below the Name box. You can set the permissions when you create the folder if you want.

> **TIP**
>
> To make the contents of the folder available to anyone, drag the slider up to the top so it is next to the Everyone (public).

10. Click in the Include your own message box, type **You can now access the contents of the One Planet folder on my SkyDrive.**, and then click **Send**. Your partner will receive an email message from you advising him or her that you have shared your One Planet folder. If your partner is completing the steps at the same time, you will receive an email message from your partner.

11. Check your email for a message from your partner advising you that your partner has shared his or her Sales folder with you. The subject of the email message will be "*Your Partner's Name* has shared documents with you."

12. If you have received the email, click the **View folder** button in the email message, and then sign in to Windows Live if you are requested to do so. You are now able to access your partner's One Planet folder on his or her SkyDrive. See **Figure D–14**.

FIGURE D–14
One Planet folder on someone else's SkyDrive

name of person who gave you permission to access the One Planet folder on his or her SkyDrive

your Windows Live name appears here

current folder

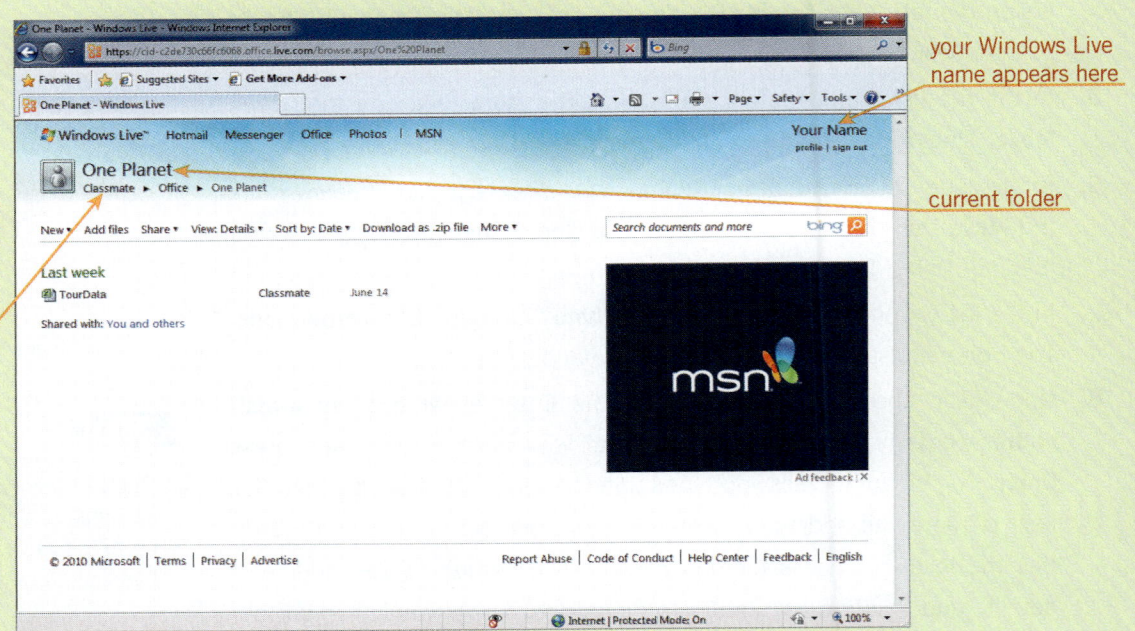

13. Leave Internet Explorer open for the next Step-by-Step.

Co-Authoring with the Excel Web App

When you work with the Excel Web App, you can use its *co-authoring* feature to simultaneously edit an Excel workbook at the same time as a colleague. When you co-author a workbook, a list of the people currently co-authoring the workbook appears at the bottom of the window. Co-authoring is not available in the Word or PowerPoint Web Apps. When you open a file in the Excel Web App, a notification appears at the right end of the status bar notifying you that two people are editing the document. See **Figure D–15**. You can click this to see the email addresses of the people currently editing the workbook.

▶ **VOCABULARY**
co-author

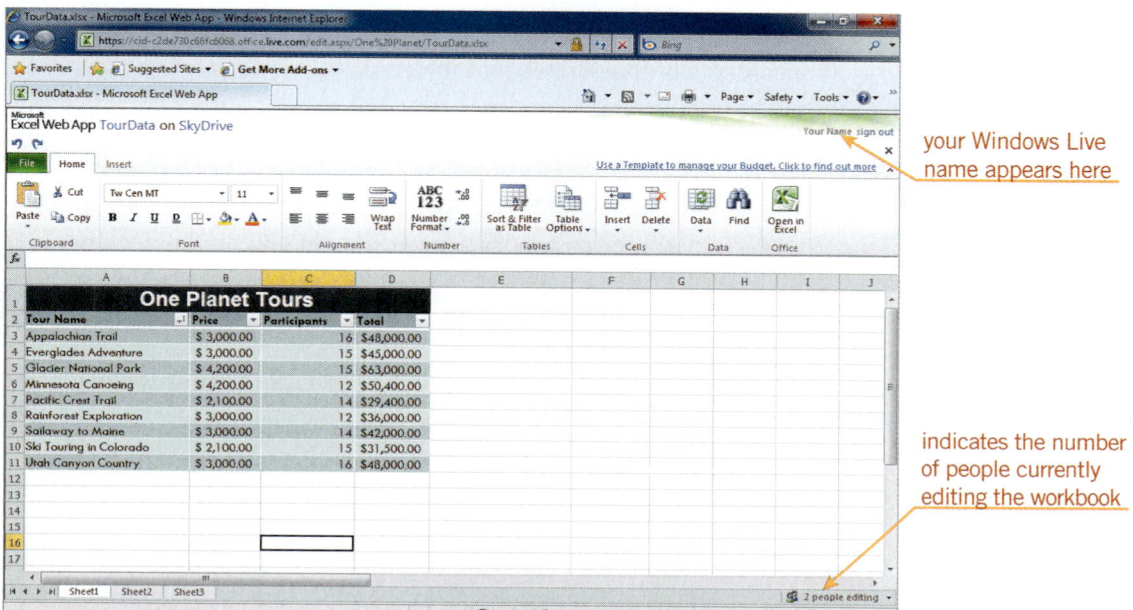

your Windows Live name appears here

indicates the number of people currently editing the workbook

FIGURE D–15 Tour Data file open in Edit mode in Excel Web App with two people editing

To complete this next Step-by-Step, you need to continue working with the partner who has permission to access the One Planet folder on your SkyDrive and who gave you permission to access his or her One Planet folder.

Step-by-Step D.10

1. Decide with your partner whether you will modify the Tour Data file stored on your SkyDrive or on his or her SkyDrive. After you decide the SkyDrive account with which you are going to work, both of you display the contents of that One Planet folder.

2. Point to **Tour Data**, and then in the list of command links, click the **Edit in browser** link.

3. In the status bar, click the **2 people editing** button. A list pops up identifying you and your partner as the two people editing the document.

   Decide with your partner which one of you will execute Step 4. The other person will then execute Step 5.

4. Either you or your partner click cell **A12**, type **Gulf Islands Sailing**, press **Tab**, type **3000**, press **Tab**, type **10**, and then press **Tab**. The formula in the other cells in column D is copied automatically to cell D12 because the data in the original Excel file was created and formatted as an Excel table. Both you and your partner see the data entered in row 12.

   If you entered the data in row 12, you partner should execute Step 5; if your partner entered the data in row 12, you should execute Step 5.

5. Either you or your partner—the person who did not execute Step 4—click cell **B12**, type **3700**, and then press **Tab**. The data entered is reformatted in the Accounting number format, and the total in cell D12 is recalculated. Again, both you and your partner see the change executed.

   Both you and your partner should execute the rest of the steps in this section.

6. Click the **File** tab, and then click **Close**. The changes you made to the Excel workbook are saved automatically on the current SkyDrive account. You are finished working with the Office Web Apps, so you can sign out of Windows Live.

7. In the upper-right of the SkyDrive window, click the **sign out** link. You are signed out of Windows Live.

8. In the title bar of your Web browser window, click the **Close** button ![X] to exit your Web browser.

OneNote Web App

The other Office Web App is OneNote. As with Word, Excel, and PowerPoint files, you can share OneNote files on SkyDrive directly from OneNote. Note that you need to click the Share tab in the navigation bar in Backstage view, and then click Web and specify Windows Live as the Web location. After you upload a OneNote file to SkyDrive, you can work with it in its corresponding Web App.

GLOSSARY

3-D reference   A reference to the same cell or range in multiple worksheets that you use in a formula.

A

Absolute cell reference   A cell reference that does not change when copied or moved to a new cell.

Action button   An interactive button that performs instructions such as going to a specific slide or other object that you can create by drawing from the Shapes gallery.

Action Center   An area in a window that displays important messages about critical security and maintenance components on a computer, such as the firewall, antivirus protection, and spyware protection.

Active cell   The cell in the worksheet in which you can type data.

Active worksheet   The worksheet that is displayed in the work area.

Address bar   An area in a window that contains the path to the current folder.

Address Book   A collection of personal and professional contact information stored in a directory.

Adjacent range   A range where all cells touch each other and form a rectangle.

Adjustment handle   A yellow diamond-shaped handle that appears on a selected object. Drag the handle to change the appearance of the object.

Align (in Excel)   To specify how the contents of a cell are lined up horizontally or vertically within the cell.

Align (in PowerPoint)   Use to arrange objects to line up with the other objects on the slide or place an object relative to other objects on the slide. Align commands include: Left, Center, Right, Top, Middle, and Bottom.

Alignment (in Excel)   The specification of how the contents of a cell are lined up within the cell.

Alignment (in Word)   The position of text between the margins.

Alphanumeric data   Data that contains numbers, text, or a combination of numbers and text.

Always-on connection   An Internet connection method, such as fiber optic, DSL, or cable, where the computer is always connected to the Internet as long as the computer is on.

And operator   An operator used in a query that selects records that match all of two or more conditions in a query.

Animation   Adds motion to an object.

Antispyware Programs that protect your computer from spyware.

Antivirus   Programs that protect your computer from viruses.

Applications software   A program used to perform a job or task; examples include word processors, databases, graphics programs, and spreadsheets.

Appointment   An Outlook activity that involves the user at a set date and time.

Archive   An electronic repository that organizes, stores, and saves old files.

Argument   The value the function uses to perform a calculation, including a number, text, or a cell reference that acts as an operand.

Ascending   A sort order that arranges records using the values in a specific field or column from A to Z or from smallest to largest.

Ascending sort   To arrange data with letters in alphabetical order (A to Z), data with numbers from lowest to highest, and data with dates from earliest to latest.

Aspect ratio   The relationship of an object's height to its width.

Attribute   A formatting feature that affects how a font looks, such as a style, the color, or an effect.

AutoComplete   A feature in Word that guesses names of calendar items, such as the days of the week and months, as you type them, and then suggests the complete word.

AutoCorrect   A feature in Word that corrects errors as you type.

AutoFilter   A menu that opens when you click the arrow on the right side of a field selector in a datasheet. The menu contains options for sorting data and for applying and clearing filters.

AutoFit   An automatic determination of the best width for a column or the best height for a row, based on its contents.

AutoFormat As You Type   A feature in Word that applies built-in formats as you type.

Automatic grammar checking   A feature in Word that checks your document for grammatical errors as you type, and flags them with a green, wavy underline.

Automatic page break   A page break Excel inserts whenever it runs out of room on a page.

Automatic spell checking   A feature in Word that checks your document for spelling errors as you type, and flags them with a red or blue wavy underline.

AutoNumber   A data type that automatically adds a unique field value to each record in a table.

Axis   A horizontal or vertical line that establishes the relationship between data in a chart.

B

Background   The area behind the text and graphics on a slide.

Backstage view   The Ribbon tab where you do "behind the scenes" tasks such as getting information about the current file, creating new files, printing the current file, sharing files with others, and defining file properties.

Bar code reader   Device used to read printed codes such as the UPC (universal product code) to track merchandise or other inventory in a store.

Best fit   The term used when a column in a datasheet is resized to the best width for the data contained in the column.

Blank Database template   A template that creates a database that contains only an empty table.

Blank presentation   A new presentation that does not have theme elements, text, or objects.

Blu-ray disc (BD)   A high-capacity optical storage media that can store full-length feature films up to 35GB of data.

Blu-ray drive   A device used to read Blu-ray discs.

Border   A line around the edges of a cell.

Bound control   A control in a form or report that is connected to a field in the record source and is used to display, enter, and update data.

Broadcast   Placing a link to a presentation on the Web to allow others to watch your presentation as you give it from a remote location through a Web browser.

Building block (in Publisher)   A collection of design and text placeholders that can be used to further enhance a publication's appearance and functionality.

Building block (in Word)   Document parts that you can store in Word and reuse.

Bullet   Any small character that appears before an item in a list.

Business information set   A collection of information about an individual. Business information sets are stored in Publisher and are associated with templates.

Button   An icon you click to choose a command, which gives the program instructions about what you want to do.

Byte   A single character of data such as a letter which is composed of eight bits.

C

Calculated field   A field in a query, form, or report that displays a value that is calculated using a combination of operators, constants, and the values in other fields.

Callout   A special type of label in a drawing that consists of a text box with an attached line to point to something in the drawing.

Category axis   The identifying labels listed on the horizontal axis in a chart.

CD (compact disc)   A durable form of removable optical storage in the form of a round flat disk that can hold 750MB of data. Used for file storage as well as audio files for music playback.

CD drive   A device used to read and write data to CDs.

Cell   The intersection of a column and a row in a table or worksheet.

Cell reference   A unique identifier for a cell, which is formed by combining the cell's column letter and row number.

Cell style   A collection of formatting characteristics you apply to a cell or range of data.

Center   To position text so that it is centered between the left and right margins.

Central processing unit (CPU)   A silicon chip, stored on the motherboard, which processes data and carries out instructions given to the computer.

Chart   A visual representation of numerical data, which can be in the form of lines, bars, wedges in pies, or other graphics. *Also called* graph.

Chart area   The entire chart and all other chart elements.

Chart layout   An arrangement that specifies which elements are included in a chart and where they are placed.

Chart sheet   A separate sheet in the workbook that stores a chart.

Chart style   Formatting applied to a chart based on the colors, fonts, and effects associated with the workbook's theme.

Clear   To remove all the formatting applied to a cell or range of cells.

Client   A personal computer that requests data from a server.

Clip art   Graphics that are stored in the Clip Organizer or available online that you can insert in any document.

Clipboard   A temporary storage place in the computer's memory, available to all the programs on your computer, which can hold only one selection at a time; to place items on the Clipboard, you use the Cut or Copy command. An item on the Clipboard can be pasted into the file. *Also called* system Clipboard.

Clock speed   The speed of the processor.

Close button   The window button that closes the open window or application.

Cloud computing   The process of using data, applications, and even resources that are stored on servers that you access over the Internet rather than on your own computer.

Co-author   To simultaneously edit a file at the same time as someone else.

Color palette   A coordinated set of colors available for use in a document.

Color scheme   A named set of four colors that work well together.

Column   Appears vertically in the worksheet; identified by letters at the top of the worksheet window.

Column chart   A chart that uses bars of varying heights to illustrate values in a worksheet.

Column heading   The column letter.

Comma-separated values (CSV)   A file format in which commas separate the field values of each record in the data source and paragraph marks separate individual records.

Comment (in Excel)   A note attached to a cell that explains or identifies information contained in the cell.

Comment (in PowerPoint)   A small note or annotation on a slide.

Common field   A field that appears in two or more tables in a database and that has the same data type and field values. A common field (also called a matching field) is used to relate tables and usually has the same field name in the related tables.

Compacting   A process that rearranges the way a database is stored on disk and optimizes the performance of the database.

Computer folder   In Windows, provides access to hard drives, removable drives and media, CD and DVD drives, network locations, and other removable media such as flash storage, cameras, and scanners.

Computer system   Includes the system unit of a computer, and all peripheral input and output devices.

Condition   In a query, a condition (also called a criterion) specifies which data to display in the query results.

Conditional formatting   Formatting that changes the look of cells that meet a specified condition.

Contact   A person, organization, or business in an Outlook Address Book.

Content control   A special placeholder designed to contain a specific type of text, such as a date or the page number.

Contextual spell checking   A feature in Word that checks your document for words that are spelled correctly, but that might be misused, and flags them with a blue, wavy underline.

Contextual tab   A tab that appears on the Ribbon only when you select certain items in a file, and they contain commands related to that item.

Control   An object in a form or report, such as a label or text box, that displays data from the record source on which the form or report is based.

Control layout   A "container" that groups together the controls in a form or report so that you can change the formatting of and move these controls as a group.

Control Panel   The command center for configuring Windows settings.

Copy   To place a copy of selected text on the Clipboard or the Office Clipboard.

Copy (in Excel)   To duplicate a cell's contents without affecting the original cell.

Copyright   The legal method for protecting the intellectual property of the author or creator. Images, text, and sound files can be copyrighted.

Criteria   A term that indicates that a query contains two or more conditions. A condition specifies which data to display in the query results.

Crop   To remove part of a picture.

Custom show   A feature that allows you to create presentations for different audiences by selecting specific slides from a presentation.

Cut   To remove selected text and place it on the Clipboard or the Office Clipboard.

Cut (in Excel)   To move cell contents from the original position and place in the new location.

D

Daily Task List   Tasks visible in Calendar Day or Week view.

Data   Information entered into and manipulated or processed by a computer.

Data and information management   Organizing and storing of data in a company or organization using computers.

Data bus   The wiring and pathways by which the CPU communicates with the peripherals and components of the computer

Data label   Text or numbers that provides additional information about a data marker.

Data marker   A symbol (such as a bar, line, dot, slice, and so forth) that represents a single data point or value from the corresponding worksheet cell.

Data series   A group of related information in a column or row of a worksheet that is plotted on the chart.

Data source (in Access)   When used with a form letter, the term given to the file that contains the records to insert in the form letter. The data source might be a Word document, an Excel workbook, or an Access database.

Data source (in Excel)   The chart data stored in a range of cells in the worksheet.

Data source (in Word)   The file used in a mail merge that contains the information that varies in each document.

Data table   A grid that displays the data plotted in the chart.

Data type   The property of a field that determines the type of data that you can enter into the field, such as numbers or text.

Database   A collection of objects that work together to store, retrieve, display, and summarize data and also to automate tasks.

Database management system (DBMS)   A program that you use to store, retrieve, analyze, and print information.

Datasheet (in Access)   Displays the data for a table or query in rows and columns, with records in rows and fields in columns.

Datasheet (in PowerPoint)   A worksheet that appears with a chart on the slide and contains the numbers for the chart.

Datasheet selector   The box in the upper-left corner of a datasheet that, when clicked, selects all fields and records in the datasheet.

Datasheet tool   An Access tool that creates a form that looks like a datasheet.

Datasheet view   The view of a database table that displays data in rows and columns.

Date and time functions   Functions that convert serial numbers to a month, a day, or a year, or that insert the current date or the current date and time.

Date Navigator   The monthly calendar shown at the top of the To-Do Bar in Outlook.

Default Value property   A field property that lets you specify the value to enter into that field for each record in a table.

Delimited data   Data that is stored in text format and separated by delimiters, such as commas.

Delimiter   A punctuation mark or other character in a text file that separates data into fields and records.

Descending sort   To arrange data with letters from Z to A, data with numbers from highest to lowest, and data with dates from oldest to newest.

Description property   An optional field property that you can use to describe the data to store in the field.

Design Checker   A feature that finds and lists potential design problems associated with your publication.

Design grid   The top half of the Table window in Design view that displays the name, data type, and optional Description property for each field in a table.

Design view (table)   The view of a table that lets you add, delete, and rearrange fields. You can also use Design view to make changes to the way that fields store data.

Desktop   The main screen and workspace that opens when Windows is started.

Desktop computer   A personal computer that includes a system unit, keyboard, and mouse that is not portable.

Destination   The location where data will appear.

Destination file   The file that an object is embedded in or linked to, such as a presentation file. *See also* source file.

Detail query   A query that shows every field in each record in the query results.

Detail section   The section in Design view for a form or report that contains the detail records from the record source.

Diagram   A visual representation of data to help readers better understand relationships among data.

Dialog box   An interactive message window that appears when more information is required before the command can be performed.

Dial-up   The oldest, slowest, and cheapest Internet access technology, where your computer has to dial out through a local phone line to get access to the Internet.

Digital Subscriber Line (DSL)   Always-on broadband Internet connection that is faster than dialup or satellite but not as fast as cable or fiber optic.

Disk Cleanup   A Windows utility that deletes temporary files from the hard disk and improves computer performance.

Document Inspector   A feature that enables you to check for hidden metadata or personal information in a presentation.

Document properties   Information about the presentation file including title, author, and keywords.

Documents folder   Stores the files you use for your projects, such as documents, presentations, spreadsheets, and other files.

Draft view   A way of viewing a document on screen that shows only the text of a document; you don't see headers and footers, margins, columns, or graphics.

Drag   To select text by positioning the I-beam pointer to the left of the first character of the text you want to select, holding down the left button on the mouse, dragging the pointer to the end of the text you want to select, and then releasing the button.

Drag-and-drop   To drag selected text from one place in a file to another.

Driver   Software that runs peripheral hardware devices or facilitates other programs. It may install automatically when new hardware is detected by your computer, or you may have to install a driver yourself.

DVD   A high-capacity, optical disc that can store up to 4.7GB of data.

DVD drive   A device used to read and write data to CDs and DVDs.

E

E-mail   An electronic message sent using a computer network.

Effects options   The Entrance, Exit, Emphasis, and Motion Path animation features such as pinwheel, diamond, and fly effects that you can use to animate objects.

Embed   To place an object that was created in another application such as Microsoft Word or Excel in a slide. When you select the object, the original program will open for editing.

Embedded chart   A chart inserted in the center of the worksheet.

ENIAC (Electronic Numerical Integrator and Computer)   One of the earliest computers; designed for military use in 1946. It could accomplish a task in 20 seconds that would normally take a human three days to complete.

Event   An Outlook activity that lasts all day long over one or more days, but does not block out time in a calendar.

Exact match condition   A condition in a query that specifies the exact condition that a record must satisfy to be displayed in the query results.

Exploded pie chart   A pie chart with one or more slices pulled away from the pie to distinguish them.

Explorer windows   Vista windows that explore a computer and navigate to items.

Export   A term used when data is saved into a different file format.

Expression   The term given to the calculation used in a calculated field that identifies the fields and operators to use in the calculated field.

F

Favorites   Area in the Navigation Pane that contains links to folders for commonly used items, including the desktop, downloads, and recently opened files and folders.

Field   A single characteristic in a table's design that appears in a datasheet as a column.

Field List pane   A pane in Design view for a form or report that displays the tables and other objects in the database and the fields they contain.

Field name   The name of a column in a database table.

Field Properties pane   The bottom half of the Table window in Design view that displays properties for the selected field in a table.

Field property   An additional description of a field beyond the field's data type that specifies how to store data in the field, such as the number of characters the field can store.

Field selector   The top of a column in a datasheet that contains the field name. Clicking a field selector selects the column.

Field Size property   The property that identifies the number of characters that a Text, a Number, or an AutoNumber field can store.

Field value   The specific data stored in a field for a record.

File extension   A series of letters Office adds to the end of a file name that identifies in which program that file was created.

Fill   The background color of a cell.

Fill handle   The black square in the lower-right corner of the active cell or range that you drag over the cells you want to fill.

Filling   Copying a cell's contents and/or formatting into an adjacent cell or range.

Filter (in Access)   A temporary rearrangement of the records in a table, query, form, or report based on one or more specified conditions.

Filter (in Excel)   To display a subset of the data that meets certain criteria and temporarily hide the rows that do not meet the specified criteria.

Filter arrow   An arrow that appears in a column heading cell that opens the AutoFilter menu.

Filter By Form   A filter that you can apply to a datasheet or form that rearranges the records based on one or more field values that you select from a list.

Filter By Selection   A filter that you can apply to a datasheet or form that rearranges the records based on a selected field value or part of a field value.

Financial functions   Functions that are used to analyze loans and investments.

Find   An Access command that lets you specify how to locate data in an object.

First-line indent   A description of the indent in a paragraph when only the first line of text in the paragraph is indented.

Floating object   An object in a document that acts as if it were sitting in a separate layer on the page, and can be repositioned anywhere on the page.

Floppy disk drive   An outdated removable magnetic storage technology that came in many formats including the 3-inch HD, which was capable of storing 1.4 megabytes (MB) of information.

Folder   An electronic directory containing files or other folders.

Font   The design of text.

Font effect   *See* text effect.

Font scheme   A named set of two fonts that are used for all of the text elements in a publication.

Font size   The height of characters in points.

Font style   A formatting feature you can apply to a font to change its appearance. Common font styles are bold, italic, and underlining.

Footer   Text that is printed at the bottom of each page.

Foreign key   When two tables in a database are related, the common field in the related table is called a foreign key.

Form   A database object that displays data from one or more tables or queries in a format that has a similar appearance to a paper form.

Form Footer section   The section in Design view for a form that contains the information that is displayed at the bottom of the form.

Form Header section   The section in Design view for a form that contains the information that is displayed at the top of the form.

Form letter   A document that contains merge fields that indicate where to insert data from a data source, such as an Access database or an Excel workbook.

Form tool   An Access tool that creates a simple form that includes all the fields in the selected table or query.

Form view   A view of a form that displays the data in the record source in a form.

Form Wizard   An Access wizard that creates a form based on a record source and using options that the user specifies to select the form's record source and layout.

Format   To change the appearance or look of text.

Format Painter   A feature that copies format attributes such as colors, borders, and fill effects from an object, text, or cell in order to apply the same formatting to another object, text, or cell.

Format property   A property for a field that specifies how to display numbers, dates, times, and text.

Formula   An equation that calculates a new value from values currently in a worksheet.

Formula AutoComplete   A tool to help you enter a formula with a valid function name and arguments.

Formula Bar   The box to the right of the Name Box that displays a formula when the cell of a worksheet contains a calculated value (or the results of the formula).

Freeze panes   To keep selected rows and/or columns of the worksheet visible on the screen as the rest of the worksheet scrolls.

Front side bus speed   The speed of the bus that connects the processor to main memory.

Full Screen Reading view   A way of viewing a document on screen that shows text on the screen in a form that is easy to read; the Ribbon is replaced by a small bar called a toolbar that contains only a few relevant commands.

Function   A shorthand way to write an equation that performs a calculation.

G

Gadget   A tool available on the Windows sidebar.

Gallery   A list of options available for a command.

Gigahertz (GHz)   One billion cycles per second. Used to measure the speed of a computer.

Graphic   A picture that helps illustrate the meaning of the text and make the page more attractive; graphics include predefined shapes, diagrams, and charts, as well as photographs and drawings.

Grid   Vertical and horizontal lines that appear on the Slide pane and help you place text and objects.

Gridline   The lines in a table that form the rows and columns.

Grouping   A feature that allows you to move, format, or resize several objects as if they were one object.

Grouping level   An option for reports that organizes data based on one or more fields into groups.

Groups   Groups are part of each tab on the Ribbon. Buttons are arranged by category in groups.

Guidelines   Vertical and horizontal lines that you can display on the Slide pane to help place objects on the slide.

Gutter margin   *See* inside margin.

H

Hacker   A person who creates and sends programs such as viruses and any malicious code to harm a computer or computer system.

Handles   Appear when an object is selected and are used to drag to resize the object.

Handout master   The master view for the audience handouts; includes placeholders for the slides, a header, footer, and the date and slide number.

Handouts   Printouts that include a small image of the slides and an area to take notes. Can be formatted in several different ways using the Handout master formatting and Backstage view print options.

Hanging indent   A description of the indent in a paragraph when the first line of text is not indented but all of the following lines in the paragraph are.

Hard drive   The main storage device for a computer; reads and writes data to and from a round magnetic platter, or disk.

Hardware   The physical components, devices or parts, of the computer such as the central processing unit (CPU), the monitor, the keyboard, and the mouse.

Header   Text that is printed at the top of each page.

Help and Support   The Windows system where information can be found using topic lists or by searching using keywords.

Home page   The first page that opens when you start your browser. *Also called* start page.

Hyperlink   Text, cell, or an object that when clicked "jumps to" another location, such as another file location or a Web site. *Also called* link.

Hyperlink (in PowerPoint)   Text or an object that when clicked "jumps to" another slide in the current slide show or another PowerPoint presentation, opens a Word, Excel, or Access file, or a browser window. *Also called* link.

I

Icon   A small graphic image that represents a file, folder, program, or program shortcut.

Identity theft   Using a person's identity without their permission.

Import   To bring any object, data, graphics, or another file into a file.

Indent (in Excel)   To shift data within a cell and insert space between the cell border and its content.

Indent (in Word)   The space between text and the margin.

Ink-jet printer   Technology used by most color printers, or photo printers; uses a spray of ink to print an image.

Inline object   An object in a document that can be repositioned as if it were a character in the line of text.

Input   Data entered into the computer through a variety of devices, such as a keyboard, microphone, or mouse.

Input device   Hardware used to enter information into a computer and interact with the user; for instance, a keyboard, microphone, or pointing device.

Insertion point   A blinking vertical line that shows where text will appear when you begin typing.

Inside margin   The right margin on the left page and the left margin on the right page when a document is set up with mirrored margins. *Also called* gutter margin.

Internet   A vast network of computers located all over the world and linked to one another.

Internet Service Provider (ISP)   A company that provides connection to the Internet by subscription.

J

Join line   The line that connects tables that have a relationship; the join line connects the common fields and indicates the relationship type.

Journal   An Outlook action that records entries and document interactions with contacts.

Jump list   A list of recently used files that appears on the Start menu when you right-click an icon.

Justify   To format a paragraph so the text is distributed evenly across the page between the left and right margins, and both the left and right edges of the paragraph are aligned at the margins.

K

Keyword   A word or phrase used in a search.

L

Label Wizard   An Access wizard that creates a report of standard or custom labels.

LAN (local area network)   Connected computers within a small geographical area such as a home, office, school, or building.

Landscape orientation   A page or worksheet rotated so it is wider than it is long.

Laptop computer   A small lightweight computer that includes monitor, keyboard, hard drive, CD/DVD storage drives, and a pointing device as one unit that folds for easy portability. *Also called* notebook computer.

Laser printer   A fast, high-quality printer that uses heat to fuse a powdery substance called toner to the page.

Layout   The way content and text placeholders are placed on the slide.

Layout guides   Guides that help you position objects in a publication.

Layout master   In the slide master, the individual layouts that determine the location of content and text placeholders for the slides.

Layout view   A view of a form or report that displays data from the record source and that lets you make certain types of changes to the form or report, such as increasing the size of a text box control.

LCD (Liquid Crystal Display) technology   Typically used by computer monitors because it enables them to provide a very sharp picture using low energy.

Leader   A solid, dotted, or dashed line that fills the blank space before a tab stop.

Left-align   To position text so that it is aligned along the left margin.

Legend   A list that identifies patterns, symbols, or colors used in a chart.

Libraries   Virtual folders that contain links to files and folders throughout your computer.

Line chart   A chart that uses points connected by a line to illustrate values in a worksheet.

Line tool   An Access tool that you can use to draw a line in a form or report.

Link   *See* hyperlink.

Linked object   A file, chart, table or other object that is created in another application such as Excel, stored in a source file, and inserted into a destination file, such as a PowerPoint slide, while maintaining a connection between the two files.

Live Preview   The Office 2010 feature that lets you point to the various choices in a gallery or palette and see the results before applying.

Logical functions   Functions that display text or values if certain conditions exist.

Logo   A symbol that represents a business and its products.

M

Magnetic tape   Removable, sequential storage medium commonly used for backing up a computer system, used by businesses.

Mail merge   A process that combines a document with information that personalizes it.

Main document   The file used in a mail merge that contains the information that does not vary from one document to the next.

Manual calculation   Lets you determine when Excel calculates formulas in the worksheet.

Manual page break   A page break you insert to start a new page.

Margin   Blank space around the top, bottom, left, and right sides of a page.

Master page   A background page that includes placeholders for text and graphics as well as layout guides.

Mathematical functions   Functions that manipulate quantitative data in a worksheet.

Maximize button   The window sizing button that enlarges a window to the full size of the screen.

Meeting   An Outlook activity that has a scheduled date and time and includes other people and a location.

Megahertz   One million cycles per second. Used to measure the speed of a computer.

Memory   The chips that store data and programs while the computer is working. Often called RAM or Random Access Memory.

Menu   A list of related commands.

Merge   To combine multiple cells into one cell.

Merge field   A placeholder in the main document in a mail merge that is replaced with data from the data source when you perform the merge.

Microsoft Office 2010 (or **Office**)   A collection of software programs, including Word, Excel, PowerPoint, Access, Outlook, and Publisher.

Mini toolbar   A floating toolbar that appears in the work area after you drag the pointer over text while holding down the left mouse button.

Minimize button   The window sizing button that reduces the window to an icon on the taskbar.

Mirrored margins   Margins on left and right pages that are identical—"mirror" each other—when facing each other; usually used in books and magazines.

Mixed cell reference   A cell reference that contains both relative and absolute references.

Modem   A device that allows computers to communicate by converting data in bytes to sound media in order to send data and then convert it back to bytes after receiving the data.

Monitor   A standard output device that includes the screen on which you view your work.

Motherboard   Located inside the system unit, a circuit board where the computer memory, power supply, the processor, and other vital electronic parts are housed.

Motion Path   A way to animate an object by drawing the path on the slide. Allows you to make an object move along a specified path on the slide.

Mouse   A hand-held device used to move a pointer on the computer screen.

Multilevel list   A list with two or more levels of bullets or numbering. *Also called* outline numbered list.

Multiple Items tool   An Access tool that creates a form that lists all the fields in the record source in a datasheet format.

Multitable query   A query that is based on the data in two or more tables.

N

Name Box   The cell reference area located below the Ribbon, which displays the cell reference of the active cell.

Navigation Pane (in Access)   The pane in Access that displays the objects in a database.

Navigation Pane (in Outlook)   Provides centralized navigation to the main Outlook components; includes view buttons and shortcut icons.

Negative indent   A description of an indent in a paragraph in which the left indent marker is past the left margin. *Also called* outdent.

Network   Two or more computers connected to share data, either by wires or using wireless technology.

Network card   A device in the system unit that allows computers to access networks.

Network software   Software used to run a network server.

Nonadjacent range   A range that includes two or more adjacent ranges and selected cells.

Normal view (in Excel)   The worksheet view best for entering and formatting data in a worksheet.

Normal view (in PowerPoint)   The view that includes the Slides/Outline tabs on the left, the Slide pane showing the selected slide in the center, and the Notes pane beneath the Slide pane. Commonly used to place objects on the slide.

Notebook computer   *See* laptop computer.

Notes   In Outlook, an electronic equivalent of a sticky note.

Notes master   The master view for the notes pages. Includes placeholders for the slide, notes, header, footer, date, and slide number.

Notes Page view   A view in PowerPoint for working on the speaker notes page; includes placeholders for the slide notes.

Notes pane   The area below the Slide pane where you can type speaker notes.

Notification area   Program icons on the task bar that provide status and notifications about programs and features, such as speaker volume or new mail.

Number format   Changes the way data looks in a cell.

O

Object   Anything that appears on the screen that you can select and work with as a whole, such as a shape, picture, or chart.

Office Clipboard (or **Clipboard**)   A special clipboard available only to Microsoft Office programs, on which you can collect up to 24 items.

Office Web Apps   Versions of Microsoft Word, Excel, PowerPoint, and OneNote that you can access online from your SkyDrive.

OneNote   An electronic notebook program included with Microsoft Office.

One-to-many relationship   A relationship between two tables in a database in which one record in the primary table can match many (zero, one, or many) records in the related table.

Operand   A constant (text or number) or cell reference used in a formula.

Operator   A symbol that indicates what mathematical operation to perform on the operands such as a plus sign (+) for addition.

Operating system   Software such as Windows 7 or Windows Vista or Mac OS X that controls the basic operations of your computer.

Or operator   An operator used in a query that selects records that match at least one of two or more conditions in a query.

Order of evaluation   The sequence used to calculate the value of a formula.

Organization chart   A SmartArt graphic used to show hierarchy and relationships of people or objects.

Orientation   Rotates cell contents to an angle or vertically.

Orphan   The last line of a paragraph at the top of a page.

Outdent   *See* negative indent.

Outline numbered list   *See* multilevel list.

Outline tab   A tab used to enter text in Normal view, located on the left side of the window in the same pane as the Slides tab.

Outline view   A way of viewing a document on screen that displays headings and text in outline form so you can see the structure of your document and reorganize easily; headers and footers, page boundaries, graphics, and backgrounds do not appear.

Output   The results of data processing; can be presented in many ways such as an image on a screen or a monitor, printed pages from a printer, or sound through speakers.

Output device   Hardware that displays the results of computer processing; for example, a monitor, printer, or speaker.

Outside margin   The left margin on the left page and the right margin on the right page when a document is set up with mirrored margins.

P

Package for CD   A feature that allows you to save a presentation to a CD to be viewed on a computer that does not have PowerPoint installed.

Page break   The place where one page ends and another begins.

Page Break Preview   The worksheet view for adjusting page breaks in a worksheet.

Page Layout view   The worksheet view that shows how the worksheet will appear on paper.

Page Navigation pane   The Page Navigation pane is placed on the left side of the document window and includes thumbnail images of each page in the publication.

Panel heading   The area provided for the title or heading of a project or section of a project.

Paste   To copy an item stored on the Clipboard or the Office Clipboard to a location in a file.

Peripheral devices   Additional hardware, such as printers and scanners, that are not essential to the computer but increase its functionality.

Personal computer   A computer used at home or in school for individual use.

Personal Digital Assistants (PDA)   A pocket-sized electronic organizer that helps you to manage addresses, appointments, expenses, tasks, and memos. Often included as part of a cell phone.

Personal folder   Stores your most frequently used folders and is labeled with by the computer user account name.

Phishing   A criminal activity that is used by people to fraudulently obtain your personal information, such as usernames, passwords, credit card details, and social security information.

Picture   A digital photograph or other image file.

Pie chart   A chart that shows the relationship of a part to a whole.

Pin To attach a program icon directly to the Start menu or task bar for easy access.

Pixel A single point in a graphic image. It is from picture element, using the abbreviation "pix" for "picture."

Placeholder A boxed outline on a slide that can be used to insert text or an object when clicked.

Plot area The graphical representation of all of the data series.

Point-and-click method In a formula, to click a cell rather than type its cell reference.

Point The unit of measurement for fonts.

Pointer The tip of a pointing device as it appears on the screen.

Pointing device A device that allow users to navigate and interact with a computer.

Portrait orientation A page or worksheet rotated so it is longer than it is wide.

PowerPoint presentation A computer slide show created in PowerPoint.

Presenter view A way to view your presentation with the speaker notes showing on one computer screen, while an audience views the presentation without viewing the speaker notes on another computer screen.

Primary key The field in a database table that contains a unique field value for each record in the table.

Primary table In a one-to-many relationship, the table that contains the records on the "one" side of the relationship.

Print area The cells and ranges designated for printing.

Print Layout view The most common way of viewing a document on screen; it shows how a document will look when it is printed, and you can work with headers and footers, margins, columns, and graphics, which are all displayed.

Print Preview A way of viewing a document on screen that enables you to see the document as it will appear when printed.

Print titles Designated rows and/or columns in a worksheet that print on each page.

Printer A type of output device that produces a paper printout of information.

Process Electronic manipulation of input or stored data by a computer in order to produce information or output.

Processing device Electronic chips inside the system unit that are used to provide results of data input or user commands.

Program A set of instructions to the computer.

Program window The rectangle that contains the open program, tools for working with the file, and the work area.

Property Identifying information about a file that is saved along with the file, such as the author's name and the date the file was created.

Public folder Used to store the files you want to share with other users on the same computer or who are connected through a network.

Publishing Placing a presentation in a format for others to use; published presentations include handouts, Package for CD, and presentations on a document management server, in a document workspace, and on the Web.

Pull quote Text copied from a document and set off in a text box.

Q

Query A database object that lets you ask the database about the data it contains.

Quick Access Toolbar A small customizable toolbar at the top of the screen with buttons for common commands such as Save and Print.

Quick Part A building block stored in the Quick Parts gallery and available when you click the Quick Parts button in the Text group on the Insert tab.

Quick Steps Predefined or user-defined shortcuts that combine multiple steps into a one-click button.

Quick Style A predefined format that you can apply by clicking a button in the Styles group on the Home tab.

R

RAM (Random Access Memory) Memory that temporarily stores programs and data when the computer is turned on but does not retain the contents when the computer is turned off.

Range A group of selected cells.

Range-of-values condition A condition in a query that specifies a range of values that a record must satisfy to be displayed in the query results.

Range reference The unique identifier for a range, which is the cell in its upper-left corner and the cell in its lower-right corner, separated by a colon.

Read-only A term used to describe data that can be viewed but not changed.

Read-only memory (ROM)   Permanent memory that stores the instructions that tell the computer how to begin to load its operating system and programs.

Reading Pane   Area where you can read an e-mail message; pane appears either at the bottom or right side of the window.

Reading view   A PowerPoint view you can use to display your presentation; very much like Slide Show view, the slide does not quite fill the screen and you can use navigation buttons on the status bar beneath the slide.

Record   The collection of field values for a complete set of data.

Record selector   The box to the left of a record in a datasheet that, when clicked, selects the entire record.

Record source   The tables or queries that contain the data used in a form or report.

Recycle Bin   Wastebasket icon on the Windows desktop where items are deleted and from which they can be restored before the Recycle Bin is emptied.

Referential integrity   A set of rules that a DBMS follows to ensure that there are matching values in the common field used to create the relationship between related tables and that protects the data in related tables to make sure that data is not accidentally deleted or changed.

Related table   In a one-to-many relationship, the table that contains the records on the "many" side of the relationship.

Relationship   The feature of a DBMS that lets you connect the data in the tables in the database so you can create queries and other objects using the data from two or more tables.

Relative cell reference   A cell reference that adjusts to its new location when copied or moved.

Report   A database object that displays data from one or more tables or queries in a format that has an appearance similar to a printed report.

Report selector   The box in the upper-left corner of a report where the horizontal and vertical rulers intersect that you can click to select the entire report.

Report tool   An Access tool that creates a simple report that includes all the fields in the selected table or query on which it is based, uses a columnar format, formats the report using a theme, and includes a title with the same name as the record source.

Report Wizard   An Access wizard that you can use to create a report by specifying a record source, layout, sort order, and grouping level.

Required property   A field property that specifies whether a value must be entered into the field.

Research task pane   A task pane that provides access to information typically found in references such as dictionaries, thesauruses, and encyclopedias.

Resolution   The clarity of an image on the screen, measured in pixels. The higher the resolution, the more pixels and the clearer the image.

Resources   In Outlook, refers to materials and/or equipment needed for a meeting, such as a conference room, computer, or large plasma screen.

Restore Down button   The window sizing button that returns the window to the size it was before the Maximize button was clicked.

Ribbon   An area at the top of an Office program window that contains commands for working with the open file; the commands are organized under tabs.

Ribbon (in Outlook)   Contains commands organized under tabs for working with an Outlook element.

Right-align   To position text so that it is aligned along the right margin.

ROM (Read-only Memory)   The memory that stays in the computer when it is turned off because it stores the programs that run the computer as it starts.

Rotation handle   A green circle that appears connected to a selection rectangle around an object and that you can drag to rotate the object.

Router   An electronic device that joins two or more networks and directs the flow of information across the network.

Row   The horizontal placement of cells in a table or worksheet.

Row heading   The row number.

Row (in Excel)   Appears horizontally in the worksheet; identified by numbers on the left side of the worksheet window.

Run   The term given to the act of opening a query and displaying the query results.

S

Scale   To resize a worksheet to print on a specific number of pages.

Scanner   A device that converts text or graphics from a printed page into code that a computer can process.

Scatter chart   A chart that shows the relationship between two categories of data; sometimes called an XY chart.

Screen clipping   The area you choose to include in a screenshot.

Screenshot   A picture of all or part of something you see on your monitor, such as a Word document, an Excel workbook, a photograph, or a Web page.

ScreenTip   A box that appears when you point to a button; contains the button's name and a description of its function as well as a link to more information and a keyboard shortcut if available.

Scroll arrows   Located at either side of a scroll bar; used to move the window contents up or down.

Scroll bar   A bar that appears on the edge of a window when there is more content than can appear in the window at its current size.

Scroll box   A slider that can be dragged to change position in a scroll bar.

Section   A part of a document where you can apply a layout, headers and footers, page numbers, margins, orientation, and other formatting features different from the rest of the document.

Select   To highlight a block of text.

Selection rectangle   The box that appears around an object when it is selected.

Server   Computer hardware and software that stores and delivers data to the other computers on a network.

Shape   Rectangles, circles, arrows, lines, flowchart symbols, or callouts that can help make a worksheet more informative.

SharePoint   A site set up by an organization, such as a school, business, or nonprofit group.

Sheet tab   The name of each worksheet at the bottom of the worksheet window.

Shortcut menu   A menu that appears when you right-click something in the program window; it contains a list of commands you are most likely to use with the item or text you right-clicked.

Sidebar   Text set off from the main body of text in a text box that provides additional information for the reader.

Signature   An electronic identifier inserted in e-mail messages that use text, hyperlinks, pictures, or an Electronic Business Card.

Simple Query Wizard   The wizard in Access that lets you create a query and indicate what you'd like to see in the query results by selecting options in dialog boxes.

Sizing handle   A square, circle, or set of three dots that appears on a selection rectangle around an object and that you can drag to resize the object.

SkyDrive   An online storage and file sharing service provided by Microsoft.

Slide layout   The placement of placeholders or objects on a slide that determines how all of the objects on a slide are arranged.

Slide master   Determines the graphics and layout for the slides in a presentation. Each theme has a slide master, and slide masters include layout masters.

Slide pane   The main work area for the selected slide in Normal view.

Slide Show view   A view in PowerPoint that shows the slides on the full screen with animations and transitions.

Slide Sorter view   A view in PowerPoint that displays a thumbnail of each slide in the order in which they appear in the presentation; used to rearrange slides, check timings, and view slide transitions.

Slide transition   The animated way in which a slide appears and leaves the screen during a slide show.

Slides tab   In Normal view, the tab on the left slide of the PowerPoint window that displays thumbnails of each slide.

SmartArt   A predesigned chart or diagram that visually illustrates text and includes formatted graphics.

SmartArt graphic   A graphic diagram that visually illustrates text and includes formatted graphics.

Smartphone   Handheld portable cellular phone that can do more than just make and receive phone calls, including features such as a full keypad for text messaging and writing notes, email, a browser for Web access, a calendar, and an address book.

Snap to   When an object is drawn to the guide or grid as though it were magnetic; used for exact placement of objects.

Software   The programs or code that run on a computer; includes programs that tells the computer how to operate its devices, how to manipulate, store, and output information, and how to accept the input you give it.

Solid state card reader   Devices that can read solid state memory cards, such as those used by digital cameras.

Sort   To arrange a list of words or numbers in ascending or descending order.

Sort (in Access)   A method of arranging the records in a table, query, form, or report using the values in one or more fields.

Sound input device   A microphone or other device that accepts speech or sounds as input for processing on a computer.

Source   The location data is being transferred from.

Source file   The file in which a linked or embedded object is stored in a presentation.

Spam   Unsolicited or junk e-mail.

Sparkline   A mini chart you can insert into a cell.

Speech recognition technology   Software that converts speech or sounds to data.

Speed   How fast the computer processes each instruction; measured in megahertz (MHz) and gigahertz (GHz).

Spell checker   A feature used to locate and correct spelling errors.

Split   To divide the worksheet window into two or four panes that scroll independently.

Split Form tool   An Access tool that creates a form using all the fields in the selected record source and splits the window into two panes, with one displaying the form in Form view and the other displaying the form in Datasheet view.

Spreadsheet   A grid of rows and columns in which you enter text, numbers, and the results of calculations.

Spyware   A program that can harm a computer by gathering user information through the user's Internet connection without his or her knowledge, usually for advertising purposes.

Start button   Centralized starting point that brings up menus and other options.

Statistical functions   Functions that are used to describe large quantities of data.

Status bar   A bar at the bottom of the program window that provides information about the current file and process.

Storage device   Hardware such as a disk drive, CD/DVD drive, flash drive, or tape drive that is used to store and retrieve data on a computer.

Storage media   Work together with storage devices to store data; includes disks, CDs, DVDs, tape, solid state storage cards, and memory sticks.

Store   The computer function that keeps the data and information available for processing or for user output.

Style   A combination of formatting characteristics such as alignment, font, font size, font color, fill color, and borders that are applied simultaneously.

Subdatasheet   When two tables are related, the datasheet for the primary table contains expand indicators for each record. Clicking an expand indicator in the primary table displays the records in the related table in a subdatasheet.

Sum button   Inserts the SUM function to add long columns or rows of numbers.

Summary query   A query that summarizes relevant data, such as adding the field values in a column that displays price data, in the query results.

System Clipboard   *See* Clipboard.

System unit   A computer case that contains the CPU, power supply, memory, and some storage devices.

Systems software   The operating system (OS) of the computer; controls data flow among computer parts, and provides the platform on which application and network software work.

T

Tab stop   An indicator in a paragraph that marks the place where the insertion point will stop when you press the Tab key. *Also called* tab.

Table   An arrangement of text or numbers in rows and columns, similar to a spreadsheet.

Tablet PC   Small portable computers that allow you to input data by writing directly on the computer screen.

Tabs   Tabs are part of the Ribbon and include buttons arranged by groups of categories.

Task   An Outlook activity involving the user that can be monitored to completion.

Task pane   A window along the left side of the program window that contains options and commands.

Taskbar   The area at the bottom of the Windows screen that contains the Start button as well as program or window buttons for open programs.

Telecommuting   When employees use computer technology to work from home or during business travel and are linked by network to the office.

Template   A predesigned file that you can use to create a new file.

Template (in Access)   An object that you can use to create a database, table, or field in a database.

Template (in Excel)   A predesigned workbook file that you can use as the basis or model for new workbooks.

Template (in PowerPoint)   A predesigned presentation that has graphics and some content, such as theme elements, text, and graphics used to create a new presentation.

Template (in Word)   A file that already contains the basic elements of a document, such as page and paragraph formatting, fonts, and text and from which you can create a new document.

Text box   A shape specifically designed to hold text.

Text effect   Formatting for text that is similar to font styles and that can help enhance or clarify text. *Also called* font effect.

Text functions   Functions that are used to format and display cell contents.

Theme   A preset collection of design elements, including fonts, colors, and other effects.

Thesaurus   A built-in reference for finding synonyms for words in a document.

Thumbnail   A small graphic image.

Title bar   The bar at the top of the program window with the names of the program and the current file.

To-Do List   Tasks visible in the To-Do Bar in Outlook.

Toggle   To switch between two options or to turn a feature on or off.

Toggle command   A command that you can select or deselect to switch between two options or to turn a feature on or off.

Toner   A powdery substance used by laser jet printers instead of ink to create printed output on paper.

Toolbar   A small bar that appears at the top or bottom of a window instead of the Ribbon; it displays buttons you can click to quickly choose a command.

Total row   The optional row in a datasheet that counts the number of values in a column. When a field contains numeric data, you can use the Total row to calculate the total, average, minimum, or maximum value in a column.

Touchpad   A digital tracking device on the keyboard of a laptop computer that allows you to control the pointer by moving your finger on a small electronic pad.

Track Changes   A tool in Word that keeps a record of any changes you or a reviewer makes in a document by formatting inserted text in a color and underlined, and deleted and moved text in a balloon in the right margin.

Trackball   A digital tracking device that has a roller ball that turns to control a pointer on the screen.

Transition   *See* slide transition.

Trigonometric functions   Functions that manipulate quantitative data in a worksheet.

Truncate   To hide text that does not fit in a cell.

U

Unbound control   A control in a form or report, such as a line, rectangle, or picture, that is not connected to the record source on which the form or report is based.

Undo   To reverse a recent action.

Uniform Resource Locator (URL)   The address of a Web page on the Web.

USB flash drive   A portable, small, solid state storage device that plugs directly into a USB port on the computer system unit and that can read and write data.

Utility software   Programs that allow you to make changes to the way hardware and software works, such as changing the screen resolution, or improving the way disk drives read and write data.

V

Value axis   The identifying numbers listed on the vertical axis in a chart.

Vertical alignment   The position of text on a page between the top and bottom margins.

View buttons   In an Office program window, buttons that you can click to change views quickly.

Virus   Malicious software program written by a hacker that can damage the programs on your computer, causing the computer to either stop working or run slowly.

W

Web browser   Special software such as Internet Explorer, Google Chrome, or Firefox, used to view Web pages.

Web Layout view   A way of viewing a document on screen that simulates the way a document will look when it is viewed as a Web page; text and graphics appear the way they would in a Web browser, and backgrounds are visible.

Web server   A computer that stores and delivers the Web pages on the Internet.

Widow   The first line of a paragraph at the bottom of a page.

Wildcard   A special character that represents other characters in a search.

Window   A work area in Windows containing a user interface.

Windows Aero   Windows Vista graphic interface that includes transparency for windows and dialog boxes.

Windows Live   A collection of services and Web applications that help users be more productive.

Windows Security Center   Windows utility that monitors the status of a computer's security components.

Windows Sidebar   A transparent panel attached to one side of the Windows desktop screen that contains gadgets.

Wireless network   Computer networks that use RF (radio frequency) technology to communicate with each other; computers are not physically connected to the network with wires or cables.

Wireless network technology   Technology that uses the airwaves to connect devices and computers.

Word processing   The use of a computer and software to enter and edit text and produce documents such as letters, memos, forms, and reports.

Word wrap   A feature in Word that automatically wraps words around to the next line when they will not fit on the current line.

WordArt   Stylized text that is treated as an object.

Workbook   The file used to store worksheets; usually a collection of related worksheets.

Workgroup collaboration   The process of working together in teams, sharing comments, and exchanging ideas for a common purpose.

Worksheet   A computerized spreadsheet in Excel.

Worksheet range   A group of adjacent worksheets.

World Wide Web (or **Web**)   A system of computers that share information by means of links on Web pages.

Wrap text   To move data to a new line when the cell is not wide enough to display all the contents.

Z

Zip disk   A portable disk that will hold 100MB, 250MB, or 750MB of data.

Zip drive   Hardware required to read and write data to a Zip disk.

Zoom   The percentage the file is magnified or reduced on the screen; 100% zoom represents the normal size; percentages higher than that mean the document appears larger on screen; percentages lower than that mean the document appears smaller on screen.

Zoom Slider   A feature on the status bar that can be dragged to change the zoom percentage of the Slide pane in the PowerPoint window.

INDEX

Index

O